U.S. Civilian Unemployment Rate, 1970–1995

Year	United States	Canada	Japan	France	(West) Germany	Italy	United Kingdom
	Civilian unemployment rate (percent)[1]						
1970	4.9	5.7	1.2	2.5	0.5	3.2	3.1
1971	5.9	6.2	1.3	2.8	0.6	3.3	3.9
1972	5.6	6.2	1.4	2.9	0.7	3.8	4.2
1973	4.9	5.5	1.3	2.8	0.7	3.7	3.2
1974	5.6	5.3	1.4	2.9	1.6	3.1	3.1
1975	8.5	6.9	1.9	4.2	3.4	3.4	4.6
1976	7.7	7.2	2.0	4.6	3.4	3.9	5.9
1977	7.1	8.1	2.0	5.2	3.4	4.1	6.4
1978	6.1	8.4	2.3	5.4	3.3	4.1	6.3
1979	5.8	7.5	2.1	6.1	2.9	4.4	5.4
1980	7.1	7.5	2.0	6.5	2.8	4.4	7.0
1981	7.6	7.6	2.2	7.6	4.0	4.9	10.5
1982	9.7	11.0	2.4	8.3	5.6	5.4	11.3
1983	9.6	11.9	2.7	8.6	6.9	5.9	11.8
1984	7.5	11.3	2.8	10.0	7.1	5.9	11.8
1985	7.2	10.5	2.6	10.5	7.2	6.0	11.2
1986	7.0	9.6	2.8	10.6	6.6	7.5	11.2
1987	6.2	8.9	2.9	10.8	6.3	7.9	10.3
1988	5.5	7.8	2.5	10.3	6.3	7.9	8.6
1989	5.3	7.5	2.3	9.6	5.7	7.8	7.3
1990	5.6	8.1	2.1	9.1	5.0	7.0	7.0
1991	6.8	10.4	2.1	9.6	4.3	6.9	8.9
1992	7.5	11.3	2.2	10.4	4.6	7.3	10.1
1993	6.9	11.2	2.5	11.8	5.7	10.2	10.5
1994	6.1	10.4	2.9	12.3	6.5	11.3	9.6
1995	5.6	9.5	3.2	11.7	6.5	12.0	8.8

[1]Civilian unemployment rates, approximating U.S. concepts. Quarterly data for France and Germany should be viewed as less precise indicators of unemployment under U.S. concepts than the annual data.

Source: Economic Report of the President, 1997, Table B-107, p. 421.

ECONOMICS
Principles and Tools

Arthur
O'SULLIVAN
Oregon State University

Steven M.
SHEFFRIN
University of California, Davis

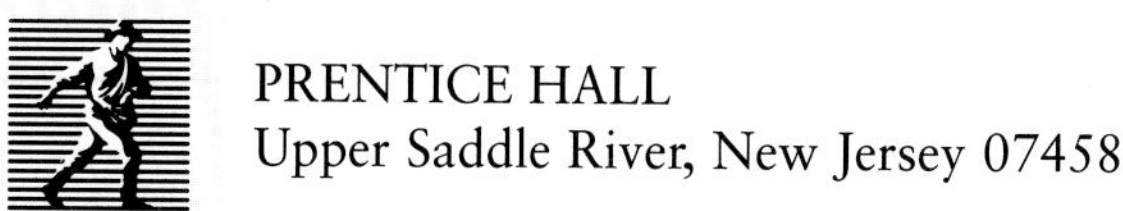

PRENTICE HALL
Upper Saddle River, New Jersey 07458

TO OUR CHILDREN: CONOR, MAURA, MEERA, AND KIRAN

Executive Editor: Leah Jewell
Development Editors: Elisa Adams and Steven A. Rigolosi
Assistant Editor: Gladys Soto
Editorial Assistant: Kristen Kaiser
Editorial Director: James Boyd
Director of Development: Steve Deitmer
Marketing Manager: Patrick Lynch
Associate Managing Editor: David Salierno
Production Coordinator: Ivy Azoff
Managing Editor: Dee Josephson
Manufacturing Supervisor: Arnold Vila
Manufacturing Manager: Vincent Scelta
Design Manager: Patricia Smythe
Interior Design: Ann France
Cover Design: Lorraine Castellano/Cheryl Asherman
Illustrator (Interior Graphs): ElectraGraphics, Inc.
Illustrator (Infographics): Batelman Illustration
Project Management/Composition: TSI Graphics
Cover Art: Warren Gebert

A Simon & Schuster Company
Upper Saddle River, New Jersey 07458

Library of Congress Cataloging-in-Publication Data
O'Sullivan, Arthur.
Economics : principles and tools / Arthur O'Sullivan, Steven M. Sheffrin. — 1st ed.
p. cm.
Includes bibliographical references and index.
ISBN 0-13-206368-9 (hardcover : alk. paper)
1. Economics. I. Sheffrin, Steven M. II. Title.
HB171.5.084 1998
330—dc21 97-26468
CIP

Prentice-Hall International (UK) Limited, London
Prentice-Hall of Australia PTY. Limited, Sydney
Prentice-Hall Canada, Inc., Toronto
Prentice-Hall Hispanoamericana, S.A., Mexico
Prentice-Hall of India Private Limited, New Delhi
Prentice-Hall of Japan, Inc., Tokyo
Simon & Schuster Asia Pte. Ltd., Singapore
Editora Prentice-Hall do Brasil, Ltda., Rio de Janeiro

Printed in the United States of America

10 9 8 7 6 5 4 3 2 1

BRIEF CONTENTS

CONTENTS

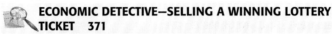

A Closer LOOK

Features

A Closer LOOK

Features (continued)

PREFACE

OUR MISSION

We wrote this book to match our teaching philosophy for a "principles" or introductory course in economics: The course should be taught as if it is the last economics course students will take. Most students don't go beyond the introductory courses in economics, so we have just one opportunity to get them thinking like economists. From our experience, the best way to teach these students is to emphasize the key principles and ideas of economics, showing them how to use these concepts in their lives and careers. In contrast, many introductory texts are virtual encyclopedias of economic doctrine, so they overwhelm students with unimportant details and obscure the essential ideas of economics.

Extensive class testing of our book has shown us that it succeeds in getting students to think like economists: By the end of the course, they use the notion of opportunity cost, weigh marginal benefits and marginal costs, think about trade-offs, and distinguish between nominal and real values. This is a major accomplishment for students who take only one or two economics courses.

This book also provides a solid foundation for further study in economics. The best way to prepare students for advanced study is to provide them with the big picture—the framework of economic reasoning. Rather than filling their heads with forgettable details, we make the key concepts unforgettable by using them repeatedly, illustrating them with intriguing examples, and giving students many opportunities to practice what they've learned. As a result, they become well prepared for the more detailed and complex analysis in later economics courses.

Our approach allows us to present sophisticated material in a way that the average student of principles can understand. For example, in microeconomics, we discuss imperfect information, price discrimination, and strategic decision-making by firms. In macroeconomics, we explain the origins of hyperinflation and even present a simplified growth model in an appendix. We wish to emphasize that students don't realize that these topics might be considered "advanced" material. To them, the material is no more difficult than the other material they encounter, and is actually less difficult than some traditional topics. Because we emphasize key concepts and use them to explain these modern topics, we can more accurately portray economics as it is practiced today.

PRINCIPLES, TOOLS, AND ACTIVE LEARNING

As our title, *Economics: Principles and Tools*, suggests, we place the principles of economics and the tools of our discipline at the center of our approach. The five principles of economics are as follows:

1. *Principle of Opportunity Cost.* The opportunity cost of something is what you sacrifice to get it. For example, the cost of a college degree includes the student's foregone earnings, and the cost of a warship purchased by Malaysia in 1992 was safe drinking water for 2.5 million people.
2. *Marginal Principle.* Pick the level of an activity at which the marginal benefit equals the marginal cost. For example, it is sensible to run an airline flight with few passengers if the marginal benefit (revenue from tickets) exceeds the marginal cost (extra costs for the crew and fuel).
3. *Principle of Diminishing Returns.* If we increase one input while holding the other inputs fixed, output will increase, but at a decreasing rate. For example, adding workers to a one-oven pizzeria increases the number of pizzas, but at a decreasing rate.
4. *Spillover Principle.* In some circumstances, decision-makers do not bear all the costs or experience all the benefits from their decisions—i.e., there are externalities. For example, a paper producer that pollutes a river imposes costs on people downstream; a contributor to public radio generates benefits for other listeners.
5. *Reality Principle.* What matters to people is the real value or purchasing power of money. For example, workers should be interested in the purchasing power of their wages, not simply the dollar value of their wages.

We believe these are the core principles of economics. They should be self-evident to students and can be easily understood without any previous training in economics. In Chapter 2 we discuss each of these principles in detail and provide examples.

The power of economics comes from the tools that can be used to analyze a wide variety of issues and problems. For example, we use supply and demand curves to explore market phenomena, and cost and revenue curves to explore firms' decisions. This book uses the key principles of economics to explain the logic underlying the most important tools of economics. This approach generates simple explanations that students can readily understand. We demystify the tools of economics, preparing students to use the tools properly.

This text is based on the notion of **active learning**. Once we've explained the logic of an economic tool and provided examples of its proper use, we give students plenty of opportunities to use the tool themselves. Most chapters have an "Economic Detective" exercise that provides a few clues into an economic puzzle or mystery and then asks students to solve the mystery. The last section of each chapter is a set of challenging "Using the Tools" questions that give students the opportunity to do their own economic analysis. Economic experiments throughout the text allow students to engage in role-playing as consumers, producers, citizens, and policymakers. At the beginning of each chapter, we capture students' attention with a story and a list of practical questions that are answered within the chapter. In combination, these active-learning features make studying economics a hands-on experience.

Our teaching experience tells us that a good example will stay with students longer than an abstract discussion. Students and instructors will find new and exciting examples throughout the text. In fact, every chapter of this book is jam-packed with relevant, interesting examples (and occasional "A Closer Look" features) that are fully integrated into each chapter's content.

For a preview of the special pedagogical features we've developed to assist both students and instructors, please turn to page xxviii.

ORGANIZATION AND PLAN

All three versions of our book (*Economics*, *Microeconomics*, and *Macroeconomics*) begin with a four-chapter preview. Part 1, "Introduction and Key Principles," includes several novel features. After an introduction to the discipline and a review of graphing techniques in Chapter 1, we develop the key principles of economics in Chapter 2. This chapter is essential reading for all students. In Chapter 3 we explain how markets naturally arise through specialization. We use the concept of specialization to explain comparative advantage and introduce the global economy, setting the stage for the international examples and topics we introduce throughout the text. We also provide an overview of the role of government in a market economy. Chapter 4 provides a thorough introduction to supply and demand, showing students how to play "economic detective" by using simple clues to solve economic mysteries and puzzles.

In our combined text, we proceed directly to microeconomics. However, we have designed the text so that instructors may proceed directly to macroeconomics after teaching the four introductory chapters.

The Plan of Microeconomics

The microeconomics part of the text begins with Part 2, "A Closer Look at Demand and Supply." Chapter 5, on elasticity, is packed with examples that breathe life into what is too often a dry topic. We also show how to use elasticity to predict changes in price, quantity, and total revenue. We begin Chapter 6 with a discussion of when markets are likely to be efficient and inefficient, then highlight the many ways that governments can intervene in markets—and the trade-offs associated with intervention. Chapter 7 explains consumer choice in a simple, intuitive way, using the marginal principle. (For those who are interested, an optional appendix on indifference curves is provided.)

The firm comes to prominence in Part 3, "Market Structure and Pricing," as we discuss cost curves, pricing, and supply decisions for individual firms and the market (Chapters 8–11). This part of the book includes several innovations. To explain the long-run cost curves, we use real cost data to draw average-cost curves and provide an intuitive explanation for their shapes. In Chapter 12 we focus on the firm's entry decision, contrasting a natural monopoly with monopolistic competition. In Chapter 13 we use simple game trees to explain the notions of price fixing and entry deterrence, and then discuss the logic of antitrust policy.

Part 4, "Market Failure: Spillovers and Information," provides a detailed exploration of market failure. Chapter 14 considers the role of government in providing goods with spillover benefits—for example, protection from threatening asteroids, wildlife conservation, and college education. It also considers the issue of public choice, contrasting three models of government behavior. Chapter 15 discusses the economic approaches to solving environmental problems, including global warming and ozone depletion. Chapter 16, on imperfect information, uses simple supply and demand concepts to explain the "lemons" problem and adverse selection, and includes discussions of the markets for used baseball pitchers, blood for transfusions, and medical insurance.

Part 5, "The Markets for Labor and Capital," explores these markets and discusses some of the most vexing problems facing society today. Chapter 17 explains why wages vary among occupations and explores the effects of imperfect information on the labor market. Chapter 18 uses supply and demand to show why interest rates vary across financial instruments. Chapter 19 provides a wealth of factual information on four current policy issues (poverty, income distribution, the aging of society, and medical care), and explores the trade-offs associated with different policy options.

The Plan of Macroeconomics

The second part of *Macroeconomics*, "The Basic Concepts of Macroeconomics," provides an overview of the discipline. The first chapter summarizes the big ideas in macro, and the second discusses measurement issues—including the most recent changes in government statistics. These chapters provide a natural building block for the rest of macroeconomics.

In the next part, "The Economy in the Long Run," we begin analysis of the long run. We start with a chapter on the economy at full employment, followed by a chapter exploring economic growth. We decided to place long-run considerations early in the text for several reasons. First, many policy debates center on long-run issues (for example, productivity growth). Second, we felt that too many students take away from the course oversimplified Keynesian notions and apply them inappropriately. For example, many students come away from a macroeconomics course believing that increased government spending will always increase output. By considering a full-employment economy first, we can bring Keynesian fiscal policy into its proper perspective. Finally, there has been a resurgence of research in economic growth in recent years, which has highlighted many interesting and exciting issues.

After discussing growth, we devote an entire part (three chapters) to "Economic Fluctuations"—specifically, the business cycle and Keynesian economics. Our discussion of the macroeconomic short run is based on the idea that output is demand determined in the short run. We illustrate the difference between the macroeconomic short run and long run with aggregate demand and supply curves. With demand determining output in the short run, the Keynesian cross is a useful tool, and we extend it to explain fiscal policy, automatic stabilizers, and the open economy.

In the two chapters that make up the next part, "Money, Banking, and Monetary Policy," we integrate these three factors into our short-run model, highlighting important policy issues and the key role of the Federal Reserve. Finally, in the last part of the macroeconomics section, "Inflation, Unemployment, and Government Deficits," we bring the long run back into the picture. First we develop a complete model that explains how the economy can, in principle, return to full employment after economic shocks or disturbances. Next we analyze inflation and unemployment in more depth, again stressing the links between the short run and the long run. In the last chapter of macroeconomics, we ask and answer ten important questions about government deficits and debt.

International Coverage

The concluding section of all three versions of the book (*Economics*, *Microeconomics*, and *Macroeconomics*) is devoted to exploring international topics in more depth. This part, "The International Economy," also covers recent issues and events, such as GATT, NAFTA, and protectionism. In *Economics* and *Macroeconomics,* we also cover the international finance system. We have designed this material so that it can be read with only a knowledge of the material in Chapters 1–4.

In addition, international examples and applications are featured in every chapter, both in "A Closer Look" features and within the text.

Alternative Course Syllabi

We have designed this book to be flexible, to allow its use by instructors with different time lines and course objectives. Several chapters may be skipped without disrupting the flow of the presentation, permitting each instructor to choose his or her ideal combination of chapters.

Microeconomics Courses

Those who teach microeconomics confront two major issues. First, if the instructor wants to emphasize supply and demand (rather than the theory of consumer or producer behavior), what chapters should be covered? Second, which chapters form the core of a traditional microeconomics course, and how many additional chapters can be covered in a quarter course or a semester course?

A Course Emphasizing Supply and Demand. This book works well in any course that emphasizes supply, demand, and the application of the market model to various policy issues. The instructor can start with Chapters 1–6, which explain the basics of supply and demand, including why markets exist, how they work, the price elasticities of supply and demand, and the market effects of government intervention. The instructor could then skip Part 3 ("Market Structure and Pricing") and go directly to the three chapters in Part 4, which consider various types of market failure. The first two chapters in Part 5 ("The Markets for Labor and Capital") cover supply and demand in factor markets, and can be used individually or in combination. The final chapter in Part 5, "Economic Challenges for the Twenty-First Century," uses supply and demand analysis to explore several current policy issues.

Core and Other Chapters in a Quarter or Semester Course. Chapters 1–8 constitute the core of a traditional microeconomics course. The number of additional chapters that can be covered depends on the pace and length of the course. An instructor should be able to cover four to six additional chapters in a quarter course, or five to eight additional chapters in a semester course.

Macroeconomics Courses

Most of those who teach macroeconomics confront a key issue: How much time should be devoted to more classical topics, such as growth and production, versus more Keynesian topics, such as economic fluctuations? Our book allows instructors to pursue either emphasis.

A Course Emphasizing Classical Themes. A course highlighting classical themes should initially concentrate on Chapters 1–4, which review the foundations of markets and supply and demand, before turning to the macroeconomic sections. The first five chapters in the macroeconomics section could then be covered in full. These chapters cover the big ideas in macroeconomics, measurement issues, full employment, growth, and aggregate demand and aggregate supply. The instructor could then discuss financial intermediation, the Federal Reserve, the money creation process, and other chapters as time permits.

A Course Emphasizing Keynesian Themes. After doing a quick overview of Chapters 1–3, the instructor could cover the first two chapters in macroeconomics, which emphasize the big ideas in macroeconomics and measurement issues. The instructor would then skip the two chapters on the long run and proceed directly to the chapter on aggregate demand and supply ("Coordinating Economic Activity: Aggregate Demand and Supply"). The instructor would then turn to the chapters titled "Keynesian Economics and Fiscal Policy," "Money, the Banking System, and the Federal Reserve," and "Monetary Policy in the Short Run." Subsequent chapters could then be included as time permits.

A Combined Microeconomics and Macroeconomics Course

Because it emphasizes use of the key economics principles throughout, our book is the ideal text for a one-semester or one-quarter course. A combined course should first cover Chapters 1–4 in detail. The instructor could then follow the different alternatives for the micro and macro courses that we sketched above.

THE TEACHING AND LEARNING PACKAGE

Each component of the teaching and learning package has been carefully crafted to ensure that the introductory economics course is a rewarding experience for both students and instructors.

Instructor's Manual with Video Guide

Two Instructor's Manuals are available—one for microeconomics (by Léonie Stone of SUNY Geneseo) and one for macroeconomics (by Stephen Perez of Washington State University). Both Instructor's Manuals reflect the textbook's organization, incorporating policy problems in case studies, exercises, extra questions, and useful Internet links. The manuals also provide detailed outlines (suitable for use as lecture notes) and solutions to all questions in the textbook. The integrated Video Guide, with suggested questions, provides real-life examples of the textbook's key economic principles. The videos are keyed by chapter.

Study Guides

The author of both Study Guides (for microeconomics and macroeconomics), Janice Boucher Breuer of the University of South Carolina, emphasizes the practical application of theory. Each Study Guide is a practicum designed to promote comprehension of economic principles and develop each student's ability to apply them to different problems.

Each chapter of the Study Guides begins with an overview of the corresponding chapter in the textbook, a checklist to provide a quick summary of material covered in the textbook and lectures, and a list of key terms. The language in the Study Guide matches that in the text. Unlike all other introductory economics study guides, the O'Sullivan/Sheffrin Study Guides contain performance enhancing tips (PETs), which are designed to help students understand economics by applying the principles and promoting analytical thinking.

Two practice exams, featuring both multiple-choice and essay questions, are included at the end of each chapter. Both exams require students to apply one or more economic principles to arrive at each correct answer. Full solutions to the multiple-choice questions are included, not only listing each correct answer but also explaining in detail why one answer is correct and the others are not. Detailed answers to the essay questions are also provided.

Test Item File

Test item files are available for both *Microeconomics* and *Macroeconomics*. These offer approximately 3,500 multiple-choice, true/false, short-answer, and problem questions, both definitional and applied. Each question is keyed by topic and coded by degree of difficulty (easy, moderate, challenging, and honors) and degree of computation involved. Both are available in printed and electronic format.

Prepared by David Figlio of the University of Oregon, the test item files offer many unique features. For example, the multiple-choice questions provide five-answer questions, as recommended in the educational testing literature. In addition, the test banks integrate selected end-of-chapter problems from the text, as well as questions and answers from the Study Guides.

Prentice Hall Custom Test

The test item files are designed for use with the Prentice Hall Custom Test, a computerized package that allows instructors to custom design, save, and generate classroom tests. The test program (in PC Windows and Macintosh formats) permits instructors to edit, add, or delete questions from the test item file; edit existing graphics and create new graphics; and export questions to various word processing programs, including WordPerfect and Microsoft Word. Graphics capability ensures that all graphs included in the test item file can be printed next to the appropriate questions.

PowerPoint Presentations

The comprehensive PowerPoint supplement for this text, prepared by Donald Balch of the University of South Carolina, is a unique accompaniment to the classroom lecture. The computer-generated slides offer summaries of important text material, and clever artwork that reinforces the concepts being presented. The slides, which may be shown on a large-screen TV, a computer projector, or an LCD panel, may be used with either the IBM or Macintosh computer platform. Each chapter of the text has a corresponding slideshow presentation.

A special feature of the PowerPoint supplement is its presentation of graphic analysis. Each analysis is sequentially structured, with each slide in a series showing one step in the progression toward completion. Along with the graphic building process, each slide highlights the most recent addition(s) to the sequence, any point(s) of reference, and corresponding values of the reference point(s).

ABC/Prentice Hall Video Library

ABCNEWS

Prentice Hall and ABC News have combined their experience in academic publishing and global reporting to provide a comprehensive video ancillary to enhance our principles of economics texts. Through its wide variety of award-winning programs—*Nightline*, *This Week With David Brinkley*, *World News Tonight*, and *20/20*—ABC offers a resource for feature and documentary-style videos related to the chapters in the text. The programs have extremely high production quality, present substantial content, and are hosted by well-versed, well-known anchors.

Video Guide

The integrated Video Guide (included as part of the Instructor's Manual) provides a summary of each of the clips in the Video Library. For each video, the guide also supplies running time, teaching notes, and discussion questions, as well as useful tips on how to use the clip in class. Each video is keyed to the appropriate topic in the text.

The New York Times
PRENTICE HALL
THEMES OF THE TIMES

The New York Times "Themes of the Times" Program

The New York Times and Prentice Hall cosponsor "Themes of the Times," a program designed to enhance student access to current information of relevance in the classroom.

Through this program, the text's core subject matter is supplemented by a collection of articles from one of the world's most distinguished newspapers, *The New York Times*. These articles demonstrate the vital, ongoing connections between what is learned in the classroom and what is happening in the world around us.

To enjoy the wealth of information of *The New York Times* daily, students and professors can take advantage of a reduced subscription rate. For information, call toll-free: 1-800-631-1222.

Economics: Principles and Tools CD-ROM

The O'Sullivan/Sheffrin CD-ROM gives students a chance to actively engage the theory and, with a seamless link to the Internet, launch into exploration of their own. The CD-ROM uses the text itself as a framework, so students can relate their activities directly to their class assignments. Its features include:

- *The entire O'Sullivan/Sheffrin text*: reformatted for easy reading and on-screen navigation.
- *Active Graphs*: an interactive learning device that enables students to explore examples and problems from the text by manipulating dynamic, active graphs.
- *Author Help*: hints and explanations in the authors' voices.
- *News Links*: articles and abstracts of current events, both on the CD-ROM and updated over the Web, through which students can explore the theory at work in the real world.
- *Exploration Links*: hyperlinks to relevant, engaging sites on the Web from the text itself.
- *Interactive Study Guide*: links students to on-line study guide.
- *Hot-linked Glossary, Index, and Table of Contents*: for quick reference and navigation.
- *FREE Internet browser.*

Online Student Review and PHLIP—Prentice Hall's Learning through the Internet Partnership (http://www.prenhall.com/osullivan)

This Web-based resource offers students another opportunity to sharpen their problem-solving skills and to assess their understanding of the text material. For each chapter, the site contains the traditional pedagogy, such as chapter objectives and multiple-choice and Internet exercises. Approximately ten questions are provided per chapter. In addition, the online study guide has a built-in grading feature. Students take the exams and receive immediate feedback.

This site also links the student to the "Take it to the Net" exercises featured in the textbook. These Web-destination exercises are keyed to each chapter and direct the student to an appropriate, updated, economics-related Web site to gather data and analyze a specific economic problem. From the O'Sullivan home page, instructors and students can access Prentice Hall's Learning on the Internet Partnership (PHLIP). Developed by Dan Cooper at Marist College, PHLIP provides academic support for faculty adopting this text. From the PHLIP Web site, instructors can download supplements and lecture aids, including the Instructor's Manuals, lecture notes, PowerPoint presentations, problem and case solutions, and chapter outlines. Electronic delivery means that you always get the very latest in support materials.

PHLIP also helps you bring current events into the classroom. Using our *PHLIPping Through the News* service, you and your students can access the most current news in economics. Twice each month (biweekly), Scott Simkins (North Carolina Agricultural and Technical State University) and Jim Barbour (Elon College) review current articles, then post summaries of those articles, along with discussion questions, group activities, and research ideas. The stories are always keyed to specific chapters in the text, providing instructors with a dynamic and invaluable teaching tool.

To get the necessary username and password to access PHLIP and our digital supplements, please call your Prentice Hall sales representative. Or contact Prentice Hall Sales directly at college_sales@prenhall.com.

ACKNOWLEDGMENTS

There is a long distance between the initial vision of an innovative principles text and the final product. Along the way we participated in a structured process to reach our goal.

After writing a first draft of the manuscript, we participated in a two-day focus group in San Francisco. We went over the entire manuscript page by page with five economics instructors, who eagerly shared their teaching experiences and expectations. Their insightful comments helped us distinguish between the strong and the weak parts of the manuscript, giving us many opportunities to improve it.

The project went through four rounds of reviews by instructors, with the staff at Prentice Hall helping us interpret the reviewers' comments and develop strategies to refine the manuscript. The manuscript was tested in classrooms at many colleges and universities, providing us with valuable feedback from instructors and students. In the final round of reviews and revisions, we focused on making improvements that would make it easier for instructors to make the transition from other textbooks to ours.

We wish to acknowledge the assistance of the many individuals who participated in this process. First, we want to thank the participants in our two-day focus group, who helped us see the manuscript from a fresh perspective:

Jeff Holt, Tulsa Junior College; Gary Langer, Roosevelt University; Tom McKinnon, University of Arkansas; Barbara Ross-Pfeiffer, Kapiolani Community College; Virginia Shingleton, Valparaiso University

Many people read all or parts of the manuscript at various stages. For their helpful criticisms, we thank:

Harjit K. Arora, Le Moyne College; Alex Azarchs, Pace University; Kevin A. Baird, Montgomery County Community College; John Payne Bigelow, Louisiana State University; Scott Bloom, North Dakota State University; Janice Boucher Breuer, University of South Carolina; Kathleen K. Bromley, Monroe Community College; Cindy Cannon, North Harris College; Katie Canty, Cape Fear Community College; David L. Coberly, Southwest Texas State University; John L. Conant, Indiana State University; Ana-Maria Conley, DeVry Institute of Technology; Peggy Crane, San Diego State University; Albert B. Culver, California State University, Chico; Norman Cure, Macomb Community College; Mousumi Duttaray, Indiana University; Ghazi Duwaji, University of Texas, Arlington; Paul C. Harris, Jr., Camden County College; Duane Eberhardt, Missouri Southern State College; David Figlio, University of Oregon; Randy R. Grant, Linfield College; Rowland Harvey, DeVry Institute of Technology; Charlotte Denise Hixson, Midlands Technical College; Jeff Holt, Tulsa Jr. College; Brad Hoppes, Southwest Missouri State University; Jonathan O. Ikoba, Scott Community College; John A. Jascot, Capital Community Technical College; George Jensen, California State University, Los Angeles; Taghi T. Kermani, Youngstown State University; Rose Kilburn, Modesto Junior College; James T. Kyle, Indiana State University; Gary Langer, Roosevelt University; Marianne Lowery, Erie Community College; Melanie Marks, Longwood College; Jessica McCraw, University of Texas, Arlington; Rahmat Mozayan, Heald College; Alex Obiya, San Diego City College; Paul Okello, University of Texas, Arlington; Charles M. Oldham, Jr., Fayetteville Technical Community College; Jack W. Osman, San Francisco State University; Randall Parker, East Carolina University; Chirinjev Peterson, Greenville Technical College; Nampeang Pingkarawat, Chicago State University; L. Wayne Plumly, Jr., Valdosta State University; Teresa M. Riley, Youngstown State University; John Robertson, University of Kentucky; Barbara Ross-Pfeiffer, Kapiolani Community College; Dennis Shannon, Belleville Area College; Virginia Shingleton, Valparaiso University; David L. Sollars, Auburn University at Montgomery; Ed Sorensen, San Francisco State University; Evan Tanner, American Graduate School of International Mgmt./Thunderbird; Robert Tansky, St. Clair County Community College; Fred Tyler, Fordham University; James R. VanBeek, Blinn College; Chester Waters, Durham Technical Community College, Shaw University; Irvin Weintraub, Towson State University; James Wheeler, North Carolina State University; Gilbert Wolfe, Middlesex Community College.

A special acknowledgment goes to the instructors who were willing to class-test drafts in different stages of development. They provided us with instant feedback on parts that worked and parts that needed changes:

John Constantine, University of California, Davis; James Hartley, Mt. Holyoke College; John Farrell, Oregon State University; Kailash Khandke, Furman College; Peter Lindert, University of California, Davis; Louis Makowski, University of California, Davis; Stephen Perez, Washington State University; Barbara Ross-Pfeiffer, Kapiolani Community College

From the start, Prentice Hall provided us with first-class support and advice. Jim Boyd, Kristen Kaiser, and Gladys Soto of Prentice Hall contributed in myriad ways to the project. We want to single out several people for special mention. Our Development Editors, Elisa Adams and Steven Rigolosi, worked with us patiently to find our "voice" in the text. They were always enthusiastic and always worked with us to support our vision. Finally, we are deeply indebted to Leah Jewell, Economics Editor at Prentice Hall. From the very beginning, her inexhaustible energy and enthusiasm propelled the project forward.

Last but not least, we must thank our families, who have seen us disappear—sometimes physically and other times mentally—to spend hours wrapped up in our own world of principles of economics. A project of this magnitude is very absorbing, and our wives have been particularly supportive in this endeavor.

Arthur O'Sullivan

Steven M. Sheffrin

A GUIDED TOUR

Economics: Principles and Tools features a number of special pedagogical features to assist students and instructors. Many of these features are designed to promote an active learning environment.

ACTIVE LEARNING

Economic Detective

Throughout the book, students are invited to play "Economic Detective" to use the tools of economics to explain puzzles or answer questions. Playing detective promotes an exciting active learning environment in the classroom.

The Mystery of the Bouncing Price of Used Newspapers

In 1987 you could sell a ton of used newspapers for $60. Five years later, anyone with a pile of used newspapers had to pay someone to take them away.[7] In other words, the price of used newspapers dropped from $60 to zero in just five years. Then the price started climbing. It reached $106 per ton in 1995, a price high enough so that thieves started stealing newspapers that people had left on the curb for recycling.[8] What explains the bouncing price of used newspapers?

We can solve this mystery with some additional information about changes over time in the quantity of used newspapers. Between 1987 and 1992, the quantity increased dramatically, so the price and quantity moved in opposite directions. Therefore, we would conclude that the decrease in price was caused by an increase in supply (the third row of Table 2). Over this five-year period, hundreds of communities adopted curbside recycling programs. These programs increased the supply of used newspapers, generating a surplus of used newspapers that decreased the equilibrium price. As shown in the left panel of Figure 13, the increase in supply was so large that the equilibrium price fell to zero.

What happened between 1992 and 1995 to increase the price from zero to $106? During this period, the equilibrium quantity of used newspapers increased: The price and the quantity moved in the same direction. Therefore, we would conclude that the increase in price was caused by an increase in demand (the first row in Table 2). During this period many states passed laws requiring paper manufacturers to make newsprint (the paper used to make newspapers) with a higher percentage of recycled fiber. In addition, the federal government, one of the world's largest paper users, now buys paper with a minimum recycled content of 20%. As shown in the right panel of Figure 13, these changes shifted the demand curve for used newspapers to the right, increasing the equilibrium price from zero to $106.

Figure 13
Bouncing Price of Used Newspapers

Between 1987 and 1992, the price of used newspapers decreased, a result of increases in supply. Between 1992 and 1995, the price increased, a result of increases in demand.

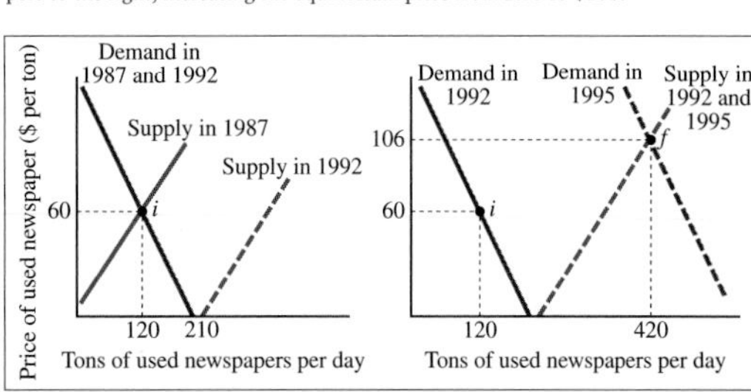

Economic Experiments

Economic experiments throughout the text involve students in experimenting with some of the key ideas in each chapter. These role-playing exercises allow students to make decisions as consumers, producers, citizens, and policymakers. Like the "Economic Detective" features, experiments provide excellent opportunities for active learning. For example, the "Market Equilibrium" experiment shows how decentralized decision-making generates an equilibrium price.

1. ECONOMIC EXPERIMENT: ***Market Equilibrium***

The simple experiment takes about 20 minutes to run. We start by dividing the class into two equal groups, consumers and producers.

- The instructor provides each consumer with a number indicating the maximum amount that he or she is willing to pay (WTP) for a bushel of apples: The WTP is a number between $1 and $100. Each consumer has the opportunity to buy 1 bushel of apples per trading period. The consumer's score for a single trading period equals the gap between his WTP and the price actually paid for apples. For example, if the consumer's WTP is $80 and he pays only $30 for apples, his score is $50. Each consumer has the option of not buying apples. This will be sensible if the best price you can get exceeds your WTP. If you do not buy apples, your score will be zero.
- The instructor provides each producer with a number indicating the cost of producing a bushel of apples (a number between $1 and $100). Each producer has the opportunity to sell 1 bushel per trading period. The producer's score for a single trading period equals the gap between the selling price and the cost of producing apples. So, if a producer sells apples for $20 and her cost is only $15, her score is $5. Producers have the option of not selling apples, which is sensible if the best price she can get is less than her cost. If she does not sell apples, her score is zero.

Once everyone understands the rules, consumers and producers meet in a trading area to arrange transactions. A consumer may announce how much he or she is willing to pay for apples and wait for a producer to agree to sell apples at that price. Alternatively, a producer may announce how much he or she is willing to accept for apples and wait for a consumer to agree to buy apples at that price. Once a transaction has been arranged, the two people (consumer and producer) inform the instructor of the trade, record the transaction, and leave the trading area.

There are several trading periods, each of which lasts a few minutes. After the end of each trading period, the instructor lists the prices at which apples sold during that period. Then another trading period starts, providing consumers and producers another opportunity to buy or sell 1 bushel of apples. After all the trading periods have been completed, each participant computes his or her score by adding the scores from each trading period.

Test Your Understanding

At several points in each chapter, "Test Your Understanding" questions help students determine whether they understand the preceding material before continuing. These are not brain-twisters; they are straightforward questions that ask students to review and synthesize what they've read. Complete answers appear at the end of each chapter.

TEST *Your Understanding*

1. True or false, and explain: The cost of a master's degree in engineering equals the tuition plus the cost of books.
2. Suppose that a nation picks 1,000 young adults at random to serve in the army. What information do you need to determine the cost of using these people in the army?
3. Explain the logic behind the economist's quip that "there is no such thing as a free lunch."
4. If a bus company adds a third daily bus between two cities, the company's total costs will increase from $500 to $600 per day and its total revenue will increase by $150 per day. Should the company add the third bus?
5. Suppose that you can save $50 by purchasing your new car in a different city. If the trip requires only $10 in gasoline, is the trip worthwhile?

MODEL ANSWERS

Test Your Understanding

1. False. This statement ignores the opportunity cost of time spent in school.
2. We need the opportunity cost of using the people in the army instead of in the civilian economy. One measure of the opportunity cost is the wages the people could have earned as engineers, teachers, doctors, lawyers, or factory workers.
3. One of the costs of a lunch is the time spent eating it. Even if someone else pays for your lunch, it is not truly free.
4. The marginal benefit is $150 and the marginal cost is only $100 ($600 – $500), so it would be sensible to add the third bus.
5. It will be worthwhile if the opportunity cost of the time spent traveling is less than $40.

Using the Tools

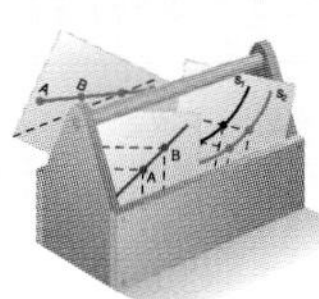

The last section of each chapter is a set of challenging "Using the Tools" questions. These are an important part of each chapter, not traditional end-of-chapter material. They are designed to stretch the students into using the ideas developed in the chapter. Complete answers are provided.

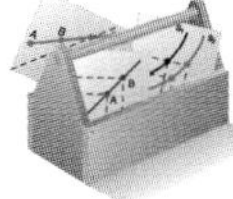

Using the **TOOLS**

In this chapter you learned how to use two of the tools of economics—the supply curve and the demand curve—to predict how a change in demand or supply will affect prices and quantities. Here are some opportunities to use these tools to do your own economic analysis.

2. College Enrollment and Housing

Consider a college town where the initial price of apartments is $400 and the initial quantity is 1,000 apartments.

a. Use supply and demand curves to show the initial equilibrium, and label the equilibrium point with an *i*.
b. Suppose that the number of students attending college increases by 20%. Use your graph to show the effects of this on the price and quantity of apartments. Label the new equilibrium point with an *f*.

3. Innovation and Phone Prices

Suppose that the initial price of a pocket phone is $100 and the initial quantity demanded is 500 phones per day. Depict graphically the effects of a technological innovation that decreases the cost of producing pocket phones. Label the starting point with an *i* and the new equilibrium with an *f*.

4. Market Effects of an Import Ban

Consider a nation that initially imports half the shoes it consumes. Use a supply and demand diagram to predict the effect of a ban on shoe imports on the equilibrium price and quantity of shoes.

DYNAMIC EXAMPLES

Examples bring economics to life. We've all heard the "dollar bill on the sidewalk" story a million times. Economics: Principles and Tools *has hundreds of fresh, new, never-before-seen examples.*

Chapter-Opening Stories

Each chapter opens with a story to motivate the chapter's subject matter, followed by a series of chapter-opening questions. These questions are revisited and answered at the end of the chapter.

CHAPTER 2

Key Principles of Economics

Emma owned some stock in Marginal Airlines, and she flew with the airline whenever she had a chance. You can imagine her dismay when she boarded a plane and saw just 30 passengers in the 120-seat airplane. How could the airline make a profit with so few passengers? She wrote a letter to the president of the airline demanding an explanation. Did the person who scheduled the flight make a mistake, or was the airline deliberately trying to lose money?

As we'll see later in the chapter, it was sensible to run the flight because the extra revenue from the flight exceeded the extra cost. This is the *marginal principle*—one of the five key principles of economics—in action.

1. What is the cost of producing military goods such as bombs and warships?
2. If a student group offers to pay $500 to use a college auditorium for an evening, should the college accept the offer?
3. As a firm hires more workers, what happens to the total output of its factory?
4. If a paper producer dumps chemical waste into a river, what is the true cost of paper?
5. Suppose that your wage doubles and that the prices of consumer goods double too. Are you better off, worse off, or about the same?

MODEL ANSWERS FOR THIS CHAPTER

Chapter-Opening Questions

1. To get a warship, we sacrifice something else, for example, safe drinking water for 2.5 million Malaysians.
2. According to the marginal principle, the college should accept the offer if the marginal cost associated with using the auditorium (for security, lighting, heat, and cleanup) is less than the marginal benefit ($500).
3. According to the principle of diminishing returns, output will eventually increase at a decreasing rate.
4. The true or economic cost of paper equals the firm's cost (for material, labor, and the paper mill) and the cost associated with the pollution generated as a byproduct of paper.
5. Your income will buy the same quantity of goods and services, so you will be equally well off.

Integration of International Examples

International examples are integrated throughout the text. Chapter 3 sets the stage early, introducing comparative advantage, exchange rates, and the language of trade and trade policy. Examples and illustrations from the global economy are then woven into every chapter thereafter.

Using the Principle: Opportunity Cost of Military Spending

We can use the principle of opportunity cost to explore the cost of military spending. Malaysia bought two warships in 1992, paying a price equal to the cost of providing safe drinking water for the 5 million Malaysians lacking it.[1] In other words, the opportunity cost of the warships was safe drinking water for 5 million people. When the Soviet Union fell apart and military tensions around the world diminished, citizens in the United States and Western Europe called for massive cuts in defense spending, with the idea of spending the "peace dividend" on social programs. The French cut their annual defense budget by billions of dollars and withdrew 50,000 troops stationed on German soil.[2] In the United States, the number of people employed by the military has decreased dramatically, and the Pentagon developed a new program, "Troops to Teachers," to help former soldiers get jobs teaching in local schools.[3] The switch from army duty to teaching reminds us that the opportunity cost of a soldier may be a teacher.

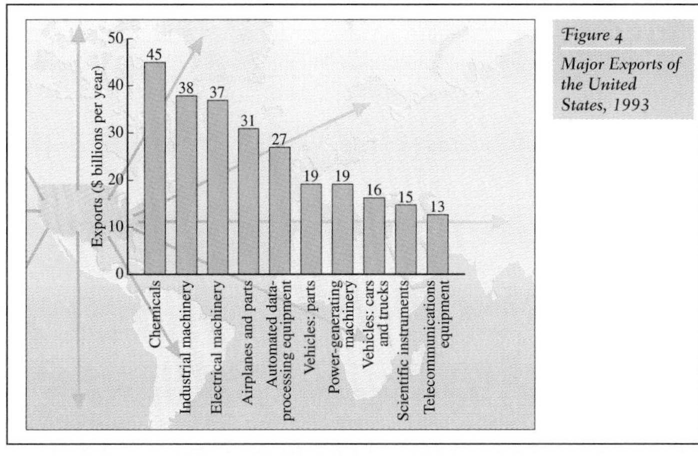

Figure 4
Major Exports of the United States, 1993

A Closer Look

"A Closer Look" features throughout the text provide brief, interesting examples of the tools and concepts discussed in the text.

A Closer LOOK

Jurassic Park and the Price of Amber

Scientists who use amber to study fossils and extinct animals were shocked when the price of amber tripled during 1993.* Because the equilibrium quantity of amber increased along with its price, the increase in price was caused by an increase in demand, not a decrease in supply. The increase in demand coincided with the release of the movie *Jurassic Park,* in which scientists use specimens from amber to clone dinosaurs. Many of the people who saw the movie bought amber specimens, and this new consumer demand increased the demand for amber. The demand curve shifted to the right, increasing the equilibrium price and quantity.

Amber contains the preserved remains of mosquitos that feasted on dinosaurs. In 1993 the price of amber tripled.

*Tim Friend, "Dino-Craze Sends Sales of Amber with Insects Buzzing," *USA Today,* June 17, 1993, p. A1.

LEARNING WITH TECHNOLOGY

Economics: Principles and Tools *offers a full technological component to stimulate active learning and retention.*

Take It to the Net

At the end of each chapter, a "Take it to the Net" feature sends students to the Prentice Hall Web site, where chapter-specific exercises are located. These exercises are updated regularly. The O'Sullivan/Sheffrin site links to PHLIP, which also offers summaries of the latest news on the economic front.

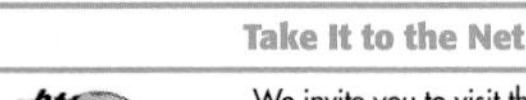

Take It to the Net

We invite you to visit the O'Sullivan/Sheffrin page on the Prentice Hall Web site at:
http://www.prenhall.com/osullivan/
for this chapter's World Wide Web exercise.

PHLIP—Prentice Hall Learning through the Internet Partnership

*PHLIP (at **http://www.phlip.marist.edu**) provides academic support for faculty adopting this text. From the PHLIP site, instructors can download supplements and lecture aids, including the Instructor's Manuals, lecture notes, PowerPoint presentations, problem and case solutions, and chapter outlines. Electronic delivery means that you always get the very latest in support materials.*

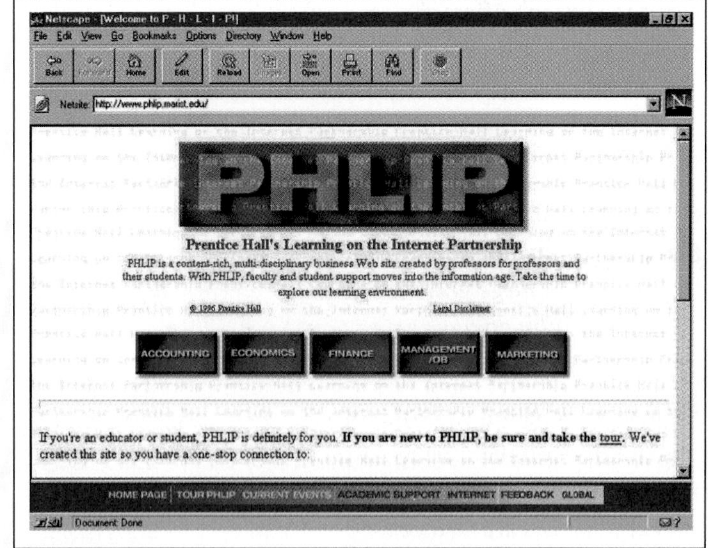

C H A P T E R

Part 1 ▮
Introduction and Key Principles

1 Introduction: What Is Economics?

Helen collapsed on her sofa after a very busy day. As she reviewed the day's events, questions kept popping into her head. That morning, she accepted one of the five job offers she received after graduating from college. She wondered why she was so lucky: Just two years earlier, the unemployment rate was much higher and most graduates were lucky to get even one job offer.

Why does the unemployment rate vary from year to year?

Helen's starting salary was about 80% higher than the salary of the typical high-school graduate and about 10 times higher than the salary in the typical developing nation. She wondered why her salary was so high.

Why do college graduates earn so much more than high-school graduates? Why do workers in the United States earn so much more than workers in developing nations?

Helen bought a three-month-old car with just 4,000 miles on it, paying about $6,000 less than she would for an otherwise identical new car. It seemed too good to be true. As she drove off the lot, she remembered her friends' warning that used cars are "lemons" and wondered if she'd made a mistake.

Why do so many used cars turn out to be lemons?

Helen was surprised at how easy it was to get a loan from a local bank to pay for her car, and she wondered about how the financial system works.

Where did the bank get the money for her auto loan?

On the way home, Helen stopped to vote in a congressional election. The biggest issue in the campaign was the size of government: One candidate promised to cut government; while the other promised to develop some new government programs. Helen wondered which candidate was right.

What is the role of government, and is it too large or too small?

s you can see from this story, economics is all around us. Our everyday experiences in the economy—as buyers, sellers, workers, and citizens—lead us to questions about the state of the national economy, about how markets operate, and about the role of government. The purpose of this book is to help answer these questions. If you are a curious person, constantly asking questions about the world around you, economics is for you. If you're not very inquisitive, give us a chance to pique your curiosity. By the end of the book, you might find yourself asking more questions and discovering some surprising answers.

In addition to helping us understand the world around us, the study of economics helps us make better decisions. Economic analysis exposes the trade-offs—the costs and the benefits—associated with a particular action, so it helps us make sensible choices. For example, Helen could compare the costs and benefits of new cars and used cars and then decide what type of car to buy. Economics also helps us decide how to vote. Political campaigns often deteriorate into vacuous sloganeering and dueling bumperstickers. Economic analysis exposes the trade-offs associated with various public policies, allowing voters to make more informed choices. In this book we discuss dozens of hotly debated policy issues, including free trade, environmental regulations, monetary policy, taxes, and government patents. These discussions will inform you about specific issues and teach you how to do your own economic analysis of other issues.

We build on what you already know about economics. You've heard news reports about the inflation rate and the unemployment rate, so you have a general idea about what they are and why they are important. In this book you'll learn why the unemployment rate and the inflation rate fluctuate and what the government can do to affect them. You've already participated in the economy, both as a buyer of consumer goods and perhaps as a seller of labor services, and your economic experience has given you an intuitive understanding of how markets work. In this book we show you how to combine your intuition with sound reasoning. In many cases, economic reasoning will generate conclusions that are at odds with your intuition and what you've heard from others. Studying economics will improve your critical thinking skills, so you'll be better equipped to discuss the economic issues of the day.

WHAT IS ECONOMICS?

Economics: The study of the choices made by people who are faced with scarcity.

Scarcity: A situation in which resources are limited and can be used in different ways, so we must sacrifice one thing for another.

Economics is the study of the choices made by people who are faced with scarcity. **Scarcity** is a situation in which resources are limited and can be used in different ways, so we must sacrifice one thing for another. Here are some examples of scarcity.

- You have a limited amount of time today. If you read this book for an hour, you have one less hour to spend on other activities, such as, studying for other courses, reading the newspaper, or exercising.
- A city has a limited amount of land. If the city uses an acre of land to build a park, there is one less acre for apartments, office buildings, or factories.

- A nation has a limited number of people, so if it forms an army, it has fewer people to serve as teachers, doctors, and clerks.

Because of scarcity, people must make difficult choices: You must decide how to spend your time; the city must decide how to use its land; and a nation must decide how to divide its people between military and civilian pursuits.

Wherever you look, we are surrounded by economic concerns. The pervasiveness of choice in the face of scarcity is reflected in the definition of economics offered by the famous economist Alfred Marshall (1842–1924): "*Economics is the study of mankind in the everyday business of life.*"

Each person is faced with dozens of decisions, including what goods to buy, what occupation to pursue, how many hours to work, and how much money to save. A firm must decide what goods to produce and how to produce them. A government must choose a set of public programs and then decide how to raise money to support the programs. Together, the choices made by individuals, firms, and governments determine society's choices and answer three basic questions.

1. ***What goods and services do we produce?*** To decide how much of each good to produce, we face some important trade-offs. For example, if we devote more resources to medical care, we have fewer resources for education and consumer goods. If we increase the number of people working in factories, we have fewer people to work on farms and in the classroom.
2. ***How do we produce these goods and services?*** We must decide how to use our resources to produce what we desire. For example, should we produce electricity with oil, solar power, or nuclear power? Should we teach college students in large lectures or in small sections? Should we produce food on large corporate farms or on small family farms?
3. ***Who consumes the goods and services that are produced?*** We must decide how the products of society are distributed among people in our society. If some people earn more money than others, should they consume more goods? How much money should we take from the rich and give to the poor?

Scarcity and the Production Possibilities Curve

Let's take a closer look at the first question, What goods and services do we produce? The resources used to produce goods and services are known as the **factors of production**. Economists distinguish between five types of factors.

1. ***Natural resources*** are things created by acts of nature and used to produce goods and services; for example, arable land, mineral deposits, oil and gas deposits, water, and naturally occurring plants. Some economists use the term *land* to refer to all types of natural resources.

2. ***Labor*** is the human effort used to produce goods and services, including both physical and mental effort. Labor is scarce because there are only 24 hours in each day: If we spend time in one activity, we have less time for other activities.

3. ***Physical capital*** is an object made by human beings and used to produce goods and services; for example, machines, buildings, equipment, roads, pencils, computers, and trucks.

4. ***Human capital*** is the knowledge and skills acquired by a worker through education and experience and used to produce goods and services. Every job requires some human capital: To be a surgeon, you must learn about anatomy and acquire surgical skills; to be an accountant, you must learn the rules of accounting and acquire computer skills; to be a taxi driver, you must know the city streets; to be a

Factors of production: The resources used to produce goods and services.

Natural resources: Things created by acts of nature and used to produce goods and services.

Labor: Human effort used to produce goods and services, including both physical and mental effort.

Physical capital: Objects made by human beings and used to produce goods and services.

Human capital: The knowledge and skills acquired by a worker through education and experience and used to produce goods and services.

musician, you must know how to play an instrument. One of the reasons for getting a college degree is to increase your human capital and thus widen your employment opportunities.

Entrepreneurship: Effort used to coordinate the production and sale of goods and services.

5. ***Entrepreneurship*** is the effort used to coordinate the production and sale of goods and services. An entrepreneur comes up with an idea for a business, decides how to produce the product, and sells the product to consumers. An entrepreneur takes risks, committing time and money to a business without any guarantee of profit.

The first step in deciding what goods and services to produce is to determine which combinations of goods and services are possible, given a society's productive resources and its technological know-how. If we simplify matters by assuming that a nation produces just two products—space missions and home computers—we can use a two-dimensional graph to illustrate the nation's options. In Figure 1 the feasible combinations of computers and space missions are shown by the shaded area. For example, one option is point *e*, with 380,000 computers and 4 space missions per year. Another option is point *i*, with 200,000 computers and 2 space missions. The set of points on the border between the shaded and unshaded area is called the **production possibilities curve** (or **production possibilities frontier**) because it separates the combinations that are attainable (the shaded area within the curve and the curve itself) from the combinations that are not attainable (the unshaded area outside the curve).

Production possibilities curve: A curve that shows the possible combinations of goods and services available to an economy, given that all productive resources are fully employed and efficiently utilized.

What's the difference between points inside the production possibilities curve and points on the curve? For any point inside the curve, we can find a point *on* the curve that generates more of both goods. For example, a move from point *i* (with 200,000 computers and 2 space missions) to point *e* (with 380,000 computers and 4 missions) would increase the number of computers *and* the number of space missions, so point *i* is clearly inferior to point *e*. An economy that reaches a point inside the curve is operating inefficiently in the sense that it could produce more of both goods. An economy could reach a point inside the curve for one of two reasons.

1. ***Resources are not fully employed.*** For example, some workers could be idle or some production facilities could be idle or underutilized.

Figure 1

Scarcity and the Production Possibilities Curve

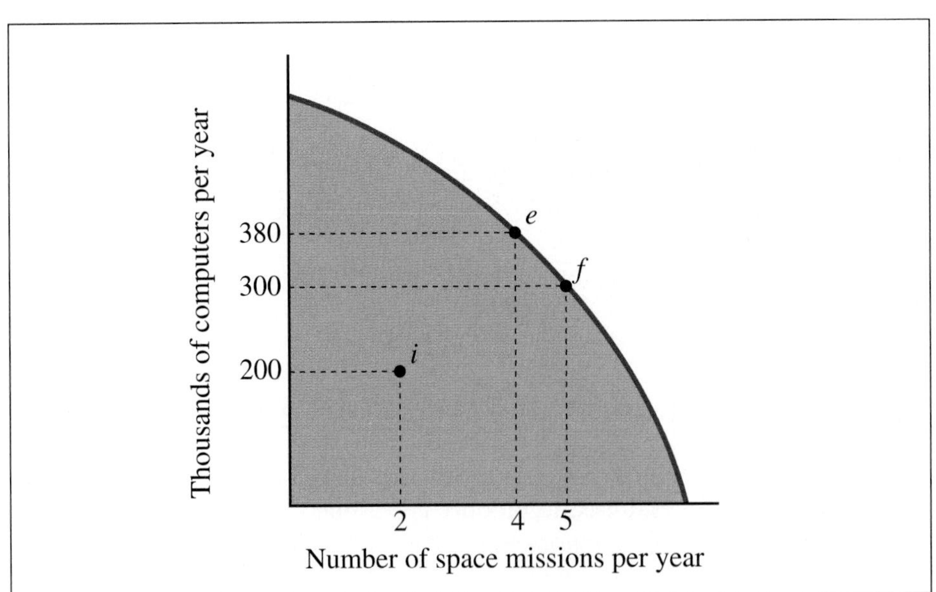

The production possibilities curve (or frontier) illustrates the notion of scarcity: With a given amount of resources, an increase in one good (space missions) comes at the expense of another (computers).

2. ***Resources are used inefficiently.*** Goods can be produced with different combinations of inputs, and if businesses pick the wrong input mixture, the economy won't produce as much output as it could.

In contrast with points inside the production possibilities curve, points on the curve are efficient in the sense that it would be impossible to increase the production of both goods. For every point on the curve, the society's resources are fully employed and used in an efficient manner.

The production possibilities curve illustrates the notion of scarcity. At a given time, a society has a fixed amount of each factor of production, so the production of one product comes at the expense of another. If we want to produce more space missions, we must switch some resources from computer production into the production of space missions. Of course, as we move resources out of computer production, the total output of computers will decrease. For example, if we move from point *e* to point *f*, we sacrifice 80,000 computers to get one more space mission.

What sort of changes would shift the entire production possibilities curve? The curve shows the production options available with a given set of productive resources, so an increase in an economy's resources will shift the entire curve outward. If an economy acquires more natural resources, labor, physical capital, human capital, or entrepreneurial ability, the economy can produce more of each good. As a result, the production possibilities curve will shift outward, as shown in Figure 2. For example, if we start at point *f* and the resources available to the economy increase, we can produce more space missions (point *g*), more computers (point *h*), or more of both goods (points between *g* and *h*). The curve will also shift outward as a result of technological innovation that allows an economy to produce more output with its existing physical resources. In Chapter 2 we discuss some of the other features of the production possibilities curve, including why it is curved.

Market: An arrangement that allows buyers and sellers to exchange things: A buyer exchanges money for a product, while a seller exchanges a product for money.

Markets

Now that we know the three questions an economy must answer, let's look at how a market-based economy answers these questions. A **market** is an arrangement that allows buyers and sellers to exchange things: a buyer exchanges money for a

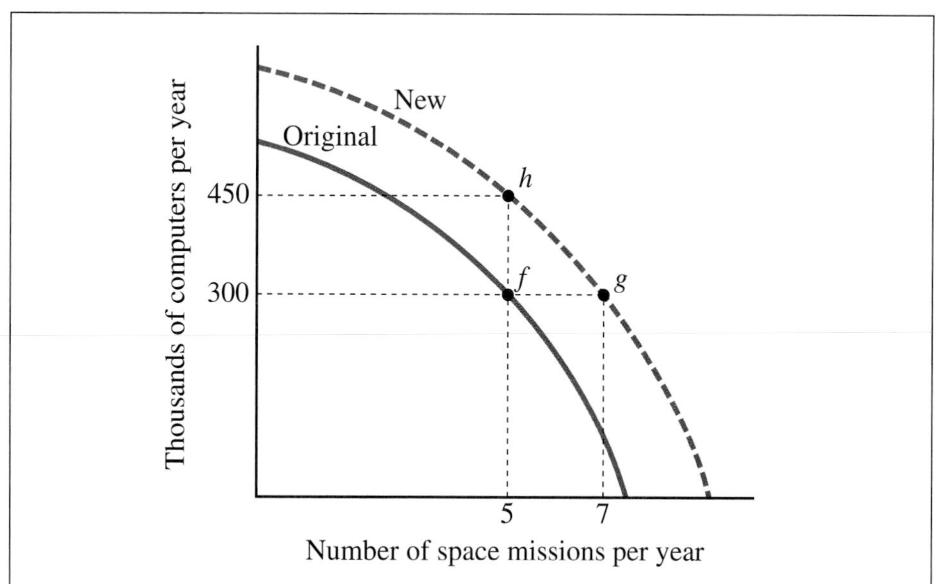

Figure 2

Shifting the Production Possibilities Curve

The production possibilities curve will shift as a result of an increase in the economy's resources or a technological innovation that increases the output from a given amount of resources.

particular product such as a car or a book, while a seller exchanges a product for money. A market provides opportunities for people to trade what they have for what they want. Here are some examples.

- The bicycle market allows bicycle consumers to come together to exchange money and bicycles: The consumer has $200 and wants a bicycle, while the producer has a bicycle and wants money, perhaps to pay its workers or the suppliers of other inputs.
- The labor market allows workers and firms to come together to exchange time and money: The firm has money and wants people to work 8 hours a day, whereas a person has time and wants the income from employment.

Later in the book we explore the role of markets in helping society answer the three basic questions of what to produce, how to produce it, and who gets the goods and services produced. Markets allow these economic decisions to be made through the interactions of millions of people, with each person making his or her own choices without direct supervision from government or a planning agency. These basic questions are not answered by a single person or entity but instead are answered by decisions made in markets. Of course, no economy relies exclusively on markets to make these economic decisions. Later in the book we take a close look at the role of government in a market-based economy.

TEST *Your Understanding*

1 List the three basic questions that we can ask about a society's economy.

2 Which of these three questions does the production possibilities curve help us answer?

PREVIEW OF COMING ATTRACTIONS: MICROECONOMICS

There are two types of economic analysis, microeconomics and macroeconomics. In this course you may study one or both of them.

Microeconomics: The study of the choices made by consumers, firms, and government, and how these decisions affect the market for a particular good or service.

Microeconomics is the study of the choices made by households, firms, and government and how these choices affect the markets for all sorts of goods and services. To understand a particular market outcome, we must explore the decisions made by all persons involved in the market. For example, to understand what's been happening in the corn market, we study the decisions made by consumers, farmworkers, farmers, and governments. For a preview of microeconomics, let's think about three ways we can use microeconomic analysis.

1. To understand how markets work
2. To make personal or managerial decisions
3. To evaluate the merits of public policies

Understand Markets and Predict Changes

One reason for studying microeconomics is to get a better understanding of how markets work. Once you know how markets operate, you can use economic analysis to predict changes in the price of a particular good and changes in the quantity of the good sold. In this book we answer dozens of practical questions about markets and how they operate. Here are some examples:

- How do environmental regulations affect the price of paper?
- Will most video rental stores disappear in the next few years?
- How does gender discrimination affect the wages of men and women?
- How would a ban on shoe imports affect the price of shoes?
- How would a tax on beer affect the number of highway deaths among young adults?

Here is a sneak preview of the answer to the last question. If the government imposes a tax on beer, that will make beer more expensive, and young adults, like other beer consumers, will consume less beer. Alcohol consumption contributes to highway accidents, and the number of highway fatalities among young adults is roughly proportional to the total beer consumption of the group. Therefore, a tax that decreases beer consumption by 10% will decrease highway deaths among young adults by about the same percentage amount.

Make Personal and Managerial Decisions

People use economic analysis to make decisions for themselves and for their employers. On the personal level, we can use economic analysis to answer the following questions:

- Should I contribute money to public radio?
- If my wage increases, should I work more or fewer hours each week?

The manager of a firm makes all sorts of choices for the firm. Here are some managerial questions that could be answered with some simple economic analysis.

- If a firm increases its price, how will its competitors respond?
- If the existing firms in a market are profitable, should your firm enter the market?

Let's take a brief look at the last question. If your firm enters a market, the competition between firms for consumers will heat up, leading to a lower price for the product. In addition, your production cost may be higher than that of the existing firms. It will be sensible to enter the market only if you expect a small drop in price and a small difference in cost. An added risk is that the existing firms may try to protect their market shares by cutting prices and mounting an aggressive advertising campaign. Indeed, entering what appears to be a lucrative market may turn out to be a financial disaster.

Evaluate the Merits of Public Policies

Although modern societies use markets to make most of the decisions concerning production and consumption, the government has several important roles in a market-based society. We can use economic analysis to determine how well the government performs its roles in the market economy. We can also explore the trade-offs associated with various public policies. Here are some of the questions that can be answered with simple economic analysis.

- What causes global warming, and what should the government do about it?
- Should the government prevent the merger of two large firms?
- Should firms be allowed to purchase the right to pollute the air and water?
- Is it sensible for the government to pay part of the cost of your college education?

For a sneak preview of the answer to the last question, think about who benefits from your college education. You get many benefits yourself, including higher lifetime income, more career options, and the thrill of learning. But other people also benefit from your education. In the modern workplace, teamwork is important, and the productivity of a team depends in part on the education level of the team members. A college education is likely to make you a better team worker, allowing your fellow workers to earn more income. In addition, your college education will make you a more intelligent citizen, which means that you'll make better choices on election day. It is sensible for the government to help pay for your college education because taxpayers (your fellow workers and citizens) benefit from your education.

Preview of Coming Attractions: Macroeconomics

Macroeconomics: The study of the nation's economy as a whole.

Macroeconomics is the study of the nation's economy as a whole. In macroeconomics we learn about important topics that are regularly discussed in newspapers and on television, including unemployment, inflation, the budget deficit, and the trade deficit. Macroeconomics explains why economies grow and change, and why economic growth is sometimes interrupted.

In the 1930s, over a quarter of the workers in the United States could not find jobs. Banks were closed, factories shut down, and the economy ground to a halt. In terms of the production possibilities curve described earlier in the chapter, the U.S. economy was inside the production possibilities curve. The economy's resources were not fully employed, leading to inefficiency: In principle, we could have used the economy's resources to produce more goods and services. Economics explains the forces that cause the economy to malfunction and provides insights into how we might try to fix the economy to allow it to grow over time.

People today enjoy a much higher living standard than did their grandparents. We eat better food, live in bigger houses, and travel routinely across the country and around the world. We can consume more of all goods and services because the economy has more of the resources needed to produce these goods and services. The production possibilities curve has shifted outward over time, reflecting increases in the economy's productive resources. Economics explains why some of these productive resources increase over time and how an increase in these resources translates into a higher standard of living. In other words, economics explains why we have a higher living standard than that of our forebears.

For a preview of macroeconomics, let's think about three ways we can use macroeconomic analysis.

1. To understand how a national economy works
2. To understand the grand debates over economic policy
3. To make informed business decisions

The standard of living has increased dramatically in the last several decades: We eat better food and live in better houses.

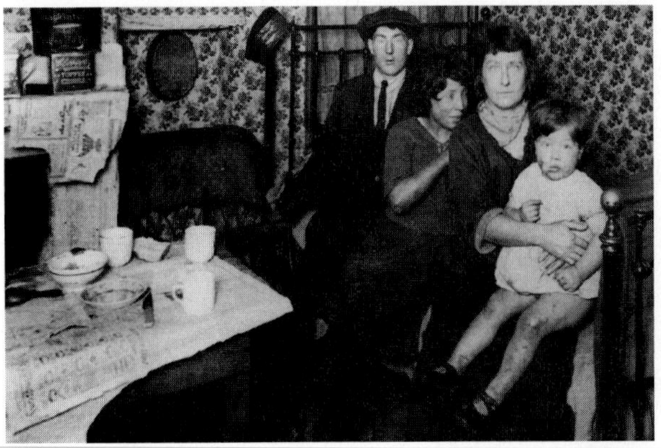

Understand How a National Economy Operates

One of the purposes of studying macroeconomics is to understand how the entire economy works. This book takes some of the mystery out of global economic affairs, answering the following questions:

- Why do the prices of most goods increase over time?
- What causes unemployment?
- Why are interest rates higher in some countries than in others?
- Why does the exchange rate between the United States and Japan—the price at which we exchange U.S. dollars for Japanese yen—change so frequently?
- Which nation has the highest standard of living, and why?
- Why does the United States seem to have a trade deficit (buying more from abroad than we sell) every year?
- Why do some countries grow much faster than others?

Here is a sneak preview of the answer to the last question. There are two main reasons why some countries grow faster than others. First, in some countries, citizens save a large fraction of the money they earn, some of which they invest in business firms, and firms then use the money saved to purchase machines and equipment. An economy with a well-equipped workforce will grow faster than one whose workers are poorly equipped. Second, a country that invents or adopts new technologies at a fast rate will have more productive workers. A country's ability to invent or adopt new technologies is closely related to the education of its workforce.

Understand the Grand Debates over Economic Policy

Macroeconomics is a policy-oriented subject that was developed as a separate subject during the 1930s, when the entire world suffered from massive unemployment. With a knowledge of macroeconomics, you can make sense of the following policy debates:

- Should we have a constitutional amendment to balance the federal budget?
- Should the United States adopt policies to encourage savings, or is it more important to encourage consumption?
- Do we need to take action to decrease our trade deficit? If we do, what type of choices do we really have?
- Should Congress and the President take action to reduce the unemployment rate?

Here is a preview of some of the factors that are relevant to the last question. If unemployment is very high, the Congress and the President may want to take action to reduce it. However, it is important not to reduce the unemployment rate too much, because a relatively low unemployment rate will cause inflation. Moreover, even in the best of circumstances, we can't reduce unemployment overnight. Therefore, it is sensible to take action only if we believe that *inaction* guarantees that a high unemployment rate will persist for a long time. In macroeconomics, we study the trade-offs associated with policies designed to combat unemployment and inflation.

As we can see from this sneak preview, macroeconomics does not give definitive answers to the questions concerning economic policy. There are usually conflicting factors—pros and cons—on each side of the debate. But studying macroeconomics will enable you to understand the positions on each side of the debate and to make up your own mind.

Make Informed Business Decisions

A third reason for studying macroeconomics is to make informed business decisions. A manager who understands how the national economy operates will make better decisions involving macroeconomic variables such as interest rates, exchange rates, the inflation rate, and the unemployment rate. Consider the following examples:

- A manager who intends to borrow money for a new production facility uses her knowledge of macroeconomics to predict the effects of current public policies on interest rates and then decide when to borrow the money.
- Exporting firms keep track of changes in exchange rates and base their marketing decisions on current and projected exchange rates.
- All firms are concerned about inflation because changes in prices affect their profits and influence their decisions about how much to charge for their products and how much to pay their workers and other suppliers.
- Firms are concerned about the unemployment rate because a low unemployment rate means that productive workers will be relatively hard to find and wages are more likely to increase over time.

A manager who studies macroeconomics will be better equipped to understand the complexities of unemployment, interest rates, inflation, and exchange rates. Although managers do not make public-policy decisions, they benefit from an understanding of how macroeconomics affects their business lives.

THE ECONOMIC WAY OF THINKING

We've seen what economics is and how it can be used, so let's take a look at how economists think. Economists have developed a particular approach to thinking about economic phenomena. This economic way of thinking is best summarized by noted economist John Maynard Keynes: *"The Theory of Economics does not furnish a body of settled conclusions immediately applicable to policy. It is a method rather than a doctrine, an apparatus of the mind, a technique of thinking which helps its possessor to draw correct conclusions."*

Let's look at some of the elements of the economic way of thinking.

Use Assumptions to Simplify

Economists use assumptions to make things simpler and to focus our attention on what really matters. Most people use simplifying assumptions in their everyday thinking and decision-making. For example, suppose that you want to travel from Seattle to San Francisco by automobile. If you use a road map to pick a travel route, you are using two assumptions to simplify your decision-making.

1. The earth is flat: The flat road map does not show the curvature of the earth.
2. The highways are flat: The standard road map does not show hills and mountains.

These two assumptions are abstractions from reality, but they are useful because they simplify your decision-making without affecting your choice of a travel route. You could plan your trip with a globe that shows all the topographical features of the alternative travel routes between Seattle and San Francisco, but you would probably pick the same travel route because the curvature of the earth and the topography of the highways are irrelevant for your trip. In this case, the assumptions underlying the standard road map are harmless.

The assumptions underlying the standard road map are not always harmless. Suppose that you've decided to travel by bicycle instead of by automobile, and you'd like to avoid pedaling up mountains. If you use the standard road map and assume that there are no mountains between Seattle and San Francisco, you are likely pick a mountainous route instead of a flat one. In this case, the simplifying assumption makes a difference. The lesson from this example is that we must think carefully about whether an assumption is truly harmless.

In this book we use simplifying assumptions to facilitate the learning process. Most of the assumptions are harmless in the sense that they simplify the analysis by eliminating irrelevant details. Although many of the assumptions are unrealistic, that does not mean that the analysis based on the assumption is incorrect. Just as we can use an unrealistic road map to plan a trip, we can use unrealistic assumptions to answer the sort of questions listed earlier in the chapter. When we use an assumption that actually affects the analysis, we alert you to this fact and explore the implications of alternative assumptions.

Most of the economic analysis in this book is based on two key assumptions, both of which are realistic in most circumstances. The first assumption is that all people act in their own self-interest, without considering the effects of their actions on other people. For example, we assume that a pizza consumer doesn't care about other people who might want to buy the pizza but only about his or her own welfare. Similarly, we assume that a pizzeria owner doesn't care about how his or her decisions affect other people but only about his or her own profit. There is solid evidence that most people act in their own self-interest in most situations, so the economic analysis in this book is relevant for a wide range of decisions. For the classic statement about self-interest, read the Closer Look box "Adam Smith on Self-Interest."

The second key assumption in economics is that people make informed decisions. For example, we assume that a consumer who is deciding what to eat for lunch knows the price of pizza and the price of tofu sandwiches and also the relevant characteristics of the two foods (taste, amount of fat, number of calories). Armed with this information, the consumer can make an informed decision about what to eat. Similarly, the manager of a pizzeria knows the cost of producing pizza. Armed with this information, the owner can make an informed decision about how many pizzas to produce and what price to charge. In most cases, consumers and producers

A Closer LOOK

Adam Smith on Self-Interest

The writings of Adam Smith (1723–1790) provide a foundation for modern economic analysis. His masterpiece, *An Inquiry into the Nature and Causes of the Wealth of Nations,* is perhaps the most famous and important economics book of all time. The book contains many insights that guide modern economic analysis, including the following gem about self-interest: "It is not from the benevolence of the butcher, the brewer, or the baker that we expect our dinner, but from their regard to their own interest. We address ourselves, not to their humanity but to their self-love, and never talk to them of our own necessities but of their advantages."

Source: Adam Smith, *Wealth of Nations* (New York: Modern Library, 1994).

A Closer LOOK

Warning Labels

Here are some warning labels from various consumer products.

- **Television set:** DO NOT POUR LIQUIDS DOWN THE BACK OF THE TELEVISION.
- **Can of tomato sauce:** TO OPEN, USE CAN OPENER.
- **Box of Pop Tarts:** PASTRY FILLING MAY BE HOT WHEN HEATED.
- **Automobile fan belt:** DO NOT CHANGE FAN BELT WHILE ENGINE IS RUNNING.
- **On the pull-top lid of a can of liquid radiator sealant:** DO NOT LICK LID.

Source: After Margie Boulé, "Holiday Reading Reveals: We're Just as Dumb as Ever," *The Oregonian*, December 1, 1992, p. B01.

---

have enough information to make informed decisions. As we'll see later in the book, there are cases in which buyers have less information than sellers (used cars and baseball pitchers), and other cases in which sellers have less information than buyers (medical insurance).

Much of the information about products comes from producers, who provide instructions on how to use their products and warnings about the dangers associated with inappropriate uses. The government also plays a role in providing information, either disseminating information itself or forcing producers to provide additional information. Some examples are information about the fuel efficiency of cars, the nutritional-content labels on food, and warning labels for drugs. As shown in the Closer Look box "Warning Labels," some producers are very thorough in their instructions to consumers.

Explore the Relationship between Two Variables

Variable: A measure of something that can take on different values.

Economists often explore the relationship between two variables. A **variable** is a measure of something that can take on different values. For example, consider a student who has a part-time job and also receives a fixed weekly allowance from her parents. The value of one variable (weekly income) is determined by the values of the other variables—the number of hours worked, the hourly wage, and the allowance. To explore the relationship between any two variables, such as work time and weekly income, we assume that the other variables (wage and allowance) do not change. For example, the student might say: "If I work one more hour this week, my income will increase by $4." In making this statement, the student is exploring the relationship between two variables (work time and income), assuming that the other two variables (wage and allowance) do not change. A complete statement is: "If I work one more hour this week, my income will increase by $4, *assuming that my wage and my allowance do not change.*"

This book contains many statements about the relationship between two variables. For example, the number of pizzas consumed by a particular person depends on the price of pizza, the price of burgers, and the person's income. Suppose that you read the following statement: "A decrease in the price of pizzas increases the quantity of pizzas consumed." In making this statement, we are exploring the relationship between two variables (the price of pizzas and the quantity of pizzas), implicitly assuming that the other two variables (the price of burgers and the person's income) do not change. Sometimes we will make this assumption explicit by adding a warning label: "A decrease in the price of pizzas increases the quantity of pizzas consumed, **ceteris paribus**." The Latin words mean "other things being equal to what they were before" or "other variables being fixed." From now on, whenever we refer to a relationship between two variables, we assume that the other relevant variables are held fixed.

Ceteris paribus: Latin for "other variables are held fixed."

Think Marginal

Economists explore the effects of small changes in the relevant variables. They often think about *marginal* or incremental changes, posing the following question: "If we increase the value of one variable *by one unit*, by how much will the value of the other variable change?" The key feature of this marginal question is that the value of one variable increases by a single unit. For the student discussing her income, the marginal question is: "If I work *one more hour* per week, by how much will my income increase?" Marginal analysis provides information that can be used to make decisions. For example, the answer to the student's question would help her make an informed decision about how many hours to work.

You will encounter marginal thinking throughout this book. Here are some other examples of marginal questions.

- If I study one more hour for my midterm, by how many points will my grade increase?
- If I spend one more year in school, by how much will my lifetime income increase?
- If I buy one more CD, how many tapes will I sacrifice?
- If a landscaper installs one more sprinkler system, by how much will his or her labor costs increase?
- If a table producer hires one more carpenter, how many more tables will be produced?

As we'll see later in the book, answering a marginal question is the first step in deciding whether or not to pursue a particular activity.

TEST *Your Understanding*

3 Two simplifying assumptions are used extensively in economics. What are they?

4 Suppose that your grade on an economics exam is affected by the number of lectures you attend. What is the marginal question about this relationship?

SUMMARY

In this chapter we've learned what economics is and why it's useful. As you move through the book, you'll see that economics is all about choices made by individuals, organizations, governments, and society as a whole. We can use economic analysis to understand how these choices affect the world around us. We can also use economics to make our own choices as consumers, workers, managers, and voters. Here are the main points of the chapter.

1. The production possibilities curve shows the combinations of goods and services available to an economy and illustrates the notion of scarcity: the production of one product comes at the expense of another. The curve will shift outward as a result of

an increase in the economy's productive resources or an improvement in technology.

2. We use microeconomics to understand how markets work, predict changes in prices and quantities, make personal or managerial decisions, and evaluate the merits of public policies.
3. Macroeconomics explains how an economy works and helps us understand the grand debates over economic policy.
4. To think like an economist, we (a) use assumptions to simplify matters; (b) explore the relationship between two variables, holding other variables fixed; and (c) think in marginal terms.
5. Two assumptions are used extensively in economics: people act in their own self-interest, and people make informed choices.

KEY TERMS

ceteris paribus, *13*
economics, *2*
entrepreneurship, *4*
factors of production, *3*
human capital, *3*
labor, *3*
macroeconomics, *8*
market, *5*
microeconomics, *6*
natural resources, *3*
physical capital, *3*
production possibilities curve, *4*
scarcity, *2*
variable, *12*

PROBLEMS AND DISCUSSION QUESTIONS

1. For some goods and services, the assumption that people have enough information to make informed choices is unrealistic. Provide a brief list of some of these goods and services.
2. For some decisions, you act altruistically rather than acting in your own self-interest. Provide a brief list of such decisions.
3. List the variables that are held fixed to make the following statement: "If I study one more hour for my economics exam, I expect my grade to increase by 3 points."
4. It's your first day on your job in the advertising department of a baseball team. Your boss wants to know whether it is sensible to run one more television advertisement encouraging people to attend an upcoming game. List the relevant marginal questions.
5. Complete the statement: As we switch resources from the production of one good to another, we ____________ the production possibilities curve; as we add resources to an economy, we ____________ the curve.

Take It to the Net

We invite you to visit the O'Sullivan/Sheffrin page on the Prentice Hall Web site at:

http://www.prenhall.com/osullivan/

for this chapter's World Wide Web exercise.

MODEL ANSWERS FOR THIS CHAPTER

Test Your Understanding

1. What goods and services do we produce? How do we produce the chosen goods and services? Who consumes the goods and services that we produce?
2. The production possibilities curve shows the combinations of goods that are available to the economy, so it helps us answer the first question.
3. People act in their own self-interest; people make informed decisions.
4. "If I attend one more lecture, by how much will my exam grade increase?"

Appendix
Using Graphs and Formulas

Using Graphs to Show Relationships
Drawing a Graph
Computing the Slope
Shifting a Curve
Negative and Nonlinear Relationships

Using Formulas to Compute Values
Computing Percentage Changes
Using Formulas to Compute Missing Values

In this appendix we review the mechanics of simple graphs and formulas. You'll recognize most of this material because it is covered in high-school mathematics. It will be useful to review it before you begin your own economic analysis.

USING GRAPHS TO SHOW RELATIONSHIPS

A graph is a visual representation of the relationship between two variables. A **variable** is a measure of something that can take on different values. For example, suppose that you have a part-time job and you are interested in the relationship between the number of hours you work and your weekly income. In this case the relevant variables are work time (hours per week) and weekly income.

Variable: A measure of something that can take on different values.

We can use a table of numbers such as Table A-1 to show the relationship between work time and income. Let's assume that your weekly allowance from your parents is $20 and your part-time job pays $4 per hour. For example, if you work 10 hours per week, your weekly income is $60 ($20 from your parents and $40 from your job). The more you work, the higher your weekly income: If you work 22 hours, your income is $108; if you work 30 hours, your income is $140.

Drawing a Graph

A graph makes it easier to see the relationship between work time and income. To draw a graph, we perform seven simple steps.

1. Draw a horizontal line to represent the first variable. In Figure A-1 on page 16 we measure work time along the horizontal axis (also known as the *x* axis). As we move to the right along the axis, the number of hours worked increases, from zero to 30 hours. The numbers along the horizontal line are spaced equally to preserve the scale of the line.
2. Draw a vertical line intersecting the first line to represent the second variable. In Figure A-1 we measure income along the vertical axis (also known as the *y* axis). As we move up along the axis, income increases from zero to $140.

Table A-1: **Relationship between Work Time and Income**

Work hours per week	0	10	22	30
Income per week	$20	$60	$108	$140

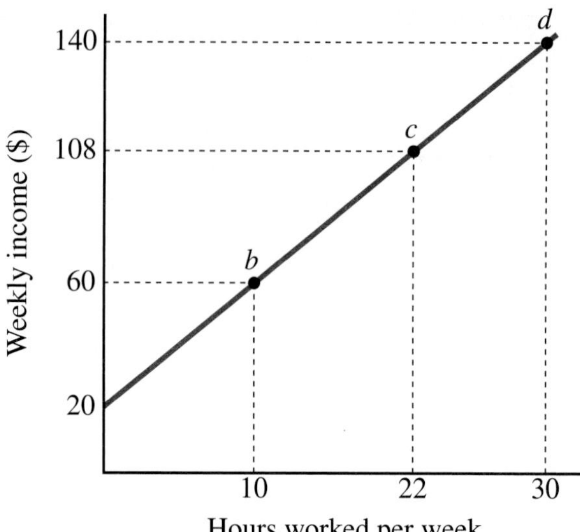

Figure A-1

Relationship between Hours Worked and Total Income

There is a positive relationship between the amount of work time and income. The slope of the curve is 4: Each additional hour of work increases income by $4.

3. Pick a combination of work time and income from the table of numbers. From the second column, for instance, work time is 10 hours and income is $60.
4. Find the point on the horizontal axis with the chosen number of work hours (for this example, 10 hours) and draw a dashed line straight up from that point.
5. Find the point on the vertical axis with the chosen income ($60) and draw a dashed line straight to the right from that point.
6. The meeting place of the dashed lines shows one combination of work hours and income. For example, point *b* shows the combination of 10 work hours and $60 income.
7. Repeat steps 3 through 6 for different combinations of work time and income from the table of numbers. Once you have a series of points on the graph (*b*, *c*, and *d*), you can connect them to draw a curve. This curve shows the relationship between work hours and income.

Positive relationship: A relationship in which an increase in the value of one variable increases the value of the other variable.

Negative relationship: A relationship in which an increase in the value of one variable decreases the value of the other variable.

There is a **positive relationship** between two variables if an increase in the value of one variable increases the value of the other variable. An increase in work time increases your income, so there is a positive relationship between the two variables. As you increase your work time, you move upward along the curve shown in Figure A-1 to higher income levels. In contrast, there is a **negative relationship** between two variables if an increase in the value of one variable *decreases* the value of the other variable. Some people refer to a positive relationship as a *direct relationship* and to a negative relationship as an *inverse relationship*.

Computing the Slope

Slope: The change in the variable on the vertical axis resulting from a one-unit increase in the variable on the horizontal axis.

How sensitive is one variable to changes in the other variable? We can use the slope of the curve to measure this sensitivity. The **slope** of a curve is defined as the change in the variable on the vertical axis resulting from a 1-unit increase in the variable on the horizontal axis. Once we pick two points on a curve, we can compute the slope as follows:

$$\text{slope} = \frac{\text{vertical difference between two points}}{\text{horizontal difference between two points}}$$

To compute the slope of a curve, we take four steps.

1. Pick two points on the curve: for example, b and c in Figure A-1.
2. Compute the vertical distance between the two points (also known as the *rise*). For points b and c, the vertical distance is 48 (108 – 60).
3. Compute the horizontal distance between the same two points (also known as the *run*). For points b and c, the horizontal distance is 12 hours (22 – 10).
4. Divide the vertical distance by the horizontal distance to get the slope. For points b and c, the slope is 4:

$$\text{slope} = \frac{\text{vertical difference}}{\text{horizontal difference}} = \frac{48}{12} = 4$$

In this case a 12-hour increase in work time increases income by $48, so the increase in income per hour of work is $4. This of course is the hourly wage.

Because the curve is a straight line, the slope is the same at all points along the curve. You can check this yourself by using points c and d.

Shifting a Curve

Up to this point we've explored the effect of change in variables that cause movement along a given curve. In Figure A-1 we see the relationship between a student's hours of work (on the horizontal axis) and her income (on the vertical axis). The student's income also depends on her allowance and her wage, so we can make two observations about the curve in Figure A-1.

1. To draw this curve, we must specify the weekly allowance ($20) and the hourly wage ($4).
2. The curve shows that an increase in work time increases the student's income, assuming that her allowance and her wage are fixed.

A change in the student's allowance will shift the curve showing the relationship between work time and income. In Figure A-2, when the allowance increases from $20 to $35, the curve shifts upward by $15. For a given work time, the student's income increases by $15. Now the income associated with 10 hours of work is $75 (point z), compared to $60 with 10 hours of work and the original allowance (point b). In general, an increase in the allowance shifts the curve upward and leftward: For a given amount of work time, the student will have more income (an upward shift); to reach a given amount of income, the student needs fewer hours of work (a leftward shift).

This book uses dozens of two-dimensional curves, each of which shows the relationship between only two variables. That is all a single curve can show. A common error is to forget that a single curve tells only part of the story. In Figure A-2 on page 18 we needed two curves to show what happened when we looked at three variables (work time, allowance, and income). Here are some simple rules that will help avoid this error.

1. A change in one of the variables shown on the graph causes movement along the curve. In Figure A-2, an increase in work time causes movement along the curve from point b to point c.
2. A change in one of the variables that is not shown on the graph (one of the variables held fixed in drawing the curve) shifts the entire curve. In Figure A-2, an increase in the allowance causes the entire curve to shift upward.

Negative and Nonlinear Relationships

We can also use a graph to show a negative relationship between two variables. Consider a consumer who has a monthly budget of $150 and buys CDs at a price of

Figure A-2

Shifting the Curve

We assume that the weekly allowance ($20) and the wage ($4) are fixed. An increase in the fixed weekly allowance from $20 to $35 shifts the curve upward by $15: For each work time, income is $15 higher.

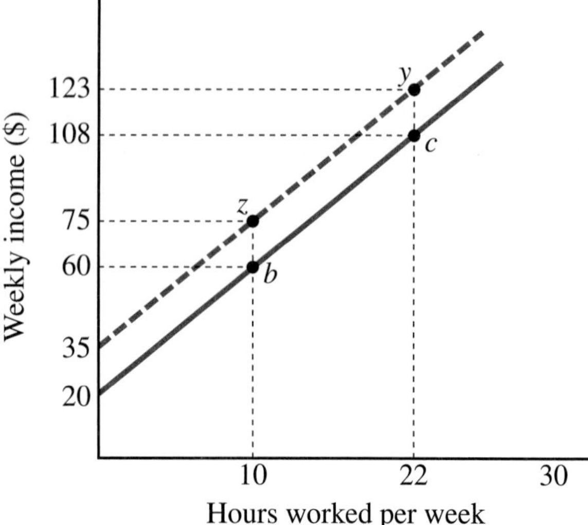

$10 per CD. Table A-2 shows the relationship between the number of CDs purchased and the amount of money left over for other goods. For example, if the consumer buys 5 CDs in a certain month, he or she will spend a total of $50 on CDs, leaving only $100 to spend on other goods. As the number of CDs increases, the leftover money decreases, from $100 for 5 CDs, to $50 for 10 CDs, to $0 for 15 CDs. Using the seven-step process outlined earlier, we can use the numbers in Table A-2 to draw a curve showing this negative relationship. In Figure A-3 the curve is negatively sloped: The more the consumer spends on CDs, the less money is left for other goods. We can use points *e* and *f* to compute the slope of the curve. The slope is –10: A 5-unit increase in CDs (the horizontal difference or the run) decreases the amount of money left over by $50 (the vertical difference or the rise):

$$\text{slope} = \frac{\text{vertical difference}}{\text{horizontal difference}} = \frac{-50}{5} = -10$$

The curve is a straight line with a constant slope of –10.

We can also use a graph to show a nonlinear relationship between two variables. Figure A-4 shows the relationship between study time and the grade on an exam. Although the exam grade increases as study time increases, the grade increases at a decreasing rate. For example, the second hour of study increases the grade by 4 points (from 6 points to 10 points), but the ninth hour of study increases the grade by only 1 point (from 24 points to 25 points). This is a *nonlinear* relationship, in that the slope of the curve changes as we move along the curve. In Figure A-4 the slope decreases as we move to the right along the curve: The slope is 4 between points *g* and *h*, but only 1 between points *i* and *j*. Another possibility for a nonlinear curve is that the slope increases (the curve becomes steeper) as we move to the right along the curve.

Table A-2: **Relationship between CD Purchases and Leftover Money**

Number of CDs purchased	0	5	10	15
Leftover income	$150	$100	$50	$0

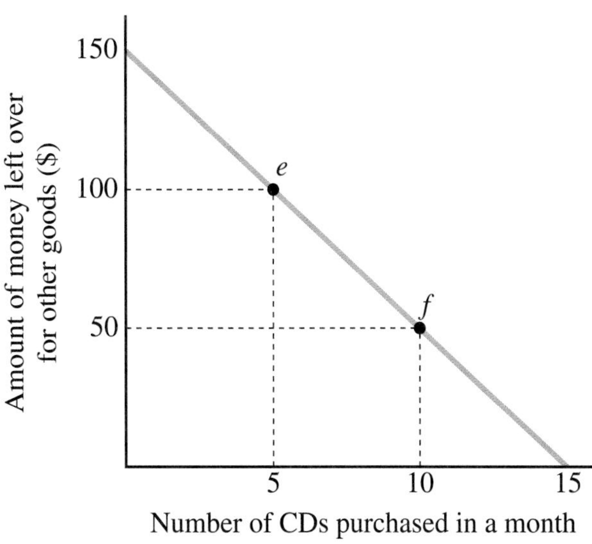

Figure A-3

Negative Relationship between CD Purchases and Leftover Money

There is a negative relationship between the number of CDs purchased and the amount of money left over for other goods. Because the price of CDs is $10, the slope of the curve is −10.

USING FORMULAS TO COMPUTE VALUES

Economists often use formulas to compute the values of the relevant variables. Here is a brief review of the mechanics of formulas.

Computing Percentage Changes

In many cases the formulas used by economists involve percentage changes. In this book we use the simple approach to computing percentage changes: We divide the absolute change in the variable by the *initial* value of the variable and then multiply by 100. For example, if the price of pizzas increases from $20 to $22, the percentage

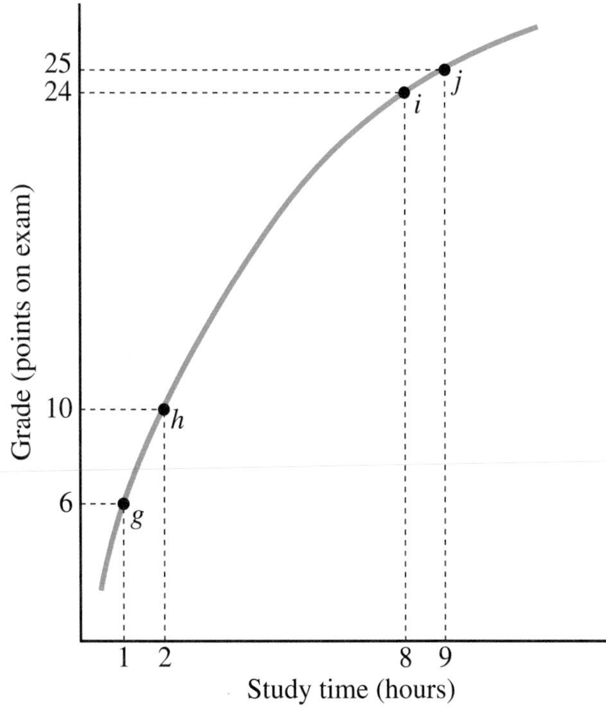

Figure A-4

Nonlinear Relationship between Study Time and Exam Grade

There is a positive and nonlinear relationship between study time and the grade on an exam. As study time increases, the exam grade increases at a decreasing rate. The second hour of study increases the grade by 4 points (from 6 to 10), but the ninth hour of study increases the grade by only 1 point.

change is 10%: The absolute change ($2) divided by the initial value ($20) is 0.10; multiplying this number by 100 generates a percentage change of 10%:

$$\text{percentage change} = \frac{\text{absolute change}}{\text{initial value}} = \frac{2}{20} = 0.10 = 10\%$$

Going the other direction, if the price decreases from $20 to $19, the percentage change is –5%: the absolute change (–$1) divided by the initial value ($20).

The alternative to the simple approach is the midpoint approach, under which the percentage change equals the absolute change in the variable divided by the *average* value or the midpoint of the variable. For example, if the price of pizza increases from $20 to $22, the computed percentage change under the midpoint approach would be 9.52381%:

$$\text{percentage change} = \frac{\text{absolute change}}{\text{average value}} = \frac{2}{(20 + 22)/2} = \frac{2}{21} = 0.0952381 = 9.52381\%$$

If the change in the variable is relatively small, the extra precision associated with the midpoint approach is usually not worth the extra effort. The simple approach allows us to spend less time doing tedious arithmetic and more time doing economic analysis. In this book we use the simple approach to compute percentage changes: If the price increases from $20 to $22, the price has increased by 10%.

What about translating percentage changes into absolute changes? We can simply add to or subtract from the initial number. For example, if we start with a price of $20 and the price increases by 10%, we add 10% of the initial price ($2 is 10% of 20) to the initial price ($20), for a new price of $22. If the price decreases by 5%, we subtract 5% of the initial price ($1 is 5% of $20) from the initial price ($20), for a new price of $19. In most of the book we keep the numerical examples simple enough that we can do the percentage changes in our heads.

Using Formulas to Compute Missing Values

It will often be useful to compute the value of the numerator (the top half of a fraction) of a particular formula. To do so, we must have values for the other two parts of the formula. For example, consider the relationship between work time and income. Suppose that the slope of the curve showing this relationship is 4. If you decide to work 7 more hours per week, how much more income will you earn? In this case we can compute the change in income by looking at the formula for the slope of the curve:

$$\text{slope} = \frac{\text{difference in income}}{\text{difference in work time}}$$

$$4 = \frac{\text{difference in income}}{7}$$

Because we know two of the three parts of the slope formula (slope = 4 and the difference in work time is 7 hours), we can figure out the third part (the difference in income) by plugging in different numbers for the numerator until we find the value that satisfies the formula. In this case the answer is $28: Plugging $28 into the numerator, the difference in income is four times the difference in work time, which is consistent with a slope of 4.

There is a more direct approach to computing the value of the numerator or denominator of a formula. We can rearrange the three parts of the formula to put the missing variable on the left side. For example, to compute the difference in income resulting from a change in work time, we can rearrange the slope formula as follows:

difference in income = slope × (difference in work time)

Plugging in the slope (4) and the difference in work time (7 hours), the change in income is $28 ($4 times 7 hours). We can use the same process to compute the value of the denominator, given values for the two other variables.

KEY TERMS

negative relationship, *16*
positive relationship, *16*
slope, *16*
variable, *15*

PROBLEMS AND DISCUSSION QUESTIONS

1. Suppose you belong to a tennis club that has a monthly fee of $100 and a charge of $5 per hour of tennis.
   a. Use a curve to show the relationship between the monthly bill from the club and the hours of tennis played.
   b. What is the slope of the curve?
   c. If you increase your monthly tennis time by 3 hours, by how much will your monthly bill increase?
2. Suppose that Terry uses three ingredients to make pizza: tomato sauce, dough, and cheese. Terry initially uses 100 gallons of tomato sauce per day and the cost of other ingredients (dough, cheese) is $500 per day.
   a. Draw a curve to show the relationship between the price of tomato sauce and the daily cost of producing pizza (for prices between $1 and $5).
   b. To draw the curve, what variables are assumed to be fixed?
   c. What sort of changes would cause the pizzeria to move upward along the curve?
   d. What is the slope of the curve?
   e. What sort of changes would cause the entire curve to shift upward?
3. Compute the percentage changes for the following changes:

Initial Value	*New Value*	*Percentage Change*
10	11	________
100	98	________
50	53	________

4. Suppose that your favorite store decreases the price of jeans by 15%. If the original price was $20, what is the new price?
5. Suppose that the slope of a curve showing the relationship between the number of burglaries per month (on the vertical axis) and the number of police officers (on the horizontal axis) is –½ or –0.50. Use the slope formula to compute the change in the number of burglaries resulting from hiring 8 additional police officers.
6. Complete the statement: A change in one of the variables shown on a graph causes movement ____________ a curve, while a change in one of the variables that is not shown on the graph ____________ the curve.

CHAPTER

2

Key Principles of Economics

Emma owned some stock in Marginal Airlines, and she flew with the airline whenever she had a chance. You can imagine her dismay when she boarded a plane and saw just 30 passengers in the 120-seat airplane. How could the airline make a profit with so few passengers? She wrote a letter to the president of the airline demanding an explanation. Did the person who scheduled the flight make a mistake, or was the airline deliberately trying to lose money?

As we'll see later in the chapter, it was sensible to run the flight because the extra revenue from the flight exceeded the extra cost. This is the *marginal principle*—one of the five key principles of economics—in action.

In this chapter we discuss five principles that provide a foundation for economic analysis. A **principle** is a simple, self-evident truth that most people readily understand and accept. These principles provide a useful starting point for a discussion of the tools of economic analysis. Just as a carpenter uses hammers and saws to make furniture, an economist uses a set of tools—including supply and demand curves—to do economic analysis. Starting in Chapter 3, we use the five principles to explain how these tools work and show how you can use them yourself. As you go through the book, you will see these principles again and again as you add tools to your economics toolbox and learn how to do your own economic analysis.

Principle: A simple truth that most people understand and accept.

In addition to providing a foundation for economic analysis, the five principles are useful in their own right. Here are some of the practical questions we answer:

1. What is the cost of producing military goods such as bombs and warships?
2. If a student group offers to pay $500 to use a college auditorium for an evening, should the college accept the offer?
3. As a firm hires more workers, what happens to the total output of its factory?
4. If a paper producer dumps chemical waste into a river, what is the true cost of paper?
5. Suppose that your wage doubles and that the prices of consumer goods double, too. Are you better off, worse off, or about the same?

THE PRINCIPLE OF OPPORTUNITY COST

The principle of opportunity cost incorporates the notion that no matter what we do, there is always a trade-off. We must trade off one thing for another because resources are limited and can be used in different ways: By acquiring something, we use up resources that could have been used to acquire something else. The notion of opportunity cost allows us to measure this trade-off.

PRINCIPLE *of Opportunity Cost*

The opportunity cost of something is what you sacrifice to get it.

In most cases the resources used to get something could have been used to get one of several alternatives. For example, if you spend an hour studying for an economics exam, you have one less hour in which to pursue various other activities. To determine the opportunity cost of something, we look at the *best* of these alternatives. For example, two of the alternatives to studying economics are playing video games and studying for a history exam. If in your mind the better alternative is to study for the history exam, we express the opportunity cost of studying economics in terms of what you sacrifice by not studying history. We ignore the video game because that's not the best alternative use of your time.

What is the opportunity cost of an hour spent studying for an economics exam? Suppose that an hour of studying history—instead of economics—would increase your grade on a history exam by 4 points. In this case the opportunity cost of studying economics is 4 points on the history exam. If the best alternative to studying economics had been to play video games, the opportunity cost would have been the pleasure you could have experienced from an hour in the video arcade. As shown in the Closer Look box "Opportunity Cost of a College Degree" on page 24 we can use the principle of opportunity cost to determine the actual cost of attending college.

The principle of opportunity cost is also applicable to decisions about how to spend a fixed money budget. For example, suppose that you have a fixed budget to spend on cookies and donuts and that a donut costs twice as much as a cookie. If you consume an additional donut, you must consume two fewer cookies: The opportunity cost of a donut is two cookies. A law firm with a fixed salary budget can increase the number of lawyers only at the expense of paralegals. If a lawyer costs three times as much as a paralegal, the opportunity cost of a lawyer is three paralegals.

Opportunity Cost and Production Possibilities

The production possibilities curve illustrates the principle of opportunity cost for an entire economy. From Chapter 1 we know that this curve shows all the possible combinations of goods and services available to an economy, assuming that all its

A Closer LOOK

Opportunity Cost of a College Degree

What is the opportunity cost of a college degree? Consider a student who spends four years in college, paying $10,000 per year for tuition and books. Part of the opportunity cost of college is the $40,000 worth of other goods that the student must sacrifice to pay for tuition and books. If instead of going to college, the student could have worked as a bank clerk for $20,000 per year, the opportunity cost of the time spent in college is $80,000. As shown below, the total opportunity cost of the student's degree is $120,000.

Tuition and books ($10,000 per year)	$ 40,000
Opportunity cost of college time (4 years at $20,000 per year)	80,000
Total opportunity cost	$120,000

You'll notice that we haven't included the costs of food or housing in our computations of opportunity cost. You'll have to eat something and live somewhere even if you don't go to college, so going to college doesn't necessarily affect your food and housing expenses. If housing or food is more expensive in college, however, we would incorporate these extra costs into our calculations of opportunity cost. We've simplified the calculations by just adding costs that are incurred at different times. Later in the book we discuss an alternative method for computing the total cost of a stream of costs.

What are the implications for your decision to attend college? As we'll see later, a college degree increases your earning power, so there are also benefits from a college degree. To make an informed decision about whether to attend college, you must compare the benefits to the opportunity costs.

The cost of a college degree includes the opportunity cost of time spent in college.

productive resources are fully employed. In Figure 1 each point on the production possibilities curve shows a feasible combination of computers and space missions. For example, one option is point *b*, with 530,000 computers and 1 space mission.

The principle of opportunity cost explains why the production possibilities curve is negatively sloped. At a given time, an economy has fixed amounts of productive resources, so the production of one product comes at the expense of another. If we start at point *b* and increase the number of space missions by one, we'll move to point *c*, with 30,000 fewer computers. So the opportunity cost of the extra space mission is the 30,000 computers that we sacrifice to get it.

Why does the production possibilities curve become steeper as we move downward along the curve? The production possibilities curve is bowed outward because the resources used to produce the two goods are not perfectly adaptable: Some resources are more suitable for the production of computers, whereas others are more suitable for space missions. As we produce more and more space missions, we are forced to switch to space missions some resources that are very well suited to producing computers but not very well suited to producing space missions. As a result, the opportunity cost of space missions increases: We sacrifice progressively more computers for each additional space mission. Notice that the opportunity cost is 30,000 computers for the second space mission (point *b* versus point *c*), but 80,000 computers for the fifth mission (point *e* versus point *f*).

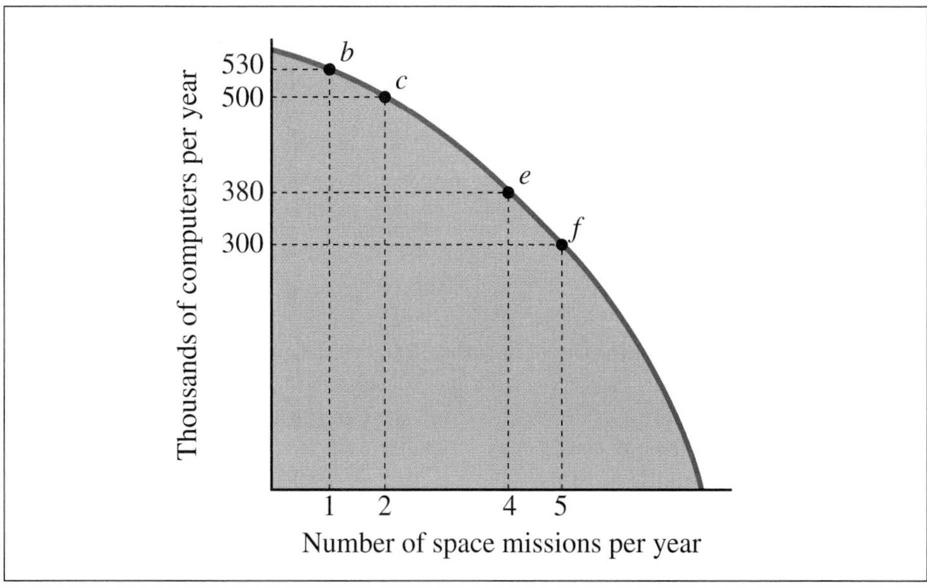

Figure 1

Production Possibilities Curve

The production possibilities curve (or frontier) is negatively sloped because a society has fixed amounts of its productive resources, and bowed outward because resources are not perfectly adaptable.

Using the Principle: Opportunity Cost of Military Spending

We can use the principle of opportunity cost to explore the cost of military spending. Malaysia bought two warships in 1992, paying a price equal to the cost of providing safe drinking water for the 5 million Malaysians lacking it.[1] In other words, the opportunity cost of the warships was safe drinking water for 5 million people. When the Soviet Union fell apart and military tensions around the world diminished, citizens in the United States and Western Europe called for massive cuts in defense spending, with the idea of spending the "peace dividend" on social programs. The French cut their annual defense budget by billions of dollars and withdrew 50,000 troops stationed on German soil.[2] In the United States, the number of people

For many developing countries, the opportunity cost of military spending is safe drinking water.

employed by the military has decreased dramatically, and the Pentagon developed a new program, "Troops to Teachers," to help former soldiers get jobs teaching in local schools.[3] The switch from army duty to teaching reminds us that the opportunity cost of a soldier may be a teacher.

THE MARGINAL PRINCIPLE

The marginal principle provides a simple decision-making rule for individuals, firms, and governments. As we saw in Chapter 1, economists think in marginal terms, considering the effect of a 1-unit change in one variable on the value of another variable. A synonym for *marginal* is *incremental,* indicating that we're considering a small increase (or an increment) in a particular variable. The marginal principle allows us to fine-tune our decisions: We can use it to determine whether a 1-unit increase in a variable would make us better off. For example, a barber could decide whether to keep his or her shop open for one additional hour.

Marginal PRINCIPLE

Increase the level of an activity if its marginal benefit exceeds its marginal cost, but reduce the level if the marginal cost exceeds the marginal benefit. If possible, pick the level at which the marginal benefit equals the marginal cost.

Marginal benefit: The extra benefit resulting from a small increase in some activity.

Marginal cost: The additional cost resulting from a small increase in some activity.

The marginal principle is based on a comparison of the marginal benefits and marginal costs of a particular activity. The **marginal benefit** of some activity is the extra benefit resulting from a small increase in the activity, for example, the revenue generated by keeping your barbershop open for one more hour. Similarly, the **marginal cost** is the additional cost resulting from a small increase in the activity, for example, the additional costs incurred by keeping a shop open for one more hour. According to the marginal principle, if the marginal benefit of some activity exceeds the marginal cost, you will be better off if you do more of the activity. You should continue to increase the activity until the marginal benefit equals the marginal cost. In other words, you should continue to fine-tune your decision as long as a change would make you better off. It's worth emphasizing that the marginal principle is based on *marginal* benefits and costs, not *total* benefits and costs.

Consider a problem facing Edward Scissorhands the barber. Suppose that on a particular day, Edward must decide whether to keep his shop open for an extra hour, for 4 hours instead of 3. To use the marginal principle, Edward must compare the marginal benefit of staying open to the marginal cost: If the marginal benefit exceeds the marginal cost, he will be better off if he stays open for the extra hour.

1. The marginal benefit of remaining open is the revenue generated during the extra (fourth) hour. For example, if Edward charges $8 for a haircut and expects to give 5 haircuts during the fourth hour, the marginal benefit of remaining open is $40.
2. The marginal cost of remaining open is the extra cost incurred during the fourth hour, including the cost of electricity to power and light the shop and the opportunity cost of Edward's time. If Edward could earn $20 per hour trimming hedges or mowing lawns, the opportunity cost of his time is $20. If the cost of electricity is $4 per hour, the extra cost for the fourth hour (the marginal cost of remaining open) is $24 ($20 + $4).

Because the marginal benefit ($40 in haircut revenue) exceeds the marginal cost ($24), it would be sensible for Edward to remain open for the extra hour.

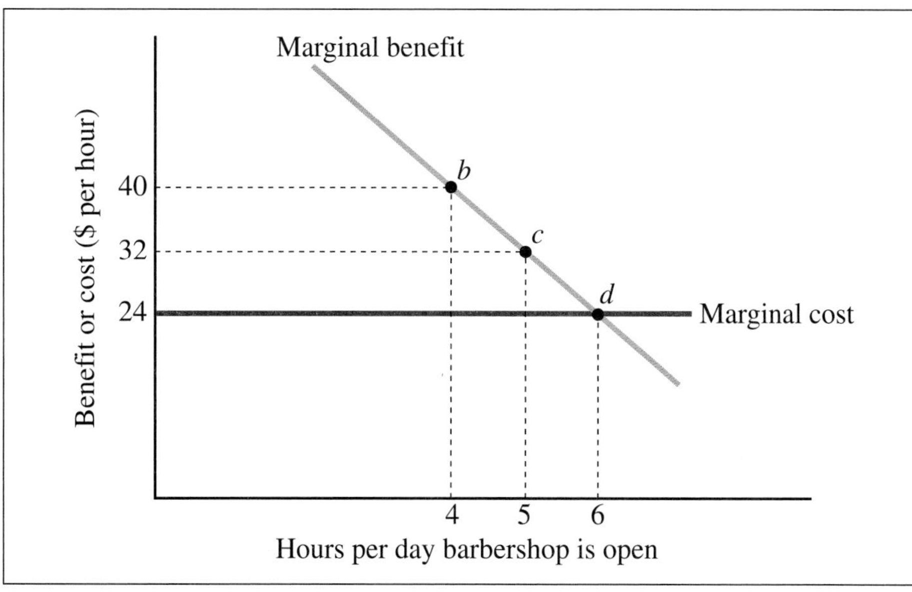

Figure 2

Marginal Principle and the Barbershop

The marginal principle suggests that Edward should operate his barbershop 6 hours per day: The marginal benefit equals the marginal cost at 6 hours per day.

The marginal principle suggests that Edward should increase his hours of operation until the marginal benefit equals the marginal cost. In Figure 2 the marginal-benefit curve is negatively sloped because Edward cuts progressively fewer heads of hair per hour (4 heads, for a total of $32, during the fifth hour; 3 heads, for a total of $24, during the sixth hour; and so on). The marginal benefit equals the marginal cost at 6 hours, so it would be sensible to remain open for 6 hours (shown by point *d*).

To use the marginal principle properly, Edward must measure his costs carefully. It is worth noting two important ideas about costs.

Fixed costs: Costs that do not change as the level of an activity changes.

Variable costs: Costs that change as the level of an activity changes.

1. Edward ignores **fixed costs**, defined as costs that do not change as the level of an activity changes. For Edward, the fixed costs are the costs that do not change when he remains open for a longer time. Edward ignores the monthly rent on his barbershop because the rent is fixed: It does not change if he keeps the shop open 4 hours instead of 3 hours. A common error in economic analysis is to include fixed costs in the calculation of marginal cost. In contrast, **variable costs** are the costs that change as the level of an activity changes, for example, the opportunity cost of Edward's time and the cost of electricity.

Explicit costs: Costs in the form of actual cash payments.

Implicit costs: The opportunity cost of nonpurchased inputs.

Economic cost: The sum of explicit and implicit costs.

2. Edward includes all the opportunity costs. Although Edward does not pay himself an hourly wage, he does incur a cost because instead of cutting hair, he could be doing something else. A common error in cost computations is to include only **explicit costs**, defined as the firm's actual cash payments for its inputs, and ignore **implicit costs**, defined as the opportunity cost of nonpurchased inputs. By including the opportunity cost of his time in his calculations, Edward measures his **economic cost**, defined as the sum of explicit and implicit costs.

The marginal principle has been part of the economic way of thinking for a very long time. For a classic explanation of the principle, read the Closer Look box on page 28, "Alfred Marshall on the Marginal Principle."

Using the Principle: Airline Flights

In the opening paragraphs of the chapter, we saw Emma's airline puzzle. Although only 30 of the 120 seats on a particular flight were filled, the airline ran the flight anyway. Here is a hypothetical reply to her letter to the president of the airline:

A Closer LOOK

Alfred Marshall on the Marginal Principle

Alfred Marshall's most famous book, *Principles of Economics,* published in 1890, was used for decades as a classroom text. Here is Marshall's explanation of the marginal principle: "When a boy picks blackberries for his own eating . . . the pleasure of eating is more than enough to repay the trouble of picking. But after he has eaten a good deal, the desire for more diminishes; while the task of picking begins to cause weariness. . . . Equilibrium is reached when at last his eagerness to play and his disinclination for the work of picking counterbalances the desire for eating. The satisfaction which he can get from picking fruit has arrived at its maximum: for up to that time every fresh picking has added more to his pleasure than it has taken away; and after that time any further picking would take away from his pleasure more than it would add."

Source: Alfred Marshall, *Principles of Economics,* 8th ed. (London: Macmillan, 1920), p. 330.

Dear Emma,

We're always pleased to hear from our stockholders. Thanks for your letter about Flight 101, which we continue to run despite its low ridership. To decide whether to run a particular flight, we compare the revenue from the flight to the "out-of-pocket" or extra costs generated by the flight. For Flight 101, we pay $1,000 to the three-person flight crew and use $1,200 worth of jet fuel, so the extra cost is $2,200. Because the flight is serviced by a ground crew that would be on duty anyway, we don't include the salaries of the ground crew in the out-of-pocket cost. Similarly, we don't include the cost of the airplane itself because we pay a fixed monthly rent on the plane no matter how many flights it makes. We usually sell 30 tickets at $100 per ticket, so the revenue from the flight is $3,000. The marginal benefit of the flight ($3,000) exceeds the out-of-pocket or marginal cost ($2,200), so it is sensible to run the flight—even though we usually have 90 empty seats on the plane.

Sincerely,

Margie Jones, President

The wisdom of running the flight can be explained by the marginal principle: The marginal benefit exceeds its marginal cost, so it is sensible to run the flight.

What about the airline's broader decision to rent the plane and hire the ground crew in the first place? Using the marginal principle, we would say that it is sensible to rent a plane and hire a crew if the extra revenue generated by *all* the flights made possible by the plane and crew (Flight 101 and other flights) exceeds the extra cost of all the flights. These extra costs include the costs of the plane and the crew. If the airline's other flights are more popular than Flight 101, the extra revenue may exceed the extra costs, and it would be sensible to rent the plane and hire the crew.

Using the Principle: Student Groups and College Facilities

Many colleges rent their facilities to student groups for events such as films, dances, and musical performances. If a student film club offers to rent an auditorium for an evening for $500, should the college accept the offer?

To decide whether to rent the auditorium, the college should determine the marginal cost of renting out the facility. In other words, the college should compute the extra costs it incurs by allowing the student group to use an otherwise vacant facility. Suppose that the extra cost is $180, including $20 for electricity and heating, $60 for cleanup, and $100 for security. It would be sensible to rent the auditorium because the marginal benefit ($500) exceeds the marginal cost ($180).

Most colleges do not use this sort of logic. Instead, they use complex formulas to compute the perceived cost of renting out the facility. In most cases, the perceived cost includes some of the fixed costs of the college, costs that are unaffected by renting out the facility for the evening. As a result, many colleges overestimate the actual cost of renting their facilities, missing opportunities to serve student groups and make money at the same time.

TEST *Your Understanding*

1. True or false, and explain: The cost of a master's degree in engineering equals the tuition plus the cost of books.
2. Suppose that a nation picks 1,000 young adults at random to serve in the army. What information do you need to determine the cost of using these people in the army?
3. Explain the logic behind the economist's quip that "there is no such thing as a free lunch."
4. If a bus company adds a third daily bus between two cities, the company's total costs will increase from $500 to $600 per day and its total revenue will increase by $150 per day. Should the company add the third bus?
5. Suppose that you can save $50 by purchasing your new car in a different city. If the trip requires only $10 in gasoline, is the trip worthwhile?

THE PRINCIPLE OF DIMINISHING RETURNS

The principle of diminishing returns states an important feature of the production process, one that is relevant for the production of all goods and services.

PRINCIPLE *of Diminishing Returns*

Suppose that output is produced with two or more inputs and that we increase one input while holding the other inputs fixed. Beyond some point—called the point of diminishing returns—output will increase at a decreasing rate.

Diminishing returns: As one input increases while the other inputs are held fixed, output increases but at a decreasing rate.

This principle is relevant when we try to produce more output in an existing production facility (a factory, a store, an office, or a farm) by increasing the number of workers sharing the facility. When we add a worker to the facility, each worker becomes less productive because he or she works with a smaller piece of the production facility: There are more workers to share the machinery, equipment, and factory space. As we pack more and more workers into the factory, total output increases, but at a decreasing rate.

Table 1 on page 30 shows some hypothetical data concerning the production of pizza. The "production facility" is the pizzeria and all the machines and equipment used to produce pizza, including the pizza oven. Suppose that the first worker in the pizzeria assembles 10 uncooked pizzas per hour and pops them into the oven as soon as they are assembled. A second worker could also assemble 10 pizzas per hour, but because he shares the pizza oven with the first worker, he will occasionally have to wait before he can pop an assembled pizza into the oven. Therefore, we

Table 1: Diminishing Returns for Pizza

Number of workers	1	2	3
Total number of pizzas produced	10	18	23
Additional pizzas from hiring the worker	10	8	5

wouldn't expect output to double. If output increases to 18 pizzas, it means that hiring the second worker increases the output by only 8 pizzas. In a three-worker pizzeria, there would be even more time spent waiting for an empty oven, so hiring the third worker increases the quantity by only 5 pizzas, from 18 to 23. As we hire more workers, output is increasing but at a decreasing rate: The first worker adds 10 pizzas, the second adds 8 pizzas, and the third adds 5 pizzas.

Short run: A period of time over which one or more factors of production is fixed; in most cases, a period of time over which a firm cannot modify an existing facility or build a new one.

Later in the book we use the principle of diminishing returns to explore the decisions made by a firm in the short run. The **short run** is a period of time over which one or more factors of production is fixed. In most cases, the short run is defined as a period of time over which a firm cannot modify an existing facility or build a new one, so a firm is stuck with its existing production facility. The length of the short run varies across industries, depending on how long it takes to build a production facility. The short run for a hot-dog stand lasts just a few days: That's how long it takes to get another hot-dog cart. In contrast, it may take a year to build a computer factory, so the short run for a computer manufacturer is one year. Although a firm can increase its output by adding workers to an existing facility, the sharing of the facility by more and more workers will eventually cause diminishing returns.

Using the Principle: Results of a Classroom Experiment

We can demonstrate the principle of diminishing returns with a simple experiment that has been performed in many economics classrooms. Here is how the experiment worked in one classroom. The instructor placed a stapler and a stack of paper on a small table and asked students from the class to produce "foldits" by folding a page of paper in thirds and stapling both ends of the folded page. As the number of students increases, by how much will the output of the production process (the number of foldits) increase?

Figure 3 shows how the number of foldits produced in a 1-minute period varied with the numbers of workers. A single worker produced 7 foldits, while a team of two workers produced 15: The second worker added more to output than the first worker. This is the case of increasing—as opposed to diminishing—returns, and occurred because each member of the team performed a distinct task: One worker folded and the other one stapled, so the team was more than twice as productive as the single worker. As the number of workers increased, however, diminishing returns eventually set in: The third worker increased output by 6 foldits (from 15 to 21), the fourth increased output by 4, and so on, until the seventh worker increased output by only one foldit. The reason for diminishing returns is that the workers shared a single stapler. As the number of workers increased, more and more time was spent waiting for the stapler.

Long run: A period of time long enough that a firm can change all the factors of production, meaning that a firm can modify its existing production facility or build a new one.

What About the Long Run?

The principle of diminishing returns is not relevant in the long run. The **long run** is defined as a period of time long enough so that a firm can change all the factors of production, meaning that it can modify its existing facility (a factory, a store, an office, or a farm) or build a new one. To increase output in the long run, a firm can build an additional production facility and hire workers for the new facility. The firm will not suffer from diminishing returns because workers won't have to share

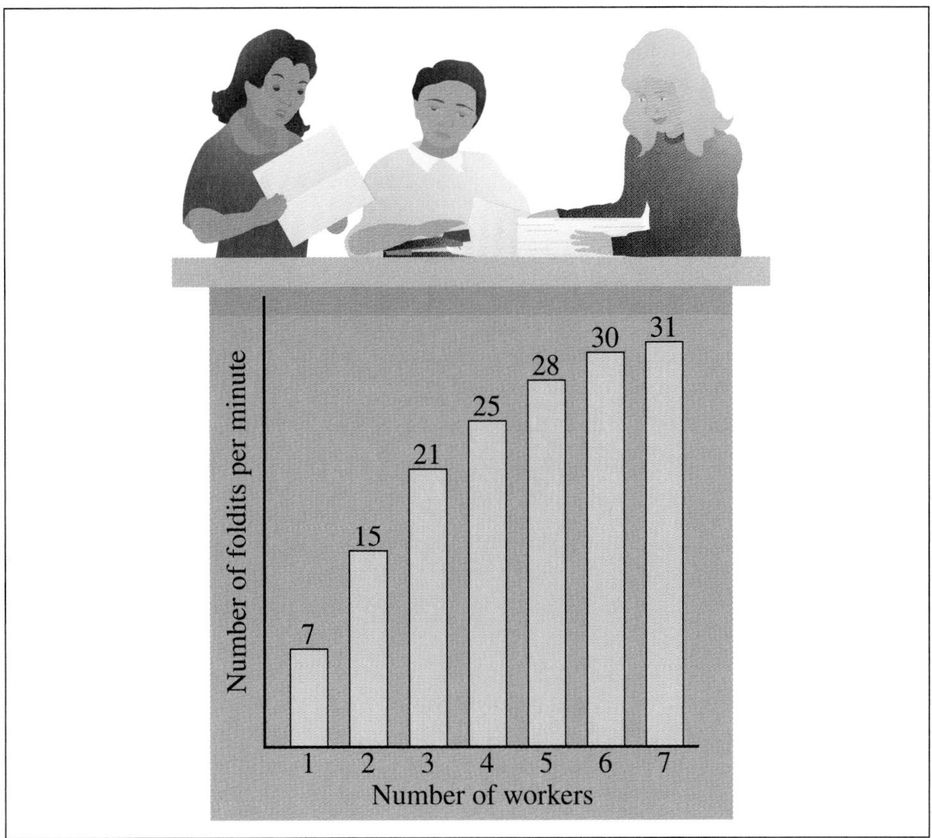

Figure 3

Diminishing Returns in a Classroom Experiment

As the number of workers increases, the number of foldits produced per minute increases, but eventually increases at a decreasing rate because workers share a single stapler.

a production facility with more and more workers. For example, if the firm builds a second factory that is identical to the first and hires the same number of workers, the firm's output will double.

THE SPILLOVER PRINCIPLE

The **spillover** (or *externality*) principle suggests that the costs or benefits of some decisions "spill over" onto people who are not involved in the decision-making process.

Spillover: A cost or benefit experienced by people who are external to the decision about how much of a good to produce or consume.

Spillover PRINCIPLE

For some goods, the costs or benefits associated with the good are not confined to the person or organization that decides how much of the good to produce or consume.

A spillover occurs when people who are external to a decision are affected by the decision, and another word for spillover is *externality.* In a market economy we rely on millions of individuals to make decisions about what to produce and what to consume. When decision-makers face all the costs and benefits of a decision, we can be confident that they will make good choices. But when there are spillovers, the people who experience the spillover benefits or costs should be involved in the decision-making process.

Let's examine spillover costs and spillover benefits separately, starting with the costs. Consider a paper mill that dumps chemical waste into a river, causing health problems for people who live downstream from the mill. The paper firm decides how much paper to produce, but some of the costs of producing paper are incurred by people who live downstream. If each ton of paper generates enough chemical waste to increase the cost of treating water (to make it suitable for drinking) by $10, the spillover cost of paper is $10 per ton. The paper firm will base its production decisions on its own costs (for example, $30 per ton for labor and materials) and will ignore the $10 spillover cost.

Most spillover costs involve air or water pollution, but there are other types of spillovers. Here are some examples:

- Freon leaks from an air conditioner, imposing a cost on the owner (he or she must replace the Freon) and other citizens (Freon released into the atmosphere depletes the protective ozone layer).
- Your neighbor stages a loud party while you are trying to study.
- When you drive your car, you release pollutants that contribute to urban smog.

In each of these examples, the decision-maker incurs some—but not all—of the costs associated with the decision. As we'll see later in the book, the challenge for policymakers is to ensure that everyone who is affected by a decision is involved in the decision-making process.

Some goods generate spillover benefits instead of spillover costs. For example, suppose that a farmer is thinking about building a dike or small flood-control dam on a river, and the dike costs $100,000. If the farmer's benefit from the dike is only $40,000, he or she won't build the dike. Other farmers could benefit, however, and if their benefits add up to at least $60,000, it would be sensible for all of them to build the dike. To make the right decision, we must get all the potential beneficiaries to participate in the decision-making process. For example, if 10 farmers each contributed $10,000 to a dike-building fund, the dike could be built.

There are many goods that generate spillover benefits. Here are a few more examples.

- If a person contributes money to public television, everyone who watches these channels benefits from the improved programming.
- If a scientist discovers a new way to treat a common disease, everyone suffering from the disease will benefit.
- If you get a college degree, you'll become a better team worker and a better citizen, so your fellow workers and citizens will benefit.

In each case some of the benefits spill over onto people not involved in the decision-making process, so a decision-maker might decide against taking an action that would be beneficial to society.

TEST *Your Understanding*

6 When a table producer hired its 20th worker, the output of its factory increased by 5 tables per month. If the firm hires 2 more workers, would you expect output to increase by 10 tables per month?

7 True or false, and explain: According to the principle of diminishing returns, an additional worker decreases total output.

8 Consider a variation on the foldit experiment. Suppose that the instructor gives each additional pair of workers an additional stapler and a separate table.

Predict the number of foldits produced with 6 workers (with 3 staplers and 3 tables). Do diminishing returns still occur? Why or why not?

9 For each of the following examples, is there a spillover benefit or a cost?

a. Your roommate plays obnoxious music on a stereo set with very loud speakers.
b. Strip mining causes oil and gas to enter the underground water system, making smoking in the bathtub hazardous to your health.
c. A person in a residential neighborhood collects and restores old cars.
d. A family contributes $5,000 to an organization that provides holiday meals to the poor.
e. A landowner preserves a large stand of ancient trees and thus provides a habitat for the spotted owl (an endangered species).

THE REALITY PRINCIPLE

One of the key ideas in economics is that people are interested not just in the amount of money they have but in how much their money will buy.

Reality PRINCIPLE

What matters to people is the real value or purchasing power of money or income, not its face value.

To illustrate this principle, suppose that you work in the college bookstore to earn extra money to pay for movies and newspapers. If your take-home pay is $10 per hour, is this a high wage or a low wage? The answer depends on the prices of the goods you buy. If a movie costs $4 and a newspaper costs $1, with one hour of work you could afford to see two movies and buy two papers. The wage may seem comfortably high to you. On the other hand, if a movie costs $8 and a newspaper costs $2, an hour of work would buy only one movie and one paper. The same $10 wage now appears rather low. This is the reality principle in action: What matters is not the dollars you earn but what those dollars will purchase.

The reality principle can explain how people choose the amount of money to carry around with them. Suppose that you typically withdraw $40 per week from an ATM machine to cover your normal expenses. Now suppose that the prices of all goods you purchase during the week double. You would have to withdraw $80 per week to make the same purchases. People choose to carry a sum that relates to the real prices they face every day.

Nominal value: The face value of a sum of money.

Real value: The value of a sum of money in terms of the quantity of goods the money can buy.

Economists use special terms to reinforce the idea behind the reality principle. The **nominal value** of a sum of money is simply its face value. For example, the nominal wage paid by the bookstore is $10 per hour. The **real value** of a sum of money is measured in terms of the quantity of goods the money can buy. To compute a real value of a sum of money, we take into account the level of prices in the economy and control for changes in the purchasing power of money. For example, the *real* value of your bookstore wage would fall as the prices of movies and newspapers increase even though your *nominal* wage stayed the same.

Using the Principle: Government Programs and Statistics

Government officials use the reality principle when they design public programs. For example, Social Security payments are increased each year to ensure that the checks received by the elderly will purchase the same amount of goods and services even if prices have increased. The government also uses the reality principle when it publishes statistics about the economy. For example, when the government issues reports about changes in "real wages" in the economy over time, these statistics take into account the prices of the goods purchased by workers and therefore state the wage in terms of its buying power as opposed to its face (or nominal) value.

TEST *Your Understanding*

10 Average hourly earnings in the United States increased between 1970 and 1993, but real wages fell. How could this occur?

11 Suppose that your wage doubles but so do the prices of consumer goods. Are you better off, worse off, or about the same?

12 Suppose that your bank pays you 4% per year on your savings account: Each $100 in the bank grows to $104 over a one-year period. If prices increase by 3% per year, how much do you really gain by keeping $100 in the bank for a year?

SUMMARY

This chapter covers five key principles of economics, defined as simple, self-evident truths that most people would readily accept. If you understand these principles, you are ready for the rest of the book, which will show you how to do your own economic analysis. In fact, if you've done the exercises in this chapter, you're already doing economic analysis.

1. *Principle of opportunity cost.* The opportunity cost of something is what you sacrifice to get it.
2. *Marginal principle.* Increase the level of an activity if its marginal benefit exceeds its marginal cost, but reduce the level if the marginal cost exceeds the marginal benefit. If possible, pick the level at which the marginal benefit equals the marginal cost.
3. *Principle of diminishing returns.* Suppose that output is produced with two or more inputs and that we increase one input while holding the other inputs fixed. Beyond some point—called the point of diminishing returns—output will increase at a decreasing rate.
4. *Spillover principle.* For some goods, the costs or benefits associated with the good are not confined to the person or organization that decides how much of the good to produce or consume.
5. *Reality principle.* What matters to people is the real value or purchasing power of money or income, not its face value.

KEY TERMS

diminishing returns, *29*
economic cost, *27*
explicit cost, *27*
fixed cost, *27*
implicit cost, *27*
long run, *30*
marginal benefit, *26*
marginal cost, *26*
nominal value, *33*
principle, *22*
real value, *33*
short run, *30*
spillover, *31*
variable cost, *27*

PROBLEMS AND DISCUSSION QUESTIONS

1. Suppose that you lend $1,000 to a friend and he or she pays you back one year later. What is the actual cost of lending the money?
2. Suppose that a sawmill buys a bunch of logs and uses the logs one year later to make lumber. What information do you need to compute the cost of using the logs?
3. True or false, and explain: "Our new stadium was built on land that was donated to our university by a wealthy alum. The university didn't have to buy the land, so the cost of the stadium equals its construction cost."
4. Suppose that another year of college will increase your lifetime earnings by about $30,000. The costs of tuition and books add up to only $8,000 for an additional year. Comment on the following statement: "Because the benefit of $30,000 exceeds the $8,000 cost, you should complete another year of college."
5. To celebrate its 50th anniversary, a gasoline station sells gasoline at the price it charged on its first day of operation: $0.10 per gallon. As you drive by the gasoline station, you notice that there is a long line of people waiting to buy gasoline. What types of people would you expect to join the line?
6. You are about to buy a personal computer and must decide how much random-access memory (RAM) to have in the computer. Suppose that each additional megabyte of RAM costs $40. For example, a 5-megabyte computer costs $40 more than a 4-megabyte computer. The marginal benefit of RAM is $640 for the first megabyte and decreases by half for each additional megabyte, to $320 for the second megabyte, $160 for the third megabyte, and so on. How much RAM should you get in your computer? Illustrate your answer with a graph.
7. You are the mayor of a large city, and you must decide how many police officers to hire. Explain how you could use the marginal principle to help make the decision.
8. Consider a city that must decide how many mobile cardiac arrest units (specially equipped ambulances designed to treat people immediately after a heart attack) to deploy. Explain how you could use the marginal principle to help make the decision.
9. Explain why the principle of diminishing returns does not occur in the long run.
10. You are the manager of a firm that makes computers. If you had to decide how much output to produce in the next week, would you use the principle of diminishing returns? If you had to decide how much output to produce ten years from now, would you still use this principle?
11. Your photocopying firm has a single copying machine. As the firm adds more and more workers, would you expect output (pages per hour) to increase at a constant rate? Why or why not?
12. Use the spillover principle to discuss the following examples. Are there spillover costs or benefits?
    a. Logging causes soil erosion and stream degradation, harming fish.
    b. An environmental group buys 50 acres of wetlands to provide a habitat for migrating birds.
    c. Your office mate smokes cigarettes.
    d. A person buys a dilapidated house in your neighborhood and fixes it up.
13. Explain this statement: The salaries of baseball players have increased in both real and nominal terms.

Take It to the Net

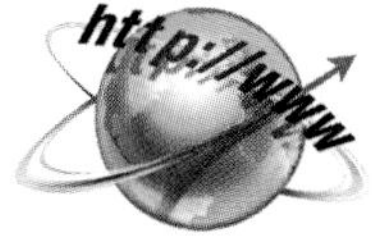

We invite you to visit the O'Sullivan/Sheffrin page on the Prentice Hall Web site at:

http://www.prenhall.com/osullivan/

for this chapter's World Wide Web exercise.

MODEL ANSWERS FOR THIS CHAPTER

Chapter-Opening Questions

1. To get a warship, we sacrifice something else, for example, safe drinking water for 2.5 million Malaysians.
2. According to the marginal principle, the college should accept the offer if the marginal cost associated with using the auditorium (for security, lighting, heat, and cleanup) is less than the marginal benefit ($500).
3. According to the principle of diminishing returns, output will eventually increase at a decreasing rate.
4. The true or economic cost of paper equals the firm's cost (for material, labor, and the paper mill) and the cost associated with the pollution generated as a byproduct of paper.
5. Your income will buy the same quantity of goods and services, so you will be equally well off.

Test Your Understanding

1. False. This statement ignores the opportunity cost of time spent in school.
2. We need the opportunity cost of using the people in the army instead of in the civilian economy. One measure of the opportunity cost is the wages the people could have earned as engineers, teachers, doctors, lawyers, or factory workers.
3. One of the costs of a lunch is the time spent eating it. Even if someone else pays for your lunch, it is not truly free.
4. The marginal benefit is $150 and the marginal cost is only $100 ($600 – $500), so it would be sensible to add the third bus.
5. It will be worthwhile if the opportunity cost of the time spent traveling is less than $40.
6. No. If the factory experiences diminishing returns, the additional output from the 21st worker will be smaller from the additional output from the 20th worker, and the extra output from the 22nd worker will be even smaller. Therefore, hiring two more workers will increase total output by less than 10 tables.
7. False. The principle says that output increases but at a decreasing rate. Its does not say that hiring another worker decreases output, although this is a possibility with a very crowded factory.
8. No. Each table will produce the same output as the two-person, one-stapler table shown in Figure 4, for a total of 120 foldits per minute.
9. a. Spillover cost. You must listen to loud music chosen by your roommate.
   b. Spillover cost. People who bathe in the contaminated water risk being burned.
   c. Spillover cost. For most people, a bunch of partly restored cars (cars jacked up on the street or in the front lawn) is an eyesore.
   d. Spillover benefit. Even non-contributors are happy if the poor receive holiday meals.
   e. Spillover benefit. Many people like the idea of preventing a species from becoming extinct.
10. The price of consumer goods increased faster than wages.
11. Your real wage hasn't changed, so you are just as well off.
12. A set of goods that cost you $100 will cost you $103 today, so you must use $3 of your $4 interest earnings to cover the higher costs, leaving you with only $1 as actual interest earnings.

NOTES

1. United Nations Development Program, *Human Development Report 1994* (New York: Oxford University Press, 1994).
2. Alan Riding, "The French Seek Their Own 'Peace Dividend,'" *New York Times,* July 15, 1990, p. 6.
3. Eric Schmitt, "Peace Dividend: Troops Turn to Teaching," *New York Times,* November 30, 1994, p. B1.

CHAPTER 3

Markets and Government in the Global Economy

Like many other consumers in the United States, Robin drives a Japanese car, wears clothes made in Hong Kong, and sits on furniture made in Canada. When he bought his new personal computer, he was happy at last to buy something from a U.S. company. You can imagine his surprise when he discovered that most of the computer's components (the hard disk, the case, and the monitor) were produced overseas. Robin learned an important lesson about living in the modern global economy: A product purchased from a domestic firm may not be a truly domestic product.

In Chapter 1 we saw that each society makes three types of economic decisions: A society must decide what products to produce, how to produce them, and who gets the products. In this chapter we provide an overview of a modern market-based economy like that of the United States, where most economic decisions are made in markets. Our overview of the modern economy explains why markets exist, how they operate, and the role that government plays in a market-based economy. You may have heard about the movement to a "global economy." We'll explain what this means and why it is happening.

In this chapter we take a close look at three facets of a modern economy—markets, government, and international trade—and the connections among them. Markets arise because individuals benefit from specializing in production and then trading with each other. But markets do not exist in isolation: We need governments to enforce basic contracts and property rights in markets, to provide goods and services not readily delivered through markets, and to deal with deficiencies that emerge from pure market transactions. In modern economies, markets and governments are not contained within national boundaries but spill over from one nation to another. Specialization and markets arise on a global scale, leading to international trade in goods and services. One of the roles of government is to develop policies to deal with trade between countries. To understand the modern economy, we must look at the three components—markets, government, and international trade—together.

The material that we cover in this chapter will help you understand how a market-based economy operates in today's global environment. Here are some of the practical questions we answer:

1. Why do both rich and poor nations benefit from trade?
2. What is a firm, and how are firms organized?
3. Which of the industrialized nations has the lowest taxes?
4. Which nations are most dependent on international trade?
5. How do governments restrict international trade?
6. What are GATT, NAFTA, and the World Trade Organization?

HOUSEHOLDS AND FIRMS IN MARKETS

In Chapter 1 we saw that a market is an arrangement that allows buyers and sellers to exchange things. A buyer exchanges money for a product (a good or service), while a seller exchanges a product for money. Before we explore how a market operates, let's think about why markets exist in the first place. In the words of Adam Smith, *"Man is the only animal that makes bargains; one dog does not exchange bones with another dog."* We use markets to make our bargains, exchanging what we have for what we want. If each person were self-sufficient, producing everything that he or she consumed, there would be no need for markets. Markets exist because we aren't self-sufficient but instead consume many products that are produced by others. To get the money to pay for these products, each of us produces something to sell: Some people grow food, others produce goods such as clothing and bicycles, and others provide services such as medical care or legal advice. Because each of us specializes in producing just a few products, we need markets to sell what we have and buy what we want. For example, the labor market allows workers to sell their work time to employers, and the bicycle market allows consumers to buy bicycles.

Market system: A system under which individuals and firms use markets to facilitate the exchange of money and products.

Absolute advantage: The ability of one person or nation to produce a particular good at a lower absolute cost than that of another person or nation.

Comparative Advantage and Specialization

A **market system** exists to facilitate exchanges among people who aren't self-sufficient but instead specialize in producing a small number of products. But why do people specialize? We can explain the rationale for specialization with an example of two people who produce and consume shirts and bread. Table 1 shows how much each person can produce in an hour. Brenda can produce either 6 loaves or 2 shirts, while Sam can produce either 1 loaf or 1 shirt. In other words, Brenda is more productive than Sam in producing both goods; in economic terms, she has an **absolute advantage** over Sam in both goods.

Suppose that each person is initially self-sufficient: Both Brenda and Sam produce their own bread and their own shirts. Would they be better off if Brenda were

Table 1: Productivity Example

	Bread per Hour	Shirts per Hour
Brenda	6	2
Sam	1	1

to specialize in bread and Sam in shirts? Let's think about what would happen if the two people reallocated some of their time in the direction of specialization: Brenda switches 1 hour from shirt production to bread production, and Sam switches 3 hours from bread production to shirt production. Here are the implications for bread and shirt production:

Brenda's production:	+6 loaves of bread	–2 shirts
Sam's production:	–3 loaves of bread	+3 shirts
Net effects	+3 loaves of bread	+1 shirt

The total amount of bread increases by 3 loaves (6 more from Brenda but 3 fewer from Sam) and the total number of shirts increases by 1 shirt (2 fewer from Brenda but 3 more from Sam). In other words, specialization increases the production of both goods, so each person could consume more of each good. Later in the book we explain how the extra output would be divided between the two people.

We can use the principle of opportunity cost to explain why specialization increases the production of both goods.

PRINCIPLE *of Opportunity Cost*

The opportunity cost of something is what you sacrifice to get it.

Let's start by computing the opportunity costs for each person and each good.

1. In an hour, Brenda can produce either 6 loaves or 2 shirts, so she sacrifices 3 loaves for each shirt she produces. In other words, the opportunity cost of a shirt is the 3 loaves of bread she could have produced instead. Conversely, her opportunity cost of bread is ⅓ of a shirt.
2. Sam sacrifices 1 loaf for each shirt, so his opportunity cost of a shirt is the 1 loaf of bread he could have produced instead. This means that his opportunity cost of bread is 1 shirt.

It is sensible for each person to produce the good for which he or she has a **comparative advantage** or lower opportunity cost than another person. Sam's opportunity cost for shirts (1 loaf) is lower than Brenda's (3 loaves), so it is sensible for Sam to produce shirts. Brenda's opportunity cost for bread (⅓ shirt) is lower than Sam's (1 shirt), so Brenda should produce bread. When they switch some production time from one good to another, each person produces more of the good for which he or she has a comparative advantage (lower opportunity cost). Therefore, to get the extra shirts from Sam, they sacrifice a small amount of bread; to get the extra bread from Brenda, they sacrifice a small number of shirts.

Comparative advantage: The ability of one person or nation to produce a good at an opportunity cost that is lower than the opportunity cost of another person or nation.

We've seen that specialization is beneficial if there are differences in opportunity costs that generate comparative advantages. This means that people will not be self-sufficient but will instead specialize and exchange what they produce for the goods and services they want to consume. For example, Sam could produce shirts and then exchange some of them for some bread produced by Brenda. In a modern economy, we don't exchange goods directly but instead use money to facilitate the exchange

The typical person is not self-sufficient, but instead specializes by working at a particular job and uses his or her income to purchase goods and services.

process. The typical person earns an income (specializing by working at a particular job) and uses this income to buy the products that he or she wants to consume.

Households and Firms

Most of the decisions about what to produce and consume in a market-based economy are made by households and firms. A *household* is one person or a group of people who live in the same housing unit. A *firm* is an organization that uses resources to produce a product, which it then sells. There are three types of firms:

1. A *sole proprietorship* is a firm owned by a single person, who earns all the firm's profit and is responsible for all the firm's debts. Although about 70% of all firms are proprietorships, most of them are small, so proprietorships generate only about 6% of total sales by firms.
2. A *partnership* is a firm owned by two or more partners, who agree on a particular division of responsibilities and profits. Each partner is responsible for the firm's debts, so if the firm fails, one partner may pay for another partner's mistakes. Partnerships make up about 8% of firms and generate about 4% of total sales by firms.
3. A *corporation* is a legal entity owned by stockholders, each of whom faces a limited liability for the firm's debts. A corporation is established by filing a corporate charter with a state government. A corporation may have hundreds or thousands of owners, each of whom receives shares of stock that entitle the stockholder to a share of the firm's profits. One advantage of a corporation is that each shareholder's responsibility for the firm's debt is limited: If the firm fails, each owner loses no more than the value of his or her stock. In contrast, a proprietor or a partner is responsible for paying all the firm's debts.

Multinational corporation: An organization that produces and sells goods and services throughout the world.

The world's largest corporations sell their goods and services throughout the world and are appropriately labeled **multinational corporations.** Table 2 lists the world's largest 20 corporations as measured by total sales. Eight of the top 20 are U.S. corporations, while five are Japanese and three are German. The other nations with corporations in the top 20 are the Netherlands, the United Kingdom, South Korea, and Italy.

Table 2: The Twenty Largest Corporations in the World Measured by Total Sales, 1993

Corporation	Country
1. General Motors	United States
2. Ford Motor	United States
3. Exxon	United States
4. Royal Dutch Shell	The Netherlands
5. Toyota	Japan
6. Hitachi	Japan
7. International Business Machines (IBM)	United States
8. Matsushita	Japan
9. General Electric	United States
10. Daimler-Benz	Germany
11. Mobil	United States
12. Nissan Motor	Japan
13. British Petroleum	United Kingdom
14. Samsung	South Korea
15. Phillip Morris	United States
16. IRI	Italy
17. Siemens	Germany
18. Volkswagen	Germany
19. Chrysler	United States
20. Toshiba	Japan

Source: FORTUNE, July 25, 1994, p. 143.

The Circular Flow

Now that we know why markets exist, we're ready to discuss how they operate. Figure 1 on page 42 is a circular flow diagram of a simple market-based economy. There are two markets where exchanges occur.

1. ***Factor or input market.*** The owners of the factors of production—natural resources, labor, physical capital (machines, buildings, and equipment), and human capital (the knowledge and skills acquired by a worker)—sell these inputs to organizations that use the inputs to produce goods and services.
2. ***Product or output market.*** The organizations that produce goods and services sell their products to consumers.

There are two types of decision-makers in the circular flow model: households and firms. Let's look at households first.

Households as Sellers and Buyers

Households own the factors of production (inputs) and firms have the know-how required to transform inputs into outputs. As shown by arrows B and C in Figure 1, the factor markets allow households and firms to exchange inputs and money: Households supply inputs to the factor market (arrow B) and firms pay households for these inputs (arrow C). There are three types of factor markets.

1. In the labor market, firms hire workers, paying them wages or salaries in exchange for the workers' time. In the United States, about three-fourths of the income earned by households comes from wages and salaries.
2. In the capital market, households use their savings to provide the funds that firms use to buy physical capital (for example, machines, buildings, and equipment). In exchange for the funds, households receive interest payments or some portion of the firm's profits. In the United States, about 20% of the income earned by households comes from interest payments and profits.
3. In the natural resource market, households sell natural resources (for example, land, minerals, or oil) to firms.

Households are also involved in the product market, where they purchase goods and services from firms. This interaction between households and firms is shown by arrows H and G in Figure 1: Households consume the products produced by firms (arrow H) and pay firms for these products (arrow G). To summarize, households are sellers in factor markets and buyers in product markets.

Firms as Sellers and Buyers

The purpose of a firm is to transform inputs into outputs and then sell its products to households. Before a firm can produce anything, it must get the inputs required for production. As shown by arrow D in Figure 1, inputs flow from the factor markets to the firm, where they're used to produce output. As shown by arrow E, the money to pay for the inputs flows from the firm to the factor market on its way to households. In other words, the firm is a buyer in the factor markets. Once the firm produces something, it brings its product to the product market (shown by arrow F) and receives money when consumers buy it (arrow I).

Figure 1 shows that economic activity is truly circular. The inner circle shows physical flows (products and inputs), while the outer circle shows monetary flows

Figure 1

Circular Flow Diagram

A circular flow diagram shows the interactions between households (the suppliers of factors of production, or inputs) and firms (the producers of products) in the factor and product markets.

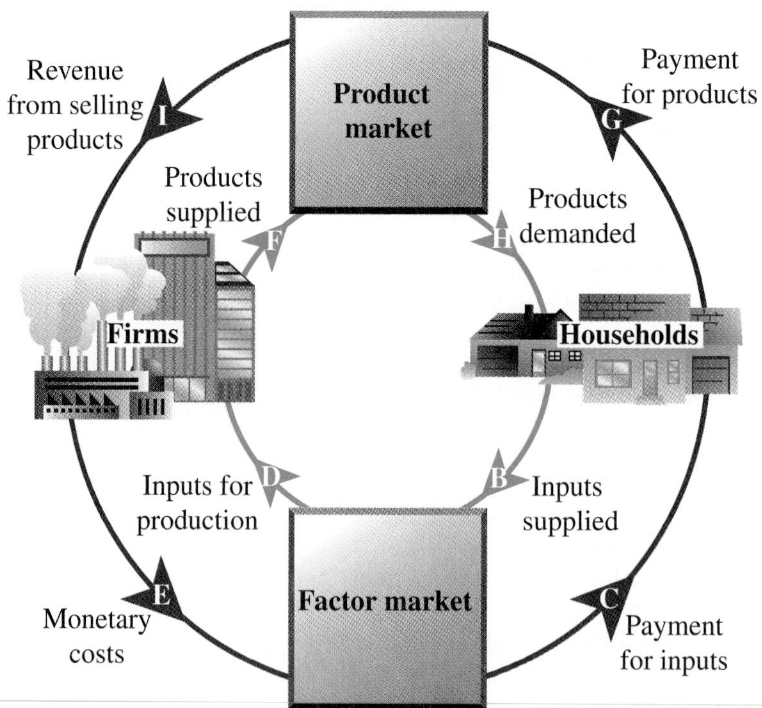

(money exchanged for inputs or products). The money firms pay to households comes back to the firms when households buy products from firms. The money that households pay to firms for products comes back to the households when the firms buy inputs from households.

This simple circular flow diagram is a useful starting point for describing how an economy works, but it is incomplete for two reasons. First, it does not show the effects of government. As we'll see in the next part of the chapter, the government is involved in many facets of a market-based economy: It provides some goods and services, redistributes income, collects taxes, and regulates firms. Second, the diagram does not show the effects of international trade, which, as we'll see, is a large and growing part of most modern economies.

TEST ***Your Understanding***

1 Tim's opportunity cost of producing chairs is 5 tables, while Carla's opportunity cost of producing chairs is 1 table. Which person should produce chairs, and which should produce tables?

2 Nation T can produce either 3 tons of wheat or 9 tons of steel, while nation H can produce 4 tons of wheat or 8 tons of steel. Which nation has a comparative advantage in producing wheat?

3 Why do markets exist?

THE ROLE OF GOVERNMENT

Now that we know how markets operate, let's discuss the role of government in a market-based economy. In most modern societies, the government has five general responsibilities.

1. ***Providing goods and services.*** The government provides all sorts of goods and services, including streets and highways, education, parks, public safety, national defense, and space exploration.
2. ***Redistributing income.*** In a market-based economy, some people earn much more income than others, and the government redistributes income to the poor.
3. ***Taxation.*** The government use taxes on various goods and services to support its spending programs.
4. ***Regulation of business practices.*** The government uses regulations to control pollution, encourage competition among firms, and improve the safety of consumer goods.
5. ***Trade policy.*** The government uses various policies to control international trade, promoting some types of trade and restricting others.

Although it's convenient to speak of "the government," it's important to recognize that there are thousands of governments in the United States, and each citizen deals with at least three levels of government. Local governments pave the streets and run the primary and secondary schools, while state governments pave the highways and run the colleges and universities. The national government provides goods and services for the nation as a whole, including national defense and space exploration. In addition, the national government has the primary responsibility for income redistribution. All three levels of government impose taxes to pay for their spending programs, and all three regulate business practices.

Government Spending Programs

How do governments in the United States spend the money they collect from taxpayers? Figure 2 shows the budget breakdown for the three levels of government.

1. There are more than 80,000 local governments in the United States, including municipalities (city governments), counties, school districts, and special districts. Local governments spend most of their money on education (kindergarten through high school), welfare and health (payments to poor households and support for public hospitals), environment and housing (recreation, sewerage, solid waste management, housing programs), public safety (fire protection, the courts, and jails), and transportation.

2. The three biggest spending programs for states are education (including colleges and universities), public welfare, and public safety (police, the courts, and prisons). The states also spend large sums of money on highways, health programs, and hospitals.

3. The two biggest spending programs for the federal government are income security (payments to the poor and the elderly) and national defense.

Criteria for a Tax System

If the government is to play a role in the market-based economy, taxes are necessary. The practical policy question is whether our current tax system is the best we can do. To most people, a good tax system is one that is fair and easy to understand and does not disrupt markets that otherwise operate effectively. Let's take a closer look at each of these criteria.

Benefit-tax approach: The idea that a person's tax liability should depend on how much he or she benefits from government programs.

There are two perspectives on the issue of fairness. The **benefit-tax approach** suggests that a person's tax liability should depend on his or her benefits from government programs. For example, the revenue from the gasoline taxes in the United States supports the construction and maintenance of highways. The more you drive, the more you use the highway system *and* the more gasoline taxes you pay. For many government programs, however, it would be difficult if not impossible to determine just how large a benefit a particular citizen receives. For example, all law-abiding citizens benefit from the criminal-justice system (police, courts, prisons), but because we don't know how much each person benefits from the system, it would be impossible to determine just how much each person should pay for it.

Horizontal equity: The notion that people in similar economic circumstances should pay similar taxes.

Vertical equity: The notion that people with higher income or wealth should pay higher taxes.

The second perspective on fairness focuses on a citizen's ability to pay. A tax is **horizontally equitable** if people in similar economic circumstances pay similar amounts in taxes. For example, under a pure income tax, each person with a given amount of income would pay the same income tax. In contrast, the idea of **vertical equity** is that people with more income or wealth should pay higher taxes. The practical policy question is *how much* more they should pay. A tax system that is vertically equitable in the eyes of one citizen may be inequitable in the eyes of another.

The second criterion for evaluating a tax system is simplicity. If you've ever filled out an income-tax form, you know that the tax system in the United States is very complex. The average household devotes about 27 hours per year to federal tax preparation.[1] Each household must contend with state and local taxes as well. Firms spend large sums of money to comply with the tax code and pass on these costs to consumers in the form of higher prices. Despite frequent calls for tax simplification, there is no sign that it will get any easier to comply with the tax system.

The third criterion for the tax system concerns its effects on market decisions. If a particular market does not generate spillover benefits or costs, there is no reason to disrupt the market. When a tax is imposed, many people try to avoid the tax

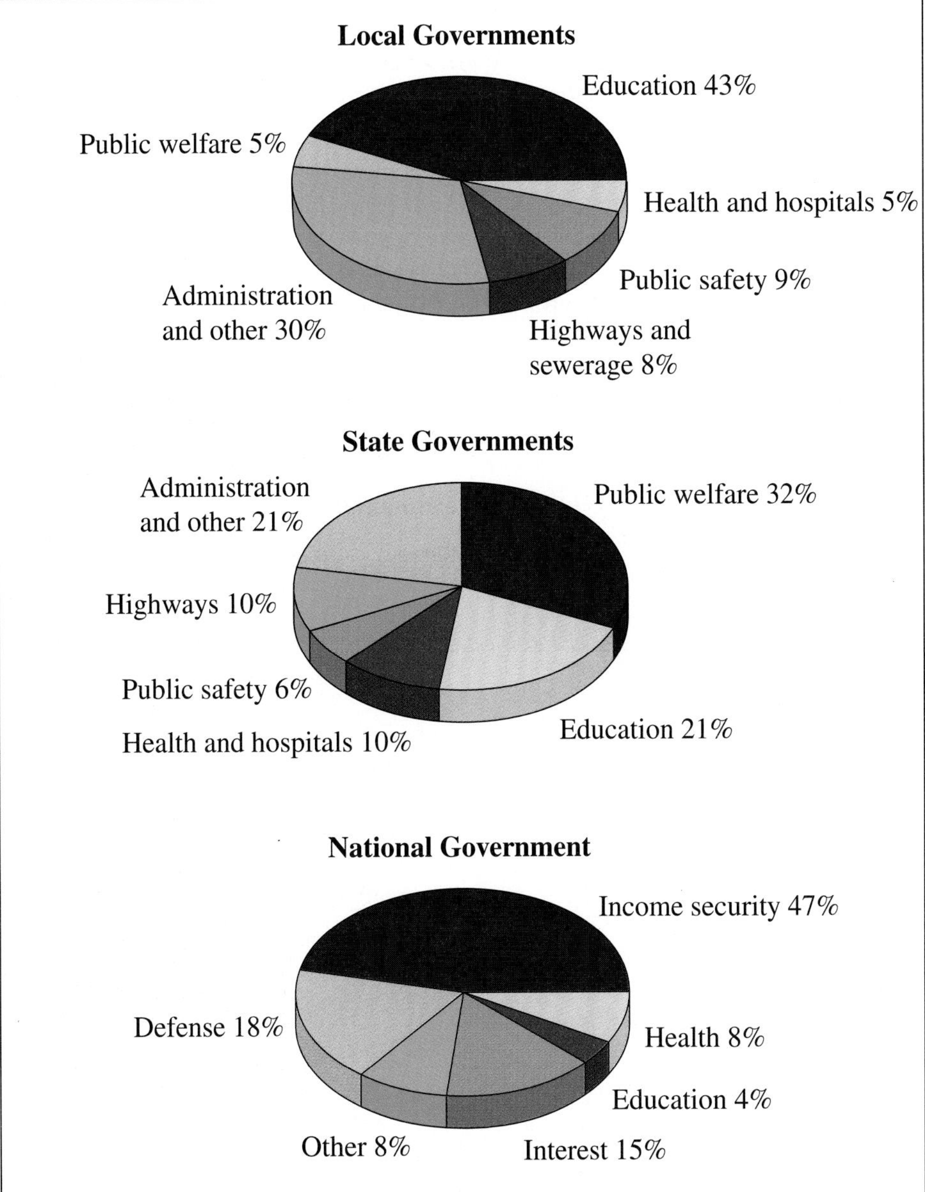

Figure 2

Percentages of Government Spending on Various Programs, 1990

Sources: U.S. Bureau of the Census, *Government Finances in 1989–90;* and *State Government Finances in 1990; Economic Report of the President* (Washington, DC: U.S. Government Printing Office, 1991).

by changing their behavior. Taxes distort people's choices and disrupt markets, and one of the objectives of tax policy is to minimize such disruptions. One implication for policy is that taxes should be spread over many goods and services rather than just a few. For example, a special tax on electricians would discourage people from becoming electricians and disrupt the market for electricians. In contrast, a general income tax would have roughly the same effect on occupations that generate the same income, so the market disruptions will be smaller.

There are many trade-offs associated with designing a tax system. A tax system that is pretty simple may not be equipped to deal with the many different circumstances of taxpayers, leading to horizontal inequities. A simple tax system may also be vertically inequitable in the eyes of many taxpayers, with high-income people paying either too much or too little. A tax that is considered vertically equitable is likely to distort peoples' decisions, causing disruptions in many markets. The challenge for policymakers is to develop a system with the appropriate balance among the three criteria.

Revenue Sources of Local, State, and Federal Governments

Now that we know the criteria for a tax system, let's look at the tax structures of the three levels of government. Figure 3 shows the revenue sources for localities, states, and the federal government.

1. The major revenue source for local governments is the property tax. The property tax is a flat percentage of the value of residential, commercial, or industrial property. For example, if the tax rate is 2% and you own a property with a market value of $100,000, your annual tax would be $2,000 (0.02 × $100,000).
2. The major revenue sources for the states are sales taxes and individual income taxes. The sales tax is a fixed percentage of the purchase price of a consumer good. A person's income-tax liability is based on how much he or she earns, with tax rates that typically increase as income increases.

Figure 3

Percentages of Government Revenue from Various Sources, 1990

Sources: U.S. Bureau of the Census, *Government Finances in 1989–90;* and *State Government Finances in 1990; Economic Report of the President* (Washington, DC: U.S. Government Printing Office, 1991).

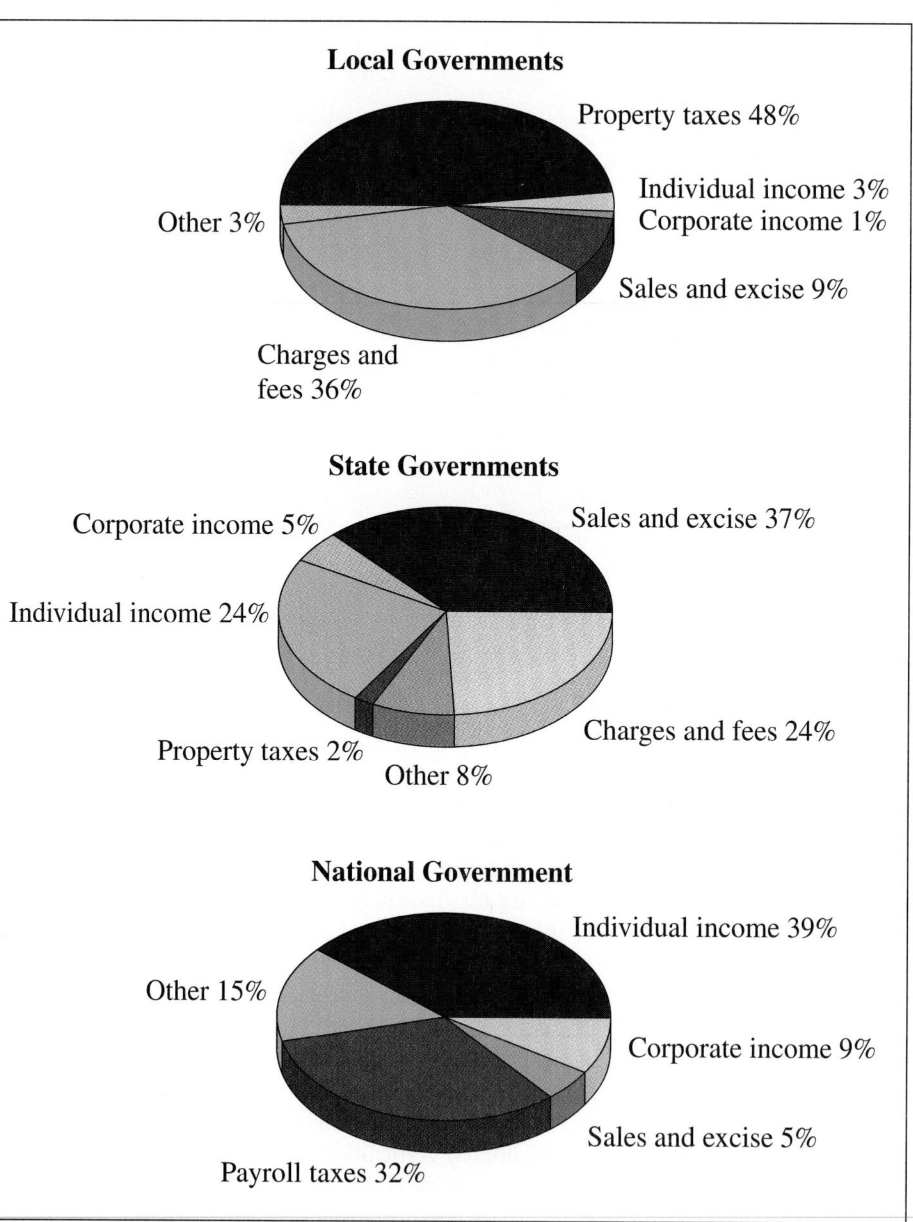

3. The major revenue sources for the federal government are individual income taxes and payroll taxes. The government uses the revenue from payroll taxes to support social security, unemployment compensation, and other programs for workers. Some payroll taxes are paid by employers, and others are paid by workers.

To see how U.S. tax rates compare to those in other industrial nations, read the Closer Look box "Tax Rates in Different Nations."

Government Regulation

It is possible to imagine a world in which the government plays no role in the economy. In such a world, all economic decisions (what products to produce, how to produce them, and who gets the products) would be made in unregulated markets. The French word for this state of affairs is *laissez-faire,* which translates roughly as "let it happen." In modern economies, however, we do not have laissez-faire. Instead, the government plays an important role in many markets.

A Closer LOOK

Tax Rates in Different Nations

Which industrialized country has the lowest tax burden? As we see in the accompanying figure, the answer is the United States. The overall tax rate (total tax revenue divided by total income) is 32%, the lowest rate among all the industrialized countries of the world. The tax rates in other countries range from 33% in Japan to 59% in Denmark. The U.S. government pays a relatively small share of its citizens' health care costs, and this is one reason for the relatively low tax rate in the United States.

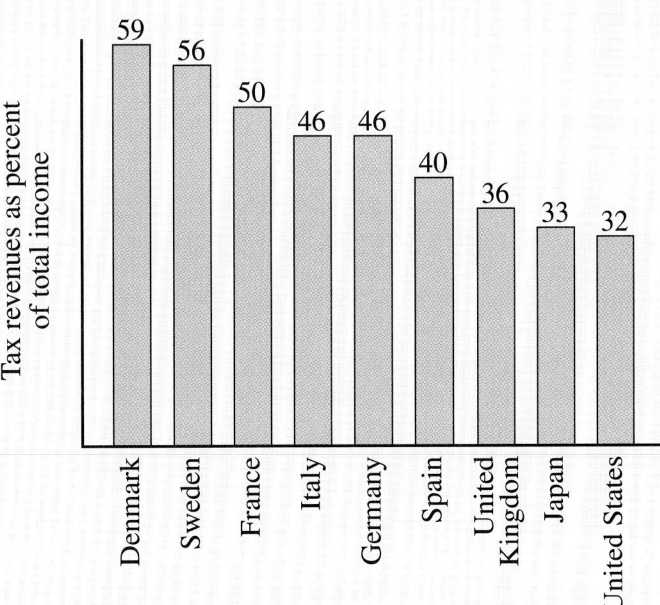

Source: Nathaniel Nash, "Europeans Shrug as Taxes Go Up," *New York Times,* February 16, 1995, p. A10; Organization of Economic Cooperation and Development.

At the most basic level, the government establishes a legal system to enforce property rights. If you buy land to build a house, you must register your purchase with the appropriate government entity and ensure that no one else has a claim on that property. The government's legal system also allows one person to write a binding contract with another. A contract facilitates a transaction because each person involved in the transaction can be confident that the other person will meet his or her part of the deal. Without the legal system to enforce contracts, it would be nearly impossible to conduct business.

Governments at all levels also regulate economic activity. Here are a few examples of government regulation at the national level. The Securities and Exchange Commission (SEC) regulates the purchase and sale of stocks in organized markets. The Federal Trade Commission (FTC) examines the mergers of large corporations to ensure that they do not result in too much power for any single corporation. The Federal Communications Commission (FCC) regulates telecommunications, broadcast television, cable television, and radio. The Food and Drug Administration (FDA) looks after the safety of food and medicines. The Occupational Safety and Health Administration (OSHA) enforces regulations about safety and working conditions. The Environmental Protection Agency (EPA) develops rules about dumping wastes into the air and water.

State and local governments regulate many economic activities within their borders. States have their own rules for air and water pollution. Among the economic activities regulated by states are banking, transportation, education, and land use. States also license many professionals, such as physicians, lawyers, pharmacists, and house builders. Local governments use zoning and other regulations to decide how land is used, and use building codes to regulate commercial and residential construction. It is difficult to think of a single area in which the government does not influence market outcomes.

Mixed economy: An economic system under which government plays an important role, including the regulation of markets, where most economic decisions are made.

Centrally planned economy: An economy in which a government bureaucracy decides how much of each good to produce, how to produce the goods, and how to allocate the products among consumers.

Because government plays such an important role in a modern economy, we have what economists call a **mixed economy**. Although most economic decisions are made in markets, these markets are regulated by the government, with regulations differing from one nation to another. This book uses economic analysis to explore the advantages and disadvantages of government regulation.

Alternative Economic Systems: Centrally Planned Economies

An alternative to a market-based economy is a **centrally planned economy**, an economic system under which production and consumption decisions are made by a central government, not by individual producers and consumers in markets. Under such a system, a central bureaucracy makes all the decisions about what products to produce, how to produce them, and who gets the products. After collecting information from consumers and state-run firms, the bureaucrats tell each firm how much it should produce. One challenge for bureaucrats is to ensure that each firm has enough raw materials and workers to meet their production goals.

Until the late 1980s, central planners ran the economies of the Soviet Union, most nations in Eastern Europe, and China. There were two major problems with these planned economies. First, workers and firms were paid bonuses for meeting or exceeding the production targets established by the bureaucrats, so there was a strong incentive for workers and firms to understate their potential production to more easily meet their quotas. Second, the bureaucrats lacked information to make the millions of decisions required to allocate raw materials and other inputs to thousands of enterprises in the economy. The result was inefficiency and waste.

Many nations have recently shifted from centrally planned economies toward a mixed economic system, with markets playing a much greater role in making economic decisions about production and consumption. These nations are engaged in the difficult **transition** to a market system based on prices and private property. To complete the transition, state firms must be **privatized**—sold to individuals—and then allowed to compete with one another in the marketplace. However, there may be only one or two firms in a certain market, so there is little competition between the privatized firms.

Transition: The process of shifting from a centrally planned economy toward a mixed economic system, with markets playing a greater role in the economy.

Privatizing: The process of selling state firms to individuals.

THE GLOBAL ECONOMY

In today's global economy, many products are produced in one country and sold in another. After introducing some of the language of international trade, we discuss two complications involved in international trade. First, many governments adopt policies to inhibit trade. Second, because each country has its own currency (for example, dollars in the United States and yen in Japan), there must be a market where one currency can be traded for another.

International Trade: Exports and Imports

From the perspective of the United States, an export is a good that is produced in the United States and sold in another country, while an import is a good that is produced elsewhere and purchased in the United States. As shown in Figure 4, the leading U.S. exports are chemicals, industrial machinery, electrical machinery, airplanes and parts, and automated data-processing equipment (primarily computers). Figure 5 on page 50 shows the major U.S. imports, including vehicles, petroleum products, electrical machinery, data-processing equipment, and clothing. You'll notice that with these broad categories of goods, some of the major exports are also major imports. For example, we export $27 billion worth of computers (automated data-processing equipment) and import computers worth $43 billion. This means that nations

Export: A good produced in the "home" country (for example, the United States) and sold in another country.

Import: A good produced in a foreign country and purchased by residents of the "home" country (for example, the United States).

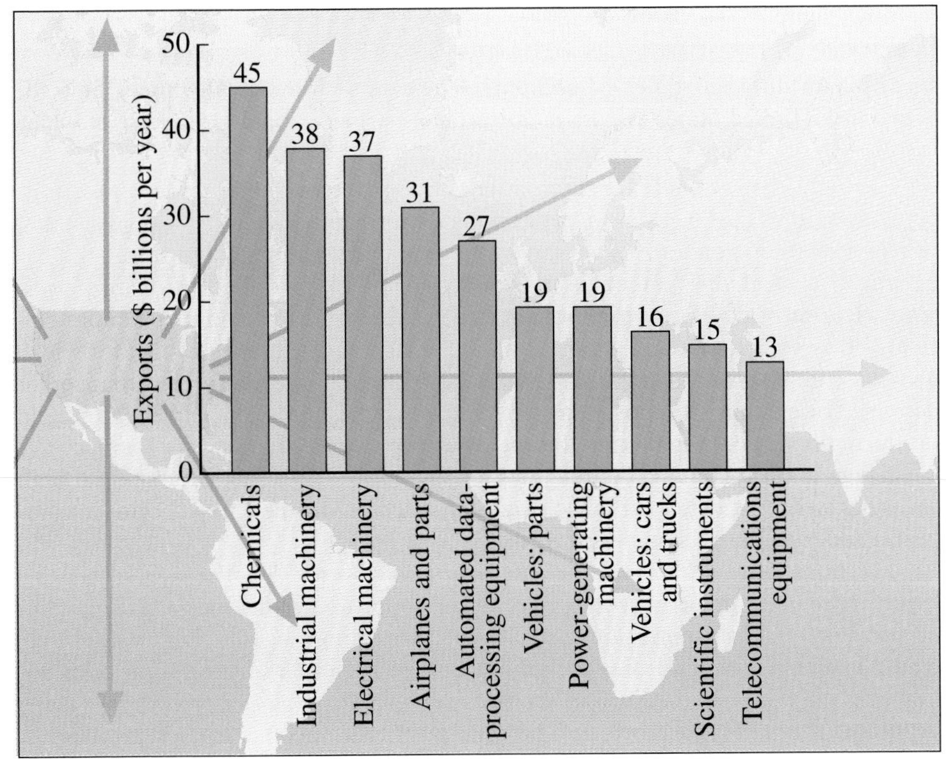

Figure 4

Major Exports of the United States, 1993

Figure 5

Major Imports of the United States, 1993

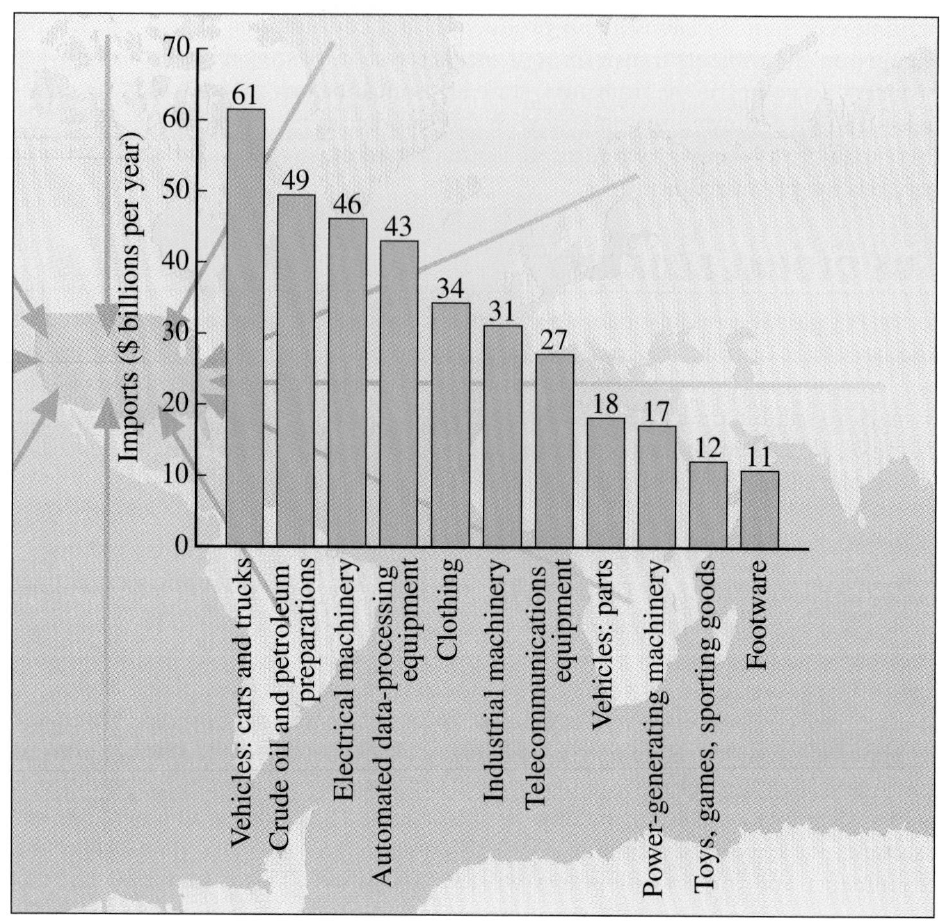

specialize in different types of computers. Figure 6 shows the volumes of trade between the United States and its major trading partners, the three largest of which are Canada, Japan, and Mexico.

What is the rationale for international trade? International trade is just trade between nations and is no more mysterious than trade between individuals, states, or regions within a nation. As we saw in the example with bread and shirts, trade is beneficial even if one person is more efficient in the production of all goods. Similarly, trade between two nations is beneficial even if one country is more efficient in the production of all goods. A nation will specialize in the product for which it has a comparative advantage, defined as a lower opportunity cost than other nations. For example, suppose that the United States is more efficient than India in producing both computers and clothing, but the United States has a comparative advantage in computers while India has a comparative advantage in clothing. Both countries would be better off if each country specialized—the United States in computers and India in clothing—and traded.

Nations differ in their reliance on international trade. Smaller nations typically rely more on trade because they have fewer opportunities for specialization within their borders. Transportation costs also play an important role. For example, we would expect a high level of trade within Europe because transportation costs are low and the countries in Europe are relatively small. Table 3 lists *export ratios,* defined as the value of exports as a percentage of total income, for several nations. In the last few decades, export ratios have increased for most nations.

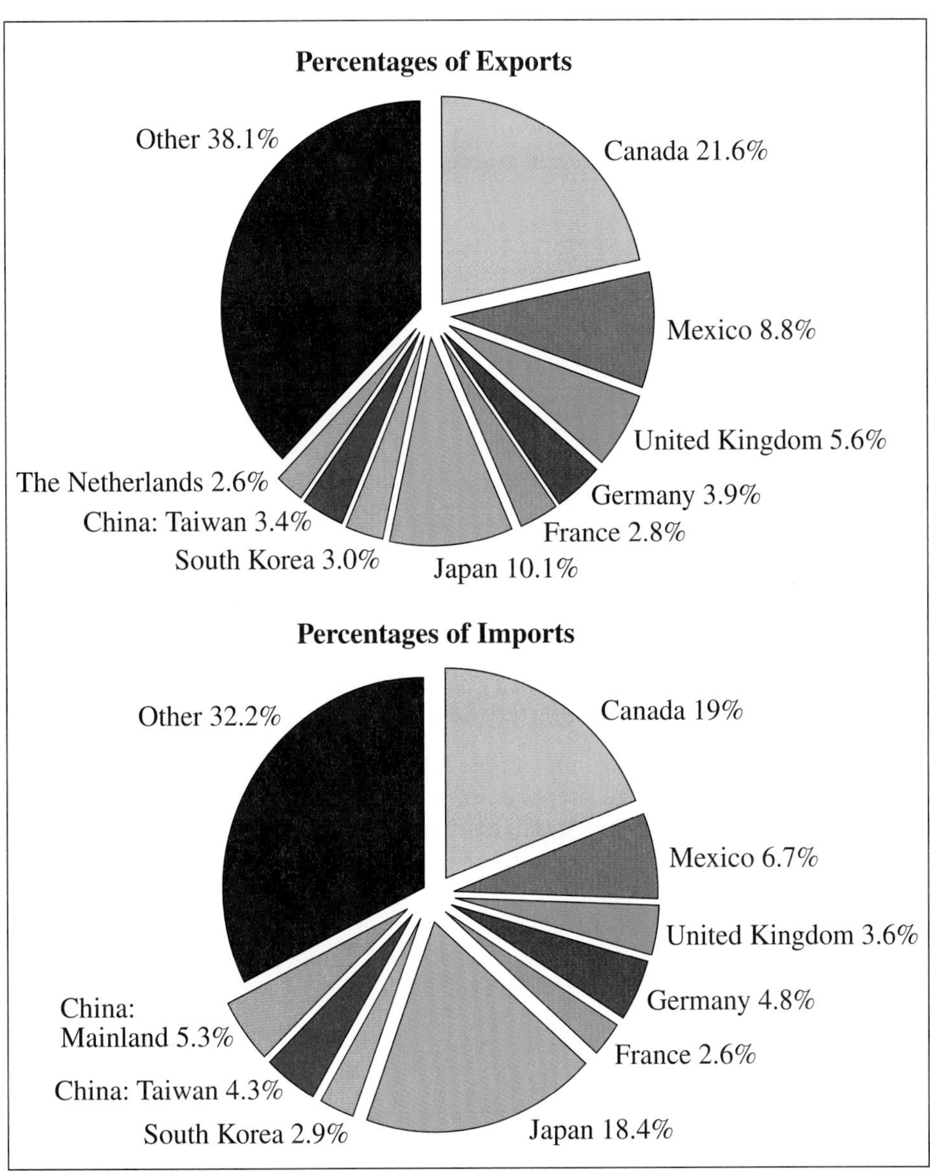

Figure 6

Major Trading Partners for the United States: Exports and Imports, 1993

Source: Statistical Abstract of the United States (Washington, DC: U.S. Government Printing Office, 1994).

Table 3: Export as a Percentage of Income, 1994

Country	*Export Ratio*
Norway	43
Canada	33
Germany	33
South Korea	30
United Kingdom	26
France	23
United States	11
India	10
Brazil	10
Japan	9

Source: International Financial Statistics Yearbook, International Monetary Fund, 1995.

We began the chapter by describing Robin's surprise when he discovered that the personal computer he purchased from a U.S. firm was not truly a domestic product. As explained in the Closer Look box "Multinational Confusion: Imports or Domestic Goods?" the global nature of production makes it difficult to distinguish between domestic and foreign goods.

Protectionist Policies

Trade barriers: Rules that restrict the free flow of goods between nations, including **tariffs** (taxes on imports), **quotas** (limits on total imports) **voluntary export restraints** (agreements between governments to limit imports), and **nontariff trade barriers** (subtle practices that hinder trade).

In the modern global economy, most nations use **trade barriers** to restrict international trade. These policies are often designed to protect domestic firms from foreign competitors, so they are labeled *protectionist* policies. Here are three common forms of protection.

1. A **quota** is an absolute limit on the volume of a particular good that can be imported into a country. For example, if a country imposed a quota on steel imports of 200,000 tons, only 200,000 tons of steel could enter the country.
2. Under a **voluntary export restraint**, one country agrees to limit the volume of exports to another country. For example, the Japanese government agreed to limit the number of Japanese cars sold in the United States and Europe. Many nations use voluntary export restraints to avoid explicit quotas, which are often prohibited by treaties.
3. A **tariff** is a special tax on imported goods. For example, a 10% tariff on imported television sets means that the tax on a $300 imported TV set is $30.

Worldwide sourcing: The practice of buying components for a product from nations throughout the world.

There are other ways to limit imports without an official trade barrier. For example, a nation may target imports for extra-strict enforcement of health and safety laws. Faced with stricter standards than domestic firms, a foreign firm may decide to stay out of the market. Alternatively, a nation may design its customs system to be inefficient and sluggish. If it takes a lot of time and effort to pass imported goods through customs, foreign firms may drop out of the market. These are examples of **nontariff trade barriers**, practices that do not show up as official laws but have the same effects as tariffs and quotas.

A Closer LOOK

Multinational Confusion: Imports or Domestic Goods?

Multinational corporations design, manufacture, and market their products around the globe. For example, U.S. automobile firms design their cars in the United States but import parts and components from Asia and assemble many of the cars sold in the United States in Canada and Mexico. According to some estimates, the Big Three carmakers buy over one-third of the Japanese auto parts imported into the United States.* The practice of using inputs (raw materials or components) from other parts of the world is known as *worldwide sourcing*. As a result, an automobile purchased from a U.S. firm is not a purely domestic product. Many other goods are produced on a global basis, including high-priced athletic shoes (designed in the United States but produced in the Far East) and personal computers (designed in the United States but assembled overseas with parts and components from the United States and other nations). Worldwide sourcing blurs the distinction between domestic and foreign goods.

*Valerie Reitman, "At the Roots of the U.S.–Japan Trade Gap," *Wall Street Journal*, October 10, 1994, p. A10.

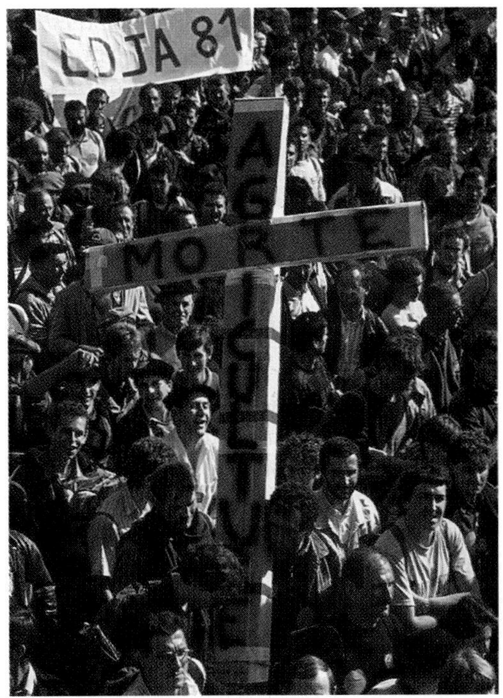

A proposal to lift trade restrictions is often met with opposition from people employed in protected domestic industries. French farmers protested against GATT.

History of Tariff and Trade Agreements

Since 1980, the average U.S. tariff has been about 5%, a rate that is close to the average tariffs in Japan and most European nations but is very low by historical standards. Under the Smoot–Hawley tariffs of the 1930s, the average tariff in the United States was a whopping 59%. The **General Agreement on Tariffs and Trade (GATT)** was initiated in 1947 by the United States and 23 other nations and now has over 100 member nations. There have been eight rounds of GATT negotiations, resulting in progressively lower tariffs for the member nations. The last set of negotiations, the *Uruguay round,* completed in 1994, decreased tariffs by about one-third. In 1995 the **World Trade Organization (WTO)** was formed to oversee GATT and other international trade agreements.

In recent years, various groups of nations have formed trade associations to lower trade barriers and promote international trade.

- The **North American Free Trade Agreement (NAFTA)**. This agreement took effect in 1994 and will be implemented over a 15-year period. The agreement will eventually eliminate all tariffs and other trade barriers between Canada, Mexico, and the United States. NAFTA may soon be extended to other nations in the western hemisphere.
- A total of 15 nations have joined the **European Union (EU)**, an organization designed to remove all trade barriers within Europe and create a single market. In addition, the nations are developing a single currency for all the member nations, labeled the *euro*.
- The leaders of 18 Asian nations formed an organization called **Asian Pacific Economic Cooperation (APEC)** and in 1994 signed a nonbinding agreement to reduce trade barriers between their nations.

General Agreement on Tariffs and Trade (GATT): An international agreement that has lowered trade barriers between the United States and other nations.

World Trade Organization (WTO): An organization that oversees GATT and other international trade agreements.

North American Free Trade Agreement (NAFTA): An international agreement that lowers barriers to trade between the United States, Mexico, and Canada (signed in 1994).

European Union (EU): An organization of European nations that has reduced trade barriers within Europe.

Asian Pacific Economic Cooperation (APEC) organization: An organization of 18 Asian nations that attempts to reduce trade barriers between their nations.

Currency Markets and Exchange Rates

Foreign exchange market: A market in which people exchange one currency for another.

Exchange rate: The price at which currencies trade for one another.

The **foreign exchange market** allows people to exchange one currency for another. Because each nation uses a different currency, international trade would not be possible without such a market. For example, a U.S. firm that sells computers in Japan is paid in yen but must pay its U.S. workers with dollars. The foreign exchange market allows the firm to exchange its yen for dollars. The **exchange rate** is defined as the rate at which we can exchange one currency for another. For example, at an exchange rate of 90 yen per dollar, if the U.S. firm sells a computer in Japan for 90,000 yen, it can exchange the yen for 1,000 U.S. dollars. For some tips on how to read the exchange rate tables found in many newspapers, read the Closer Look box "How to Read a Foreign Exchange Table."

We can use the exchange rate between two currencies to determine the actual cost of a good produced in another nation. Suppose that you are planning a trip to Japan and want to determine the actual cost of staying in a hotel. If a hotel room in Japan costs 9,000 yen per night and the exchange rate is 90 yen per dollar, the hotel room will cost you $100: To get the 9,000 yen to pay for the room,

A Closer LOOK

How to Read a Foreign Exchange Table

Foreign exchange rates are quoted in two equivalent ways. First, the value of a currency in dollars tells us how many dollars 1 unit of the currency will buy. For example, on November 1, 1996, the value of a German mark was $0.6603, meaning that 1 mark could be exchanged for $0.6603. Second, the units per dollar tells us how many units of the currency are necessary to buy 1 dollar. For example, to get 1 dollar, you needed 1.5144 marks.

Nation	*Currency*	*Value in Dollars*	*Units per Dollar*	*Nation*	*Currency*	*Value in Dollars*	*Units per Dollar*
Argentina	peso	1.0000	1.0000	Japan	yen	0.0088	113.6400
Australia	dollar	0.7913	1.2637	Mexico	new peso	0.1247	8.0200
Belgium	frank	0.0320	31.2020	The Netherlands	guilder	0.5889	1.6980
Brazil	real	0.9732	1.0275	New Zealand	dollar	0.7063	1.4158
Canada	dollar	0.7464	1.3398	Norway	krone	0.1567	6.3800
Chile	peso	0.0024	420.000	Peru	new sol	0.3906	2.5600
Costa Rica	colon	0.0046	215.4600	Philippines	peso	0.0381	26.2400
Denmark	krone	0.1720	5.8146	Portugal	escudo	0.0065	153.1600
Finland	markka	0.2207	4.5315	Saudi Arabia	rial	0.2666	3.7503
France	franc	0.1957	5.1107	Singapore	dollar	0.7097	1.4090
Germany	**mark**	**0.6603**	**1.5144**	Spain	peseta	0.0078	127.6200
Great Britain	pound sterling	1.6262	0.6149	South Korea	won	0.0012	824.0000
Greece	drachma	0.0042	237.9400	Sweden	krona	0.1524	6.5619
Hong Kong	dollar	0.1293	7.7315	Switzerland	franc	0.7950	1.2578
India	rupee	0.0281	35.6000	Taiwan	dollar	0.0363	27.5200
Ireland	punt	1.6285	0.6141	Thai	baht	0.0392	25.5050
Israel	shekel	0.3058	3.2703	Venezuela	bolivar	0.0021	470.2600
Italy	lira	0.00066	1,515.3600				

Source: The Oregonian, November 1, 1996, p. B5. Data from U.S. Bank of Oregon Treasury Division.

you must give up $100. If the exchange rate were 200 yen per dollar instead, the hotel room would cost you only $45 a night: To get the 9,000 yen, you would need only $45. A Japanese hotel room might seem expensive when the exchange rate is 90 yen per dollar but a real bargain when the exchange rate is 200 yen per dollar. Later in the book we'll see how exchange rates are determined in the foreign exchange market.

TEST *Your Understanding*

4 Match each trade restriction with its description.

Restriction	*Description*
A. Tariffs	1. Limits on total imports.
B. Quotas	2. Hidden impediments to trade.
C. Voluntary export restraints	3. Agreements between nations to restrict trade.
D. Nontariff trade barriers	4. Taxes on imports.

5 Complete the statement with *GATT* or *NAFTA*: The ____________ is a worldwide trade agreement whereas ____________ applies to a single continent.

6 Complete the statement with *more* or *less*: If the exchange between U.S. dollars and French francs went from 5 francs per dollar to 3 francs per dollar, this would tend to make French goods ____________ expensive to U.S. citizens.

SUMMARY

This chapter has provided an overview of a market-based economy. In the factor markets, households provide labor and capital to firms in exchange for money. In the product markets, firms provide goods and services to households in exchange for money. The government has several roles in the market-based economy: It provides some goods and services, collects taxes, redistributes income, and regulates firms. In recent years, international trade agreements have lowered the barriers to trade, hastening the move to a truly global economy. Here are the main points from the chapter.

1. Most people are not self-sufficient, but instead specialize to earn income, which they use to buy goods and services from others.
2. A system of international specialization and trade is sensible because people and nations have different opportunity costs of producing goods, giving rise to comparative advantage.
3. The free flow of goods can be hampered by barriers to trade, including tariffs, quotas, voluntary export restraints, and nontariff trade barriers. There are many international agreements designed to reduce trade barriers, including GATT, NAFTA, and the European Union.
4. The foreign exchange market allows people to exchange one currency for another, facilitating international trade.

KEY TERMS

absolute advantage, *38*
Asian Pacific Economic Cooperation (APEC), *53*
benefit-tax approach, *44*
centrally planned economy, *48*
comparative advantage, *39*
European Union (EU), *53*
exchange rate, *54*
export, *49*
foreign exchange market, *54*
General Agreement on Tariffs and Trade (GATT), *53*

horizontal equity, *44*
import, *49*
market system, *38*
mixed economy, *48*
multinational corporation, *40*
nontariff trade barriers, *52*
North American Free Trade Agreement (NAFTA), *53*
privatizing, *49*
quota, *52*
tariff, *52*
trade barriers, *52*
transition, *49*
vertical equity, *44*
voluntary export restraints, *52*
World Trade Organization (WTO), *53*
worldwide sourcing, *52*

PROBLEMS AND DISCUSSION QUESTIONS

1. Use the notion of comparative advantage to explain why two countries, one of which is less efficient in producing all products, will still find it advantageous to trade.
2. Some studies have suggested that industries in countries that receive protection from foreign trade are less efficient than the same industries in other countries that do not receive protection. Can you explain this finding?
3. Suppose that the prices of goods in Mexico and the United States remain unchanged while the exchange rate increases from 10 pesos per dollar to 20 pesos per dollar.
   a. Take the perspective of a U.S. consumer. Are Mexican goods more or less attractive?
   b. Take the perspective of a Mexican consumer. Are U.S. goods more or less attractive?

Take It to the Net

We invite you to visit the O'Sullivan/Sheffrin page on the Prentice Hall Web site at:

http://www.prenhall.com/osullivan/

for this chapter's World Wide Web exercise.

MODEL ANSWERS FOR THIS CHAPTER

Chapter-Opening Questions

1. Comparative advantage makes trade between two nations beneficial for both nations.
2. A firm is an organization that uses resources to produce a product, which it then sells. There are three types of firms: a sole proprietorship, a partnership, and and a corporation.
3. As shown in A Closer Look: Tax Rates in Different Nations, the answer is the United States.
4. As shown in Table 3, some nations with relatively high export ratios are Norway, Canada, Germany, South Korea, Britain, and France.
5. The most common forms of protection are quotas, voluntary export restraints, and tariffs.
6. GATT is an international agreement that has lowered trade barriers between the United States and other nations. WTO is the new organization that oversees GATT and other international trade agreements. NAFTA is an international agreement that lowers barriers to trade between the United States, Mexico, and Canada (signed in 1994).

Test Your Understanding

1. Carla has a lower opportunity cost of chairs, so she should produce chairs. Tim has a lower opportunity cost of tables (⅓ of a chair), so he should produce tables.
2. Nation H has a comparative advantage in wheat: The opportunity cost of wheat is 2 tons of steel, compared to 3 tons in nation E.
3. They facilitate the exchanges made necessary by specialization.
4. 1B, 2D, 3C, 4A
5. GATT, NAFTA
6. more

NOTES

1. Marsha Blumenthal and Joel Slemrod, "The Compliance Cost of the U.S. Individual Income Tax System: A Second Look after Tax Reform," *National Tax Journal*, vol. 45, no. 2, June 1992, pp. 185–202.

CHAPTER

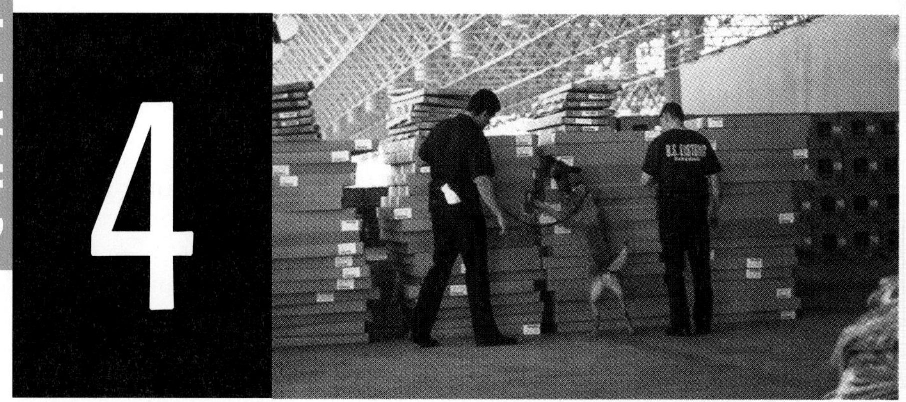

Supply, Demand, and Market Equilibrium

Ted Koppel, host of the ABC news program *Nightline,* once made the following statement[1]: "Do you know what's happened to the price of drugs in the United States? The price of cocaine, way down, the price of marijuana, way down. You don't have to be an expert in economics to know that when the price goes down, it means more stuff is coming in. That's supply and demand." According to Koppel, the price of drugs dropped because the government's efforts to control the supply of illegal drugs had failed.

We know from earlier chapters that a market is an arrangement that allows buyers and sellers to exchange money and products. In this chapter we use a model of supply and demand, the most important tool of economic analysis, to see how markets work. We can use the model of supply and demand to see how the prices of goods and services are affected by all sorts of changes in the economy, including bad weather, higher income, technological innovation, taxes, regulation, and changes in consumer preferences. This chapter will prepare you for the dozens of applications of supply and demand you'll see in the rest of the book.

This chapter will also prepare you to do your own economic analysis. You'll learn how to predict whether a specific change in a market will cause the price to rise or fall. You'll also learn how to play economic detective, using clues from the market to explain past changes in market prices. If Ted

Koppel had read this chapter before making his comment about the price of drugs, he might not have been so glib about the connection between drug prices and the government's antidrug policies. The facts on the drug market suggest a very different conclusion.

Perfectly competitive market: A market with a very large number of firms, each of which produces the same standardized product and is so small that it does not affect the market price of the good it produces.

In this chapter we use the model of supply and demand to explain how a perfectly competitive market operates. A **perfectly competitive market** has a very large number of firms, each of which produces the same standardized product and is so small that it does not affect the market price of the good it produces. The classic example of a perfectly competitive firm is a wheat farmer, who produces a tiny fraction of the total supply of wheat. No matter how much wheat the farmer produces, the market price of wheat won't change.

The chapter includes many practical applications of supply and demand analysis. Here are some of the practical questions we answer:

1. How would an antismoking campaign affect the price of cigarettes and the amount of smoking?
2. What's the connection between the war in Bosnia and the price of raspberries in the Pacific Northwest?
3. How does technological innovation affect the price of computers?
4. Over the last few decades, the consumption of poultry (chicken and turkey) increased dramatically. Why?
5. Why has the price of used newspapers bounced around so much during the last decade?

MARKET DEMAND

On the demand side of a product market, consumers buy goods or services from firms. The principal question for the buyer or demand side of the market is: How much of a particular product are consumers willing to buy during a particular time period? A consumer who is "willing to buy" a particular product is willing to sacrifice enough money to purchase the good. In other words, the consumer doesn't merely have a desire to buy the good but is willing to sacrifice something to get it. Note that demand is defined for a particular time period, for example, a day, a week, or a year.

The answer to the demand question is "it depends," and here is a list of the variables that affect consumers' decisions, using the market for apples as an example:

- The price of the product, for example, the price of apples
- Consumer income
- The price of related goods, for example, the prices of bananas and ice cream
- The number of potential consumers (population)
- Consumer tastes and advertising
- Consumer expectations about future prices

These variables are the determinants of demand: Together, they determine how much of a particular product consumers are willing to buy.

Demand curve: A curve showing the relationship between price and the quantity that consumers are willing to buy during a particular time period.

The Demand Curve and the Law of Demand

The **demand curve** shows the relationship between the price of a good and the quantity that consumers are willing to buy during a particular time period. To show this relationship for apples, we assume that the other variables that affect the demand for apples (consumer income, the prices of related goods, population, tastes, and expectations about future prices) are fixed. To draw a *demand curve*, we use the data shown in a demand schedule, which is just a table showing, for each price, the quantity that consumers are willing to buy. Figure 1 shows a demand schedule and the associated demand curve. The quantity demanded is 14,000 pounds per day at a price of $0.80 (point *j*) but 20,000 pounds at a price of $0.60 (point *e*) and 26,000 pounds at a price of $0.40 (point *c*).

As the price of apples changes and we move along the demand curve, the quantity demanded changes. According to the **law of demand**, the lower the price, the larger the quantity demanded. To see why this is sensible, let's think about how you as a consumer make choices among the wide variety of goods and services available and how these choices are affected by a drop in price.

Law of demand: The lower the price, the larger the quantity demanded.

1. ***Substitution effect.*** When you buy apples, you have less money to spend on other products, such as bananas, bread, music, books, and travel. The price of apples determines exactly how much of these other goods you sacrifice to get a pound of apples. Suppose that the price of apples is $2 per pound and the price of bananas is $0.50 per pound. In this case you'll sacrifice 4 pounds of bananas for every pound of apples, and the large trade-off between the two goods will discourage you from buying very many apples. If the price of apples drops to $0.50, however, you'll sacrifice only 1 pound of bananas for each pound of apples: The price of apples has decreased relative to the price of bananas. Given the smaller sacrifice associated with consuming apples, you are likely to buy more apples, substituting apples for other goods such as bananas.

Substitution effect: The change in consumption resulting from a change in the price of one good relative to the price of other goods.

2. ***Income effect.*** A decrease in the price of apples means that a given amount of money will buy more of all goods, including apples and any other goods you purchase. For example, suppose that you have $5 per week to spend on fruit and you buy 1 pound of apples at a price of $2 and spend $3 on other fruit. If the price of apples drops to $0.50, your original basket of fruit will cost only $3.50, so you'll

Income effect: The change in consumption resulting from an increase in the consumer's real income.

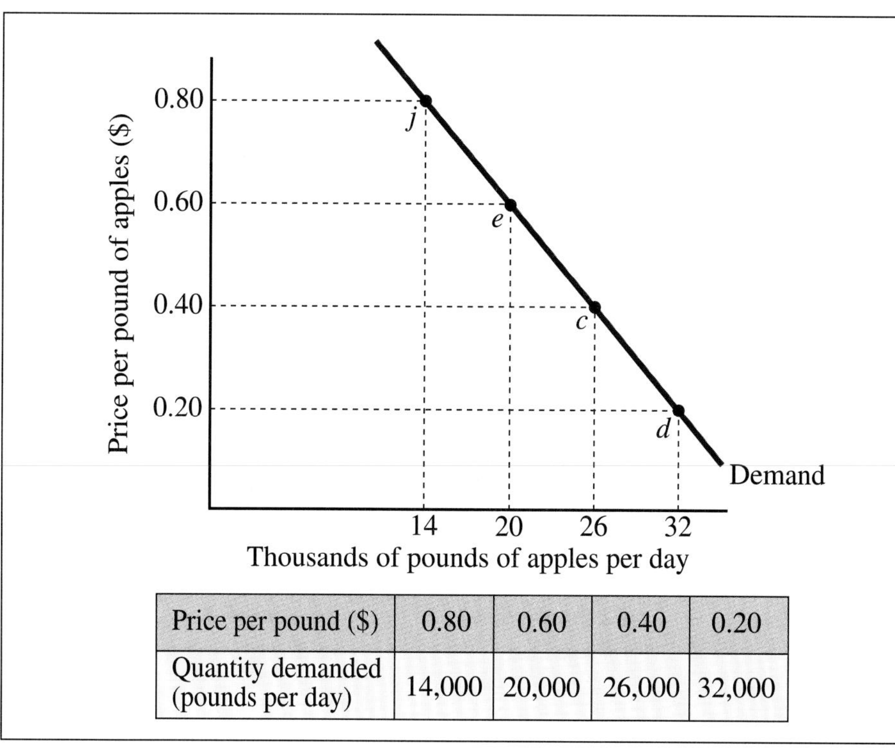

Price per pound ($)	0.80	0.60	0.40	0.20
Quantity demanded (pounds per day)	14,000	20,000	26,000	32,000

Figure 1

Demand Schedule and Demand Curve

According to the law of demand, the lower the price, the larger the quantity demanded. Therefore, the demand curve is negatively sloped: When the price decreases from $0.80 to $0.60, the quantity demanded increases from 14,000 pound per day to 20,000.

have $1.50 left to spend as you please. In other words, the drop in price increases your real income, defined as your income in terms of the goods the money can buy. As your real income increases, you are likely to consume more apples—and more of other goods as well.

Change in quantity demanded: A change in quantity resulting from a change in the price of the good; causes movement along a demand curve.

There is some special jargon associated with movement along a demand curve: A **change in quantity demanded** is defined as a change in quantity resulting from a change in the price of the good.

Trying to Draw a Demand Curve with Incomplete Data

What sort of data do we need to draw a market demand curve? The market demand curve shows the relationship between the price and quantity of a particular good, *everything else being equal*. If we have data on prices and quantities, we cannot draw a demand curve unless we are certain that the other variables that affect the market demand (the prices of other goods, income, tastes, and the number of consumers) are held fixed.

A common error is to use incomplete data to attempt to draw a market demand curve. Table 1 shows two years of data on gasoline consumption in a hypothetical city. It might be tempting to plot these two combinations of price and quantity, draw a line between the two points, and call the resulting curve a demand curve. We cannot do that because the data are incomplete: They do not show what happened to the other variables that affect the demand for gasoline between 1996 and 1997. To draw a demand curve with these data, we must have additional data that convince us that these other variables did not change.

SHIFTING THE DEMAND CURVE

We've seen that changes in price cause movement along the demand curve, but what about the other determinants of demand? What are the implications of a change in consumer income, the price of a related good, population, consumer tastes and advertising, or expectations about future prices?

If any of these other variables changes, the entire demand curve will shift. Recall that when we draw the demand curve—the relationship between the quantity demanded and the price—we assume the other variables that affect the demand for apples are fixed. If any of these other variables changes, the relationship between price and quantity changes, so the demand curve shifts. In the jargon of economics, this is called a **change in demand.** A new demand curve means that at each price, the quantity demanded will be either larger or smaller. We'll discuss several sources of change in demand.

Change in demand: A change in quantity resulting from a change in something other than the price of the good; causes the entire demand curve to shift.

Change in Income

The demand for a particular good depends on consumer income, and a change in income will shift the entire demand curve. In Figure 2 the original demand curve for

Table 1: Price and Quantity of Gasoline

Year	*Gasoline Price (per gallon)*	*Quantity Consumed (millions of gallons)*
1996	1.20	400
1997	1.40	350

apples is labeled D_1. If consumer income increases, consumers are likely to spend at least some of their extra income on apples. Therefore, the demand curve will shift to the right, from D_1 to D_2: At each price, consumers will buy more apples. For example, at a price of $0.60, the quantity demanded increases from 20,000 pounds to 30,000 pounds. This is an example of a **normal good:** An increase in income increases demand for that good.

Normal good: A good for which an increase in income *increases* demand.

The most dramatic illustrations of the relationship between income and consumption come from developing countries. Between 1978 and 1992, per capita income in China more than tripled. During the same period, the per capita consumption of many products increased: The percentage increase was 19% for grain, 135% for pork, 56% for sugar, 400% for bicycles, and 92% for housing.[2] The number of television sets per 1,000 people increased from 3 to 195. The tripling of per capita income was certainly a major factor in these increases in consumption, although changes in prices may also have played a role.

For an **inferior good,** an increase in income decreases demand, shifting the demand curve to the left. In most cases an inferior good is an inexpensive good (for example, margarine) that has an expensive alternative (butter). As income increases, many consumers switch from relatively inexpensive inferior goods to the more expensive good. As a result, the demand curve for an inferior good shifts to the left: At each price, a smaller quantity is demanded. Some other examples of inferior goods are potatoes, intercity bus travel, and used clothing.

Inferior good: A good for which an increase in income *decreases* demand.

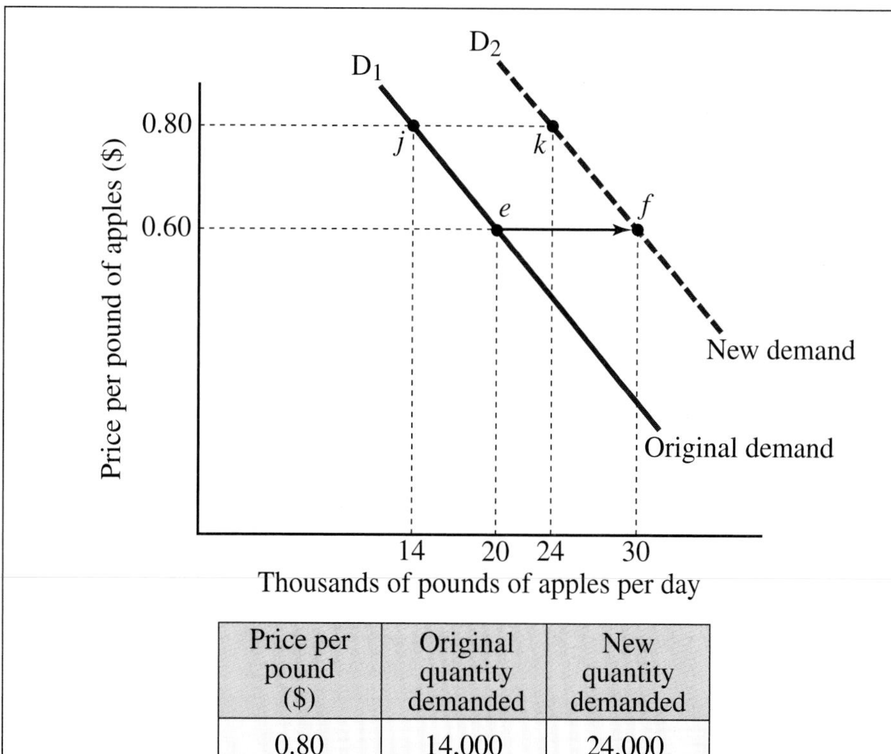

Price per pound ($)	Original quantity demanded	New quantity demanded
0.80	14,000	24,000
0.60	20,000	30,000

Figure 2

Increase in Income Shifts the Demand Curve

An increase in income shifts the demand curve for a normal good to the right, from D_1 to D_2: At each price, a larger quantity is demanded. For example, at a price of $0.60, the quantity demanded increases from 20,000 pounds (point *e*) to 30,000 pounds (point *f*).

Changes in the Price of a Related Good

Substitutes: Two goods for which an increase in the price of one good increases the demand for the other good.

Complements: Two goods for which an increase in the price of one good decreases the demand for the other good.

The demand for a particular good is also affected by the prices of related goods. Two goods are **substitutes** if an increase in the price of one good increases the demand for the other good. In most cases, substitutes can be used in place of one another. In contrast, two goods are **complements** if an increase in the price of one good decreases the demand for the other good. Complements are typically consumed together.

Let's start by looking at substitute goods. In Figure 3 an increase in the price of bananas shifts the demand for apples to the right, from D_2 to D_3: at every price, more apples will be demanded. This is sensible because when bananas become more expensive relative to apples, some consumers will substitute apples for bananas. Some other examples of substitute goods are compact disks (CDs) and audio tapes, different brands of personal computers, and pencils and pens. In general, an increase in the price of a substitute increases demand, shifting the demand curve to the right. For another example of substitute goods, read the Closer Look box "Infant Airline Seats and Safety."

Consider next the effects of changing the price of a complementary good. In Figure 3 an increase in the price of ice cream (often consumed with apple pie) shifts the demand curve for apples to the left, from D_2 to D_1. This is sensible because an increase in the price of ice cream increases the cost of apple pie and ice cream together, causing some consumers to switch to other types of food. Other examples of complementary goods are CD players and CDs, personal computers and printers, and tennis rackets and tennis balls. In general, an increase in the price of a complementary good increases the cost of the bundle of goods, causing people to demand less of both goods.

Light bulbs and electricity are complementary goods, so a consumer's choice of light bulbs depends in part on the price of electricity. The recent development of the compact fluorescent lamp (CFL) provides an alternative to the traditional incandescent bulb. Although a CFL is much more expensive than a traditional bulb, it is much more energy efficient, using only 25% as much electricity. It's not surprising that CFLs are most popular in nations with high electricity prices. For example, the

Figure 3

Shifting the Demand Curve

An increase in the price of a substitute shifts the demand curve to the right, from D_2 to D_3: At each price, a larger quantity is demanded. An increase in the price of a complement shifts the demand curve to the left, from D_2 to D_1: At each price, a smaller quantity is demanded.

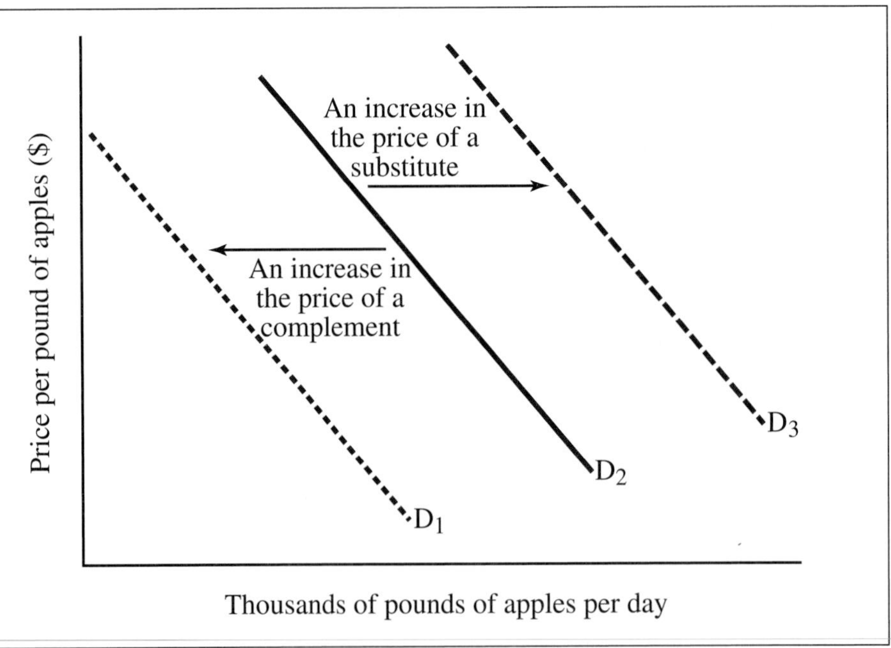

A Closer LOOK

Infant Airline Seats and Safety

Should parents traveling by airplane be allowed to hold their infants in their laps, or should they be required to buy separate tickets for infants and strap them into safety seats? A law requiring separate tickets and seats for infants would generate good news and bad news.

1. *Good news.* Fewer infants would die in airline crashes because infants are safer in their own seats.
2. *Bad news.* More people would die in car crashes. A law requiring parents to buy two tickets instead of one would increase the cost of traveling by air, causing some parents to switch from flying to driving, a more dangerous travel mode.

After several studies concluded that the bad news would dominate the good news, the Federal Aviation Commission ruled in 1992 that parents would be allowed to hold their infants in their laps.*

The simple lesson is that consumers respond to changes in prices. An increase in the price of one good (air travel) causes some consumers to switch to a substitute good (highway travel), leading to some unexpected results.

* "U.S. Won't Require Infant Seats on Planes," *New York Times*, September 15, 1992, p. A18.

An increase in the price of air travel will cause some consumers to switch to highway travel, which is actually more dangerous.

Japanese, who pay 65% more for electricity than do their U.S. counterparts, get 80% of their home lighting from CFLs.[3]

Other Factors Affecting Demand

We've seen that changes in income or the prices of related goods shift the market demand curve. Three other sorts of changes affect the relationship between price and quantity, shifting the demand curve.

1. ***Population.*** An increase in the number of people means that there are more potential apple consumers, so we expect the demand curve to shift to the right: At each price, a larger quantity is demanded.

2. ***Consumer tastes and advertising.*** Changes in consumer preferences will shift the demand curve for apples. The preferences of an individual consumer are

influenced by other people, often through advertising campaigns. A successful advertising campaign will shift the market demand curve to the right. In general, consumers' desires for a particular good change over time, causing the demand curve to shift.

3. ***Consumer expectations about future prices.*** A change in expectations about prices will shift the demand curve as consumers decide to buy more or less of a product today. For example, if consumers think that next month's price will be higher than they had initially expected, they will buy a larger quantity today and a smaller quantity next month. This will shift the demand curve to the right today, with an offsetting leftward shift next month.

TEST *Your Understanding*

1 Which of the following items go together?

A. Change in demand
B. Change in quantity demanded
C. Change in price
D. Movement along the demand curve
E. Shifting the demand curve
F. Change in income

2 True or false, and explain: An increase in income will shift the demand curve for a normal good to the left.

3 Complete the statement with *right* or *left*: An increase in the price of cassette tapes will shift the demand curve for CDs to the __________; an increase in the price of CD players will shift the demand curve for CDs to the __________.

4 From the following list of variables, circle those that change as we move along the market demand curve for pencils, and cross out those that are assumed to be fixed: *quantity of pencils, number of potential consumers, price of pencils, price of pens, consumer income.*

MARKET SUPPLY

On the supply side of a product, market firms sell their products to consumers. Recall that a perfectly competitive market has a very large number of firms, each of which is so small that it does not affect the market price of the good it produces. The principal question for the seller or supply side of the market is: How much of a particular product are firms willing to sell? Here is a list of variables that affect the decisions of sellers, using the market for apples as an example:

- The price of the product, for example, the price of apples
- The cost of the inputs used to produce the product, for example, the wage paid to farmworkers and grocery clerks, the cost of fertilizer, and the cost of apple-processing equipment
- The state of production technology, for example, the knowledge used in growing and processing apples
- The number of producers, for example, the number of apple farmers
- Producer expectations about future prices

These variables are the determinants of supply: Together, they determine how much of a particular product producers are willing to sell.

The Supply Curve and the Law of Supply

The **supply curve** shows the relationship between the price of a good and the quantity of the good that producers are willing to sell during a particular time period. To show this relationship for apples, we assume that the other variables that affect the supply of apples (input costs, technology, and the number of producers) are fixed. To draw a supply curve, we use the data shown in a *supply schedule,* which is a table showing the quantities supplied at different prices. Figure 4 shows a supply schedule and the associated supply curve. The quantity supplied is 10,000 pounds per day at a price of $0.40 (point *b*), but 20,000 pounds at $0.60 (point *e*).

Supply curve: A curve showing the relationship between price and the quantity that producers are willing to sell during a particular time period.

As the price of apples changes and we move along the supply curve, the quantity supplied changes. According to the **law of supply,** the higher the price, the larger the quantity supplied. This is sensible because an increase in price makes the production of apples more profitable, leading to two responses.

Law of supply: The higher the price, the larger the quantity supplied.

1. Existing firms will supply more apples, squeezing more apples out of their production facilities (farms and stores).
2. New firms will enter the industry by setting up production facilities.

In the jargon of economics, a **change in quantity supplied** is defined as a change in quantity resulting from a change in the price of the good and results in movement along the supply curve.

Change in quantity supplied: A change in quantity resulting from a change in the price of the good; causes movement along a supply curve.

Shifting the Supply Curve

What sort of changes would shift the entire supply curve? Recall that when we draw the supply curve—the relationship between the quantity supplied and the price—we assume that the other variables that affect the supply of apples (input costs, technology, and the number of producers) are fixed. If any of these other variables changes, the entire supply curve will shift, indicating a change in the relationship between

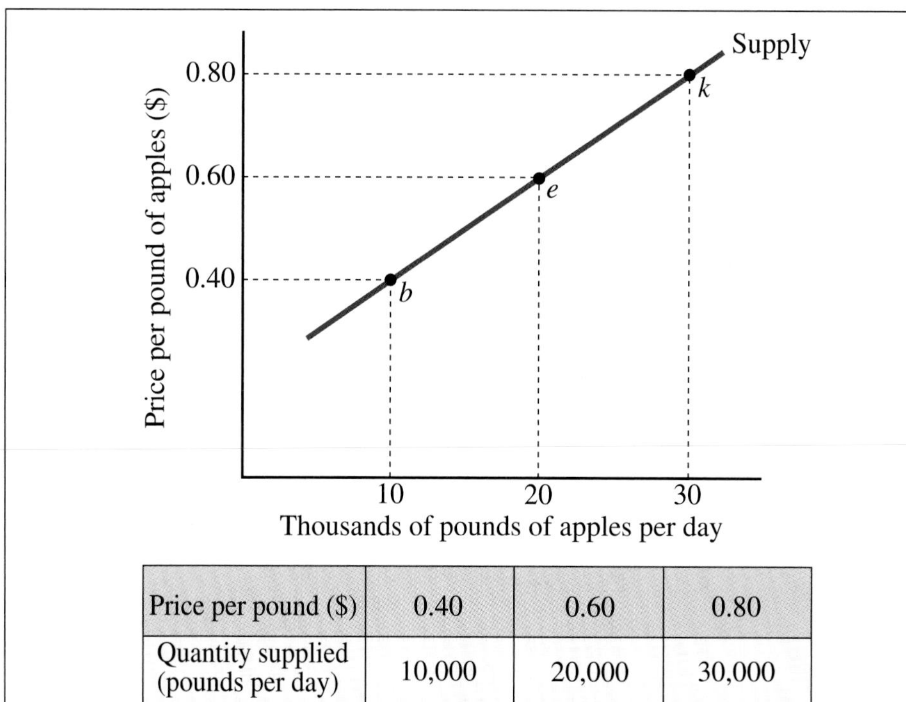

Price per pound ($)	0.40	0.60	0.80
Quantity supplied (pounds per day)	10,000	20,000	30,000

Figure 4

Supply Schedule and Supply Curve

According to the law of supply, the higher the price, the larger the quantity supplied. Therefore, the supply curve is positively sloped: When the price increases from $0.40 to $0.60, the quantity supplied increases from 10,000 pounds per day to 20,000.

Change in supply: A change in quantity resulting from a change in something other than the price of the good; causes the entire supply curve to shift.

price and quantity. In the jargon of economics, this is called a **change in supply.** A new supply curve means that at each price, the quantity supplied will be either larger or smaller. We'll discuss several sources of change in supply.

Figure 5 shows an increase in supply, represented as a rightward shift of the supply curve from S_1 to S_2. At each price, producers are willing to supply more apples. For example, at a price of \$0.40, the quantity supplied increases from 10,000 pounds (shown by point *b*) to 16,000 pounds (shown by point *h*). Here are some of the changes that would shift the supply curve to the right.

1. A decrease in the cost of one or more inputs (for example, labor or fertilizer) will make apple production more profitable at a given price, so producers will be willing to supply more apples at that price.
2. A technological advance that makes it possible to produce apples at a lower cost will make apple production more profitable, so producers supply more apples.
3. An increase in the number of producers.
4. A change in price expectations, with producers expecting future prices to be lower than they had expected before.

Of course, the supply curve could also shift to the left, reflecting a decrease in supply. For example, an increase in input costs makes the production of apples less profitable, so producers will be willing to supply fewer of them. Another reason for a leftward shift of the supply curve is a tax imposed on apple producers, which has the same effect as an increase in production costs: Profits from apple production will fall, so firms will produce fewer apples. The supply curve will also shift to the left if the number of firms drops or producers expect future prices to be higher than they had expected before.

Figure 5

Shifting the Supply Curve

An increase in supply shifts the supply curve to the right, from S_1 to S_2: At each price, a larger quantity is supplied. Supply will increase as a result of (1) a decrease in input prices, (2) a technological innovation that decreases production costs, or (3) an increase in the number of producers.

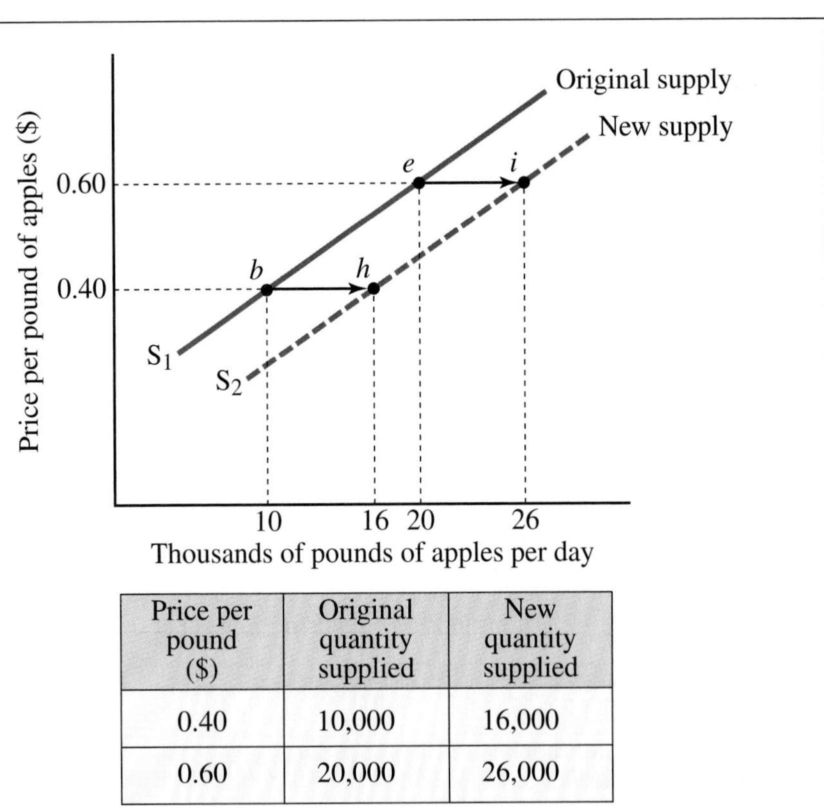

Price per pound (\$)	Original quantity supplied	New quantity supplied
0.40	10,000	16,000
0.60	20,000	26,000

TEST *Your Understanding*

5 Which of the following items go together?

A. Change in quantity supplied
B. Change in production cost
C. Change in supply
D. Shifting the supply curve
E. Change in price
F. Movement along the supply curve

6 True or false, and explain: An increase in the wage of computer workers will shift the supply curve for computers to the left.

7 From the following list of variables, circle those that change as we move along the market supply curve for housing, and cross out those that are assumed to be fixed: *quantity of housing, number of potential consumers, price of wood, price of houses, consumer income.*

MARKET EQUILIBRIUM

A **market equilibrium** is a situation in which the quantity of a product demanded equals the quantity supplied, so there is no pressure to change the price. For example, if apple firms produce exactly the quantity of apples that consumers are willing to buy, there will be no pressure to change the price of apples. The equilibrium price is shown by the intersection of the supply and demand curves. In Figure 6 on page 68, at a price of $0.60, the supply curve shows that firms will produce 20,000 pounds, which is exactly the quantity that consumers are willing to buy at this price.

Market equilibrium: A situation in which the quantity of a product demanded equals the quantity supplied, so there is no pressure to change the price.

If the price is less than the equilibrium price, there will be a shortage of the product. A **shortage** occurs when consumers are willing to buy more than producers are willing to sell. In Figure 6 there is a shortage at a price of $0.40: Consumers are willing to buy 26,000 pounds of apples (point *s*), but producers are willing to sell only 10,000 pounds (point *r*). As a result, the price of apples will increase: Firms will increase the price on their limited supply of apples, and anxious consumers will gladly pay the higher price to get one of the few apples that are available. As the price rises, the market moves upward along both the demand curve (the quantity demanded decreases) and the supply curve (the quantity supplied increases), so the gap between the quantities demanded and supplied will shrink. The price will continue to rise until the shortage is eliminated: At a price of $0.60, the quantity supplied equals the quantity demanded.

Shortage: A situation in which consumers are willing to buy more than producers are willing to sell.

What happens if the price exceeds the equilibrium price? A **surplus** occurs when producers are willing to sell more than consumers are willing to buy. This is shown by points *k* and *j* in Figure 6: At a price of $0.80, producers are willing to sell 30,000 pounds, while consumers are willing to buy only 14,000 pounds. The price of apples will decrease as firms cut the price to sell their leftover apples. As the price drops, the market moves downward along both the demand curve (the quantity demanded increases) and the supply curve (the quantity supplied decreases). The price will continue to decrease until the surplus is eliminated: At a price of $0.60, the quantity supplied equals the quantity demanded.

Surplus: A situation in which producers are willing to sell more than consumers are willing to buy.

Market Effects of Changes in Demand

Now that we know how to find the market equilibrium, we can explore the effects of changes in demand on the equilibrium price and quantity of a particular good. In Figure 7 on page 68 an increase in the demand for apples shifts the demand curve to the right, from D_1 to D_2. At the original price of $0.60, there will be a shortage of apples, as indicated by points *e* and *g*: Consumers are willing to buy 28,000 pounds

Figure 6
Supply, Demand, and Market Equilibrium

At the market equilibrium (point *e*, with price = \$0.60 and quantity = 20,000), the quantity supplied equals the quantity demanded. At a price below the equilibrium price (for example, \$0.40), there is a shortage, while at a price above the equilibrium price (for example, \$0.80), there is a surplus.

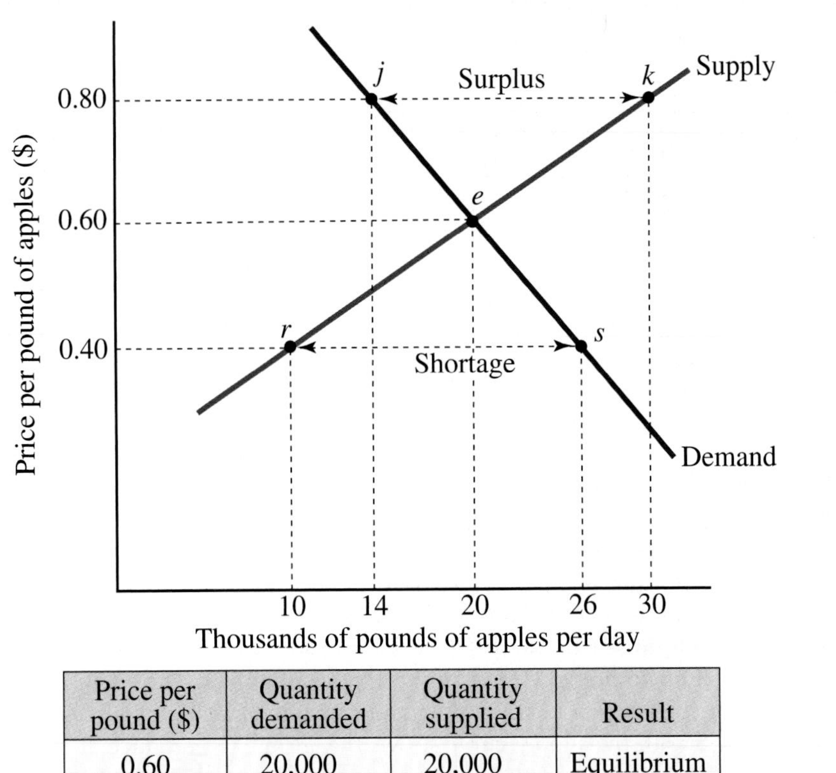

Price per pound ($)	Quantity demanded	Quantity supplied	Result
0.60	20,000	20,000	Equilibrium
0.80	14,000	30,000	Surplus
0.40	26,000	10,000	Shortage

Figure 7
Market Effects of an Increase in Demand

An increase in demand shifts the demand curve to the right, causing a shortage at the original price. To eliminate the shortage, the price increases, in this case from \$0.60 to \$0.70.

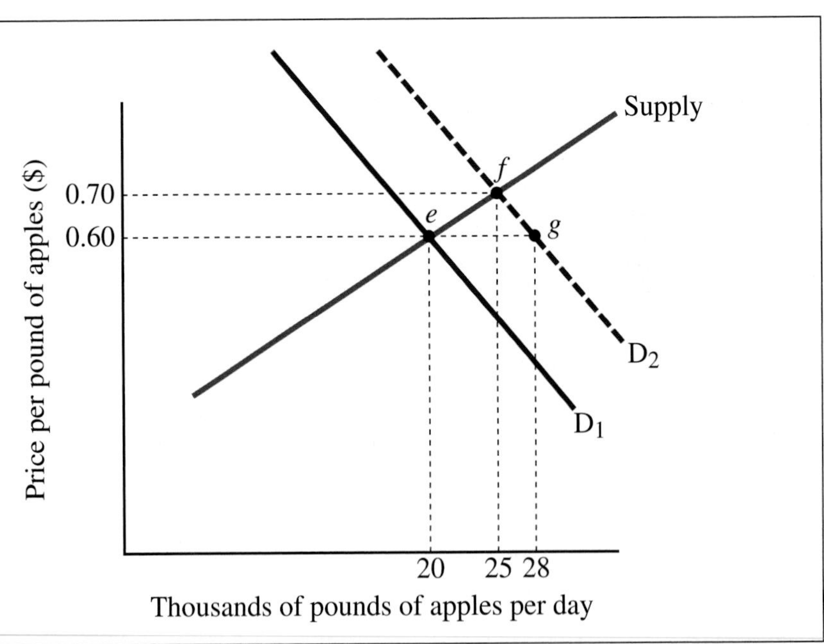

(point *g*), but producers are willing to sell only 20,000 pounds (point *e*). The resulting increase in price will eliminate the shortage. The supply curve intersects the new demand curve at point *f*, so the new equilibrium price is $0.70 (up from $0.60) and the new equilibrium quantity is 25,000 pounds (up from 20,000).

We've seen how an increase in demand affects the price of a good, but what about a decrease in demand? Suppose that a government uses an antismoking campaign to decrease the demand for cigarettes. In Figure 8 the initial (precampaign) equilibrium is shown by point *i:* The price is $2 per pack and the quantity is 100,000 packs per day. A successful antismoking campaign will shift the demand curve for cigarettes to the left: At each price, fewer cigarettes will be demanded. At the initial price of $2, there will be a surplus of cigarettes, and the resulting decrease in price will eliminate the surplus. Equilibrium is restored at point *f*, with a price of $1.80 and a quantity of 80,000 packs per day. The same sort of changes will occur when the demand for any product decreases: Both the price and the quantity decrease.

What other sort of changes in demand would affect the equilibrium price? As we saw earlier in the chapter, the demand curve will shift as a result of a change in consumer income, the price of a related good, the number of consumers, and consumer preferences. To predict the market effects of a change in demand, we draw a supply–demand diagram, shift the demand curve to the right or the left, and see what happens to the equilibrium price. If you try this a few times, you'll discover that demand and price move in the same direction: An increase in demand increases price, but a decrease in demand decreases the price.

Market Effects of Changes in Supply

Now that we've seen the market effects of changes in demand, we can discuss the effects of changes in supply. Let's think about how a technological innovation affects the equilibrium price of personal computers. Figure 9 on page 70 shows the initial equilibrium in the computer market: The supply curve intersects the demand curve at point *i*, so the equilibrium price is $1,000. As we saw earlier, a technological innovation that decreases production costs will increase supply and shift the supply curve to the right. At the original price, there will be a surplus, so the price decreases, eliminating the surplus. In Figure 9 the market reaches a new equilibrium at point *f*, with a new price of $800.

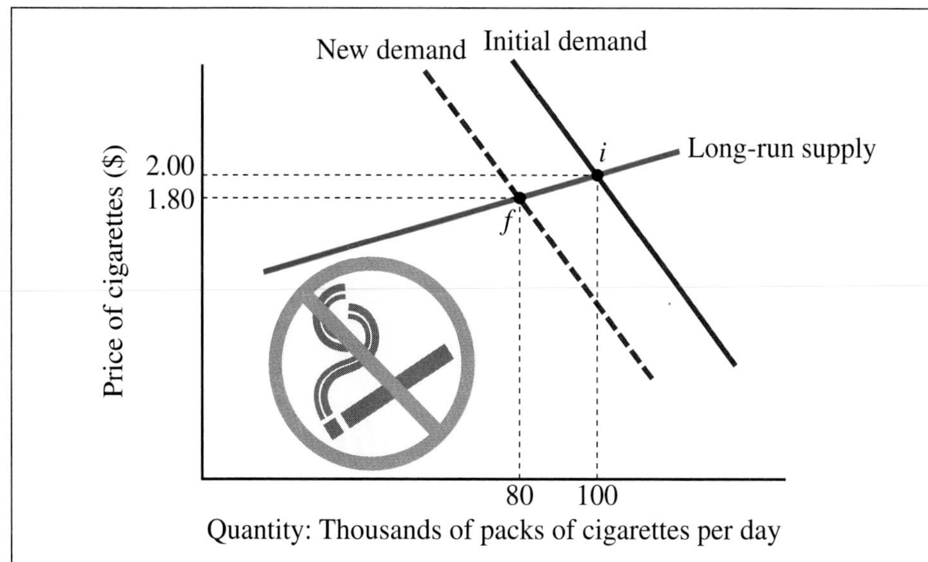

Figure 8

Market Effects of an Antismoking Campaign

An antismoking campaign shifts the demand curve for cigarettes to the left. At the initial price ($2), there is a surplus: The quantity supplied exceeds the quantity demanded. The price decreases until equilibrium is restored at point *f*.

Figure 9

Effects of Technological Innovation on the Market for Personal Computers

Technological innovation decreases production costs, shifting the supply curve to the right. The equilibrium price decreases and the equilibrium quantity increases.

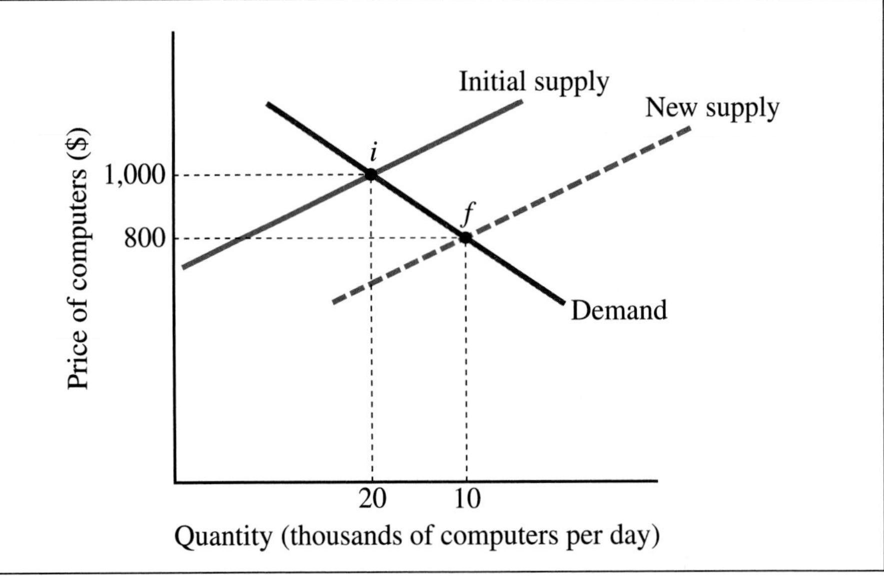

Technological innovations increase supply and decrease equilibrium prices. Recent innovations in the design of computers, calculators, and communication devices have decreased prices. There are many examples from the distant past as well. In fact, many of the goods we consume today were made affordable by technological innovations that decreased production costs and prices.

How does poor weather affect the supplies of agricultural goods and their prices? In 1992 several events combined to decrease the world supply of coffee and increase its price. Poor weather and insect infestations in Brazil and Colombia decreased the coffee-bean harvest by about 40%.[4] In addition, a slowdown by dockworkers at Santos, Brazil's main coffee port, decreased the amount supplied to the world market. In Figure 10 the initial equilibrium is shown by point *i*, with a price of

Figure 10

Effects of Bad Weather on the Coffee Market

Bad weather decreases the supply of coffee beans, shifting the supply curve to the left. At the initial price ($0.60), there is a shortage. The price increases until equilibrium is restored at point *f*.

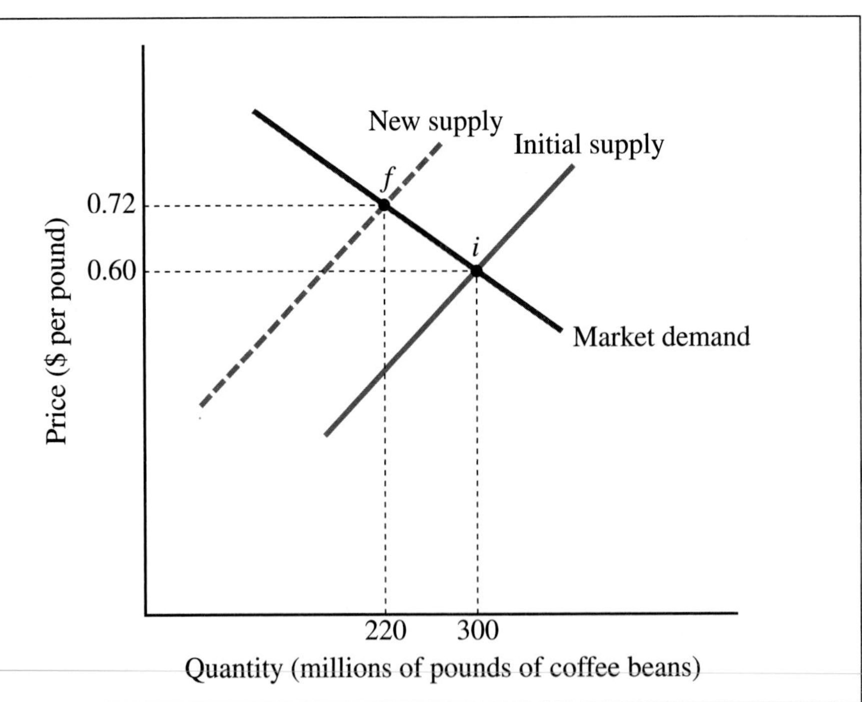

A Closer LOOK

War in Bosnia and the Price of Raspberries

What's the connection between war in Bosnia and the price of raspberries? In 1993, a United Nations' trade embargo against the combatants in the Bosnian war decreased Yugoslavian raspberry exports to a trickle. U.S. food companies that normally import berries from Yugoslavia were forced instead to compete for berries available from the Cascadia region: Washington, Oregon, and British Columbia. Wholesale prices that had been running about 50 cents a pound suddenly shot up to 60 cents a pound. "Berries aren't getting out of Yugoslavia, so it's as if one of the world's biggest producers had a crop failure," said Ann Seegere, manager of the Washington Red Raspberry Commission in Bellingham, Washington.

What are the implications of the trade embargo for the farmers in the Cascadia region? In 1994, raspberry farmers in the state of Washington produced 43 million pounds, farmers in British Columbia produced 23 million pounds, and farmers in Oregon produced 16 million pounds. The UN trade embargo increased the price of raspberries by 10 cents per pound, increasing the income of farmers in Cascadia by $7.9 million.

Source: After John Davies, "War Helps NW Raspberry Growers," *Corvallis Gazette-Times,* January 19, 1994, p. A3. Permission to use granted by the *Journal of Commerce,* Baltimore, MD.

$0.60 per pound. The poor weather, insect infestations, and other supply disruptions shifted the supply curve to the left, generating a shortage at the initial price: The quantity demanded exceeded the quantity supplied. The price of coffee increased, eliminating the shortage and leading to a new equilibrium at point *f*, with a price of $0.72.

There are many other changes in supply that affect prices. As we saw earlier, a number of changes will shift the market supply curve, including changes in input prices, the cost of the production facility, and the number of firms. To predict the market effects of a change in supply, we draw a supply–demand graph, shift the supply curve to the right or the left, and see what happens to the equilibrium price. If you try this a few times, you'll discover that supply and price move in the opposite directions: An increase in supply decreases price, while a decrease in supply increases the price. For another example of the market effects of a change in supply, read the Closer Look box "War in Bosnia and the Price of Raspberries."

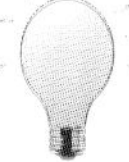

TEST *Your Understanding*

8 Complete the statement: The market equilibrium is shown by the intersection of the ____________ curve and the ____________ curve.

9 Complete the statement with *less* or *greater:* A shortage occurs when the price is ____________ than the equilibrium price, while a surplus occurs when the price is ____________ than the equilibrium price.

10 Draw a supply–demand diagram to illustrate the Bosnian raspberry situation depicted in the Closer Look box. Use all the price data contained in the box.

ECONOMIC DETECTIVE

We have discussed several examples of how changes in supply or demand affect equilibrium prices and quantities. We observed a change in supply or demand and used supply and demand curves to predict the market effects. Table 2 on page 72 summarizes what we've learned so far about changes in prices and quantities.

Table 2: Market Effects of Changes in Demand or Supply

Change in Demand or Supply	*Change in Price*	*Change in Quantity*
Increase in demand	Increase	Increase
Decrease in demand	Decrease	Decrease
Increase in supply	Decrease	Increase
Decrease in supply	Increase	Decrease

When demand changes, price and quantity change in the same direction. For example, an increase in demand increases both the price and the quantity. In contrast, when supply changes, price and quantity change in opposite directions. For example, an increase in supply decreases price and increases quantity.

We can use the information in Table 2 to play economic detective. Suppose that we observe changes in the equilibrium price and quantity of a particular good, but we don't know what caused these changes. It could have been a change in demand or a change in supply. We can use the information in Table 2 to work backward to discover the reason for the changes in price and quantity. For example, suppose that we observe increases in both price and quantity. Looking at the first row of the table, we would conclude that these changes were caused by an increase in demand. We discuss three cases for the economic detective: a decrease in the price of cocaine, an increase in the consumption of poultry products, and a bouncing price of used newspapers.

The Mystery of Falling Cocaine Prices

As we saw in the beginning of the chapter, Ted Koppel observed a decrease in drug prices and concluded that the supply of drugs had increased. What does the information in Table 2 suggest about the Koppel explanation? In the third row of the table, an increase in supply will decrease the price and increase the quantity. Therefore, the Koppel explanation of lower prices is correct only if the quantity of drugs increased at the same time that the price decreased. In fact, according to the U.S. Department of Justice, the quantity of drugs consumed actually decreased during the period of dropping prices,[5] so Koppel's explanation is incorrect. The correct explanation for the falling prices is shown in the second row of Table 2 and Figure 11: A decrease in demand (a leftward shift of the demand curve) decreased both the price and the quantity of drugs demanded. Lower demand—not a failure of the government's drug policy—was responsible for the decrease in drug prices.

The simple lesson from this example is that we shouldn't jump to conclusions based on limited information. A change in price could result from either a change in supply or a change in demand. To draw any conclusions, we need information about both price and quantity.

The Mystery of Increasing Poultry Consumption

Why has the consumption of poultry (chicken and turkey) increased so dramatically over the last several decades? One possibility is that consumers have become more health conscious and have switched from red meat to poultry as part of an effort to eat healthier food. In other words, the demand curve for poultry may have shifted to the right, increasing the quantity of poultry consumed. Of course, an increase in demand will increase the price too, so if this explanation is correct, we should also observe higher prices for poultry.

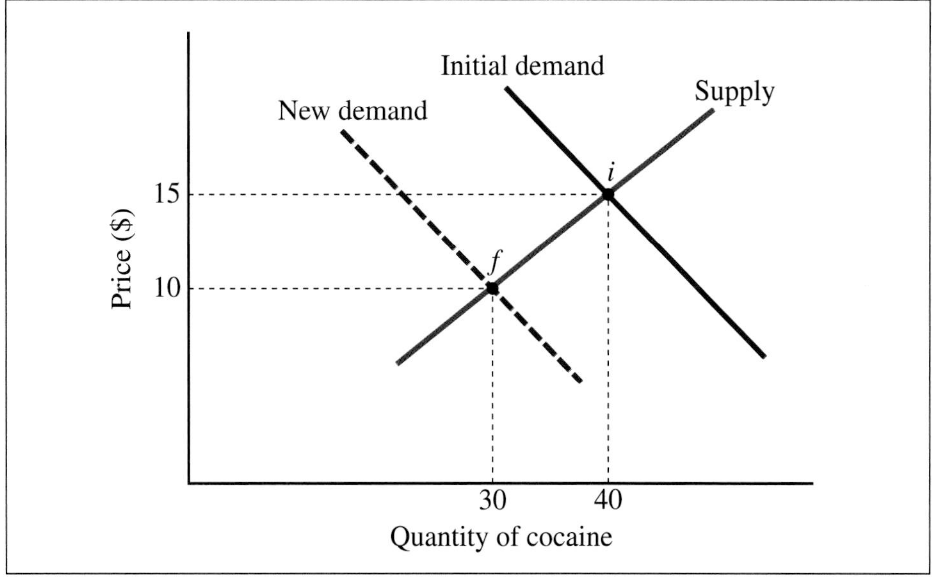

Figure 11

What Caused the Decrease in the Price of Illegal Drugs?

A decrease in demand for cocaine decreases the price and decreases the quantity consumed.

According to the U.S. Department of Agriculture, this popular explanation is incorrect.[6] In fact, the increase in poultry consumption was caused by an increase in supply, not an increase in demand. This conclusion is based on the fact that poultry prices have been decreasing, not increasing. Between 1950 and 1990, the real price of poultry (adjusted for inflation) decreased by about 75%. In Figure 12 and the third row of Table 2, an increase in supply increases the quantity and decreases the price. The supply of poultry increased because innovations in poultry processing decreased the cost of producing poultry products.

There may be a grain of truth in the popular explanation. It is possible that both demand and supply increased, shifting both curves to the right. Because the price of poultry decreased, however, we know that the shift of the supply curve (which tends to decrease the price) overwhelmed any shift of the demand curve (which tends to increase the price). Although changes in consumer preferences might

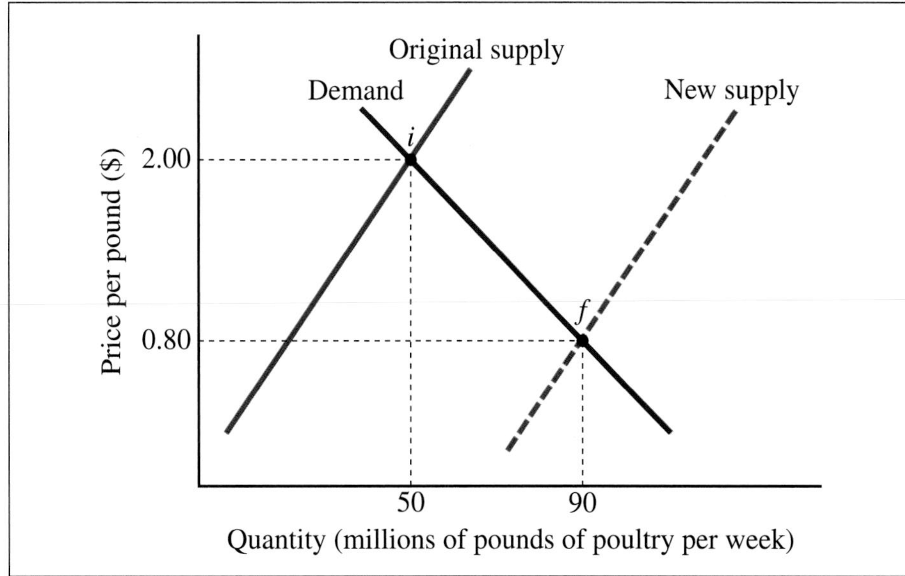

Figure 12

What Caused the Increase in the Consumption of Poultry?

An increase in the supply of poultry decreases the price and increases the quantity consumed.

contribute to increasing poultry consumption, the changes on the supply side of the market are much more important.

The Mystery of the Bouncing Price of Used Newspapers

In 1987 you could sell a ton of used newspapers for $60. Five years later, anyone with a pile of used newspapers had to pay someone to take them away.[7] In other words, the price of used newspapers dropped from $60 to zero in just five years. Then the price started climbing. It reached $106 per ton in 1995, a price high enough so that thieves started stealing newspapers that people had left on the curb for recycling.[8] What explains the bouncing price of used newspapers?

We can solve this mystery with some additional information about changes over time in the quantity of used newspapers. Between 1987 and 1992, the quantity increased dramatically, so the price and quantity moved in opposite directions. Therefore, we would conclude that the decrease in price was caused by an increase in supply (the third row of Table 2). Over this five-year period, hundreds of communities adopted curbside recycling programs. These programs increased the supply of used newspapers, generating a surplus of used newspapers that decreased the equilibrium price. As shown in the left panel of Figure 13, the increase in supply was so large that the equilibrium price fell to zero.

What happened between 1992 and 1995 to increase the price from zero to $106? During this period, the equilibrium quantity of used newspapers increased: The price and the quantity moved in the same direction. Therefore, we would conclude that the increase in price was caused by an increase in demand (the first row in Table 2). During this period many states passed laws requiring paper manufacturers to make newsprint (the paper used to make newspapers) with a higher percentage of recycled fiber. In addition, the federal government, one of the world's largest paper users, now buys paper with a minimum recycled content of 20%. As shown in the right panel of Figure 13, these changes shifted the demand curve for used newspapers to the right, increasing the equilibrium price from zero to $106.

For another mystery that can be solved with a few clues and some simple economic analysis, consider the market for amber, a semiprecious material made of fossilized resin from prehistoric trees. Some pieces of amber contain the preserved remains of plants and animals from millions of years ago—including mosquitoes, who may have feasted on dinosaurs during the Jurassic period. The market price of amber tripled during 1993. Why? For the answer, read the Closer Look box "Jurassic Park and the Price of Amber."

Figure 13

Bouncing Price of Used Newspapers

Between 1987 and 1992, the price of used newspapers decreased, a result of increases in supply. Between 1992 and 1995, the price increased, a result of increases in demand.

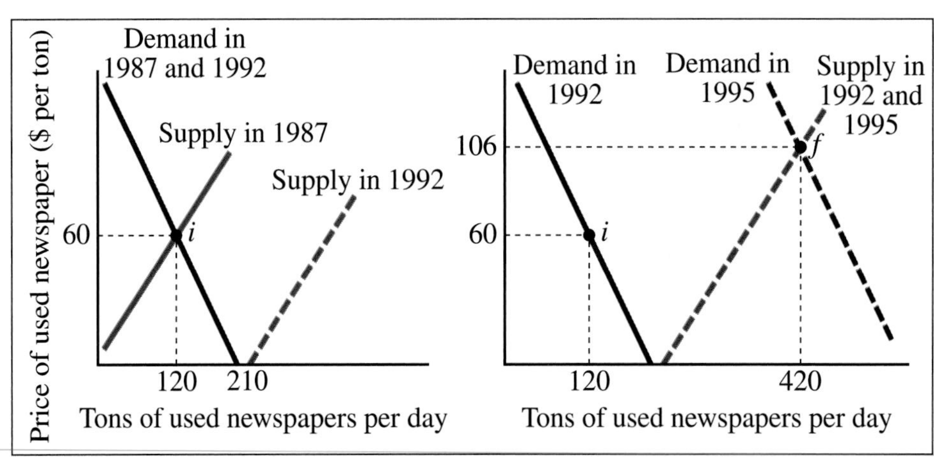

A Closer LOOK

Jurassic Park and the Price of Amber

Scientists who use amber to study fossils and extinct animals were shocked when the price of amber tripled during 1993.* Because the equilibrium quantity of amber increased along with its price, the increase in price was caused by an increase in demand, not a decrease in supply. The increase in demand coincided with the release of the movie *Jurassic Park,* in which scientists use specimens from amber to clone dinosaurs. Many of the people who saw the movie bought amber specimens, and this new consumer demand increased the demand for amber. The demand curve shifted to the right, increasing the equilibrium price and quantity.

*Tim Friend, "Dino-Craze Sends Sales of Amber with Insects Buzzing," *USA Today,* June 17, 1993, p. A1.

Amber contains the preserved remains of mosquitos that feasted on dinosaurs. In 1993 the price of amber tripled.

TEST *Your Understanding*

11 Complete the statement with *supply* or *demand:* If the price and quantity change in the same direction, ____________ is changing; if the price and quantity change in opposite directions, ____________ is changing.

12 Suppose that between 1997 and 1999, the equilibrium price and the equilibrium quantity of amber both decrease. Draw a supply–demand diagram that explains these changes.

SUPPLY AND DEMAND IN THE GLOBAL ECONOMY

As we saw in Chapter 3, a large and increasing share of goods and services are produced in one country and purchased in another. We can use the model of supply and demand to show how changes in one country affect producers and consumers in another.

The demands for export goods are affected by changes in other countries. Here are some examples of changes in the demand for products exported by the United States.

- The United States exports wheat to Russia. An increase in per capita income in Russia will increase the demand for U.S. wheat, shifting the demand curve to the right and increasing the equilibrium price.
- The Airbus (an airplane produced in Europe) is a substitute for airplanes produced by Boeing, a U.S. producer. Therefore, a decrease in the price of the Airbus will decrease the demand for Boeing airplanes.
- The United States exports wood to Japan, and some of the exported wood is used to produce housing. An increase in income in Japan will increase the demand for housing, increasing the demand for U.S. wood. The demand curve will shift to the right, increasing the equilibrium price.

The supplies of imported goods are affected by changes in other countries. Here are some examples of changes in the supply of products imported by the United States.

- The United States imports carpets from India. An increase in the wages of Indian workers will decrease the supply of carpets to the U.S. market, shifting the supply curve to the left and increasing the equilibrium price.
- The United States imports telephones from Japan. A technological innovation that decreases the cost of producing telephones will increase the supply of telephones to the U.S. market, shifting the supply curve to the right and decreasing the equilibrium price.
- The United States imports oil from Russia. A new oil discovery will increase the supply of oil to the U.S. market and shift the supply curve to the right, decreasing the equilibrium price.

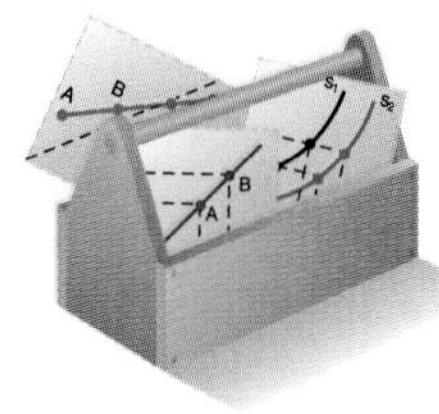

Using the **TOOLS**

In this chapter you learned how to use two of the tools of economics—the supply curve and the demand curve—to predict how a change in demand or supply will affect prices and quantities. Here are some opportunities to use these tools to do your own economic analysis.

1. ECONOMIC EXPERIMENT: *Market Equilibrium*

The simple experiment takes about 20 minutes to run. We start by dividing the class into two equal groups, consumers and producers.

- The instructor provides each consumer with a number indicating the maximum amount that he or she is willing to pay (WTP) for a bushel of apples: The WTP is a number between $1 and $100. Each consumer has the opportunity to buy 1 bushel of apples per trading period. The consumer's score for a single trading period equals the gap between his WTP and the price actually paid for apples. For example, if the consumer's WTP is $80 and he pays only $30 for apples, his score is $50. Each consumer has the option of not buying apples. This will be sensible if the best price you can get exceeds your WTP. If you do not buy apples, your score will be zero.
- The instructor provides each producer with a number indicating the cost of producing a bushel of apples (a number between $1 and $100). Each producer has the opportunity to sell 1 bushel per trading period. The producer's score for a single trading period equals the gap between the selling price and the cost of producing apples. So, if a producer sells apples for $20 and her cost is only $15, her score is $5. Producers have the option of not selling apples, which is sensible if the best price she can get is less than her cost. If she does not sell apples, her score is zero.

Once everyone understands the rules, consumers and producers meet in a trading area to arrange transactions. A consumer may announce how much he or she is willing to pay for apples and wait for a producer to agree to sell apples at that price. Alternatively, a producer may announce how much he or she is willing to accept for apples and wait for a consumer to agree to buy apples at that price. Once a transaction has been arranged, the two people (consumer and producer) inform the instructor of the trade, record the transaction, and leave the trading area.

There are several trading periods, each of which lasts a few minutes. After the end of each trading period, the instructor lists the prices at which apples sold during that period. Then another trading period starts, providing consumers and producers another opportunity to buy or sell 1 bushel of apples. After all the trading periods have been completed, each participant computes his or her score by adding the scores from each trading period.

2. College Enrollment and Housing

Consider a college town where the initial price of apartments is $400 and the initial quantity is 1,000 apartments.

a. Use supply and demand curves to show the initial equilibrium, and label the equilibrium point with an *i*.

b. Suppose that the number of students attending college increases by 20%. Use your graph to show the effects of this on the price and quantity of apartments. Label the new equilibrium point with an *f*.

3. Innovation and Phone Prices

Suppose that the initial price of a pocket phone is $100 and the initial quantity demanded is 500 phones per day. Depict graphically the effects of a technological innovation that decreases the cost of producing pocket phones. Label the starting point with an *i* and the new equilibrium with an *f*.

4. Market Effects of an Import Ban

Consider a nation that initially imports half the shoes it consumes. Use a supply and demand diagram to predict the effect of a ban on shoe imports on the equilibrium price and quantity of shoes.

SUMMARY

In this chapter we've seen how supply and demand determine market prices. You should be able to predict the effects of changes in demand or supply on prices. Here are the main points of the chapter.

1. To draw a market demand curve, we must be certain that the other variables that affect demand (consumer income, prices of related goods, tastes, and number of consumers) are held fixed.
2. To draw a market supply curve, we must be certain that the other variables that affect supply (input costs, technology, and the number of producers) are held fixed.
3. An equilibrium in a market is shown by the intersection of the demand curve and the supply curve. When a market reaches an equilibrium, there is no pressure to change the price.
4. A change in demand changes price and quantity in the same direction: An increase in demand increases both price and quantity; a decrease in demand decreases both price and quantity.
5. A change in supply changes price and quantity in opposite directions: An increase in supply decreases price and increases quantity; a decrease in supply increases price and decreases quantity.

KEY TERMS

change in demand, *60*
change in quantity demanded, *60*
change in quantity supplied, *65*
change in supply, *66*
complements, *62*
demand curve, *58*
income effect, *59*
inferior good, *61*
law of demand, *59*
law of supply, *65*
market equilibrium, *67*
normal good, *61*
perfectly competitive market, *58*
shortage, *67*
substitutes, *62*
substitution effect, *59*
supply curve, *65*
surplus, *67*

PROBLEMS AND DISCUSSION QUESTIONS

1. Figure A shows the supply and demand curves for CD players. Complete the following statements.
   a. At the market equilibrium (shown by point ___________), the price of CD players is ___________ and the quantity of CD players is ___________.
   b. At a price of $100, there would be a ___________ of CD players, so we would expect the price to ___________ (fill in with *increase* or *decrease*).
   c. At a price exceeding the equilibrium price, there would be a ___________ of CD players, so we would expect the price to ___________ (fill in with *increase* or *decrease*).
2. The following table shows the quantities of corn supplied and demanded at different prices.

Price per Ton	*Quantity Supplied*	*Quantity Demanded*	*Surplus (+) or Shortage (–)*
$ 80	600	1,200	______
$ 90	800	1,100	______
$100	1,000	1,000	______
$110	1,200	900	______

   a. Complete the table.
   b. Draw the demand curve and the supply curve.
   c. What is the equilibrium price of corn?
3. Consider the market for personal computers. Suppose that the demand is stable: The demand curve doesn't change. Predict the effects of the following changes on the equilibrium price of computers. Illustrate your answer with a supply and demand diagram.
   a. The cost of memory chips (one component of a computer) decreases.
   b. The government imposes a $100 tax on personal computers.
4. Draw a supply–demand diagram to illustrate the effect of an increase in income on the market for restaurant meals.
5. Suppose that the tuition charged by public universities increases. Draw a supply–demand diagram to illustrate the effects of the tuition hike on the market for private college education.
6. Suppose that the government imposes a tax of $1 per pound of fish and collects the tax from fish producers. Draw a supply–demand diagram to illustrate the market effects of the tax.
7. As summer approaches, the weekly rent of beach cabins increases and the quantity of cabins rented increases. Draw a supply–demand diagram that explains these changes.

Take It to the Net

We invite you to visit the O'Sullivan/Sheffrin page on the Prentice Hall Web site at:

http://www.prenhall.com/osullivan/

for this chapter's World Wide Web exercise.

Figure A

Supply and Demand for CD Players

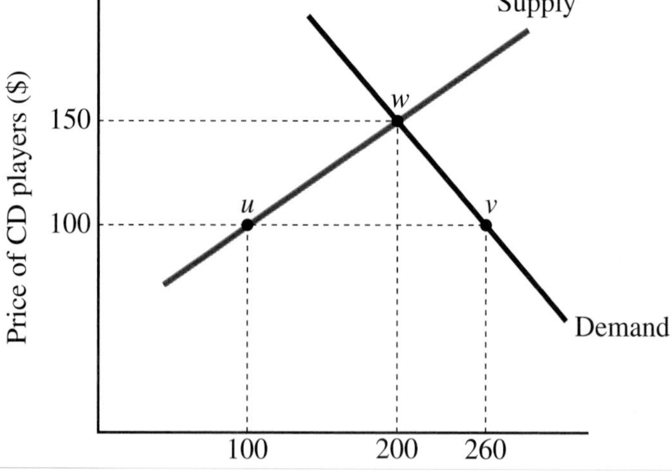

MODEL ANSWERS FOR THIS CHAPTER

Chapter-Opening Questions

1. As shown in Figure 8 (page 69), the campaign will decrease the demand for cigarettes, decreasing both the quantity consumed and the price.
2. As shown in the Closer Look box "War in Bosnia and the Price of Raspberries" (page 71), a UN embargo decreased the supply of raspberries from Yugoslavia, raising the world price of raspberries.
3. As shown in Figure 9 (page 70), technological innovation increases the supply of computers, leading to a lower equilibrium price.
4. Innovations in poultry processing decreased the cost of producing poultry products. The resulting increase in supply decreased the equilibrium price, causing consumers to buy more poultry products.
5. Curbside recycling rapidly between 1987 and 1992, increasing the supply of used newspapers and decreasing the price. Between 1992 and 1995, the implementation of laws requiring the use of recycled fiber increased demand, increasing the price.

Test Your Understanding

1. One group is A, E, and F; another group is B, C, and D.
2. False. The demand curve will shift to the right, with a larger quantity at each price.
3. right, left
4. Circle *quantity of pencils, price of pencils.* Cross out *number of potential consumers, price of pens, consumer income.*
5. One group is A, E, and F; another group is B, C, and D.
6. True. An increase in the wage increases production cost, so fewer computers will be supplied at each price.
7. Circle *quantity of housing, price of houses.* Cross out *number of potential consumers, price of wood, consumer income.*
8. supply, demand
9. less, greater
10. The supply curve shifts to the left, increasing the equilibrium price and decreasing the equilibrium quantity.
11. demand, supply
12. The demand decreases (an end to the Jurassic Park fad buying?), decreasing both the price and the quantity.

Using the Tools

2. College Enrollment and Housing
   a. See Figure B (page 80).
   b. See Figure B. The demand curve shifts to the right by 15%. Equilibrium is restored at point *f*, with a higher price and a larger quantity.
3. Innovation and Phone Prices

   See Figure C (page 80). The supply curve shifts to the right, so the innovation decreases the equilibrium price from $100 to $90 and increases the equilibrium quantity.
4. Market Effects of an Import Ban

   See Figure D (page 80). The import ban eliminates half the producers in the market, so the supply curve shifts to the left. The decrease in supply will increase the equilibrium price and decrease the equilibrium quantity.

NOTES

1. Kenneth R. Clark, "Legalize Drugs. A Case for Koppel," *Chicago Tribune,* August 30, 1988, sec. 5, p. 8. © Copyrighted Chicago Tribune Company. All rights reserved. Used with permission.
2. Megan Ryan and Christopher Flavin, "Facing China's Limits," Chapter 7 in *The State of the World,* edited by Lester R. Brown (New York: W.W. Norton, 1995).
3. World Bank, *World Development Report 1992* (New York: Oxford University Press, 1992).
4. "Coffee Prices Surge Again; Fear of Tight Supply Grows," *New York Times,* November 14, 1992, p. 44.
5. U.S. Department of Justice, *Drugs, Crime, and the Justice System* (Washington, DC: U.S. Government Printing Office, 1992), p. 30.
6. Mark R. Weimar and Richard Stillman, *Market Trends Driving Broiler Consumption,* Livestock and Poultry Situation and Outlook Report LPS-44 (Washington, DC: U.S. Department of Agriculture, Economic Research Service, November 1990).
7. Kim Munsinger, "Supply and Demand in the Market for Used Newsprint," *The Margin,* Fall 1992, p. 56.
8. Bryan Denson, "Snatching Paper Money," *The Oregonian,* August 7, 1995, p. B1.

Figure B

College Enrollment and Apartment Rent

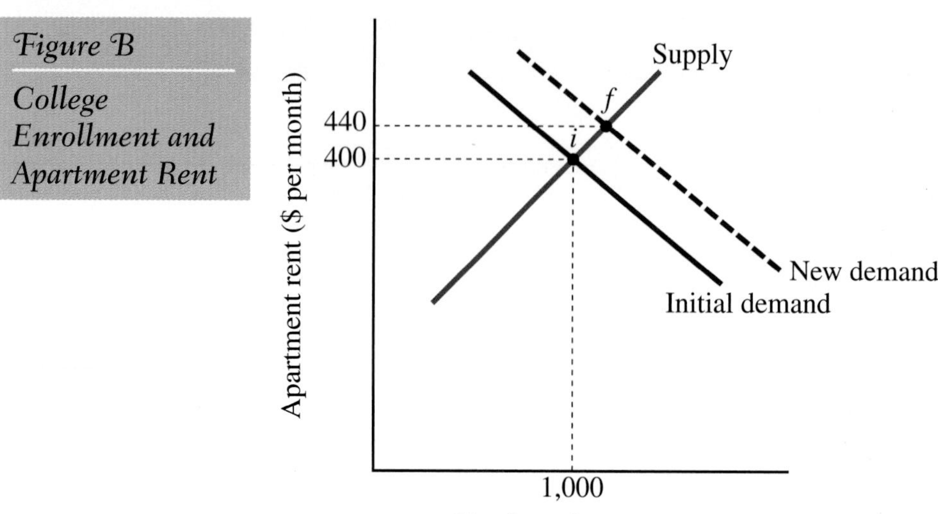

Figure C

Effects of Technological Innovation on the Market for Pocket Phones

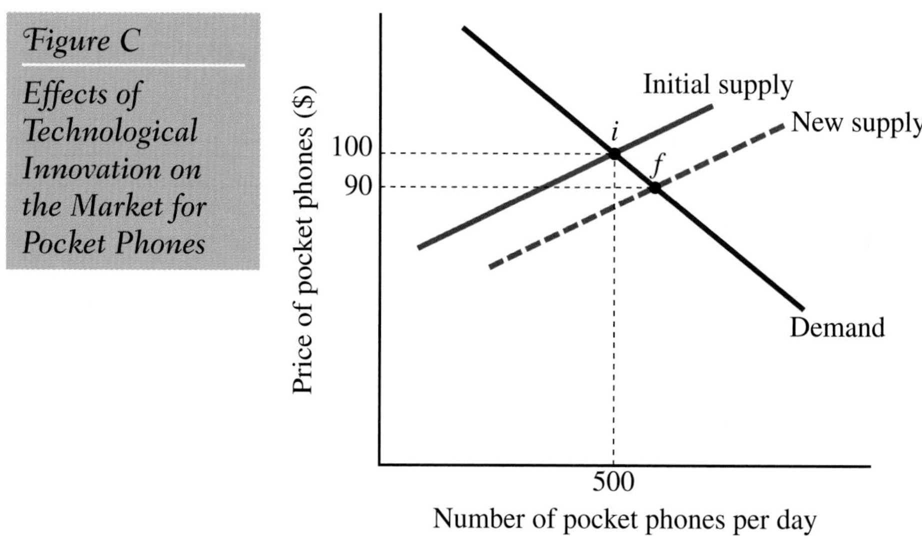

Figure D

Market Effects of an Import Ban

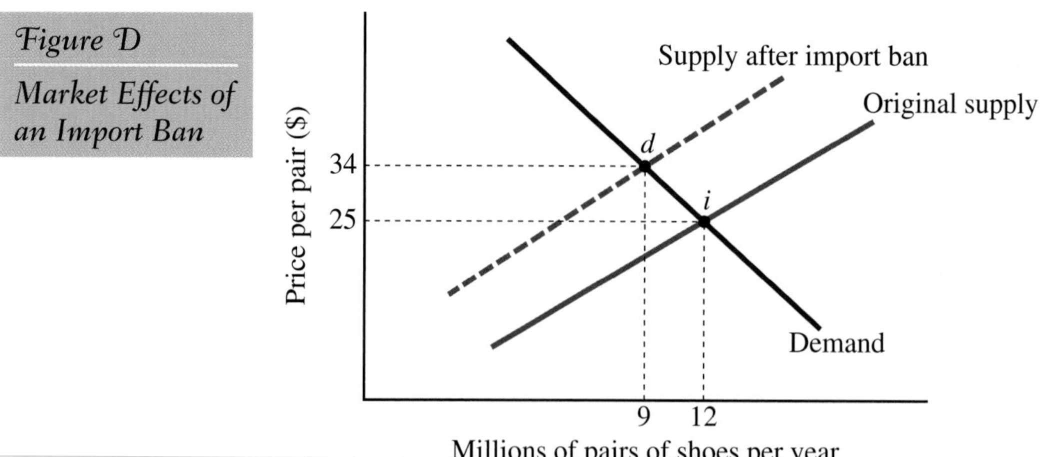

5 Elasticity: A Measure of Responsiveness

As Carly drove through the state of Virginia, she was surprised by the large number of "vanity" license plates. Hundreds of cars had license plates with personal messages, many of which hinted at the occupation of the drivers. Her favorites were SAY CHZ (a photographer), EDUC8R (a teacher), and DR X KV8R (a dentist). Carly's experience raises some questions about vanity plates.

1. Why are vanity plates so numerous in Virginia? Are Virginians unusually vain, or is there some other explanation?
2. How much should the state charge for its vanity plates? If the state raised its price, would the total revenue from the plates increase or decrease?

In Chapter 4, we saw how consumers and producers respond to changes in price. We can summarize their responses in two laws of economics:

- *Law of demand.* The lower the price of a good, the larger the quantity demanded.
- *Law of supply.* The higher the price of a good, the larger the quantity supplied.

These laws tell us the direction of a response to a change in price—a larger quantity demanded with a lower price, and a larger quantity supplied at a higher price—but they don't tell us how large the response is. In many cases it will be useful to know just *how much* more consumers will demand at a lower price or *how much* more producers will supply at a higher price. The following examples illustrate the importance of knowing the numbers behind the laws of supply and demand.

1. Before a computer firm cuts its prices, it should predict how many more computers it will sell at the lower price.
2. Before the state of Virginia raises its price for vanity plates, it should predict how many fewer vanity plates it will sell at the higher price.
3. Before a transit authority cuts its bus fares, it should predict how many more riders it will serve at the lower price.
4. Before a government sets a minimum price above the equilibrium price, it should predict how much more of the product will be supplied at the higher price.

Economists use the concept of *elasticity* to measure the responsiveness of people to changes in economic variables. Let's think about consumers first. For some goods, consumers are very responsive to changes in price: A small decrease in price increases the quantity demanded by a large amount. In this case we say that demand is *elastic* or *highly elastic*. In contrast, if consumers are not very responsive to changes in price, we say that demand is *inelastic*. On the other side of the market, we say that supply is elastic if producers are very responsive to changes in price, producing much more when the price rises. On the other hand, we say that supply is inelastic if producers are not very responsive.

This chapter contains many applications of the elasticity concept. Here are some of the practical questions we answer:

1. How would a tax on beer affect the number of highway deaths among young adults?
2. Why is a bumper crop bad news for farmers?
3. If a firm wants to increase its total revenue, should it raise or lower its price?
4. Why do policies that limit the supply of illegal drugs increase the number of burglaries and robberies?
5. If the demand for a product increases, what information do we need to predict the resulting change in the equilibrium price?

THE PRICE ELASTICITY OF DEMAND

Price elasticity of demand: A measure of the responsiveness of the quantity demanded to changes in price; computed by dividing the percentage change in quantity demanded by the percentage change in price.

One of the key questions about consumer behavior concerns the responsiveness of consumers to changes in prices. When the price of a good decreases, consumers will buy more of the good, but *how much* more will they buy? The **price elasticity of demand** (E_d) measures the responsiveness of consumers to changes in price.

We compute the elasticity by dividing the percentage change in the quantity demanded by the percentage change in price:

$$E_d = \frac{\text{percentage change in quantity demanded}}{\text{percentage change in price}}$$

As we saw in the appendix to Chapter 1, the simple way to compute the percentage change in a variable is to divide the absolute change in the value of the variable by the initial value. Let's compute the percentage changes in price and quantity when the price of milk increases from \$2.00 (point *d* on the demand curve in Figure 1) to \$2.20 (point *e*).

- The percentage change in price equals the absolute change (\$0.20) divided by the initial price (\$2.00), or 10% (\$0.20 divided by \$2.00).

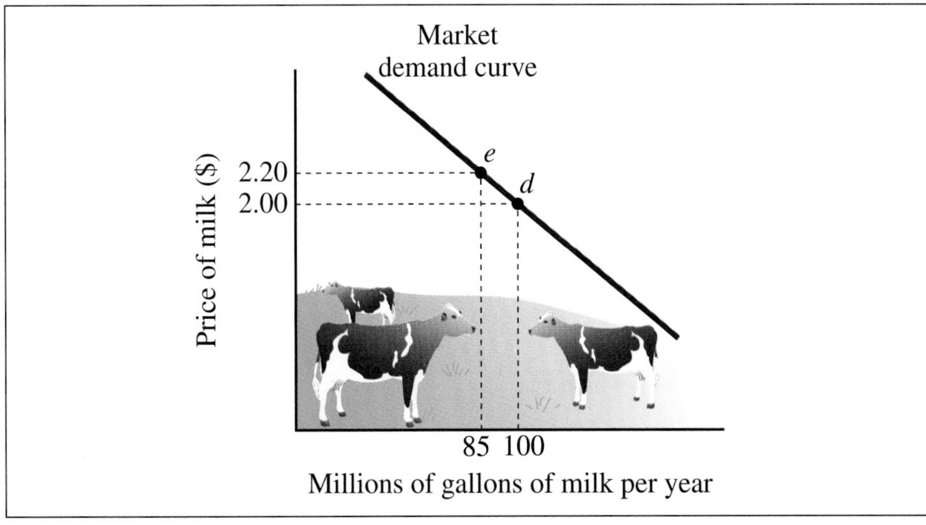

Figure 1

Market Demand Curve and Price Elasticity of Demand

A 10% rise in the price of milk (from $2 to $2.20) decreases the quantity demanded by 15% (from 100 to 85), so the price elasticity of demand is 1.50 = 15%/10%.

- The percentage change in quantity demanded equals the absolute change (–15 million) divided by the initial quantity (100 million), or –15% (–15 divided by 100).

To compute the price elasticity, we take the absolute value of each percentage change: In effect, we ignore any minus signs. Plugging these percentage changes into the formula, the price elasticity for this example is 1.50:

$$E_d = \frac{\text{percentage change in quantity demanded}}{\text{percentage change in price}} = \frac{15\%}{10\%} = 1.50$$

We can use the concept of price elasticity of demand to divide consumer goods into three groups.

1. ***Elastic.*** If the price elasticity of demand for a particular good is greater than 1.0, we say that demand is elastic. This is sensible because if the elasticity is greater than 1.0, the percentage change in quantity exceeds the percentage change in price, meaning that consumers are very responsive to changes in price.
2. ***Inelastic.*** If the price elasticity of demand is less than 1.0, consumers are not very responsive, and we say that demand is inelastic.
3. ***Unitary elastic.*** If the elasticity equals 1.0, we say that demand is unitary elastic.

Elasticity and Substitutes

The price elasticity of demand for a particular good is influenced by the availability of substitutes. Consider two goods, insulin, a medicine for diabetics, and cornflakes. There are no good substitutes for insulin, so demand is inelastic: Consumers are not very responsive to changes in price. In contrast, there are many substitutes for cornflakes, including different types of corn cereal and cereals made from other grains (wheat, rice, oats). Therefore, a small increase in the price of cornflakes will cause a relatively large decrease in quantity demanded as consumers switch to other types of cereal. In other words, if substitutes are plentiful, demand is relatively elastic.

The estimated price elasticities of demand in Table 1 on page 84 illustrate the importance of substitutes in determining the price elasticity of demand. Given the lack of substitutes for water and salt, it's not surprising that the demand for these goods is relatively inelastic. For example, the price elasticity of demand for water

Table 1: Estimated Price Elasticities of Demand for Selected Products

Product	Price Elasticity of Demand
Salt	0.1
Water	0.2
Coffee	0.3
Cigarettes	0.3
Shoes and footwear	0.7
Housing	1.0
Automobiles	1.2
Foreign travel	1.8
Restaurant meals	2.3
Air travel	2.4
Motion pictures	3.7
Specific brands of coffee	5.6

Sources: Frank Chaloupka, "Rational Addictive Behavior and Cigarette Smoking," *Journal of Political Economy,* August 1991, pp. 722–742; Gregory Chow, *Demand for Automobiles in the United States* (Amsterdam: North-Holland, 1957); David Ellwood and Mitchell Polinski. "An Empirical Reconciliation of Micro and Grouped Estimates of the Demand for Housing," *Review of Economics and Statistics,* vol. 61, 1979, pp. 199–205; H. F. Houthakker and Lester B. Taylor, *Consumer Demand in the United States: Analysis and Projections,* 2nd ed. (Cambridge, MA: Harvard University Press, 1970); John R. Nevin, "Laboratory Experiments for Estimating Consumer Demand: A Validation Study," *Journal of Marketing Research,* vol. 11, August 1974, pp. 261–268; Herbert Scarf and John Shoven, *Applied General Equilibrium Analysis* (New York: Cambridge University Press, 1984).

(0.20) suggests that a 10% increase in the price of water would decrease the quantity demanded by only 2%:

$$E_d = 0.20 = \frac{\text{percentage change in quantity of water demanded}}{\text{percentage change in price of water}} = \frac{2\%}{10\%}$$

The demand for cigarettes, an addictive good, is also relatively inelastic: The elasticity of 0.30 suggests that a 10% increase in price would cause a 3% decrease in quantity demanded. Although the demand for coffee is relatively inelastic (0.30), the demand for a specific brand of coffee is very elastic (between 5.6 and 8.9). An elasticity of 5.6 suggests that a 10% increase in price of a specific brand would decrease the quantity demanded by 56%. The specific brands of coffee are substitutes for one another, but there are few good substitutes for coffee.

For another example of the price elasticity of demand, consider the demand for trash disposal. Until recently, most cities charged a fixed monthly fee for trash collection. Under an alternative approach, called a "pay-to-throw" plan, the more trash a household generates, the higher its trash bill. In 1991, the city of Charlottesville, Virginia, switched 75 households from a fixed monthly fee to a price of \$0.80 per 32-gallon bag of trash. The new pricing plan caused the following changes among the households participating in the experiment.[1]

1. The volume of trash collected decreased by 37%, to 0.46 bags per person per week. The price elasticity of demand with respect to the volume of trash was 0.23.

2. The weight of trash collected decreased by 14%, to 9.37 pounds per person per week. The weight decreased by a relatively small amount because of the "Seattle stomp," a technique that allows a person to pack more trash into each bag. (It gets its name from the location of an early experiment in pay-to-throw pricing.) The price elasticity of demand with respect to the weight of trash was 0.08.
3. The weight of recyclable materials (collected at no cost to the household) increased by 16%, to 4.27 pounds per person per week.
4. Illegal dumping (littering and dumping household trash in commercial dumpsters) is difficult to measure. It appears that it may have increased by about 0.5 pounds per person per week.

This study has some important lessons for other communities considering a pay-to-throw plan: Although the total volume of trash would decrease, the total weight would decrease by a relatively small amount, and illegal dumping would increase.

Other Determinants of Elasticity

The availability of substitute goods is an important factor in determining the elasticity of demand. There are, however, three other factors that influence the price elasticity.

A Closer LOOK

Using the Midpoint Formula to Compute Price Elasticity

As we saw in the appendix to Chapter 1, the midpoint formula provides a second way to compute percentage changes. Under the midpoint approach, we divide the absolute change in the variable by the *average* value of the variable. We can use this approach to compute the price elasticity associated with points *d* and *e* in Figure 1.

- **The percentage change in price equals the absolute change ($0.20) divided by the average price ($2.10), or 9.52%:**

$$\text{percentage change} = \frac{\text{absolute change}}{\text{average value}} = \frac{0.20}{(2.00 + 2.20)/2} = \frac{0.20}{2.10} = 0.0952 = 9.52\%$$

- **The percentage change in quantity demanded equals the absolute change (–15) divided by the average quantity (92.5), or –16.22%:**

$$\text{percentage change} = \frac{\text{absolute change}}{\text{average value}} = \frac{-15}{(100 + 85)/2} = \frac{-15}{92.5} = -0.1622 = -16.22\%$$

$$E_s = \frac{\text{percentage change in quantity supplied}}{\text{percentage change in price}} = \frac{20\%}{10\%} = 2.0$$

Plugging these percentage changes into the formula, the price elasticity for this example is 1.70:

$$E_d = \frac{\text{percentage change in quantity demanded}}{\text{percentage change in price}} = \frac{16.22\%}{9.52\%} = 1.70$$

Why is this elasticity different from the elasticity we computed with the simple approach (1.50)? The midpoint approach measures the percentage changes more precisely, so we get a more precise measure of price elasticity. In this case the percentage changes are relatively small, so the two elasticity numbers aren't too far apart. If the percentage changes were larger, however, the elasticity numbers generated by the two approaches would be quite different and it would be wise to use the midpoint approach.

1. *Time.* Because it takes time to change consumption habits and find substitute goods, the more time we give consumers to respond to a price change, the larger their response. When the price of gasoline increases, consumers' immediate response is limited by the fact that they cannot promptly buy more fuel-efficient cars or move closer to their workplaces. The passage of time allows consumers to change cars and to relocate, so we would expect a much larger reduction in gasoline consumption in the longer run. As time passes, demand becomes more elastic because consumers have more options. For another example of the role of time, read the Closer Look box "The Demand for International Telecommunications."

2. *Importance in budget.* If a good represents a small part of the budget of the typical consumer, demand for it is relatively inelastic. If the price of pencils increases by 10% (from $0.50 to $0.55), there will be a relatively small decrease in the quantity demanded because the price change is trivial relative to the income of the typical consumer. In contrast, a 10% increase in the price of cars (from $10,000 to $11,000) will generate a much larger response because the change in price is large relative to consumer income.

3. *Necessities versus luxuries.* For necessities such as bread, rice, and potatoes, demand is relatively inelastic. For luxury goods such as restaurant meals and air travel, demand is relatively elastic. This is sensible because it is easier to do without luxury goods.

Elasticity along a Linear Demand Curve

If a demand curve is linear, does that mean that the elasticity of demand is the same at all points on the curve? As shown in Figure 2, the demand elasticity increases as we move downward along a linear demand curve.

A Closer LOOK

The Demand for International Telecommunications

International telecommunication plays a vital role in today's global economy. In the last decade, the prices of international telephone services have dropped considerably: technological innovations have decreased the cost of providing telephone service, and deregulation has increased competition among companies providing the service. How have consumers responded to these lower prices? A study of telephone service between Sweden and the United States suggests that the price elasticity of demand is 0.51 in the short run (one year) and 1.18 in the long run (several years).* In other words, a 10% drop in price increases the quantity demanded by 5.1% in the short run and 11.8% in the long run. The demand elasticities for Sweden's other major trading partners—Germany and the United Kingdom—reflected the same pattern, with the long-run elasticities higher than the short-run elasticities.

In recent years, the price of international telephone service has dropped, increasing the quantity of telephone service demanded.

*Peter Hackl and Anders H. Westlund, "Demand for International Telecommunication: Time Varying Price Elasticity," *Journal of Econometrics*, vol. 70, 1996, pp. 243–260.

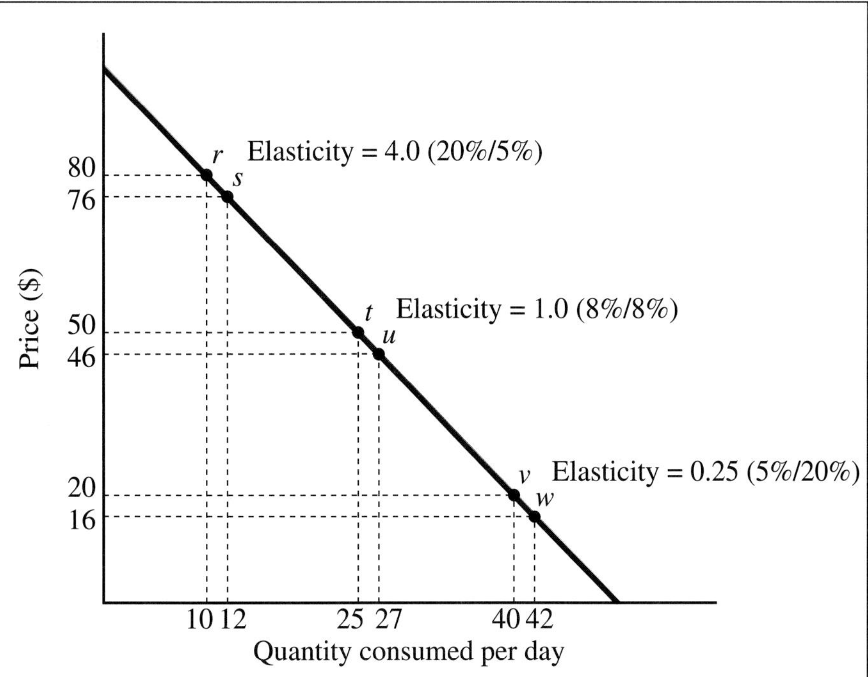

	Percentage decrease in price	Percentage increase in quantity	Elasticity
Point *r* to point *s*	4/80 = 5%	2/10 = 20%	20%/5% = 4.0
Point *t* to point *u*	4/50 = 8%	2/25 = 8%	8%/8% = 1.0
Point *v* to point *w*	4/20 = 20%	2/40 = 5%	5%/20% = 0.25

Figure 2

Price Elasticity along a Linear Demand Curve

The price elasticity of demand decreases as we move downward along a linear demand curve. Demand is elastic on the upper part of the demand curve, and inelastic on the lower part.

1. On the upper part of a linear demand curve, demand is elastic. Moving from point *r* to point *s*, the percentage change in quantity (20% = 2/10) is four times the percentage change in price (5% = 4/80), so the elasticity is 4.0.
2. In the middle of a linear demand curve, the price elasticity is unitary elastic. Moving from point *t* to point *u*, the percentage change in quantity (8% = 2/25) equals the percentage change in price (8% = 4/50), so the elasticity is 1.0.
3. On the lower part of a linear demand curve, demand is inelastic. Moving from point *v* to point *w*, the percentage change in quantity (5% = 2/40) is one-fourth of the percentage change in price (20% = 4/20), so the elasticity is 0.25.

Why does the price elasticity vary along a linear demand curve? Because the linear curve has a constant slope, it's tempting to conclude that the elasticity is constant. The problem with this logic is that elasticity is measured by *percentage* changes, not absolute changes. As we move downward along the demand curve to larger quantities, the same absolute change in quantity (2 units) becomes a smaller *percentage* change in quantity. Between points *r* and *s*, the percentage change in quantity is 20% (2/10), compared to only 5% (2/40) between points *v* and *w*. At the same time, the movement downward along the curve leads to a *larger* percentage change in price. As a result, the elasticity becomes smaller and smaller.

TEST ***Your Understanding***

1. Complete the statement: To compute the price elasticity of demand, we divide the percentage change in ____________ by the percentage change in ____________.

2. Complete the statement: If a 10% increase in price decreases the quantity demanded by 12%, the price elasticity of demand is ____________.

3. Explain why the demand for prerecorded audio tapes is more elastic in the long run than in the short run.

4. If we are on the upper portion of the market demand curve and the price increases by 10%, will the quantity demanded decrease by more than 10% or by less than 10%?

USING THE PRICE ELASTICITY OF DEMAND

The price elasticity of demand is a very useful tool for economic analysis. We know from the law of demand that a decrease in price will increase the quantity demanded. If we know the elasticity of demand for a particular good, we can predict just how much more of a good will be sold at the lower price. In addition, we can predict whether an increase in price will increase or decrease total spending on the good.

Predicting Changes in Quantity Demanded

We can use an estimate of the elasticity of demand to predict what happens to the quantity demanded when the price increases. The formula for the elasticity has three components: The elasticity of demand equals the percentage change in quantity divided by the percentage change in price. If we know two of the three components, we can compute the third. For example, suppose that you run a campus film series and you've decided to increase your admission price by 15%. If you know the elasticity of demand for your movies, you could use the elasticity formula to predict how many fewer tickets you'll sell at the higher price. For example, if the elasticity of demand is 2.0, a 15% price hike will decrease the quantity demanded by 30%:

$$2.0 = \frac{\text{percentage change in quantity}}{15\%} = \frac{30\%}{15\%}$$

Applications: College Education, Highway Deaths

Here are some other examples of using the elasticity of demand to predict changes in quantity.

1. ***Tuition and college enrollment.*** Suppose that the price elasticity of demand for education at a certain university is 1.40. We can use this fact to predict the change in enrollment resulting from an increase in tuition. Suppose that a university increases its tuition by 10%, from $4,000 to $4,400. Using the elasticity formula, we predict that enrollment will decrease by 14%:

$$1.40 = \frac{\text{percentage change in quantity}}{10\%} = \frac{14\%}{10\%}$$

2. ***Beer tax and highway deaths.*** The price elasticity of demand for beer among young adults (age 18 to 24) is about 1.30, and the number of highway deaths is roughly proportional to the group's beer consumption.[2] If a state imposes a beer tax that increases the price of beer by 20%, what will happen to the number of highway deaths among young adults? Using the elasticity formula, we predict that beer consumption will decrease by 26%:

$$1.30 = \frac{\text{percentage change in quantity}}{20\%} = \frac{26\%}{20\%}$$

If the number of highway deaths among young adults is proportional to their beer consumption, the number of highway deaths will also decrease by 26%. Of course, if young adults switch from beer to other alcoholic beverages, the number of highway deaths will decrease by a smaller amount.

If the price of medical care increases, how will consumers respond? The rising cost of medical care has forced many nations to take a closer look at programs that subsidize medical care for their citizens. If prices are increased to cover more of the costs of providing medical care, how will this affect poor and wealthy households? For an answer, read the Closer Look box "The Pricing of Medical Care in Developing Countries."

Predicting Changes in Total Revenue

If a firm increases its price, will its total sales revenue increase or decrease? The answer depends on the elasticity of demand for the good. If we know the elasticity, we can determine whether a price hike will increase or decrease the firm's total revenue.

Let's return to the example of the campus film series. An increase in the ticket price generates good news and bad news.

A Closer LOOK

The Pricing of Medical Care in Developing Countries

Many developing nations subsidize medical care, charging consumers a small fraction of the cost of providing the services. If a nation increased the price of medical care, how would this affect its poor and wealthy households? In Côte d'Ivoire in Africa, the price elasticity of demand for hospital services is 0.47 for poor households and 0.29 for wealthy households.* This means that a 10% increase in the price of hospital services would cause poor households to cut back their hospital care by 4.7%, while wealthy households would cut back by only 2.9%. In Peru, the differences between poor and wealthy households are even larger: The price elasticity is 0.67 for poor households but only 0.03 for wealthy households. The same pattern occurs in the demand for the medical services provided by physicians and health clinics. The poor are much more sensitive to price, so when prices increase, they experience much larger reductions in medical care.

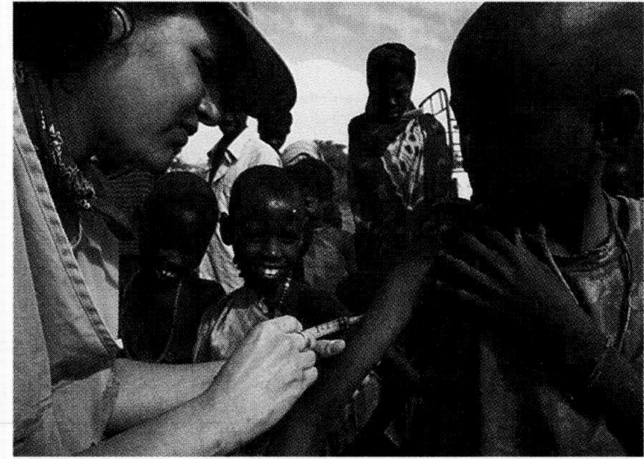

In developing nations, the poor are relatively sensitive to changes in the price of medical care.

*Paul Gertler and Jacques van der Gaag, *The Willingness to Pay for Medical Care: Evidence from Two Developing Countries* (Baltimore: Johns Hopkins University Press, 1990).

1. ***Good news.*** You get more money for each ticket sold.
2. ***Bad news.*** You sell fewer tickets.

Your total revenue will decrease if the bad news—fewer tickets sold—dominates the good news—more money per ticket. The elasticity of demand tells us whether the good news will dominate the bad news.

An increase in price will decrease total revenue if the demand for the good is elastic. In the film example, the elasticity of demand is 2.0, meaning that the percentage decrease in quantity is twice the percentage increase in price. In this case, consumers are very responsive to changes in price, so the bad news (fewer tickets sold) will dominate the good news (more money per ticket). For example, if you increase the admission price by 10%, from $4.00 to $4.40, the quantity of tickets will decrease by 20%, from 100 to 80. Therefore, your total revenue will be $352 ($4.40 times 80), compared to $400 at the old price and quantity ($4 times 100). In general, an elastic demand means that the percentage change in quantity will exceed the percentage change in price, so an increase in price will decrease total revenue.

We get the opposite result if the demand for the good is inelastic. In this case, an increase in price *increases* total revenue. If demand is inelastic, consumers are not very responsive to an increase in price, so the good news (more money per unit sold) dominates the bad news (fewer units sold). For example, suppose that the campus bookstore starts with a textbook price of $50 and a quantity of 100 books. If the bookstore increases its price by 10% (from $50 to $55 per book) and the elasticity of demand for textbooks is 0.40, the quantity of textbooks sold will decrease by only 4% (from 100 to 96). Therefore, the store's total revenue will be $5,280 ($55 times 96), compared to only $5,000 at the lower price ($50 times 100). In general, an inelastic demand means that the percentage change in quantity will be smaller than the percentage change in price, so an increase in price will increase total revenue.

Table 2 summarizes the revenue effects of changes in prices for different types of goods.

1. ***Elastic demand.*** There is a negative relationship between price and total revenue: An increase in price decreases total revenue; a decrease in price increases total revenue.
2. ***Inelastic demand.*** There is a positive relationship between price and total revenue: An increase in price increases total revenue; a decrease in price decreases total revenue.

The relationship between elasticity and total revenue provides a simple test of whether demand is elastic or inelastic. Suppose that a music store increases the price of its CDs and its total revenue from CDs then falls. The negative relationship

Table 2: Elasticity and Total Revenue

Type of Demand	*Value of* E_d	*Change in Quantity versus Change in Price*	*Effect of* Increase *in Price on Total Revenue*	*Effect of* Decrease *in Price on Total Revenue*
Elastic	Greater than 1.0	Larger percentage change in quantity	Total revenue decreases	Total revenue increases
Inelastic	Less than 1.0	Smaller percentage change in quantity	Total revenue increases	Total revenue decreases
Unitary elastic	Equal to 1.0	Same percentage changes in quantity and price	Total revenue does not change	Total revenue does not not change

between price and total revenue suggests that demand for the store's CDs is elastic. In contrast, suppose that a city increases the price it charges for water and the total revenue from water sales increases. The positive relationship between price and total revenue suggests that the demand for the city's water is inelastic.

Applications: Vanity Plates, Property Crime

Recall the discussion of vanity license plates at the beginning of the chapter. Suppose that the state of Virginia is thinking about increasing the price of its vanity plates by 10%. Your job is to predict whether the price hike will increase or decrease the state's revenue from vanity plates. According to a recent study,[3] the price elasticity of demand for vanity plates in Virginia is 0.41. Without doing any calculations, you can safely predict that the price hike will increase total revenue from vanity plates: Because demand is inelastic, the good news (more money per plate) will dominate the bad news (fewer plates sold).

What's the connection between antidrug policies and property crimes such as robbery, burglary, and auto theft? The government uses search-and-destroy tactics to restrict the supply of illegal drugs. If this approach succeeds, drugs become scarce and the price of drugs increases. Because the demand for illegal drugs is inelastic, the increase in price will increase total spending on illegal drugs. Many drug addicts support their habits with property crime, so the increase in total spending on drugs is bad news for the victims of property crimes committed by addicts.[4] To support their more expensive drug habits, addicts will commit more burglaries, robberies, and auto thefts.

ECONOMIC DETECTIVE– *The Video Elasticity Mystery*

You've been called in by the manager of a video-rental store to solve a puzzle. According to national studies of the video-rental market, the price elasticity of demand for video rentals is 0.80: A 10% increase in price decreases the quantity of videos demanded by about 8%. Based on this information, the manager of a video store increased her price by 20%, expecting to rent fewer videos because video consumers obey the law of demand. Based on the national studies suggesting that demand is inelastic, she also expected to get more total revenue. When her total revenue decreased instead of increasing, she was puzzled. Your job is to solve this mystery.

The key to solving this mystery is to recognize that the manager can't use the results of a national study to predict the effects of increasing her own price. The national study suggests that if *all* video stores in the nation increased their prices by 10%, the nationwide quantity of videos demanded would drop by 8%. But when a single video store in a city increases its price, consumers can easily switch to other video stores in the city. As a result, a 10% increase in the price of one store will decrease the quantity sold by the store by much more than 8%. The demand facing the store is elastic, so an increase in price will *decrease* total revenue.

TEST *Your Understanding*

5. Complete the statement: If the price elasticity of demand is 0.60, a 10% increase in price will ____________ (fill in with *increase* or *decrease*) the quantity demanded by ____________%.

6. If an increase in the price of accordions does not change total revenue from accordion sales, what can we infer about the price elasticity of demand for accordions?

7 In 1987, the price elasticity of demand for vanity plates in the state of Ohio was 2.60. If the state's objective was to maximize its revenue from vanity plates, should it have picked a higher price or a lower one?

THE PRICE ELASTICITY OF SUPPLY

Price elasticity of supply: A measure of the responsiveness of the quantity supplied to changes in price; computed by dividing the percentage change in quantity supplied by the percentage change in price.

While the price elasticity of demand measures the responsiveness of consumers to changes in price, the **price elasticity of supply** measures the responsiveness of producers. We compute the supply elasticity by dividing the percentage change in quantity supplied by the percentage change in price:

$$E_s = \frac{\text{percentage change in quantity supplied}}{\text{percentage change in price}}$$

In Figure 3, when the price of milk increases from \$2.00 to \$2.20, the quantity supplied increases from 100 million gallons to 120 million gallons. In other words, a 10% increase in price increased the quantity supplied by 20%, so the price elasticity of supply is 2.0:

$$E_s = \frac{\text{percentage change in quantity supplied}}{\text{percentage change in price}} = \frac{20\%}{10\%} = 2.0$$

Time is an important factor in determining the price elasticity of supply. When the price of a particular product increases, the immediate response is that existing firms produce more output in their current production facilities (for example, factories, stores, offices, or restaurants). Although firms will certainly produce more output, the response will be relatively small because the firms' facilities have limited capacities. Over time, however, firms can enter the market and build new production facilities, so there will be a larger response. As time passes, supply becomes more elastic because more and more firms have the time to build production facilities and produce more output.

The milk industry provides a nice example of the difference between short-run and long-run supply elasticities. The price elasticity of supply over a one-year period is 0.12: If the price of milk increases by 10% and stays at the higher level for a year, the quantity of milk supplied will rise by only 1.2%.[5] In the short run, dairy

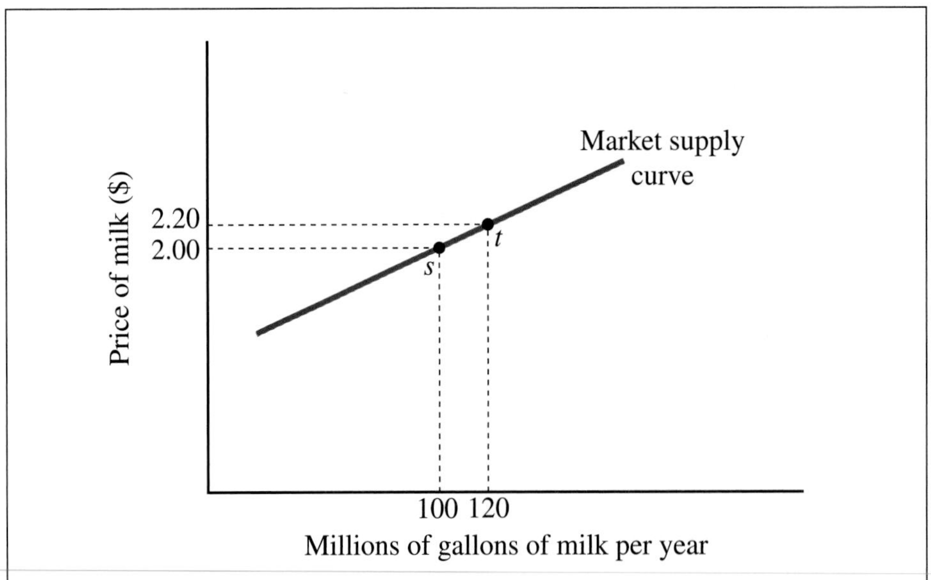

Figure 3

Market Supply Curve and Price Elasticity of Supply

A 10% rise in the price of milk (from \$2 to \$2.20) increases the quantity demanded by 20% (from 100 million gallons to 120 million), so the price elasticity of supply is 2.0 = 20%/10%.

farmers can squeeze a little more output from their existing production facilities. In contrast, over a 10-year period, the price elasticity is 2.5: The same 10% rise in price will increase the quantity supplied by 25%. In the long run, dairy farmers can expand existing facilities and build new ones, so there is a larger response to a higher price.

We can use the price elasticity of supply to predict the effect of price changes on the quantity supplied. For example, suppose that the elasticity of supply is 0.80 and the price increases by 5%. Using the elasticity formula, we would predict a 4% increase in quantity supplied:

$$0.80 = \frac{\text{percentage change in quantity}}{5\%} = \frac{4\%}{5\%}$$

As we'll see in Chapter 6, many governments establish minimum prices for agricultural products. The higher the minimum price, the larger the quantity supplied, consistent with the law of supply. If we know the price elasticity of supply, we can predict just how much more will be supplied at the higher price. For example, if the minimum price of cheese increases by 10% and the price elasticity is 0.60, the quantity of cheese supplied will rise by 6%:

$$0.60 = \frac{\text{percentage change in quantity}}{10\%} = \frac{6\%}{10\%}$$

PREDICTING PRICE CHANGES USING ELASTICITIES

When supply or demand changes, we can draw a supply and demand diagram to predict whether the equilibrium price will increase or decrease. In many cases, the simple diagram will tell us all we need to know about the effects of a change in supply or demand. But what if we want to predict *how much* a price will increase or decrease? We can use a simple formula to predict the actual change in price resulting from a change in supply or demand.

As shown in Figure 4, an increase in demand shifts the demand curve to the right and increases the equilibrium price. When will the increase in price be relatively small? When demand increases, the immediate effect is a shortage: At the original price, the quantity demanded exceeds the quantity supplied. As the price increases, both consumers and producers help to eliminate the shortage: Consumers buy less

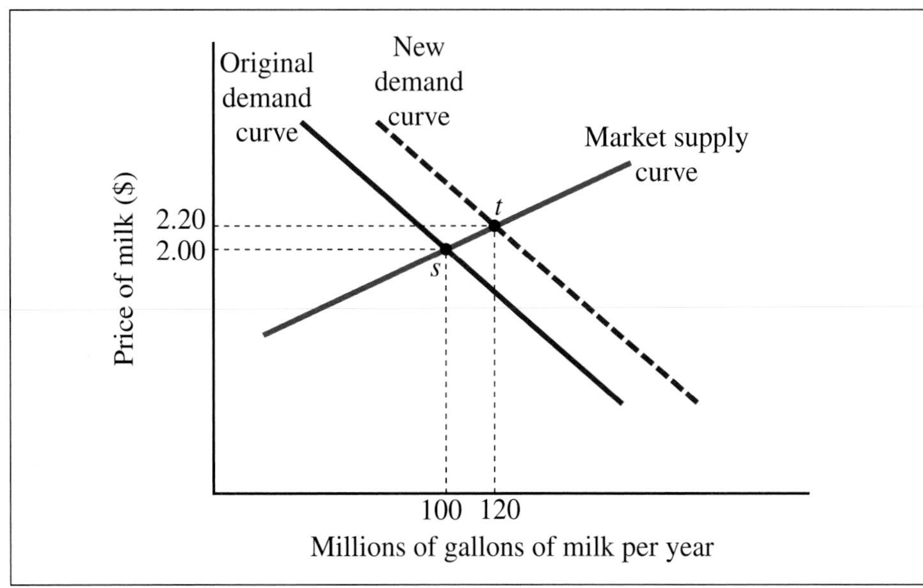

Figure 4

Increase in Demand Increases the Equilibrium Price

An increase in demand shifts the demand curve to the right, increasing the equilibrium price. In this case, a 35% increase in demand increases the price by 10%: 10% = 35%/(2.0 + 1.5).

(the law of demand), and firms produce more (the law of supply). If both consumers and producers are very responsive to changes in price, it will take a relatively small increase in price to eliminate the shortage. In other words, an increase in demand will cause a small increase in price if both demand and supply are elastic.

We can use the following **price-change formula** to predict the change in price resulting from a change in demand. We just divide the percentage change in demand by the sum of the price elasticities of supply and demand:

$$\text{percentage change in price} = \frac{\text{percentage change in demand}}{E_s + E_d}$$

The numerator (the upper half of the fraction) is the rightward shift of the demand curve in percentage terms. The two elasticities appear in the denominator (the lower half of the fraction). This is sensible because if consumers and producers are very responsive to changes in price (the elasticities are large numbers), a shortage will be eliminated with a relatively small increase in price. For example, suppose that demand increases by 35% (the demand curve shifts to the right by 35%), the supply elasticity is 2.0, and the demand elasticity is 1.5. In this case, the predicted change in price is 10%:

$$\text{percentage change in price} = \frac{\text{percentage change in demand}}{E_s + E_d} = \frac{35\%}{2.0 + 1.5} = 10\%$$

If either demand or supply were less elastic (if either of the elasticity numbers were smaller), the predicted change in price would be larger. For example, if the supply elasticity is 0.25 instead of 2.0, we would predict a 20% increase in price (35%/1.75).

This formula is designed to be used with a supply–demand diagram. The formula shows the size of the change in the equilibrium price, but it does not show the direction of the price change. To determine the direction of the price change, we draw a simple supply–demand diagram, shift the demand curve in the appropriate direction, and see what happens to the equilibrium price. Then we can plug the appropriate numbers into the price-change formula and compute the percentage change in price.

We can use a slightly different version of the price-change formula to predict the change in price resulting from a change in supply. As explained in Chapter 3, a change in supply results from changes in something other than the price of the product, for example, a change in the cost of an input such as labor, material, or production facilities, a change in production technology, or a change in the number of firms. To predict the change in price resulting from a change in supply, we just substitute *supply* for *demand* in the numerator:

$$\text{percentage change in price} = \frac{\text{percentage change in supply}}{E_s + E_d}$$

An increase in supply causes a surplus that is eliminated by a decrease in the market price. If consumers are very responsive to changes in price, the surplus will be eliminated by a relatively small decrease in price. Once you've used a supply–demand diagram to determine the direction of a price change, you can use the price-change formula to predict just how large the price change will be.

TEST *Your Understanding*

8 Complete the statement: If a 10% increase in price increases the quantity supplied by 15%, the price elasticity of supply is ____________.

9 Suppose the price elasticity of a supply of cheese is 0.80. If the price of cheese rises by 20%, by what percentage will the quantity supplied change?

10 Suppose that the elasticity of demand for chewing tobacco is 0.70 and the elasticity of supply is 2.30. If an antichewing campaign decreases the demand for chewing tobacco by 30%, in what direction and by what percentage will the price of chewing tobacco change?

11 Suppose that the elasticity of demand for motel rooms in a town near a ski area is 1.0 and the elasticity of supply is 0.50. If the population of the surrounding area increases by 30%, in what direction and by what percentage will the price of motel rooms change?

Using the **TOOLS**

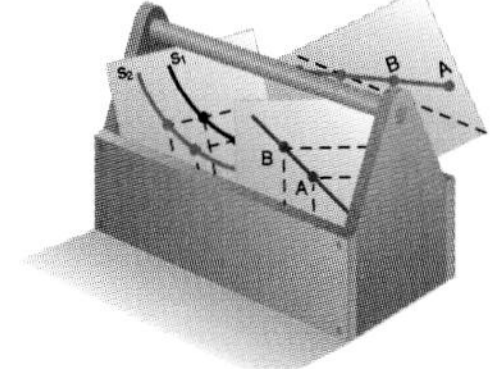

This chapter introduced two tools of economics, the price elasticity of demand and the price elasticity of supply. We also learned how to use a simple formula to predict the actual change in price resulting from a change in supply or demand. Here are some opportunities to use these tools to do your own economic analysis.

1. Projecting Transit Ridership

As a transit planner, you must predict how many people ride commuter trains and how much money is generated from train fares. According to a recent study,[6] the short-run demand for commuter rail is 0.62 and the long-run elasticity is 1.59. The current ridership is 100,000 people per day. Suppose that the transit authority decides to increase its fares by 10%.

a. Predict the changes in train ridership over a one-month period (the short run) and a five-year period (the long run).

b. Over the one-month period, will total revenue increase or decrease? What will happen in the five-year period?

2. Bumper Crops

Your job is to predict the total revenue generated by the nation's corn crop. Last year's crop was 100 million bushels, and the price was $4.00 per bushel. This year's weather was favorable throughout the country, and this year's crop will be 110 million bushels, or 10% larger than last year's. The price elasticity of demand for corn is 0.50.

a. Predict the effect of the bumper crop on the price of corn, assuming that the entire crop is sold this year.

b. Predict the total revenue from this year's corn crop.

c. Did the favorable weather increase or decrease the total revenue from corn? Why?

3. Washington, DC, Gas Tax

You are a tax analyst for the city of Washington, DC, and have been asked to predict how much revenue will be generated by the city's gasoline tax. The initial quantity of gasoline is 100 million gallons per month, and the price elasticity of demand for gasoline in the typical large city is 4.0. The tax, which is $0.10 per gallon, will increase the price of gasoline by 5%.

a. How much revenue will the gasoline tax generate?

b. In 1980, tax analysts in Washington, DC, based their revenue predictions for a gasoline tax on the elasticity of demand for gasoline in the United States as a whole (1.0). Would you expect the national elasticity to be larger or smaller than the elasticity for the typical large city? Would you expect the analysts to overestimate or underestimate the revenue from the gasoline tax?

4. College Enrollment and Housing

Consider a college town where the initial price of apartments is $400 and the initial quantity is 1,000 apartments. The price elasticity of demand for apartments is 1.0 and the price elasticity of supply of apartments is 0.50.

a. Use supply and demand curves to show the initial equilibrium, and label the equilibrium point with an *i*.

b. Suppose that an increase in college enrollment is expected to increase the demand for apartments in a college town by 15%. Use your graph to show the effects of the increase in demand on the apartment market. Label the new equilibrium point with an *f*.

c. Predict the effect of the increase in demand on the equilibrium price of apartments.

SUMMARY

This chapter deals with the numbers behind the laws of demand and supply. The law of demand tells us that an increase in price will decrease the quantity demanded. If we know the price elasticity of demand, we can determine just how much less will be sold at the higher price. Similarly, armed with the price elasticity of supply, we can determine just how much more will be supplied at a higher price. Here are the main points of the chapter.

1. The price elasticity of demand—defined as the percentage change in quantity demanded divided by the percentage change in price—measures the responsiveness of consumers to changes in price.
2. Demand is relatively elastic if there are good substitutes.
3. If demand is elastic, there is a negative relationship between price and total revenue. If demand is inelastic, there is a positive relationship between price and total revenue.
4. The price elasticity of supply—defined as the percentage change in quantity supplied divided by the percentage change in price—measures the responsiveness of producers to changes in price.
5. If we know the elasticities of supply and demand, we can predict the percentage change in price resulting from a change in demand or supply.

KEY TERMS

price-change formula, *94*

price elasticity of demand, *82*

price elasticity of supply, *92*

PROBLEMS AND DISCUSSION QUESTIONS

1. When the price of compact disks (CDs) increased from $10 to $11, the quantity of CDs demanded decreased from 100 to 87. What is the price elasticity of demand for CDs? Is demand elastic or inelastic?
2. Explain why the demand for residential natural gas (gas used for heating, cooling, and cooking) is more elastic than the demand for residential electricity.
3. Would you expect the demand for a specific brand of running shoes to be more elastic or less elastic than

the demand for running shoes in general? Why?

4. For each of the following goods, indicate whether you expect demand to be inelastic or elastic, and explain your reasoning: opera, foreign travel, local telephone service, video rentals, and eggs.
5. You observe a positive relationship between the price your store charges for CDs and the total revenue from CDs. Is the demand for your CDs elastic or inelastic?
6. Suppose that the price elasticity of demand for a campus film series is 1.40. If the objective of the film society is to maximize its total revenue (price times the number of tickets sold), should it increase or decrease its price?
7. As the head of a state chapter of MADD (Mothers Against Drunk Driving), you are to speak in support of policies that discourage drunk driving. The number of highway deaths among young adults, which is roughly proportional to the group's beer consumption, is initially 100 per year. You have scheduled a news conference to express your support for a beer tax that will increase the price of beer by 10%. The price elasticity of demand for beer is 1.30. Complete the following statement: "The beer tax will decrease the number of highway deaths among young adults by about ____________ per year."
8. When the price of paper increases from $100 per ton to $104 per ton, the quantity supplied increased from 200 tons per day to 220 tons per day. What is the price elasticity of supply?
9. Suppose that the government restricts logging to protect an endangered species. The restrictions increase the price of wood products and shift the supply curve for new housing to the left by 4%. The initial price of new housing is $100,000, the elasticity of demand is 1.0, and the elasticity of supply is 3.0. Predict the effect of the logging restriction on the equilibrium price of new housing. Illustrate your answer with a graph that shows the initial point (labeled with an *i*) and the new equilibrium (labeled with an *f*).

Take It to the Net

We invite you to visit the O'Sullivan/Sheffrin page on the Prentice Hall Web site at:

http://www.prenhall.com/osullivan/

for this chapter's World Wide Web exercise.

MODEL ANSWERS FOR THIS CHAPTER

Chapter-Opening Questions

1. A beer tax will increase the price of beer, decreasing beer consumption. Highway deaths are roughly proportional to beer consumption, so the tax will also decrease highway deaths. The actual change in highway deaths depends on the price elasticity of demand for beer.
2. As shown in Using the Tools: Bumper Crops, a bumper crop of corn decreases the equilibrium price of corn by a relatively large amount because the demand for corn is inelastic. Although corn farmers will sell more bushels, they will receive much less per bushel, so total revenue will drop.
3. If demand is elastic, the firm should lower its price. If demand is inelastic, the firm should raise its price.
4. The policies increase the price of the illegal drug, which increases total spending on the drug because demand is inelastic. If drug addicts support their habits with property crime, they must commit more crime to support their more expensive habits.
5. The percentage change in demand, the price elasticity of supply, and the price elasticity of demand.

Test Your Understanding

1. quantity, price
2. 1.20
3. An increase in the price of tapes will cause some consumers to buy CD players and switch from tapes to CDs, but this takes some time.
4. On the upper portion, demand is elastic, so quantity will decrease by more than 10%.
5. decrease, 6
6. The price elasticity is 1.0 (neither elastic nor inelastic).

7. Demand is elastic, so a decrease in price would increase total revenue.
8. 1.50 = 15%/10%.
9. The quantity supplied will increase by 16%.
10. Using the price-change formula, the price will decrease by 10% = 30%/3.
11. Using the price-change formula, the price will increase by 20% = 30%/1.50.

Using the Tools

1. Projecting Transit Ridership
   a. Using the elasticity formula, ridership will decrease by 6.2% in the short run (a loss of 6,200 riders) and 15.9% in the long run (a loss of 15,900 riders).
   b. Demand is inelastic in the short run, so total revenue will increase. Demand is elastic in the long run, so total revenue will eventually decrease.
2. Bumper Crops
   a. Using the price elasticity formula, to sell an additional 10% of corn, the price must decrease by 20%, to $3.20.
   b. Total revenue is 110 million × $3.20, or $352 million.
   c. Total revenue last year was $400 million, so the bumper crop decreased total revenue. This occurs because demand is inelastic, so the price decreases by a large amount.
3. Washington, DC, Gas Tax
   a. Using the price elasticity formula, the 5% increase in price will decrease the quantity demanded by 20%, from 100 million gallons to 80 million gallons. The revenue is the tax per gallon ($0.10) × the quantity (80 million gallons), or $8 million.
   b. They will overestimate the revenue from the tax because they will underestimate the change in quantity demanded by the tax. Specifically, they will predict a quantity of 95 million gallons instead of 80 million gallons, and revenue of $9.5 million instead of $8 million. Because it is relatively easy to buy gasoline in a nearby city, the demand for gasoline will be relatively elastic at the city level.
4. College Enrollment and Housing
   a. See Figure B in Chapter 4 (page 80).
   b. See Figure B in Chapter 4. The demand curve shifts to the right by 15%. Equilibrium is restored at point *f*, with a higher price and a larger quantity.
   c. Use the price-change formula: The price increases by 10% = 15%/(0.50 + 1.0).

NOTES

1. Don Fullerton and Thomas Kinnaman, "Household Responses to Pricing Garbage by the Bag," *American Economic Review,* vol. 86, no. 4, 1996, pp. 971–984.
2. Henry Saffer and Michael Grossman, "Beer Taxes, the Legal Drinking Age, and Youth Motor Vehicle Fatalities," *Journal of Legal Studies,* vol. 41, June 1987.
3. Neil O. Alper, Robert B. Archibald, and Eric Jensen, "What Price Vanity: An Econometric Model of Personalized License Plates," *National Tax Journal,* vol. 40, 1987, pp. 103–109.
4. L. P. Silverman and N. L. Sprull, "Urban Crime and the Price of Heroin," *Journal of Urban Economics,* vol. 4, 1977, pp. 80–103.
5. Richard Klemme and Jean-Paul Chavas, "The Effects of Changing Milk Price on Milk Supply and National Dairy Herd Size," *Economic Issues,* University of Wisconsin, June 1985.
6. Richard Voith, "The Long Run Elasticity of Demand for Commuter Rail Transportation," *Journal of Urban Economics,* vol. 30, 1991, pp. 360–372.

Appendix
Other Elasticities of Demand

Income Elasticity

Cross Elasticity

In Chapter 4 we saw that the demand for a product depends on several variables, including the price of the product, consumer income, and the price of related goods. In this chapter we've seen that the price elasticity of demand measures the responsiveness of the quantity of a particular good demanded to changes in the price of that good. How do we measure the responsiveness of consumers to changes in the other variables that affect demand?

INCOME ELASTICITY

We can use the **income elasticity of demand** to measure the responsiveness of consumers to changes in income. This elasticity is defined as the percentage change in quantity demanded divided by the percentage change in income:

$$E_i = \frac{\text{percentage change in quantity demanded}}{\text{percentage change in income}}$$

Income elasticity of demand: A measure of the responsiveness of the quantity demanded to changes in consumer income; computed by dividing the percentage change in the quantity demanded by the percentage change in income.

For a normal good, there is a positive relationship between income and the quantity demanded, so the income elasticity is positive. We say that demand is income elastic if the income elasticity is larger than 1.0. In contrast, demand is income inelastic if the income elasticity is less than 1.0. For inferior goods such as intercity bus travel and used clothing, there is a negative relationship between income and quantity demanded, so the income elasticity is negative.

CROSS ELASTICITY

We can use the **cross elasticity of demand** to measure the responsiveness of consumers to changes in the price of a related good. This elasticity is defined as the percentage change in quantity demanded of one good (X) divided by the percentage change in the price of a related good (Y):

$$E_{xy} = \frac{\text{percentage change in quantity of } X \text{ demanded}}{\text{percentage change in price of } Y}$$

Cross elasticity of demand: A measure of the responsiveness of the quantity demanded to changes in the price of a related good; computed by dividing the percentage change in the quantity demanded of one good (X) by the percentage change in the price of another good (Y).

As we saw in Chapter 4, there is a positive relationship between the quantity demanded of one good and the price of a substitute goods. For example, an increase in the price of bananas increases the demand for apples as consumers substitute apples for the more expensive bananas. In this case, the cross elasticity is positive. In contrast, there is a negative relationship for complementary goods. For example, an increase in the price of ice cream increases the cost of apple pie with ice cream, causing consumers to demand fewer apples. In this case, the cross elasticity is negative.

KEY TERMS

CHAPTER

6 Government Intervention in Markets

Fionna took the envelope from her uncle, a retiring taxi driver, and thanked him politely. She knew the envelope contained a taxi medallion, a license to earn enormous profits operating a taxi in New York City. The problem was that Fionna didn't want to drive a taxi; she wanted to go to college. When she opened the envelope, she found the taxi medallion and a small slip of paper with a phone number written on it. She rushed to a phone and dialed the number. A voice answered with, "Medallion Brokers—Do you want to buy or sell a medallion?" Yipeeeee! Fionna sold the medallion for $150,000 and used the money to pay for her college education.

We know from earlier chapters that the actions of consumers and producers lead to a market equilibrium, with the quantity demanded equal to the quantity supplied. In this chapter we see what happens when the government intervenes in a market, picking an alternative price or quantity. In the taxi example, the city government controls the quantity of taxi service by issuing a small number of taxi medallions. This policy hurts taxi consumers, who pay a high price because there are so few taxis in the market. The policy helps the people who get a medallion—and with it the right to charge an artificially high price for taxi service. Fionna benefits from the policy because she sells her medallion for a price that reflects the large profits that can be earned with it.

In this chapter we explore the effects of government intervention in perfectly competitive markets. Recall that a perfectly competitive market has a very large number of firms, each of which is so small that it takes the market price as given. A key feature of a perfectly competitive market is that firms are free to enter or exit the market. Whenever there is an opportunity to make a profit—that is, whenever the price of a product exceeds the cost of producing it—firms will enter the market and supply more of the product. The quantity supplied will continue to increase until the opportunity for profit is eliminated, which happens when the price is just high enough to cover the cost of providing the product, but no higher.

We'll see that it is sensible for the government to intervene in a market if there are spillover benefits or costs, but not sensible otherwise. We also explore the positive and negative consequences of government intervention in competitive markets. Here are some of the practical questions we answer:

1. If consumers and producers are guided only by self-interest and we reach a market equilibrium, can we do any better?
2. If a college town uses a rent-control policy to cut the monthly rent on apartments, will some students be harmed by the policy?
3. Who bears the cost of restrictions on textile imports, and what is the cost per textile job saved?
4. Why do governments assume the responsibility for providing dams, national defense, and law enforcement?
5. If paper mills dump chemical wastes into rivers, should the government intervene in the paper market?

EFFICIENT OR INEFFICIENT MARKETS?

Before we explore the effects of government intervention, let's think about whether a market is efficient or inefficient. The market equilibrium for a particular product involves thousands of transactions, with people buying and selling the product at its equilibrium price. A market is **inefficient** if once we reach the market equilibrium, there is an additional transaction that would benefit a buyer, a seller, and any third parties affected by the transaction. The purpose of a market is to facilitate mutually beneficial transactions, so a market that fails to execute some beneficial transactions fails to do its job and is considered inefficient. In contrast, a market is **efficient** if it executes all the potential transactions that would benefit a buyer, a seller, and any third parties affected by the transactions.

Inefficient market: A market in which there is an additional transaction that would benefit a buyer, a seller, and any third parties affected by the transaction.

Efficient market: A market in which there are *no* additional transactions that would benefit a buyer, a seller, and any third parties affected by the transactions.

The Efficiency of a Market Without Spillovers

Consider a market that does not generate spillover costs or benefits. In other words, the costs of producing the good are confined to the people who decide how much to produce, and the benefits of consuming the good are confined to the people who decide how much to consume. If there are no spillovers, there are no third parties who would be affected by market transactions, so we say that the market is efficient if there are no additional transactions that would benefit a buyer and a seller.

We can use the market for rental housing as an example of a market without spillovers. Figure 1 on page 102 shows the supply and demand curves for a hypothetical housing market in a college town. The market equilibrium is shown by point *i*: The price is $400 per month and the equilibrium quantity is 800 apartments. In other words, housing firms supply 800 apartments, charging $400 to each

Figure 1

Market Equilibrium and Efficiency

The market equilibrium is shown by point *i*: There are 800 apartments provided at a price of $400 per month. The equilibrium is efficient because it is impossible to arrange a transaction between a nonbuyer and a potential housing producer.

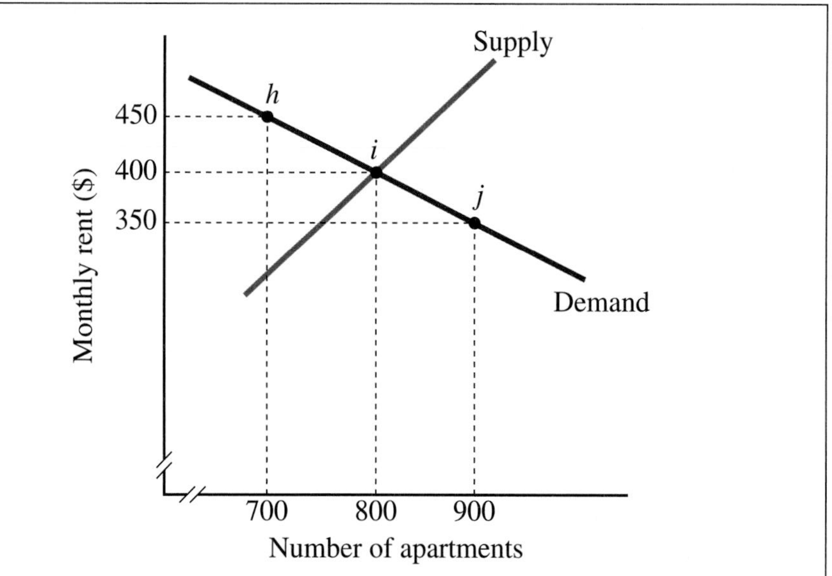

of the 800 students who rent apartments. To prove that the apartment market is efficient, we must show that it would be impossible to arrange an additional transaction that would benefit a buyer (a student) and a seller (a housing firm).

Let's look first at the consumer side of the market. The market demand curve shows how much money consumers are willing to pay for apartments. At a price of $450, the quantity of apartments demanded is 700 (point *h*), but at a slightly higher price, the quantity demanded is only 699 apartments. In other words, to persuade the 700th student to rent an apartment, the price must drop from $451 to $450. This means that the 700th student is willing to pay $450 for an apartment, but no more. Moving downward along the demand curve, we see that students on the lower portion of the demand curve are willing to pay much less for apartments: For example, the student at point *j* is willing to pay only $350. Students on the lower part of the demand curve are not willing to pay the market price ($400), so they don't participate in the market.

Let's look next at the producer side of the market. In a perfectly competitive market for apartments, there are no restrictions on the number of apartments supplied. Whenever there is an opportunity to make a profit—that is, whenever the price exceeds the cost of producing an apartment—firms will supply more apartments. The quantity supplied will continue to increase until the opportunity for profit is eliminated, which happens when the price is just high enough to cover the cost of providing apartments, but no higher.

We can use the supply curve in Figure 1 to determine the cost of providing the 800th apartment. At a price of $400, a total of 800 apartments are supplied, suggesting that a price of $400 is just high enough to cover the cost of providing the 800th apartment ($400). To see why the cost of the 800th apartment must be $400, think about the implications of either a lower cost or a higher cost.

- If the cost were lower than $400, say $390, there would be a $10 profit to be made on additional apartments, so more than 800 apartments would be supplied. But the supply curve tells us that only 800 apartments are supplied at a price of $400.
- If the cost were higher than $400, say $415, a firm supplying the 800th apartment would lose $15 on the apartment, so no one would supply the

apartment. But the supply curve tells us that at a price of $400, the 800th apartment is in fact supplied.

Putting these two observations together, the cost of providing the 800th apartment must be $400.

What about the cost of providing one more apartment, the 801st apartment? Because firms don't provide the 801st apartment when the price is $400, the cost of the additional apartment must be greater than $400. Although it's not shown in Figure 1, housing producers would supply the 801st apartment if the price rose to $401. This price is just high enough to cover the cost of providing the apartment, so the cost of producing the 801st apartment is $401.

Let's see if we can arrange a transaction between a student who does not participate in the market and a potential housing producer. The student who is at point *j* on the demand curve is willing to pay only $350 for an apartment. This student would occupy the 801st apartment, which we know would cost $401 to produce. Because this student is not willing to pay the cost of producing the additional apartment, it is impossible to arrange a transaction between the student and a potential housing producer. This is true for all the students on the lower portion of the demand curve. Each of these students is willing to pay *less* than the equilibrium price, while each potential producer has a cost that is *greater* than the equilibrium price. As a result, we cannot arrange a transaction that would benefit both people. In general, once we reach the market equilibrium, there are no additional transactions that would benefit a buyer and a seller. This means that the market is efficient.

The same conclusion emerges from other markets. A consumer will decide not to buy a particular good if he or she is not willing to pay the market price. A firm will decide not to produce the good if the cost of producing it exceeds the market price. It would be impossible to arrange a transaction between a nonbuyer and a nonseller because the consumer is willing to pay less than the cost of producing the good.

Efficiency and the Invisible Hand

It is truly remarkable that a market with thousands of buyers and sellers may reach an efficient outcome. Instead of using a bureaucrat to coordinate the actions of everyone in the market, we can rely on the actions of individual consumers and producers, each guided only by self-interest. Adam Smith used the metaphor of the **invisible hand** to explain how a market generates an efficient outcome.

Invisible hand: The phenomenon that leads individual consumers and producers to the market equilibrium, which is efficient in some circumstances.

> It is not from the benevolence of the butcher, the brewer, or the baker that we expect our dinner, but from their regard to their own interest. We address ourselves, not to their humanity but to their self-love, and never talk to them of our own necessities but of their advantages. [Man is] led by an invisible hand to promote an end which was no part of his intention. . . . By pursuing his own interest he frequently promotes that of the society more effectually than when he really intends to promote it.
>
> Adam Smith, *Wealth of Nations* (New York: Modern Library, 1994)

It's important to note that in referring to the idea that a person may promote the social interest, Smith used the word *frequently*, not *always*. Smith recognized that sometimes an individual gains at the expense of society as a whole. Later in the chapter we show that if there are spillover costs or benefits, the market equilibrium will be inefficient and government intervention will be sensible.

The experience of the former Soviet Union demonstrates the importance of prices and the power of Adam Smith's ideas. The Soviet economy was a planned economy in the sense that bureaucrats—not individual producers—decided how much of each good to produce. There were no prices to guide the decisions of producers. When the Soviets discovered a persistent mismatch between what they were producing and what consumers wanted, they asked a team of experts to propose a solution to the problem. The experts told the bureaucrats to figure out the prices that would have occurred *if* the Soviet economy were a market economy instead of a planned one, and to base their production decisions on these fabricated prices. In other words, the experts told the bureaucrats to base their decisions on the prices that would have emerged from a market economy.

Inefficiency with Spillovers or Imperfect Competition

What can we say about the efficiency of a market that generates spillover costs or benefits? If there are spillovers, third parties will be affected by market transactions, and we can't determine whether or not the market is efficient until we know how a transaction would affect a buyer, a seller, *and* the third parties. As we'll see later in the chapter, a market with spillover benefits or costs may be inefficient: Starting from the market equilibrium, there may be additional transactions that would benefit a buyer, a seller, and some third parties.

It's important to note that our conclusions about market efficiency apply only to perfectly competitive markets. In a perfectly competitive market, each firm is such a small part of the market that it takes prices as given. In contrast, firms in an **imperfectly competitive market** are large enough to affect market prices. Later in the book we'll see that the equilibrium in such a market will be inefficient even if there are no spillover benefits or costs.

Imperfectly competitive market: A market in which firms are large enough that they affect market prices.

TEST *Your Understanding*

1 Complete the statement with *greater* or *less*: If there are no spillover costs or benefits, the market equilibrium is efficient because a potential consumer is willing to pay ____________ than the equilibrium price, while a potential producer requires a price ____________ than the equilibrium price.

2 According to Ida, "I'm willing to buy a CD player for $50, but I can't find anyone willing to sell me one for that price." Does that mean that the market for CD players is inefficient?

3 The conclusion that a market equilibrium is efficient is based on two assumptions. What are they?

MAXIMUM PRICES

Now that we know that a perfectly competitive market without spillovers is efficient, we can discuss the effects of government intervention in such a market. We first examine the effects of a maximum price for a particular good. If a government passes a law that sets a maximum price below the equilibrium price (also known as a **price ceiling**), the price of the good will drop. If you are a consumer, a price cut may sound like a great idea, but the maximum price will actually harm some consumers. Here are some examples of goods that have been or may be subject to maximum prices.

Price ceiling: A maximum price; transactions above the maximum price are outlawed.

- *Rental housing.* A rent control program establishes a maximum monthly rent.
- *Gasoline.* Price controls in the 1970s established a maximum price.
- *Medical goods and services.* Some proposals to control medical costs include price controls.

We will use rent control to explain the market effects of a maximum price, but the lessons apply to other markets that are subject to maximum prices.

Market Effects of Rent Control

Rent control: A policy under which the government specifies a maximum rent that is below the equilibrium rent.

A **rent-control** law specifies a maximum price (a maximum monthly rent) on rental dwellings. During World War II, the federal government instituted a national system of rent controls. Although New York City was the only city to retain rent controls after the war, rent control returned to dozens of cities during the 1970s, including Boston, Cambridge, Los Angeles, Washington, DC, Albany, Berkeley, and Santa Monica. In recent years, several states, including New York, California, and Massachusetts, have weakened rent control by passing laws that limit the ability of individual cities to control rents. It remains to be seen whether this new activism on the part of state government will lead to the elimination of rent control as a policy instrument.

Figure 2 shows the long-run effects of rent control in a hypothetical city. Point *i* shows the initial equilibrium: the price is $400 per month and the equilibrium quantity is 800 apartments. Suppose that the government picks a maximum price of $360 per month. Housing producers obey the law of supply, and they respond to the price cut by supplying fewer apartments: The quantity supplied drops from 800 (point *i*) to 760 (point *s*). The decrease in quantity means that some of the city's households must either live elsewhere or share apartments with other households.

Why does rent control decrease the quantity of apartments supplied? In a perfectly competitive market for apartments, the price is just high enough to cover the cost of supplying apartments. Because rent control decreases the price, some firms will now lose money on their apartments and will withdraw their apartments from the market, either by converting their apartments to condominiums (fleeing from the

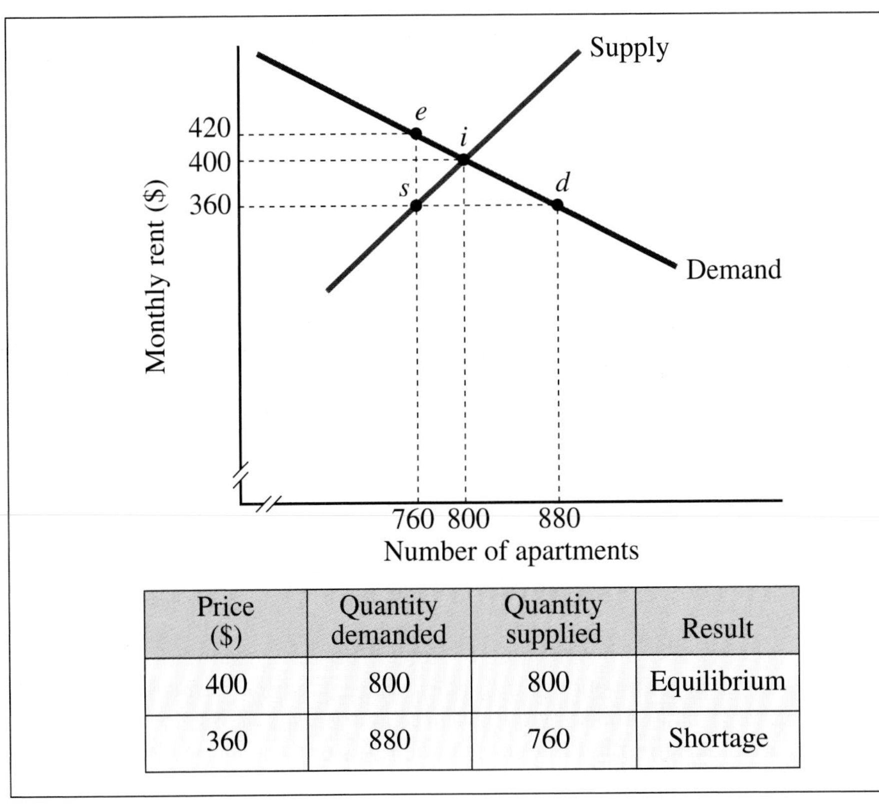

Price ($)	Quantity demanded	Quantity supplied	Result
400	800	800	Equilibrium
360	880	760	Shortage

Figure 2

Market Effects of Rent Control

Rent control decreases the price of apartments from $400 to $360, decreasing the quantity supplied from 800 (point *i*) to 760 (point *s*) and increasing the quantity demanded to 880 (point *d*). The shortage is 120 apartments.

regulated rental market to an unregulated one) or by allowing the apartments to deteriorate to the point that they are not habitable. In addition, housing producers will build fewer new apartments to replace old apartments because the maximum price is not high enough to cover the cost of building a new apartment.

Rent control may also decrease the *quality* of the remaining apartments. To maintain a dwelling at a given quality level, the property owner must spend money on routine maintenance and repair. In a city without rent control, the property owner will spend money on maintenance to keep the apartment at a quality level high enough to justify a $400 rent. When the rent drops to $360, there is no reason to keep the quality level at the $400 level because the government does not allow anyone to pay $400 for the apartment. Rent control decreases the rewards from maintenance, so the property owner will spend just enough to justify a rent of $360.

There is plenty of evidence that rent control decreases spending on routine maintenance and decreases the quality of housing. A study of the housing market in Cambridge, Massachusetts, found that rent control decreased maintenance spending per apartment by $50 per year.[1] One study of the housing market in New York City suggests that rent control decreased the quality and quantity of rental housing[2]: Between 1960 and 1967, the inventory of "dilapidated" housing increased by 44%; and the inventory of "deteriorating" housing increased by 37%. Another study of New York City showed that rent-controlled buildings are more likely than uncontrolled buildings to be in a "dilapidated" or "deteriorating" condition.[3] For another view of the effects of rent control, read the Closer Look box "Rent Control in Vietnam."

Maximum Prices and Market Efficiency

We know that a maximum price moves the market away from the market equilibrium, but so what? The problem with a maximum price is that it outlaws transactions that would benefit both a buyer and a seller. The maximum price prevents the market from doing its job, so it replaces an efficient outcome (the market equilibrium) with an inefficient one.

Let's see how rent control prevents beneficial transactions in the housing market. Some of the consumers who are shut out of the market would gladly pay more than the maximum price to get an apartment. The frustrated consumers are on the demand curve between points *e* and *d* in Figure 2: They are willing to pay between $360 and $420 for an apartment. On the producer side, the cost of producing one additional apartment (the 761st apartment) is shown by point *s*: This apartment wouldn't be supplied at a price of $360, but it would be supplied at a price of $361, so the cost of providing this apartment is $361. Here is a transaction that would benefit a buyer and a seller.

- The consumer at point *i* is willing to pay $400 for an apartment.
- A producer could provide the 761st apartment at a cost of $361.
- The two people agree on a price of $380, so the consumer receives a net benefit of $20 and the producer receives a net benefit of $19.

Because there is an additional transaction that would benefit both people, the outcome under the maximum price is not efficient. The same logic applies to any price other than the equilibrium price: We could find an additional transaction that would benefit a buyer and a seller.

Actual experiences with rent control suggest that this example is not so far-fetched. Consumers in some rent-control cities willingly pay extra money to property owners to outbid other consumers for scarce apartments. These extra payments are often disguised as nonrefundable security deposits or "key money" (hundreds of dollars to get the key to the apartment when a consumer signs a lease).

A Closer LOOK

Rent Control in Vietnam

Following the Vietnam war, the city of Hanoi used rent control to keep the price of rental housing low. In an interview with *Fortune* magazine, Foreign Minister Nguyen Co Thach said that because of rent control, fewer rental units were available and most of the available units were in poor condition. Recalling the massive bombing of Hanoi during the Vietnam war, the foreign minister made the following comment: "The Americans couldn't destroy Hanoi, but we have destroyed our city by very low rents. We realized that it was stupid and that we must change policy."

Source: After "Rent Control: It's Worse Than Bombing," *FORTUNE*, February 27, 1989, p. 134. © 1989 Time Inc. All rights reserved.

Rent control in Hanoi decreased the quantity and quality of rental housing.

If you've ever looked for an apartment in a city with rent control, you're aware of a second inefficiency caused by a maximum price. Rent control causes a shortage of housing: In Figure 2, at a price of $360, there are 880 people who want to rent apartments, but only 760 apartments are available. The housing shortages caused by rent control force consumers to spend much more time searching for apartments. One of the subtle costs of rent control is the opportunity cost of the extra time spent searching for apartments. Another example comes from price controls for gasoline during the 1970s: Gasoline consumers spent hours waiting in line to buy gasoline, using time that could have been spent working, studying, or having fun.

Rent Control and the Poor

Some people defend rent control on the grounds that it helps poor people by cutting the price of rental housing. There are many anecdotes about wealthy and famous people who benefit from rent control,[4] suggesting that rent control is a very blunt instrument for helping the poor: You don't have to be poor to qualify for a rent-controlled apartment. As we explain later in the book, there are other policies that can be used to improve the economic situation of the poor.

MINIMUM PRICES

The government's motivation for the second type of price control—a minimum price—is that the equilibrium price seems to be too low rather than too high. Governments around the world set minimum prices (also known as **price floors**) for agricultural products, a policy known as a **price-support program.** In the United States there are price supports for all sorts of agricultural products, including wheat, corn, dairy products, and cotton. The European Community has price

Price floor: A minimum price; transactions below the minimum price are outlawed.

Price-support program: A policy under which the government specifies a minimum price above the equilibrium price.

supports for grains, dairy products, livestock, and sugar. Japan uses price supports for dairy products and sugar. Most governments combine price supports with a variety of other policies that affect the supply and demand for agricultural products. We explain the effects of a minimum price with a simple policy under which the government establishes a minimum price and then buys any surplus output at the minimum price. Later in the book we look at a minimum price for labor, the minimum wage.

Market Effects of Price Supports

To explain the market effects of a minimum price, consider a price-support program for corn. The lessons from the corn market apply to other markets subject to a minimum price. In Figure 3, point *i* shows the initial long-run equilibrium in our hypothetical corn market: The price is \$100 per ton and the quantity is 1,000 tons per day. When the government establishes a minimum price of \$110 per ton, the quantity supplied increases from 1,000 (point *i*) to 1,200 (point *s*) and the quantity demanded decreases from 1,000 (point *i*) to 900 (point *d*). At this artificially high price, there is a surplus of corn: The quantity supplied exceeds the quantity demanded by 300 tons. With a minimum price of \$110, the government buys the surplus corn at a total cost of \$33,000.

Why does the minimum price increase the quantity of corn supplied? In a perfectly competitive corn market, the price is just high enough to cover all the costs of producing corn. The price-support policy increases the price, and farmers respond by producing more corn. The higher price allows farmers to outbid other activities for the inputs used to produce corn (capital, labor, land). The quantity of corn increases, and the market moves upward along the supply curve from point *i* to point *s*.

Figure 3

Market Effects of Corn Price Support

A price support for corn (a minimum price) increases the quantity supplied from 1,000 (point *i*) to 1,200 (point *s*) and decreases the quantity demanded to 900 (point *d*). The surplus (the gap between quantity supplied and demanded) is 300 tons.

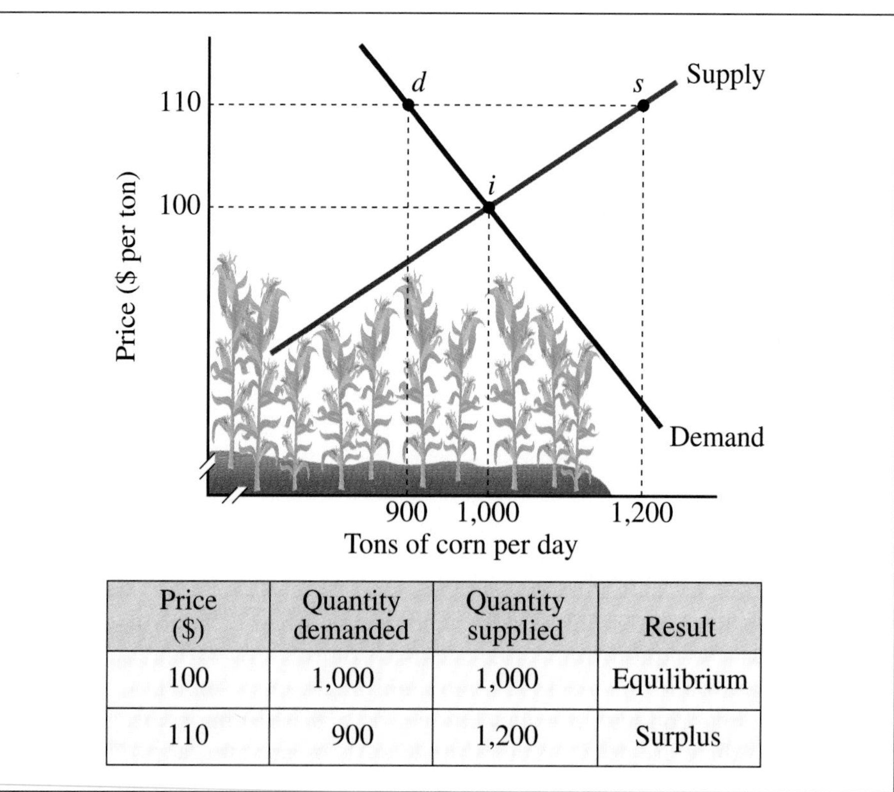

Price ($)	Quantity demanded	Quantity supplied	Result
100	1,000	1,000	Equilibrium
110	900	1,200	Surplus

A minimum price like an agricultural price support moves the market away from the market equilibrium. We know that if there are no spillovers, the competitive market equilibrium is efficient. Because the minimum price prevents the market from doing its job, it causes inefficiency.

Winners, Losers, and the Politics of Price Supports

Who wins and who loses as a result of price supports? Let's take a look at the facts on price-support programs.

- *Corporate farmers.* In the United States, most payments from price-support programs go to corporate farmers.[5] In 1990 about 38% of farm subsidies went to the 5% of farms with annual incomes exceeding $200,000.
- *Family farmers.* Few of the payments from U.S. price-support programs go to small family farmers.[6] In 1990, only 3% of farm subsidies went to the 59% of farms with annual incomes of less than $20,000.

These facts suggest that small family farms receive a relatively small share of the payments under the price-support program. Because the markets for most agricultural products are perfectly competitive, any increase in farm profits resulting from a price-support program will quickly be dissipated as firms enter the market and bid up the price of agricultural land. As a result, the bulk of the benefits from price-support programs go to the owners of agricultural land. The big losers from price supports are the people who pay higher prices for agricultural products and pay taxes to buy the surplus agricultural products.

As explained in the Closer Look box "Range War over Sugar Price Supports," a price-support program can lead to conflict within the farming community. The farmers growing a crop covered by price supports can outbid other farmers for farmland, leading to dramatic changes in farming communities.

In 1996, after several decades of agricultural price supports, the U.S. Congress voted to end the price-support program. Between 1996 and 2003, farmers will receive steadily declining *market adjustment payments* to ease the transition to a free-market agricultural system.[7] The supporters of the legislation suggested that it's time for the markets for agricultural products to operate freely. The opponents

A Closer LOOK

Range War over Sugar Price Supports

The U.S. price-support program for sugar caused a modern range war in Minnesota in 1990. The world price of sugar was at 12 cents per pound, and the government guaranteed sugar-beet farmers (known as "beeters" in Minnesota) a price of 22 cents per pound. At this price the profit per acre from sugar beets was about four times the profit per acre from grains such as corn, wheat, and soybeans. As a result, beeters outbid grain farmers for thousands of acres of land.

The range war started after a displaced grain farmer returned from a trip to Washington, DC, where he had protested the sugar price supports. Some beeters dumped sugar into the gas tank of the farmer's tractor and spray-painted his pickup truck with graffiti like "We Love Sugar." Some grain farmers responded in kind, timing their spraying of herbicide to ensure that the wind carried it into sugar-beet fields.

Source: After Bruce Ingersoll, "Range War: Small Minnesota Town Is Divided by Rancor over Sugar Policies," *Wall Street Journal*, June 26, 1990, p. 1. Reprinted by permission of the *Wall Street Journal*, © 1990 Dow Jones & Company, Inc. All Rights Reserved Worldwide.

expressed their fears that if the market prices of agricultural products dropped, farmers would be harmed. It remains to be seen whether other nations will follow the lead of the United States and eliminate their price-support programs.

TEST *Your Understanding*

4 In Figure 2 (page 105) suppose that the maximum rent were $380 instead of $360. Compute the shortage of apartments assuming that the supply curve and the demand curve are linear.

5 Complete the statement: Suppose that a price-control program for gasoline decreases the price by 8%. If the price elasticity of supply of gasoline is 2.0, the quantity of gasoline supplied will decrease by ______________ %.

6 Draw a supply and demand diagram for the gasoline market. Suppose that the equilibrium price is $2.00 and the government sets a maximum price of $1.60. Show the effects of the maximum price on the quantity supplied and quantity demanded.

7 Complete the statement with *increases* or *decreases*: A policy that establishes a maximum price ______________ the quantity supplied, while a policy that establishes a minimum price ______________ the quantity supplied.

8 Suppose that a price-support program increases the price of cheese by 6%. If the elasticity of supply of cheese is 1.5, by what percentage will the quantity supplied increase?

9 Suppose that when the government establishes price support for a particular agricultural product, the government ends up buying a huge amount of the product. What can we infer about the elasticity of supply for the product?

QUANTITY CONTROLS: LICENSING AND IMPORT RESTRICTIONS

We've learned what happens when the government controls the *price* of a good, but what happens when the government controls the *quantity* instead? We'll consider two policies that control quantities. In the domestic economy, many state and local governments limit the number of firms in particular markets by limiting the number of business licenses. In the global economy, national governments use a wide variety of policies to restrict imports, including import bans, import quotas, tariffs, and voluntary export restraints.

Licensing: Taxi Medallions

Taxi medallion: A license to operate a taxi.

You may be surprised at the extent of business licensing programs used by state and local governments. There are limits on the number of taxicabs, dry cleaners, tobacco farms, liquor stores, bars selling liquor, appliance repairers, and dog groomers. Some people defend licensing schemes on the grounds that they protect consumers from high prices and low-quality goods and services. The studies of licensing suggest that most licensing programs increase prices without improving the quality of service.[8] We use **taxi medallions** to explain the market effects of licensing, but the analysis applies to other markets in which the government uses licenses to limit the number of firms.

To show the market effects of taxi medallions, let's first look at an unregulated taxi market. In Figure 4, point *i* shows the initial equilibrium: The industry provides

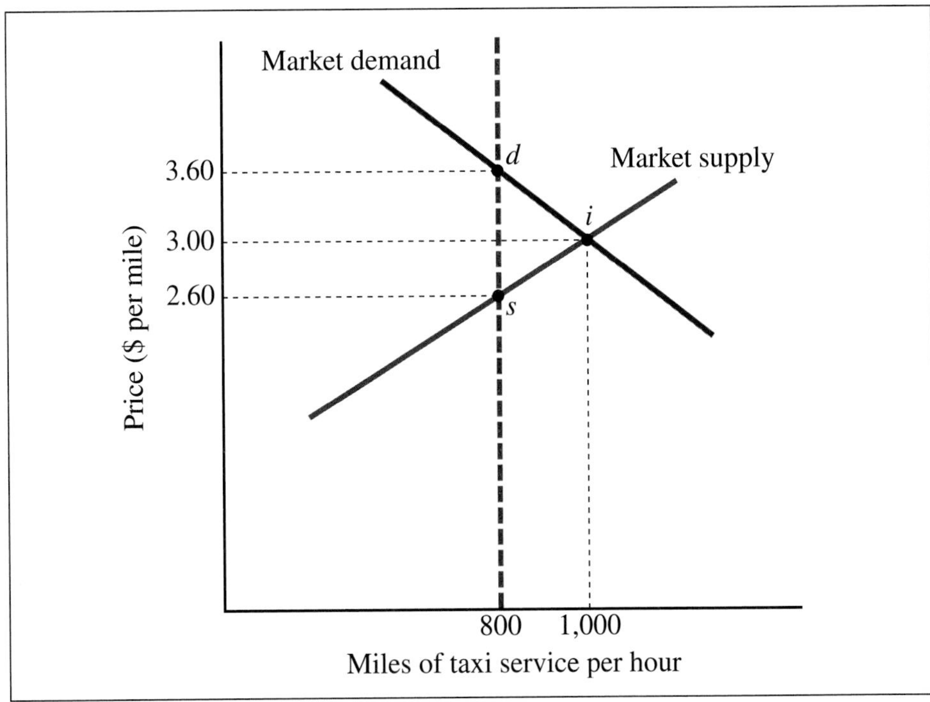

Figure 4

Market Effects of Taxi Medallions

In the absence of government interference, the market equilibrium is shown by point *i* (price = $3.00 and quantity = 1,000 miles per hour). A medallion policy that fixes the number of taxis at 80 fixes the quantity of taxi service at 800 miles per hour (10 miles per taxi) and increases the price to $3.60 (point *d*).

1,000 miles of taxi service at a price of $3.00. Each taxi produces 10 miles of service per hour, and there are 100 taxicabs in the market.

Suppose that the city passes a law requiring each taxicab to have a medallion and then gives 80 taxi medallions to the first 80 people who show up at city hall. In Figure 4 the dashed vertical line at 800 miles of service shows that this policy fixes the quantity of taxi service at 800 miles (80 taxis times 10 miles per taxi). The medallion policy creates an artificial shortage of taxi service: At the original price ($3.00), the quantity demanded is 1,000 miles, but the city's 80 taxicabs provide only 800 miles of service. The shortage increases the price of taxi service: The market moves upward along the demand curve to point *d*, with a price of $3.60. In other words, the medallion policy increases the price of taxi service.

Winners and Losers from Taxi Medallions

Who benefits and who loses from the city's medallion policy? The losers are consumers, who pay more for taxi rides. The winners are the people who receive a free medallion and the right to charge an artificially high price for taxi service. In some cities, people buy and sell medallions, and the market value of a medallion reflects the profits that a medallion owner can earn. The market price of a medallion is over $150,000 in New York City and over $100,000 in Toronto.[9] In cities such as Chicago, where medallions are more plentiful, the market price is much lower.

To be a winner in the medallion game, you must have received a medallion free of charge from the government. If you were to buy a medallion at the current market price (for example, $150,000), you won't benefit from the medallion policy because the price you pay will be just high enough to offset any profits you'll earn with the medallion. In fact, you would be a big loser if the city issues more medallions. An increase in the number of medallions—and taxis—will decrease the price and profits of taxi service, decreasing the market price of your medallion. One reason that medallion schemes persist is that the current owners of medallions would lose a lot of money if the government allowed additional taxis to enter the market.

Licensing and Market Efficiency

Because a licensing scheme moves the market away from the market equilibrium, it causes inefficiency. If there are no spillover costs or benefits, the market equilibrium is efficient: There are no additional transactions that would benefit a buyer and a seller. In contrast, the medallion policy excludes some consumers and producers from the market, and these people would gladly exchange money and taxi service. As shown by the points between *d* and *i* on the demand curve, many consumers are willing to pay between \$3.00 and \$3.60 for taxi service. Although there are plenty of drivers who would be willing to provide taxi service at these prices, they can't do so without a medallion. Because the medallion policy prevents these people from participating in the market, the policy causes inefficiency.

Our analysis of the inefficiency of taxi medallions applies to other markets that are subject to quantity controls. State and city governments use licensing to limit many small businesses. Other cities limit the number of housing units by limiting the number of building permits. These policies decrease the quantity supplied, increase prices, and cause inefficiency. Although some producers are willing to supply the good at a lower price, the government does not allow them to do so.

Import Restrictions

We've seen that the government can control the quantity of a good produced by issuing a limited number of business licenses to producers. Another way to control the quantity is to limit the imports of a particular good. Like a licensing scheme, an **import restriction** increases the market price.

Import restriction: A law that prohibits the importation of a particular good.

To show the market effects of import restrictions, let's start with an unrestricted market. Figure 5 shows the market equilibrium in a hypothetical sugar market when there is free trade. The domestic supply curve shows the quantity supplied by domestic (U.S.) firms. Looking at point *m*, we see that U.S. firms will not supply any sugar unless the price is at least 18 cents per pound. The total supply curve, which shows the quantity supplied by both domestic and foreign firms, lies to the right of the domestic curve. At each price, the total supply exceeds the domestic supply because foreign firms also supply sugar. Point *i* shows the free-trade equilibrium: the demand curve intersects the total supply curve at a price of 12 cents and a quantity

Figure 5

Market Effects of an Import Ban

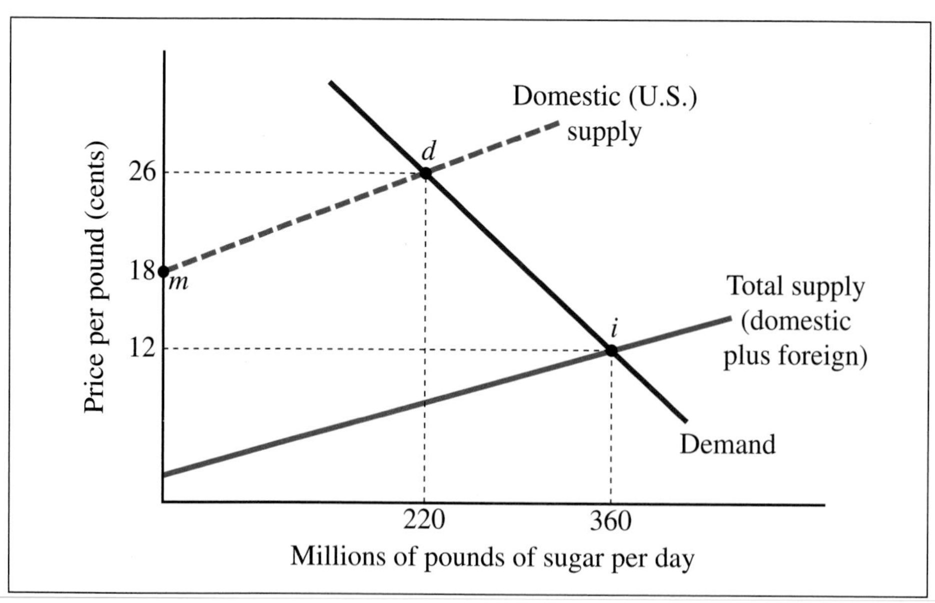

In the free-trade equilibrium, demand intersects the total supply curve at point *i*, with a price of 12 cents and a quantity of 360 million pounds. If sugar imports are banned, the price increases to 26 cents.

of 360 million pounds. Because this price is below the minimum price for domestic firms, domestic firms do not supply any sugar.

What would happen if the United States bans sugar imports? Foreign suppliers will disappear from the market, so the total supply of sugar will be just the domestic supply. In Figure 5 the new equilibrium is shown by point *d*: The demand curve intersects the *domestic* supply curve at a price of 26 cents and a quantity of 220 million pounds. In other words, the decrease in supply resulting from the import ban increases the price and decreases the quantity. Domestic firms produce all the sugar for the domestic market: The import ban resurrects the U.S. sugar industry.

How would the analysis change if the government restricts imports but does not eliminate them? Starting from the free-trade equilibrium at point *i*, an import quota will shift the total supply curve to the left: At each price there will be a smaller quantity of imported sugar because foreign suppliers cannot supply as much. The new total supply curve will lie between the domestic supply curve and the original total supply curve. The new equilibrium price (shown by the intersection of the demand curve and the new total supply curve) will be between 12 cents (the free-trade price) and 26 cents (the price under the import ban).

Winners and Losers from Import Restrictions

Import restrictions are often defended on the grounds that they increase employment in the protected industries. The protection of these jobs increases consumer prices, so there is a trade-off: We have more jobs in the protected industry, but consumers pay higher prices. According to one study, import restrictions in force in 1993 protected 56,464 jobs in the U.S. textile and apparel industries at a cost to consumers of about $178,000 per job, and 3,419 jobs in the motor-vehicle industry at a cost of about $271,000 per job.[10] For an example of how Japan's ban on apple imports protected its domestic apple growers at the expense of consumers, read the Closer Look box on page 114, "Taking a Bite Out of the Trade Gap."

ECONOMIC DETECTIVE– *The Case of Cheaper Medallions*

You've been hired by a New Yorker who owns 20 taxi medallions and is puzzled by recent changes in the market price of medallions. In the last two years, the price of medallions dropped—along with the price of taxi service. In contrast, the total quantity of taxi service did not change. The medallion owner suspects that the city issued more medallions during the last two years but isn't sure about this. Your job is to explain why prices have dropped: Has the city issued more medallions, or is there some other explanation?

The key to solving this mystery is the fact that the quantity of taxi service hasn't changed. This means that the city hasn't issued any more permits. In the example shown in Figure 4, the market is still operating along the vertical dashed line, with 800 miles of service per hour. An increase in the number of medallions would shift this line to the right and increase the quantity of service. Therefore, the price decreases must have been caused by a decrease in the demand for taxi service. The demand curve shifted to the left, decreasing the price of taxi service. The lower price will decrease the profits earned with a medallion and decrease the market price of medallions.

TEST *Your Understanding*

10 Suppose that the demand for taxi service decreases and the new demand curve intersects the supply curve at a quantity of 700 miles. If the government doesn't change the number of medallions, what happens to the price of a medallion?

A Closer LOOK

Taking a Bite Out of the Trade Gap

Between 1972 and 1995, it was illegal to import apples into Japan. The import ban protected domestic apple growers from foreign competition, leading to prices that were so high (up to $3 per apple) that apples were considered a luxury good, not a casual snack. When the import ban ended in 1995, farmers in Washington state responded by shipping 5,000 tons of apples to Japan, about 1% of Japan's annual apple consumption. The Washington apples sell at a fraction of the price of Japanese apples.

Washington apple growers are trying to change Japanese apple-eating habits. The traditional apple etiquette requires a person to peel and cut the apple into small pieces before eating it. Apple growers are promoting apples as a casual snack. In the words of Brent Evans, a marketing manager of the Washington Apple Commission, "We want millions of Japanese to pick up a nice big juicy apple and just bite it." The slogan for the growers' advertising campaign is "An Apple Biting Culture Dawns." To get consumers to take that first bite, the growers are staging apple-biting contests and giving prizes to the person who makes the loudest crunch.

The lifting on the Japanese import ban on apples will decrease the price of apples and perhaps change eating habits.

Source: After Alan K. Ota, "Apple Ban Ends with a Crunch," *The Oregonian,* January 10, 1995, p. B16.

11 In Figure 5 (page 112) how much sugar will domestic firms produce at a price of $0.15?

12 Complete the statement with *increases* or *decreases*: An import ban ______________ the price of sugar, ______________ the quantity of sugar, and ______________ the output of the domestic sugar industry.

SPILLOVER BENEFITS AND COSTS

We've seen that a market without spillovers is efficient and government intervention in such a market prevents people from executing beneficial transactions. In this part of the chapter we'll see that a market with spillover benefits or costs is *inefficient.* In this case, government intervention can improve matters by making beneficial transactions happen.

Spillover Benefits and Public Goods

Spillover benefit: The benefit from a good experienced by people who do not decide how much of the good to produce or consume.

To illustrate the idea of **spillover benefits,** consider a dam built for flood-control purposes. Recall the spillover principle. The benefits of a flood-control dam are experienced by everyone in the valley below the dam, not just those who pay for the dam. As we'll see, a good that generates spillover benefits may not be provided by a market, even if the benefits of the good exceed the cost. The government can facilitate collective decision-making and ensure that such a good is provided.

Spillover **PRINCIPLE**

For some goods, the costs or benefits associated with the good are not confined to the person or organization that decides how much of the good to produce or consume.

We can use a simple numerical example to illustrate the role of government in providing a good with spillover benefits. Suppose that each person in a city of 100,000 would benefit from a flood-control dam that would cost \$200,000 and each person is willing to pay \$5 for the dam. Although the total benefit of the dam (\$500,000 = 100,000 times \$5) exceeds the cost, no single person would build the dam because the cost exceeds his or her personal benefit. In other words, if we rely on the forces of supply and demand, with each person considering only the personal benefits and costs of a dam, no dam will be built.

The government can solve this problem by arranging some transactions between its citizens. Suppose that the government offers to build the dam and pay for it with a tax of \$2 per person. The tax is just high enough to pay for the dam: \$2 times 100,000 citizens is \$200,000. Each citizen will support this proposal because the tax is less than his or her personal benefit from the dam (\$5). In effect, the government uses its taxing power to arrange a transaction between the citizens and the dam builder. By relying on collective decision-making rather than the forces of supply and demand, we can provide a good that would otherwise not be provided.

The dam is an example of a **public good**, a good that is available for everyone to consume, regardless of who pays and who doesn't. In contrast, a **private good** is consumed by a single person or household. For example, only one person can eat a hot dog. If a government hands out free cheese to the poor, is the free cheese a public good or a private good? Although anyone can get in line for the cheese, only one person can actually consume a particular piece of cheese, so the free cheese is a private good that happens to be available free of charge from the government. Similarly, an apartment in a public housing project can be occupied by a single household, so it is a private good that is provided by the government.

Public good: A good that is available for everyone to consume, regardless of who pays and who doesn't.

Private good: A good that is consumed by a single person or household.

We can be more precise about the difference between public and private goods. Private goods are *rival in consumption* (only one person can consume the good) and *excludable* (it is possible to exclude a person who does not pay for the good). In contrast, public goods are *nonrival in consumption* (available for everyone to consume) and *nonexcludable* (it is impractical to exclude people who don't pay). Here are some other examples of public goods:

- National defense
- Law enforcement
- Space exploration
- Preservation of endangered species
- Protecting the earth's ozone layer
- City streets and highways

If someone refuses to pay for one of these public goods, it would be impractical to prevent that person from consuming the good. The role of government is to use its taxing power to collect the money to pay for a public good from citizens who consume the good. If a person or a firm tried to provide a public good, the effort is likely to fail because most people would refuse to pay for the good.

Public Goods and the Free-Rider Problem

Most public goods are supported by taxes. What would happen if we eliminated taxes and asked people to contribute money to pay for national defense, dams, city streets, and the police? Would people contribute enough money to support these programs at their current levels?

Free-rider problem: Each person will try to get the benefit of a public good without paying for it, trying to get a free ride at the expense of others.

The problem with using voluntary contributions to support public goods is known as the **free-rider problem**. Each person will try to get the benefits of a public good without paying for it, thus getting a free ride at the expense of others. Of course, if everyone tries to get a free ride, no one will contribute any money to support the public good, so it won't be provided. The flip side of the free-rider problem is the chump problem: No one wants to be the chump (the person who gives free rides to other people), so no one contributes any money. The free-rider problem suggests that the replacement of taxes with voluntary contributions would force the government to cut back or eliminate many programs. Later in the book, we discuss some experimental evidence for the free-rider problem.

Spillover Costs and Market Inefficiency

The government also has an important role to play in markets with spillover *costs*. For example, if paper mills dump their chemical wastes into a river, some of the costs of producing paper are incurred by people who use the river for recreation and drinking water. When there are spillover costs, the market will be inefficient because the people making the decisions about how much paper to produce ignore the costs they impose on others.

We can use the paper market to illustrate the inefficiency that occurs in a market with spillover costs. Suppose that there are several paper mills along a river, and a city downstream from the mills uses river water for drinking. The city's water-treatment costs depend on the volume of chemical waste from the paper mills: If paper production decreased by 1 ton, the city's water-treatment cost would decrease by $20. There are spillover costs because the decision-makers in the paper mills ignore the costs incurred by people in the city.

Starting from the market equilibrium in the paper market, could we arrange some transactions that would benefit a paper buyer, a paper seller, and city dwellers? Figure 6 shows the market equilibrium: The supply curve intersects the demand curve at point *i*, so the equilibrium price is $60 and the equilibrium quantity is 100 tons per day. Let's see if we can get everyone to agree to produce 1 less ton of paper.

- *Paper producers.* Recall that in a perfectly competitive market, the price of a product is just high enough to cover the cost of producing it. If a paper firm

Figure 6

Equilibrium in the Paper Market

The market equilibrium, which is shown by point *i*, is inefficient because there are additional transactions that would benefit a buyer, a seller, and third parties affected by the transaction.

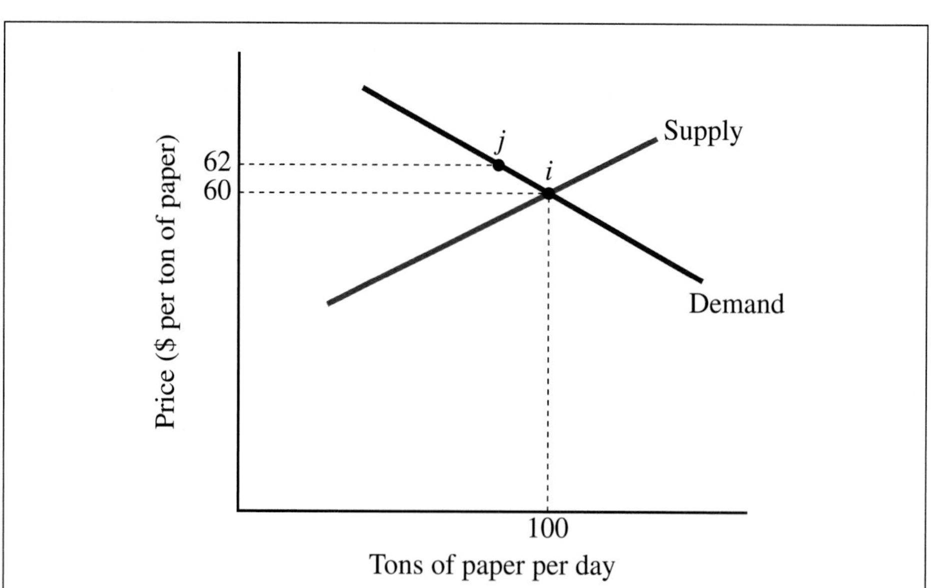

did not produce the 100th ton of paper, the firm would lose $60 in revenue but would also save $60 in production costs. The firm would agree to produce 1 less ton if the city paid the firm a small amount, say $1.

- *Paper consumers.* Recall that the demand curve shows how much consumers are willing to pay for a particular product. Suppose that Margie is willing to pay $62 for a ton of paper, as shown by point *j* on the market demand curve. If the market price is $60, her net benefit from buying a ton of paper is $2. If the city gave her a slightly larger amount (for example, $3), she would agree not to consume a ton of paper.
- *City government.* The decrease in paper production would decrease the city's water-treatment cost by $20. To get a 1-ton reduction in paper production, the city could pay $1 to a paper producer and $3 to Margie the consumer and still have a net savings of $16. If the city cut its taxes by $16, taxpayers would go along with the deal.

This series of transactions benefits everyone involved, including the third parties who experience the spillover costs from paper production. Because we can do better than the market equilibrium, the paper market is inefficient.

Spillover Costs and Public Policy

What is the role of government in a market that generates spillover costs? Later in the book we explore several policy responses to pollution problems.

- *Pollution tax.* To an economist, the obvious response is to impose a tax on each unit of waste generated. The idea behind a pollution tax is to force firms to pay for the waste they generate, just as they pay for labor, raw materials, and their production facilities.
- *Regulations.* A second response is to directly control the pollution generated by specific firms, directing them to install abatement equipment and decrease the volume of waste generated.
- *Marketable pollution permits.* A third option is to issue a fixed number of pollution permits and allow firms to buy and sell the permits.

As we'll see in Chapter 15, there are some trade-offs with each of these policies. We'll also explore some of today's most important environmental challenges, including global warming, ozone depletion, acid rain, and urban smog.

TEST *Your Understanding*

13 In the dam example (page 115), suppose that the dam costs $600,000 and each of the 100,000 citizens is willing to pay $5 for the dam. Will people in the city support the building of the dam? Explain.

14 Explain the difference between a private good and a public good.

15 Which of the following goods are private goods, and which are public goods? Explain.

- Pizza
- Fireworks
- Lighthouse
- Clean air
- Public television
- Apartment

16 Suppose that Hiram is one of the consumers on the upper part of the demand curve for paper, willing to pay $85 for a ton of paper. Is it possible to involve Hiram in a voluntary transaction to decrease paper production by 1 ton?

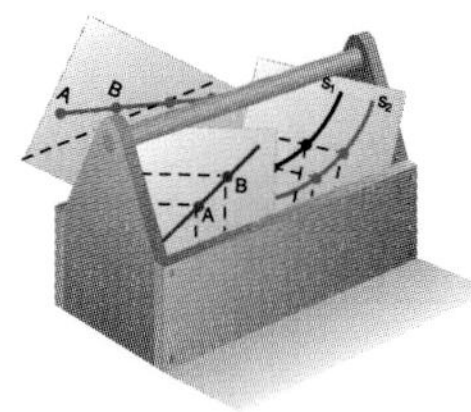

Using the **TOOLS**

In this chapter we used two of the tools of economics—the supply curve and the demand curve—to study the effect of government intervention in efficient markets. We also explored the role of government in markets that generate spillover benefits and costs. Here are some opportunities to use these tools to do your own economic analysis.

1. ECONOMIC EXPERIMENT: *Government Intervention*

Recall the market-equilibrium experiment from Chapter 4. We can modify the experiment to the show the various forms of government intervention in the market. After several trading periods without any government intervention, you can change the rules as follows:

- The instructor sets a maximum price for apples.
- The instructor sets a minimum price for apples.
- The instructor issues licenses to a few lucky producers.
- The instructor divides producers into domestic producers and foreign producers, and some of the foreign producers are excluded from the market.

2. Price Controls for Medical Care

Suppose that in an attempt to control the rising costs of medical care, the national government imposes price controls on visits to physicians. The maximum price for a physician visit is 10% less than the equilibrium price. Assume that the price elasticity of demand for physician visits is 0.60 and the price elasticity of supply is 1.5.

a. By what percentage will the quantity of medical care supplied decrease?
b. By what percentage will the quantity of medical care demanded increase?
c. Illustrate your answer with a graph.
d. What sort of inefficiencies will occur as a result of the maximum price?
e. Would you expect patients and physicians to find ways around the maximum price?

3. Daily Profit from a Barber License

Consider a city in which the initial price of a haircut is $6 and the initial quantity is 200 haircuts per day. The demand curve for haircuts is linear, with 200 haircuts demanded at a price of $6 and 100 haircuts demanded at a price of $12. Initially, there are 20 barbers, each of whom produces 10 haircuts per day. Suppose that the city passes a law requiring all barbers to have a license and then issues only 15 barber licenses. Each licensed barber continues to provide 10 haircuts per day. Predict the new equilibrium price of haircuts and illustrate your answer with a supply–demand diagram.

4. Market Effects of a Pollution Tax

Consider the paper market depicted in Figure 6. Suppose that the national government imposes a pollution tax on the paper industry: For each gallon of waste dumped into the river, a paper firm pays a tax.

a. Use a supply and demand graph to show how the market effects the tax. What happens to the equilibrium price of paper?
b. What are the trade-offs associated with the tax?

SUMMARY

In this chapter we explored the conditions under which the market equilibrium is efficient and discussed the consequences of government intervention in different types of markets. In some markets the government prevents people from executing beneficial transactions, and this is inefficient. In other markets, the government makes beneficial transactions happen and thus promotes efficiency. Here are the main points of the chapter.

1. A market is inefficient if there are additional transactions that would benefit a buyer, a seller, and any third party affected by the transaction, and efficient if there are no such transactions.
2. The equilibrium in a perfectly competitive market will be efficient if there are no spillover costs or benefits.
3. Government intervention in an efficient market moves the market away from the (efficient) market equilibrium and prevents some transactions that would benefit a buyer and a seller.
4. Price controls cause either a shortage (from a maximum price) or a surplus (from a minimum price).
5. A licensing scheme that limits the number of firms increases the price and decreases the quantity consumed.
6. An import restriction decreases supply and increases the price of the protected good.
7. If a good generates spillover benefits or costs, the market equilibrium will be inefficient: It would be possible to arrange an additional transaction that would benefit a buyer, a seller, and any third parties affected by the transaction.

KEY TERMS

efficient market, *101*
free-rider problem, *116*
imperfectly competitive market, *104*
import restriction, *112*
inefficient market, *101*
invisible hand, *103*
price ceiling, *104*
price floor, *107*
price-support program, *107*
private good, *115*
public good, *115*
rent control, *105*
spillover benefit, *114*
taxi medallion, *110*

PROBLEMS AND DISCUSSION QUESTIONS

1. What assumptions do we make to ensure that the market equilibrium in a perfectly competitive market is efficient? For each assumption, provide an example of a good for which the assumption is likely to be violated.
2. Your city just announced a new rent-control program under which the maximum rent on apartments will be 20% below the equilibrium price. The price elasticity of supply of apartments is 0.50.
   a. Use a supply–demand diagram to show the effects of the rent-control program on the rental housing market. The initial price is \$300 and the initial quantity is 10,000. Label the initial equilibrium point with an *i* and the point that shows the quantity supplied under rent control with an *s*.
   b. By what percentage will the quantity of apartments increase or decrease?
3. You are responsible for finding storage space for the surplus to be generated by a new price-support program. Before the new program, the equilibrium quantity of dairy products is 50 billion pounds. The minimum price under the price-support program is 5% above the equilibrium price. The price elasticity of supply of dairy products is 2.0 and the price elasticity of demand is 0.80. Predict the surplus for next year (in billions of pounds).

4. Suppose that the federal government is considering the elimination of price supports for dairy products. Your job is to predict the effects of this change in policy on the quantity of dairy products consumed. The current minimum price support exceeds the market price by 20%. Here are the elasticities of demand for various dairy products:

Fresh milk:	$E_d = 0.63$
Butter:	$E_d = 0.73$
Cheese:	$E_d = 0.52$
Cottage cheese:	$E_d = 1.10$

For each dairy product, predict the percentage change in consumption that would occur if the dairy price supports were eliminated.

5. Predict the effect of each of the following policies on the price of the relevant good. Then draw a supply–demand diagram to defend your answer.
   a. Licenses for dry cleaners
   b. Limit on building permits for housing
   c. Import restrictions on clothing
6. Suppose that initially there are no restrictions on importing kiwi fruit. The supply curves are the same as the supply curves for sugar shown in Figure 5 (page 112). The initial price of kiwi fruit is 12 cents. When imports are banned, the equilibrium price increases to 22 cents. Draw a market demand curve consistent with these numbers.
7. Why are local rent controls (a maximum price on rental housing in a city) more common than a maximum price on food or clothing sold in a city?
8. In an attempt to promote the glass recycling, the state of California established a minimum price for used glass that was about 20% higher than the equilibrium price. Use a supply–demand diagram to show the effects of this policy on the market for used glass. Would you expect the policy to increase or decrease the amount of glass recycled? If it's obvious to you that this policy will decrease—not increase—the volume of recycling, why do you suppose the state adopted the policy?
9. In the example in the text of taxi medallions, suppose the city announced that it would issue 101 medallions instead of 80. Predict the market price of taxi service and the market price of medallions.

Take It to the Net

We invite you to visit the O'Sullivan/Sheffrin page on the Prentice Hall Web site at:

http://www.prenhall.com/osullivan/

for this chapter's World Wide Web exercise.

MODEL ANSWERS FOR THIS CHAPTER

Chapter-Opening Questions

1. If there are no spillovers in a perfectly competitive market, once we reach an equilibrium, there are no additional transactions that would benefit a buyer and a seller.
2. The rent-control policy decreases the quantity of apartments supplied, forcing some students out of the market.
3. Consumers pay higher prices, and the cost per job saved is about $178,000.
4. There are spillover benefits that make the market equilibrium inefficient: the government can intervene to make beneficial transactions happen.
5. Because of spillover costs, the market equilibrium is inefficient, so the government could arrange some transactions that would make everyone better off.

Test Your Understanding

1. less, greater
2. No. The market is inefficient if there is another transaction that benefits both a buyer and a seller. Although Ida would benefit from a transaction at a price of $50, apparently no seller would benefit from a transaction at this price.
3. (1) No spillover costs or benefits (2) perfect competition (each firm is a price taker).
4. The quantity supplied would be 975 (halfway between 950 and 1,000), and the quantity demanded would be 1,050 (halfway between 1,000 and 1,100), so the shortage is 75 apartments.
5. 16%. Use the elasticity formula: 2.0 = 16% / 8%.
6. The supply curve intersects the demand curve at $2.00. A maximum price of $1.60 causes the

market to move downward along the supply curve, causing a shortage, just as in the case of rent control.

7. decreases, increases
8. 9%. Use the elasticity formula: 1.50 = 9% / 6%.
9. The supply elasticity is relatively large. A large supply elasticity means that a small increase in price increases the quantity supplied by a large amount, so the surplus will be relatively large. Another possible reason for the huge surplus is that demand is very elastic. In this case, consumers respond to the higher price by purchasing a much smaller quantity, so there is a large surplus.
10. Although the government offers 80 medallions, only 70 will actually be used. The price of taxi service equals the market equilibrium price, and the price of taxi medallions is zero.
11. Zero. This is below the minimum domestic price.
12. increases, decreases, increases
13. No. The per capita cost ($6) exceeds the per capita benefit ($5).
14. A public good is available for everyone to consume, regardless of who pays and who doesn't, while a private good can be consumed by only one person, the person who pays for it.
15. Public goods: clean air, fireworks, public television, lighthouse. Private goods: pizza and apartment. If a lighthouse supplier can force people to pay to use the lighthouse, it will be a private good.
16. His net benefit is $25, which exceeds the benefits experienced by river users ($20). Therefore, river users would not be willing to pay Hiram enough to persuade him not to consume a ton of paper.

Using the Tools

2. Price Controls for Medical Care
   a. Using the supply elasticity formula, the quantity of doctor visits supplied will decrease by 15%: 1.5 = 15% / 10%.
   b. Using the demand elasticity formula, the quantity of doctor visits demanded will increase by 6%: 0.60 = 6% / 10%.
   c. In Figure A below, the initial equilibrium point (before the maximum price) is shown by point *i*: The price is $50 and the quantity is 1,000 visits. The maximum price is $45, so the new quantity supplied is 850 (point *s*), and the new quantity demanded is 1,060 (point *d*).
   d. The policy outlaws transactions that would benefit a buyer and a seller and causes a shortage that will increase the time spent waiting for doctors.
   e. Perhaps doctors can increase the prices charged for other services (x-rays, stitches, vaccinations, other office procedures).
3. Daily Profit from a Barber License

   See Figure B on page 122. If there are 15 licenses, the maximum quantity is 150 haircuts per day. This quantity is halfway between 100 (at which the price is $6) and 200 (at which the price is $12), so the new price is $9.
4. Market Effects of a Pollution Tax
   a. See Figure C on page 122. The tax increases the cost of producing paper because a producer must either pay the tax or spend money on pollution-control methods to avoid dumping the waste into the river. The increase in

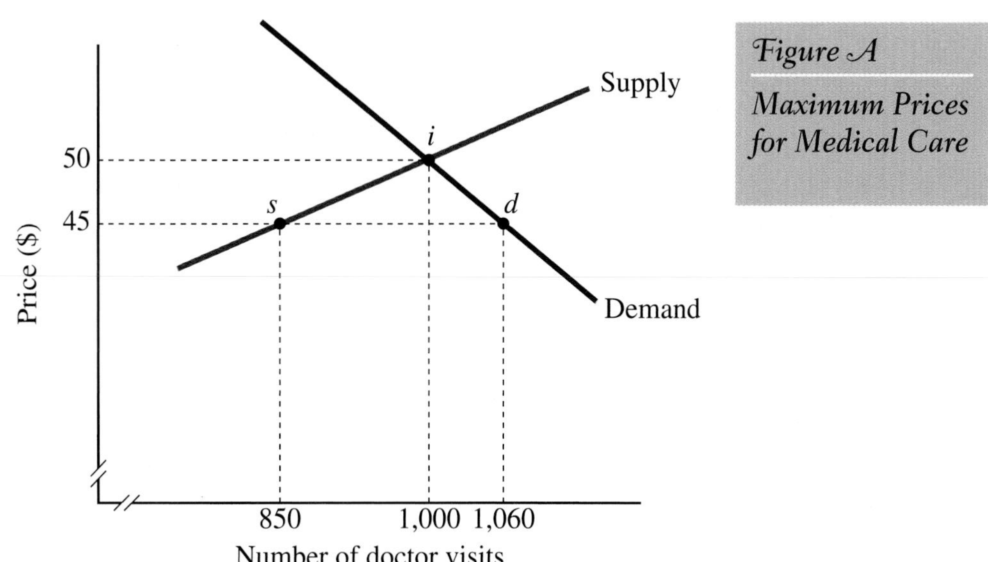

Figure A

Maximum Prices for Medical Care

production costs shifts the supply curve to the left, and the market moves from point *i* to point *f*, where the demand curve intersects the new supply curve. The price of paper increases from \$60 to \$68 per ton, and consumers respond by decreasing the quantity of paper demanded, from 100 tons per day to 80.

b. On the benefit side, the volume of waste decreases as the volume of paper decreases, so the river water is cleaner and more favorable for aquatic life, recreation, and drinking. The bad news is that consumers pay more for each ton of paper and get less of it: The price increases by \$8 and the quantity decreases by 20 tons.

Figure B

Market Effects of Barber Licenses

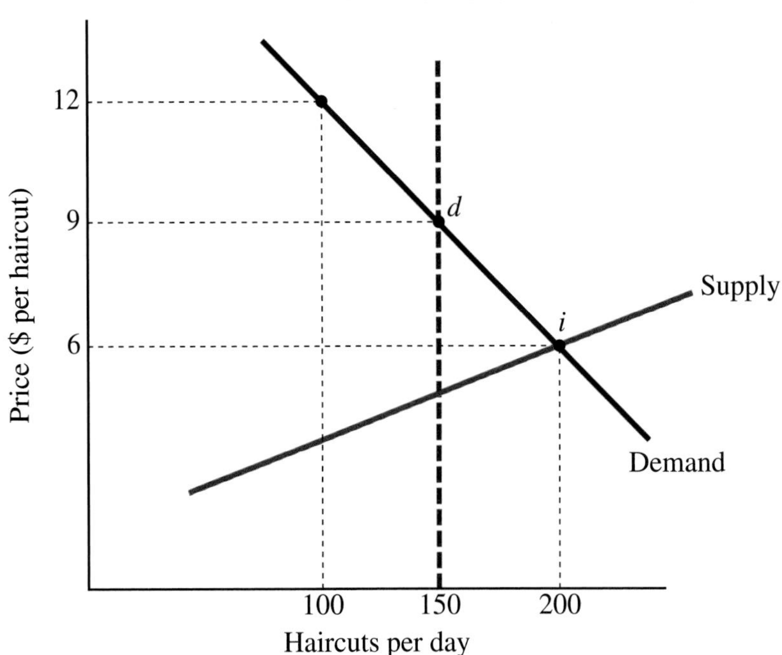

Figure C

Pollution Tax and the Paper Market

The pollution tax shifts the supply curve to the left, increasing the equilibrium price from \$60 to \$68 and decreasing the equilibrium quantity from 100 tons to 80 tons.

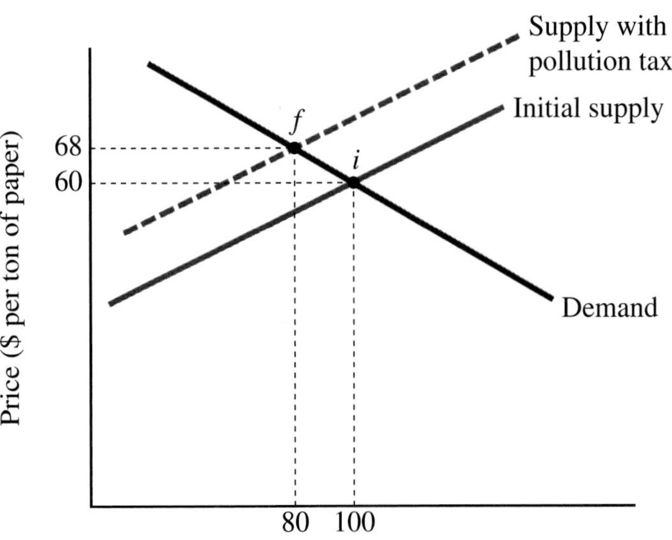

NOTES

1. Peter Navarro, "Rent Control in Cambridge, Massachusetts," *The Public Interest,* 1987, pp. 83–100.
2. Joseph Gyourko and Peter Linneman, "Rent Controls and Rental Housing Quality: A Note on the Effects of New York City's Old Controls," *Journal of Urban Economics*, vol. 27, 1990, pp. 398–409.
3. "The Effects of Rent Control on Housing in New York City," in *Rental Housing in New York City: Confronting the Crisis,* RM-6190-NYC (Santa Monica, CA: Rand Corporation, 1970).
4. William Tucker, "A Model for Destroying a City," *Wall Street Journal,* March 12, 1993, p. A8.
5. U.S. Department of Agriculture, *Economic Indicators of the Farm Sector: National Financial Summary* (Washington, DC: U.S. Government Printing Office, 1990), p. 44.
6. U.S. Department of Agriculture, *Economic Indicators of the Farm Sector.*
7. "Senate Passes Compromise Bill to End Farmers' Price Supports," *New York Times,* March 29, 1996, p. A10.
8. J. K. Smith, "An Analysis of State Regulations Governing Liquor Store Licensees," *Journal of Law and Economics,* October 1982, pp. 301–319; David Kirp and Eileen Soffer, "Taking Californians to the Cleaners," *Regulation,* September/October 1985, pp. 24–26; D. W. Taylor, "The Economic Effects of Direct Regulation of Taxicabs in Metropolitan Toronto," *Logistics and Transportation Review,* June 1989, pp. 169–182.
9. Taylor, "The Economic Effects of Direct Regulation of Taxicabs in Metropolitan Toronto."
10. *The Economic Effects of Significant U.S. Import Restraints* (Washington, DC: U.S. International Trade Commission, initial report in 1993; update in 1996).

CHAPTER

7 Consumer Choice

Carla and Otto were in the library doing research for a project on energy consumption in different countries when they discovered that the typical consumer in the United States uses much more gasoline than consumers in other industrialized countries. For example, the typical U.S. driver uses 7 times as much gasoline as the typical Italian, 6 times as much as the typical Japanese, and 1.3 times as much as the typical Canadian. What explains these large differences in gasoline consumption?

In this chapter we study the behavior of consumers, the people who buy the goods and services produced by firms and other organizations. As we saw in Chapter 4, the market demand curve shows the relationship between the price of a good and the quantity that consumers are willing to buy. The demand curve is negatively sloped, reflecting the law of demand: The lower the price, the larger the quantity that consumers will buy. In this chapter we discuss the logic behind the market demand curve and the law of demand. We start by exploring the decisions of individual consumers and then show the connection between these individual decisions and the market demand curve.

In this chapter we use some key principles of economics to explain the law of demand. Once we understand the logic behind the law, we can answer some practical questions about consumer behavior.

1. What explains the large differences in gasoline consumption in different countries?
2. How should a consumer divide his or her income among the alternative goods and services?
3. How do copayments for medical services (a nominal fee the patient pays for service when insurance covers the rest) affect the consumption of medical care?

4 Why do college students who live—and eat—in dormitories gain more weight than their counterparts who live in apartments?

THE INDIVIDUAL DEMAND CURVE

As we saw in Chapter 3, the market demand curve for a particular good represents the decisions of all the people who buy the good. We start our analysis of demand with the decisions of an individual consumer. The **individual demand curve** shows the relationship between the price of a good and the quantity that a single consumer is willing to buy (the quantity demanded) during a particular time period. After we explain the individual demand curve, we discuss the connection between individual and market demand.

Individual demand curve: A curve that shows the relationship between the price of a good and the quantity that a single consumer is willing to buy (the quantity demanded).

To make things concrete, we consider a hypothetical market for burgers and examine the decisions made by Bob, the typical consumer. He has a fixed income ($30 per month), which he spends entirely on two goods, burgers and tacos. Bob must decide how many burgers and tacos to consume each month. His consumption of burgers is determined by a number of factors, including the price of burgers, the price of tacos, his income, and his underlying tastes or preferences for the two goods.

The demand curve in Figure 1 shows the quantity of burgers Bob is willing to buy (demand) at each price. To find each point on the demand curve, we pick a price, say $3, and answer the question, "How many burgers does Bob buy at this price?" If the answer is 8 burgers per month, point *b* (with $3 on the price axis and 8 burgers on the quantity axis) is on Bob's demand curve. We can find a different point on the demand curve by choosing a different price, say $2, and asking the same question. If the answer is 11 burgers per month, point *c* ($2 on the price axis and 11 on the quantity axis) is on Bob's demand curve. We can find other points in the same way.

It's important to note that to draw Bob's demand curve, we change only one of the variables that affects his demand for burgers. We change the price of burgers, but all the other variables that influence Bob's consumption decision (the price of tacos, his income, and his tastes) remain unchanged. Therefore, we can be sure the points we've plotted show the true relationship between the price and the quantity of burgers. This is Bob's demand curve.

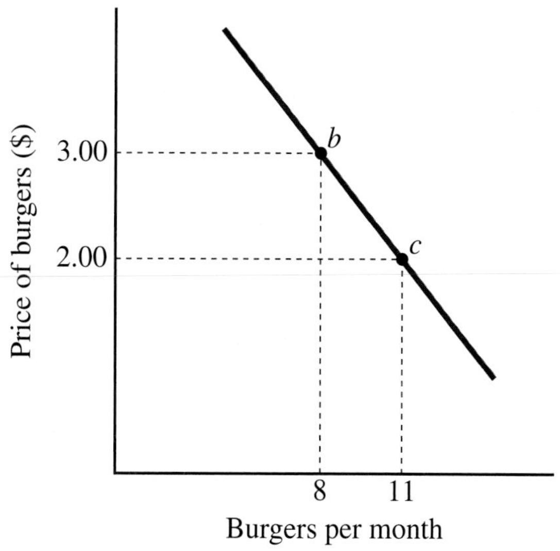

Figure 1

Individual Demand Curve

The individual demand curve is negatively sloped, consistent with the law of demand: The higher the price, the smaller the quantity demanded. If the price of burgers is $3, Bob consumes 8 burgers per month (point *b*). At a price of $2, he consumes 11 burgers per month (point *c*).

The Demand Curve and the Rational Consumer

Each point on the individual demand curve is the result of a rational choice by the consumer. To decide how many burgers to consume, Bob considers the benefits and costs of each burger. The benefit is the satisfaction or pleasure Bob experiences when he eats the burger. The principle of opportunity cost helps us think logically about the cost of a burger:

PRINCIPLE *of Opportunity Cost*

The opportunity cost of something is what you sacrifice to get it.

The opportunity cost of a burger is determined by how many tacos Bob sacrifices to get the burger. For example, if the price of burgers is $3 and the price of tacos is $1, Bob sacrifices 3 tacos for each burger. Therefore, the opportunity cost of a burger is the pleasure Bob could experience by eating 3 tacos (at a price of $1 each) instead of the single burger (at a price of $3).

Why does Bob consume exactly 8 burgers? Let's start with the first burger and work our way up. Bob eats the first burger because the pleasure from eating it exceeds the potential pleasure from the 3 tacos that he could have eaten instead. The same is true for the second through the eighth burgers. Bob stops at 8 burgers because the potential pleasure from the ninth burger is less than the pleasure from the three tacos he can eat instead. Later in the chapter we'll see how to measure the benefits and costs of consumption and then find a point on the individual demand curve.

Income and Substitution Effects

The negatively sloped demand curve in Figure 1 is consistent with the law of demand. The lower the price, the more burgers Bob demands. For example, when the price decreases from $3 to $2, Bob consumes 11 burgers instead of just 8. Earlier in the book, we saw that a decrease in price generates a substitution effect and an income effect, both of which tend to increase the quantity demanded. Let's take a closer look at each of these effects.

Substitution effect: The change in consumption resulting from a change in the price of one good relative to the price of other goods.

Let's look first at the **substitution effect**, the change in consumption resulting from a change in the price of one good relative to the prices of other goods. At the original price of $3, Bob consumed only 8 burgers because the potential benefit from the ninth burger was less than the opportunity cost. When the price drops to $2, the price of burgers decreases relative to the price of tacos, decreasing the opportunity cost of the ninth burger: To get the ninth burger, Bob now sacrifices only 2 tacos, not 3. If the benefit from the ninth burger now exceeds the opportunity cost, Bob will consume the ninth burger. Because he consumes the ninth burger instead of the 2 tacos he could have consumed instead, we say that he substitutes a burger for some tacos. For Bob, a decrease in the relative price of burgers decreases the opportunity cost of burgers, so he substitutes burgers for tacos.

The substitution effect cuts both ways: It is also relevant for an increase in price. For an example of consumers' response to an increase in price, read the Closer Look box "Copayments for Medical Care."

Real income: Consumer's income measured in terms of the goods it can buy.

The second response to a decrease in price is called the *income effect.* At the original price of $3, Bob buys 8 burgers (at a cost of $24) and 6 tacos (at a cost of $6), for a total cost of $30. A decrease in the price of burgers will increase Bob's purchasing power: Given the lower price, he can buy more burgers *and* more tacos. A consumer's **real income** is measured in terms of the goods the money can buy.

A Closer LOOK

Copayments for Medical Care

Insurance companies understand the substitution effect and design their insurance policies accordingly. Under one type of medical insurance, the company simply collects a fixed annual fee from each policyholder and there are no additional charges for medical care. A second option is to combine a lower annual fee with a copayment: Every time the policyholder gets some medical care, he or she pays a small fee or copayment, for example, $10 for each visit to a physician. Copayments are very effective in decreasing the quantity of medical care demanded. In one study, a switch to a copayment system decreased the quantity of medical care demanded (the number of doctor visits) by about 20%.*

People who have copayments go to the doctor less frequently because of the substitution effect. If there is no copayment, the opportunity cost of a doctor visit is zero: From the consumer's perspective, there is no trade-off between medical care and other goods. A switch to a copayment system increases the opportunity cost of medical care—a consumer who pays $10 for a doctor visit has $10 less to spend on other goods—and decreases the quantity of medical care demanded. This is the substitution effect in action.

*Charles E. Phelps, *Health Care Costs: The Consequences of Increased Cost Sharing* (Santa Monica, CA: Rand Corporation, November 1982).

When the price of burgers decreases, Bob's $30 buys more burgers and more tacos, so his real income is higher. For example, the cost of purchasing his original burger–taco combination decreases to $22, leaving him $8 of leftover money to spend any way he wishes. He could spend this leftover money on more burgers, more tacos, or more of both. The decrease in price gives him more options, so his real income is higher.

An increase in real income causes a consumer to buy more of most—but not all—goods. For a **normal good**, the amount consumed increases as real income rises. As its name implies, most goods are normal, so the consumption of most goods increases with the consumer's income. In contrast, for an **inferior good**, the amount consumed decreases as income rises. Some examples of inferior goods are used clothing, intercity bus travel, and potatoes. In all three cases, consumers switch to more expensive goods (new clothing, air travel, and meat) as their incomes increase.

Normal good: A good for which the demand increases as real income rises.

Inferior good: A good for which demand decreases as real income rises.

Income effect: The change in consumption resulting from an increase in the consumer's real income.

The change in consumption resulting from an increase in the consumer's real income is known as the **income effect**. Suppose that a burger is a normal good for Bob. When the price of burgers decreases, Bob's real income increases, so he buys more burgers. Of course, he may buy more tacos as well, but we are interested in the effect of the price change on his burger consumption.

For normal goods, the law of demand is sensible because the income and substitution effects reinforce one another. A decrease in the price of burgers increases Bob's burger consumption because (1) the opportunity cost of burgers is lower, so Bob substitutes burgers for tacos (the substitution effect), and (2) Bob can afford more of all goods, including burgers (the income effect).

For inferior goods, the case for the law of demand is not so transparent. When the price of an inferior good decreases, there are two conflicting effects: The substitution effect tends to increase consumption, while the income effect tends to decrease consumption. In almost every case, the substitution effect is stronger than the income effect, so the law of demand is correct and the demand curve is negatively sloped.

TEST *Your Understanding*

1. Complete the statement: The individual demand curve shows the relationship between ____________ and ____________.

2. List the variables that are held fixed in drawing an individual demand curve.

3. Suppose that Tammy consumes only 50 lipsticks per year. What does this suggest about the opportunity cost of a 51st lipstick?

4. Will an increase in the price of a good increase or decrease the opportunity cost of consuming the good?

THE MARKET DEMAND CURVE

Now that we understand the logic behind the individual demand curve, we're ready to discuss the market demand curve. The market demand curve shows, for each price, the quantity of a particular good demanded by *all* consumers. Later in the chapter we'll see how firms and other organizations use the market demand curve to predict how consumers will respond to changes in price.

If we have information about the demands of individual consumers, it's easy to draw a market demand curve. All we do is add up the quantities demanded by all consumers. The following three-step process is illustrated in Figure 2.

1. Pick a price for the good, say $3.
2. For the chosen price, use the individual demand curves to determine the quantity demanded by each consumer. For example, at a price of $3, Betty buys 4 burgers (point *g*) and Bob buys 8 burgers (point *b*).
3. For the chosen price, the market quantity is the sum of the quantities demanded by all the consumers. At a price of $3, the market quantity is 12 burgers (4 plus 8), so point *j* is on the market demand curve.

We can repeat this process for other prices. For each price, we get another point on the demand curve. In effect, we are summing the individual demand curves horizontally, picking a price and adding up the quantities (the variable on the horizontal or *x* axis).

In most markets there are thousands of consumers, not just two. Nonetheless, the logic behind the market demand curve is exactly the same. At each price, the quantity demanded in the market is just the sum of the quantities demanded by the individual consumers. Figure 3 shows the market demand curve for a market with many consumers. At a price of $3, the quantity demanded is 250 (point *b*); at a price of $2, the quantity demanded is 1,000 (point *c*).

The market demand curve is drawn under the assumption that everything except the price of the good is held fixed. For the market demand, these other variables include all the variables held fixed for the individual demand curve (the prices of other goods, income, and tastes) and one more variable, the number of consumers. In other words, the market demand curves shows the relationship between the price and the quantity of a particular good, all else being fixed.

The market demand curve is negatively sloped, consistent with the law of demand. It suggests that the lower the price of a particular good, the larger the quantity demanded, everything else being equal. In the beginning of the chapter, we discussed the puzzling facts about gasoline consumption in different countries. The typical U.S. driver uses 7 times as much gasoline as the typical Italian, 6 times as much as the typical Japanese, and 1.3 times as much as the typical Canadian. As

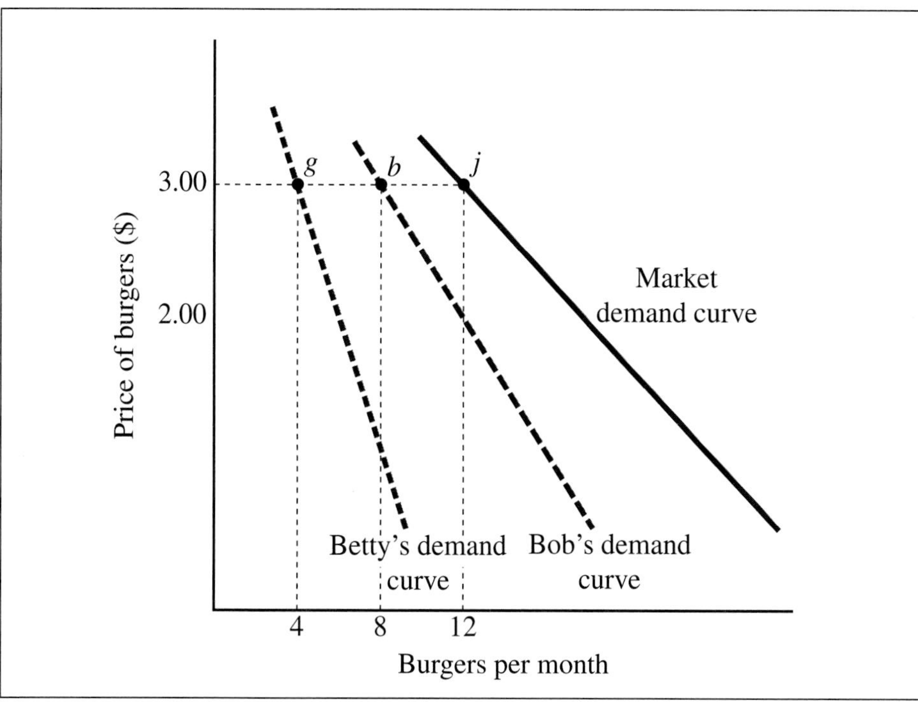

Figure 2

Market Demand Curve with Two Consumers

To determine the market demand at a given price, we add the quantities demanded by all consumers. For example, at a price of $3, Betty consumes 4 burgers (point *g*) and Bob consumes 8 burgers (point *b*), so the total quantity demanded is 12 (point *j*).

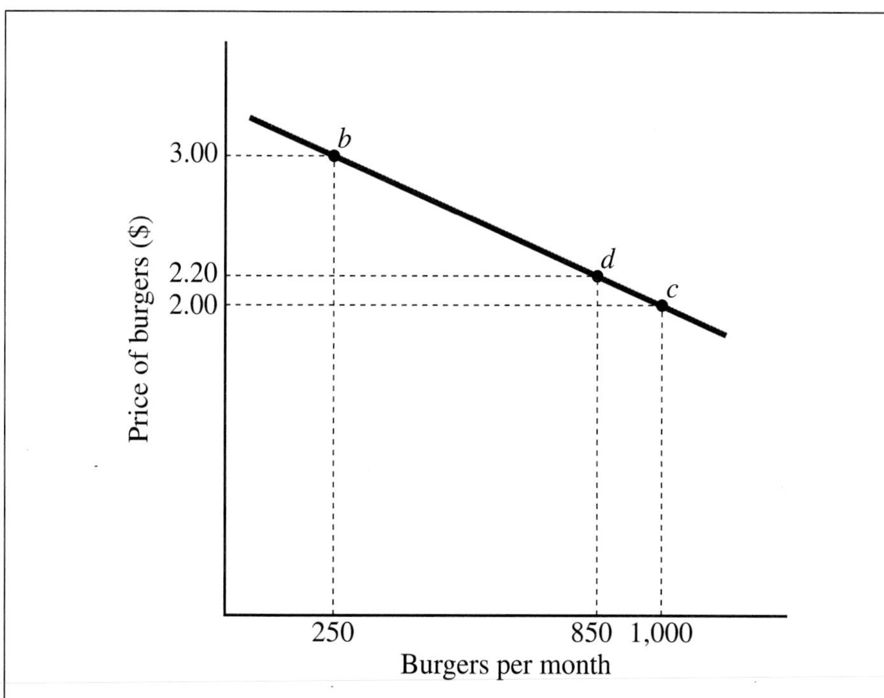

Price ($)	Quantity demanded
3.00	250
2.20	850
2.00	1,000

Figure 3

Market Demand Curve with Many Consumers

The market demand curve shows, for each price, the quantity of the good demanded by all consumers. A decrease in the price of burgers from $3 to $2 increases the total quantity demanded from 250 (point *b*) to 1,000 (point *c*).

Figure 4

Price of Gasoline in Various Nations

Source: Alfred A. Marcus, *Controversial Issues in Energy Policy*, Volume 2 (New York: Sage Publications, 1992), Table 2.

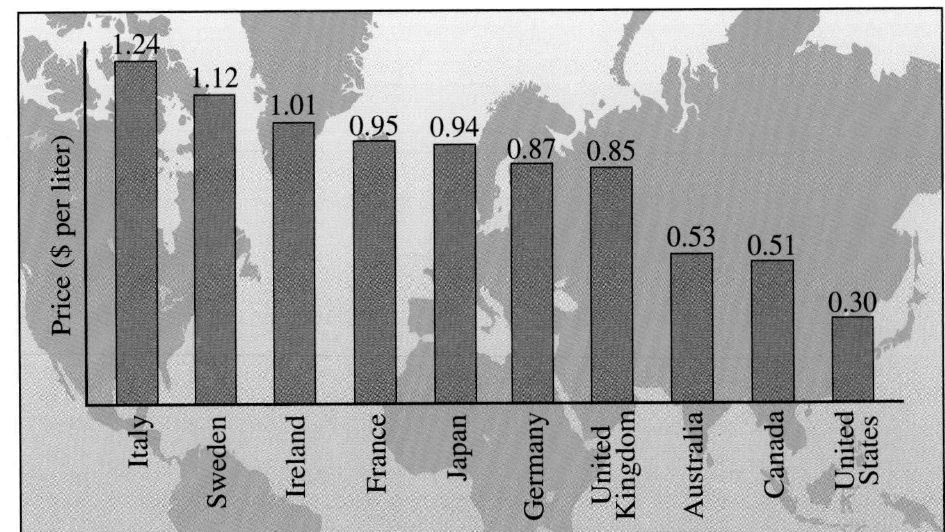

shown in Figure 4, gasoline prices in the United States are much lower than those in other industrialized nations, so it's not surprising that gasoline consumption is so high. The differences in prices reflect differences in gasoline taxes: Gas is cheap in the United States because gasoline taxes are much lower than they are in other nations. Of course, other factors contribute to higher gasoline consumption in the United States—including higher income and lower population density—but the differences in price are the most important factor.

UTILITY THEORY AND CONSUMER DEMAND

Earlier in the chapter we suggested that each point on the individual demand curve is the result of a rational choice by the consumer, a choice based on the benefits and costs of consuming the good. We can use the marginal principle to show how consumers incorporate benefits and costs into their consumption decisions.

Marginal PRINCIPLE

Increase the level of an activity if its marginal benefit exceeds its marginal cost, but reduce the level if the marginal cost exceeds the marginal benefit. If possible, pick the level at which the marginal benefit equals the marginal cost.

Bob's activity is eating burgers, so he should pick the quantity of burgers at which the marginal benefit of burgers equals the marginal cost.

Total and Marginal Utility

Utility: The satisfaction or pleasure the consumer experiences when he or she consumes a good, measured as the number of utils.

Before we use the marginal principle, let's think about how to measure the benefit of consuming a particular good. The benefit is the **utility** generated by consuming the good, which is the satisfaction or pleasure the consumer experiences when he or she consumes the good. Although the benefit is easy to define, it is difficult to measure: We can't hook Bob up to a pleasure meter to determine how much happier he is after eating his burgers. Nonetheless, let's suppose that we can measure the consumer's benefit as the number of *utils* (a util is 1 unit of utility or satisfaction) generated by the good.

Panel A of Figure 5 shows the relationship between Bob's total utility from burgers and his burger consumption. As the number of burgers increases, Bob's total

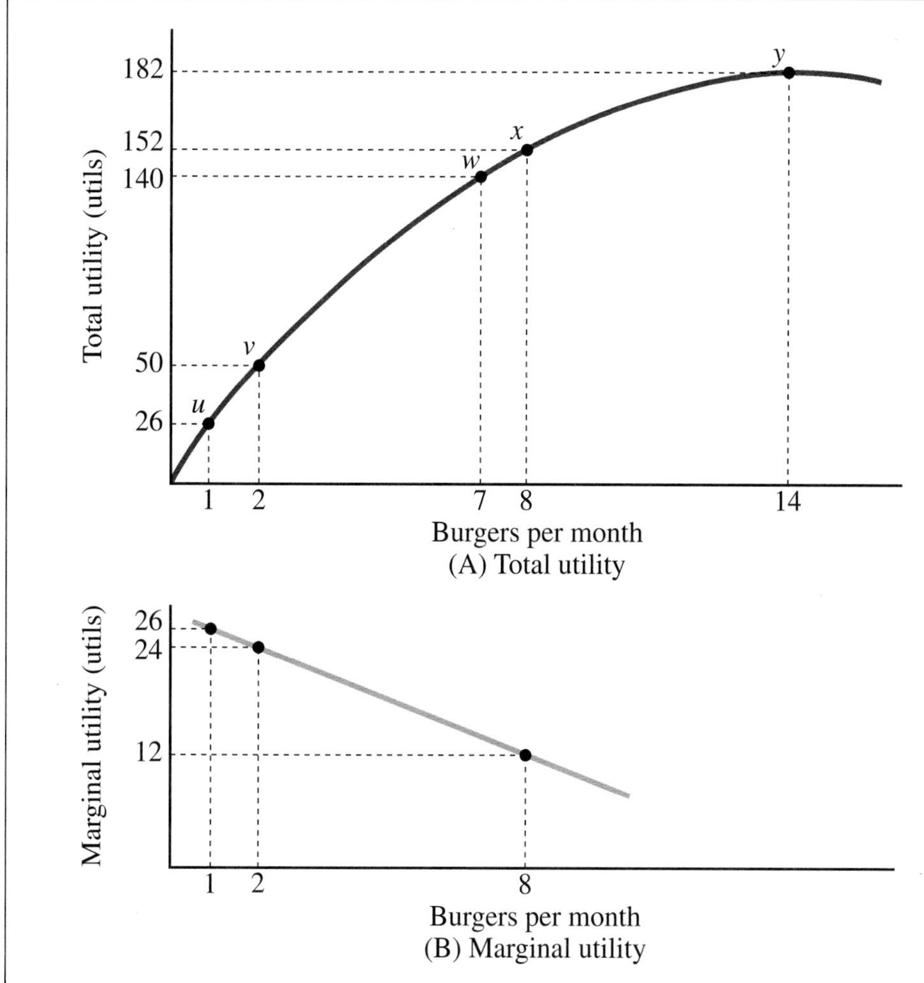

Figure 5

Total and Marginal Utility

In panel A, as the quantity of burgers consumed increases, the utility or satisfaction increases at a decreasing rate, and eventually falls. In panel B, as the quantity of burgers increases, the marginal utility (the change in utility from one more burger) decreases. Both curves reflect the law of diminishing marginal utility.

utility increases, but at a decreasing rate. When Bob eats his first burger, his total utility increases from zero to 26 utils (point *u* along the total utility curve). When he eats the second burger, his utility increases to 50 utils (point *v*), so although utility is higher, the second burger adds less utility than the first. Moving upward along the curve, the eighth burger increases Bob's utility by only 12 utils (152 minus 140). Eventually, additional burgers actually decrease Bob's utility level, as shown by the points beyond point *y* on the curve.

Panel B of Figure 5 shows Bob's marginal-utility curve. **Marginal utility** is defined as the change in utility resulting from one additional unit of the good. According to the **law of diminishing marginal utility**, as the consumption of a particular good increases, marginal utility decreases. This is shown in panel B of Figure 5: The marginal utility drops from 26 utils for the first burger, to 24 utils for the second burger, and 12 utils for the eighth burger.

Marginal utility: The change in utility from one additional unit of the good.

Law of diminishing marginal utility: As the consumption of a particular good increases, marginal utility decreases.

To use the marginal principle, we must compute the marginal benefits for different quantities of burgers. Bob's benefit from burgers is the utility level he achieves with different quantities, so his marginal benefit is the same as his marginal utility. The second column of Table 1 (page 132) shows the marginal benefits for the fifth through the tenth burgers, with the numbers consistent with Figure 5. The marginal benefit is 18 utils for the fifth burger, 16 utils for the sixth burger, and so on, down to 8 utils for the tenth burger.

Table 1: Marginal Utility and the Marginal Principle

Number of Burgers	Marginal Benefit of Burgers = Marginal Utility of Burgers (utils)	Number of Tacos	Marginal Utility of Tacos (utils)	Marginal Cost of Burgers = 3 times the Marginal Utility of Tacos (utils)
5	18	15	1	3
6	16	12	2	6
7	14	9	3	9
8	12	6	4	**12**
9	10	3	5	15
10	8	0	6	18

Finding a Point on the Demand Curve

The marginal cost of burgers is simply the opportunity cost of burgers, which we defined earlier as the pleasure Bob could experience by eating three tacos (at a price of $1 each) instead of a single burger (at a price of $3). We can use the data in Table 1 to compute the marginal cost for different quantities of burgers.

1. The third column shows the number of tacos Bob can buy given his $30 budget and the number of hamburgers listed in the first column. For example, if Bob buys 5 burgers at $3 each, he has $15 left to buy 15 tacos at $1 each. As we move down in the table, the number of tacos decreases as the number of burgers increases.

2. The fourth column shows the marginal utility of tacos, defined as the additional satisfaction from consuming one additional taco. For example, if Bob has 15 tacos, the marginal utility is 1 util: If he ate one more taco, his utility would increase by 1 util; if he ate one less, his utility would decrease by 1 util. As we move down the column, the marginal utility of tacos increases, consistent with the law of diminishing marginal utility: The fewer tacos Bob consumes, the larger the marginal utility of a taco.

3. In the fifth column we compute the marginal cost of a burger by multiplying the number of tacos sacrificed per burger (3) by the marginal utility of a taco. In the first row, the marginal utility of a taco is 1 util, so the marginal cost of the fifth burger is 3 utils (3 tacos times 1 util per taco). As the number of burgers increases and the number of tacos decreases, the marginal utility of tacos increases, so the marginal cost increases to 6 utils for the sixth burger, 9 utils for the seventh burger, and so on.

To satisfy the marginal principle, Bob should consume 8 tacos. For each of the first 8 burgers, the pleasure from eating the burger (the marginal benefit) is greater than or equal to the potential pleasure from the 3 tacos he could have eaten instead (the marginal cost). In the first row of Table 1, the marginal benefit of the fifth burger is 18 utils, compared to 3 utils for the 3 tacos he could have eaten instead. Similarly, the marginal benefit is greater than or equal to the marginal cost for the sixth, seventh, and eighth burgers. Bob stops at 8 burgers because the marginal benefit of the ninth burger (10 utils) is less than the marginal cost (15 utils from the 3 tacos he could eat instead).

We can use Figure 6 to summarize our application of the marginal principle to Bob's decision-making. The two curves are based on the numbers in Table 1. The marginal benefit equals the marginal cost at 8 burgers (and 6 tacos), so this is the best Bob can do.

We've seen that one point on the demand curve is the result of rational choice by the consumer. When the price of burgers is $3, Bob consumes 8 burgers because that is the quantity that satisfies the marginal principle. If he started out with any other quantity, he could make himself better off by consuming 8 burgers instead. If

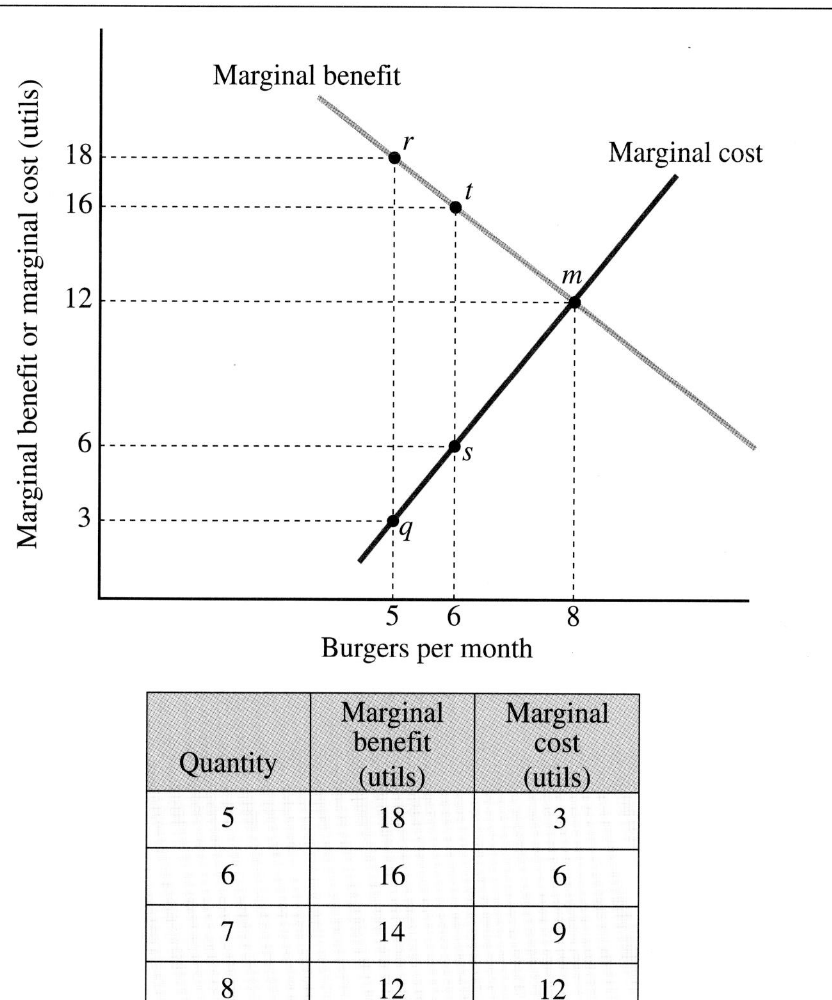

Quantity	Marginal benefit (utils)	Marginal cost (utils)
5	18	3
6	16	6
7	14	9
8	12	12

Figure 6

Marginal Principle and Demand

The marginal benefit of burgers equals the marginal cost at 8 burgers, so the marginal principle is satisfied at point *m*.

we repeated this exercise with different prices, we'd find that each point on the demand curve satisfies the marginal principle and therefore is a rational choice, given the price of the good.

Is it possible to actually measure the satisfaction or utility generated by consuming a good or service? For a discussion of one attempt to quantify the concept of utility, see the Closer Look box on page 134, "Measuring Utility."

The Utility-Maximizing Rule

We can use utility theory to introduce a general rule for consumer decisions. According to the **utility-maximizing rule**, The consumer will maximize his or her utility by picking the affordable combination of consumer goods that makes the marginal utility per dollar spent on one good equal to that of a second good. In our example of burgers and tacos, this means that

$$\frac{\text{marginal utility of burgers}}{\text{price of burgers}} = \frac{\text{marginal utility of tacos}}{\text{price of tacos}}$$

Utility-maximizing rule: Pick the affordable combination of consumer goods that makes the marginal utility per dollar spent on one good equal to that of a second good.

Looking back at the numbers in Table 1, we see that Bob's choice of 8 burgers and 6 tacos satisfies the utility-maximizing rule: The marginal utility per dollar spent

A Closer LOOK

Measuring Utility

During the nineteenth century, some philosophers believed that it was actually possible to measure the well-being or *utility* that individuals received from consuming goods and services. The idea was to hook a person up to some sort of machine, let the consumer eat a pie, and then read from the machine's gauges the amount of "happiness," or utility, generated by the pie. Because such a machine has not been invented, it is impossible to measure utility. Jeremy Bentham, one of these "utilitarians," died in London in 1832. He helped establish University College, London, and his fully clothed skeleton—with a wax head—is kept in a glass case there.

Is it possible to measure the utility or satisfaction a person gets from consuming one more unit of a good?

on burgers is 4 utils (12 utils for the eighth burger divided by a price of $3), which is the same as the marginal utility per dollar spent on tacos (4 utils for the sixth taco divided by a price of $1). The utility-maximizing rule is consistent with the marginal principle.

To see the logic behind the utility-maximizing rule, let's see what would happen if Bob picked a different combination of burgers and tacos. Would it be wise to pick 5 burgers and 15 tacos? In this case the marginal utility per dollar spent on burgers is 6 utils (18 divided by $3), while the marginal utility per dollar spent on tacos is only 1 util (1 divided by $1). In other words, he gets a bigger marginal utility per dollar or a bigger "bang per buck" for the money he spends on burgers. Therefore, it would be sensible to spend more money on burgers and less on tacos. To maximize his utility he should increase his burger consumption as long as it generates a larger bang per buck (a larger marginal utility per dollar). He should stop at 8 burgers and 6 tacos because the bang per buck of the ninth burger (3.33 utils) would be less than the bang per buck of tacos (5 utils).

TEST *Your Understanding*

5 Betty bought 5 books in January, 6 books in February, and 7 books in March. Her utility level was 30 utils in January, 45 utils in February, and 54 utils in March. Are these utility numbers consistent with the law of diminishing marginal utility?

6 As a person's consumption of a particular good increases, what happens to the marginal benefit of consumption? Relate your answer to the law of diminishing marginal utility.

7 Suppose that Bob initially consumes 6 burgers and 12 tacos. Use the numbers in Table 1 (page 132) to compute the marginal utility per dollar spent for each good. Which good generates the largest bang per buck?

CONSUMER SURPLUS

Why do most consumers say "thank you" when they purchase a good or service? Perhaps they are simply being polite to the person selling the good, but perhaps they really mean it. If you say "thank you" when you buy a CD for $10, it could mean that you're willing to pay much more for the CD and are delighted to get it at that price. **Consumer surplus** is the difference between the maximum amount a consumer is willing to pay for a product and the price that he or she pays for the product. For example, if you are willing to pay $21 for a CD that you buy for $10, your consumer surplus is $11.

Consumer surplus: The difference between the maximum amount a consumer is willing to pay for a product and the price the consumer pays for the product.

The Demand Curve and Consumer Surplus

Let's start our discussion of consumer surplus with another look at the demand curve, which we can use to show how much consumers are willing to pay for a product. In Figure 7 on page 136, Oscar's demand curve shows that he won't buy any CDs at a price of $24 (point *t*), but he will buy one CD if the price drops to $21 (point *u*). This suggests that Oscar is willing to pay up to $21 for the first CD, but no more: The first CD is worth buying at a price of $21 but not worth buying if the price is over $21. Moving down the demand curve to point *v*, Oscar will buy a second CD when the price drops to $18, suggesting that he is willing to pay up to $18 for the second CD. As we continue to move downward along the demand curve, Oscar is willing to pay less and less for each additional CD.

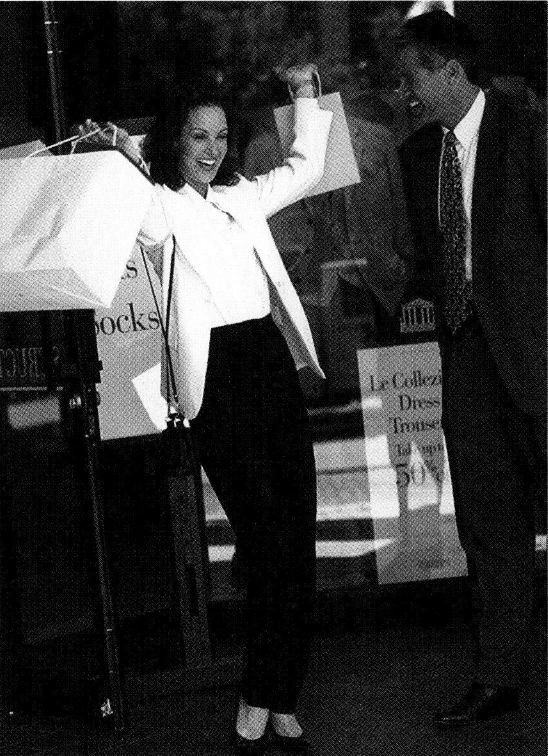

The price a consumer pays for a good is usually less than the amount he or she is willing to pay. Consumer surplus measures the bonus or surplus received by the consumer.

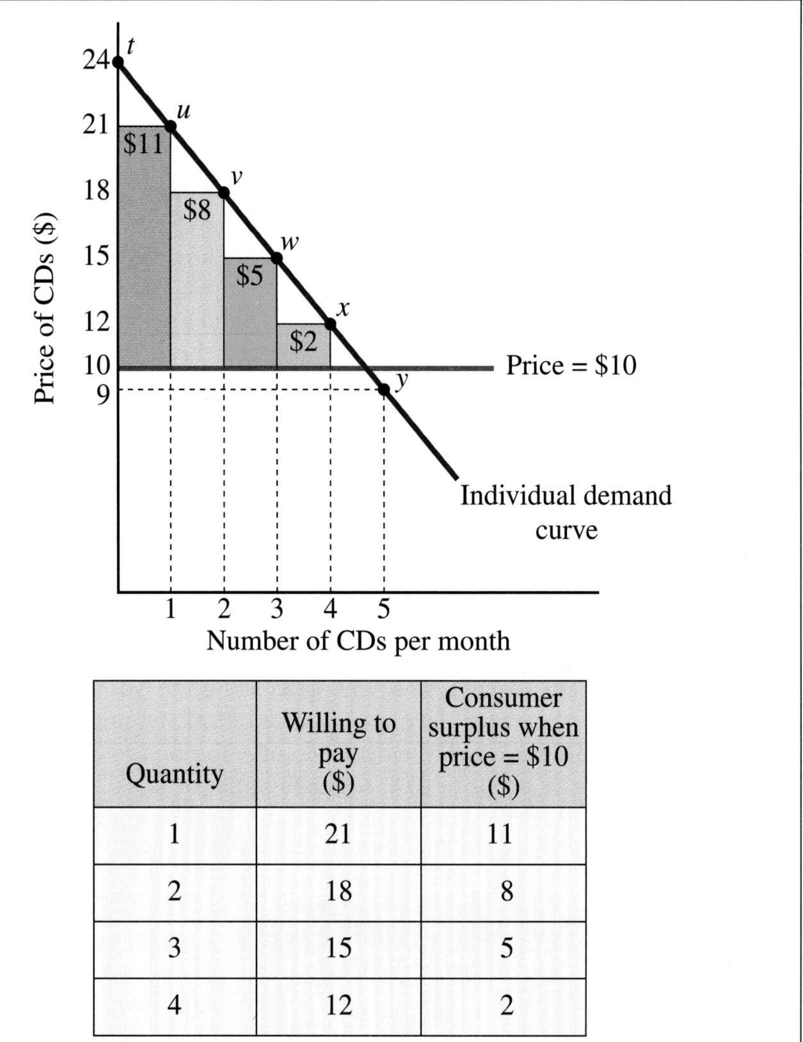

Quantity	Willing to pay ($)	Consumer surplus when price = $10 ($)
1	21	11
2	18	8
3	15	5
4	12	2

Figure 7

Consumer Surplus for an Individual Consumer

The individual demand curve shows how much a consumer is willing to pay for each unit of the good; for example, $21 for the first CD, and $18 for the second CD. Consumer surplus equals the difference between the amount a consumer is willing to pay and the price; for example, $11 for the first CD, and $8 for the second.

We can use the demand curve to measure just how much of a bonus or surplus a consumer gets from buying a particular product. If the price of CDs is $10, Oscar's consumer surplus for the first CD is $11, the amount he is willing to pay ($21) minus the price. We can compute Oscar's consumer surplus from CDs by adding up the surpluses from each of the CDs he actually purchases at the market price. For example, at a price of $10, Oscar will actually buy 4 CDs: He doesn't buy a fifth CD because he is willing to pay only $9 for it (point *y*). His consumer surplus is $8 for the second CD, $5 for the third, and $2 for the fourth. Therefore, at a price of $10, his consumer surplus from CDs is $26.

We can also compute the consumer surplus for an entire market. Like an individual demand curve, the market demand curve shows how much consumers are willing to pay for a particular product. In Figure 8, when the price of CDs drops from $20.01 to $20, someone buys the 100th CD. It is worthwhile to purchase the 100th CD at $20, but not worthwhile at a higher price, meaning that the consumer who buys the 100th CD is willing to pay up to $20 for the CD. Similarly, the consumer who purchases the 200th CD is willing to pay up to $15 for it (point *i*). Each point on the market demand curve shows the amount that a consumer is willing to pay for a particular CD.

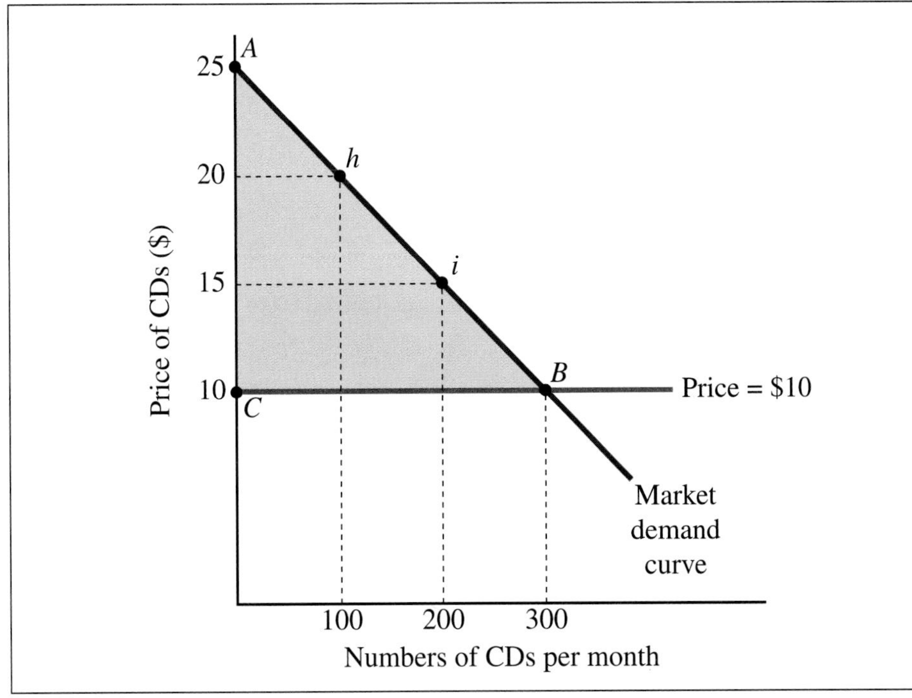

Figure 8

Consumer Surplus for the CD Market

The market demand curve shows how much a marginal consumer is willing to pay for the product. The market consumer surplus is equal to the area between the demand curve and the horizontal price line.

We can use the market demand curve to compute the consumer surplus for the entire market. At a price of $10, the consumer surplus is $10 for the 100th CD, $5 for the 200th CD, and so on. Once we compute the consumer surplus for each CD, we could add up these surpluses to compute the total consumer surplus for the market. Fortunately, there is a shortcut: The consumer surplus is shown by the area between demand curve and horizontal price line, that is, the area of triangle *ABC*. Using the formula for the area of a triangle (one-half the height times the base), if the price is $10, the consumer surplus is $2,250.

Price Changes and Consumer Surplus

How would a change in price affect the consumer surplus in a particular market? If the price of CDs increased, Oscar would get a smaller surplus for each CD he buys. For example, if the price rose from $10 to $14, his surplus from the first CD would drop from $11 to $7. At the market level, each consumer will get a smaller surplus, so the total consumer surplus will drop. In Figure 9 on page 138, at a price of $10, the consumer surplus is shown by triangle *ABC*, while at a price of $14, the consumer surplus is shown by the smaller triangle *ADE*. The price hike decreases the consumer surplus by the area of the trapezoid *EDBC*. Later in the book we use the concept of consumer surplus to explore the effects of changes in prices on the well-being of consumers.

ECONOMIC DETECTIVE– *The CD Club Mystery*

Madeline owns a music store and charges $16 for each CD. Each of her customers has the same demand curve as Oscar (see Figure 7) and buys 2 CDs per month at this price. Madeline decided to start a CD club: Each person who pays a monthly club fee can buy up to 4 CDs per month at a special reduced price of $13. Madeline decided to have a monthly fee of $5, reasoning that this was just below the monthly savings that each club member would enjoy (a $3 savings on each of 2 CDs purchased). Much to her dismay, her marketing department made a mistake in their

Figure 9

Increase in Price Decreases Consumer Surplus

The consumer surplus at a price of $10 is shown by triangle *ABC*. The consumer surplus at a price of $14 is shown by the smaller triangle *ADE*. The loss of consumer surplus is shown by the trapezoid *EDBC*.

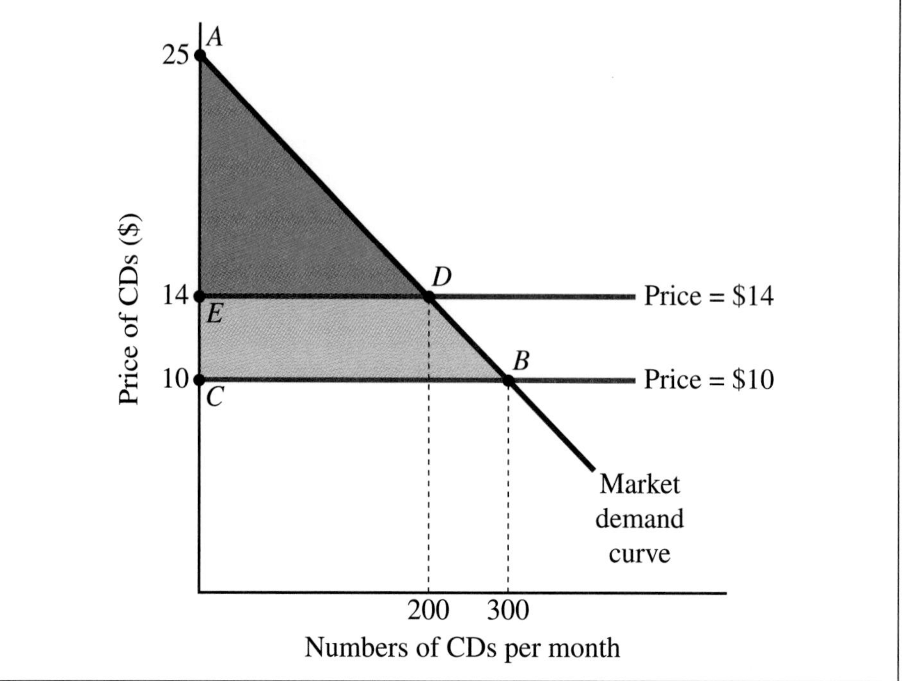

advertising campaign, announcing that the membership fee was $7 per month. The puzzle is that all of Madeline's customers joined the CD club anyway. Your job is to solve this mystery: Why did everyone join a club with a $7 membership fee and what appears to be a savings of only $6 per month?

The key to solving this mystery is the law of demand. At the lower price ($13), each customer will buy 3 CDs instead of just 2. Each consumer is willing to pay $15 for the third CD, which is less than the regular price ($16) but higher than the club price ($13). In addition to saving $3 on each of the first 2 CDs, each member will get a consumer surplus of $2 from the third CD. Therefore, the benefit of joining the club is $8, not $6 as Madeline had assumed. The benefit exceeds the $7 monthly fee, so it is sensible to join the club.

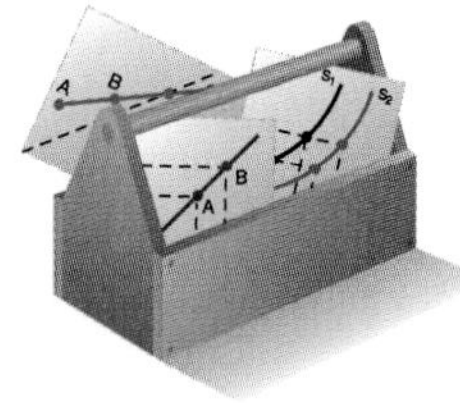

Using the **TOOLS**

In this chapter we use some of the key principles of economics to explain the logic behind consumer choice and the law of demand. Here are some opportunities to do your own economic analysis.

1. Gaining Weight in the Dormitories

As a nutrition consultant for a university, you have the task of explaining why students who live—and eat—in dormitories gain so much weight during their first year on campus. The typical dorm student gains about 15 pounds, compared to just 3 pounds for the typical student living in an apartment. So far, you have concluded that dorm students gain more weight because they eat more food.

a. How do dorm students pay for food? How does this differ from the way students in apartments pay for food?

b. What is the opportunity cost of 1 unit of dorm food (one slice of bread or meat loaf)? What is the opportunity cost of apartment food?

c. How might these differences in opportunity cost explain the larger weight gain for dorm students?

2. Consumer Metrics

You are the economist for Consumer Metrics, a consumer research firm that has developed a new device that measures the satisfaction level of a consumer before and after consuming a particular product. The company has an annual holiday party at which people eat food and drink punch (free of charge). By the end of the party, everything has been consumed. Your job is to determine whether the company spent its party budget wisely. If you could hook the new device to the typical person at the party, what information would you collect, and how would you use it? What additional information would you need to determine whether the firm's chosen combination of food and punch maximized the utility of the typical partier?

3. Pollution and Consumer Surplus

Consider a city that dumps sewage into Fish Lake, a popular spot for sport fishing. Fishers pay a fixed fee of $10 per day to fish in the lake, and the initial number of fishers is 200 per day. Suppose that the city builds a sewage-treatment plant, meaning that less waste is dumped into the lake and the quality of the lake's water improves.

a. Use a graph to show the effects of the sewage-treatment plant on (i) the number of fishers and (ii) the consumer surplus generated by Fish Lake.

b. Use your graph to show how much the fishers would be willing to pay to have the sewage-treatment plant built.

SUMMARY

In this chapter we've seen that the market demand curve represents the rational decisions of individual consumers. We've also used utility theory to think about how people make consumption decisions. Here are the main points of the chapter.

1. The market demand curve for a normal good is negatively sloped because the substitution effect reinforces the income effect.
   a. Substitution effect: the change in consumption resulting from a change in the price of one good relative to the price of other goods.
   b. Income effect: the change in consumption resulting from an increase in the consumer's real income.
2. Each point on the demand curve satisfies the marginal principle.
3. To maximize utility, a consumer should pick the affordable combination of goods that makes the marginal utility per dollar spent on one good equal to that of a second good.
4. Consumer surplus measures the net benefit of consumption, equal to the difference between the amount that a consumer is willing to pay for a product and the price that he or she actually pays.

KEY TERMS

consumer surplus, *135*
income effect, *127*
individual demand curve, *125*
inferior good, *127*
law of diminishing marginal utility, *131*
marginal utility, *131*
normal good, *127*
real income, *126*
substitution effect, *126*
utility, *130*
utility-maximizing rule, *133*

PROBLEMS AND DISCUSSION QUESTIONS

1. Recall the market demand curve in Figure 2 (page 129). Suppose that Popeye, whose demand curve is identical to Betty's demand curve, joins the market. Draw a new market demand curve.
2. Suppose that the price of muffins is $2 and the price of cookies is $1. Complete the following table and then determine how many muffins Betty will consume (given a budget of $60).

Number of Muffins	*Marginal Benefit of Muffins = Marginal Utility of Muffins*	*Number of Cookies*	*Marginal Utility of Cookies*	*Marginal Cost of Muffins ($)*
5	11	50	3	_____
6	8	48	4	_____
7	5	46	5	_____
8	3	44	6	_____

3. Suppose that you have a fixed monthly budget for audio tapes and CDs. The price of CDs is $10 and the price of tapes is $5. Given your current choice of CDs and tapes, your marginal utility of CDs is 60 and your marginal utility of tapes is 15. Are you doing the best you can with your music budget? If not, should you buy more CDs (and fewer tapes) or more tapes (and fewer CDs)? Relate your answer to the marginal principle and the utility-maximizing rule.
4. Suppose that you have a fixed budget of $3,000 per year to spend on food and music. The price of food is $1 per pound and the price of music is $10 per CD. You currently spend $2,400 on food and $600 on music. If you want to determine whether you are spending your money wisely, what questions must you ask yourself?
5. List the variables that are held fixed in drawing the market demand curve.
6. Use the utility-maximizing rule to discuss the following statement: "My car can use either gasoline or gasohol (a mixture of methanol and gasoline). I use whatever fuel has a lower price per gallon." Is this a good rule for deciding what type of fuel to use in a car? If not, develop a rule that is consistent with the utility-maximizing rule.
7. Use Figure 8 (page 137) to answer this question. Suppose that each consumer buys either 1 CD per month or none. If the price of CDs drops from $20 to $15, by how much does the total consumer surplus change? Is the change in consumer surplus greater than, equal to, or less than the money saved by the original consumers (those who purchased CDs at a price of $20)?
8. According to Oscar Wilde, "A cynic is someone who knows the price of everything but the value of nothing." Use the notion of consumer surplus to discuss this statement.
9. A state is considering the construction of a new highway between two cities. Otto travels between the two cities, and the following equation describes the relationship between the number of trips he takes per month (T) and the price of travel in cents (P), which includes monetary and time costs:

$$T = 40 - P$$

If the new highway is built, the cost per trip will decrease from 30 cents to 20 cents.

a. Draw Otto's demand curve for travel between the two cities and compute the number of trips he takes at the original price (30 cents) and the potential new price (20 cents).
b. If the highway is built, Otto's taxes will increase by $1.25 per month. Will Otto support the construction of the new highway? Explain.

Take It to the Net

We invite you to visit the O'Sullivan/Sheffrin page on the Prentice Hall Web site at:

http://www.prenhall.com/osullivan/

for this chapter's World Wide Web exercise.

MODEL ANSWERS FOR THIS CHAPTER

Chapter-Opening Questions

1. The much higher consumption in the United States is caused in large part by low prices, a result of low gasoline taxes.
2. According to the utility-maximizing, the consumer should pick the affordable combination of consumer goods that makes the marginal utility per dollar spent on one good equal to that of a second good.
3. Copayments increase the opportunity cost of medical care, causing a substitution effect that decreases the consumption of medical care.
4. For students in dormitories, the opportunity cost of food is zero, so they tend to eat more food than students in apartments, who face a positive opportunity cost.

Test Your Understanding

1. price, quantity demanded by a single consumer
2. The fixed variables are income, tastes, and price of other goods.
3. The opportunity cost must exceed the benefit.
4. It will increase the opportunity cost.
5. The marginal utility drops from 15 for the sixth book to 9 for the seventh book, consistent with the law of diminishing marginal utility.
6. The marginal benefit equals the marginal utility, which according to the law of diminishing marginal utility, decreases as consumption increases.
7. For burgers, 5.33 utils (16 utils divided by $3); for tacos, 3 utils (3 utils divided by $1). Burgers generate a larger bang per buck.

Using the Tools

1. Gaining Weight in the Dormitories
   a. The typical dorm student pays a fixed monthly fee for food, while a student in an apartment pays according to how much food he or she consumes.
   b. The opportunity cost of one more unit of dorm food (e.g., a slice of meatloaf or a scoop of ice cream) is zero: There is no trade-off between food and other goods. For a student living in an apartment, food comes at the expense of other goods: The more food the student eats, the less money she has to spend on other goods, such as movies, travel, and books.
   c. The substitution effect says that the lower the opportunity cost of food, the greater the consumption of food. Therefore, the dorm student—with a zero opportunity cost for food—will eat more food and gain more weight.
2. Consumer Metrics

   You could use the device to determine the marginal utility of food (the change in utility or satisfaction from eating the last ounce) and the marginal utility of punch (the change in utility or satisfaction from drinking the last ounce). If you get information on the prices of food and punch (prices per ounce), you could compute the marginal utility per dollar (bang per buck) for both food and punch. To maximize utility, the firm should equate the bang per buck on the two goods.
3. Pollution and Consumer Surplus

   See Figure A on page 142. The improvement in water quality will increase the demand for fishing—and shift the demand curve to the right—for two reasons. The fish population is likely to increase, making it more likely that fishers will actually catch some fish. In addition, fishers will presumably get more enjoyment from the sights and smells of the outdoors when the lake is cleaner. The rightward shift of the demand curve will increase the number of fishers at the fixed price of $10. It will also increase the consumer surplus associated with the fixed price. The increase in consumer surplus is shown by the area between the old and new demand curves above the horizontal price line. This is the amount that fishers would be willing to pay for the sewage-treatment plant.

Figure A

Consumer Surplus for Fish Lake

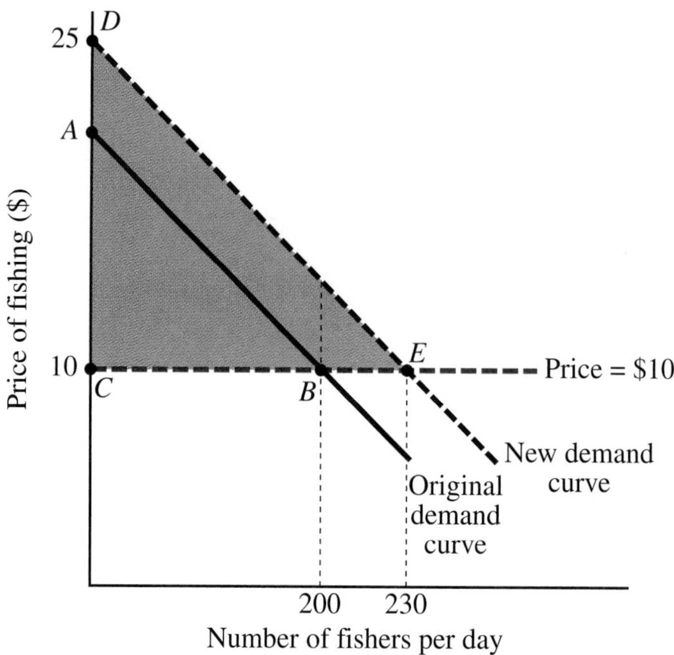

Appendix

Consumer Choice Using Indifference Curves

The Budget Set and Budget Line

Indifference Curves

Maximizing Utility

The Tangency Condition and the Marginal Principle

Drawing the Demand Curve

In Chapter 7 we used utility theory to show that each point on the demand curve is the result of a rational choice by the consumer. In this appendix we use a different model of consumer behavior to explain how the consumer makes this rational choice. The model is based on the notion that the consumer's objective is to maximize his or her *utility* given the limitations dictated by his or her income and the prices of consumer goods. In contrast to the old-style utility theory discussed earlier, this modern approach does not require the measurement of utility or satisfaction. It just requires us to determine the rate at which a consumer is willing to trade one good for another. The modern approach is more realistic and useful because a consumer can easily answer the question, "How many tacos are you willing to give up to get one more burger?"

THE BUDGET SET AND BUDGET LINE

Bob's ability to purchase burgers and tacos is limited by his income and the prices of the two goods. Bob's **budget set** includes all the combinations of burgers and tacos that he can afford, given his income and the prices of burgers and tacos. The **budget line** shows all the combinations that exhaust his budget. Let's assume that Bob has $30 per week to spend on burgers and tacos and that the price of burgers is $3, while the price of tacos is $1. In Figure A-1 the budget line connects points *y* and *x*: at point *y*, Bob spends his entire budget on tacos, getting 30 tacos ($30 = $1 times 30 tacos); at point *x*, he spends his entire budget on burgers, getting 10 burgers ($30 = $3 times 10 burgers). If Bob spends some money on each good, he can reach the points between *y* and *x*. For example, he could reach point *e* (8 burgers and 6 tacos) by spending $24 on burgers and $6 on tacos. The budget set is the shaded area below the budget line.

Budget set: A set of points that includes all the combinations of two goods that a consumer can afford, given the consumer's income and the prices of the two goods.

Budget line: The line connecting all the combinations of two goods that exhaust a consumer's budget.

The slope of the budget line is the market trade-off between burgers and tacos. It shows the rate at which the consumer can trade burgers for tacos, given the market prices of the two goods. Starting from any point on the budget line, if Bob buys 1 more burger, he uses $3 that he could have used instead to buy 3 tacos. The market trade-off is the ratio of the two prices (the price of burgers divided by the price of tacos), and the slope is the negative of the price ratio, −3.0 in our example.

INDIFFERENCE CURVES

We can represent the consumer's preferences or tastes with indifference curves. An **indifference curve** shows the combinations of the two goods that generate the same level of utility or satisfaction. In Figure A-2 on page 144 the indifference curve passing through point *e* divides the combinations of burgers and tacos into three groups.

Indifference curve: The set of combinations of two goods that generate the same level of utility or satisfaction.

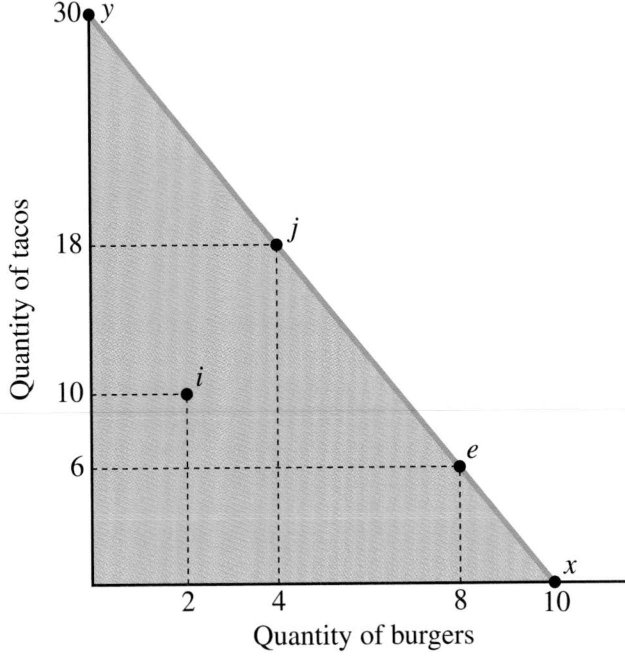

Figure A-1

Budget Set and Budget Line

The budget set (the shaded triangle) shows all the affordable combinations of burgers and tacos, and the budget line (with endpoints *x* and *y*) shows the combinations that exhaust the budget.

Figure A-2

Indifference Curve and the Marginal Rate of Substitution

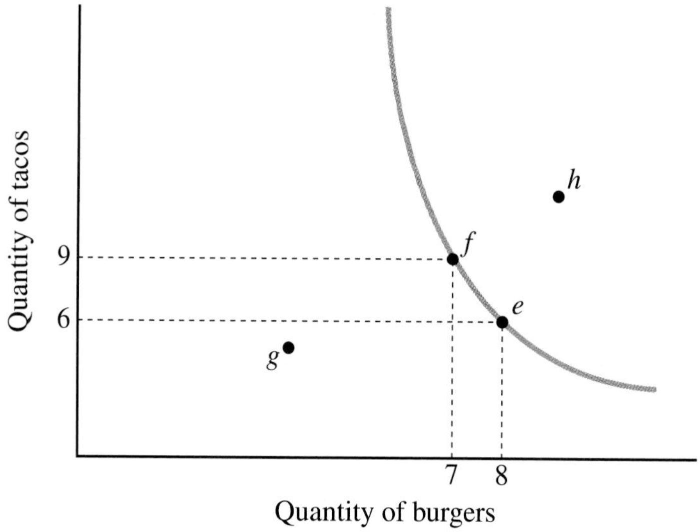

The indifference curve shows the different combinations of burgers and tacos that generate the same utility level. The slope (3.0 between points *e* and *f*) is the marginal rate of substitution between the two goods.

1. ***Superior combinations.*** All the combinations above the indifference curve generate more satisfaction (higher utility) than combinations on the curve. For example, Bob would prefer point *h* to point *e* or *f* because he gets more of both goods with point *h*.
2. ***Inferior combinations.*** All the combinations below the indifference curve generate less satisfaction (lower utility) than do combinations on the curve. For example, Bob would prefer point *e* to point *g* because he gets more of both goods with point *e*.
3. ***Equivalent combinations.*** All combinations along the indifference curve generate the same satisfaction (the same utility) as combination *e*. For example, Bob would be indifferent between combinations *e* and *f*.

An indifference curve shows the subjective preferences of an individual consumer, so indifference curves vary from one consumer to another. Nonetheless, the indifference curves of all consumers share two characteristics: They are negatively sloped, and they become flatter as we move downward along an individual curve.

Marginal rate of substitution (MRS): The rate at which a consumer is willing to substitute one good for another.

Why is the indifference curve negatively sloped? If we give Bob an additional burger, he would be happier if he continued to consume the same number of tacos. To keep him at the same level of utility or satisfaction, we must take away some tacos. In other words, there is a negative relationship between burgers and tacos, so the indifference curve is negatively sloped. The slope of the curve is the **marginal rate of substitution (MRS)** between the two goods. It shows the rate at which Bob is willing to substitute one good for another. In Figure A-2 if Bob starts at point *f* and we give him 1 more burger, we must take away 3 tacos to keep him on the same indifference curve. Therefore, the marginal rate of substitution near point *f* is 3.0.

The indifference curve becomes flatter as we move downward along the curve because of diminishing marginal utility. As we move down Bob's indifference curve, burger consumption increases and taco consumption decreases. The marginal rate of substitution decreases for two reasons.

1. The larger the number of burgers, the lower the marginal utility of burgers, so we can take away fewer tacos to offset each additional burger.
2. The smaller the number of tacos, the higher the marginal utility of tacos. Therefore, each taco we take away has a larger negative effect on the utility level, so we can offset any given increase in utility by taking away fewer tacos.

On the upper portion of the curve, Bob has many tacos and just a few burgers, so he is willing to trade several tacos to get another burger: The MRS is large and the curve is steep. On the lower portion of the curve, he has many burgers and just a few tacos, so he is not willing to trade very many tacos to get another burger: The MRS is small and the curve is flat.

An *indifference map* is a set of indifference curves. Figure A-3 shows three indifference curves, C1, C2, and C3. As Bob moves from a point on indifference curve C1 to any point on C2, his utility increases. This is sensible because he can get more of both goods on C2, so he will be better off. In general, Bob's utility increases as he moves in the northeasterly direction to higher indifference curve (from C1 to C2 to C3, and so on).

MAXIMIZING UTILITY

The consumer's objective is to maximize his or her utility, given the consumer's budget and the market prices. Bob can pick from many affordable combination of burgers and tacos, and he will pick the one that generates the highest level of utility or satisfaction. In graphical terms, Bob will reach the highest indifference curve possible, given his budget set.

In Figure A-4 on page 146, Bob will choose point *e* (8 burgers and 6 tacos) and will achieve the utility level associated with indifference curve C2. Why does he choose point *e* instead of point *i*, *j*, or *k*?

- Point *i*. Bob doesn't choose this point for two reasons. First, it is not on the budget line, so it does not exhaust his budget. Second, it is on a lower indifference curve (and thus generates less utility) than point *e*.
- Point *j*. Although point *j* exhausts Bob's budget, *j* lies on a lower indifference curve than *e*, so it generates less utility than point *e*. Starting from point *j*, Bob could reallocate his budget and buy more burgers and fewer tacos. As he moves down his budget line, he moves to progressively higher indifference curves, ultimately reaching point *e* and indifference curve C2.
- Point *k*. Although point *k* generates a highest utility level (it's on a higher indifference curve), it lies outside Bob's budget set, so he cannot afford it.

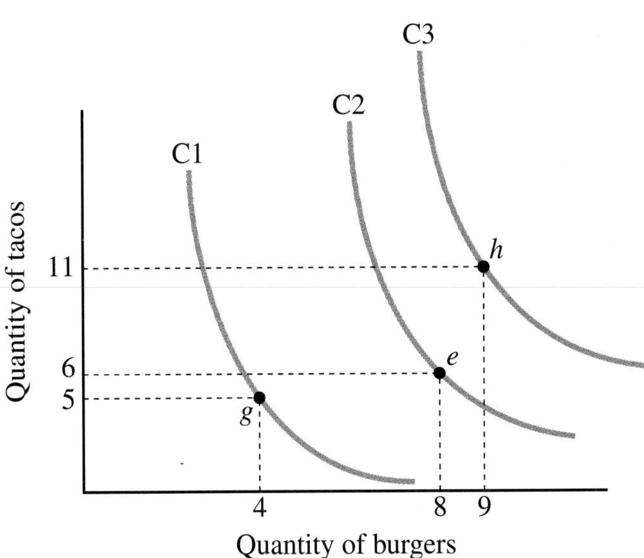

Figure A-3
Indifference Map

An indifference map shows a set of indifference curves, with utility increasing as we move northeasterly to higher indifference curves.

Figure A-4

Consumer Maximizes Utility at Tangency of Indifference Curve and Budget Line

To maximize utility, the consumer finds the combination of hamburgers and tacos which an indifference curve is tangent to the budget line, meaning that the marginal rate of substitution equals the price ratio.

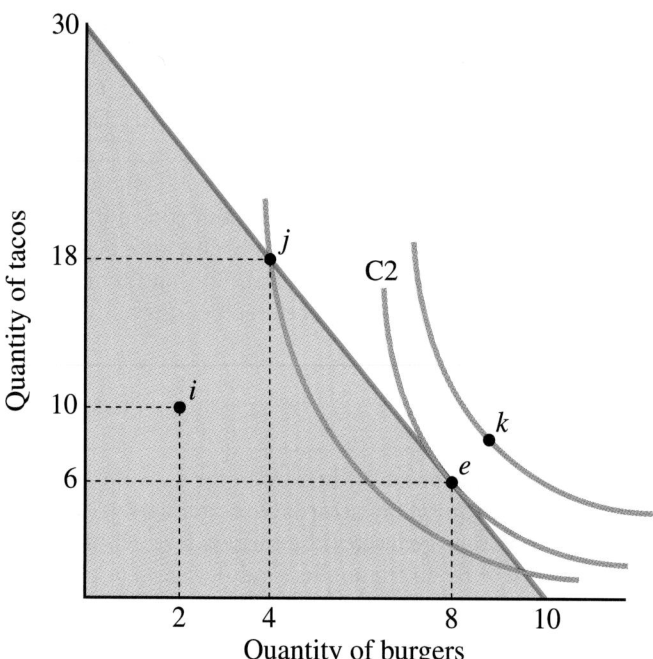

At point *e*, Bob reaches the highest indifference curve possible, given his budget set. The indifference curve touches—but does not pass through—the budget line: The indifference curve is tangent to the budget line. If an indifference curve cuts through the budget line at some point (e.g., at point *j*), the consumer could increase his utility by reallocating his budget between the two goods. A tangency occurs at the combination that generates the highest possible utility.

What is the economic interpretation of the tangency condition? The slope of the indifference curve (the MRS) equals the slope of the budget line (the price ratio). Therefore, the consumer's subjective trade-off between the two goods (the MRS) equals the market trade-off (the price ratio). At any other combination, the MRS would not be equal to the price ratio, so the consumer could reallocate his budget and increase his utility. For example, starting at point *j*, Bob's MRS (the slope of the indifference curve) is 7.0: He is willing to give up 7 tacos to get 1 burger. Given the prices of the two goods, the price ratio is 3.0, so Bob must give up only 3 tacos to get 1 burger. Therefore, he will increase his utility by purchasing more burgers and fewer tacos. He will continue to reallocate his budget until the MRS equals the price ratio (until the slope of the indifference curve equals the slope of the budget line). This occurs at point *e*, where MRS = 3.

THE TANGENCY CONDITION AND THE MARGINAL PRINCIPLE

The tangency condition is consistent with the marginal principle. In Chapter 7 we saw that the marginal principle is satisfied when the marginal benefit of burgers equals the marginal cost. The marginal benefit equals the marginal utility of burgers. The marginal cost is the opportunity cost of burgers, which equals the number of tacos sacrificed per burger times the marginal utility of tacos. We can use the following equation to represent this application of the marginal principle:

marginal utility of burgers = (number of tacos per burger) × (marginal utility of tacos)

The number of tacos sacrificed per burger is the market trade-off or the slope of the budget line (the price of burgers divided by the price of tacos), so we can rewrite the equation as follows:

$$\text{marginal utility of burgers} = \frac{\text{price of burgers}}{\text{price of tacos}} \times \text{marginal utility of tacos}$$

If we divide each side by the marginal utility of tacos, we get the following expression:

$$\frac{\text{marginal utility of burgers}}{\text{marginal utility of tacos}} = \frac{\text{price of burgers}}{\text{price of tacos}}$$

The ratio on the left is the marginal rate of substitution—the consumer's subjective trade-off between the two goods. For example, if an additional burger generates three times as much additional utility as an additional taco, the ratio on the left will be 3.0: The consumer will be willing to substitute 3 tacos for 1 burger (the MRS is 3.0). Therefore, we can rewrite the equation for the marginal principle as follows:

$$\text{MRS} = \frac{\text{price of burgers}}{\text{price of tacos}}$$

At the utility-maximizing combination of burgers and tacos, the slope of the indifference curve equals the slope of the budget line.

DRAWING THE DEMAND CURVE

We can use the consumer choice model to draw Bob's demand curve for burgers. We've already derived one point on his demand curve: In Figure A-4, when the price of burgers is \$3, he consumes 8 burgers. To find another point on the demand curve, we change the price of burgers and find the new utility-maximizing combination of burgers and tacos.

Figure A-5 on page 148 shows what happens to the budget line when the price of burgers decreases to \$2. The decrease in price tilts the budget line outward. The original vertical intercept (point *y*) is still in the budget set: If Bob spends his entire budget on tacos, he would be unaffected by the decrease in the price of burgers. The horizontal intercept moves outward from *x* (10 burgers) to *z* (15 burgers) because a given budget will buy more burgers. If Bob buys burgers and tacos (he chooses some point between the horizontal and vertical intercepts), he can afford more combinations of the two goods because he spends less money per burger.

How will Bob respond to the lower price of burgers? Given the new budget line and the same set of indifference curves, Bob picks point *n*, where one of his indifference curves is tangent to the new budget line. In other words, he responds to the decrease in price by consuming 11 burgers instead of 8.

In Figure A-6 on page 148, we can draw a second point on the demand curve: When the price is \$2, Bob consumes 11 burgers. We can find other points on the demand curve by repeating this process for other prices: Draw the new budget line and find the point at which an indifference curve is tangent to the new budget line. When we do this we'll find that the demand curve is negatively sloped, consistent with the law of demand: The lower the price, the larger the quantity demanded.

We've used the consumer choice model to find two points on the individual demand curve. For each price we found the quantity of burgers that generated the highest possible utility level, given the consumer's budget and the price of the other good (tacos). We have drawn a true demand curve because we changed the price of burgers but did not change the consumer's income or the prices of other goods.

Figure A-5

Consumer's Response to a Decrease in Price

A decrease in the price of burgers tilts the budget line outward. The indifference curve is tangent to the budget line at a larger quantity of burgers (11 instead of 8). This is the law of demand: A decrease in price increases the quantity demanded.

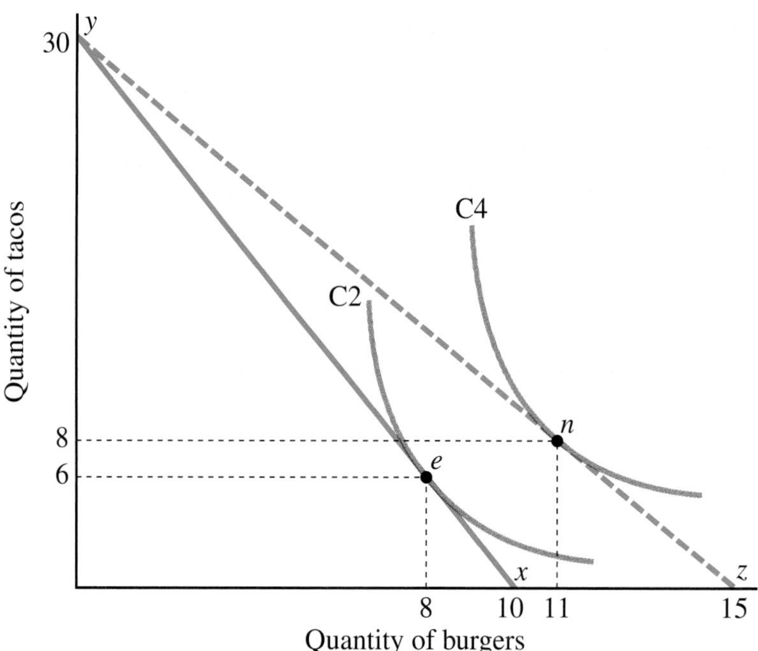

Figure A-6

Individual Demand Curve

At a price of $3, Bob maximizes his utility with 8 burgers (point *e* in Figure A-5 and point *b* in Figure A-6); at a price of $2, Bob maximizes his utility with 11 burgers (point *n* in Figure A-5 and point *c* in Figure A-6).

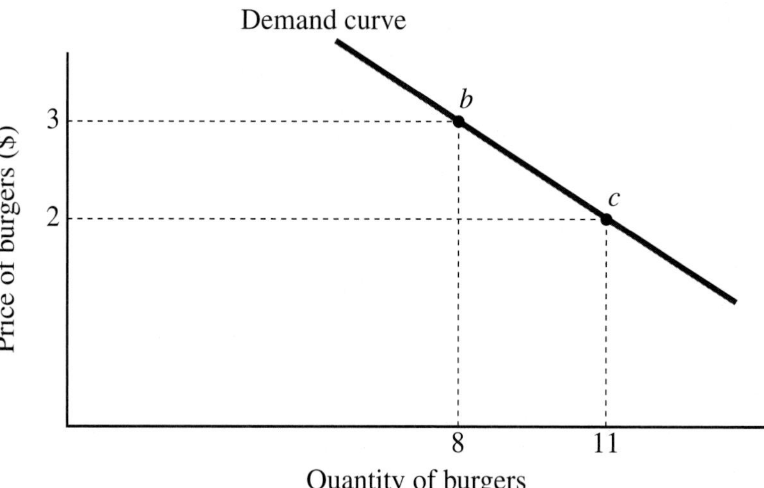

SUMMARY

We've used a model of consumer behavior to show how a consumer decides how much of a particular good to consume. The consumer's objective is to maximize his or her utility, given an income and the prices of consumer goods. Here are the main points of the appendix.

1. To maximize utility, the consumer finds the point at which an indifference curve is tangent to the budget line.
2. At the utility-maximizing combination of two goods, the marginal rate of substitution (the consumer's subjective trade-off between the two goods) equals the price ratio (the market trade-off).
3. The tangency condition (MRS = the price ratio) is consistent with the marginal principle.

KEY TERMS

budget line, *143*
budget set, *143*
indifference curve, *143*
marginal rate of substitution (MRS), *144*

PROBLEMS AND DISCUSSION QUESTIONS

1. Consider a person who spends a total of $200 on hats and violets. The price of hats is $20 and the price of violets is $5. Draw a budget line with hats on the horizontal axis and violets on the vertical axis.
   a. What is the slope of the budget line?
   b. Draw an indifference curve that intersects the budget line. Explain why the consumer can reach a higher utility level than the level shown by this indifference curve.
   c. Draw a second indifference curve showing the highest possible utility level.
   d. Complete the statement: To maximize utility, the consumer finds the combination of hats and violets such that ____________ equals 4.
2. Mistletoe Inc. spent $500 on food and drink for this year's party. At the end of the party, there were no leftovers. The price of food (per ounce) is three times the price of drink. Your task is to figure out whether the firm could have spent the $500 more wisely.
   a. If you could conduct an exit poll as the employees leave the party, what question (only one) would you ask them?
   b. Provide an answer to your question that would suggest the firm should have spent more on food and less on drink.
3. Carla has a fixed budget for a new car and has tentatively decided to buy a car with 80 horsepower (hp) and 100 cubic feet (cf) of interior space. Given the current selection of cars, the price of horsepower is one-third the price of cubic feet. After some prompting from the used-car salesperson, Carla said, "To get an additional unit of horsepower, I would be willing to sacrifice 2 cubic feet of interior space." Does her tentative choice (80 hp and 100 cf) maximize her utility subject to her auto budget? If not, should she choose an auto with more or fewer horsepower?

8

The Firm's Short-Run and Long-Run Cost Curves

Your small city is about to replace its 800-bed hospital with either another 800-bed hospital or two 400-bed hospitals. In a public hearing before the city council concerning the merits of the two options, an economic consultant made the following statement: "A big hospital is much more efficient than a small one, so it would be silly to build two 400-bed hospitals rather than a single 800-bed hospital. In fact, the cost per bed in an 800-bed hospital is about one-third of the cost per bed in a 400-bed hospital."

Before the city council decides whether to build one or two hospitals, it should take a careful look at the cost of providing hospital services with small and large hospitals. If a small hospital has a higher cost per bed, how much higher is it? Similarly, before a firm builds a production facility, it must determine the cost of producing its output in facilities of different sizes. If production costs are lower in a large factory, how much lower are they? Once a production facility is built, a firm must decide how much output to produce in the facility, and this decision is based in part on the cost of producing different quantities of output.

This chapter is about the cost of production and how it varies with the size of the production facility and the quantity of output produced in a given facility. We explain the shapes of the firm's cost curves and show the actual cost curves for several goods and services, including electricity generation, aluminum production, truck freight, and hospital services. We can use the hospital cost curve to check the accuracy of the consultant's claim about the costs of large and small hospitals. We'll see how to use cost curves to answer the following practical questions:

1. If the government breaks up a large aluminum producer into two smaller firms, by how much will the average cost of producing aluminum increase?
2. Are large trucking firms more efficient than smaller ones? If so, how much more efficient?
3. Why is the typical short-run average cost curve shaped like the letter U, while the typical long-run average cost curve is shaped like the letter L?
4. Suppose that one electric utility has three times as many customers as a second utility. Which firm has a higher unit cost of electricity, and how large is the cost difference?

DEFINITIONS

Before we can discuss the firm's cost curves, we must define some terms and concepts. We start with alternative definitions of costs and then discuss the difference between short run and long run.

Economic versus Accounting Profit

Our discussion of the firm's costs is based on the notion of economic cost. You may be surprised to hear that accountants and economists compute costs differently. As we see in Table 1, an accountant computes the firm's **explicit costs**, defined as the firm's actual cash payments for its inputs. For example, if the firm spends a total of $60,000 per year on labor, materials, rent, and machinery, its explicit costs would be $60,000, and this is the firm's total accounting cost.

Explicit costs: The firm's actual cash payments for its inputs.

The key principle underlying the computation of economic cost is opportunity cost.

PRINCIPLE *of Opportunity Cost*

The opportunity cost of something is what you sacrifice to get it.

To compute the firm's costs, the economist includes the firm's **implicit costs**, defined as the opportunity costs of nonpurchased inputs such as the entrepreneur's time or money.

Implicit costs: The opportunity costs of nonpurchased inputs.

1. ***Opportunity cost of the entrepreneur's time.*** A person who runs a firm has less time to pursue other activities, and we include the opportunity cost of the time spent running the firm. For example, if the entrepreneur could earn $30,000 per year in another job, the opportunity cost of his or her time is $30,000 per year.

Table 1: Accounting versus Economic Cost

	Accounting Approach	*Economic Approach*
Explicit cost (purchased inputs)	$60,000	$ 60,000
Implicit: opportunity cost of entrepreneur's time		30,000
Implicit: opportunity cost of funds		10,000
Total cost	$60,000	$100,000

2. *Opportunity cost of funds.* Many entrepreneurs use their own funds to set up and run their businesses, and we include the opportunity cost of these funds. For example, if an entrepreneur withdraws some money from his or her bank account and sacrifices $10,000 of interest income per year, the opportunity cost of the funds invested in the firm is $10,000 per year.

Economic cost: The sum of explicit and implicit costs.

In this case, the implicit cost is $40,000 per year, and the **economic cost**—defined as the sum of the explicit and implicit costs—is $100,000. The economic cost is higher because the economist includes implicit costs but the accountant does not. When we refer to the firm's production cost, we mean the economic cost of production, including both implicit and explicit costs.

Short-Run versus Long-Run Decisions

The firm's cost curves help the firm make two types of decisions. First, a firm that already has a production facility must decide how much output to produce in its facility. This is a short-run decision because one of the factors of production (the facility) is fixed. The second decision concerns what type of production facility to build in the first place. This is a long-run decision because none of the factors of production are fixed: The firm is starting from scratch and can choose any size or type of facility and any size of workforce.

In most cases the long run is the time required for a firm to build a production facility and start producing output. For example, if it takes a year to build a chair factory, the long run is one year, and the short run is any time less than a year. The long run varies across industries. If it takes one day to get a hot-dog cart and start selling hot dogs, the long run is a day. In contrast, it takes several years to design and build a computer chip factory, so the long run in that industry is several years.

SHORT-RUN COST CURVES

Let's start with the firm's short-run cost curves. The short run is a period of time over which at least one input to the production process is fixed. For most firms, the fixed input is capital, meaning that the firm cannot modify its production facility (a factory, farm, office, or store) or build a new facility. To increase its output in the short run, the firm must instead add more labor and materials to its existing facility. As we'll see in Chapter 9, the firm can use its short-run cost curves to decide how much output to produce in an existing facility.

We can explain the firm's short-run cost curves with an example of a hypothetical computer-chip manufacturer. Suppose that the firm spent $1 billion on a computer-chip factory. The firm has two types of costs.

1. *Fixed costs.* The cost of the production facility is fixed in the sense that it does not depend on how much output the firm produces. We're not interested in the total output of the facility over its 10-year life, but in its output per unit of time: for example, the output per hour, per day, or per year. If we're looking at the output per hour, we must translate the one-time $1 billion expense into the hourly cost of the production facility, for example, $7,200 per hour.

2. *Variable costs.* The costs of labor and materials depend on how many chips the firm produces: The larger the quantity of chips, the more workers and materials the firm needs.

The short-run total cost is the sum of the fixed and variable costs.

Diminishing Returns and Marginal Cost

The key principle behind the firm's short-run cost curves is the principle of diminishing returns.

PRINCIPLE *of Diminishing Returns*

Suppose that output is produced with two or more inputs and we increase one input while holding the other inputs fixed. Beyond some point—called the point of diminishing returns—output will increase at a decreasing rate.

As we saw earlier in the book, a firm experiences diminishing returns because its workers share a fixed production facility. When the firm adds a worker, each worker becomes less productive because he or she works with a smaller piece of the production facility: There are more workers to share the machinery, equipment, and factory space. Here are some examples of diminishing returns from Chapter 2.

1. *Pizza production.* Workers share a pizza oven. As the number of workers increases, pizza output increases at a decreasing rate because workers spend more and more time waiting to pop their assembled pizzas into the oven.
2. *Foldit experiment.* Workers share a stapler. Adding workers increases output at a decreasing rate because the workers spend more time waiting for the stapler.

In our chip factory example, as the firm packs more and more workers into the factory, total output increases, but at a decreasing rate. Flipping this statement around, as the firm steadily increases its output—from 100 chips to 101 chips to 102 chips—the firm requires more and more workers to increase its output by a single chip.

We can use the hypothetical data in Table 2 to show the effects of diminishing returns on the firm's short-run costs. Consider the first two columns in the table. If the firm starts with a small quantity of chips (100), the production of one more chip (the 101st chip) would require 2 additional hours of labor. If the firm starts with a medium quantity (300), the production of one more chip (the 301st chip) would require 6 additional hours of labor. Because workers share the production facility and experience diminishing returns, workers in a 300-chip factory are less productive than workers in a 100-chip factory, so it takes more additional labor to produce the 301st chip than it does to produce the 101st chip. It takes even more additional labor to produce the 401st chip. In general, the more chips the firm produces, the larger the amount of labor required to produce one additional chip.

The last three columns of Table 2 show the connection between diminishing returns and the firm's marginal cost. The **short-run marginal cost** is the change in total cost resulting from a 1-unit increase in the output of an existing production facility. In our example, the marginal cost of production is the amount of money the

Short-run marginal cost (SMC): The change in total cost resulting from a 1-unit increase in output from an existing production facility.

Table 2: Diminishing Returns and Increasing Marginal Cost

Quantity of Chips	*Additional Labor Hours*	*Additional Labor Cost*	*Additional Material Cost*	*Marginal Cost*
Small: 100	2	$16	$10	$26
Medium: 300	6	48	10	58
Large: 400	10	80	10	90

firm must spend to get enough additional labor and materials to produce one more chip. If the firm starts with a small quantity of chips (100) and wants to produce one more chip, it must spend $16 for additional labor (2 hours of labor times an hourly wage of $8). The firm also needs $10 worth of additional materials, so the marginal cost of the 101st chip is $26.

The marginal cost of production increases as we move to progressively larger output levels. If the firm starts with a medium quantity (300), it takes $48 worth of labor—along with $10 worth of materials—to produce one more chip. Because it takes more labor to produce the 301st chip than it does to produce the 101st chip, the marginal cost of the 301st chip ($58) is higher than the marginal cost of the 101st chip ($16). For the same reason, the marginal cost of the 401st chip is even higher. Figure 1 shows the marginal-cost curve associated with the numbers in Table 1. The marginal cost increases as the quantity produced increases, reflecting diminishing returns.

The U-Shaped Average Total Cost Curve

Short-run average total cost (SATC): Short-run total cost divided by the quantity of output.

Now that you understand the shape of the marginal cost curve, let's think about the average cost of production. The **short-run average total cost (SATC)** equals the total cost divided by the quantity of output, or the cost per unit of output.

Table 3 shows how to compute the short-run average total cost for the computer-chip firm. *Total cost* is the sum of fixed costs, labor costs, and material

Figure 1

Short-Run Marginal and Average Cost Curves

The short-run marginal cost curve is positively sloped because of diminishing returns. The short-run average total cost curve is U-shaped, a result of two conflicting forces. An increase in output decreases the fixed cost per chip, pulling down average cost. In constrast, diminishing returns increase labor cost per chip, pulling up the average cost.

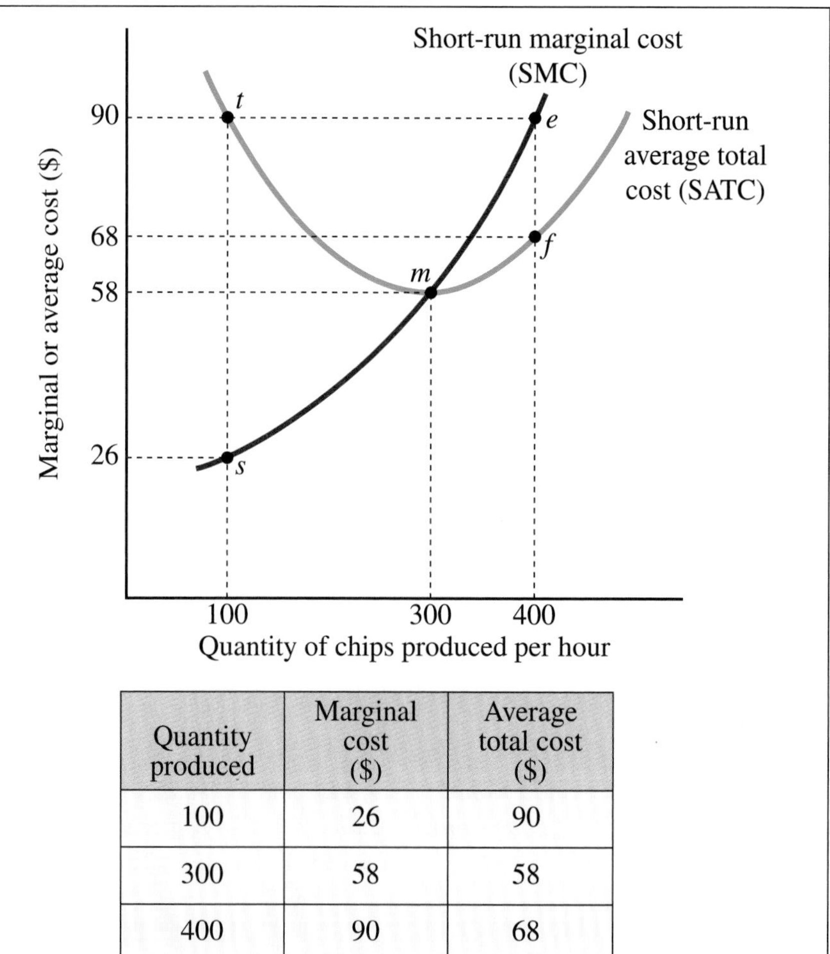

Quantity produced	Marginal cost ($)	Average total cost ($)
100	26	90
300	58	58
400	90	68

Table 3: Short-Run Average Total Cost

Quantity of Chips	Fixed Cost per Chip	Labor Hours	Labor Cost	Labor Cost per Chip	Material Cost per Chip	Average Total Cost
Small: 100	$72	100	$ 800	$ 8	$10	$90
Medium: 300	24	900	7,200	24	10	58
Large: 400	18	2,000	16,000	40	10	68

costs, so the average total cost is the sum of the fixed cost per chip, the labor cost per chip, and the material cost per chip.

1. ***Fixed cost per chip.*** The fixed cost is $7,200 (the cost of the production facility on an hourly basis). The fixed cost *per chip* depends on how many chips the firm produces. In the second column of Table 3, the fixed cost per chip is $72 for a small quantity ($7,200 divided by 100 chips). As the number of chips increases, this fixed cost is spread over more chips, so the fixed cost per chip decreases to $24 for the medium quantity and $18 for the large quantity.

2. ***Labor cost per chip.*** The third column in Table 3 shows the amount of labor required to produce different quantities of chips. For example, a small quantity (100 chips) requires only 100 hours of labor. The medium quantity, with three times as many chips, requires nine times as much labor (900 hours). This is the principle of diminishing returns in action: As the firm packs more and more workers into its factory, workers become less productive, so it takes a relatively large number of workers to triple the firm's output. For the small quantity, the total labor cost is $800 (the $8 wage times 100 hours), and the labor cost per chip is $8 ($800 divided by 100 chips). Because of diminishing returns, the labor cost per chip increases as chip production increases: The labor cost per chip is $24 for the medium quantity and $40 for the large quantity.

3. ***Material cost per chip.*** Suppose that each chip requires the same amount of material. In the sixth column in Table 3, the material cost per chip is constant at $10 per chip.

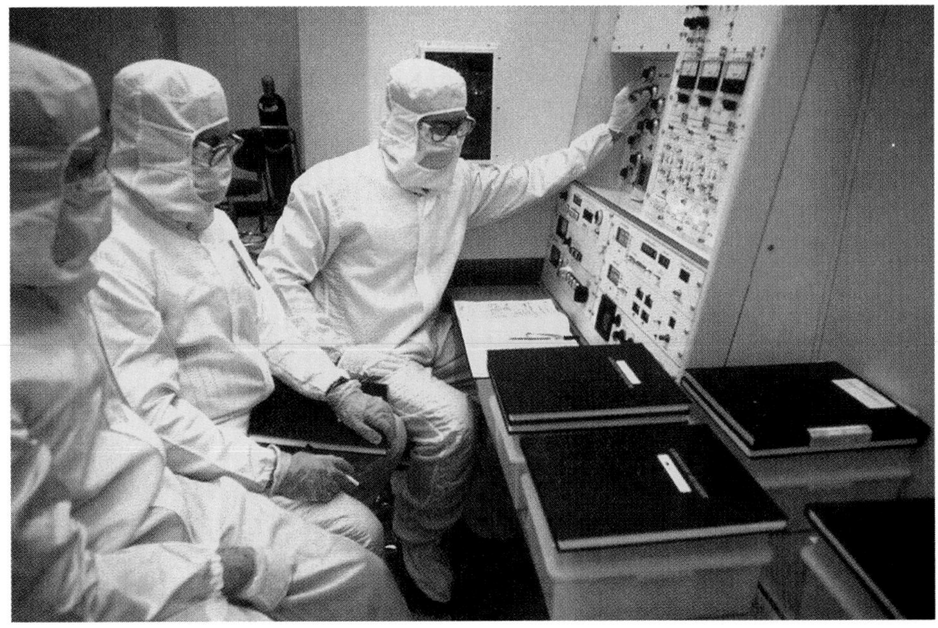

Like most production facilities, a computer chip factory has a U-shaped short-run average total cost curve.

To compute the short-run average total cost, we just add the three components of average cost: the fixed cost per chip, the labor cost per chip, and the material cost per chip. In the last column of Table 3, the average total cost of producing 100 chips is \$90 (\$72 + \$8 + \$10). The cost per chip is \$58 for the medium quantity and \$68 for the large quantity. Figure 1 shows the SATC curve for the computer-chip firm. The SATC curve is shaped like the letter U: As the quantity of chips increases, the average cost first decreases, but eventually it increases.

Why is the SATC curve U-shaped? When a firm increases its output, there is good news and bad news.

1. ***Good news.*** Fixed costs are spread out. The fixed cost of the firm's production facility (\$7,200 in our example) is spread over more chips, from \$72 per chip for the small quantity, to \$24 per chip for the medium quantity, to \$18 per chip for the large quantity. The decrease in the fixed cost per chip pulls down the average cost of producing chips.
2. ***Bad news.*** Productivity decreases because of diminishing returns. When the firm adds workers to increase output, each worker becomes less productive because he or she works with a smaller piece of the production facility. Therefore, the labor cost per chip increases, from \$8 per chip for the small quantity, to \$24 per chip for the medium quantity, to \$40 per chip for the large quantity. The increase in the labor cost per chip pulls up the average cost of producing chips.

Now that we know the good news and bad news associated with increasing output, we're ready to explain why the average cost curve is U-shaped. Let's look at the trade-offs associated with increasing output for two cases.

1. ***Switch from a small quantity to a medium quantity.*** The good news dominates the bad news. The good news is that the fixed cost per chip decreases from \$72 to \$24. The bad news is that labor cost per chip increases from \$8 to \$24. The net effect is that the average cost decreases from \$90 to \$58. A firm that starts with a small quantity will have a lower average cost because there are large benefits from spreading its fixed costs, and diminishing returns are moderate in an uncrowded production facility.
2. ***Switch from a medium quantity to a large quantity.*** The bad news dominates the good news. The good news is that the fixed cost per chip decreases from \$24 to \$18. The bad news is that labor cost per chip increases from \$24 to \$40. The net effect is that the average cost increases from \$58 to \$68. A firm that starts with a medium quantity will have a higher average cost because there are small benefits from spreading its fixed costs, and diminishing returns are severe in a crowded production facility.

The Relationship between Marginal and Average Total Cost

As we've seen, one feature of the SATC curve is that it is U-shaped. A second feature is that the marginal cost curve intersects the SATC curve at the minimum point of the average curve. We can use some simple logic to explain why this happens. Suppose that you start the term with a cumulative GPA of 3.0 (a B average) and enroll in a history course this term (your only course). If you receive a grade of C (2.0 for computing your GPA), your GPA will drop below 3.0. Your GPA decreases because the grade in the "marginal" course (the history course) is less than the "average" grade (the starting GPA). Suppose that you take an economics class the following term and get an A (4.0 for computing your GPA). In this case your GPA will increase because the marginal grade (in economics) is higher than your average (your GPA). An increase in the average (your GPA) means that the marginal grade is greater than the average grade.

In Figure 1 (page 154) the SATC curve is negatively sloped for the first 300 chips. Using the arithmetic of averages, the fact that the average cost is decreasing means that the marginal cost is less than the average cost. In contrast, the SATC curve is positively sloped for more than 300 chips, which means that the marginal cost exceeds the average cost. If the average cost is neither increasing nor decreasing, the marginal cost must equal the average cost. In Figure 1 the SATC curve reaches its minimum point at a quantity of 300 chips (point *m*), so the average cost is neither increasing nor decreasing. As a result, the marginal cost equals the average cost at the minimum point of the SATC curve.

The Average Variable Cost Curve

We can get a different perspective on the U-shaped average total cost curve by looking at two other average cost curves. Recall that total cost is the sum of **fixed costs** (the cost of the production facility) and **variable costs** (the costs of labor and materials). Therefore, average total cost is the sum of two averages:

short-run average total cost = average fixed cost + short-run average variable cost

The **average fixed cost (AFC)** equals the fixed cost divided by the quantity produced. The **short-run average variable cost (SAVC)** equals the total variable cost divided by the quantity produced. Using the acronyms for the cost curves, we can rewrite the expression for SATC as

$$SATC = AFC + SAVC$$

Fixed cost: Costs that do not depend on the quantity produced.

Variable costs: Costs that vary as the firm changes its output.

Average fixed cost (AFC): Fixed cost divided by the quantity produced.

Short-run average variable cost (SAVC): Variable cost divided by the quantity produced.

Figure 2 on page 158 shows the three average-cost curves and the numbers that go with the curves. We've already seen the SATC curve. The AFC curve is the negatively sloped curve with points *u, p,* and *h*. By definition, the firm's fixed cost doesn't depend on the quantity produced, so the average fixed cost decreases as the quantity increases: As output increases, the firm spreads out its fixed costs over more units. The fixed cost of the chip manufacturer is $7,200, so the average fixed cost decreases from $72 for 100 chips, to $24 for 300 chips, and so on. In our chip example, total variable cost equals the cost of labor and materials, so the SAVC curve shows the sum of labor cost per chip and material cost per chip. The SAVC is $18 for 100 chips (point *v*), $34 for 300 chips (point *n*), and $50 for 400 chips (point *g*).

What is the relationship between average variable cost and average total cost? The firm's total cost is the sum of its fixed cost and its variable cost, so the difference between average total cost and average variable cost is average fixed cost. As output increases, the average fixed cost decreases, so the gap between the average total cost and average variable cost decreases. In Figure 2 the fixed cost is $7,200, so the average fixed cost decreases from $72 for 100 chips to $24 for 300 chips. Therefore, the gap between the SATC and the SAVC curves is $72 for 100 chips but only $24 for 300 chips. As output increases, the gap between the two curves narrows as fixed costs are spread over more and more units of output.

ECONOMIC DETECTIVE– *The Cost of Pencils*

Mr. Big wants to enter the pencil-making business. He gathered some information from two existing pencil manufacturers, Sharp Inc., and Pointy Inc. The two firms have identical factories, pay the same wage to their workers, and pay the same prices for materials. Although Sharp produces 1,000 pencils per minute and Pointy produces 2,000 per minute, they each have a short-run average total cost of 10 cents per pencil. After building a factory identical to the ones used by Sharp and Pointy, Mr. Big hired enough workers and bought enough materials to produce 2,500 pencils per minute. Based on the experience of Sharp and Pointy, he expected to produce

Figure 2

Short-Run Average Cost Curves

The gap between short-run average total cost (SATC) and short-run average variable cost (SAVC) is average fixed cost (AFC).

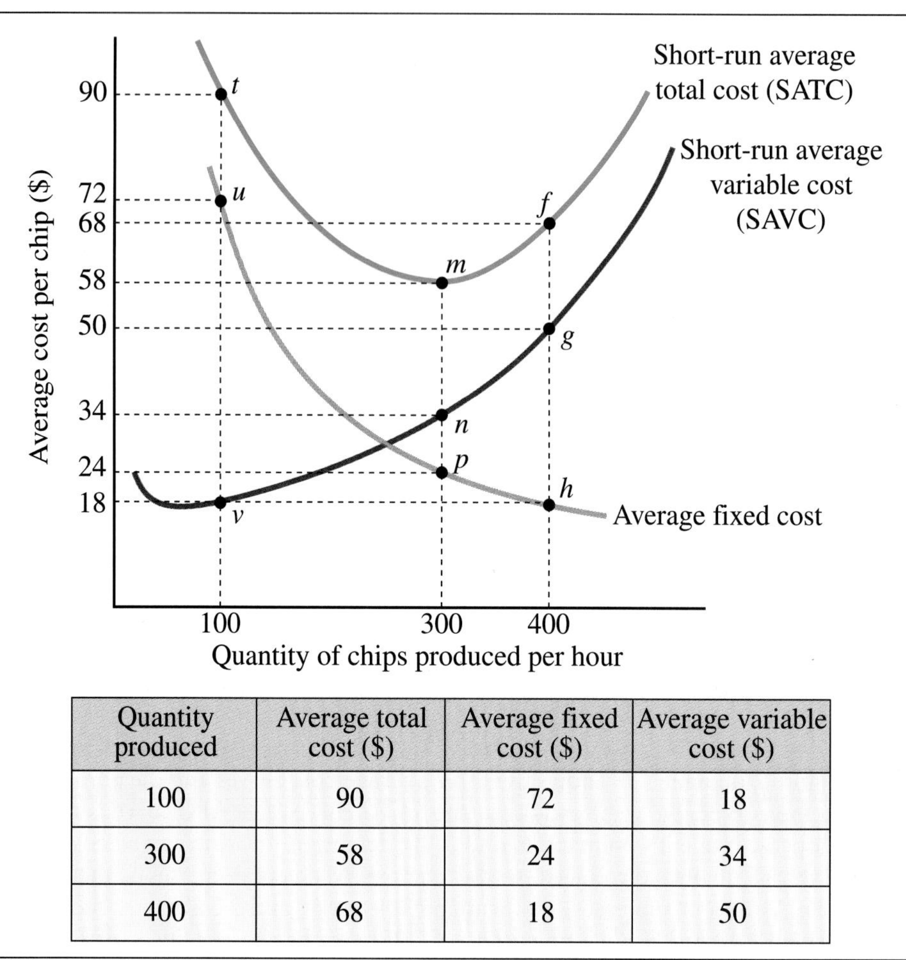

Quantity produced	Average total cost ($)	Average fixed cost ($)	Average variable cost ($)
100	90	72	18
300	58	24	34
400	68	18	50

at an average cost of 10 cents per pencil. After all, he thought, that's the average cost for 1,000 pencils and 2,000 pencils, so it should also be the average cost for 2,500 pencils. Much to his dismay, his average cost was 14 cents per pencil.

We can solve this mystery with a quick look at a typical short-run average total cost curve. In Figure 3 the U-shaped average cost curve shows the same average cost (10 cents) for Sharp (1,000 pencils) and Pointy (2,000 pencils). Sharp produces on the negatively sloped portion of the average cost curve, while Pointy produces on the positively sloped portion. In contrast, Mr. Big produces 2,500 pencils at an average cost of 14 cents. Mr. Big thought that because Sharp and Pointy had the same average cost, the average cost curve must be horizontal. In fact, the average cost curve is U-shaped. Along a U-shaped curve, it is possible to have the same average cost for two different quantities of output. Unfortunately for Mr. Big, it's not possible to have the same average cost for three different quantities.

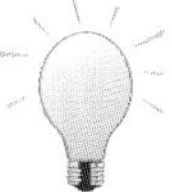

TEST *Your Understanding*

1 What key principle explains why the short-run marginal cost curve is positively sloped?

2 True or false, and explain: If the labor cost per table is $20 and the material cost per table is $30, the short-run average total cost is $50.

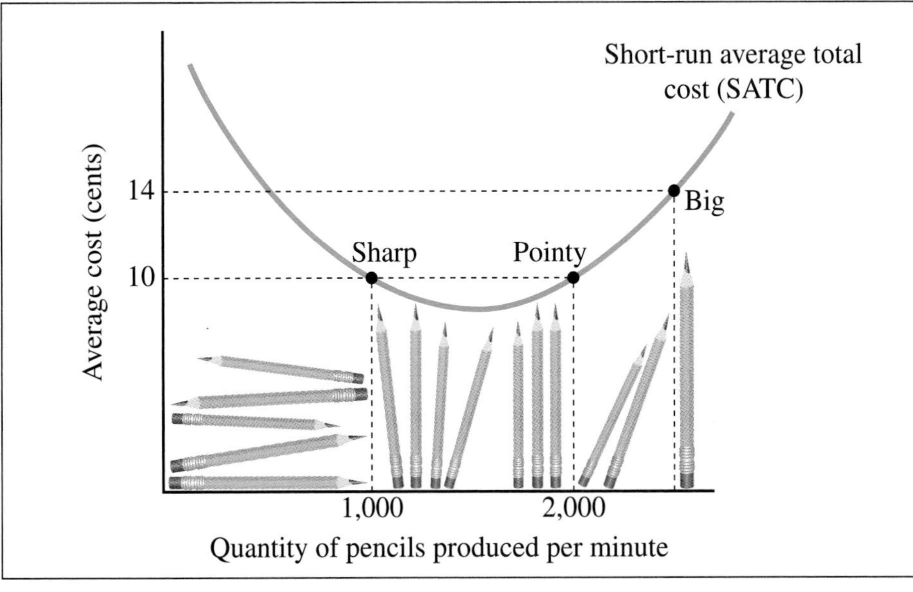

Figure 3
The Cost Mystery

The short-run average total cost curve is U-shaped, so it is possible to have the same average cost at two different quantities. Mr. Big produces at a higher average cost because Pointy is on the positively sloped portion of the curve and Mr. Big produces more output than Pointy.

3 Critically appraise the following statement: "We're planning on increasing the output of our rubber-chicken factory by 10%. It's obvious that our average cost will decrease because we'll spread out our fixed costs over more chickens."

4 According to the foreman in your chair factory, the marginal cost of chairs is less than the short-run average cost. If you increase your output of chairs, will your average cost increase or decrease?

5 Complete the statement with *average* or *marginal*: The marginal cost curve intersects the average cost curve at the minimum point of the ___________ cost curve.

LONG-RUN AVERAGE COST

Up to this point we've been exploring short-run cost curves, which show the cost of producing different quantities of output in a given production facility. Let's turn next to long-run curves, which show the cost of producing different quantities of output in facilities of different sizes. The long run is defined as a period of time over which a firm is perfectly flexible in its choice of inputs. In the long run a firm can build a new production facility (factory, store, office, or restaurant) or modify an existing facility, hire a workforce, and buy raw materials. The **long-run average cost (LAC)** of production is defined as total cost divided by the quantity of output when the firm can choose a production facility of any size.

Long-run average cost (LAC): Total cost divided by the quantity of output when the firm can choose a production facility of any size.

What does the typical long-run average cost curve look like? Figures 4 through 7 (pages 160–161) show the actual long-run average cost curves for several goods and services: electricity generation, aluminum production, truck freight, and hospital services. The figures are based on careful studies of the relevant industries. Each of the average cost curves is negatively sloped for small quantities of output and relatively flat (almost horizontal) over a large range of output. In addition, each curve has a slight positive slope for large quantities of output. In other words, these curves are L-shaped. Other studies suggest that the long-run cost curves of a wide variety of goods and services have the same shape.[1]

Economies of scale: A situation in which an increase in the quantity produced decreases the long-run average cost of production.

Why is the typical long-run average cost curve L-shaped? The initial range of decreasing average cost results from **economies of scale**. If an increase in output

Figure 4

LAC Curve for Electricity Generation

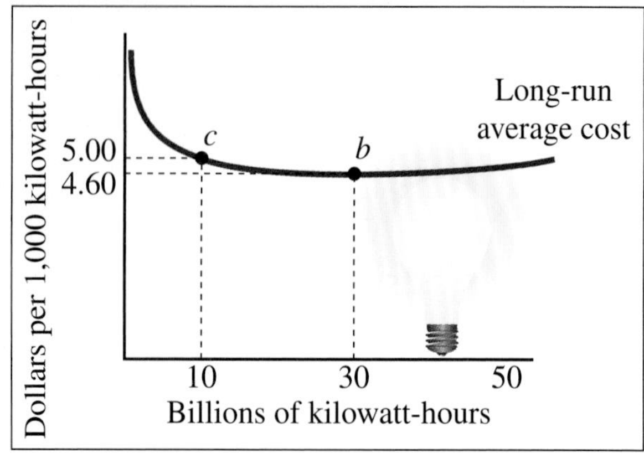

Source: Laurits Christensen and William H. Greene, "Economies of Scale in U.S. Electric Power Generation," *Journal of Political Economy,* vol. 84, 1976, pp. 655–676. Reprinted by permission of The University of Chicago Press.

decreases the average cost of production, there are some *economies* (cost savings) associated with *scaling up* the firm's operation (adding more capital, labor, and materials to produce more output). There are two reasons for economies of scale and decreasing average cost: spreading the cost of indivisible inputs and input specialization. Let's look at each of them, starting with indivisible inputs.

Economies of Scale from Indivisible Inputs

Indivisible input: An input that cannot be scaled down to produce a small quantity of output.

Consider first the benefits associated with spreading the cost of **indivisible inputs.** An input is indivisible if it cannot be scaled down to produce a small quantity of output. For example, a railroad company offering freight service between two cities must lay a set of tracks between them. The company cannot scale down the tracks

Figure 5

LAC Curve for Aluminum Production

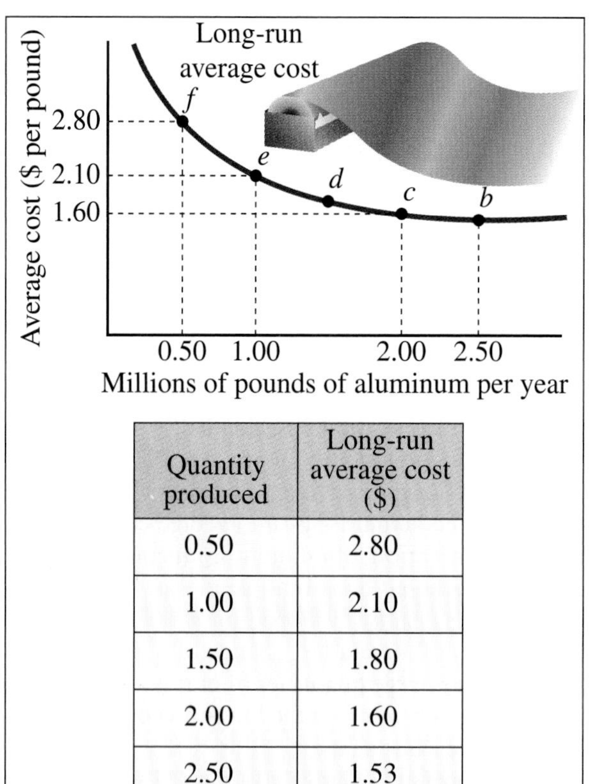

Quantity produced	Long-run average cost ($)
0.50	2.80
1.00	2.10
1.50	1.80
2.00	1.60
2.50	1.53

Source: Joel P. Clark and Merton C. Flemings, "Advanced Materials and the Economy," *Scientific American,* vol. 255, October 1986, pp. 51–60. Copyright © 1986 by Scientific American, Inc. All rights reserved.

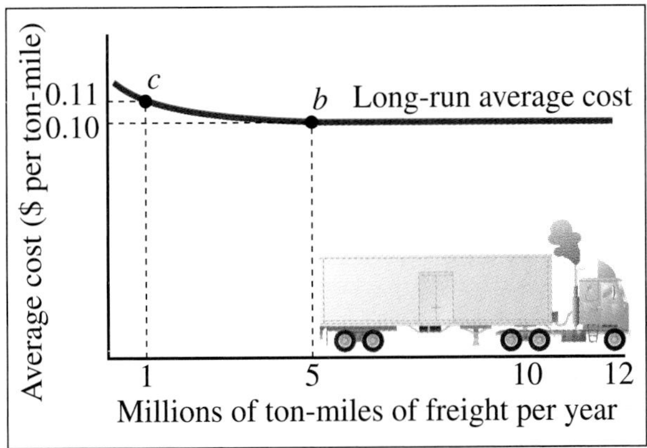

Figure 6

LAC Curve for Truck Freight

Source: Figure 2 of "Optimal Scale and the Size Distribution of American Trucking Firms," by Roger Koenker, *Journal of Transport Economics and Policy,* January 1977, p. 62.

by laying a half set of tracks (a single rail) because trains can't ride on a single track. As the railroad's output increases, the cost per unit of output decreases because the firm spreads out the cost of the track over more units of output. In other words, the long-run average cost curve is negatively sloped. For example, if the cost for one set of tracks is $5 million, the track cost per ton of freight is $5,000 if the firm produces 1,000 tons of freight service ($5 million divided by 1,000) but only $5 per ton if the firm produces 1 million tons.

Another example of an indivisible input is an industrial mold, which firms use to make multiple copies of the same item. A firm must make or buy a mold to produce the first unit of output, so the average cost of the first unit of output is very high. As the firm's output increases, the cost of the mold is spread over more and more units of output, so the average cost of production decreases. For an example of

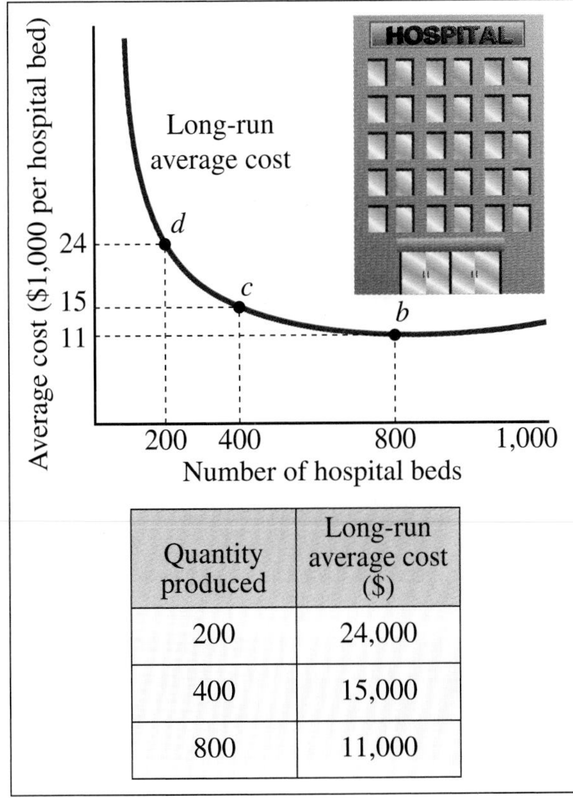

Quantity produced	Long-run average cost ($)
200	24,000
400	15,000
800	11,000

Figure 7

LAC Curve for Hospital Services

Source: Harold A. Cohen, "Hospital Cost Curves with Emphasis on Measuring Patient Care Output," in *Empirical Studies in Health Economics,* edited by Herbert E. Klarman (Baltimore: Johns Hopkins University Press, 1970).

how the use of molds affects production costs, see the Closer Look box "Indivisible Inputs and the Cost of Fake Killer Whales."

Most production processes have at least one indivisible input. Here are some other examples of firms and their indivisible inputs.

- A computer-chip factory uses *clean rooms* and sophisticated machines and testing equipment.
- A transatlantic shipper uses a large ship to carry TV sets from Japan to the United States.
- A cable-TV firm uses a cable running throughout its territory.
- A steel mill uses a large furnace.
- A freight hauler uses a freight truck.
- A software designer uses a personal computer.
- A pizzeria uses a pizza oven.

A Closer **LOOK**

Indivisible Inputs and the Cost of Fake Killer Whales

Sea lions off the Washington coast eat steelhead and other fish, depleting some species that are threatened with extinction and decreasing the harvest of the commercial fishing industry. Rick Funk, a plastics manufacturer, thinks that a variation on the old scarecrow routine would solve the sea lion problem. Killer whales love to eat sea lions, and Funk says that he could build a life-sized fiberglass killer whale, mount it on a rail like a roller coaster, and then send the whale diving through the water to scare off the sea lions. According to Funk, it would cost about $16,000 to make the first whale. Once the mold is made, however, each additional whale would cost an additional $5,000: It would cost a total of $21,000 for two whales, $26,000 for three whales, and so on.

This little story provides a nice illustration of the effects of indivisible inputs on the firm's cost curves. The cost of the first whale ($16,000) includes the cost of the mold (the indivisible input). Once the firm has the mold, the additional cost for each whale is only $5,000, so the average cost per whale decreases as the number of whales increases. The average cost curve is shown below left.

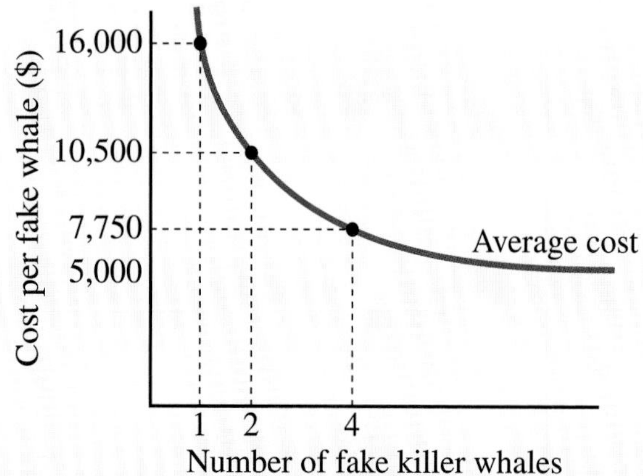

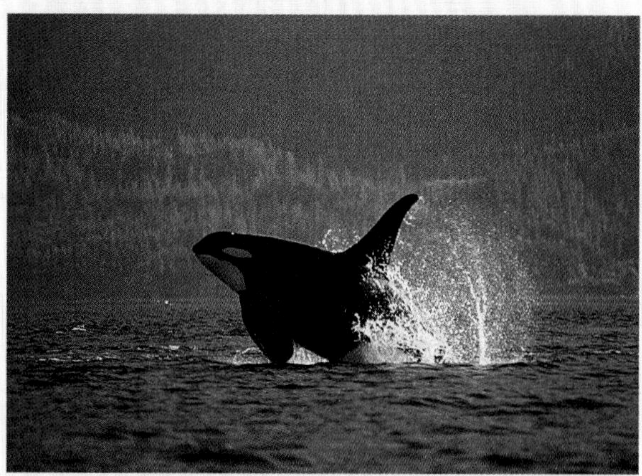

How much would it cost to make fake killer whales to scare away sea lions that feast on steelheads and other fish?

Source: After Sandi Doughton, "Killer Whale Latest Idea on Sea Lions," *The Oregonian*, January 7, 1995.

These inputs are indivisible in the sense that they cannot be scaled down to produce a smaller quantity of output. For example, it may be impractical to produce computer chips in a production facility costing less than $1 billion, just as it its impractical to transport a TV set across the ocean in a rowboat.

A firm that spends a large sum of money on its indivisible inputs will experience relatively large economies of scale. In other words, the average cost curve of such a firm will be negatively sloped—and relatively steep—over a large range of output. Some examples of goods and services with large economies of scale are computer chips, steel, automobiles, computer chips, and cable-TV service. In these cases, each firm must spend a large sum of money on indivisible capital inputs (machinery and equipment), so the average cost decreases rapidly as output increases. For example, if the cost of a computer-chip facility is $1 billion, the average cost decreases from $1 billion for the first chip to $500 million for the second chip, and so on.

A firm that spends a relatively small amount on its indivisible inputs will have relatively small scale economies. Some examples of goods and services with relatively small scale economies are truck-freight service, software design, and pizza. In these cases the typical firm doesn't spend much money on machinery and equipment, so the average cost curve isn't very steep.

Economies of Scale from Specialization

The second reason for economies of scale is input specialization. In a small operation with just a few workers, each worker performs a wide variety of production tasks. In a large operation with many workers, each worker specializes in one or two tasks and is more productive than his or her counterpart in the small operation for two reasons. First, repetition increases productivity: Each worker becomes more proficient in the one or two tasks that he or she performs. Second, workers spend less time switching from one task to another, so more time is spent working rather than switching between tasks. Higher productivity (more output per worker) means lower costs (lower labor cost per unit of output), so specialization decreases production costs. As the operation expands and the workers become more specialized and more productive, the average cost decreases.

Two centuries ago, Adam Smith used the making of pins to illustrate the benefits from specialization.[2]

> A workman . . . could scarce, perhaps with his utmost industry, make one pin a day, and certainly could not make twenty. But the way in which this business is now carried on . . . one man draws out the wire, another straightens it, a third cuts it, a fourth points it, a fifth grinds the top for receiving the head; to make the head requires two or three distinct operations. . . . The . . . making of a pin is, in this manner, divided into about eighteen distinct operations. . . . I have seen a small manufactory of this kind where ten men . . . make among them . . . upward of forty eight thousand pins in a day.

The idea of specialization is summarized in the old saying that a person who is a jack of all trades is a master of none. In a small operation, each worker is a jack of many tasks and is not very productive at any particular task. As the operation expands, each worker can concentrate on just a few tasks and become a master at those tasks. As productivity increases, the average cost of production decreases.

Minimum Efficient Scale

Minimum efficient scale: The output at which the long-run average cost curve becomes horizontal.

One way to quantify the extent of scale economies in the production of a particular good is to determine the **minimum efficient scale** for producing the good, defined as the output at which the long-run average cost curve becomes horizontal. If a firm starts out with an output below the minimum efficient scale, an increase in output will decrease its average cost. In contrast, a firm that increases its output beyond the minimum efficient scale will not experience lower average cost.

Economists have estimated the minimum efficient scale for various industries. In Great Britain, the minimum efficient scale is 1 million tons for sulfuric acid (about 30% of the British market), 9 million tons for steel (about 33% of the British market), 10 million tons for oil (10% of the British market), and 300,000 tons for ethylene (9% of the British market).[3] In the United States, the minimum efficient scale for automobiles is between 200,000 and 400,000 autos per year.[4] This means that a production facility serving between 3 and 6% of the U.S. market would be large enough to fully exploit the economies of scale in auto production. As shown in the Closer Look box "Bigger Breweries," the minimum efficient scale for beer is 4.5 million barrels per year.

Diseconomies of Scale

Diseconomies of scale: A situation in which an increase in the quantity produced increases the long-run average cost of production.

We've seen that as a firm scales up its operation, its long-run average cost may drop. Is it possible that the long-run average cost will rise instead? If a firm's average cost curve is positively sloped, we say that the firm experiences **diseconomies of scale**. In this case, an increase in output increases the average cost of production, so diseconomies (a higher average cost) accompany a scaling up of the firm's operation (adding more of all inputs). Diseconomies of scale may arise for two reasons.

1. *Coordination problems.* One of the problems of a large organization is that it requires several layers of management (a bureaucracy) to coordinate the activities of the different parts of the organization. If an increase in the firm's output requires additional layers of management, the average cost curve may be positively sloped.

2. *Increasing input costs.* When a firm increases its output, it will demand more of each of its inputs and may be forced to pay higher prices for some of these inputs. An increase in input prices will increase the average cost of production, generating a positively sloped average cost curve.

A Closer LOOK

Bigger Breweries

Why has the average size of breweries increased so dramatically in the last few decades? Between 1963 and 1992, the number of breweries with capacities exceeding 4 million barrels per year increased from 3 to 22, while the number of smaller breweries decreased from 176 to 28. Changes in brewing technology have increased the minimum efficient scale of breweries, allowing larger breweries to produce at a lower average cost than their smaller competitors. By 1992, the minimum efficient scale had grown to about 4.5 million barrels. One reason for economics of scale in brewing is the use of indivisible packaging machinery: Modern canning lines process 2,000 cans per minute, and it takes a huge brewery to utilize this equipment fully. Large plants also benefit from the automation of brewing and warehousing operations, leading to lower labor costs.

Source: After Kenneth G. Elzinga, "Beer," Chapter 5 in *The Structure of the American Economy,* 9th ed., edited by Walter Adams and James W. Brock (Upper Saddle River, NJ: Prentice Hall, 1995).

The cost curves shown in Figures 4 through 7 suggest that diseconomies of scale are relatively mild. Once we reach a large quantity of output, the average cost curves have a slight positive slope. The studies of other goods and services generate the same sort of L-shaped curves, suggesting that diseconomies of scale are not very severe, at least in the range output firms actually produce. This is sensible because if a firm experienced diseconomies of scale, it would decrease its output and decrease its average cost.

The experience of General Motors suggests there are diseconomies of scale in the production of automobiles, largely because of coordination problems.[5] General Motors, which is one-third bigger than Ford and larger than the two largest Japanese automakers combined (Toyota and Nissan), produces automobiles at an average cost that is between $200 and $2,000 higher than the average cost of Ford, Chrysler, and the Japanese. The Saturn project—an independent manufacturing operation with its own production facilities and its own input suppliers—is General Motor's response to these diseconomies of scale. By dividing its production into smaller pieces, General Motors hopes to avoid the high costs resulting from diseconomies of scale.

Firms recognize the possibility of diseconomies of scale and adopt various strategies to avoid them. For a description of the strategy used by 3M, read the Closer Look box, "Avoiding Diseconomies of Scale at 3M."

Application: Hospital Services

In the opening paragraph of the chapter, an economic consultant claims that the average cost per bed in a 800-bed hospital would be one-third the cost per bed in each 400-bed hospital. The long-run cost curve in Figure 7 suggests that the consultant has overstated the scale economies in hospital services. The average cost for the 800-bed hospital is $11,000 per bed (point *b*), compared to an average cost of $15,000 for each of the 400-bed hospitals (point *c*). In other words, the larger hospital is more efficient, but the difference in cost is not as large as suggested by the consultant.

Short-Run versus Long-Run Cost

Why is the firm's short-run average cost curve U-shaped, while the long-run average cost curve is L-shaped? Each curve is negatively sloped at small quantities of output because an increase in output allows the firm to spread out some type of costs (the costs of indivisible inputs in the long run and the cost of the production facility in the short run). For large quantities of output, the short-run curve is

A Closer LOOK

Avoiding Diseconomies of Scale at 3M

For an example of a firm that adjusts its operations to avoid diseconomies of scale, consider Minnesota Mining & Manufacturing, also known as 3M. According to Gordon Engdahl, the company's vice president for human resources, "We made a conscious effort to keep our units as small as possible because it keeps them flexible and vital. When one gets too large, we break it apart. We like to say that our success in recent years amounts to multiplication by division." On average, 3M's manufacturing plant has just 270 employees, and many of its management teams have just five people.

Source: Frederick C. Klein, "At 3M Plants, Workers Have Flexibility, Involvement—and Their Own Radios," *Wall Street Journal,* February 5, 1982, p. 1.

positively sloped because of diminishing returns and the resulting increases in the labor cost per unit of output. In the long run, the firm can scale up its operation by building a larger production facility, so the firm does not suffer from diminishing returns. If there are no diseconomies of scale, the long-run average cost curve will be negatively sloped or horizontal. If the firm experiences some diseconomies of scale, the long-run curve will eventually be positively sloped, but the short-run curve will be much steeper.

TEST *Your Understanding*

6 Draw a line connecting each item on the left with the appropriate item on the right.

• Diseconomies of scale	• Negatively sloped long-run average cost curve
• Economies of scale	• Positively sloped long-run average cost curve
• Indivisible inputs	
• Input specialization	
• Coordination problems	

7 When you mention that most firms have L-shaped long-run average cost curves, your new boss says: "Are you crazy? Haven't you heard of the principle of diminishing returns?" How should you respond?

8 As a kid, you recorded the costs of your lemonade stand and drew your long-run average cost curve. Now you work in a computer-chip factory. Would you expect any similarities between the lemonade cost curve and the cost curve for the chip factory? Would you expect any differences?

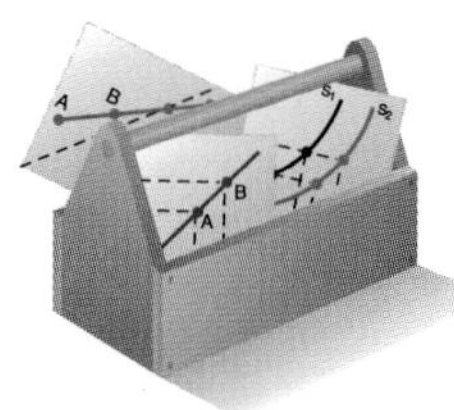

Using the TOOLS

You've learned all about the firm's short- and long-run cost curves. Here are some opportunities to use these tools to do your own economic analysis.

1. Production Consultant

You've just been hired by a hammer manufacturer to advise the firm on its production costs. In your first meeting with production managers, you hear the following statements. Are they true or false? Explain.

a. "If the production process is subject to diminishing returns, the long-run average cost curve will be positively sloped."

b. "At the current output level, this factory is subject to diminishing returns. Therefore, the firm is operating along the upward-sloping portion of its short-run marginal cost (SMC) curve."

c. "At the current output level, this factory is subject to diminishing returns. Therefore, the firm is operating along the upward-sloping portion of its short-run average cost (SATC) curve."

d. "The short-run average total cost of producing 250 hammers is less than the average cost of producing 260 hammers. Therefore, the marginal cost of 260 hammers is less than the average cost of 260 hammers."

2. Cost of Breaking Up an Aluminum Firm

Consider a large aluminum firm that initially produces 2 million pounds of aluminum per year. Suppose that an antitrust action breaks up the firm into two smaller firms, each of which produces half as much as the original firm. Use the information in Figure 5 (page 160) to predict the effects on the average cost of producing aluminum.

3. Deregulation and the Cost of Trucking

The public hearing on a proposal to deregulate a truck-freight market was packed. The market is currently served by a single regulated firm. If the market is deregulated, several new firms will enter the market. At the public hearing, the manager of the regulated firm issued a grim warning to the regulatory authorities. "If you deregulate this market, four or five firms will enter the market and the unit cost of truck freight will at least triple. There are big economies of scale in trucking services, so a single large firm is much more efficient than several small firms. If you want firms in your city to pay three times as much for their truck freight, go ahead and deregulate this market." Use the information in Figure 6 (page 161) to appraise this statement.

SUMMARY

In this chapter we looked at the cost side of a firm, explaining the shapes of the firm's short- and long-run cost curves. We use these curves later in the book to explore a firm's decisions about whether to enter a market, how much to produce, and whether to shut down an unprofitable operation. Here are the main points of the chapter.

1. The short-run marginal cost curve is positively sloped because of diminishing returns.
2. The short-run average total cost curve is U-shaped because of the conflicting effects of (a) fixed costs being spread over a larger quantity of output and (b) diminishing returns and increasing labor cost per unit of output.
3. The long-run average cost curve is L-shaped because of the benefits of spreading the cost of indivisible inputs and input specialization.
4. Diseconomies of scale arise if there are coordination problems or higher input costs in a larger organization.

KEY TERMS

average fixed cost (AFC), *157*
diseconomies of scale, *164*
economic cost, *152*
economies of scale, *159*
explicit costs, *151*
fixed cost, *157*
implicit costs, *151*
indivisible input, *160*
long-run average cost (LAC), *159*
minimum efficient scale, *163*
short-run average total cost (SATC), *154*
short-run average variable cost (SAVC), *157*
short-run marginal cost (SMC), *153*
variable costs, *157*

PROBLEMS AND DISCUSSION QUESTIONS

1. Suppose that the indivisible inputs used in the production of shirts have a cost per day of \$400. To produce 1 shirt per day, the firm must spend a total of \$5 on other inputs (labor, materials, and other capital), and the firm incurs the same additional cost for each additional shirt. Compute the

average cost for 40 shirts, 100 shirts, 200 shirts, and 400 shirts. Draw the long-run average cost curve for 40 to 400 shirts per day.

2. Consider a shirt producer that is stuck with its existing production facility. The wage is $4 per hour and each shirt requires $1 worth of materials. Complete the following table.

	For One More Shirt			
Quantity of Shirts	Additional Labor Hours	Additional Labor Cost	Additional Material Cost	Marginal Cost
50	2	_____	$1	_____
150	4	_____	1	_____
250	7	_____	1	_____

Is the production of shirts subject to diminishing returns and increasing marginal cost?

3. Consider a table producer that is stuck with its existing production facility. The wage is $10 per hour and each table requires $20 worth of materials. Complete the following table.

	Number of Tables		
	10	30	50
Fixed cost ($)	1,200	_____	_____
Fixed cost per table ($)	_____	_____	_____
Labor hours	25	225	625
Labor cost ($)	_____	_____	_____
Labor cost per table ($)	_____	_____	_____
Material cost per table ($)	_____	_____	_____
Average cost ($)	_____	_____	_____

4. Consider a firm that experiences constant marginal returns. For example, the first worker is just as productive as the second, who is just as productive as the third, and so on. The same is true for all the firm's inputs.
   a. Draw the firm's short-run marginal cost curve.
   b. Explain why this firm's cost curve differs from the conventional marginal cost curve.
5. Beaverduck Bus Company wants to compute the cost of adding a third daily bus between Eugene and Corvallis. Critically appraise the following statement of Abby Abacus, the company accountant: "If we add the third bus, our total cost would increase from $700 to $780. Therefore, the marginal cost of the third bus is $260 ($780 divided by 3)."
6. You want to know the marginal cost of producing a Chevrolet Caprice. Critically appraise the following quote from an analyst in the production department. "The marginal cost of a Caprice, given our current volume, is $12,500. Of course, the actual marginal cost depends on the number of cars produced: The larger the number produced, the lower the unit cost because we will spread out our design and tooling costs over more cars."
7. Explain the difference between diseconomies of scale and diminishing returns. Based on the cost curves we've seen in this chapter, which is more pervasive?
8. Suppose that one firm generates 30 billion kilowatt-hours of electricity, which is about three times the output of a second electricity firm. Which firm will have a higher cost per kilowatt-hour? Use the information in Figure 4 to predict the gap between the average costs of the two firms.

Take It to the Net

We invite you to visit the O'Sullivan/Sheffrin page on the Prentice Hall Web site at:

http://www.prenhall.com/osullivan/

for this chapter's World Wide Web exercise.

MODEL ANSWERS FOR THIS CHAPTER

Chapter-Opening Questions

1. As shown in Figure 5 (page 160), the average cost for the large firm is $1.60 per pound (point *c*), compared to an average cost of $2.10 for each of the small firms.
2. As shown by Figure 6 (page 161), although a larger trucking firm has lower average costs than a small one, the difference is relatively small, except for very small firms.
3. The short-run curve reflects diminishing returns,

which pulls up average cost as output increases. There are no diminishing returns in the long run.

4. In Figure 4 (page 160), the larger firm (30 billion kwh) has an average cost that is 8 percent lower than the smaller firm (10 billion kwh).

Test Your Understanding

1. It is the principle of diminishing returns.
2. False. To compute the average cost, we also need the fixed cost per table.
3. It's not obvious that average cost will decrease because diminishing returns pull up average cost as output increases. If the starting output is large enough, the bad news associated with increasing output (diminishing returns) will dominate the good news (spreading out the fixed costs), so average cost will increase.
4. If the marginal is less than the average, the marginal pulls down the average, so the average cost curve is negatively sloped. Therefore, average cost will decrease, at least for small increases in output.
5. average
6. Draw lines from "diseconomies of scale" and "coordination problems" to "positively sloped long-run average cost curve." Draw lines from "economies of scale," "indivisible inputs," and "input specialization" to "negatively sloped long-run average cost curve."
7. Diminishing returns occur when we increase output in an existing production facility. The principle of diminishing returns is applicable in the short run, not in the long run. To draw the long-run curve, we assume that we can change the size of the production facility.
8. There are some indivisible inputs for the lemonade stand (the pitcher, nondisposable cups, sign), just as there are for the chip factory (testing equipment, clean room). Therefore, both operations will have negatively sloped long-run average cost curves. Of course, the cost of these indivisible inputs is tiny for the lemonade stand and huge for the chip factory. Therefore, the average cost curve for the chip factory will be negatively sloped over a large range of output. If your lemonade stand was a one-person operation, you probably never experienced the benefits from input specialization. In contrast, input specialization will be important in the chip factory.

Using the Tools

1. Production Consultant
   a. False. The principle of diminishing returns is applicable to the short-run cost curves, not the long-run curves.
   b. True. Diminishing returns imply increasing marginal cost.
   c. False. Diminishing returns imply increasing marginal cost but do not imply increasing average cost. If the output is small enough, the spreading of fixed costs will generate a negatively sloped average-cost curve even if there are diminishing returns.
   d. False. The first sentence implies that the average-cost curve is positively sloped. This means that the marginal cost exceeds the average cost.
2. Cost of Breaking Up an Aluminum Firm

   In Figure 5 (page 160) the average cost for the large firm is \$1.60 per pound (point *c*), compared to an average cost of \$2.10 for each of the small firms.
3. Deregulation and the Cost of Trucking

   The cost curve for trucking service in Figure 6 (page 161) suggests that the manager has overstated the effects of deregulation on the average cost of trucking services. Suppose that the regulated firm provides 5 million ton-miles of trucking services per year at an average cost of \$0.10 (point *b*). The entry of five firms would decrease the output per firm to 1 million ton-miles per year, increasing the cost per ton-mile to \$0.11 (point *c*). In other words, deregulation would increase the average cost by only \$0.01 per ton-mile.

NOTES

1. John Johnson, *Statistical Cost Analysis* (New York: McGraw-Hill, 1960).
2. Adam Smith, *The Wealth of Nations* (New York: The Modern Library, 1937), pp. 4–5.
3. Aubrey Silberson, "Economies of Scale in Theory and Practice," *Economic Journal,* vol. 82, 1972, pp. 369–391.
4. Walter Adams and James W. Brock, "Automobiles," Chapter 4 in *The Structure of the American Economy,* 9th ed., edited by Walter Adams and James W. Brock (Upper Saddle River, NJ: Prentice Hall, 1995).
5. Adams and Brock, "Automobiles."

CHAPTER

9 Perfect Competition in the Short Run

The wheat farmer delivered the bad news to his workers:

> The price of wheat is very low this year, and the most I can get from the crop is $35,000. If I paid you the same amount as last year ($30,000), I'd lose money, because I also have to worry about the $20,000 I paid three months ago for seed and fertilizer. I'd be crazy to pay a total of $50,000 to harvest a crop I can sell for only $35,000. If you are willing to work for half as much as last year ($15,000), my total cost will be $35,000, so I'll break even. If you don't take a pay cut, I won't harvest the wheat.

As the farmworkers passed around the ballots for the vote on the pay cut, Shantelle did some quick calculations and then spoke up:

> The farmer is bluffing. He'll harvest the crop even if we don't take a pay cut, because his total revenue ($35,000) will exceed the variable cost ($30,000 for us). I vote against the pay cut.

Is Shantelle right? Is the farmer bluffing, or will the farmworkers lose their jobs if they reject the proposed pay cut?

In this chapter we look at the decisions made by firms in a **perfectly competitive market,** defined as a market with a very large number of firms, each of which produces the same standardized product and takes the market price as given. Another label for a perfectly competitive firm is *price-taking firm.* The classic example of a perfectly competitive firm is a wheat farmer, who produces a tiny fraction of the total supply of wheat. No matter how much wheat the farmer produces, the market price of wheat won't change.

Perfectly competitive market: A market with a very large number of firms, each of which produces the same standardized product and takes the market price as given.

For another example of a perfectly competitive market, think about the stocks traded on major exchanges like the New York Stock Exchange. As a result of the communications revolution, stock markets around the world are now linked together, leading to a global stock market with literally millions of potential buyers and sellers. A growing number of U.S. investors are buying and selling foreign stocks, and more and more foreigners are trading U.S. stocks. In such a market, each person is a tiny part of the market and takes stock prices as given. Of course, everyone *hopes* that prices will increase once he or she buys some stock.

In this chapter you'll learn how firms use data on revenues and costs to make production decisions. One decision is whether to shut down an unprofitable operation such as the wheat farmer's. We'll see that the farmer is indeed bluffing when he claims he'll shut down if the workers don't take a pay cut. Here are some other practical questions we answer:

1. What information do you need to decide how much output your firm will produce?
2. Suppose that the price of chairs is $36. At your current production level, the marginal cost of production is $24. Should you increase, decrease, or not change your production level?
3. On your first day on your new job, your boss tells you that the firm's objective is to maximize its profit margin (price minus average cost). You know that this is inappropriate, but how can you explain it to your boss?
4. According to your firm's accountant, you are losing money. Should you close your business or continue to operate at a loss?

FOUR TYPES OF MARKETS

This is the first of several chapters on decision-making by firms in different market settings. Table 1 on page 172 shows the characteristics of four types of markets. On the left is the extreme case of perfect competition, the topic for this chapter. The other markets differ from a perfectly competitive market in several respects, the most important of which is the number of firms in the market.

1. ***Monopolistic competition.*** There are many firms, each of which sells a differentiated product. Some examples are restaurants, retail stores, gas stations, and clothing. This contrasts with perfect competition, in which each firm sells a standardized product. Because the products sold by different firms in a monopolistically competitive market are not perfect substitutes, each firm has some control over its price: If a firm increased its price, not all of its consumers would switch to other firms. There are no barriers to entering the market, so there are many firms.

2. ***Oligopoly.*** There are just a few firms in the market, a result of two sorts of barriers to entry. First, if there are large economies of scale, a large firm can produce at a much lower cost than a small firm, and this limits the number of firms that can earn a profit. In a market with many small firms, each firm would produce at a high cost and

Table 1: Characteristics of Different Types of Markets

	Perfect Competition	*Monopolistic Competition*	*Oligopoly*	*Monopoly*
Number of firms	Very large number	Many	Few	One
Type of product	Standardized	Differentiated	Standardized or differentiated	Unique
Control over price	None	Slight	Considerable	Considerable if not regulated
Entry conditions	No barriers	No barriers	Large barriers from economies of scale or government policy	Large barriers from economies of scale or government policy
Examples	Wheat, soybeans	Restaurants, retail stores, clothing	Automobiles, air travel, breakfast cereal	Local phone and electricity service, patented drugs

would not be able to charge a price high enough to cover its costs. Second, the government may limit the number of firms in the market. Some examples are automobiles, airline travel, and breakfast cereals.

3. *Monopoly*. A single firm serves the entire market. A monopoly occurs when the barriers to entry are very strong, which could result from very large economies of scale or a government limit on the number of firms. Some examples of goods with large scale economies are local phone service and electric power generation. Some examples of monopolies established by government policy are drugs covered by patents and concessions in national parks.

We take a close look at these other types of markets later in the book.

If you're thinking that the model of perfect competition is not very realistic, you're correct. In contrast with the price-taking firm in a perfectly competitive market, most firms have some control over their prices. The typical firm can cut its price to sell more output or increase its price to sell less. Nonetheless, it is sensible to study perfect competition as a first step. The decision-making process of a price-taking firm is very simple and easy to understand because the firm doesn't have to worry about picking a price—it just decides how much to produce given the market price. Once we master this simple case, we can move on to the more complex decisions of firms in other types of markets.

THE OUTPUT DECISION

Total revenue: The money the firm gets by selling its product; equal to the price times the quantity sold.

Economic profit: Total revenue minus the total economic cost (the sum of explicit and implicit costs).

Before we explore the firm's output decision, let's define some terms and concepts. A firm's **total revenue** is the money the firm gets by selling its product and is equal to the price times the quantity sold. For example, the total revenue for a farmer who sells 100 bushels of corn at $2 per bushel is $200. We know from Chapter 8 that a firm's total economic cost is the sum of its explicit costs (the firm's actual cash payments for its inputs) and implicit costs (the opportunity costs of nonpurchased inputs such as the entrepreneur's time or money). A firm's **economic profit** equals total revenue minus total economic cost. For example, if our corn farmer has an economic cost of $180, his profit would be $20.

If you were a manager of a perfectly competitive firm, one of your key decisions would be how much output to produce. How would you choose your output level? One approach is to experiment, trying out different quantities of output and computing your economic profit from each quantity. You could continue to experiment until you found a quantity that generates a reasonable profit. Although you may eventually find a profitable quantity, it could take a long time to do so, and you couldn't be sure that you'd found the level of output that generates the highest possible profit. As we'll see in this chapter, you could be more systematic in your search for the best quantity of output.

The Marginal Principle and the Output Decision

The marginal principle provides a general rule for making decisions. A perfectly competitive firm can use the principle to decide how much output to produce.

Marginal PRINCIPLE

Increase the level of an activity if its marginal benefit exceeds its marginal cost, but reduce the level if the marginal cost exceeds the marginal benefit. If possible, pick the level at which the marginal benefit equals the marginal cost.

The firm's activity is producing output, so to use the principle, the firm must compute the marginal benefit and the marginal cost of producing output.

Let's look at the benefit side of the marginal principle first. The marginal benefit of a firm's activity is the extra revenue earned by selling one more unit of output. The firm's *marginal revenue* is defined as the change in total revenue that results from selling 1 more unit of output. A perfectly competitive firm can sell as much as it wants at the market price, so if the firm sells 1 more unit of output, its total revenue will increase by the market price. *For a perfectly competitive firm, marginal revenue equals the market price.* For example, if our corn farmer sells 101 bushels instead of just 100 bushels, total revenue will increase from $200 to $202. The marginal revenue associated with the 101st bushel ($2) is the same as the price.

We learned about the marginal cost of production in Chapter 8, so we're ready to apply the marginal principle to the output decision of a perfectly competitive firm. The marginal principle suggests that the firm should pick the quantity of output at which marginal revenue equals marginal cost:

$$\text{marginal revenue} = \text{marginal cost}$$

In other words, the firm should continue to increase its output as long as the extra revenue from 1 unit of output exceeds the extra cost. For a perfectly competitive (price-taking) firm, marginal revenue equals the market price, so the firm should pick the quantity of output at which the price equals the marginal cost:

$$\text{price} = \text{marginal cost}$$

Table 2 on page 174 has some hypothetical data for a chair manufacturer. The first column shows different output levels, and the two other columns show prices and marginal costs. The firm is a price taker, so the price is fixed at $36 per chair. In contrast, the marginal cost of production increases as output increases, reflecting diminishing returns. Reading down the table, we see that the marginal principle is satisfied with an output of 25 chairs: At this quantity, the price equals the marginal cost. In Figure 1 (also on page 174), the profit-maximizing choice is shown by point *e*, where the horizontal price line intersects the positively sloped marginal cost curve. In other words, the firm will maximize its profit by producing 25 chairs.

To see that an output of 25 chairs maximizes the firm's profit, let's think about what would happen if the firm picked some other quantity, for example, 20

Table 2: Picking the Profit-Maximizing Output Level

Output (chairs per hour)	*Marginal Revenue = Price*	*Marginal Cost*
14	$36	$12
17	36	18
20	36	24
25	36	36
27	36	43

chairs per hour. Could the firm do better? To determine whether the firm should produce one more chair (21 instead of 20), we must answer two questions.

1. What is the extra cost associated with producing the 21st chair? Point *b* tells us that the marginal cost of the 20th chair is $24, so the marginal cost of the 21st chair must be just over $24.
2. What is the extra benefit associated with producing the 21st chair? The price of chairs is fixed at $36, so the marginal benefit (marginal revenue) of the 21st chair is $36.

Because the extra revenue from the 21st chair (price = $36) exceeds the extra cost (marginal cost), the production and sale of the 21st chair increases the firm's total profit. Therefore, it is sensible to produce the 21st chair. The same logic applies, with different numbers for marginal cost, for the 22nd chair, the 23rd chair, and so on up to 25 chairs.

Figure 1

Short-Run Cost Curves and Profit-Maximizing Output

Using the marginal principle, the profit-maximizing output is the output at which price equals the marginal cost (point *e*): The firm produces 25 chairs per hour. Economic profit equals the gap between price and average cost ($10 = $36 – $26) times the quantity produced (25), or $250 per hour.

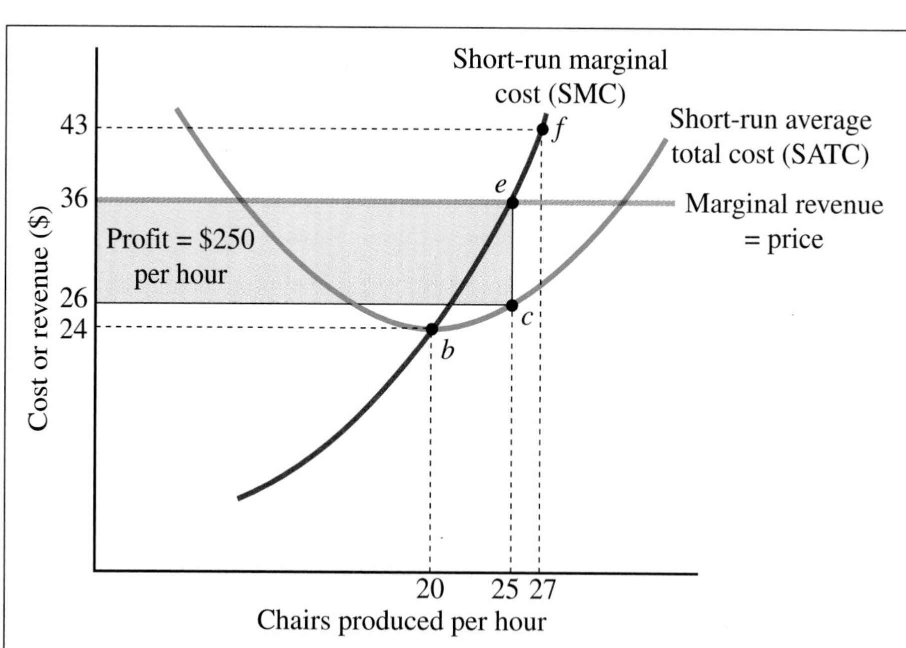

Quantity	Marginal revenue = price	Marginal cost	Average cost	Profit
25	$36	$36	$26	$250

The same logic applies for a tentative output choice exceeding 25 chairs per hour, for example, 27 chairs per hour. Would the firm be better off producing one less chair per hour (26 instead of 27)? From Table 2 and the marginal cost curve in Figure 1, we see that the extra cost from the 27th chair is $43 (point *f*), which exceeds the marginal revenue (price) of $36. Therefore, the 27th chair adds more to cost ($43) than it adds to revenue ($36), so it is clearly unprofitable to produce the chair. For the same reason, it is unprofitable to produce the 26th chair. The marginal principle suggests that the firm should pick point *e*, with an output of 25 chairs per hour.

Economic Profit and Accounting Profit

We've seen that the firm maximizes its profit by producing the quantity at which marginal revenue (price) equals marginal cost, but just how much profit does the firm earn? The firm's total economic profit equals its total revenue minus its total cost. The easiest way to compute a firm's total profit is to multiply the average profit (the gap between the price and the average cost) by the quantity produced:

$$\text{total profit} = (\text{price} - \text{average cost}) \times \text{quantity}$$

In Figure 1 the average cost of producing 25 chairs is $26 (point *c*), so the average profit is $10 per chair ($36 – $26) and the firm's total profit is $250 ($10 × 25):

$$\text{total profit} = (\$36 - \$26) \times 25 = \$10 \times 25 = \$250$$

In Figure 1 the firm's profit is shown by the area of the shaded rectangle: the height of the rectangle is the average profit ($10), and the width of the rectangle is the quantity produced (25 chairs).

When will the firm's economic profit be zero? The chair producer will earn zero economic profit if the market price equals the average cost of production. In Figure 2 this occurs if the price is $24: At this price, the firm satisfies the marginal principle (price = marginal cost) at point *b*, with 20 chairs. At this quantity, the price also equals *average* cost, so economic profit is zero. We know from Chapter 8 that the marginal cost equals the average cost at the minimum point of the average cost curve. Therefore, the firm will earn zero economic profit if the horizontal price line goes through the minimum point of the average cost curve. In other words, profit

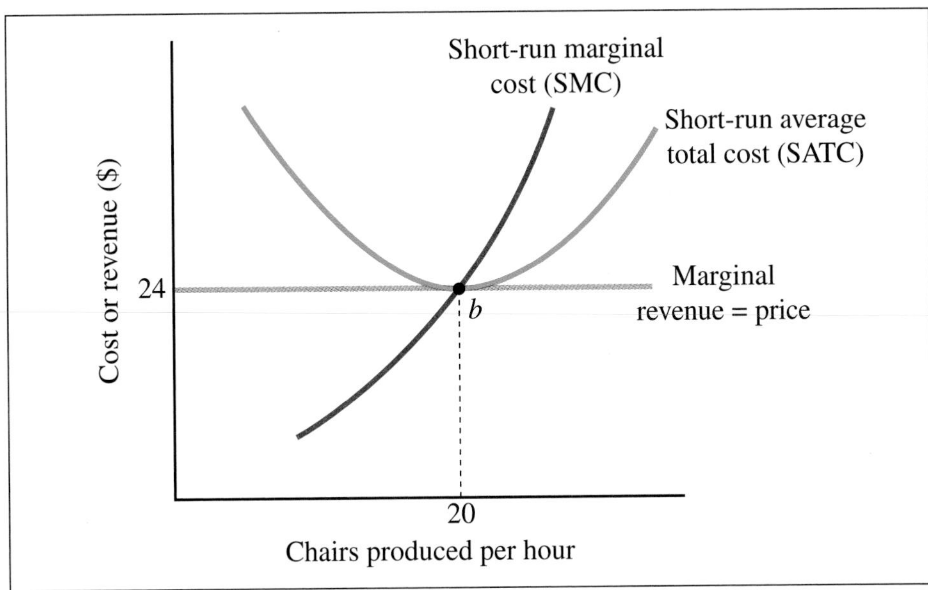

Figure 2

Economic Profit Is Zero at the Minimum Point of the SATC

Using the marginal principle, if the price is $24, the firm equates the price and marginal cost at point *b* and produces 20 chairs per hour. Since point *b* is the minimum point of the average cost curve, marginal cost equals average cost, so price equals average cost and economic profit is zero.

will be zero if price equals the minimum average cost. In this case, the best the firm can do is to earn zero economic profit.

Accounting profit: Total revenue minus explicit costs.

Normal accounting profit: An accounting profit equal to the firm's implicit costs.

When a firm earns zero economic profit, it earns a normal level of accounting profit. A firm's **accounting profit** is defined as its total revenue minus its explicit costs. The computation of accounting profit ignores the firm's implicit costs, so when economic profit is zero, accounting profit will be positive. When this happens, we say that the firm is earning a **normal accounting profit**. Its accounting profit is normal in the sense that it is just high enough to cover the firm's implicit costs. For example, suppose that when the firm in our example produces 20 chairs, its explicit cost is $400 and its implicit cost is $80 for the opportunity cost of the entrepreneur's time. With a price of $24, the firm's economic profit would be zero: The total revenue of $480 equals the sum of the explicit and implicit costs. The firm's accounting profit would be $80 ($480 – $400), which is just high enough to cover the firm's implicit costs.

Application: Questions for Managers

The marginal principle provides a simple framework for a manager who wants to determine whether a firm is maximizing its profit. The manager could compute the marginal cost of production by asking two questions of the firm's employees.

1. To produce 1 more unit of output in our production facility, how much additional labor and materials would we need? Presumably, the firm's production engineer could answer this question.
2. How much would we pay for each additional unit of labor and each additional unit of materials? Presumably, the firm's accountant could answer this question.

For example, suppose that an additional unit of output would require 3 hours of labor and 6 units of materials. If the wage is $10 per hour and the price of materials is $1 per unit, the firm would pay a total of $36 for the inputs required to produce 1 more unit of output. This is the marginal cost of production.

To apply the marginal principle, the manager must compare the marginal cost of production to the firm's marginal revenue (the price). The firm should increase its output if the price exceeds the marginal cost. In our example, if the price is greater than $36, it would be sensible to produce more output. Alternatively, if the price is less than $36, it would be sensible to produce less. If the price equals $36, the firm is doing the best it can, and it would be sensible to keep output at its current level.

ECONOMIC DETECTIVE– *The Turnaround Artist*

Emilio has a reputation as a person who knows how to turn an unprofitable company into a profitable one. His latest project was a hammer manufacturer that was losing $1,000 per day. The firm produced 100 hammers per day at a total cost of $3,000 and sold them for $20 apiece. Emilio was called in on Monday, and he asked the firm to produce 101 hammers on Tuesday. On Wednesday, he gave his advice to the firm and then disappeared. One week later, the firm was producing fewer hammers but making a profit of $200 per day. Your job is to figure out Emilio's secret formula for success. Why did he ask the firm to produce one more hammer? What advice did he give the firm? What is the logic behind his advice?

The key to answering these questions is the marginal principle. To determine whether the firm was maximizing its profit, Emilio needed to figure out the firm's marginal cost. One way to do this is to compare the total cost of producing 101 hammers with the total cost of producing only 100. Emilio's little experiment must have shown that the firm's marginal cost was greater than the market price, because he apparently told the firm to decrease its output. If the marginal cost exceeds the price, a decrease in output will increase the firm's profit. Emilio's formula for success is the marginal principle.

TEST *Your Understanding*

1. Explain why a perfectly competitive firm takes prices as given.
2. Complete the statement: A perfectly competitive firm will produce the quantity of output at which ____________ equals ____________.
3. Suppose that an additional unit of output would require 3 additional hours of labor and 4 additional units of materials. If the wage is $10 per hour and the price of materials is $1 per unit, what is the marginal cost of production?
4. Suppose that the market price of sugar is 22 cents per pound. If a sugar farmer produces 100,000 pounds, the marginal cost of sugar is 30 cents per pound. Is the farmer maximizing profit? If not, should the farmer produce more sugar or less sugar?

THE SHUT-DOWN DECISION

Consider next a problem faced by a firm that is losing money. Suppose the market price is so low that the firm's total revenue is less than its total cost, despite the fact that the firm has used the marginal principle to pick the best quantity of output, given the price. The question for an unprofitable firm is: Should we continue to operate at a loss, or shut down our production facility? At first glance this may seem like a silly question. Why would any firm continue to operate a facility that is losing money? As we'll see, it will be sensible to operate at a loss if the firm would lose *even more* money by shutting down.

Figure 3 on page 178 shows the situation faced by an unprofitable firm. Suppose that the market price of chairs drops to $18. If the firm continues to operate, it will produce 17 chairs per hour [point *z*, where the marginal revenue (price) equals marginal cost]. The problem is that the average total cost of producing this quantity is $26 (shown by point *t*), which exceeds the market price. The average cost exceeds the price by $8, so the firm will lose $136 per hour ($8 × 17 chairs). Should the firm continue to operate at a loss, or shut down the production facility?

Total Revenue versus Variable Cost

The firm should continue to operate an unprofitable facility if the benefit of operating the facility exceeds the cost. The benefit equals the total revenue generated by the facility, or the price times the quantity produced. In Figure 3 the firm can sell 17 chairs at a price of $18 per chair, so the revenue from operating the facility is $306. The firm's cost of operating—as opposed to shutting down—the facility is equal to the firm's variable cost (the cost of its labor and materials). Point *u* tells us that when the firm produces 17 chairs, its average variable cost is $14. Therefore, its total variable cost is $238 ($14 × 17 chairs). Because the benefit of operating the facility (total revenue of $306) exceeds the variable cost ($238), it is sensible to continue to operate the facility.

We can use a shortcut to determine whether total revenue exceeds the variable cost. Total revenue is the price times the quantity produced, and the variable cost is the average variable cost times the quantity produced. Therefore, if the price exceeds

Figure 3

Shut-Down Decision

With a price of \$18, the marginal principle suggests that the firm should pick point *z*. Total cost (\$442 = \$26 × 17) exceeds total revenue (\$306), so the firm will lose \$136 per hour. The average variable cost is \$14, so the variable cost for 17 chairs is \$238. The firm should operate because total revenue (\$306) exceeds variable cost (\$238).

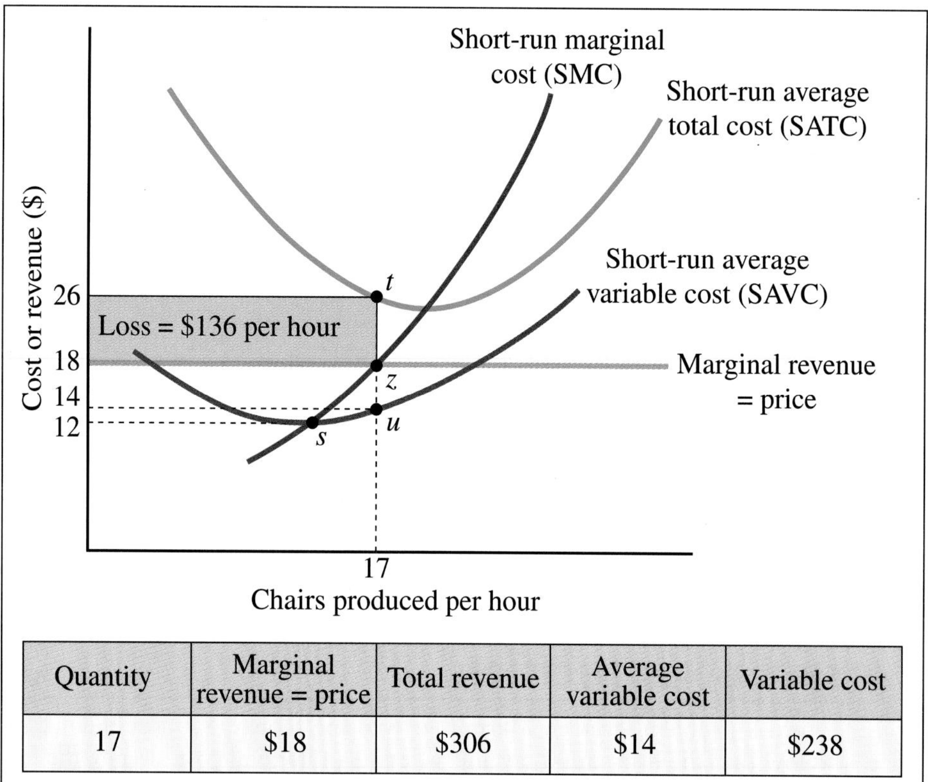

Quantity	Marginal revenue = price	Total revenue	Average variable cost	Variable cost
17	\$18	\$306	\$14	\$238

the average variable cost, the total revenue exceeds the variable cost. The firm should continue to operate if price exceeds the average variable cost, but it should shut down otherwise.

Operate:	price > average variable cost
Shut down:	price < average variable cost

In Figure 3 the price is \$18 and the average variable cost of 17 chairs is \$14, so it is sensible to continue operating the facility, even at a loss.

Why Operate an Unprofitable Facility?

Sunk cost: The cost a firm has already paid—or has agreed to pay some time in the future.

If the idea of operating an unprofitable facility is puzzling, think about what would happen if the firm shut down its facility. Although the firm would no longer pay for labor and materials, it would still pay for its idle production facility. The cost of the facility is a **sunk cost**, defined as a cost the firm has already paid—or has agreed to pay some time in the future. For example, a firm with a \$1 million production facility has a sunk cost of \$1 million, regardless of whether the firm paid for the facility in the past or will pay for it in the future. What matters is that the firm cannot do anything about this sunk cost. Let's assume that the sunk cost is the same as fixed cost (the cost of the firm's production facility). In most cases, this is a realistic assumption.

If a firm shuts down its production facility, it will still pay its sunk (or fixed) costs—the cost of the production facility. Because the firm won't sell any output, it will lose an amount of money equal to its fixed cost. How do we compute the firm's fixed cost per period? We know that the total cost equals the fixed cost plus the variable cost, so the fixed cost equals the total cost minus the variable cost. For example, the firm's total cost with 17 chairs is \$442 and the variable cost is \$238, so the fixed

A firm should shut down an unprofitable facility if its total revenue is less than variable cost.

cost is $204. Therefore, the firm will lose $204 per hour if it shuts down. If the firm operates the facility, it will lose only $136 per hour. The firm loses less money if it operates because the total revenue ($306) exceeds the variable cost ($238), leaving $68 to cover part of the firm's fixed cost.

How can a firm operate a facility that doesn't generate enough revenue to pay all its bills? Let's think about how a small entrepreneur deals with an unprofitable operation. Imagine that you own a chair firm and are personally responsible for paying all the bills. Your production facility operates at a loss of $136 per hour, and you cover your losses by withdrawing money from your savings account. If you shut down your facility, you still have to pay your sunk (fixed) cost of $204 per hour, so you would be forced to withdraw even more money from your savings account to cover your losses. Therefore, you should stay in business. The same logic applies to a firm that uses the revenue from some profitable facilities to cover the losses of an unprofitable one. The firm would pay $204 per hour if it shut down the unprofitable facility but only $136 per hour if it continued to operate the facility. As long as the total revenue from an unprofitable facility exceeds its variable cost, the firm will earn more profit in total if it continues to operate the facility.

How long will the firm continue to operate at a loss? Let's think about what happens when the firm must decide whether to build a new facility. The firm will build a new facility—and stay in the market—only if the price exceeds the average *total* cost of production. In other words, the firm will stay in the market only if the price is high enough to cover all the costs of production, including the cost of a new facility. In our example a price $14 is not high enough to cover the full cost of production, so as soon as the facility wears out, the firm will leave the market.

Application: Shantelle the Farmworker

The opening paragraphs of this chapter describe a possible shut-down situation: The farmer threatens to plow the crop under rather than harvesting it. The farmer claims that he would lose money by harvesting the wheat: His revenue would be $35,000, compared to a cost of $50,000 ($20,000 for seed and fertilizer purchased three months ago, and $30,000 for workers). The manager is bluffing: His total revenue

($35,000) exceeds the *variable cost* ($30,000 for the farmworkers). The $20,000 paid for seed and fertilizer was incurred months ago, and it is a sunk cost that will be ignored in the decision about whether to harvest the crop. Because his total revenue exceeds his variable cost, the farmer will harvest the crop even if the workers don't accept a wage cut.

The Shut-Down Price

Shut-down price: The price at which the firm is indifferent between operating and shutting down.

If the price of a firm's product is low enough, it will be sensible to shut down an unprofitable facility. If total revenue is less than variable cost (if price is less than average variable cost), the benefit of operating the facility is less than the cost, so it would be irrational to continue operating the facility. In Figure 3 this will occur if the price is less than $12. The **shut-down price** is the price at which the firm is indifferent between operating and shutting down, and is shown by point *s*. If the price equals average variable cost, total revenue equals variable cost, so the benefit of operating the facility equals the cost and the firm is indifferent about operating the facility. For any higher price it will be sensible to operate the facility because the total revenue will exceed the variable cost; for any lower price it will be sensible to shut down.

TEST ***Your Understanding***

5 Complete the statement with a number: If a lamp producer can sell 40 lamps per day at a price of $20 per lamp, the benefit of operating its production facility is ____________ per day.

6 Complete the statement with *operate* or *shut down*: Consider a firm with total revenue of $500, total cost of $700, and variable cost of $400. The firm should ____________ its production facility.

7 Complete the statement: A firm should continue to operate an unprofitable facility if the market price exceeds ____________.

SHORT-RUN SUPPLY CURVES

Now that we've explored the output decision of a price-taking firm, we're ready to show how firms respond to changes in the market price of output. We'll summarize the relationship between price and quantity supplied with two supply curves, one for the individual firm and one for the entire industry. We saw the industry supply curve early in the book, before we knew anything about the firm's cost curves. We can now use these cost curves to provide a more thorough explanation of the supply curve.

Firm's short-run supply curve: A curve showing the relationship between price and the quantity of output supplied by a firm.

Short-run marginal cost curve: A curve showing the change in cost from producing just one more unit of output in an existing facility.

The Short-Run Supply Curve of the Firm

The **firm's short-run supply curve** shows the relationship between the market price and the quantity supplied by the firm. In the case of chair producers, the firm's supply curve answers the following question: At a given price of chairs, how many chairs will the firm produce? We have already answered this question for three different prices ($18, $24, and $36). For each price we used the marginal principle to pick the profit-maximizing quantity of chairs (the quantity at which price equals marginal cost). Therefore, if we know the price, we just read the quantity supplied from the marginal cost curve.

The firm's short-run supply curve is the part of the firm's **short-run marginal cost curve** above the shut-down price. This is shown in Figure 4. Suppose that the firm's shut-down price is $12: The firm will shut down its facility if the price of chairs drops below $12. For any price above the shut-down price, the firm will use the marginal principle (price = marginal cost) to pick the quantity of output, so we can read the quantity supplied from the marginal cost curve. For example, if the price is $18, the firm will produce 17 chairs (point *z*). As the price increases, the firm responds by supplying more chairs: For example, the firm produces 20 chairs when the price is $24 (point *b*) and 25 chairs when the price is $36.

What about prices below the shut-down price? In our example, the shut-down price, shown by the intersection of the marginal cost curve and the average variable cost curve, is $12. If the price drops below the shut-down price, the firm's total revenue will not be high enough to cover the variable cost, so the firm will shut down its facility and produce no output. In Figure 4 the firm's supply curve starts at point *s*, indicating that the quantity supplied is zero for any price less than $12. For another example of the short-run supply curve, read the Closer Look box on page 182, "Supply Decisions of a Corn Farmer."

The Market Supply Curve

The **short-run market supply curve** shows the relationship between the market price and the quantity supplied by the entire industry. We've been assuming that each perfectly competitive firm takes the price of output and the price of inputs as given. To draw the short-run market supply curve, we assume that input prices are

Short-run market supply curve: A curve showing the relationship between price and the quantity of output supplied by an entire industry.

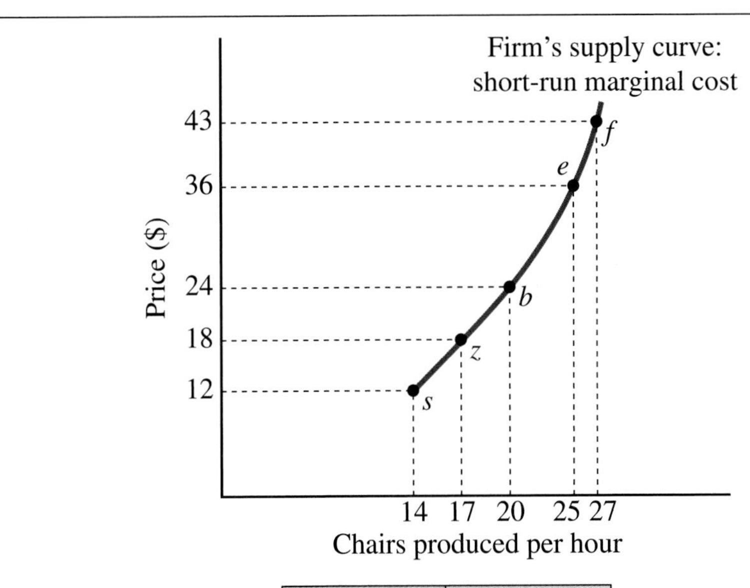

Price ($)	Quantity supplied
12	14
18	17
24	20
36	25
43	27

Figure 4

Firm's Short-Run Supply Curve

The short-run supply curve of the individual firm shows the quantity supplied at each price. The supply curve is the part of the marginal cost curve above the shut-down price ($12). For prices below the shut-down price, the firm shuts down, so the quantity supplied is zero.

A Closer LOOK

Supply Decisions of a Corn Farmer

What's the shut-down price for a corn farmer? What's the break-even price? We can answer these questions with the actual short-run cost curves for corn farmers shown in the figure at right (in 1971 dollars). The break-even or zero-profit price is $0.72: At any higher price, the farmer will make a profit. For example, if the price is $1.00, the farmer will produce 53,000 bushels at an average cost of about $0.74 and earn a profit of about $10,700. The shut-down price is $0.44: At prices between $0.44 and $0.72, the farmer will lose money but will continue to operate at a loss because the price exceeds the average variable cost; at prices below $0.44, the farmer will shut down the unprofitable operation.

Source: *The Structure of the American Economy,* 8th ed., Walter Adams, ed., © 1990. Adapted by permission of Prentice-Hall, Inc., Upper Saddle River, NJ.

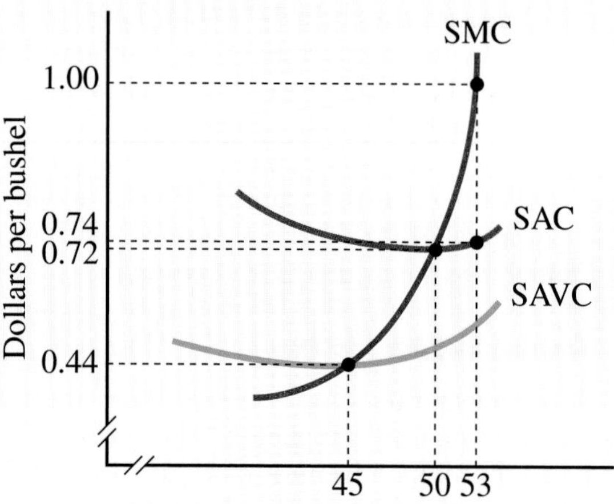

unaffected by changes in the total output of the industry: As the chair industry grows, the prices of labor and raw materials do not change. This assumption is realistic if the chair industry is just a small part of the relevant input markets, so that an increase in chair output won't affect the demand for labor or materials by very much.

Figure 5 shows the short-run market supply curve when there are 50 identical chair firms. For each price we get the quantity supplied per firm from the supply curve of the typical firm and multiply this number by 50 to get the quantity supplied by the industry as a whole. For example, at a price of $24, each firm produces 20 chairs (point *b* in Figure 4), so the industry as a whole produces 1,000 chairs (point *w*). If the price increases to $43, each firm produces 27 chairs, so the industry produces 1,350 (point *y*).

What happens if firms are not identical? In this case we must draw a supply curve for each firm in the industry. To compute the market supply at a particular price, we would use the individual supply curves to determine how much output each firm will produce at that price, and then add these quantities to get the total supply for the industry. Because a perfectly competitive industry has dozens—or hundreds—of firms, the picture showing the supply curves of all the individual firms and the market supply curve is a mess. The assumption that firms are identical is harmless: It makes it easier to go from the firm's supply curve to the market supply curve, but it does not change the analysis in a substantive way.

MARKET EQUILIBRIUM AND EFFICIENCY

We can use what we've learned about short-run supply curves to discuss the concept of equilibrium in a perfectly competitive market. Figure 6 shows the market for chairs from two perspectives. In panel B the market demand curve intersects the market supply curve at a price of $24 and a quantity of 1,000. In panel A each of the 50 chair firms takes the market price as given, so the typical firm produces the

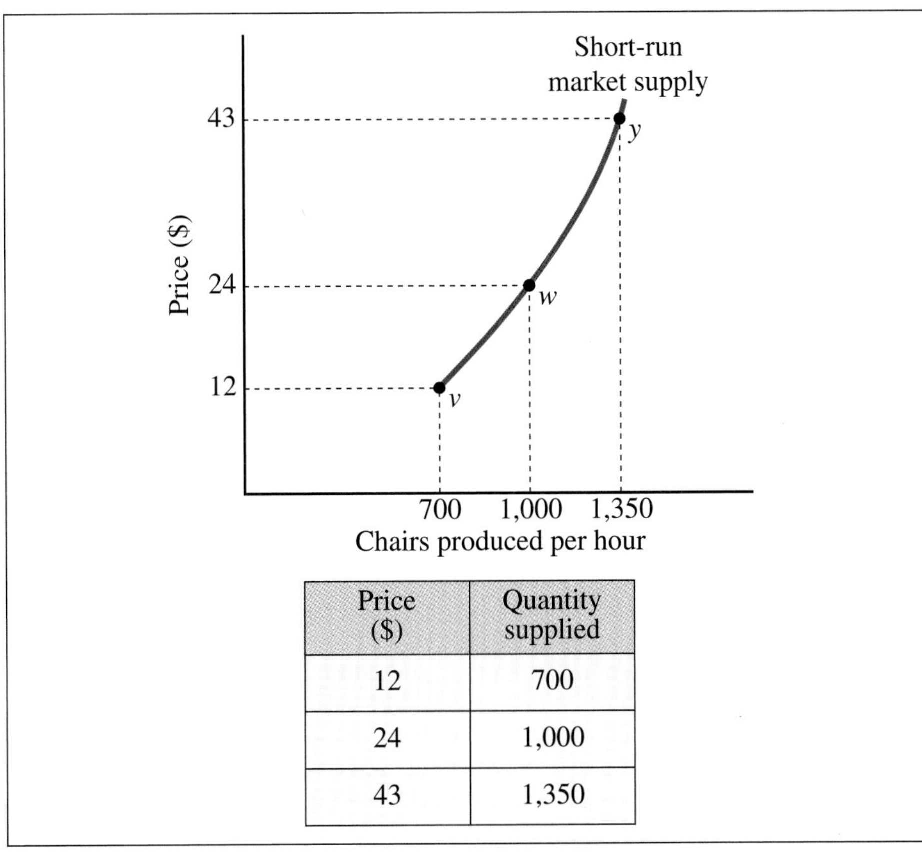

Price ($)	Quantity supplied
12	700
24	1,000
43	1,350

Figure 5

Short-Run Market Supply Curve

If there are 50 identical chair firms, the short-run industry supply at a given price is 50 × the supply from the typical firm. For example, at a price of \$24, each firm supplies 20 chairs (point *b* in Figure 4), so the market supply is 1,000 chairs (point *w* in Figure 5).

quantity at which price equals marginal cost, or 20 chairs (point *b*). Because the price equals the average cost at the chosen quantity, each firm makes zero economic profit. In other words, total revenue is just high enough to cover all the firm's cost. This is an equilibrium in the sense that there is no incentive for additional firms to enter the market or existing firms to leave.

Market Effects of a Change in Demand

Figure 7 on page 184 shows what happens when the demand for chairs increases. The market demand curve shifts to the right and intersects the market supply curve at a price of \$36. In panel A the increase in price causes each of the 50 firms to produce

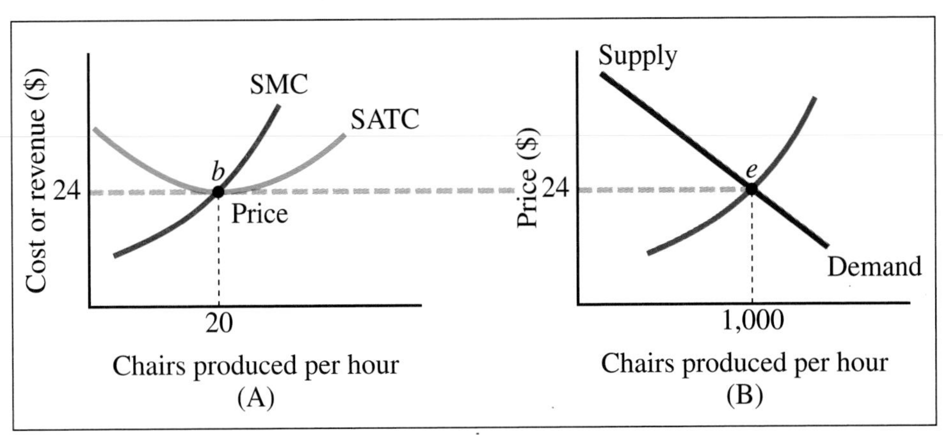

Figure 6

Market Equilibrium

The market demand curve intersects the short-run market supply curve at a price of \$24. The typical chair firm satisfies the marginal principle at point *b*, producing 20 chairs per day. Economic profit is zero.

Figure 7

Effect of Increased Demand

An increase in demand increases market price to $36, causing the typical firm to produce 25 chairs instead of 20. Price exceeds the average cost at the chosen quantity, so economic profit is positive.

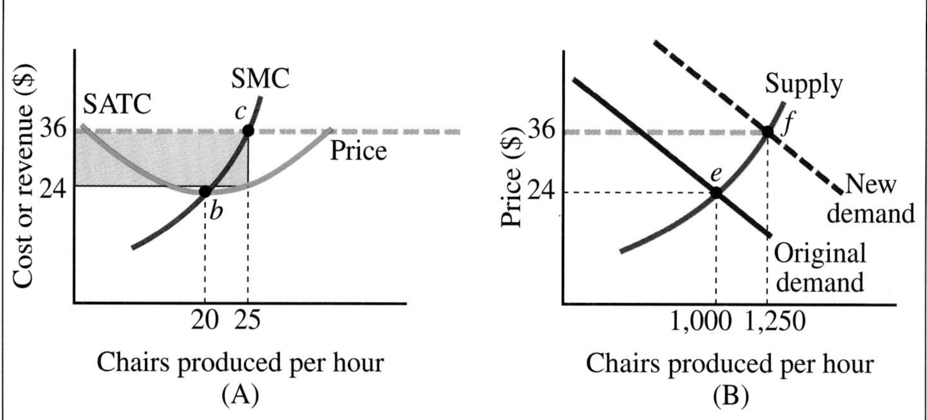

more output: The new price equals marginal cost at 25 chairs, and this is the new quantity supplied per firm. The market price now exceeds the average cost at the chosen quantity, and the economic profit of the typical firm is shown by the shaded rectangle.

The situation shown in Figure 7 is not a long-run equilibrium because each firm is making a positive economic profit. As we'll see in Chapter 10, in the long run, firms will enter this profitable market, and entry will continue until the price drops to the point at which economic profit is zero. At that point each firm will be earning just enough revenue to cover all its costs. Economic profit provides a vital role in markets: It encourages firms to enter markets that have experienced an increase in demand, accommodating consumers who are willing to buy more of a particular product.

Producer Surplus

Producer surplus: The difference between the market price of a product and the minimum amount a producer is willing to accept for that product; alternatively, the difference between the market price and the marginal cost of production.

Earlier in the book we used the concept of consumer surplus to measure the benefits that consumers get from participating in a market. Producers also benefit from the market, and we use the concept of producer surplus to measure their benefits. **Producer surplus** is defined as the difference between the market price of a product and the minimum amount a producer is willing to accept for that product. For example, if you are willing to produce a chair for as little as $24 but the market price of chairs is $36, your producer surplus from producing the chair is $12. Of course, the minimum amount a producer is willing to accept is the extra or marginal cost of producing the good. So we can also define producer surplus as the difference between the market price and the producer's marginal cost.

Let's start our discussion of producer surplus with another look at the market supply curve. The supply curve in Figure 8 shows how many chairs firms will supply at each price and also the minimum amount a producer is willing to accept for each chair. For example, point *w* indicates that the 1,000th chair will be produced if the price of chairs is $24 but won't be produced if the price is lower, say $23.99. A price of $24 is just high enough to cover the marginal cost of producing the chair, so that's the minimum amount a producer is willing to accept for the chair. As we move upward along the supply curve, the marginal cost of chairs increases, so the minimum amount producers are willing to accept for a chair also increases.

We can use the market supply curve to measure just how much of a bonus or surplus producers get from participating in a market. Suppose that the price of chairs is $36. The firm that produces the 1,000th chair is willing to accept as little as $24 for the chair, so the producer surplus for that chair is $12. Similarly, a firm

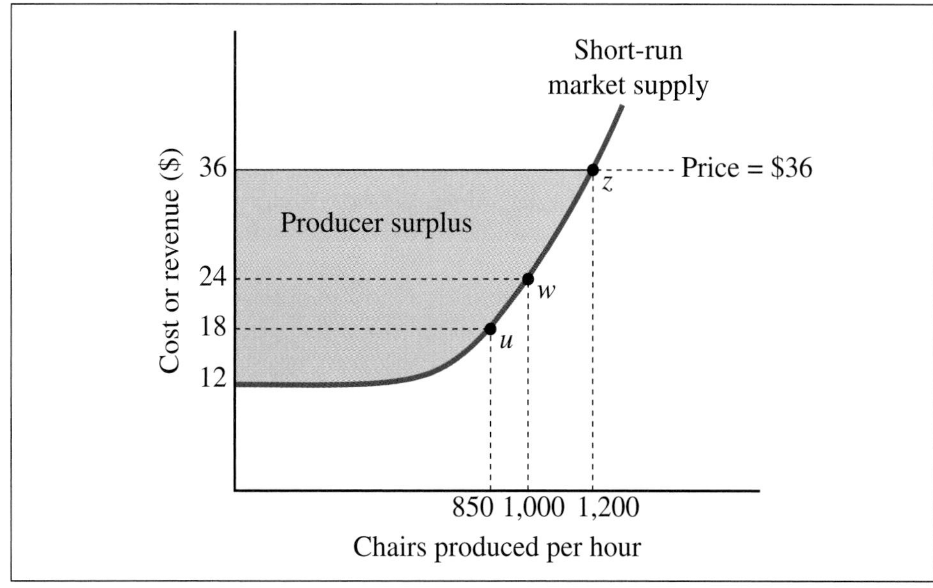

Figure 8

Market Supply Curve and Producer Surplus

The producer surplus for a particular chair equals the difference between the market price and the minimum amount producers are willing to accept for it, or the difference between price and marginal cost.

is willing to accept as little as $18 to produce the 850th chair (point *u*), so with a market price of $36, the producer surplus for that chair is $18. To get the producer surplus for the market, we just add the surpluses for each chair produced. For the market as a whole, the producer surplus is shown by the shaded area between the supply curve and horizontal price line.

How would a change in price affect the producer surplus in a particular market? A decrease in the price of chairs will decrease the producer surplus for two reasons. First, there will be a smaller gap between what producers are willing to accept and what they get, so the producer surplus for each chair will be smaller. Second, at the lower price, firms produce fewer chairs, so we would add up the surpluses of fewer chairs.

The price a producer receives for a good may be greater than the amount he or she is willing to accept. Producer surplus measures the bonus or surplus received by the producer.

Another Look at Market Efficiency

Earlier in the book we saw that if there are no spillovers in a perfectly competitive market, the market equilibrium is efficient because there are no additional transactions that would benefit a buyer and a seller. We've developed some tools in last few chapters that allow us to take a closer look at the issue of market efficiency.

Total value of a market: The sum of the net benefits experienced by consumers and producers; equal to the sum of consumer surplus and producer surplus.

The **total value of a market** equals the sum of consumer surplus and producer surplus. An individual's consumer surplus equals the difference between the maximum amount that the consumer is willing to pay for a product and the amount that he or she actually pays for it. At the market level, consumer surplus is shown by the area between the market demand curve and the horizontal price line. In Figure 9 the equilibrium price of chairs is $36. At this price the consumer surplus is shown by the lightly shaded area. Producer surplus is shown as the darker shaded area, so the total value of the market is shown by the two shaded areas.

The market equilibrium maximizes the total value of the market. To see why, let's look at the total value of the market when the price is less than the equilibrium price. In Figure 10 suppose that the government imposes a maximum price of $24. As shown by point *w*, firms supply only 1,000 chairs at this price. The producer surplus is shown by the darkly shaded area between the price line and the supply curve. Consumers can buy only as much as producers are willing to sell, so to compute the consumer surplus we add up the surpluses for the first 1,000 chairs: The consumer surplus is shown by the lightly shaded area. The total value of the market is shown by the two shaded areas.

How does the imposition of a maximum price affect the total value of the market? Comparing Figure 10 to Figure 9, we see that the total value of the market is smaller under the maximum price. The difference is shown by the area bounded by points *d*, *z*, and *w*. Although the maximum price increases consumer surplus, it decreases producer surplus by a larger amount, so the total value decreases.

The market equilibrium maximizes the total value of the market because all the potentially beneficial transactions are executed. Once we reach the market

Figure 9

Producer Surplus and Market Supply Curve

The producer surplus for a particular chair equals the difference between the market price and the minimum amount producers are willing to accept for it, or the difference between price and marginal cost. At the market level, the producer surplus is shown by the area between the horizontal price line and the supply curve.

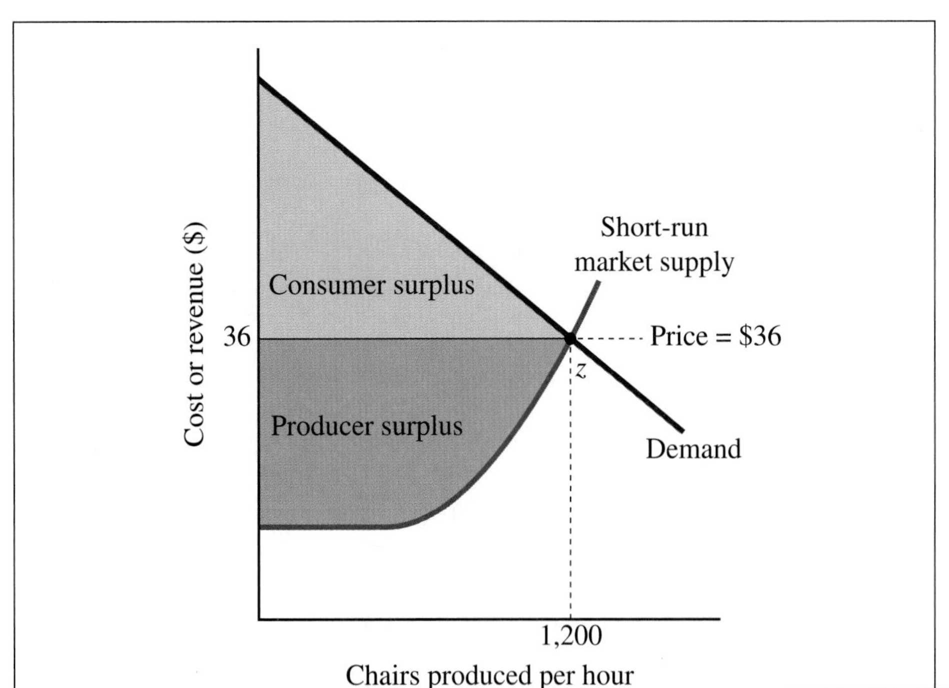

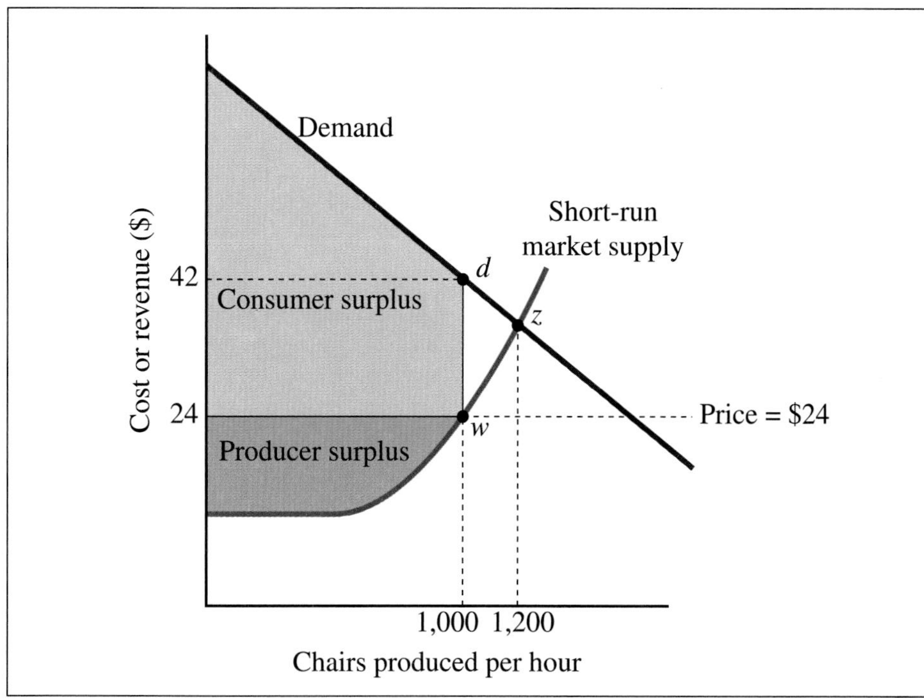

Figure 10

Maximum Price Decreases the Total Value of the Market

A maximum price below the equilibrium price decreases the total value of the market, with the loss equal to the area bounded by points *d*, *z*, and *w*.

equilibrium at point *z* in Figure 9, there are no additional transactions that would benefit a buyer and a seller. The demand curve tells us that the potential buyer of the 1,201st chair is willing to pay less than $36 for the chair. But the supply curve tells us that the potential seller of the 1,201st chair would incur a cost of more than $36. This transaction doesn't happen because the potential buyer is not willing to pay the full cost of producing the good.

In contrast, at any outcome other than the market equilibrium, some potentially beneficial transactions will not be executed. In Figure 10 when there is a maximum price of $24, the market will be stuck at 1,000 chairs. The demand curve tells us that a potential buyer is willing to pay just below $42 for the 1,001st chair (point *d* on the demand curve), while firms can produce the chair at a cost of just above $24 (point *w* on the supply curve). If a consumer and a producer split the difference, agreeing on a price of $33, each would benefit from the transaction: The buyer would get a surplus of about $9 and the seller would get a surplus of about $9. The execution of this transaction would move the market closer to the market equilibrium and increase the total value of the market by about $18.

We've seen that the imposition of a maximum price decreases the total value of a market. If the government instead imposed a minimum price, that would also decrease the value of the market. The difference between the two policies is that under a maximum price, consumers gain and producers lose, whereas under a minimum price, producers gain and consumers lose. In both cases, however, the policy decreases the total value of the market because the policy blocks some mutually beneficial transactions.

TEST *Your Understanding*

8. Complete the statement: The firm's short-run supply curve shows the relationship between ____________ and ____________.

9. Suppose that you want to draw the firm's short-run supply curve. What information do you need?

10 Complete the statement with a number: Suppose that there are 100 identical firms in a perfectly competitive industry. If the typical firm supplies 50 units of output at a price of $30, the quantity supplied by the industry will be ______________.

11 Why do most sellers say "thank you" when they sell you a product?

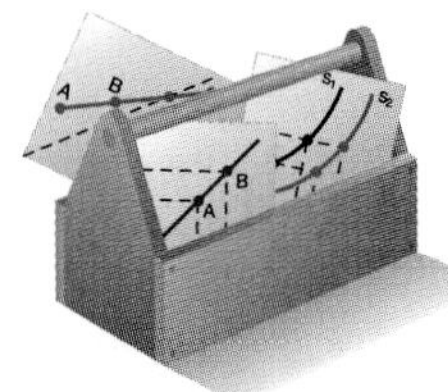

Using the TOOLS

You've learned how a perfectly competitive firm can use its cost curves to decide how much to produce and whether to continue operating an unprofitable operation. You've also learned how to use cost curves to draw the supply curves for a firm and the entire industry. Here are some opportunities to use these tools to do your own economic analysis.

1. Advice for an Unprofitable Firm

You've been hired as an economic consultant to a price-taking firm that produces shirts. The firm already has a shirt factory, so it is operating in the short run. The price of shirts is $5, the hourly wage is $12, and each shirt requires $1 worth of material. At the current level of output (70 shirts per hour), the firm is losing money: Its total cost exceeds its total revenue. The firm has experimented with different numbers of workers and discovered the following facts.

- To produce 70 shirts per hour (the current level of output), the firm uses 20 workers. A 21st worker would increase shirt production by 2 shirts per hour.
- To produce 60 shirts per hour, the firm uses 15 workers. A 16th worker would increase shirt production by 3 shirts per hour.

Your job is to tell the firm what to do, picking one of the following four options.

- Option 1: Shut down the unprofitable operation.
- Option 2: Continue to produce 70 shirts per hour.
- Option 3: Produce more shirts.
- Option 4: Produce fewer shirts.

2. Maximizing the Profit Margin

According to the marginal principle, the firm should pick the output at which price equals marginal cost. A tempting alternative is to maximize the firm's profit margin, defined as the difference between price and short-run average total cost. For example, if the price is $36 and the average cost of producing 20 chairs is $24, the profit margin is $12. Use the cost curves shown in Figure 1 (page 174) to critique this approach. Draw the firm's short-run supply curve and compare it to the supply curve of a firm that maximizes its profit.

SUMMARY

In this chapter we explored the decisions made by perfectly competitive firms and the implications of these decisions for a market. A perfectly competitive firm faces two types of decisions. First, the firm uses the marginal principle to decide how much output to produce. Second, the firm compares the price to the average variable cost to decide whether to continue operating an unprofitable facility. We used what we've learned about consumer and producer surplus to take a closer look at market efficiency. Here are the main points of the chapter.

1. A price-taking firm should produce the quantity of output at which the marginal revenue (the price) equals the marginal cost of production.
2. The firm should continue to operate an unprofitable production facility if its total revenue exceeds the variable cost—if the price exceeds the average variable cost.
3. We can use the short-run marginal cost curve of the typical firm to draw the short-run industry supply curve.
4. If there are no spillovers in a perfectly competitive market, the market equilibrium maximizes the total value of the market, defined as the sum of consumer surplus and producer surplus.

KEY TERMS

accounting profit, *176*
economic profit, *172*
firm's short-run supply curve, *180*
normal accounting profit, *176*
perfectly competitive market, *171*
producer surplus, *184*
short-run marginal cost curve, *180*
short-run market supply curve, *181*
shut-down price, *180*
sunk cost, *178*
total revenue, *172*
total value of a market, *186*

PROBLEMS AND DISCUSSION QUESTIONS

1. The following table shows short-run marginal costs for a perfectly competitive firm:

Output	100	200	300	400	500
Marginal cost	$5	$10	$20	$40	$70

   a. Use these data to draw the firm's marginal-cost curve.
   b. Suppose that the shut-down price is $10. Draw the firm's short-run supply curve.
2. Suppose that there are 100 identical firms like the one discussed in problem 1. Draw the short-run industry supply curve.
3. Suppose the wage for workers in a table factory is $5 per hour. In the table below, fill in a number wherever you see a _____. Then use the data to draw the short-run supply curve for tables.
4. You've been hired by an unprofitable firm to determine whether it should shut down its unprofitable operation. The firm currently uses 70 workers to produce 300 units of output per day. The daily wage (per worker) is $100, and the price of the firm's output is $30. The cost of other variable inputs is $500 per day. Although you don't know the firm's fixed cost, you know that it is high enough that the firm's total cost exceeds its total revenue. Should the firm continue to operate at a loss?
5. Consider the choices facing an unprofitable (and perfectly competitive) firm. The firm currently produces 100 units per day at a price of $22. The firm's total cost is $3,000 per day and its variable cost is $2,500 per day. At the current output level, the marginal cost of production is $45.
   a. Critically appraise the following statement from the firm's accountant: "Given our current production level, our variable cost ($2,500) exceeds our total revenue ($2,200). We should shut down our production facility."

Tables per Hour	*Number of Workers*	*Additional Workers*	*Additional Labor Cost*	*Additional Material Cost*	*Marginal Cost*
3	15				
4	18	_____	$_____	$20	$_____
5	23	_____	_____	20	_____
6	33	_____	_____	20	_____

b. Illustrate your answer with a graph showing the standard short-run cost curves and the revenue curve of a perfectly competitive firm.

6. Consider a firm that uses the following rule to decide how much output to produce: If the profit margin (price minus short-run average total cost) is positive, the firm will produce more output.
   a. Using the cost curves shown in Figure 1 (page 174), appraise this rule. If the price is $36, how much output will the firm produce? How much profit will the firm earn? If the price drops to $24, how much will the firm produce, and how much profit will it earn?
   b. Use the cost curves shown in Figure 1 to draw the firm's short-run supply curve. How does the firm's supply curve compare to the supply curve of a profit-maximizing firm?

7. Suppose that the government imposes a minimum price on chairs of $42. Use a graph to show the consumer and producer surplus under this policy.

Take It to the Net

We invite you to visit the O'Sullivan/Sheffrin page on the Prentice Hall Web site at:

http://www.prenhall.com/osullivan/

for this chapter's World Wide Web exercise.

MODEL ANSWERS FOR THIS CHAPTER

Chapter-Opening Questions

1. To use the marginal principle, you need the price (marginal benefit or marginal revenue) and the marginal cost of production for different levels of output.
2. Using the marginal principle, the marginal benefit (the price of $36) exceeds the marginal cost ($24), so you should increase your output.
3. The profit-margin approach is misguided because it looks at only one part of the profit picture: total profit equals the profit margin times the quantity produced. The firm will earn more total profit if it uses the marginal principle.
4. It would be sensible to close (shut down) if your total revenue is less than your variable cost, and sensible to continue operating otherwise.

Test Your Understanding

1. The firm is such a tiny part of the market that no matter how much output it produces, it will not affect the market price.
2. marginal revenue (or price), marginal cost
3. The marginal cost is $34, including $30 for labor ($10 times 3 hours) and $4 for materials ($1 times 4 units).
4. The farmer is not maximizing profit because the marginal revenue (price) is less than the marginal cost. The farmer should produce less sugar, moving down the marginal cost curve until marginal cost equals the price.
5. $800 ($20 times 40 lamps)
6. operate
7. average variable cost
8. price, quantity supplied
9. You need the short-run marginal cost curve and the shut-down price. If you have the average variable cost curve and the marginal cost curve, you can figure out the shut-down price by finding the price at which the two curves intersect.
10. 5,000 (50 units per firm times 100 firms)
11. A seller receives a producer surplus equal to the difference between the price and the minimum amount they are willing to accept.

Using the Tools

1. Advice for an Unprofitable Firm

   At the current output level (70 shirts), the marginal cost of production is $7: To produce one more shirt, the firm must use 0.50 hour of labor, which would cost $6 (half of the hourly wage) and $1 worth of material. Because the marginal cost exceeds the price ($5), the firm is not maximizing its profit.

   At an output level of 60 shirts, the marginal cost of production is only $5: To produce one more shirt, the firm must use one-third of an hour of labor, which would cost $4 (one-third of the hourly wage) and $1 worth of material. At this level of output, price equals marginal cost, so the firm is maximizing profit. Total revenue

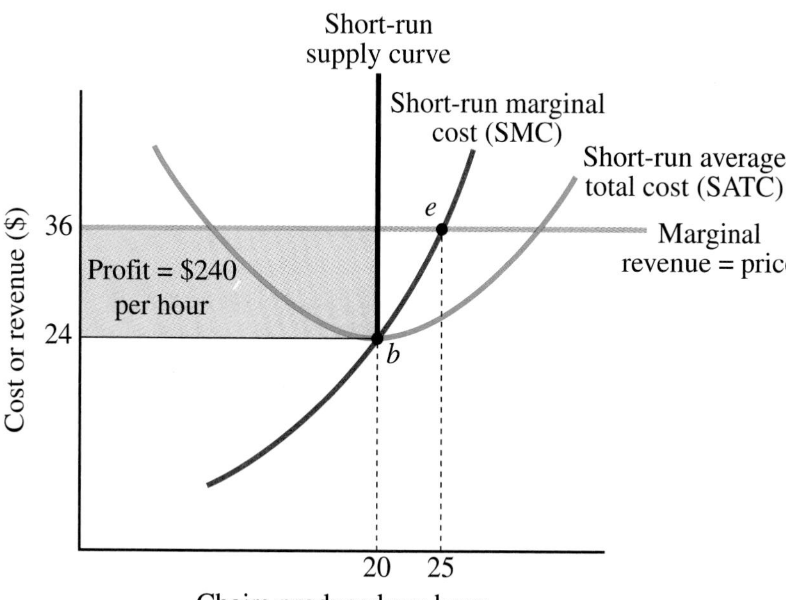

Figure A

Short-Run Supply Curve with Maximizing the Profit Margin

($300 = $5 times 60 shirts) exceeds variable cost ($240 = $180 for labor [$12 times 15 hours]) plus $60 for materials ($1 times 60 shirts), so it is sensible to continue to operate, even if total cost exceeds total revenue.

2. Maximizing the Profit Margin

To maximize the profit margin, the firm will pick the quantity that generates the largest possible gap between the price and average cost, and this occurs at the minimum point of the average cost curve. In Figure 1 (page 174) the average cost curve reaches its minimum point at point *b*, with a quantity of 20 and an average cost of $24. Therefore, the firm would produce 20 chairs per hour and earn a profit of $240 per hour.

As shown in Figure 1, at a price of $36, the firm would earn more profit by using the marginal principle. The price equals marginal cost with 25 chairs and profit is $250. The profit-margin approach is misguided because it looks at only one part of the profit picture: Total profit equals the profit margin times the quantity produced. Although the profit margin will be lower with 20 chairs, total profit will be higher.

As shown in Figure A above, the supply curve is a vertical line starting at the minimum point of the average-cost curve. Suppose that the firm will shut down if the profit margin is negative. At any price less than $24, price will be less than average cost, so the profit margin will be negative and the firm will shut down. To maximize the gap between price and average cost, the firm will pick the quantity associated with the minimum point of the average cost curve (20 chairs), regardless of the price of chairs. Therefore, as long as the price exceeds $24, the firm will produce 20 chairs. In contrast, the supply curve of a profit-maximizing firm is the marginal cost curve above the shut-down price.

CHAPTER 10

Long-Run Supply and Market Dynamics

As usual, Bob returned home from his monthly fishing trip on the Columbia River without any fish. He was a happy man, however, because he was $30 richer, thanks to a squawfish bounty program that paid him $3 for every squawfish he caught. The squawfish is an environmental pest that eats salmon smolts (young salmon) and thus contributes to the depletion of chinook and sockeye salmon, two species that are threatened with extinction. When the state of Washington started its squawfish bounty program in 1990, the bounty was $1 per fish, and sport fishers caught just a few fish. The state increased the bounty to $3 the following year, and sport fishers responded by catching almost 74,000 squawfish. The average fisher caught 4 squawfish per day, and one person caught 174, earning $522 for a single day of fishing.[1]

In Chapter 9 we explored the short-run decisions of perfectly competitive firms. We saw that when the price of a product increases, existing firms produce more output from their production facilities, so the total output of the industry rises. In this chapter we'll see that in the long run, an increase in price will increase total output as new firms enter the industry and existing firms expand their production facilities. In other words, the law of supply also works in the long run.

The law of supply applies to other sorts of activities, as illustrated by the response of sport fishers to the squawfish bounty. When the price of squawfish increased from $1 to $3, sport fishers responded by catching more fish. Similarly, when the price of a consumer good such as chairs increases, firms respond by producing more chairs.

In this chapter we use some of the key principles of economics to explain the logic behind the law of supply and the long-run supply curve. As in Chapter 9, the analysis applies to a perfectly competitive market, defined as one with a large number of firms, each of which takes prices as given. Once we understand the long-run supply curve, we can answer some practical questions about the supply side of a perfectly competitive market.

1 Why is the long-run supply curve flatter than the short-run curve? In other words, why are producers more responsive in the long run than they are in the short run?

2 When the monthly rent on apartments increases, the number of apartments doesn't increase by very much, even in the long run. Why?

We'll use what we learn about supply curves to develop a deeper understanding of market equilibrium. Here are some practical questions about markets that we answer:

3 How did Hurricane Andrew affect the price of ice?

4 When the demand for a particular product decreases, the price drops, often by a large amount, but then rises. Why?

THE LONG-RUN SUPPLY CURVE

The market supply curve shows the quantity of a product supplied at different prices. We can use the supply curve to see how firms in the market respond to changes in price. For example, an increase in the market price will increase the quantity supplied, and the supply curve tells us how much more will be produced. In the long run, firms can enter or leave an industry, and existing firms can modify their facilities or build new facilities. The **long-run supply curve** shows the relationship between price and quantity supplied over a period of time long enough that firms can enter or leave the market and firms can modify their production facilities.

Long-run supply curve: A curve showing the relationship between price and quantity supplied in the long run.

Production Cost and the Size of the Industry

Let's use the chair-industry example from Chapter 9 to explain the long-run supply curve. Suppose that the typical firm produces 20 chairs per hour, using a standard set of inputs, including a factory, some workers, and some wood. In a perfectly competitive industry, there are no restrictions on entry, so anyone can use the standard set of inputs to produce 20 chairs per hour.

Table 1 on page 194 shows some hypothetical data on the cost of producing chairs. Let's start with the first row, which shows the firm's production costs in an industry with 25 firms and 500 chairs (20 chairs per firm). To compute the total cost for the typical firm, we add the cost of the firm's production facility (the cost of the chair factory), the cost of labor, and the cost of materials. In the first row, the total cost of the typical firm is $400. The average cost per chair equals the total cost divided by the number of chairs produced by the typical firm (20 chairs). For example, if the industry produces a total of 500 chairs, each firm incurs a cost of $400 per hour to produce 20 chairs per hour, so the average cost is $20 per chair ($400/20).

What happens to the average cost of production as the industry grows? In the last column of Table 1, the average cost increases as the industry grows: The average cost is

Table 1: Industry Output and Average Production Cost

Number of Firms	*Industry Output*	*Chairs per Firm*	*Total Cost for Typical Firm*	*Average Cost per Chair*
25	500	20	$400	$20
50	1,000	20	480	24
75	1,500	20	560	28

$20 in an industry that produces 500 chairs, $24 in an industry that produces 1,000 chairs, and so on. The average cost increases as the industry grows for two reasons.

1. ***Increasing input prices.*** As an industry grows, it competes with other industries for limited amounts of various inputs, and this competition drives up the prices of these inputs. For example, suppose that the chair industry competes against other industries for a limited amount of special wood. To get more wood to produce more chairs, firms in the chair industry must outbid other industries for the limited amount available, and this competition drives up the price of wood.

2. ***Less productive inputs.*** A small industry will use only the most productive inputs, but as the industry grows, firms may be forced to use less productive inputs. For example, a small chair industry will use only the most skillful carpenters. As the industry grows, however, it will have to rely on less skillful workers. As the average skill level of the industry's workforce decreases, the average cost of production increases: In a large chair industry, it will take more hours of labor—and more money—to produce each chair. Another example is the mining of metals such as gold and silver. In a small industry, firms extract these metals from high-grade ore near the surface of the earth. As the industry grows, firms will be forced to use low-grade ore from deposits far below the surface. As a result, the average cost per ton of metal will increase as the industry grows. A final example is the production of agricultural products such as sugar. Because of variation in climate and soil conditions, it is cheaper to grow sugar in some areas than in others. As the quantity of sugar produced increases, growers are forced to produce sugar in areas with higher costs.

Drawing the Long-Run Market Supply Curve

The long-run supply curve tells us how much output will be produced at each price. If we pick a price, we determine the total output of the industry by multiplying the output per firm (20 chairs in our example) by the number of firms in the industry. So the key question for the long-run supply curve is: How many firms will enter the market?

Let's think about the incentive for a firm to enter the market. We know that a firm's economic profit is the firm's total revenue minus its economic cost, which includes all the costs of production, both implicit and explicit. Profit is positive when total revenue exceeds total cost, or when price exceeds the average cost. Whenever there is an opportunity to make a profit—that is, whenever the price exceeds average cost—firms will enter the market. Firms will continue to enter the market until economic profit is zero, which happens when the price equals average cost. In this case the firm's revenue is high enough to cover all its costs—including the opportunity cost of all its inputs—but not high enough to cause additional firms to enter the market. In other words, each firm makes just enough money to stay in business, so there is no incentive for new firms to enter the market and no incentive for existing firms to leave.

As a starting point, suppose that the price of chairs is $24. Recall that there are no restrictions on entry into the industry: Anyone can use the standard set of inputs to produce 20 chairs per hour. The information in Table 1 suggests that 50 firms will enter the market. To explain why the magic number is 50 firms, think about what would happen if there were either fewer firms or more firms.

1. *Fewer firms.* If there were fewer than 50 firms, the average cost would be less than the price ($24). For example, if there were only 25 firms (producing a total of 500 chairs per hour), the average cost would be only $20, so the profit per chair would be $4 (a price of $24 minus a cost of $20). Firms would start to enter this profitable market, and they would continue to enter until the average cost reached the market price. This occurs with 50 firms and total output of 1,000 chairs.
2. *More firms.* If there were more than 50 firms, the average cost would exceed the price ($24). For example, if there were 75 firms (producing a total 1,500 chairs per hour), the average cost would be $28, so each firm would lose $4 per chair (a cost of $28 minus a price of $24). Firms would start to leave this unprofitable market, and they would continue to leave until the average cost dropped to the market price, which occurs with 50 firms and 1,000 chairs.

To find the number of firms in the market, we find the quantity of chairs at which the average cost equals the market price ($24). If the price equals the average cost, each of the 50 firms makes zero economic profit, so there is no incentive for new firms to enter the market and no incentive for existing firms to leave.

The long-run supply curve shows the quantity of chairs supplied at different prices. To find a point on the market supply curve, we pick a price and then determine how many chairs the industry will produce at that price. At a price of $24, there will be 50 firms and 1,000 chairs, so one point on the supply curve, which we show in Figure 1(page 196), is point *h*. To find the other points on the long-run supply curve, we pick other prices and use the data in Table 1 to determine the quantity at which price equals the average cost of production. At a price of $20, the quantity is 500 chairs (point *e*), and at a price of $28, the quantity is 1,500 (point *i*).

The supply curve in Figure 1 is positively sloped, providing another example of the law of supply. The higher the price of chairs, the larger the quantity supplied. An increase in the price of chairs makes chair production more profitable, so firms enter the market, increasing the total output of the industry. Firms will continue to enter the market until the average cost per chair reaches the market price. In other words, each firm gets just enough revenue to cover its production costs, so economic profit is zero. For another example of the law of supply, read the Closer Look box on page 196, "The Supply of Wolfram during World War II."

Application: The World Supply of Sugar

Does the world sugar market obey the law of supply? If the price of sugar is only 11 cents per pound, sugar production is profitable in areas with relatively low production costs, including the Caribbean, Latin America, Australia, and South Africa.[2] At a price of 11 cents, the world supply of sugar equals the amount produced in these areas. As the price increases, sugar production becomes profitable in areas with higher production costs, and the quantity of sugar supplied increases as these other areas join the world market. For example, at a price of 14 cents, sugar production is profitable in the European Community, and at a price of 24 cents, production is profitable even in the United States. The law of supply works in the world sugar market: The higher the price, the larger the number of areas that produce sugar, so the larger the quantity of sugar supplied.

Figure 1

Long-Run Market Supply Curve

The long-run market supply curve shows the relationship between the price and quantity supplied when firms can enter or leave the industry. At each point on the supply curve, the price of output equals the average cost of production.

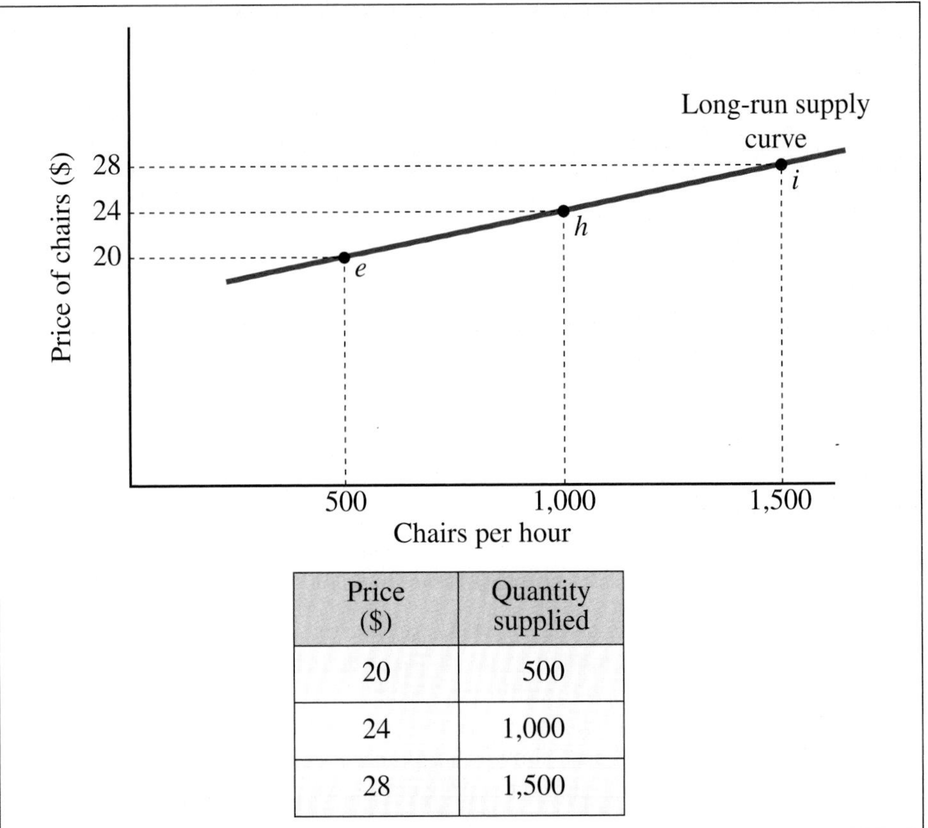

Price ($)	Quantity supplied
20	500
24	1,000
28	1,500

A Closer LOOK

The Supply of Wolfram during World War II

For an example of the law of supply, let's look at what happened to the supply of wolfram during World War II.* Wolfram is an ore of tungsten, an alloy required to make heat-resistant steel for armor plate and armor-piercing shells. During World War II the Allied powers used a "preclusive buying" program to buy the wolfram produced in Spain, thus denying the Axis powers (Germany and Italy) access to Spanish wolfram. The idea was to hamper the Axis war effort by denying them a vital input to the production of military equipment and weapons. The preclusive buying program was very costly to the Allied powers for two reasons.

1. The Allied powers had to outbid the Axis powers for the Spanish wolfram, and the price of wolfram increased from $1,144 per ton to $20,000 per ton.

2. Spanish firms responded to the higher prices by supplying more wolfram. Workers poured into the Galatia area in Spain, using simple tools to gather wolfram from the widely scattered outcroppings of ore. The quantity of wolfram supplied increased tenfold. Because wolfram miners obeyed the law of supply, the Allied powers were forced to buy a huge amount of wolfram, much more than they had expected.

*D. I. Gordon and R. Dangerfield, *The Hidden Weapon* (New York: Harper & Brothers, 1947), pp. 105–116.

TEST *Your Understanding*

1. Complete the statement: The long-run supply curve shows the relationship between ____________ (on the horizontal axis) and ____________ (on the vertical axis).

2. Use Table 1 (page 194) to compute the average cost in a 100-firm industry, assuming that the total cost of the typical firm in such an industry is $640.

3. Explain why the average cost of chair production increases as the industry grows.

HOW STEEP ARE THE SUPPLY CURVES?

The law of supply tells us that supply curves are positively sloped, but it does not tell us how steep they are. Suppose that the price of a particular good increases and we want to predict how much more of the good will be produced. To make a prediction, we must know how steep the supply curve is.

How Steep Is the Long-Run Supply Curve?

The law of supply suggests that an industry won't produce more output unless the price increases. In Figure 1, if we start with a price of $24, the chair industry will produce 1,000 chairs (point *h*), but no more. To get the industry to produce 1,500 chairs, the price must rise to $28 (point *i*). To get more output, the price must increase to cover the higher average cost experienced by firms in a larger industry. In other words, the long-run supply curve will be positively sloped if the average cost of production increases as the industry grows. As we saw earlier, this occurs if the expansion of the industry increases input prices or forces firms to use less productive inputs.

An industry with a positively sloped long-run supply curve is called an **increasing-cost industry**, indicating that the average cost of production increases as the industry grows. The supply curve will be relatively steep if the average cost increases rapidly as the industry grows. In an industry with rapidly increasing average cost, we need a relatively large increase in price to get firms in the industry to produce more output. For an example of an increasing-cost industry, read the Closer Look box on page 198, "Why Is the Supply Curve for Rental Housing So Steep?"

Increasing-cost industry: An industry in which the average cost of production increases as the industry grows, so the long-run supply curve is positively sloped.

Constant-Cost Industries

An industry with a horizontal long-run supply curve is called a **constant-cost industry**, indicating that the average cost of production is constant. As a constant-cost industry grows, it can continue to buy its inputs at the same prices, and these inputs are just as productive as the inputs in the smaller industry. For this to happen, the industry must be a small part of the relevant input markets, meaning that the industry does not affect the prices of its inputs. Therefore, the long-run supply curve is horizontal at the constant average cost.

Constant-cost industry: An industry in which the average cost of production is constant, so the long-run supply curve is horizontal.

As an example of a constant-cost industry, consider the taxi industry in a particular city. As the taxi industry grows, it will use more gasoline. But will the price of gasoline increase as the taxi industry grows? The price of gasoline is determined in the national gasoline market, and the city's taxi industry consumes a tiny fraction of the nation's gasoline. Therefore, the growth of the city's taxi industry will not affect the price of gasoline. Similarly, the taxi industry is a small part of the labor market,

A Closer LOOK

Why Is the Supply Curve for Rental Housing So Steep?

A common observation among people living in apartments is that housing producers are not very responsive to changes in price. An increase in the monthly rent (the price of rental housing) does not increase the quantity of apartments supplied by very much. According to one study,* the long-run elasticity of supply of apartments is about 0.50, meaning that a 10% increase in the monthly rent increases the number of apartments supplied by only 5%. In other words, the supply curve for apartments is relatively steep, even in the long run.

The supply curve is relatively steep because local governments use land-use zoning to restrict the amount of land available for apartments. When housing producers decide to build more apartments, there is fierce competition for the small amount of land zoned for apartments, so the cost of land—and the cost per apartment—increases rapidly. When the monthly rent increases by 10%, new apartments will continue to be built until the cost per apartment increases by 10% too. Because of zoning, the cost per apartment increases rapidly, so housing producers build a relatively small number of apartments.

The supply of rental housing is relatively inelastic because most local governments restrict the amount of land available for building apartments.

*Frank De Leeuw and Nkanta Ekanem, "The Supply of Rental Housing," *American Economic Review*, vol. 61, 1971, pp. 806–817.

so although the growing taxi industry hires more workers, the wage paid to cab drivers will not increase.

Figure 2 shows the long-run supply curve for the constant-cost taxi industry. Suppose that the average cost per mile of taxi service is $3. This cost includes the cost of gasoline, the cost of the taxicab, and the cost of a driver. Because the growth of the taxi industry does not affect the prices of cars, labor, or gasoline, the average cost is constant, and the long-run supply curve is horizontal at $3. At any lower price, the quantity supplied would be zero because no rational firm would provide taxi service at a price less than the average cost of providing the service. At any higher price, firms would enter the taxi industry in droves, and entry would continue until the price drops to the constant average cost of taxi service ($3).

Decreasing-cost industry: An industry in which the average cost of production decreases as the industry grows.

We've seen the supply curves for an increasing-cost industry and a constant-cost industry, but what about a **decreasing-cost industry**? If the average cost of production decreases as the industry expands, we say that the industry experiences decreasing costs. Suppose that the growth of a particular industry is concentrated in a single city. As the number of firms in the city increases, the firms that supply inputs to the industry may also find it advantageous to locate near the city. If so, the cost of inputs will drop, pulling down the industry's costs. Reversing the logic we used to show the positively sloped supply curve for an increasing-cost industry, the supply curve of a decreasing-cost industry is negatively sloped. It's important to note that decreasing-cost industries are rare, so most supply curves are either horizontal (constant-cost industry) or positively sloped (increasing-cost industry).

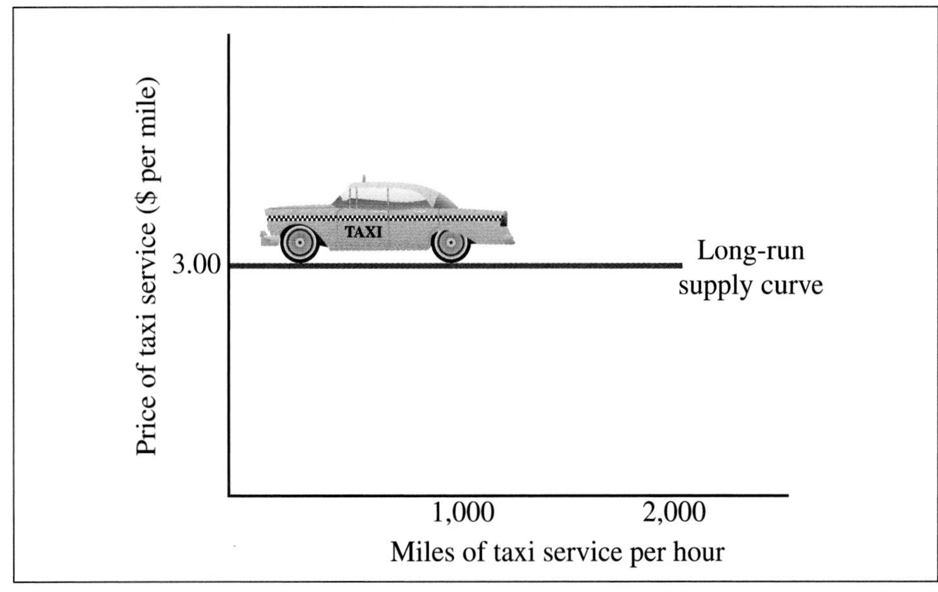

Figure 2

Long-Run Supply Curve for a Constant-Cost Industry

In a constant-cost industry, input prices do not change as the industry grows, so the average production cost is constant and the long-run supply curve is horizontal. For the taxi industry, the cost per mile of taxi service is constant at $3.00, so the supply curve is horizontal at $3.00 per mile of service.

SHORT-RUN VERSUS LONG-RUN SUPPLY CURVES

We're ready to compare the short-run supply curve from Chapter 9 to the long-run curve we've developed in this chapter. In Figure 3 the short-run curve intersects the long-run curve at point *h*, with a price of $24 and a quantity of 1,000 chairs per hour. There are 50 firms, each of which produces 20 chairs per hour. As we saw in Chapter 9, this point is on the short-run supply curve: If the price is $24, each firm produces 20

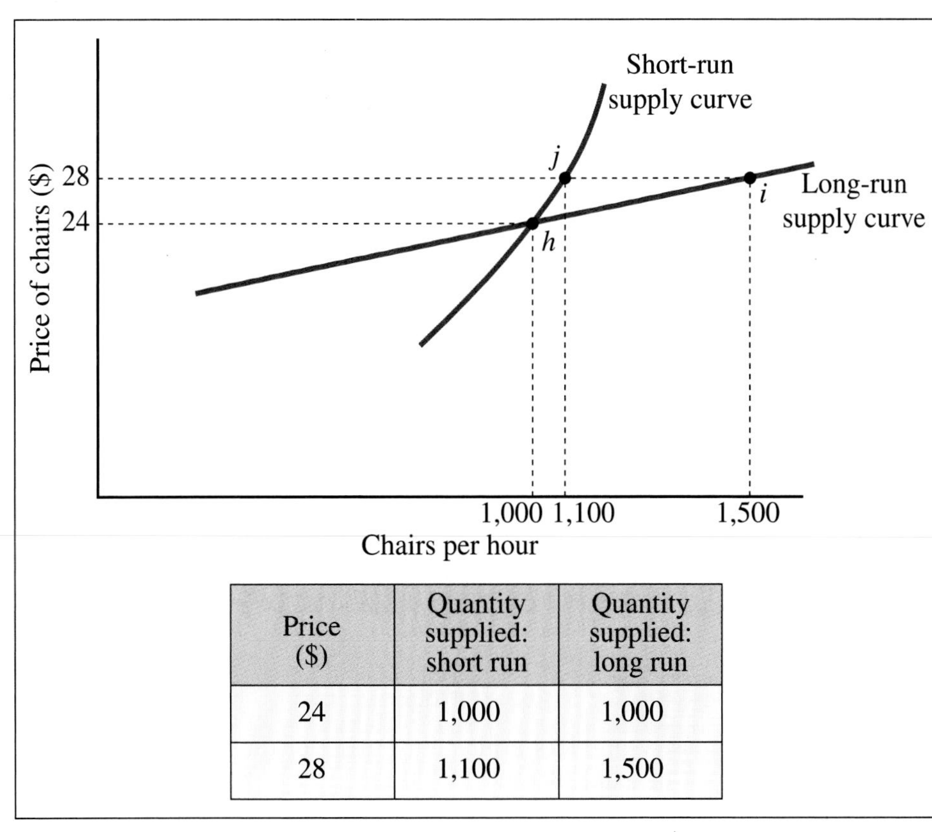

Price ($)	Quantity supplied: short run	Quantity supplied: long run
24	1,000	1,000
28	1,100	1,500

Figure 3

Long-Run versus Short-Run Market Supply Curves

The short-run supply curve is steeper than the long-run supply curve because there are diminishing returns in the short run. In the short run, an increase in price from $24 to $28 increases the quantity supplied from 1,000 (point *h*) to 1,100 (point *j*). In the long run, the same increase in price increases the quantity supplied to 1,500 (point *i*).

chairs per hour (that's the quantity at which price equals marginal cost). This point is also on the long-run supply curve: If the price is $24, the price equals the average cost with 50 firms and 1,000 chairs per hour (see the first row in Table 1).

The two supply curves in Figure 3 show that the long-run response to a change in price is much greater than the short-run response. Suppose that the price of chairs increases from $24 to $28. In the short run, the industry moves upward along the short-run supply curve to a larger quantity: Each of the 50 firms produces 22 chairs instead of 20, and the quantity increases from 1,000 to 1,100 (point *j*). In the long run the industry moves upward along the long-run supply curve to a larger quantity because new firms enter the market. The quantity increases from 1,000 to 1,500 (point *i*) because at the higher price there are 75 firms, each of which produces 20 chairs per hour. The long-run supply curve is flatter than the short-run curve, meaning that the quantity of chairs increases by a larger amount in the long run.

What explains the difference between the short- and long-run curves? The short-run supply curve is relatively steep because of diminishing returns. In the short run, the number of firms is fixed and each firm is stuck with its production facility, so it is very costly to increase chair production. When the price increases from $24 to $28, the quantity of chairs supplied doesn't increase by very much. In contrast, the long-run supply curve is relatively flat because firms enter the industry and build new factories, so there are no diminishing returns. The average cost per chair increases slowly as the industry grows, so a small increase in price generates a large increase in quantity.

We can use the concept of price elasticity of supply to measure the difference between the short- and long-run responses to a change in price. The change in price is 16.67% (4 divided by 24). For the short-run response, the percentage change in quantity is 10%, so the short-run elasticity of supply is 0.60. For the long-run response, the percentage change in quantity is 50%, so the long-run elasticity of supply is 3.0.

TEST *Your Understanding*

4 Circle the three items in the following list that go together: *positively sloped supply curve, horizontal supply curve, increasing-cost industry, increasing average cost of production, constant average cost of production.*

5 In a certain industry the average cost increases rapidly as the industry grows. Will the industry have a relatively steep supply curve or a relatively flat one?

6 Explain why the short-run supply curve is steeper than the long-run supply curve.

MARKET EQUILIBRIUM REVISITED

We can use what we've learned about short- and long-run supply curves to get a deeper understanding of perfectly competitive markets. Let's use the two supply curves to explore the short- and long-run effects of a change in demand.

Increase in the Demand for Video Rentals

The video rental industry provides a nice illustration of the short- and long-run effects of increases in demand. Between 1980 and 1990, the percentage of U.S. households with videocassette recorders (VCRs) increased from 1% to 70%.[3] The rapid growth in the number of VCRs increased the demand for video rentals. How did this increase in demand affect the price of video rentals in both the short run and long run?

Figure 4 shows the short-run effects of the increase in demand for video rentals. Point *i* shows the initial equilibrium, with a price of $2 per video. The increase in the number of VCRs shifted the demand curve for video rentals to the right, causing a shortage: At the original price ($2), the quantity of videos demanded exceeded the quantity supplied. In the short run, the number of firms is fixed, so the supply curve is relatively steep and the price increases by a large amount, from $2 to $6 (shown by point *s*). At this higher price, video stores earned huge profits.

Figure 5 on page 202 uses a long-run supply curve to show why the price of videos decreased gradually over time. In the long run, firms can enter the market, so the long-run supply curve is relatively flat. The short-run increase in the price of video rentals caused thousands of firms to enter the lucrative market: the number of video stores in the United States increased from 5,000 in 1980 to 25,000 in 1990.[4] The competition among the growing number of video stores decreased prices and profits until a long-run equilibrium was established with a typical price just above $2 per night. Point *f* shows the new long-run equilibrium: The new demand curve intersects the long-run supply curve at a price of $2.15.

The lesson from Figure 5 is that an increase in demand causes a large upward jump in prices, followed by a slide downward to the new long-run equilibrium price. In the short run an industry responds to an increase in price by squeezing more output from the existing production facilities. Because of diminishing returns, it is costly to increase output in the short run, so the price increases by a relatively large amount. The high price causes firms to enter the industry, and the price gradually drops to the point at which each firm makes zero economic profit. In the long run, the price is just high enough for each firm to cover all its production costs, including the costs of labor, materials, and the production facility.

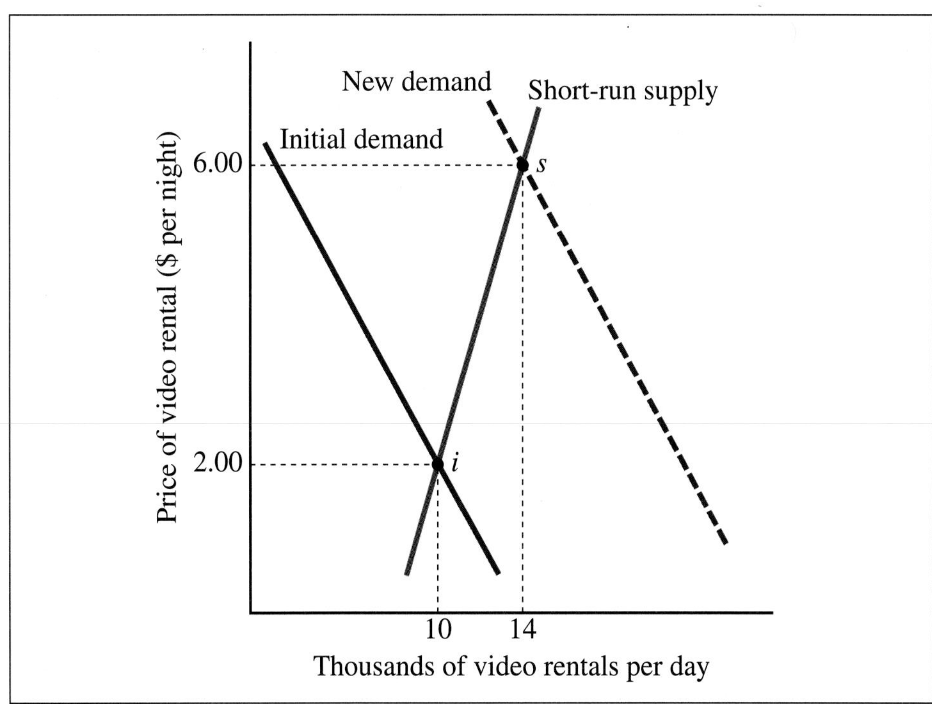

Figure 4

Short-Run Effects of an Increase in Demand for Video Rentals

In the short run, the number of firms in an industry is fixed, so the supply curve is relatively steep. An increase in demand increases price by a relatively large amount.

Figure 5

Long-Run Effects of an Increase in Demand for Video Rentals

In the long run, firms can enter or leave an industry, so the supply curve is relatively flat. At a price of $6, video rental outlets earn large profits, so new firms enter the market, and the price drops. Eventually, we reach a new long-run equilibrium with a price just above the initial price.

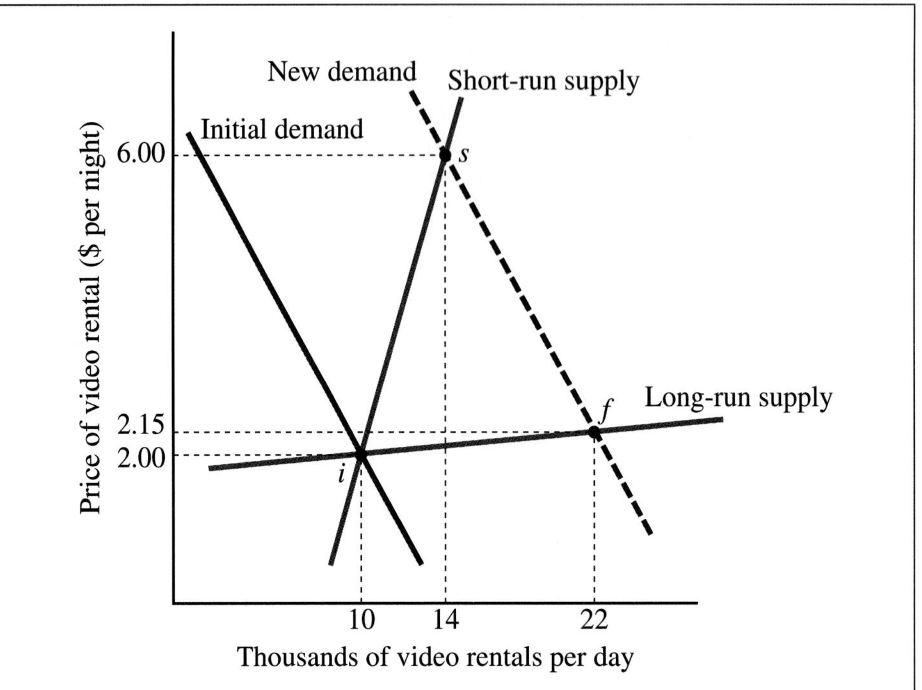

Hurricane Andrew and the Price of Ice

For another example of the short- and long-run effects of an increase in demand, let's look at the short- and long-run effects of a hurricane. In 1992, Hurricane Andrew struck the southeastern United States, causing millions of people to be without electricity for several days. Figure 6 shows the short- and long-run effects of the hurricane on the price of ice, which was used to cool and preserve food in areas without electricity. Before the hurricane, the market was at point *i*, with a price of $1 per bag. In the short run (a few days), the supply of ice is relatively inelastic, and the increase in demand caused by the hurricane moved the market to point *s*, with

Figure 6

Effects of a Hurricane on the Price of Ice

A hurricane increases the demand for ice, shifting the demand curve to the right. In the short run, the supply curve is relatively steep, so the price jumps up by a large amount. In the long run, firms enter the industry, so the supply curve is relatively flat. There is a downward slide to the new long-run equilibrium price.

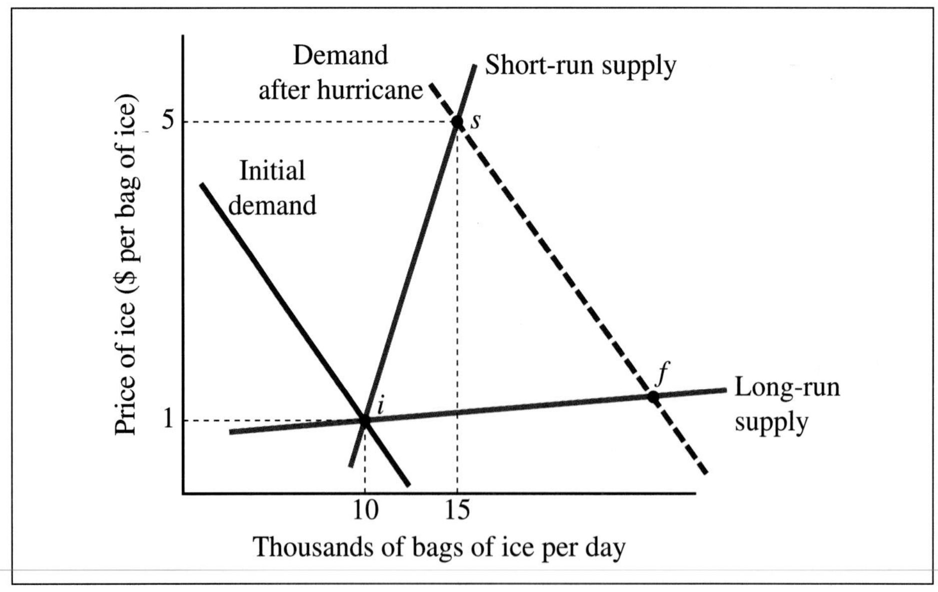

Hurricane Andrew increased the demand for ice and its price, causing entry into the market by roadside ice vendors.

a price of $5 per bag.[5] In the long run, firms responded to the higher price by entering the market, with many people selling ice from trucks parked on streets and highways. As these firms entered the ice market, the price of ice gradually dropped until the market reached the intersection of the new demand curve and the long-run supply curve (point *f*), with a price slightly higher than the pre-hurricane price.

This pattern of price changes was observed in many markets. Immediately following the hurricane, $200 chain saws were sold for $900, but the price dropped steadily as new "roadside" firms entered the market. The same sort of price changes occurred for bottled water, tarpaper (for repairing roofs), and plywood. The basic pattern was a large upward jump in price followed by a downward slide to the long-run equilibrium price.

ECONOMIC DETECTIVE– *Butter Prices*

Several years ago, people became concerned about the undesirable health effects of eating butter. The demand for butter dropped, decreasing its price. Some time later, the price of butter started rising steadily despite the fact that demand hadn't changed in the meantime. Based on several months of price hikes, it appeared that the price of butter would return to the level prevailing before demand decreased. According to a consumer watchdog organization, the rising price of butter was evidence of a conspiracy on the part of butter producers. Is there an alternative explanation?

The key to solving this puzzle is the distinction between the short run and the long run. In the short run, a decrease in demand will cause a relatively large decrease in price as the market moves downward along a relatively steep short-run supply curve. In the short run, not many firms will leave the market even when the price drops, so the decrease in demand will cause a relatively large price drop. Although many of the remaining firms will lose money, they will stay in the market if their total revenue covers their operating or variable cost. In the long run, however, unprofitable firms will leave the market, and as they do, the market price will rise. The pattern of a large price drop followed by a gradual increase in price is a normal pattern for a perfectly competitive market. If the butter industry is a constant-cost industry, the price will eventually reach the price that prevailed before demand decreased. If it is an increasing-cost industry, the price will stop rising before it reaches the original level.

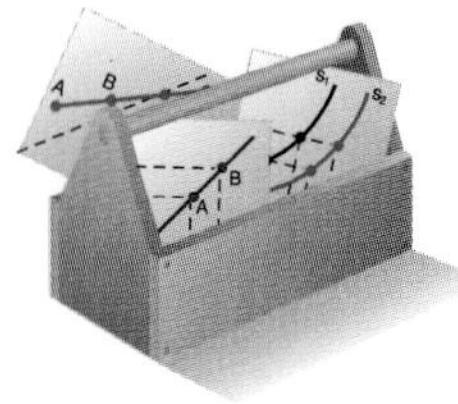

Using the **TOOLS**

In this chapter we use some of the key principles of economics to explain the long-run supply curve and show why the long-run curve is flatter than the short-run curve. We've used these tools to explore the short- and long-run effects of changes in demand. Here are some opportunities to use these tools to do your own economic analysis.

1. Market Effects of an Increase in Housing Demand

Consider the market for apartments in a small city. In the initial equilibrium, the monthly rent (the price) is $500 and the quantity is 10,000 apartments. Suppose that the population of the city suddenly increases by 24%. The price elasticity of demand for apartments is 1.0, while the short-run price elasticity of supply is 0.20 and the long-run price elasticity of supply is 0.50.

a. Depict graphically the short- and long-run effects of the increase in population.
b. By what percentage will the price increase in the short run? (Use the price-change formula from Chapter 5.)
c. By what percentage will the price increase in the long run?

2. Recycling and a Minimum Price for Cullet

To produce glass bottles, bottle manufacturers can use virgin materials (soda ash and sand), cullet (recycled bottles), or a mixture of virgin material and cullet. Cullet is supplied by households and firms when they give their used bottles to recyclers. Suppose that the equilibrium price of cullet is $60 per ton and the equilibrium quantity is 100 tons per day. The price elasticity of supply of cullet (from households and firms) is 2.0, and the price elasticity of demand (from bottle manufacturers) is 1.0.

a. Draw the initial supply curve for cullet and label the starting point (with price = $60 and quantity = 100 tons) with an *s*.
b. Suppose that the state of California wants to promote glass recycling and imposes a minimum price for cullet of $66 per ton. In other words, the state outlaws the sale of cullet at any price below $66. Predict the effect of this minimum price on the quantity of cullet supplied and the quantity demanded.
c. Does the policy achieve its objective of increasing the volume of recycling?

3. Supply Curve for Gasoline

Consider the following data on the relationship between the price of gasoline (in real terms, adjusted for inflation) and the quantity of gasoline sold per day in the city of Ceteris Paribus.

Year	*Price*	*Gallons per Day*
1995	1.00	50,000
1996	1.10	53,000

If possible, draw the industry supply curve and compute the price elasticity of supply.

SUMMARY

In this chapter we've seen that the market supply curve represents the decisions made by individual producers. The law of supply summarizes the relationship between price and quantity supplied: The higher the price, the larger the quantity supplied. In the long run, an increase in price causes new firms to enter the market, so the quantity supplied increases by a relatively large amount. Here are the main points of the chapter.

1. The long-run supply curve will be positively sloped if the average cost of production increases as the industry grows.
2. The long-run supply curve is flatter than the short-run curve because there are diminishing returns in the short run, but not in the long run.
3. An increase in demand causes a large upward jump in price, followed by a downward slide to the new long-run equilibrium price.

KEY TERMS

constant-cost industry, *197*
decreasing-cost industry, *198*
increasing-cost industry, *197*
long-run supply curve, *193*

PROBLEMS AND DISCUSSION QUESTIONS

1. Suppose that each lamp manufacturer produces 10 lamps per hour. In the following table, fill in a number wherever you see a ______. Then use the data in the table to draw the long-run supply curve for lamps.

Number of Firms	*Industry Output*	*Total Cost for Typical Firm*	*Average Cost per Lamp*
40	______	$300	$______
80	______	360	______
120	______	420	______

2. Use the data in Table 1 (page 194) to answer the following question: If the price of chairs is $32, how many chairs will be supplied? Explain your reasoning.
3. Suppose that a new technology decreases the amount of labor time required to produce a particular good. Would you expect all firms eventually to adopt the new technology?
4. Explain the difference between an increasing-cost industry and a constant-cost industry.
5. Draw a long-run supply curve for haircutting that is consistent with this statement: "The haircutting industry in our city uses a tiny fraction of the electricity, scissors, and commercial space available on the market. In addition, the industry uses only about 100 of the 50,000 of people who could cut hair."
6. Draw a long-run supply curve for pencils and explain why you drew it as you did.
7. Explain the difference between the short- and long-run supply curves. Why should we care?

Take It to the Net

We invite you to visit the O'Sullivan/Sheffrin page on the Prentice Hall Web site at:

http://www.prenhall.com/osullivan/

for this chapter's World Wide Web exercise.

MODEL ANSWERS FOR THIS CHAPTER

Chapter-Opening Questions

1. In the short run, the number of firms is fixed and firms cannot change their production facilities. Because of diminishing returns, it takes a relatively large increase in price to increase the quantity supplied. In the long run, firms can enter an industry and build new factories, so there are no diminishing returns. An increase in price will increase the quantity supplied by a relatively large amount.
2. Local governments use zoning policies to limit the amount of land available for apartments, so when demand increases, the competition for apartment land raises the cost of apartments rapidly.
3. Hurricane Andrew knocked out electricity, increasing the demand for ice for preserving food. In the short run, the supply of ice was relatively inelastic, so the price increases by a relatively large amount. Over time, the price dropped as new firms entered the ice market.
4. As in the case of butter, the large drop in price is a short-run effect, reflecting the relatively inelastic supply in the short run. As firms drop out of the market and production drops, the price starts rising.

Test Your Understanding

1. quantity supplied, price
2. The average cost per chair is \$32 (\$640/20).
3. The chair industry competes against other industries for a limited amount of special wood. Firms in the chair industry can increase output only by outbidding other industries for the limited amount available.
4. The related terms are *positively sloped supply curve*, *increasing-cost industry*, and *increasing average cost of production.*
5. The supply curve will be relatively steep.
6. There are diminishing returns in the short run but not in the long run. Because the number of firms is fixed and each firm is stuck with its production facility, it is relatively costly to increase chair production.

Using the Tools

1. Market Effects of an Increase in Housing Demand
   a. See Figure A below.
   b. Use the price-change formula from Chapter 5:

$$\text{percentage change in price} = \frac{\%\text{ change in demand}}{E_s + E_d} = \frac{24}{1.20} = 20\%$$

   c. Percentage change in price = 24/1.50 = 16%.
2. Recycling and a Minimum Price for Cullet
   a. See Figure B on page 207.
   b. Using the elasticity formula, we would predict that the minimum price will increase the supply

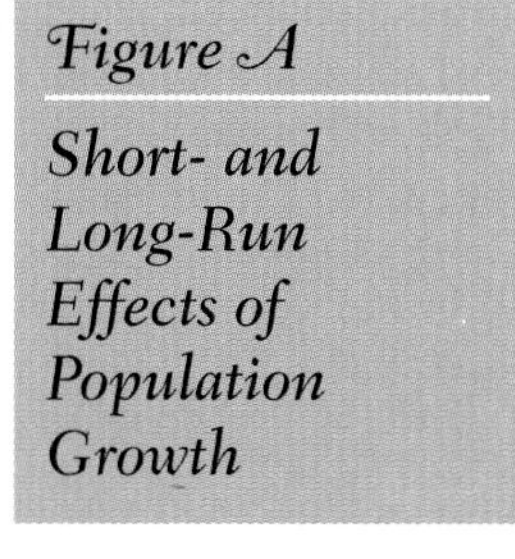

Figure A

Short- and Long-Run Effects of Population Growth

The initial equilibrium is shown by point *i*. The increase in demand moves the market to point *s* in the short run and to point *l* in the long run.

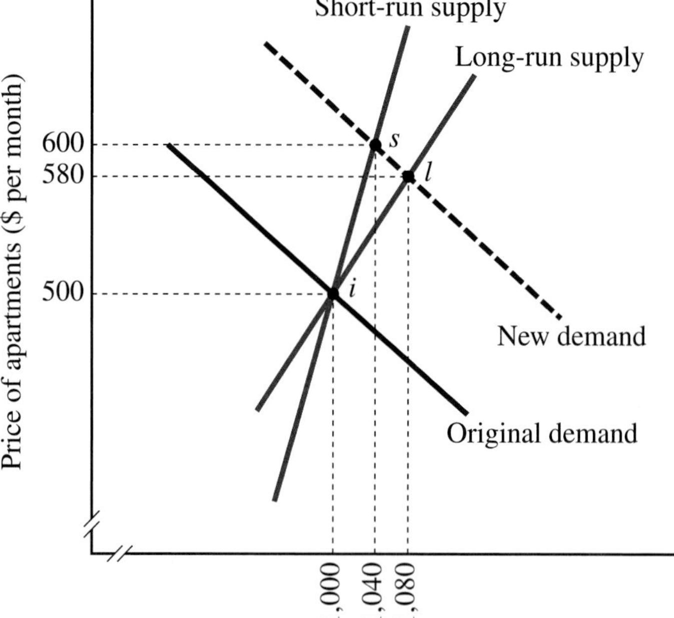

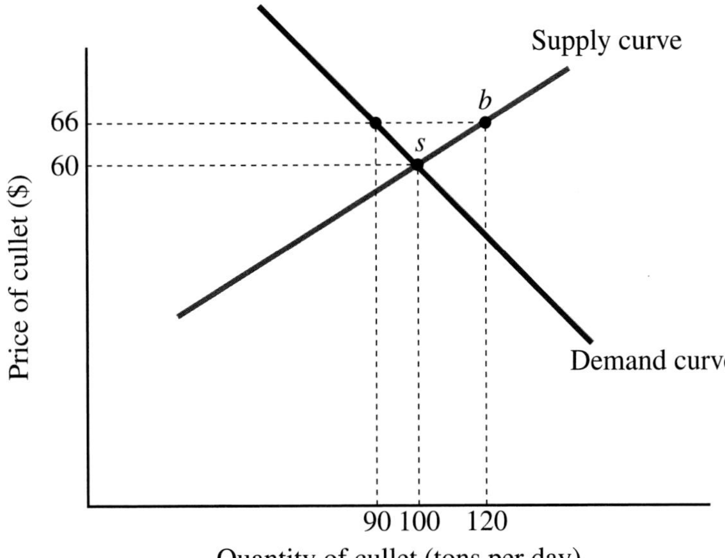

Figure B

Effect of Minimum Price for Cullet

of cullet by 20%. In Figure B we move upward along the supply curve from point *s* (price = $60 and quantity = 100 tons) to point *b* (price = $66 and quantity = 120 tons). At the same time, the quantity demanded decreases by 10%, from 100 tons to 90 tons.

c. The quantity supplied is 120 while the quantity demanded is only 90 tons, so there is a surplus of cullet of 30 tons per day. The amount of cullet actually reused to make bottles is 90 tons, down from 100 tons before the minimum-price policy. In the state of California, the surplus cullet generated by the minimum-price policy was actually dumped in landfills. After several years, the minimum-price policy was abandoned.

3. Supply Curve for Gasoline

We cannot draw a supply or compute a price elasticity of supply because we cannot be certain that the other variables that affect the supply of gasoline did not change over this period.

NOTES

1. Bill Monroe, "Squawfish Bounty Program Is Booming," *The Oregonian,* July 14, 1991, p. D6.
2. Frederic L. Hoff and Max Lawrence, *Implications of World Sugar Markets, Policies, and Production Costs for U.S. Sugar,* Agricultural Economic Research Report 543 (Washington, DC: U.S. Department of Agriculture, Economic Research Service, November 1985).
3. Timothy Tregarthen, "Supply, Demand, and Videotape," *The Margin,* September/October, 1990, p. 29.
4. Tregarthen, "Supply, Demand, and Videotape."
5. Joseph B. Treaster, "Rising Complaints of Price Gouging," *New York Times,* August 30, 1992, p. 1.

CHAPTER 11

Monopoly and Price Discrimination

The day after his 60th birthday, George took his granddaughter to the movies. He was pleased to get a 50% senior-citizen discount for admission but surprised when he discovered that he would have to pay the full price for popcorn. George's experience raises two questions about the pricing decisions of firms.

1. **Is a senior-citizen discount an act of generosity or of profit maximization?**
2. **If a senior discount is sensible for admission to a movie, why isn't it sensible for popcorn?**

In Chapters 9 and 10 we explored the decisions made by firms in a perfectly competitive market, one with dozens or hundreds of firms. This chapter deals with the opposite extreme, a **monopoly**, which is a market that is served by a single firm. In contrast with a perfectly competitive or price-taking firm, a monopolist can pick any price it wants. Of course, the higher the price it charges, the smaller the quantity it will sell, because consumers obey the law of demand. We'll see that some firms charge different prices for different types of consumers, a practice known as **price discrimination**. One example of price discrimination is a discount for senior citizens. Another example is a discount for students.

Monopoly: A market in which a single firm serves the entire market.

Price discrimination: The process under which a firm divides consumers into two or more groups and picks a different price for each group.

A monopoly occurs when there is some barrier to entry that prevents other firms from entering a market. Here is a list of possible entry barriers.

1. A **patent** is granted by the government and gives an inventor the exclusive right to sell a new product for some period of time. Before 1995, U.S.

patents were issued for 17 years from the date the patent was issued. Under a GATT agreement that took effect in 1995, patents in the United States and other GATT nations are now issued for 20 years from the time the inventor applies for a patent. To receive a patent, the inventor must prove that the product is useful and novel (a true innovation, not just a slight modification of an existing product) and must provide a working model. Patent holders in many European countries pay an annual renewal fee for their patents, and the longer an inventor holds a patent, the higher the annual fee. In the United States there are no renewal fees, so by paying a one-time fee, an inventor can prevent anyone else from selling the product for 20 years.

Patent: The exclusive right to sell a particular good for some period of time.

2. In some cases the government implicitly grants monopoly power by allowing industrial associations to restrict the number of firms in the market. For example, the U.S. government allows sports associations such as major league baseball to restrict the number and location of teams.

3. Under a **franchise** or **licensing scheme**, the government designates a single firm to sell a particular good. Here are some examples of franchise and licensing schemes:

Franchise or **licensing scheme:** A policy under which the government picks a single firm to sell a particular good.

- Some cities select a single firm to provide off-street parking.
- The National Park Service picks a single firm to sell food and other goods in Yosemite National Park.
- The Federal Communications Commission issues licenses for individual radio and television stations.

4. In some markets there are large economies of scale in production (average cost decreases as the firm's output increases), so a single firm will be profitable, but a pair of firms would lose money. A **natural monopoly** occurs when the entry of a second firm would make price less than average cost, so a single firm serves the entire market. We discuss natural monopolies in Chapter 12.

Natural monopoly: A market in which there are large economies of scale, so a single firm will be profitable but a pair of firms would lose money.

To explain how a monopoly works, we'll use an example of a monopoly that results from a patent, but the analysis applies to monopolies generated by other barriers to entry as well. We'll see that a monopolist can use the marginal principle to find the price that generates the highest possible profit. Here are some of the practical questions we answer:

1. What are the trade-offs associated with patents and other policies that grant monopoly power?
2. When the patent on a popular pharmaceutical drug expires, what happens to the price of the drug?

We also explain why some firms charge different prices to different consumers. The analysis of price discrimination applies to monopolies as well as firms that share the market with other firms, but it is easiest to explain with a monopoly. Here are some practical questions about price discrimination.

3. Why do faculty members pay more than students for on-campus movies?
4. Why are hardback books so much more expensive than paperback books?

THE MONOPOLIST'S OUTPUT DECISION

A monopolist must decide what price to charge and how much output to produce. Like other firms, the monopoly's objective is to maximize profit, defined as the difference between total revenue and total cost. We learned about production costs in an earlier chapter, so we start our discussion with the revenue side of the monopolist's profit picture. Then we show how a monopolist picks a price and a quantity.

Total Revenue and Marginal Revenue

A firm's *total revenue* is the money the firm gets by selling its product, and is equal to the price times the quantity sold. For example, a firm that sells 2 units of output for $12 each gets $24 in total revenue. Table 1 shows how to use a demand schedule (shown in the first two columns) to compute a firm's total revenue (in the third column). At a price of $16, the firm doesn't sell anything, so its total revenue is zero. To sell the first unit, the firm must cut its price to $14, so its total revenue is $14. When the firm drops its price to $12, it will sell a second unit and increase its total revenue to $24. As the firm continues to cut its price, its total revenue increases for awhile but then starts falling. Selling the fifth unit decreases total revenue from $32 to $30, and selling the sixth unit decreases total revenue to $24. The upper panel in Figure 1 shows the relationship between total revenue and the quantity sold.

The firm's *marginal revenue* is defined as the change in total revenue that results from selling 1 more unit of output. In Table 1 we compute marginal revenue by taking the difference between the total revenue from selling a certain quantity of output (for example, 3 units), and the total revenue from selling 1 less unit of output (for example, 2 units). Looking at the fourth row in the table, the total revenue from selling 3 units is $30 and the total revenue from selling 2 units is only $24, so the marginal revenue from selling the third unit is $6. As shown in the table and in the lower panel of Figure 1, marginal revenue is positive for the first 4 units of output. Beyond that point, selling an additional unit actually decreases total revenue, so marginal revenue is negative. For example, the marginal revenue for the fifth unit is –$2 and the marginal revenue for the sixth unit is –$6.

Table 1 and Figure 1 illustrate the trade-offs associated with cutting a price to sell a larger quantity. When the firm cuts its price from $12 to $10, there is good news and bad news.

1. ***Good news.*** The firm collects $10 from the new customer (the third), so revenue increases by $10.
2. ***Bad news.*** The firm cuts the price for all its customers, so it gets less revenue from the customers would have been willing to pay the higher price ($12). Specifically, the firm collects $2 less from each of the two original customers, so revenue decreases by $4.

The combination of good news and bad news leads to a net increase in total revenue of only $6, an amount equal to the $10 gained on the additional customer minus the $4 lost on the first two customers. Because of the bad news associated with selling an additional unit of output, a firm's marginal revenue is always less than its price.

Table 1: Demand, Total Revenue, and Marginal Revenue

Price	*Quantity Sold*	*Total Revenue*	*Marginal Revenue*
$16	0	0	—
14	1	$14	$14
12	2	24	10
10	3	30	6
8	4	32	2
6	5	30	–2
4	6	24	–6

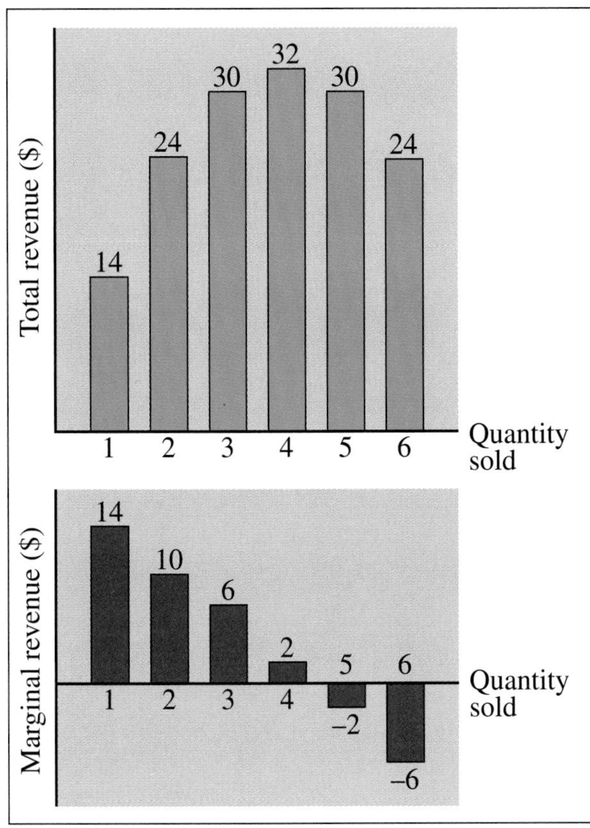

Figure 1

Total Revenue and Marginal Revenue

As the firm cuts its price to sell more output, its total revenue rises for the first 4 units sold, then decreases for the fifth and sixth units. Therefore, marginal revenue is positive for the first 4 units, then becomes negative.

Figure 2 on page 212 shows the demand curve and marginal revenue curve for the data shown in Table 1. Because the firm must cut its price to sell more output, the marginal revenue curve lies below the demand curve. For example, the demand curve shows that the firm will sell 3 units at a price of $10 (point *d*), but the marginal revenue for this quantity is only $6 (point *i*). For quantities of 5 units and greater, marginal revenue is actually negative because when the firm cuts its price to sell 1 additional unit, the bad news dominates the good news: The amount the firm loses on its original customers exceeds the amount it gains on the new one, so total revenue drops.

The Marginal Principle and the Output Decision

We use a simple example to explain how a monopolist decides how much output to produce. Sneezy, who holds a patent on a new drug that cures the common cold, must decide how much of the drug to produce and what price to charge for it. These two decisions are related because consumers obey the law of demand: The higher the price, the smaller the quantity demanded. Sneezy can use the marginal principle to choose how much to produce and what price to charge.

Marginal PRINCIPLE

Increase the level of an activity if its marginal benefit exceeds its marginal cost, but reduce the level if the marginal cost exceeds the marginal benefit. If possible, pick the level at which the marginal benefit equals the marginal cost.

Figure 2

Demand Curve and Marginal Revenue Curve

Marginal revenue is less than price: To increase the quantity sold, a firm cuts its price and receives less revenue on the units that could have been sold at the higher price. Therefore, the marginal revenue curve lies below the demand curve.

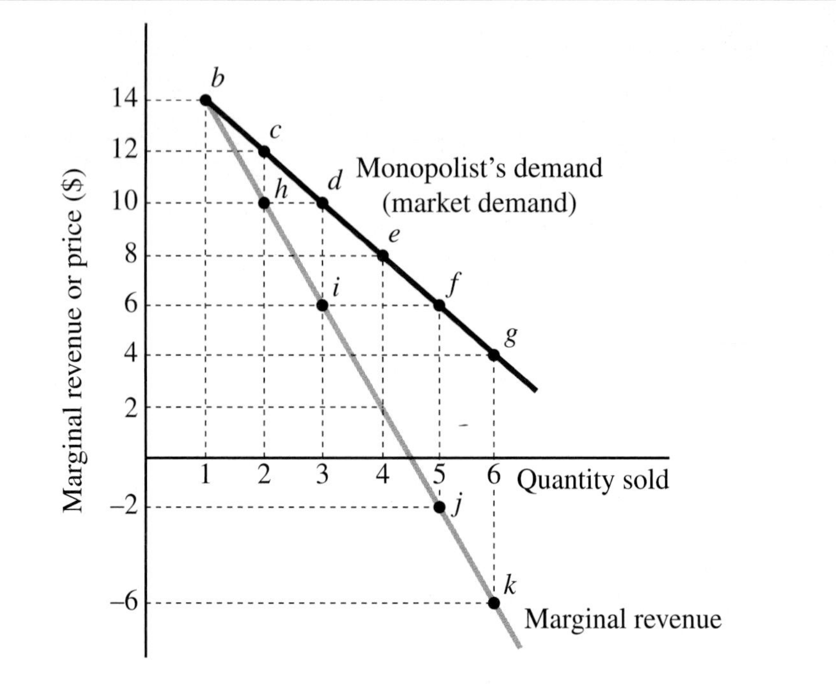

Sneezy's activity is producing the cold drug, and he will pick the quantity at which the marginal revenue (the marginal benefit) equals the marginal cost:

marginal revenue = marginal cost

The first two columns of numbers in Table 2 show the relationship between the price of the cold drug and the quantity demanded. We can use these numbers to draw the market demand curve, as shown in Figure 3. Because Sneezy is a monopolist (the only seller of the drug), the market demand curve shows how much he will sell at each price. The demand curve is negatively sloped, consistent with the law of demand. For example, at a price of $18, the quantity demanded is 600 doses per hour (point *h*), compared to 900 doses at a price of $15 (point *m*).

Like other monopolists, Sneezy must cut his price to sell a larger quantity. Therefore, marginal revenue is less than price, as shown in the third column of numbers in Table 2. In Figure 3 the marginal revenue curve lies below the demand curve. For example, with a price of $18, Sneezy will sell 600 doses (point *h*), and the marginal revenue for this quantity is $12 (point *i*). In other words, if he cuts his

Table 2: Using the Marginal Principle to Pick a Price and Quantity

Price	*Quantity Sold*	*Marginal Revenue*	*Marginal Cost*
$18	600	$12	$6
17	700	10	6
16	800	8	6
15	**900**	**6**	**6**
14	1,000	4	6
13	1,100	2	6
12	1,200	0	6

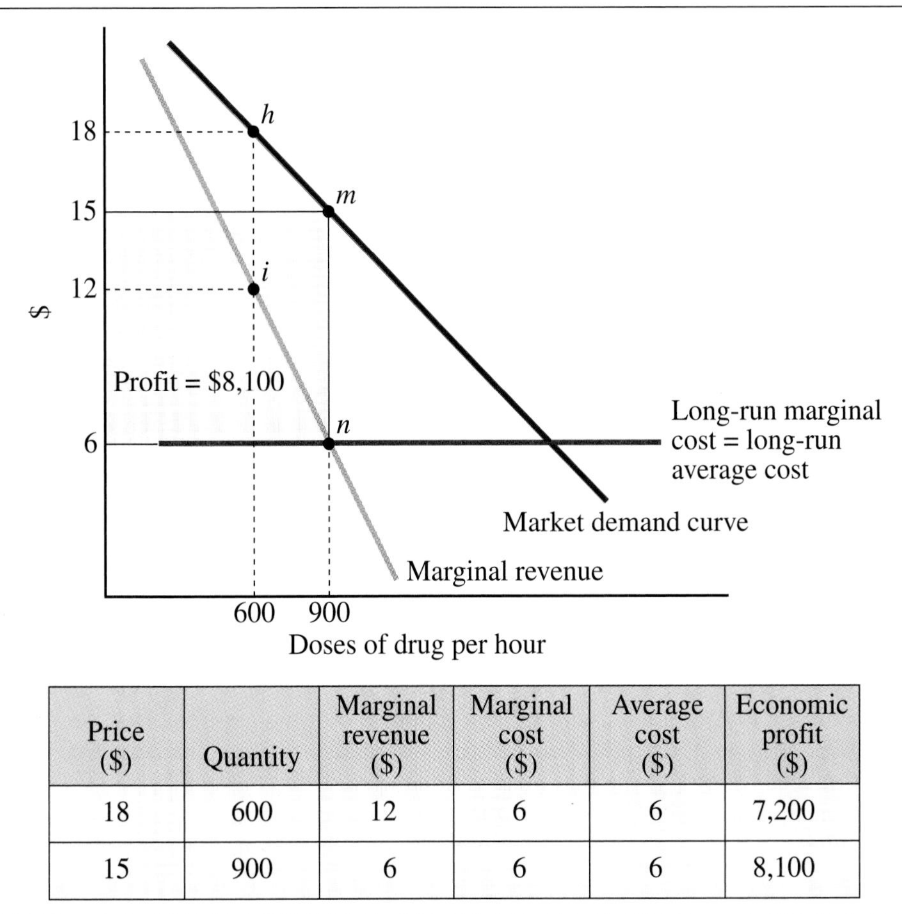

Price ($)	Quantity	Marginal revenue ($)	Marginal cost ($)	Average cost ($)	Economic profit ($)
18	600	12	6	6	7,200
15	900	6	6	6	8,100

Figure 3

Monopolist Picks a Quantity and a Price

To maximize profit, the monopolist picks point *n*, where marginal revenue equals marginal cost. The price is $15 and the quantity is 900. Economic profit equals the gap between price and average cost ($9) times the quantity produced (900), or $8,100.

price by an amount large enough to sell just one more dose, his total revenue would increase by $12. Similarly, with a price of $15, he will sell 900 doses (point *m*) and the marginal revenue for this quantity is $6 (point *n*).

Figure 3 also shows some of Sneezy's long-run cost curves. We'll assume that Sneezy hasn't built his production facility yet, so he makes a long-run decision: Once he picks a quantity to produce, he'll build a production facility to produce that quantity. He'll use his long-run cost curves to make this long-run decision. We know from Chapter 8 that the long-run average cost curve is L-shaped. If the scale economies in the production of the cold drug are small relative to the market demand for the drug, the long-run average cost curve becomes horizontal at a relatively small quantity of output. In Figure 3 we've shown just the horizontal portion of the average cost curve, ignoring the negatively sloped portion.

If the average cost curve is horizontal, the marginal cost will equal the average cost. We can use the arithmetic of averages to explain this. Suppose that you start the term with a cumulative grade-point average (GPA) of 3.0 (a B average) and take a single course. If you get a B in the new course (3.0 for the purposes of computing your GPA), your GPA will not change. Your GPA doesn't change because the grade in the "marginal" course (the new course) equals the "average" grade (your starting GPA). As long as you continue to get a B in each additional course you take, your GPA won't change. For the firm's cost curves, if the marginal cost is the same as the average cost, the average cost won't change. In Figure 3 the marginal cost and the average cost curves are horizontal at a cost of $6 per dose.

Picking a Price and Quantity

We're ready to show how a monopolist can use the marginal principle to pick a quantity and price. Sneezy should produce the quantity at which the marginal revenue equals marginal cost. Looking at the numbers in Table 2, this happens in the fourth row, with a quantity of 900 doses and a price of $15. In Figure 3 the marginal revenue curve intersects the marginal cost curve at point *n*, so the appropriate quantity is 900 doses per hour. To get consumers to buy this quantity, the price must be $15 (point *m* on the demand curve). The average cost of production is $6, so the profit per dose is $9 ($15 minus $6), and Sneezy's profit is $8,100 per hour ($9 per dose times 900 doses).

To show that a price of $15 and a quantity of 900 doses maximizes Sneezy's profit, let's see what would happen if he picked some other quantity. For example, suppose that he tentatively picks a price of $18 and a quantity of 600 (point *h* on the demand curve). To decide whether to drop his price enough to sell one more dose, Sneezy should ask himself two questions.

1. What is the extra cost associated with producing dose number 601? As shown by the marginal cost curve, the marginal cost is $6.
2. What is the extra revenue associated with dose number 601? As shown by point *i* on the marginal revenue curve, the marginal revenue is $12.

If Sneezy wants to maximize his profit, he should produce the 601st dose because the extra revenue ($12) exceeds the extra cost ($6), so his profit will increase by $6. The same argument applies, with different numbers for marginal revenue, for doses 602, 603, and so on, up to 900 doses. Sneezy should continue to increase the quantity produced as long as the marginal revenue exceeds the marginal cost. The marginal principle is satisfied at point *n*, with a total of 900 doses.

Why should Sneezy stop at 900 doses? Beyond that point, the marginal revenue from an additional dose will be less than the marginal cost. Although Sneezy could cut his price and sell a larger quantity, an additional dose would add less to revenue than it adds to cost, so his profit would decrease. As shown in the fifth row in Table 2, Sneezy could sell 1,000 doses at a price of $14, but the marginal revenue for this quantity is only $4, while the marginal cost is $6. Therefore, producing the 1,000th dose would decrease Sneezy's profit by $2. For any quantity exceeding 900 doses, the marginal revenue is less than the marginal cost, so Sneezy should produce only 900 doses.

Formula for Marginal Revenue

There are two ways to compute a firm's marginal revenue. The first approach, shown in Table 1, involves computing the total revenue from selling two different quantities of output. The second approach uses a simple formula that incorporates the good news and bad news associated with a price cut:

$$\text{marginal revenue} = \text{initial price} - (\text{initial quantity} \times \text{slope of demand curve})$$

The first part of the formula's right side shows the good news. If a firm cuts its price by just enough to sell 1 more unit, the firm's revenue increases by an amount just below the initial price. To keep things simple, we'll use the initial price as an approximate value of the good news. Recall that the bad news equals the initial quantity sold times the price cut. The slope of the demand curve is the change in price per unit change in quantity, or the price cut required to sell just one more unit of output. Therefore, the bad news equals the initial quantity times the slope of the demand curve.

We can use our earlier example to show how to use the marginal revenue formula. At point *h* on Sneezy's demand curve, the price is $18 and the quantity is 600. The slope of the demand curve is $0.01: Using points *h* and *m*, the *rise* is

\$3 (\$18 – \$15) and the *run* is 300 doses (900 – 600), so the slope is \$0.01 (\$3/300). This means that to sell one more dose, Sneezy must cut his price by \$0.01. We can plug these values into the marginal revenue formula:

$$\text{marginal revenue} = \text{price} - (\text{quantity} \times \text{slope of demand curve})$$
$$= \$18 - (600 \times \$0.01) = \$12$$

This is shown by point *i* on the marginal revenue curve: For a quantity of 600 doses, the marginal revenue is \$12. This formula provides an approximate value for marginal revenue because it uses the initial price (\$18) instead of the new price (\$17.99). As long as the difference between the initial price and the new price is relatively small, the formula provides a good approximation of the true marginal revenue.

TEST *Your Understanding*

1 Why is a monopolist's marginal revenue less than the price?

2 Complete the statement with a number: At a price of \$15, a firm sells 80 CDs per day. If the slope of the demand curve is \$0.10, marginal revenue is ________.

3 You want to determine the quantity of output produced by a monopolist. What information do you need, and how would you use it?

4 At a price of \$18, the marginal revenue of a CD seller is \$12. If the marginal cost of CDs is \$9, should the firm increase or decrease its price?

THE COSTS OF MONOPOLY

What are the trade-offs—the costs and benefits—associated with a monopoly? This is an important question because in many cases, a monopoly results from government policy. If the costs exceed the benefits, it may be sensible to remove the barriers to entry and allow other firms to enter the market. We discuss the costs of monopoly in this part of the chapter and explore the benefits in the next part.

Monopoly versus Perfect Competition

How does a monopoly differ from a perfectly competitive market? To show the difference, let's imagine that the technology for producing the cold drug is available to everyone, not just to Sneezy. If there are no barriers to entry, firms will enter a profitable market, and entry will continue as long as there is an economic profit to be made. If dozens of firms enter the cold-drug market, each firm would be so small that it would take the market price as given. In other words, the market for the drug would be perfectly competitive.

In Figure 4 on page 216, the long-run supply curve of the perfectly competitive drug industry is a horizontal line. We're assuming that the cold-drug industry is a constant-cost industry: Input prices do not change as the industry grows, so the long-run market supply curve is the same as the horizontal long-run average cost of producing the drug. The long-run supply curve intersects the demand curve at point *p*, with an equilibrium price of \$6 and an equilibrium quantity of 1,800. The monopoly outcome is shown by point *m*: The monopoly has a higher price (\$15) and a smaller quantity (900).

Because the monopolist charges a higher price than we'd have in a perfectly competitive market, consumers are obviously worse off. We can use the concept of consumer surplus to determine just how much worse off they are. As we saw earlier

Figure 4
Monopoly versus Perfect Competition

The horizontal long-run supply curve of a perfectly competitive industry intersects the demand curve at point *p*, generating a price of \$6 and a quantity of 1,800. The monopolist stops at point *m*, producing half the output of a perfectly competitive market.

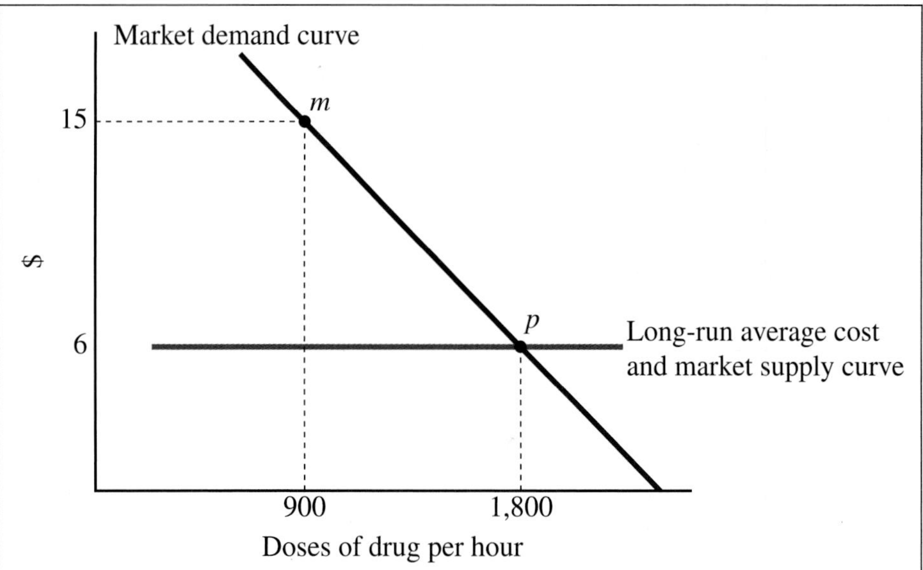

in the book, consumer surplus is shown by the area between the demand curve and the horizontal price line. In Figure 5, the monopoly price is \$15, so the consumer surplus associated with the monopoly is shown by triangle *C*. In contrast, the perfectly competitive price is \$6, so the consumer surplus associated with perfect competition is shown by the larger triangle consisting of triangle *C*, rectangle *M*, and triangle *D*. In other words, a switch from perfect competition to monopoly would decrease consumer surplus by the areas *M* and *D*.

Let's take a closer look at the loss of consumer surplus associated with a monopoly.

- Rectangle *M*. A switch from perfect competition to monopoly increases the price by \$9 per dose. Consumers buy a total of 900 doses at the higher price, so the extra cost to consumers is \$8,100.
- Triangle *D*. A switch to monopoly decreases the quantity consumed because the monopolist charges a higher price and consumers obey the law of demand. Consumers lose the consumer surplus that they would have experienced on the 901st through 1,800th doses, and this loss is shown by triangle *D*.

How much better off are firms under a monopoly situation? Under perfect competition, each firm makes zero economic profit, while a monopolist earns positive economic profit. In Figure 5 the monopolist's profit is shown by rectangle *M*: The profit margin is \$9 (a price of \$15 minus an average cost of \$6) and the quantity is 900 doses per hour, for a profit of \$8,100 per hour. The monopolist gains the rectangle *M* at the expense of consumers: They pay \$9 extra on each dose, while the monopolist gets a profit of \$9 per dose.

Only part of the loss experienced by consumers is recovered by the monopolist, so there is a net loss from monopoly. Consumers lose rectangle *M* and triangle *D*, but the monopolist only gains rectangle *M*, leaving triangle *D* as the net loss or *deadweight loss* associated with monopoly. Consumers lose this triangle because in a perfectly competitive market, they would receive some consumer surplus from the 901st through 1,800th doses, which of course are not produced by the monopolist. The lesson is that monopoly is inefficient because it generates less output than that generated by a perfectly competitive market.

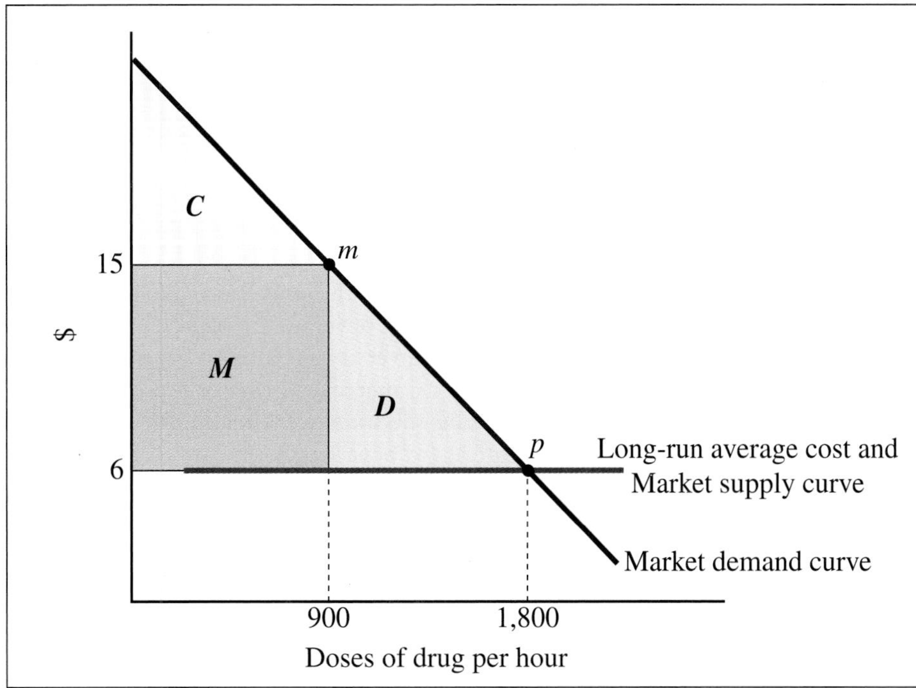

Figure 5

Gains, Losses, and Inefficiency of a Monopoly

A switch from a perfectly competitive market to a monopoly increases the price from \$6 to \$15, decreases consumer surplus by the areas *M* and *D*, and increases profits by rectangle *M*. The net loss or deadweight loss of monopoly is shown by triangle *D*.

Rent Seeking: Using Resources to Get Monopoly Power

Another source of inefficiency from a government-sanctioned monopoly is that firms use resources to acquire monopoly power. A firm that gets a monopoly on a particular product will earn a large profit, so firms are willing to spend large sums of money in an effort to persuade the government to erect barriers to entry (licensing, franchises, and industrial associations). In Figure 5 a firm would be willing to spend up to \$8,100 per hour to get a monopoly on the cold drug. One way to get monopoly power is to hire lobbyists to make the case for monopoly to legislators and other policymakers. This is known as **rent seeking.**

Rent seeking: The process under which a firm spends money to persuade the government to erect barriers to entry and pick the firm as the monopolist.

Rent seeking is inefficient because it uses resources that could be used in other ways. For example, the people employed as lobbyists could instead produce goods and services. In Figure 5 if a monopolist spent all its potential profit (\$8,100 per hour) on rent-seeking activity, the net loss to society would be areas *M* and *D*, not just area *D*. The classic study of rent seeking found that firms in some industries spent up to 30% of their total revenue to get monopoly power.[1] For an example of rent seeking, read the Closer Look box on page 218, "Paying for Monopoly Power on Campus."

PATENTS AND MONOPOLY POWER

Are there benefits associated with a government-sanctioned monopoly? As we'll see, a patent or another entry barrier encourages innovation because the innovator knows that he or she will earn monopoly profits on a new product for some period of time. If the monopoly profits are large enough to offset the substantial research and development costs of a new product, a firm will develop the product.

Incentives for Innovation

Let's use Sneezy's cold drug to show why a patent encourages innovation. Suppose that Sneezy hasn't yet developed the drug and he computes the potential benefits and costs of developing the drug as follows.

A Closer LOOK

Paying for Monopoly Power on Campus

In 1994, the Coca-Cola Company gave several million dollars to a large state university, enabling the university to build a new scoreboard for its football stadium and remodel its student center. Was this an act of generosity or profit maximization? In return for the multimillion-dollar payment, the university granted Coca-Cola the exclusive right to sell beverages on campus until the year 2006. Coca-Cola will use its new monopoly power to increase the price of beverages, so the money for the scoreboard and student center will actually come out of the pockets of students.

This beverage contract raises some interesting questions about monopoly power and the pricing of education.

1. Why doesn't the university allow competition among beverage suppliers?
2. If the university needs to raise money, why doesn't it increase tuition or fees rather than raising the money indirectly through higher prices for beverages?

Source: After Jeannie Donnelly, "OSU Beverages Will Be Provided Exclusively by Coca-Cola," *The Daily Barometer,* May 27, 1994, p. 1.

1. The cost of research and development would be $14 million.
2. The annual profit from a monopoly will be $2 million (in today's dollars).
3. It will take Sneezy's competitors three years to develop and produce their own versions of the drug, so if he isn't protected by a patent, his monopoly will last only three years.

Based on these numbers, Sneezy won't develop the drug unless he receives a patent that lasts at least seven years. That's the length of time he needs to recover his research and development costs ($2 million per year times seven years is $14 million). For example, if there is no patent and he loses his monopoly in three years, he will earn a profit of $6 million, which is less than his research and development costs. On the other hand, with a 20-year patent he will earn $40 million, which is more than enough to recover his costs.

Trade-offs from Patents

Is the patent for Sneezy's drug beneficial from the social perspective? The patent grants monopoly power to Sneezy, and he responds by charging a relatively high price and producing half the quantity that would be produced in a perfectly competitive market (900 doses per hour instead of 1,800). From society's perspective, 1,800 doses would be better than 900 doses, but we don't have that choice. Sneezy won't develop the drug unless a patent protects him from competition for at least seven years. Therefore, society's choice is between 900 doses (the patent and monopoly outcome) and zero doses. Because 900 doses is clearly better than none, the patent is beneficial from society's perspective.

What about a product that would be developed even without a patent? For example, suppose that Flo could develop a new drug with a research and development project costing $5 million. If Flo does not have a patent for her new drug, she would earn monopoly profits of $2 million per year for three years, a total of $6 million. Because her research and development costs are relatively low, a three-year monopoly will generate enough profit to cover her costs, so she will develop the new drug even without a patent. Therefore, if the government issues a 20-year patent, the only effect is to prolong Flo's monopoly, meaning that the patent would be inefficient from society's perspective.

What are the general conclusions about the merits of the patent system? As usual, there are some trade-offs. It is sensible to grant a patent for a product that would otherwise not be developed, but not sensible to grant one for a product that would be developed even without a patent. Unfortunately, we don't know in advance whether a particular product would be developed without a patent, so we can't be selective in granting patents. Therefore, some patents will merely prolong a firm's monopoly power and generate higher prices. There is no consensus among economists on whether the benefits of patents (from the development of new products) exceed the costs (from prolonging monopoly power).

What happens when a patent expires? New firms will enter the market and the resulting competition for consumers will decrease prices. Nonetheless, the original firm continues to benefit from its innovation: It often charges a higher price than its competitors but still keeps a large part of the market. For an example of this phenomenon, read the Closer Look box "Do Doctors Care about Prices?"

Do the Benefits Exceed the Costs?

We cannot make a clear-cut case for or against a government-sanctioned monopoly on efficiency grounds. As usual, there are both benefits and costs associated with using patents, licenses, franchises, and industrial associations to establish monopolies. On the cost side, a monopolist produces less output than a perfectly competitive market, and people waste resources trying to get and keep monopoly power. On the benefit side, a patent or a license increases the payoff from research and development, and firms respond by developing new products. In some cases—when research and development costs are substantial and other firms could quickly imitate a new product—the benefits will dominate the costs, and public policies that support a monopoly are sensible. In other cases it would be more efficient to eliminate the artificial barriers to entry.

A Closer LOOK

Do Doctors Care about Prices?

Generic drugs sell for about half as much as name-brand drugs. Why do so few physicians prescribe generic drugs to their patients?

When the patent for a popular pharmaceutical drug expires, other firms introduce generic versions of the drug. The generics are virtually identical to the original or branded drug, but they sell at a much lower price. In response to competition from generics, the producer of the branded drug usually decreases its price, but the price of the branded drug is typically about twice the price of generic drugs. Despite this large difference in price, generic drugs capture only about one-fourth of the typical market.

To explain why generics capture such a small part of the market, think about how physicians choose between a branded drug and its generic equivalent. Like other consumers, physicians have some brand loyalty, so we'd expect many of them to continue prescribing branded drugs even when generics become available. In addition, physicians make their choices with little information about the prices of branded and generic drugs. Many physicians don't check price lists before they prescribe drugs, so they are often ill-equipped to make economical choices for their patients.

Source: After Richard E. Caves, Michael D. Whinston, and Mark A. Hurwitz, "Patent Expiration, Entry, and Competition in the U.S. Pharmaceutical Industry," *Brookings Papers: Microeconomics* (Washington, DC: The Brookings Institution, 1991), pp. 1–50.

TEST *Your Understanding*

5 If you want to determine the socially efficient quantity of output, what information do you need?

6 Your city will select a single firm to provide off-street parking. Your long-run average cost is $30 per parking space per day and you'd charge a price of $35 per space per day for a total of 500 spaces. How much would you be willing to pay for the monopoly?

7 For each of the following changes in the Sneezy example, determine whether Sneezy will develop the cold drug without a patent.

a. The cost of research and development is $3 million instead of $14 million.

b. In the absence of a patent, Sneezy will have a monopoly for five years rather than three years.

8 Critically appraise the following statement: "I just invented a new product. I could do the research and development required to bring the product to the market, but it would cost me $100 million. Once other firms develop imitations of my product, I will earn an annual profit of only $1 million. If I don't have a patent, I would be crazy to develop this product."

9 In the United States you cannot patent a gambling device such as a slot machine. Can you think of any rationale for this policy?

PRICE DISCRIMINATION

Up to this point, we've assumed that a monopolist charges the same price to all consumers. In some markets, firms divide consumers into two or more groups and pick a different price for each group, a practice known as *price discrimination.* One approach is to offer a discount (resulting in a lower price) to some types of consumers. The firm identifies a group of customers who are not willing to pay the regular price and then offers a discount to people in that group.

Here are some real-life examples of price discrimination involving discounts for certain groups of consumers.

1. Discounts on airline tickets for travelers who spend Saturday night away from home. An airline passenger who spends a Saturday night away from home is likely to be a tourist, not a business traveler. The typical tourist is not willing to pay as much for air travel as is the typical business traveler.
2. Discount coupons for groceries and restaurant food. The typical coupon-clipper is not willing to pay as much as the typical consumer.
3. Manufacturers' rebates for appliances. A person who takes the trouble to mail a rebate form to the manufacturer is not willing to pay as much as the typical consumer.
4. Senior-citizen discounts on airline tickets, restaurant food, drugs, and entertainment.
5. Student discounts on movies and concerts.

The only legal restriction on price discrimination is that a firm cannot use it to drive rival firms out of business. We discuss this process, known as *predatory pricing,* in Chapter 13.

Price discrimination is not always possible. A firm has an opportunity for price discrimination if three conditions are met.

1. ***Market power.*** The firm must have some control over its price. Therefore, price discrimination does not occur in a perfectly competitive market, where each firm takes the market price as given.

2. ***Different consumer groups.*** Consumers must differ in their willingness to pay for the product or in their responsiveness to changes in price (as measured by the price elasticity of demand).

3. ***Resale is not possible.*** It must be impractical for one consumer to resell the product to another consumer. As a counterexample, suppose that a bar sells drinks to women at a discount price and women can easily resell drinks to men. In this case, women are likely to buy extra drinks and sell them to men, so the bar won't sell many drinks at the regular price and price discrimination won't be profitable. In general, the possibility of resale causes price discrimination to break down, so a firm will be better off with a single price.

Senior Discounts in Restaurants

We can explain the mechanics of price discrimination with an example of a restaurant that offers discounts to senior citizens. Suppose that there is a single restaurant in a particular town, so we're dealing with a monopoly. Of course, price discrimination also occurs in markets with more than one firm. It is easier to explain price discrimination by a monopolist, but the conclusions apply to other markets as well.

Suppose that restaurant patrons can be divided into two groups, senior citizens and others. In Figure 6 the demand curve for senior citizens is lower than the demand curve for other citizens, reflecting the assumption that the typical senior is willing to pay less than the typical nonsenior. What happens if the restaurant picks a single price for the two groups? Suppose that the most profitable single price is \$5. At this price, the restaurant will have 100 seniors (point *s*) and 300 nonseniors (point *n*), for a total of 400 customers per day. In Figure 6 the average cost of production is constant at \$1 per customer, so the profit per customer is \$4 and the restaurant's total profit is \$1,600 (\$4 times 400).

Under a price-discrimination scheme, the restaurant will divide its customers into two groups and offer a lower price to senior citizens. This is sensible because the two groups have different demands for restaurant meals, so the restaurant should treat them differently. Panel A of Figure 6 shows how to pick a price for

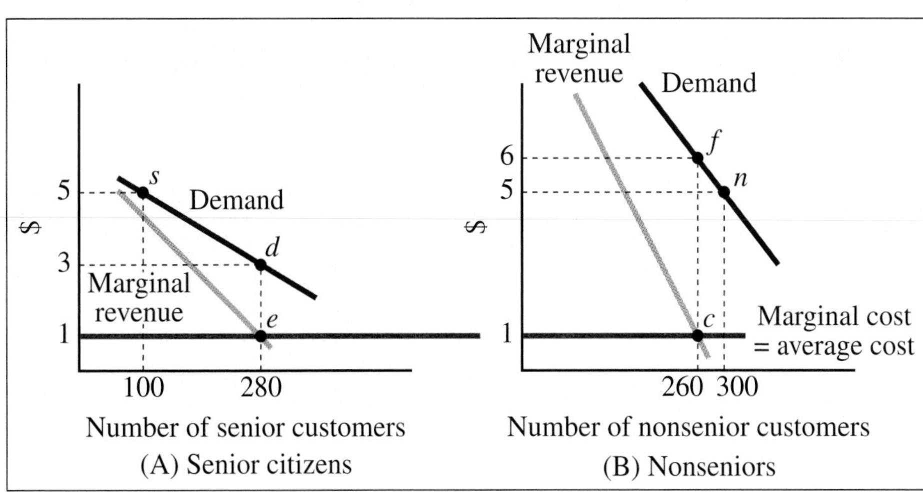

Figure 6

Price Discrimination

Under a single-price policy, the firm picks a single price of \$5 and reaches point *n* on the nonsenior demand curve (300 customers) and point *s* on the senior demand curve (100 customers). Under a price-discrimination scheme, the price for nonseniors is \$6 (point *f*) and the price for the seniors is \$3 (point *d*).

senior citizens. The marginal principle (marginal revenue = marginal cost) is satisfied at point *e*, with 280 seniors per day. Therefore, the appropriate price for seniors is \$3 (point *d* on the senior demand curve). The profit per senior is \$2 [\$3 minus \$1 (the average cost)] and the restaurant's profit from its senior customers is \$560 per day (\$2 times 280). In contrast, the profit from seniors under the single-price policy is only \$400 per day (\$4 per customer times 100 seniors).

We can also use the marginal principle to find the appropriate price for nonseniors. In panel B of Figure 6, the marginal principle is satisfied at point *c*, with 260 nonsenior customers per day. Therefore, the restaurant should charge \$6 for nonseniors (point *f* on the demand curve), twice the price charged to seniors. The profit per nonsenior is \$5 (\$6 minus the average cost of \$1) and the restaurant's profit from nonseniors is \$1,300 per day (\$5 times 260), compared to only \$1,200 from nonseniors under the single-price policy (\$4 per customer times 300 nonseniors).

By treating the two groups of consumers differently, the restaurant can earn more profit and serve more consumers. The switch from a single-price policy to price discrimination increases the restaurant's profit in both segments of the market, so its total profit increases from \$1,600 to \$1,860 per day (\$560 from seniors plus \$1,300 from nonseniors). In addition, the total number of customers increases from 400 to 540 (280 seniors and 260 nonseniors).

Price Discrimination and the Elasticity of Demand

We can use the concept of price elasticity of demand to explain why price discrimination increases the restaurant's profit. Compared to other consumers, senior citizens have more elastic demand for restaurant meals, in part because they have lower income and more flexible schedules that give them more time to shop around for low prices. In other words, seniors are more responsive to changes in price. Let's start with a single-price policy (\$5 for each customer) and assume that the demand for restaurant meals by nonseniors is inelastic, while the demand by seniors is elastic.

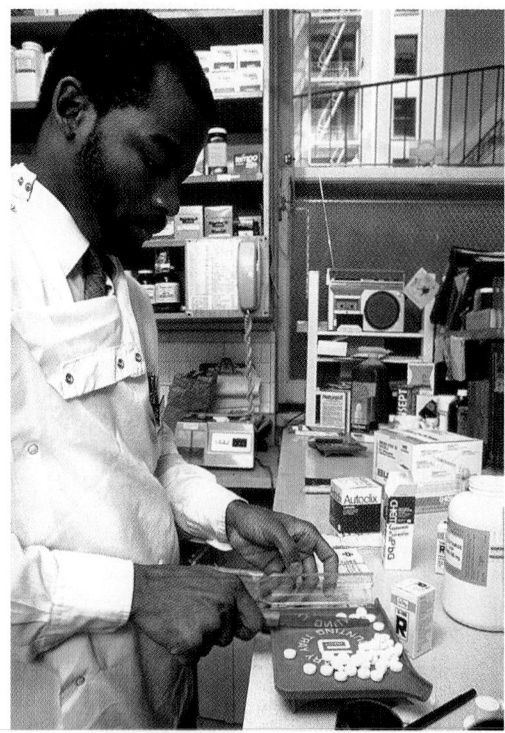

Local pharmacies pay up to five times as much as hospitals for common drugs, a result of price discrimination.

Why does an increase in the price for nonseniors increase the restaurant's profit? We know from Chapter 5 that if demand is inelastic, an increase in price will increase total revenue: The good news (more revenue per customer) dominates the bad news (fewer customers). Therefore, an increase in the nonsenior price will increase the revenue from nonseniors. At the same time, the restaurant will have fewer nonsenior customers, so its costs will decrease. Because the restaurant's nonsenior revenue increases while its cost decreases, its profit will increase.

Why does a *decrease* in the price for senior customers increase the restaurant's profit? If the demand by seniors is elastic, a decrease in price will increase the revenue from seniors: The good news (more customers) dominates the bad news (less revenue per customer). At the same time, the restaurant's total cost will increase because it will serve more meals to seniors. If demand is very elastic, however, the increase in revenue will more than offset the increase in cost, so the restaurant's profit from senior citizens will increase.

The same logic applies to other cases of price discrimination. A firm will charge a higher price to consumers with relatively inelastic demand. For example, local pharmacies pay up to five times as much as hospitals for common drugs.[2] The demand for drugs by pharmacies is relatively inelastic because pharmacies stock a wide variety of drugs to fill individual prescriptions, and they buy much smaller quantities of each drug. The inelastic demand by pharmacies encourages pharmaceutical firms to discriminate against them. For an example of international price discrimination, read the Closer Look box "International Price Discrimination: Korean TV Sets."

Dumping: The practice under which a firm charges a lower price in a foreign market.

A Closer LOOK

International Price Discrimination: Korean TV Sets

In the 1980s, the worst place to buy a Korean TV set was Korea, where consumers paid 52% more than their U.S. counterparts paid for identical Korean sets.* Why did Korean firms charge their fellow citizens so much more for TV sets?

The Korean firms engaged in price discrimination, selling for a higher price in the market with relatively inelastic demand. Demand was inelastic in Korea because the firms had a virtual monopoly in the home market: Consumers did not have the option of buying imported TV sets, so they were not very responsive to changes in the price of Korean TV sets. In contrast, the Korean firms competed with dozens of firms in the U.S. market, so demand was relatively elastic. In this case the Korean firms discriminated against their fellow citizens and in favor of foreigners. International price discrimination—selling for a higher price in the home country—known as *dumping*, is illegal under international trade agreements. We return to the issue of dumping later in the book.

As a result of price discrimination by Korean producers, Korean consumers paid 52% more than U.S. consumers for identical TV sets.

*Taeho Bark, "The Korean Consumer Electronics Industry: Reaction to Antidumping Actions," Chapter 7 in *Antidumping: How It Works and Who Gets Hurt,* edited by J. Michael Finger (Ann Arbor, MI: University of Michigan Press, 1993).

Application: Movie Admission and Popcorn

We're ready to answer the two questions in the opening paragraph of the chapter. A senior discount for movie admission is not an act of generosity but part of a pricing strategy designed to increase profit. Senior citizens are typically willing to pay less than other citizens for movies, so a theater divides its consumers into two groups—seniors and others—and offers a discount to seniors. This price discrimination in favor of senior citizens increases the theater's profit. Why don't theaters offer a senior discount for popcorn? Unlike admission to the theater, popcorn can be easily transferred from one customer to another. If senior citizens could buy popcorn at half the regular price, many nonseniors would get seniors to buy popcorn for them, so the theater wouldn't sell as much popcorn at the regular price. Therefore, price discrimination will not be profitable.

ECONOMIC DETECTIVE– *Why Are Hardback Books So Expensive?*

Most novels are published in two forms: hardback and paperback. The cost of producing a hardback book is only about 20% higher than the cost of producing a paperback book, but the price of a hardback book is about three times the price of a paperback book. Why is the price difference so large when the cost difference is so small?

The key to solving this puzzle is the fact that hardback novels are published first, followed several weeks or months later by the paperback edition. Booksellers use hardbacks and paperbacks to distinguish between two types of consumers, those willing to pay a lot and those willing to pay a little. The people who are willing to pay the most are eager to read the book as soon as it comes out, so they pay $18 for a hardback book. The people who are willing to pay less are more patient and wait a few weeks or months for the $6 paperback version. In other words, the pricing of hardback and paperback books is another example of price discrimination.

TEST *Your Understanding*

10 Why is the aspirin sold in airports so much more expensive than the aspirin sold in grocery stores?

11 Complete the statement with *increase* or *decrease*: Suppose that a firm starts with a single price and then switches to a price-discrimination scheme. The firm will ____________ the price for the group of consumers with relatively inelastic demand and ____________ the group with relatively elastic demand.

12 Many bars that impose cover charges have lower cover charges for women. Why?

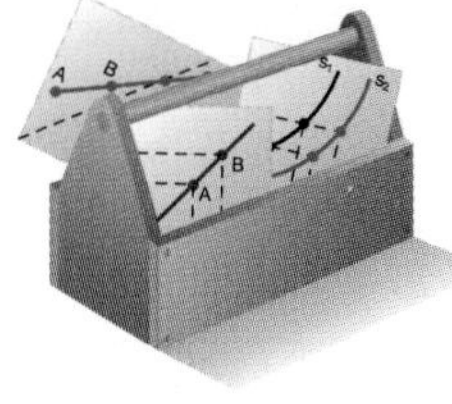

Using the TOOLS

We've seen how a monopolist uses its revenue and cost curves to decide how much to produce and what price to charge. We've also looked at price discrimination as a strategy to increase profit. Here are some opportunities to do your own economic analysis.

1. ECONOMIC EXPERIMENT: *Price Discrimination*

Here is an experiment that shows how a monopolist—a museum—picks different prices for different consumer groups. Some students play the roles of consumers, and others play the roles of museum managers. Here is how the experiment works.

- The instructor picks a small group of students (three to five people) to represent the museum. There is a fixed marginal cost of each museum patron (for ticket-takers, ushers, cleanup, and other tasks).
- There are 40 consumers (potential museum patrons), half of whom are senior citizens with senior-citizen cards. Each consumer receives a number indicating how much he or she is willing to pay for a trip to a museum.
- In each round of the experiment, each museum posts two prices, one for senior citizens and one for nonseniors. Consumers then decide whether to buy a ticket at the relevant posted price.
- A consumer's score in a particular round equals the difference between his or her WTP and the amount actually paid for a museum admission.
- A museum's score equals its profit, equal to its total revenue minus its total cost ($2 times the number of patrons).

The experiment is run for five rounds. At the end of the experiment, each consumer computes his or her score by adding up his or her consumer surpluses. The museum's score equals the sum of the profits from the five rounds.

2. Textbook Pricing: Publishers versus Authors

Consider the problem of setting a price for an economics textbook. The marginal cost of production is constant at $20 per book. The publisher knows from experience that the slope of the demand curve is $0.20: Starting with a price of $48, a price cut of $0.20 will increase the quantity of books demanded by 1 book. For example, here are some combinations of price and quantity:

Price	$44	$40	$36	$32	$30
Quantity	80	100	120	140	150

a. What price will the publisher choose?

b. Suppose that the author receives a royalty payment equal to 10% of the total sales revenue from the book. If the author could choose a price, what would it be?

c. Why do the publisher and the author disagree about the price for the book?

d. Design an alternative author-compensation scheme under which the author and the publisher would choose the same price.

3. Price Discrimination in a Campus Film Series

You manage a campus film series and charge different prices to students and faculty members. The current prices and numbers of viewers are as follows:

	Price	*Number of viewers*	*Slope of demand curve*
Students	$3	100	0.01
Faculty	$4	50	0.10

The marginal cost of another viewer is zero. Does the current pricing scheme maximize your total revenue? If not, how should you change your prices?

4. Pricing First-Run Movies and Early Apples

If you see a movie when it first comes out, you pay much more than you would if you waited a month or two for the movie to appear at a second-run movie theater. If you buy apples early in the harvest season, you pay more than you would if you waited until the middle of the harvest season. Are both movies and apples subject to price discrimination?

SUMMARY

In this chapter we've seen some of the subtleties of monopolies and their pricing policies. Most people realize that a monopolist charges a high price and produces a relatively small quantity of output, but they don't realize that a lot of resources are wasted in the process of seeking monopoly power. On the positive side, some of the products we use today might never have been invented without the patent system and the monopoly power it grants. We've also seen that senior-citizen discounts and other forms of favorable price discrimination are not acts of generosity but are designed to increase the firm's profits. Here are the main points of the chapter.

1. Compared to a perfectly competitive market, a market served by a monopolist will have a higher price and a smaller quantity of output.
2. A switch from perfect competition to monopoly decreases consumer surplus by more than it increases profits, so there is a net loss or a deadweight loss to society.
3. Some firms spend money and use resources to acquire monopoly power, a process known as rent-seeking.
4. Patents protect innovators from competition, leading to higher prices for new products but a greater incentive to develop new products.
5. To engage in price discrimination, a firm divides its customers into two groups and charges a lower price to the group with the more elastic demand.

KEY TERMS

dumping, *223*
franchise, *209*
licensing scheme, *209*
monopoly, *208*
natural monopoly, *209*
patent, *208*
price discrimination, *208*
rent seeking, *217*

PROBLEMS AND DISCUSSION QUESTIONS

1. Consider a restaurant that charges $10 for all you can eat and has 30 customers at this price. The slope of the demand curve is 0.10 and the marginal cost of providing a meal is $3. What price will satisfy the marginal principle and maximize the restaurant's profit?
2. The National Park Service grants a single firm the right to sell food and other goods in Yosemite National Park. Discuss the trade-offs associated with this policy.
3. Since 1963, many state governments that outlaw commercial lotteries have introduced state lotteries to raise revenue for state and local governments. In 1994, the net revenue from these lotteries was about $10 billion. Would you expect the state lotteries to have higher or lower paybacks (total prize money divided by the total amount of money collected) than commercial games like horse racing and slot machines? Explain.
4. Consider the Slappers, a hockey team that plays in an arena with 8,000 seats. The only cost associated with staging a hockey game is a fixed cost of $6,000: The team incurs this cost regardless of how many people attend a game. The demand curve for hockey tickets has a slope of 0.001 ($1 divided by 1,000): Each $1 increase in price decreases the number of tickets sold by 1,000. For example, here are some combinations of price and quantity:

Price	$4	$5	$6	$7
Quantity	8,000	7,000	6,000	5,000

   The owner's objective is to maximize the profit per hockey game (total revenue minus the $6,000 fixed cost).
   a. What is the appropriate price?
   b. If the owner picks the price that maximizes profit, how many seats in the arena will be empty? Is it rational to leave some seats empty?
5. The government allows professional sports associations (collections of teams) to restrict the number of teams. How do these barriers to entry affect the

price of tickets to professional sporting events and the number of tickets sold? If we eliminated these barriers to entry, what would happen to ticket prices and total attendance at sporting events?

6. Consider an airline that initially has a single price ($300) for all consumers. At this price it has 120 business travelers and 80 tourists. The airline's marginal cost is $100. The slope of the business demand curve is 2.0 and the slope of the tourist demand curve is 1.0. Does the single-price policy maximize the airline's profit? If not, how should it change its prices?
7. Suppose that you are the marketing manager for the Slappers, the hockey team discussed in an earlier problem. Outline a price-discrimination scheme that would increase the team's ticket sales and profit.
8. Appraise the following statement from a member of a city council: "Several of the merchants in our city offer discounts to our senior citizens. These discounts obviously decrease the merchants' profits, and we should decrease the merchants' taxes to offset their losses on senior-citizen discounts."
9. An advertisement for an early-bird sale at a fabric store notes that people who buy fabric between 6 and 7 A.M. receive a 40% discount, while people who shop between 7 and 8 A.M. receive a 20% discount. What is the rationale for such a pricing scheme?
10. Why are senior-citizen discounts common for services such as admission to museums and other entertainment but uncommon for consumer goods such as hardware, appliances, and automobiles?

Take It to the Net

We invite you to visit the O'Sullivan/Sheffrin page on the Prentice Hall Web site at:

http://www.prenhall.com/osullivan/

for this chapter's World Wide Web exercise.

MODEL ANSWERS FOR THIS CHAPTER

Chapter-Opening Questions

1. The bad news is that a monopolist charges a higher price. The good news is that monopoly profits encourage innovation.
2. In response to competition from generics, the producer of the branded drug usually decreases its price, but the price of the branded drug is still about twice the price of generic drugs.
3. Compared to students, faculty members are willing to pay more for campus movies (their demand is less elastic), so a profit-maximizing monopolist will charge them a higher price.
4. Consumers who are eager to read a book are willing to pay a lot, and end up buying the expensive hardback version because it comes out first. People who are willing to pay less wait for the cheaper paperback version a few months later.

Test Your Understanding

1. To sell 1 more unit, the monopolist must cut the price. The marginal revenue equals the price minus the revenue lost from selling goods at a lower price to the original customers.
2. MR = $15 – (80 × $0.10) = $7.
3. You need the marginal revenue curve and the marginal cost curve. The monopolist will pick the quantity at which the two curves intersect.
4. Marginal revenue exceeds marginal cost, so the firm should increase its output by cutting its price.
5. The socially efficient quantity is shown by the intersection of the long-run supply and demand curve, so you need these two curves. If the industry is a constant-cost industry, the supply curve will be the same as the (horizontal) long-run average cost curve.
6. The profit per space is $5 ($35 – $30), so the daily profit is $2,500 ($5 per space × 500 spaces). You are willing to pay up to $2,500 per day for the monopoly.
7. a. With the lower cost of research, Sneezy will make enough profit in the first three years ($6 million) to cover the research and development cost, so he will develop the drug.
   b. Sneezy's monopoly profit lasts five years, for a total of $10 million. This is less than the cost

of the research and development project ($14 million), so he won't develop the drug.

8. It will be sensible to develop the product even without a patent if the inventor maintains his monopoly position long enough. Suppose it takes other firms five years to develop an imitation product and the original inventor earns a profit of $30 million per year. In this case the monopoly profit will more than cover the research and development costs.
9. The absence of a patent will discourage innovation in gambling devices. Perhaps this is an indirect way of discouraging gambling.
10. People looking for aspirin in airports usually have a headache or expect one. They are willing to pay more than a headache-free grocery shopper: The airport shopper has a less elastic demand. Firms engage in price discrimination, charging a higher price to the group of consumers with the less elastic demand (airport customers).
11. increase, decrease
12. If women are willing to pay less than men for admission into a bar (or if they have a more elastic demand), price discrimination may increase the bar's profit. A discounted cover charge works well because the good purchased (admission) cannot be transferred to men.

Using the Tools

2. Textbook Pricing: Publishers versus Authors
   a. To maximize profit, the publisher picks the quantity at which marginal revenue equals marginal cost. Using the marginal revenue formula, we can compute the marginal revenue at each price and quantity. Here are the numbers for marginal revenue:

Price	$44	$40	$36	$32	$30
Quantity	80	100	120	140	150
MR	$28	$20	$12	$ 4	$ 0

   If the marginal cost is $20, the publisher will pick a price of $40 and a quantity of 100 books.
   b. The author's objective is to maximize total revenue (price times quantity), not profit (total revenue minus total cost). From the author's perspective, the marginal cost of selling another book is zero, so to satisfy the marginal principle, the author will choose the price at which marginal revenue is zero. In this case the author would choose a price of $30.
   c. They disagree because the authors ignore production costs.
   d. If the author received a share of profits instead of a share of revenue, he or she would choose the same price as the publisher.
3. Price Discrimination in a Campus Film Series

   At the current prices, the marginal revenue for students is $2 = $3 − (100 × 0.01), which exceeds the marginal cost, so you should decrease the price. In contrast, the marginal revenue for faculty is −$1 = $4 − (50 × 0.10). Marginal revenue is negative, so an increase in price will increase total revenue.
4. Pricing First-Run Movies and Early Apples

   The price pattern for movies is another example of price discrimination. Eager moviegoers are willing to pay a large amount of money for a movie when it first comes out, while patient moviegoers are willing to wait for the movie to appear in a second-run theater at a lower price.

   The price pattern for apples is unlikely to be a case of price discrimination because the apple market is perfectly competitive, with each farmer taking the market price as given. Price discrimination isn't possible unless the firm has some control over its price. The price pattern for apples reflects the forces of supply and demand: Early in the harvest season, there aren't many apples available for sale, so the equilibrium price is relatively high. As supply increases over the course of the harvest season, the price drops. At the end of the season, the price rises again.

NOTES

1. Richard A. Posner, "The Social Costs of Monopoly and Regulation," *Journal of Political Economy,* vol. 83, 1975, pp. 807–827.
2. William Comanor and Stuart O. Schweitzer, "Pharmaceuticals," Chapter 7 in *The Structure of the American Economy,* 9th ed., edited by Walter Adams and James W. Brock (Upper Saddle River, NJ: Prentice Hall, 1995).

CHAPTER

Entry Decisions:

Natural Monopoly and Monopolistic Competition

Tweeter has just inherited a large sum of money, enough to start her own business. Tweeter knows that Whoofer, who owns the only car-stereo store in town, sells stereos at a price of $230 and an average cost of $200 per stereo, for a profit of $30 per stereo. Should Tweeter use her inheritance to open her own car-stereo store? If she does, will she make $30 per stereo, just like Whoofer?

Tweeter wants to become a successful entrepreneur. An **entrepreneur** is a person who comes up with an idea for a business and coordinates the production and sale of goods and services: The entrepreneur builds a production facility, buys raw materials, and hires workers. An entrepreneur takes risks, committing time and money to a business without any guarantee that the business will be profitable.

Entrepreneur: A person who has an idea for a business and coordinates the production and sale of goods and services, taking risks in the process.

Like entrepreneurs around the world, Tweeter has a difficult decision to make. Before she decides whether to enter the car-stereo market, she must predict the price of car stereos and her average cost of production. Although there is initially a $30 gap between price and average cost, the gap will certainly be smaller after she enters the market: The price will fall as Whoofer and Tweeter compete for customers, and Tweeter may also have a higher average cost. If the price dropped below her average cost, Tweeter would lose money, so it would be unwise to enter the market. In this chapter we explore the entry decisions of entrepreneurs such as Tweeter.

This chapter is about market entry—when it happens and when it doesn't. Our discussion of the entry process leads to an important question about markets:

Why do some markets have more firms than others?

We'll see that if there are relatively large economies of scale in production, the market will support a single firm, one that is large enough to exploit the large economies of scale. In contrast, if there are relatively small economies of scale, the market can support many firms. Here are some of the practical questions we answer:

1. Should the government allow an electric utility (a monopolist in the market for electricity) to charge any price it wants?
2. Why are video rental stores likely to disappear in the next few years?
3. It costs about $3.4 billion to set up the satellites for a global pocket phone network. How many firms are likely to set up such a network and provide pocket-phone service?
4. How did the deregulation of the trucking industry affect the price of trucking service and the profits of trucking firms?

The analysis in this chapter is based on three assumptions. First, we assume that there are no artificial barriers to entry: There are no patents or government licensing programs that limit the number of firms. Second, we assume that firms do not act strategically: Each firm acts on its own, taking the actions of other firms as given. This means that existing firms do not try to prevent other firms from entering the market and do not engage in *price fixing* (a collective agreement to raise prices). Later in the book we discuss both entry deterrence and price fixing. Third, we assume that firms have perfect information about what the other firms in the market are doing and what they intend to do.

NATURAL MONOPOLY

Natural monopoly: A market in which the entry of a second firm would make price less than average cost, so a single firm serves the entire market.

In this chapter we explain when entry happens and when it doesn't. In the case of **natural monopoly**, the entry of a second firm would make the market price less than the average cost of production, so a single firm will serve the entire market. In a natural monopoly, a single firm is profitable but a pair of firms would lose money, so entry stops after the first firm enters the market. The classic examples of natural monopolies are public utilities (sewerage, water, and electricity generation) and

Because the indivisible inputs required to generate electric power are very costly, there are large economies of scale in power generation.

transportation services (railroad freight and mass transit). We'll use the example of electricity generation to explain why a natural monopoly occurs.

Cost and Revenue Curves

As we saw in Chapter 11, a monopolist can use its revenue and cost curve to decide how much to produce and what price to charge. A firm entering a market makes a long-run decision, deciding what size and type of production facility to build. Therefore, the long-run cost curves—which show production costs for a firm that hasn't committed to a particular production facility—are relevant for the entry decision. Figure 1 shows the long-run average cost curve for electricity generation, using real data from Chapter 8. The curve is negatively sloped and relatively steep, reflecting the large economies of scale associated with generating electric power. These economies of scale occur because the indivisible inputs required to generate power (the power plant or hydroelectric dam) are very costly.

What about the long-run marginal cost of generating electricity? As we learned in Chapter 8, if the average value of a variable is decreasing, the marginal value is less than the average value. If your cumulative GPA (the average) drops as a result of taking a certain class, your grade in the class (the marginal) must be less than your starting GPA. Similarly, if the average cost decreases as output increases (the average cost curve is negatively sloped), the marginal cost must be less than the average cost. To keep things simple, we've assumed that marginal cost is constant, so the marginal cost curve in Figure 1 is horizontal and lies below the average cost curve.

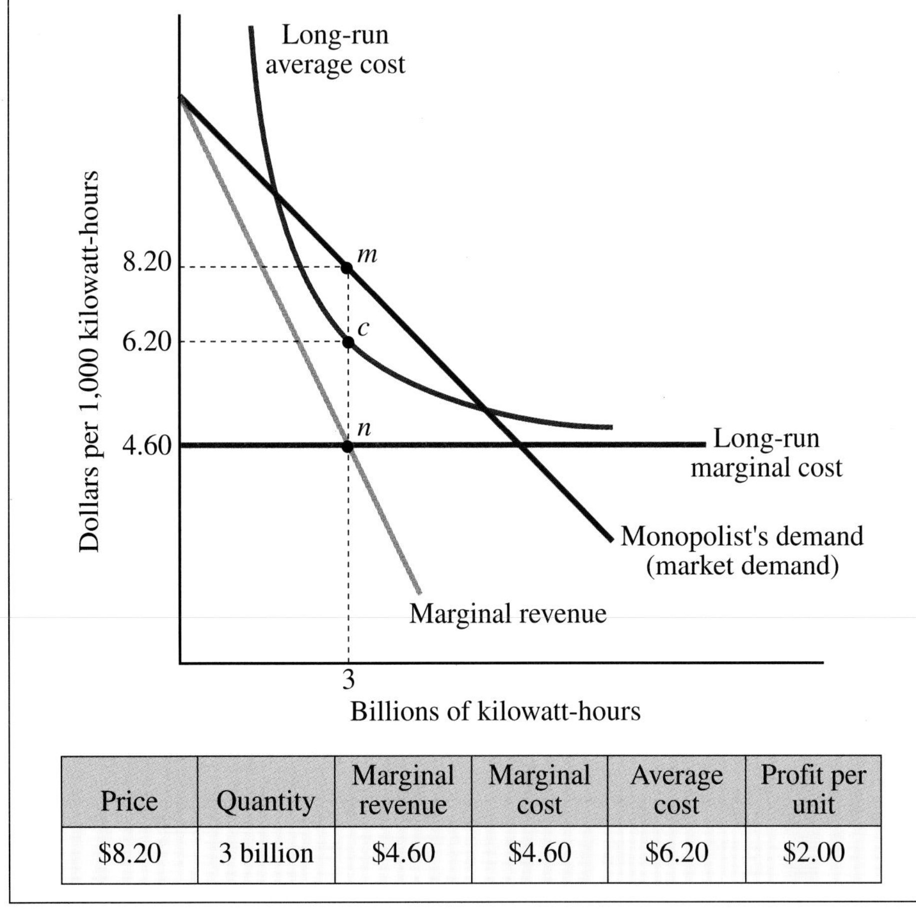

Price	Quantity	Marginal revenue	Marginal cost	Average cost	Profit per unit
$8.20	3 billion	$4.60	$4.60	$6.20	$2.00

Figure 1

Monopolist Uses the Marginal Principle to Pick a Price and Quantity

The long-run average cost curve is negatively sloped because of the benefits of spreading the cost of indivisible inputs. The monopolist chooses point *n* (where marginal revenue equals marginal cost), supplying 3 billion kilowatt-hours at a price of $8.20 (point *m*) and an average cost of $6.20 (point *c*). The profit per unit is $2.00.

Figure 1 shows the monopolist's revenue curves. If a single firm provides electricity, the firm's demand curve is the same as the market demand curve: To determine how much electricity the monopolist will sell at a particular price, we look at the market demand curve. The demand curve is negatively sloped, consistent with the law of demand: The lower the price, the larger the quantity demanded. We know from Chapter 11 that a monopolist's marginal revenue is less than its price, so the marginal revenue curve lies below the demand curve.

The Entry Decision

Let's look first at the output and pricing decisions of an electric company that has a monopoly in the generation of electricity. As we saw in earlier chapters, a firm can use the marginal principle to decide how much to produce and what price to charge.

Marginal PRINCIPLE

Increase the level of an activity if its marginal benefit exceeds its marginal cost, but reduce the level if the marginal cost exceeds the marginal benefit. If possible, pick the level at which the marginal benefit equals the marginal cost.

The company's activity is generating electricity, and it picks the quantity at which the marginal revenue equals the marginal cost. In Figure 1 the marginal principle is satisfied at point *n*, with 3 billion kilowatt-hours (kWh) of electricity. The price associated with this quantity is $8.20 (shown by point *m*) and the average cost is $6.20 (shown by point *c*), so the profit per unit of electricity is $2.00. The price exceeds the average cost, so the electric company will earn a profit.

What would happen if a second firm entered the market? In Figure 2 the entry of a second firm would shift the demand curve facing the first firm to the left, from

Figure 2

Why Won't a Second Firm Enter the Market?

The entry of a second electricity firm would shift the demand curve for the typical firm to the left: The firm's demand curve is no longer the same as the market demand curve. In this example, the firm's demand curve lies entirely below the long-run average cost curve. No matter what price the firm charges, it will lose money. Therefore, the second firm will not enter the market.

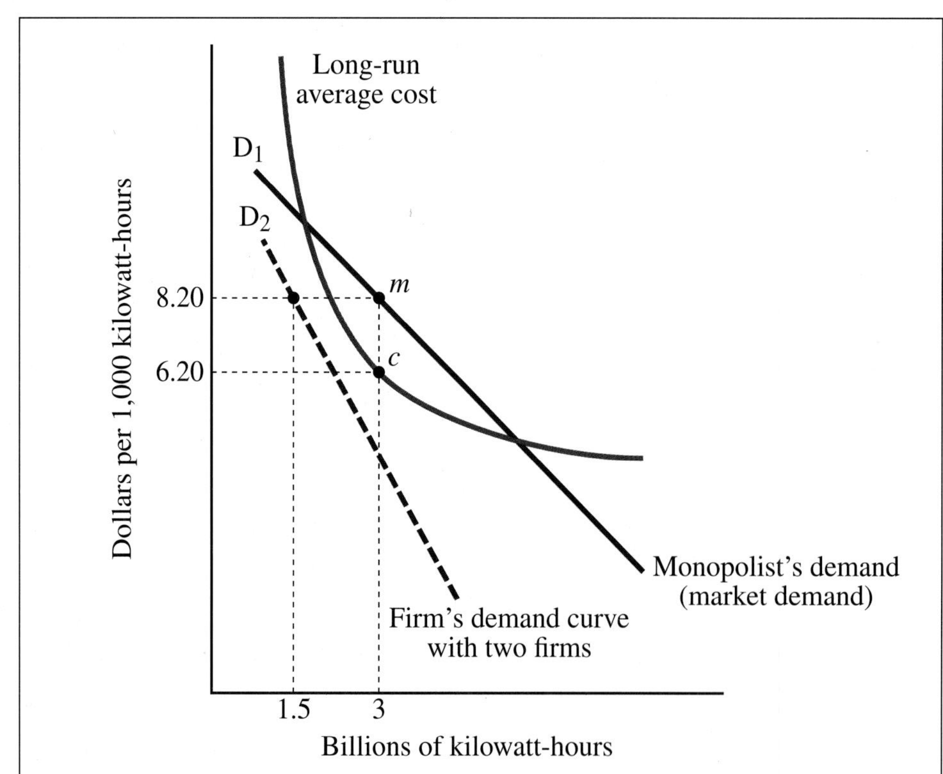

D_1 to D_2: At each price, the first firm will sell a smaller quantity of electricity because it now shares the market with another firm. For example, at a price of \$8.20, the total quantity of electricity sold is 3 billion kWh, or 1.5 billion kWh for each firm. In general, the larger the number of firms, the lower the demand curve facing the typical firm. D_2 is the demand curve for the typical firm in a two-firm market, so it is also the demand curve for the potential entrant.

Will a second firm enter the electricity market? The demand curve of the typical firm in a two-firm market lies entirely below the long-run average-cost curve, so there is no quantity at which the price exceeds the average cost of production. No matter what price the typical firm charges, the firm will lose money. The firm's demand curve lies below the average cost curve because the average cost curve is relatively steep, reflecting the large economies of scale in generating electricity. A second firm—with half the market—would have a very high average cost and wouldn't be able to charge a price high enough to cover its high average cost. Therefore, the second firm will not enter the market, so there will be a single firm, a natural monopoly. For an example of a potential global natural monopoly, read the Closer Look box "A Global Pocket-Phone Monopoly?"

Price Controls for a Natural Monopoly

When a monopoly is inevitable—the case of natural monopoly—the government often sets a maximum price for the monopolist. There are many examples of natural monopolies subject to maximum prices. Local governments regulate utilities and firms that provide water, electricity, and local telephone service. State governments use public utility commissions (PUCs) to regulate the electric-power industry.

Let's use the electricity market to explain the effects of government regulation of a natural monopoly. Suppose that the government sets a maximum price for electricity and forces the electric company to serve all the consumers willing to

A Closer LOOK

A Global Pocket-Phone Monopoly?

Irridium Inc. plans to launch a series of 66 satellites to allow people to talk over pocket phones anywhere in the world. Each satellite would be loaded with computerized switching equipment to receive a call from one spot on the planet and relay the signals to companion satellites around the world. The companion satellite would then relay the signal to another pocket phone on the earth. In theory, a call made by a person with a pocket phone in Tuscaloosa could travel directly to another pocket phone in Siberia without going through a land-based telephone network. The total cost of the global wireless network will be \$3.4 billion, an amount to be raised with the help of Motorola, the firm that set up Irridium.*

The pocket-phone satellite network is a potential natural monopoly. Given the large cost of setting up the satellite system, there are large economies of scale in pocket-phone communication services. Once the system is in place, the marginal cost of relaying phone signals is relatively low. If the demand for pocket-phone communication is not large enough to support more than one satellite system, there will be a global natural monopoly.

Another possibility is that other firms will launch their own satellites and enter the pocket-phone communication market. This will occur if the demand for pocket phones increases to the point where the market can support more than one \$3.4 billion satellite system.

*Edmund L. Andrews, "Motorola Raises \$1.57 Billion toward Goal of Satellite Telephone Network," *The Oregonian*, September 22, 1994, p. E2.

Average-cost pricing policy: A regulatory policy under which the government picks the point on the demand curve at which price equals average cost.

pay the maximum price. In other words, the government—not the firm—picks a point on the market demand curve. Under an **average-cost pricing policy**, the government picks the price at which the demand curve intersects the average cost curve. In Figure 3 the original average cost curve intersects the demand curve at point *i*, with a price of $5.20. Although consumers would prefer a lower price, the electric company would lose money at any price less than $5.20, so lower prices are not feasible.

How will this regulatory policy affect the firm's production costs? Under average cost pricing, a change in the firm's production cost will not affect the firm's profit because the government will adjust the regulated price to keep the price equal to the average cost. The government will increase the regulated price when the firm's cost increases, and decrease the price when the firm's cost decreases. Because there is no reward for cutting its costs and no penalty for higher costs, the firm has little incentive to control its cost, so its costs will increase, pulling up the regulated price.

The average-cost policy causes the market to move along the market demand curve in two steps.

1. ***Downward slide.*** Starting from the unregulated monopoly outcome (point *m*), we slide down the demand curve to point *i* (here *i* stands for impossible dream), the point that would occur if regulation did not increase the firm's cost.
2. ***Upward climb.*** As the regulated firm's cost increases, the price rises to cover the extra costs associated with regulation, so we climb part way back up the market demand curve, from point *i* to point *r*.

Figure 3

Regulation Using Average Cost Pricing

Under an average cost pricing policy, the government chooses the price at which the demand curve intersects the average cost curve. Regulation shifts the average cost curve upward, so the government picks point *r*, with a price of $6.00.

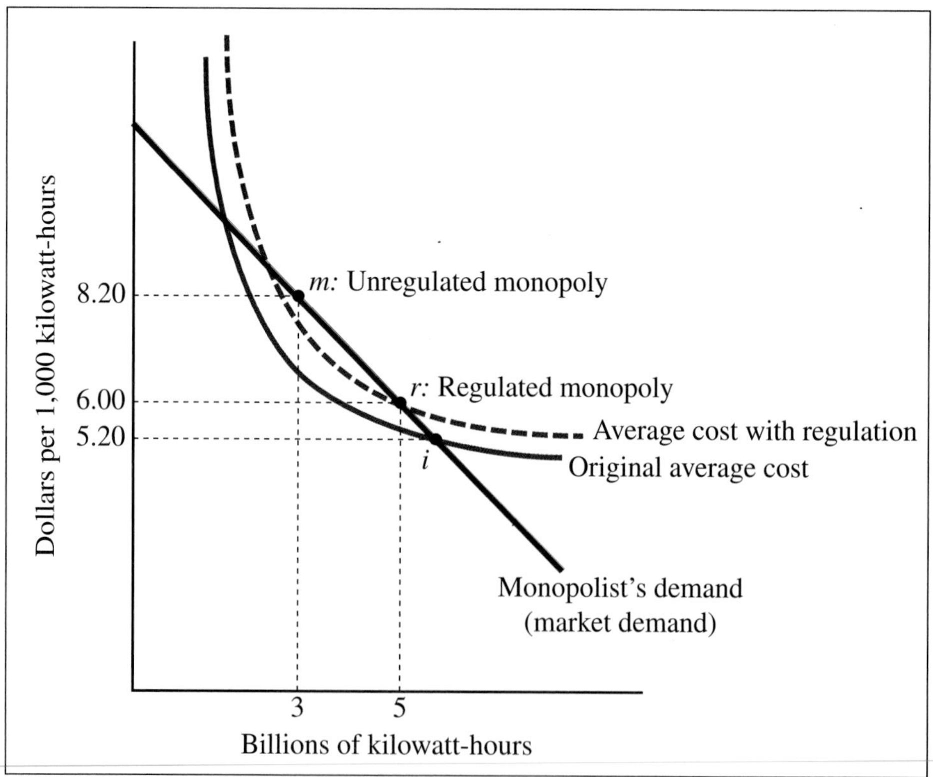

The net effect of this regulatory policy is a lower price of electricity ($6.00 instead of $8.20) and a larger quantity (5 billion kilowatt-hours instead of 3 billion). In other words, the regulatory policy moves the market down the market demand curve, from point *m* to point *r*.

TEST *Your Understanding*

1 Complete the statement: A monopolist picks the quantity of output at which __________ equals __________.

2 Explain the effects of the entry of a second firm on the demand curve facing the typical firm.

3 Complete the statement with *above* or *below*: A natural monopoly occurs when the long-run cost curve lies entirely __________ the demand curve of the typical firm in a two-firm market.

MONOPOLISTIC COMPETITION

Now that we know the features of a natural monopoly, let's think about a market that accommodates more than one firm. The extreme case of entry is **monopolistic competition**, a market with the following characteristics.

Monopolistic competition: A situation in which each firm has a *monopoly* in selling its own differentiated product, but *competes* with firms selling similar products.

1. *Many firms.* Because there are relatively small economies of scale, small firms can produce at about the same average cost as large firms. Therefore, even a small firm can cover its costs, and the market can support many firms.
2. *Differentiated product.* The firms sell slightly different products, with differentiation with respect to physical characteristics, location, services, and the aura or image associated with the good.
3. *Slight control over price.* When a firm increases its price, some of its customers will switch to firms that sell slightly different products.
4. *No artificial barriers to entry.*

In a market subject to monopolistic competition, each firm has a *monopoly* in selling its own differentiated product, but it *competes* with firms selling similar products. A key feature of a monopolistically competitive market is product differentiation. Firms differentiate their products in several ways.

1. *Physical characteristics.* A firm can distinguish its products from others by offering a different size, color, shape, texture, or taste. Some examples of goods differentiated by their physical characteristics are athletic shoes, toothpaste, dress shirts, appliances, and pens.
2. *Location.* Some products are differentiated by where they are sold. Some examples are gas stations, music stores, grocery stores, movie theaters, and ice-cream parlors. In each case, firms sell the same product at different locations.
3. *Services.* Some products are distinguished by the services that come with them. For example, some stores provide helpful sales people, while others require consumers to make decisions on their own. Some other examples of services that can differentiate products are home delivery (for appliances and pizza) and free technical assistance (for computer hardware and software).

4. *Aura or image.* Some firms use advertising to make their products stand out from a group of virtually identical products. In this case, product differentiation is a matter of perception rather than reality. Some examples are aspirin, designer jeans, and motor oil.

We'll use music stores in a hypothetical city to explain monopolistic competition. Most of the music stores in your city sell the same CDs at about the same price. The stores differentiate their products by selling them at different locations. Everything else being equal, you are likely to patronize the closest store, but if a store across town offers lower prices, you may purchase your CDs there instead. In other words, each music store has a monopoly in its own neighborhood but competes with music stores in the rest of the city.

Short-Run and Long-Run Equilibrium

Suppose that we start with a single music store in the city. We can use the hypothetical cost and revenue curves in Figure 4 to see whether other firms will enter the market. There are relatively small scale economies in music retailing, so the long-run average cost curve becomes horizontal at a relatively small quantity of output (300 CDs sold per hour). We know that if the average value of some variable is constant, the marginal value equals the average value. If your cumulative GPA doesn't change as a result of taking a particular class, the marginal grade must be the same as your starting GPA. Similarly, if the average cost is constant (the average curve is horizontal), the marginal cost must be equal to the average cost. In Figure 4, for more than 300 CDs per hour, the marginal cost is the same as the average cost.

The demand curve facing a monopolist is the market demand curve. The marginal principle is satisfied at point *n*, where the marginal revenue curve intersects the

Figure 4

Short-Run Equilibrium in Monopolistic Competition: A Single Music Store

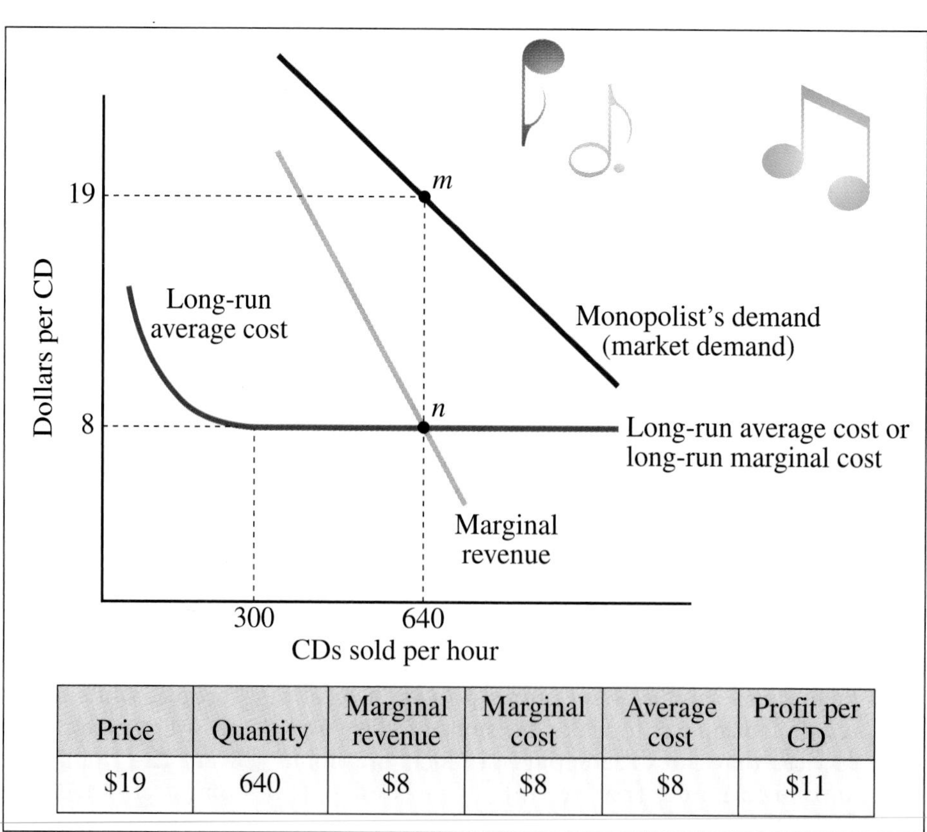

Price	Quantity	Marginal revenue	Marginal cost	Average cost	Profit per CD
$19	640	$8	$8	$8	$11

Along the horizontal portion of the long-run average-cost curve, the average cost equals the marginal cost. The single music store (a monopolist) picks point *n* (where marginal revenue equals marginal cost), supplying 640 CDs per hour at a price of $19 (point *m*) and an average cost of $8 (point *n*). The profit per CD is $11.

marginal cost curve. Therefore, the monopolist will sell 640 CDs per hour. The price of CDs is \$19 (point *m*) and the average cost is \$8 (point *n*), so the monopolist's profit per CD is \$11.

Will a second music store enter this lucrative market? In Figure 5 the entry of a second firm will shift the demand curve facing the typical firm to the left from D_1 to D_2. The marginal principle is satisfied at point *f*, where the marginal cost curve intersects the new marginal revenue curve. Therefore, each firm will produce 440 CDs per hour at a price of \$18 (point *e*) and an average cost of \$8 (point *f*). The entry of the second store decreases the price of CDs as firms compete for customers, and the profit per CD decreases from \$11 (\$19 – \$8) to \$10 (\$18 – \$8).

Because there are no artificial barriers to entering the market, firms will continue to enter the market until each music store makes zero economic profit. Figure 6 on page 238 shows the long-run equilibrium from the perspective of the typical store. As more stores enter the market, the market share of the typical firm decreases, so its demand curve shifts to the left. The typical firm satisfies the marginal principle at point g and sells 70 CDs per hour at a price of \$14 (point *h*) and an average cost of \$14. The price equals the store's average cost, so the typical firm makes zero economic profit. The firm's revenue is high enough to cover all its costs—including the opportunity cost of all its inputs—but not enough to cause additional firms to enter the market. In other words, the firm makes just enough money to stay in business.

The entry of firms into the music market drives economic profit to zero. As the number of firms increases, the profit per CD decreases for two reasons.

1. ***Lower price.*** The stores compete for customers by cutting their prices: the larger the number of stores, the greater the competition and the lower the price.
2. ***Higher average cost.*** The stores share the market, and the larger the number of stores, the fewer CDs sold per store and the higher the average cost in the typical store. As more and more firms enter the market, we eventually move upward along the negatively sloped portion of the average-cost curve to a higher average cost.

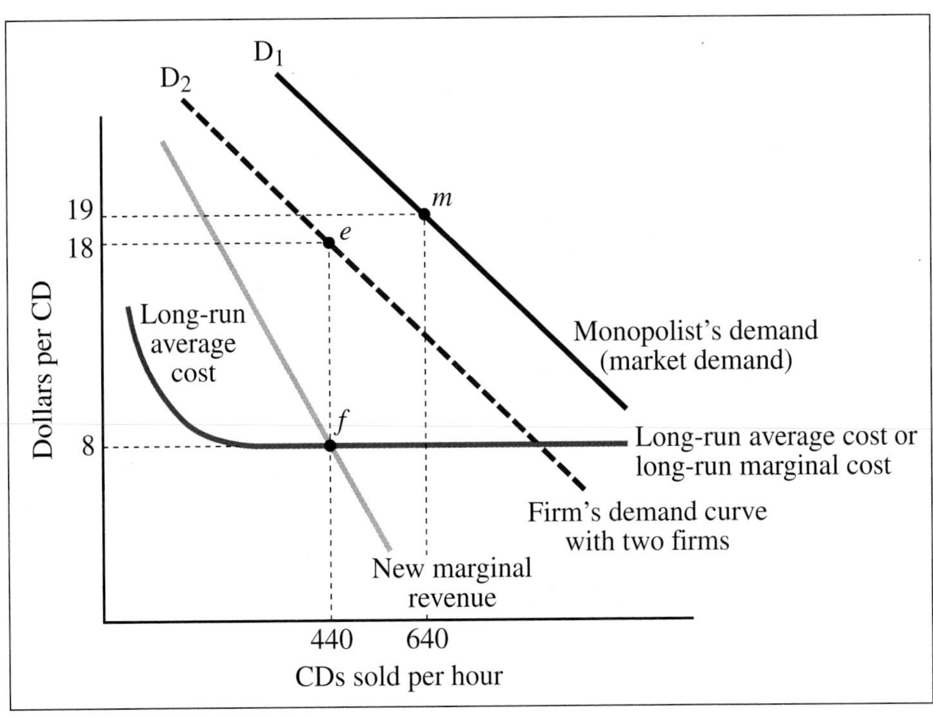

Figure 5

Why Does a Second Music Store Enter the Market?

The entry of a second music store will shift the demand curve for the typical store to the left: The firm's demand curve is no longer the same as the market demand curve. In this example the firm's demand curve lies above the long-run average cost curve, so there is an opportunity to make a profit. Therefore, the second firm will enter the market.

Figure 6

Long-Run Equilibrium with Monopolistic Competition: Music Stores

In a monopolistically competitive market, entry continues until economic profit is zero. The typical firm chooses the quantity at which its marginal revenue equals marginal cost (point *g*). Economic profit is zero because the price equals the average cost (shown by point *h*).

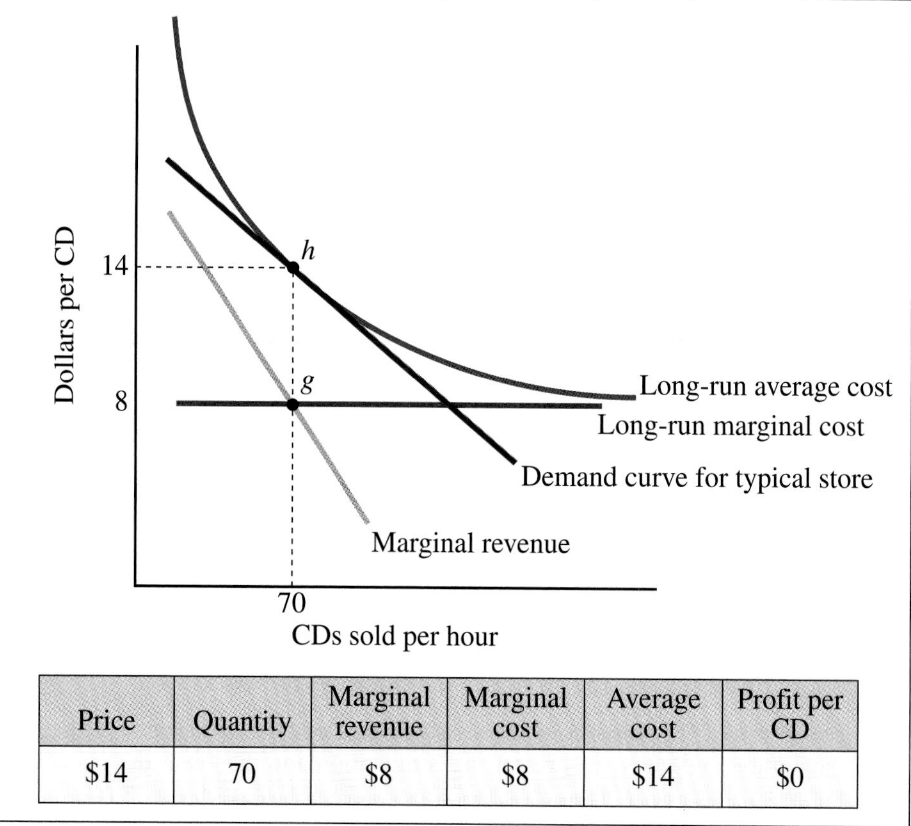

Price	Quantity	Marginal revenue	Marginal cost	Average cost	Profit per CD
$14	70	$8	$8	$14	$0

The entry of the additional store squeezes profit from both sides: The price decreases while the average cost increases.

For an example of the effects of entry on price, cost, and profit, recall Tweeter's entry decision described in the opening paragraph of the chapter. Whoofer the monopolist initially sells 10 stereos per day at a price of $230 and an average cost of $200. Suppose that if Tweeter enters the market, the price will drop to $225 and her average cost will be $205, so she could earn a profit of $20 per stereo. Although Tweeter's entry squeezes profit from both sides—decreasing the price and increasing the average cost—there is still some profit to be made, so she will enter the market. Of course, other firms may also enter the market, so she should not count on making a $20 profit per stereo for too long.

Entry, Prices, and Profit

Empirical studies of real markets provide overwhelming evidence that entry decreases prices and profit.[1] In one study of the retail pricing of tires, a market with only two tire stores had a price of $55 per tire, compared a price of $53 in a market with three stores, $51 with four stores, and $50 with five stores.[2] In other words, the larger the number of stores, the lower the price of tires.

A recent change in public policy shows what happens when the government eliminates artificial barriers to entry. The Motor Carrier Act of 1980 eliminated the government's entry restrictions on the trucking industry, most of which had been in place since the 1930s. New firms entered the trucking market and freight prices dropped by about 22%.[3] The market value of a firm's trucking license reflects the profit the firm can earn in the market. As a result of increased competition and lower prices from deregulation, the average value of a trucking license dropped from $579,000 in 1977 to less than $15,000 in 1982.[4]

European nations are also deregulating their markets. Until recently, most nations in Western Europe had national monopolies in telecommunication equipment and services. That changed in 1988, when the European Union deregulated telecommunication markets, starting with the market for data communication in 1990, followed by the market for voice communication in 1998. European and U.S. companies are preparing to enter the deregulated markets, with many of the companies forming transatlantic alliances. For example, Deutsche Telekom and France Telecom have an alliance with Sprint (the third largest U.S. long-distance carrier), while MCI and AT&T have their own alliances with other European companies. The increase in competition is expected to improve service and decrease prices, perhaps cutting the cost of international calls by as much as 50%.[5]

Trade-offs with Monopolistic Competition

There are some important trade-offs associated with monopolistic competition and product differentiation. Let's compare the monopoly outcome (Figure 4) with the long-run equilibrium under monopolistic competition (Figure 6). The proliferation of music stores generates good news and bad news.

1. ***Good news:*** lower price. The competition among music stores decreases the price of CDs.
2. ***Good news:*** lower travel costs. The larger the number of music stores, the shorter the distance each consumer must travel to the nearest store.
3. ***Bad news:*** higher average cost. As the output per store decreases, the average cost of the typical store increases.

Given these trade-offs, it's impossible to make a clear-cut case for or against monopolistic competition on efficiency grounds. Although a city with many music stores has lower prices and travel costs, it also has a higher average cost of production because there are more buildings (stores), cash registers, and other equipment used to sell CDs. Looking at the trade-offs from the other perspective, a city that used zoning laws to limit the number of music stores to one would have a lower average cost of providing CDs, but prices would be higher and consumers would spend more time and money traveling to buy CDs.

Product Differentiation and Monopolistic Competition

There are many differentiated products sold in monopolistically competitive markets. We've seen that CDs from different stores are differentiated according to location or accessibility. This sort of differentiation occurs for other retail products that require travel on the part of consumers, such as groceries, hardware, drugs, dry cleaning, and bank services. Different firms sell essentially the same product at different locations. We have the same trade-offs: an increase in the number of retail outlets decreases price and travel costs, but increases average cost. As explained in the Closer Look box on page 240, "Good-Bye Video Rental Stores?", the market for video rentals is subject to monopolistic competition, but this is likely to change in the next few years.

Products can also be differentiated according to the characteristics of the product itself. Some examples are restaurant food and clothing. The typical city has dozens of Italian restaurants, each of which has a slightly different menu and prepares its food in slightly different ways. In this case, the benefit of product differentiation is variety: Consumers can pick from a wide variety of menus and preparation techniques. Although a city with a single Italian restaurant would have a lower average

A Closer LOOK

Good-Bye Video Rental Stores?

If you enjoy cruising the aisles of your neighborhood video store, you'd better savor your next cruise because you may not have many left. If you don't like cruising, relief is in sight. According to some experts, most of these video stores will disappear in the next five or six years, to be replaced by video-on-demand (VOD), a system that allows consumers to view any movie at any time in their own homes.

The market for video rentals is subject to monopolistic competition. The scale economies associated with renting videos are very small—to supply video rentals, all you need is a set of videos and a cash register—so the typical city can support dozens of video stores. The VOD system, which has been tested in several markets, uses fiber-optic technology to deliver movies on demand, just as a phone system delivers voice signals on demand. There are substantial fixed costs in setting up the fiber-optic technology: The fiber-optic cable must be laid throughout a city, so the typical city will be able to support only one or two VOD providers. Dozens of video rental stores will be replaced by one or two VOD firms, probably the local cable-TV company and the local phone company. In other words, a market subject to monopolistic competition will be replaced by a monopoly or a duopoly (two firms).

The development of video on demand (VOD) may cause video rental outlets to disappear.

cost of Italian food, there would be less variety for restaurant patrons. The same logic applies to articles of clothing such as jeans and shirts, which are differentiated according to their fit, color, design, durability, and the aura associated with the label. There is a trade-off between production cost and variety: If we all wore uniforms, the average cost of producing clothing would be lower, but most people prefer to wear a variety of clothes.

ECONOMIC DETECTIVE– *How Many Gas Stations?*

Consider a city that initially allowed only one gasoline station to operate in the city. When Jane, a staff member of a local employment agency, heard that the city had decided to relax its restrictions and allow more gasoline stations to operate in the city, she decided to identify some unemployed workers who could apply for the new station-manager jobs. She knew that the city's single gas station pumped 20,000 gallons of gasoline per hour and that the typical gas station reaches the horizontal portion of its average cost curve with an output of 5,000 gallons per hour. Therefore, Jane reasoned, the city would soon have a total of four gas stations (20,000 gallons divided by 5,000 gallons per station) and would need three new station managers.

You can imagine Jane's surprise when she discovered that there would be five new gas stations instead of three. Therefore, she had to find five unemployed workers to apply for the new manager jobs. Your job is to solve this puzzle. Why did Jane underestimate the number of new gasoline stations?

There are two keys to solving the gas-station puzzle. The first is the law of demand. The entry of firms will increase competition in the gasoline market, so the market price will drop and the quantity of gasoline demanded will rise. In other words, the total quantity of gasoline demanded will exceed the initial quantity of 20,000 gallons per hour. The second key to solving the puzzle concerns the output per gas station. The typical firm operates along the negatively sloped portion of its average cost curve, not the horizontal portion, so we would expect each gas station to pump less than 5,000 gallons per hour. If the total demand is greater than 20,000 and the output per station is less than 5,000, there will be more than four stations. For example, suppose that the total quantity demanded rises to 24,000 gallons per hour and each station pumps only 4,000 gallons per hour. In this case, there will be six gas stations (24,000 divided by 4,000) instead of just four.

TEST *Your Understanding*

4 Explain the logic behind the label *monopolistic competition*. What's monopolistic, and what form does the competition take?

5 Complete the statement with *increases* or *decreases*: The entry of an additional firm ____________ the profit per unit of output because entry ____________ the price and ____________ the average cost of production.

6 Explain the trade-offs associated with monopolistic competition and product differentiation.

Using the TOOLS

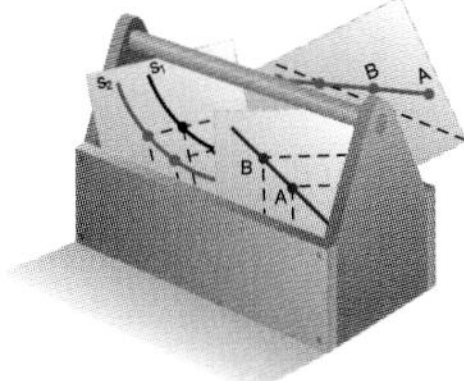

We've used the tools of economics to explore the firm's entry decision, showing that a firm will enter a market if the price will exceed the average cost of production. Here are some opportunities to use these tools to do your own economic analysis of markets.

1. ECONOMIC EXPERIMENT: *Business Licenses*

Here is an experiment that shows the effects of entry on prices and average cost. Students play the role of entrepreneurs who must decide whether to enter a market and how much to pay for a business license.

- The class is divided into groups of three to five students, each of whom represents a firm that has the option of buying a business license to produce and sell tables.
- The following table shows how the market price, the quantity per firm, and the average cost of production vary with the number of firms in the market.

Number of Firms	*Price*	*Quantity per Firm*	*Average Cost*
1	$20	10	$ 9
2	18	9	10
3	16	8	11
4	14	7	12
5	12	6	13
6	10	5	14
7	8	4	15

- A business license allows a firm to operate the business for one day. Each license will be auctioned to the highest bidder. Each firm can buy only one license.
- In the first round of the experiment, the instructor auctions up to seven business licenses. The instructor will continue to auction licenses as long as someone bids a positive amount for one of the licenses.
- Once the license auction is complete (everyone who wants to buy a license gets one), each firm can use the table to compute its daily profit: the profit per unit of output (price minus average cost), times the quantity produced, minus the price paid for the license.
- The license auction is repeated five times. In the first three rounds, the instructor auctions up to seven licenses. In the last two rounds, the instructor auctions only two licenses.
- At the end of the experiment, we compute the profit of each firm by adding up its profit over the five rounds.

2. How Many Music Stores?

Consider the city of Discville, where zoning laws limit the number of music stores to one. The city's only music store sells compact disks (CDs) at a price of $20 and an average cost of $12. Suppose that the city eliminates its restrictions on music stores, allowing additional stores to enter the market. According to an expert in the music market, "Each additional music store will decrease the price of CDs by $2 and increase the average cost of selling CDs by $1." How many music stores will enter the market?

3. Opposition to a New Drugstore

The city of Drugville is evaluating a request by a drugstore chain to open a new drugstore in the city. Consider the following statement from a citizen at a public hearing: "The output of the typical drugstore in our city is about 80% of the output at which its long-run average cost is minimized, so the average cost of drugs is higher than the minimum cost. The new drugstore would increase the average cost of production even further, so all our drugstores—including the new one—would be unprofitable, and consumers would pay higher prices for drugs." Assume that the citizen is correct in stating that the typical drugstore produces at 80% of the output at which average cost is minimized. Do the citizen's conclusions (all stores will be unprofitable and consumers will pay higher prices) follow logically from the facts?

4. ECONOMIC EXPERIMENT: *Fixed Costs and Entry*

Here is an experiment that shows the implications of entry for prices and profits. Students play the role of entrepreneurs who must decide whether to enter the market for lawn cutting. If they enter the market, they must then decide how much to charge for cutting lawns.

- There are eight potential lawn-cutting firms (each represented by one to three students). There are two sorts of costs for firms: a fixed cost per day, and a marginal cost of cutting each lawn. Each firm can cut up to two lawns per day.
- There are 16 potential consumers who are willing to pay different amounts to have their lawns cut.
- The experiment has two stages. In the first stage, each potential firm decides whether to enter the market. The entry decision is sequential: The instructor

will go down the list of potential firms and give each firm the option of entering the market. The entry decisions are public knowledge. When a firm enters the market, it incurs a fixed cost of $14.

- Each firm in the market posts a price for lawn cutting, and consumers shop around and decide whether to purchase lawn care at a posted price. Each trading period lasts several minutes, and each firm can change its posted price up to three times (a total of three prices per trading period).
- A consumer's score in a trading period equals the difference between the amount that he or she is willing to pay for lawn care and the price actually paid.
- A firm's score equals its profit, which is its total revenue minus its total cost (the fixed cost of $14 plus the variable cost equal to $3 per lawn times the number of lawns cut).

SUMMARY

This chapter is about market entry—when it happens and when it doesn't. A second firm won't enter a market if a firm with half the market won't be able to charge a price high enough to cover its cost of production. In some markets, scale economies are relatively small, so a firm with just a small part of the market can earn a profit. Here are the main points of the chapter.

1. A natural monopoly occurs when scale economies in production are relatively large, so that the market can support only one firm.
2. Under an average cost pricing policy, the government sets the maximum price for a natural monopoly equal to the average cost of production.
3. Firms subject to average cost pricing have less incentive to control their production costs, so their costs are relatively high.
4. As firms enter a market, profit is squeezed from both sides: The market price decreases and the average cost of production increases.
5. In a market with monopolistic competition, firms sell slightly different products and continue to enter the market until each firm makes zero economic profit.
6. There are some trade-offs associated with monopolistic competition and product differentiation: An increase in the number of firms decreases price and increases variety, but it also increases the average cost of production.

KEY TERMS

average-cost pricing policy, *234*
entrepreneur, *229*
monopolistic competition, *235*
natural monopoly, *230*

PROBLEMS AND DISCUSSION QUESTIONS

1. Consider a natural monopolist. Here are some data on prices and quantities.

Price	$20	$19	$18	$17	$16
Quantity	100	120	140	160	180
Marginal revenue	___	___	___	___	___

a. Complete the table: For each quantity, use the formula for marginal revenue (see Chapter 11) to compute the marginal revenue.
b. Draw the monopolist's demand curve and its marginal revenue curve.
c. Suppose that the firm's long-run marginal cost is $9. How much output should the firm produce?

2. Consider the city of Discville, where zoning laws limit the number of video arcades to one. The city's only video arcade has a price of 50 cents per game and a long-run average cost of 34 cents per game. Suppose that the city eliminates its restrictions on video arcades, allowing additional firms to enter the market. According to an expert in the arcade market, "Each additional video arcade will decrease the price of games by 2 cents and increase the average cost of providing video games by 3 cents." What is the equilibrium number of video arcades?
3. Sinead is thinking about opening a wig store in her town. Jean-Luc owns the only wig store in town, and he sells 30 wigs per week at a price of $70 and an average cost of $35. Some experts have reported the following facts on the wig market: (i) The average cost of wig selling increases by $2 for every 1-unit decrease in the number of wigs sold. For example, if Jean-Luc sold only 29 wigs per week, his average cost would be $37. (ii) The price of wigs decreases by $1 for every 1-unit increase in the number of wigs sold: the slope of the market demand curve is $1. Suppose that Sinead opens a second wig store and sells wigs at a price of $60. If Jean-Luc sells wigs at the same price as Sinead, will the profit per firm be positive or negative?
4. The city of Zoneville currently uses zoning laws to restrict the number of pizzerias. Under a proposed law, the restrictions on pizzerias would be eliminated. Consider the following statement by an expert in the pizza industry: "A pizzeria reaches the horizontal portion of its long-run average cost curve at an output of about 1,000 pizzas per day. The city's existing pizzeria sells 3,000 pizzas per day. Based on these facts, I predict that if the city eliminates the restrictions on pizzerias, we will soon have three pizzerias (3,000 divided by 1,000 pizzas per outlet)." Let's assume that the expert's facts about production costs are correct. Is the expert's conclusion (three pizzerias) correct?
5. The Bonneville Power Administration (BPA) is a regulated monopoly that uses dozens of hydroelectric dams to generate electricity. The dams block the path of migrating fish and thus contribute to the decline of several species of fish. Suppose that BPA spends $100 million to make its hydroelectric dams less hazardous for migrating fish. Who will bear the cost of this program?

Take It to the Net

We invite you to visit the O'Sullivan/Sheffrin page on the Prentice Hall Web site at:

http://www.prenhall.com/osullivan/

for this chapter's World Wide Web exercise.

MODEL ANSWERS FOR THIS CHAPTER

Chapter-Opening Questions

1. An unregulated monopolist will charge a relatively high price, so the government often sets a maximum price. The idea is to move the market down the market demand curve to a lower price and a larger quantity.
2. The VOD system uses fiber-optic technology to deliver movies on demand. There are substantial fixed costs in setting up the fiber-optic technology, so the typical city will be able to support only one or two VOD providers.
3. The substantial fixed cost means that the market will be able to support only a few firms.
4. Prices dropped by about 22% and profit per license decreased dramatically.

Test Your Understanding

1. marginal revenue, marginal cost
2. The firm's demand curve shifts to the left: At each price, firm sells a smaller quantity.
3. below
4. Each firm has a monopoly in the sale of its differentiated product, but the firms compete with firms selling similar products.
5. decreases, decreases, increases
6. The more numerous the firms, the greater the accessibility to retailers (the lower the travel cost) and the greater the variety of consumer goods.

Using the Tools

2. How Many Music Stores?

   Based on the information from the expert, we expect two additional firms to enter the market. The following table shows price and average cost for different numbers of music stores:

Number of stores	1	2	3	4
Price	$20	$18	$16	$14
Average cost	$12	$13	$14	$15

   In a three-store market, price exceeds average cost by $2. In a four-store market price is $1 less than average cost. Therefore, we would expect three firms in the music market.

3. Opposition to a New Drugstore

   In all the examples we have conside, the typical firm operates along the negatively sloped portion of its long-run average cost curve, yet profit is still positive. A firm will voluntarily enter the market only if it expects to earn a positive profit, so the statement that the new drugstore would make profit negative for all drugstores is puzzling. We know that entry decreases prices as firms compete for customers, so the statement that consumers would pay higher prices is also puzzling.

NOTES

1. Leonard W. Weiss, ed., *Concentration and Price* (Cambridge, MA: MIT Press, 1989).
2. Timothy F. Bresnahan and Peter C. Reiss, "Entry and Competition in Concentrated Markets," *Journal of Political Economy,* vol. 99, October 1991, pp. 977–1009.
3. Theodore E. Keeler, "Deregulation and Scale Economies in the U.S. Trucking Industry: An Econometric Extension of the Survivor Principle," *Journal of Law and Economics,* vol. 32, October 1989, pp. 229–253.
4. Thomas Gale Moore, "Rail and Truck Reform—The Record So Far," *Regulation,* November/December 1983.
5. Richard L. Hudson, "European Companies Speed Shift to Phone Competition," *Wall Street Journal,* June 24, 1994, p. B4. Reprinted by permission of the *Wall Street Journal*, © 1994 Dow Jones & Company, Inc. All Rights Reserved Worldwide.

CHAPTER 13

Oligopoly and Antitrust Policy

The class of 1950 was holding its 40-year reunion and everyone flew in for the occasion. The discussion among the classmates eventually turned to the cost of their airline tickets. Although everyone traveled about the same distance to the reunion, they paid very different prices for their airline tickets.

- **Bertha is puzzled and upset: "Culbert and I both live in cities that are served by a single airline, but Culbert paid \$370 and I paid \$400." Why is the price lower in Culbert's city?**
- **Dermot is puzzled and upset too: "Emily and I both live in cities that are served by two airlines, but Emily paid \$350 and I paid \$400." Why is the price higher in Dermot's city?**

In this chapter we explain these puzzling differences in prices. The monopolist in Culbert's city could be charging a low price to discourage other firms from entering the market. The two airlines in Dermot's city could have a price-fixing scheme under which they do not compete with one another but, instead, collude and charge the same high price.

This is the fifth and last chapter on decision-making by firms. In earlier chapters, we looked at perfect competition (many firms selling a homogeneous product), monopoly (a single firm), and monopolistic competition (many firms selling differentiated products). In this chapter we look at **oligopolies**, markets with just a few firms. Economists use **concentration ratios** to measure the degree of concentration in a market. For example, a four-firm concentration ratio is the percentage of output produced by the four largest firms. In Table 1, the four-firm concentration ratio for cigarettes is 93%, indicating that the

Oligopoly: A market served by a few firms.

Concentration ratio: A measure of the degree of concentration in a market; the four-firm concentration ratio is the percentage of output produced by the four largest firms.

largest four firms produce 93% of the cigarettes in the United States. According to one rule of thumb, if the four-firm concentration ratio is greater than 40%, the market is considered an oligopoly.

In this chapter we explore the decisions of oligopolists and the role of public policy in markets with just a few firms. Here are some of the practical questions we answer:

1. You've probably heard an advertisement that goes like this: "If you buy a stereo from us and find it somewhere else for a lower price, we'll pay you the difference in price." Does this refund policy lead to higher or lower stereo prices?
2. Suppose that two airlines agree to charge the same high price for air travel between two cities. Will the pricing agreement persist?
3. In some states students can purchase textbooks from off-campus booksellers: A student orders a book over the phone and UPS delivers the book two days later. How will your favorite monopoly—the campus bookstore—respond to these off-campus sellers?
4. Why does the government sometimes prevent two firms from merging into a single firm?
5. How did the deregulation of air travel affect competition among airlines?

You may be surprised by the answers to some of these questions. Perhaps you should write down your own answers now and look at them after you've read the chapter.

The key feature of an oligopoly is that firms act strategically. The firms in an oligopoly are interdependent because they sell similar products and consumers can easily switch from one firm to another. As a result, the actions of one firm affects the profits of other firms in the oligopoly. For example, if one airline cuts its fares, the other airlines in the market will either lose customers to the low-price airline or be forced to cut their prices. We'll discuss two types of strategies used by oligopolists: price fixing (conspiring to keep prices high) and entry deterrence (preventing

Table 1: Concentration Ratios in Selected Manufacturing Industries

Industry	*Four-Firm Concentration Ratio (%)*	*Eight-Firm Concentration Ratio (%)*
Cigarettes	93	Not available
Guided missiles and space vehicles	93	99
Beer and malt beverages	90	98
Batteries	87	95
Electric bulbs	86	94
Breakfast cereals	85	98
Motor vehicles and car bodies	84	91
Greeting cards	84	88
Engines and turbines	79	92
Aircraft and parts	79	93

Source: U.S. Bureau of the Census, *1992 Census of Manufacturing, Concentration Ratios in Manufacturing* (Washington, DC: U.S. Government Printing Office, 1995).

additional firms from entering the market). We'll also discuss the merits of public policies designed to prevent these anti-competitive strategies.

Most firms in an oligopoly earn large profits, yet additional firms do not enter the market. An oligopoly—with just a few profitable firms—occurs for three reasons.

1. ***Economies of scale in production.*** As we saw in Chapter 12, a natural monopoly occurs when there are relatively large economies of scale in production, so a large firm can produce at a much lower cost than a small firm. In some cases, scale economies are not large enough to generate a natural monopoly but are large enough to generate a natural oligopoly, with a few firms serving the entire market.

2. ***Artificial barriers to entry.*** As we saw in Chapter 11, government may limit the number of firms in a market by issuing patents or controlling the number of business licenses.

3. ***Advertising campaign.*** In some markets, a firm cannot enter without a substantial investment in an advertising campaign. The result is the same as economies of scale in production: Just a few firms will enter the market.

CARTEL PRICING AND THE DUOPOLISTS' DILEMMA

One of the virtues of a market economy is that firms compete with one another for customers, and this leads to lower prices. But in some markets, firms cooperate instead of competing with one another. The eighteenth-century economist Adam Smith recognized the possibility that firms would conspire to raise prices: "People of the same trade seldom meet together, even for merriment and diversion, but the conversation ends in a conspiracy against the public, or in some contrivance to raise prices."[1] We'll see that raising prices is not simply a matter of firms getting together and agreeing on higher prices. An agreement to raise prices is likely to break down unless the firms find some way to punish a firm that violates the agreement.

We'll use a market with two firms—a *duopoly*—to explain the key features of an oligopoly. The basic insights from a duopoly apply to oligopolies with more firms. Consider a duopoly in the market for air travel between two hypothetical cities. The two airlines can compete for customers on the basis of price, or they can cooperate and conspire to raise prices. In Figure 1, if the firms compete with one another, the market reaches point *d* on the demand curve, with a price of $350 and a quantity of 200 passengers per day (100 per airline). To keep things simple, let's assume that the average cost of providing air travel is constant at $300 per passenger, as shown by the horizontal average cost curve in Figure 1. Therefore, each firm will earn a profit of $5,000 per day (a profit of $50 per passenger times 100 passengers per day).

What would happen if the two firms reached an agreement to raise their prices? A **cartel** is a group of firms that coordinate their pricing decisions, often by charging the same price. In our airline example, the two airlines could form a cartel and act as one, choosing the price that would be chosen by a monopolist. This is also known as **price fixing**. As we'll see later in the chapter, cartels and price-fixing are illegal under U.S. antitrust laws.

Cartel: A group of firms that coordinate their pricing decisions, often by charging the same price.

Price fixing: An arrangement in which two firms coordinate their pricing decisions.

In Figure 1 the cartel or price-fixing outcome is shown by point *m* on the demand curve. The price is $400, and the two airlines serve a total of 150 passengers per day (point *m*), 75 passengers per airline. The profit per passenger is $100 ($400 minus the constant average cost of $300), so each airline earns a daily profit of $7,500 ($100 per passenger times 75 passengers). The cartel profit exceeds the profit when the two airlines compete with one another ($5,000), so there would be a large payoff from forming a cartel and fixing prices.

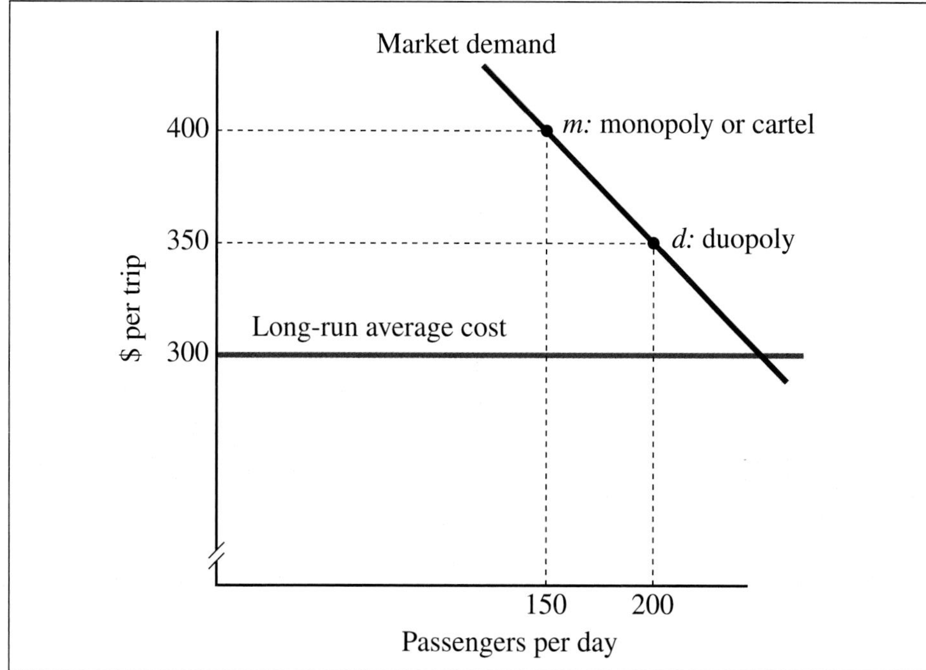

Figure 1

Cartel versus Duopoly

Point *m* shows the outcome with a successful cartel. The total output is 150 and the price is $400, so each firm serves 75 passengers at an average cost of $300 and earns a profit of $7,500. Point *d* shows the outcome with a duopoly: Total output is 200 and the price is $350, so each firm serves 100 passengers at an average cost of $300 and earns a profit of $5,000.

The Game Tree

Each firm would earn more profit under a price-fixing agreement, but will the firms reach such an agreement? We can answer this question with the help of a **game tree**, a graphical tool that provides a visual representation of the consequences of alternative strategies. Each firm must choose a price for airline tickets, either a high price (the cartel price of $400) or a low price (the duopoly price of $350). Each firm can use the game tree to develop a pricing strategy, knowing that the other firm is also choosing a price.

Game tree: A visual representation of the consequences of different strategies.

Figure 2 on page 250 shows the game tree for the price-fixing game. Let's call the managers of the airlines "Jack" and "Jill." The game tree has three components.

1. The squares are decision nodes. For each square there is a player (Jack or Jill) and a list of the player's options. For example, the game starts at square X, where Jill has two options: the high price or the low price.

2. The arrows show the path of the game from left to right. Jill chooses her price first, so we move from square X to one of Jack's decision nodes, either square Y or Z. For example, if Jill chooses the high price, we move from square X to square Y. Once we reach one of Jack's decision nodes, he chooses a price (high or low), and then we move to one of the rectangles. For example, if Jack chooses the high price too, we move from square Y to rectangle 1.

3. The rectangles show the profits for the two firms. When we reach a rectangle, the game is over, and the players receive the profits shown in the rectangle.

There is a profit rectangle for each of the four possible outcomes of the price-fixing game.

We've already computed the profits for two profit rectangles. The first rectangle shows what happens when each firm chooses the high price. This is the cartel or price-fixing outcome, with each firm earning $7,500. The fourth rectangle shows what happens when each firm chooses the low price. This is the duopoly outcome, with each firm earning $5,000.

Figure 2

Game Tree for Price-Fixing Game

The path of the game is square X to square Z to rectangle 4: Each firm picks the low price and earns a profit of $5,000. The duopolists' dilemma is that each firm would make more profit if they both picked the high price, but neither firm will do so, fearing that the other firm would pick the low price.

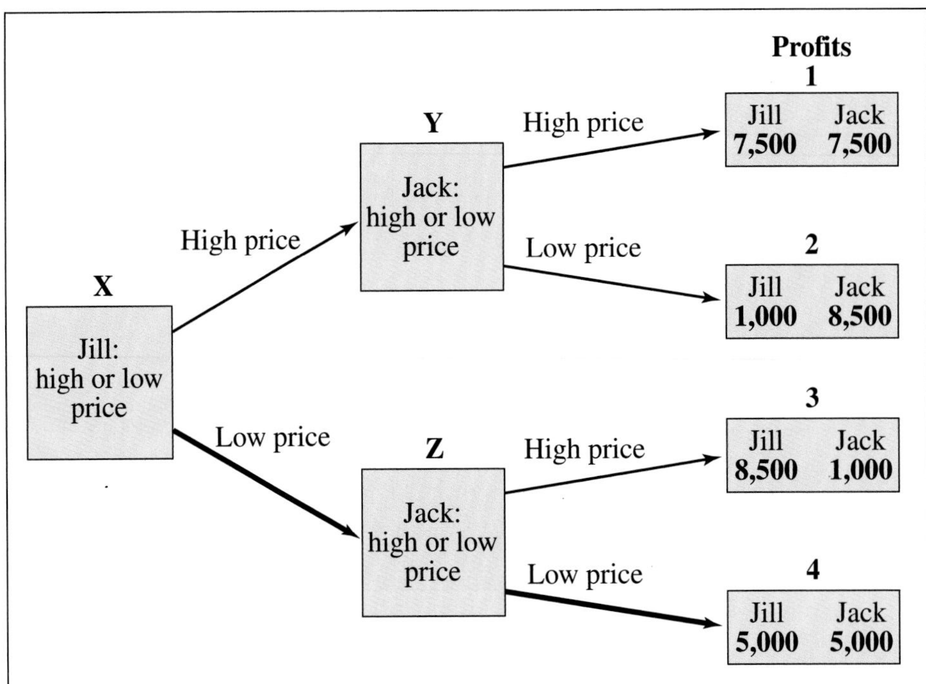

What would happen if the two firms chose different prices? If Jill chooses the low price and Jack chooses the high price, Jill will capture a large share of the market and gain at Jack's expense. In the first column of Table 2, Jill serves 170 passengers at a price of $350 and an average cost of $300, so her profit is $8,500 (a $50 profit per passenger times 170). In the second column, Jack serves only 10 passengers at a price of $400 and the same average cost, so his profit is $1,000 (a $100 profit per passenger times 10). This is shown by rectangle 3 in Figure 2: The path of the game is square X to square Z to rectangle 3. The other underpricing outcome is shown by rectangle 2. In this case Jill chooses the high price and Jack chooses the low price, so Jack gains at Jill's expense. The roles are reversed, and so are the numbers in the profit rectangle.

The Outcome of the Price-Fixing Game

We can predict the outcome of the price-fixing game by a process of elimination. We'll eliminate the rectangles that would require one or both of the firms to act irrationally, leaving us with the rectangle showing the outcome of the game.

Table 2: Profits When Firms Choose Different Prices

	Jill: Low Price	*Jack: High Price*
Price	$350	$400
Quantity	170	10
Average cost	$300	$300
Profit per passenger	$50	$100
Profit	$8,500	$1,000

- If Jill chooses the high price, we'll move along the upper branches of the tree and eventually reach rectangle 1 or 2, depending on what Jack does. Although Jill would like Jack to choose the high price too, this would be irrational for Jack, because he can make more profit by choosing the low price. Therefore, we can eliminate rectangle 1.
- If Jill chooses the low price, we'll move along the lower branches of the tree, eventually reaching rectangle 3 or 4, depending on Jack's choice. Jack won't choose the high price because then Jill would gain at his expense. Therefore, we can eliminate rectangle 3.

We've eliminated the two rectangles involving a high price for Jack. This means that the low price is a **dominant strategy** for Jack: Regardless of what Jill does, Jack will choose the low price.

Dominant strategy: An action that is the best choice under all circumstances.

There are two rectangles left (2 and 4), and Jill's action will determine which rectangle we'll reach. Jill knows that Jack will choose the low price regardless of what she does, so she can either choose a high price and allow Jack to gain at her expense (rectangle 2) or choose the low price too (rectangle 4). It would be irrational for Jill to allow herself to be underpriced, so we can eliminate rectangle 2. The remaining rectangle shows the outcome of the game: Each person chooses the low price. The thick arrows show the path of the game, from square X to square Z to rectangle 4.

Both firms will be unhappy with this outcome because they could each earn a higher profit with rectangle 1. To get there, however, each firm must choose the high price. The **duopolists' dilemma** is that although both firms would be better off if they chose the high price, each firm chooses the low price. Jill won't choose the high price because Jack would underprice her and gain at her expense. Jack won't choose the high price because then Jill would gain at *his* expense. As we'll see later, the firms can avoid this dilemma, but only if they find some way to punish a firm that underprices the other. For a description of how one cartel tried to enforce a price-fixing arrangement, read the Closer Look box on page 252, "Agents Turn Bakers in Battle against Italian-Bread Cartel."

Duopolists' dilemma: A situation in which both firms would be better off if they chose the high price but each chooses the low price.

The duopolists' dilemma is similar to the famous prisoners' dilemma. Consider two people, Bonnie and Clyde, who have been accused of committing a crime. The police confront the two with the game tree shown in Figure 3 on page 253. If both people confess, they will move along the lower branches of the tree and each receive a prison term of five years. If neither one confesses, they move along the upper branches and each receive two years (the police can convict them on a lesser charge without any confession). If only one person confesses, he or she will be rewarded by a short prison term (one year), while the other person will serve 10 years. The rational choice for each person is to confess, so they each serve five years. Although both criminals would be better off if they both kept quiet, they implicate each other because the police reward them for doing so. There is an incentive for "squealing" just as there is an incentive for one duopolist to underprice the other.

Guaranteed Price Matching

The duopolists' dilemma occurs because the two firms are unable to coordinate their pricing decisions and act as one. Each firm has an incentive to underprice the other firm because the low-price firm will capture a large share of the market and earn a larger profit. To eliminate the incentive for underpricing, one firm can guarantee that it will match its competitors' price. Suppose that Jill places the following advertisement in the local newspaper: "If you buy a plane ticket from me and then discover that Jack offers

A Closer LOOK

Agents Turn Bakers in Battle against Italian-Bread Cartel

For years, law-enforcement officials heard complaints about a small group of unscrupulous bakers trying to corner the Italian-bread market in parts of New York City. Using threats of violence, investigators were told, the cartel controlled the distribution of fresh Italian bread to small grocery stores in Brooklyn and Staten Island, inflating prices and eliminating competition.

But investigators found that bakers and store owners were reluctant to cooperate. The only way to get to the heart of the Italian-bread racket, they decided, was to open a bakery themselves. So a team of a half-dozen undercover detectives opened a storefront at 327 West 11th Street in Greenwich Village in early 1993 and called it Louis Basile's. Wearing bakers' whites, they pretended to bake several dozen loaves of bread each day, taking turns getting up at 3 A.M. to drive to New Jersey to buy the real stuff, and wrapping the loaves in the customized white paper sleeves that are the signature of authentic, fresh Italian bread. It was not long after the investigators began trying to sell the bread to neighborhood grocery stores in Manhattan and Brooklyn that they heard from the Association of Independent Bakers and Distributors of Italian Bread. Over drinks at the White Horse Tavern on Hudson Street, investigators say, a detective posing as a baker was told by two members of the association that violence could come to Basile's and its employees if they did not play by association rules.

The rules involved fixed prices for bread—a system of distribution that forced a store to buy from a single baker, said the Manhattan District Attorney, Robert M. Morgenthau, who announced yesterday the indictment of four officials of the association on price-fixing charges. If a store wanted to shift to another baker, he said, the association had to be consulted and cash paid to the former baker.

Daniel J. Castleman, head of investigations in Mr. Morgenthau's office, said that association members included about 50 bakeries that supplied Italian bread to more than 1,000 small grocery stores and delicatessens in the city. As an example of the association's activity, Mr. Morgenthau cited a decision in 1990 to raise the retail price of bread from 75 cents to 85 cents. Five cents of the increase went to the bakers and the other five was divided between the bread deliverers and the store owners, he said. "Because the association had a lock on the market, consumers had no choice but to pay the increase," Mr. Morgenthau said. All the association members printed the new price on their bread sleeves, he noted. While Mr. Morgenthau said he could not estimate how much the association and its members profited from illegal operations, Mr. Castleman said the 1990 price increase cost consumers millions of dollars.

Source: Adapted from Seth Faison, "Agents Turn Bakers in Battle against Italian-Bread Cartel," *New York Times,* July 14, 1994, p. A1.

---

the same trip at a lower price, I will pay you the difference between my price and Jack's price. If I charge you $400 and Jack's price is only $350, I will pay you $50." This pricing scheme is known as **guaranteed price matching:** Jill guarantees that she will match Jack's price. It is also known as a *meet-the-competition policy*. Jill's promise to match Jack's lower price is credible because she announces it in the newspaper.

Guaranteed price matching: A scheme under which a firm guarantees that it will match a lower price by a competitor; also known as a meet-the-competition policy.

How will Jack respond to Jill's price-matching scheme? In effect, Jill tentatively chooses the high price but will instantly switch to the low price if Jack picks the low price. After a $50 refund, Jill's price would be $350, the same as Jack's. Jack will respond to Jill's price-matching scheme in one of two ways.

1. Choose the high price. If Jack matches Jill's announced high price, each firm will earn a profit of $7,500 (rectangle 1 in the game tree in Figure 2).
2. Choose the low price. If Jack tries to underprice Jill, she will switch to the low price, and each firm will earn a profit of only $5,000 (rectangle 4 in the game tree).

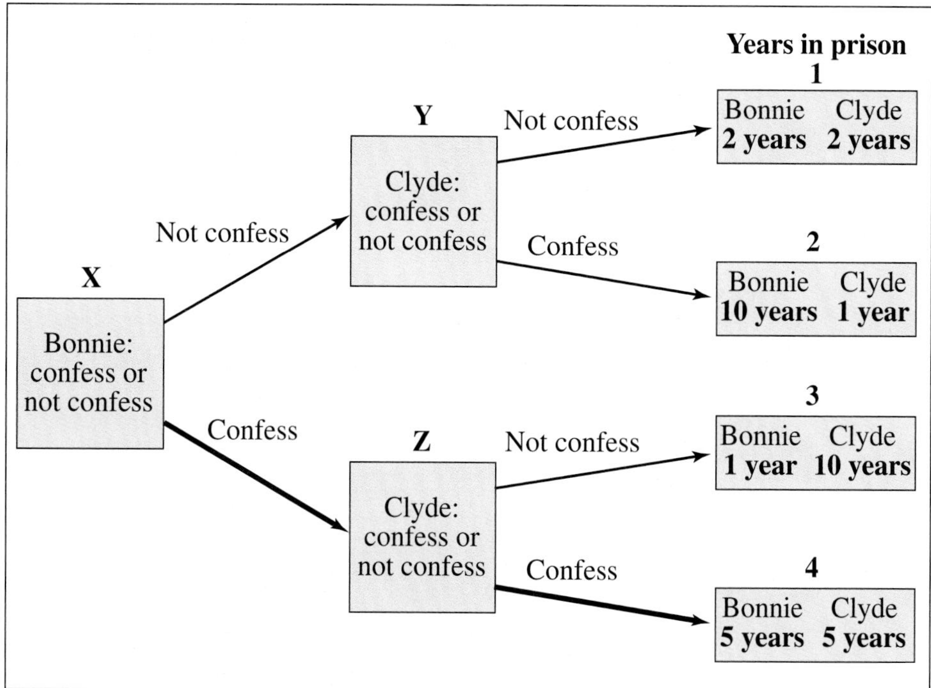

Figure 3

Game Tree for Prisoners' Dilemma

The path of the game is square X to square Z to rectangle 4: Each person confesses and gets five years in prison. The prisoners' dilemma is that each person would be better off if neither confessed, but neither person will do so, fearing that the other person would confess.

Jack's decision is easy: A pair of high prices is more profitable than a pair of low prices, so he will choose the high price, just like Jill.

Jill's price-matching scheme eliminates the duopolists' dilemma and makes cartel pricing possible, even without a formal cartel. The duopolists' dilemma disappears because underpricing is no longer possible. The motto of the price-matching scheme is: "High for one means high for all, and low for one means low for all." It would be irrational for Jack to choose the low price because he knows that Jill would match it. Once the possibility of underpricing has been eliminated, the duopoly will be replaced by an informal cartel, with each firm charging the price that would be charged by a monopolist.

To most people, the notion that guaranteed price matching leads to higher prices is surprising. After all, Jill promises to give refunds if her price exceeds Jack's, so we might expect her to keep her price low to avoid giving out a lot of refunds. In fact, she doesn't have to worry about refunds because she knows that Jack will also choose the high price. In other words, Jill's promise to issue refunds is an *empty promise*. Although consumers might think Jill's refund policy will protect them from high prices, the policy *guarantees* that they will pay the high price. The illustration on page 254 demonstrates this practice.

Application: Different Ticket Prices

One of the puzzles in the beginning of the chapter is that Dermot paid more than Emily for his plane ticket even though they both live in cities that are served by two airlines. The two airlines in Emily's city may suffer from the duopolists' dilemma: Although they would prefer the high price ($400), they both choose the low price ($350). In contrast, an airline in Dermot's city could use a guaranteed price-matching scheme, promising to refund the difference between its price and the price of the other airline. The price-matching scheme eliminates underpricing, so each airline will choose the high price ($400). Dermot pays a higher price because the price-matching scheme allows the airlines in his city to engage in cartel pricing (price fixing).

Many stores advertise their guaranteed price-matching policies. Focus Camera goes beyond matching a lower price, promising to refund the difference plus 10%. This empty promise promotes price fixing by camera stores.

At **FOCUS CAMERA**, we guarantee you the lowest prices. If you purchase a camera from us and within 30 days find the same camera at a lower price, we'll **REFUND** the difference **PLUS** 10%. For example, if you buy a camera from us for $300 and find it elsewhere for $280, we'll give you $22, making our actual price only $278!

TEST *Your Understanding*

1 Complete the statement with *d* or *m*: Rectangle 1 in Figure 2 (page 250) is associated with point ____________ in Figure 1, while rectangle 4 is associated with point ____________.

2 Use Figure 2 (page 250) to complete the statement: If each firm picks the low price, the path of the game is square ____________ to square ____________ to rectangle ____________, and each firm earns a profit of ____________.

3 Suppose Jack promises that if Jill chooses the high price, he will too. If Jack's objective is to maximize his profit, what will he do after Jill chooses the high price?

4 If you were Jill, would you believe Jack's promises to choose the high price? Which price would you choose?

5 Complete the statement with a number: Suppose that Jack offers plane tickets for $350. Under Jill's price-matching scheme, she would give each of her customers a refund of ____________.

6 Have you ever encountered a guaranteed price-matching scheme? If so, did you think it was good news or bad news for consumers? What do you think now?

REPEATED PRICING AND RETALIATION FOR UNDERPRICING

Up to this point we've assumed that the price-fixing game is played only once. Each firm chooses a price and sticks with that price for the lifetime of the firm. What happens when two firms play the price-fixing game repeatedly, setting prices over an extended period of time? We'll see that repetition makes price fixing more likely because firms can punish a firm that cheats on a price-fixing agreement.

Retaliation Strategies

Firms use several strategies to maintain a price-fixing agreement. We explore three, all of which involve punishing a firm that underprices the other firm. To continue the airline example, suppose that Jack and Jill choose their prices at the beginning of each month. Jill chooses the cartel price ($400) for the first month and then waits to see what price Jack chooses. Jill could use one of the following schemes to punish Jack if he underprices her.

1. ***Duopoly price.*** Jill continues to choose the high price until Jack underprices her. Once that happens, she chooses the duopoly price ($350 in our example) for the remaining lifetime of her firm. Jill allows herself to be underpriced only once and then abandons the idea of cartel pricing and accepts the duopoly outcome, which is less profitable than the cartel outcome but more profitable than being underpriced by the other firm.

2. ***Grim trigger.*** When Jack underprices Jill, she responds by dropping her price to a level at which each firm will make zero economic profit forever. This is called the grim-trigger strategy because "grim" consequences are "triggered" by Jack's underpricing.

Grim trigger: A strategy under which a firm responds to underpricing by choosing a price so low that each firm makes zero economic profit.

3. ***Tit-for-tat.*** Starting in the second month, Jill chooses whatever price Jack chose the preceding month. As long as Jack chooses the cartel price, the cartel arrangement will persist, but if Jack underprices Jill, the cartel will break down. In Figure 4 on page 256, Jack underprices Jill in the second month, so Jill chooses the low price for the third month, resulting in the duopoly outcome. To restore the cartel outcome, Jack must eventually choose the high price, allowing Jill to underprice him for one month. This happens in the fourth month, so the cartel is restored in the fifth month. Although Jack can gain at Jill's expense in the second month, if he wants to restore cartel pricing, he must allow Jill to gain at his expense for a month.

Tit-for-tat: A strategy under which the one firm starts out with the cartel price and then chooses whatever price the other firm chose in the preceding period.

These three pricing schemes promote cartel pricing by penalizing the underpricer. To decide whether to underprice Jill, Jack must weigh the short-term benefit against the long-term cost.

- The short-term benefit is the increase in profit in the current period. If Jack underprices Jill, he can increase his profit from $7,500 (Jack's profit if both firms pick the high price) to $8,500 (Jack's profit if he chooses the low price and Jill chooses the high price). Therefore, the short-term benefit of underpricing is $1,000.

Figure 4

Tit-for-Tat Pricing

Under a tit-for-tat retaliation scheme, the leading firm (Jill the square) chooses whatever price the other firm (Jack the circle) chose the preceding month.

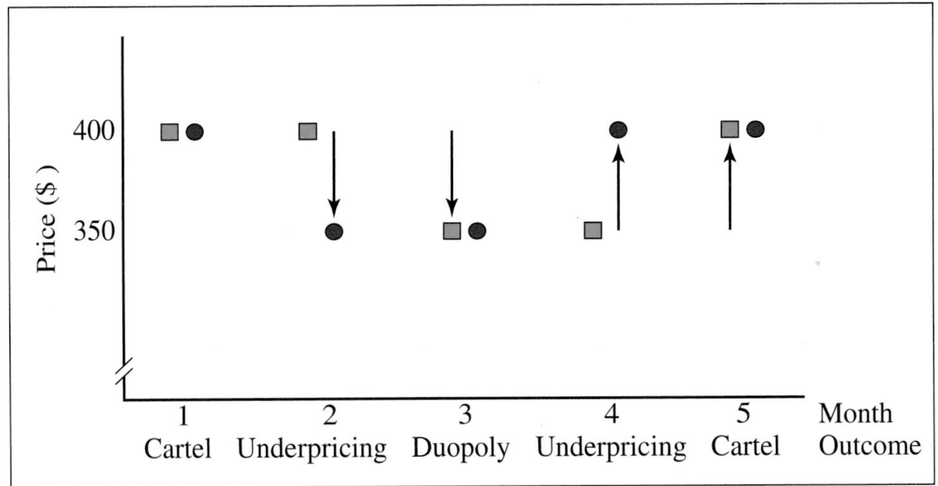

- The long-term cost is the loss of profit in later periods. Jill will respond to Jack's underpricing by cutting her price, and this decreases Jack's profit. For example, if Jill pulls the grim trigger, Jack will lose the opportunity for a monthly profit of $7,500 for the remaining lifetime of his firm.

If the two firms expect to share the market for a long time, the long-term cost of underpricing will exceed the short-term benefit, so underpricing is less likely. The threat of punishment makes it easier to resist the temptation to cheat on the cartel.

Price Fixing and the Law

Under the Sherman Anti-Trust Act of 1890 and subsequent legislation, explicit price fixing is illegal. It is illegal for firms to discuss their pricing strategies or their methods of punishing a firm that underprices other firms. In one of the early price-fixing cases (Addyston Pipe, 1899), six manufacturers of cast-iron pipe met to fix prices in certain geographical areas. Several months after the Supreme Court ruled that their cartel pricing was illegal, the firms merged into a single firm, so instead of acting like a monopolist, which was illegal, they became a monopolist. Here are some other examples of price fixing.

1. ***GE/Westinghouse*** (1961). General Electric and Westinghouse were convicted of fixing prices for electrical generators, resulting in fines of over $2 million and imprisonment or probation for 30 corporate executives.

2. ***Coca-Cola*** (1986). The Coca-Cola Bottling Company of North Carolina paid a fine and issued discount coupons to its customers to settle a case involving a conspiracy to fix the prices of soft drinks.

3. ***Infant formula*** (1993). The three major producers of infant formula (together serving 95% of the market) paid a total of $200 million to wholesalers and retailers to settle lawsuits claiming that they had conspired to fix prices.

4. ***Plastic wrap in Japan*** (1993). A Tokyo court found eight Japanese companies guilty of conspiring to fix the prices of the plastic film used for wrapping food. The companies received fines of $54,000 to $73,000, and 15 executives were given suspended jail sentences of six months to one year.

5. ***Airline pricing*** (1994). In an antitrust lawsuit filed in 1992, the U.S. Justice Department alleged that the nation's airlines used advanced price listing to fix airline ticket prices. Before an airline increased its price, it could post a "suggested" price on a central computer and see if the other airlines would increase their prices. By

March 1994, eight of the nation's largest airlines (United Airlines, USAir Group, American Airlines, Delta Airlines, Northwest Airlines, Continental Airlines, Trans-World Airlines, and Alaska Air) had agreed to drop this practice. According to Ann Bingaman of the antitrust division of the Justice Department, the advance price listing system allowed airlines to fix prices at an artificially high level, costing consumers an extra $1.9 billion for airline tickets.[2]

6. ***Steel beam pricing in Europe*** (1994). The European Union Commission fined 16 steel companies a total of 104 million European currency units ($116 million) for conspiring to fix the price of steel beams.

7. ***Carton board pricing in Europe*** (1994). The European Union Commission fined 19 manufacturers of carton board a total of 132 million European currency units ($165 million) for operating a cartel that fixed prices at secret meetings in luxury Zurich hotels.

Price Leadership

Because explicit price fixing is illegal, firms often rely on implicit pricing agreements to fix prices at the monopoly level. Under a **price leadership** arrangement, a group of firms selects a firm to serve as a price leader and then matches the price of the leader. If successful, these implicit agreements allow firms to cooperate without actually discussing their pricing strategies.

Price leadership: An arrangement under which one firm sets a price and other firms in the market match the leader's price.

The problem with an implicit pricing agreement is that it relies on indirect signals that are often garbled and misinterpreted. For example, suppose that two firms have cooperated for several years, both sticking to the cartel price. When one of the firms suddenly drops its price, the second firm could interpret the price cut in one of two ways.

1. ***Change in market conditions.*** Perhaps the first firm has observed a change in demand or production cost and decides that both firms would benefit from a lower price.
2. ***Underpricing.*** Perhaps the first firm is trying to increase its market share and profit at the expense of the second firm.

The first interpretation would probably cause the second firm to match the lower price of the first firm, and price fixing would continue at the lower price. In contrast, the second interpretation could trigger a price war that destroys the price-fixing agreement. Because firms often pull the grim trigger when a more moderate response would be appropriate, implicit pricing agreements are difficult to maintain.

Kinked Demand Curve

The **kinked demand model** of oligopoly gets its name from its assumptions about how firms in an oligopoly respond when one firm changes its price. Figure 5 on page 258 shows the demand curve facing Kirk, one of the oligopolists. Suppose that each firm starts out with a price of $6, so Kirk sells 30 units of output (point *k*).

Kinked demand model: A model under which firms in an oligopoly match price reductions by other firms but do not match price increases.

1. If Kirk increases his price, the other firms will not change their prices. Kirk will have a higher price than the other firms, so his quantity will decrease by a large amount (from 30 to 10).
2. If Kirk decreases his price, the other firms will decrease their prices. Kirk will have the same (lower) price as other firms, so his quantity will increase by a small amount (from 30 to 33).

These assumptions mean that the demand curve of the typical firm has a kink at the prevailing price: It is relatively flat (elastic) for higher prices because other firms

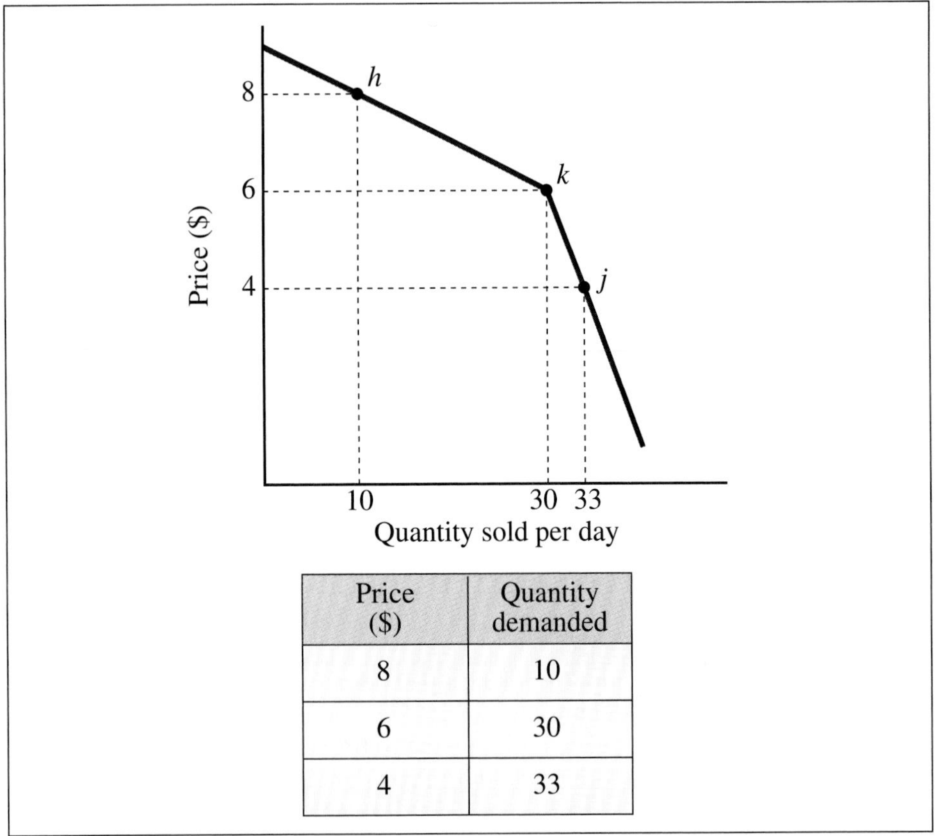

Price ($)	Quantity demanded
8	10
6	30
4	33

Figure 5

Kinked Demand Curve Model

Under the kinked demand model, when one firm increases its price, the other firms don't change their prices, but when one firm decreases its price, the other firms cut their prices. Therefore, there is a kink in the demand curve facing an individual firm.

won't match a higher price, but relatively steep (inelastic) for lower prices because other firms will match a lower price. Once a price has been established, it will tend to persist because there is a large penalty for increasing the price (a large decrease in the quantity sold) and a small benefit for decreasing the price (a small increase in the quantity sold).

This is really a model of pessimism. Each firm assumes the worst about how its fellow oligopolists will respond to a change in price: The other firms will not go along with a higher price, but will match a lower price. Although this model may have some intuitive appeal, there is no evidence that firms really act this way. Starting in 1947, various studies of oligopolies have failed to find compelling evidence to support the kinked-demand model of oligopoly.[3]

TEST *Your Understanding*

7 Which retaliation strategy, the duopoly price or the grim trigger, provides a greater incentive to maintain cartel pricing? Explain.

8 Suppose that Jack and Jill use a tit-for-tat scheme to encourage cartel pricing and Jill chooses the low price for a single month. How long will the two firms deviate from cartel pricing? Explain.

9 Complete the statement with *cost* or *benefit*: If two firms expect to be in the market together for a long time, the ____________ of underpricing will be large relative to the ____________.

ENTRY DETERRENCE BY AN INSECURE MONOPOLIST

We've seen what happens when two duopolists try to act as one, fixing the price at the monopoly level. Now let's think about how a monopolist might try to prevent a second firm from entering its market. In other words, we look at a potential oligopoly. To explain the notion of **entry deterrence**, we use the numbers from our airline example, although we look at a different city with a different cast of characters.

Entry deterrence: A scheme under which a firm increases its output and accepts a lower price to deter other firms from entering the market.

Suppose that Jane initially has a secure monopoly in the market for air travel between two cities. When there is no threat of entry, Jane uses the marginal principle (marginal revenue = marginal cost) to pick a quantity and a price. In Figure 6 on page 260 we start at point *m*, with a quantity of 150 passengers per day and a price of $400. Her profit per passenger is $100 ($400 – the average cost of $300), so her daily profit is $15,000. If Jane discovers that the manager of a second airline is thinking about entering the market, what will she do? Now that she has an **insecure monopoly**, she has two options: She can be passive and allow the second airline to enter the market, or she can try to prevent the second airline from entering.

Insecure monopoly: A monopoly faced with the possibility that a second firm will enter the market.

Game Tree for the Entry Game

Let's look at the passive strategy first. By producing a small quantity of output, Jane will leave room in the market for the second airline. If the second airline enters the market, Jane will be forced to cut her price to compete with the new airline for customers. In Figure 6 the market will move downward along the demand curve from point *m* to point *d* (the duopoly outcome). The price is lower ($350 instead of $400) and Jane will have only 100 passengers per day (half of the 200 passengers served at a price of $350). Her profit per passenger will be $50 ($350 minus the average cost of $300), so her daily profit will be $5,000. In Figure 7 on page 260 the path of the game is square X to square Y to rectangle 1: If Jane is passive, Dick will enter the market and each firm will receive a profit of $5,000.

What must Jane do to prevent Dick from entering the market? One possibility is to buy a large fleet of airplanes and sign labor contracts that force her to hire a large workforce. These actions would commit Jane to serve a large number of passengers at a low price. If Dick enters the market, he will be forced to charge a low price too, and both firms would lose money. This is shown in the lower branches of the game tree in Figure 7.

- If Jane produces a large quantity and Dick enters anyway, the total output of the two firms will be very large. In Figure 6 the market would move downward along the demand curve to point *h*, with a price of $290 and a quantity of 260. Consumers would be happy with this outcome, but the two firms would not: The price would be less than the average cost of each firm, so each firm would lose $1,300 (rectangle 3 in Figure 7).
- If Jane produces a large quantity and Dick stays out of the market, the total output of the market will be 180, as shown by point i in Figure 6. Jane's profit would be $12,600 ($70 per passenger × 180 passengers). This outcome is shown by rectangle 4 in Figure 7.

The Outcome of the Entry Game

Let's use a process of elimination to predict the outcome of the entry-deterrence game. We've already eliminated rectangle 2: If Jane is passive and chooses a small quantity, Dick will enter. We've also eliminated rectangle 3: If Jane produces a large quantity, Dick would lose money in the market, so he will stay out.

Figure 6

Entry Deterrence and Limit Pricing

Moving downward along the demand curve, point *m* shows the secure monopoly, point *i* shows the insecure monopoly, and point *d* shows the duopoly. Point *h* shows what happens if the insecure monopolist produces a large quantity but a second firm enters anyway.

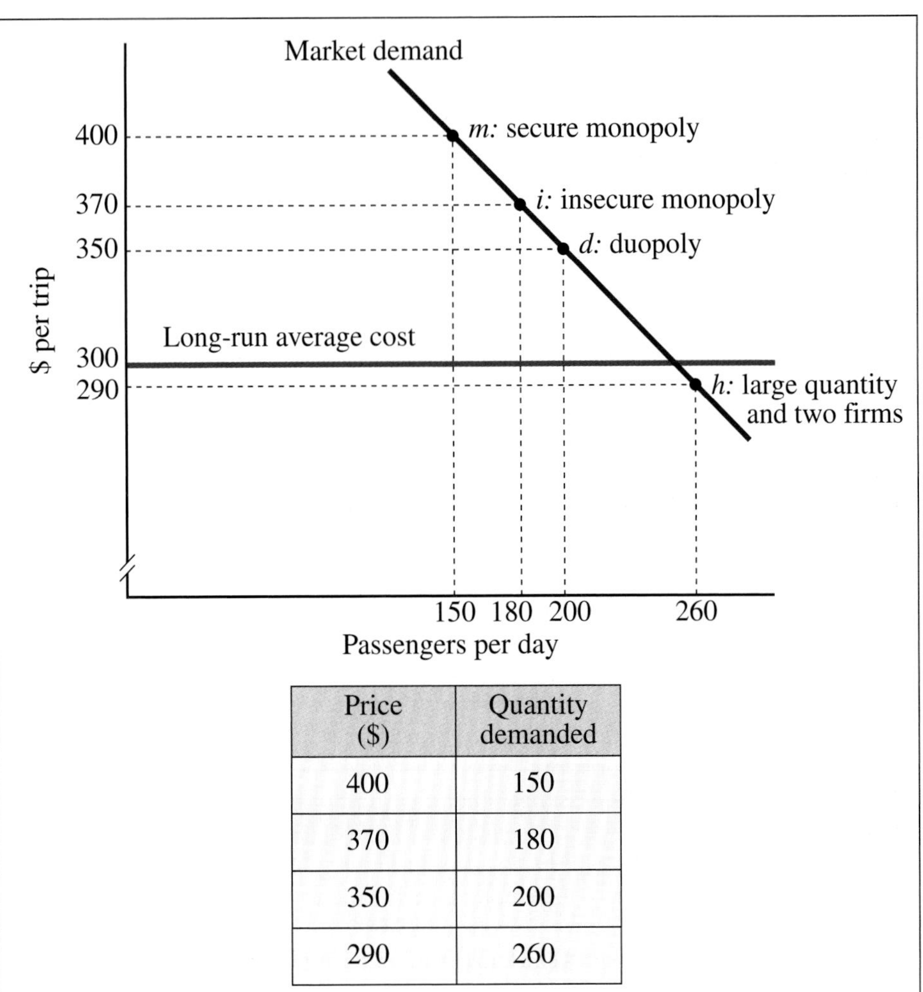

Price ($)	Quantity demanded
400	150
370	180
350	200
290	260

Figure 7

Game Tree for the Entry Game

The path of the game is square X to square Z to rectangle 4: Jane chooses a large quantity, so Dick decides to stay out. Jane earns a profit of $12,600, and Dick gets nothing.

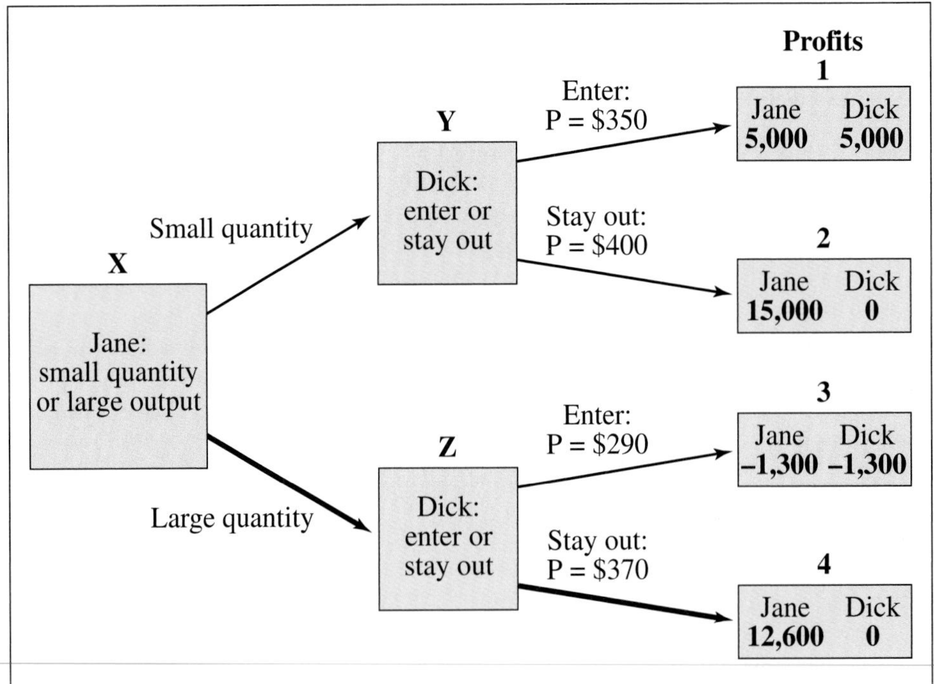

There are two rectangles left (1 and 4), and Jane's action will determine which rectangle we'll reach. If Jane produces a large quantity, she can prevent Dick from entering the market, but is this sensible? Jane's profit from the passive approach (rectangle 1) is lower than the profit from entry deterrence (rectangle 4), so we can eliminate rectangle 1. The remaining rectangle shows the outcome of the game: Jane will maintain her insecure monopoly by producing a large quantity. The thick arrows show the path of the game, from square X to square Z to rectangle 4.

The entry-deterrence game generates a market price that is between the price of a secure monopolist and the duopoly price. Before Dick threatened to enter the market, Jane was a secure monopolist and charged $400 (point *m* in Figure 6). Once Dick threatens to enter the market, point *m* will no longer be an option because if Jane continues to act like a secure monopolist (choosing a small quantity of output), Dick will enter the market and the price will fall to $350 (point *d*). Jane can avoid sharing the market by committing herself to produce a large quantity and accepting the lower price associated with an insecure monopolist ($370, as shown by point *i*).

Although our example shows that deterrence is the best strategy for Jane, it won't be the best strategy for all monopolists. Suppose that Clyde could prevent Bonnie from entering his market, but only if he increased his output by a very large amount and thus accepted a much lower price. A low price means a small profit, so the deterrence strategy could generate less profit than simply sharing the market with Bonnie. In general, deterrence will not be profitable if the price required to prevent entry is relatively low. For some examples of when deterrence is sensible and when it's not, read the Closer Look box "To Deter or Not to Deter: Aluminum and Ball-Point Pens."

Applications: Ticket Prices, Campus Bookstore Monopoly

One of the puzzles in the beginning of the chapter is that Bertha paid more than Culbert for her plane ticket even though they both live in cities that are served by a single airline. If the monopolist in Bertha's city is secure (there is no threat of entry),

A Closer LOOK

To Deter or Not to Deter: Aluminum and Ball-Point Pens

As the following examples demonstrate, sometimes entry deterrence is sensible and sometimes it's not.

- *Aluminum.** Between 1893 and 1940, the Aluminum Company of America (Alcoa) had a monopoly on primary aluminum production in the United States. During this period, Alcoa kept other firms out of the market by producing a large quantity and keeping its price relatively low. Although a higher price would have generated more profit in the short run, other firms would have entered the market, so Alcoa's profit would have been lower in the longer run.
- *Ball-point pens.*† In 1945, Reynolds International Pen Corporation introduced a revolutionary product, the ball-point pen. This simple technology could be copied easily by other producers, so the price required to deter entry would have been so low that it was better to pick a high price and squeeze out as much profit as possible from a short-lived monopoly. Reynolds sold its pens at a price of about $16, which was 20 times the average production cost of $0.80. By 1948, a total of 100 firms had entered the ball-point market, and Reynolds dropped out of the market.

*Leonard W. Weiss, *Economics and American Industry* (New York: Wiley, 1963) pp. 189–204.

†Thomas Whiteside, "Where Are They Now?" *New Yorker*, February 17, 1951, pp. 39–58.

the airline will charge the normal monopoly price of $400. In contrast, an insecure airline in Culbert's city prevents a second airline from entering the market by committing itself to produce a large quantity and accepting a low price. Culbert pays a lower price because he buys his ticket from an insecure monopolist.

We can apply the notion of entry deterrence to your favorite monopoly—your campus bookstore. On most college campuses the campus bookstore has a monopoly on the sale of textbooks. Other organizations are prohibited from selling textbooks on campus, usually by the state government or the college. In some states, students have another option: They can order a book by phone from an off-campus bookseller and either pick up the book at a local copy shop or have it delivered by UPS.[4] An off-campus bookseller charges much less than the campus bookstore, and the growth of these firms threatens the campus bookstore monopoly. If your campus bookstore suddenly feels insecure about its monopoly position, it could cut its prices to prevent off-campus booksellers from extending their services to your state. If so, you would pay lower prices even if the off-campus seller does not actually sell books in your state.

Entry Deterrence and Contestable Markets

We've seen that an insecure monopolist may cut his or her price to prevent other firms from entering the market. The threat of entry moves the market price closer to the price that would occur in a market with two firms. The same logic applies to a monopolized market that could potentially have many firms: The threat of entry will force the monopolist to charge a price that could be close to the one that would occur in a market with many firms. The mere existence of a monopoly does not guarantee high prices and large profits. To protect its monopoly, a monopolist may act like a firm in a market with many firms, picking a low price and earning a small profit.

Contestable market: A market in which the costs of entering and leaving are very low, so the firms in the market are constantly threatened by the entry of new firms.

The threat of entry underlies the theory of market contestability. A **contestable market** is one in which firms can enter and leave the market without incurring large costs. The few firms in a contestable market will be threatened constantly by the entry of new firms, so prices and profits will be relatively low. In the extreme case of perfect contestability, firms can enter and exit a market at zero cost. In this case, the price will be the same as the price that would occur in a perfectly competitive market, one with dozens of firms. Although few markets are perfectly contestable, many markets are contestable to a certain degree, and the threat of entry tends to decrease prices and profits.

ECONOMIC DETECTIVE– *The Pricing of Copying Machines*

In 1959, Xerox Corporation introduced the Xerox 914, a copying machine that used xerography, an alternative to electrofax technology. Xerography involves a more complex copying process and more costly machinery, but xerographic copies can be made on plain paper, while electrofax technology requires the use of expensive coated paper. Xerox produced copy machines for two different markets and adopted quite different pricing strategies.

- *Low-volume market* (fewer than 5,000 copies per month). Xerox charged a relatively high price for its low-volume machines and earned a large profit per machine.
- *High-volume market.* Xerox charged a relatively low price for its high-volume machines and earned a moderate profit per machine.

Why did Xerox adopt such different pricing strategies in the two markets? Why did the company pick such a high price for the low-volume market?

The key to solving this puzzle is the fact that xerography had a large cost advantage over electrofax technology in the high-volume market but not in the

Xerox introduced the first machines based on xerography technology, one for the low-volume market and another for the high-volume market. Why were the pricing strategies for the two markets so different?

low-volume market. In both markets, there is a trade-off between paper costs (higher with electrofax technology) and machine costs (higher with xerographic technology).

- In the low-volume market, a copy machine uses a relatively small amount of paper each month, so the monthly cost of a xerographic machine was about the same as the monthly cost of an electrofax machine. Although Xerox could have deterred other firms from entering the market, the price required to do so would have been very low, so Xerox wouldn't have earned much profit on each machine. Therefore, the firm charged a high price for its machines and earned a large annual profit, recognizing that other firms would eventually enter the market and decrease its profits. Between 1961 and 1967, a total of 29 firms entered the low-volume market with electrofax machines.[5]
- In the high-volume market, a copy machine uses a large amount of paper per month, so the monthly cost of a xerographic machine was much lower than the monthly cost of an electrofax machine. Xerox charged a relatively low price for its copiers, which discouraged entry but still left Xerox with a moderate profit per machine. Between 1961 and 1967, only four firms entered the high-volume market with electrofax machines.[6]

TEST *Your Understanding*

10 Complete the statement: Suppose that Jane picks a small quantity of output. In Figure 7 (page 260) the path of the game would be square ____________ to square ____________ to rectangle ____________.

11 In Figure 7 (page 260) Jane would prefer rectangle 2 to rectangle 4. Why can't she get to rectangle 2?

12 Why does a secure monopolist charge a higher price than an insecure monopolist?

CONTROLLING THE NUMBER OF FIRMS: ANTITRUST POLICY

What is the role of government in markets that are dominated by a small number of large firms? In the United States the government uses antitrust policy to regulate the business practices of firms in such markets. The basic objective of these policies is to prevent a few firms from dominating a market and charging relatively high prices.

Market Concentration and Antitrust Policy

Before we look at antitrust policies, let's think about how a firm might try to increase its share of the market in an attempt to dominate the market. A firm can increase its market share in a number of ways, three of which are subject to government scrutiny.

Trust: An arrangement under which the owners of several companies transfer their decision-making powers to a small group of trustees, who then make decisions for all the firms in the trust.

Merger: A process in which two or more firms combine their operations.

Predatory pricing: A pricing scheme under which a firm decreases its price to drive a rival out of business, and increases the price when the other firm disappears.

1. *Trust*. To form a trust, the owners of several companies transfer their decision-making powers to a small group of trustees, who then make decisions for all the firms in the trust. For example, the Standard Oil Trust was formed in 1882 when the owners of 40 oil companies empowered nine trustees to make the decisions for all 40 companies. The firms in a trust act as a single large firm, so an industry that appears to have many firms may in fact be a virtual monopoly.

2. *Merger*. The merging of two firms increases market concentration: A duopoly becomes a monopoly, a three-firm market becomes a duopoly, and so on.

3. *Predatory pricing*. Here is how predatory pricing works.

a. One firm (the predator) sets its price low enough that both the predator and its prey (a second firm) lose money.

b. The second firm goes out of business.

c. The first firm (the predator) increases its price to restore its profits.

The government uses a number of policies to limit the size or the market shares of firms in highly concentrated markets. Table 3 provides a brief summary of the history of antitrust policy. The first legislation was the Sherman Antitrust Act of 1890, which made it illegal to monopolize a market or to engage in

Table 3: Brief History of Antitrust Legislation

Year	Legislation
1890	*Sherman Act*: made it illegal to monopolize a market or to engage in practices that resulted in a restraint of trade.
1914	*Clayton Act*: outlawed specific practices that discourage competition, including tying contracts, price discrimination for the purpose of reducing competition, and stock-purchase mergers that would substantially reduce competition.
1914	*Federal Trade Commission*: established to enforce antitrust laws.
1936	*Robinson–Patman Act*: prohibited selling products at "unreasonably low prices" with the intent of reducing competition.
1950	*Celler–Kefauver Act*: outlawed asset-purchase mergers that would substantially reduce competition.
1980	*Hart–Scott–Rodino Act*: extended antitrust legislation to proprietorships and partnerships.

practices that resulted in a restraint of trade. Because the act did not specify which practices were illegal, it led to conflicting court rulings: The courts decided that Standard Oil Trust and the American Tobacco Trust violated the act but that some companies that appeared to be engaging in anticompetitive practices did not.

Many of the ambiguities of the Sherman Act were resolved in the Clayton Act of 1914. This act outlawed specific practices that discourage competition, including tying contracts (preventing a customer from buying one product without buying a second product) and price discrimination for the purpose of reducing competition. The act also outlawed mergers resulting from the purchase of a competitor's stock when such a merger would substantially reduce competition. Also in 1914, the Federal Trade Commission was established to enforce antitrust laws.

More recent legislation has clarified and extended antitrust law. The Robinson–Patman Act of 1936 prohibited selling products at unreasonably low prices with the intent of reducing competition. The Celler–Kefauver Act of 1950 closed a loophole in the Clayton Act by outlawing mergers through the purchase of another firm's physical assets (for example, buildings and equipment) when such a merger would reduce competition substantially. The Hart–Scott–Rodino Act of 1980 extended antitrust legislation to proprietorships and partnerships. Before this act, antitrust legislation applied only to corporations.

What is the rationale for government policy that limits market concentration? We know that an increase in the number of firms causes movement downward along the market demand curve, so a merger causes movement in the opposite direction, upward along the market demand curve to a higher price. The idea behind blocking a merger is prevent higher prices. Similarly, the idea behind breaking up a monopoly into two or more competing firms is to increase competition and decrease prices. As explained in the Closer Look box "The Price Effects of Mergers," two mergers in the microfilm market increased prices.

The government also intervenes when a specific business practice increases market concentration in an already concentrated market. For example, Microsoft Corporation receives royalties from computer makers that install Microsoft operating

A Closer LOOK

The Price Effects of Mergers

In 1981, the Federal Trade Commission brought an antitrust suit against Xidex Corporation for its earlier acquisition of two of its rivals in the microfilm market. By acquiring Scott Graphics, Inc. in 1976 and Kalvar Corporation in 1979, Xidex increased its market share of the U.S. microfilm market from 46% to 71%. As a result, the price of microfilm increased: The price of one type of microfilm (diazo) increased by 11%, and the price of a second type (vesicular) increased by 23%. These price hikes were large enough that Xidex recovered the cost of acquiring its two rivals ($4.2 million for Scott Graphics and $6 million for Kalvar) in less than two years.

This is a classic case of a merger that leads to higher prices and more profits for a dominant firm. To settle the antitrust lawsuit, Xidex agreed to license its microfilm technology—at bargain prices—to other firms. The idea is that if other firms have access to the microfilm technology, the competition between Xidex and the competing firms will decrease the price of microfilm.

Source: After David M. Barton and Roger Sherman, "The Price and Profit Effects of Horizontal Merger: A Case Study," *Journal of Industrial Economics,* vol. 33, December 1984, pp. 165–177.

software on their computers. The curious—and illegal—feature of the original royalty arrangement was that Microsoft received a royalty for every computer made by a computer firm, even if the computer employed operating software from another software company. This royalty scheme discouraged computer makers from using software from Microsoft's rivals and was declared illegal by the courts.

Trade Barriers and Market Concentration

One way to increase competition and decrease prices is to remove trade barriers, allowing firms in other nations to compete with domestic firms. In the last 40 years, European nations have systematically decreased tariffs and trade barriers. The process started in 1957 with the formation of the European Economic Community (EEC). The EEC eliminated all tariffs between the member nations (France, West Germany, Italy, the Netherlands, Belgium, and Luxembourg), who agreed on a common set of tariffs for products coming from the outside world. The European Union—a modern version of the EEC, with 15 member nations—has eliminated even more trade barriers between European nations. The elimination of the trade barriers has increased competition. For example, many firms that were monopolies in their own countries now face competition from foreign firms. In other words, national monopolies have become international oligopolies,[7] leading to lower prices.

Airlines: Deregulation and Concentration

The recent experience with deregulating air travel shows some of the complexities associated with regulations and antitrust policies. Before 1978, the Civil Aeronautics Board (CAB) regulated interstate air travel by limiting entry into the market and controlling prices. About 90% of the markets were monopolized, with prices that were between 30 and 50% higher than would have occurred in a more competitive environment.[8] The Airline Deregulation Act of 1978 eliminated most of the entry restrictions and price controls, and the CAB eventually disappeared. In the first few years following deregulation, a large number of firms entered the market, and competition among airlines serving individual markets (individual routes) increased. Controlling for inflation, the price of air travel dropped from about 20 cents per passenger mile in 1981 to about 14 cents in 1986.[9]

Most observers expected deregulation to increase competition, with more firms providing service between each pair of cities. Much to their surprise, the industry is now less competitive. Most of the firms that entered the market just after deregulation have disappeared: Some firms went out of business and others merged with other airlines. Between 1986 and 1992, the percentage of U.S. passenger miles controlled by the largest eight firms increased from 72 percent to 90 percent.[10] In some markets, the share of the market served by the dominant firm has increased dramatically. Here are some examples: In Atlanta, Delta's market share increased from 50 percent to 87 percent; in Pittsburgh, USAir's share increased from 48 percent to 89 percent; in Minneapolis, Northwest's share increased from 40 percent to 81 percent.[11] In markets dominated by just a few firms, fares are actually higher than they were before deregulation.[12]

Why did deregulation increase concentration in the airline industry? There are three main reasons.

1. *Mergers.* The U.S. Department of Transportation surprised everyone by supporting every merger proposed by the airlines. Alfred Kahn, the former chairman of the Civil Aeronautics Board and an early proponent of deregulation, characterized this as an "abysmal dereliction."[13] Many of the mergers decreased competition and are likely to lead to higher prices.

2. *Airport gates.* Under the old regulatory policy, the rights to use particular airport gates were granted to certain airlines. These airlines can prevent new firms from entering a market by denying them access to airport gates.
3. *Mileage bonus and frequent flier programs.* The large airlines give free trips to travelers who accumulate mileage with an individual airline. These bonus programs encourage consumers to do all their travel on a single airline and make it difficult for new firms to enter the market.

The experience with airline deregulation provides some important lessons for policymakers. Although fares are generally lower, they are higher in markets that are now dominated by just a few firms. The deregulation of air travel eliminated the government's artificial barriers to entry, but other barriers have led to increased concentration in some markets. The obvious policy response is to allow all airlines to compete for the available gates and to provide additional gates. The government could also use antitrust policy to oppose mergers that reduce competition and eliminate other anticompetitive practices, such as mileage bonus programs.

TEST *Your Understanding*

13 Why did the elimination of government barriers to entry in the airline industry increase market concentration?

14 Complete the statement with *upward* or *downward*: A merger will cause movement ____________ along the demand curve.

Using the TOOLS

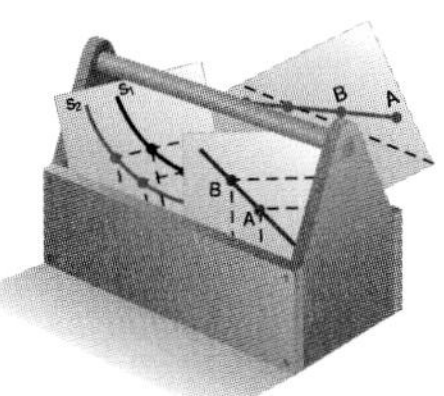

We've used one of the tools of economics—the game tree—to predict the outcomes of price-fixing and entry-deterrence games. Here are some opportunities to use this tool to do your own economic analysis of markets.

1. Price-Fixing Game for the Classroom

Here is a price-fixing or cartel game for the classroom. You'll have an opportunity to conspire to fix prices in a hypothetical market with five firms.

- The instructor divides the class into five groups. Each group represents one of five firms that produce a particular good.
- Each group must develop a pricing strategy for its firm, recognizing that the other groups are choosing prices for their firms at the same time. There are only two choices: a high price (the cartel price) or a low price.
- The profit of a particular firm depends on the price chosen by the firm and the prices chosen by the four other firms. Here is the profit matrix:

Number of High-Price Firms	*Number of Low-Price Firms*	*Profit for each High-Price Firm*	*Profit for each Low-Price Firm*
0	5	—	$ 50
1	4	$ 20	70
2	3	40	90
3	2	60	110
4	1	80	130
5	0	100	—

From the second row, if one of the five firms chooses the high price and the other four firms choose the low price, the high-price firm earns a profit of $20, and each low-price firm earns a profit of $70.

- The game is played for several rounds. In the first three rounds, the firms make their choices without talking to each other in advance. In the fourth and fifth rounds, the firms discuss their strategies, disperse, and then make their choices.
- The group's score equals the profit earned by the firm.

2. Advertising and Price Fixing

Consider two sellers of CD players (Cecil and Dee) who suffer from the duopolists' dilemma. Although both firms would be better off if they both chose the high price, they both choose the low price. Cecil recently discovered that Dee is planning a big advertising campaign, the purpose of which is to increase her sales at Cecil's expense (without changing her price). Suppose that Cecil has the opportunity to launch his own advertising campaign before Dee starts hers. What sort of advertising campaign should he launch?

3. Entry Deterrence

Your firm sells a very popular children's toy. The manager of another firm is thinking about introducing a similar toy. You have the following facts.

a. Your average cost of production is constant at $2.
b. At the current monopoly price of $5, you sell 120 toys per day.
c. You could prevent the entry of the second firm by increasing your output to 150 toys per day and cutting your price to $4.
d. If the second firm enters the market, your price would decrease to $3 and you would sell only 80 toys per day.

Should you prevent entry of the second firm?

SUMMARY

In this chapter we've seen that when a few firms share a market, they have an incentive to act strategically. Firms may use cartel pricing or price fixing to avoid competition and keep prices high. If there is a threat of entry into a market , a monopoly may cut its price to discourage other firms from entering a market. The government uses antitrust policies to discourage price fixing and to control the number of firms in a market. Here are the main points of the chapter.

1. Each firm in an oligopoly has an incentive to underprice the other firms, so price fixing (cartel pricing) will be unsuccessful unless firms have some way of enforcing a price-fixing agreement.
2. One way to maintain cartel pricing (price fixing) is a guaranteed price-matching scheme: One firm chooses the high price and promises to match a lower price offered by its competitor.
3. Cartel pricing is more likely to occur if firms choose prices repeatedly and can punish a firm that chooses a price below the cartel price.
4. To prevent a second firm from entering the market, an insecure monopolist may commit itself to produce a relatively large quantity and accept a relatively low price.
5. The purpose of antitrust policy is to prevent a few firms from dominating a market and charging high prices.

KEY TERMS

cartel, *248* **concentration ratio,** *246* **contestable market,** *262*

dominant strategy, *251*
duopolists' dilemma, *251*
entry deterrence, *259*
game tree, *249*
grim trigger, *255*
guaranteed price matching, *252*
insecure monopoly, *259*
kinked demand model, *257*
merger, 264
oligopoly, *246*
predatory pricing, *264*
price fixing, *248*
price leadership, *257*
tit-for-tat, *255*
trust, *264*

PROBLEMS AND DISCUSSION QUESTIONS

1. Suppose that two firms, Speedy and Hustle, provide land transportation from the downtown area to the airport (airporter service). The practice of guaranteed price matching is illegal.
   - If the two firms act independently (they do not engage in price fixing or any other collusive behavior), each firm will serve 100 passengers per day at a price of $20 and an average cost of $15.
   - Under a price-fixing or cartel arrangement, each firm would serve 75 passengers at a price of $28 and an average cost of $18.
   - If one firm charges $20 and the other firm charges $28, the low-price firm will earn a profit of $900 and the high-price firm will earn a profit of $400.

   Speedy chooses a price first, followed by Hustle. Draw a game tree for the price-fixing game and predict the outcome.
2. Recall the example of the repeated pricing game between Jack and Jill. Suppose that each firm uses the grim-trigger strategy to punish underpricing. Each person expects to go out of business in one month, meaning that each person is about to choose a price for the last time. Which price will each person choose?
3. Many firms have "going out of business" sales with remarkable bargains. What insights does the material in this chapter provide about such sales?
4. Consider the example of entry deterrence shown in Figure 7 (page 260). Suppose that just one number changes: If Jane chooses a large quantity and Dick stays out, Jane's profit would be $4,500. All the other numbers are the same as those shown in Figure 7. Draw a new game tree and predict the outcome: Will Jane choose a large or a small quantity, and will Dick enter or stay out?

Take It to the Net

We invite you to visit the O'Sullivan/Sheffrin page on the Prentice Hall Web site at:

http://www.prenhall.com/osullivan/

for this chapter's World Wide Web exercise.

MODEL ANSWERS FOR THIS CHAPTER

Chapter-Opening Questions

1. It is likely to lead to higher prices because it eliminates the possibility of underpricing. The promise to issue refunds is an empty promise.
2. The price fixing arrangement is more likely to persist if the airlines pick prices repeatedly over a long period of time, giving the airlines the opportunity to punish anyone who cheats on the price-fixing agreement.
3. The growth of the off-campus firms threatens the campus bookstore monopoly, and the bookstore might cut its prices to prevent off-campus booksellers from extending their services to your state.
4. A merger decreases competition and leads to higher prices.
5. Deregulation actually made the airline industry less competitive, a result of mergers, a limited number of airport gates, and airline promotions such as frequent-flier programs that discourage consumers from switching airlines.

Test Your Understanding

1. *m*, *d*
2. X, Z, 4, $5,000
3. He will choose the low price and gain at Jill's expense.

4. Jack's promise is not credible because once Jill chooses the high price, he will earn more profit by choosing the low price. Jill should ignore the incredible promise and choose the low price.
5. \$50 (\$400 – \$350)
6. They are common in appliance and electronics stores and in hardware stores. Many grocery stores honor the coupons of other stores. Although these schemes appear to be good news for consumers, they actually facilitate price-fixing and lead to higher prices.
7. The grim trigger makes profit zero, while the duopoly price leaves each firm with a positive profit. The costs of underpricing are higher with the grim trigger, so there is a greater incentive to charge the cartel price.
8. Two months. In the first month, Jill underprices Jack. In the second month, Jill chooses the high price but is underpriced by Jack, who is punishing her for underpricing him in the first month. In the third month, they both choose the high price.
9. cost, benefit
10. X, Y, 1
11. If she chooses a small quantity, Dick will enter.
12. To prevent the entry of a second firm, an insecure monopolist commits itself to produce a large quantity of output and accepts a low price. A secure monopolist doesn't have to worry about other firms entering the market.
13. The large airlines used mergers, airline gate rights, and bonus mileage programs to increase their market shares.
14. upward

Using the Tools

2. Advertising and Price Fixing

   The first option is the duopolist strategy. To prevent losing sales to Dee, Cecil could "neutralize" Dee's advertising campaign with an identical campaign of his own. Cecil and Dee would probably continue to sell about the same quantities at the same prices, but their profits would be lower because the advertising campaign costs money. The second option is a guaranteed price-matching scheme. Cecil could advertise the monopoly price and promise to match any lower price by Dee. If Dee recognizes the opportunity for price fixing, she will also advertise the monopoly price, and both firms will earn more profit.
3. Entry Deterrence

   The profit from entry deterrence is \$300 per day: Profit is the quantity (150) times the gap between price and average cost (\$2 = \$4 minus \$2). The profit from allowing entry is only \$80 per day: The profit is the quantity (80) times the gap between price and average cost (\$1 = \$3 minus \$2). The deterrence strategy generates a higher price and a larger quantity with no change in average cost, so profits are higher.

NOTES

1. Adam Smith, *Wealth of Nations* (New York: Modern Library, 1994).
2. Sharon Walsh, "Six Airlines to Halt Advance Price Listing," New York Times News Service, printed in *The Oregonian*, March 18, 1994, p. B1.
3. George Stigler, "The Kinked Oligopoly Demand Curve and Rigid Prices," *Journal of Political Economy*, vol. 55, 1947, pp. 432–449.
4. Michelle Mahoney, "Firm's Success a Textbook Case," *The Denver Post*, September 5, 1990, p. C1.
5. Erwin A. Blackstone, "Limit Pricing and Entry in the Copying Machine Industry," *Quarterly Review of Economics and Business*, vol. 1, Winter 1972, pp. 57–65.
6. Blackstone, "Limit Pricing and Entry in the Copying Machine Industry."
7. Hideki Yamawaki, Leo Sleuwaegen, and Leonard W. Weiss, "Industry Competition and the Formation of the European Common Market," Chapter 6 in *Concentration and Price*, edited by Leonard W. Weiss (Cambridge, MA: MIT Press, 1989).
8. William G. Shepherd and James W. Brock, "Airlines," Chapter 10 in *The Structure of American Industry*, edited by Walter Adams and James W. Brock (Upper Saddle River, NJ: Prentice Hall, 1995).
9. Steven Morrison and Clifford Winston, *The Evolution of the Airline Industry* (Washington, DC: The Brookings Institution, 1994).
10. Morrison and Winston, *The Evolution of the Airline Industry*.
11. Shepherd and Brock, "Airlines."
12. Paul MacAvoy, *Industry Regulation and the Performance of the American Economy* (New York: W.W. Norton, 1992).
13. Alfred E. Kahn, "Airline Deregulation—A Mixed Bag but a Clear Success Nonetheless," *Transportation Law Journal*, vol. 16, 1988, pp. 229–252.

CHAPTER

Part 4 ▮

Market Failure: Spillovers and Information

Public Goods, Taxes, and Public Choice

Here is the text from a TV newscast in the year 2070:

> Boomer, the 200-meter asteroid on a collision path with the earth, is expected to land at about 10:00 tomorrow in the heart of the world's breadbasket, the American midwest. The energy to be released by Boomer's impact exceeds the total explosive yield of all the nuclear weapons on the planet. Although Boomer is much smaller than the asteroid that caused the extinction of the dinosaurs about 65 million years ago, it is large enough to cause significant changes in the world's climate. The collision will generate a stratospheric dust cloud that will inhibit photosynthesis and retard plant growth, resulting in lower agricultural yields throughout the world. According to scientists, the earth's total agricultural output will decrease by about 20% over the next decade, increasing the price of food by about 35%.
>
> Could this catastrophe have been averted? Yes, according to scientists at the National Aeronautics and Space Administration. In 1996, scientists developed the technology for an asteroid-diversion system: large optical telescopes would detect an asteroid on a collision course with the earth, and an orbiting gossamer mirror of coated polyester would focus a tight beam of sunlight on the asteroid, vaporizing enough of the asteroid's surface to change the asteroid's path. In the UN

debate over the asteroid-diversion system, everyone agreed that the potential benefits of the system would outweigh the costs, but no one was willing to pay for the system. Why couldn't the nations of the world agree on such an important program, one that would have prevented tomorrow's catastrophe?

In Chapter 6 we saw that if a particular good generates spillover benefits, government intervention can make beneficial transactions happen. For example, the cost of an asteroid-diversion program is so high that no single person would provide such a program. We will never have such a program—even if the benefits exceed the costs—unless we make a collective decision about what sort of diversion program to develop and how to pay for it. The purpose of government is to help us make this sort of collective decision. The text of the hypothetical newscast suggests that some sort of multinational arrangement will be necessary to launch an asteroid-diversion program.

In this chapter we explore the special economic challenges associated with providing—and paying for—goods that generate spillover benefits. We also take a look at some alternative theories on how governments operate. Here are some of the practical questions we answer:

1. What is the rationale for subsidizing college education?
2. Should we eliminate taxes and finance government programs with voluntary contributions instead?
3. Is it sensible to pay landowners to host endangered wildlife such as wolves and spotted owls?
4. How will an $80 tax on apartments affect the monthly rent on apartments?
5. It often seems that there is little difference between the candidates in an election. Why?

THE ROLE OF GOVERNMENT

In Chapter 3 we saw that governments in the United States spend money on many goods and services, including education, public safety, highways, and national defense. In this chapter we explore the rationale for using government to provide these and other goods and services. In Chapter 19 we look at government programs that redistribute income to poor households.

Public Goods

Public good: A good that is available for everyone to consume, regardless of who pays and who doesn't.

Private good: A good that is consumed by a single person or household.

As we saw in an earlier chapter, one of the roles of government is to provide public goods such as dams for flood protection. Although the total benefit of a dam may exceed the cost, no single person would build the dam because no one has a benefit large enough to exceed the full cost of the dam. A dam is a **public good**, defined as a good that is available for everyone to consume, regardless of who pays and who doesn't. In contrast, a **private good** is consumed by a single person or household. As we explained in Chapter 6, the fact that a good is provided free of charge by the government does not make it a public good. For example, only one person can actually drink a free cup of milk, just as only one household can actually occupy a free apartment in a public-housing project. These are private goods that are provided by the government.

We can be more precise about the difference between public and private goods. Private goods are *rival in consumption* (only one person can consume the good) and *excludable* (it is possible to exclude a person who does not pay for the good). In contrast, public goods are *nonrival in consumption* (they are available for everyone to consume) and *nonexcludable* (it's impractical to exclude people who don't pay). Here are some other examples of public goods:

- National defense
- Law enforcement
- Space exploration
- Preservation of endangered species
- Protection of the earth's ozone layer
- City streets and highways

Spillover Benefits and Inefficiency

Spillover benefit: The benefit from a good experienced by people who do not decide how much of the good to produce or consume.

In addition to providing public goods, governments use various means to encourage the production and consumption of other goods that generate **spillover benefits**. As we saw in Chapter 3, state and local governments spend large sums of money on education. Recall the spillover principle:

Spillover PRINCIPLE

For some goods, the costs or benefits associated with the good are not confined to the person or organization that decides how much of the good to produce or consume.

For example, a college education generates some benefits for the graduate—including higher earning power and the thrill of learning—and two types of spillover benefits.

1. *Workplace spillovers.* In most workplaces, people work in groups, and teamwork is important. A person with a college education understands instructions more readily and is more likely to suggest ways to improve the production process. Therefore, if one member of a team gets a college degree, everyone on the team will become more productive. In other words, a college degree generates spillover benefits for the graduate's fellow workers.
2. *Civic spillovers.* Citizens in a democratic society make collective decisions by voting in elections, and each citizen must live with these decisions. A person with a college education is likely to vote more intelligently, so there are spillover benefits for the graduate's fellow citizens.

We know from Chapter 6 that if a good generates spillover benefits, the market equilibrium will be inefficient. Figure 1 on page 274 shows the market for college degrees in a small state. Let's assume that college education is a constant-cost industry, with a constant cost of $40,000 per degree. Point *i* shows the market equilibrium: The demand curve intersects the horizontal supply curve with a price of $40,000 and a quantity of 8,000 college degrees per year. As explained earlier, the way to show that the market equilibrium is inefficient is to find an additional transaction that would benefit a buyer, a seller, and some third parties.

The key to finding an additional transaction is to involve the citizens who experience the spillover benefits from college education. Suppose that the spillover benefit per college degree is $15,000: This is the amount that taxpayers are collectively willing to pay for each college degree, recognizing the workplace and civic externalities that come with a degree. Let's pick the potential college student who is positioned at point *d* on the demand curve. Heidi is willing to pay $30,000 for a college degree: If the price is less than this amount, she will get a degree; if the price exceeds this amount, she won't. The market price is $40,000, so Heidi won't get a degree under the market equilibrium.

Figure 1

Market for College Degrees

The equilibrium number of degrees is shown by the intersection of the demand curve and the horizontal supply curve. A student at point *d* will not get a degree in the market equilibrium, but will get a degree if he or she receives a subsidy equal to the spillover cost of college education ($15,000 in our example).

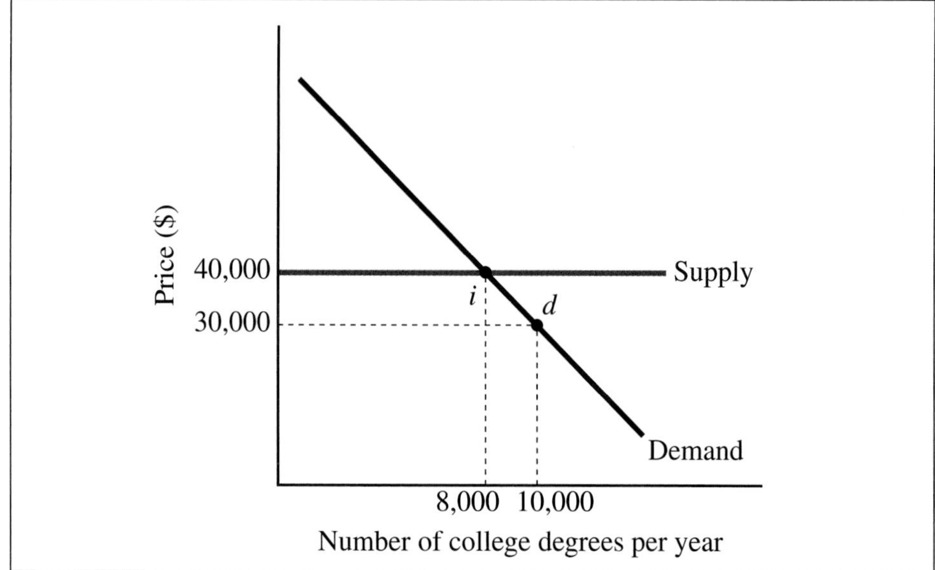

Here are some transactions between Heidi and her fellow citizens that would benefit everyone.

- If taxpayers give Heidi $11,000 to cover part of the cost of college, her net cost of college is only $29,000 ($40,000 in tuition less the $11,000 subsidy). This is less than the amount she is willing to pay, so she'll get a degree.
- Because Heidi's tuition covers the cost of educating her, the college would agree to educate Heidi if it received an additional token amount, say $100.

The citizens benefit from these transaction because they pay $11,100 and get a spillover benefit of $15,000. We've found a series of transactions that benefits everyone, so the market equilibrium is inefficient. We can use government subsidies for education to improve upon the market equilibrium.

The market equilibrium is inefficient because consumers and producers ignore the spillover benefits from college degrees. Although the Heidi transaction would be beneficial from society's perspective, it doesn't happen because Heidi considers only her personal benefits from a degree. The invisible hand—with each person guided by self-interest—does not lead to an efficient quantity of college education. The visible hand of government can arrange additional transactions that benefit everyone.

Subsidies to Guide the Market

The government can use tuition subsidies to increase the equilibrium number of college degrees. Suppose that each student receives a subsidy equal to the spillover benefit of a college degree ($15,000 in our example). The student will then consider the spillover benefits when he or she decides whether to attend college. Another term for *spillover benefit* is **external benefit**: Some of the benefits of consuming a particular good are external to the person who decides how much to consume. In the language of economics, an education subsidy *internalizes the externality*: The spillover benefit of $15,000 is now internal to the decision-maker. The subsidy eliminates the spillover problem, so we can rely on potential students—each acting in his or her own self-interest—to make efficient choices. If the sum of the personal and spillover benefits of a degree exceeds the cost ($40,000), a person will get a degree.

External benefit: Another term for *spillover benefit.*

How do the education policies of local, state, and federal governments actually work? State and local governments charge students at public colleges and universities a fraction of the cost of providing education, so there is an implicit subsidy for college education. In addition, the federal government provides financial aid to students in both public and private schools. Local governments provide grade-school and high-school education free of charge, so there is a 100% subsidy for primary and secondary education.

The government subsidizes other goods that generate spillover benefits. For example, many firms use government subsidies to support on-the-job training and education. This is sensible because some of the benefits of education and training go to other firms: When a worker trained by one firm switches to another firm, the second firm also benefits. This is the rationale for subsidizing some types of education and training programs. Another example is research at universities and other non-profit organizations. If a research project provides knowledge or technology that leads to the development of new products or the improvement of old ones, the benefits from the project spill over onto consumers and producers. This is the rationale for subsidizing basic research in the sciences.

Government Failure?

Does government always make efficient choices concerning public goods and subsidies? The government can use its taxing power to make beneficial transactions happen and thus improve the efficiency of the economy. The government will, however, sometimes make inefficient decisions. There are three reasons for government inefficiency.

1. ***Inadequate information.*** To decide whether to provide a public good, policymakers must compare the benefits to the costs. It is often difficult to estimate the benefits because people have a strong incentive to either understate or overstate their personal benefits. One person might overstate his benefit to make it more likely that the government will provide the public good, while another might understate her benefit to avoid paying a large tax for the public good.
2. ***Inflexible tax systems.*** If we want everyone to approve an efficient public good, we should match benefits and tax liabilities: A person with a large benefit should pay a higher tax than someone with a small benefit. Most tax systems are not flexible enough to allow a close matching of taxes and benefits. As a result, voters will reject some efficient public projects and approve some inefficient ones.
3. ***Special-interest groups.*** If a few people reap large benefits from a project but many people bear small costs, the project may be approved, even if the total cost exceeds the total benefit. For example, suppose that a dam protects just a few farms but will be financed with taxes from a million people. The farmers have a strong incentive to spend time and money to convince policymakers to build the dam. In contrast, if the tax is only $1 per capita, not many taxpayers will make their preferences known to policymakers. If politicians listen to people who express their preferences and contribute money to political campaigns, the inefficient project may be approved. This is an example of a special-interest group (farmers) who manipulate government at the expense of a larger group (taxpayers). In general, when a few people share the benefit from a project and a large number of people share the cost, government is more likely to approve inefficient projects.

Government failure: A situation in which the government fails to make an efficient choice in providing public goods or subsidies.

For these three reasons, the government may fail to make efficient choices. This is sometimes known as **government failure**. For an example of the role of special-interest groups in Europe, read the Closer Look box on page 276, "The European Union and Lobbyists."

A Closer LOOK

The European Union and Lobbyists

The European Union (EU), with 15 member nations, makes decisions that affect people and firms throughout Europe. As the power of the union has grown, so has the number of lobbyists expressing their points of view. By 1995 there were 10,000 lobbyists trying to influence decision-makers on the European Commission (the executive branch), the Council of Ministers (the representatives of member states), and the European Parliament (popularly elected representatives).* The fear of manipulation by lobbyists representing special interests has led some officials to advocate a formal registration process: Each lobbyist would be required to provide a list of his or her clients and the amount of money spent on the behalf of each client. Under a second proposal, lobbyists would be issued color-coded entry badges that would allow them to enter only certain parts of the parliament building, limiting their access to officials of the EU.

*Charles Goldsmith, "The EU Is Beset by Swarms of Lobbyists," *Wall Street Journal,* April 14, 1995, p. A6. Reprinted by permission of the *Wall Street Journal,* © 1995 Dow Jones & Company, Inc. All Rights Reserved Worldwide.

TEST *Your Understanding*

1. Explain the difference between the two types of benefit spillovers from education: a civic spillover and a workplace spillover.
2. Do you and your family pay the full cost of your college education? If not, who pays the rest? Are the spillover benefits from your education large enough to justify the subsidy?
3. Suppose that Lowell is one of the consumers on the lower part of Figure 1's demand curve for college education and is willing to pay $8,000 for a college education. Is it possible to involve Lowell in a voluntary transaction to increase the number of college degrees by one?

VOLUNTARY CONTRIBUTIONS AND THE FREE-RIDER PROBLEM

Free-rider problem: Each person will try to get the benefit of a public good without paying for it, trying to get a free ride at the expense of others.

What would happen if we replaced taxes with a system of voluntary contributions for public goods and subsidies? As we learned in Chapter 6, any attempt to replace taxes with voluntary contributions will be frustrated by the **free-rider problem.** If a person tries to get the benefits of a public good without paying for it, no one will contribute any money to support the public good, so it won't be provided.

Classroom Experiment in Free Riding

Do people really try to get free rides, or would most people contribute at least some money to support a public good? Here are the results of a classroom experiment that answers this question.

1. The instructor selected 10 students at random and gave each student 10 dimes ($1 per student).
2. Each student had an opportunity to contribute money to support a public good by dropping some or all of the dimes into a "public-good" pot. The

contributions were anonymous: None of the students knew how much the other students contributed.

3. For each dime in the pot, the instructor added two dimes. For example, if the students contributed a total of 40 dimes, the instructor added 80 dimes, so there was a total of $12 in the pot.
4. The instructor divided the money in the public-good pot equally among the 10 students. For example, if there was $12 in the pot, each student received $1.20.

Each person received one-tenth of the money in the public-good pot, regardless of how much he or she contributed to the pot. There was a large social payoff from contributing to the public good (a $0.10 contribution grows to $0.30), but each person had an incentive to free ride (not contribute).

Table 1 shows the results of this experiment in an introductory economics class. There were three free riders (students who contributed nothing) and the other students contributed between one and six dimes. The students contributed a total of $2.20, so the instructor added $4.40 to the pot and each student received $0.66 from the pot ($6.60 divided by 10). The bottom row of Table 1 shows how much money each student had at the end of the experiment. Each noncontributor ended up with $1.66 (the initial $1 plus the $0.66 share of the pot). At the other end of the table, the student who contributed six dimes ended up with only $1.06 (the initial $1 minus the $0.60 contribution plus the $0.66 share of the pot). As we saw earlier, if each student had contributed $1, each student would have ended up with $3.

This experiment suggests that people will voluntarily contribute some money to support a public good, but much less than the amount that would maximize the per capita benefit from the public good. On average, students in the experiment contributed 22% of the amount required to maximize the benefit. Other experiments on free riding generate the same result: People contribute some money but less than the amount that would maximize the payoff per person.[1]

What does this experiment tell us about the effects of using voluntary contributions to support real public goods? Suppose that a city government eliminates its taxes and asks its citizens to contribute voluntarily to a fund that would pay for local schools, the police, and fire protection. Our experiment suggests that some citizens would not contribute at all, even if they benefit from the public services. Other citizens would contribute some money to the fund, but the contributions would be small relative to the benefits these citizens receive from the public services. In general, we would expect the city to raise only a fraction of the amount required to maximize the per capita benefit from public goods.

Overcoming the Free-Rider Problem

Many organizations raise money through voluntary contributions, including public radio and television, religious organizations, and charitable organizations. It appears that some people overcome their inclination to engage in free riding and contribute voluntarily to organizations that provide public goods. The successful organizations use a number of techniques to encourage people to contribute.

Table 1: Free Riding in a Classroom Experiment

Contribution	$0	$0.10	$0.20	$0.30	$0.40	$0.50	$0.60
Number of students	3	1	2	1	2	0	1
Money at end	$1.66	$1.56	$1.46	$1.36	$1.26	$1.16	$1.06

1. Give contributors private goods such as coffee mugs, books, musical recordings, and magazine subscriptions. People are more likely to contribute if they get something for it.
2. Arrange matching contributions. You are more likely to contribute if you know that your $30 contribution will be matched with a contribution from another person.
3. Appeal to peoples' sense of civic or moral responsibility.

It's important to note, however, that these organizations are only partly successful in mitigating the free-rider problem. Public radio is one of the more notable success stories, but the typical public-radio station gets contributions from less than a quarter of its listeners. Moreover, as discussed in the Closer Look box "The Cost of Fundraising," there are large costs associated with collecting voluntary contributions.

ECONOMIC DETECTIVE– *The Mystery of the Three-Sided Clock Tower*

Back in the days before the inexpensive wristwatch, most people did not carry their own timepieces. Many towns built clock towers in the center of town to help their citizens keep track of time, and used voluntary contributions to raise the money to build the clock towers. One town in the northeastern United States built a four-sided tower but put clock faces on only three sides of the tower. To most people, this seems bizarre: If you build a clock tower, why not put faces on all four sides?

The key to solving this puzzle is the free-rider problem. It turns out that one of the town's wealthy citizens refused to contribute money to help build the clock tower, and the town officials decided to punish him by not putting a clock face on the side of the tower facing his house. In other words, the citizen tried—unsuccessfully—to get a free ride. The problem is that other citizens on the same side of town suffered too. In this case, preventing a free ride by one citizen caused problems for other citizens.

TEST *Your Understanding*

4 Explain why the free-rider problem occurs for public goods but not for private goods.

5 Margie, one of the students participating in the free-rider experiment, thinks in marginal terms and poses the following question: "If I contribute one dime, how will that affect my payoff from the experiment?" Answer her question.

6 Suppose that Margie uses the marginal principle to make all her decisions. Will she contribute the extra dime?

APPLICATIONS: ASTEROIDS AND WILDLIFE

Now that we've discussed some of the economic challenges associated with providing public goods, let's think about two unconventional public goods, the diversion of asteroids and the preservation of wolves.

Asteroid Diversion

How do we apply the concepts of public goods to the issue of protecting the earth from catastrophic collisions with asteroids? On average, the earth is hit by a 200-meter asteroid every 10,000 years, by a 2-kilometer asteroid every million years, and

A Closer LOOK

The Cost of Fundraising

Many organizations rely on voluntary contributions for financial support. Organizations such as United Way, the Sierra Club, and public television stations spend a lot of money on fundraising campaigns. According to the Council of Better Business Bureaus, the cost of a fundraising campaign should be no more than 35% of the money raised in the campaign. Using this rule of thumb, the typical organization will spend about $35 to raise $100, leaving only $65 to support the organization. In some cases, fundraising costs are much higher. In 1992, the primary public-television station in New York spent $2.3 million on a telemarketing campaign that raised only $2.8 million, leaving just $500,000 for the station.* Although a fundraising campaign may diminish the free-rider problem, it can be very costly.

*Marvine Howe, "Fund-Raising by Channel 13 Proves Costly," *New York Times*, June 27, 1992, p. 29.

by a 10-kilometer asteroid every 100 million years.[2] An asteroid collision generates a large stratospheric dust cloud that inhibits photosynthesis and retards plant growth. It seems that an asteroid collision 65 million years ago led to catastrophic climatic changes and probably the extinction of dinosaurs. If a large asteroid struck the earth today, similar changes would result in the deaths of millions of people. According to scientists, we already have the technology for an asteroid-diversion system. We could use large optical telescopes to detect an asteroid on a collision course with the earth and then change its path in one of two ways. First, an orbiting gossamer mirror of coated polyester could focus a tight beam of sunlight on the asteroid, vaporizing enough of the asteroid's surface to change the path.[3] Second, a series of nuclear explosions near the threatening asteroid could deflect the asteroid.

The diversion of asteroids is a public good in the sense that it is available for everyone to consume, regardless of who pays and who doesn't. As with any public good, the key to a developing an asteroid-diversion program is to collect money to pay for the program. According to NASA scientists, the program would require several new telescopes, which would cost about $50 million to install and about $10 million per year to operate.[4] The cost of the gossamer mirror or the nuclear weapons required to change the path of the asteroid would be $100 million to $200 million. Although it would be sensible to finance the program with contributions from all earthlings, it may be impossible to collect money from everyone. A more likely outcome is that one or more developed countries will finance their own diversion systems.

Preservation of Wolves

We can also apply the concepts of public goods and free riding to the issue of preserving wildlife. There are some trade-offs associated with preserving wolves and other wildlife in Yellowstone Park. To environmentalists, wolves are a part of the ecosystem, and the purpose of preserving wolves is to maintain the natural ecosystem. Ranchers, whose livestock is often eaten by wolves, consider the wolf a pest that should be eliminated or tightly controlled. In other words, there are costs as well as benefits associated with the preservation of wolves, just as there are both costs and benefits associated with other public goods, such as dams, fireworks, national defense, and space exploration.

One response to the wolf-preservation problem comes from Defenders of Wildlife, an environmental group in Montana. The organization collects money

Some organizations treat the preservation of species such as the wolf as a public good.

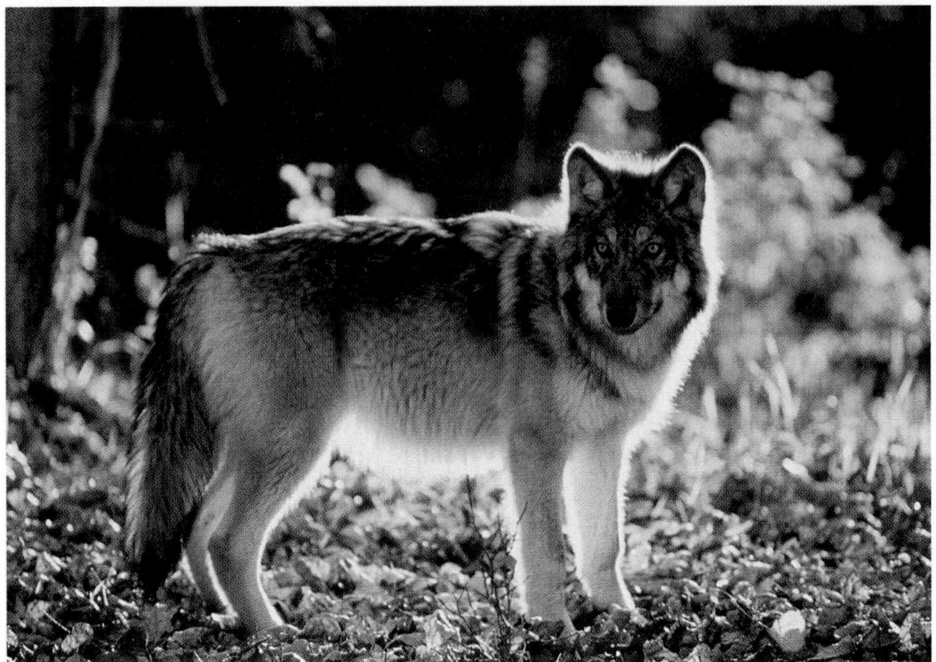

from its members and then uses the money to reward landowners who allow wolves to live on their properties: The "host" landowner receives a payment of $5,000 for each litter of wolf pups that is reared on the property.[5] In addition, the organization compensates ranchers for livestock killed by wolves. As a result of these programs, ranchers in the Yellowstone area are more likely to support efforts to maintain the wolves as part of the ecosystem of Yellowstone Park. The programs treat preservation as a public good, one that is supported by money collected from the people who benefit from preservation.

FINANCING GOVERNMENT: TAXES

So far, we've discussed the rationale for government spending programs. As we saw in Chapter 3, the government raises money to pay for these programs by imposing taxes on all sorts of goods and services. We'll look at two important questions about taxes.

1. Who really bears the burden of a tax? As we'll see, it is not necessarily the person who actually pays the tax to the government.
2. Is the total burden of a tax equal to the revenue collected by the government? As we'll see, a tax changes peoples' behavior, so the total burden actually exceeds the revenue collected.

We start with the issue of who bears the tax burden and then discuss the total burden of taxes.

Tax Shifting: Forward and Backward

We can use supply and demand curves to look at the market effects of taxes. Suppose that your city imposes a tax of $80 per apartment and collects the tax from housing firms. You may think that the burden of the tax falls exclusively on the housing firm, because after all, that's who mails the check to the government. But some simple supply and demand analysis will show why this is incorrect. The housing firm will charge more for apartments and pay less for his or her inputs, so the tax will actually be paid by consumers and input suppliers.

Figure 2 shows the market effects of a $80 tax on apartments. We learned in Chapter 4 that an increase in the cost of producing a good shifts the supply curve to the left. In a perfectly competitive industry, in the long run the equilibrium price equals the average cost of production, so each firm makes just enough money to stay in the market. The original price of $200 was just high enough to cover the monthly cost of providing an apartment. The tax increases the average cost per apartment by $80, so the original price is now less than the average cost. At the original price, housing firms will lose money on their apartments, so they will withdraw some apartments from the market and build fewer new apartments to replace old ones. As a result, the supply curve will shift to the left: At each price, fewer apartments will be supplied.

The leftward shift of the supply curve increases the equilibrium price of apartments. At the original price, there will be a shortage of apartments, and the price will increase to eliminate the shortage. In Figure 2 the market moves from point *i* to point *f*: The demand curve intersects the new supply curve at a price of $230, compared to $200 before the tax. In other words, housing firms shift part of the tax forward to consumers. Although housing firms pay the tax in a legal sense, they get some of the money to pay the tax by charging consumers more for apartments.

The tax also affects the people who supply inputs to the housing industry. The tax decreases the output of the industry, so the industry needs smaller quantities of all the inputs used to produce apartments. Therefore, the tax causes a surplus of each of the inputs to housing, for example labor and land. To eliminate the surpluses, input prices drop, meaning that part of the tax is shifted backward to input suppliers: Housing firms pay lower wages and less for land. Although housing firms pay the apartment tax in a legal sense, they get some of the money to pay the tax by paying less to workers and landowners.

So who really pays the apartment tax? Although the housing firm actually sends the money to the government, the firm collects more money from consumers and pays less money to input suppliers, so consumers and input suppliers indirectly pay the tax. Recall that at every point on the long-run supply curve, economic profit per firm is zero. This means that each housing firm makes zero profit before *and*

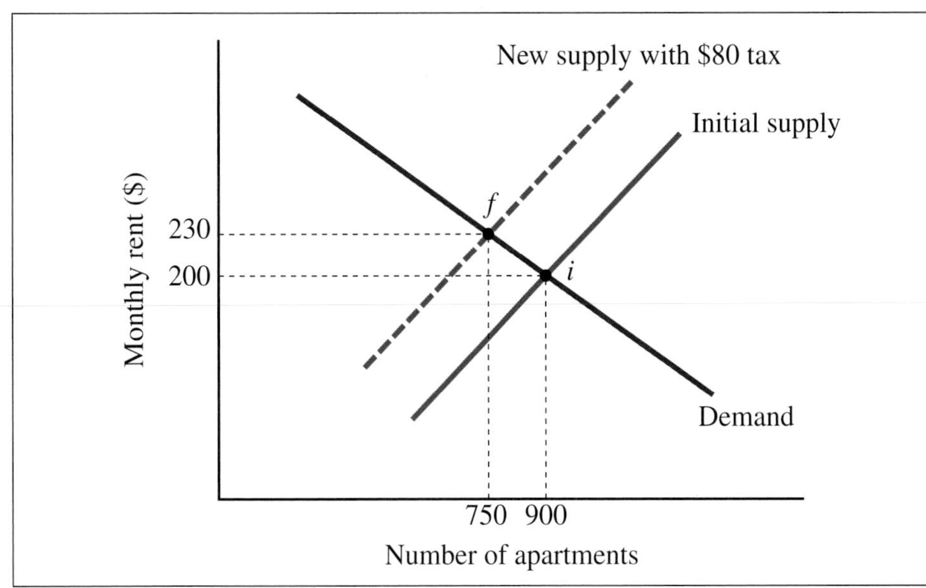

Figure 2

Market Effects of an Apartment Tax

A tax of $80 per apartment shifts the supply curve to the left, increasing the equilibrium price by $30 and decreasing the equilibrium quantity to 750.

after the tax. This is possible because the firm shifts part of the tax forward to consumers and part of the tax backward to input suppliers.

We can use Figure 2 to show just how the apartment tax is split between consumers and input suppliers. After the tax is imposed, the typical apartment owner charges $230 to consumers, pays a tax of $80 to the government, leaving $150 to pay all the people who supply the inputs required to produce the apartment. In contrast, before the tax, the apartment owner charged $200 and gave it all to input suppliers. Therefore, the tax makes input suppliers worse off by $50 per apartment ($200 minus $150). If we add the $50 burden imposed on input suppliers to the $30 price hike experienced by consumers, we get a total of $80, an amount equal to the apartment tax.

Predicting the Amount of Forward Shifting

How much of a tax will be shifted forward to consumers, and how much will be shifted backward to input suppliers? No one likes to pay taxes, so everyone will try to avoid paying a particular tax by changing his or her behavior. We've already seen that housing firms avoid paying the tax by shifting part of the tax to consumers. Firms can do this because they produce fewer apartments, causing a shortage of apartments that increases the price of apartments. If consumers want to avoid paying too much of the tax, they must change their behavior.

The amount of forward shifting to consumers depends on the price elasticity of demand. If the demand for apartments is relatively inelastic—if consumers are not very responsive to price changes—we need a large price hike to eliminate the shortage of housing caused by the tax. Therefore, consumers will experience a relatively large increase in price and thus pay the bulk of the tax. This is shown in panel A of Figure 3: Demand is inelastic, so the demand curve is relatively steep and a $5 tax increases the equilibrium price by $4 (from $10 to $14). In other words, consumers pay four-fifths of the tax. In contrast, if demand is relatively elastic, the demand curve will be relatively flat, and consumers will pay a relatively small part of the tax. This is shown in panel B of Figure 3: A $5 tax increases the equilibrium price by only $1 (from $10 to $11), so consumers pay only one-fifth of the tax.

The amount of backward shifting to input suppliers depends on their responsiveness to changes in input prices. We know that a tax causes a surplus of inputs, requiring a drop in input prices to eliminate the surplus. If input suppliers are not

Figure 3

Elasticities of Demand and Tax Effects

If demand is relatively inelastic (panel A), a tax will increase the market price by a relatively large amount, so consumers will bear a large share of the tax. If demand is relatively elastic (panel B), price increases by a relatively small amount and consumers bear a small share of the tax.

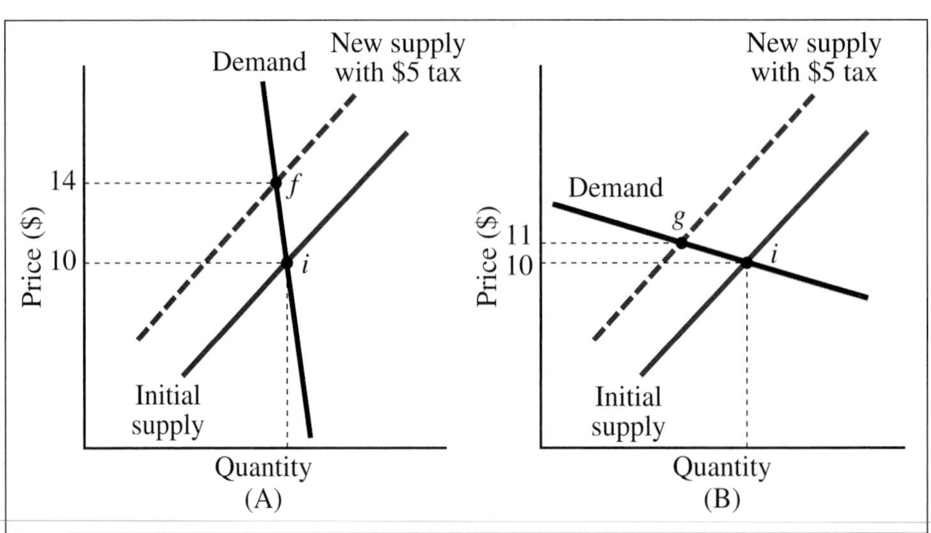

very responsive to price changes (if the supply of inputs is very inelastic), we need a large decrease in input prices to eliminate the surplus of inputs caused by the tax. Therefore, input suppliers will experience relatively large decreases in price and thus pay the bulk of the tax.

Suppose that you are asked to predict which side of the market will pay the bulk of a particular tax. To make a prediction, you must determine which side of the market—demand or supply—is less responsive to changes in price. Here are some examples of taxes for which we can make some predictions.

1. ***Housing tax.*** Land-use zoning policies limit the amount of land available for rental housing, so the supply of apartment land is not very responsive to changes in price. Therefore, land owners will pay the bulk of a tax on rental property.
2. ***Food tax.*** The demand for basic food items such as bread and milk is relatively inelastic, so consumers will pay the bulk of a tax on basic foods.
3. ***Income tax.*** As we'll see later in the book, the supply of labor is not very responsive to changes in the wage, so workers (suppliers) will pay a large part of an income tax.

Why should we care about tax shifting? Taxes are inevitable because without them we couldn't provide any public goods. An important policy question is: Who actually pays the taxes that support public goods? We've seen that the easy answer—the people who are legally responsibility for paying the tax—is often wrong. A tax increases consumer prices and decreases input prices, so we must look beyond the taxpayer to determine who actually bears the cost of a tax. The subtleties of tax shifting are often missed by the people who design our tax policy and the media folks who report on it.

Applications: Cigarette Tax and Luxury Tax

We can use what we've learned about tax shifting to discuss two recent episodes in tax policy. The first is the response of the U.S. Congress to a proposed increase in the cigarette tax, and the second is the unexpected effect of a tax on luxury goods. These episodes remind us that part of a tax will be shifted backward onto input suppliers.

In 1994, President Clinton proposed an immediate $0.75 per pack increase in the cigarette tax. The tax had two purposes: to generate revenue for Clinton's health-care reform plan, and to decrease medical costs by discouraging smoking. Figure 4 on page 284 shows the effects of the proposed tax on the cigarette market. The tax would decrease the supply of cigarettes and increase the equilibrium price from $2.00 per pack to $2.45. Cigarette producers would charge $2.45 per pack and pay a tax of $0.75, leaving only $1.70 to pay input suppliers, including the owners of tobacco-growing land. This is less than input suppliers received before, so some of the $0.75 tax would come out of the pockets of people who own land that is suitable for growing tobacco.

It appears that tobacco farmers and landowners understand the economics of cigarette taxes. Led by a group of representatives and senators from tobacco-growing areas in North Carolina, Kentucky, and Virginia, the Congress scaled back Clinton's proposed tax hike to $0.05. Although the government would collect the tax from cigarette producers, savvy tobacco farmers realized that the tax would decrease their income and the price of the land used to grow tobacco. The representatives of tobacco-growing areas, acting on behalf of tobacco farmers and landowners, used their power in Congress to scale back the President's proposed tax hike.

Figure 4

Market Effects of a Cigarette Tax

A tax of $0.75 per pack of cigarettes shifts the supply curve to the left, increasing the equilibrium price from $2.00 to $2.45.

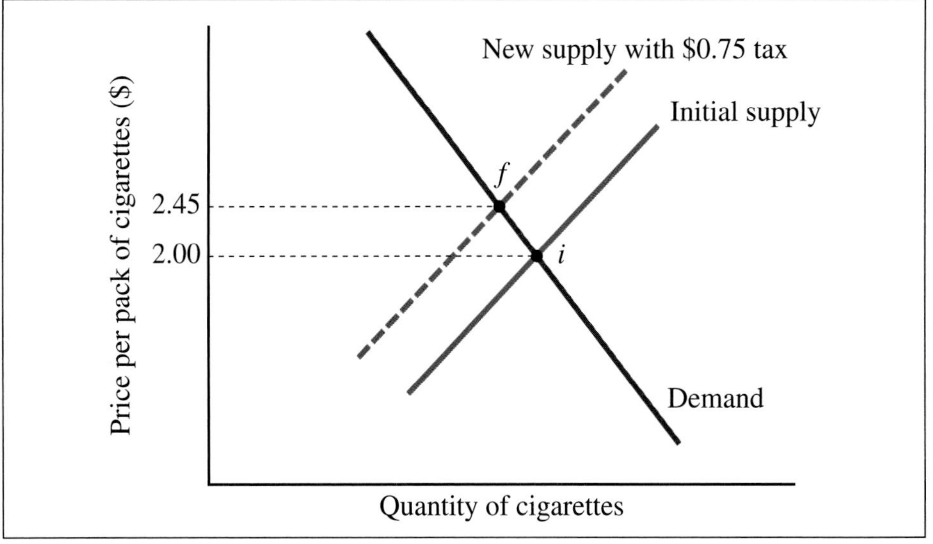

Another lesson on backward shifting comes from a special luxury tax passed by the U.S. Congress in 1990. The idea was to raise money from wealthy consumers by taxing luxury goods such as expensive boats. For example, the luxury tax on a $300,000 boat was $20,000. In fact, the luxury tax was shared by consumers and input suppliers, including people who worked in boat factories and boat yards. The tax decreased the quantity of boats produced, so the boat industry needed fewer workers, leading to layoffs and lower wages for the remaining workers. Although the idea behind the luxury tax was to "soak the rich," the tax actually harmed low-income workers in the boat industry.

A luxury tax on expensive boats will harm both wealthy consumers and people who work in boat factories and boat yards.

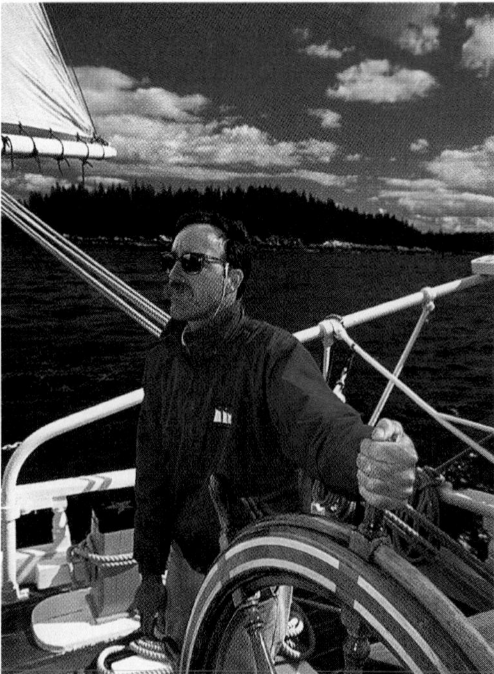

The Total Burden of a Tax

We've seen that people respond to a tax by changing their behavior, causing the tax to be shifted to other people. These changes in behavior also have important implications for the *total* burden of a tax. If people change their behavior in response to a tax, the total burden of a tax will exceed the amount of money the government actually collects from the tax. To see why, suppose that the government imposes a tax on No. 3 pencils, and the tax is large enough that everyone who initially used No. 3 pencils switches to other types of pencils or other writing implements. If no one purchases No. 3 pencils, the tax won't raise any revenue for the government, but the tax generates a burden because some people who would prefer to use No. 3 pencils have switched to other writing implements.

We'll use the fish market to explore the total burden of a tax. In Figure 5 the initial supply curve for fish is a horizontal line, indicating that the fish market is a constant-cost industry. In other words, input prices don't change as the industry grows or shrinks. The demand curve intersects the initial supply curve at point *i*, so the price is $2 and the quantity is 60,000 pounds of fish per day. If the government imposes a tax of $1 per pound of fish, the supply curve will shift upward by $1. In addition to paying $2 for the inputs required to produce 1 pound of fish, the fish producer must also pay a $1 tax, so the price required to cover all expenses is now $3 instead of $2.

In Figure 5 the fish tax increases the equilibrium price of fish from $2 to $3. Why does the price increase by an amount equal to the tax? In a constant-cost industry, input prices are fixed, so there is no opportunity to shift the tax backward onto input suppliers: They get the same prices for their inputs, regardless of how much output is produced. Therefore, it makes sense that consumers bear the full cost of the tax.

We can use the concept of consumer surplus to determine just how much consumers lose as a result of the tax. Before the fish tax, the consumer surplus is shown by the area between the initial supply curve and the demand curve, or areas *T*, *R*, and *E*. When the price increases to $3, the consumer surplus shrinks to the area of triangle *T*, so the loss of consumer surplus is shown by rectangle *R* and triangle *E*. Let's take a closer look at these two areas.

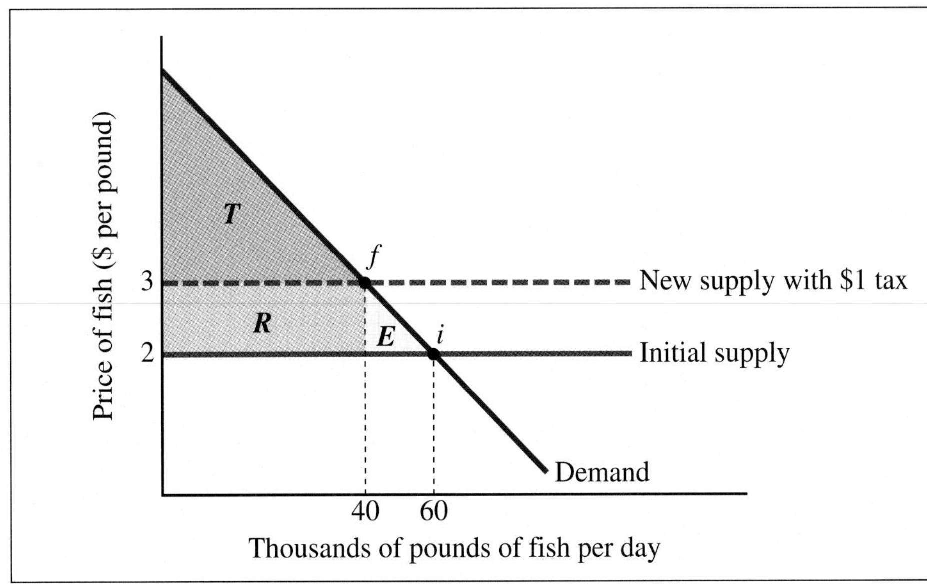

Figure 5

Total Burden of a Tax

In a constant-cost industry, a tax increases the equilibrium price by the tax ($1 per pound in this example). Consumer surplus decreases by areas *R* and *E*. Total tax revenue is shown by rectangle *R*, so the total burden exceeds tax revenue by triangle *E*, sometimes known as the deadweight loss or excess burden of the tax.

- Rectangle *R* shows the extra money consumers must pay for the 40,000 pounds of fish they purchase. The tax increases the price by $1, so consumers pay an extra $40,000.
- Triangle *E* shows the loss of consumer surplus on the fish *not* consumed because of the tax. Consumers obey the law of demand, so when the price rises, they cut their fish purchases by 20,000 pounds. As a result, they give up the consumer surplus they would have received on these fish.

How does the total burden of the tax compare to the tax revenue raised by the government? The total tax revenue is the tax per pound ($1) times the quantity consumed (40,000 pounds), or $40,000. This is shown by rectangle *R*: Part of the loss experienced by consumers is a revenue gain for government. In addition to losing rectangle *R*, consumers also lose triangle *E*, so the total burden of the tax exceeds the tax revenue. Triangle *E* is sometimes known as the **deadweight loss from taxation** or the **excess burden** of the tax. Because the tax causes consumers to change their behavior—consuming less fish at the higher price—there is a deadweight loss or excess burden.

Deadweight loss from taxation: The difference between the total burden of a tax and the amount of revenue collected by the government.

Excess burden: The difference between the total burden of a tax and the amount of revenue collected by the government.

TEST *Your Understanding*

7 Complete the statement with *right* or *left*: A tax on a particular good shifts the market supply curve to the ____________.

8 How will a tax on backpacks affect the price and quantity of backpacks?

9 Complete the statement with *surplus* or *shortage*: A tax on chairs will cause a ____________ in the market for chairs and a ____________ in the markets for the inputs used to make chairs.

10 The demand for coffee is very inelastic (about 0.30). Which side of the market—consumers or input suppliers—will pay a larger part of a coffee tax?

PUBLIC CHOICE

Earlier in the chapter we discussed the challenges associated with providing and paying for goods that generate spillover benefits. We use governments to make collective decisions about public goods, subsidies, and taxes. In this part of the chapter we look at how governments actually operate and explore some of the policy issues raised by a field in economics known as **public choice**. We explore the three contrasting views of government that have emerged from public-choice economics.

Public choice: A field of economics that explores how governments actually operate.

Governments Take Actions to Promote Efficiency

The public-interest view of government is based on the idea that governments make the economy more efficient. For example, governments throughout the world subsidize education. As we saw earlier in this chapter, education generates spillover benefits, so education subsidies are necessary to achieve economic efficiency. Similarly, governments provide all sorts of public goods, including dams, national defense, and space exploration. Because of the free-rider problem, a system of voluntary contributions for public goods is unlikely to raise enough money to support public goods at the efficient levels. The alternative to voluntary contributions is to give government the power to collect taxes.

Voters Tell Governments What to Do

The second view of government focuses on voters and how they affect government decisions. We vote directly on ballot measures and budget elections, both of which may impose constraints on government. We also vote for people to represent our viewpoints in legislative bodies (city councils, state legislatures, Congress) and in executive positions (mayor, governor, president). The basic idea of a democracy is that the government will take actions that are approved by the majority of citizens. If governments are responsive to voters, the voting public ultimately makes all the important decisions, and the actions of government reflect the preferences of voters.

One of the key results of public choice economics is known as the **median-voter rule**. According to this rule, the choices made by government will reflect the preferences of the median voter, defined as the voter who splits the voting population into two halves, with one half wanting more of something (for example, a larger government budget) and the other half wanting less (a smaller government budget). As we'll see, this rule has some interesting implications for decision-making and politics.

Median-voter rule: A rule suggesting that the choices made by government will reflect the preferences of the median voter.

To see the logic of this rule, consider a state where there are two candidates for governor—Penny and Buck—and the only issue in the election is how much the state should spend on education. Each citizen will vote for the candidate whose proposed education budget is closest to the citizen's preferred budget. Figure 6 shows citizens' preferences for education spending, with different preferred budgets on the horizontal axis and the number of voters with each preferred budget on the vertical axis. For example, 2 citizens have a preferred budget of \$1 billion, 4 have a preferred budget of \$2 billion, and so on. The median budget, which splits the rest of the voters into two equal groups (20 voters on either side), is \$5 billion.

Suppose that the two candidates start out with very different proposed education budgets. Penny proposes a budget of \$3 billion, and Buck proposes \$7 billion. The 20 citizens with preferred budgets less than or equal to \$4 billion will vote for Penny because her proposed budget is closest to their preferred budgets. Similarly, the 20 citizens with preferred budgets greater than or equal to \$6 billion will vote for Buck. The two candidates will split the 10 voters with a preferred budget of \$5 billion (halfway between the two proposed budgets), so each candidate will get a total of 25 votes, resulting in a tie.

Penny could increase her chance of being elected by increasing her proposed budget. Suppose that she proposes \$4 billion instead of \$3 billion. The voters with a

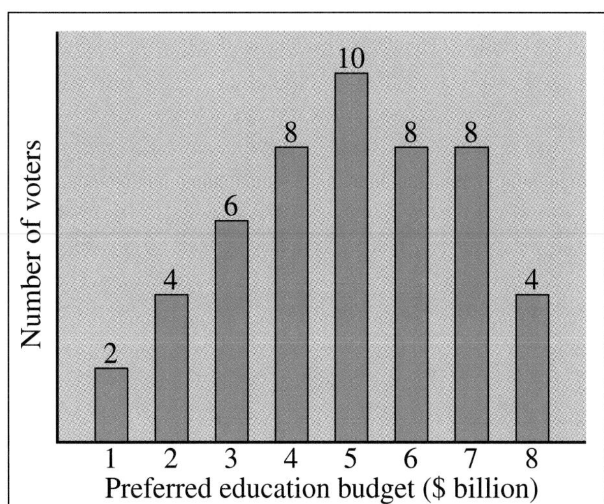

Figure 6

Median Voter Rule

If Penny proposes a \$3 billion budget and Buck proposes a \$7 billion budget, the election will result in a tie. By moving toward the median budget, Penny can increase her chance of being elected. Both candidates will propose a budget close to the preferred budget of the median voter (\$5 billion).

preferred budget of $5 billion will switch to Penny because Penny's $4 billion proposal is now closer than Buck's $7 billion. Penny won't lose any of her other votes, so she will win the election by a vote of 30 (2 + 4 + 6 + 8 + 10) to 20 (8 + 8 + 4). If Buck is smart, he will realize that he could get more votes by moving toward the median budget. For example, if he decreases his proposed budget to $6 billion, the election would result in a tie vote again. Penny and Buck will continue to move their proposed budget toward the median budget ($5 billion) until they both actually propose budgets that are very close to the median budget.

There are powerful forces pulling the two candidates toward the preferences of the median voter. As long as Penny proposes a smaller budget than Buck, the people with small preferred budgets will continue to vote for her. The benefit of moving toward the median is that she can get some votes from Buck. Similarly, Buck doesn't have to worry about people with large preferred budgets but can concentrate instead on the battle for voters in the middle. The result is that by election day, the two candidates have adopted virtually the same position on the education budget. In other words, there isn't much of a choice.

One logical problem with the median-voter rule is that voters do not usually have an opportunity to vote separately on each issue. Some economists and political scientists stress the role of political parties in putting together packages of issues to attract support. In this case, voters influence the government's decisions, but each spending or tax program will not necessarily reflect the preferences of the median voter.

It is also possible to "vote with your feet." The economist Charles M. Tiebout suggested that a household's choice of a community is based in part on the tax and spending policies of different communities. Households express their preferences by moving to communities that offer the best package of services and taxes. A community with inefficient public services will experience a loss in population, perhaps causing the local officials to make the public services more efficient.

It is clear that people vote with both ballots and their feet. In both cases, citizens can express their preferences for public goods, taxes, and public policies. These two sources of citizen power limit the ability of governments to take actions that are inconsistent with the preferences of most voters.

Government Officials Pursue Their Own Self-Interest

Several economists, including Nobel laureate James Buchanan, have suggested a model of government that focuses on the selfish behavior of government officials. According to this view, politicians and bureaucrats pursue their own narrow interests, which of course may differ from the public interest. For example, politicians or bureaucrats may gain prestige from starting a new spending program even if the cost of the program exceeds its social benefit. Because voters don't have much information about the costs and benefits of public services, they may not be in a position to evaluate the actions of politicians or bureaucrats and vote accordingly.

The self-interest theory of government explains why voters sometimes approve explicit limits on taxes and government spending. For example, most states have limits on the amount of property taxes that can be raised, and many states also limit total government spending. According to the self-interest theory of government, limitations on taxes and spending are necessary safeguards against politicians and bureaucrats who benefit from larger budgets.

The theory of rent seeking, which we described in Chapter 11, also applies to governments. Since governments can transfer resources from one group of citizens to another, individuals and groups may try to persuade government officials to transfer these resources their way. Resources are expended in the attempts to influence the decisions of politicians and bureaucrats, and from a social point of view, much of this expenditure is wasteful. This can be an important inefficiency in the operation of government.

Which Theory Is Correct?

Which of these three theories best describes the actual practices of governments? This is a very difficult question. Economists and political scientists have studied many dimensions of the decision-making processes underlying tax and spending policies. There is evidence that people do indeed vote with ballots and their feet and that these two forms of voting make a difference. There is also evidence that government officials sometimes pursue their own interests. The field of public choice is a very active area of research involving both economists and political scientists.

Using the **TOOLS**

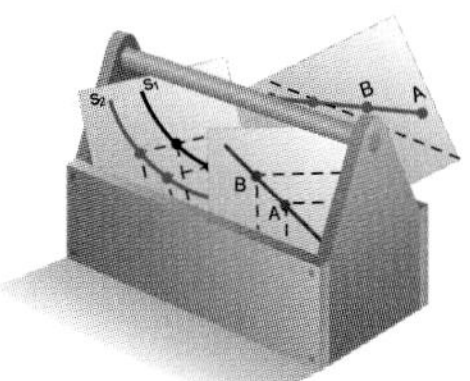

In this chapter we explain why the government provides public goods and subsidizes other goods that generate spillover benefits. Because of the free-rider problem, we can't rely on voluntary contributions to support public goods and subsidies, so we use taxes to support public programs. Here are some opportunities to do your own economic analysis of public goods and taxes.

1. ECONOMIC EXPERIMENT: *Voluntary Contributions*

In this voluntary-contribution experiment, students play the role of citizens who have the opportunity to contribute money to support public education. Here is how the experiment works.

- The class is divided into groups of three to five students, with each group representing a citizen. Each group starts with $30.
- Each day each citizen decides how much to contribute to public education. The maximum contribution is $10 per time period. The group records this amount on its report card.
- The instructor computes the total contributions to public education. Each dollar contributed to public education decreases the cost of the city's welfare system and criminal-justice system by $3, so the city's budget savings from the contributions equals the total contributions times 3.0. The tax refund per citizen equals the budget savings divided by the number of citizens. Here are some examples of contributions and tax refunds for a city with 20 citizens:

Total Contributions	*Decrease in Budget*	*Tax Refund per Citizen*
$ 20	$ 60	$ 6
100	300	30
200	600	60

- The experiment is run for five periods. A group's score for the experiment equals the amount of money it has at the end of five periods.

2. Stream Preservation

Suppose that a trout stream is threatened with destruction by a nearby logging operation. Each of the 10,000 local fishers would be willing to pay $5 to preserve the stream. The owner of the land would incur a cost of $20,000 to change the logging operation to protect the stream.

a. Is the preservation of the stream efficient from the social perspective?
b. If the landowner has the right to log the land any way he wants, will the stream be preserved?
c. Propose a solution to this problem. Describe a transaction that would benefit the fishers and the landowner.
d. Will your proposed solution work?

3. Shifting a Housecleaning Tax

Consider a city where people from poor households clean the houses of rich households. Initially, firms charge households $10 per hour, keep $1 per hour for administrative costs, and pay their workers $9 per hour. Like many luxury goods, the demand for housecleaning service is very elastic. In contrast, workers are not very responsive to changes in the wage.

a. Use supply and demand curves to show the initial equilibrium in the market for cleaning services (price = $10 per hour and quantity = 1,000 hours per week), and label the equilibrium point with an *i*.
b. Suppose that the city imposes a unit tax of $3 per hour of cleaning services, and one-third of the tax is shifted forward to consumers. Use your graph to show the effects of the tax on the cleaning market. Label the new equilibrium point with an *f*. What is the new price?
c. Is it reasonable that only one-third of the tax is shifted forward? Explain.
d. Suppose that firms continue to keep $1 per hour for administrative costs. Predict the new wage.
e. Who bears the bulk of the housecleaning tax, wealthy or poor households?

SUMMARY

In this chapter we've seen that governments can solve the problems caused by spillover benefits. Another insight from this chapter is that taxes affect the prices of consumer goods and inputs, so we must look beyond the taxpayer to determine who actually bears the cost of a tax. We've also examined three different views on how governments actually operate. Here are the main points of the chapter.

1. If the cost of a particular good exceeds its per capita benefit, the good will not be provided by a market, even if the total benefit exceeds the total cost. We can use government—with its taxing authority—to make a collective decision about whether to provide such a good.
2. The government can use subsidies to encourage the people who consume goods with spillover benefits to make decisions that are efficient from society's perspective.
3. A system of voluntary contributions suffers from the free-rider problem: People will contribute a small fraction of the amount that would be generated under a collective decision supported by taxes.
4. The bulk of a tax will be paid by the side of the market—supply or demand—that is less responsive to changes in price.
5. Because a tax causes people to change their behavior, the total burden of the tax exceeds the revenue generated by the tax.

KEY TERMS

deadweight loss from taxation, *286*
excess burden, *286*
external benefit, *274*
free-rider problem, *276*
government failure, *275*

median-voter rule, *287*
private good, *272*
public choice, *286*
public good, *272*
spillover benefit, *273*

PROBLEMS AND DISCUSSION QUESTIONS

1. Consider a three-person city that is considering a fireworks display. Bertha is willing to pay $100 for the proposed fireworks display, while Marian is willing to pay $30, and Sam is willing to pay $20. The cost of the fireworks display is $120.
   a. Will any single citizen provide the display on his or her own?
   b. If the cost of the fireworks display is divided equally among the citizens, will a majority vote in favor of the display?
   c. Describe a transaction that would benefit all three citizens.
2. Suppose that the students in the free-rider experiment make the following agreement: If any single person does not contribute the full 10 cents, all the contributions will be returned, with each contributor receiving a refund equal to the amount that he or she contributed. How will this agreement affect the outcome of the experiment?
3. Churches collect substantial sums of money through voluntary contributions. What explains their ability to overcome the free-rider problem at least partially?
4. The spotted owl is an endangered creature that lives in old-growth forests. Logging in the old-growth forests destroys the habitat of the owls. Explain how the lessons from the wolf-preservation program might be applied to the issue of preserving the spotted owl.
5. Suppose that each of the 80,000 citizens in a particular county would be willing to pay $0.10 to increase the number of wolf litters by one. Each litter of wolves imposes costs on ranchers (from livestock losses) of $5,000.
   a. Is the provision of an additional litter of wolves efficient from the social perspective?
   b. If ranchers have the right to kill any wolves on their property, will an additional litter in fact be provided?
   c. Propose a solution to this problem. Describe a transaction that would benefit the wolf-lovers and ranchers.
6. Can you think of any goods that generate spillover benefits but are not subsidized by government? If so, starting from the market equilibrium, describe a transaction that would benefit a buyer, a seller, and a third party.
7. Contributions to organizations such as United Way and the American Cancer Society are tax deductible: For each dollar contributed, a person's tax liability decreases by $0.15 to $0.31. Explain the rationale for this tax policy.
8. Under a special luxury tax passed by Congress in 1990, buyers of expensive cars pay a 10% tax on the portion of the purchase price above $30,000.
   a. Will the luxury car tax be paid exclusively by the wealthy consumers who buy expensive cars?
   b. What information do you need to determine the share of the tax paid by wealthy consumers?
9. In the words of Will Rogers, "The trouble with land is that they're not making it any more." In other words, the supply of land is fixed, and the supply curve is a vertical line.
   a. If the government imposes a tax on land, which side of the market—land consumers or landowners—will pay a larger part of the tax?
   b. Will the land tax generate a deadweight loss?
10. Consider the example of the governor's election shown in Figure 6 (page 287). Suppose that 18 new people move into the state and that each newcomer has a desired education budget of $9 billion.
    a. Will the two candidates change their proposed education budget? If so, how much will each candidate propose?
    b. How would your answer to part a change if each newcomer had a desired budget of $15 billion instead of $9 billion?

Take It to the Net

We invite you to visit the O'Sullivan/Sheffrin page on the Prentice Hall Web site at:

http://www.prenhall.com/osullivan/

for this chapter's World Wide Web exercise.

MODEL ANSWERS FOR THIS CHAPTER

Chapter-Opening Questions

1. A college education generates two sorts of spillover benefits: workplace spillovers (fellow workers are more productive) and civic spillovers (a graduate may vote more intelligently).
2. A system based on voluntary contributions would suffer from the free-rider problem, with few people contributing money to support the public good.
3. The payments to "host" landowners treat preservation as a public good, one that is supported by money collected from the people who benefit from preservation.
4. The housing firm collects more money from consumers (the price of apartments is higher) and pays less money to input suppliers (the prices of inputs are lower), so consumers and input suppliers indirectly pay the tax.
5. A liberal candidate that moves toward the center won't lose the votes of liberal citizens, but will gain some votes from moderate citizens. Similarly, a conservative candidate who moves toward the center won't lose conservative votes, but will gain moderate votes. As a result, both candidates are likely to adopt moderate positions.

Test Your Understanding

1. A civic spillover benefits everyone in society, while a workplace spillover benefits fellow workers.
2. Most students receive some sort of implicit or explicit subsidy from the government.
3. If taxpayers paid the full spillover benefit associated with Lowell's education ($15,000), the net cost to Lowell would be $25,000. Because this exceeds the amount he is willing to pay ($8,000), he wouldn't get the degree.
4. The producer of a private good collects money from each consumer, so if you don't pay, you don't get the good. In contrast, it is impossible to prevent nonpayers from consuming a public good.
5. If Margie adds a dime to the pot, the instructor adds 20 cents and then divides the 30 cents equally among the 10 students, so Margie gets back 3 cents for every dime she puts in.
6. She will not contribute the extra dime because the marginal benefit (3 cents) is less than the marginal cost (10 cents).
7. left
8. The equilibrium price increases and the quantity decreases.
9. shortage, surplus
10. Consumers are not very responsive to changes in price, so they will pay a large part of the tax.

Using the Tools

2. Stream Preservation
   a. The benefit is $50,000 (10,000 fishers × $5 per fisher), which exceeds the cost of $20,000. Since the benefit exceeds the cost, the preservation of the stream is socially efficient.
   b. No. If the landowner is also a fisher, the cost ($20,000) exceeds the benefit ($5).
   c. The citizens could contribute to a stream-preservation fund to cover the landowner's cost. For example, if each fisher contributed $3 (60% of his or her benefit), they could raise a total of $30,000. The landowner would be better off by $10,000, and each fisher would be better off by $2.
   d. The free-rider problem may make it difficult to raise enough money to pay off the landowner.
3. Shifting a Housecleaning Tax
   a. See Figure A on page 293.
   b. See Figure A. The tax shifts the supply curve to the left, and the new price is $11.
   c. We know that demand is very elastic and input suppliers are not very responsive, so a one-third shift is reasonable.
   d. The firm collects $11 from consumers, pays the $3 tax, pays its $1 administrative cost, leaving only $7 for workers. In other words, the wage decreases from $9 to $7.
   e. Workers experience a wage cut of $2 per hour, while consumers pay an additional $1 per hour for cleaning services.

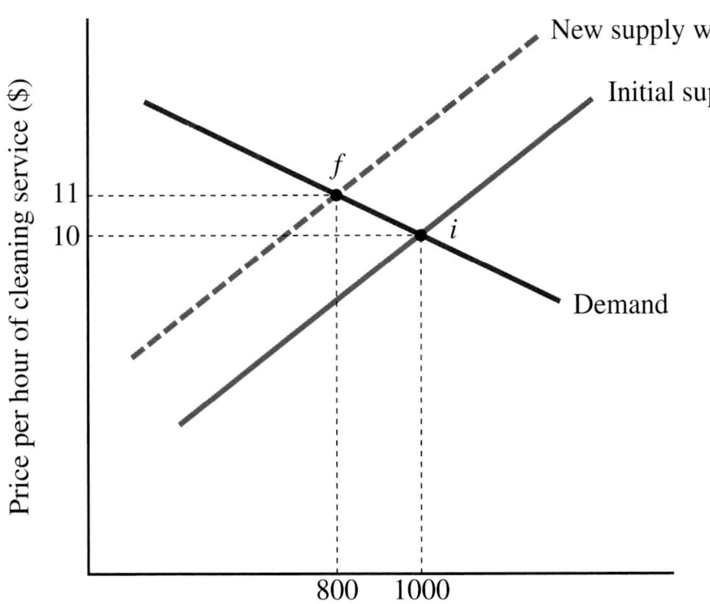

Figure A

Market Effects of Cleaning Tax

NOTES

1. R. Mark Isaac and James M. Walker, "Communication and Free-Riding Behavior: The Voluntary Contribution Mechanism," *Economic Inquiry,* vol. 26, no. 4, October 1988.
2. Carl Sagan, "A Warning for Us?" *Parade,* June 5, 1994, p. 8.
3. "Mirror Beam Could Deflect Killer Asteroid, Theory Says," *New York Times,* November 9, 1994, p. C6.
4. John Boudreau, "Collision Course: Scientists Say There's a Big Asteroid Bank in Our Future," *Washington Post,* April 6, 1994, p. C1.
5. Terry L. Anderson, "A Carrot to Save the Wolf," *The Margin,* Spring 1992, p. 28.

CHAPTER

15

Environmental Problems and Public Policy:

Global Warming, Ozone Depletion, Acid Rain, and Urban Smog

Under the Climate Control Accord of 1994, electric utilities in the United States agreed to do their part in the battle against global warming. Arizona Public Service provides electricity to the rapidly growing population in the southwestern United States. Although the utility could decrease its emissions of the pollutants responsible for global warming, it would be very costly to do so. Instead, the utility indirectly paid for projects that will decrease air pollution in India, China, and other developing countries, where pollution abatement is relatively cheap.[1] In addition, the utility paid for a reforestation project in Mexico, which will help in the battle against global warming because forests absorb some of the pollutants responsible for global warming.

This story of Arizona Public Service provides an introduction to recent innovations in environmental policy. In more and more cases, the government sets a target pollution level and lets the polluters decide how to meet the target. This approach contrasts sharply with the traditional regulatory policy under which the government gets involved in the details of pollution abatement. In the case of global warming, Arizona Public Service can meet its pollution-abatement responsibility by paying for abatement projects elsewhere, even projects in other countries. Indeed, our most pressing environmental problems—global warming, the depletion of the ozone layer, and acid rain—cross international boundaries, and so do the solutions.

We know from earlier chapters that if a particular good generates spillover costs, the market equilibrium will be inefficient. In this chapter we explore several environmental problems that result from spillover costs. You've seen the headlines and read the stories about global warming, the hole in the ozone layer, acid rain, and urban smog. Now you'll learn why these problems occur and what we can do about them. Here are some of the practical questions we answer:

1. How does a pollution-control policy affect the equilibrium price of a polluting good?
2. Would a switch from a traditional regulatory policy to a pollution tax make both environmentalists and business people happy?
3. How is global warming affected by pollution from power plants and the destruction of tropical rain forests?
4. Why do we want to protect the ozone layer in the upper atmosphere but get rid of ozone (also known as smog) near the earth's surface?
5. What is the rationale for the "cash for clunkers" program, under which firms buy old cars and destroy them?

TAX ON POLLUTION

In Chapter 6 we used the paper market as an example of a market that generates spillover costs. The paper market is perfectly competitive: Each firm is small enough that it takes the price of paper as given. The market equilibrium is shown in Figure 1: The supply curve intersects the demand curve at point *i*, so the equilibrium price of paper is \$60 and the equilibrium quantity is 100 tons per day. Paper mills generate chemical wastes as part of their production process and dump some of these wastes

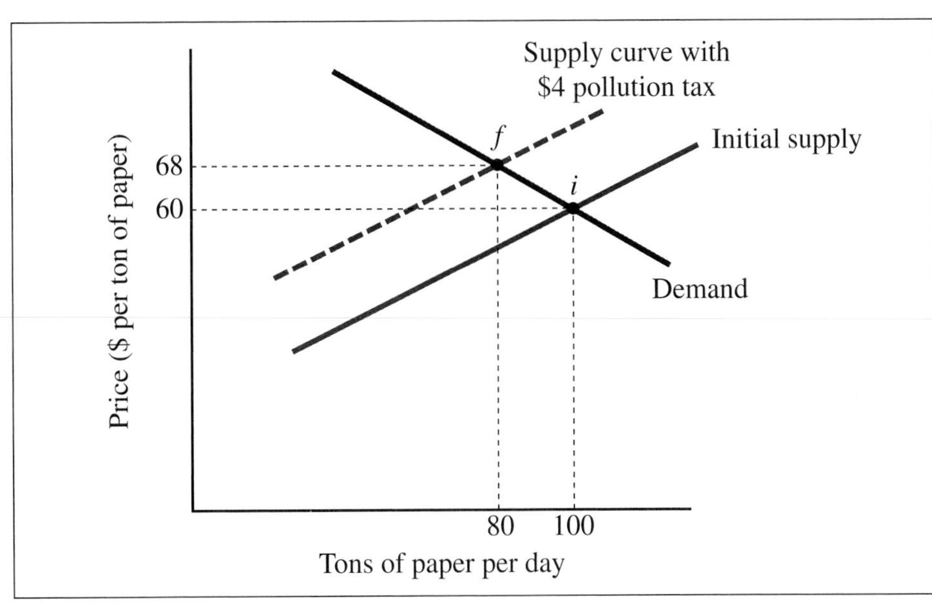

Figure 1

Market Effects of a Pollution Tax

The pollution tax increases the cost of producing paper, shifting the market supply curve to the left. The tax increases the equilibrium price and decreases the equilibrium quantity.

into rivers. Suppose that a city downstream from the paper mills treats the river water to make it safe for drinking and that each gallon of waste increases the city's water-treatment costs by $4.

Pollution tax: A tax or charge equal to the spillover cost per unit of waste.

External cost: The part of production cost that is external to the organization that decides how much of a particular good to produce.

An obvious policy response to the pollution problem is to impose a **pollution tax**, a tax equal to the spillover cost per unit of waste. For example, because each gallon of waste increases the city's water-treatment costs by $4, the pollution tax would be $4 per gallon of waste. The pollution tax forces firms to pay for their use of river water, just as they pay for labor, materials, and their production facilities. Another word for *spillover cost* is **external cost**, defined as the part of production cost that is incurred by someone outside or external to the organization that decides how much to produce. A pollution tax *internalizes the externality* associated with producing paper: If a paper firm pays $4 per gallon of waste, the cost of polluting the river is internal to the firm, not external.

The Firm's Response to a Pollution Tax

Most polluting firms can control the amount of waste they dump into the environment. For example, a paper firm could install filters and other abatement equipment, or it could switch to raw materials that generate less chemical waste. The first two columns of Table 1 show a hypothetical relationship between the volume of waste generated and the cost of producing a ton of paper. For example, the cost per ton is $60 if the firm generates 5 gallons of waste, but $61 if the firm generates only 4 gallons of waste. In other words, when the firm decreases its waste by 1 gallon, the production cost per ton increases by $1. As the firm continues to decrease its waste, it becomes progressively more expensive to do so. This is sensible because the firm must use progressively more sophisticated and expensive abatement equipment to decrease the volume of waste. For example, the cost of eliminating the last gallon of waste is $30 ($116 minus $86).

The third and fourth columns of Table 1 show the tax cost and the total cost per ton of paper with different volumes of waste. The tax is $4 per gallon of waste, so the tax cost is $20 if the firm generates 5 gallons of waste per ton of paper, but only $16 for 4 gallons, $12 for 3 gallons, and so on. The fourth column of Table 1 shows the firm's total cost per ton of paper, equal to the sum of the production cost per ton and the tax cost per ton. If the firm generates 5 gallons of waste, the production cost will be $60 and the tax cost will be $20, so the total cost per ton is $80. As the firm continues to decrease the volume of waste, the production cost increases while the tax cost decreases. The total cost per ton initially decreases (from $80 to $77 to $76), but eventually increases, reaching $116 if the firm generates no waste.

Table 1: Cost per Ton of Paper with Varying Amounts of Pollution

Waste per Ton (gallons)	*Production Cost per Ton*	*Tax Cost per Ton*	*Total Cost per Ton*
5	$ 60	$20	$ 80
4	61	16	77
3	64	12	76
2	71	8	79
1	86	4	90
0	116	0	116

How will the typical paper firm respond to a pollution tax? The question for the firm is: Should we continue to generate 5 gallons of waste per day and pay $20 in pollution taxes, or should we spend some money to reduce our waste? In Table 1 the total cost per ton is minimized at $76 with 3 gallons of waste. Therefore, the typical firm will decrease its waste from 5 gallons to 3 gallons.

We can use the marginal principle to explain why it is sensible to generate only 3 gallons of waste.

Marginal PRINCIPLE

Increase the level of an activity if its marginal benefit exceeds its marginal cost, but reduce the level if the marginal cost exceeds the marginal benefit. If possible, pick the level at which the marginal benefit equals the marginal cost.

In this case, the activity is reducing waste, so the firm should continue to cut its waste as long as the marginal benefit (the $4 savings in taxes) exceeds the marginal cost (the extra production cost from cutting waste by 1 gallon). Starting with 5 gallons of waste, it is sensible to cut back to 4 gallons because the marginal benefit ($4) exceeds the marginal cost ($1). Similarly, it is sensible to cut back to 3 gallons because although the marginal cost is higher ($3), the marginal benefit still exceeds the marginal cost. The firm will not cut back to 2 gallons because the marginal cost is $7, an amount that exceeds the marginal benefit ($4).

The Market Effects of a Pollution Tax

We're ready to study the market effects of a pollution tax. Suppose that each firm produces 1 ton of paper and has the production costs shown in Table 1. Figure 1 shows the effects of the $4 pollution tax on the industry supply curve. In a perfectly competitive industry, the equilibrium price equals the average cost of production, so each firm makes just enough money to stay in the market. The original price of $60 was just high enough to cover the cost of producing paper without the pollution tax. The tax increases the cost of producing paper because the typical firm pays some pollution taxes *and* incurs some costs when it cuts back its pollution from 5 gallons to 3 gallons per ton of paper. Therefore, the old price will not be high enough to cover the higher production costs, and some firms will leave the market. As a result, the supply curve will shift to the left: At each price, a smaller quantity of paper will be supplied.

The leftward shift of the supply curve increases the equilibrium price of paper. In Figure 1 the market moves from point *i* to point *f*, where the demand curve intersects the new supply curve. The price of paper increases from $60 to $68 per ton, and consumers respond by decreasing the quantity of paper demanded, from 100 tons per day to 80. Like other taxes, the pollution tax is partially shifted to consumers in the form of a higher price, and they respond by consuming less paper. When consumers face the full cost of producing paper, they decide to consume less of it.

How does the pollution tax affect the total volume of waste dumped into the river? The volume of waste decreases for two reasons.

1. ***Abatement.*** There is less waste per ton of paper (3 gallons per ton instead of 5).
2. ***Lower output.*** The industry produces less paper (only 80 tons per day instead of 100).

In this example, the volume of water pollution decreases from 500 gallons per day (100 tons of paper times 5 gallons per ton) to 240 gallons per day (80 tons times

3 gallons). In general, we can clean up the environment by producing less of a polluting good *and* generating less waste per unit of the good.

In some cases, it is government rather than industry that generates spillover costs and makes inefficient choices. One example is explained in the Closer Look box "Spillover Costs from Rock Salt."

TEST *Your Understanding*

1 As the volume of waste decreases, the production cost per ton of paper increases at an increasing rate. Why?

2 Suppose that the pollution tax is $8 instead of $4. Use the information in Table 1 to determine how many gallons of waste (per ton of paper) the typical firm will generate.

3 Complete with *increases* or *decreases*: A pollution tax ____________ the equilibrium price of the polluting good, ____________ the equilibrium quantity, and ____________ the volume of waste.

A Closer LOOK

Spillover Costs from Rock Salt

Local governments in northern states use rock salt to melt ice on streets and highways during the winter. The problem is that rock salt is corrosive: It causes metal objects such as cars and bridges to rust, and it also harms roadside vegetation. According to a study by New York State, each ton of rock salt generates $1,600 worth of damage. An alternative deicer, calcium magnesium acetate (CMA), generates no spillover costs. If all the local governments in Minnesota switched from rock salt to CMA, the total cost of deicing the streets and highways—including corrosion costs—would decrease by about $244 million per year.

Why don't local governments switch from rock salt to CMA? A small local government is concerned only about the budgetary costs of melting the ice on its streets. Local governments use rock salt because it is cheaper—selling for $20 per ton, compared to $400 per ton for CMA. Like a paper mill that ignores the spillover costs of paper production, the local government ignores the spillover costs of rock salt. One solution to this problem is a pollution tax equal to the spillover cost of rock salt. If the state of Minnesota imposed a tax of $1,600 per ton of rock salt, the net price of rock salt ($1,620) would exceed the price of CMA ($400), so local governments would to switch to CMA.

The rock salt used to melt ice on streets and highways causes corrosion and requires costly repairs for cars and bridges.

Source: After David Morris, "A Free Market Demands Accurate Prices," *Building Economic Alternatives*, Fall 1990, p. 4.

Regulation and Marketable Pollution Permits

To an economist, the obvious response to a pollution problem is to impose a pollution tax, forcing firms—and consumers—to pay for the waste they generate. An alternative response is to use regulations to control the amount of pollution. Let's look at two forms of regulation, a traditional policy under which the government gets involved in most of the details of pollution abatement, and a modern policy involving marketable pollution permits.

Traditional Regulation: Command and Control

The label for a traditional regulatory policy is a **command-and-control policy**. The government *commands* each firm to produce no more than a certain volume of pollution and *controls* the firm's production process by forcing the firm to use a particular pollution-control technology. In our paper example, the government would tell each firm to produce no more than 4 gallons of chemical waste *and* force each firm to install a particular type of filter to meet the pollution target.

Command-and-control policy: A pollution-control policy under which the government *commands* each firm to produce no more than a certain volume of pollution and *controls* the firm's production process by forcing the firm to use a particular pollution-control technology.

One problem with this approach is that the mandated abatement technology (the *control* part of the policy) is unlikely to be the most efficient technology. There are two reasons for this.

1. The regulatory policy specifies a single abatement technology for all firms. Because the producers of a polluting good often use different materials and production techniques, an abatement technology that is efficient for one firm is likely to be inefficient for others.

2. The regulatory policy decreases the incentives to develop more efficient abatement technologies. The *command* part of the policy specifies a maximum volume of waste for each firm (for example, 4 gallons), and there is no incentive to cut the volume of waste below the maximum volume. There is a relatively small benefit from developing new technology because there is no payoff from using it. In contrast, a pollution tax provides the right incentives: If the firm develops a new technology that cuts the firm's waste below 4 gallons, the firm will pay less in pollution taxes.

Because a command-and-control policy causes firms to use relatively inefficient abatement technology, the policy will increase firms' costs by a relatively large amount.

Figure 2 on page 300 shows the market effects of a command-and-control policy. Let's assume that the maximum volume of waste is 4 gallons per firm (4 gallons per ton of paper). The policy increases the cost of producing paper, so it shifts the market supply curve to the left. For the reasons explained earlier, the mandated technology will be less efficient—and more costly—than the technology developed under a pollution tax, so the supply shift resulting from the regulatory policy will be larger than the supply shift from the pollution tax. To see this, compare Figure 2 to Figure 1. The regulatory policy has a larger supply shift even though firms generate more waste (4 gallons per ton instead of just 3 under the tax). In Figure 2 the new supply curve intersects the demand curve at point *f*: The price increases to \$74 and the quantity decreases to 70 tons per day. The total volume of pollution is 280 gallons per day (70 tons times 4 gallons per ton).

Why do people on both sides of the environmental debate gripe about environmental policy? If we compare the regulation outcome in Figure 2 with the pollution-tax outcome in Figure 1, we can see why everyone will be unhappy with the command-and-control policy.

- Consumers will be unhappy because the price is higher (\$74 instead of \$68 with the tax).

Figure 2

Command and Control

The command-and-control policy increases the cost of producing paper, shifting the market supply curve to the left. Because the mandated technology is less efficient than the technology that would emerge from a pollution-tax policy, the supply curve shifts by a larger amount, increasing the equilibrium price by a larger amount.

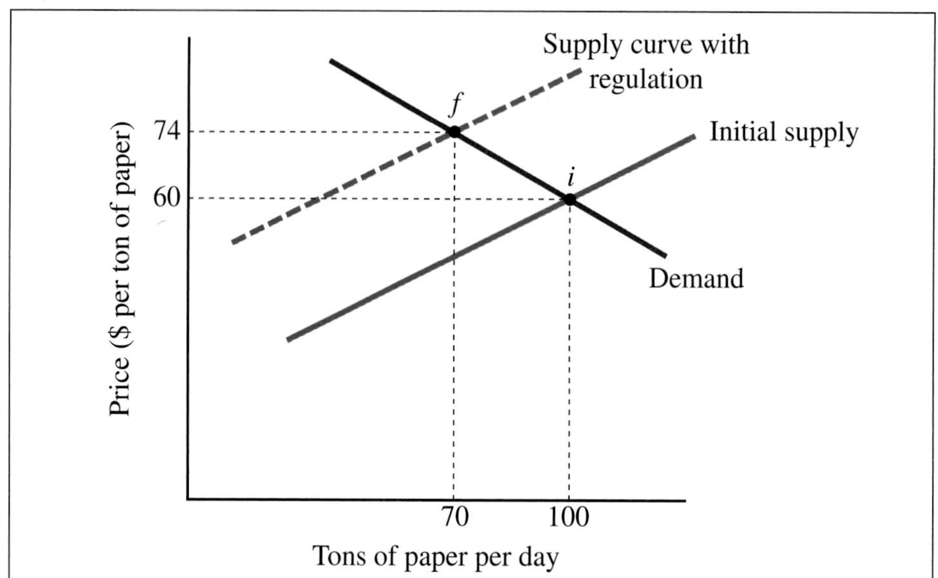

- Firms will be unhappy because they produce less paper (70 tons per day instead of 80 with the tax).
- Environmentalists will be unhappy because there is more pollution (280 gallons per day instead of 240).

Everyone is unhappy with the command-and-control policy because the mandated abatement technology is inferior—and more costly—than the technology developed under the tax policy. Therefore, we get less pollution abatement at a higher cost to firms and consumers.

An added bonus from the tax policy is that it generates tax revenue. The money raised from a pollution tax could be used to cut other taxes or increase spending on public programs. In several European nations—Germany, France, and the Netherlands—the revenue from pollution taxes is used to clean up polluted rivers.

A command-and-control policy has one advantage over a pollution tax. The response to a command-and-control policy is predictable: The policy specifies how much waste each firm can produce, so we can predict the total volume of waste. In contrast, we don't know how firms will respond to the pollution tax—they could pollute a little or a lot, depending on the tax and the cost of abating pollution—so it is difficult to predict the total volume of waste. As we'll see, a system of marketable pollution permits has the best features of a pollution tax (efficiency) and traditional regulatory policy (predictability).

Marketable pollution permits system: A system under which the government picks a target pollution level for a particular area, issues just enough pollution permits to meet the pollution target, and allows firms to buy and sell the permits.

Marketable Pollution Permits

In recent years, policymakers have developed a new approach to environmental policy. Under a **marketable pollution permits system,** the government picks a target pollution level for a particular area, issues just enough pollution permits to meet the pollution target, and allows firms to buy and sell the permits. For example, if the target pollution level in the paper industry is 400 gallons of waste per day, the government would issue a total of 400 permits, each of which entitles a firm to generate 1 gallon of waste per day. The key innovation is that these permits are marketable: Firms can buy and sell the permits. In fact, an environmental group could decrease the amount of pollution by purchasing a permit and then retiring it.

To explain the effects of marketable pollution permits, let's extend our example of the paper industry in three ways.

1. There are 100 paper mills (firms) in the market, each of which produces 1 ton of paper per day and initially generates 5 gallons of waste per day.
2. Half the paper mills can abate pollution at a relatively low cost, as shown in the second column of Table 2. For example, the production cost per ton is $61 with 4 gallons of waste, compared to $60 with 5 gallons of waste.
3. Half the paper mills have relatively high abatement costs, as shown in the third column of Table 2. For example, if a high-cost firm generates 4 gallons of waste, the cost per ton is $67, compared to $61 for a low-cost firm generating the same volume of waste.

Suppose that the government decides to decrease the volume of waste to 400 gallons per day. To do so, the government issues four marketable permits to each of the 100 paper firms. If a particular firm wants to generate 5 gallons of waste per day, it can buy a fifth permit from another firm. Of course, a firm that sells one of its permits can generate only 3 gallons of waste per day.

Each low-cost firm will sell a permit to a high-cost firm. Such an exchange benefits the buyer and the seller because the buyer is willing to pay more than the seller requires for a permit. In other words, the buyer's willingness to pay exceeds the seller's willingness to accept. Let's look at the willingness to pay first, then the willingness to accept.

1. Each high-cost firm is willing to pay up to $7 for a permit. If a high-cost firm gets a fifth permit, it can generate 5 gallons of waste and produce a ton of paper for $60, compared to a cost of $67 with only four permits. In other words, getting a fifth permit saves the firm $7, so the firm will be better off if it gets an additional permit for any amount less than $7.
2. Each low-cost firm is willing to accept any amount above $3. If a low-cost firm gives up one of its four permits, it could generate only 3 gallons of waste, so its production cost would increase by $3 (from $61 to $64). The firm will be better off if it sells a permit for any amount greater than $3.

The actual price of the permit depends on the negotiating skills of the two firms. A plausible outcome of the bargaining process is a price halfway between the willingness to pay ($7) and the willingness to accept ($3), or $5.

Table 2: Abatement Costs: Low-Cost versus High-Cost Firm

Waste per Ton (gallons)	*Production Cost per Ton: Low Cost*	*Production Cost per Ton: High Cost*
5	$ 60	$ 60
4	61	67
3	64	82
2	71	112
1	86	172
0	116	300

Abatement Costs: Marketable versus Nonmarketable Permits

The first row of Table 3 shows the costs of abatement with marketable permits. If each of the high-cost firms purchases a permit from a low-cost firm, each high-cost firm will generate 5 gallons of waste and spend nothing on pollution abatement. In contrast, each of the low-cost firms will generate only 3 gallons of waste and incur an abatement cost of $4 per ton of paper ($64 minus $60). Therefore, the total cost of cutting pollution from 500 gallons to 400 gallons is $200 ($4 times 50 firms).

The alternative to marketable permits is a system of nonmarketable permits. If the government issues four permits to each firm and outlaws trading, the total cost of pollution abatement will be much higher. Let's look at the costs incurred by the two types of firms.

1. *High-cost firms.* Each firm incurs a cost of $7 to abate 1 gallon of waste: The production cost per ton increases from $60 to $67. There are 50 high-cost firms, so the total abatement cost for these firms is $350 ($7 per firm times 50 firms).
2. *Low-cost firms.* Each firm incurs a cost of $1 to abate 1 gallon of waste: The production cost per ton increases from $60 to $61. There are 50 low-cost firms, so the total abatement cost for these firms is $50 ($1 per firm times 50 firms).

The total abatement cost under the traditional permit policy is $400, the sum of the $350 incurred by high-cost firms and the $50 incurred by low-cost firms. As shown in the last column of Table 3, a system of nonmarketable permits costs twice as much as a system of marketable permits.

Why is the total cost of abatement lower with marketable permits? By allowing firms to trade their permits, the government exploits the differences in abatement costs, relying on low-cost firms to do all the abatement. As a result, we can achieve the same volume of pollution abatement (100 gallons) at a much lower cost. In a perfectly competitive market, these cost savings will be passed on to consumers in the form of a lower price of paper.

Experiences with Marketable Permits

The first program of marketable pollution permits, started in 1976 by the U.S. Environmental Protection Agency, allowed limited trading of permits for several airborne pollutants. Trading was later extended to lead in gasoline (in 1985) and the chemicals responsible for the depletion of the ozone layer (in 1988). The 1990 Clean Air Act established a trading system for sulfur dioxide, which is responsible for acid rain. In the early 1990s, a trading system was introduced in the Los Angeles Basin for the pollutants responsible for urban smog.

The first sale of a pollution permit occurred in 1977, and thousands of exchanges have occurred since then. Here are some examples.

1. Duquesne Light Company paid $3,750,000 to Wisconsin Power and Light for the rights to dump 15,000 tons of sulfur dioxide. In this transaction, the price of a ton of sulfur dioxide emissions was $250.

Table 3: Differences in Total Abatement Costs

	Gallons Abated	Abatement Costs		
		High-Cost Firms	*Low-Cost Firms*	*Total*
With trading	100	0	$200	$200
Without trading	100	$350	50	400

2. Mobil Oil Corporation paid $3,000,000 for the rights to dump 900 pounds of reactive vapors per day. Mobile paid this sum to the city of Torrence, California, which had earlier acquired the pollution rights from General Motors.
3. A firm in Los Angeles installed a new incinerator that decreased its hydrocarbon emissions by 100 tons per year and offered to sell the rights to emit 100 tons of hydrocarbons for $400,000.

A system of marketable permits may lead to severe pollution in some areas. For example, if you live in Torrence, California, you probably don't like the idea that Mobil Oil will use a marketable permit to generate more pollution at its refinery. You probably don't care that the marketable permit system is more efficient than a command-and-control system that would limit the refinery's pollution to its current level. This "hot spot" problem suggests that the marketable permit system may be inappropriate for pollutants that generate large local effects. Alternatively, the number of permits issued for a particular geographical area could be limited to prevent severe pollution.

The government can use marketable permits to reduce air and water pollution over time. A common practice is to issue marketable permits with a one-year life and then decrease the number of permits issued each year. For example, under an air-quality management plan for the Portland metropolitan area, the number of permits will decrease by 10% each year. This approach was also used by the Environmental Protection Agency to phase out lead in gasoline and the chemicals responsible for the depletion of the ozone layer.

ECONOMIC DETECTIVE– *No Market for Marketable Permits*

A state issued some marketable permits for sulfur dioxide emissions to several electricity generators and set up a special marketing office to help firms buy and sell the permits. Most of the permits were given to the utilities with the oldest generating facilities. One year later, none of the permits had been bought or sold. This was puzzling to the state officials and the people in the marketing office, because the idea of issuing marketable permits was to get a market going. Your job is to solve this mystery. Why didn't the marketable-permit program work? How could the program be changed to encourage trading?

A careful reading of the description of the permit policy reveals a clue that will help solve this mystery. Old electricity-generating facilities usually have old pollution-abatement technology, so they have relatively high abatement costs. When a utility sells one of its permits, it must reduce its emissions, and this would be relatively costly for old facilities with high abatement costs. By issuing most of the permits to old facilities with high abatement costs, the state inadvertently gave most of the permits to the utilities that had the greatest incentive to keep them. These utilities kept all their permits rather than selling them.

A simple example will show why a utility with high abatement costs will hold on to its permit. Suppose that a 1-ton reduction in sulfur dioxide emissions would increase abatement costs by $1,000 in an old facility, but by only $200 in a new facility. In this case the old facility would be willing to accept no less than $1,000 for one of its pollution permits, while a new facility would be willing to pay no more than $200 for a permit. The two utilities can't make a deal because the minimum amount the old facility is willing to accept exceeds the maximum amount the new facility is willing to pay. To encourage trading, the state could redesign its permit policy to spread the permits more evenly among old and new facilities.

TEST ***Your Understanding***

4 Complete the statement with *low* or *high*: Under a system of marketable pollution permits, a firm with relatively ____________ abatement costs will buy permits from a firm with relatively ____________ abatement costs.

5 Why will a switch to marketable pollution permits decrease total abatement costs?

6 Looking back at Table 2 (page 301), suppose that for the low-cost firm, the production cost per ton with 3 gallons of waste is $69 (instead of $64). If the government issues four permits per firm, will trading still occur? Explain.

7 Looking back at Table 2 (page 301), suppose that after the high-cost and low-cost firms finish buying and selling permits, an environmental group appears. If the group is willing to pay $10 for each gallon of waste reduction, how many permits will the group purchase?

GLOBAL WARMING AND PUBLIC POLICY

Now that we've discussed the policy options for dealing with environmental problems, we are ready to discuss some of today's most important problems. We look at global warming first and then discuss ozone depletion, acid rain, and urban smog.

The Causes of Global Warming

Here is a simple experiment that explains global warming. On a warm day, park your car in a sunny spot, roll up the windows, and wait. Solar energy in the form of visual and ultraviolet light will come through the car windows and heat the air in the car. This is the greenhouse effect: If all the windows are closed, there is no way for the heat to escape, so the temperature in the car (or in a greenhouse) will increase.

The windows of the car are like earth's atmosphere. Solar energy comes through the atmosphere and heats the air near the earth's surface. Certain types of gases in the atmosphere (called *greenhouse gases*) trap this heat close to the earth's surface and are beneficial: Without these gases, the earth's surface temperature would be far below freezing, so most forms of life would die off. Unfortunately, we are pumping more of these greenhouse gases into the atmosphere, so the earth's temperature is increasing. Just as rolling up a window in a parked car increases the temperature in the car, increasing the volume of greenhouse gases increases the temperature near the earth's surface.

Carbon dioxide is by far the most important greenhouse gas. To explain why the volume of carbon dioxide is increasing, let's look at the carbon cycle, the movement of carbon between the earth's atmosphere and the plant material on the earth's surface. When a plant grows, it converts carbon dioxide from the atmosphere into carbon and stores this carbon in its tissue. When we burn oil, coal, and gas (the fossilized remains of old plants), the carbon stored in the plant material combines with oxygen to form carbon dioxide, which is released back into the atmosphere. To put it bluntly, plants suck in carbon dioxide, and we blow it back out when we burn plant material. In the last century we have blown out more carbon than plants have been able to suck in, and the volume of carbon dioxide in the atmosphere has increased by about 25%. By digging up stored carbon and burning it, we've thrown the carbon cycle out of whack, and the resulting increase in greenhouse gases has increased global temperatures.

How does the destruction of tropical rain forests affect global warming? The plants in these forests absorb some of the carbon dioxide we generate when we burn fossil fuels. Their destruction has two effects:

1. If trees and plants are burned to clear the land, the carbon stored in these plants is converted into carbon dioxide.
2. Once the forest is cleared, there is less plant material to convert carbon dioxide into stored carbon.

As we'll see later in the chapter, one approach to dealing with global warming is to protect existing rain forests and promote the recovery of damaged forests.

The Consequences of Global Warming

The accumulation of greenhouse gases and the resulting warming of the earth will have far-reaching consequences. The volume of atmospheric carbon dioxide is now about 25% above the preindustrial level, and it is increasing at a rate of about 1.6% per year,[2] so the volume of greenhouse gases will double in about 60 years. There is a consensus among scientists that a doubling of atmospheric carbon dioxide will increase the average global temperature by 2 to 5°C.[3] Not all scientists agree with this prediction, however: Because we know so little about how the earth's ecosystems will respond to such a rapid increase in carbon dioxide, the actual change in temperature could be much larger or much smaller.

How will the accumulation of greenhouse gases and an increase in temperatures affect the earth's environment and the global economy? Total rainfall will increase, with some areas getting more and others getting less. The increase in carbon dioxide will make all plants—crops and weeds alike—grow faster. Overall, the net effect on agriculture is likely to be negative because scientists expect less rainfall in areas with fertile soil and more rainfall in areas with less productive soil. For a discussion of some of the implications of global warming for U.S. agriculture, read the Closer Look box on page 306, "Would Global Warming Be Good for U.S. Agriculture?"

An increase in global temperatures will also melt glaciers and the polar ice caps, increasing sea levels. As a result, a large amount of land currently used for agriculture or living space will be inundated. Of course, we could build dikes to protect low-lying areas, but such protective measures are very expensive. According to a recent report from the Climate Institute, by the year 2070 much of the metropolitan area in Manila, Philippines, could be under 1 meter of water, and rising sea levels could force the relocation of 3.3 million people in Jakarta, Indonesia.[4]

A Carbon Tax

The economist's response to global warming is to impose a tax on fossil fuels. The burning of these fuels generates spillover costs on a global scale, and a tax would force people who use the fuels to pay the full cost of using them. The spillover cost of a particular fuel depends on how much carbon dioxide is released into the atmosphere, so the **carbon tax** for a particular fuel would be determined by the fuel's carbon content.

Carbon tax: A tax based on a fuel's carbon content.

Figure 3 on page 306 shows the effects of a carbon tax on the market for coal in China. Coal provides about three-fourths of the primary energy in China and is used in small industrial boilers, household stoves, and room heaters. In contrast, most of the coal consumed in developed countries such as the United States is used to generate electricity. A carbon tax will add to the expenses incurred by coal producers, so some of them will lose money at the initial price ($35) and some suppliers will leave the market. The resulting decrease in the supply of coal will shift the supply

A Closer LOOK

Would Global Warming Be Good for U.S. Agriculture?

According to the conventional view, global warming would be a disaster for U.S. agriculture, with crop losses of about $20 billion per year. This view is based on several studies that study the effects of climatic changes on the U.S. heartland, where we grow cool-weather crops such as corn and wheat.

A recent study challenges this conventional view and suggests that global warming may actually be beneficial for U.S. agriculture. Specifically, the changes in climatic conditions are expected to increase total revenue from crops by about $1.5 billion per year. This new study differs from the older studies in two ways.

1. The new study explores the effects of climatic changes on the entire United States, not just the heartland. The crop losses in the heartland will be more than offset by gains in warm-weather crops grown elsewhere (cotton, fruit, vegetables, rice, hay, and grapes).
2. The old studies were based on the "dumb farmer" assumption: Farmers were assumed to use the same inputs to grow the same crops, regardless of the climatic conditions. In contrast, the new study recognizes that farmers will respond to changes in climate by changing the way they grow a given crop (changing seeds, fertilizer, or growing techniques) and switching to crops that are more suited to the new climate.

The old studies generate erroneous conclusions because they ignore the good news from global warming and assume that farmers are inflexible.

Source: Robert Mendelsohn, William D. Nordhaus, and Daigee Shaw, "The Impact of Global Warming on Agriculture: A Ricardian Analysis," *American Economic Review,* vol. 84, no. 4, September 1994, pp. 253–771.

curve to the left. In Figure 3 the coal tax leads to a higher price ($42 instead of $35) and a smaller quantity (78 tons per day instead of 100).

Table 4 shows some of the effects of two carbon taxes—a low one and a high one—on the prices of fossil fuels. For example, the high tax would more than double the price of coal (a fuel with a high carbon content), but it would increase the price of gasoline by only 23%.

Figure 3

Market Effects of a Carbon Tax on Coal

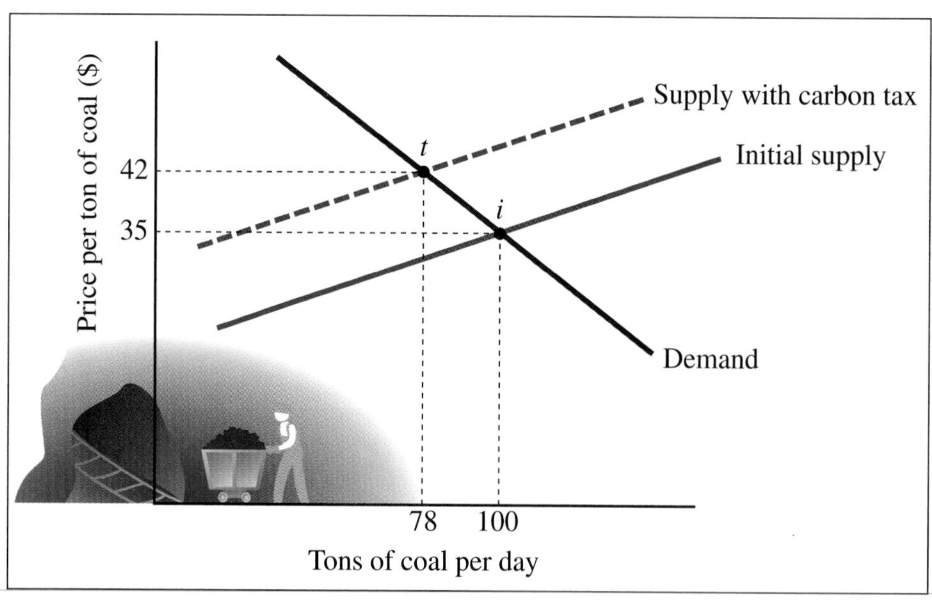

A carbon tax of $10 per ton of carbon will increase the price of coal by about 20%, from $35 per ton to $42 per ton, and decrease the equilibrium quantity, from 100 tons per day to 78.

Table 4: Effects of Different Carbon Taxes

	Low Tax	*High Tax*
Tax per ton of carbon	$5.00	$100.00
Effect on price of coal		
Tax per ton	$3.50	$70.00
Percentage increase	10	205
Effect on price of oil		
Tax per barrel	$0.58	$11.65
Percentage increase	2.8	55
Effect on price of gasoline		
Tax per gallon	$0.014	$0.28
Percentage increase	1.2	23
Percentage reduction in greenhouse emissions	10	43
Total tax revenue per year, U.S. (billions)	$10	$125

Source: William D. Nordhaus, "Economic Approaches to Greenhouse Warming," in *Global Warming: Economic Policy Responses,* edited by Rudiger Dornbusch and James M. Poterba (Cambridge, MA: MIT Press, 1991).

In Table 4 we see that a carbon tax of $100 would decrease greenhouse emissions by 43%, a result of three types of changes.

1. The tax will increase the price of energy and increase the cost of producing energy-intensive goods. Consumers will respond by demanding smaller quantities of these goods, in part by switching to goods produced with less energy.
2. Some energy producers will switch to noncarbon energy sources such as the wind, the sun, and geothermal sources.
3. Energy producers will improve the efficiency of carbon-based fuels, squeezing out more energy per ton of coal or oil.

How would the money from a carbon tax be spent? In Table 4 we see that the low carbon tax would generate $10 billion per year, while the high tax would generate $125 billion. We could use this money to cut income or payroll taxes. Alternatively, we could use the money to mitigate the problems caused by global warming. For example, we could build dikes to protect low-lying areas or pay to relocate people to higher ground. Another option is to increase the earth's capacity to absorb carbon dioxide by protecting the tropical rain forests or planting trees in other areas. The tax revenue could also be used to develop new technologies to generate energy from noncarbon sources or squeeze more energy from each unit of fossil fuel we use.

Worldwide Marketable Permits?

To solve the global warming problem, the nations of the world must cooperate. One possibility is to issue carbon permits to each nation and then let each nation decide how to meet its carbon target. Some nations would probably use a carbon tax, while others might subsidize noncarbon fuels or preserve forests that absorb carbon from the atmosphere.

A system of marketable carbon permits would allow trades that decrease the cost of meeting the planet's carbon target. For example, suppose that by modernizing China's electric power plants, we could decrease carbon dioxide emissions at a cost of $30 per ton, compared to a cost of $70 in the United States. If the United States buys a permit for $50, China could use the money to decrease carbon dioxide emissions by a ton and still have $20 left over. The United States would pay $50 instead of $70 for pollution abatement, a savings of $20. In general, as long as there are differences in abatement costs, a system of marketable permits will lead to trades that benefit both countries.

TEST ***Your Understanding***

8 Use a supply and demand diagram to show the effects of a carbon tax on the market for an energy-intensive good such as aluminum or steel.

9 Explain how a carbon tax would decrease the total volume of greenhouse gases.

10 In Chapter 14 you learned the rationale for subsidizing goods that generate spillover benefits. Does the same sort of reasoning apply to trees?

OTHER ENVIRONMENTAL PROBLEMS

The problem of global warming is not the only environmental problem that we face today. There are many other problems, including the depletion of the ozone layer, acid rain, and urban smog. Let's look at each of these problems separately.

Ozone Depletion

A layer of ozone in the upper atmosphere prevents most of the sun's harmful ultraviolet light from reaching the surface of the earth. Ultraviolet light causes living cells to mutate, causing skin cancer and eye disease in humans and the death of marine organisms at the base of the food web. It also disrupts plant growth and hastens the decay of plastics. The ozone layer in the upper atmosphere is essential to life on the planet because it protects us from the harmful effects of ultraviolet light.

A 1991 report suggests that human-made chemicals had depleted the ozone layer by about 3% overall, with a 50% depletion in the atmosphere over Antarctica. The primary culprit is a family of chemicals known as chlorofluorocarbons (CFCs), which were used in refrigeration, air conditioning, spray products, foam injection, and industrial solvents. When these chemicals reach the upper atmosphere, they act as catalysts, converting ozone into oxygen, which does not block ultraviolet light. The depletion over Antarctica is much greater because the presence of ice crystals accelerates this chemical reaction.

The nations of the world have agreed to stop producing CFCs altogether. Under the Montreal Protocol (of 1990), the production of these chemicals will stop by 2010. Because CFCs take a long time to break down, however, scientists expect the depletion of the ozone layer to continue for at least 50 more years.

The ban on CFCs will increase the equilibrium prices of the goods that were produced with these chemicals. For example, refrigerator producers will switch from CFCs to other chemicals that don't harm the ozone layer but are more expensive and less efficient as coolants. The resulting increase in production costs will increase the equilibrium price of refrigerators. In the case of CFCs, an outright ban is sensible because the good news (greater protection from ultraviolet light) dominates the bad news (higher prices for refrigerators and other products). The bad news isn't too bad because there are good substitutes for CFCs.

Acid Rain

In the 1970s and 1980s, there were persistent reports of sterile lakes and withering trees in the northeastern United States, eastern Canada, Scandinavia, and Germany. The sulfur dioxide emissions of coal-burning power plants combined with nitrogen oxides and other chemicals in the atmosphere to form acid rain. The rainfall in the areas downwind from the power plants changed the acidity of soil and water, causing problems for trees, fish, and other forms of aquatic life. Power plants in the eastern and midwestern United States caused acid rain in the northeastern United States and eastern Canada, while power plants in the United Kingdom and Germany caused acid rain in Scandinavia.

The Clean Air Act of 1990 established a system of marketable pollution permits for sulfur dioxide. Each utility will receive enough permits to generate between 30% and 50% of the volume of sulfur dioxide it produced 10 years earlier. Overall, the permit system will decrease sulfur dioxide emissions by about 10 million tons per year, a reduction of about 40%. Under the first permit trade, a Wisconsin utility sold permits to the Tennessee Valley Authority at a price of $250 per ton of sulfur dioxide. A report from the National Acid Precipitation Assessment Program (NAPAP) estimated the cost of reducing sulfur dioxide emissions under two alternative systems, one with marketable permits and one with nonmarketable permits. The cost with marketable permits is 15% to 20% lower.[5]

Urban Smog

Urban smog is one of our most persistent environmental problems. Smog results from the mixing of several pollutants, including nitrogen oxides, sulfur dioxide, and volatile organic compounds. Another name for *smog* is *ground-level ozone.* Although atmospheric ozone is beneficial because it blocks harmful ultraviolet light, ozone is harmful when it comes in contact with living things, as it does at ground level. Smog causes health problems in human beings and other animals. It also retards plant growth and decreases agricultural productivity. The Environmental Protection Agency (EPA) has established standards for the concentrations of urban smog. About a third of the U.S. population lives in areas where the concentrations of smog often exceed the EPA standards.

The automobile is by far the most important source of the pollutants that lead to smog. We currently use a command-and-control approach to regulate automobile pollution: The Environmental Protection Agency tells automakers what emissions equipment to install in cars. There are several problems with this approach.

1. If a car is not properly maintained, the emissions equipment quickly loses its effectiveness. Although many states have inspection programs to monitor emissions equipment, the programs are not very effective.
2. Many of the cars on the road were built before the emissions controls were implemented, and these cars are responsible for a large share of automobile emissions.
3. The emissions equipment does not control the total emissions of the car, just the emissions per mile driven. If people drive more miles in a cleaner car, total emissions can actually increase.

An alternative to the current policy is to levy an annual pollution tax on each car.[6] At the end of the year, a car would be tested to determine the volume of pollution per mile driven. The tax per mile would equal the volume of pollution per mile times a tax per unit of pollution. The annual tax would be computed by multiplying the tax per mile by the number of miles driven in the last year. For example, if a car generated 5 units of pollution per mile and the tax per unit of pollution were $0.01, the tax per mile would be $0.05. If the car were driven 10,000 miles each year, the annual pollution tax would be $500. The pollution tax would encourage people to buy cleaner cars, maintain their emissions equipment, drive less, and use alternative modes of transportation. The tax is consistent with the idea that people should pay the full cost of driving, including the spillover costs.

We saw earlier that one of the problems with the current policy is that it does nothing to decrease the pollution from cars that don't have pollution-control equipment. To see how the Environmental Protection Agency would like to deal with this problem, read the Closer Look box "Cash for Clunkers."

TEST *Your Understanding*

11 Use a supply demand diagram to show the effects of a ban on CFCs on the market for refrigerators.

12 Explain how a carbon tax will affect the urban smog problem.

13 The policy of buying and destroying heavy polluting cars is called "Cash for Clunkers," not "Cash for Cars." Why?

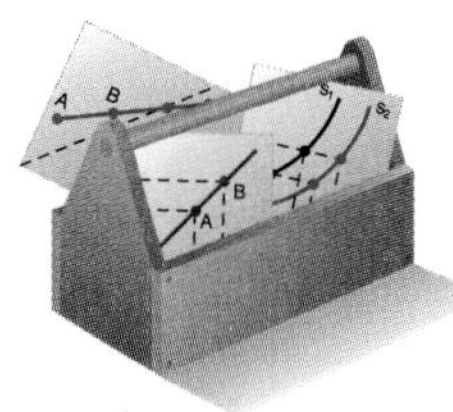

Using the TOOLS

You've learned about several environmental policies, including a pollution tax, pollution regulations, and marketable pollution permits. Now you can use what you've learned to do your own economic analysis of environmental problems.

1. Market Effects of a Carbon Tax

Consider the market for gasoline. In the initial equilibrium, the price is $2.00 per gallon and the quantity is 100 million gallons. The price elasticity of demand is 1.0 and the price elasticity of supply is 2.0. Suppose that the government

A Closer LOOK

Cash for Clunkers

In 1992, the Environmental Protection Agency (EPA) designed a program that would allow many types of firms to meet their pollution-abatement responsibilities by purchasing and destroying old cars. A disproportionate amount of automobile air pollution comes from cars built before modern emissions equipment was required. For example, 38% of the cars on the road in 1992 were built before 1980, but these cars were responsible for 86% of the emissions of carbon monoxide and volatile organic compounds.* The EPA has a booklet that shows how much pollution each type of car generates. Under a cash-for-clunkers program, a firm can meet its pollution abatement responsibility by retiring enough cars so that the volume of automobile pollution avoided equals the amount the firm would otherwise abate itself. There have been several successful experiments with cash-for-clunkers programs, in Los Angeles, Denver, and the state of Texas.

Older cars are responsible for a relatively large share of automobile pollution.

*Marshall Ingwerson, "Bush's Clunkers for Cash: Plan for Pollution Control," *Christian Science Monitor*, March 20, 1992, p. 3.

imposes a carbon tax and the tax is expected to shift the gasoline supply curve to the left by 24%.

a. Use a supply–demand diagram to show the market effects of the carbon tax.

b. Predict the new equilibrium price and quantity of gasoline.

2. Predict the Price of Pollution Permits

Consider the example of marketable pollution permits discussed in the chapter. Suppose that instead of issuing 400 permits, the government issues only 300 permits (three permits to each of the 100 firms).

a. How much money is each high-cost firm willing to pay to get one additional permit?

b. How much money is each low-cost firm willing to accept in exchange for one of its permits?

c. If firms split the difference between the willingness to pay and the willingness to accept for a permit, what will be the price of a permit?

3. *Hot Rod, Motor Trend,* and Cash for Clunkers

Several car-hobby magazines, including *Hot Rod* and *Motor Trend,* have run editorials in opposition to the "cash-for-clunkers" program. Why would car-hobby magazines oppose the program? Can you imagine any way to overcome their objections?

4. ECONOMIC EXPERIMENT: *Pollution Permit*

In the pollution-permit experiment, students play the role of paper firms that buy or sell pollution permits. The experiment, which involves five trading periods, works as follows.

- The class is divided into groups of three to five students, with each group representing a firm that produces 1 ton of paper per period. The instructor provides each firm with data about the firm's cost of production. The cost depends on how much waste the firm generates: The smaller the volume of waste, the higher the production cost. Here is an example:

Gallons of waste	2	3	4
Production cost per ton	\$66	\$56	\$50

- Each firm receives three pollution permits for each of the five trading periods. A firm that does not sell any of its permits to other firms has the right to generate 3 gallons of waste in that period. A firm that sells one of its three permits can generate only 2 gallons of waste, and a firm that buys a permit from another firm can generate 4 gallons of waste.
- At the beginning of each trading period, firms meet in the trading area to buy or sell pollution permits for that day. Each firm can buy or sell one permit per day. Once a transaction has been arranged, the two firms (a buyer and a seller) inform the instructor of the transaction, record the transaction on their report cards, and then leave the trading area.
- In each trading period, we compute the firm's profit with the following equation:

profit = price of paper – production cost +
revenue from permit sold – cost of permit purchased

In each period, a firm will either buy or sell a permit, so we compute the firm's profit with just three numbers. For example, using the production-cost numbers from the table above, if the price of paper is $70 and a firm buys a permit for $5, the firm's profit is

profit = $70 – $50 + 0 – $5 = $15

If another firm sold a permit for $12, the firm's profit would be $16:

profit = $70 – $66 + $12 – 0 = $16

- For the fourth and fifth trading periods, several environmental groups have the option of buying pollution permits. Each environmental group is given a fixed sum of money to spend on permits, and the objective is to get as many permits as possible, reducing the total volume of pollution in the process.

SUMMARY

We started this chapter by showing the market effects of a pollution tax. Because a traditional command-and-control policy discourages innovation in pollution abatement technology, it is less efficient—and more costly—than a pollution tax or a system of marketable permits. Here are the main points from the chapter.

1. A pollution tax, which forces firms to pay for pollution, decreases the total volume of pollution because firms produce less of the polluting good and generate less pollution for each unit produced.
2. Compared to a pollution tax, a command-and-control policy is likely to lead to higher consumer prices and more pollution.
3. A system of marketable permits is predictable (the government issues just enough permits to reach a target level of pollution) and efficient (abatement will come from the firms with the lowest abatement cost).
4. Global warming occurs because burning fossil fuels releases more carbon dioxide than plants are able to absorb.
5. The ban on chlorofluorocarbons (CFCs) is sensible because they destroy the protective ozone layer and there are good substitutes for CFCs.
6. The problem of acid rain is being handled with marketable permits for sulfur dioxide.
7. Urban smog is a continuing problem, in part because we use command-and-control policies. An annual pollution tax would be more effective at reducing smog.

KEY TERMS

carbon tax, *305*
command-and-control policy, *299*
external cost, *296*
marketable pollution permits system, *300*
pollution tax, *296*

PROBLEMS AND DISCUSSION QUESTIONS

1. Use a supply–demand graph to show a situation in which the equilibrium quantity of a polluting good is 20 tons, but a pollution tax decreases the equilibrium quantity of the good to zero. Is this situation likely to occur?
2. Suppose that paper firms have access to the abatement technology shown in the first two columns of Table 1 (page 296) and the government imposes a pollution tax of $8 per gallon of waste.

a. Compute new values for the third and fourth columns of the table. How much waste will the typical firm generate?
b. Use a supply–demand diagram to show the market effects of the tax.
c. Would you expect the volume of pollution to be larger or smaller than the volume generated with the $4 tax (shown in Figure 1, page 295)?

3. Suppose the government adopts a zero-tolerance pollution policy for the production of paper. In other words, the government requires each paper mill to eliminate all its water pollution. Suppose that paper firms have access to the abatement technology shown in the first two columns of Table 1 (page 296).
a. What is the production cost per ton under the zero-tolerance policy?
b. Suppose that the government uses a pollution tax to implement its zero-tolerance policy. What is the smallest tax that would cause the typical firm to pick zero pollution voluntarily?
4. To predict the market price of a marketable pollution permit, what information do you need? Explain how you would use this information.
5. Use a supply–demand diagram to show the market effects of a cash-for-clunkers program on the market for used cars.
6. Consider the use of marketable pollution permits for the control of sulfur dioxide emissions from two electric utilities, Old Power and Light (OPL) and Young Power and Light (YPL). The following table shows the production cost for the two utilities with different volumes of sulfur dioxide emissions.

Tons of Sulfur Dioxide	*Production Cost for OPL*	*Production Cost for YPL*
10	$1,000	$1,000
9	1,100	1,020
8	1,300	1,060
7	1,600	1,120

Suppose that the government issues 10 marketable pollution permits to OPL and eight marketable permits to YPL.
a. Will any permits be traded? Explain.
b. Suppose that the government had issued nine permits to YPL and nine permits to OPL. Will any permits be traded? If so, predict the equilibrium price for a permit.
7. One of the objections to a carbon tax is that it would be regressive: Poor people would pay a large fraction of their incomes for carbon taxes. How could we overcome this objection?
8. You are the economic consultant to a member of Congress. Someone has just introduced a bill that would impose a $50 carbon tax, which will of course affect the market for home-heating oil. Would you expect the entire tax to be paid by consumers? Why or why not? Your job is to determine which side of the market—consumers or input suppliers—will pay the larger part of the tax. What additional information do you need?

Take It to the Net

We invite you to visit the O'Sullivan/Sheffrin page on the Prentice Hall Web site at:
http://www.prenhall.com/osullivan/
for this chapter's World Wide Web exercise.

MODEL ANSWERS FOR THIS CHAPTER

Chapter-Opening Questions

1. Pollution-control policies increase the cost of producing the polluting good, either through a tax or regulations that affect the firm's production process. The increase in production cost decreases supply, leading to higher prices.
2. As shown in Figures 1 and 2 (pages 295 and 300), compared to a command-and-control policy, a tax policy generates a lower price of paper, more output, and less pollution.
3. The burning of fossil fuels releases the carbon stored in plants into the atmosphere, increasing the level of carbon dioxide. The destruction of tropical rain forests releases more carbon into the atmosphere and decreases the amount of plant material available to absorb carbon dioxide. The

increase in the level of carbon dioxide contributes to global warming.

4. Atmospheric ozone is beneficial because it blocks harmful ultraviolet light. Ozone is harmful when it comes in contact with living things, as it does at ground level.
5. A disproportionate amount of automobile air pollution comes from cars built before modern emissions equipment was required. The "cash for clunkers" program removes these heavy-polluting cars from the road.

Test Your Understanding

1. The unit production cost increases at an increasing rate because the firm must use progressively more sophisticated and expensive abatement equipment to decrease the volume of waste.
2. The marginal benefit of abatement would be \$8 (the tax savings per gallon abated), so the firm would generate only 2 gallons: The marginal cost from abating the third gallon of waste is only \$7, but the marginal cost from abating the second gallon of waste is \$15.
3. increases, decreases, decreases
4. high, low
5. Under a system of marketable permits, low-cost firms do most of the abating.
6. No. The low-cost firm is willing to accept any amount greater than \$8 (the difference between the cost of 4 gallons and 3 gallons), which exceeds the willingness to pay by the high cost firm.
7. The group will buy one permit from each low-cost firm (the willingness to accept for one of the firm's three permits is \$7) and one from each of the high-cost firms (the willingness to accept for one of the firm's five permits is \$7).
8. The tax will increase production costs, shifting the supply curve to the left. The new supply curve will intersect the demand curve at a higher price and a smaller quantity.
9. Consumers will buy a smaller quantity of the good. Energy producers will switch to noncarbon energy sources and improve the efficiency of carbon fuels.
10. A tree decreases the volume of carbon dioxide in the atmosphere and diminishes the problem of global warming, so there is a spillover benefit. A subsidy internalizes the externality, encouraging people to plant and maintain trees.
11. The tax will increase production costs, shifting the supply curve to the left. The new supply curve will intersect the demand curve at a higher price and a smaller quantity.
12. The tax will increase the price of gasoline, causing people to drive fewer miles and generate smaller volumes of the pollutants that cause urban smog.
13. The word "clunker" suggests an old car in poor repair, which is the sort of car that is likely to be destroyed under the policy.

Using the Tools

1. Market Effects of a Carbon Tax
   a. See Figure A below.
   b. Using the price-change formula from Chapter 6, the percentage change in price is 8% = 24%/(1.0 + 2.0). Therefore, the price increases from \$2.00 to \$2.16. Using the formula for

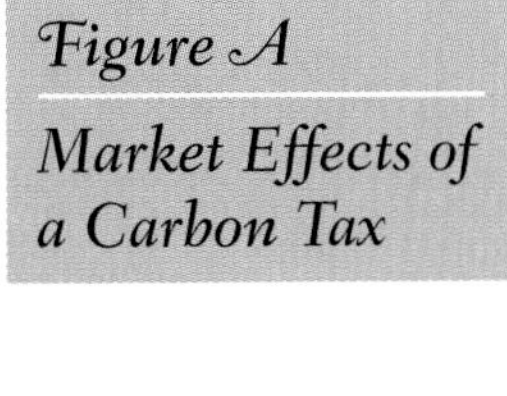

Figure A

Market Effects of a Carbon Tax

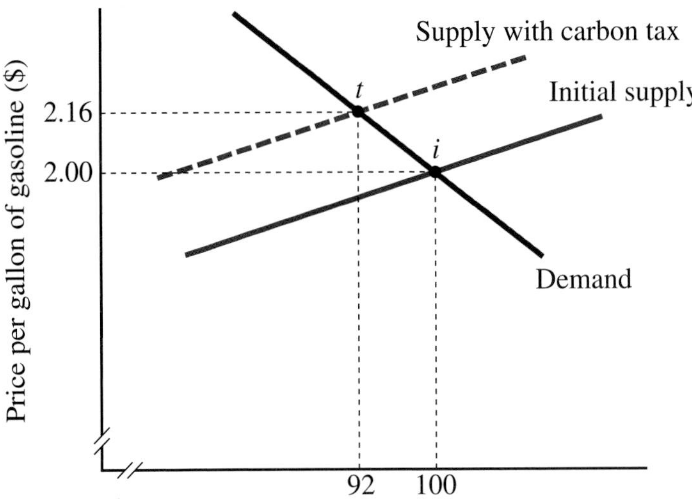

demand elasticity (the tax causes the market to move upward along the supply curve), the percentage change in quantity is also 8%: 1.0 = 8%/8%. Therefore, the quantity decreases from 100 million gallons to 92 million gallons.

2. Predict the Price of Pollution Permits
   a. A high-cost firm is willing to pay up to $15 for one more permit, one that would allow the firm to generate 4 gallons (with production cost = $67) instead of 3 gallons (production cost = $82).
   b. A low-cost firm is willing to accept any amount greater than $7 for one of its three permits. If the firm sold one of its permits, the firm could produce only 2 gallons of waste and its production cost would increase from $64 to $71.
   c. A price of $11 is halfway between the willingness to pay ($15) and the willingness to accept ($7).
3. *Hot Rod, Motor Trend,* and Cash for Clunkers

   The hobby magazines are written for car hobbyists, many of whom like to buy old cars and fix them up—or at least try to fix them. The cash-for-clunkers program will decrease the supply of fix-up cars and increase their price. This would make the car-restoration hobby more expensive, so we would expect fewer people to buy old cars and hobby magazines. One way to overcome this problem would be to use the clunkers program to destroy only the engine of the high-pollution cars, giving hobbyists the opportunity to buy the rest of the car and install a cleaner engine.

NOTES

1. Peter Pasell, "For Utilities, New Clean-Air Plan," *New York Times,* November 18, 1994, p. C1; Brad Knickerbocker, "Trading Pollutants Is a Big First Step toward Cleaner Air," *Christian Science Monitor,* November 22, 1994, p. 12.
2. Andrew R. Solow, "Is There a Global Warming Problem?" in *Global Warming: Economic Policy Responses,* edited by Rudiger Dornbush and James M. Poterba (Cambridge, MA: MIT Press, 1991).
3. William D. Nordhaus, "Economic Approaches to Greenhouse Warming," in *Global Warming: Economic Policy Responses,* edited by Rudiger Dornbusch and James M. Poterba (Cambridge, MA: MIT Press, 1991).
4. Eduardo Lachica, "Asia Faces Increasing Pressure to Act as Global Warming Threatens Its Coasts," *Wall Street Journal,* August 22, 1994, p. A5C.
5. *1990 Integrated Assessment Report* (Washington, DC: U.S. National Acid Precipitation Assessment Program, 1991).
6. Edwin S. Mills and Lawrence J. White, "Government Policies towards Automobile Emissions Control" in *Approaches to Air Pollution Control,* edited by Anne Frielaender (Cambridge, MA: MIT Press, 1978).

CHAPTER

16

Imperfect Information and Disappearing Markets

Otto is about to buy his first car. He has decided to buy the same make, model, and model year as all of his friends, a 10-year-old model X. According to several consumer magazines, about half the model X cars on the road are lemons, defined as a car that breaks down frequently and generates large repair bills. Based on this information, Otto figures that there is a 50% chance that he will get a lemon. Before he buys his own car, Otto asks his friends about their experiences with their model X cars. Much to his surprise, nine of 10 friends purchased cars that turned out to be lemons. Given the conflicting information from the consumer magazines and his friends, Otto doesn't know what to think. Is there a 50% or a 90% chance of getting a lemon?

In this chapter we show why Otto is likely to buy a lemon, just like most of his friends. Although half the model X cars on the road may be high-quality cars, few of them will be offered for sale in our hypothetical used-car market, so most buyers will get lemons. To explain this, think about who is more likely to sell a used car, a person with a lemon or a person with a plum (a high-quality car). Because people with lemons are more likely to sell their cars, most of the cars on the market will be lemons. Buyers realize this, so they won't be willing to pay very much for used cars, and the price of used cars will be relatively low. The low price makes the owners of high-quality used cars even less likely to sell their cars, so the average quality of cars decreases further. This downward spiral continues until most of the cars on the market are lemons.

We'll see that a market will break down if either buyers or sellers are unable to distinguish between low- and high-quality goods. As we saw earlier in the book, the model of supply and demand is based on several key assumptions, one of which is that buyers and sellers have enough information to make informed choices. In a world of fully informed buyers and sellers, markets operate smoothly, generating an equilibrium price and an equilibrium quantity for each good. In a world with imperfect information, however, some goods will be sold in very small numbers or not sold at all.

This chapter explores the effect of imperfect information on several types of markets. Here are some of the practical questions we answer.

1. What questions should you ask before joining a commercial dating service?
2. Why do some used car sellers offer money-back guarantees?
3. Why do we rely on volunteer blood donors instead of paying people to donate blood?
4. Why do professional baseball pitchers who switch teams spend so much time on the disabled list, nursing their injuries instead of playing?
5. Why did insurance companies recently change their pricing schemes for medical insurance?

THE MIXED MARKET FOR USED CARS

The classic example of a market with imperfect information is the market for used cars.[1] Suppose that prospective buyers cannot distinguish between low-quality cars (lemons) and high-quality cars (plums). Although a buyer can get some information about a particular car by looking at the car and taking it for a test drive, this information is not sufficient to determine whether the car is a lemon or a plum. In contrast, the seller (the current owner of a used car) knows from experience whether the car is a lemon or a plum. We say that there is **asymmetric information** in a market if one side of the market—either buyers or sellers—has better information than the other. For example, the sellers of used cars know more than buyers. Because buyers cannot distinguish between lemons and plums, there will be a single market for the two types of used cars. Lemons and plums will be sold together in a mixed market for the same price.

Asymmetric information: One side of the market—either buyers or sellers—has better information about the good than the other.

We start our discussion of the used-car market with an extreme case, a market in which all the cars on the market will be lemons. This extreme case is unrealistic, but it provides a useful starting point for a discussion of the implications of asymmetric information. It shows that one possibility is the disappearance of the market for the high-quality good. As we'll see later, a more realistic case is a situation in which most—but not all—the used cars are lemons, so there is a small chance that a buyer will get a high-quality good.

Ignorant Consumers and Knowledgeable Sellers

How much is a consumer willing to pay for a used car that could turn out to be either a lemon or a plum? To determine the price in a mixed market, we must answer three questions.

1. How much is the consumer willing to pay for a plum (a high-quality car)?
2. How much is the consumer willing to pay for a lemon (a low-quality car)?
3. What is the chance that a used car purchased in the mixed market will turn out to be a lemon?

Suppose that the typical buyer is willing to pay $4,000 for a plum and $2,000 for a lemon. In addition, the consumer has neutral expectations about the used-car market: She assumes that half the used cars are lemons and the other half are plums, so there is a 50% chance of getting a lemon. How much is she willing to pay for a car that has a 50% chance of being a lemon? A reasonable assumption is that she is willing to pay the average value of the two types of cars, or $3,000.

In contrast with buyers, the sellers of used cars are knowledgeable. The current owner of a used car knows from experience whether his car is a lemon or a plum. Given a single market price for all used cars—lemons and plums alike—each current owner must decide whether or not to sell his car. We can use the supply curves for lemons and plums to show how many plums and lemons will be supplied at a particular price.

Figure 1 shows two hypothetical supply curves, one for plums and another for lemons. The minimum price for plums is $2,500: At any price less than $2,500, there will be no plums supplied. As shown by the plum supply curve, the number of plums supplied increases with the price of used cars. For example, 4 plums will be supplied at a price of $3,000 (point *n*). The minimum price for lemons is $500: At any price less than $500, no lemons will be supplied. Lemons

Figure 1

Market for Used Cars

If buyers cannot distinguish between low-quality cars (lemons) and high-quality cars (plums), the two goods are sold together in a mixed market. At a price of $3,000, the supply of plums is 4 (point *n*) and the supply of lemons is 16 (point *m*). At a price of $2,000, only lemons will be supplied (9 lemons, as shown by point *p*).

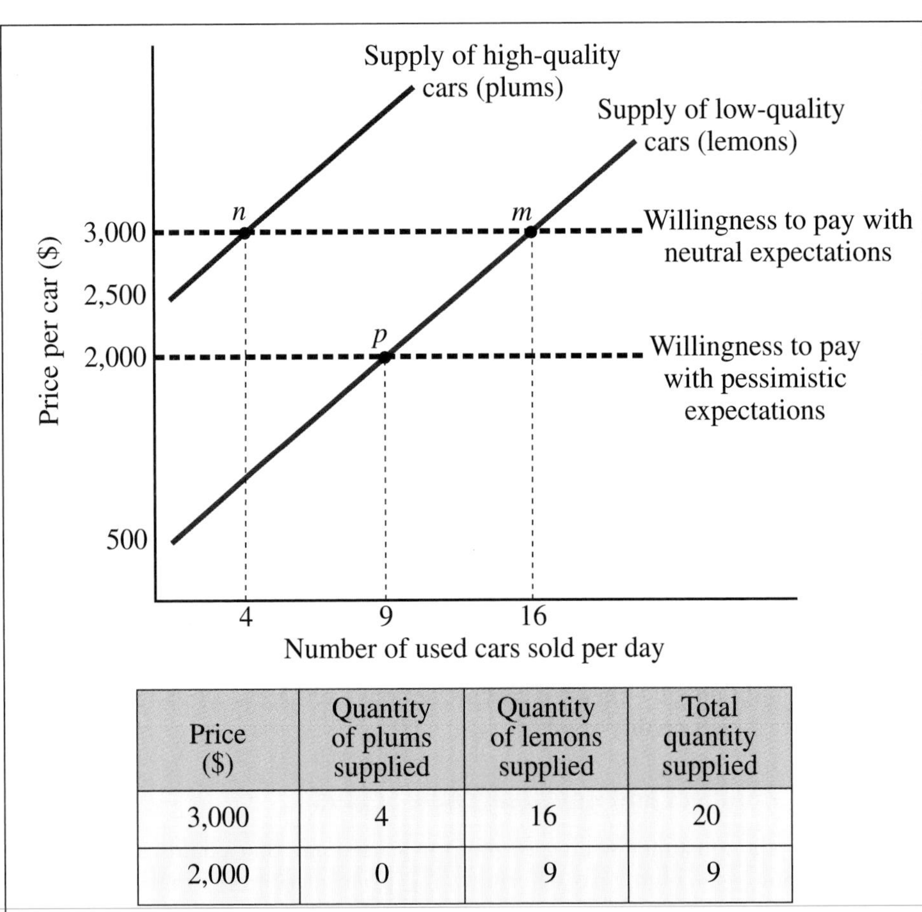

Price ($)	Quantity of plums supplied	Quantity of lemons supplied	Total quantity supplied
3,000	4	16	20
2,000	0	9	9

have a lower minimum price because they are worth less to their current owners. As shown by the lemon supply curve, the number of lemons supplied increases with the price of used cars. For example, 16 lemons will be supplied at a price of $3,000 (point *m*).

Equilibrium in the Mixed Market

Table 1 shows two scenarios for our hypothetical used-car market, with numbers consistent with the supply curves shown in Figure 1. In the first column we assume that consumers have neutral expectations about the chance of getting a lemon. If consumers assume that half the used cars on the market are lemons and half are plums, the typical buyer will be willing to pay $3,000 for a used car. At this price, 4 plums and 16 lemons will be supplied, so 80% of the used cars (16 of 20) are lemons. In this case, consumers underestimate the chance of getting a lemon.

What will consumers do when they realize that they've underestimated the chance of getting a lemon? They certainly won't be willing to pay $3,000 for a used car. In general, the greater the chance of getting a lemon, the smaller the amount that consumers are willing to pay. As a result, the price of used cars will decrease. We learned earlier in the book that a market reaches an equilibrium when there is no pressure to change the price. Therefore, the scenario in the first column is obviously not an equilibrium.

Suppose that after observing the outcome in the first column, buyers become very pessimistic: They assume that all the used cars on the market are lemons. Under this assumption, the typical consumer will be willing to pay only $2,000 (the value of a lemon) for a used car. This price is less than the minimum price for plums ($2,500), so plums will disappear from the used-car market. This is shown in Figure 1: At a price of $2,000, the quantity of plums supplied is zero, but the quantity of lemons is 9 (point *p*). In other words, all the used cars will be lemons: consumers' pessimism is justified. Because consumers' expectations are consistent with their actual experiences in the market, the equilibrium price of used cars is $2,000. The equilibrium in the used-car market is shown in the second column of Table 1.

In the equilibrium of our hypothetical market, no plums are bought or sold, so every buyer will get a lemon. The domination of the used-car market by lemons is an example of the **adverse-selection problem**. The uninformed side of the market (buyers in this case) must choose from an undesirable or adverse selection of goods (used cars). The asymmetric information in the market generates a downward spiral of price and quantity: A decrease in price decreases the quantity of high-quality cars supplied, decreasing the price further when buyers realize the lower average quality of cars on the market, which leads to even fewer high-quality cars on the market. In

Adverse-selection problem: The uninformed side of the market must choose from an undesirable or adverse selection of goods.

Table 1: All Used Cars Are Lemons

	Neutral Expectations	*Pessimistic Expectations*
Assumed chance of lemon	50%	100%
Willingness to pay for lemon	$2,000	$2,000
Willingness to pay for plum	$4,000	$4,000
Willingness to pay for used car	$3,000	$2,000
Number of lemons supplied	16	9
Number of plums supplied	4	0
Total number of used cars	20	9
Actual chance of lemon	80%	100%

the extreme case, this downward spiral continues until all the cars on the market are lemons, so every buyer will get a lemon.

The problem of adverse selection occurs whenever one side of the market has better information than the other. As explained in the Closer Look box "Should You Join a Commercial Dating Service?" people who join a commercial dating service may encounter an adverse selection of companions.

ECONOMIC DETECTIVE– *Low Prices for Young Cars*

Mona bought a new car in January and was forced to sell it one month later, after driving the car for just 900 miles. She was surprised when the highest price she could get was about 30% less than the price she paid one month—and only 900 miles—earlier. Why was the resale value of her virtually new car so low?

To solve this puzzle, put yourself in the shoes of a car buyer. Suppose that you are considering two cars, a brand-new one from a car dealer, and Mona's car, which appears to be identical except for the 900 miles on the odometer. Like most consumers, you might suspect that there is something wrong with Mona's car. Otherwise, why would she want to sell it after only 900 miles? Although some people are forced to sell their high-quality cars after just a few months of driving, many of the people selling young cars are trying to get rid of low-quality cars. The price of young cars is low because there is an adverse selection of young cars in the market. If you buy a young car, there is a chance that you'll get a high-quality car at a bargain price, but there is also a chance that you'll get a lemon.

A Closer LOOK

Should You Join a Commercial Dating Service?

Imagine yourself in 10 years, working 50 hours per week in a high-pressure job that leaves little time to search for a husband, wife, or partner. You could join a commercial dating service, but is it worth the $1,000 price tag?

Our discussion of imperfect information and adverse selection provides a framework for thinking about whether to join a dating service. Here are some questions you should answer before joining.

1. **Will the dating service provide an adverse selection of potential partners, with a large number of lemons and just a few plums? If a person is willing to pay $1,000 to meet potential partners, what does this mean about the person? Do the clients of dating services have personality problems that make it difficult for them to initiate and maintain relationships with other people? Or are they just too busy to meet new people on their own?**
2. **Given your expectations about the mixture of lemons and plums, is the $1,000 fee worthwhile?**

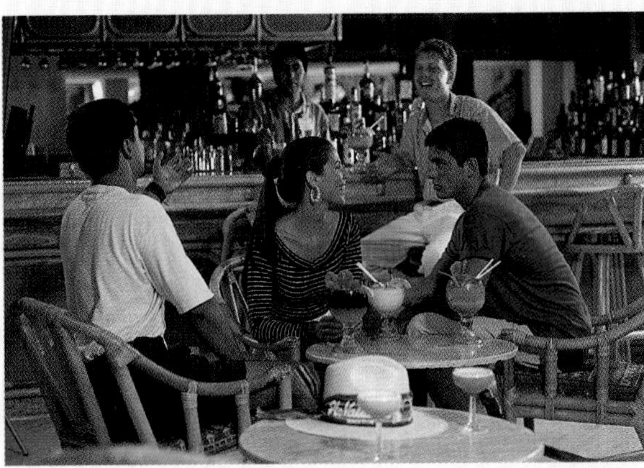

Commercial dating services provide introductions to potential companions.

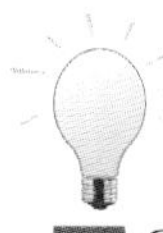

TEST *Your Understanding*

1. Complete the statement with *buyers* or *sellers*: There is asymmetric information in the used car market because ____________ cannot distinguish between lemons and plums but ____________ can.

2. Suppose that the typical consumer is willing to pay $3,000 for a plum and $1,000 for a lemon. If there is a 50% chance of getting a lemon, how much is the consumer willing to pay for a used car?

3. Why do goods of different qualities (such as used cars) sell for the same price, but goods of different sizes (such as apples) sell for different prices?

4. When buyers assume that there is a 40% chance of getting a lemon, 8 lemons and 2 plums are supplied. Is this an equilibrium? Explain.

5. Complete the statement: The fact that a buyer must pick a used car from an undesirable selection of cars is called the ____________ problem.

REVIVING THE HIGH-QUALITY MARKET

The disappearance of high-quality cars from our hypothetical market is an extreme—and unrealistic—case. In most used-car markets, some high-quality cars are offered for sale, so there is at least a small chance that a buyer will get a high-quality car. There are some high-quality cars on the market because some plum owners are willing to sell their cars at a relatively low price, a result of changes in their transportation needs or a desire to buy a new car.

Thin Market for Plums

In our earlier example, the market for high-quality used cars disappears because informed suppliers refuse to participate in the mixed market for used cars. Specifically, the minimum price for high-quality cars is so high ($2,500) that no plums are supplied at the equilibrium price of $2,000. If the minimum price for plums were lower, say $1,800, some plums will be supplied when the market price is $2,000. Although most of the used cars will be lemons, some lucky buyers will get plums. In this case we say that asymmetric information generates a **thin market**: Some high-quality goods are sold, but fewer than would be sold in a market with perfect information.

Thin market: A market in which some high-quality goods are sold but fewer than would be sold in a market with perfect information.

We can use a simple example to show how we get a thin market for plums. In Table 2, consumers assume that there is a 90% chance of getting a lemon (worth

Table 2: Thin Market for Plums

Assumed chance of lemon	90%
Willingness to pay for lemon	$2,000
Willingness to pay for plum	$4,000
Willingness to pay for used car	$2,200
Number of lemons supplied	18
Number of plums supplied	2
Total number of used cars	20
Actual chance of lemon	90%

$2,000 to the consumer) and a 10% chance of getting a plum (worth $4,000 to the consumer). Let's assume that each consumer is willing to pay $2,200 for a used car under these circumstances. Consumers are willing to pay a little more than the value of a lemon because there is a small chance of getting a plum. Figure 2 shows the supply curves for this example: At a price of $2,200, there will be 2 plums (shown by point *s*) and 18 lemons (shown by point *t*). In this case, consumers accurately assess the chance of getting a lemon: 90% of the used cars sold (18 of 20) turn out to be lemons. Therefore, the equilibrium price of used cars is $2,200 and the equilibrium quantity is 20 cars, 10% of which are plums.

Applications: Otto's Puzzle, the Supply of Blood

The opening paragraphs of this chapter describe Otto's puzzle. Is there a 50% chance of getting a lemon, as suggested by a casual reading of the data from consumer magazines, or a 90% chance, as suggested by the experiences of Otto's friends? As we see in Table 2 and Figure 2, the answer is 90%: To assess his chances of getting a lemon, Otto should listen to his friends. The price of model X cars is so low that just a few plum owners sell their cars.

For another example of a good with asymmetric information, think about blood used for transfusions. The supplier of blood has more information about his or her health history than the potential recipient. As explained in the Closer Look box "The Blood Supply in the United States and Japan," this asymmetrical information means that paying for blood may actually decrease the quality of the blood supply.

Money-Back Guarantees and Warranties

The domination of the used-car market by lemons provides an opening for clever suppliers. Consumers are willing to pay $4,000 for a true plum, and some plum owners would gladly supply cars if they could get more than $2,200 for them. This

Figure 2

Thin Market for Plums

If buyers assume that there is a 90% chance of getting a lemon, they are willing to pay $2,200 for a used car. At this price, the supply of plums is 2 (point *s*) and the supply of lemons is 18 (point *t*), so the actual chance of getting a lemon is 90%, the same as the assumed chance of getting a lemon.

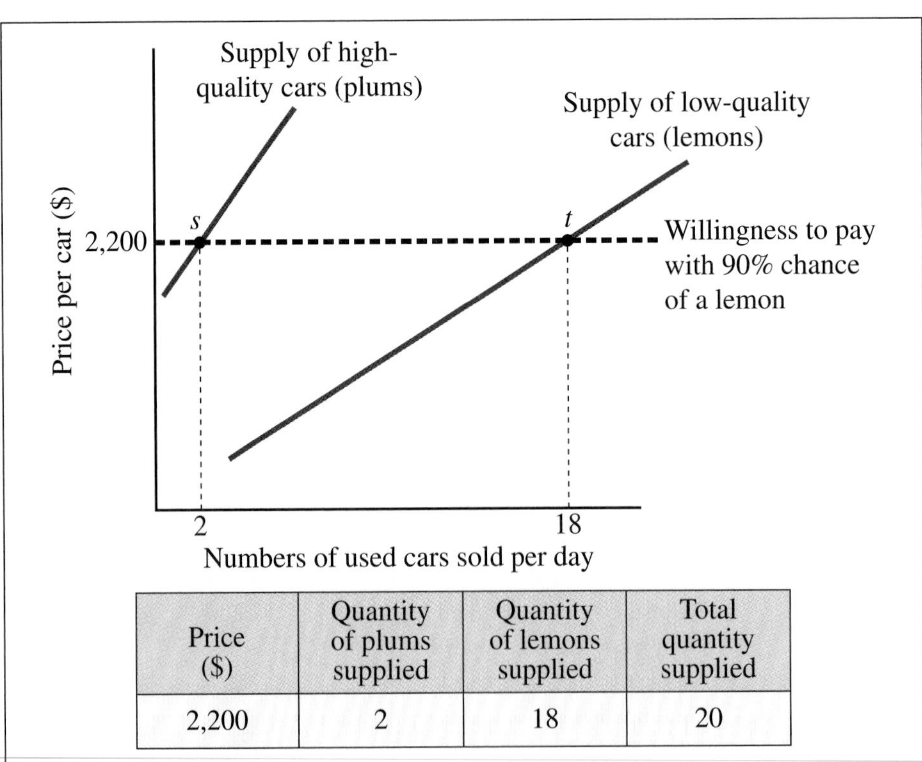

Price ($)	Quantity of plums supplied	Quantity of lemons supplied	Total quantity supplied
2,200	2	18	20

A Closer **LOOK**

The Blood Supply in the United States and Japan

About 30 years ago, a large fraction of the blood used for transfusions in the United States came from paid donors ("commercial" blood). Today, all the blood for transfusions comes from volunteer donors. During the 1960s, Japan made similar changes in its blood supply system, moving from a largely commercial supply to one that relies to a much greater extent on volunteer donors.* What explains these shifts away from commercial blood supply in favor of a volunteer supply? The answer is *adverse selection.*

Hospitals cannot always distinguish between bad blood (from donors with infectious disease such as hepatitis) and good blood. Thirty years ago, 30% of heart-surgery patients contracted hepatitis from tainted blood. According to Dr. Harvey G. Klein, the chief of the department of transfusion medicine at the National Institutes of Health, an important factor in the hepatitis problem was the reliance on paid blood donors.† The monetary incentives caused a relatively large number of people with "bad" blood to give blood—and be less than completely honest about their health histories. The elimination of paid donors in the last 30 years has decreased the chance of contracting hepatitis during heart surgery to only 2%.

*Alvin W. Drake, Stan N. Finkelstein, and Harvey M. Sapalsky, *The American Blood Supply* (Cambridge, MA: MIT Press, 1982).

†Oz Hopkins Koglin, "U.S. Blood 'Extremely Safe' as Volunteer Donors Cut Risks," *The Oregonian*, November 7, 1994, p. B1.

large gap between the willingness to pay and the willingness to accept provides a profit opportunity for clever entrepreneurs who can somehow persuade a skeptical consumer that a particular used car is truly a plum, not a lemon.

A supplier could identify a particular car as plum in a sea of lemons by offering one of the following guarantees.

1. *Money-back guarantee.* The supplier could promise to refund the $3,500 price if the car turned out to be a lemon. Because the car is in fact a plum (a fact known by the seller), the buyer will not ask for a refund, and both buyer and seller will be happy with the transaction.
2. *Warranties and repair guarantees.* The supplier could promise to cover any extraordinary repair costs for a one-year period. Because the car is a plum, there won't be any extraordinary repair costs, so both buyer and seller will be happy with the transaction.

Car consumers also have an incentive to get information about the quality of used cars. A consumer who identified a true plum could buy the high-quality car for a price that is much less than his or her willingness to pay ($4,000). In other words, there is a big payoff from information that enables the consumer to distinguish between lemons and plums. It may be rational for a car consumer to hire a mechanic to inspect a particular car for defects.

TEST *Your Understanding*

6 When buyers assume that there is a 70% chance of getting a lemon, 7 lemons and 3 plums are supplied. Is this an equilibrium? Explain.

7 Explain why it would not be rational for a lemon owner to offer a buyer a money-back guarantee.

8 Suppose that the minimum price of plums decreases. Would you expect the market to become "thinner" or "thicker"?

9 Explain why there are profit opportunities in a thin market.

APPLICATIONS

The most important lesson of this chapter is that if one side of a market cannot distinguish between high- and low-quality goods, the mixed market will be dominated by low-quality goods. In other words, imperfect information causes the adverse-selection problem. Let's look at three other examples of mixed markets that suffer from the adverse-selection problem: used baseball pitchers, malpractice insurance, and medical insurance.

Used Baseball Players

Professional baseball teams compete with each other for players. After six years of play in the major league, a player has the option of becoming a free agent and offering his services to the highest bidder. A player is likely to switch teams if the new team offers him a higher salary than his original team. One of the puzzling features of the free-agent market is that pitchers who switch teams are more prone to injuries than pitchers who don't. On average, pitchers who switch teams spend 28 days per season on the disabled list, compared to only 5 days per season for pitchers who do not switch teams.[2] This doesn't mean that all the switching pitchers are lemons: Many of them are injury-free and are terrific additions to their new teams. But on average, the switching pitchers spend five times longer recovering from injuries.

Baseball pitchers who switch teams are more prone to injuries than those who don't switch.

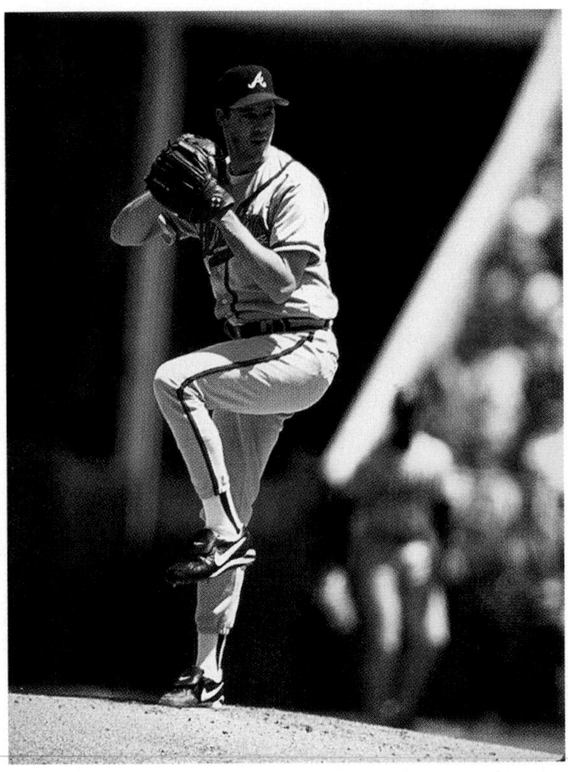

This puzzling feature of the free-agent market is explained by asymmetric information and adverse selection. Because the coaches, physicians, and trainers from the player's original team have interacted with the player on a daily basis for several years, they know from experience whether he is likely to suffer from injuries that prevent him from playing. In contrast, the new team has much less information: Its physicians can examine the pitcher, but a single exam is not the same as several years of daily experience with the pitcher. Suppose that the market price for pitchers is $1 million per year and a pitcher who is currently with the Chicago Cubs is offered this salary by another team. If the Cubs think the pitcher is likely to spend a lot of time next season recovering from injuries, they won't try to outbid the other team for the pitcher but will let the pitcher switch teams. On the other hand, if the Cubs think the pitcher will be injury-free and productive, he will be worth more than $1 million to the Cubs, so they will outbid the other team and keep the pitcher. In general, an injury-prone pitcher is more likely to switch teams: Like the used-car market, there are many "lemons" on the used-pitcher market. The market for other baseball players does not suffer from the adverse selection, perhaps because the injuries that affect their performance are easier for a potential new team to detect.

Although you may think it's bizarre to compare baseball pitchers to used cars, people in baseball don't think so. They recognize the similarity between the two markets. Jackie Moore, who managed a free-agent camp where teams looking for players can see free agents in action, sounds like a used-car salesman[3]: "We want to get players off the lot. We want to cut a deal. How many camps can you go into where you can look at a player and take him home with you?"

Malpractice Insurance

So far, we've discussed markets in which sellers have better information than buyers, but what happens when buyers are better informed than sellers? Let's think about the market for insurance. A person who buys an insurance policy knows much more about his or her risks and needs for insurance than the insurance company. For example, when you buy an auto-insurance policy, you know much more than your insurance company about your driving habits and your chances of getting in an accident. We'll see that insurance markets suffer from the adverse-selection problem: Insurance companies must pick from an adverse or undesirable selection of customers.

Let's look at the market for malpractice insurance. To keep things simple, suppose that there are just two types of physicians, careful and reckless. On average, the cost of settling malpractice suits against careful doctors is $4,000 per doctor per year, while the cost of settling malpractice suits against reckless doctors is $30,000 per doctor per year. If the doctor is insured, these costs are covered by an insurance company. Uninsured physicians will pay these costs themselves. Suppose that insurance companies cannot distinguish between careful and reckless doctors, but that each doctor knows whether he or she is careful or reckless. In other words, there is asymmetric information in the insurance market: Buyers (physicians) have better information than sellers (insurance companies).

If insurance companies cannot distinguish between careful and reckless physicians, there will be a mixed market and a single price for malpractice insurance. Suppose that all insurance companies are initially neutral in their expectations about what type of doctors will get malpractice insurance. In other words, insurance companies assume that half the doctors who buy insurance are careful and half are reckless. If the typical insurance company gets equal numbers of careful and reckless doctors, the average cost of providing insurance will be $17,000 per doctor. Therefore, if the insurance company charges $17,000 per year for insurance and its expectations about the mixture of careful and reckless doctors are correct, the company's total revenue will cover its total cost. In other words, the company will earn zero economic profit (normal accounting profit).

The expectations of the insurance company are unlikely to be realized. At a price of $17,000, none of the careful physicians will buy malpractice insurance because the premium is over four times the average cost of settling malpractice suits against a careful doctor, so malpractice insurance is not a very good deal. A careful doctor would rather take the risk, knowing that he or she will pay an average of $4,000 per year to settle malpractice suits. This is the adverse-selection problem: Insurance companies get an undesirable (adverse) selection of doctors. To ensure zero economic profit, the price of insurance must increase to $30,000, the average cost of serving the reckless physicians.

In this example, careful physicians do not buy malpractice insurance because insurance companies are unable to distinguish between careful and reckless doctors. The reckless doctors in the mixed market inflate the cost of providing insurance and increase the price of insurance. In fact, insurance companies try to identify careful doctors and offer them lower insurance rates. When a doctor applies for an insurance policy, the insurance company gathers information about the doctor and the history of his or her medical practice. Although these actions help insurance companies to distinguish between careful and reckless physicians, they are by no means perfect, so the adverse-selection problem persists.

The problem of adverse selection occurs in many insurance markets. As explained in the Closer Look box "Deposit Insurance in the United States and Argentina," one response to this problem is to make insurance mandatory rather than voluntary.

Pricing Health Insurance

Community rating: In a given community or metropolitan area, every firm pays the same price for medical insurance.

Our discussion of adverse selection provides some insights into recent changes in the pricing of medical insurance. Until recently, most insurance prices were based on **community rating.** In a given community or metropolitan area, every firm paid the same price for medical insurance, with the price equal to the average cost of providing medical coverage to the entire community. A firm providing medical

A Closer LOOK

Deposit Insurance in the United States and Argentina

Suppose that you deposit some money in a bank savings account and then the bank fails (goes bankrupt). Because most banks in the United States participate in a federal program that provides deposit insurance (run by the Federal Deposit Insurance Corporation or FDIC), the first $100,000 of your deposit is safe: If the bank goes bankrupt, you'll still get your money back. The widespread participation in the FDIC program keeps insurance costs low.

Some recent events in Argentina illustrate the effects of nationwide deposit insurance. In April 1995, fears of widespread bank failures and a collapse of the nation's banking system prompted the government to implement a new nationwide deposit-insurance program. The new insurance program restored confidence in the banking system, in large part because it is a nationwide program, one that will not suffer from the adverse-selection problem.[†]

[†]"Argentine Stocks, Bonds Rise on News about Banks," *Wall Street Journal*, April 24, 1995, p. A9; "Argentina Moves to Stem Bank Losses," *New York Times*, April 15, 1995, p. 32.

coverage to its employees through an insurance company would pay the insurance company an amount equal to the number of employees times the community price.

Most insurance companies now use **experience rating** to set their prices. Under this system, they charge different prices to different firms, depending on the past medical bills of the firm's employees. A firm whose employees have relatively low medical bills pays a relatively low price for its employees' insurance. The switch from community rating to experience rating occurred when insurance companies were able to identify those employers with relatively low medical costs. As the low-cost firms were switched to experience-rated plans, the cost of serving the remaining high-cost firms increased, forcing insurers using community rating to increase their prices. Eventually, most insurance companies switched to experience rating.[4]

Experience rating: Each firm pays a different price for medical insurance, depending on the past medical bills of the firm's employees.

Experience rating gives firms an incentive to decrease the health costs of their workers. Firms are more likely to invest in safety and health programs for their workers. Firms will also make a greater effort to avoid hiring applicants with health problems. Under experience rating, a firm that hires a worker with above-average medical costs will experience an increase in the price of its insurance. Among the workers who might suffer as a result are older workers and the disabled.

TEST *Your Understanding*

10 Your favorite baseball team just announced that it signed two pitchers from the free-agent market. What's your reaction?

11 Complete the statement with numbers: Suppose that the average annual malpractice cost is $40,000 for reckless physicians and $2,000 for careful physicians. If half the doctors insured by an insurance company are reckless, the company will earn zero economic profit if the price of insurance is ____________. If careful doctors are not willing to pay any more than $5,000 for insurance, the price required for zero economic profit is ____________.

Using the TOOLS

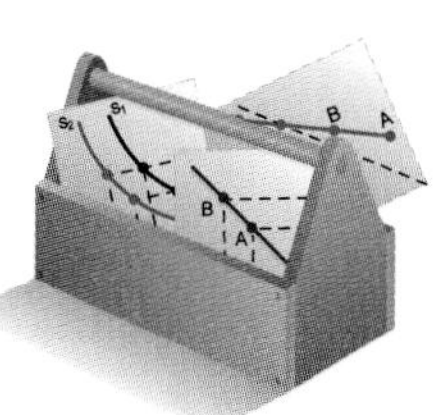

We've seen what happens when one side of the market—buyers or sellers—has better information than the other side. In a market for a used good, sellers know more than buyers, and the market will be dominated by low-quality goods. In an insurance market, buyers know more than sellers, and the market will be dominated by high-risk consumers. Here are some opportunities to do your own economic analysis of markets with asymmetric information.

1. ECONOMIC EXPERIMENT: *Lemons*

In this lemons experiment, students play the role of consumers purchasing used cars. Over half the used cars on the road (57%) are high-quality cars (plums), and the remaining cars (43%) are low-quality cars (lemons). Each consumer offers a price for a used car and then rolls a pair of dice to find out whether he or she gets a lemon or a plum. In general, rolling a big number is good news: To get a high-quality car, you need to roll a big number. The higher the price you offer, the smaller the number you must roll to get a plum. Here is how the experiment works.

- Each consumer tells the instructor how much he or she is offering for a used car and then rolls the dice.

- The instructor uses a secret formula (reflecting the mixture of lemons and plums offered for sale at the price the consumer has offered) to tell the consumer whether the number she rolled is large enough to get a plum. If the number is not large enough, she gets a lemon.
- The consumer's score equals the difference between the maximum amount she is willing to pay for the type of car she got ($1,200 for a plum and $400 for a lemon) and the price she actually paid. For example, if Otto offers $500 and gets a plum, his score would be $700. If Carla offers $600 and gets a lemon, her score would be –$200.
- The instructor announces the result of each transaction to the class.
- There will be three to five buying periods. At the end of the last trading period, each consumer adds up his or her surpluses.

2. Rising Insurance Rates

At a large state university, an insurance company provides group medical coverage for university employees. When the company discovered that some of the younger employees had switched to insurance companies with lower rates, the company increased its rates. This is puzzling because you might think that the insurance company would drop its rates to prevent other employees from switching to other companies. Indeed, the rate hike caused *more* employees to switch. Did the insurance company act irrationally?

3. Purchasing a Fleet of Used Cars

Suppose that you are responsible for buying a fleet of 10 used cars for your employees and must pick either brand B cars or brand C cars. For your purposes, the two brands are identical except for one difference: Based on your market experience with the two brands, you figure that 50% of B cars are lemons, and only 20% of C cars are lemons. Suppose that you are willing to pay $1,000 for a known lemon and $3,000 for a known plum. If the price of B cars is $1,800 and the price of C cars is $2,200, which brand of car should you pick?

4. State Auto Insurance Pool

Consider a state in which automobile drivers are divided equally into two types of drivers: careful and reckless. The average annual auto-insurance claim is $400 for a careful driver and $1,200 for a reckless driver. Suppose that the state adopts an insurance system under which all drivers are placed in a common pool and allocated to insurance companies randomly. An insurance company cannot refuse coverage to any consumer it is assigned, but a consumer who is unhappy with the insurance company has the option of being reassigned (randomly) to another. By law, each insurance company must charge the same price to all its customers. Predict the price of auto insurance under two alternative policy scenarios.

a. Auto insurance is mandatory.

b. Auto insurance is voluntary.

5. ECONOMIC EXPERIMENT: *Bike Insurance*

This experiment shows the effect of asymmetric information on the market for bicycle insurance. Consider a city with two types of bike owners, some that face a relatively high probability of bike theft, and others that face a relatively low probability of bike theft. Bike owners know from experience whether they face a high or low probability of theft, but the insurance company cannot distinguish between the two types of owners. For the city as a whole, 20% of bicycles are stolen every year. Here is how the experiment works.

- The class is divided into small groups, each of which represents an insurance company that must pick a price at which the firm will offer bike theft insurance. The insurance company must pay $100 for each insured bike that is stolen.
- The instructor has a table showing, for each price of bike insurance, how many owners of each type (high probability and low probability) will purchase insurance. Using the numbers supplied by the instructor, each insurance company can compute its total revenue (price times the number of customers), the number of bikes stolen, and the company's total replacement cost.
- The group's score for a trading period equals the company's profit, which is the total revenue less total replacement cost.
- The experiment runs for several trading periods, and a group's score equals the sum of its profits over these trading periods.

SUMMARY

In this chapter, we've seen what happens when one of the assumptions underlying most supply and demand analysis—that people make informed decisions—is violated. If either buyers or sellers don't have reliable information about a particular good or service, the market will suffer from the adverse-selection problem. The uninformed side of the market picks from an adverse selection of goods or customers. Here are the main points of the chapter.

1. If one side of the market cannot distinguish between high- and low-quality goods, both goods will be sold in a mixed market at the same price.
2. The markets for many used goods suffer from the adverse-selection problem because sellers have better information than buyers.
3. If sellers of high-quality goods have a relatively low minimum price, some high-quality goods will be sold but the market will be "thin."
4. Insurance markets suffer from adverse selection because buyers have better information than sellers.

KEY TERMS

adverse-selection problem, *319*
asymmetric information, *317*
community rating, *326*
experience rating, *327*
thin market, *321*

PROBLEMS AND DISCUSSION QUESTIONS

1. Use the notion of adverse selection to explain a classic quip from Groucho Marx: "I won't join any club that is willing to accept me as a member."
2. The table at the top of page 330 shows some scenarios for different used-car markets. Which markets are in equilibrium? Graph each equilibrium, using Figure 1 on page 318 as a model.

	Scenario		
	A	*B*	*C*
Assumed chance of lemon	60%	80%	95%
Willingness to pay for used car	$6,000	$5,000	$4,500
Number of lemons supplied	70	40	90
Number of plums supplied	30	10	10
Total number of used cars	100	50	100

3. You are thinking about buying a used camera, the price of which is $60. You are willing to pay $20 for a lemon (low quality) and $100 for a plum (high quality).
   a. Under what circumstances would it be wise to buy a used camera?
   b. Are these circumstances likely to occur? Explain.
4. Suppose that both buyers and sellers of used cars are ignorant: No one can distinguish between lemons and plums. Would you expect the market to be dominated by lemons?
5. Suppose that a new lie detector is 100% accurate. Discuss the implications for the adverse-selection problem in the used-car market.
6. When a person applies for life insurance, the insurance agent asks the applicant about his or her occupation. Why should this matter to the insurance company?
7. Scientists have recently developed new genetic tests that could be used by an insurance company to determine whether a potential customer is likely to develop certain diseases. Discuss the trade-offs associated with allowing insurance companies to use these tests.
8. On the campus of Bike University, half the bikes are expensive (replacement value = $100) and half are cheap (replacement value = $20). There is a 50% chance that any particular bike—expensive or cheap—will be stolen in the next year. Suppose that a firm offers bike-theft insurance for $40 per year: The firm will replace any insured bike that is stolen. If the firm sells 20 insurance policies, will the firm make a profit? Explain.

Take It to the Net

We invite you to visit the O'Sullivan/Sheffrin page on the Prentice Hall Web site at:

http://www.prenhall.com/osullivan/

for this chapter's World Wide Web exercise.

MODEL ANSWERS FOR THIS CHAPTER

Chapter-Opening Questions

1. Will the service generate an adverse selection of dates? Given your expectations of the mix of lemons and peaches, is the service worth the fee you'd pay?
2. They are trying to distinguish their high-quality cars from low-quality cars.
3. Hospitals cannot always distinguish between bad blood (from donors with infectious disease like hepatitis) and good blood, and monetary incentives for blood caused a relatively large number of people with "bad" blood to give blood—and be less than completely honest about their health histories.
4. Like the used-car market, the used-pitcher market has asymmetric information: the pitcher's original team has more information than the new team. A team is more likely to be outbid by another team for a pitcher's services, if the pitcher has health problems that make him worth less to the original team.
5. Insurance companies started identifying employers with relatively low medical costs, and offered them cheaper "experience-rated" insurance. As the low-cost firms were switched to experience-rated plans, the cost of serving the remaining firms increased, forcing insurers using the old rating system to increase their prices. Eventually, most insurance companies switched to experience rating.

Test Your Understanding

1. buyers, sellers
2. $2,000, the average value of the two types of cars
3. It is easy to determine the size of an apple but not easy to determine the quality of a car.

4. No. 80% of the used cars are lemons, meaning that consumers underestimate the chance of getting a lemon.
5. adverse-selection
6. Yes. 70% of the cars are lemons.
7. The buyer will eventually return the car and get a full refund, perhaps after putting a lot of miles on it or abusing it.
8. Thicker: The lower the minimum price, the larger the quantity supplied at each price, so the more plums in the market.
9. There will be a large gap between the amount a buyer is willing to pay for a true plum and the amount a plum owner is willing to accept.
10. You may be skeptical about the new player because free-agent pitchers who switch teams spend a relatively long time on the disabled list. Before reading this chapter, you might have been more optimistic about the pitchers.
11. $21,000 (the average of the two cost figures), $40,000 (the cost for reckless doctors)

Using the Tools

2. Rising Insurance Rates

   The medical costs of younger employees are usually lower than the average medical cost for all university employees. When the youngsters switched to a different insurance company, the average age—and the average medical costs—of the original insurance company increased. The insurance company increased its rates to cover its higher costs, fully anticipating that this would cause other low-cost employees to switch to other companies. The insurance company faced a progressively more adverse selection of customers in the firm, and the higher price of medical insurance reflects the adverse selection.

3. Purchasing a Fleet of Used Cars

   The table in the next column shows how to compute the benefits and costs of the two brands. For brand B, you expect half the cars to be lemons and half to be plums, so the total value of a brand B fleet is $20,000 (5 lemons worth a total of $5,000 and 5 plums worth a total of $15,000). At a price of $1,800, the total cost of a B fleet is $18,000 ($1,800 times ten cars). Therefore, the value of a B fleet exceeds its cost by $2,000. We can do the same computations for the C fleet. The only difference is that you would get 2 lemons and 8 plums with a C fleet. The value of a C fleet exceeds its cost by $4,000, so the C fleet is a better deal. Although you pay $400 more per C car, the extra cost is more than offset by the smaller number of lemons in the C fleet.

	Brand B	*Brand C*
Number of lemons	5	2
Value of lemons	$5,000	$2,000
Number of plums	5	8
Value of plums	$15,000	$24,000
Total value of fleet	$20,000	$26,000
Total cost of fleet	$18,000	$22,000
Surplus (value – cost)	$2,000	$4,000

4. State Auto Insurance Pool

   Under the pooling policy, there will be a single mixed market and a single price for auto insurance. If auto insurance is mandatory, the pooling policy will increase the price to $800 (the average cost per driver for each insurance company).

   If auto insurance is voluntary, the long-run equilibrium price will exceed $800 and may even approach $1,200. If insurance companies initially have neutral expectations about the mixture of careful and reckless drivers, the price will be $800. If this price exceeds the maximum price of some careful drivers, they will drop out of the market, so more than 50% of the insured drivers will be reckless. Given the larger percentage of reckless (high cost) drivers, insurance companies will lose money at a price of $800, so they will increase the price to restore zero economic profit. The price of insurance will increase until the expectations of the insurance company are realized. If all the careful drivers drop out of the market, the price of insurance will increase to $1,200 (the cost per reckless driver).

NOTES

1. George Akerlof, "The Market for 'Lemons': Quality Uncertainty and the Market Mechanism," *Quarterly Journal of Economics*, August 1970, pp. 488–500.
2. Kenneth Lehn, "Information Asymmetries in Baseball's Free Agent Market," *Economic Inquiry*, vol. 22, January 1984, pp. 37–44.
3. Chris Sheridan, "Free Agents at End of Baseball's Earth," Associated Press, printed in *Corvallis Gazette-Times*, April 15, 1995, p. B1.
4. Henry J. Aaron, "Issues Every Plan to Reform Health Care Financing Must Confront," *Journal of Economic Perspectives*, vol. 8, no. 3, Summer 1994, pp. 31–43.

CHAPTER

Part 5
The Markets for Labor and Capital

17

The Labor Market

Several recent reports on the earnings of college graduates have made the jobs of college recruiters much easier. Here are some facts.

- In 1972, the typical college graduate earned about 43% more than a high-school graduate.
- In 1992, the typical college graduate earned about 82% more than a high-school graduate.[1]

These facts raise two questions. First, why do college graduates earn so much more than high-school graduates? Second, why did the earnings gap between high-school and college graduates almost double in the last 20 years?

In this chapter we use a model of supply and demand to answer these and other practical questions about the labor market. You may be surprised by the answers. Here are some of the other issues we address:

1. Do individual workers obey the law of supply? If the wage increases, will people work longer hours?
2. If a worker switches from a relatively safe factory job to a job in a steel mill, by how much will his or her wage increase?
3. Why do women, on average, earn about 75% as much as men?
4. Would an increase in the minimum wage help everyone who is currently paid the minimum wage?
5. In 1913, Henry Ford increased the wage of his autoworkers from $3 per day to $5. Was this an act of generosity or a calculated move to decrease his cost and increase his profit?

THE LABOR MARKET IN THE LONG RUN

We can use supply and demand curves to show how wages are determined and how public policies affect wages and employment. We start with a discussion of the labor market in the long run, a period of time over which firms can enter or leave the market and existing firms can change all their inputs, including their production facilities. On the supply side of the market, the long run is the period of time over which people can change occupations and/or migrate from one city to another.

When we speak of a labor market, we are referring to the market for a specific occupation in a specific geographical area. We explain the labor market with an example: the market for nurses in the city of Florence. On the demand side of the market, nursing services are used by dozens of firms and organizations in a city, including hospitals, doctors' offices, schools, emergency clinics, and nursing homes. On the supply side of the market, we must think about how many nurses are in the city and how many hours each nurse works.

The Long-Run Supply Curve

The principal question about labor supply is: How many hours of labor will be supplied at each wage? Before we look at the market supply curve, let's think about the supply decisions of individual workers. Suppose that each nurse in the city of Florence initially works 36 hours per week at an hourly wage of $10, and the wage increases to $12. Here are three plausible responses to the increase in the wage.

1. For Lester: less labor and more leisure time. If Lester works 30 hours instead of 36 hours, he gets 6 hours of extra leisure time and still earns the same income per week ($360 = 30 × $12).
2. For Sam: same amount of labor and more income. If Sam continues to work 36 hours per week, he gets an additional $72 of income ($2 × 36 hours) and the same amount of leisure time.
3. For Maureen: more labor, less leisure time, and much more income. If Maureen works 43 hours instead of 36 hours, she sacrifices 7 hours of leisure time and earns a total of $516, compared to only $360 at a wage of $10.

Empirical studies of the labor market confirm that each of these responses is plausible: When the wage increases, some people work more, others work less, and others work about the same amount.[2] You may notice that only one of our hypothetical workers—Maureen—obeys the law of supply, working more hours when the wage increases.

Now that we know something about how individuals respond to an increase in the wage, we're ready to discuss the **market supply curve for labor**, which shows the relationship between the wage and the quantity of labor supplied by all workers for a particular occupation. In Figure 1 on page 334 the market supply curve is positively sloped, consistent with the law of supply: The higher the wage (the price of labor), the larger the quantity supplied. An increase in the wage affects the quantity of nursing supplied in three ways.

Market supply curve for labor: A curve showing the relationship between the wage and the quantity of labor supplied.

1. *Change in hours per worker.* When the wage increases, some nurses will work more hours, while others will work fewer hours, and others will work the same number of hours. We don't know for certain whether the average time per worker will increase, decrease, or stay the same, but the change in the average time is likely to be relatively small.

Figure 1

Supply, Demand, and Market Equilibrium

At the market equilibrium (point *e*, with wage = $15 and quantity = 16,000 hours), the quantity supplied equals the quantity demanded, so there is neither a surplus nor a shortage of labor.

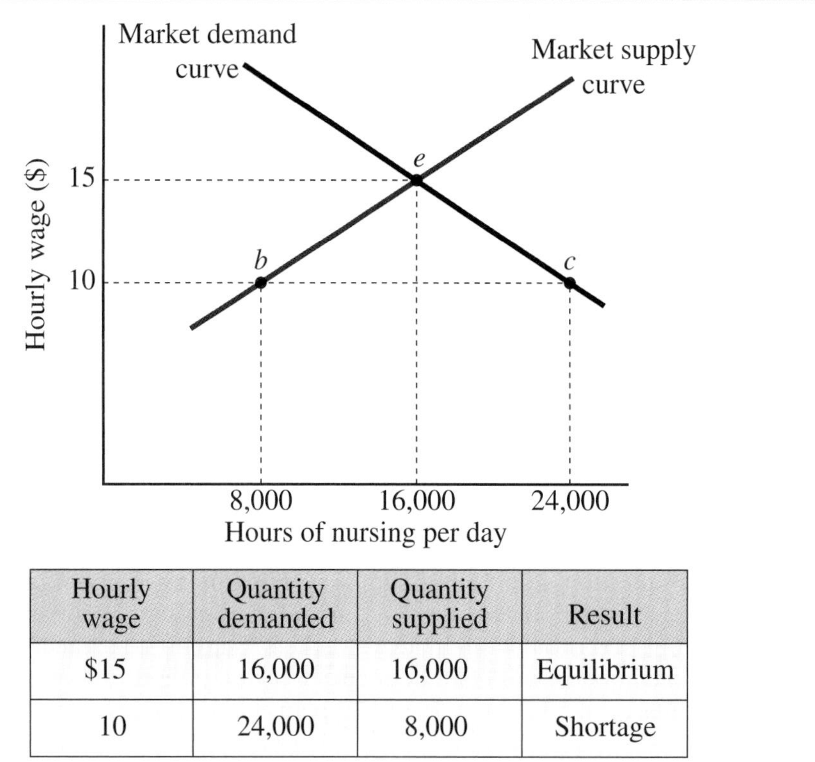

Hourly wage	Quantity demanded	Quantity supplied	Result
$15	16,000	16,000	Equilibrium
10	24,000	8,000	Shortage

2. *Occupational choice.* An increase in the nursing wage will cause some workers to switch from other occupations to nursing and more new workers to pick nursing over other occupations.
3. *Migration.* Some nurses in other cities will move to Florence to earn higher wages.

The second and third effects reinforce one another, so an increase in the wage causes movement upward along the market supply curve. For example, if the wage of Florence nurses increases from $10 to $15, the quantity supplied increases from 8,000 hours per day (point *b*) to 16,000 hours per day (point *e*). Although individual workers may violate the law of supply, the supply curve is positively sloped because an increase in the wage changes workers' occupational choices and causes migration.

The Long-Run Demand Curve

Derived demand: The demand for an input such as labor is derived from the demand for the final product.

Long-run demand curve for labor: A curve showing the relationship between the wage and the quantity of labor demanded in the long run.

Let's turn from the supply side of the market to the demand side. Firms use labor and other inputs to produce goods and services, so the demand for labor is a **derived demand** in the sense that it is derived from the demand for the final product. The **long-run demand curve for labor** shows the relationship between the wage and the quantity of labor demanded in the long run, when firms can change their production facilities. In Figure 1 the demand curve is negatively sloped, consistent with the law of demand: The higher the wage, the smaller the quantity of labor demanded. At a wage of $15 per hour, the quantity demanded is 16,000 nursing hours per day, compared to 24,000 hours at a wage of $10.

Why is the market demand curve negatively sloped? An increase in the wage will decrease the quantity of labor demanded for two reasons.

1. The **output effect**. An increase in the wage will decrease the quantity of output (medical services) sold by firms that use nurses. An increase in the wage increases production costs, and firms will pass on at least part of the higher cost to their consumers: Prices will increase. According to the law of demand, an increase in price decreases the quantity demanded, so firms will sell less output at the higher price and they will need less of all inputs, including labor. In our example, an increase in the nursing wage will increase the cost of medical services, causing people to spend less time in hospitals, so hospitals won't need as many nurses.

Output effect: The change in the quantity of labor demanded resulting from a change in the quantity of output.

2. The **input-substitution effect**. Firms will substitute other inputs for labor. Suppose that a nursing home initially uses nurses to cook and serve food, administer medicine, and monitor the health of the patients. When the wage increases, the firm could substitute other inputs for nurses by (1) purchasing food from outside vendors and (2) installing cameras and other monitoring equipment to allow a single nurse to monitor more than one patient. The increase in the wage causes the firm to substitute other inputs for relatively expensive nurses.

Input-substitution effect: The change in the quantity of labor demanded resulting from a change in the relative cost of labor.

The output effect reinforces the input-substitution effect, so the market demand curve is negatively sloped.

You may recall that we used similar logic in earlier chapters to explain why the demand curves for consumer goods (burgers, CDs, shoes) are negatively sloped. An increase in price decreases the consumer's real income, causing consumers to buy less of all "normal" goods. This income effect for consumer goods is analogous to the output effect for labor. An increase in price also causes consumers to substitute other goods for the good experiencing the increase in price. This substitution effect for consumer goods is analogous to the input-substitution effect for labor.

The notion of input substitution applies to other labor markets as well. For the most graphic examples of factor substitution, we can travel from a developed country such as the United States, Canada, France, Germany, or Japan, to a less developed country in South America, Africa, or Asia. Wages are much lower in the less developed countries, so production tends to be much more labor intensive. In other words, labor is cheap relative to machinery and equipment, so labor is substituted for these other inputs. Here are some examples.

1. *Mining*. U.S. firms use huge earth-moving equipment to mine for minerals, while some firms in less developed countries use thousands of workers, digging by hand.
2. *Furniture*. Firms in developed countries manufacture furniture with sophisticated machinery and equipment, while some firms in less developed countries make furniture by hand.
3. *Accounting*. Accountants in developed countries use computers and sophisticated software programs, while some accountants in less developed countries use simple calculators and ledger paper.

Market Equilibrium

Now that we know about the supply and demand curves for labor, we can think about the equilibrium in the labor market. A market equilibrium is a situation in which there is no pressure to change the price of a good or service. Figure 1 shows the equilibrium in the market for nurses. The supply curve intersects the demand curve at point *e*, so the equilibrium wage is $15 and the equilibrium quantity is 16,000 hours of nursing per day. At this wage, there is neither a shortage nor a surplus of labor, so the market has reached an equilibrium.

How would a change in demand affect the equilibrium wage of nurses? We know from Chapter 4 that a change in demand causes price and quantity to move in the same direction: An *increase* in demand *increases* the price and quantity, while a *decrease* in demand *decreases* the price and quantity. For example, suppose that the demand for medical care increases. Nurses are used in the provision of medical care, so an increase in the quantity of medical care will shift the demand curve for nurses to the right: At each wage, firms will demand more hours of nursing. As shown in Figure 2, an increase in demand increases the equilibrium wage and the equilibrium quantity of nursing services.

How would a change in supply affect the equilibrium wage of nurses? We know from Chapter 4 that a change in supply causes price and quantity to move in opposite directions: An *increase* in supply *decreases* the price but *increases* the quantity, while a *decrease* in supply *increases* the price but *decreases* the quantity. For example, suppose that a new television program makes nursing look like an attractive occupation, causing a large number of youngsters to become nurses rather than accountants, lawyers, or doctors. The supply curve will shift to the right: At each wage there will be more nursing hours supplied. The equilibrium wage will decrease and the quantity will increase. For another example of the market effects of a change in supply, read the Closer Look box "Nannies versus Au Pairs."

TEST *Your Understanding*

1 Your objective is to earn exactly $120 per week. If your wage decreases from $6 to $4, how will you respond?

2 Each worker in a certain occupation works exactly 40 hours per week, regardless of the wage. Does this mean that the market supply curve is vertical (a fixed quantity, regardless of the wage)?

3 Complete the statement with *increase* or *decrease*: According to the output effect, a decrease in the wage will ____________ production costs, so the price of final goods will ____________. The quantity of final goods produced will ____________, so the demand for labor will ____________.

4 Explain the input-substitution effect associated with a decrease in the wage.

Figure 2

Market Effects of an Increase in Demand for Labor

An increase in the demand for nursing services shifts the demand curve to the right, increasing the equilibrium wage from $15 to $17. The equilibrium quantity increases from 16,000 hours to 19,000 hours.

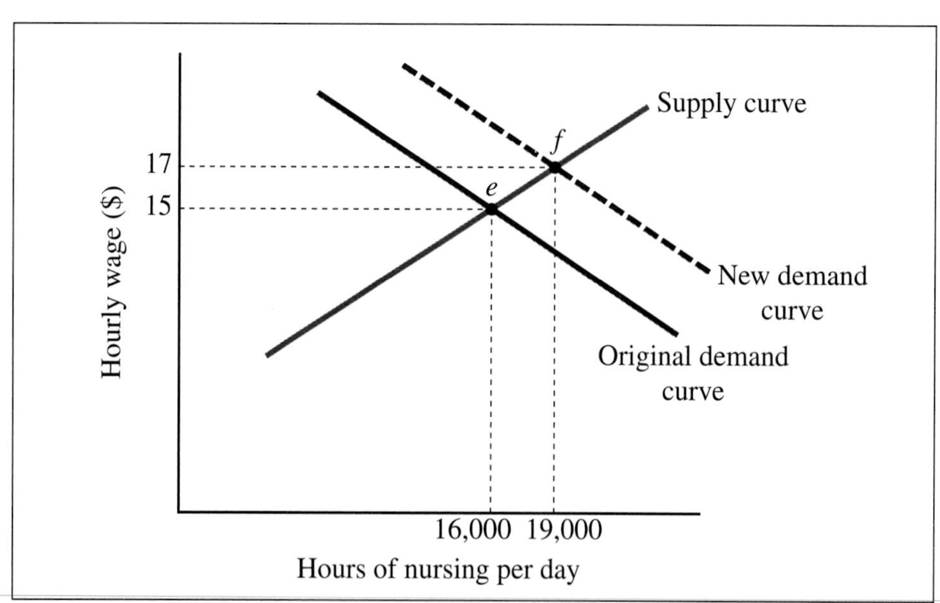

A Closer LOOK

Nannies versus Au Pairs

In 1992, the Network of American Nanny Agencies (NANA) asked the U.S. Congress to impose strict limits on the number of European women participating in cultural exchange programs. Why? Each year about 8,000 European women participate in the "au pair" program, coming to the United States for one-year stints to learn about the country, improve their English, and provide child care. NANA claimed that the au pairs provide "unfair competition" and depress the wages of domestic nannies.

How would the elimination of the au pair program affect the wage of nannies? As shown in the figure on the right, the supply curve for child-care services would shift to the left: At each wage, fewer workers would provide child-care services. As a result, the equilibrium wage for child-care workers would increase, from $800 per month to $840 per month in this example.

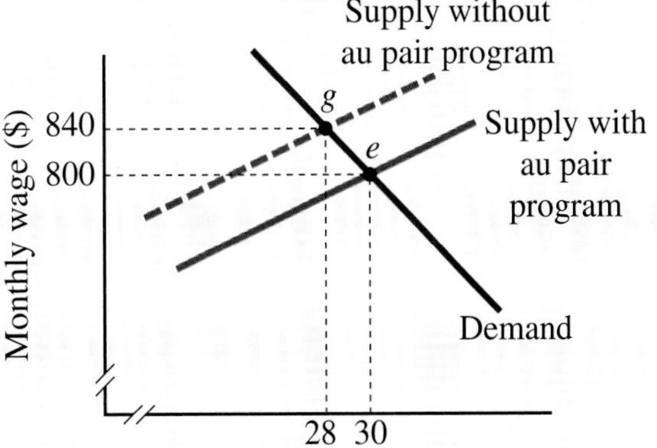

Source: After Brent Bowers, "Nanny Agencies Say Threat from 'Au Pairs' Isn't Kid Stuff," *Wall Street Journal,* May 28, 1992, p. B1. Reprinted by permission of the *Wall Street Journal,*

THE LABOR MARKET IN THE SHORT RUN

Now that we've seen how the labor market works in the long run, let's think about how it might be different in the short run. The short run is the time during which there is a fixed number of firms, and at least one input—for example, the production facility—cannot be changed. New production facilities cannot be built and existing facilities cannot be modified. We start our discussion of the short-run analysis with the hiring decisions of an individual employer.

Labor Demand and the Marginal Principle

We use two of the key principles of economics to explain the short-run demand for labor by an individual firm. Recall the marginal principle:

Marginal PRINCIPLE

Increase the level of an activity if its marginal benefit exceeds its marginal cost, but reduce the level if the marginal cost exceeds the marginal benefit. If possible, pick the level at which the marginal benefit equals the marginal cost.

For a firm, the relevant activity is hiring labor to produce output, so the firm will pick the quantity of labor at which the marginal benefit of labor equals its marginal cost. Suppose that the firm is a price taker: It is small enough that it does not affect the prices of inputs or outputs. The firm can hire as many workers as it wants at the market wage, so the marginal cost of labor is the hourly wage. For example, if the wage is $10, the extra cost associated with one more hour of labor (the marginal cost) is $10, regardless of how much labor the firm hires.

Marginal product of labor: The change in output per unit change in labor.

Marginal revenue product of labor (MRP): The extra revenue generated from 1 more unit of labor; equal to price of output times the marginal product of labor.

What is the marginal benefit of labor? The firm hires labor to produce output, so the marginal benefit equals the monetary value of the output produced with an additional hour of labor. For example, suppose that a car wash initially uses 19 hours of labor per day. When the firm hires one more hour of labor (the 20th hour), the firm washes 3 additional cars per day. In other words, the **marginal product of labor**, defined as the change in output per unit change in labor, is 3 cars. If the firm charges $5 per car, the marginal benefit of labor is $15 ($5 × 3 cars). In general, the marginal benefit of labor is the **marginal revenue product of labor (MRP)**, which equals the price of the firm's output times the marginal product of labor:

marginal benefit = marginal revenue product (MRP) = price × marginal product

Figure 3 shows the marginal revenue product curve for our hypothetical firm. It is negatively sloped because of the principle of diminishing returns.

PRINCIPLE *of Diminishing Returns*

Suppose that output is produced with two or more inputs and that we increase one input while holding the other inputs fixed. Beyond some point—called the point of diminishing returns—output will increase at a decreasing rate.

As a firm adds workers to an existing production facility, each worker uses a smaller piece of the firm's production facility, so total output increases at a decreasing rate. In other words, as the quantity of labor increases, the marginal product of labor decreases. Look back at the formula for marginal revenue product. If the marginal product of labor decreases and the price of output is fixed, the MRP decreases too. For example, the 20th hour of labor increases the output of the car wash by

Figure 3

Firm's Short-Run Labor Demand Curve

The short-run labor demand curve for an individual firm is the marginal revenue product curve (the marginal benefit curve).

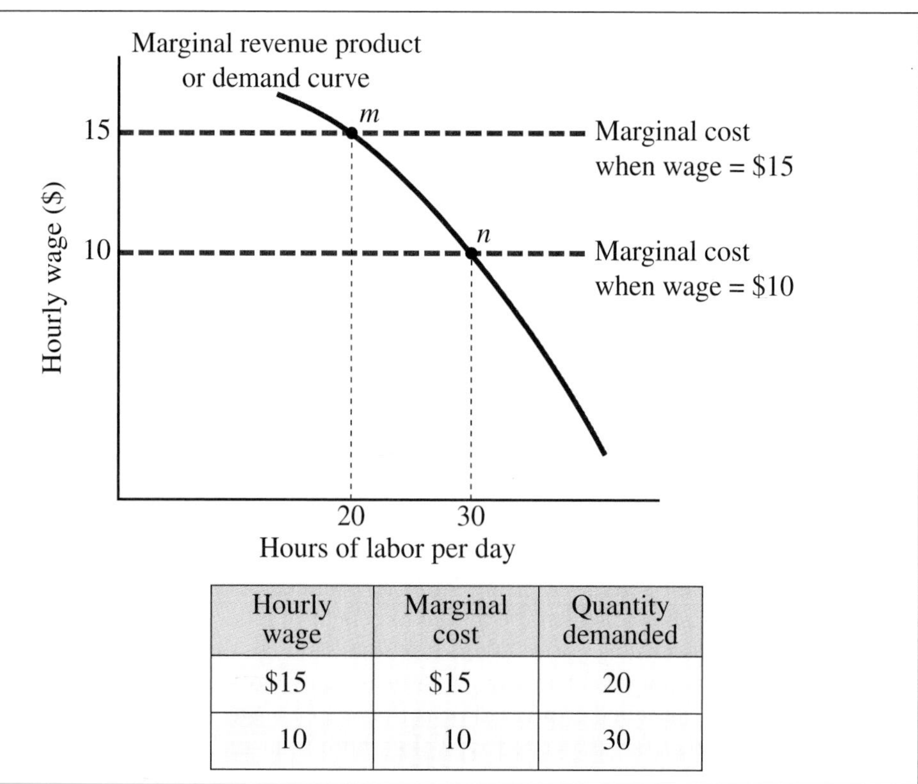

Hourly wage	Marginal cost	Quantity demanded
$15	$15	20
10	10	30

3 cars (MRP = $15), but the 30th hour increases the output by only 2 cars (MRP = $10). This means that the MRP curve must be negatively sloped: The larger the quantity of labor, the lower the MRP.

A firm can use its MRP curve to decide how much labor to hire at a particular wage. In Figure 3, if the wage (the marginal cost of labor) is $15, the marginal principle is satisfied at point *m*, where the marginal cost equals the marginal revenue product. The firm will hire 20 hours of labor because for the first 20 hours, the marginal benefit (the MRP) is greater than or equal to the marginal cost (the $15 wage). It would not be sensible to hire another hour because the additional revenue from the 21st hour would be less than the additional cost ($15). If the wage drops to $10, the firm will satisfy the marginal principle at point *n*, hiring 30 hours of labor instead of just 20.

Short-Run Labor Demand Curve

The MRP curve is the firm's **short-run demand curve for labor**, which shows the relationship between the wage and the quantity of labor demanded in the short run. The demand curve answers the following question: At each wage, how many hours of labor does the firm want to hire? We've already used the MRP curve to answer this question for two different wages ($15 and $10), and we can do the same for any other wage. Because the MRP curve is a marginal-benefit curve and the firm uses the marginal principle to decide how much labor to hire, the MRP curve is the same as the firm's demand curve. If you pick a wage, the MRP curve tells you exactly how much labor the firm will demand.

Short-run demand curve for labor: A curve showing the relationship between the wage and the quantity of labor demanded in the short run.

What sort of changes would cause the demand curve to shift? We know that a change in anything held fixed in drawing a curve will shift the entire curve. To draw the labor demand curve, we fix the price of the output and the productivity of workers. An increase in the price will increase the MRP of workers, shifting the entire demand curve to the right: At each wage, the firm will hire more workers. Similarly, if workers become more productive, the increase in the marginal product of labor will increase the MRP and shift the demand curve to the right. Conversely, a decrease in price or labor productivity would shift the demand curve to the left.

Market Demand and Equilibrium

To draw the market demand curve for labor, we add the labor demands of all the firms that use a particular type of labor. In the simplest case, all firms are identical and we multiply the number of firms by the quantity of labor demanded by the typical firm. For example, if there were 100 firms, each of which employs 20 hours of labor at a wage of $15, the market demand for labor would be 2,000 hours. This is shown by point *m* in Figure 4 on page 340. Similarly, if the typical firm demands 30 hours per day at a wage of $10, the market demand would be 3,000 hours.

Figure 4 shows the market equilibrium with short-run demand and supply curves. The supply curve is relatively steep because in the short run, workers cannot change occupations or migrate from one location to another. The only supply response to a change in the wage is that existing workers change the number of hours they work. We know that when the wage increases, some workers work more, others work less, and others work about the same number of hours. The net effect of these changes in work hours varies from one occupation to another. In Figure 4 we're assuming that there is a weak positive relationship between the wage and the hours worked, so the supply curve is relatively steep. In the market equilibrium (point *n*), the wage is $10 and the quantity is 3,000 hours of labor per day.

Figure 4

Market Equilibrium in the Short Run

The short run market equilibrium is shown by the intersection of the short-run market demand and the short-run market supply curve.

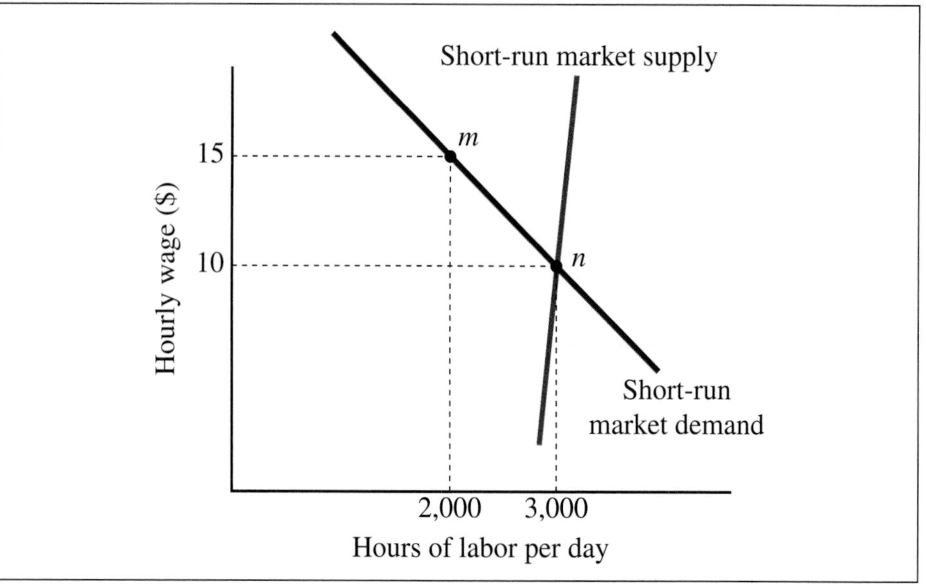

EXPLAINING DIFFERENCES IN WAGES AND INCOME

Now that we know how the equilibrium wage for a particular occupation is determined, we're ready to explain why wages vary from one job to another. Let's think about why some occupations pay more than others, why women earn less than men, and why college graduates earn more than high-school graduates.

Why Do Wages Differ Across Occupations?

There is substantial variation in wages across occupations. Most professional athletes earn more than medical doctors, who in turn earn more than college professors, who earn more than janitors. We'll see that the wage for a particular occupation will be relatively high if the supply of workers in that occupation is small relative to the demand for workers. This is shown in Figure 5: the supply curve intersects the demand curve at a relatively high wage.

The supply of workers in a particular occupation could be relatively small for three reasons.

1. ***Few people with the required skills.*** To play professional baseball, a person must be able to hit balls that are pitched at about 90 miles per hour. The few people who have this skill receive high wages because firms (baseball teams) compete with one another for skillful players and bid up the wage in the process. The same argument applies to other professional athletes, musicians, and actors. The few people who have the skills required for these occupations receive high wages.

2. ***High training costs.*** The skills required for some occupations can only be acquired through education and training. For example, the skills required of a medical doctor can be acquired in medical school, and legal skills can be acquired in law school. If it is costly to acquire these skills, a relatively small number of people will do so, and those people will receive high wages. The higher wage compensates workers for their training costs.

3. ***Undesirable job features.*** Some occupations are dangerous, and a relatively small number of people are willing to work in dangerous occupations. The workers with the greatest risk of dying on the job are lumberjacks, boilermakers, taxicab drivers, bartenders, and mine workers.[3] The workers who choose dangerous occupations

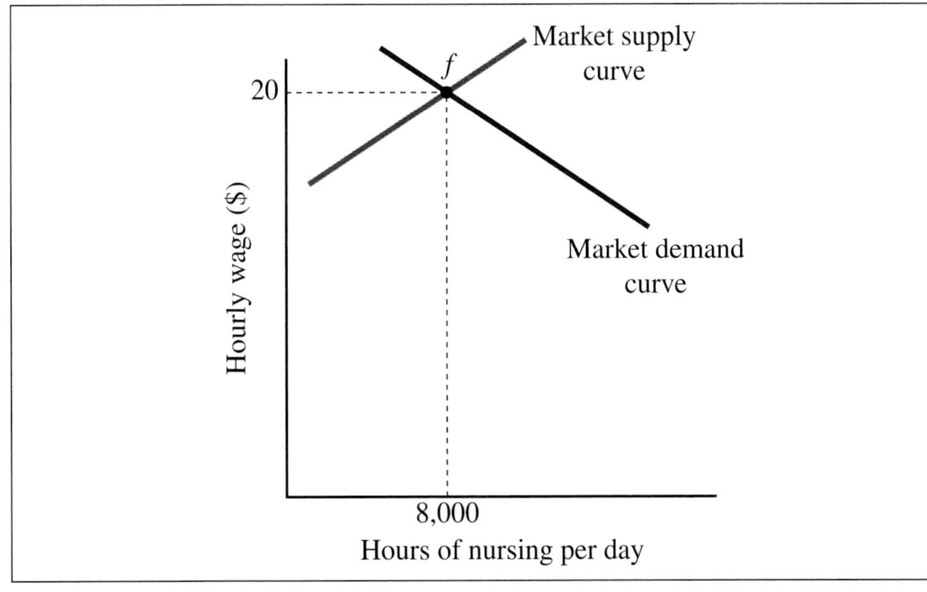

Figure 5

Supply Is Low Relative to Demand

If supply is low relative to demand, the equilibrium wage will be relatively high.

receive relatively high wages, so they are compensated for the danger associated with their jobs. The same logic applies to other undesirable job features. For example, wages are higher for jobs that are stressful or dirty or that force people to work at odd hours.

4. ***Artificial barriers to entry***. As we'll see later, government and professional licensing boards restrict the number of people in certain occupations, and unions restrict their membership. These supply restrictions increase wages.

For some facts on wages in dangerous jobs, read the Closer Look box "High Wages for Steel Workers, Coal Miners, and Bartenders."

A Closer LOOK

High Wages for Steel Workers, Coal Miners, and Bartenders

Why do steel workers earn more than other manufacturing workers? Studies of the labor market have shown that more dangerous jobs pay higher wages.[4] Let's compare the wage for a very safe manufacturing job to the wage in a steel mill. Each year, 1 in 10,000 steel workers is killed on the job. To compensate for the higher risk of dying on the job, steel workers receive a wage premium of 3.7%. If a worker switched from a safe job to an otherwise equivalent job in a steel mill, his or her annual income would increase by about $700. The worker's income would increase by a larger amount if the worker switched to an even more dangerous job, such as coal mining, logging, or bartending.

People with dangerous jobs receive higher wages to compensate for the greater risk of injury.

Why do women, on average, earn less than men? Figure 6 shows the hourly earnings of women as a percentage of the hourly earnings of men in different nations. In the United States the typical woman earns about 75% as much as the typical man. The "gender gap" is smaller in European nations but much larger in Japan.

Why is the gender gap so large? Part of the gender gap is explained by differences in skills and productivity. On average, women in many occupations have less education and less work experience, so they are less productive and are paid less. Another reason for the wage gap is occupational discrimination: Women have been denied access to many occupations, causing them to flood a small number of "female-dominated" occupations such as teaching, nursing, and clerical work. Given the plentiful supply of workers in these female-dominated occupations, wages are relatively low.

What about differences in earnings by race? In 1995, black males who worked full time earned 73% as much as their white counterparts,[4] while black females earned 86% as much as their white counterparts. Hispanic males earned 62% as much as white males, while Hispanic females earned 73% as much as white females. For both males and females, part of the earnings gap is caused by differences in productivity: On average, whites have more education and work experience, so they receive higher wages.

Part of the wage gap is caused by racial discrimination. Some black and Hispanic workers receive lower wages for similar jobs, and others are denied opportunities to work in some high-paying jobs. According to one widely cited study, racial discrimination is responsible for about half the wage gap for males and about 60% of the wage gap for females.[5] If we eliminated racial discrimination in the workplace, black men would earn 86% as much as white men, and black women would earn 96% as much as white women.

Figure 6

Gender Gap: Average Wage of Women as a Percentage of the Average Wage of Men, Selected Nations

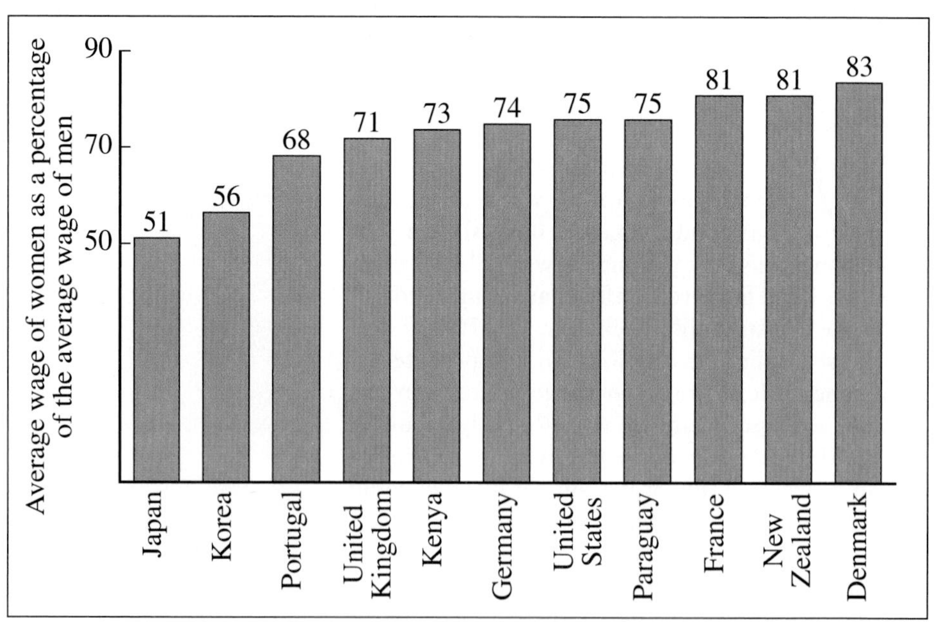

Sources: *Yearbook of Labour Statistics* (Geneva: International Labour Organization, 1994); U.S. Department of Labor, *Employment and Earnings*, vol. 43, no. 1, January 1996.

Why Do College Graduates Earn Higher Wages?

In 1992, the typical college graduate earned 82% more than the typical high-school graduate. Over the last 20 years, this wage gap or "college premium" has almost doubled. There are two explanations for the college premium.

The first explanation uses some simple supply and demand analysis. A college education provides the skills necessary to enter certain occupations, so a college graduate has more job options than a high-school graduate. Both types of workers can fill jobs that require only a high-school education, so the supply of workers for these low-skilled jobs is plentiful and the equilibrium wage for these jobs is relatively low. In contrast, there is a smaller supply of workers for jobs that require a college education, so the wages in these high-skill jobs are relatively high. This is the **learning effect** of a college education: Students learn the skills required for certain occupations.

Learning effect: The increase in a person's wage resulting from the learning of skills required for certain occupations.

The second explanation of the college premium requires a different perspective on college and its role in the labor market. Suppose that there are certain skills required for a particular job but an employer cannot determine whether a potential worker has these skills. For example, most managerial jobs require the worker to manage her time efficiently, but it is impossible for an employer to determine whether a potential worker is a good manager of time. Suppose that these skills are also required to complete a college degree. For example, to get passing grades in all your classes, you must be able to use your time efficiently. When you get your college degree, firms will conclude that you have some of the skills they desire, so they may hire you instead of an equally skilled high-school graduate.

This second explanation of the college premium relies on the **signaling** or **screening effect** of college. The idea is that the completion of college provides a signal to employers about the skills of a potential worker. In other words, colleges indirectly screen job applicants, separating the admissible workers (college graduates) from the inadmissible ones (people who don't complete a degree). This second explanation suggests that colleges don't teach anything but simply provide an environment in which students can reveal their skills to potential employers.

Signaling or **screening effect:** The increase in a person's wage resulting from the signal of productivity provided by completing college.

Both explanations for the college premium are correct. A college education provides new skills and refines other skills, so the learning effect contributes to higher wages for college graduates. In addition, a college education provides a signal to employers about a potential worker's skills, so firms will often choose college graduates instead of high-school graduates. Although it is clear that both the learning effect and the signaling effect contribute to higher earnings for college graduates, it's not clear which of these two effects is more important.

As we saw in the opening paragraph of the chapter, the college premium has almost doubled in the last 20 years. The most important factor in the growing college premium is technological change, which has increased the demand for college graduates relative to the demand for other workers. In all sectors of the economy, firms are switching to sophisticated machinery and equipment that requires highly skilled workers. The share of jobs that require the skills of a college graduate has increased steadily, increasing the demand for college graduates and increasing their wages. Another factor in the growing college premium is the pace of technological change. Workers with more education can more easily learn new skills and new jobs, so firms are willing to pay more for college graduates.

TEST *Your Understanding*

5 The coach of a professional basketball team wants to hire a new player for $3 million per year. Under what circumstances would it be sensible to hire the player?

6 Complete the statement with *demand* or *supply*: The wage for a particular occupation will be relatively low if ____________ is small relative to ____________.

7 The wages of police officers vary from city to city. What could explain the wage differences?

8 In some countries it is customary to tip restaurant waiters. What are the implications for wages of waiters?

9 Would you expect people who work the night shift (midnight to 8 A.M.) to earn higher or lower wages? Explain.

PUBLIC POLICY AND LABOR MARKETS

We can use the model of the labor market to show the effects of public policies on wages and employment. We'll look at three policies: the minimum wage, comparable worth, and occupational licensing. Each of these policies affects one side of the labor market—supply or demand—leading to changes in the equilibrium wage and total employment. We'll also look at the effects of redistribution policies on poverty rates in several industrial nations.

Effects of the Minimum Wage

In 1991, the federal minimum wage increased from $3.80 to $4.25. Figure 7 shows the effects of a minimum wage on the market for restaurant workers. The market equilibrium is shown by point *e*: Supply equals demand at a wage of $4.00 and a quantity of 50,000 hours per day. Suppose that a minimum wage is established at

Figure 7

Market Effects of Minimum Wage

The market equilibrium is shown by point *e:* The wage is $4.00 and the quantity of labor is 50,000 labor hours per day. A minimum wage of $4.40 decreases the quantity of labor demanded to 49,000 hours per day. Although some workers receive a higher wage, others lose their jobs or work fewer hours.

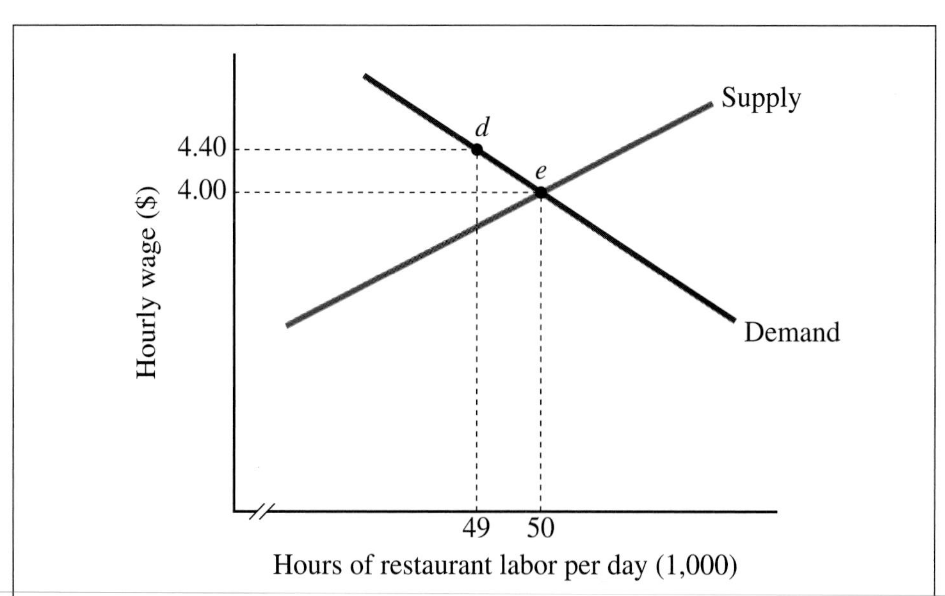

$4.40 per hour. At this wage, the quantity of labor demanded is only 49,000 hours (point *d* on the demand curve). In other words, the minimum wage decreases the quantity of labor used by restaurants by 1,000 hours per day.

What are the trade-offs associated with the minimum wage? From the perspective of restaurant workers, there is good news and bad news.

1. ***Good news for workers.*** Some workers keep their jobs and receive a higher wage ($4.40 per hour instead of $4.00).
2. ***Bad news for workers.*** Some workers lose their jobs. For example, if the typical workday for restaurant workers is 5 hours, the loss of 1,000 hours of restaurant work per day translates into a loss of 200 jobs.

From the perspective of consumers, there is some additional bad news.

3. ***Bad news for consumers.*** The increase in the wage increases the cost of producing restaurant meals, increasing their price.

There are clearly winners and losers from the minimum wage: Workers who keep their jobs gain at the expense of other workers and consumers. For a discussion of the actual effects of a higher minimum wage, read the Closer Look box "The Minimum Wage and the Working Poor."

Comparable Worth

We saw earlier that there is a large gap between the average hourly earnings of men and women. One response to the gender gap is a policy called **comparable worth**, under which the government specifies a minimum wage for some occupations, typically the occupations with a disproportionate number of women. We know that a minimum wage increases the wage of some workers but causes other workers to lose their jobs. The same is true of comparable-worth: Some women in female-dominated occupations would earn higher wages, but others would lose their jobs. In addition, consumers would pay higher prices, just as they will with a minimum wage.

Comparable worth: A policy under which the government specifies a minimum wage for some occupations.

A Closer LOOK

The Minimum Wage and the Working Poor

How would an increase in the minimum wage affect the working poor? The conventional rule of thumb is that a 10% increase in the minimum wage decreases the number of minimum-wage jobs by about 1%. In 1996, Congress considered a 20% increase in the minimum wage, from $4.25 to $5.15. According to the rule of thumb, such a boost in the minimum wage would decrease the number of minimum-wage jobs by 2%, about 120,000 jobs. On the other hand, the 98% of minimum-wage workers who kept their jobs would earn more income: The annual income of a full-time minimum-wage worker would increase from about $8,500 to about $10,300. About two-thirds of minimum-wage workers are adults over 25, and many of these workers provide a large fraction of their families' incomes.[†] For families supported by minimum-wage workers, a boost in the minimum wage is a mixed blessing: It's good news if the workers keep their jobs, but bad news otherwise.

*David Neumark and William Wascher, "Employment Effects of Minimum and Subminimum Wages: Panel on State Minimum Wage Laws," *Industrial and Labor Relations Review,* October 1992, pp. 55–81.

[†]Louis Uchitelle, "Minimum Wage and Jobs," *New York Times,* January 12, 1995, p. C1.

A more direct approach to the problem of the gender gap is to combat occupational discrimination. If the government eliminated the barriers that have excluded women from some occupations, the market would then eliminate the artificial wage gap generated by occupational discrimination. One way to facilitate the movement of women into traditional male occupations is to ensure that the education system provides both men and women with the skills required to work in these occupations.

Occupational Licensing

In some occupations the number of workers is limited by government-sanctioned licensing boards. A licensing board establishes requirements for working in a particular occupation. For example, a person may be prohibited from working in an occupation unless she (1) completes a given educational program, (2) passes an examination, (3) has a certain amount of work experience, and/or (4) has lived in a particular area for some time. Among the workers who are subject to occupational licensing are physicians, dentists, beauticians, plumbers, and pharmacists. In the United States there are over 1,500 occupational licensing boards.[6]

Occupational licensing is controversial. In principle, the licensing requirements are designed to protect consumers from incompetent workers. However, occupational licensing has been criticized on three grounds.

1. ***Weak link between performance and licensing requirements.*** In many cases the licensing requirements seem arbitrary, and there is a relatively weak link between the requirements and the likely performance of the worker.

2. ***Alternative means of protection.*** There are other ways to protect consumers from incompetent workers. The government could provide consumers with information about the past performance of workers. Alternatively, consumers can spread the word about workers' performance, just as they do for other goods and services. Of course, the dissemination of information will work better for some occupations (for example, plumbers and beauticians) than for others (doctors).

3. ***Entry restrictions.*** The licensing requirements increase the cost of entering the occupation, decreasing the supply of workers and increasing the wage.

Figure 8 shows the market effects of occupational licensing for retail pharmacists. Most of the drugs dispensed by retail pharmacists have already been compounded by drug companies, so the principal tasks for a retail pharmacist are counting pills and pasting labels on bottles. To be licensed as a retail pharmacist, a worker can complete a five-year baccalaureate or a six-year doctorate. The market equilibrium with this educational requirement is shown by point *e* in Figure 8: The wage of retail pharmacists is $15 per hour.

What would be the market effects of increasing the educational requirement for retail pharmacists? In 1991, three labor organizations representing over 170,000 pharmacists proposed changes in the licensing of pharmacists that would force all new pharmacists to complete the six-year doctorate program.[7] The increase in the education requirement (from five years to six) would increase the cost of entering the occupation, shifting the supply curve to the left: At every wage, fewer pharmacist hours would be supplied. In Figure 8, the market would move from point *e* to point *g*, increasing the equilibrium wage to $17. In addition, the increase in the wage would increase the cost of producing and selling drugs, increasing the price of drugs. The general lesson is that occupational licensing increases wages, production costs, and prices.

If occupational licensing leads to higher prices, why does it persist for workers such as plumbers, beauticians, and retail pharmacists? Perhaps consumers

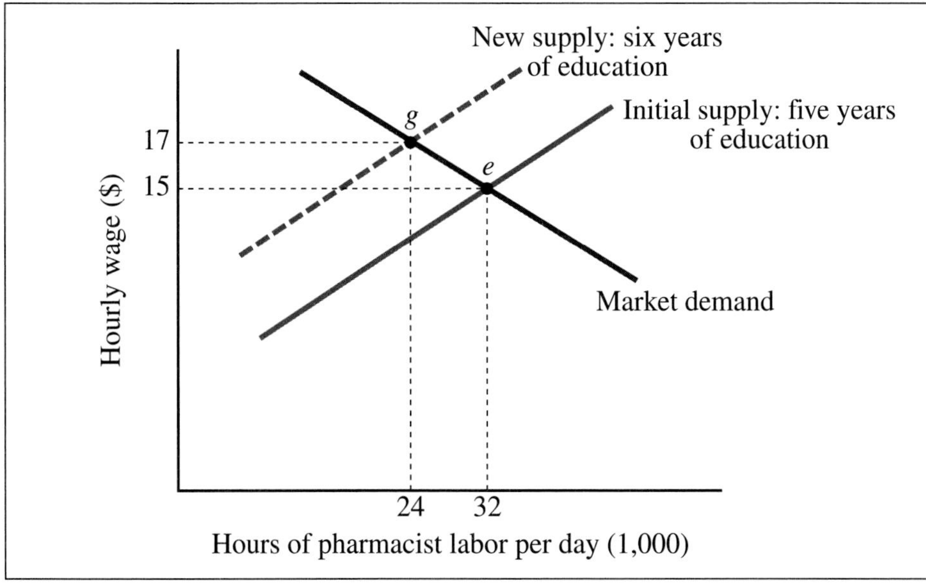

Figure 8

Market Effects of Occupational Licensing

Occupational licensing increases the cost of entering an occupation, shifting the supply curve to the left. Here, an increase in the required education for pharmacists increases the equilibrium wage from $15 to $17 and decreases the equilibrium quantity from 32,000 to 24,000.

believe that licensing protects them from incompetent and unscrupulous workers, and consumers are willing to pay higher prices for this perceived protection. Alternatively, the workers who receive higher wages may be better organized than consumers and thus more effective in influencing public policy. This could be another example of public policy that benefits special-interest groups at the expense of the general public.

TEST *Your Understanding*

10 Imelda works 20 hours per week in a shoe store and is paid the minimum wage. When the government increases the minimum wage by $1, she rejoices, saying "I will be better off by $20 per week." Is her calculation correct?

11 Suppose that your state has a referendum on a new comparable-worth policy for state workers. For any job in which at least 60% of the workers are women, the wage would increase by 15%. Would you vote for or against this policy? Explain the logic behind your vote.

12 Complete the statement with *increases* or *decreases*: Occupational licensing increases the cost of entering an occupation, so it ____________ supply, ____________ the wage, and ____________ the price of goods produced by the licensed occupation.

LABOR UNIONS

We've used a simple model of supply and demand to explain differences in wages and explore the effects of public policies. Our analysis is based on the assumption that workers take the market wage as given. A **labor union** is an organized group of workers, the main objective of which is to improve working conditions, wages, and fringe benefits. In other words, workers in a union do not take wages as given, but try to increase them.

Labor union: An organized group of workers, the main objective of which is to improve working conditions, wages, and fringe benefits.

Brief History of Labor Unions in the United States

Today about one-sixth of all workers in the United States belong to a union, down from about one-third of workers 40 years ago. There are two types of unions.

Craft union: A labor organization that includes workers from a particular occupation, for example, plumbers, bakers, or electricians.

Industrial union: A labor organization that includes all types of workers from a single industry, for example, steelworkers or autoworkers.

- A **craft union** includes workers from a particular occupation, for example, plumbers, bakers, or electricians.
- An **industrial union** includes all types of workers from a single industry, for example, steel workers or autoworkers.

There are also umbrella organizations that include many individual unions. The largest of these "unions of unions" is the AFL–CIO (the American Federation of Labor–Congress of Industrial Organizations).

Let's take a brief look at the history of labor organizations in the United States. In the nineteenth century, there were all sorts of craft unions, and the main umbrella organizations were the Knights of Labor (founded in 1869) and the AFL (founded in 1881). The CIO (formed in 1931) was a collection of industrial unions that represented semiskilled workers involved in mass production, including workers in the automobile, rubber, and steel industries. The CIO merged with the AFL in 1955. The most important recent trend has been the expansion of unions serving workers in the public sector. In the last 30 years, the number of government workers in unions and employee associations has more than doubled.

Labor unions get their power to influence labor markets from the states and the national government. Let's take a brief look at the most important pieces of labor legislation.

- The Wagner Act (1935) guaranteed workers the right to join unions and required each firm to bargain with a union formed by a majority of its workers. The National Labor Relations Board (NLRB) was established to enforce the provisions of the Wagner Act.
- The Taft–Harley Act (1947) gave government the power to stop strikes that "imperiled the national health or safety" and gave the states the right to pass "right-to-work" laws. These laws, which are currently in force in 21 states, outlaw *union shops*, defined as a workplace where union membership is required.
- The Landrum–Griffin Act (1959) was a response to allegations of corruption and misconduct by union officials. The act guaranteed union members the right to fair elections, made it easier to monitor union finances, and made the theft of union funds a federal offense.

How does participation in unions vary across developed nations? As shown in Figure 9, 16% of U.S. workers belong to unions, compared to 29% in Canada, 40% in Italy, and 87% in Sweden.

Labor Unions and Wages

One of the goals of a union is to increase the wages of its members, and there is evidence that unions do indeed raise wages. The definitive study of unions concluded that unionized workers earn between 20 and 30% more than their nonunion counterparts.[8] Let's look at three ways a union could try to increase the wages of its members.

The first approach is to organize workers and negotiate a higher wage. Suppose that workers in a particular industry form an industrial union and agree on a union wage that exceeds the equilibrium wage. Like a minimum wage imposed by a government, a union wage generates a trade-off between wages and

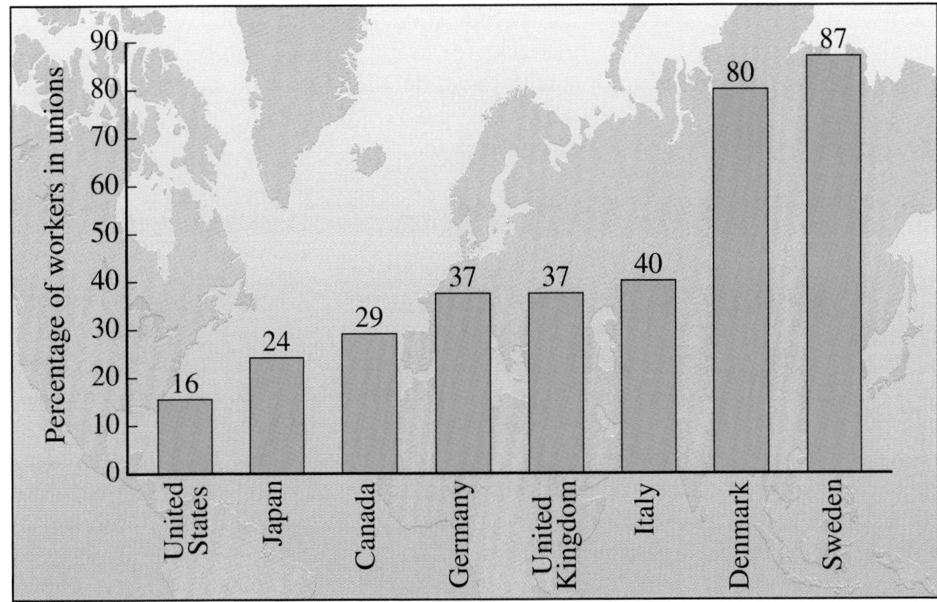

Figure 9

Union Membership in Various Countries, 1994

Union membership varies across developed nations, from 16% in the United States to 87% in Sweden.

Source: U.S. Department of Labor, *Foreign Labor Trends, Selected Countries* (Washington, DC: U.S. Government Printing Office, 1995).

total employment: Although some workers will earn higher wages, other people who would be willing to work will not have the opportunity to do so. To deal with this problem, the union can restrict membership or share the smaller number of jobs among its members.

A second way to increase the wage of union workers is to promote the products produced by union workers. You've probably seen advertisements encouraging people to "buy products with the union label." The demand for labor is a derived demand, so an increase in the demand for a final good will increase the demand for labor, increasing the equilibrium wage. This approach can be used together with a union wage to prevent an excess supply of labor at the higher wage.

A third approach—which may or may not increase wages—is to impose work rules that increase the amount of labor required to produce a given quantity of output. One example of "featherbedding" is a minimum crew size, which forces a firm to hire more workers than it needs to perform a particular task. For example, the typical unionized airline hires three workers to guide an airplane into the gate, while nonunion airlines use only two workers. In the past, railroad unions forced railroads to use firemen (whose job is to shovel coal) on diesel-powered engines.

Featherbedding may or may not increase the demand for labor. Although featherbedding forces the firm to use more labor per unit of output, it also decreases the quantity of output. A firm suffering from featherbedding hires workers it doesn't need, so its production costs will be relatively high. Firms will increase their prices to cover these extra production costs, and consumers will respond by purchasing less output. Therefore, the direct effect of featherbedding (an increase in the amount of labor for a given quantity of output) will be at least partly offset by a decrease in output. The demand for labor is derived from the demand for the final good, so featherbedding may actually decrease the demand for labor, decreasing the wage and total employment.

A different approach to managing union employment comes from Volkswagen A.G., Europe's largest automaker. In 1993, the firm got its labor unions to switch to a 4-day, 28-hour workweek, down from a 5-day, 36-hour workweek. If workers hadn't accepted the shorter workweek and lower pay, Volkswagen would have eliminated 30,000 of its 100,000 jobs in Germany. In other words, the switch to the shorter workweek preserved 30,000 union jobs in the automobile industry.[9] Some analysts suggest that shorter workweeks for union workers will become more common as European unions grapple with lower demand for their workers.

Do Labor Unions Increase Productivity?

We've seen that unions lead to higher wages and work rules that are designed to decrease labor productivity. In other words, there are some costs associated with labor unions. Are there any positive aspects of unions?

Unions may increase productivity by facilitating communication between workers and managers. If a worker is unhappy with his or her job, one option is to quit. From the firm's perspective, this is costly because the firm loses an experienced worker and must train a new one. A dissatisfied worker who belongs to a union has a second option: The worker can use the union as an intermediary to discuss job issues with managers. This sort of communication can solve problems before they become so severe that the worker quits. There is evidence that union firms have lower turnover rates, in part because they facilitate communication between workers and managers.[10] These lower turnover rates lead to lower training costs and a more experienced workforce, so there are some positive aspects of unions. There is no consensus among economists whether the benefits associated with better communication dominate the costs of unions (higher wages and disruptive work rules).

OTHER IMPERFECTIONS IN THE LABOR MARKET

So far, our analysis of the labor market has been based on two key assumptions. First, there is perfect information in the labor market. Second, employers take the market wage as given. Let's see what happens when these assumptions are not satisfied.

Imperfect Information and Efficiency Wages

What happens when workers have better information than their employers? Workers differ in their skill levels and the amount of effort they exert on the job. Employers cannot always distinguish between skillful and unskillful workers or between hard workers and lazy ones. In other words, there is asymmetric information in the labor market.

We know from our discussion of the market for used cars that asymmetric information causes high- and low-quality goods to be sold in a mixed market at a single price. Suppose that there are two types of workers: low skill (marginal revenue product = \$100 per day) and high skill (marginal revenue product = \$200 per day), and the employer cannot distinguish between them. Employers will offer a single wage, realizing that they will probably hire some workers of each type.

What is the appropriate wage? Suppose that the opportunity cost of high-skill workers is \$130 and a firm offers a wage of \$110. Because the wage is less than the opportunity cost of high-skill workers, only low-skill workers will apply for jobs. The firm will lose money because the wage (\$110) exceeds the marginal revenue product of the low-skill workers (\$100). To get some high-skill workers, the employer must pick a wage that exceeds their opportunity cost (\$130). As the firm increases its wage, it will attract more high-skill workers, and the average productivity of its workforce will increase. Depending on the responses of the two types of workers to the higher wage, a firm could actually make more profit by offering a higher wage. This is known as *paying efficiency wages*: The firm pays a higher wage to increase the average productivity of its workforce.

Another reason for paying relatively high wages is to encourage employees to work hard. Firms realize that their employees can vary their work efforts, with the extremes being working hard and hardly working (shirking). To encourage their employees to work hard, employers fire workers who are caught shirking. The penalty associated with being fired will be much greater if the firm pays a wage above the worker's opportunity cost. For example, suppose that a worker could earn $80 per day in another job. If the firm pays its workers $100 per day, a worker who is fired—and then immediately gets a job with another firm—would take a pay cut of $20 per day. This is another example of paying efficiency wages: By increasing the wage, the firm increases the work effort of its employees and increases the average productivity of its workforce.

ECONOMIC DETECTIVE- *Higher Wages at Ford Motor Company*

In the early days of the automobile industry, the prevailing wage for autoworkers was $3 per day. The assembly-line jobs were repetitive and tedious, and the turnover rate of workers was very high. When Henry Ford decided to increase the daily wage for his workers from $3 to $5, most observers were baffled. They figured that Ford's labor costs would be almost twice as high as his rivals, so he would lose a lot of money and quickly go out of business. The wage hike appeared to be a great act of generosity—but very bad business. You can imagine their surprise when Ford's profit doubled from $30 million to $60 million. How was this possible? How can higher wages lead to higher profits?

The key to solving this puzzle is the concept of efficiency wages. When Ford raised the wage, the average productivity of Ford workers increased dramatically, a result of several changes in the workforce.[11]

- The pool of job applicants improved, so Ford could choose better workers.
- Fewer workers were fired for shirking.

People were baffled when Henry Ford increased the daily wage for his assembly workers from $3 to $5.

- Fewer workers quit voluntarily.
- The rate of absenteeism decreased.

In the words of Henry Ford, "There was no charity in any way involved. . . . The payment of five dollars a day for an eight-hour day was one of the finest cost cutting moves we ever made."

Monopsony Power

Monopsony: A market in which there is a single buyer of an input.

We've assumed that each employer is such a small part of the labor market that it takes the market wage as given. Although this is true for many labor markets, in some markets there is a single employer. For example, if your city has a single hospital, there will be a single employer of surgical nurses. This is the case of **monopsony:** There is a single buyer of a particular input.

A monopsonist faces a positively sloped supply curve for labor. It is the only employer, so its hiring decisions affect the market wage. If the firm decides to hire more workers, it must pay a higher wage to attract them away from other firms. Similarly, if the firm decides to hire fewer workers, it can pay the remaining workers a lower wage. In other words, a monopsonist picks a point along the market supply curve for labor. The monopsonist will control its labor costs by picking a relatively low wage, in the process hiring a relatively small quantity of labor.

You may have noticed the similarity between a monopsonist and a monopolist. A monopolist (a single seller) uses its market power to *increase the price of output*, while a monopsonist (a single buyer) uses its market power to *decrease the wage*. The monopolist produces an artificially small quantity of *output*, while the monopsonist hires an artificially small quantity of a particular *input* (labor). Table 2 summarizes the key features of a monopolist and a monopsonist.

What is the role of a labor union in a labor market with a single buyer? Monopsony leads to an artificially low wage and a union leads to an artificially high wage. A market with both a union and a monopsonist will have a wage somewhere between the two extremes, depending on the bargaining power of the two sides. In other words, it may be sensible to counteract market power on the demand side of the market (a monopsony) with market power on the supply side (a union).

TEST *Your Understanding*

13 Explain how an increase in the wage can increase the average productivity of the firm's workforce.

14 Suppose that a union's objective is to maximize total employment in a certain occupation and it cannot affect the demand for labor. The firms in the market take the wage as given. What should the union do?

Table 2: Monopoly versus Monopsony

Monopoly	*Monopsony*
Single seller of output	Single buyer of input
High price of output	Low price of input
Small quantity of output	Small quantity of input

15 Suppose that a union's objective is to maximize the total income of nurses (total money spent by firms on nurses). At the current wage, the price elasticity of demand for nurses is 1.50. Should the union increase or decrease the union wage? Explain.

16 Complete the statement with *high* or *low*: A monopolist sells its output at a relatively ____________ price, while a monopsonist buys its inputs at a relatively ____________ price.

Using the **TOOLS**

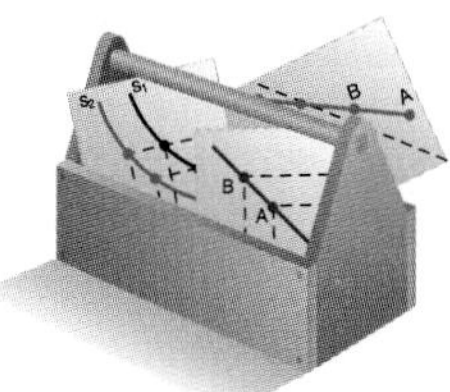

You've learned how to use supply and demand curves to explain differences in wages and predict the effects of public policy on the equilibrium wage and employment. You've also learned about effects of unions and the rationale for paying a wage above the equilibrium wage. Here are some opportunities to do your own economic analysis.

1. Market Effects of Immigration

In the initial equilibrium, the wage for farmworkers is $5 per hour. The elasticity of supply of farmworkers is 2.0 and the elasticity of demand for farmworkers is 1.0. Suppose that immigration increases the supply of farmworkers by 12%: The supply curve shifts to the right by 12%.

a. Predict the effect of immigration on the wage paid to farmworkers: By how much will the wage increase or decrease?

b. How will immigration affect the cost of producing food and the equilibrium price of food?

2. Effects of a Nurses' Union

Suppose that the nurses in the city of Florence form a union: To work as a nurse, you must belong to the union. The nurses do not allow new nurses to join the union, so the supply of nurses decreases by 3% per year as old nurses retire. The initial equilibrium (before the union) is shown in Figure 1 (page 334): The wage is $15 and the quantity is 16,000 hours per day.

a. Depict graphically the effect of the union on the nursing market.

b. If the price elasticity of demand for nursing is 1.5, by what percentage will the wage of nursing increase each year?

3. Demand for Newskids

Consider the market for newspaper delivery kids in Kidsville. Each newskid receives a piece rate of $2 per subscriber per month and has a fixed territory that initially has 100 subscribers. The price elasticity of demand for subscriptions is 2.0. Suppose that the new city council of Kidsville passes a law that establishes a minimum piece rate of $3 per subscriber per month. As a result, the publisher increases the monthly price of a subscription by 20%. How will the new law affect the monthly income of the typical newskid?

4. Equilibrium with Efficiency Wages

Consider a labor market with asymmetric information: Each worker knows his or her marginal revenue product, but firms cannot distinguish between low- and high-skill workers. Each low-skill worker has an opportunity cost of $80 and a marginal revenue product of $100, and each high-skill worker has an opportunity cost of $130 and a marginal revenue product of $200. The workforce is divided equally between the two types of workers. Your job is to predict the equilibrium wage in the market given that each firm takes the price as given and earns zero economic profit. Try the following wages: (a) $90, (b) $100, (c) $140, (d) $150, (e) $170.

SUMMARY

We've seen how wages are determined in perfectly labor competitive markets and why wages differ from one occupation to another. We've also explored the effects of various market imperfections—public policies, unions, and imperfect information—on wages and employment. Here are the main points of the chapter.

1. The wage in a particular occupation will be relatively high if supply is small relative to demand. This will occur if (a) few people have the skills required for the occupation, (b) training costs are relatively high, or (c) the job is relatively dangerous or stressful.
2. College graduates earn more than high-school graduates because a college education provides new skills and allows people to reveal their skills to employers.
3. There are trade-offs with a minimum wage or a union wage: Some workers earn higher income, but others lose their jobs.
4. Occupational discrimination decreases the wage of women and minorities.
5. Occupational licensing increases the wage of the licensed occupation and increases the price of the good produced by that occupation.
6. A firm that increases its wage may increase the average productivity of its workers and increase its profit.

KEY TERMS

comparable worth, *345*
craft union, *348*
derived demand, *334*
industrial union, *348*
input-substitution effect, *335*
labor union, *347*
learning effect, *343*
long-run demand curve for labor, *334*
marginal product of labor, *338*
marginal revenue product of labor, *338*
market supply curve for labor, *333*
monopsony, *352*
output effect, *335*
short-run demand curve for labor, *339*
signaling or **screening effect,** *343*

PROBLEMS AND DISCUSSION QUESTIONS

1. You are an economic consultant to a city that just imposed a payroll tax of $1 per hour of work. This payroll tax is paid by workers through a payroll deduction: For each hour of work, the employer deducts $1 and sends the money to the city government. The initial wage (before the tax) is $10, and total employment is 20,000 hours per day. Use a graph to show the effect of the tax on the equilibrium wage and employment.
2. We discussed the response of three hypothetical workers (Lester, Sam, and Maureen) to an increase in the wage. Which person's response is closest to your own? If your wage increased, would you work more hours, fewer hours, or about the same number of hours?
3. Critically appraise the following statement from Mr. Chuckles: "The law of supply says that an increase in price increases the quantity supplied.

A decrease in the income tax rate will increase the worker's net wage, so each worker will work more hours. As a result, the revenue from the income tax will increase."

4. Draw two supply curves for carpenters, one for the city of Portland and one for the United States. Explain any differences between the two curves.
5. The advocates of higher salaries for teachers point out that most teachers have college degrees, and that the teaching of our children is an important job.
   a. Why aren't teachers' salaries higher given the importance of the job and the education required?
   b. Suppose that a law is passed that requires teachers to be paid the same hourly wage as college graduates who work in business. Predict the effects of this law on the market for teachers.
6. Appraise the following statement: "There is no substitute for an airline pilot: Someone has to fly the plane. Therefore, an increase in the wage of airline pilots will not change the number of pilots used by the airlines."
7. Suppose that a new government program improves worker safety in coal mines. Use a graph to predict the effect of the program on the equilibrium wage for coal workers.
8. Under some occupational licensing laws, licensed members of an occupation write licensing exams. An example is the bar exam for licensing lawyers. How might this practice limit entry into an occupation?

Take It to the Net

We invite you to visit the O'Sullivan/Sheffrin page on the Prentice Hall Web site at:

http://www.prenhall.com/osullivan/

for this chapter's World Wide Web exercise.

MODEL ANSWERS FOR THIS CHAPTER

Chapter-Opening Questions

1. When the wage increases, some people work more, others work less, and others work about the same amount.
2. As shown in A Closer Look: High Wages for Steel Workers, Coal Miners, and Bartenders, the worker's income would increase by about 3.7%, or about $700.
3. The gender gap results from differences in skills and productivity and occupational discrimination.
4. An increase in the wage decreases the quantity of labor demanded, so some workers will lose their jobs, and others will be forced to work fewer hours.
5. Henry Ford described the wage hike as "one of the finest cost cutting moves we ever made."

Test Your Understanding

1. You will work 30 hours per week instead of 20 hours.
2. No. An increase in the wage will increase the number of workers because of changes in occupational choices and migration.
3. decrease, decrease, increase, increase
4. As the wage increases, the firm will substitute other inputs for the relatively expensive labor.
5. If the marginal revenue product of the new player exceeds $3 million. If the player increased attendance and increased the revenue from ticket sales by $4 million, it would be sensible to hire the player.
6. demand, supply
7. Wages are higher in cities where police officers face a greater chance of being killed on the job.
8. Waiters in tipping countries will have lower wages than those in nontipping countries.
9. Working the night shift disrupts sleeping and eating patterns and a person's social life. Because of these undesirable consequences, we except night-shift workers to receive higher wages than their day-shift counterparts.
10. Imelda's statement could be incorrect for three reasons. First, she may lose her job as a result of the higher minimum wage. Second, if she keeps her job, her employer may ask her to work fewer hours per week. Third, as a consumer, she will pay higher prices for the goods produced by minimum-wage workers, partly offsetting any increase in income she experiences.

11. Obviously, a person's vote is determined by the perceived personal benefits and costs as well as personal preferences concerning equity and fairness. The policy will increase taxes and may decrease the number of workers hired by the state but will also generate benefits for some state workers.
12. decreases, increases, increases
13. The firm will attract better applicants and workers are less likely to shirk.
14. Total employment is maximized at the intersection of supply and demand, so the union should do nothing and let the market reach equilibrium.
15. We know that if demand is elastic, an decrease in price will increase total expenditures (total revenue, total income). Therefore, the union should decrease its wage.
16. high, low

Using the Tools

1. Market Effects of Immigration
   a. Immigration will shift the supply curve to the right, decreasing the equilibrium wage. We can use the price-change formula for an increase in supply explained in Chapter 5 to predict the change in the equilibrium wage (the price of labor):

$$\% \text{ change in price} = \frac{\% \text{ change in supply}}{E_s + E_d}$$

$$= \frac{12\%}{2+1} = 4\%$$

   The wage will decrease from $5.00 to $4.80.

   b. The cost of producing food will decrease, so the price of food will decrease.
2. Effects of a Nurses Union
   a. The union causes movement upward along the market demand curve as the number of nurses decreases by 3% per year.
   b. The quantity of labor decreases by 3% per year. To compute the resulting change in price, we can use the formula for price elasticity of demand:

$$E_d = \frac{\% \text{ change in quantity}}{\% \text{ change in price}}$$

$$1.50 = \frac{3\%}{2\%}$$

   To be consistent with an elasticity of 1.5, a 3% decrease in quantity generates a 2% increase in the wage.
3. Demand for Newskids

   The elasticity of demand is 2.0, so a 20% increase in price will decrease the quantity demanded by 40%:

$$E_d = \frac{\% \text{ change in quantity}}{\% \text{ change in price}}$$

$$2.0 = \frac{40\%}{20\%}$$

   To be consistent with an elasticity of 2.0, the percentage change in quantity must be twice the percentage change in price. In other words, the number of subscribers per newskid will decrease from 100 to 60. The income of the typical newskid will decrease from $200 ($2 × 100 subscribers) to $180 ($3 × 60 subscribers). This is the output effect in action.
4. Equilibrium with Efficiency Wages
   a. Wage = $90. Each firm will get all low-skill workers, each with a marginal revenue product (MRP) of $100. Each firm will make a profit, so this is not an equilibrium. Competition among the firms will bid up the wage.
   b. Wage = $100. Each firm will get all low-skill workers, each with a MRP of $100. Each firm will make zero economic profit, so this is an equilibrium wage.
   c. Wage = $140. Each firm will get half low-skill workers and half high-skill workers, so the average MRP will be $150. Each firm will make a profit, so this is not an equilibrium. Competition among the firms will bid up the wage.
   d. Wage = $150. Each firm will get half low-skill workers and half high-skill workers, so the average MRP will be $150. Each firm will make zero economic profit, so this is an equilibrium.
   e. Wage = $170. Each firm will get half low-skill workers and half high-skill workers, so the average MRP will be $150. Each firm will lose money, so this is not an equilibrium.

NOTES

1. W. Michael Fox and Beverly J. Fox, "What's Happening to Americans' Income?" *The Southwest Economy*, Federal Reserve Bank of Dallas, Issue 2, 1995, pp. 3–6.
2. Mark Killingsworth, *Labor Supply* (New York: Cambridge University Press, 1983).
3. Craig Olson, "An Analysis of Wage Differentials Received by Workers on Dangerous Jobs," *Journal of Human Resources*, vol. 16, Spring 1981, pp. 167–85.
4. U.S. Department of Labor, Employment and Earnings (Washington, DC: U.S. Government Printing Office, 1996).
5. Mary Corcoran and Greg J. Duncan, "Work History, Labor Force Attachment, and Earnings Differences Between the Races and Sexes," *Journal of Human Resources*, 14, Winter 1979.
6. Werner Hirsch, *Law and Economics: An Introductory Analysis*, 2nd ed. (San Diego, CA: Academic Press, 1988), pp. 347–350.
7. Lawrence J. McQuillan, "Pharmacists' Proposal Will Raise Costs of Medicine," *The Margin*, Spring 1993, p. 52.
8. Richard B. Freeman and James Medoff, *What Do Unions Do?* (New York: Basic Books, 1985).
9. Ferdinand Protzman, "VW Plan for 4-Day Workweek Is Adopted," *New York Times*, November 26, 1993, p. D11; Tyler Marshall, "VW, Unions, OK 20% Reduction in Work Week," *Los Angeles Times*, November 26, 1993, p. A1; "Worldwire," *Wall Street Journal*, July 8, 1994, p. A5.
10. Freeman and Medoff, *What Do Unions Do?*
11. J. R. Lee, "So-Called Profit Sharing System in the Ford Plant," *Annals of the American Academy of Political and Social Science*, May 1915, pp. 297–310; David Halberstam, *The Reckoning* (New York: William Morrow, 1986), pp. 91–92; Daniel M. G. Graff and Lawrence H. Summers, "Did Henry Ford Pay Efficiency Wages?" *Discussion Paper 1287*, December 1986, Harvard Institute of Economic Research.

CHAPTER 18

Interest Rates and Present Value

A group of scientists use the "doomsday clock" to indicate their assessment of the likelihood of nuclear war. As the likelihood of nuclear war increases, the time on the clock moves closer to midnight, the time at which nuclear war is a virtual certainty. In 1984, the clock showed 3 minutes before midnight, reflecting the accelerating arms race and tensions between the United States and the Soviet Union. By the end of 1991, the Soviet Union had collapsed and the Strategic Arms Reduction Treaty had been signed. To reflect the smaller likelihood of nuclear war, the scientists who operate the clock moved the time back to 17 minutes before midnight. How will the decrease in the threat of nuclear war affect the amount of money people save? How will it affect interest rates?

People save money with the idea of spending their savings—along with the accumulated interest—some time in the future. The threat of nuclear war discourages saving because people realize that they might not be alive to spend their savings—or if they survive, there might not be anything to buy. As the threat of nuclear war diminishes, people will save more money to prepare themselves for a more secure future, and interest rates will decrease.[1] The cost of borrowing money will decrease, so firms will build more production facilities and more families will be able to afford their own houses.

The threat of war is only one of the factors that affects interest rates. We'll use a model of supply and demand to show how interest rates are determined and explain why a savings account earns a lower interest rate than a *bond* (a promissory note issued by a corporation or a government when it borrows money). We also explain a simple rule that you can use to decide how to invest your money. Here are some of the practical questions we answer:

1. Why do the rules used for awarding financial aid to college students discourage their families from saving money?
2. Which industrial nation has the highest saving rate, and which nation has the lowest?
3. Which is riskier, a corporate bond or a share of corporate stock?
4. You currently pay $360 per year for cable-TV service, but you could switch to a digital satellite system (DSS) with a one-time hook-up fee of $700 and an annual fee of $200. Should you switch?
5. Suppose that the cost of your college degree is $140,000. If the degree increases your annual income by $20,000, is it worthwhile?

THE MARKET FOR LOANABLE FUNDS AND INTEREST RATES

Let's start with a discussion of the market forces—supply and demand—that determine interest rates. In the **market for loanable funds**, the suppliers are people who save money, and the demanders are people who borrow money. The price of loanable funds is the **interest rate**, the amount of money paid for the use of a dollar for a year. In some cases, banks act as financial intermediaries in the market for loanable funds: They pay interest to people who deposit funds in bank accounts, and charge interest to people and corporations who borrow the money. We start our discussion of the market for loanable funds with suppliers (savers), and then turn to demanders (borrowers).

Market for loanable funds: A market in which savers (the suppliers of funds) and borrowers (the demanders of funds) interact to determine the equilibrium interest rate (the price of loanable funds).

Interest rate: The amount of money paid for the use of a dollar for a year.

The Market Supply Curve

The principal question about saving is: How much money will people save at each interest rate? Let's think about how individual savers respond to an increase in the interest rate. Suppose that the interest rate is 4% and each person saves $1,000 per year in a savings account. At the end of a year, each person will have $1,040 in his or her savings account ($1,040 = $1,000 + $40 in interest). If the interest rate increases to 10%, people will respond in three ways.

1. ***Party now.*** Save less and spend more this year. The higher interest rate means that each dollar saved earns more interest ($1.10 instead of just $1.04), so a person can save less than $1,000 and still have the same amount of money to spend next year. Specifically, a person who saved only $946 would have over $1,040 one year later, so there would be $54 for a party this year ($1,000 – $946 = $54).

2. ***Party later.*** Save the same amount this year and spend more next year. The higher interest rate means that a person who continues to save $1,000 this year will have more money to spend next year ($1,100 instead of $1,040), so there would be $60 for a party next year.

3. ***Party hearty later.*** Save more this year and spend much more next year. A person who saves more than $1,000 will have much more money to spend next year. For example, a person who saves $1,200 will have $1,320 instead of just $1,040, so there would be $280 for a party next year.

Each of these choices is plausible, so an increase in the interest rate could increase, decrease, or not change the amount of money saved by an individual.

Supply curve for loanable funds: A curve that shows the relationship between the interest rate and the quantity of loanable funds supplied by savers.

The **supply curve for loanable funds** shows the relationship between the interest rate and the total amount of money saved—and available to be loaned. To find a point on the supply curve, we pick an interest rate and then add up the amounts saved by each person in the economy at that interest rate. In Figure 1 the market supply curve is positively sloped, consistent with the law of supply: The higher the price (the interest rate), the larger the quantity supplied. An increase in the interest rate causes some people to save less and others to save more. Empirical studies of saving behavior suggest that on average, people save more at higher interest rates, so the supply curve is positively sloped.[2] For example, an increase in the interest rate from 4% to 6% increases the amount saved from $500 million (point *e*) to $550 million (point *h*).

What matters to potential savers is the net benefit from saving money. If there were no taxes, the net benefit would be determined exclusively by the market interest rate. Because taxes decrease the net benefit from savings, they decrease the amount of money saved, decreasing the supply of loanable funds. For another example of a public policy that discourages savings, read the Closer Look box "Financial Aid and Household Savings."

The Market Demand Curve

The demand for loanable funds comes from households, firms, and government. Households borrow money to purchase expensive goods such as houses and cars. Firms borrow money to purchase production facilities such as buildings, machines, and

Figure 1

Equilibrium in the Market for Loanable Funds

At the market equilibrium (point *e*, with interest rate = 4% and quantity = $500 million per year), the amount of funds supplied (savings) equals the amount demanded (borrowing).

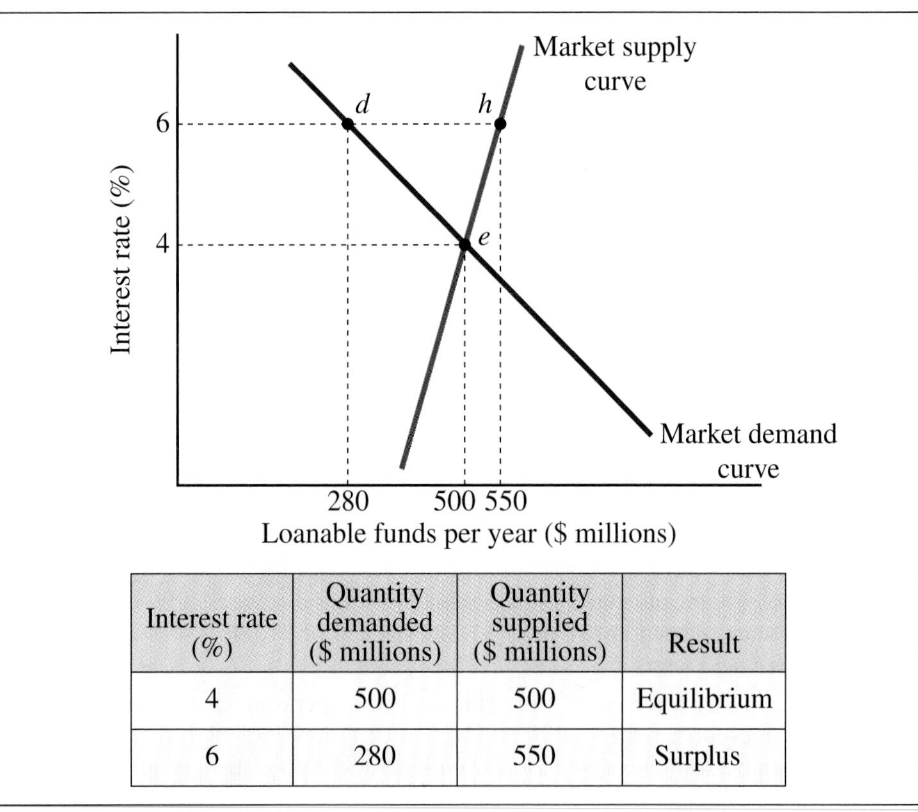

Interest rate (%)	Quantity demanded ($ millions)	Quantity supplied ($ millions)	Result
4	500	500	Equilibrium
6	280	550	Surplus

A Closer LOOK

Financial Aid and Household Savings

According to a recent study, the rules used to award financial aid to college students cause families with college-bound children to save less money.* These rules cut the accumulated savings of the typical family in half, from $46,000 to $23,000. What's the connection between financial aid and savings?

Most U.S. colleges provide financial aid to needy students. To determine the financial need of a particular student, colleges use a two-step process.†

1. The suggested parental contribution depends on the family's income and the value of its assets (the family home, bank accounts, stocks, and bonds).
2. The student's financial need equals the annual cost of attending college minus the parental contribution and a $3,000 student contribution.

For example, if the suggested parental contribution is $8,000 and the annual cost of attending college is $15,000, the student's financial need is $4,000. Most colleges provide financial aid equal to the student's financial need.

How does this method of determining financial aid affect the saving behavior of families with college-bound students? If a family places $1,000 in a money-market account with an interest rate of 5%, the family will earn $50 in the first year. If the family has a student in college, however, the $1,000 increase in the family's assets will decrease the student's "financial need," so the college will cut its financial aid by about $20 per year, leaving the family with a net benefit of only $30 ($50 in interest − $20 in extra college costs). The financial-aid rules decrease the net return from saving from 5% to 3%, and households respond by saving less money.

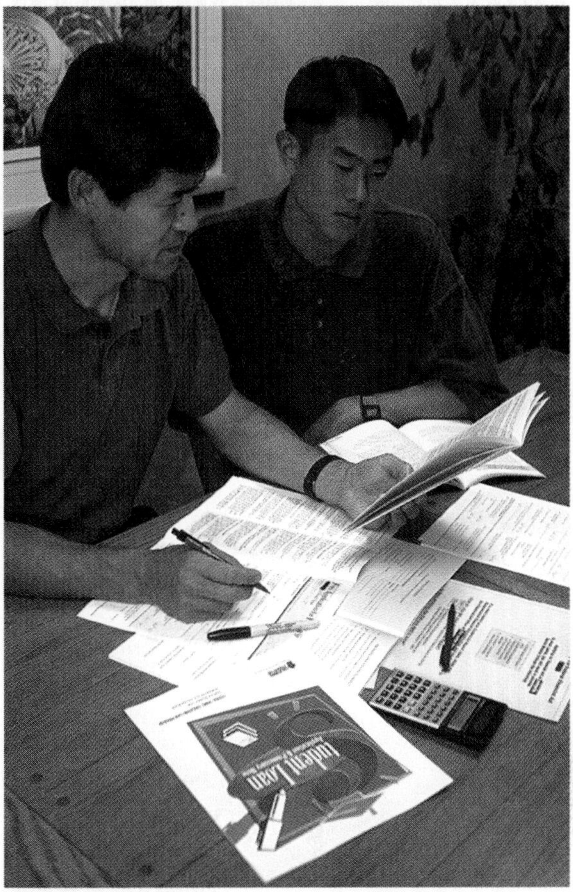

The rules for financial aid to college students discourage saving by the families of college students.

*Martin Feldstein, "College Scholarship Rules and Private Saving," *American Economic Review*, vol. 85, June 1995, pp. 552–556.

†Aaron S. Edlin, "Is College Financial Aid Equitable and Efficient?" *Journal of Economic Perspectives*, vol. 7, Spring 1993, pp. 143–158.

equipment. Governments borrow money to build public facilities such as highways, schools, dams, and prisons. The federal government borrows money to cover the difference between its tax revenue and its expenditures. We'll see that when the price of loanable funds (the interest rate) increases, households, firms, and government will be willing to borrow less money.

Demand curve for loanable funds: A curve that shows the relationship between the interest rate and the quantity of loanable funds demanded by borrowers.

The **demand curve for loanable funds** shows the relationship between the interest rate and the amount of loanable funds demanded. In Figure 1 the demand curve is negatively sloped, consistent with the law of demand: The higher the interest rate, the smaller the amount of funds demanded. For example, at an interest rate of 4%, the quantity demanded is $500 million (point *e*), compared to only $280 million at an interest rate of 6% (point *d*). To explain the negative slope, let's think about how potential borrowers respond to an increase in the interest rate.

1. *Consumers will borrow less.* An increase in the interest rate increases the cost of borrowing money to purchase houses, cars, and other expensive goods. Households will respond by delaying the purchase of these goods or buying less expensive goods, so they will borrow less money.

2. *Firms will borrow less.* An increase in the interest rate increases the cost of borrowing money to build production facilities, and firms will pass on at least part of the higher cost to their consumers in the form of higher prices. According to the law of demand, an increase in price will decrease the quantity demanded, so firms will sell less output and need fewer production facilities—or smaller ones. As a result, firms will borrow less money.

3. *Government will borrow less.* An increase in the interest rate will increase the cost of borrowing money for public facilities such as schools and prisons, and this tends to decrease spending on these facilities and to decrease government borrowing.

Market Equilibrium

The market equilibrium is shown by the intersection of the supply and demand curves. In Figure 1 the supply curve intersects the demand curve at point *e*, so the equilibrium interest rate is 4% and the equilibrium quantity is $500 million per year. At this interest rate, there is neither a shortage nor a surplus of funds, so the market has reached an equilibrium.

How do changes in supply and demand affect the equilibrium interest rate? Let's look at two changes, one on the demand side and another on the supply side.

1. *Increase in demand.* Economic growth increases the demand for all goods in the economy. Firms will respond to the increase in demand by expanding their production facilities, so the demand curve will shift to the right: At each interest rate, firms will demand more funds. As shown in Figure 2, the increase in demand increases both the price (the interest rate) and the quantity (the quantity of loanable funds).

2. *Increase in supply.* Suppose a widely publicized government report suggests that the social security benefits for people who retire in the next 40 years will be much lower than expected. If current workers decide to save more of their current income for retirement, the supply curve for loanable funds will shift to the right: At each interest rate, more money will be saved. As shown in Figure 3, the increase in supply decreases the price (the interest rate) and increases the quantity (the quantity of loanable funds).

We can use the same approach to predict the effects of other changes in supply and demand. Here are some other changes that will affect the equilibrium interest rate.

1. *Government spending.* If the government increases its spending without increasing taxes, it must borrow money to finance the new spending program. This deficit spending increases the demand for loanable funds and increases the equilibrium interest rate.

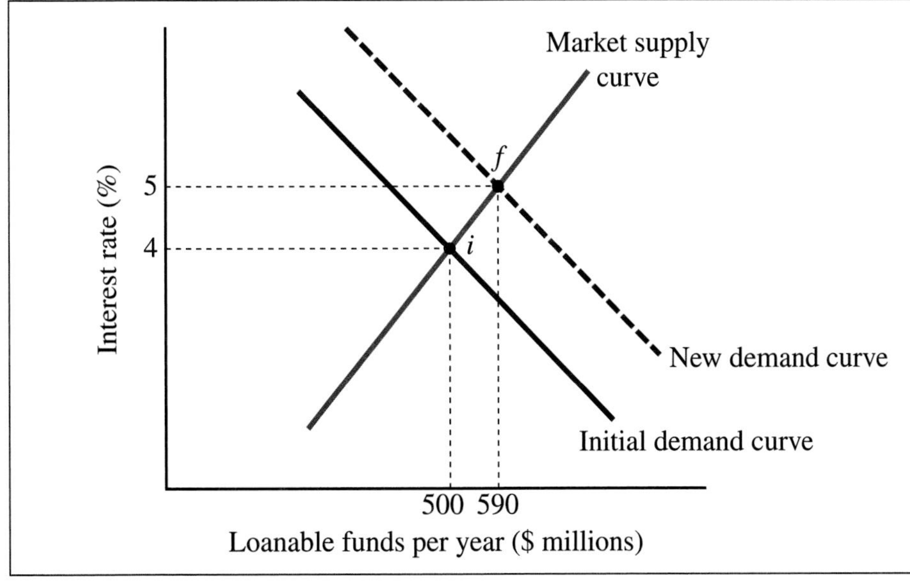

Figure 2

Market Effects of an Increase in Demand

An increase in demand (a rightward shift of the demand curve) increases the equilibrium interest rate and the quantity of loanable funds.

2. ***Investment subsidy.*** If the government provides a subsidy for spending on production facilities (buildings, machines, and equipment), firms will borrow more money to spend on facilities, and the equilibrium interest rate will increase.
3. ***Tax on interest income.*** A tax on interest income decreases the benefit of saving: For each dollar saved, the individual saver gets to keep only part of the interest income. The decrease in the benefit of saving will decrease the supply of loanable funds and increases the equilibrium interest rate.
4. ***Change in time preferences.*** If people become more patient (more willing to delay consumption), the supply of savings will increase and the equilibrium interest rate will decrease.

Recall the discussion of the doomsday clock in the opening paragraph of the chapter. How will a decrease in the threat of nuclear war affect the market for

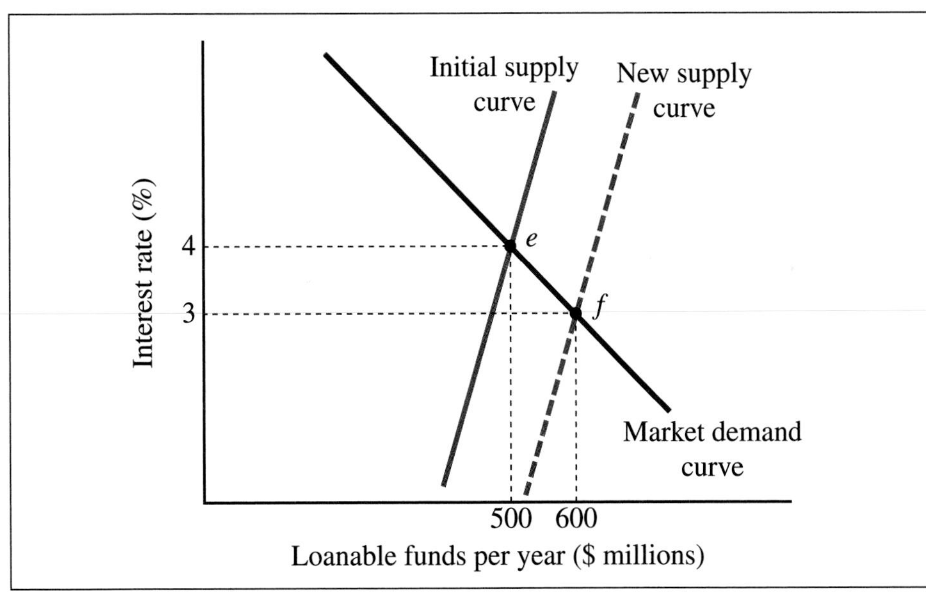

Figure 3

Market Effects of an Increase in Supply

An increase in supply (a rightward shift of the supply curve) decreases the equilibrium interest rate and increases the quantity of loanable funds.

loanable funds? People save for future consumption, either for themselves or for their heirs. As the threat of war decreases, people will save more money because there is a better chance they will be around to spend their savings. As the setting on the doomsday clock moves away from midnight, the supply curve for loanable funds will shift to the right. In Figure 3 an increase in supply decreases the equilibrium interest rate.

Personal Savings in Different Nations

How do personal savings rates differ among developed countries? Figure 4 shows personal savings as a percentage of after-tax income for six nations. Japan's saving rate (18.1%) is over four times as large as the U.S. rate (4.1%). The European nations have saving rates between 12% and 15%, about three times the U.S. rate. The differences in savings rates reflect many differences between these nations, including differences in the taxation of interest income and personal thrift.

TEST *Your Understanding*

1. If the interest rate increased, would you save more, less, or about the same? In other words, what type of person are you, a "party now," a "party later," or a "party hearty later"? (If you don't currently save money, picture yourself in about 10 years, when you will probably have an opportunity to save.)
2. You just received a check for $1,000 and must save enough money to have $550 in one year. If the interest rate drops from 10% to 8%, will you save more or less money?
3. Complete the statement: The market supply curve for loanable funds shows the relationship between ____________ and ____________.
4. Complete the statement with "increases" or "decreases": An increase in the demand for loanable funds ____________ the equilibrium interest rate, while an increase in supply ____________ the equilibrium interest rate.

Figure 4

Savings Rates in Various Nations, 1993

Source: Data from "Savings by Nation," *Wall Street Journal*, April 5, 1993, p. A1. Reprinted by permission of the *Wall Street Journal*, © 1993 Dow Jones & Company, Inc. All Rights Reserved Worldwide.

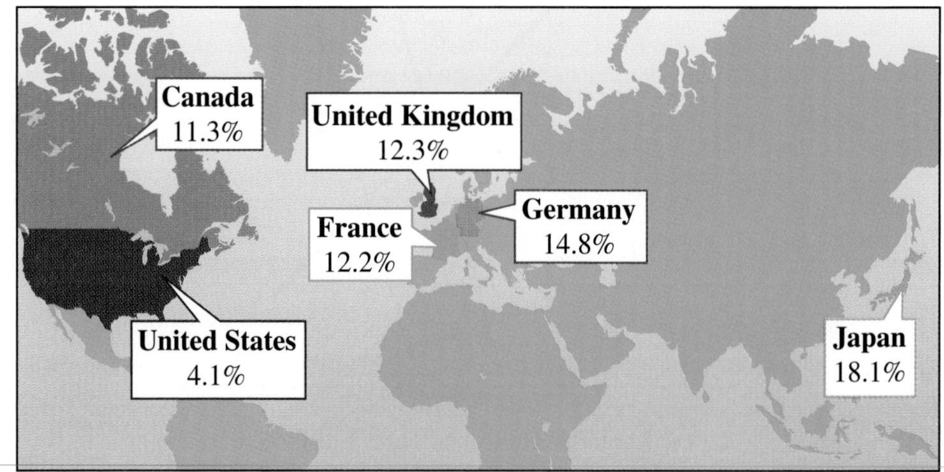

EXPLAINING DIFFERENCES IN INTEREST RATES

Up to this point we've discussed the market for loanable funds in very general terms, which may lead you to believe that there is a single market for loanable funds and a single interest rate. Of course, there are many types of loanable funds and many different interest rates. We'll compare a simple savings account to other financial instruments.

Savings Accounts and Bonds

You are probably familiar with a *savings account*. You can open a savings account in a savings and loan, a bank, or a credit union. The federal government insures savings accounts for amounts up to $100,000 per depositor. Therefore, a savings account is virtually free of risk: If the bank, savings and loan, or credit union goes bankrupt, the federal government will repay its depositors. As long as you deposit no more than $100,000, you can be sure that you won't lose your money.

One alternative to a bank savings account is a **corporate** or **government bond**, a promissory note issued by a corporation or a government when it borrows money. When you buy a bond from the government or a corporation, you purchase the right to receive a fixed amount of money at some future date (the *face value* of the bond) and an annual interest payment. For example, if a $5,000 bond "matures" in the year 2010 and pays 10% per year, you will receive $500 per year until the year 2010, when you receive $5,000 back to redeem the bond.

Corporate or government bond: A promissory note issued by a corporation or a government when it borrows money.

The purchase of a bond is risky because the issuer may default on the bond. This happens when the bond issuer doesn't have enough money to repay all its bondholders, so it pays back less than the face value of the bonds. For example, if a firm goes bankrupt and pays bondholders only 50 cents per dollar of face value, you would receive only $2,500 on your $5,000 bond. Government bonds are less risky than corporate bonds because the government is less likely to declare bankruptcy. The risk associated with corporate bonds depends on the financial health of the firm: The more profitable the firm, the lower the risk of default.

Differences in Interest Rates

Why is the interest rate for a bank savings account less than the interest rate for a corporate bond? In panel A of Figure 5 on page 366, the equilibrium interest rate for savings accounts is 3%. If corporate bonds were offered to investors at the same interest rate, no one would buy corporate bonds because a bank savings account provides the same rate of return with virtually no risk. In panel B of Figure 5, the supply curve for funds invested in corporate bonds intersects the vertical axis at an interest rate of 5%, meaning that the quantity of funds invested in corporate bonds is zero for any interest rate less than or equal to 5%. The supply curve for investment in corporate bonds intersects the demand curve at an interest rate of 6%, so the equilibrium interest rate for corporate bonds is 6%. The higher interest rate for corporate bonds compensates investors for the greater risk associated with investing in corporate bonds.

The same logic applies to other financial instruments such as government bonds. The greater the risk associated with the financial instrument, the higher the interest rate required to compensate investors for the risk they face. For example, corporate bonds are more risky than government bonds, so corporate bonds have higher interest rates.

Figure 5

Equilibrium Interest Rates for Bank Savings Accounts and Corporate Bonds

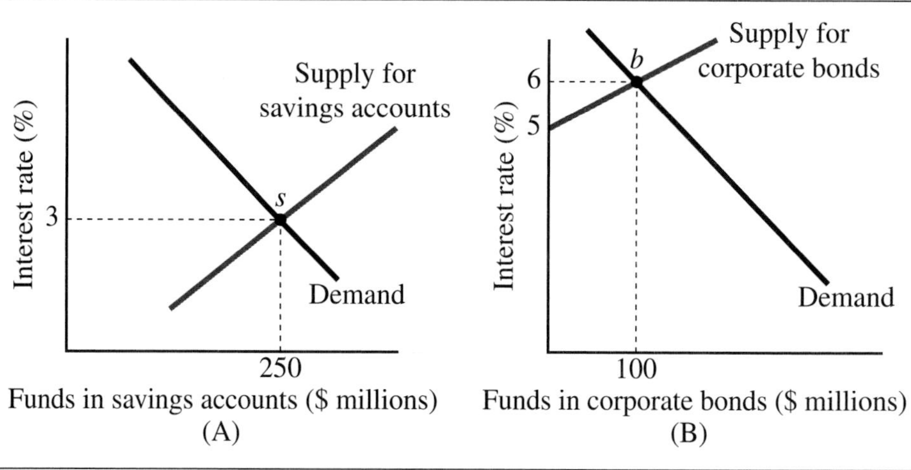

The equilibrium interest rate for corporate bonds (6% at point *b*) exceeds the interest rate for savings accounts (3% at point *s*) because bonds are riskier.

Corporate Stocks

Corporation: A legal entity that is owned by people who purchase stock in the corporation.

Corporate stock: A certificate that reflects ownership in a corporation and gives the holder the right to receive a fraction of the corporation's profit.

Dividends: The part of a corporation's profit paid to stockholders.

Another alternative to putting your money in a bank savings account is to buy corporate stock. A **corporation** is a legal entity that is owned by people who purchase stock in the corporation. When you buy a share of **corporate stock** (1 unit of ownership), you receive a certificate reflecting your ownership in the corporation and gain the right to receive a fraction of the firm's profit. For example, if you buy 1 of 100 shares of a corporation's stock, you have the right to receive 1% (1/100) of the corporation's profit. There are two potential benefits from buying stock.

1. ***Dividends.*** Most corporations pay part of their profits as **dividends** to their stockholders. Dividends are typically paid four times a year (quarterly), and the size of the dividend depends on the corporation's profit: The higher the profit, the larger the dividend per share of stock. Dividends are analogous to interest payments on savings accounts and bonds.
2. ***Capital gains.*** If the market price of the stock increases, you can sell your stock for more than you paid for it.

The purchase of a share of stock is risky because the firm may turn out to be less profitable than expected. If so, the dividends will be smaller than expected and the market price of the stock may decrease. If the price of the stock decreases, you may be forced to sell your stock for less than you paid for it.

Corporate stocks are bought and sold on stock markets. Most newspapers publish data on transactions in major stock markets such as the New York Stock Exchange. If you want to learn how to interpret this stock-market data, take a look at the Closer Look box "How to Read the Stock Pages."

How does the rate of return on stocks (the percentage yield) compare to the interest rates on savings accounts and bonds? We know that investors demand higher rates of return to compensate for the risk they face. Because of the laws concerning bankruptcy, corporate stocks are more risky than corporate bonds: When a firm goes bankrupt, it sells its assets and then pays its bondholders first; stockholders are paid only if there is money left over after the firm pays its bondholders. The greater risk associated with corporate stocks is reflected in higher rates of return on corporate stocks.

A Closer LOOK

How to Read the Stock Pages

The fragment of table shown below is a representative sample of information from the stock pages of the *New York Times* for July 14, 1995. Let's use the first row (showing Kmart stock) to show how to interpret this information. The first two columns show the highest and lowest prices of the stock over the last year, expressed in dollars per share: The highest price was $18.625 (18⅝) and the lowest price was $11.875. The column labeled "Div" shows the dividend per share over the last year: A person who held a share of Kmart stock received $0.48 in dividend payments over the preceding year. In the column labeled "Yld %," we see the annual yield on the stock, which is computed by dividing the dividend by the day's closing price (shown in the column marked "Last"): the dividend of $0.48 is 3.3% of the closing price of $14.625.

The column labeled "PE Ratio" (price–earnings ratio) shows the price of the stock divided by the corporation's total earnings per share, which includes dividends as well as profit that is retained by the corporation. The PE ratio for Kmart was 32. The column labeled "Sales 100s" shows how many hundreds of shares of stock were sold during the day's trading (1,151,400). The next two columns show the range of prices during the day's trading: The highest price was $15.00 and the lowest price was $14.625. The column labeled "Last" shows the price of the stock for the last transaction of the day (also known as the closing price), which in the case of Kmart is the same as the low price. In the column labeled "Chg." we see the change in the closing price from the closing price of the preceding day.

52 Week				*Yld*	*PE*	*Sales*				
High	*Low*	*Stock*	*Div*	*%*	*Ratio*	*100s*	*High*	*Low*	*Last*	*Chg.*
18⅝	11 ⅞	Kmart	.48	3.3	32	11514	15	14 ⅝	14 ⅝	–¼
26	20 ½	KanPip	2.20	9.5	11	222	23 ⅝	22 ⅞	23 ¼	+⅜
24 ¼	19 ¾	KCPL	1.52	6.9	12	1054	22 ½	22 ⅛	22 ⅛	–¼
73 ⅞	51 ⅛	Kellog	1.44	2.0	22	2169	71 ⅜	70	71	+1 ⅛

Source: From the *New York Times*, July 14, 1995, pp. D6–D8. Copyright © 1995 by The New York Times Co. Reprinted by Permission.

Imperfect Information and Credit Rationing

When a person borrows money, there is no guarantee that he or she will repay the loan. There is asymmetric information in the market for loanable funds: The borrower has better information than the lender about whether the loan will be repaid. Earlier in the book, we discussed the effects of asymmetric information in the markets for consumer goods (used cars), insurance, and labor. Let's look at the implications for lending and borrowing.

Asymmetric information leads to an adverse-selection problem for lenders. To keep matters simple, let's assume that there are two types of borrowers, those who intend to repay their loans and those who don't (people who default on the loan). Suppose that a lender charges an interest rate of 10% and loans money to anyone who is willing to pay this interest rate. Suppose that the default rate is 20% (one in five borrowers fails to repay his or her loan), but the lender still makes a small profit: The total revenue (interest plus repaid principal) exceeds the total cost (including the cost of covering the defaults). Could the lender make even more money if he or she charged a higher interest rate?

A higher interest rate is likely to increase the default rate. As the interest rate increases, the cost of repaying a loan will increase, and some of the people who would repay a loan will decide not to borrow money. In contrast, a higher interest rate doesn't discourage a person who intends to default on a loan, because he or she won't repay the principal or the interest. As the people who would repay their loans drop out of the market, the default rate will increase. Therefore, the lender may actually lose money at the higher interest rate. This is the adverse-selection problem: The higher the interest rate, the more undesirable (adverse) the selection of borrowers.

Credit rationing: The practice of limiting the amount of credit available to individual borrowers.

In response to the adverse-selection problem, most lenders engage in **credit rationing**, the practice of limiting the amount of credit available to individual borrowers. For example, your bank or credit union specifies the maximum amount you can charge on your credit card. If you borrow money to pay for college, a car, or a house, the lender will specify the maximum amount you can borrow. In the extreme case, credit rationing means that a particular person will be unable borrow any money. The key feature of credit rationing is that people would be willing to pay a higher interest rate for the right to borrow more money, but the lender won't increase the rate and lend more money.

Why doesn't a lender accommodate people who are eager to borrow more money, even at a higher interest rate? As we saw earlier, an increase in the interest rate will lead to a more adverse selection of borrowers, increasing the default rate. To control the default rate, lenders must keep interest rates low to retain the people who are likely to repay their loans. To deal with the excess demand for credit, lenders limit the amount of credit issued to each individual, with the limit determined by the borrower's financial circumstances.

TEST *Your Understanding*

5 List the two potential benefits from buying a share of stock.

6 What do you get when you buy a bond from the government or a firm?

7 Complete the statement with *higher* or *lower*: The greater the risk associated with the financial instrument, the ____________ the interest rate.

8 Suppose that you regularly loan money to your fellow students, charging an interest rate of 6%. Explain why you might make more profit if you charged only 4%.

PRESENT VALUE AND INVESTMENT DECISIONS

There are many alternatives to investing your money in a savings account or a bond, including investments in property (land or housing), machines and equipment, and firms. The alternative investments do not pay interest, so it's not obvious how to measure the payoffs from these investments. Fortunately, we can use the market interest rate as a sort of benchmark with which to compare the payoffs from alternative investments.

As an example of an investment, consider your decision to get a college degree. You are incurring some costs today, including tuition, book costs, and the income sacrificed by studying instead of working. You're willing to pay these costs because you expect some future benefits from a college degree, including higher wages for the rest of your life. Are the benefits greater than the costs? To answer this question, we must compare your current costs to your future benefits. We can use the market interest rate to make this comparison and evaluate the wisdom of your college investment decision. Other investors use the same logic to decide how to invest their money.

Opportunity Cost and Present Value

Suppose that a friend wants to borrow money from you today, and promises to pay you $110 in one year. How much are you willing to lend her? In other words, how much are you willing to pay today for the right to receive $110 in one year?

The **present value** of a payment to be received in the future is the maximum amount a person is willing to pay *today* for such a payment. Recall the principle of opportunity cost.

Present value: The maximum amount a person is willing to pay today for a payment to be received in the future.

PRINCIPLE *of Opportunity Cost*

The opportunity cost of something is what you sacrifice to get it.

Let's think about how much you are willing to pay today for the right to receive $110 in one year. Suppose that you can earn 10% per year in a savings account or money-market account.

1. How about $105? If you withdraw $105 from your bank account and lend it to your friend, you will sacrifice $105 *and* the interest you could have earned on the $105 for the next year ($10.50 is 10% of $105), for a total cost of $115.50. The opportunity cost exceeds the $110 benefit, so it would be unwise to give up $105 today for $110 in a year.
2. How about $90? In this case, the opportunity cost is only $99 (the $90 you pay today and $9 of interest sacrificed), it would be wise to give up $90 today for $110 in a year.
3. How about $100? In this case, the opportunity cost is $110 (the $100 you pay today and $10 of interest sacrificed), which is equal to the benefit.

You are willing to pay up to $100 for the right to receive $110 in one year, so the present value of $110 in a year is $100.

Formulas for Present Value

A simple formula shows the present value of a future payment. If you will receive $R in t years and the interest rate is i, the present value (PV) of the future payment is

$$\text{PV} = \frac{R}{(1+i)^t}$$

In our example, the payment (R) is $110, the interval of time (t) is one year, and the interest rate (i) is 0.10. Using the present-value formula, the present value of $110 in one year is $100:

$$\text{PV} = \frac{R}{(1+i)^t} = \frac{110}{(1+0.10)^1} = 100$$

This is the maximum amount that you are willing to pay today to receive $110 in one year.

How much would you be willing to pay for a payment to be received two years from now? The present value of $110 in two years is only $91:

$$\text{PV} = \frac{R}{(1+i)^t} = \frac{110}{(1+0.10)^2} = \frac{110}{1.21} = 91$$

This is sensible because the more distant the payment, the greater the interest income you sacrifice between now and the time of the payment. In this case, if you pay \$91 today, you sacrifice a total of \$110 over the next two years: \$91 today, \$9 of forgone interest in the first year, and \$10 of forgone interest in the second year. Therefore, the opportunity cost equals the benefit. You'll notice that the more remote the payment, the lower the present value: The longer the time you wait for a payment, the more interest you sacrifice.

Many investments pay the investor a stream of money over some period of time. For example, if you buy some land and rent it out, your tenant will pay rent every year. If a firm buys a machine that produces output over a 10-year period, the firm receives revenue from the machine for 10 years. To compute the present value of a stream of payments, we just add up the present values of each payment. For example, if you receive \$110 per year for two years, with the first payment one year from now, the present value is

$$\text{PV} = \frac{R_1}{(1+i)^1} + \frac{R_2}{(1+i)^2} = \frac{110}{(1+0.10)^1} + \frac{110}{(1+0.10)^2} = \frac{110}{1.21} = 100 + 91 = \$191$$

If this annual stream of \$110 lasts for 10 years, the present value is \$675:

$$\text{PV} = 100 + 91 + 83 + 75 + 68 + 62 + 56 + 51 + 47 + 42 = \$675$$

The longer the stream lasts, the smaller the increment in the present value per year because the more remote the payment, the smaller its value.

Applications: Investment Choices, College Degrees

We can use present value to help us make investment decisions. Let's think about a project for which we incur a cost today and experience benefits in the future. Here is a simple investment rule for such a project.

> *Investment Rule*: Invest in a project if the cost you incur today is less than the present value of the future payments from the project.

In our first present-value example, the "project" pays \$110 in one year, and the present value (given an interest rate of 10%) is \$100. Therefore, if the cost of the project (incurred today) is less than \$100, the project is worthwhile. We can apply the investment rule to our other examples:

1. Project 2 pays \$110 in two years. If the cost of the project is less than \$91 (its present value), the project is worthwhile.
2. Project 3 pays \$110 for two consecutive years. If the cost of the project is less than \$191 (its present value), the project is worthwhile.
3. Project 4 pays \$110 per year for 10 years. If the cost of the project is less than \$675 (its present value), the project is worthwhile.

Let's return to the issue of the benefits and costs of attending college. Suppose that your cost of getting a college degree at a hypothetical university is \$140,000, including \$80,000 in four years of forgone earnings and \$60,000 for tuition, books, and other expenses. If a college degree will increase your annual income by \$20,000, is the degree worthwhile? To simplify the calculations, suppose you incur all the costs today and the annual benefit lasts for

40 years. If the interest rate is 10%, the present value of $20,000 per year is about $196,000, which exceeds the total cost. Given these numbers, getting a college degree is a good idea.

We can use present value to compare a sum of money paid today with a payment to be received some time in the future. As explained in the Closer Look box "Do Lawyers Know about Present Value?," the results of such a comparison have important implications for personal decisions concerning corporate stocks.

ECONOMIC DETECTIVE– *Selling a Winning Lottery Ticket*

Lulu had been lucky all her life, so no one was really surprised they found out that she held the winning ticket in the state's lottery. Lulu's ticket entitled her to $2 million per year for the next 30 years, or a total of $60 million. Everyone was shocked when she promptly sold the lottery ticket to someone else for only $21 million and put the money in a bank account earning 10% per year. What explains this puzzling behavior? Is Lulu lucky but stupid, or just generous?

A Closer LOOK

Do Lawyers Know about Present Value?

A recent takeover battle between two corporate giants—Time and Paramount—provides a good lesson in present value.* In 1989, the price of Time's stock was $148 per share. When Paramount tried to take over Time by offering to buy Time stock for $200 per share, the stockholders of Time were overjoyed, anticipating an instant profit of $52 per share. The executives of Time opposed the takeover bid, arguing that they had a new strategic plan that would increase the price of Time stock to $250 in about five years. One part of the strategic plan was the acquisition of Warner, another corporate giant.

If you were a Time stockholder, would you support or oppose the Paramount takeover? Let's assume that the price of Time stock will indeed be $250 in five years. With an interest rate of 10%, the present value of $250 in five years is only $155. Therefore, a stockholder would clearly be better off getting $200 immediately rather than waiting five years to get $250. To put it in different terms, if a stockholder who received $200 today invested the money in an account earning 10% per year, the sum would grow to $292 after five years. Therefore, getting $200 immediately would be better than waiting five years to get $250. The logic of present value explains why many Time stockholders were upset when Time executives blocked the takeover bid by Paramount. With the approval of the Maryland Supreme Court, Time acquired Warner, causing Paramount to withdraw its offer of $200 per share of Time stock.

The concept of present value is relevant to many legal disputes, for example, the takeover battle between Time and Paramount.

*Bill Saporito, "The Inside Story of Time Warner," *FORTUNE*, November 20, 1989, pp. 164–166.

The key to solving this puzzle is the concept of present value. It will be sensible to sell the lottery ticket if the price Lulu can get for the ticket exceeds the present value of the payout from the ticket ($2 million per year for 30 years). If the interest rate is 10%, the present value of the payout is about $18.85 million. We get this number by adding up the present value of $2 million in one year, another $2 million in two years, and so on for 30 years. In this case the present value of the prize is less than a third of the $60 million prize, and Lulu will be better off by accepting $21 million now rather than getting $2 million per year for the next 30 years. Another way to see why it's a good idea to sell the ticket is to notice that Lulu will get $2.1 million per year forever from her bank account, compared to just $2 million per year for 30 years. It turns out that Lulu is lucky *and* smart.

Would it be wise for you to buy a $1 lottery ticket that may give you a prize with a present value of $18.85 million? It depends on your chances of winning the lottery. In the typical state lottery, your chance of winning a $60 million lottery prize (with a present value of $18.85 million) would be about 1 in 120 million. You can decide for yourself whether the $1 ticket is a good deal or a bad one.

TEST *Your Understanding*

9 If the interest rate is 10%, the present value of $55 in one year is ____________.

10 If the interest rate is 5%, the present value of $400 per year forever is ____________.

11 You could pay $7,000 today for a project that will generate $400 per year forever. If the interest rate is 5%, should you make the investment? Explain.

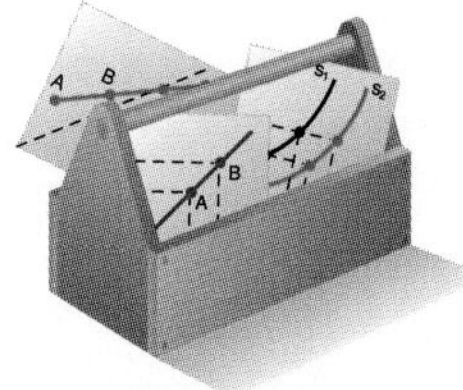

Using the **TOOLS**

You've learned how to use supply and demand curves to show why interest rates change and why there are different interest rates for savings accounts, government bonds, and corporate bonds. You've also learned how to compute the present value of a future payment and to use present value to make investment decisions. Here are some opportunities to do your own economic analysis.

1. Effects of Eliminating Federal Deposit Insurance

Suppose that the federal government eliminates its insurance program for savings deposits. The current interest rate on savings account is 3%. Use a graph to show the effect of this new policy on the equilibrium interest rate on savings deposits.

2. Cable TV versus Digital Satellite System

A digital satellite system (DSS) is an alternative to cable-TV service. A satellite transmits signals to small satellite dishes mounted on individual homes, and a digital receiver then decodes the signals, allowing digital sound and pictures to be displayed on a regular television set. Suppose you could participate in a DSS by paying a one-time hookup fee of $700 (for the dish and receiver) and an annual fee of $200. For equivalent cable-TV service, you would pay an annual fee of

$360. Assume that the DSS equipment lasts for 10 years and the annual fees for the two systems won't change. If the interest rate is 10%, which system is a better deal?

3. Effects of an Investment Tax Credit

Your firm is thinking about purchasing a machine that would produce $500 worth of output each year for five years. The current interest rate is 10%.

a. If the price of the machine is $2,000, should you buy it?
b. Suppose that the government introduces a 20% investment tax credit that will decrease your tax liability by $2 for each $10 you spend on machinery. Should you buy the machine?

SUMMARY

In this chapter we've seen that interest rates are determined by the interactions of savers (who supply loanable funds) and borrowers (who demand loanable funds). Because investors must be compensated for risk, interest rates are higher on financial instruments that are relatively risky. We've learned how to use present value to make investment decisions for projects that do not pay interest. Here are the main points of the chapter.

1. An increase in the interest rate may increase, decrease, or not change the amount of money saved by the typical person.
2. An increase in the interest rate decreases the amount of loanable funds demanded because households and firms borrow less money.
3. A bank savings account has a lower interest rate than a corporate bond because the savings account is less risky.
4. The present value of a dollar to be received in a year is less than a dollar.

KEY TERMS

corporate bond, *365*
corporate stock, 366
corporation, *366*
credit rationing, *368*
demand curve for loanable funds, *362*
dividends, *366*
government bond, *365*
interest rate, *359*
market for loanable funds, *359*
present value, *369*
supply curve for loanable funds, *360*

PROBLEMS AND DISCUSSION QUESTIONS

1. Imagine yourself in 10 years with a full-time job and enough income so that you can save some money each year. At an interest rate of 6%, you save $1,000 per year. If the interest rate increases from 6% to 8%, will you save more, less, or about the same amount?
2. Consider an economy with three people who save different amounts at different interest rates:

Interest Rate (%)	*Abe's Annual Saving*	*Bertha's Annual Saving*	*Caitlyn's Annual Saving*
4	$2,000	$2,000	$2,000
6	1,800	2,000	2,500
8	1,600	2,000	3,000

Draw the market supply curve for savings.

3. Suppose that you win a lottery that pays you $10 million each year for five years. If the interest rate is 10%, what is the present value of your prize?
4. You could insulate your house with $2,000 withdrawn from a savings account with an interest rate of 5% per year. The insulation would decrease the energy costs of your house by $120 per year forever.
   a. Should you insulate your house?
   b. If the interest rate were 10% instead of 5%, would the insulation still be sensible?
5. Recall the example of the present value of a college degree. Suppose that a college degree increases your annual earnings by only $10,000 per year (instead of $20,000). If the other numbers are the same, is a college degree still worthwhile? Explain.

Take It to the Net

We invite you to visit the O'Sullivan/Sheffrin page on the Prentice Hall Web site at:

http://www.prenhall.com/osullivan/

for this chapter's World Wide Web exercise.

MODEL ANSWERS FOR THIS CHAPTER

Chapter-Opening Questions

1. The larger the family's savings, the smaller the financial aid awarded to the student. The financial-aid rules decrease the net return on savings, so families save less.
2. As shown in Figure 4 (page 364), Japan has the highest saving rate and the United States has the lowest savings rate.
3. Corporate stocks are more risky than corporate bonds because when a firm goes bankrupt, it sells its assets and then pays its bondholders first. Stockholders are paid only if there is money left over after the firm pays its bondholders.
4. With an interest rate of 10%, the present value of the DSS is $1,929, compared to $2,212 for the cable system.
5. With an interest rate of 10 percent, the present value of $20,000 per year is about $196,000, meaning that the benefit exceeds the cost.

Test Your Understanding

1. It depends on personal preferences. Some people will save more, while others will save less, and others will save the same amount.
2. If you save $500, you'll earn $20 in interest (4% of $500), so you'll have $520 in one year. To meet your target of $520, you must save more today because each dollar saved will earn less money. If you save $510, you'll earn just over $10 in interest, so you'll hve just over $520.
3. the interest rate, quantity of funds supplied
4. increases, decreases
5. The potential benefits are dividends and capital gain.
6. You get a payment equal to the bond's face value and an annual interest payment.
7. higher
8. The decrease in the interest rate will make borrowing money more attractive to people who are likely to repay the loan. Therefore, your default rate will be lower and your total profit may be higher.
9. $50 ($55/1.10)
10. $8,000 (400/0.05)
11. The present value of $400 forever is $8,000, which exceeds the cost, so you should make the investment.

Using the Tools

1. Effects of Eliminating Federal Deposit Insurance

   The elimination of federal insurance would shift the supply curve for savings deposits to the left: A smaller amount of funds will be supplied at each interest rate. The equilibrium interest rate will increase, reflecting the greater risk associated with savings accounts.

2. Cable TV versus Digital Satellite System

   At an interest rate of 10%, DSS is a better deal. The present value of DSS is $1,929 [the present value of the $200 annual fee for 10 years ($1,229) plus the $700 hookup fee]. The present value of the $360 annual cable fee for 10 years is $2,212. DSS has a lower present value, so it is a better deal.

3. Effects of an Investment Tax Credit
   a. The present value of $500 for five years is $1,895, so it would not be sensible to buy the $2,000 machine.
   b. The net cost of the machine will be only $1,600 (spending $2,000 cuts your taxes by $400), so it would be sensible to buy it.

NOTES

1. Joel Slemrod, "Saving and the Fear of Nuclear War," *Journal of Conflict Resolution*, vol. 30, September 1986, pp. 403–419.
2. Michael J. Boskin, "Taxation, Saving, and the Rate of Interest," *Journal of Political Economy*, vol. 86, April 1978, pp. S3–S28.

CHAPTER 19

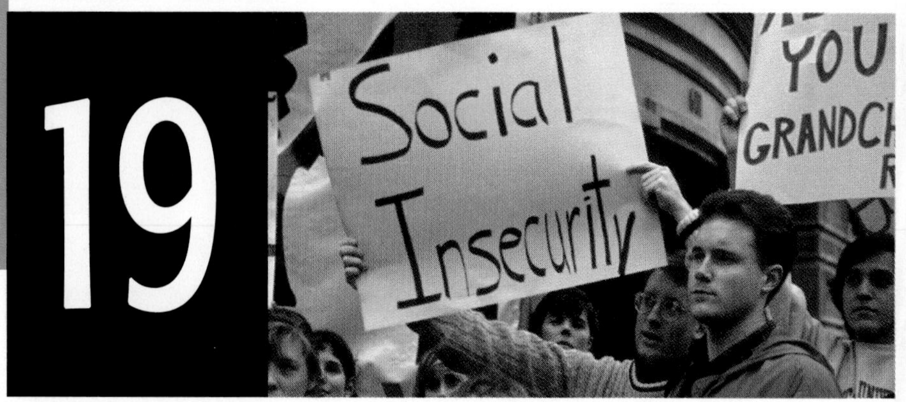

Economic Challenges for the Twenty-First Century

Ethena Jones has just graduated with an honors degree in computer engineering and is pleased with the high salary she will earn on her new job. But she wonders about her classmates from high school who did not go to college and are either earning low wages or even living in poverty. She also wonders whether her older brother, who recently lost his job, will be able to have any health insurance. She is concerned about her parents, who are near retirement age; they do not have much saved because they spent a lot of money for their children's college tuition. Are the stories true that the Social Security trust fund will run out of money, and how might her parents be affected?

As we begin to enter the twenty-first century, economic problems are still with us. True, the material aspects of our lives are remarkably enriched compared to a century ago, and we enjoy vastly higher living standards. Yet we still worry about economic concerns.

In this chapter we look at four challenges that the United States and other developed countries will face in the next century. Two concern the distribution of income. Poverty remains a stubborn problem and there are important controversies over its causes and remedies. More generally, inequality has been growing in our society in recent years as more educated and better skilled persons seem to be doing much better economically than those with less education and skills.

Our society is also getting older. In the next century, the proportion of the population over 65 years of age will increase sharply. This will create tensions around our current system for supporting the elderly. To compound the problem, the costs of health care have been rising steadily. This not only makes it more difficult to support the elderly, who are large consumers of health care, but also makes it more difficult for all of us to afford the type of health care we have grown to expect.

We explore the policy choices we will face as we try to deal with these issues in the twenty-first century. We first look at the possible causes of poverty and inequality and the policy options that are available to deal with them. We then turn to the problems generated by the aging of the population and the high costs of providing adequate health care. As you read this chapter, you will appreciate that the fundamental problem in economics—scarcity of resources—is still with us.

After reading this chapter, you will be able to answer the following real-world questions:

1. How effective are U.S. poverty programs in reducing poverty among children?
2. What can explain the growing gap between the wages of skilled and unskilled workers?
3. What are the advantages and disadvantages from privatizing the Social Security system?
4. Why does the cost of health care continue to rise?

POVERTY AND PUBLIC POLICY

In every society, there are people who do not earn enough income to provide what most of their fellow citizens would consider a reasonable amount of food, clothing, housing, medical care, and other goods. For example, there were over 39 million poor Americans in 1993. In this part of the chapter, we explain why some people are poor, discuss the current set of antipoverty policies, and examine some recent proposals and changes in law to reform the welfare system.

Who Are the Poor?

The Census Bureau defines a **family** as a group of two or more people related by birth, marriage, or adoption who live in the same housing unit. A **household** is a group of related family members and unrelated persons who live in the same housing unit. According to the U.S. government, a poor family is one whose total income is less than the amount required to satisfy the family's "minimum needs." The government estimates a minimum food budget for each type of family (such as single-parent or two-parent) and multiplies the food budget by three to get the official **poverty budget**. For example, in 1993 the poverty budget was $7,363 for an individual, $9,414 for a two-person family, and $14,763 for a four-person family.[1] A family with less income than the official poverty budget is considered poor.

The first column of numbers in Table 1 (page 378) shows the makeup of the nation's poor population. In total, there were 39.3 million poor people, about half of whom were white (18.9 million) and a quarter of whom were black (10.9 million). About a third of the poor lived in single-parent families headed by women

Family: A group of two or more individuals related by birth, marriage, or adoption who live in the same housing unit.

Household: A group of related family members and unrelated individuals who live in the same housing unit.

Poverty budget: The minimum amount the government estimates that a family needs to avoid being in poverty.

Table 1: The Poverty Populations in 1993

Group	Persons in Poverty (millions)	Poverty Rate (%)
All persons	39.3	15.1
Race		
White	18.9	9.9
Black	10.9	33.3
Hispanic	8.1	30.6
Asian	1.1	15.3
Family type		
Two-parent	9.5	9.1
Single-parent, male	1.2	22.1
Single-parent, female	13.6	48.0
Age		
Over 65	3.8	12.2
Under 18	15.3	22.7
Education level		
No high school diploma	8.2	25.6
High school graduate	6.0	10.4
Some college	2.6	7.0
College graduate	1.1	3.0

Source: U.S. Bureau of the Census, *Current Population Reports*, P60-188 (Washington, DC: U.S. Government Printing Office, 1994).

(13.6 million). Perhaps the most startling numbers are for the old and the young: Only about 10% of the poor were over 65 years of age (3.8 million), while 40% of the poor were children (15.3 million).

The second column of numbers shows the poverty rates for various groups. The poverty rate equals the percentage of people in a particular group who live in households below the official poverty line. Poverty rates differ sharply by groups:

1. ***Race.*** The poverty rates for blacks (33.3%) and Hispanics (30.6%) are over three times the white rate (9.9%).
2. ***Family type.*** The poverty rate for single-parent families is much higher than the rate for two-parent families. The poverty rate for single-parent families headed by women is over five times the rate of two-parent families and over twice the rate of single-parent families headed by men.
3. ***Age.*** One of the recent successes in the battle against poverty was the decrease in poverty among the elderly: their poverty rate dropped from 35% in 1959 to 12.2% in 1993, largely as a result of increased Social Security benefits. In contrast, the poverty rate for children is over 22%.
4. ***Education.*** The poverty rate of high-school dropouts is over twice the rate for high-school graduates and over eight times the rate of college graduates.

What Causes Poverty?

To put it simply, poverty results from the failure of the adults in a household to earn enough money to provide for the household's basic needs. Some adults are unable to work because of health problems, disabilities, or age. Others have limited work options because they are responsible for raising small children. A common perception is that most poor adults don't work, but this is incorrect: In fact, about two-thirds of poor households have at least one part-time worker, and one-fifth of poor households have a full-time worker.[2] For these "working poor," the problem is low wages and part-time employment, not the lack of a job.

For a single-earner household to avoid poverty, the worker must earn far above the minimum wage. A single parent with two children needs an hourly wage of about $7.30 to avoid poverty, an amount that reflects the cost of child care and taxes. Many single parents don't have the skills required to earn this wage, so their families are poor. Of course, it's easier to avoid poverty if there are two earners in the family. For example, if the primary earner in a two-parent family earns an hourly wage of about $6.30 and the second worker earns the minimum wage in a part-time job, the family's income will be just above the poverty line.[3]

The problems of the working poor have gotten worse over the last few decades. Between 1973 and 1993, the average wage for workers without college education dropped in real terms, with the largest losses experienced by high-school dropouts and workers with limited work experience.[4] Wages dropped because the demand for low-skilled workers decreased; technological innovation has often made it possible to replace low-skilled workers with "smart" machines. A second reason is the globalization of the economy and the growth of international trade: If a foreign nation has a comparative advantage in producing goods using low-skilled labor, an increase in imports at home will decrease the demand for low-skilled labor in the home country. As we'll see later in the chapter, while wages for low-skilled labor have decreased, wages for highly skilled labor have actually increased.

Antipoverty Programs

Table 2 shows recent spending on the major antipoverty programs in the United States. An *antipoverty program* is defined as a program that is available only to the poor. Spending on antipoverty programs accounted for about 14% of the federal budget, compared to 32% for Social Security and Medicare and 18% for national defense.

Table 2: Major Redistribution Programs

Program	*Number of Participants (millions)*	*Total Cost (billions per year)*	*Annual Cost per Participant*
Cash assistance			
Aid to Families with Dependent Children (AFDC)	14.2	$ 25.9	$1,823
Supplemental Security Income (SSI)	6.4	27.3	4,265
Noncash assistance			
Medicaid	34	143.6	4,223
Food stamps	28.9	27.4	948
Housing assistance	4.8	26.1	5,437

Source: *Statistical Abstract of the United States* (Washington, DC: U.S. Government Printing Office, 1996). Data are for 1994.

Aid to Families with Dependent Children (AFDC): A government poverty program that provides assistance to families with children under the age of 18.

Supplemental Security Income (SSI): A special program for the aged, the blind, and the permanently disabled.

Medicaid: A program that provides medical services to the poor.

Let's look first at the programs that provide cash assistance to poor households. As its name indicates, **Aid to Families with Dependent Children (AFDC)** provides assistance to families with children under 18 years of age. In most states, AFDC is limited to families in which one parent is either absent or disabled, and almost all AFDC families are headed by women. In 1994, there were 14.2 million people in the AFDC program and the annual cost was $25.9 billion, or $1,823 per participant. AFDC has become less generous in recent years. For a typical four-person family, the real AFDC payment decreased by about 43% between 1970 and 1993.[5] **Supplemental Security Income (SSI)** is a special program for the aged, the blind, and the permanently disabled. There were 6.4 million SSI participants in 1994 and the cost per participant was $4,265.

A second set of antipoverty programs provides noncash assistance to the poor. These programs cost three times as much as cash assistance programs. By far the biggest noncash program is **Medicaid**, which provides medical care to many households below the poverty line, including those who participate in SSI and AFDC. In 1994, the cost of the Medicaid program was $143.6 billion, or $4,223 per participant. In recent years spending on Medicaid has increased rapidly, a result of general increases in the cost of medical care and higher costs for providing long-term nursing home care for the elderly and disabled. The other noncash programs are much smaller than Medicaid: The cost of the food stamps program was $27.4 billion, and the cost of housing assistance was $26.1 billion. In recent years, food stamp assistance has become more generous, but increases in food stamps only partly offset decreases in AFDC payments: Between 1970 and 1994, the sum of AFDC and food stamp assistance for the typical four-person family decreased by about 25%.[6]

Figure 1

Years of AFDC Participation for Women

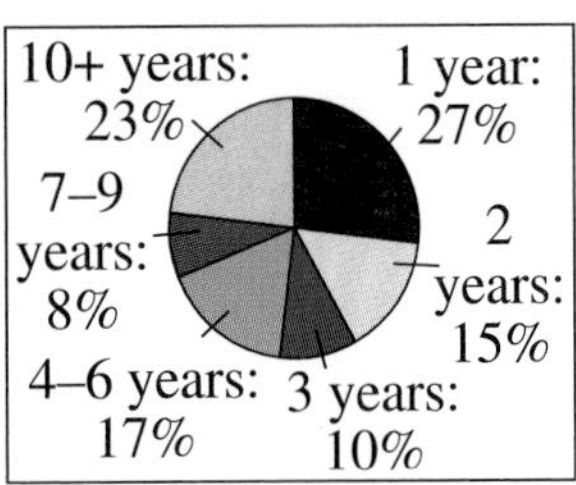

Source: Rebecca M. Blank, *Changing Poverty: Complex Problems and Effective Policies* (Princeton, NJ: Princeton University Press, 1996).

How do the antipoverty programs affect the work effort of poor households? One way to answer this question is to see what happens when a parent's AFDC payment decreases. Economists estimate that a $1,000 decrease in the annual AFDC payment would cause an AFDC parent to work approximately 20 additional hours per year.[7] Because AFDC recipients earn relatively low wages, there would still be a net decrease in the family's net income. Another way to answer the work-effort question is to see what happens when the government drops a family from the AFDC program. A study by the U.S. General Accounting Office suggests that a parent dropped from the program would work longer hours, but the additional earnings would not be large enough to offset the loss of AFDC: On average, the family's income would still drop by between 12 and 26%.[8]

One of the concerns about antipoverty programs is that they may be "addictive" in the sense that once a family gets on AFDC, it is very difficult to get off. Figure 1 shows the total time spent on AFDC for women who are in the program at some point in their lives. About a quarter (27%) of AFDC women participate for just one year, and over half (52%) participate for three years or less. At the other extreme, about a quarter (23%) spend 10 or more years in the program. Most long-time users cycle on and off the program: When their economic circumstances improve they leave the program, but they return when their circumstances change for the worse.[9]

Income Redistribution and Poverty Rates in Industrial Nations

How effective are government redistribution programs in decreasing poverty? Figure 2 provides a "before" and "after" picture of poverty in the United States and several other industrial nations in the late 1980s. The U.S. poverty rate was 19.9% before considering the effects of taxes and transfers, and 13.1% after. Looking at

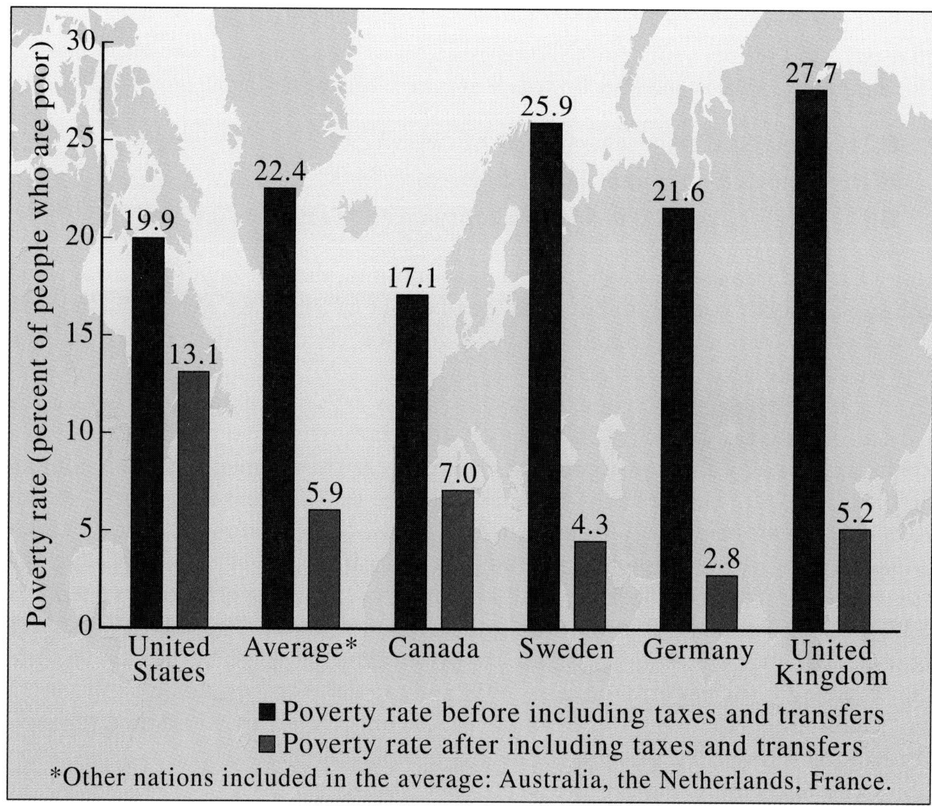

Figure 2

Effects of Public Policy on Poverty Rates

Source: Timothy M. Smeeding, "Why the U.S. Antipoverty System Doesn't Work Very Well," *Challenge*, January/February 1992, Table 3, pp. 30–35.

the next two bars, we see that the average poverty rate in eight nations (the five nations shown in the figure plus Australia, the Netherlands, and France) was 22.4% before considering transfers and taxes, but only 5.9% after. Although the United States had a lower "before" poverty rate than the average, it had a much higher "after" rate. The other nations were more effective in decreasing poverty, largely because they spend more money on redistribution programs and target the money to the households that need it the most.

Antipoverty programs in the United States are particularly ineffective in reducing poverty among children. The U.S. poverty rate among children was 22.3% before considering taxes and transfers, and 20.4% after. The average poverty rate among children in the eight nations was 16.7% before considering taxes and transfers, but only 7.4% after. The "after" poverty rate for U.S. children is about three times the average child poverty rate. Other countries spend much more money on programs that lift children out of poverty.

Challenge: Welfare Reform

Given widespread dissatisfaction with welfare programs, the challenge for policymakers is to develop a set of policies that are more efficient and effective. Let's first look at three problems with the traditional system that was in effect through 1996 and then explore some alternative policies. We conclude this section with a discussion of some of the changes to the traditional system that began in 1997.

The first problem is that the traditional system discourages participants from working and earning an income. To explain the trade-offs between welfare and working, let's see what happens when an AFDC mother who initially receives

$4,800 per year in AFDC and $2,500 in food stamps decides to take a part-time job that pays $5,000 per year (1,000 hours per year at $5 per hour). The good news is the $5,000 increase in income, but there are three bits of bad news.[10]

- The family's AFDC payment decreases by $2,218.
- The family's food stamp allotment decreases by $1,294.
- The family pays $380 in Social Security taxes on the earnings.

The bad news sums to $3,892 per year, meaning that the payoff from working is just $1,108 per year, or an hourly wage of about $1.11. If we were to include the cost of child care (about $2,500 per year for two children), the net payoff from working would actually be negative.

Earned income tax credit (EITC): A tax subsidy given to low-wage workers with children.

There is one bit of good news that partly offsets this picture. Under the **earned income tax credit (EITC)**, a poor household with two children receives a refundable tax credit of 40 cents per dollar of earned income, with a maximum credit of $3,560. This credit is refundable in the sense that if a worker does not earn enough money to pay federal income taxes, the government issues a check equal to 40% of the worker's earnings. In our example, the good news from the tax credit is a refund check of $2,000. Therefore, the payoff from working is $3,108, which translates into a net hourly wage of about $3.11. Of course, the cost of child care would decrease the payoff and the net wage: If the cost of child care is $2,500, the payoff would be $608 and the net wage would be about $0.61 per hour. The lesson from this example is that under the current system, the payoff from working is very small, so there is little incentive to work.

The EITC has expanded in recent years, and its budgetary cost is close to the total cost of AFDC. While some policymakers have proposed scaling the EITC back to reduce the federal budget deficit, others have proposed that it be maintained—or even expanded—to encourage work effort among AFDC recipients. The outcome of this debate will determine the future of the EITC.

The second problem with the current system is the lack of child support from absent fathers. Fewer than one-fourth of poor mothers receive child-support payments from absent fathers, and the average payment among the recipients is only about $1,900 per year.[11] Under one reform proposal, the government would specify a minimum child support payment (for example, $1,500 per child) and collect the minimum payment from absent fathers who can afford it. To collect money from absent fathers, the government could extend the federal tax withholding system to include child support payments. For absent fathers who cannot afford the full payment, the government would collect what it can and cover the difference between the amount collected and the minimum support payment. This sort of guaranteed child support program provides an alternative to AFDC. Because the child support payment would not drop as the mother's income increased, it would not discourage work effort among poor families.

The third problem is that the current welfare system is inflexible in dealing with people who need assistance. A person entering the system is immediately asked to fill out a stack of forms to determine whether he or she is eligible for assistance. An alternative approach is to carefully screen each person who asks for assistance to see which of three types of assistance they should receive:[12]

1. ***Short-term assistance.*** Many people enter the welfare system when they lose their jobs because of temporary setbacks such as a broken-down car, a medical problem, or the loss of housing. In some cases, a small amount of cash or other assistance would allow them to keep their jobs.

2. *Assistance combined with education, training, or job search.* For people who are currently unemployed but employable, the government could provide cash and noncash assistance. In return for the assistance, the recipient would participate in programs involving education, job training, and job search.
3. *Assistance for the unemployable.* For people who are unemployable because of poor health (physical or mental), drug problems, or disabilities, the government could provide financial assistance.

For an example of a program requiring work in exchange for assistance, read the Closer Look box "Welfare Reform in Wisconsin."

In 1996, President Bill Clinton signed a bill that would make major changes in the welfare system starting in 1997. The new law would end the federal guarantee to families under AFDC. States would take over the responsibility for families with dependent children, assisted by block grants from the federal government. Lifetime welfare benefits would be limited to five years, although states could exempt 20% of families on grounds of hardship. In addition to this five-year lifetime limit, adults would be required to work within two years of receiving benefits or the benefits would be lost.

Supporters of the new law hope that the states will take the initiative in designing new policies to assist welfare recipients in joining the labor force. They point to the creative approaches taken by many states, such as Wisconsin, in developing new approaches. Opponents of the bill, however, worry that the 61-year-old federal guarantee of federal aid to dependent children is being ended without any ultimate safeguards. They also express doubt about whether welfare recipients will be able to find work in the numbers that are required. The next several years will provide economists with evidence on how this new approach actually works.

In designing a welfare program, or any social program, it is important to recognize that none will operate with complete efficiency. The economist Arthur Okun, who worked as a presidential adviser and at the Brookings Institution in Washington, DC, coined the term *leaky bucket* to describe the inefficiencies that

A Closer LOOK

Welfare Reform in Wisconsin

The state of Wisconsin developed a plan that would replace AFDC with a program under which poor mothers would work in exchange for government aid. In announcing the new program, Governor Tommy Thompson said, "Finally, we are caring enough about these children and families to free them from the welfare trap, instead of just handing them a check and walking away." Under the program, poor mothers would work 28 to 40 hours per week in exchange for several types of assistance:

1. **Job training and help finding jobs**
2. **Subsidies for employers who hire women who would otherwise not be hired**
3. **Enrollment in a health-maintenance organization**
4. **Child care subsidies of up to $100 per month**
5. **Food stamps**

The state's objective is to put all able-bodied welfare mothers to work by the year 2000.

Source: After "Moms Will Work for Welfare in Wisconsin," *The Oregonian,* March 15, 1996.

could occur as society engages in transfer programs for the poor. Transfer programs, like leaky buckets, will inevitably waste some funds as they operate. Designing social programs to avoid too many "leaks" is an important objective.

TEST *Your Understanding*

1 Which of the following statements are true, and which are false?

a. Most of the poor are black, and very few are white.

b. The poverty rate among the elderly exceeds the poverty rate among children.

c. Most poor households have at least one part-time worker.

d. A single parent can avoid poverty by getting a full-time job at the minimum wage.

2 Comment on the following statement: "In the last two decades, welfare programs (AFDC and food stamps) have become more generous, and this has contributed to the rapid increase in the number of female-headed households."

3 Explain in a few sentences why the traditional AFDC program discourages work effort among the participants.

THE DISTRIBUTION OF INCOME

In 1992 the average family income in the United States was $39,000, but this simple average tells only part of the income story. Some families earn much more income, and others earn much less. In this part of the chapter we discuss the extent of income inequality in the United States and explore some of the reasons why families with the highest income are receiving a larger and larger share of the nation's total income.

Income Distribution Facts

Let's start with the facts about the distribution of income in the United States. It's obvious that income is not distributed equally: Some families have much higher incomes than others. The question is: How unequally is income distributed? Table 3 shows the distribution of income without considering the effects of taxes or noncash transfers such as food stamps, public housing, or medical care. Cash transfers from government redistribution programs are included in these figures. To compute the numbers in the table, we take four steps.

Table 3: Percent of Income Earned by Different Groups, 1993

Income Group	*Income Range*	*Percent of Total Income*
Lowest fifth	0–$16,952	4.2
Second fifth	$16,953–$30,000	10.1
Middle fifth	$30,001–$45,020	15.9
Fourth fifth	$45,021–$66,794	23.6
Highest fifth	$66,795 and greater	46.2

Source: *Statistical Abstract of the United States* (Washington, DC: U.S. Government Printing Office, 1995), Table 733.

1. Rank the nation's families according to income: The family with the lowest income is at the top of the list, and the family with the highest income is at the bottom of the list.

2. Divide the families into five groups: the first fifth includes the poorest 20% of the families (the top 20% of the list); the second fifth is the next poorest 20% (the next 20% of the list), and so on. The second column of the table shows the income ranges for each of the five groups: The lowest fifth includes families with income up to $16,952, the second fifth includes families with income between $16,953 and $30,000, and so on.

3. Compute each group's income by adding up the income received by all the families in the group.

4. Compute each group's percentage of total income (the number in the table) by dividing the group's income by the nation's total income.

Let's look at the two ends of the income distribution. The wealthiest families obviously have more income than the poorest families, but how much more? Each group in the table has the same number of families, so we can answer this question by dividing the percent of income received by the highest fifth (46.2%) by the percent of income received by the lowest fifth (4.2%). The typical family in the highest fifth has 11 times as much income as the typical family in the lowest fifth (46.2 divided by 4.2).

What explains the differences in the incomes of U.S. families? There are five key factors.

1. ***Differences in labor skills and effort.*** Some people have better labor skills than others, so they earn higher wages. Labor skills are determined in part by education and in part by the person's innate ability. In addition, some people work longer hours or at more demanding jobs, so they earn more income.
2. ***Inheritances.*** Some people inherit large sums of money and earn income by investing this money.
3. ***Luck and misfortune.*** Some people are luckier than others in investing their money, starting a business, or picking an occupation. Among the unlucky people are those who develop health problems that make it difficult to earn an income.
4. ***Discrimination.*** Some people are paid lower wages because of their race or gender.
5. ***Redistribution programs.*** The government uses various redistribution programs (Social Security, AFDC, SSI) to give money to individual families.

So far, our discussion of inequality has examined the distribution of income, which is the amount of money a family receives each year. We should also consider the distribution of wealth. A household's wealth is the value of the things it owns. For a discussion of the distribution of wealth, read the Closer Look box on page 386, "The Distribution of Wealth in Different Nations."

Recent Changes in the Distribution of Income

Figure 3 (page 386) shows the changes in the distribution of income between 1980 and 1993. The share of the top fifth rose from 41.5% to 46.2%, while the share of every other group dropped. By historical standards, these changes in the distribution of income were very rapid. What caused these changes in the distribution in income?

One reason is that the income of highly skilled workers increased relative to the income of low-skilled workers. Figure 4 on page 387 shows the relative incomes of workers with different educational backgrounds, using the income earned by a

A Closer **LOOK**

The Distribution of Wealth in Different Nations

Which of the developed nations has the most concentrated distribution of wealth? A *household's wealth* is defined as the value of its assets (stocks, bonds, houses, motor vehicles, and other assets) *minus* its debts (mortgages, consumer loans, and other debts). During the 1980s, the United States became the most economically stratified of the industrial nations. The wealthiest 1% of U.S. households now own nearly 40% of the nation's wealth. To fit into this elite category, your net worth or wealth must be at least $2.3 million. In contrast, the wealthiest 1% of British households own about 18% of Britain's wealth. The wealthiest 20% in the United States, defined as people with a net worth of at least $180,000, own 80% of the nation's wealth. This is a much larger percentage than we find in other industrialized countries.

Source: Edward N. Wolff, *Top Heavy: A Study of Increasing Inequality of Wealth in America* (New York: Twentieth Century Fund, 1995).

high-school graduate as a basis for comparison. For example, in 1972 a college graduate earned 1.43 times as much as a high-school graduate: The "college premium" was 43%. By 1992 the college premium increased to 82%. Similarly, the premium for attending some college over a high graduate increased from 10% to 25%. While the people with advanced degrees earned 1.72 times as much as a high-school graduate in 1972, by 1992 they earned 2.54 times as much. At the other end of the chart, high-school dropouts fell even further behind workers with more education.

Why did the earning power of more educated workers increase so dramatically in the last two decades? There are two main reasons.

Figure 3

Changes in the Distribution of Income, 1980–1993

Source: Statistical Abstract of the United States (Washington, DC: U.S. Government Printing Office, 1995), Table 733.

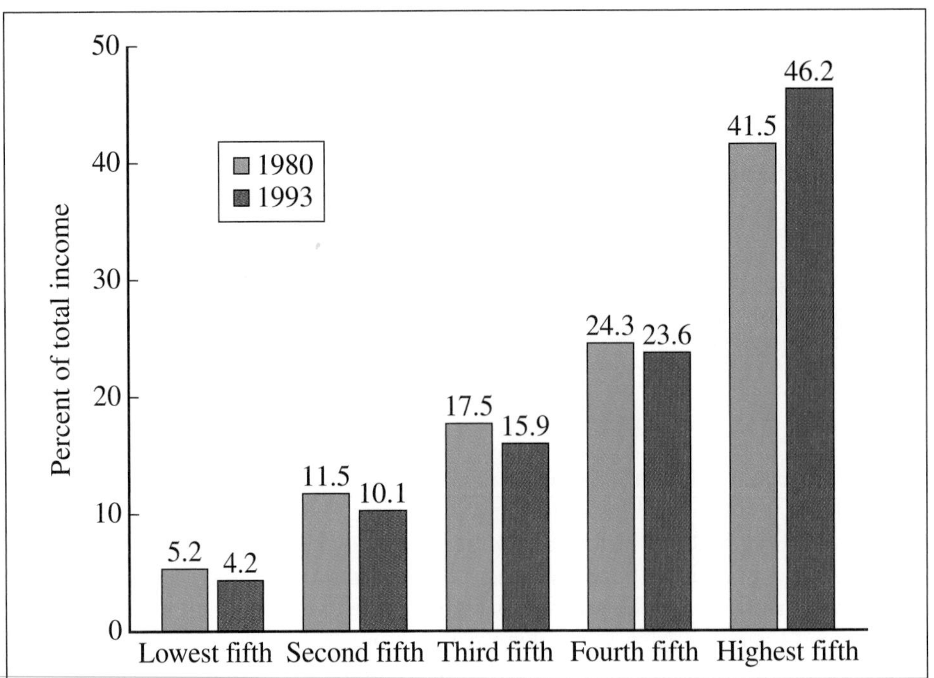

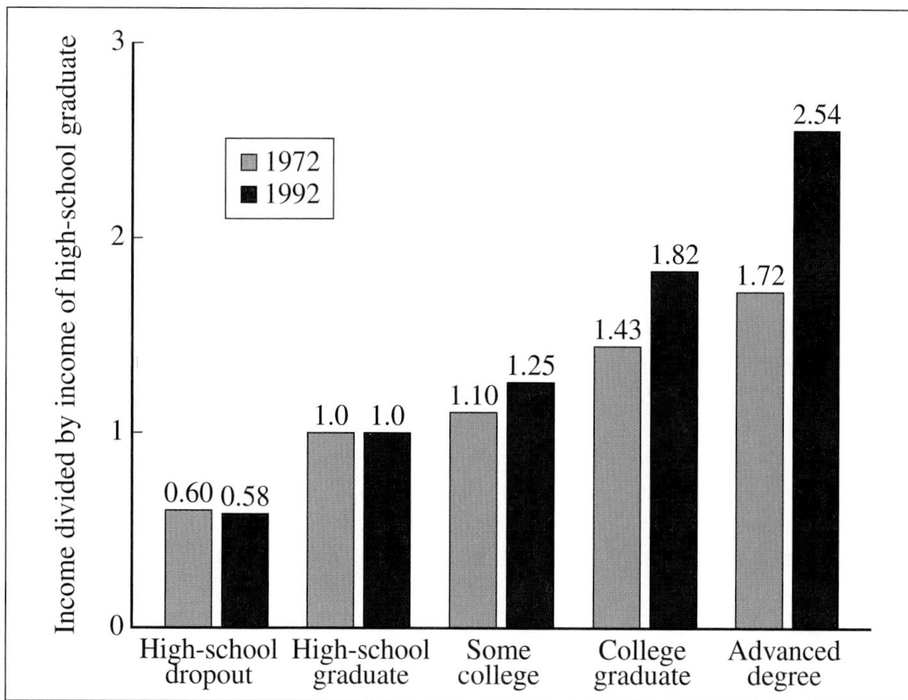

Figure 4

Changes in the Incomes for Different Education Levels, 1972–1992

Source: W. Michael Fox and Beverly J. Fox, "What's Happening to Americans' Income?" *The Southwest Economy*, Issue 2, 1995 (Dallas, TX: Federal Reserve Bank of Dallas, 1995).

1. ***Technological change.*** Advances in technology have simultaneously decreased the demand for less educated workers (high-school dropouts and graduates) and increased the demand for college graduates and people with advanced degrees. While the new technology has made it possible to replace many low-skilled workers with "smart" machines and computers, it has also increased the demand for workers who have the education and skills required to produce the new technology and use it. For example, the wage for a job that requires the use of a computer is about 19% higher than for similar jobs that don't require computer use.[13]

2. ***Globalization and international trade.*** The United States has a comparative advantage in producing goods using highly skilled labor, and some foreign nations have comparative advantages in producing goods with low-skilled labor. An increase in trade will increase exports from the United States, and this increases the demand for highly skilled labor in the United States and increases its wage. In contrast, an increase in imports will decrease the demand for low-skilled labor in the United States and lead to lower wages for low-skilled labor.

Policy Challenges

What are the policy implications of the recent changes in relative incomes and the distribution of income? We can expect some lively debate among policymakers about what, if anything, to do about these changes. Here are some potential policy responses.

- ***Education policy.*** The payoff from a college education is much higher than it was 10 or 20 years ago, and we can expect the demand for college education to increase. There may be pressure on state governments to accommodate the larger number of people seeking a college education by spending more money on public universities and college. In addition, state and local governments may decide to modify the curriculum of grade schools, middle schools, and high schools to better prepare students for the rigors of college.

- ***Redistribution policy.*** If the share of income going to the lowest four-fifths of the population continues to drop, the federal government may adjust its tax and spending programs to offset these changes. This would mean decreasing the tax burden on lower-income individuals and raising the burden on middle- and higher-income individuals.
- ***Welfare policy.*** The decrease in the share of income going to the lowest fifth may lead to changes in antipoverty programs. The earned income tax credit (EITC) could be modified to offset falling wages for high-school dropouts and graduates and at the same time encourage work effort among the poor.

Take a moment to reflect on these options. If you could pick a set of public policies to deal with the problem of growing income inequality, what policies would you choose? Using the policies listed above as a starting point, develop your own policy recommendations. Do not forget the principle of opportunity cost. If your recommendations involve additional government spending, think about where the government will get the money for the additional programs. Will taxes increase, or will other programs be cut? In addition, you should think about the other trade-offs (good news and bad news) associated with each of your recommendations.

TEST *Your Understanding*

4 In 1993 the typical family in the highest fifth of the income distribution earned ____________ times as much as the typical family in the lowest fifth, up from ____________ in 1980.

5 Between 1980 and 1993, which group of families (which fifth) experienced the largest decrease in its share of income?

6 Explain briefly why the relative wages of more educated workers have increased in the last two decades.

THE AGING OF SOCIETY

In 1950 there were seven people aged 24 to 64 (prime working age) for every person 65 years and older. By 1990, that ratio had fallen to 4.8. Current projections indicate that by the year 2030, there will be only 2.8 people of working age for every person over retirement age. In this part of the chapter we examine how this dramatic change in the age distribution in our society will force us to reexamine our social programs.

These changes are not occurring only in the United States. Many countries around the world, both developed and developing, are facing an aging society in the future. Figure 5 presents projections of the **dependency ratios**, the ratio of the population over 65 years of age to the population between 20 and 65. As the figure indicates, by the year 2050, the United States is projected to have a dependency ratio of 37%, while Japan is projected to have a much higher dependency ratio of 60.1%. This means that in the year 2050, there will be only 1.66 (1/0.601) people between the ages of 20 and 65 for every person over the age of 65.

Dependency ratio: The ratio of the population over 65 years of age to the population between 20 and 65.

Structure of the Social Security System

Social Security: A government program that provides retirement, survivor, and disability benefits.

As we saw earlier in the chapter, the poverty rate among the elderly is much lower than the poverty rate for other age groups in our society. The reason for this low rate of poverty is the familiar **Social Security** system. Started in 1935 during the

Since women live longer than men, a higher proportion of the elderly will be women.

depths of the Great Depression, the Social Security system provides retirement and health benefits to the elderly. It is one of our most popular social programs and has widespread support throughout the entire political system.

The Social Security system is actually quite complex and has many different provisions. Here is a basic overview. Over 92% of the civilian workforce is included in the Social Security system today. (Not all employment is covered by Social

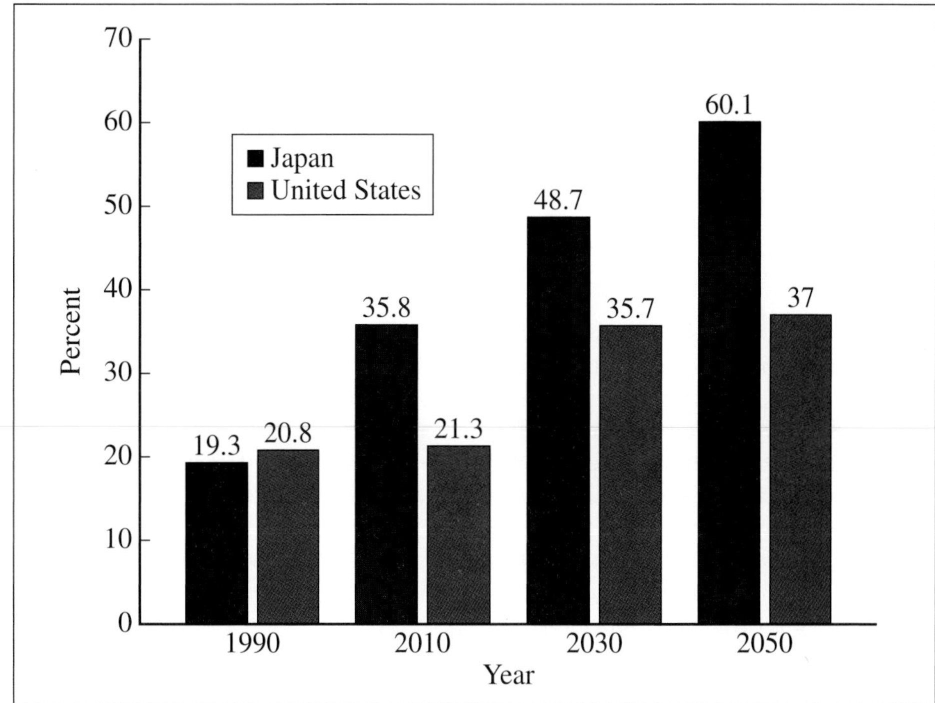

Figure 5

Dependency Ratios for Japan and the United States

The dependency ratio is the ratio of the population over 65 to the population between 20 and 65.

Source: Congressional Budget Office.

Security, and there are minimum earning requirements.) Workers included in Social Security receive either retirement benefits at the age of 65 or reduced benefits at the age of 62. A recipient with a dependent wife, husband, or child receives 50% more than a recipient without dependents. If the worker dies, survivor benefits are provided to the family. Social Security also provides disability payments for workers who suffer from an illness that prevents them from working for a minimum of a year.

Medicare: A government program that provides health benefits to those over 65 years of age.

In addition to these retirement provisions, the other major part of the Social Security system is **Medicare**, health coverage for the elderly. Medicare consists of both hospital insurance and supplementary medical insurance for doctor services and other services outside the hospital. Medicare hospital benefits are provided automatically to workers and their married partners when they reach the age of 65. Supplementary medical insurance is voluntary and requires monthly payments, but most elderly buy the insurance since their payments only cover about one-fourth of the true cost of the insurance. Widows or widowers of deceased workers are also covered at the age of 65.

The Social Security system (except for supplementary medical insurance) is financed through flat payroll taxes on both employees and employers. Each contributes one-half the total tax. For all parts of the system except the hospital portion of Medicare, there is a yearly maximum amount (or "cap") beyond which a worker need not contribute in a given year.

The retirement, survivor, and disability benefits that Social Security pays are determined by an average of the wages the worker earned during employment. The Social Security system calculates a "replacement rate" for each worker, which is the fraction of their average wage they will receive. An important feature of the system is that replacement rates are higher for workers who earned lower wages. Therefore, the Social Security system redistributes income to retirees who had low wages and away from retirees who had higher wages. Thus, despite the fact that it is financed with a flat payroll tax, the system as a whole redistributes income toward low-wage workers.

Social insurance: A system that compensates individuals for bad luck, low skills, or misfortune.

Because the Social Security system redistributes income toward low-wage persons, provides survivor benefits to widows and children, and provides income to disabled workers and their families, it is sometimes viewed as a **social insurance** system, a program that takes care of those who have had bad luck, possess low skills, or experience misfortunes. Although Social Security is a universal program and not restricted to the poor, it does have important redistributive features built in.

The Coming Financing Crisis

Pay-as-you-go: A retirement system that pay benefits to the old with taxes currently levied on the young.

From virtually the beginning of the Social Security system until quite recently, the payroll taxes paid by employees and employers in any given year went to finance the benefits received by retirees in that same year. Thus the payments that an employer and an employee made did not go into an account earmarked for that worker's retirement. Instead, these dollars were paid out immediately to current recipients. This type of financing mechanism is called a **pay-as-you-go** system.

In the early days of the Social Security system, pay-as-you-go worked quite well. As long as the elderly population is small relative to the working population, it does not take a high level of payroll taxes to finance retirements. Throughout much of its history, retirees under Social Security received vastly more in benefits than they paid in taxes. In fact, the first recipient paid $22 in Social Security taxes, lived to the age of 99, and collected $20,000 in benefits.[14]

However, for two distinct reasons, the easy times for Social Security are behind us. First, as we discuss later in the chapter, medical costs have risen very rapidly and these increases are projected to continue. Sharply rising medical costs dramatically increase the costs of Medicare. Second, the age distribution in the next century will not be favorable, as the ratio of the working age to the retiree population decreases.

To provide the same benefit structure for Social Security and Medicare into the next century, at a time when we face rising health costs and a larger percentage of the population over 65 years of age, sharp increases in payroll taxes will be required. How high must these taxes go? Projections far into the future are risky, but a typical estimate is that the combined employer–employee payroll tax rates, now 15.3%, may have to rise to approximately 26%.[15] Income taxes and other taxes come on top of these payroll taxes. Assuming that federal and state income taxes stay in the same range, this would mean that the average worker could easily face total taxes between 50 and 60% of his or her income. While some European countries have tax rates this high, such rates would bring about a dramatic change in our fiscal system.

Challenge: Financing the Elderly

What are the options we face to deal with this problem? There are essentially three approaches we could take:

1. Preserve Future Benefits but Invest More Today

If we increased our rate of investment today, we could increase the living standards of the next generation. With higher living standards, the next generation would be better able to bear the burden of financing Social Security and Medicare payments. Indeed, we could view this as a generational compact or deal: Workers today will provide the next generation with higher living standards by consuming less and investing more, as long as the next generation provides Social Security and Medicare benefits to the members of the current generation when they retire.

Although this may seem like a reasonable bargain, higher living standards for future generations will not reduce the tax rates they face. As increased investment by today's generations raises real GDP over time, retirement benefits will rise since they are largely determined by wages near retirement. Thus, if current generations save more, they will receive larger retirement benefits. Total tax rates for the average worker in future generations could still range between 50 and 60%. Looking back, will future workers remember their bargain, or will they just be dissatisfied with the high rates of taxation? Raising the standard of living for future generations does nothing to alleviate the redistributions between generations that will occur if the system is not changed.

2. Cut Benefits

A second possibility is to reduce benefits. Obviously, reducing benefits for current retirees or those just nearing retirement would be perceived as unfair. However, it is possible to cut future benefits. For example, the retirement age is already scheduled to be increased in the twenty-first century, and further increases are possible. In addition, unlike private retirement plans, Social Security benefits are currently fully adjusted for inflation. Reducing the inflation adjustment could provide important long-run savings.

But we should not underestimate the degree of difficulty in even making these changes. Retirement ages, for example, have drifted down in recent years from an average age of 65 to 62. Workers anticipating an earlier retirement will not want to see benefits held off until a later age. Similarly, many elderly worry that they will not have sufficient assets and that their only benefits will be from Social Security. If these benefits are not protected against inflation, will the elderly be forced into poverty?

3. Privatize the Entire System

A third dramatic alternative would be to change the entire system fundamentally and make the benefits received by any person depend directly on his or her own contribution. In other words, we could privatize the entire system. The government would require everyone to make at least a minimum contribution, but they would be free to direct their funds as they saw fit among an approved set of alternatives. Upon retirement, the person could draw upon his or her accumulated savings. Chile recently replaced its pay-as-you-go system with a fully funded privatized system.

Proponents of a privatized system point to several advantages. First, it would alleviate future workers from the burden of paying excessive taxes. Second, workers could earn higher returns by investing, for example, in the stock market than they could earn through traditional Social Security. Finally, total saving and investment in the economy are likely to increase as workers save for their own retirements rather than simply waiting to receive Social Security benefits as in the current system.

Nonetheless, there are important disadvantages to replacing our current system. First, there are transition problems. Consider, for example, a woman who is now 50 years old and anticipates retiring in 15 years. During her working career she did not save very much because she knew she would receive Social Security; all that time, she paid taxes that financed the retirement of others. If we suddenly privatized the system, she would only have 15 years to save for her retirement, which is not a sufficient time to set aside funds for her old age. Clearly, we would not think this was fair and would have to design some transition system that would supplement her savings. Still, she gets a raw deal: In the past she paid for others to retire, and now she must pay for part of her own retirement as well. There is no way to escape this problem. During a transition, some groups in society will have to pay both for their own retirement as well as for the retirement of others.

Second, full privatization of the Social Security system would effectively end our current system of social insurance. Under the system, if the breadwinner in the household dies, the family receives survivor benefits. Under full privatization, these benefits would not be available unless the government created a new program. Similarly, if a worker made a series of poor investments with his retirement funds and then died, would the widow have to live in poverty?

The funding of Social Security and Medicare will be the grand debate as we enter the twenty-first century. Indeed, the debate has already started. In 1996 an advisory council to the Social Security Administration reported on alternative solutions to the challenges of funding future benefits. Their report discussed several options, including partial or total privatization as well as investing some of the payroll taxes in the stock market. The group had to confront the issues we've raised, including the role of the Social Security system in providing social insurance as well as difficult transition issues. As you can see, some fundamental aspects of the nature of our society are at stake in this debate.

TEST *Your Understanding*

7 True or false, and explain. Since Social Security is financed by a flat payroll with a cap, lower-wage workers are hurt by the system relative to higher-wage workers.

8 Explain why the age distribution in a society matters for a pay-as-you-go system.

9 Name two advantages and two disadvantages of privatizing the Social Security system.

HEALTH CARE

As we have seen, the cost of health care plays an important role both in our programs for the poor (Medicaid) and in our programs for the elderly (Medicare). In recent years the federal government and states have faced increasing challenges in meeting these obligations as health care costs have risen sharply. At the same time, workers and businesses in the private sector find themselves struggling to afford health care. In the last part of the chapter we look at our health care system and the challenges we face in controlling costs and providing care.

Two Problems with Our Health System

Despite the availability of the latest technology, many social scientists believe that our health system has serious difficulties. There are two basic problems: cost and access. Over the last 40 years, real spending per person on medical care has risen at a rate of over 4% a year. Such rapid growth has meant that we are devoting an increasing fraction of our output to health care. From 1960 to 1992 the share of our gross domestic product devoted to health care has risen from 6% to 13.6%. As Figure 6 on page 394 illustrates, the United States spends a much higher fraction of its GDP here than do comparable countries. Germany, for example, devotes 8.7% of its GDP to health care, and Canada spends 10.3%.

In principle, there is no reason why such a high level of spending might not be worthwhile. But most observers believe that much of our spending is not in fact worthwhile. In making spending decisions, we should be guided by the marginal principle.

Marginal PRINCIPLE

Increase the level of an activity if its marginal benefit exceeds its marginal cost, but reduce the level if the marginal cost exceeds the marginal benefit. If possible, pick that level at which the marginal benefit equals the marginal cost.

In the health sector, however, we constantly violate the marginal principle: We make expenditures of little marginal value that have substantial marginal costs. For example, studies suggest that as many as one-fourth of common medical procedures for the elderly are of very low or dubious value.[16] Physicians have traditionally been trained to heal the sick, not make economic decisions.

The second problem in our health system is that not everyone has health insurance. In 1994, approximately 40 million persons were not covered by health

Figure 6

Health Expenditure as Percent of GDP, 1992

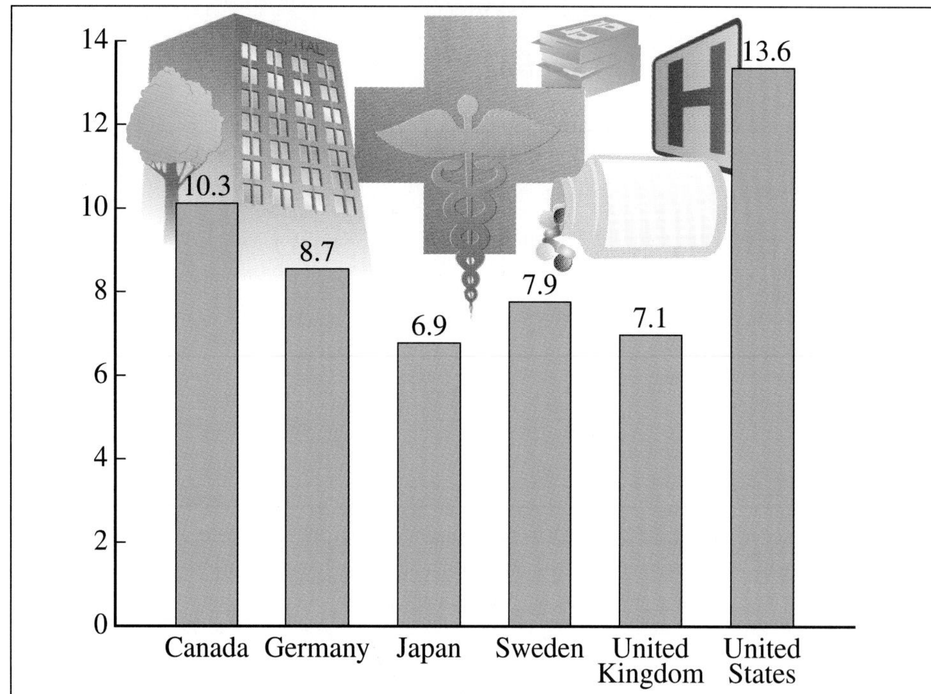

Source: "Health System Performance in OECD Countries," *Health Affairs*, Fall 1994.

insurance. Almost all the elderly are covered through Medicare, and many of the poor are covered under Medicaid. Most U.S. workers receive their health insurance through their employers. The uninsured are those people and their families who do not receive insurance through their employers, are unemployed or between jobs, or are poor but do not qualify for Medicaid in their state. Persons who do not have health insurance obtain care for emergencies but fail to receive routine, and less costly, preventive care. Without health insurance, people do not use the medical system efficiently.

Two Sources of Difficulties

Why do we have these problems with our health system? Two areas that cause us particular difficulties are coping with all the effects of insurance and our management of technological advance. Two different types of problems arise from health insurance. First, under traditional insurance policies in which insurance companies pay for any treatment, patients and physicians have few incentives to contain costs. If doctors and hospitals are fully reimbursed for their expenses, patients with insurance can demand expensive care even if the marginal benefit of that care is extremely low. Doctors and hospitals will supply this care since they are fully reimbursed. In recent years, many employers have required their employees to join health-maintenance organizations (HMOs) in which physicians are paid a fixed amount per patient regardless of the treatments that are actually provided. Under this type of system, doctors and hospitals have an increased incentive to contain costs. Since they are paid a fixed amount per patient, their profits increase as they reduce their costs. A health system in which HMOs and similar organizations compete for patients is commonly known as **managed competition.**

Managed competition: A health system in which organizations such as HMOs compete for patients.

A second problem is that insurance companies want to avoid providing insurance to high-risk, therefore costly, persons. If an insurance company is providing insurance to the employees of a large firm, it probably has a good idea of the total risk it faces because the employees of the large firm are likely to be a typical cross section of the labor force. But if it offers insurance policies to individuals, those at high risk (whom the insurance company cannot easily distinguish from those at low risk) will have the greatest incentives to purchase the policies. The insurance companies recognize this problem and charge high rates for individual policies or to small firms. Because of these high costs, many people simply do not buy insurance at all. Thus the insurance market does not provide as good coverage for individuals or small firms as it does for large companies.

The other major problem we face is our inability to cope with technological advances in medicine. We are tempted to adopt any technological advance regardless of its cost. We should, instead, be guided by the marginal principle and adopt a technological advance only if its marginal benefit exceeds its marginal costs. Patients and physicians, however, are reluctant to use this reasoning and often choose high-cost treatments even when their advantage over lower-cost treatments is minimal. The fact that insurance policies will pay for these treatments removes the incentive to measure costs and benefits.

Challenge: Reforming the System

It appears there is little chance of an immediate, radical, sweeping reform of the health system. During 1993–1994, the Clinton administration tried to provide universal coverage, in part by requiring all firms to provide health insurance to their employees. This plan was soundly defeated because of its sheer complexity and the difficulties of developing policies to subsidize small firms so that they

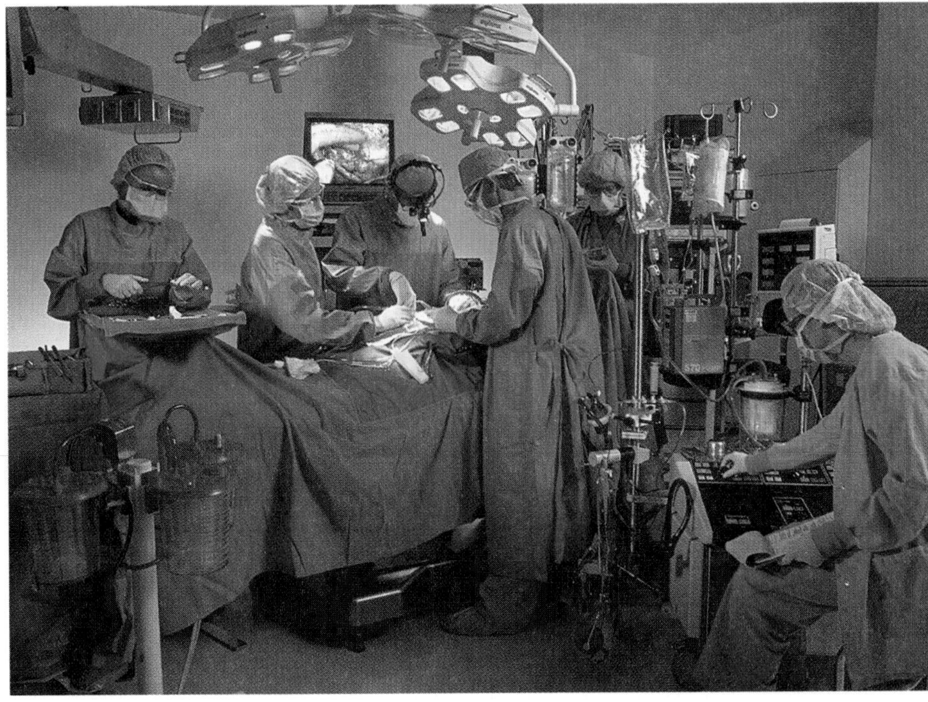

Complex and expensive heart operations are commonplace today.

could provide insurance to their employees. However, as the costs of health care continue to grow and large numbers of people remain uninsured, there will be pressures for change. Let's look at some of the key issues that will be debated in the next century.

1. Work Toward Universal Coverage

The problem of large numbers of uninsured persons does not show any signs of improving. Although the defeat of the Clinton health plan probably means that universal coverage cannot be achieved by requiring employers to provide health insurance for all workers, there may be other solutions. Stanford health economist Victor Fuchs has suggested a voucher plan in which everyone would receive a health voucher to purchase insurance.[17] The difficulties with any voucher plan, however, is that new taxes would be necessary to finance it. While it would be possible to raise rates on existing taxes to finance such a plan, most European countries that provide universal coverage have a broad-based value-added tax. (A value-added tax is essentially a sales tax levied on all the stages in the production process.) Clearly, introducing a new tax or raising existing tax rates to finance a voucher plan would be very controversial and require a broad political consensus that health reform is absolutely necessary.

2. Reform Medicare

Some politicians and policymakers have suggested that managed competition needs to be introduced into Medicare to provide incentives to reduce costs. This would be a major departure from the current system since relatively few of the elderly are currently enrolled in HMOs. Because Medicare expenses directly affect the federal budget, politicians are keenly aware of the need to reduce costs and have been discussing this option, despite resistance among the elderly, who want to ensure that the treatment they would receive from HMOs matches the quality of their current care.

3. Reform Insurance Markets

How can we ensure that everyone has access to some type of health insurance? What types of new laws or regulations are needed to address some of the problems in the market for insurance? Several states have experimented with plans to require insurance companies to provide broad coverage. However, this has proven to be difficult for states because large firms that self-insure (that is, provide their own insurance to their employees) are, by federal law, exempt from state insurance laws. Federal legislation may be needed in this highly contentious area.

Even with market reforms, some economists believe that subsidies would be required to entice many of the uninsured to purchase insurance. Many young and healthy people would rather take their chances and hope they stay healthy rather than pay for health insurance.

4. Manage Technological Change

How can we benefit from technological advance in medicine without bankrupting our society? Can the private market handle this problem, or should the government play an active role in evaluating and monitoring technology? Fuchs suggested that there is a strong need for some mechanism to assess new technologies. He proposed that a small tax be levied on all health providers to fund a private institute devoted to assessing new medical technologies. Ideally, this institution would be able to uncover the technological advances for which marginal benefits truly exceed marginal costs.

Using the **TOOLS**

1. ECONOMIC DETECTIVE– *Wages of College and High-School Graduates*

During the 1980s and 1990s, the supply of college graduates increased faster than the supply of less educated workers. Everything else being equal, we would expect the wage of college graduates to decrease relative to the wage of high-school graduates. Yet the relative wage of college graduates actually increased. Solve this mystery and use a supply and demand diagram to support your answer.

2. Chile's Transition to a Private Pension System

When Chile made the transition from a pay-as-you-go social security system to a private system, it had a very young population. Compared to the United States, the ratio of working-age persons to retirees was three times as high. How did the age structure in Chile make it easier to move to a private system?

3. Evaluating Medical Technology

Suppose that new technology enables patients of heart surgery to return to work one week earlier. The new technology is as safe as the old but very expensive. Hospitals and patients both want to use this new technology, and the government must decide whether to allow Medicare to reimburse them. What would you need to know to give the government proper advice?

SUMMARY

In this chapter we explored four policy issues that the United States and other countries will face in the next century. We will continue to grapple with poverty and inequality. At the same time, the aging of the population and the continued escalation of the cost of health care will pose new and difficult challenges.

As we think through each of these policy issues, we face three tasks. First, we must apply the correct economic analysis. For example, if we want to understand the problems of welfare recipients not working, we must consider the incentives they face. If the returns to working are small, or even negative, we should not expect people to leave welfare easily.

Second, we must clearly try to evaluate the causes of the problems. For example, is lack of education truly the culprit behind low wages? Would more education be a profitable investment? The type of analysis we used in this book needs to be applied to policy problems to discover their real sources.

Third, all policy issues involve values or judgments about what we think is right and fair. For example, some people believe that everyone is entitled to the same level of health care, despite its cost. Others believe that health care is no different from any other good or service and that some inequality is inevitable. We need to recognize when our values enter the picture.

The reason that policy analysis is so interesting is that it combines economic analysis, a search for the facts, and value judgments. We have seen in this chapter that economics can contribute significantly to the analysis of the policy issues we will face in the twenty-first century.

KEY TERMS

Aid to Families with Dependent Children (AFDC), *380*
dependency ratio, *388*
earned income tax credit (EITC), *382*
family, *377*
household, *377*
managed competition, *394*
Medicaid, *380*
Medicare, *390*
pay-as-you-go, *390*
poverty budget, *377*
social insurance, *390*
Social Security, *388*
Supplemental Security Income (SSI), *380*

PROBLEMS AND DISCUSSION QUESTIONS

1. Suppose that the government replaced AFDC with a system of guaranteed child supports and enforced it by verifying paternity at the time of birth and collecting child support from absent fathers. Would you expect the frequency of births to teenagers to change? Why or why not?
2. During the 1980s, the wages of older less educated workers (those in their 40s) increased relative to the wages of young less educated workers (those in their 20s). Explain why this could occur.
3. Suppose that state governments increased the funding for state colleges and universities, allowing the nationwide college enrollment to increase by 20%. Predict the effect of the increase in enrollment on the wages of college graduates relative to the wage of high-school graduates.
4. Suppose that the birth rate begins to fall. How would this affect a pay-as-you-go social security system?
5. What is a disadvantage of having employers provide health insurance?
6. Explain why an HMO might encourage pregnant women to have regular appointments.
7. Why might replacing a pay-as-you-go system with private pensions increase total savings?

Take It to the Net

We invite you to visit the O'Sullivan/Sheffrin page on the Prentice Hall Web site at:

http://www.prenhall.com/osullivan/

for this chapter's World Wide Web exercise.

MODEL ANSWERS FOR THIS CHAPTER

Chapter-Opening Questions

1. Compared to other countries, U.S. poverty programs are not effective in reducing poverty among children. The U.S. poverty rate among children was 22.3% before considering taxes and transfers, and 20.4 % after.
2. There are two explanations for the growing wage gap between the skilled and unskilled. First, technological change has increased the demand for skilled workers and decreased the demand for unskilled workers. Second, increases in world trade shift demand in a similar way because the United States exports skill-intensive goods and imports goods with lower skill content.
3. Privatizing Social Security may increase savings and investment in the economy. On the other hand, it would weaken the social insurance features of the current system.
4. Technological change has offered many opportunities for improving our health. However, society has not weighed the benefits from medical advances against their costs—the result has been continuing increases in costs.

Test Your Understanding

1. The false statements are the following: a (about a fourth are black and almost half are white); b (children have a higher poverty rate); and d (a

minimum wage is not high enough to avoid poverty). The only true statement is c.

2. This statement is obviously false because during this period, the real value of AFDC and food stamps actually decreased by about 25%.
3. As the family's earned income increases, the AFDC payment decreases, so the payoff per hour (the net wage) is less than the market wage.
4. eleven, eight
5. The third fifth experienced the largest absolute decline, from 17.5% to 15.9%, a drop of 1.6 percentage points.
6. The combination of technological change and growing trade increased the demand for more educated workers (college graduates and people with advanced degrees) and decreased the demand for less educated workers (high-school dropouts and graduates).
7. False. The benefit structure redistributes income because the replacement rates are higher for lower-wage workers.
8. The age structure matters because the more workers there are relative to the elderly population, the lower the tax rate needs to be to transfer income.
9. Advantages: higher rates of return on investment and increased saving for society; disadvantages: costs of making the transition and a loss of social insurance.

Using the Tools

1. Economic Detective: Wages of College and High-School Graduates

   In each market, the supply curve shifted to the right, with a larger shift in the market for college graduates. At the same time, the demand curve for college graduates shifted to the right (an increase in demand resulting from technological change and greater exports) and the demand shift was large enough to offset the supply shift. As a result, the wage for college graduates increased. In the market for high-school graduates, the demand curve for high-school graduates shifted to the left (lower demand because of technological change and an increase in imports), leading to lower wages. Because the college wage increased and the high-school wage decreased, the relative wage of college graduates increases.
2. Chile's Transition to a Private Pension System

   During any transition period from a pay-as-you-go system, it will be necessary to provide support for the retired and those near retirement. Managing this transition is easier if there is a young population since the necessary tax rate will be lower as more workers will be contributing.
3. Evaluating Medical Technology

   You need to compare the marginal benefit of the new technology and the marginal cost. The marginal benefit is value of returning people to work one week earlier. The marginal cost is the extra cost of this procedure over the original procedure. If there are no other considerations, the new technology should be used only if the marginal benefit exceeds the marginal cost.

NOTES

1. *Statistical Abstract of the United States* (Washington, DC: U.S. Government Printing Office, 1995), Table 746.
2. Blank, Rebecca M., *Changing Poverty: Complex Problems and Effective Policies* (Princeton, NJ: Princeton University Press, 1996).
3. Blank, *Changing Poverty.*
4. John Bound and George Johnson, "Changes in the Structure of Wages in the 1980's: An Evaluation of Alternative Explanations," *American Economic Review,* vol. 82, no. 3, June 1992, pp. 371–392.
5. Rebecca M. Blank, "The Employment Strategy: Public Policies to Increase Work and Earnings," in *Confronting Poverty,* edited by Sheldon H. Danziger, Gary D. Dandefur, and Daniel H. Weinburg (Cambridge, MA: Harvard University Press, 1994).
6. Blank, "The Employment Strategy."
7. Robert A. Moffitt, "Incentive Effects of the U.S. Welfare System: A Review," *Journal of Economic Literature,* vol. 30, 1992, pp. 1–61.
8. U.S. General Accounting Office, *An Evaluation of the 1981 AFDC Changes: Final Report* (Washington, DC: U.S. Government Printing Office, 1985).
9. Blank, *Changing Poverty.*
10. The computations are based on a welfare program under which the first $1,080 of income does not affect the AFDC payment or the food stamp allotment, but additional income decreases the AFDC payment by 67 cents per dollar and decreases the food stamp allotment by 33 cents.
11. *Statistical Abstract of the United States* (Washington, DC: U. S. Government Printing Office, 1995), Table 616.

12. Blank advocates this three-tiered approach in *Changing Poverty.*
13. Alan B. Kreuger, "How Computers Have Changed the Wage Structure: Evidence from Microdata, 1984–1989," *Quarterly Journal of Economics,* vol. 108, 1993, pp. 33–60.
14. "Your Stake in the Fight," *Consumer Reports,* September 1981, pp. 503–510.
15. For estimates of future tax rates, see Henry Aaron, Barry Bosworth, and Gary Burtless, *Can America Afford to Grow Old?* (Washington, DC: Brookings Institution, 1989).
16. For a discussion of inefficient spending in the health care system, see David Cutler, "Cutting Costs and Improving Health Care," in *The Problem That Won't Go Away,* edited by Henry Aaron (Washington, DC: Brookings Institution, 1996) pp. 250–265.
17. Victor Fuchs, "Economics, Values, and Health Reform," *American Economic Review,* March 1996, pp.1–26.

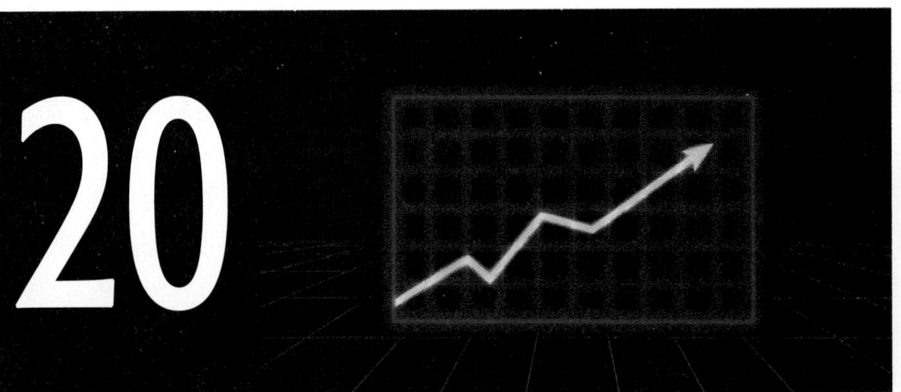

20 The Big Ideas in Macroeconomics

Last week, Tom listened to the business news on television. The announcer said that "GDP growth soared" in the fourth quarter, pulling the economy "out of the trough of the recession." She also said that some analysts feared that there would be "sharp increases in the inflation rate" in coming months. Tom was vaguely familiar with all these expressions, but he wondered what they really meant and how they would affect his day-to-day life.

This chapter begins our study of **macroeconomics**, the branch of economics that deals with the nation's economy as a whole. This is the field that focuses on the economic issues you most often see discussed in newspapers or hear on the radio or on television programs: unemployment, inflation, growth, trade, and the gross domestic product.

Macroeconomics: The branch of economics that looks at the economy as a whole.

Macroeconomic issues are at the heart of our political debates. Every newly elected president of the United States must learn a quick lesson in macroeconomics. The president's advisors explain that the chief executive's prospects for reelection will depend crucially on how well the economy performs during his or her term of office. If the public believes that the economy has performed well, the president will be reelected. But if the public thinks that the economy has not performed well, they are unlikely to support the incumbent. Democrats such as Jimmy Carter as well as Republicans such as George Bush have failed in their bids for reelection because of the economic concerns of the voting public.

Macroeconomic events profoundly affect our everyday lives. For example, if the economy fails to create enough jobs, workers will become unemployed throughout the country and millions of lives will be disrupted.

Similarly, slow economic growth will mean that standards of living will not increase rapidly in the future. Or if prices for all goods start increasing rapidly, people will find it difficult to maintain their standard of living.

Businesses are also keenly interested in macroeconomic developments. For example, they would like to know how the cost of borrowing and the value of the dollar abroad may change so they can make the most effective plans for the future. Businesses also want to know which economies in the world are most likely to grow in the future so that they can decide where to invest most profitably. Managers also want to be able to evaluate the economic policies that governments pursue so that they can estimate the economic consequences for their enterprises.

In this chapter we introduce you to the major ideas in macroeconomics. After reading it, you will be able to answer the following questions:

1 How does macroeconomics differ from microeconomics?
2 What is the gross domestic product?
3 What are economic growth and labor productivity?
4 What is a recession?
5 How do we calculate the unemployment rate in an economy?
6 What is the inflation rate?
7 What are classical and Keynesian economics?

As we learn the answers to these questions, we will build the necessary foundation for studying macroeconomics.

WHAT IS MACROECONOMICS?

The two branches of economics, microeconomics and macroeconomics, use similar tools and share common reasoning. But they focus on different aspects of the economy.

Microeconomics studies the behavior of individual consumers, firms, and markets. For example, in microeconomics, you might analyze how consumers would respond to an increase in the price of gasoline by driving less or buying more fuel efficient cars. Similarly, you might study how a firm that had a monopoly on the production of a new drug sets the price for that drug. Above all, you study how prices are arrived at in individual markets.

As we discussed in Chapter 1, *macroeconomics* steps back from the details of individual markets and looks at the economy as a whole. To understand the difference between microeconomics and macroeconomics, consider a few examples:

1. In microeconomics, you might study what determines the number of computers produced in the United States. In macroeconomics, you will study what determines the total output of the entire U.S. economy.
2. In microeconomics, you might study why there are unemployed workers in the aerospace industry. In macroeconomics, you study what determines the total amount of unemployment in the entire economy.
3. In microeconomics, you might study why the price of corn rises if farmers have bad weather and a smaller crop than usual. In macroeconomics, you study why all prices might be rising at 5% per year.
4. In microeconomics, you might study how an individual bank attempts to make a profit by taking deposits and making loans. In macroeconomics, you study how the entire banking system operates throughout the country.

Of course, there is not a hard-and-fast line between macroeconomics and microeconomics. For example, sometimes macroeconomists do study the effects of price changes in individual markets. In both 1973 and 1979, oil prices increased sharply around the world. These price increases had important macroeconomic consequences and were the focus of much investigation.

Macroeconomics developed as a subject with the aim of improving economic policy for the country as a whole. The first modern macroeconomist was John Maynard Keynes (pronounced *Canes*), who is best known as the father of "Keynesian" economics. Keynes was a renowned British economist and writer who taught at Cambridge University in England. During the dismal 1930s when all the major economies of the world suffered massive unemployment, Keynes wrote a book entitled *The General Theory of Employment, Interest and Money.* This formidable book, still hard reading today, started the field of modern macroeconomics as we now know it. Although it has been 60 years since Keynes published his major work, its influence continues to be felt throughout the world, as we shall see in our chapter on "Keynesian Economics and Fiscal Policy."

Macroeconomics today differs in some important respects from the ideas promoted by Keynes during the 1930s. Since Keynes was writing during a period of massive unemployment, he developed his theories to explain why economic times were so bad and how we could cure the worldwide crisis following the Great Depression. He emphasized the short-run benefits of increased government spending to reduce the amount of unemployment in the country. Such government spending to reduce unemployment might be new highway construction or the employment of additional teachers.

Modern macroeconomics, however, does not just focus on short-term crises. It also takes a longer view. For example, it tries to understand how government spending affects the economy when there is not massive unemployment and we are not in a deep crisis. It also studies how economies can grow over long periods of time, raising the standard of living for members of the society.

The distinction between the short- and long-run effects of economic policy is crucial. Policies that may be beneficial in the short run may not be beneficial in the long run. An analogy can help make this point. Suppose that you are recovering from a severe cold and now have a deep and annoying cough that keeps you awake at night. The doctor may prescribe some cough medicine laced with codeine to help

The desperate economic times of the Great Depression drove many of the unemployed to sell apples on the street, as this man did in "Hobo Jungle" in New York City.

you sleep. The medicine works in the short run to ease your cough and the codeine lets you sleep. But this would be bad medicine in the long run. If you kept renewing your prescription you could easily become addicted to the codeine and suffer painful consequences.

We will encounter many examples in which the short-run effects of policies differ from the long-run effects. For example, actions that decrease unemployment today may raise inflation in the future. Similarly, higher government spending today may raise the level of output in the economy today but actually reduce it in the future.

Here are just a few of the policy questions that modern macroeconomics tries to address:

1. Suppose the economy begins to experience sudden increases in unemployment. Should the government increase its spending? If so, is it better for the government to pay for its spending by raising taxes or by borrowing some of the funds from the public?
2. Suppose we want to raise the rate at which an economy grows. Are there any government policies that will help?
3. Suppose the prices of all goods start to rise at a rapid rate. How should the government react?
4. Suppose the rate at which you can trade U.S. dollars for Japanese yen starts to fall suddenly so that you get fewer yen for the dollar. What actions, if any, should the government take?

To address these policy issues, we first need to become familiar with the basic concepts of macroeconomics. In this chapter we introduce key concepts that we use throughout the book, identifying many important terms that you have encountered in the newspapers and heard on television. These concepts are developed more fully in the next chapter, where we concentrate in more detail on how economists measure them. We conclude the chapter with a discussion of two prominent, and contrasting, strands of thought in macroeconomics: classical and Keynesian economics.

A modern economy produces vast numbers of different goods and employs workers in thousands of different industries. For us to understand and comprehend the entire economy, we need to find some way to reduce its complexity. To assist in this task, economists have developed special measures for total output, total unemployment, and total prices in the economy. Let's look at each.

THE OUTPUT OF THE ECONOMY

We begin our overview of macroeconomics by studying the total level of output for an economy. First, we learn the way that total output is measured. Then we learn about growth rates, productivity, and economic fluctuations.

Measuring Total Output

Gross domestic product (GDP): The total market value of all the final goods and services produced within an economy in a given year.

The most common measure of the total output of an economy is **gross domestic product (GDP)**, the total market value of all the final goods and services produced within an economy in a given year. All the words in this definition are important. "Total market value" means that we take the quantity of goods produced and multiply them by their respective prices and then add up the totals. For example, if an economy produced two cars at $15,000 a car and three computers at $3,000 a computer, the total value of these goods and services would be:

$$(2 \times \$15,000) + (3 \times \$3,000) = \$39,000$$

The reason we multiply the goods by their prices is that we cannot simply add together the number of cars and the number of computers. Using prices allows us to express the value of everything in a common unit of measurement, in this case dollars. (In countries other than the United States, we would express the value in terms of the local currency.)

"Final goods and services" in the definition of GDP means those goods and services that are sold to ultimate or final purchasers. For example, the two cars that were produced would be final goods if they were sold to households or to a business. However, in producing the cars, the automobile manufacturer bought steel that went into the body of the cars. This steel would not be counted as a final good or service in GDP. It is an example of an **intermediate good**, a good that is used in the production process and is not a final good or service.

Intermediate good: Goods used in the production process that are not final goods or services.

The reason that we do not count intermediate as well as final goods is to avoid double-counting. The price of the car already reflects the price of the steel that is contained in it. We do not want to count the steel twice. Similarly, the large volumes of paper used by an accounting firm are also intermediate goods because they become part of the final product delivered by the accounting firm to its clients.

The final words in our definition of GDP are "in a given year." GDP is expressed as a rate of production; that is, as so many dollars per year. In 1995, for example, GDP in the United States was $7,248 billion. Goods produced in prior years, for example used cars, would not be included in GDP this year.

Since we measure GDP using the current prices for goods and services, GDP will increase if prices increase even if the physical amount of goods that are produced remains the same. For example, suppose that in the very next year the economy again produces two cars and three computers but now all the prices in the economy have doubled, so that the price of cars is $30,000 and the price of computers is now $6,000. GDP will now also be twice as high, or $78,000, (2 × $30,000) + (3 × $6,000), even though the same physical production occurs.

Now let's apply one of our five basic principles of economics, the reality principle:

Reality PRINCIPLE

What matters to people is the real value or purchasing power of money or income, not its face value.

We would like to have another measure of total output in the economy that does not increase just because prices increase. It is precisely for this reason that economists have developed the concept of **real GDP**, a measure of GDP that controls for price changes.

Real GDP: A measure of GDP that controls for changes in prices.

Nominal GDP: The value of GDP in current dollars.

In the next chapter, we explain precisely how real GDP is calculated. But the basic idea is quite simple. We call GDP that is measured using current prices **nominal GDP**. Nominal GDP can increase for one of two reasons: Either the production of goods and services has increased, or the prices of those goods and services has increased. To calculate real GDP, we essentially recalculate GDP but hold prices constant. This enables us to measure how much change there has been in real production or output in the economy.

To take a simple example, suppose that an economy produced a single good, computers. In year 1, 10 computers were produced and each sold for $1,000. In year 2, 12 computers were produced and each sold for $1,100. Nominal GDP would be $10,000 in year 1 and $13,200 in year 2. Nominal GDP would have increased by a factor of 1.32.

We can measure real GDP by recalculating GDP using year 1 prices. In year 1, real GDP would be (10 × $1,000) = $10,000 and in year 2 it would be

(12 × $1,000) = $12,000, which is greater by a factor of 1.2. The key idea is that we construct a measure using the *same prices* for both years and thus control for price changes. In principle, we could also have measured real GDP using year 2 prices for the calculation. As we will see in the next chapter, the actual measures of real GDP that the U.S. government uses are a combination of year 1 and year 2 prices.

Figure 1 plots real GDP for the U.S. economy for the years 1930–1995. The data for real GDP are constructed so that nominal and real GDP are set equal for a single year, in this case 1992. For both earlier and later years, the data for real GDP control for changes in prices and thus capture movements in real output only.

Economic growth: Sustained increases in the real production of an economy over a period of time.

The graph shows that real GDP has grown substantially over this period. This is what economists term **economic growth,** sustained increases in the real production of an economy over a period of time. In later chapters we also look at the growth of GDP per person, or per capita GDP. Differences in economic growth between countries and changes in economic growth over time are among the most important issues in macroeconomics.

TEST *Your Understanding*

1. True or false: Real GDP measures the value of goods and services using current-year prices.
2. Intermediate goods are excluded in calculating GDP to avoid ____________.
3. Give a precise definition of GDP.
4. Why do we distinguish between real and nominal GDP?

Figure 1

U.S. Real GDP, 1930–1995

Source: U.S. Department of Commerce.

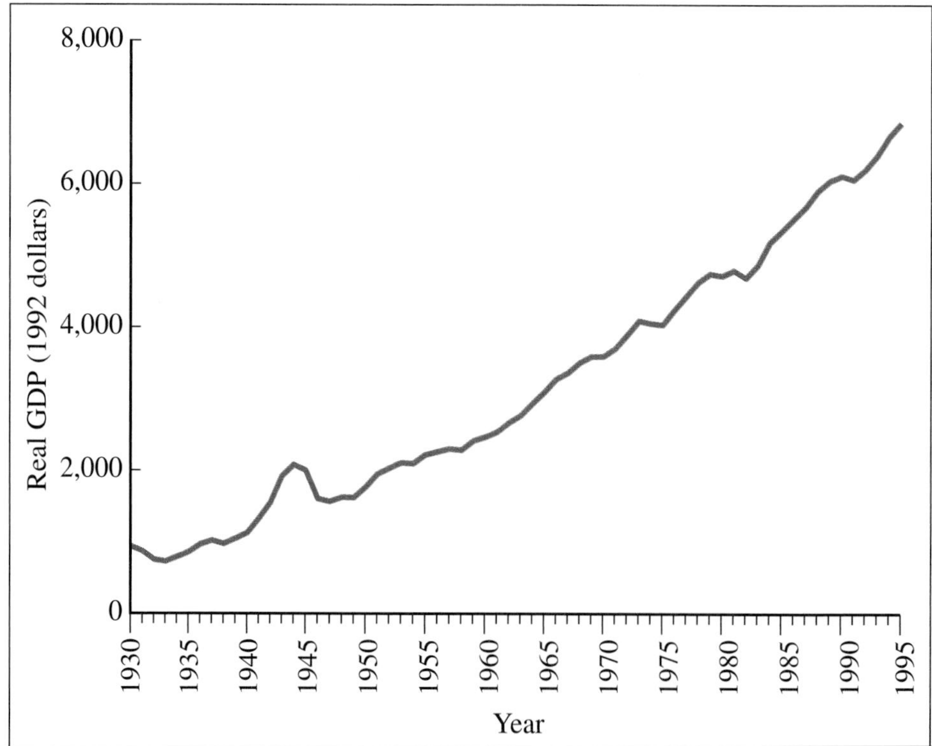

Growth Rates

GDP and prices typically grow over time. To have a convenient way to describe the changes in GDP and prices, economists frequently calculate growth rates. The **growth rate** of a variable is the *percentage change in the variable from one period to another*. Let's illustrate the idea of a growth rate with an example from real GDP. Consider calculating the growth rate of real GDP between years 1 and 2. Suppose that real GDP was 100 in year 1 and 104 in year 2. Then the growth rate of real GDP between these years would be

Growth rate: The percentage rate of change of a variable.

$$\begin{aligned}\text{growth rate} &= \text{percentage change}\\ &= \frac{\text{change in GDP}}{\text{initial GDP}}\\ &= \frac{\text{GDP year 2} - \text{GDP year 1}}{\text{GDP year 1}}\\ &= \frac{104 - 100}{100}\\ &= \frac{4}{100} = 0.04 \text{ or } 4\%\end{aligned}$$

Real GDP grew by 4%.

Growth rates can be negative. If GDP fell between years 1 and 2, the percentage change or growth rate would be negative. Suppose that real GDP was 104 in year 1 and 100 in year 2. In this case, the growth rate of real GDP would be

$$\begin{aligned}\text{growth rate} &= \frac{\text{GDP year 2} - \text{GDP year 1}}{\text{GDP year 1}}\\ &= \frac{100 - 104}{104}\\ &= \frac{-4}{104} = -0.038 \text{ or } -3.8\%\end{aligned}$$

In this case, real GDP fell by 3.8% between years 1 and 2. The growth of real GDP will be negative whenever real GDP falls.

If we know the growth rate and the initial value for GDP, we can also calculate the value for the next period. Here is the simple formula that links the growth rate, g, and the values of GDP for the initial and next periods:

$$\text{GDP year 2} = (1 + g) \times \text{GDP year 1}$$

That is, GDP in the second year is 1 plus the growth rate times GDP in the first year.

For example, suppose the growth rate for GDP were equal to 0.04 (4%) and GDP in year 1 were equal to 100. Then

$$\begin{aligned}\text{GDP year 2} &= (1 + 0.04)(100)\\ &= 104\end{aligned}$$

GDP in year 2 is 104.

We can apply the formula for growth rates for longer periods of time. Suppose that an economy started at a level of 100 in year 1 and grew at a rate g for two periods. In the second year output would be $(1 + g)(100)$. Between the second and third years output would again grow by a factor of $(1 + g)$. To calculate output in the third year, we need to multiply $(1 + g)$ times output in the second year, or

$$(1 + g)\,[(1 + g)(100)] \quad \text{or} \quad (1 + g)^2\,(100)$$

For example, if the economy grew at 4% for two years, then in the second year real GDP would be (1 + 0.04)(100), or 104. In the third year real GDP would be (1.04) [(1.04) (100)], or 108.2.

We can use this idea repeatedly if the economy grows at the same rate for several years. If, for example, the economy started at 100 and grew at rate g for n years, then the formula for real GDP after n years would be

$$\text{GDP}[n \text{ years later}] = (1 + g)^n(100)$$

Let's illustrate this formula with an example. Suppose that the economy starts at 100 and grows at a rate of 4% a year for 10 years. Output after 10 years will be

$$\begin{aligned}\text{GDP}[10 \text{ years later}] &= (1 + 0.04)^{10}(100) \\ &= 148\end{aligned}$$

nearly 50% higher than in the first year.

Seemingly small differences in growth rates can lead to significant differences over time. In this example, a growth rate of 4% led to nearly a 50% increase in real GDP after 10 years. If the growth rate were only 1% over those 10 years, output would have grown by only 11%.

Finally, a very useful rule of thumb can help you understand the power of growth rates. Suppose that you knew the constant growth rate of real GDP but wanted to know how many years it would take until the level of real GDP doubled. The answer is given by the *rule of 70*:

$$\text{years to double} = \frac{70}{\text{percentage growth rate}}$$

As an example, suppose an economy had the good fortune to grow at 5% a year. Then it would take only

$$\frac{70}{5} = 14 \text{ years}$$

for real GDP to double. Figure 2 shows how long it took for several countries to double their output starting in 1960. Japan grew the most rapidly; its output doubled in only eight years.

Productivity

We have just seen that economic growth rates can differ across countries. They also can differ over long periods of time within a single country. In the United States, for example, economic growth has slowed down over time. From 1950 to 1973, real GDP grew at an annual rate of 3.58%. However, from 1974 to 1995, real GDP grew at the slower annual rate of 2.66%.

Labor productivity: The amount of output produced per worker.

This decline in the growth rate of real GDP in the United States was also associated with a decline in the growth of **labor productivity**, the amount of output produced per worker. Labor productivity is a useful measure in economics because it gives us an idea of how much is produced by the average worker. Living standards can rise over time only if more output is produced from each worker in the economy. As we discuss in our chapter on economic growth, labor productivity will depend on the amount of machines, buildings, and equipment in the economy as well as the state of technology.

Figure 3 plots a standard measure of labor productivity, total output per hour of work, for the United States for 1959–1995. As you can see in the figure, although

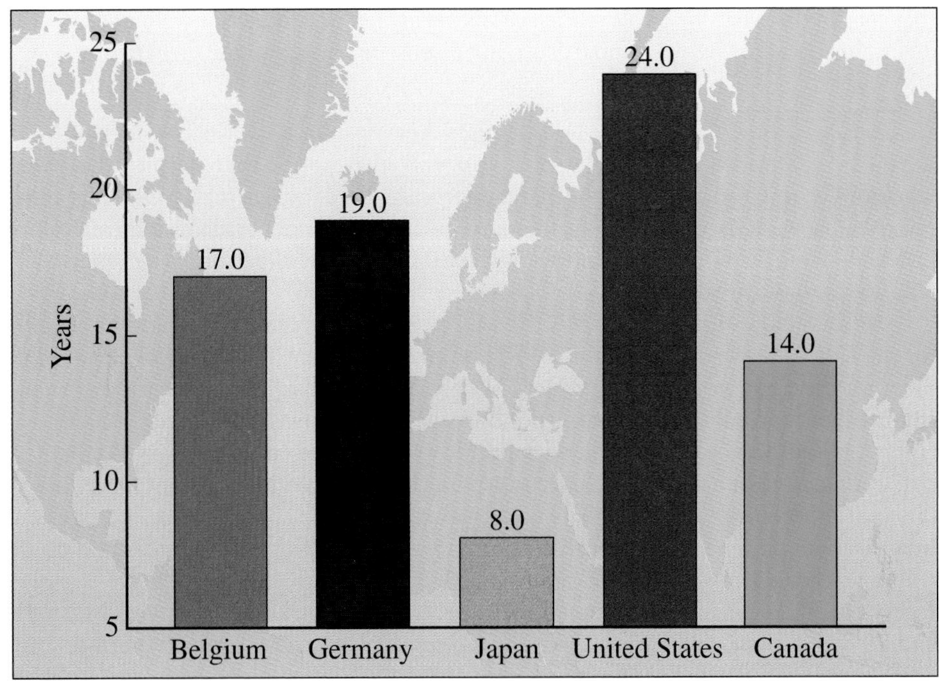

Figure 2

How Many Years It Took for GDP to Double Starting in 1960

Source: Angus Maddison, *Dynamic Forces in Capitalist Development* (New York: Oxford University Press, 1991).

productivity continued to grow over this period, after 1973 it grew at a slower rate. This phenomenon, commonly known as the *productivity slowdown*, occurred throughout the world during this period. The productivity slowdown also means that since 1973, wages and salaries in the United States have not grown as fast as

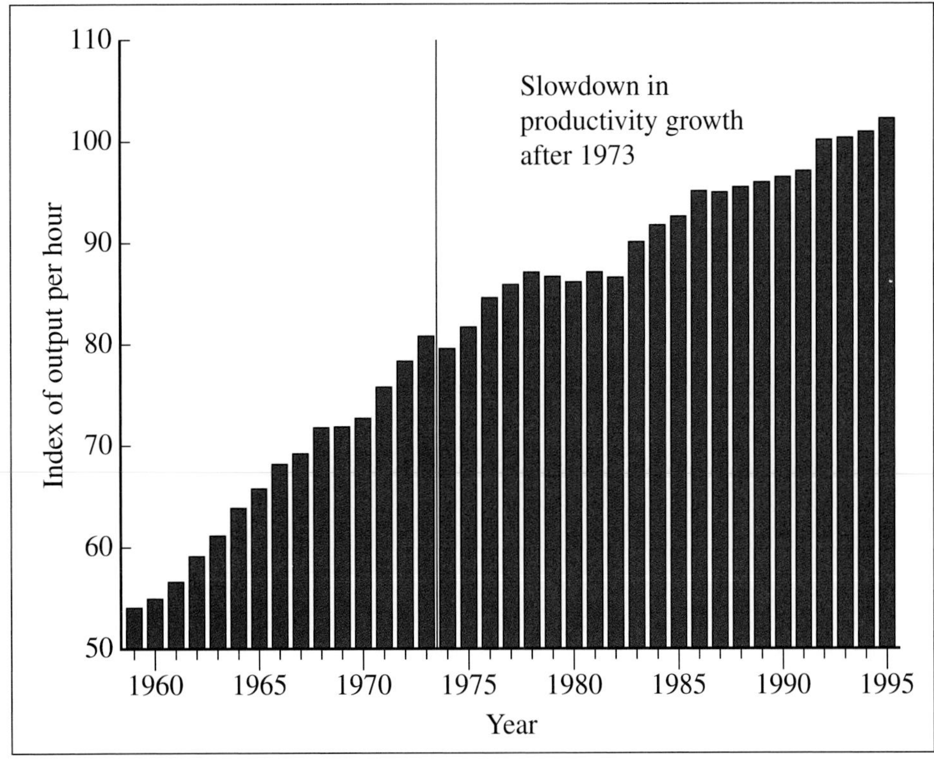

Figure 3

Labor Productivity in the United States, 1959–1995

Source: Data from *Economic Report of the President* (Washington, DC: U.S. Government Printing Office, 1996).

they had in the past. We explore the possible reasons for productivity slowdown and its implications for living standards in our discussion of economic growth.

Economic Fluctuations

If you take another look at Figure 1 you will also notice that despite the overwhelmingly upward trend in the data, there are times when real GDP falls temporarily. As we look more closely, fluctuations are even more evident. Figure 4 plots real GDP from 1967 to 1995. In this figure there are several periods when real GDP fell, for example around 1974.

A final close-up in Figure 5 is even more revealing. This figure plots real GDP for the United States from 1978 to 1983. Notice that in 1979 and in 1981 real GDP falls, and the growth rates of real GDP become negative at these times as well. (Remember that falling GDP corresponds to negative growth rates.)

Recession: Six consecutive months of negative economic growth.

Peak: The time at which a recession begins.

Trough: The time at which output stops falling in a recession.

A **recession** is a period when economic growth is negative (real GDP falls) for two consecutive quarters. A quarter is a period of three consecutive months during the year; therefore, a recession is a period when real GDP falls for at least six months. The date at which the recession starts is called the **peak** and the date at which output starts to increase again is called the **trough**. In Figure 5 we see two recessions; the peaks and troughs of the recessions are marked respectively by a "P" and a "T" on the graph. After a trough, the economy enters a recovery period.

Since World War II, the United States has experienced nine recessions. Table 1 contains the dates of the peaks and troughs of the recessions as well as the percent decline in real GDP from the peak to the trough. The sharpest decline in output occurred during the recession from 1973 to 1975, which was precipitated by a sharp rise in worldwide oil prices. Since 1982 there has been only one recession in the United States—and the recession that began in July 1990 was relatively mild by postwar standards.

Figure 4

U.S. Real GDP, 1967–1995

Source: U.S. Department of Commerce.

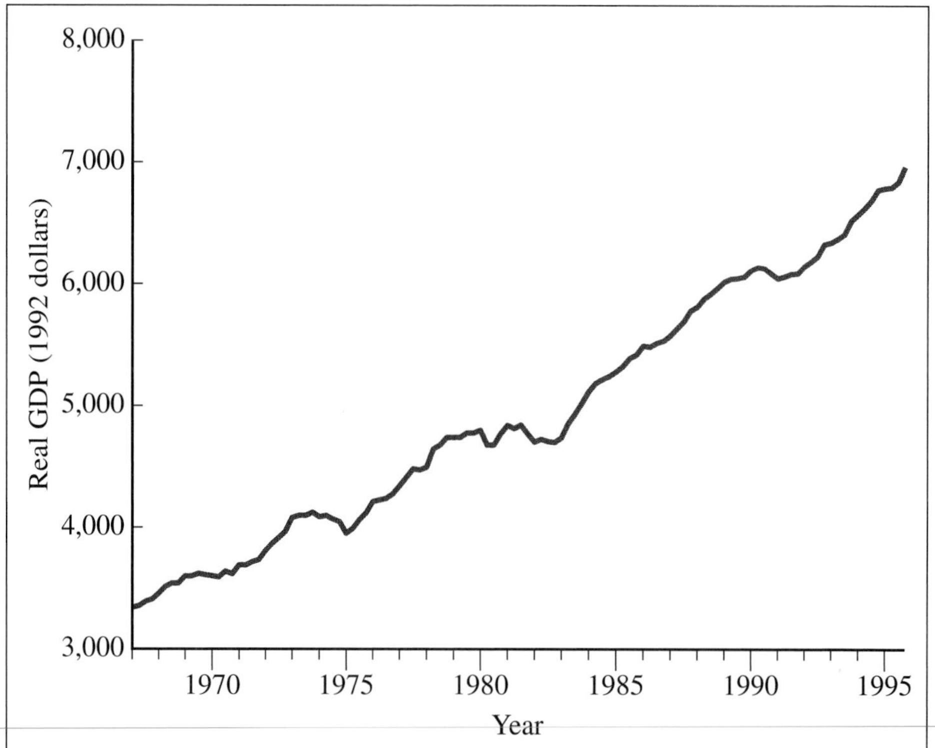

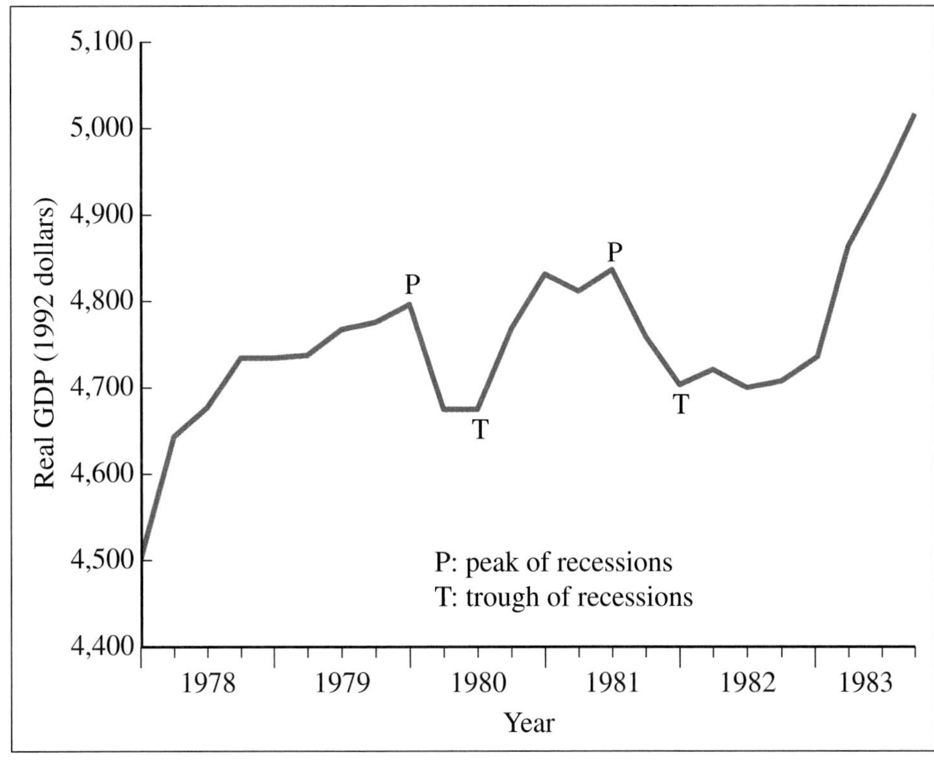

Figure 5

U.S. Real GDP, 1978–1983

Source: U.S. Department of Commerce.

Throughout U.S. history there have been other periods of economic downturns. According to scholars of the business cycle, from 1860 up to World War II there have been 20 downturns in economic activity. Not all these downturns were very pronounced, and in some, unemployment hardly changed. However, some of these downturns, such as those in 1893 and 1929, were particularly severe.

Depression is the common term for a severe recession. In the United States, the Great Depression refers to the 1929–1933 period, in which real GDP fell by over 33%. It created the most severe economic dislocations that the United States has experienced in the twentieth century. Throughout the country, and indeed the world, banks closed, businesses failed, and many people lost their life savings. Unemployment rose sharply. In 1933, over 25% of people looking for work failed to find jobs.

Depression: The common name for a severe recession.

Although the United States has not experienced a depression recently, other countries have not been as fortunate. During the 1980s and early 1990s, several countries

Table 1: Nine Postwar Recessions

Peak	*Trough*	*Percent Decline in Real GDP*
November 1948	October 1949	1.5
July 1953	May 1954	3.2
August 1957	April 1958	3.3
April 1960	February 1961	1.2
December 1969	November 1970	1.0
November 1973	March 1975	4.9
January 1980	July 1980	2.5
July 1981	November 1982	3.0
July 1990	March 1991	1.4

that were former members of the Soviet Union, as well as several Latin American countries, experienced severe economic disruptions that should be viewed as depressions.

Recessions and depressions can occur for a variety of reasons. Economists have identified a wide variety of factors that can cause recessions or depressions. As we study macroeconomics, we'll see how changes in technology, disruptions to the financial system, increases in prices of key commodities, and government policies (either deliberate or inadvertent) can all trigger recessions. As we noted, increases in oil prices helped initiate the 1973 recession, while the 1982 recession was largely a result of government policies taken to reduce the rate of price increases in the economy.

TEST ***Your Understanding***

5 Define *growth rate of a variable.*

6 Complete the statement with *risen* or *fallen*: Negative growth between two periods means that output has actually ____________.

7 If real GDP grows at a rate of 7%, how many years will it take output to double?

8 How many quarters of negative growth are required for a recession?

9 How does a depression differ from a recession?

UNEMPLOYMENT

Unemployed: People who are looking for work but do not have jobs.

Labor force: The employed plus the unemployed.

Unemployment rate: The fraction of the labor force that is unemployed.

One of the primary reasons that we want to avoid recessions and depressions is that they impose costs on individuals. During a recession, not only does GDP fall but fewer people are able to find work. Economists define the **unemployed** as those individuals who do not currently have a job but who are actively looking for work. The total **labor force** in an economy consists of all the people in an economy who either have jobs or are currently looking for jobs. The **unemployment rate** is the number of unemployed divided by the total labor force. For example, if 100 people are employed and 8 are unemployed, the unemployment rate will be: $8/(100 + 8) = 0.074$ or 7.4%.

Table 2 contains some international data on unemployment for 1995. Notice the sharp differences between countries; for example, Japan had a 3.4% unemployment rate while Spain had an unemployment rate of 22.7%.

Figure 6 plots the overall U.S. unemployment rate for the period 1950–1995. This figure has two noticeable features. First, there are periods when unemployment rises sharply over time. Second, even in the best of times there is unemployment. Let's consider each of these phenomena in turn.

Cyclical unemployment: The component of unemployment that accompanies fluctuations in real GDP.

Frictional unemployment: The part of unemployment associated with the normal workings of the economy, such as searching for jobs.

Unemployment rises sharply during recessions and falls when the economy improves. In Figure 6 there are eight times when the unemployment rate noticeably increases. All correspond to times in which the economy was in a recession. During recessions or periods of falling GDP, firms will not want to employ as many workers as they do in good times because they are not producing as many goods and services. They will lay off or fire some current workers and will be more reluctant to add new workers to their payrolls. The result will be fewer workers with jobs and rising unemployment. Economists call the unemployment that accompanies fluctuations in real GDP **cyclical unemployment.** Cyclical unemployment rises during recessions and falls when the economy improves.

Some unemployment occurs even when there are no recessions. Throughout the period 1974–1995, unemployment did not fall below 5% of the labor force. Unemployment that is not associated with recessions is either frictional unemployment or structural employment. **Frictional unemployment** is the

Table 2: Unemployment Rates Around the World, 1995

Country	Unemployment Rate
Canada	9.4
United States	5.6
Belgium	14.5
Sweden	7.8
France	11.9
Italy	12.0
Spain	22.7
United Kingdom	8.0
Netherlands	7.0
Japan	3.4
Australia	8.1

Source: OECD Employment Outlook (Paris: Organization for Economic Cooperation and Development, 1996).

unemployment that occurs naturally during the normal workings of an economy. It can occur for a variety of reasons. People change jobs, move across the country, get laid off from their current jobs and search for new opportunities, or take their time after they enter the labor force to find an appropriate job. Suppose that when you graduate from college, you take six months to find a job that you like. During the six months in which you are looking for a good job, you experience frictional unemployment. Searching for a job, however, makes good sense. It would not be wise to take the first job you were offered if it had low wages, poor benefits, and no future.

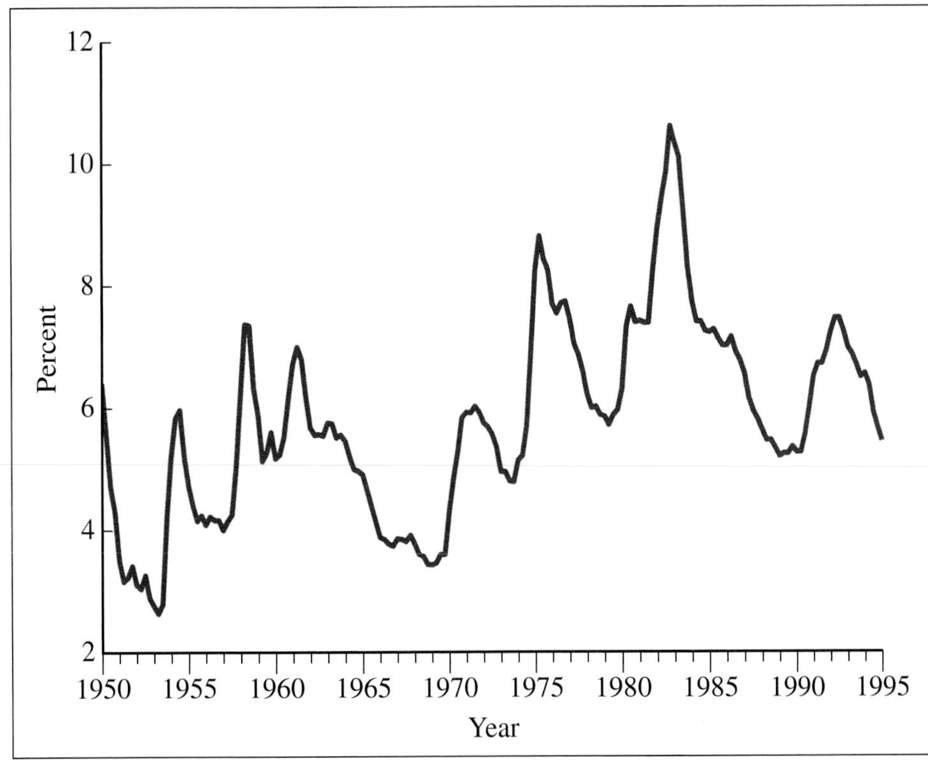

Figure 6

U.S. Unemployment Rate, 1950–1995

Source: Bureau of Labor Statistics.

Structural unemployment: The part of unemployment that results from the mismatch of skills and jobs.

Structural unemployment occurs because of a mismatch between the jobs that are available in the economy and the skills of workers seeking jobs. Workers with low skills may not find opportunities for employment. If the government requires employers to pay wages, taxes, and benefits that exceed the contribution of these workers, firms will not be likely to hire them. Similarly, workers whose skills do not match the employment opportunities in their area may be unemployed. Aerospace engineers in California will not find jobs in their area if the aerospace industry relocates to Alabama.

The line between frictional and structural unemployment is sometimes hard to draw. Suppose a highly skilled steel worker is laid off because his company shuts down its plant and moves it overseas. The worker would like to find a comparable job, but only low-wage, unskilled work is available in his town. Jobs are, however, available, and the steel company will never return. Is this person's unemployment frictional or structural? There really is no correct answer to this question: You might think of the steel worker as experiencing either frictional or structural unemployment.

Natural rate of unemployment: The level of unemployment at which there is no cyclical unemployment.

Full employment: The level of employment that occurs when the unemployment rate is at the natural rate.

Total unemployment in an economy is composed of cyclical, frictional, and structural unemployment. The level of unemployment at which there is no cyclical unemployment is called the **natural rate of unemployment**. It consists of only frictional and structural unemployment. The natural rate of unemployment is the economist's notion of **full employment**. It may seem strange at first to think that workers can still be unemployed even when the economy is at full employment. But economists choose to consider the economy to be at "full employment" when there is no cyclical unemployment, even when there is frictional and structural unemployment. The economy needs some frictional unemployment to operate efficiently so that workers and firms find the right matches.

In the United States today, economists estimate that the natural rate of unemployment is between 5.0 and 6.5%. The natural rate of unemployment can vary over time and will differ across countries. In Europe, for example, estimates of the natural rate of unemployment place it between 7 or 10%. In a later chapter we explore why the natural rate is higher in Europe than in the United States.

The actual unemployment rate can be either higher or lower than the natural rate. During a recession there will be positive cyclical unemployment, and unemployment can far exceed the natural rate. For example, in Figure 6 we can see that in 1983 unemployment exceeded 10% of the labor force. When the economy grows very rapidly for a sustained period, unemployment can fall below the natural rate. With sustained rapid economic growth, employers will be extremely aggressive in hiring workers. During the late 1960s, for example, unemployment rates fell below 4%; the natural rate then was over 5%. In this case, cyclical unemployment is negative.

Just as a car will overheat if the engine is overworked, so the economy will "overheat" if economic growth is too rapid. At very low unemployment rates, firms will find it difficult to recruit workers, and competition between firms will lead to increases in wages. As wages increase, prices soon follow. The sign of this overheating will be a general rise in prices for the entire economy, what we commonly call *inflation*. As we discuss in later chapters, when the unemployment rate falls below the natural rate, inflation will increase.

Voters are very sensitive to both unemployment and inflation, as the Closer Look box "Presidential Approval and Economic Performance" explains.

INFLATION

Price level: An average of all the prices in the economy.

In any large economy there are thousands of prices for individual goods and services. In macroeconomics we concentrate on an average of all the prices in the economy, which we call the **price level**. There are several different ways that economists calculate the price level.

A Closer LOOK

Presidential Approval and Economic Performance

Political scientists and economists have shown statistically what all presidents know: Presidential approval ratings in the polls are very sensitive to economic conditions. Higher unemployment and rising inflation both lead to lower approval ratings among all categories of voters, as measured by the Gallup Poll. A fall in approval ratings translates into a loss of votes at the polls.

Democratic voters tend to be more sensitive than Republican voters to increases in unemployment, while Republicans are more sensitive to inflation than Democrats. One study by political scientist Douglas Hibbs estimated the "trade-offs" that Democratic and Republican voters make between unemployment and inflation. In the face of a 1% increase in inflation, Democratic voters would require a drop in the unemployment rate of 0.9 points to keep their approval ratings constant. Republicans, however, would require a decrease in the unemployment rate of 1.5 points to make up for the same 1% increase in the inflation rate.

Hibbs also found that Democratic presidents, in line with the views of their political party, are more aggressive in trying to lower unemployment and less concerned about inflation than Republican presidents. Unemployment has been lower under Democratic presidents than under Republican presidents, but inflation has been higher under the Democrats as well. Thus the party affiliation of a president conveys important information about the administration's economic goals.

Low unemployment and low inflation paved the way for President Clinton's re-election.

Source: After Douglas Hibbs, *The American Political Economy* (Cambridge, MA: Harvard University Press, 1987) p. 177.

We look initially at a **chain-type price index for GDP**, an index that measures the average of the prices of the goods and services that are contained in GDP. Starting in 1996, a chain-type price index for GDP replaced the GDP deflator (a related measure) as the principal index reported by the U.S. Department of Commerce. In the next chapter, we look at another important measure of average prices in the economy, the Consumer Price Index (CPI), which is designed to measure changes in the cost of living.

Chain-type price index for GDP: A measure of the average level of prices of the goods and services contained in GDP.

A chain-type price index is constructed so that it has a value of 100 in a given year, called the base year. The important information in the value of this index for any other year is contained in its relation to the base year. For example, if a chain-type price index for GDP in one year is 105, this means that prices have increased by 5% [(105 – 100)/100] since the base year. By using a chain price index, we can see how the overall level of prices changes from one year to the next and over longer periods of time.

To understand how a price index works, let's consider our earlier example where the economy produced only a single good, computers. In year 1 there were 10 computers produced and each sold for $1,000. In year 2 there were 12 computers produced and each sold for $1,100.

If we choose year 1 as the base year, the price index for GDP will be 100 (by definition). In this example, the price of the single good in this economy, computers, rose by a factor of 1.1 ($1,100/$1,000 = 1.1). The price index in year 2 is equal to the value of the index in year 1 (100) times the factor by which prices increased

(1.1), or (100)(1.1) = 110. In subsequent years the price index will be increased by the factor by which prices have increased. Of course, in any actual economy there are thousands of goods and services, so we need to calculate the *average* rate that prices increase from one year to the next. In the next chapter, we look in more detail at how the U.S. government computes a chain-type price index for GDP.

To gain some historical perspective, Figure 7 plots a price index for GDP from 1875 to 1995. As you can see from the figure, from 1875 to the period just preceding World War I, there was virtually no change in the price level. The price level rose during World War I, fell after the war ended, and also fell sharply during the early 1930s. However, the most pronounced feature of the figure is the sustained rise in prices beginning around the 1940s. Unlike the earlier periods, in which the price level did not have a trend, after 1940 the price level increases sharply. By 1995, the price level increased by a factor of 12 over its value in 1940.

Inflation: The percentage rate of change of the price level in the economy.

To study movements in the price level, we calculate the *rate of inflation.* Just as economic growth was measured by the percentage rate of change in real GDP, **inflation** is the *percentage rate of change in the price level.* Let's return to our simple example in which a chain-type price index for GDP increased from 100 in year 1 to 110 in year 2, for a 10% increase. Since the inflation rate is defined as the percentage change in the price level, in this example the inflation rate would be 10%.

In everyday language people sometimes confuse the *level of prices* with inflation. You might hear someone say that inflation is high in San Francisco because rents on apartments are very high, but this is not a correct use of the term *inflation.* Inflation refers not to the level of prices, whether they are high or low, but to their percentage change. If rents were high in San Francisco but remained constant between two years, there would be no inflation in rents during this time.

Taking a closer look at the period following World War II, Figure 8 plots the inflation rate, the percentage change in the price index, for 1954–1995 in the United

Figure 7

Price Index for U.S. GDP, 1875–1995

Sources: R. J. Gordon, *Macroeconomics* (New York: HarperCollins, 1993); U.S. Department of Commerce.

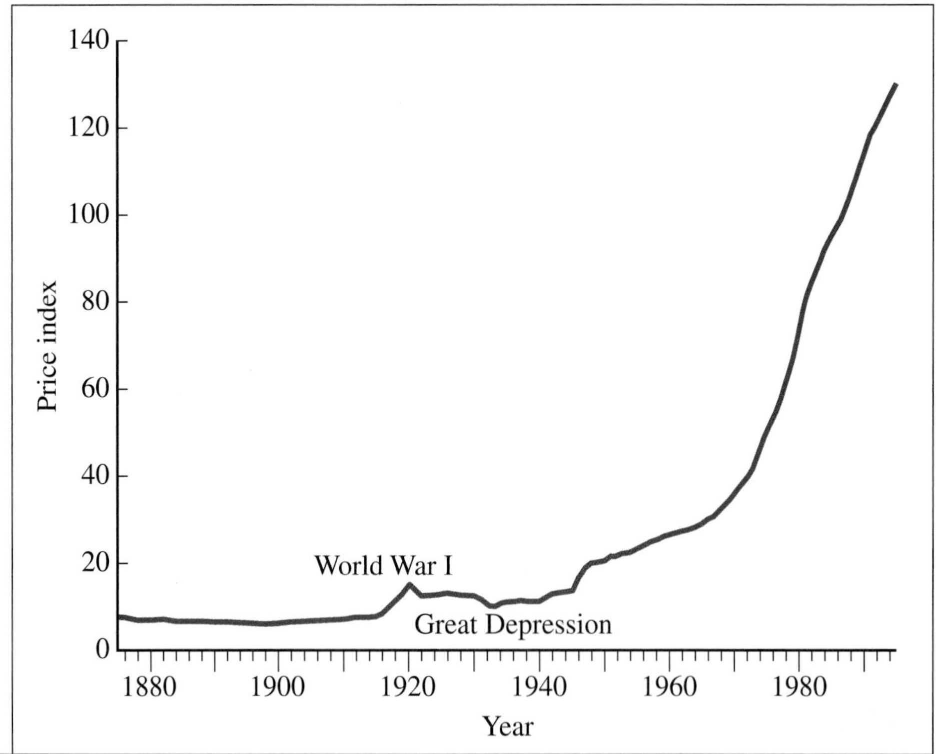

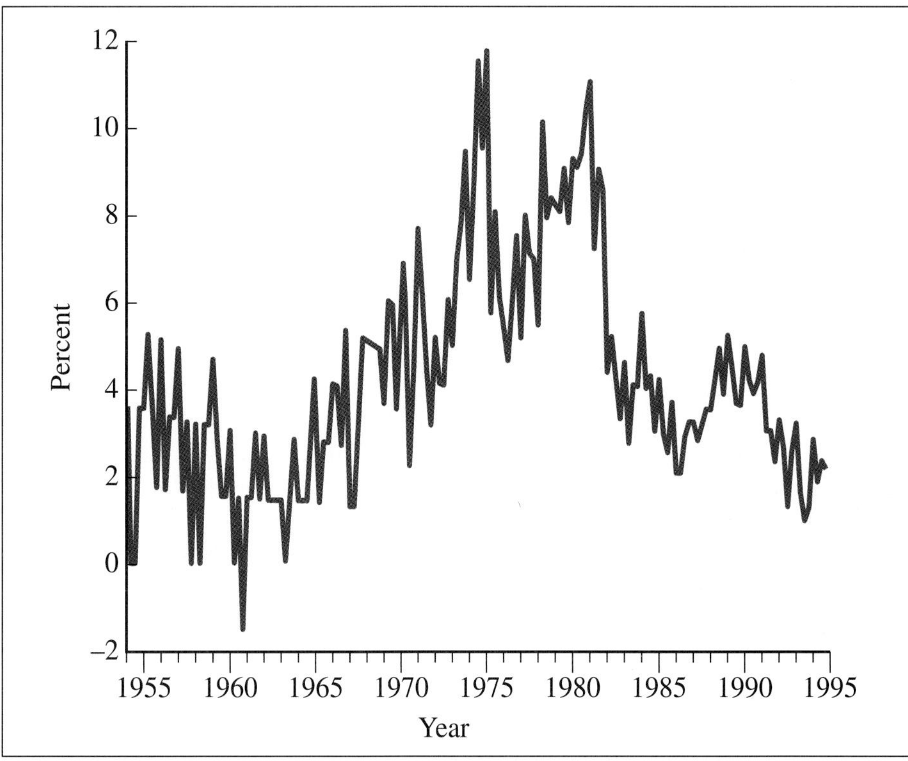

Figure 8

U.S. Inflation Rate, 1954–1995, Based on Chain-Type Price Index

Source: U.S. Department of Commerce.

States. In the 1950s and 1960s there were a few short periods where the inflation rate was negative. Since the inflation rate is defined as the percentage change in the price level, a negative inflation rate means that the price level actually fell during these times.

Those periods of zero or negative inflation quickly disappeared. The inflation rate was substantially higher in the 1970s, reaching nearly 12%. In recent years, the inflation rate has subsided and now is approximately 3% a year. Although falling prices are rare now, as the Closer Look box on the next page, "Deflations and Depressions," shows, prices have actually fallen quite sharply at times in U.S. history.

TEST *Your Understanding*

10 True or false: The unemployment rate is the total number of unemployed divided by the total number of employed.

11 Complete the statement with *recessions* or *booms*: Cyclical unemployment increases during ____________.

12 What do economists mean by *full employment*?

13 Give an example of frictional and structural unemployment.

14 True or false: Inflation must be high in New York because it is very expensive to live there.

15 Looking at Figure 7, approximately what was the average inflation rate between 1875 and the years prior to World War I?

A Closer LOOK

Deflations and Depressions

If you were born after 1952, you have never lived in a year without the price level rising, that is, without inflation. You might think it would be great if prices fell and we experience what economists call a *deflation.* In actuality, you should hope that we never do.

During the Great Depression the United States underwent a deflation, with the average level of prices falling 33% between 1929 and 1933. Wages fell along with prices during this period. The biggest problem caused by a deflation is that people cannot pay their debts. Imagine that you owe $40,000 for your education and expect to be able to pay it off over several years if you earn $20,000 a year. If a massive deflation caused your wages to fall to $10,000, you might not be able to pay your debt. You would be forced to default on your loan, as millions did during the Great Depression.

When people fail to pay interest and principal on their loans, banks get into trouble because they are no longer earning any money. In the 1930s, banks failed in the United States and throughout the world, including Austria, Hungary, Czechoslovakia, Romania, Poland, and Germany. These bank failures helped to make the Great Depression a worldwide phenomenon.

CLASSICAL AND KEYNESIAN ECONOMICS

In macroeconomics we develop models and tools to help us understand the economy. The types of models often depend on the topics or questions that we want to address. For some purposes it will be useful to analyze the economy without considering business cycles or economic fluctuations; that is, we will want to look at the economy when it is operating at or near full employment. For example, when we study economic growth or look at the causes of extremely high inflation rates, it is much easier to analyze the problem by assuming that the economy is operating at full employment. In these cases we do not significantly improve our understanding by considering economic fluctuations. As in all areas of economics, we can understand the issues more clearly if we focus on the essential aspects of a problem and not on all the details. As a useful shorthand, we call the study of the economy when it operates at or near full employment, **classical economics**.

Classical economics: The study of the economy when it operates at or near full employment.

Keynesian economics: The study of business cycles and economic fluctuations.

At other times, however, our principal concern will be business cycles, economic fluctuations, and sharp changes in unemployment rates. For these issues we want to understand how the economy can deviate from full employment. As another useful shorthand, we will call the study of business cycles and economic fluctuations that we develop **Keynesian economics** (after John Maynard Keynes, who made fundamental contributions to macroeconomics.) Our understanding of economic fluctuations today has progressed substantially since Keynes's initial writings and incorporates many different perspectives, including those of economists who were highly critical of Keynes. Our use of the term *Keynesian economics* is therefore just convenient shorthand for our study of economic fluctuations.

In this book we use insights from both classical and Keynesian economics and integrate them into our story of how the macro economy works. In particular, we will see that the factors stressed by Keynes and the tradition that followed him are useful for understanding the behavior of the economy in the short run, when the economy can be far away from full employment. However, in the long run, there are forces pushing the economy back to full employment. When the economy reaches full employment, the insights from classical economics become valuable.

Our discussions will span the full ranges of classical and Keynesian analysis. We will study why the economy can deviate from full employment in the short run and the process by which the economy returns (sometimes slowly) back to full employment. To preview our analysis, we will see that it is the slow adjustment of the price level that allows the economy to deviate from full employment. When the level of prices has adjusted fully, the economy will return to full employment.

Sometimes the words *classical* and *Keynesian* are used to refer to two different schools of economic thought. Classical economists, although recognizing that economic fluctuations do occur (and often developing their own theories of fluctuations), believe that the economy has a strong tendency to return to full employment. They therefore place great importance on studying the behavior of the economy at or near full employment. Keynesian economists, on the other hand, believe that the economy returns to full employment only slowly (if at all) and emphasize the role of economic fluctuations. In this book we draw freely on the ideas of both schools because both have important perspectives that we need to understand the full range of macroeconomic phenomena. As we will see, one of the principal disagreements among macroeconomists is about precisely how strong the forces are that push the economy back to full employment.

Using the **TOOLS**

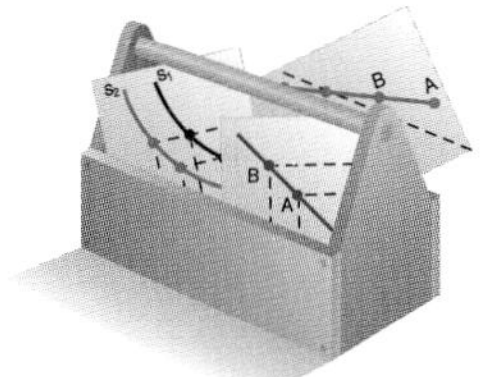

In this chapter we developed a number of useful concepts in macroeconomics and demonstrated how to calculate a variety of economic statistics. Here is an opportunity to test your understanding of these ideas.

1. Interpreting Korean Economic Statistics

Here is some data for Korea from the International Monetary Fund:

	1990	*1991*
Nominal GDP	172,724	207,517
Real GDP	131,503	142,591

What were the growth rates of nominal and real GDP between 1990 and 1991 for Korea? Which is bigger? What explains the difference?

2. ECONOMIC DETECTIVE– *Nominal and Real GDP*

Economists observed that in one country, nominal GDP increased two years in a row, but real GDP fell over the two years. How can this have occurred? Construct a numerical example to illustrate this possibility.

3. The Effects of Inflation over Time

A country has been experiencing an inflation rate of 8% a year. How many years will it take before the average price level in the country has doubled? How many years would it take for the price level to double if the inflation rate were only 4%?

4. Interpreting Worldwide Unemployment Statistics

A student looking at Table 2 on unemployment around the world argues that Spain must be experiencing a recession because its unemployment rate was 22.7% in 1995, whereas the unemployment rate in the United States was only 5.6%. Explain why the student might not be correct.

SUMMARY

Macroeconomics is the study of the nation's economy. To study the entire economy and interpret its performance, we develop concepts to measure output, prices, and employment for the economy as a whole. Here are the main points of the chapter.

1. To measure the level of output and prices in the economy, we use three interrelated concepts: Nominal GDP measures the value of currently produced output in current prices; real GDP measures the value of GDP controlling for prices; and the chain-type price index for GDP is a measure of the average level of prices of the goods contained in GDP.
2. The growth rate, or percentage rate of change, is an extremely useful tool in economics. We use growth rates to calculate the growth of real output and prices.
3. Economic growth does not always occur smoothly; sometimes the economy grows faster than average and at other times the economy fails to grow at all. Recessions occur when economic growth is negative for six consecutive months.
4. The three types of unemployment are cyclical, frictional, and structural. Cyclical unemployment is positive during periods of recession and negative during booms. However, frictional and structural unemployment still remain when the economy returns to full employment.
5. We measure inflation as the rate of change in the overall price level.
6. Sometimes we want to study the behavior of the economy when it operates at or near full employment. The study of the economy at full employment is known as Classical economics. Other times, we want to study economic fluctuations, which is the subject of Keynesian economics. In this book we draw on the insights of both approaches to study macroeconomic problems.

KEY TERMS

chain-type price index for GDP, *415*
classical economics, *418*
cyclical unemployment, *412*
depression, *411*
economic growth, *406*
frictional unemployment, *412*
full employment, *414*
gross domestic product (GDP), *404*
growth rate, *407*
inflation, *416*
intermediate good, *405*
Keynesian economics, *418*
labor force, *412*
labor productivity, *408*
macroeconomics, *401*
natural rate of unemployment, *414*
nominal GDP, *405*
peak, *410*
price level, *414*
real GDP, *405*
recession, *410*
structural unemployment, *414*
trough, *410*
unemployed, *412*
unemployment rate, *412*

PROBLEMS AND DISCUSSION QUESTIONS

1. How does macroeconomics differ from microeconomics?
2. Should we care more about the growth of real GDP or nominal GDP?
3. How can the growth rate of real GDP be negative in any year?
4. One humorist defined a recession as a time when other people are unemployed but a depression as a time when *you* are unemployed. What are the correct definitions of recessions and depressions?
5. In any city there are always some vacant apartments as well as people looking for apartments. Explain why this is always true and relate your answer to unemployment.
6. Suppose someone told you that the level of the chain-type price index for GDP in a country was 120. Why does this fact not convey much information to you?
7. Critically evaluate: "Tokyo is a very expensive place to live. They must have a high inflation rate in Japan."
8. When oil prices increased sharply in the 1970s, some economists argued that frictional unemployment also increased. Explain the logic of their argument.

Take It to the Net

We invite you to visit the O'Sullivan/Sheffrin page on the Prentice Hall Web site at:

http://www.prenhall.com/osullivan/

for this chapter's World Wide Web exercise.

MODEL ANSWERS FOR THIS CHAPTER

Chapter-Opening Questions

1. Macroeconomics is concerned with the aggregate or total economy while microeconomics is concerned with individual markets.
2. The gross domestic product is the value of all final goods and services produced in a given year.
3. Economic growth is sustained increases in real (inflation-corrected) gross domestic product. Labor productivity is output per worker.
4. A recession is two quarters of negative economic growth.
5. The unemployment rate is the ratio of the total number of unemployed to the labor force. The labor force consists of the employed plus the unemployed.
6. The inflation rate is the percentage rate of change in the price level.
7. Classical economics is the study of the economy as it operates at or near full employment while Keynesian economics is the study of business cycles and economic fluctuations.

Test Your Understanding

1. False.
2. double-counting
3. GDP is the value of final goods and services produced within a given year.
4. Real GDP controls for changes in prices and provides a better measure of the physical production in the economy.
5. It is the percentage rate of change.
6. fallen
7. It will take 10 years.
8. Two quarters are required.
9. A depression is the common name for a very severe recession.
10. False.
11. recessions
12. Full employment means no cyclical unemployment, only frictional and structural unemployment.
13. Frictional unemployment: taking time to find a job after graduating; structural unemployment: a highly skilled steel worker living in a town where the only jobs available require computer programming skills.
14. False.
15. The inflation rate was approximately zero since there was approximately no change in the price level.

Using the Tools

1. Interpreting Korean Economic Statistics

   The growth in nominal GDP is (207,517 – 172,724)/172,724 = 0.201 = 20.1%. The growth in real GDP is (142,591 – 131,503)/131,503 = 0.084 = 8.4%. Nominal GDP grew at a faster rate than real GDP. The difference in the two growth rates arises because of inflation. Recall that nominal GDP measures output in current prices while real GDP controls for price changes.
2. Economic Detective: Nominal and Real GDP

   Nominal GDP can increase while real GDP falls if prices increase sufficiently. Suppose that in a one good economy, production of cars falls from 10 to 5 but prices rise from $10,000 to $30,000. Then nominal GDP will increase from $100,00 to $150,000 but real GDP (using year 1 prices) will fall from $100,000 to $50,000.
3. The Effects of Inflation over Time

   Use the rule of 70. At an 8% inflation rate, it would take 70/8 = 8.75 years; at a 4% rate it would take 70/4 = 17.5 years.
4. Interpreting Worldwide Unemployment Statistics

   The student assumed that the high unemployment rate in Spain was due to cyclical unemployment. It may be largely frictional and structural unemployment; that is, Spain may have a higher natural rate of unemployment than the United States.

CHAPTER

21

Behind the Economic Statistics

Imagine this late-night dialogue between a foreign exchange student from France and a college student in the United States:

U.S. student: "Let's face it: The United States is the best country. We have the highest GDP per capita in the world."

French student: "But GDP per capita is not everything. In our country everyone takes four weeks vacation every year. In August, the only people in Paris are tourists! GDP does not measure the quality of life."

U.S. student: "Well, our unemployment rate is much lower than yours. We typically have unemployment rates near 6% and yours are closer to 12%."

French student: "True enough, but in the United States a higher fraction of people are actually in the labor force. Is that good? Is work the only part of life?"

U.S. student: "Well, I'm still sure we're the best. But maybe those macroeconomic statistics aren't as clear as I thought."

Macroeconomic statistics can be confusing and misleading. To be an informed citizen and not be misled, you should know how macroeconomic statistics are constructed and what they really measure. As we continue our study of the key concepts of macroeconomics—gross domestic product, unemployment, and inflation—we will realize that no single measure of an entire economy is perfect. In this chapter we will see both the strengths and the weaknesses of our standard measures of the macroeconomic economy.

Here are some of the questions you will be able to answer after reading this chapter:

1. Who buys the gross domestic product, and who gets the income that is produced in the economy?
2. Do the standard GDP calculations measure the value of our leisure time or the quality of our environment? Should they?
3. What groups suffer the most unemployment? Can the unemployment statistics tell us the answer?
4. How accurately can we measure inflation in the economy? If we don't do a good job, what impact does our inaccuracy have?

UNDERSTANDING GROSS DOMESTIC PRODUCT

Remember that we defined gross domestic product (GDP) as the market value of all final goods and services produced in the economy in a given year. To calculate GDP, we took all the final goods and services produced in a given year, multiplied them by their respective prices, and added up all the totals. Final goods and services were those sold to ultimate consumers; intermediate goods, such as steel used in production of automobiles or flour used in the production of bread, were excluded to avoid double counting.

Economists recognize that there are two interconnected sides to GDP. When firms produce output that is included in GDP, they also generate income. For example, when a computer manufacturer produces new computers, those computers are counted in GDP. At the same time, the manufacturer also generates income through its production. It pays wages to workers, perhaps pays rent on buildings, and pays interest on borrowed money. Whatever is left over after paying for the cost of production is the firm's profit and is income to the owners of the firm. Wages, rents, interest, and profits are all different forms of income.

Figure 1 on the next page illustrates the two sides of GDP with a simple diagram of the circular flow that we introduced in Chapter 3. In this highly simplified economy, there are only households and firms, which make transactions in both factor markets and product markets. In the factor markets, the households supply inputs to production. The primary inputs are labor and capital, what economists call **factors of production**. Households supply labor by working for firms. As owners of firms, households supply **capital** (that is, buildings, machines, and equipment) to the firms. In the factor markets, they are paid by the firms for the supply of these factors: wages for their work and interest, dividends, and rents for supplying capital. The households then take their income and purchase the goods and services produced by the firms in the product markets. The payments the firm receives from the sale of its products are used to pay for the factors of production. The important part of this diagram is that production generates income; corresponding to the production of goods and services in the economy are flows of income to households.

Factors of production: Labor and capital used to produce output.

Capital: The buildings, machines, and equipment used in production.

Based on this logic, economists typically ask two basic questions about GDP. Who purchases the final goods and services that are produced? And who gets the income that is generated from the production of GDP?

Who Purchases GDP?

Economists divide GDP into four broad categories that correspond to different types of purchasers of GDP. These categories and purchasers are:

Figure 1

Circular Flow

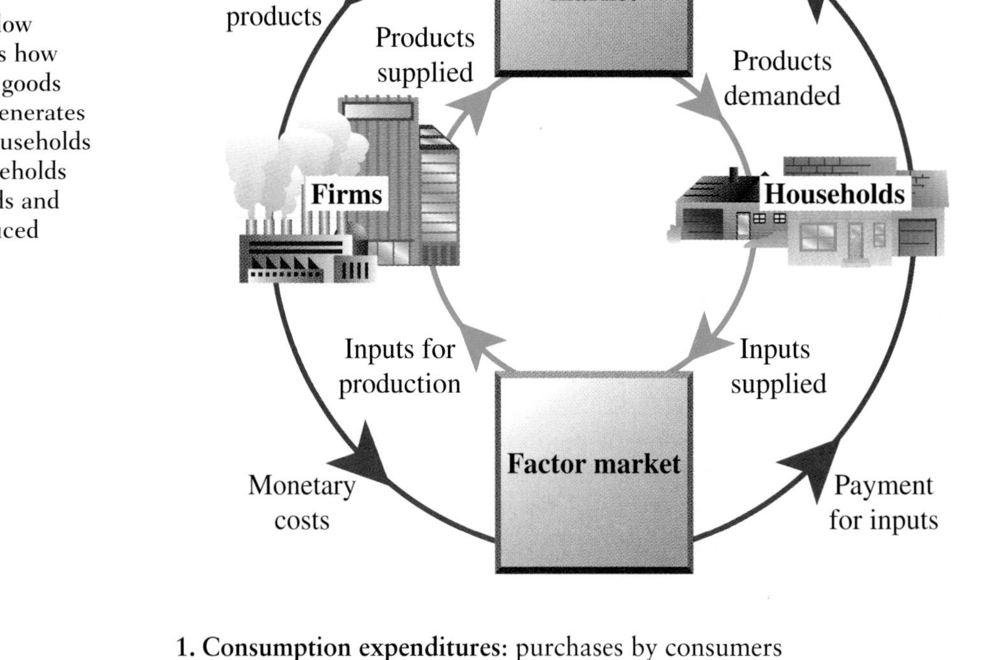

The circular flow diagram shows how production of goods and services generates income for households and how households purchase goods and services produced by firms.

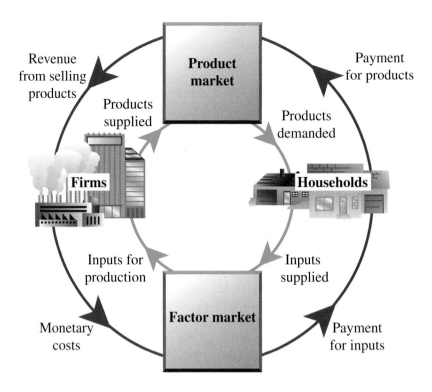

Consumption expenditures: Purchases of newly produced goods and services by households.

Private investment expenditures: Purchases of newly produced goods and services by firms.

Government purchases: Purchases of newly produced goods and services by all levels of government.

Net exports: Exports minus imports.

Durable goods: Goods that last for a long period of time, such as household appliances.

Nondurable goods: Goods that last for short periods of time, such as food.

1. **Consumption expenditures**: purchases by consumers
2. **Private investment expenditures**: purchases by firms
3. **Government purchases**: purchases by federal, state, and local governments
4. **Net exports**: net purchases by the foreign sector or exports minus imports

Before discussing these categories in more detail, let's look at some data for the U.S. economy to get a sense of the sizes of the different components. Table 1 shows the figures for GDP for a recent period. In 1995, GDP was $7,297 billion or approximately $7.3 trillion. To get a sense of the magnitude, consider that the U.S. population is approximately 255 million people. GDP per person is thus approximately $28,600.

Now let's consider each of the components of GDP in turn.

Consumption Expenditures

Consumption expenditures are purchases by consumers of currently produced goods and services, either domestic or foreign. These purchases include TV sets, VCRs, automobiles, clothing, hair-styling services, jewelry, movie tickets, food, and all other consumer items. We can break down consumption into durable goods, nondurable goods, and services. **Durable goods** are those that last for a longer period of time, such as automobiles or refrigerators. **Nondurable goods**, such as food,

Table 1: Composition of U.S. GDP, Third Quarter 1995 (billions of dollars expressed at annual rates)

GDP	*Consumption Expenditures*	*Private Investment Expenditures*	*Government Purchases*	*Net Exports*
7,297	4,965	1,067	1,366	–101

last for short periods of time. **Services** reflect work done in which people play a prominent role in delivery (such as a dentist filling a cavity); they range from haircutting to health care. Services are the fastest-growing component of consumption. Overall, consumption spending is the single most important component of GDP, constituting about 68% of total purchases.

Services: Reflect work done in which people play a prominent role in delivery, ranging from haircutting to health care.

Private Investment Expenditures

Private investment expenditures in GDP consist of three components. First, there is spending on new plants and equipment during the year. If a firm builds a new factory or purchases a new machine, that is included in GDP. Purchasing an existing building or buying a used machine does *not* count in GDP because the goods were not produced during the year. Second, newly produced housing is included in investment spending. The sale of an existing home to a new owner is not counted because the house was not built in the current year. Finally, if firms add to their stock of inventories, the increase is included in GDP. For example, if a hardware store had $1,000 worth of nuts and bolts on its shelves at the beginning of the year and $1,100 at the end, its inventory investment would be $100 ($1,100 – $1,000). The $100 increase in inventory investment is included in GDP.

We call the total of new investment expenditures **gross investment.** During the year some of the existing plant, equipment, and housing will deteriorate or wear out. This wear and tear is called **depreciation.** If we subtract depreciation from gross investment, we obtain **net investment.** Net investment is the true addition to the stock of plant, equipment, and housing in a given year.

Gross investment: Actual investment purchases.

Depreciation: The wear and tear of capital as it is used in production.

Net investment: Gross investment minus depreciation.

This distinction between gross and net investment is economically important. Consider the $1,067 billion in total investment spending for third quarter of 1995, a period in which there was $681 billion in depreciation. That means that there was only ($1,067 – $681) = $386 in net investment by firms in that year. Sixty-four percent of gross investment went to make up for depreciation of existing capital.

An important warning: In this book, and in economics generally, we use the term *investment* in a different way than we do in ordinary life. For an economist, investment in the GDP accounts means purchases of *new* final goods and services by firms. In everyday conversation we talk, for example, about "investing" in the stock market, or "investing" in gold. Buying a stock on the stock market is a purchase of an existing financial asset; it is not the purchase of new goods and services by firms. The same is true of purchasing a gold bar. In GDP accounting, investment denotes the purchase of new capital. Be careful not to confuse common usage with the definition of investment as we use it in the GDP accounts.

Government Purchases

This category refers to the purchases of newly produced goods and services by federal, state, and local governments. It includes any goods the government purchases, plus the wages and benefits of all government workers (paid when the government purchases their services as employees). The majority of spending in this category actually comes from state and local governments: $848 billion of the total $1,366 billion in 1995. Some of the government purchases are really investment goods, such as new schools or government buildings. However, these purchases are classified as government expenditures in the GDP accounts and not as private investment expenditures.

This category does *not* include all the spending that is done by governments. It excludes **transfer payments,** funds paid to individuals that are not associated with the production of goods and services. For example, payments for Social Security, welfare, and interest on government debt are all considered transfer payments and are not included in government purchases in GDP. The reason they are excluded is

Transfer payments: Payments to individuals from governments that do not correspond to the production of goods and services.

Spending on new bridges, such as San Francisco's Golden Gate Bridge, are included as government expenditures in the National Income Accounts.

that nothing is being produced in return for the payment. On the other hand, wage payments to the police, postal workers, and the staff of the Internal Revenue Service are included because they do correspond to services currently being produced.

Because transfer payments are excluded from GDP, a vast portion of the budget of the federal government is not part of GDP. In 1995 the federal government spent approximately $1,514 billion, of which only $517 billion (about one-third) was counted as federal government purchases. Transfer payments are important, however. They affect both the income of individuals and their consumption and savings behavior. They also affect the size of the federal budget deficit, which we will study in a later chapter. At this point, keep in mind the distinction between government purchases (which are included in GDP) and total government spending or expenditure (which may not be).

Net Exports

The United States has an open economy, which means that it trades with other economies. As you recall from Chapter 3, goods we buy from other countries are called imports. We also sell to other countries goods made here, which are called exports. Net exports are total exports minus total imports. In Table 1 we saw that net exports in the third quarter of 1995 were –$101 billion. The reason net exports were negative is that our imports exceeded our exports.

In creating a measure of GDP, we try to measure the goods produced in the United States. Consumption, investment, and government purchases include all purchases by consumers, firms, and the government, whether or not the goods were produced in the United States. But purchases of foreign goods by consumers, firms, or the government should be subtracted when we calculate GDP because these goods were not produced in the United States. At the same time, we must add to GDP any goods produced here that are sold abroad. For example, supercomputers made in the United States but sold in Europe should be added to GDP. By including net exports as a component of GDP, we correctly measure U.S. production by adding exports and subtracting imports.

Consider a few examples. Suppose that someone in the United States buys a $25,000 Toyota made in Japan. If we look at final purchases, we will see that consumption spending rose by $25,000 because consumers made a purchase of a consumption good. Net exports fell by $25,000, however, because the value of the import was subtracted from total exports. Notice that total GDP did not change with the purchase of the Toyota. This is exactly what we want in this case, because there was no U.S. production.

Now suppose the United States sells a car for $18,000 to a resident of Spain. In this case, net exports would increase by $18,000 since the car was an export. GDP would also be a corresponding $18,000 higher because this sale represents U.S. production.

For the United States in 1995, net exports were –$101 billion dollars. In other words, in that year the United States bought $101 billion more goods from abroad than it sold abroad. When we buy more goods from abroad than we sell, we have a **trade deficit.** A **trade surplus** occurs when our exports exceed our imports.

Trade deficit: The excess of imports over exports.

Trade surplus: The excess of exports over imports.

Figure 2 shows the U.S. trade surplus as a share of GDP from 1950 to 1995. While at times the United States had a trade surplus, in the 1980s the United States ran a trade deficit that often exceeded 3% of GDP. What are the consequences of such large trade deficits?

When the United States runs a trade deficit, U.S. residents are spending more on goods and services than they are currently producing. Although the United States does sell many goods abroad (supercomputers, movies, records, and CDs), it buys even more goods and services from abroad (Toyotas, VCRs, German machine tools).

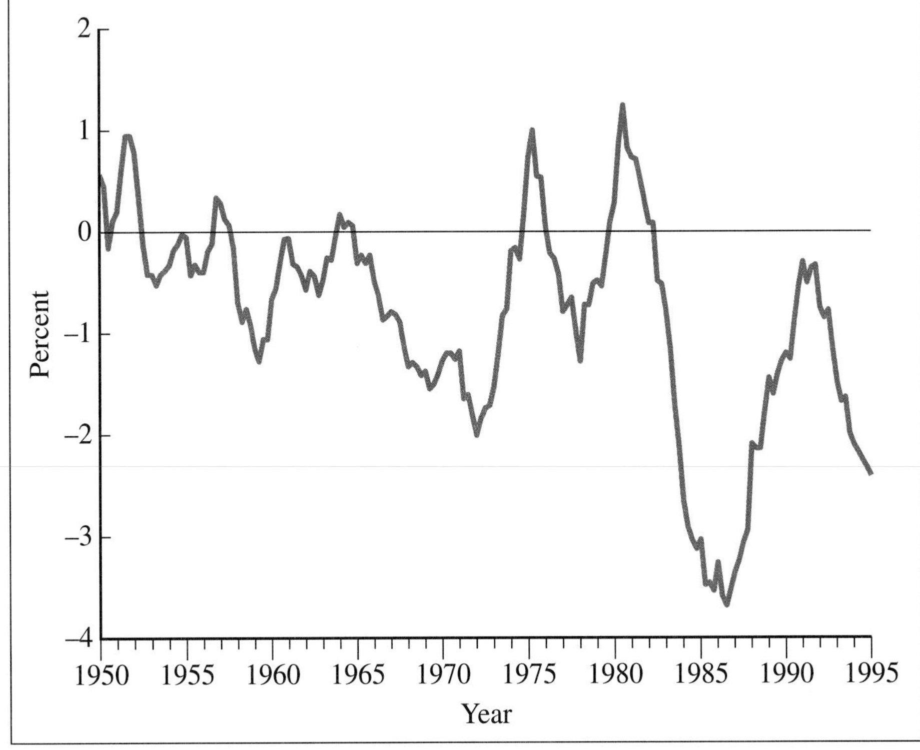

Figure 2

U.S. Trade Surplus as a Share of GDP, 1950–1995

Source: U.S. Department of Commerce.

The result of this is that the United States is forced to sell some of its assets to individuals or governments in foreign countries. Here is how it works: When U.S. residents buy more goods abroad than they sell, they give up more dollars for imports than they receive from the sale of exports. These dollars end up in the hands of foreigners and then can be used to purchase U.S. assets such as stocks, bonds, or real estate. For example, several years ago, Japanese investors purchased the famous Pebble Beach golf course in California and a large movie studio. This should not have been terribly surprising since we had been running large trade deficits with the Japanese. They were willing to sell us more goods than we were selling to them and, in the process, they accumulated U.S. dollars with which they could purchase U.S. assets.

Although this example with Japan is illustrative, what truly matters is a country's trade deficit or surplus with all the countries in the world, not just with a single country. It is the total trade surplus with all the other countries in the world that determines the amount of foreign assets that a single country will acquire. If a country ran a trade surplus with one country and an equally large trade deficit with another, it would not add to its stock of foreign assets. Japan was running a trade surplus on balance with the countries in the rest of the world and thus could add to its stock of foreign assets.

Figure 3 shows the trade surplus as a percent of GDP for a variety of other countries. For these countries, Chile had the largest trade surplus as a share of GDP, followed by Japan. On the other hand, as you can see, the United States was not alone in running a trade deficit. In later chapters we study the various impacts that trade deficits can have on an economy.

TEST *Your Understanding*

1 What are the four components of GDP?

2 The circular flow describes the process by which GDP generates ____________, which is in turn spent on goods.

Figure 3

Trade Surpluses as Percent of GDP, 1994

Source: *International Financial Statistics,* International Monetary Fund, 1996.

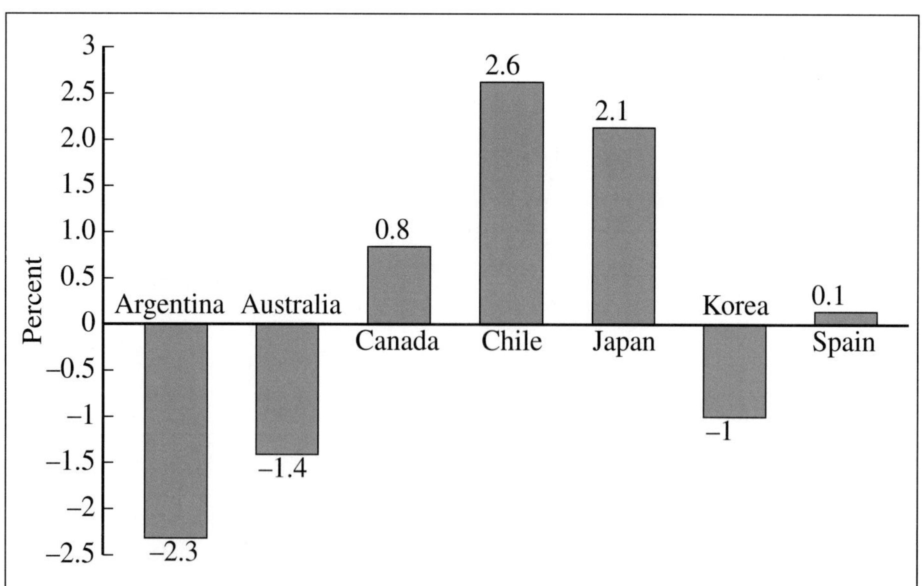

3 What part of government spending is excluded from GDP because it does not correspond to goods or services produced currently?

4 What is the difference between gross and net investment?

5 Define *net exports.*

Who Gets the Income?

Recall from the circular flow that when GDP is produced, income is created. The income that flows to the private sector is called **national income**. To obtain a measure of national income, economists first make a few adjustments to GDP. First, we add to GDP the net income earned by U.S. firms and residents abroad. To make this calculation, we add to GDP any income earned abroad by U.S. firms or residents and subtract any income earned in the United States by foreign firms or residents. For example, we add the profits earned by U.S. multinational corporations that are sent back to the United States but subtract the profits from Japanese firms operating in the United States that are sent back to Japan. The result of these adjustments is the total income earned worldwide by U.S. firms and residents. This is called the **gross national product** (GNP). For the United States, the actual difference between GDP and GNP is very small. But as the Closer Look box "GDP versus GNP" demonstrates, the differences are large for some countries.

National income: Net national product less indirect taxes.

Gross national product (GNP): GDP plus net income earned abroad.

The second adjustment we make on the way to calculating national income is to subtract depreciation from GNP. Recall that depreciation is the wear and tear on plant and equipment that occurred during the year. In a sense, our income is reduced because our buildings and machines are wearing out. When we subtract depreciation from GNP, we reach **net national product** (NNP), where the term *net* means after depreciation.

Net national product (NNP): GNP less depreciation.

Finally, the last adjustment we make to reach national income is to subtract **indirect taxes**, which are sales or excise taxes on products. If a store sells you a product for $1.00 and the sales tax is $0.08, the total bill is $1.08. However, only $1.00 of that purchase goes back to the store to pay wages or be available for profits. The

Indirect taxes: Sales and excise taxes.

A Closer LOOK

GDP versus GNP

For most countries in the world, the distinction between what they produce within their borders (GDP) and what their citizens earn (GNP) is not that important. For the United States, the difference between GDP and GNP is typically just two-tenths of 1%. In some countries, however, these differences are much larger. Turkey, for example, sends to Germany as "guest workers" many of its people, who send money back to their families that is included in the calculation of Turkey's GNP. For Turkey, foreign earnings in 1991 accounted for nearly 1.5% of GNP or total worldwide income.

The country of Kuwait earned vast amounts of income from its oil riches, which it invested abroad. Earnings from these investments are included in GNP; in 1994, they constituted over 13% of the total income in Kuwait. What is the best measure of a country's status in the world: its production or its earnings?

Source: International Financial Statistics, International Monetary Fund, 1996.

remainder goes to the government but is not part of private-sector income. When we have made these adjustments, we reach national income. Table 2 shows these adjustments (ignoring a few minor items) for the third quarter of 1995.

National income is divided among five basic categories: compensation of employees (wages and benefits), corporate profits, rental income, proprietor's income (income of unincorporated business), and net interest (interest payments received by households from business and from abroad). Table 3 presents U.S. data for the third quarter of 1995, and Figure 4 shows the percentages in the various categories. Approximately 72% of all national income goes to workers in the form of wages and benefits. For most of the countries in the world, wages and benefits are the single largest part of national income.

Value added: The sum of all the income (wages, interest, profits, rent) generated by an organization.

One way in which GDP statisticians measure national income is to look at the **value added** of each firm in the economy. Economists define the value added of a firm as the sum of all the income (wages, profits, rents, and interest) that it generates. By adding up the value added for *all* the firms in the economy (plus nonprofit and governmental organizations), we can calculate national income.

We measure the value added for a typical firm by starting with the value of its total sales and subtracting the value of any inputs it purchases from other firms. The amount of income that remains is the firm's value added, which is then distributed as wages, rents, interest, and profits. In calculating national income in this manner, it is important to include all the firms in the economy, including those that produce intermediate goods.

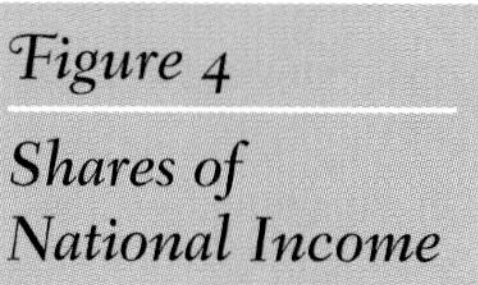

Figure 4

Shares of National Income

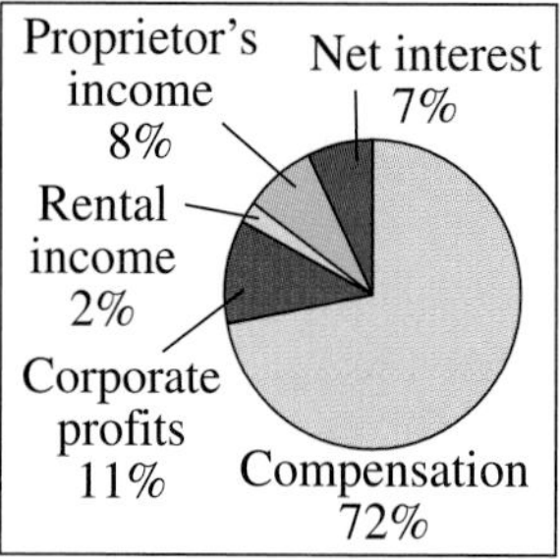

For example, suppose an economy consists just of two firms: an automobile firm that sells its cars to consumers and a steel firm that sells only to the automobile firm. If the automobile company sells $2,000 to consumers and purchases $800 from the steel firm, it has $1,200 in value added which can then be distributed as wages, rents, interest, and profits. If the steel firm sells $800 but does not purchase any inputs from other firms, its value added is $800, which is also is paid out in the form of wages, rents, interest, and profits. Total value-added in the economy is thus $2,000 ($1,200 + $800), which is the sum of wages, rents, interest, and profits for the entire economy.

Personal income: Income (including transfer payments) that is received by households.

In addition to national income, which measures the income earned in a given year by the entire private sector, we are sometimes interested in determining the total payments that flow directly into the hands of households, a concept known as **personal income.** Even though households ultimately own firms, they do not receive all the profits earned by firms in any given year because a portion is typically retained by firms for their investments. In addition, households receive transfer

Table 2: From GDP to National Income, Third Quarter 1995 (billions)

Gross domestic product	$7,297
plus net income earned from abroad =	
Gross national product	7,281
minus depreciation =	
Net national product	6,452
minus indirect taxes (and other adjustments) =	
National income	5,845

Source: Economic Report of the President (Washington, DC: U.S. Government Printing Office, 1996).

Table 3: Composition of U.S. National Income, Third Quarter 1995 (billions)

National income	$5,845
Compensation of employees	$4,233
Corporate profits	614
Rental income	118
Proprietor's income	480
Net interest	400

Source: Economic Report of the President (Washington, DC: U.S. Government Printing Office, 1996).

payments from the government. Personal income includes labor income, transfer payments, and the part of capital income paid to individuals. The amount of personal income that households keep after paying taxes is called **personal disposable income.**

Personal disposable income: Personal income after taxes.

In summary, we can look at GDP from two sides: We can ask who buys the output that is produced, or we can ask who gets the income that is created through the production process. From the spending side, we see that nearly 70% of GDP consists of consumer expenditures. On the income side, we see that nearly three-fourths of national income is paid in wages and benefits.

TEST *Your Understanding*

6 What do we add to GDP to reach GNP?

7 What is the largest component of national income?

8 Complete the statement with *households* or *firms*. Personal income and personal disposable income refer to payments ultimately flowing to ________.

What GDP Does Not Measure

GDP is our best single measure of the value of output produced by an economy. But it is not a perfect measure. There are several well-recognized flaws in the construction of GDP of which you need to be aware. They suggest that we should be cautious if we want to interpret GDP as a measure of economic welfare. First, GDP ignores transactions that do not take place in organized markets. The most important example is services performed in the home, such as cleaning, cooking, and providing free child care. Since these services are not transferred through markets, GDP statisticians cannot measure them. This probably has led us to overestimate the growth in GDP. In the last three decades, there has been a dramatic increase in the percentage of women in the labor force. Since more women are now working, there is naturally a demand for more meals in restaurants, more cleaning services, and more paid child care. All this new demand shows up in GDP, but the services that were provided (free) earlier did not. This naturally overstates the true growth in GDP.

Underground economy: Economic activity that should be in the GDP accounts but does not show up because the activity is either illegal or unreported.

Second, GDP ignores the **underground economy,** where transactions occur that are not reported to official authorities. These transactions can be legal, but to evade taxes, people fail to report the income they have generated. For example, waiters and waitresses may not report all their tips, and owners of flea markets may make "under the table" cash transactions with their customers. There are also illegal transactions that result in unreported income, such as profits from the illegal drug trade. In parts of northern California, the Census figures understate true incomes because income from the production and sale of marijuana is not included in the official measures.

In the United States, the Internal Revenue Service estimates that about $100 billion in income from the underground economy escapes federal taxes each year. If the average federal income tax rate in the country is about 20%, this means that approximately $500 billion ($100/0.20) in income escapes the GDP accountants from the underground economy every year, about 7% of GDP.

Third, GDP does not value changes in the environment that arise through the production of output. Suppose that a factory produces $1,000 of output but pollutes a river and lowers its value by $2,000. Instead of recording a loss to society of $1,000, GDP will show a $1,000 increase. This is an important limitation of GDP accounting as a measure of our economic well-being because changes in the environment are important. In principle, we can make appropriate adjustments to try to correct for this deficiency.

The U.S. Department of Commerce, which collects the GDP data, has begun a project to try to account for environmental changes. In 1994 it released a report on the first phase of the study, in which it focused on the value of mineral resources (oil, gas, coal, etc.) in the United States. The government first measured *proven reserves* of minerals from 1958 to 1991, those reserves of minerals that can be extracted given current technology and current economic conditions. They decrease when minerals are extracted and increase when new investments (such as oil wells or mines) are made.

The question the department asked was whether the stock of proven reserves had been depleted (that is, depreciated) over time. If it had, the reduction in the value of the stock of minerals should be included as part of depreciation and subtracted from GDP to measure national income correctly. It is important to note that this calculation focuses only on proven reserves, not the total stock of minerals in

The death of a loon from an oil spill, as well as other effects from pollution, are not considered in the standard GDP accounting.

the earth. The reason the Commerce Department counts only proven reserves is that some mineral deposits are simply too expensive to extract under current economic conditions. Changes in proven reserves alone correspond most closely to changes in our current economic well-being.

Figure 5 depicts one of the measures of the value of mineral resources that the Commerce Department created. The value of mineral resources, measured in constant 1987 dollars, did not change substantially from 1958 to 1991: It decreased by only $26 billion (or less than $1 billion a year). Subtracting $1 billion a year from GDP would have little effect on total GDP for a $7 trillion economy.

But mineral stocks are only part of our environment. The second phase of the Commerce Department study will include other renewable resources, such as forests and fish. The same methods can be applied to these resources, although the data may not be as accurate as for minerals. The hardest part will be the third phase of the study, where the Commerce Department will try to value changes in clean air and clean water. Has our environment improved or deteriorated as we experienced economic growth? Finding the answer to this question will pose a real challenge for the next generation of economic statisticians.

BEHIND THE UNEMPLOYMENT STATISTICS

Recall how we defined the unemployed: those people who are looking for work but do not currently have jobs. Let's take a closer look at the strengths and weaknesses of our measures of unemployment.

Labor-force participation rate: The fraction of the population over 16 years of age that is in the labor force.

Figure 6 on the next page places the unemployment statistics into perspective. The entire box represents the population over 16 years of age. This population is divided into two groups: those who are in the labor force and those who are not. The fraction of the population that is in the labor force is called the **labor-force participation**

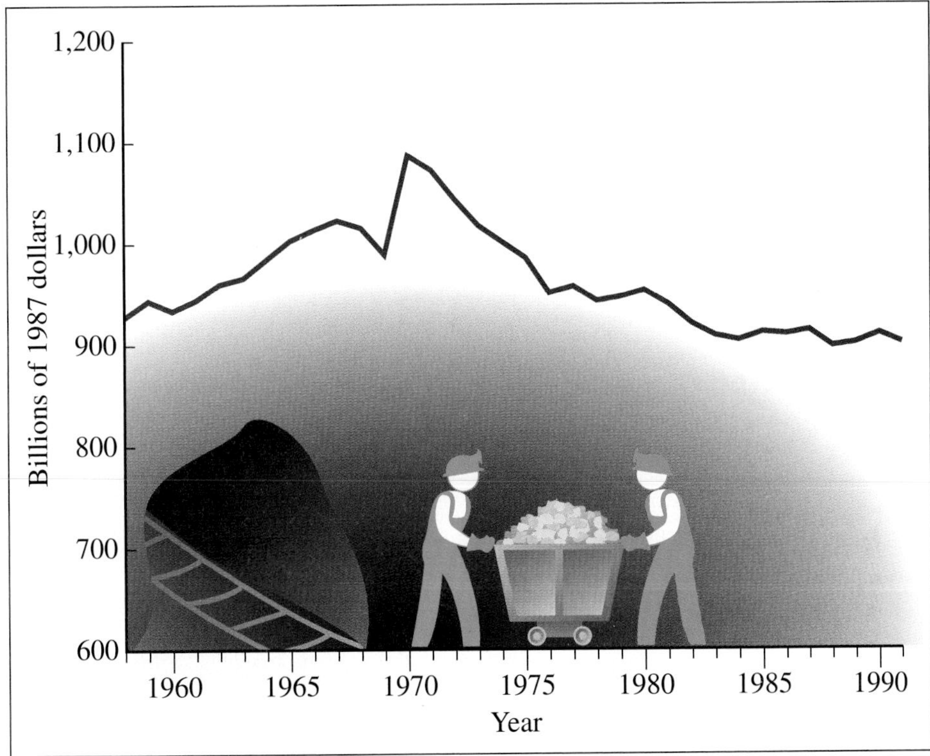

Figure 5

Value of U.S. Mineral Resources, 1958–1991

Source: U.S. Department of Commerce.

Figure 6

Unemployment Data, 1995

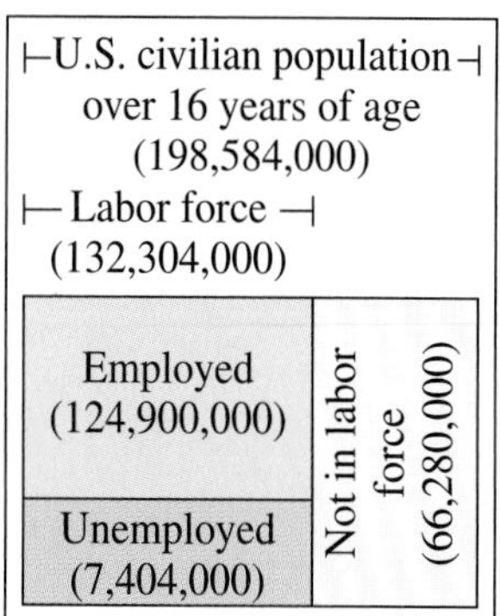

Source: Economic Report of the President (Washington, DC: U.S. Government Printing Office, 1996).

rate. In 1995, the U.S. labor-force participation rate was 66%. The labor force itself is then divided into two groups: the employed and the unemployed. In 1995, nearly 125 million people were employed and about 7.4 million were unemployed.

It is relatively straightforward in principle to determine who is employed: Just count the people who are working. What is more difficult is to distinguish between those who are unemployed and those who are not in the labor force. How is this done? Each month the Bureau of Labor Statistics directs its staff to interview a large sample of households. It asks about the employment situation of all members of households over 16 years of age. If someone in a household is not working, the interviewer asks whether the person is "actively looking for work." If so, he or she is classified as unemployed, but if not, the person is classified as not being in the labor force.

Obviously, it is difficult for an interviewer to determine whether someone is truly looking for work. Without knowing whether someone in the household actually made any effort to look for a job during the interview period, the interviewer must rely on good-faith responses to the questions.

What about those people who were looking for work sometime in the recent past but did not find any opportunities and have stopped looking? These persons are termed **discouraged workers**. They are not included in the official count of the unemployed.

Discouraged workers: Workers who left the labor force because they could not find jobs.

Underemployed: Workers who hold a part-time job but prefer to work full time or hold jobs that are far below their capabilities.

The Bureau of Labor Statistics (BLS) has long recognized that it is difficult to distinguish between the unemployed and those not in the labor force. In 1994 its interviewers actually changed the way they asked questions to avoid biasing responses in the direction of not being in the labor force. Careful study revealed that these changes did not have much effect on the overall unemployment rate but did raise the unemployment rate somewhat for older workers.

In addition, some workers may hold a part-time job but prefer to work full time. Other workers may hold jobs that are far below their capabilities. Workers in either of these situations are called **underemployed.** It is very difficult for the government to distinguish between employed and underemployed workers.

Another important fact about unemployment is that different groups experience different amounts of unemployment. Table 4 contains some unemployment statistics for selected groups for 1995. Adults have substantially lower unemployment rates than teenagers. Minorities have higher unemployment rates, with African-American

Table 4: Selected U.S. Unemployment Statistics, Unemployment Rates for December 1995

Total	5.6
Male, 20 years and over	4.8
Female, 20 years and over	4.7
Both sexes, 16–19	18.0
White	4.9
African American	10.2
White, 16–19 years	15.4
African American, 16–19 years	35.0
Married men	3.2
Married women	3.8
Women maintaining families	6.8

Source: Bureau of Labor Statistics, *Employment and Earnings,* U.S. Department of Labor, December 1996.

teenagers having extremely high unemployment rates. On average, men and women have roughly the same unemployment rates, but the unemployment rates for married men and women are lower than those of women who maintain families alone.

These relative differentials among unemployment rates do vary somewhat as GDP rises and falls. Teenage and minority employment rates often rise very sharply in recessions. In better times, however, there is typically a reduction of unemployment for all groups. Nonetheless, teenage and minority unemployment, most of which is frictional and structural, remains high at all times.

TEST *Your Understanding*

9 Complete the statement with *discouraged workers* or *unemployed*: People who stopped looking for work because they could not find jobs are called ______.

10 Define *labor-force participation rate.*

11 Complete the statement with either *higher* or *lower*: If a large number of workers are classified as being out of the labor force when they are really looking for work, this will lead to an official unemployment rate that is ______ than the true unemployment rate.

12 How does the Bureau of Labor Statistics estimate the unemployment rate?

MEASURING CHANGES IN OUTPUT AND PRICES

In this section we first take a closer look at how the U.S. government actually calculates real GDP and the chain-type price index for GDP. We then examine another important price index and discuss the biases that can occur as we try to measure price changes in our complex economy.

Real GDP and the Chain-Type Price Index for GDP

In the last chapter we introduced the idea of real GDP, which is GDP controlling for prices, and the *chain-type price index for GDP*, a measure of the average price level for the goods and services contained in GDP. To illustrate how the government actually calculates real GDP and the chain-type price index for GDP, let's consider an example of a simple economy.

In this economy there are only two goods, cars and computers, which are produced in the years 2000 and 2001. The data for this economy, the prices and quantities produced for each year, are shown in Table 5. The production of both cars and computers increased but the production of computers increased more rapidly. The price of cars rose while the price of computers remained the same. Cars therefore became more expensive relative to computers in the year 2001.

Table 5: GDP Data for a Simple Economy

	Quantity Produced		*Price*	
Year	*Cars*	*Computers*	*Cars*	*Computers*
2000	4	1	$10,000	$5,000
2001	5	3	12,000	5,000

The underlying idea behind our calculations for real GDP and the chain-type price index is straightforward. We know that nominal GDP can change over time either because prices of goods have changed or because the quantities of goods have changed. If we recalculate GDP holding *prices* constant, we can find a measure for the change in quantities. This will allow us to compute real GDP. Similarly, if we recalculate GDP holding the *quantities* produced constant, we can measure how much prices have changed. This will allow us to find the chain-type price index for GDP.

Let's first calculate nominal GDP for this economy. Nominal GDP is the total value of goods and services produced in each year. Using the data in the table, we can see that nominal GDP for the year 2000 is

$$(4 \times \$10{,}000) + (1 \times \$5{,}000) = \$45{,}000$$

Growth factor: 1 plus the growth rate.

Similarly, nominal GDP for 2001 is $75,000. The **growth factor** (1 plus the growth rate) of nominal GDP is simply the ratio of the two numbers, or $75,000/$45,000 = 1.66. We will use the idea of the growth factor several times in our calculations.

Now we'll find real GDP. To compute real GDP, we recalculate GDP using *constant prices*. In the top part of Table 6, we show how to calculate the values for GDP in both years using prices that prevailed in the year 2000. For example, the value of GDP in 2001 using year 2000 prices is (5 × $10,000) + (3 × $5,000) = $65,000. The ratio of GDP in year 2001 to GDP in year 2000 using constant year 2000 prices is the growth factor for real GDP. The growth factor in this case is 1.444. However, it is also possible to measure real GDP using prices from the year 2001, as we show in the bottom part of Table 6. The growth factor using year 2001 prices is 1.415.

Notice that we got slightly different answers for the total growth of real GDP depending on whether we used constant 2000 or 2001 prices. What government statisticians now do is to take a geometric average of the two figures to arrive at a final result. (A geometric average is the square root of the product of two numbers.) In this case, the growth factor for real GDP based on this average is 1.43.

Why does the government take an average of two different numbers? If the government just used prices in the year 2000, it would *overstate* the growth of real GDP. In our example, computers grew more rapidly than cars between 2000 and 2001 in part because the price of computers fell relative to the price of cars. Using prices for the year 2000 (when computer prices were higher relative to cars), we would exaggerate the effects of computer growth on GDP. By taking an average of two years, we can avoid this bias.

For future years (2002, 2003, etc.) the government would follow exactly the same method, calculating real growth between successive years as an average of

Table 6: Calculating Real GDP Holding Prices Constant

GDP in Year 2000 Using 2000 Prices	GDP in Year 2001 Using 2000 Prices
(4 × $10,000) + (1 × $5,000) = $45,000	(5 × $10,000) + (3 × $5,000) = $65,000
Growth factor = $\frac{\$65{,}000}{\$45{,}000}$ = 1.444	
GDP in Year 2000 Using 2001 Prices	**GDP in Year 2001 Using 2001 Prices**
(4 × $12,000) + (1 × $5,000) = $53,000	(5 × $12,000) + (3 × $5,000) = $75,000
Growth factor = $\frac{\$75{,}000}{\$53{,}000}$ = 1.415	
Geometric average of growth factors = 1.43	

growth factors using constant prices in neighboring years. For example, to calculate real GDP in 2002, we would first calculate the average growth factor between 2001 and 2002 (using 2001 and 2002 prices). Then we would multiply this growth factor by the value of real GDP in 2001, the number we calculated previously. This method, known as a **chain index**, was introduced for the first time in the United States in 1996 in official GDP accounts. The reason it is called a chain index is that it builds up an entire set of numbers for real GDP using growth factors from neighboring years, much like links in a chain.

Chain index: A method for calculating the growth in real GDP or the chain-type price index for GDP that uses data from neighboring years.

Now that we have computed real GDP, let's turn to the chain-type price index for GDP. First, let's choose the year 2000 as the base for which the chain-type price index for GDP equals 100. We then need to determine how much prices have increased on average to determine the chain-type price index for GDP for the year 2001.

To measure the average change in prices, we use a strategy very similar to the one we used to calculate real GDP. We recalculate GDP for each year, *holding quantities constant*. By holding quantities constant, we ensure that any change in GDP must come from changes in prices.

In Table 7 we illustrate this method for our economy. Now the top part of the table shows GDP recalculated using the quantities from the year 2000. The bottom part recalculates GDP using the quantities from the year 2001. Below each we show the growth factor in prices. Finally, at the bottom, we see that the geometric average of the two growth factors is 1.16. The chain-type price index for GDP for the year 2001 would thus be 100 × 1.16 = 116. In subsequent years the chain-type price index for GDP would be calculated based on an average of price changes using constant quantities for neighboring years.

As you have probably recognized, nominal GDP, real GDP, and the chain-type price index for GDP are all closely related. As we discussed, changes in nominal GDP over time reflect changes in both quantities and prices. If we hold prices constant, we can measure the change in real GDP. If we hold quantities constant, we can measure the change in prices. In fact, there is a simple formula with the new chain indexes that relates total changes in nominal GDP, real GDP, and the chain-type price index for GDP:

$$\text{growth factor in nominal GDP} = \text{growth factor in real GDP} \times \text{growth factor in prices}$$

This formula states that the growth factor of nominal GDP is the product of the growth factor in real GDP and the growth factor in prices. In our example, the

Table 7: Calculating a Chain-Type Price Index Holding Quantities Constant

GDP in Year 2000 Using 2000 Quantities	GDP in Year 2001 Using 2000 Quantities
(4 × $10,000) + (1 × $5,000) = $45,000	(4 × $12,000) + (1 × $5,000) = $53,000
Growth factor for prices = $\frac{\$53{,}000}{\$45{,}000}$ = 1.17	
GDP in Year 2000 Using 2001 Quantities	**GDP in Year 2001 Using 2001 Quantities**
(5 × $10,000) + (3 × $5,000) = $65,000	(5 × $12,000) + (3 × $5,000) = $75,000
Growth factor for prices = $\frac{\$75{,}000}{\$65{,}000}$ = 1.15	
Geometric average of growth factors = 1.16	

growth factor in nominal GDP between 2000 and 2001 was 1.66. This is equal to the product of the growth factor in real GDP (1.43) and the growth factor in prices (1.16). This formula emphasizes that we can "decompose" changes in nominal or dollar GDP into changes in real quantities and real prices.

Consumer Price Index and Biases in Measuring Prices

Consumer Price Index (CPI): A price index that measures the cost of a fixed basket of goods chosen to represent the consumption pattern of individuals.

Economists use other price indexes besides the chain-type price index for GDP. The best known of these is the **Consumer Price Index (CPI)**. The CPI is widely used by both government and the private sector to measure changes in prices facing consumers. The CPI measures changes in a fixed "basket of goods," a collection of items chosen to represent the purchasing pattern of a typical consumer. We first find out how much this basket of goods costs in a base year and then ask how much it costs in other years. The CPI index for a given year is then defined as

$$\text{CPI} = \frac{\text{cost in today's prices}}{\text{cost in the base year}} \times 100$$

Let's consider an example. Suppose a basket of goods costs \$200 in the base year of 1987 and \$300 in 1997. Then the CPI for 1997 would be $(300/200) \times 100 = 150$. The CPI in 1987, the base year, would be 100 by definition. The CPI rose from 100 in 1987 to 150 in 1997 in this example, a 50% increase over this period.

Each month the Bureau of Labor Statistics sends its employees out to sample prices for over 90,000 specific items around the entire country in order to compile the CPI. Figure 7 shows the broad categories that are used in the CPI and the importance of each category in household budgets. Rent and food and beverages account for 44% of total spending by households.

Figure 7

Components of the CPI

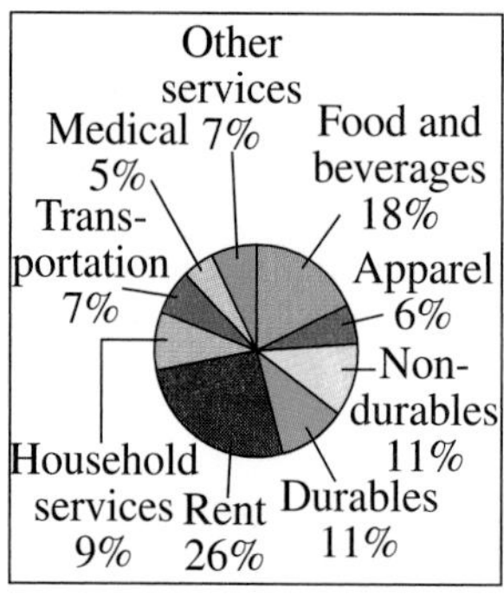

Source: Bureau of Labor Statistics Handbook (Washington, DC: U.S. Government Printing Office, 1992).

The CPI and chain-type price index for GDP are both measures of average prices, but they differ in several ways. First, the CPI measures the costs of a typical basket of goods for consumers and includes goods produced in prior years (such as older cars) as well as imports. The chain-type price index for GDP does not measure price changes from either used goods or imports. It is based on the calculation of GDP, which measures only goods and services produced currently in the United States.

Second, unlike the chain-type price index for GDP, the CPI asks how much a *fixed* basket of goods costs in the current year compared to a base year. Since consumers will tend to buy less of goods whose prices have risen, the CPI will tend to overstate true inflation. Most economists believe that in reality *all* the indexes overstate actual inflation. In other words, true inflation is probably less than the reported indexes tell us. The primary reason is that we have a difficult time measuring quality improvements. Suppose that each year the new computers that are sold to consumers become more powerful and more efficient. Furthermore, suppose that the dollar price of a new computer remains the same each year. Even though the prices remain the same, the computers in later years will be of much higher quality. If we looked simply at the prices of computers and did not take into account the change in quality, we would say that there was no price change for computers. But in later years we are getting more computer power for the same price. If we failed to take the quality change into account, we would not see that the price of computer power has fallen.

Government statisticians do try to adjust for quality when they can. But quality changes are so commonplace in our economy and products evolve so rapidly that it is impossible to keep up with all that is occurring. As a result, most economists believe that we overestimate the inflation rate by between 0.5 and

1.5% each year. This actually has important consequences. Some government programs (such as Social Security) automatically increase payments when the CPI goes up. Some union contracts also have **cost-of-living adjustments** or automatic wage changes based on the CPI. If the CPI overstates inflation, the government and employers might be overpaying Social Security recipients and workers for changes in the cost of living, as the Closer Look box "Costly Biases in the Price Indexes?" explains.

Cost-of-living adjustments: Automatic increases in wages or other payments that are tied to a price index.

LOOKING AHEAD

Now that we have learned the basic vocabulary of macroeconomics, we can begin to understand how the overall economy works. We start in the next chapter with classical economics and explain how real GDP is determined by the supply of capital and labor when the economy is at full employment. We then discuss economic growth. In subsequent chapters we explain how, when prices are fixed, changes in the total demand for goods and services can cause economic fluctuations: booms and recessions. As we noted in the last chapter, we'll call the study of how changes in demand can affect the economy *Keynesian economics.*

We then integrate classical and Keynesian economics by showing how an economy can return to full employment following a boom or recession through the adjustment of wages and prices. In the short run, when prices are fixed, changes in demand can affect the level of output, but in the long run, when prices adjust, supply considerations ultimately predominate. Throughout these discussions we emphasize how the actions taken by our public officials can—for better or worse—affect economic growth, inflation, and unemployment. We continue to highlight the increasing importance of the global economy in our economic affairs.

A Closer LOOK

Costly Biases in the Price Indexes?

Each year the federal government increases Social Security payments to the elderly by the rate of inflation as measured by the Consumer Price Index. The reason for this adjustment is to make sure that the elderly, whose other income tends to be fixed, do not suffer from inflation. But as we have seen, the CPI does not fully account for quality changes, so that true inflation is less than inflation as measured by the CPI. Since Social Security payments are increased by the CPI, we overcompensate the elderly for inflation and actually increase their benefits in real terms.

How much extra are we paying the elderly because of the bias in the CPI? Economists believe that the CPI overstates actual inflation by between .5 and 1.5% a year. Assume that we overstate inflation by 1%. According to the Congressional Budget Office, if we reduced the inflation adjustment for Social Security by 1%, it would save $42 billion dollars over a five-year period! As you can tell, not accounting for technical change is a costly bias in our price indexes.

Defenders of the elderly claim that this is a misleading argument. While the CPI may overstate inflation in general, it probably understates the rate of inflation facing the elderly. The elderly consume more medical care than do average citizens in the United States and prices for medical care have increased faster than other prices in the economy. Regardless of which side of the debate we favor, it is evident that many dollars rest on precise calculation of the CPI.

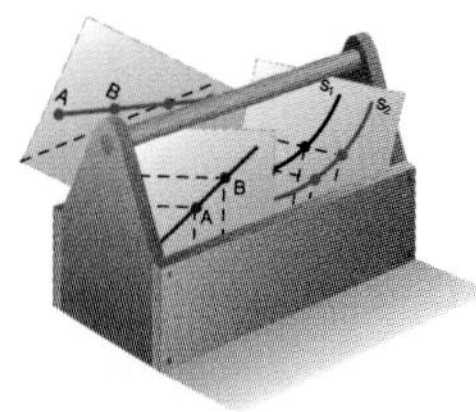

Using the **TOOLS**

In this chapter we looked in detail at the way we measure the economy. Test your ability to use the basic idea in this chapter by answering the following problems.

1. Computers and GDP

In the 1980s, as the economy began to use more computers, government statisticians noticed that the computers depreciated rapidly and that total depreciation in the economy increased.

a. Why do you think computers depreciate rapidly?

b. How does higher depreciation affect the relationship between gross and net investment? How does it affect the relationship between GDP and national income?

2. The Missing Piece

Between 1987 and 1990, a country's nominal GDP grew by 25% and its inflation rate (based on the chain-type price index for GDP) was 13%. How fast did real GDP grow over this period?

3. Fish and National Income

Suppose that you were worried that national income did not adequately take into account the depletion of the stock of fish in the economy. Describe how you would advise the Commerce Department to take this into their calculation.

4. ECONOMIC DETECTIVE– *Suspicious Unemployment Statistics*

Suppose that after a long period of high unemployment in the economy, government statisticians noticed that the labor force was lower than it was prior to the spell of unemployment. Is there any reason that you might be suspicious of these numbers?

SUMMARY

In this chapter we took a closer look at our economic statistics to explain their strengths and weaknesses. Developing meaningful statistics for the entire economy is a difficult task. As we have seen, while our statistics contain important information, they do not necessarily convey all the information that is needed. Here are some of the main points to remember:

1. The circular flow helps to emphasize the idea that GDP produces income and that income goes toward the purchase of goods.
2. GDP is divided into consumption, investment, government purchases, and net exports. Consumption is the single largest component.
3. National income is obtained from GDP by adding net income from abroad, then subtracting depreciation and indirect taxes.
5. GDP does not include nonmarket transactions, the underground economy, or changes to the environment.
6. Unemployment rates vary across groups. It is often difficult to distinguish between the unemployed and those not in the labor force.
7. Economists believe that most price indexes overstate true inflation because they fail to capture quality improvements.

KEY TERMS

capital, *423*
chain index, *437*
Consumer Price Index (CPI), *438*
consumption expenditures, *424*
cost-of-living adjustments, *439*
depreciation, *425*
discouraged workers, *434*
durable goods, *424*
factors of production, *423*
government purchases, *424*
gross investment, *425*
gross national product (GNP), *429*
growth factor, *436*
indirect taxes, *429*
labor-force participation rate, *433*
national income, *429*
net exports, *424*
net investment, *425*
net national product (NNP), *429*
nondurable goods, *424*
personal disposable income, *431*
personal income, *430*
private investment expenditures, *424*
services, *425*
trade deficit, *427*
trade surplus, *427*
transfer payments, *425*
underemployed, *434*
underground economy, 431
value added, *430*

PROBLEMS AND DISCUSSION QUESTIONS

1. Carefully review the dialogue between the French and American student at the beginning of the chapter. How serious do you think are the points raised by the French student?
2. Give two reasons why the federal budget is not the proper measure of government purchases in the GDP accounts.
3. A student once said, "Trade deficits are good because we are buying more goods than we are producing." What is the downside to trade deficits?
4. Why is there an upward bias in most measures of inflation?
5. Prior to 1996, the government measured real GDP using 1987 prices. Explain why the rapid growth in computers and the fall in computer prices after 1987 would tend to overstate real GDP growth compared to using constant prices from a later year.
6. The quantity of fish caught off the coast of New England fell drastically in the 1990s due to constant overfishing. How should this be reflected in our national accounts?
7. Sometimes at the beginning of an economic boom, total employment increases sharply but the unemployment rate does not fall. Why might this occur?
8. A publisher buys paper, ink, and computers to produce textbooks. Which of these purchases is included in investment spending?

Take It to the Net

We invite you to visit the O'Sullivan/Sheffrin page on the Prentice Hall Web site at:

http://www.prenhall.com/osullivan/

for this chapter's World Wide Web exercise.

MODEL ANSWERS FOR THIS CHAPTER

Chapter-Opening Questions

1. Gross domestic product is bought by consumers, firms, the government and foreign sector. The income that is produced is paid in wages, corporate profits, rents, interest, and income to the self-employed.
2. The standard GDP calculations do not measure the value of our leisure time nor do they account for the quality of the environment. Measures to include some environmental considerations in GDP accounting are currently being developed.
3. Teenagers and minorities have the highest unemployment rates.
4. It is difficult to measure the inflation rate because

we cannot easily measure the quality of goods and services as they change over time. Since many government programs and private contracts are connected to measures of the inflation rate, distorted measures can be quite costly.

Test Your Understanding

1. The four components are consumption, investment, government spending, and net exports.
2. income
3. Transfer payments are excluded.
4. The difference is depreciation.
5. Net exports are exports minus imports.
6. We add net income earned abroad.
7. The largest component is compensation of employees.
8. households
9. discouraged workers
10. It is the fraction of the population that is in the labor force.
11. lower
12. The Bureau of Labor Statistics conducts a household survey.

Using the Tools

1. Computers and GDP
   a. Depreciation always accompanies rapid technological progress. Computers depreciate in value and are eventually scrapped because new computers become available at lower prices and with more computing power.
   b. Higher depreciation means that for any level of gross investment (actual purchases), net investment is lower. Similarly, for any level of GDP, national income is also lower.
2. The Missing Piece

   If nominal GDP grew by 25%, its total growth was 1.25. If inflation was 13%, the total growth in prices was 1.13. Using the formula relating the growth factor in nominal GDP, real GDP, and prices, we find that the growth factor for real GDP was 1.25/1.13 = 1.11. This means real GDP grew by 11%.
3. Fish and National Income

   Follow the same procedure as for mineral wealth. First, estimate (at appropriate prices) the value of all the fish in the sea at the beginning of the year and the end of the year. Then calculate the change in the value of the stock of fish. If the value of the stock of fish decreased, this is similar to depreciation and should be subtracted from GDP to obtain national income. If it increased it should be added to national income. Note that there may be problems with national boundaries. Whose GDP is affected if the stock of fish decline in the middle of the Atlantic or Pacific oceans?
4. Economic Detective: Suspicious Unemployment Statistics

   Following a spell of high unemployment, there may be an increase in discouraged workers. This means that there may be people who would like to find jobs but have stopped looking because of the prolonged unemployment. These persons may eventually return to the labor force.

CHAPTER

Part 7 ■

The Economy in the Long Run

22 Classical Economics: The Economy at Full Employment

John Maynard Keynes used the term *classical economists* to refer to his predecessors. He believed they lacked his insights about macroeconomics. For many years, the term was often one of disrepute. Today, however, many economists are proud to call themselves classical economists and embrace many of the insights of classical economics.

In this chapter we explain how the amount of capital and labor determine GDP when an economy is producing at full employment. The study of how the economy operates at full employment is commonly known as **classical economics**. As we will see, classical economics is based on the principle that prices will adjust in the long run to bring the markets for goods and labor into equilibrium.

Classical economics: The study of the economy as it operates at full employment.

The classical economists believed that there were strong forces pushing the economy back to full employment after any external shocks that temporarily caused excessive unemployment. Although they did not deny that the economy could experience booms or busts, classical economists believed these episodes were transitory and that the economy would return to full employment.

There are several important reasons for studying classical economics. First, many of the most important issues in macroeconomics concern the long run. Consider two examples: Suppose that the government increases spending for several years to fight a major war or rehabilitate our cities. What effects will this have on the level of consumption or investment in the economy?

Or suppose we are concerned about low real wages in the economy. What public policy actions can we take to raise the level of wages in the economy in the long run? The classical model we develop in this chapter provides the appropriate tool to answer these questions.

Second, many economic debates occurring today can best be analyzed with the tools of classical economics. As an example, we use these tools to explore some of the ideas of **supply-side economics**, a school of thought that emphasizes how changes in taxes can affect economic activity.

Supply-side economics: The school of thought that emphasizes the importance of taxation for influencing economic activity.

Finally, even though there are economic fluctuations—booms and recessions—we will see in later chapters that the economy fluctuates around full employment and eventually returns to full employment after a shock, that is, a disturbance to the economy. Thus, by studying the economy at full employment we will be able to determine the average or typical level of output that we can normally expect in the economy. The classical model will provide the foundation for our study of economic fluctuations.

When the economy is at full employment, there are still unemployed workers. Recall the distinction between frictional, structural, and cyclical unemployment. Frictional unemployment occurs naturally in the labor market as workers search for jobs, while structural unemployment arises from a mismatch of skills and jobs. Cyclical unemployment is the part of unemployment that rises and falls with economic fluctuations. It can be either positive (in a recession) or negative (in a boom). Full employment corresponds to zero *cyclical* unemployment; that is, when the economy is at full employment, the only unemployment is frictional and structural.

Here are some real-world issues we can address with tools we develop in this chapter:

1. How does increased immigration affect wages and the level of output in the economy?
2. What are the benefits of increased investment?
3. What happens to wages, employment, and GDP if employers must pay higher taxes for hiring labor?
4. If governments spend more, does this mean we must have a lower level of consumption or investment in the economy?

As we develop the classical model in this chapter, it is important to keep in mind one key assumption. In the classical model, wages and prices are assumed to adjust freely and quickly to all changes in demand and supply. It is precisely this flexibility in wages and prices that distinguishes the classical model from the Keynesian models we examine in later chapters.

THE PRODUCTION FUNCTION FOR THE ECONOMY

In all of economics, we use abstractions and make simplifying assumptions. In macroeconomics we make use of extreme simplifying assumptions, since our goal is to explain the behavior of an *entire* economy. Macroeconomics is not for the timid!

One of the most fundamental abstractions in macroeconomics is the aggregate production function. The **aggregate production function** explains the relationship of the total inputs that are used throughout the economy to the total level of production in the economy or GDP. In the spirit of macroeconomics, we typically assume that there are two primary factors of production: capital and labor. The **stock of capital** comprises all the machines, equipment, and buildings in the entire economy.

Aggregate production function: Shows how much output is produced from capital and labor.

Stock of capital: The total of all the machines, equipment, and buildings in the entire economy.

Labor consists of the efforts of all the workers in the economy. Symbolically, we write the aggregate production function as:

Labor: The total effort of all workers in an economy.

$$Y = F(K,L)$$

where Y is total output or GDP, K is the stock of capital, and L is the labor force. This notation emphasizes that total output is produced from both capital and labor. The production function $F(K,L)$ tells us how much output is produced from the inputs to production, K and L. More inputs of either capital or labor lead to higher levels of output.

The stock of capital that a society has at any point in time is given to us by past investments. Any actions taken today will have little immediate effect on the total stock of machines, equipment, and buildings in existence. It takes time for investment to change the stock of capital. In this chapter we assume primarily that the stock of capital is fixed at a constant level which we call K^*. However, we consider some changes in the stock of capital as well.

With the stock of capital fixed at the constant level K^*, only variations in the amount of labor can change the level of output in the economy. Figure 1 plots the relationship between the amount of labor used in an economy and the total level of output with a fixed stock of capital. This is called the **short-run production function.**

Short-run production function: Shows how much output is produced from varying amounts of labor, holding the capital stock constant.

Figure 1 shows that as labor inputs are increased from L_1 to L_2, output increases from Y_1 to Y_2. The relationship between output and labor exhibits the principle of diminishing returns.

PRINCIPLE *of Diminishing Returns*

Suppose that output is produced with two or more inputs and that we increase one input while holding the other inputs fixed. Beyond some point—called the point of diminishing returns—output will increase at a decreasing rate.

In this case we are adding labor to a fixed stock of capital for the entire economy.

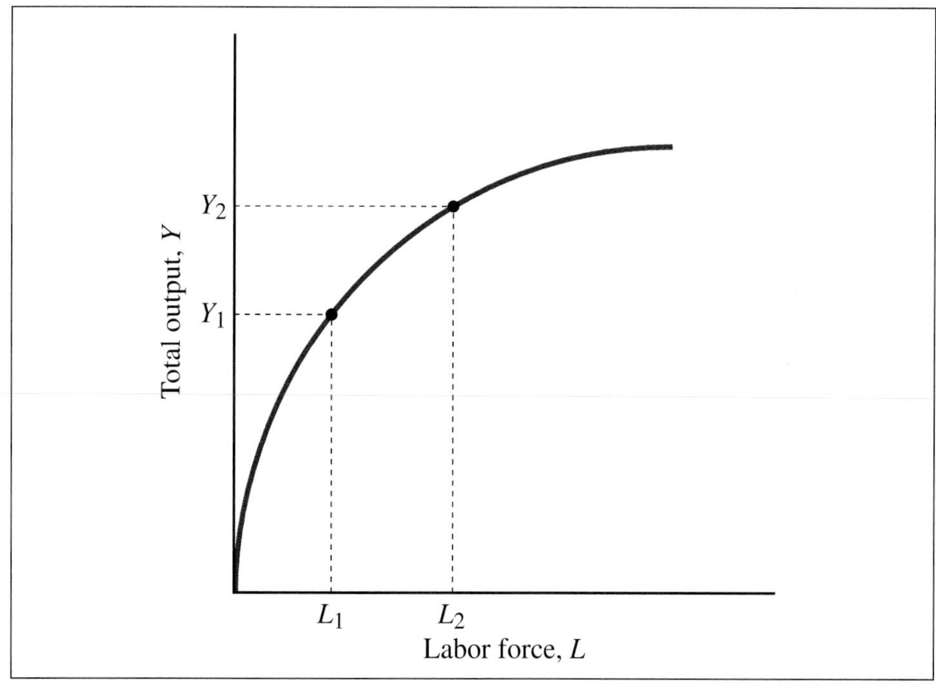

Figure 1

Relationship between Labor and Output with Fixed Capital

With capital fixed, output increases with labor input but at a decreasing rate.

To illustrate this point, let's look at the data in Table 1 from a typical production function. The table shows the amount of output that can be produced from different amounts of labor inputs. The stock of capital is held constant. First, notice that as the amount of labor increases, so does the amount of output that is produced. Second, note that whereas output increases, it does so at a diminishing rate. For example, as labor input increases from 3 to 4, output increases by 5 units, from 10 to 15. But as labor input increases from 4 to 5, output only increases by 4 units, from 15 to 19.

What happens if the stock of capital increases, say from K^* to K^{**}? Figure 2 shows the effects. When the stock of capital increases, the entire short-run production function shifts upward. At any level of labor input, more output can now be produced than before. As we add more capital, we move to the higher curve, where workers become more productive and can produce more output. For example, consider an office in which five staff members must share one copier. They will inevitably waste some time waiting to use the machine. Adding another copier will allow the staff to be more productive. The benefit of additional capital is a higher level of output from any level of labor input.

TEST *Your Understanding*

1 What is an aggregate production function?

2 Complete the statement with *an increasing* or *a decreasing*: With the stock of capital fixed, output increases with labor input but at ____________ rate.

3 Complete the statement with *upward* or *downward*: An increase in the stock of capital shifts the production function ____________.

THE DEMAND AND SUPPLY FOR LABOR

We've just seen that with the amount of capital fixed, the level of output in the economy will be determined exclusively by the amount of labor employed. In this section we study how the amount of employment is determined in an economy by the demand and supply for labor.

Figure 3 presents the essential features of the demand and supply for labor. Firms hire labor to produce output and make profits. The amount of labor they will hire, however, depends on the **real wage rate**—the wage rate adjusted for inflation— that they have to pay. To understand the demand for labor, we use the marginal principle.

Real wage rate: The wage rate paid to workers adjusted for inflation.

Table 1: Output and Labor Output

Y *(Output)*	L *(Labor Input)*
10	3
15	4
19	5
22	6

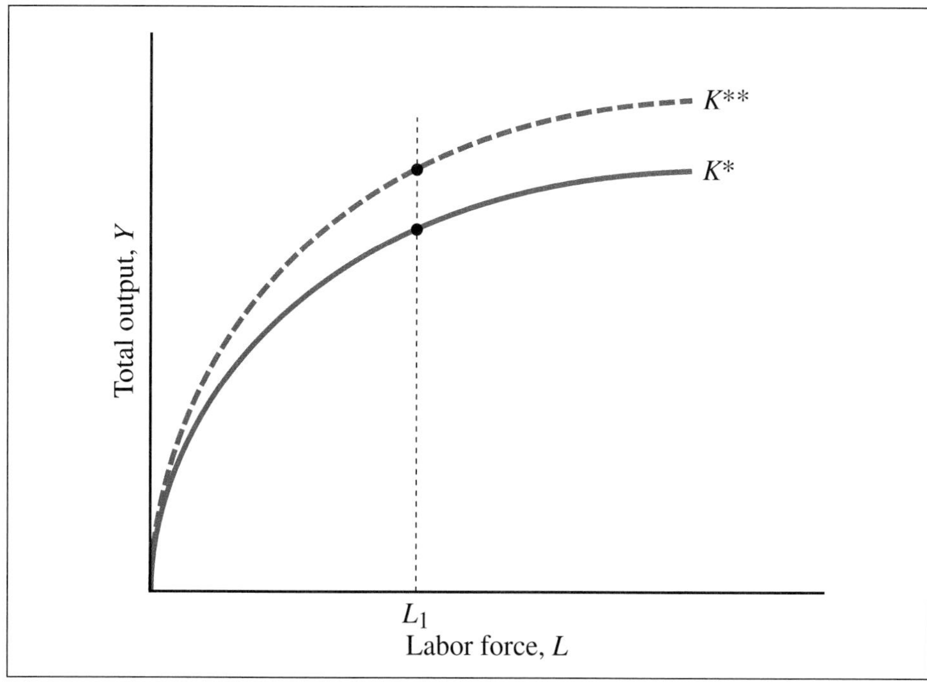

Figure 2

Increase in the Stock of Capital

When capital increases from K^* to K^{**} the production function shifts up. At any level of labor input, the level of output increases.

Marginal PRINCIPLE

Increase the level of an activity if its marginal benefit exceeds its marginal cost, but reduce the level if the marginal cost exceeds the marginal benefit. If possible, pick the level at which the marginal benefit equals the marginal cost.

The marginal benefit that a firm receives from hiring an additional worker is the extra output the worker produces. The marginal cost of the worker is the real wage a firm pays the worker for additional effort. The firm will continue to hire workers as long as the marginal benefit exceeds the marginal cost. For example, if the real wage rate for an hour of work is $20 per hour, a firm will hire workers until the marginal benefit from an additional hour of work equals $20.

If the real wage falls, the marginal cost of labor falls. The firm will therefore hire additional labor until the marginal benefit again equals marginal cost. For example, suppose that initially the real wage and the marginal benefit from an

Figure 3

Demand for and Supply of Labor

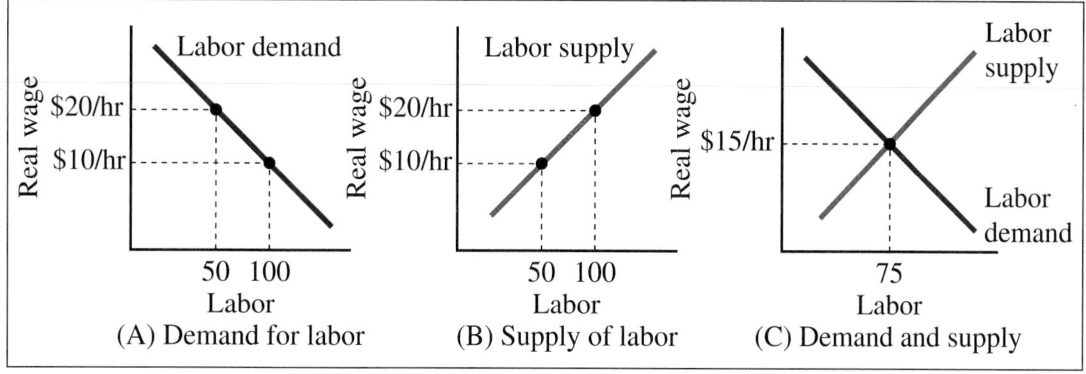

extra hour of work were each $20. If the wage rate now falls below $20 to, say, $10, the marginal benefit to the firm will exceed the wage. The firm will respond by hiring more labor until the marginal benefit from hiring an additional worker equals $10.

Thus, as the real wage rate falls, firms will hire more labor. The labor demand curve in Figure 3 is therefore downward sloping. In panel A we see that as the real wage falls from $20 per hour to $10 per hour, the firm will want to increase the amount of labor it hires from 50 to 100 workers.

The labor supply curve is based on the decisions of workers. They must decide how many hours they wish to work versus how much leisure they wish to enjoy. Changes in wage rates have two different effects on workers' decisions. First, an increase in the real wage rate will make working more attractive and raise the opportunity cost of not working. Called the **substitution effect**, this leads to workers wanting to supply more hours. Second, a higher wage rate raises a worker's income for the amount of hours that he or she is currently working. As income rises, a worker may choose to enjoy more leisure and work fewer hours. This is known as the **income effect**.

Substitution effect: An increase in the wage rate increases the opportunity cost of leisure and leads workers to supply more labor.

Income effect: An increase in the wage rate raises a worker's income at the current levels of hours of work and may lead to more leisure and a decreased supply of labor.

The substitution effect and the income effect work in opposite directions. In principle, a higher wage rate could lead workers to supply *either* greater or fewer hours of work. In our analysis we assume that the substitution effect dominates. Thus a higher wage rate will lead to increases in the supply of labor. In panel B we see that while 50 people would like to work at $10 per hour, at $20 per hour the number grows to 100.

Panel C puts the demand and supply curves together. At a wage of $15 per hour, the amount of labor that firms want to hire (75) will be equal to the number of people (75) who want to work. This is the labor market equilibrium. When the market is in equilibrium, the demand and supply for labor together determine the level of employment in the economy and the level of real wages.

When firms add additional capital, they find that the marginal benefit from hiring workers increases since each worker becomes more productive with additional capital. For example, if the marginal benefit of an additional hour of work were initially $15, an increase in the supply of capital might raise it to $20. Firms will therefore want to hire additional workers at the existing wage until the marginal benefit again equals the marginal cost. Since the demand for labor increases at any real wage rate, the labor demand curve shifts to the right. Panel A of Figure 4 shows the effects of an increase in labor demand. The new market equilibrium moves from *E* to *E*′. Real wages increase and the amount of labor employed in the economy increases as well. Having more capital in the economy is beneficial for workers.

We also can analyze the effect of an increase in the supply of labor that might come, for example, from immigration. If the population increases, we would expect that more people would want to work at any given wage. This means that the labor supply curve would shift to the right. Panel B of Figure 4 shows that with an increase in the supply of labor, the labor market equilibrium moves from *E* to *E*′. Real wages have fallen and the amount of labor employed has increased. Existing workers suffer because real wages have fallen.

These two simple thought experiments provide important insights. We can now see why existing workers might be reluctant to support increased immigration. The additional supply of labor will tend to decrease real wages. Our model also explains why workers would like to see increases in the supply of machines and equipment as long as full employment can be maintained. The increased supply of capital increases labor demand and leads to higher real wages.

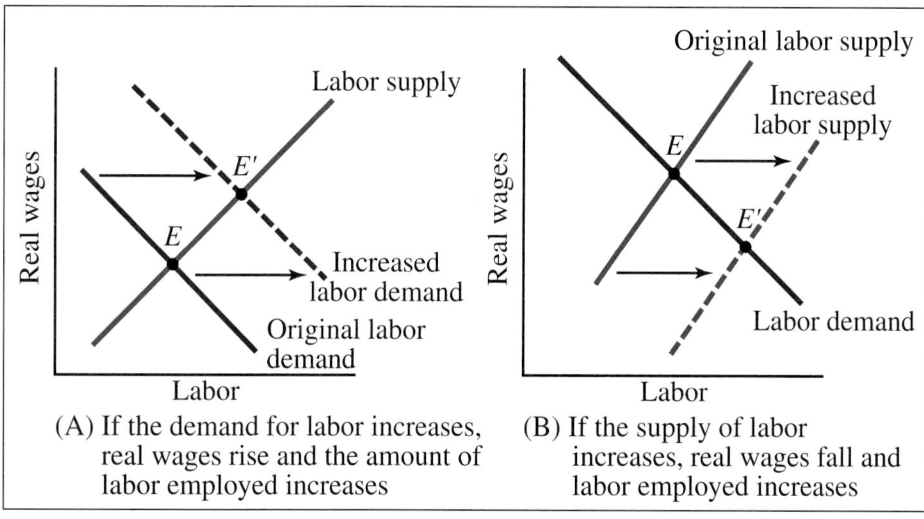

(A) If the demand for labor increases, real wages rise and the amount of labor employed increases

(B) If the supply of labor increases, real wages fall and labor employed increases

Figure 4

Shifts in Demand and Supply

Finally, our model can also help us understand the very different behavior of real wages in the United States and Europe during the 1980s. Although GDP grew at roughly the same rate in both, in the United States there was a substantial increase in new jobs, whereas in Europe very few jobs were created. In both countries the labor demand curve shifted to the right as the stock of capital increased. However, labor supply in the United States grew at a faster rate than the labor supply in Europe. The supply curve for labor shifted to the right more in the United States than in Europe. We would expect that this would mean higher employment growth but slower growth in real wages in the United States. This is precisely what

When this new computer and others like it are installed, they raise the productivity of the work force and lead to increases in real wages.

happened. For example, real wages in Germany rose by over 12% from 1980 to 1990, whereas in the United States they fell by 6%. Over the same period, however, industrial employment grew by 22% in the United States but did not grow at all in Germany.

TEST *Your Understanding*

4 Labor market equilibrium occurs at a real wage where the demand for labor equals the ____________ of labor.

5 Explain why the demand curve for labor is negatively sloped and the supply curve of labor is positively sloped.

6 Complete the statement with *right* or *left*: An increase in the amount of capital in the economy will shift the demand for labor curve to the ____________, leading to higher real wages and employment.

7 Complete the statement with *right* or *left*: Increased immigration is likely to lead to a shift in the labor supply schedule to the ____________.

8 Draw the supply and demand graphs to illustrate the differences in employment and wage growth between Europe and the United States in the 1980s.

LABOR MARKET EQUILIBRIUM AND FULL EMPLOYMENT

We now reach one of the principal objectives of this chapter, to show exactly how much output the economy can produce when it is operating at full employment. To do this we combine the short-run production function with the demand and supply for labor. The model we develop will also help us to understand how taxes on employers affect the level of output and to understand the debate about supply-side economics.

Figure 5 brings the model of the labor market together with the short-run production function. Panel B depicts equilibrium in the labor market, which we saw in Figure 3. The demand and supply for labor determine the real wage rate W^* and identify the level of employment L^*. Panel A plots the short-run production function. With the level of employment determined at L^* in panel B, we move vertically up to panel *A* and use that level of employment to determine the level of production at Y^*. **Full-employment output** is the level of output that is produced when the labor market is in equilibrium. It is also known as **potential output**.

Full-employment output or **potential output:** The level of output that results when the labor market is in equilibrium.

How do economists typically measure the level of full employment or potential output? They start with an estimate of what the unemployment rate would be if cyclical unemployment were zero, that is, if the only unemployment were due to frictional or structural factors. For the United States in recent years, most economists have estimated this to be between 5.0 and 6.5%. They then estimate how many workers will be employed and use the short-run production function to determine potential output. In a worldwide economy, there may be additional complications in measuring full employment, as the Closer Look box "Global Production and Potential Output" explains.

The level of potential output in an economy changes as the supply of labor increases or the stock of capital increases. As we discussed earlier, an increase in the supply of labor, perhaps from immigration, would shift the labor supply curve to the

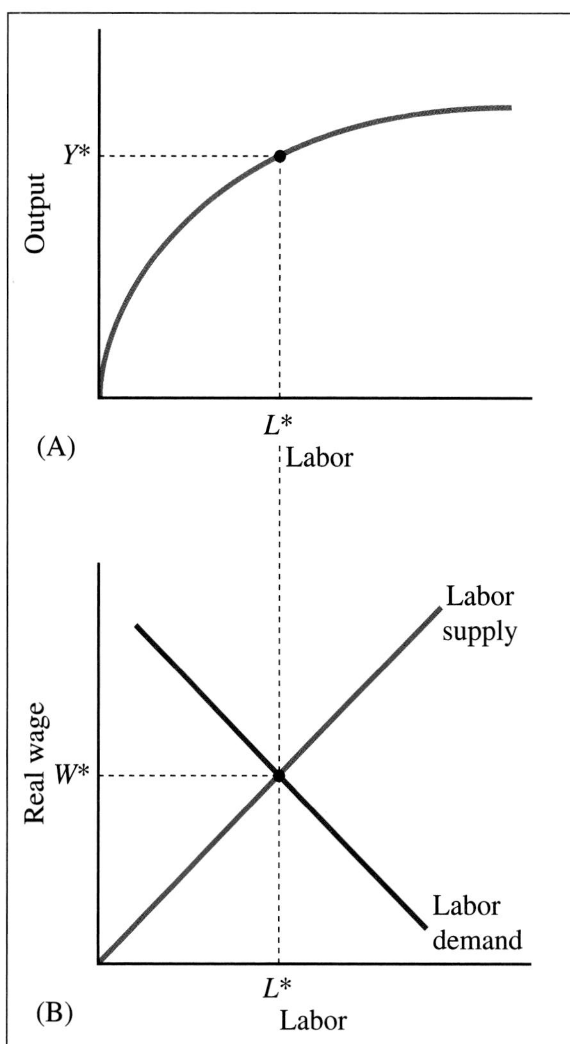

Figure 5

Determining Full-Employment Output

Panel B determines the equilibrium level of employment at L^* and the real wage rate at W^*. Full employment output in panel A is Y^*.

right and lead to a higher level of employment in the economy. With a higher level of employment, the level of full employment output will increase.

Other factors can affect the level of potential output as well. Our commitment to a clean environment may come at some cost, as the Closer Look box "Environmental Protection and Potential Output" explains.

THE DEBATE ABOUT SUPPLY-SIDE ECONOMICS

Supply-siders: Economists who believe that taxes have strong adverse affects on the economy.

All economists recognize that understanding taxes may be important for analyzing how the macroeconomy behaves. One group of economists, the **supply-siders**, have strongly emphasized the adverse effects that taxation can have on potential output. The ideas of supply-siders were very influential and helped to provide the rationale for tax cuts in the early 1980s.

Laffer curve: A relationship between tax rates and tax revenues that illustrates that high tax rates may not always lead to high tax revenues if high tax rates discourage economic activity.

The Laffer Curve

To illustrate how taxes can have important effects, let's consider a simple example, the **Laffer curve**, named after the economist Arthur Laffer. The Laffer curve shows the relationship between the tax rate that a government levies and the total tax

A Closer **LOOK**

Global Production and Potential Output

When government statisticians and business economists try to estimate potential output, they look at plant capacity as well as unemployment. If factories are fully utilizing all their plant and equipment, the economy is producing at its potential. But with U.S. firms manufacturing products throughout the world, some economists argue that traditional notions of capacity are obsolete.

For example, in 1994 the "big three" automobile manufacturers—Ford, Chrysler, and General Motors—had the capacity to produce 14 million vehicles from plants within the United States. However, using plants in Canada and Mexico, another 4.5 million vehicles could be produced. The automobile manufacturers plan their production on a global basis and could meet a U.S. demand for 18.5 million vehicles from their North American operations.

When do we reach potential output for the big three—at 14 or at 18.5 million vehicles? Economists try to pinpoint potential output by determining the level of demand for cars at which automobile manufacturers sharply raise their prices, because at that level of output they cannot easily produce any more cars. But as production becomes increasingly global, it is ever more difficult to estimate potential output.

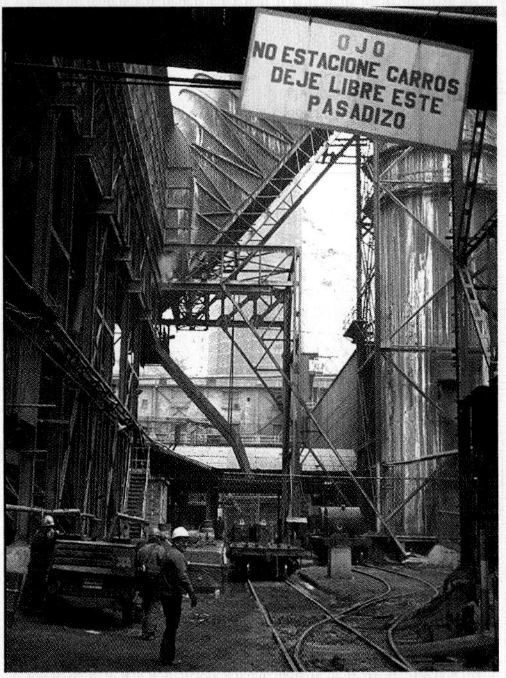

The copper that is processed in this Peruvian plant will find its way into products produced throughout the globe.

Source: Data from Louis Uchitelle, "Economic Growth Slows from Peak, Renewing Debate," *New York Times,* September 12, 1994, pp. A1, C5.

revenue that a government collects. The total amount of revenue that a government collects depends on both the tax rate and the level of economic activity. The point of the Laffer curve is to illustrate the idea that high tax rates may not bring in much revenue if economic activity decreases because tax rates are too high.

Figure 6 depicts the Laffer curve. Suppose the government imposes a tax on the wages of workers. If the tax rate is zero, the government will collect no revenue, although many people may seek jobs. As the government increases the tax rate, it starts to collect some revenue. In Figure 6 we can see that tax revenue increases as the tax rate increases from zero. At the same time, however, higher tax rates will discourage some people from seeking employment. As the government continues to increase tax rates, it will find that tax revenues begin to fall. High rates of taxation will eventually discourage so many people from seeking work that the total tax base falls dramatically. In the extreme case of a 100% tax rate, the government would take everything and no rational person would ever work! In this case the government would again collect no revenue, not because the rate was zero but because the rate was so high that economic activity would disappear.

A Closer LOOK

Environmental Protection and Potential Output

The Clean Air and Clean Water acts required U.S. firms to make investments that improved the quality of the air and water. These investments were quite substantial. In 1992, for example, over $100 billion was spent for pollution control and abatement.*

When a substantial fraction of investment is devoted to fighting pollution, less is available for adding to our regular stock of capital. In 1992, the $100 billion constituted nearly 13% of total gross investment. The net result is that potential output for the economy is reduced. Typical estimates are that the decrease in investment could lead to a decline in potential output as large as 6%.

Although pollution abatement has come at a cost, it may be worth the price. As citizens, we must weigh the benefits of pollution reduction against the loss of higher levels of output.

*The Bureau of Economic Analysis of the U.S. Department of Commerce publishes estimates of expenditures on pollution control and abatement.

The Laffer curve can provide a useful reminder to governments that extreme rates of taxation can damage an economy and be counterproductive. For example, if tariff rates (taxes on imports) become too high, importers will stop bringing goods into the country. In an extreme case, revenues from tariffs could actually be increased if the government cuts tariff rates.

Supply-siders did not, however, limit themselves to these cases. They believed that even in less extreme cases, high taxes could have important and adverse effects on the level of potential output. To understand the full economic effect of taxation and evaluate some of the claims of the supply-siders, we need to move beyond the Laffer curve.

Taxes and Potential Output

We use our model of potential output in Figure 5 to study the effects of a tax paid by employers for hiring labor, an important tax in the U.S. economy. Supply-siders use similar arguments to study a variety of taxes, including personal and corporate

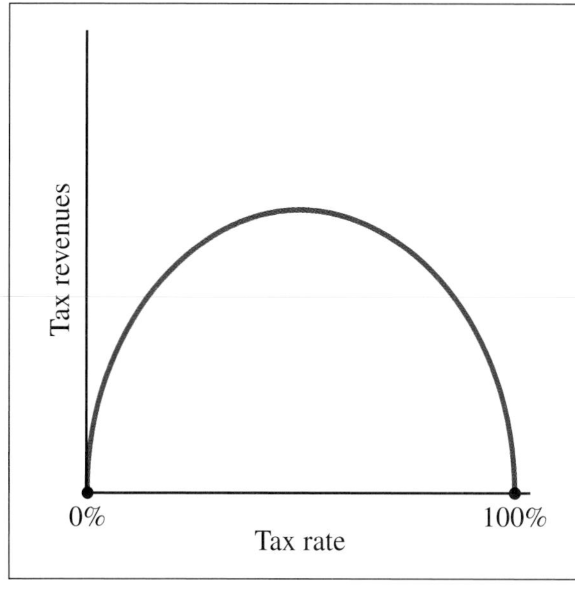

Figure 6

Laffer Curve

At a zero tax rate, the government collects no revenue. As tax rates rise, revenues increase. But at some point, the disincentives from higher taxes cause revenues to fall. At a tax rate of 100%, no one will work and tax revenues will disappear.

income taxes. A tax on labor will make labor more expensive and raise the marginal cost of hiring workers. For example, with a 10% tax, an employer who had been paying \$10 an hour for workers will now find that labor costs \$11. Since the marginal cost of hiring workers has gone up but the marginal benefit has not changed, employers will respond by hiring fewer workers at any given wage. In panel A of Figure 7, the labor demand curve shifts to the left with the tax. The market equilibrium moves from E to E' with lower real wages and lower employment.

This is the heart of the supply-side story. Higher taxes lead to less employment. With reduced employment, potential output in the economy will be reduced as we move down the short-run production function. Higher taxes therefore lead to lower output. The size of this effect, however, depends critically on the slope of the labor supply curve. The slope of the labor supply curve indicates how sensitive labor supply is to changes in real wages. Panel B in Figure 7 shows the effect of the same tax but with a vertical labor supply curve. A vertical labor supply curve means that workers will supply the same amount of labor regardless of the wage. For example, a single parent might work a full 40 hours a week regardless of the wage. His or her supply curve will be vertical. If other workers in the economy put in the same hours regardless of the wage, the supply curve for labor in the economy will be vertical. In panel B we see that with a vertical supply curve, the tax will reduce wages but have no effect on employment or therefore output.

This example illustrates that taxes have important effects. In both cases, either output or wages were lowered when the tax was imposed. However, the extent of the decline in output depends on the slope of the labor supply curve. Thus, to understand the effects of taxes on output, we need to have information about the slope of the labor supply curve.

There have been many studies of labor supply. Most studies show that full-time workers do not change their hours very much when wages change. There is some evidence that part-time workers or second earners in a family are more sensitive to changes in wages and do vary their labor supply when wages change. But the bulk of the evidence suggests that the supply curve for the economy as a whole is close to vertical. Thus it is more likely that higher taxes will reduce wages and not have pronounced effects on output.

The entire area of taxation and economics is an important and active branch of research today. Economists such as Martin Feldstein of Harvard University have studied the effects of many different types of taxes that affect employment, saving,

Figure 7

Effects of Employment Taxes

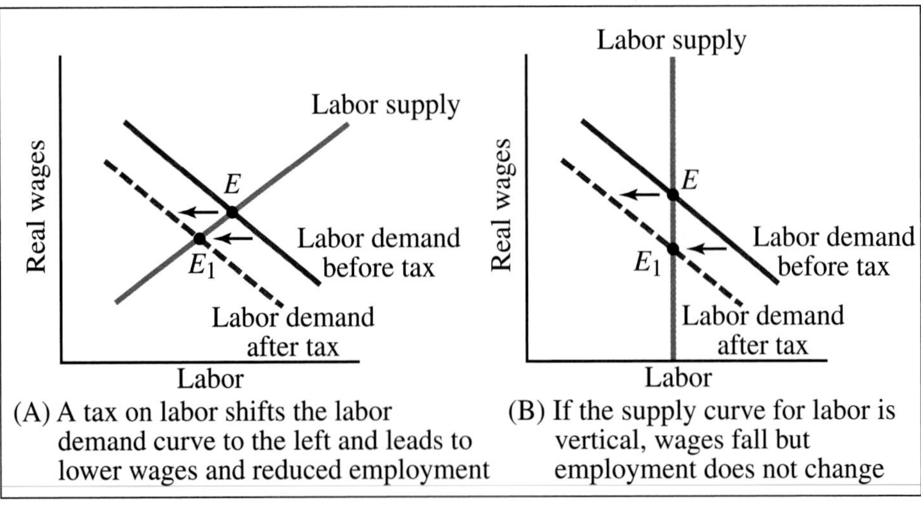

(A) A tax on labor shifts the labor demand curve to the left and leads to lower wages and reduced employment

(B) If the supply curve for labor is vertical, wages fall but employment does not change

and production. In all these areas, economists use models to try to measure these effects, just as we did for the employment tax.

THE DIVISION OF OUTPUT AMONG COMPETING USES

Our model of full employment is based entirely on the supply of factors of production. The demand for and supply of labor determine the real wage and total employment in the economy. Together, labor and the supply of capital determine the level of output through the production function. Thus, in a full-employment economy, total GDP is determined by the supply of factors of production.

Full-employment GDP must, however, be divided among competing uses in the economy. As we discussed in the last two chapters, economists think of GDP as being composed of consumption, investment, government purchases, and net exports, or, in symbols, $C + I + G + NX$. In this section we first discuss how different societies divide total GDP among these uses. Since governments often wish to increase the level of spending for many different reasons, we would like to know how this would affect other types of spending. We will see how increases in government spending must reduce other types of expenditures when the economy is operating at full employment. This phenomenon is called **crowding out.**

Crowding out: Reductions in consumption, investment, or net exports caused by an increase in government purchases.

Some Comparative Data

It is important to recognize that countries divide GDP among its uses in very different ways. Table 2 presents data on the percent of GDP in alternative uses for five countries in 1989. We chose that year because all these countries were then producing near full employment. All the entries in the table are expressed as a percent of each country's GDP. Recall that consumption (C), investment (I), and government purchases (G) refer to total spending by residents of that country. Net exports (NX) are the difference between exports (sales of goods to foreign residents) and imports (purchases of goods abroad). If a country has positive net exports (Japan, Singapore, and Germany), it is selling more goods abroad than it is buying. If a country has negative net exports (United States), it is buying more goods abroad then it is selling. One other point should be mentioned. These data are from the *International Financial Statistics*, which is published by the International Monetary Fund (IMF). In these statistics, government purchases only include government consumption (for example, military spending or wages for government employees). Government investment (for example, spending on bridges or roads) is included in the investment category (I).

The table reveals a considerable diversity among countries. The United States consumes a higher fraction of its GDP (66%) than any of the other countries. A

Table 2: Alternative Uses of GDP for 1989 (percent of total GDP)

	C	I	G	NX
Japan	57	31	9	3
United States	66	16	17	–2
France	60	21	18	0
Singapore	47	37	11	7
Germany	53	21	19	7

Source: International Financial Statistics, International Monetary Fund, 1994.

comparison with Singapore is particularly striking; Singapore consumes only 47% of its GDP. The United States also invests a much smaller fraction of GDP than do the other countries. Japan and Singapore invest over 30% of GDP, whereas the United States invests only 16%. Japan and Singapore have a smaller fraction of GDP devoted to government consumption than do Germany, France, and the United States. Finally, as we noted, the countries differ in the size of net exports relative to GDP.

The wide diversity of experience naturally poses challenges to economists to explain these differences. We have been only partly successful in this task. Some have suggested that Japan has a high saving rate, that is, a relatively low percent of GDP devoted to consumption, because it has a relatively fast growing population and young adults tend to be a high-saving part of the population. Other economists have suggested that high payroll taxes in Singapore reduce workers' incomes and their ability to consume. But not all economists accept these explanations, and there are no obvious purely *economic* reasons why the United States, France, and Germany should exhibit such different behavior.

Crowding Out in a Closed Economy

Although the economies of the world differ in their uses of GDP, we still want to know what would happen if a country increased its share of government purchases in GDP. Since the level of full employment output is given by the supply of factors in the economy, an increase in government spending must come at the expense of, or *crowd out,* other uses of GDP. This is an example of the principle of opportunity cost.

PRINCIPLE ***of Opportunity Cost***

The opportunity cost of something is what you sacrifice to get it.

At full employment, the opportunity cost of increased government spending is some other component of GDP.

Closed economy: An economy without international trade.

To understand crowding out, it is useful first to consider what will happen in an economy without international trade, which economists call a **closed economy.** In a closed economy, full employment output is divided among just three uses: consumption, investment, and government purchases. We can write this as

$$\text{output} = \text{consumption} + \text{investment} + \text{government purchases}$$
$$Y = C + I + G$$

Since we are considering the economy at full employment, the supply of output (Y) is fixed. Increases in government spending must reduce (crowd out) either consumption or investment, and in general both are affected.

One important example of crowding out occurred in the United States during World War II as the share of government spending in GDP rose sharply. Figures 8 and 9 show that shares of consumption and investment spending in GDP fell as the share of government spending rose during the war.

Crowding Out in an Open Economy

Open economy: An economy with international trade.

In an **open economy**, full-employment output is divided among four uses: consumption, investment, government purchases, and net exports (exports-imports):

$$Y = C + I + G + NX$$

In an open economy, increases in government spending need not crowd out either consumption or investment. There is one other possibility: Increased government

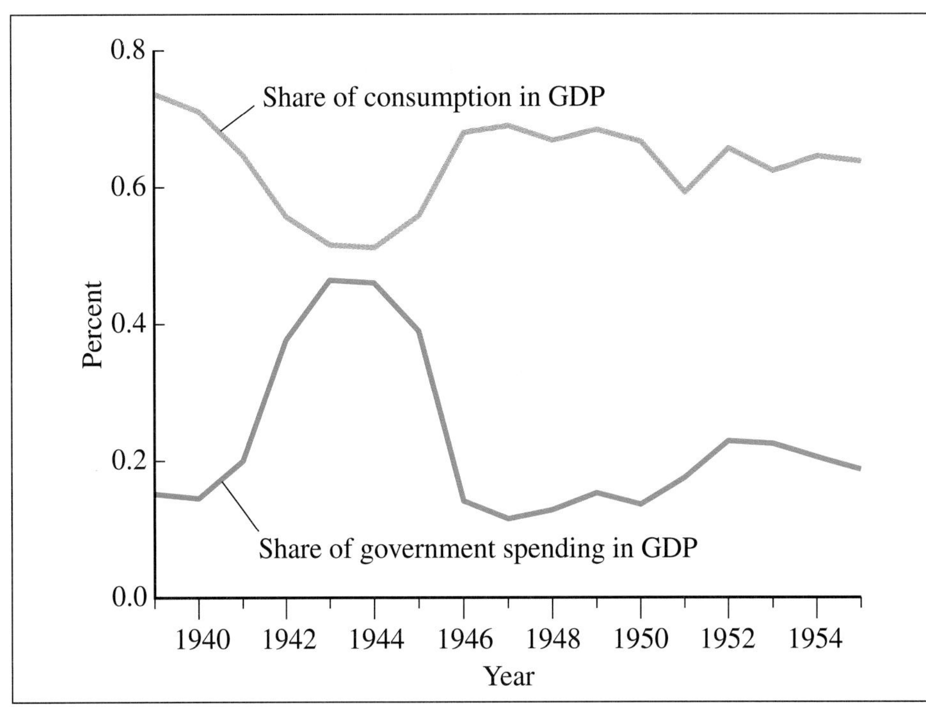

Figure 8

Increased Government Spending Crowds Out Consumption

Source: U.S. Department of Commerce.

spending could lead to reduced exports and increased imports. In other words, net exports could be crowded out.

Here is how this might happen. Suppose the U.S. government began buying goods that used resources previously devoted to producing consumer goods. If consumers wanted to maintain their previous consumption level, they could purchase goods previously sold abroad (exports) and goods sold by foreign countries

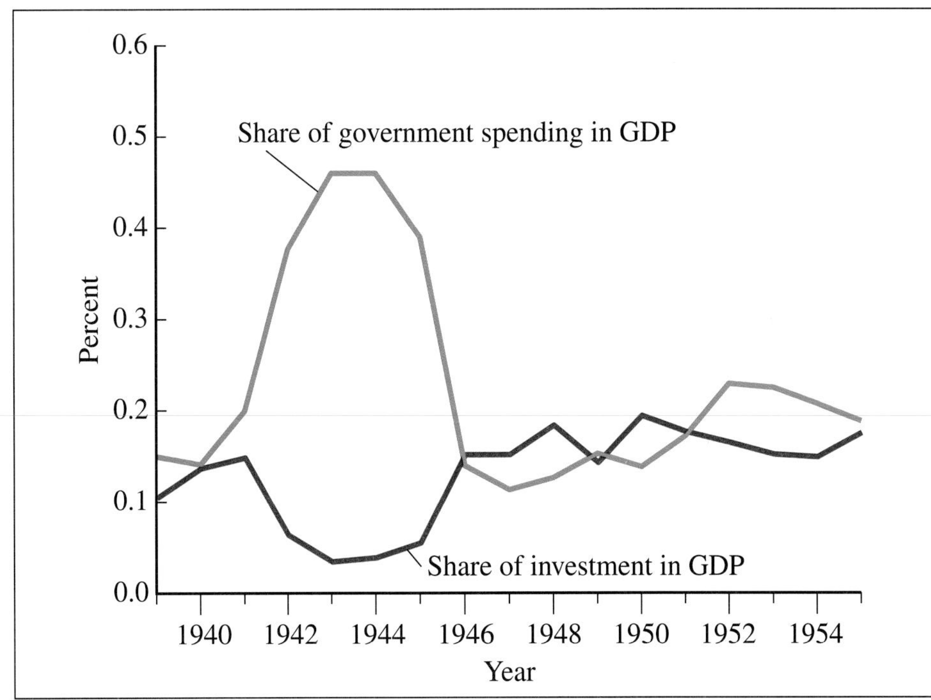

Figure 9

Increased Government Spending Also Crowds Out Investment

Source: U.S. Department of Commerce.

(imports). The result would be a decrease in the amount of goods exported and an increase in imports, that is, a decrease in net exports. In practice, increases in government spending in an open economy would crowd out consumption, investment, and net exports.

A Possibility of Crowding In?

Although it is not often discussed, it is actually possible for certain types of government spending to crowd in (or increase) some types of investment spending. Suppose, for example, that the government spent money on infrastructure such as bridges or roads. The improved transportation network might make it more profitable for firms to ship goods throughout the country. Firms might want to expand their plants to take advantage of their higher profits, and as a consequence, they might increase their investment spending. In this case the government infrastructure investment would crowd in some types of investment spending in the economy.

To understand how government spending crowds out (or in) some other component of GDP, we need to know the precise nature of the increased government spending. If the government spent more on medical care, we might think that consumers would spend less and thus consumption would be crowded out. As we saw in Figures 8 and 9, increases in military spending crowd out both consumption and investment. Increases in infrastructure spending could crowd in some types of investment while crowding out consumption, net exports, or other investment.

TEST *Your Understanding*

9 True or false: When the economy operates at full employment, an increase in government spending must crowd out consumption.

10 In an open economy, increases in government spending can crowd out consumption, investment, or ____________.

11 Compared to other countries, does the United States have a relatively high or low share of consumption spending in GDP?

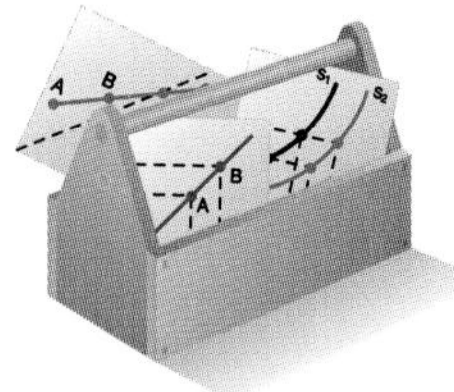

Using the TOOLS

In this chapter we developed several tools, including labor demand, labor supply, and the short-run production function. Using these tools, we developed a complete model of potential output. Here are four problems that test and extend your understanding of the tools developed in this chapter.

1. Payroll Tax for a Health Program

Suppose that to finance a universal health care program, the government places a 10% payroll tax on all labor that is hired.

a. Show how this shifts the demand for labor.

b. Assuming that the labor supply function is vertical, what are the effects on real wages, output, and employment? Explain why economists say that labor bears the full burden of the tax in this case.

c. If the labor supply is horizontal, what will be the effects on wages, output, and employment?

2. ECONOMIC DETECTIVE– *Missing Evidence?*

A journalist noticed that wages had fallen and wrote that the quantity of labor demanded must have fallen. As the economic detective, you think he may have jumped to a premature conclusion. What key piece of evidence would help you determine whether he was right or wrong?

3. Twin Deficits

In the early 1980s in the United States, government spending increased and taxes decreased, resulting in government budget deficits. Soon a trade deficit emerged. These two deficits (government budget and trade deficits) were called the "twin deficits." Explain how the spending increases and tax cuts that caused the budget deficit might cause a trade deficit to emerge. (We return to this topic in our later chapter on government deficits).

4. Would a Subsidy for Wages Necessarily Increase Employment?

Suppose the government paid a subsidy to firms for hiring workers; that is, it actually paid them an amount for every worker they hired. Using supply and demand diagrams, show how this could possibly lead to higher wages but no increase in employment. Under what circumstances would employment increase the most?

SUMMARY

In this chapter we analyzed the classical model of full employment. In this model the level of GDP is determined by the supply of factors of production, labor, and capital. We focused on how the economy operates when it is at full employment; in later chapters we consider economic fluctuations. Here are the main points from this chapter.

1. Full employment or potential output is the level of GDP produced from a given supply of capital when the labor market is in equilibrium. Potential output is fully determined by the supply of factors of production in the economy.
2. Increases in the stock of capital raise the level of full-employment output and real wages.
3. Increases in the supply of labor will raise the level of full-employment output but lower the level of real wages.
4. Supply-side economists stress that taxes on employment will reduce real wages and reduce potential output. Output will not decrease, however, if workers' supply of labor is not sensitive to the real wage.
5. At full employment, increases in government spending must come at the expense of other components of GDP. In a closed economy, either consumption or investment must be crowded out. In an open economy, net exports can be crowded out as well. Government infrastructure investment can possibly crowd in some types of private investment spending.

KEY TERMS

aggregate production function, *444*
classical economics, *443*
closed economy, *456*
crowding out, *455*
full-employment output, *450*
income effect, *448*
labor, *445*
Laffer curve, *451*
open economy, *456*
potential output, *450*
real wage rate, *446*
short-run production function, *445*
stock of capital, *444*
substitution effect, *448*
supply-side economics, *444*
supply-siders, *451*

PROBLEMS AND DISCUSSION QUESTIONS

1. Supply-side economists often discuss the labor market in Europe, which has high payroll taxes and has had low employment growth. Why are supply-siders interested in this case?
2. Suppose economist A claims that the natural rate of unemployment is 6% and economist B claims it is 5%. Which economist will estimate a higher value for potential output?
3. Explain why labor unions might be interested in limiting the employment of young workers.
4. Why do increases in government spending have to crowd out some other component of GDP when the economy operates at full employment?
5. Studies have shown that cities with a higher inflow of new immigrants have lower wages. Explain this fact.
6. Draw a diagram that shows how labor market equilibrium and the short-run production function determine potential output.
7. Some Japanese economists have said that we should limit credit cards in the United States to increase our rate of investment. Explain this comment.
8. A country cut its tariff rates but found that its total revenue from tariff collections increased. How could this happen?

Take It to the Net

We invite you to visit the O'Sullivan/Sheffrin page on the Prentice Hall Web site at:

http://www.prenhall.com/osullivan/

for this chapter's World Wide Web exercise.

MODEL ANSWERS FOR THIS CHAPTER

Chapter-Opening Questions

1. Increased immigration will typically lower real wages while increasing the level of output in the economy.
2. Increased investment will mean a higher capital stock in the future. The higher stock of capital will allow a higher standard of living.
3. If employers are required to pay higher taxes for hiring labor, wages will fall and typically employment and GDP will fall as well. As the chapter explains, the amount that employment and GDP fall depend on how sensitive labor supply is to real wages.
4. In a closed economy (not open to trade) operating at full employment, increased government spending must lead to reduced spending on either consumption or investment. In an open economy (which allows for trade), higher government spending could lead to a reduction in net exports.

Test Your Understanding

1. An aggregate production function shows the relationships between inputs and outputs in the economy.
2. a decreasing
3. upward
4. supply
5. The demand curve slopes downward because when wages are lower the firm will want to hire more labor. The supply curve slopes up because at higher wages, more people will seek employment.
6. right
7. right
8. Draw two graphs in which the demand curve shifts equally to the right in both but the supply curve shifts more to the right in the graph for the United States.
9. False.
10. net exports
11. It is high.

Using the Tools

1. Payroll Tax for a Health Program
   a. The tax will shift the labor demand curve to the left. At any wage, the employer's cost is 10%

greater. The employer will hire less labor at any wage since labor has become more expensive.

b. The demand for labor shifts to the left, lowering the real wage. Since the labor supply curve is vertical, the amount of labor supplied does not change nor does total output. Labor bears the full burden of the tax because wages fall by the total amount of the tax.

c. If the supply of labor were horizontal, the decrease in labor demand would not reduce real wages but would reduce employment. Full-employment output would fall as well. This would be an extreme supply-side story.

2. Economic Detective: Missing Evidence?

The piece of evidence you would like to have is the change in the quantity of employment. If the quantity of employment fell along with wages, the demand curve shifted to the left and the demand of labor fell. But if the quantity of employment increased along with the fall in wages, this is best explained by an increase in the supply of labor, that is, a rightward shift in the labor supply curve.

3. Twin Deficits

The increase in government spending would crowd out net exports. The tax cut would also lead to higher consumer spending on imports. The result is less exports and more imports, or a trade deficit.

4. Would a Subsidy to Wages Necessarily Increase Employment?

A subsidy is just the reverse of a tax. A subsidy for hiring labor would shift the firm's demand curve to the right. If the supply of labor were vertical (that is, not sensitive to the real wage), the subsidy would raise wages but not employment. The subsidy would be most effective in raising employment if the supply curve for labor were relatively flat.

CHAPTER

23

Why Do Economies Grow?

To understand what economic growth really means, consider how the typical American lived in 1783, seven years after the Declaration of Independence. According to economic historian Stanley Lebergott, an average U.S. home at that time had no central heat, only one fireplace, no plumbing, no hot water, and toilets that were outside shacks surrounding a hole in the ground. The lack of plumbing meant that hygiene suffered: Well into the nineteenth century, a typical farmer would take a bath only once a week. Houses had no electricity or gas and used only a single candle at night to provide light. With no electricity there were no refrigerators, toasters, or other appliances. Bedrooms contained no furniture other than a bed (no springs) and two people slept in a single bed. The plight of a housewife was particularly hard. She was expected to bake over half a ton of bread a year. She also had to kill chickens and butcher pigs as well as prepare all vegetables. Canned foods were not readily available until a century later. And you really don't want to hear about medical "science" in those days.[1]

Our living standards are dramatically different today because there has been a remarkable growth in GDP per person. Growth in GDP is perhaps the most critical aspect of a country's economic performance. Over long periods of time, there is no other way to raise the standard of living in an economy.

Here are some real-world questions we can address with the tools developed in this chapter:

1. What countries have the highest standard of living today?
2. Do countries with high saving rates grow at faster rates?
3. Do trade deficits help or hinder economic growth?
4. What factors determine technological progress?

The chapter begins by looking at some data from both rich and poor countries over the last 30 years. We will see how GDP per capita (that is, per person) and experiences with economic growth compare over this period.

We then turn to understanding the process through which growth occurs. Economists believe that there are two basic mechanisms by which GDP per capita can increase over the long term for an economy. The first way is through increases in an economy's stock of capital—its total stock of plant and equipment—relative to its work force. Economists call an increase in the stock of capital per worker **capital deepening**.

Capital deepening: Increases in the stock of capital per worker.

The second mechanism by which economies can grow is **technological progress**. Economists use this term in a very specific way: It means that an economy operates more efficiently, so that it produces more output, but without using any more inputs in production. In other words, the economy gets more output without any more capital or labor. This may seem too good to be true. Fortunately, however, technological progress does occur and is a key element of economic growth. We examine different theories of the origins of technological progress and discuss how to measure its overall importance for the economy.

Technological progress: An increase in output without increasing inputs.

The appendix to this chapter contains a simple model of capital deepening known as the Solow model. It shows, in more detail, how increases in capital per worker lead to economic growth. It will also allow us to better understand the role of technological progress in promoting sustained economic growth.

THE DIVERSITY OF ECONOMIC EXPERIENCE

Throughout the world, there are vast differences in standards of living and in rates of economic growth. Before turning to look at data, let's review a few key concepts. First, real GDP measures the total value of final goods and services in a country in constant prices. Since countries differ in the size of their populations, we often want to know what real GDP is per person in a country, or **real GDP per capita**.

Real GDP per capita: Inflation-adjusted gross domestic product per person. It is the usual measure of living standards across time and between countries.

Second, a growth rate is the percentage change between two periods. The growth rate in real GDP per capita in any country is the percentage change in real GDP per capita between two periods. Over long periods of time, we usually express growth rates as an average annual percentage. For example, we may say that from 1960 to 1993, real GDP per capita grew at an average annual rate of 1.5%. In some years the rate may have been higher, and in other years the rate may have been lower. But on average, the economy grew at this rate each year.

Making comparisons of real GDP across countries is extremely difficult. Every country has its own currency and its own price system. Whereas we quote prices in dollars, the French use francs, the British use pounds, and the Israelis use shekels. In addition, consumption patterns are very different across countries. For example, land is scarce in Japan, and people live in much smaller spaces than do residents of the United States.

Fortunately, a team of economists led by Robert Summers and Alan Heston of the University of Pennsylvania has devoted decades to developing methods for measuring real GDP across countries. They have published statistics that take into account the difficulties in comparing real GDP across countries with different currencies and different consumption patterns. Their methods are designed to measure true variations in the cost of living across countries.

How do they do it? Teams of economists collect vast amounts of data on prices of comparable goods in all countries. They try to ensure that the goods are of identical quality, but if not, they make appropriate adjustments. They then use the prices of all these goods in different countries to express the GDP of each country in U.S. prices.

Let's consider a simplified example of their procedure. Suppose that in the United States 1 gallon of milk costs $2.00, while in Germany 1 gallon of milk costs 4.0 marks (marks are the currency of Germany). With respect to a gallon of milk, $2.00 in the United States is equivalent to 4.0 marks in Germany, and $0.50 is equivalent to 1 mark ($2.00/4 marks = $0.50/mark). If German consumers spend 10 million marks on milk in a given year, this is equivalent to spending $5 million (10 million marks × $0.50 /mark) in U.S. prices. German consumption of milk is then $5 million measured in U.S. currency.

We can do similar calculations for all final goods and services in Germany, taking each good one at a time. Each calculation converts German purchases of goods and services in marks to an equivalent amount in U.S. dollars. Adding up all the final goods and services gives us German GDP in U.S. prices. If we do these calculations using constant U.S. prices (say from 1993), we obtain measures of real German GDP in constant U.S. dollars. This method, using vast amounts of price data and proceeding on a commodity by commodity basis, is viewed by most economists as the best method for comparing standards of living across countries.

Using these measures, the country with the highest level of income in the world in 1993 was Luxembourg, with real GDP per capita of $29,510. The United States ranked second with real GDP per capita of $24,750. It is important to use correct methods to compare living standards across countries, as the Closer Look box "Why Switzerland Is *Not* Number One" explains.

Exchange rate: The rate at which one currency trades for another.

Table 1 presents real GDP per capita for 11 selected countries for 1993. The table also presents the average annual growth rate of real GDP per capita for these 11 countries between 1960 and 1993. In Table 1, Japan follows the United States

A Closer LOOK

Why Switzerland Is Not *Number One*

Every so often an economist will say that the United States has fallen drastically behind other countries in per capita GDP, and Switzerland is often used as an example. Here is how the economist might argue: In 1991, GDP per capita in Switzerland was 48, 159 Swiss francs. The *exchange rate* (the rate at which one currency trades for another) between the U.S. dollar and Swiss francs in that year was 1.434 Swiss francs per dollar. Using this exchange rate, Swiss GDP per capita in U.S. dollars is $33,583 (48,159 Swiss francs/1.434 Swiss francs per dollar). This is nearly 50% higher than the 1991 U.S. GDP per capita of $22,461.

This calculation is misleading and wrong. The problem comes in using the exchange rate between the two currencies to translate Swiss GDP to U.S. dollars. As we will discuss in a later chapter, exchange rates are determined in financial markets and reflect the demand and supply for goods that are *traded* between countries as well as financial flows between countries, such as the purchases of stocks and bonds. They do not reflect the value of important goods that determine living standards that are not traded, such as housing. Moreover, the Swiss exchange rate is typically high because Switzerland tries to attract foreign funds through its efficient and secure banking system.

Using the preferred methods, which account for both goods that are traded and those that are not, Switzerland has a GDP per capita today about 93% that of the United States. This is a very high level by world standards, but still less than that of the United States.

Table 1: GDP per Capita and Economic Growth

Country	*GDP per Capita in 1993 Dollars*	*Average per Capita Growth Rate, 1960–1993 (%)*
United States	$24,750	1.86
Japan	21,090	5.06
France	19,440	2.72
Italy	18,070	3.13
United Kingdom	17,750	1.88
Mexico	7,100	2.09
Costa Rica	5,580	2.18
Pakistan	2,110	2.09
Zimbabwe	1,900	1.02
India	1,250	1.09
Zambia	1,170	–0.86

Sources: *The World Bank Atlas 1995* (Washington, DC: The World Bank) and Summers and Heston, *Penn World Tables* (National Bureau of Economic Research).

with a GDP per capita in 1993 of $21,090. Not far behind are the United Kingdom, France, and Italy. Mexico and Costa Rica were more representative of typical countries in the world. Their GDPs per capita in 1993 were $7,100 and $5,580, respectively. This is less than one-third of GDP per capita in the United States. The very poor countries of the world have extremely low figures for GDP per capita. India, for example, had a GDP per capita in 1993 of only $1,250. This is only one-twentieth the GDP per capita of the United States.

Perhaps what is most intriguing about Table 1 are the differences in growth rates. Consider the case of Japan. In 1960, Japan had a GDP per capita that was only one-half that of France and almost one-fourth that of the United States. But Japanese GDP per capita grew at the extremely rapid rate of 5.06% per year, compared to 1.86% for the United States and 2.72% for France. To place Japan's growth rate for this period into perspective, recall the rule of 70. If an economy grows at an average annual rate of x percent a year, it takes $70/x$ years for output to double. In Japan's case, per capita output was doubling every 70/5.06 years, or approximately every 14 years. At this rate, from the time someone is born to the time that person reaches the age of 28, living standards have increased by a factor of 4! This is an extraordinary rate of growth.

One question that economists ask is whether poorer countries can close the gap between their level of GDP per capita and that of richer countries, termed **convergence**. To do so, poorer countries have to grow at more rapid rates than those of richer countries. Since 1960, Japan, Italy, and France all have grown more rapidly than the United States and have narrowed the gap in per capita incomes.

Convergence: The process by which poorer countries "catch up" with richer countries in terms of real GDP per capita.

For a more extensive look at the evidence, Figure 1 on the next page plots the average growth rate for 16 currently developed countries from 1870 to 1979 versus the level of GDP in 1870. As you can see, the best-fitting line through the points slopes downward. This means that countries with higher levels of GDP in 1870 grew more slowly than countries with lower levels of GDP; in other words, there was a tendency for countries with lower levels of initial income to grow faster and thus catch up. Although the evidence is somewhat sensitive to the precise selection of countries, there is a general consensus that convergence has occurred among the currently developed countries.

Comparing the less developed countries to the advanced industrial economies, the picture is less clear. While Pakistan grew at a faster rate than the United States,

Figure 1

Countries with Lower Income in 1870 Grew Faster

Source: M. Obstfeld and K. Rogoff, *Foundation of International Macroeconomics* (Cambridge, MA: MIT Press, 1996), Table 7.1.

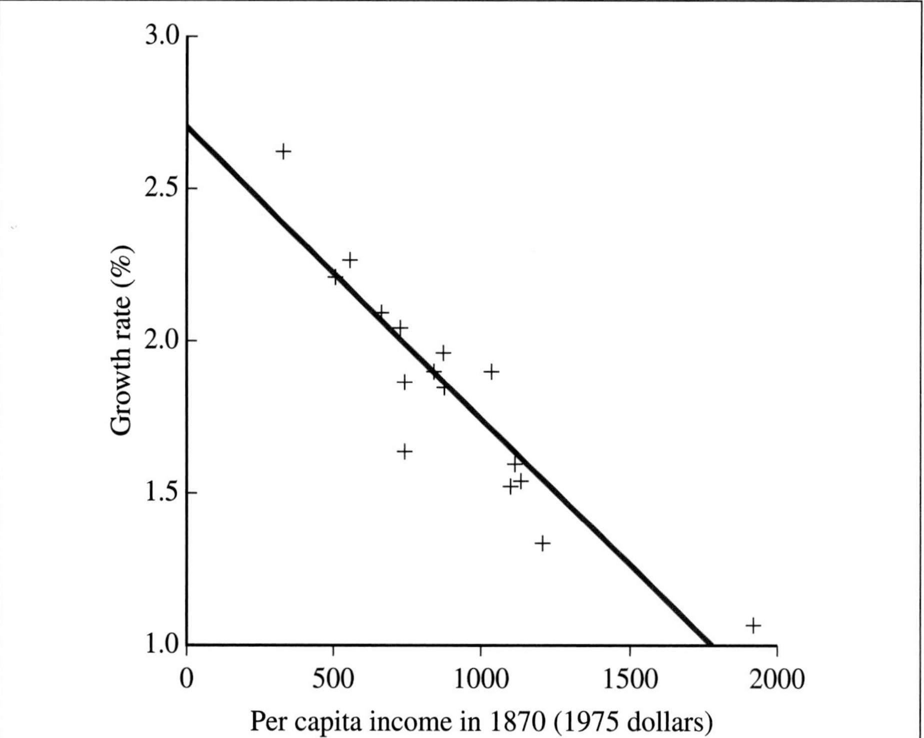

its neighbor India grew only 1.09% per year and fell further behind advanced economies. In Africa, GDP per capita actually fell substantially in Zambia, while in Zimbabwe GDP per capita grew at a slower rate than the U.S. rate.

Economists who have studied the process of economic growth in detail find, at best, only weak evidence that poorer countries are closing the gap in per capita income with richer countries. On average, it does not appear that poorer countries grow at rates substantially higher than those of richer countries. Although there are some success stories, such as Japan and other Asian economies, including Hong Kong and Singapore, there are also economies such as Zambia's that have actually regressed.

The rule of 70 reinforces how important small differences in economic growth are. A growth rate for per capita GDP of 5% a year means that living standards double in 14 years. With only 1% growth, that same growth takes 70 years. Because economic growth is so important, economists have studied it in some detail. Let's turn to some of the mechanisms of growth that economists have identified.

TEST *Your Understanding*

1. What measure of output do we use to measure living standards across countries with populations of different sizes?
2. How would we convert spending on TV sets in France to U.S. dollars?
3. True or false: Economists who have studied economic growth find only weak evidence for convergence.
4. At a 2% annual growth rate in GDP per capita, how many years would it take for GDP per capita to double?

As an indication of changing patterns of economic growth, the world's tallest building today is the Petronas Twin Towers in Kuala Lumpur, Malaysia.

THE PROCESS OF CAPITAL DEEPENING

One of the most important mechanisms of economic growth that economists have identified is increases in the amount of capital per worker in the economy. Recall that the increase in capital per worker is called capital deepening.

In the previous chapter we studied the effects of an increase in capital in a full-employment economy. Figure 2 on the next page shows the consequences. For simplicity, the supply of labor is assumed not to be affected by real wages and is drawn as a vertical line. The additional capital shifts up the production function because more output can be produced from the same amount of labor. In addition, firms increase their demand for labor since the marginal benefit from employing labor will increase.

Panel B shows how the increase in capital raises the demand for labor and increases real wages. As firms increase their demand and compete for the fixed supply of labor, they will bid up real wages in the economy. In panel A we show how the increase in the amount of capital in the economy shifts the production function up and allows more output to be produced for any level of labor input. With a given supply of labor, increases in the stock of capital both raise real wages and lead to increases in output.

An economy is better off with an increase in the stock of capital. With additions to the stock of capital, workers will enjoy higher wages and total GDP in the economy will increase. Workers are more productive because each worker has more capital at his or her disposal. But how does an economy increase its stock of capital per worker?

Saving and Investment

Let's begin with the simplest case. Consider an economy with a constant population that is producing at full employment and has no government or foreign sector. In this simplified economy, output can be purchased only by consumers or by firms. In other words, output can go only for consumption or investment. Output also equals income. Any income that is not consumed we call **saving**. Since output consists only of

Saving: Total income minus consumption.

Figure 2

Increase in the Supply of Capital

An increase in the supply of capital will shift up the production function and increase the demand for labor. Real wages will increase from W^* to W^{**} and potential output will increase from Y^* to Y^{**}.

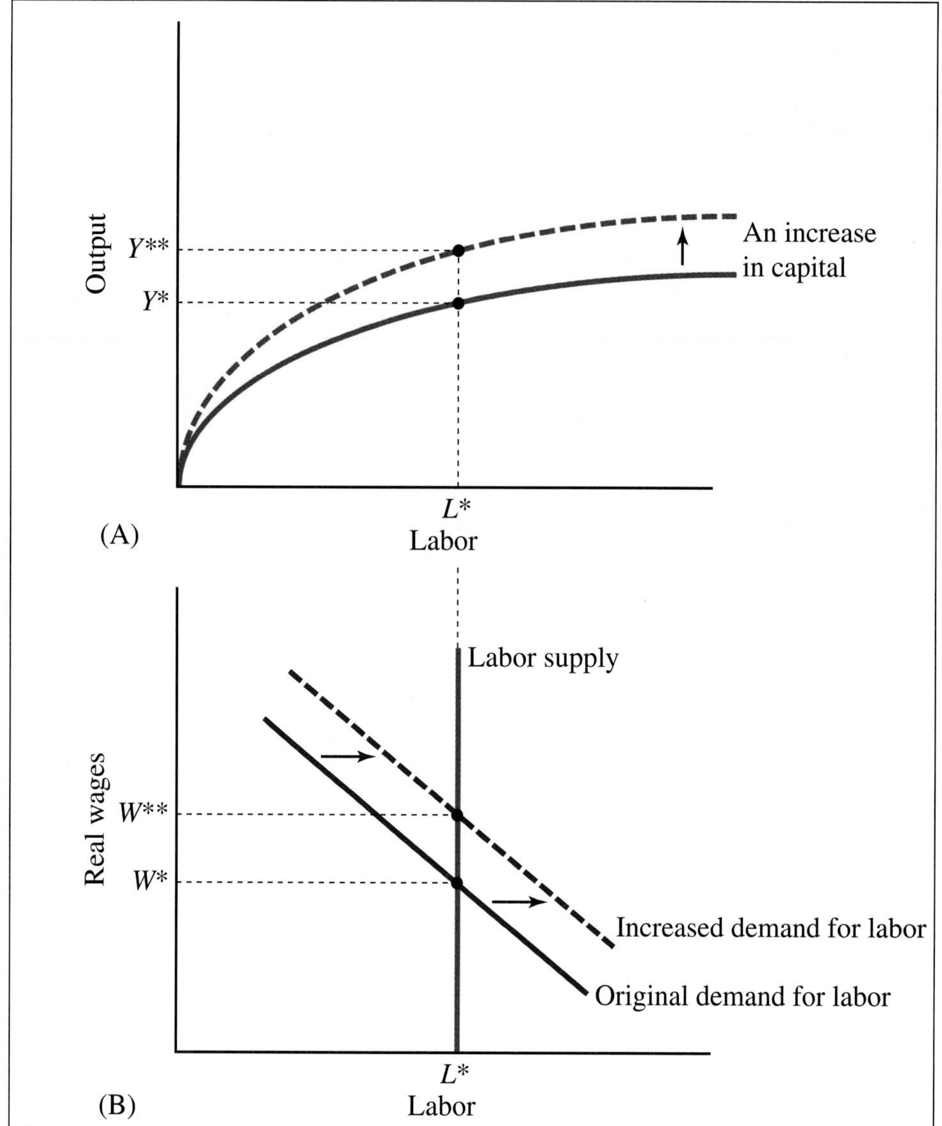

consumption and investment, whatever is not consumed must be invested. Therefore, in this economy, saving is equal to investment.

Next, we need to link the level of investment in the economy to the stock of capital. The stock of capital in the economy depends on two factors. It increases with any gross investment spending but decreases with any depreciation. For example, suppose the stock of capital at the beginning of the year is $100. During the year, if there were $10 in gross investment and $4 in depreciation, the capital stock at the end of the year would be $106 ($100 + $10 – $4).

It may be helpful to make an analogy with a bathtub. The level of water in a bathtub (the stock of capital) depends on the flow into the bathtub through the faucet (gross investment) minus the flow out of the bathtub through the drain (depreciation). As long as the flow in exceeds the flow out, the water level in the bathtub (the stock of capital) will increase.

Higher saving, which leads to higher gross investment, will therefore tend to increase the stock of capital available for production. As the stock of capital grows, however, there typically will be more depreciation, since there is more capital to depreciate. It is the difference between gross investment and depreciation, net investment, that ultimately determines the change in the stock of capital for the economy and therefore the level of real wages and real output. In our example, net investment was $10 – $4 = $6.

Population Growth, Government, and Trade

So far we've considered a very simplified economy. Let's go on to consider population growth, government, and trade. First, consider the effects of population growth. A larger labor force will allow the economy to produce more total output. But with a fixed amount of capital, the amount of *capital per worker* will be less. With less capital per worker, *output per worker* will also tend to be less because each worker has fewer machines to use. This is an illustration of the principle of diminishing returns.

PRINCIPLE *of Diminishing Returns*

Suppose that output is produced with two or more inputs and that we increase one input while holding the other inputs fixed. Beyond some point—called the point of diminishing returns—output will increase at a decreasing rate.

Consider the case of India, the country with the world's second largest population. Although India has a large labor force, the amount of capital per worker is low. With sharp diminishing returns to labor, per capita output in India will tend to be low.

The government can affect the process of capital deepening in several ways through its policies of spending and taxation. Suppose the government taxed its citizens so it could fight a war, or pay its representatives higher salaries, or give foreign aid to needy countries. The higher taxes will reduce total income. If consumers save a fixed fraction of their income, total private saving will fall. In these cases the government is not investing the funds it collects and putting them into capital formation. Instead, it is draining saving from the private sector that would be used for capital deepening. The overall result is a reduction of total investment in the economy and less capital deepening. In these examples the government is taxing the private sector to engage in consumption spending, not investment.

On the other hand, suppose the government took all the tax revenues and invested them in valuable infrastructure: for example, roads, buildings, and airports. Suppose consumers were saving 20% of their incomes. If the government took a dollar away in taxes, private saving would fall by 20 cents. On the other hand, government investment would increase by $1. The net result is an increase in total social saving of 80 cents. This *would* promote capital deepening—in this case the government is taxing its citizens to provide investment.

Finally, the foreign sector can make important contributions to capital deepening. An economy can run a trade deficit and import investment goods to aid the process of capital deepening. The United States, Canada, and Australia built their vast railroad systems in the nineteenth century by running trade deficits and borrowing from abroad to finance the large amount of capital necessary. In these cases the large trade deficits that resulted from importing capital goods were valuable for the economy. They enabled growth to occur at more rapid rates through the process of capital deepening. Eventually, these economies had to pay back the funds that were borrowed from abroad. But since economic growth raised GDP and the wealth of the economy, it was profitable for the country to borrow from abroad.

Not all trade deficits promote capital deepening, however, or are good for the economy. Suppose a country ran a trade deficit because it wanted to buy more consumer goods. In this case the country would also be borrowing from abroad. But there would be no additional capital deepening, just additional consumption spending. When the country was forced to pay back the funds, there would be no additional GDP to help foot the bill. Society will be poorer in the future when it must pay the bill for its current consumption.

Limits to Capital Deepening

There are natural limits to growth through capital deepening. To understand these limits, let's recall that the stock of capital increases only when there is positive net investment. Net investment, in turn, is equal to gross investment minus depreciation. Gross investment depends on the rate of saving in the economy. Depreciation depends on the total stock of capital that the economy has in place.

As the economy accumulates capital and the stock of capital increases, there naturally will be an increase in the total amount of depreciation of capital in the economy. As we show in the appendix to this chapter, as the stock of capital increases, the economy eventually reaches a point at which gross investment equals depreciation. At this point, net investment becomes zero and the stock of capital will no longer increase.

Therefore, there is a natural limit to growth through capital deepening as depreciation eventually catches up to the level of gross investment. While a higher rate of saving can increase the level of real GDP, eventually the process of growth through capital deepening comes to a halt. However, it takes time—on the order of decades—for this point to be reached. Thus capital deepening can be an important source of economic growth for a long time.

TEST *Your Understanding*

5 Explain why saving must equal investment without government or the foreign sector.

6 Holding everything else equal, how does an increase in the size of the population affect total and per capita output?

7 If the private sector saves 10% of its income and the government raises taxes by \$200 to finance public investments, by how much will total investment—private and public—increase?

8 True or false: If a country runs a trade deficit to finance increased current consumption, it will have to reduce consumption in the future to pay back its borrowings.

THE KEY ROLE OF TECHNOLOGICAL PROGRESS

The other important mechanism for economic growth is technological progress. As noted earlier in the chapter, economists use the term *technological progress* in a very specific way: It means that an economy operates more efficiently by producing more output without using any more inputs.

In practice, technological progress can take many forms. The invention of the light bulb made it possible to read and work indoors at night; the invention of the thermometer assisted doctors and nurses in their diagnoses; and the invention of disposable diapers made life easier at home. All these examples—and you could provide many more—enable society to produce more output without having to use more labor or more capital. With higher output per person, we enjoy a higher standard of living.

Technological progress can be thought of as the birth of new ideas. These new ideas enable us to rearrange our economic affairs and make us more productive. It is important to note that not all technological innovations are necessarily major scientific breakthroughs. Suppose that good commonsense ideas from the workers or managers of a business allow it to make more effective use of its capital and labor and to deliver a better product to its consumers at the current price. This is also technological progress. As long as new ideas, inventions, and new ways of doing things are forthcoming, the economy can become more productive and per capita output can increase on a regular basis.

How Do We Measure Technological Progress?

We all believe that we see technological progress in our everyday lives. But suppose that someone asked you how much of the increase in our standard of living were due to technological progress. How would you answer the question?

Robert Solow, a Nobel laureate in economics from the Massachusetts Institute of Technology, developed a method for measuring the importance of technological progress in an economy. As is usually the case with good ideas, his theory was relatively simple. It was based on the idea of a production function.

Recall from the previous chapter that the production function links inputs to outputs. For example, we may have

$$Y = F(K,L)$$

where output (Y) is produced from capital (K) and labor (L), which are linked through the production function F. What Solow did was to modify the production function so that it included some measure of technological progress, A.

$$Y = F(K,L,A)$$

Increases in A represent technological progress. Higher values of A mean that more output is produced from the same level of inputs K and L. If we could find some way to measure A, we could estimate the importance of technological progress.

Solow noted that over any time period we can observe increases in capital, labor, and output. Using these, we can measure technological progress indirectly. We first ask how much of the change in output can be explained by contributions from the changes in the amount of inputs that are used, capital and labor. Whatever growth we cannot explain must have been caused by increases in technological progress. The method that Solow developed for determining the contributions to economic growth from increased capital, labor, and technological progress is called **growth accounting**.

Following this basic approach, Table 2 on the next page contains a breakdown of the sources of growth for the U.S. economy for 1929–1982. Figure 3 shows the relative contributions of the sources of growth based on these data. Over the 1929–1982 period, total output grew at a rate of nearly 3%. Since capital and labor growth are measured at 0.56 and 1.34%, respectively, the remaining portion of output growth, 1.02%, must be due to technological progress. Thus, approximately 35% of output growth comes directly from technological progress.

Figure 3

Percentage Contributions to Real GDP Growth

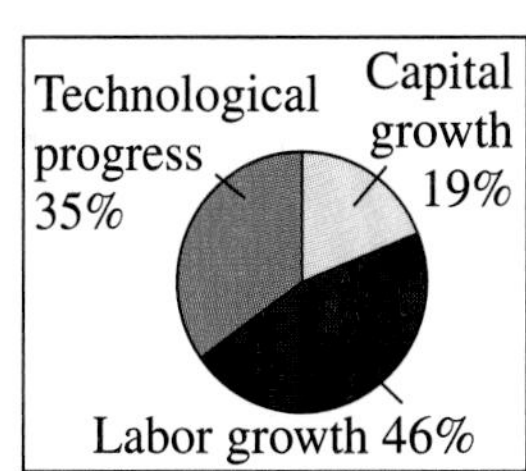

Source: Data from Edward F. Denison, *Trends in Economic Growth 1929–82* (Washington, DC: The Brookings Institution, 1985).

Growth accounting: A method to determine the contribution to economic growth from increased capital, labor, and technological progress.

Table 2: Sources of Real GDP Growth, 1929–1982 (average annual percentage rates)

Due to capital growth	0.56
Due to labor growth	1.34
+ technological progress	1.02
Output growth	2.92

Source: Edward F. Denison, *Trends in Economic Growth 1929–82* (Washington, DC: The Brookings Institution, 1985).

TWO EXAMPLES OF GROWTH ACCOUNTING

Growth accounting has proven to be a very useful tool for understanding different aspects of economic growth. Here are two examples of how economists use growth accounting.

Singapore and Hong Kong

Singapore and Hong Kong have both had phenomenal postwar economic growth. From 1980 to 1985, each grew at a rate of approximately 6% a year. But a closer examination, by Alwyn Young of the Boston University, revealed that the sources of growth were very different.[2] In Singapore, virtually all the growth was accounted for by increases in labor and capital. In particular, the ratio of investment to GDP reached as high as 43% in 1983.

Hong Kong, on the other hand, had a much lower investment rate—approximately 20% of GDP—and technological progress made an important contribution. This meant that the residents of Hong Kong could enjoy the same level of GDP but consume, not save, a higher fraction of GDP. Thus, residents of Hong Kong were actually enjoying higher consumption than residents of Singapore, despite the similarity in growth rates.

The difference in the sources of economic growth between Singapore and Hong Kong may also have important implications for future growth. As we discussed, there are natural limits to growth through capital deepening. Singapore increased its GDP by increasing its labor inputs and increasing its stock of capital. Eventually, however, it will find it difficult to keep increasing inputs to production. Economic leaders in Singapore today are concerned that unless they start to have faster increases in technological progress, their rapid growth could come to an end.

In Hong Kong, there is a different concern. With Hong Kong now part of China, residents hope the Chinese will allow them to maintain their free and open economy in which technological progress has flourished. Technological progress has been the driving force for growth in Hong Kong and there is a strong desire to maintain the system that produced technological innovation.

Labor productivity: Output per hour of work.

ECONOMIC DETECTIVE– *Explaining the Slowdown in Labor Productivity*

One of the common statistics reported about the U.S. economy is **labor productivity**, which is defined as output per hour of work. This is a simple measure of how much a typical worker can produce given the amount of capital in the economy and the state of technological progress. Since 1973 there has been a slowdown in the growth of labor productivity in the United States and other countries in the world. Table 3 shows U.S. productivity growth for different time periods since World War II. As the table indicates, productivity growth first slowed during the oil price shocks of the 1970s and has not recovered to its prior levels. Productivity growth in the United States is approximately 1% today, compared to growth rates over 2% in the 1950s and 1960s.

Similar patterns have been observed in other countries. Zvi Grilliches, a Harvard economist and expert on productivity, compared the growth of output per hour in the manufacturing sectors for 12 countries over different time periods.[3] If we use his data and compare the periods 1960–1973 and 1979–1986, we find that productivity growth slowed in 11 of 12 countries. For example, productivity growth in Japan fell from 10.3% to 5.6%, while in Canada it fell from 4.5% to 1.4%. Only the United Kingdom exhibited any increase in productivity growth over those periods, and that increase was only from 4.3% to 4.4%.

The slowdown in productivity growth has been of great concern because it has also meant slower growth in real wages and in GDP in the United States since 1973. Figure 4 on the next page plots real hourly earnings for U.S. workers. As the figure indicates, real hourly earnings have actually fallen since 1973. Total compensation, which includes employee benefits such as health insurance, did continue to rise through the 1980s as employers received lower wages but higher benefits. But the rate of growth of total compensation was clearly less than the growth of real hourly earnings in the pre-1973 period.

The decrease in the growth of labor productivity was the primary factor behind this pattern of real wages, because wages can only rise with a growing labor force if output per worker continues to increase. What can explain this decrease in the growth rate? Economists are not short of possible answers. Among the factors they have discussed are declines in the education and skills of the workforce, lower levels of investment and thus a lower level of capital, less spending on infrastructure (such as highways and bridges), the belief that managers of companies are more concerned with short-term profits than longer-term profitability for their enterprises, and a host of other economic and sociological factors as well.

Growth accounting has been used to sort through these possible explanations. Using growth accounting methods, economists typically find that the slowdown in labor productivity, both in the United States and abroad, *cannot* be explained by reduced rates of capital deepening. Nor can they be explained by changes in the quality or experience of the labor force. Either a slowdown in technological progress or other factors not directly included in our analysis, such as

Table 3: U.S. Annual Productivity Growth, 1947–1994 (percent)

Years	*Annual Growth Rate*
1947–1955	2.9
1955–1968	2.5
1968–1973	1.5
1973–1980	0.4
1980–1986	1.1
1986–1994	1.0

Source: *Economic Report of the President* (Washington, DC: U.S. Government Printing Office, 1996).

Figure 4

Real Hourly Earnings and Total Compensation in the United States

Total compensation is an index whose value is set equal to real hourly earnings in 1980.

Source: Data from *Economic Report of the President* (Washington, DC: U.S. Government Printing Office, yearly).

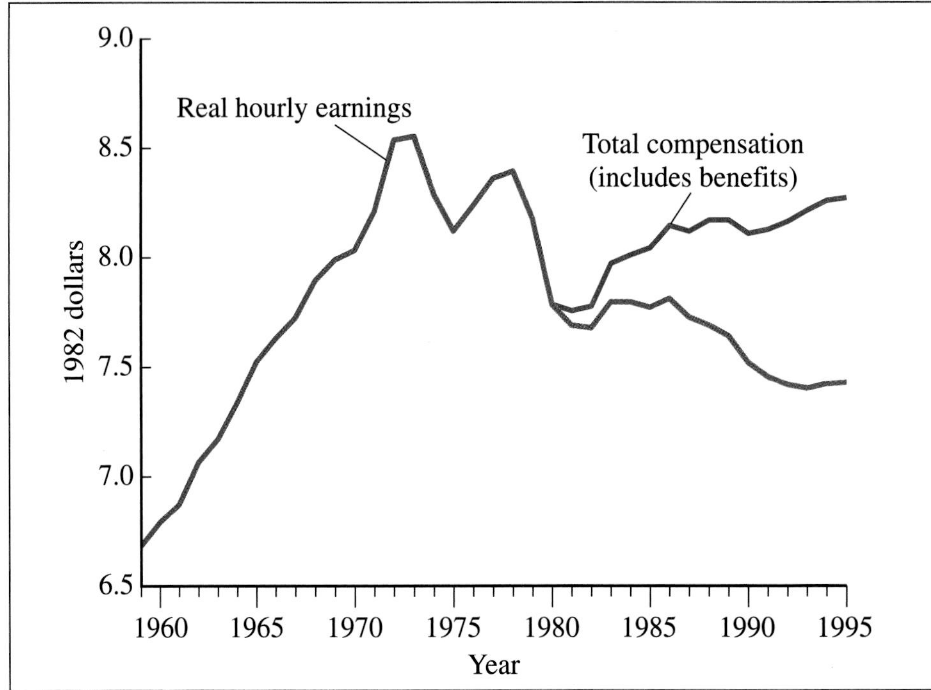

higher worldwide energy prices, must be responsible for the slowdown. Moreover, since the slowdown has been worldwide, it is plausible that factors which affect all countries (such as higher energy prices) are responsible rather than factors specific to a single country. Dale Jorgenson, another Harvard economist, has conducted extensive research attempting to link higher energy prices to the slowdown in productivity growth. Not all economists accept this view, however, and the productivity slowdown remains a bit of a mystery.

There is actually another mystery surrounding productivity that has preoccupied many economists. In the last decade there has been rapid growth in the use of computers and, more broadly, in advanced information technology. By 1996, nearly 40% of all equipment investment has been in information technology. Yet despite this introduction of modern technology, we have yet to see the gains in terms of productivity. There are several explanations for the failure of productivity growth to increase in the face of this rapid investment in new technology. First, it may take much longer, for example decades, before new technology is used in ways that really increase our output. Paul David, an economic historian who teaches at Oxford and Stanford, has noted that it took nearly 40 years after the introduction of the electric dynamo in the 1880s before there were significant productivity gains in the economy.[4]

Second, and a related point, is that at the current time, computers may be useful but they have not revolutionized our lives as did the introduction of electricity, automobiles, or the airplane. Although computers may allow us to process information rapidly, for many people computers are just another gadget.

Third, it may be that computers have improved productivity but we are failing to measure it. Economists find it difficult to measure the quality of outputs in the service industries, which is where much of the investment in computers has occurred. For example, most of us now obtain cash from cash machines without waiting in long lines inside a bank. Yet this increase in convenience is difficult to measure in conventional GDP accounting. As in all cases in which we have plausible but competing explanations, the truth is still a mystery.

WHAT CAUSES TECHNOLOGICAL PROGRESS?

Since technological progress is such an important source of growth, we would like to know how technological progress occurs and what government policies can do to promote it. Economists have studied this topic and identified a variety of factors that may influence the pace of technological progress in an economy.

1. Research and Development in Fundamental Science

One way to induce more technological progress in an economy is to pay for it. If the government or large firms employ workers and scientists to advance scientific frontiers in physics, chemistry, or biology, their work can lead to more technological progress in the long run. Figure 5 presents data on the spending on research and development as a percent of GDP for six major countries for 1990. Although the United States spends the most in total on research and development, as a percent of GDP it spends somewhat less than Germany and Japan. Moreover, unlike the case in those countries, an important fraction of U.S. spending on research and development is in defense-related areas. The United States does have the highest percentage of scientists and engineers in the labor force in the world.

Ideas must be put into practice before they raise output for an economy. To bring innovations to the marketplace, it is important to have both scientists and engineers. But not all technological progress is "high tech." An employee of a soft-drink company who accidentally discovers a new and popular flavor for a soft drink is also engaged in the process of technological progress.

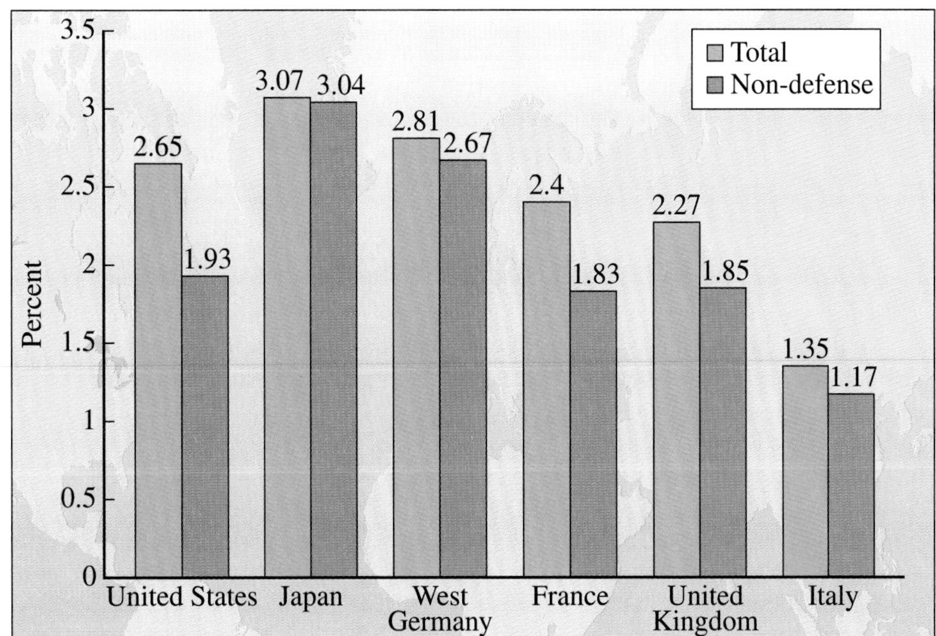

Figure 5

Research and Development as a Share of GDP, 1990

Source: *National Patterns of Research and Development Resources* (Washington, DC: National Science Foundation, 1992).

2. Monopolies That Spur Innovation

The radical notion that monopolies spur innovation was put forth by the famous economist Joseph Schumpeter. In Schumpeter's view, a firm will try to come up with new products and more efficient ways to produce products only if it reaps a reward. The reward a firm seeks is high profit from its innovations. This can only be obtained if the firm is the sole seller or monopolist for the product. Other firms will try to break its monopoly through more innovation—a process Schumpeter called **creative destruction**. By allowing firms to compete to be monopolies, society benefits from increased innovation.

Creative destruction: The process by which competition for monopoly profits leads to technological progress.

The government does allow temporary monopolies for new ideas by issuing patents. A patent allows the inventor of a product to have a monopoly until the term of the patent expires, which in the United States is now 20 years. With a patent we tolerate some monopoly power in the hope of spurring innovation.

A related idea, which is becoming increasingly important in modern society, is the need to protect intellectual property rights. Publishers of both books and computer software face problems of unauthorized copying, particularly in some developing countries. While the residents of those countries clearly benefit from inexpensive copied software or books, the firms producing them will face reduced incentives to enter the market. Large and profitable firms with secure domestic markets may continue to produce despite unauthorized copying, but other firms may be discouraged. The United States has made piracy and unauthorized reproduction an issue in recent trade talks with several countries.

3. The Scale of the Market

The famous economist Adam Smith stressed that the size of a market was important for economic development. In larger markets, there are more incentives for firms to come up with new products and new methods of production. Just as Schumpeter suggested, the lure of profits guides the activities of firms, and larger markets enable firms the opportunity to make larger profits. This provides another rationale for free trade. With free trade, markets are larger and there is more incentive to engage in technological progress.

4. Induced Innovations

Some economists have argued that innovations may be induced deliberately; that is, they may come about through inventive activity designed specifically to reduce costs. For example, during the nineteenth century in the United States, the largest single cost in agriculture was wages. Ingenious farmers and inventors came up with many different machines and methods to cut back on the amount of labor required.

5. Education and the Accumulation of Knowledge

Education can contribute to economic growth in several ways. Increased knowledge and skills can be thought of as a form of **human capital**. Society can increase output through the addition of both physical capital—plants and equipment—and human capital, investments in education for individuals. Many economists, including Nobel laureate Gary Becker from the University of Chicago, have studied the process of human capital formation in detail.

Human capital: Investments in education and skills.

Education can enable the workforce in an economy to use its skills to develop new ideas or even to copy new ideas from abroad. Consider a developing country today. In principle it has at its disposal the vast accumulated knowledge of the developed economies, both scientific and practical. If it could find a way to tap into this knowledge, it could speed the adaptation of technological progress to its own economies. But this probably requires a broadly educated and sophisticated workforce. As the Closer Look box "The Best Investment" explains, the returns to education in developing countries are very high.

Just as in all areas of life, the principle of opportunity cost operates for technological progress.

PRINCIPLE *of Opportunity Cost*

The opportunity cost of something is what you sacrifice to get it.

Resources used to promote technological progress must come from somewhere else in the economy. Here are some examples of the trade-offs a society faces: If the government raises taxes to employ workers to engage in basic scientific research, there will be fewer workers in the private sector seeking new ideas. Funds for education will inevitably compete with funds for scientific research. Monopolies may cause distortions in the economy by charging prices that are too high, but we may need to tolerate them to spur innovation. In evaluating policies designed to promote technological progress, it is important to keep such trade-offs in mind.

A Closer **LOOK**

The Best Investment

The poorest developing countries in the world lack many things: good sanitation systems, effective transportation systems, and capital investment for agriculture and industry. However, the best use of investment funds may not be for bridges, sewer systems, and roads but for human capital and education. Studies demonstrate that the returns from investing in education are extremely high in developing countries. The gains from elementary and secondary education, in particular, often exceed those from more conventional investments. In developing countries, an extra year in school can often raise wages by 15 to 20% a year.*

The returns to investing in the education of females in developing countries are often higher than for men. This is particularly true in the poorest countries, where female literacy rates are often less than 10%. Women's health in developing countries is closely tied to their education. Education promotes not only productivity but basic social development as well. For these reasons, the World Bank has focused attention on the crucial role that increased female education can play in promoting economic development.

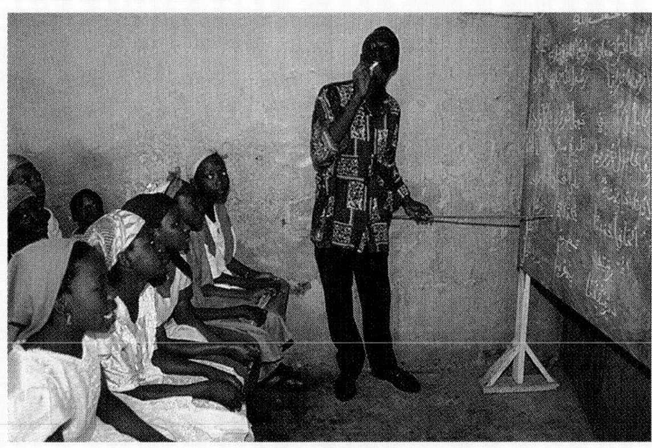

The rate of return to elementary school education in Ghana probably exceeds the rate of return to investments in machines or buildings.

*See T. Paul Schultz, "Investment in Schooling and Health of Women and Men," *Journal of Human Resources*, vol. 27, no.4, Fall 1993, pp. 694–734.

TEST *Your Understanding*

9 True or false: Technological progress means that we produce more output without using any additional inputs.

10 Explain how economists estimate the contribution of technological change to the growth of output.

11 Who invented the theory of creative destruction?

12 Define *human capital.*

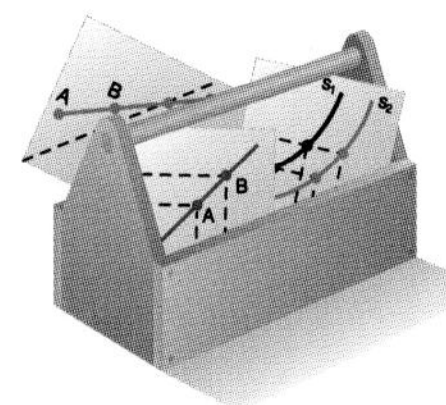

Using the **TOOLS**

In this chapter we studied the process of economic growth. Here are some opportunities to do your own economic analysis.

1. Shorten the Length of Patents?

A group of consumer activists claim that drug companies earn excessive profits because of the patents they have on drugs. They advocate cutting to five years the length of time that a drug company can hold a patent. They argue that this will lead to lower prices for drugs because competitors will enter the market after the five-year period. Are there any drawbacks to this proposal?

2. Capital Deepening

Which of the following will promote economic growth through capital deepening?

a. Higher taxes used to finance universal health care.
b. Increased imports to purchase new VCRs for consumers.
c. Increased imports to purchase supercomputers for industry.

3. Future Generations

Some economists have said that economic growth involves a trade-off between current generations and future generations. If a current generation raises its saving rate, what does it sacrifice? What will be gained for future generations?

4. Will the Poorer Country Catch Up?

Suppose one country has a GDP that is a mere one-eighth that of its richer neighbor. But the poorer country grows at 10% a year while the richer country grows at 2% a year. In 35 years, which country will have a higher GDP? (*Hint*: Use the rule of 70.)

SUMMARY

In this chapter we explored the mechanisms of economic growth. Although economists do not have a complete understanding of the processes that lead to growth, they have highlighted increases in capital per worker, technological progress, and human capital as key factors. In this chapter we discussed these factors in detail. Here are the main points to remember:

1. There are vast differences in per capita GDP throughout the world. There is lively debate about whether poorer countries in the world are converging to richer countries.
2. The two basic mechanisms by which economies grow are capital deepening and technological progress. Capital deepening is an increase in capital per worker. Technological progress is an increase in output with no additional increases in inputs.
3. Ongoing technological progress will lead to sustained economic growth.
4. A variety of alternative theories try to explain the origins of technological progress and determine how we can promote it. They include spending on research and development, creative destruction, the scale of the market, induced inventions, and education and the accumulation of knowledge.

KEY TERMS

capital deepening, *463*
convergence, *465*
creative destruction, *476*
exchange rate, *464*
growth accounting, *471*
human capital, *476*
labor productivity, *472*
real GDP per capita, *463*
saving, *467*
technological progress, *463*

PROBLEMS AND DISCUSSION QUESTIONS

1. Describe briefly how we can compare GDP per capita in the United Kingdom with GDP per capita in the United States even though the British measure GDP using their own currency, pounds.
2. Explain why the expansion of markets from free trade can lead to increased technological innovation.
3. If we cannot measure every invention or new idea, how can we possibly measure the contribution of technological progress?
4. Even with a high saving rate, there is a natural limit to the process of capital deepening. Why is there a limit?
5. The United States ran large trade deficits during the 1980s. How would you determine whether these trade deficits led to increased or decreased capital deepening?
6. If you were a leader of developing country, what policies do you think might be most effective in increasing technological progress in your economy? Would the leaders of the most highly developed countries want to pursue the same policies for their countries?

Take It to the Net

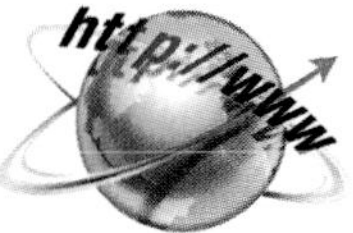

We invite you to visit the O'Sullivan/Sheffrin page on the Prentice Hall Web site at:

http://www.prenhall.com/osullivan/

for this chapter's World Wide Web exercise.

MODEL ANSWERS FOR THIS CHAPTER

Chapter-Opening Questions

1. Countries with the highest standard of living today include the United States, Luxembourg, Japan, and Germany.
2. Countries with higher savings rates can grow faster for some period of time although the growth of per capita income in the long run is determined by the rate of technical progress.

3. A trade deficit that is used to finance investment can lead to higher growth; however, a trade deficit that is used to finance consumption will allow higher consumption now but require lower consumption in the future.
4. Technological progress depends on a number of factors including research and development, the process of creative destruction, the scale of the market, induced innovations, and education and the accumulation of knowledge.

Test Your Understanding

1. We use per capita real GDP.
2. Use the prices of identical TV sets in both countries to obtain an "exchange rate" for TV sets. Use this exchange rate to convert French spending on TV sets to U.S. dollars.
3. True.
4. It would take 35 years (70/2).
5. Output is divided into consumption and investment. Output also equals income. Income is either consumed or saved. Thus saving must equal investment.
6. Total output increases while per capita output falls.
7. $180. Government investment is $200, but with a saving rate of 10%, the $200 in taxes reduces private saving (and private investment) by $20.
8. True.
9. True.
10. The contribution from technological progress is estimated by determining how much of the growth in output cannot be explained by the growth in inputs.
11. Joseph Schumpeter.
12. Human capital includes investments in education and skills.

Using the Tools

1. Shorten the Length of Patents?

   The drawback to the proposal is that the shorter patent life will reduce the incentive of drug companies to invest in the discovery of new drugs. As Schumpeter emphasized, firms need incentives in the form of monopoly profits to engage in long-term research. However, prices are clearly higher as long as a single firm has a patent.
2. Capital Deepening

   Only (c) increased imports to purchase supercomputers for industry add to capital deepening. The others will not increase the stock of capital.
3. Future Generations

   A country that increases its saving rate must cut back on its consumption. The long-run benefit will be a higher stock of capital for future generations. The current generation, however, will have to make a sacrifice, in terms of reduced consumption, to provide the additional capital. Therefore, there will be a trade-off between the present generation and the future generations.
4. Will the Poorer Country Catch Up?

   After 35 years, GDP in the initially poorer country will exceed the GDP of its slower growing neighbor. Since the poorer country grows at 10% a year, the rule of 70 implies that its GDP doubles every seven years. In 35 years its GDP will have doubled five times. This means that its GDP will have grown by a factor of 32 over the 35-year period. Using the rule of 70, the richer country, growing at 2% a year, will only double its GDP in 35 years.

   This implies that the country that was poorer initially will have a higher level of GDP after 35 years even though it started at one-eighth the level of the richer country. To see this, suppose the poorer country had a GDP of 1 and the richer country had a GDP of 8. After 35 years, the initially poorer country would now have a GDP of 32 while the initially richer country would have a GDP of 16.

NOTES

1. Stanley Lebergott, *The Americans* (New York: W.W. Norton, 1984) pp. 65–68.
2. Alwyn Young, "A Tale of Two Cities: Factor Accumulation and Technical Change in Hong Kong and Singapore," in *NBER Macroeconomic Annual 1992*, edited by Olivier Blanchard and Stanley Fischer, Cambridge, MA: MIT Press 1992, pp. 1–53.
3. Zvi Grilliches, "Productivity Puzzles and R&D: Another Nonexplanation," *Journal of Economic Perspectives*, vol. 2, Fall 1988, pp. 9–21.
4. Paul David, "The Dynamo and the Computer: An Historical Perspective on the Modern Productivity Paradox," *American Economic Review*, May 1990, pp. 355–361.

Appendix

Model of Capital Deepening

This appendix presents a simple model of capital deepening that shows explicitly the links among saving, depreciation, and capital deepening. The model will also help us to understand more fully the critical role that technological progress must play in economic growth. Originally developed by Nobel laureate Robert Solow of the Massachusetts Institute of Technology, this model is called the Solow model. In developing this model, we rely on one of our basic principles of economics to help explain the model as well as make a few simplifying assumptions. We assume the population is constant and that there is no government or foreign sector. In the chapter we discussed the qualitative effects of population growth, government, and the foreign sector on capital deepening. Here we focus solely on the relationships between saving, depreciation, and capital deepening.

Figure A-1 plots the relationship in the economy between output and the stock of capital, holding the labor force constant. Notice that output increases as the stock of capital increases but at a decreasing rate. This is an illustration of the principle of diminishing returns.

PRINCIPLE *of Diminishing Returns*

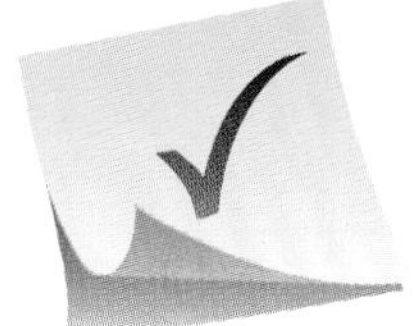

Suppose that output is produced with two or more inputs and that we increase one input while holding the other inputs fixed. Beyond some point—called the point of diminishing returns—output will increase at a decreasing rate.

Increasing the stock of capital while holding the labor force constant will increase output, but at a decreasing rate.

As Figure A-1 indicates, output increases with the stock of capital. But what increases the stock of capital? As we discussed in the chapter, the capital stock will increase as long as gross investment exceeds depreciation. Thus we need to be able to determine the level of gross investment and the level of depreciation in order to see how the capital stock changes over time.

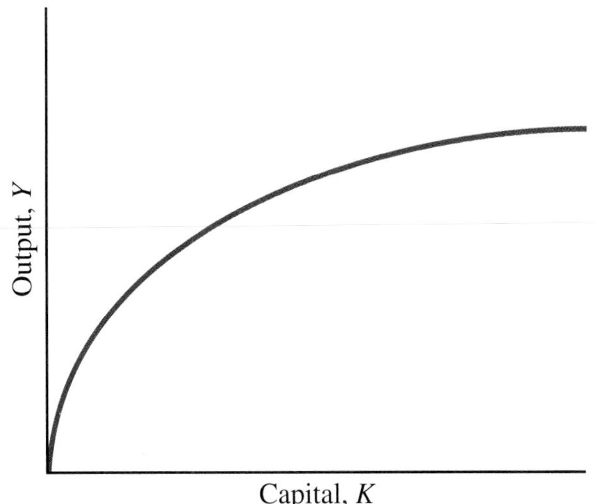

Figure A-1

Diminishing Returns to Capital

Holding labor constant, increases in the stock of capital increases output but at a decreasing rate.

Recall that without government or a foreign sector, saving equals gross investment. To make our model specific, we need to specify how much of output is consumed and how much is saved. We will assume that a fraction s of total output (Y) is saved. For example, if $s = 0.20$, then 20% of GDP would be saved and the remaining 80% would be consumed. Total saving will be sY, which is the product of the saving rate and total output.

In panel A of Figure A-2, the top curve is total output as a function of the stock of capital. The curve below it represents saving as a function of the stock of capital. Since saving is a fixed fraction of total output, the saving curve is just a constant fraction of the output curve. If the saving rate is 0.2, saving will always be 20% of output for any level of the capital stock. Total saving increases in the economy with the stock of capital, but at a decreasing rate.

To complete our model, we also need to determine depreciation. We will assume that the capital stock depreciates at a constant rate of d per year. For example, if $d = 0.03$, the capital stock would depreciate at 3% a year. If the capital stock were 100 at the beginning of the year, depreciation would be equal to 3. Total depreciation can be written as dK, where K is the stock of capital.

Panel B of Figure A-2 plots total depreciation as a function of the stock of capital. The larger the stock of capital, the more total depreciation there will be. Since the depreciation rate is assumed to be constant, total depreciation as a function of the stock of capital will be a straight line through the origin. Again, suppose the depreciation rate is 3%. Then if there is no capital, there will be no depreciation; if the stock of capital is 100, depreciation will be 3; if the stock of capital is 200, the depreciation rate will be 6. Plotting these points will give a straight line through the origin.

We are now ready to see how the stock of capital changes:

$$\begin{aligned}\text{change in the stock of capital} &= \text{saving} - \text{depreciation}\\ &= sY - dK\end{aligned}$$

The stock of capital will increase (that is, the change will be positive) as long as total saving in the economy exceeds depreciation.

Figure A-3 shows how the Solow model works by plotting output, saving, and depreciation all on one graph. Suppose that the economy starts with a capital stock K_0. Then we can see that total saving will be given by point A on the saving schedule. Depreciation at the capital stock K_0 is given by point B. Since point A lies above point B, total saving exceeds depreciation and the capital stock will increase. As the capital stock increases, we experience economic growth through capital deepening. With more capital per worker in the economy, output is higher and real wages increase. The economy benefits from the additional stock of capital.

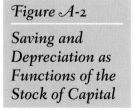

Figure A-2

Saving and Depreciation as Functions of the Stock of Capital

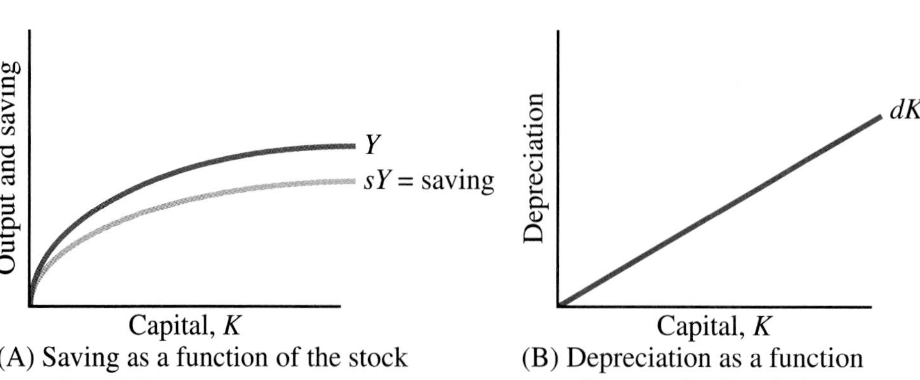

(A) Saving as a function of the stock of capital

(B) Depreciation as a function of the stock of capital

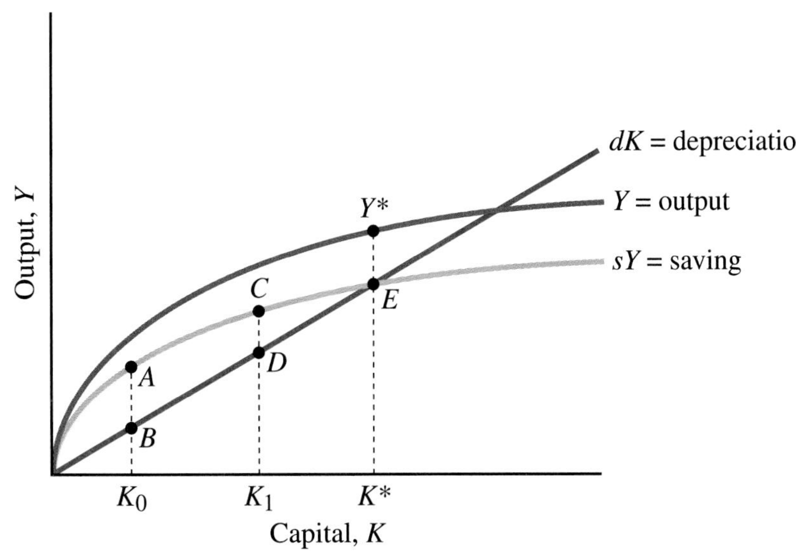

Figure A-3

Basic Growth Model

Starting at K_0, saving exceeds depreciation. The stock of capital increases. This process continues until the stock of capital reaches its long-run equilibrium at K^*.

Using the diagram we can trace the future for this economy. As the stock of capital increases, we move to the right. When the economy reaches K_1, total saving is at point C and total depreciation at point D. Since C is still higher than D, saving exceeds depreciation and the capital stock continues to increase. Economic growth continues. Eventually, after many years, the economy reaches capital stock K^*. The level of output in the economy now is Y^*, and the saving and depreciation schedules intersect at point E. Since total saving equals depreciation, the stock of capital no longer increases. The process of economic growth through capital deepening has stopped.

In this simple model, the process of capital deepening must eventually come to an end. As the stock of capital increases, output increases, but at a decreasing rate because of diminishing returns. Since saving is a fixed fraction of output, it will also increase, but also at a diminishing rate. On the other hand, total depreciation is proportional to the stock of capital. As the stock of capital increases, depreciation will always catch up with total saving in the economy. In practice it may take decades for the process of capital deepening to come to an end. But as long as total saving exceeds depreciation, the process of economic growth through capital deepening will continue.

What would happen if a society saved a higher fraction of its output? Figure A-4 on the next page shows the consequences of a higher saving rate. Suppose the economy were originally saving at a rate s_1. Eventually, the economy would reach E_1, where saving and depreciation meet. If the economy had started to save at the higher rate s_2, saving would exceed depreciation at K_1 and the capital stock would increase until the economy reached K_2. At that point, the saving line again crosses the line representing depreciation. Output is higher than it was initially, but the process of capital deepening comes to rest at this higher level of output.

If there is ongoing technological progress, however, economic growth can continue. If technological progress raises GDP, saving will increase as well, since saving increases with GDP. This will lead to a higher stock of capital. In Figure A-5 on the next page, technological progress is depicted as an upward shift of the saving function. The saving function shifts up because saving is a fixed fraction of output and we have assumed that technological progress has raised the level of output.

With a higher level of saving, the stock of capital will increase. If the stock of capital were originally at K_0, the upward shift in the saving schedule will lead to increases in the stock of capital to K_1. If there are further gains in technological process, capital deepening will continue.

Figure A-4

Increase in the Saving Rate

A higher saving rate will lead to a higher stock of capital in the long run. Starting from an initial capital stock of K_1, the increase in the saving rate leads the economy to K_2.

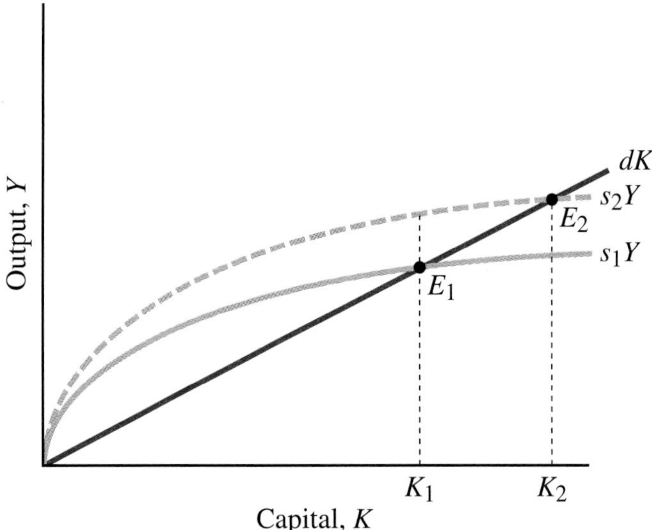

Technological progress conveys a double benefit to a society. Not only does the increased efficiency directly raise per capita output, it also leads to additional capital deepening. Therefore, output increases for two reasons.

Let's summarize the basic points of the Solow model:

1. Capital deepening, an increase in the stock of capital per worker, will occur as long as total saving exceeds depreciation. As capital deepening occurs, we experience economic growth and increased real wages.
2. Eventually, the process of capital deepening will come to a halt as depreciation catches up with total saving.
3. A higher saving rate will promote capital deepening. If a country saves more, it will have a higher output. But eventually the process of economic growth through capital deepening alone comes to an end, even though this may take decades to occur.
4. Technological progress not only directly raises output but allows capital deepening to continue.

Figure A-5

Technological Progress and Growth

Technological progress shifts up the saving schedule and promotes capital deepening.

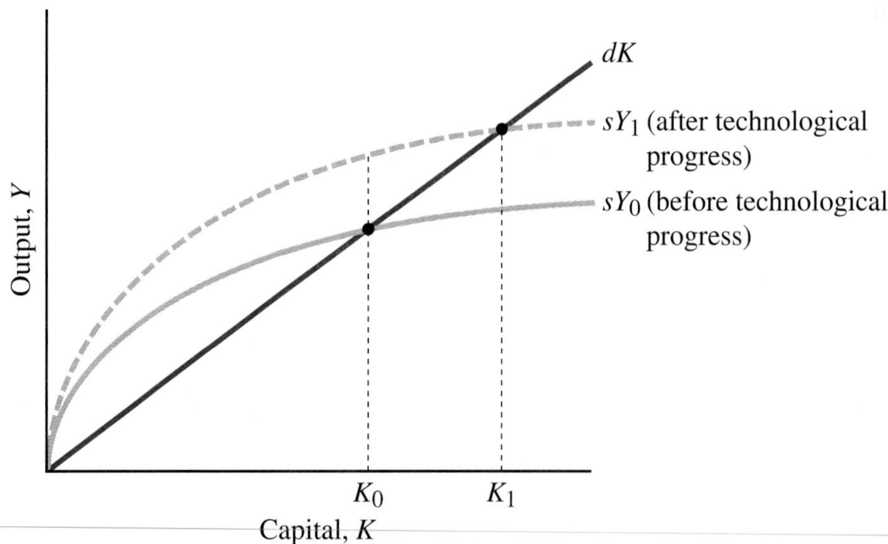

It is possible to relax our assumptions and allow for population growth, government taxes and spending, and the foreign sector. In more advanced courses, these issues are treated in detail. Nonetheless, the underlying message is essentially the same. There is a natural limit to economic growth through capital deepening. Technological progress is required to ensure that per capita incomes grow over time.

TEST *Your Understanding*

1. What two factors determine how the stock of capital changes over time?
2. Why does capital deepening come to an end?
3. Does a higher saving rate lead to a permanently higher rate of growth?

Using the TOOLS

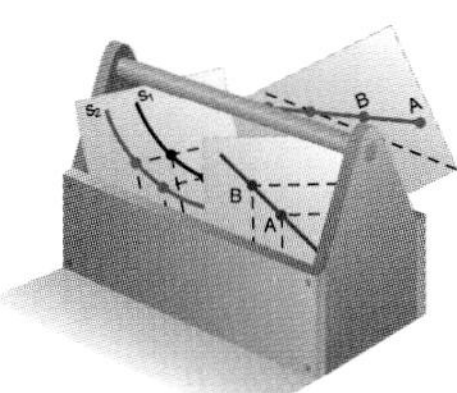

1. Germany and Japan after World War II

The economies of Japan and Germany had much of their stock of capital destroyed during World War II. Both economies had high saving rates. Use the Solow model to explain why after the war, growth in those economies was higher than in the United States.

2. Faster Depreciation

Suppose a society switches to equipment that depreciates rapidly. Use the Solow model to show what will happen to the stock of capital and output if the rate of depreciation increases.

MODEL ANSWERS FOR THIS APPENDIX

Test Your Understanding

1. The factors are gross investment and depreciation.
2. Depreciation eventually catches up with saving.
3. No. A higher saving rate will raise the level of output, but eventually, capital deepening and economic growth comes to an end.

Using the Tools

1. Germany and Japan after World War II

   Both Germany and Japan started after World War II with a low capital stock and a high saving rate. They would both be expected to have high rates of capital deepening. The United States, however, would be closer to the long-run position where capital deepening would cease in the absence of technological progress.
2. Faster Depreciation

   If the rate of depreciation increases, the line from the origin that gives total deprecation will rotate to the left. This will reduce the stock of capital.

Coordinating Economic Activity: Aggregate Demand and Supply

During the Great Depression nearly one-fourth of the U.S. labor force was unemployed. Unemployed workers could not afford to buy goods and services from factories, so factories were shut down because there was no demand for their products. As factories shut down, more workers in turn became unemployed. Clearly, there was a failure of coordination between workers and factories. How could this vicious cycle be broken?

This chapter begins our study of recessions and economic fluctuations. Economies do not always operate at full employment or grow smoothly over time. At times, real GDP grows below its potential or falls precipitously, as it did in the Great Depression. Recessions and excess unemployment occur when GDP falls. At other times, GDP grows too rapidly, and unemployment falls below the natural rate of unemployment. The inevitable result of too-rapid growth in GDP is an increase in the rate of inflation. Both too slow and too rapid GDP growth are examples of **economic fluctuations**, movements of GDP away from potential output. Economic fluctuations, also called **business cycles**, are the subject of this part of the book.

Economic fluctuations: Movements of GDP above or below normal trends.

Business cycles: Another name for economic fluctuations.

After reading this chapter, you will be able to answer the following real-world questions:

1 How does inflation interfere with the operation of the price system?

2 Why may some firms not change their prices even when the demand for their product changes?

3 Why doesn't the economy always operate at full employment?

4 Why can a sharp decrease in government spending cause a recession?

5 How do changes in the demand for goods and services affect prices and output in the short run and long run?

This chapter begins by discussing the effect of real shocks to the economy, such as an oil price increase or a change in technological progress. We then turn to the problems that arise from a failure of coordination among the millions of people in a modern economy.

During the Great Depression, there was a fundamental failure in coordination. Factories would have produced more output and hired more workers if there had been more demand for their products. In turn, the newly employed workers would have been able to afford to buy the additional goods that the firms produced.

Insufficient demand for goods and services was a key problem that Keynes identified during the Great Depression. Since then, economists have found it useful to view GDP as determined by demand in the short run. As we discuss, the **short run in macroeconomics** is the period of time when prices are fixed. In the next several chapters, we examine **Keynesian economics**, models based on the idea that demand determines output in the short run.

Short run in macroeconomics: The period of time that prices are fixed.

Keynesian economics: Models in which demand determines output in the short run.

In this chapter we develop important tools for analyzing economic fluctuations. We introduce the aggregate demand and aggregate supply curves, which will assist us in understanding some of the key aspects of business cycles. The aggregate demand and supply curves will set the stage for our more in-depth investigations of economic fluctuations in later chapters.

REAL SHOCKS TO THE ECONOMY

Economic fluctuations can occur for a variety of reasons, one of which is large shocks that sometimes hit the economy. Consider a few examples. A developing country that is highly dependent on agriculture can suffer a loss of its cash crop if there is a prolonged drought. As economic historian Stanley Lebergott reminds us, the nineteenth-century U.S. agricultural-based economy was rocked by grasshopper invasions in North Dakota in 1874–1876 and by the boll weevil migration from Mexico to Texas in 1892. Sharp increases in the price of oil can hurt modern economies that use oil in production, as was the case in both 1973 and 1979. Wars can devastate entire regions of the world, and natural disasters, such as earthquakes or floods, can cause sharp reductions in GDP.

Major shifts in technology can also cause economic fluctuations. To illustrate this idea, consider some economic developments in the nineteenth century. In the early part of that century, there were large investments in textile mills and steam power. The birth of the steel industry and railroads dominated the last half of the century. And the end of the century witnessed the birth of new industries based on chemical manufacturing, electricity, and the automobile. It is inconceivable that the vast change in technology that led to the creation of these new industries would not have profound effects on the economy, particularly because these changes in technology often came in short bursts.

Economic fluctuations can also occur because a number of small shocks all hit the economy at the same time. For example, a country that primarily produces tea might face a sudden shift of consumer preferences throughout the world to coffee.

Real business cycle theory: The economic theory that emphasizes the role of technology shocks as a cause of economic fluctuations.

Or a series of small improvements to technology in a variety of industries could cause output to rise. One school of economic thought known as **real business cycle theory** emphasizes the role that shocks to technology can play in causing economic fluctuations. Led by Edward Prescott of the University of Minnesota, this group of scholars has developed models that integrate technology shocks into the classical models of the preceding chapters.

The idea behind real business cycle theory is very simple. Changes in technology will usually change the level of full employment or potential output. For example, if there is a significant technological improvement, society will be able to produce more output and potential output will rise. Similarly, if there are adverse technological developments (such as would occur if the Internet were to crash, for example) or adverse shocks to the economy, the level of potential output will fall.

Unlike the Keynesian models that we will develop, real business cycle theory has a different view of economic fluctuations. It portrays economic fluctuations as movements *in* potential output, not as deviations *away* from potential output. As an example, if real GDP falls by 2%, real business cycle theorists analyze this as if potential output fell by 2% and not as a 2% decrease in output below potential output.

This school of thought has been influential with some academic economists but is generally viewed as quite controversial and, to this point, has not had a major impact on current macroeconomic policy. Critics of the theory find it difficult to understand how many of the post–World War II recessions could be explained by adverse changes in technology. Nonetheless, real business cycle theory is currently an active area of research and has had an important influence in the economics profession.

PRICES AND ECONOMIC COORDINATION

Beginning with John Maynard Keynes, economists have identified an important reason for economic fluctuations: difficulties in coordinating economic affairs. Think of the vast complexity of modern economies. Millions of workers produce vast numbers of distinct goods and services. Coordinating these activities is a mammoth task. As might be expected, the coordination process sometimes breaks down. The results of such breakdowns are economic fluctuations. But before studying failures in coordination, let's take a look at how the market system successfully coordinates economic activity.

The price system allows our society to coordinate its extremely complex economy. To understand how the price system serves this function, consider the following simple demand and supply example. Suppose that individuals in the economy enjoy two types of recreation: tennis and roller blading. Panels A and B in Figure 1 show the demand and supply curves for the markets in tennis racquets and roller blades. Consider the market for tennis racquets. The demand curve shows the quantity of tennis racquets that would be purchased for different prices of racquets. It is downward sloping because as tennis racquets become cheaper, more people will purchase them. The supply curve shows the quantity of racquets that would be produced for different prices. It is upward sloping because at higher prices, firms will find it profitable to produce more tennis racquets.

At a price P_0 the quantity of tennis racquets demanded equals the quantity supplied. The market for tennis racquets is in equilibrium. The amount that individuals wish to purchase is equal to the amount that producers wish to sell. The quantity of racquets produced is Q_0.

A similar story unfolds in the market for roller blades. At a price of roller blades of P_1 the market is in equilibrium. At that price the quantity of roller blades

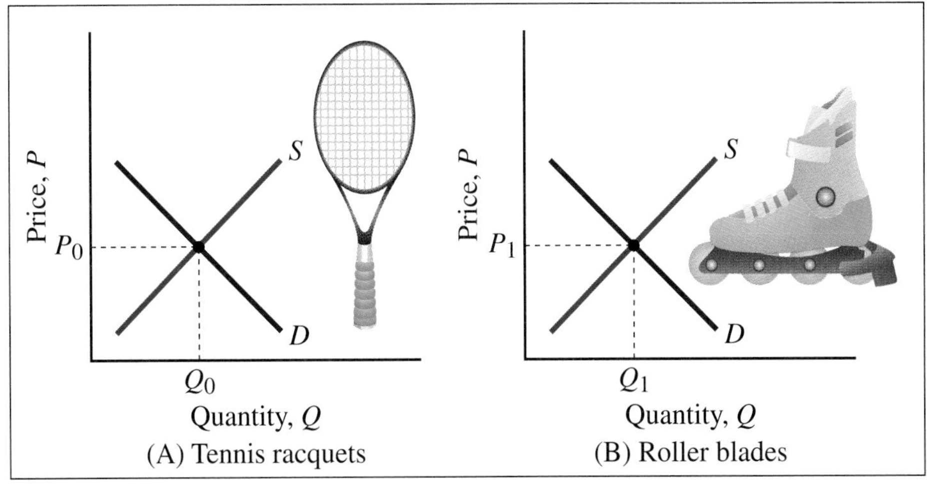

Figure 1

Initial Pattern of Demand and Prices

The initial pattern of demand and prices for racquets and roller blades.

demanded is equal to the quantity of roller blades supplied. The quantity of roller blades produced is Q_1.

Now suppose that tastes change and roller blading becomes more popular than tennis. (Perhaps some tennis players have lost interest in their sport and now want to roller blade.) Panels A and B in Figure 2 show this case. The demand for roller blades shifts to the right as shown by the demand curve D_B. At any price, more people now want to purchase roller blades. The demand for tennis racquets shifts to the left as shown by the demand curve D_A. At any price, fewer people now wish to purchase tennis racquets.

Prices rise to P_B in the market for roller blades and fall to P_A in the market for tennis racquets. On the other hand, the quantity of roller blades sold increases to Q_B while the quantity of tennis racquets sold falls to Q_A. The change in tastes from tennis to roller blading has caused the economy to produce more roller blades and fewer tennis racquets.

The economy is able to accomplish this feat through the use of prices. When roller blading became more popular than tennis, the price of roller blades rose and the price of tennis racquets fell. The producers of roller blades were given a signal to step up their production. Similarly, the producers of tennis racquets were given a signal to cut back their production. The producers of roller blades and tennis racquets

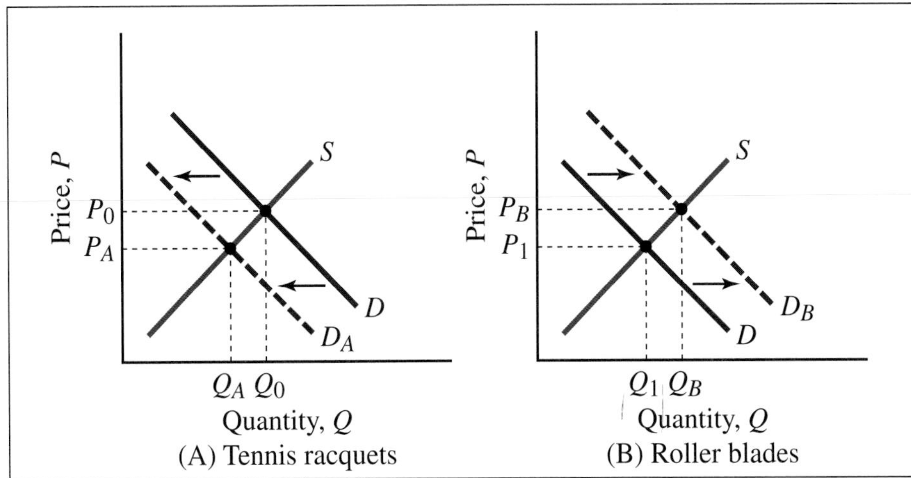

Figure 2

Demand and Prices after Changes in Tastes

Suppose that roller blading starts to replace tennis. Demand shifts to D_A in the market for tennis racquets and to D_B in the market for roller blades. Prices of roller blades will rise to P_B, and prices of tennis racquets will fall to P_A.

did not have to conduct national opinion surveys on the popularity of their sports. Nor was there was a need for any government agency to help coordinate their activities. The change in the prices of their goods told producers what to do: Prices coordinated their activities. Producers of roller blades expanded their activities when the price of roller blades increased and producers of tennis racquets contracted their activities when the price of tennis racquets decreased.

To expand production, the producers of roller blades have to expand their workforce. The producers of tennis racquets have to reduce their workforce because they are not producing as many racquets. Workers will therefore leave the tennis racquet industry to be employed in the roller blade industry. Workers still have the opportunity to be employed, but in a different industry. This feat is also coordinated by the price system. The increase in price of roller blades told managers in that industry to expand production and hire new workers. The fall in the price of tennis racquets told managers in that industry to cut back production and use fewer workers.

In microeconomics we learn that the price system also helps to coordinate activities to make the economy produce as efficiently as possible. Prices give the correct signals to all producers in the economy so that resources in the society are used efficiently and without waste. Under ideal circumstances, there is no need for a central planner for the economy; the price system coordinates economic activity efficiently. The process by which individual consumers and producers reach a market equilibrium that is efficient in some circumstances is known as the **invisible hand**. In some unusual cases, economic activity can be coordinated without prices, as the Closer Look box "Focal Points" explains.

Invisible hand: The term that economists use to describe how the price system can efficiently coordinate economic activity without central government intervention.

THE LIMITS OF COORDINATION THROUGH PRICES

It would be surprising if any social device to coordinate human affairs worked perfectly. As you may expect, there are some limits to the coordination of economic affairs through the price system.

In macroeconomics, we focus on problems with the price system that can lead to fluctuations in total output. The three problems we highlight are:

1. There may be too few prices.
2. Prices may not contain enough information.
3. Prices may be "sticky."

Too Few Prices

In the tennis and roller blade example, prices provided the proper signal to expand production of roller blades and cut production of tennis racquets. The price of roller blades increased and the price of tennis racquets fell. But suppose there are not enough prices, or signals, in the economy?

For example, suppose that a large number of consumers in an economy decide that they do not want to spend all the income they currently earn but wish to save some of their income to purchase goods in the future. In particular, suppose they cut back on consumption of both tennis racquets and roller blades to purchase automobiles five years later.

For the economy to work efficiently, the automobile industry must now begin to invest in building new plants and adding new equipment to meet consumer demands five years from now. On the other hand, the tennis racquet and roller blade industries need to contract. The economy as a whole must shift from producing goods for current consumption (tennis racquets and roller blades) to producing investment goods (plant and equipment for the automobile industry). To prevent a

A Closer LOOK

Focal Points

Sometimes economic and social affairs can be coordinated without the use of prices or even any explicit communication. Let's consider a famous example developed by the economist and game theorist, Thomas Schelling. Suppose that you had agreed to meet a friend of yours in Washington, DC at 2:00 P.M. on a particular day. You both forgot, however, to say *where* in the city you would meet. You are both traveling and cannot contact each other. Where would you go to meet your friend?

A majority of people would choose the Washington Monument as the place to meet. The reason people choose the monument is that it seems to be the most obvious place that you both might choose. Economists call obvious points of agreement, such as the Washington Monument, *focal points*. If there are obvious focal points, social activities can sometimes be coordinated. If you were meeting your friend in Paris, most people would choose the Eiffel Tower. However, in some cities, even this question is problematic: Where would you meet your friend in Los Angeles?

In most economic situations, focal points are not enough. It is not enough, for example, for a tennis racquet producer to know that young people had collectively switched from tennis to roller blading. The producer must know how many have switched and how many racquets he should produce. Only prices can easily supply this answer.

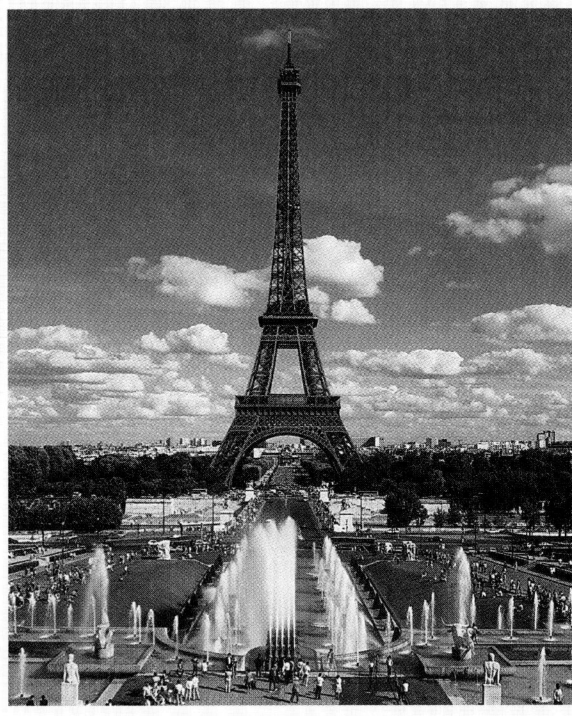

In Paris, the obvious place to meet your friend is at the Eiffel tower.

decrease in total output or GDP, the decrease in the production of consumption goods must be met by an increase in the production of investment goods.

Focal points: Obvious points of agreement in bargaining situations.

The price system in this case does not work as simply as it did in our tennis racquet–roller blade example. There is no "price" for automobiles to be delivered five years from now, so automobile producers do not receive any direct signals that consumers wish to purchase automobiles in the future. Nor does the current price of automobiles reflect the demand five years from now. Therefore, there is a risk that the automobile producers will not invest sufficiently for the future. Only a few commodities can be traded for future delivery in worldwide markets, as the Closer Look box on the next page, "Prices for the Future," explains.

As Keynes emphasized, decisions about saving and investment are made by different groups in the economy. Households decide what fraction of their income they desire to save, while firms decide on the type and number of investment projects they wish to undertake. Without explicit prices for goods in the future, this coordination is extremely difficult.

In the chapter "Investment and Financial Intermediation," we will see how the economy can partly coordinate consumers' decisions to save and firms' decisions to

A Closer LOOK

Prices for the Future

Although prices do not currently exist for 1999 cars or 1999 computers, some goods *can* be purchased for the future. The accompanying newspaper clip from the *Wall Street Journal** shows the prices of copper, gold, and platinum in organized *futures markets*. In these markets it is possible to buy or sell contracts to deliver commodities in the future at a price to be set now.

To understand how these contracts work, consider the futures market for gold. In this market, participants buy and sell contracts to deliver 100 troy ounces at a particular time in the future. For example, if you look at contracts for February 1997 in the market, you will see a price of $388.80 per troy ounce. Individuals who in September 1996 believed the price of gold in February of 1997 would be higher than this would have bought gold contracts, while those who believed the price would be lower would have sold gold contracts.

The price in the market represents the average belief about where prices will be in the future. Looking ahead to December 2000, market participants believe the price will be $453.00. This is substantially above the range of $380 to $390 that prevailed in 1996. Market participants expect the price of gold to increase over the next several years.

There are also markets for many agricultural commodities. These markets allow farmers, as well as large purchasers of agricultural commodities, to plan their activities for the future based on prices in the market today. Futures markets operate on a worldwide basis with important markets in London, Chicago, New York, Montreal, and Sydney.

*September 19, 1996, p. C16. Reprinted by permission of the *Wall Street Journal*, © 1996 Dow Jones & Company, Inc. All Rights Reserved Worldwide.

price

METALS AND PETROLEUM

COPPER-HIGH (Cmx.Div.NYM)-25,000 lbs.; cents per lb.								
Sept	89.30	91.80	89.00	90.80	+ 2.00	121.30	82.70	3,752
Oct	88.50	90.80	88.50	90.25	+ 1.80	119.00	85.00	2,130
Nov	89.90	89.90	89.90	90.05	+ 1.85	116.90	85.00	1,476
Dec	88.00	90.50	87.70	89.65	+ 1.75	118.80	82.80	25,332
Ja97	89.10	89.10	89.10	89.25	+ 1.65	115.00	84.20	1,071
Feb		....	....	89.05	+ 1.75	112.90	84.20	832
Mar	87.30	89.50	87.00	88.85	+ 1.85	115.30	83.00	8,107
Apr	89.00	89.00	89.00	88.65	+ 1.85	112.50	83.50	500
May	87.25	87.25	87.25	88.65	+ 1.85	113.70	83.50	2,820
June		....	....	88.55	+ 1.75	112.50	82.50	667
July	88.00	89.00	88.00	88.55	+ 1.75	113.65	83.00	2,805
Aug		....	....	88.45	+ 1.65	112.50	84.10	485
Sept		....	....	88.45	+ 1.65	113.70	83.00	1,851
Oct		....	....	88.45	+ 1.65	112.00	84.50	429
Nov		....	....	88.45	+ 1.65	112.00	84.50	398
Dec	87.80	89.00	87.80	88.45	+ 1.65	110.80	83.75	2,184
Ja98		....	....	88.45	+ 1.65	95.00	85.20	79
Feb		....	....	88.45	+ 1.65	94.80	85.50	111
Mar		....	....	88.45	+ 1.45	113.00	85.00	625
July		....	....	88.45	+ .95	88.00	86.00	238
Est vol 12,000; vol Tu 8,884; open int 56,052, +20.								
GOLD (Cmx.Div.NYM)-100 troy oz.; $ per troy oz.								
Sept		....	....	383.00	+ .20	389.00	383.10	1
Oct	383.20	383.60	382.70	383.40	....	432.20	382.00	8,454
Dec	386.60	386.60	385.50	386.30	+ .20	447.50	379.60	103,915
Fb97	388.50	389.10	388.40	388.80	+ .20	428.00	387.20	13,026
Apr	390.80	391.50	390.70	391.30	+ .30	428.00	390.00	8,023
June	394.30	394.30	394.30	393.90	+ .40	456.00	393.00	11,123
Aug		....	....	396.50	+ .40	414.50	395.00	4,749
Oct		....	....	399.20	+ .40	426.50	398.40	243
Dec	401.90	401.90	401.90	402.00	+ .40	477.00	400.90	10,788
Fb98		....	....	404.90	+ .40	424.00	404.20	682
Apr		....	....	407.50	+ .40	408.40	408.40	1,136
June	410.50	410.50	410.00	410.40	+ .40	489.50	410.00	5,651
Dec	419.00	419.00	419.00	419.00	+ .40	505.00	418.50	5,294
Ju99		....	....	427.40	+ .40	520.00	429.50	5,661
Dec		....	....	435.80	+ .40	506.00	437.40	3,604
Ju00		....	....	444.40	+ .40	473.50	444.00	3,700
Dec		....	....	453.00	+ .40	474.50	450.50	5,054
Ju01		....	....	461.70	+ .40	....	....	885
Est vol 28,000; vol Tu 16,032; open int 191,988, −1,742.								
PLATINUM (NYM)-50 troy oz.; $ per troy oz.								
Oct	391.00	393.40	390.50	392.50	+ 1.60	441.00	388.60	13,668
Ja97	393.00	395.00	392.50	394.40	+ 1.70	442.00	390.70	9,705
Apr	395.80	398.00	395.80	396.90	+ 1.70	426.00	394.00	5,670
July		....	....	399.90	+ 1.70	418.00	397.00	604
Est vol 2,654; vol Tu 10,487; open int 29,670, −833.								
SILVER (Cmx.Div.NYM)-5,000 troy oz.; cnts per troy oz.								
Sept	505.0	505.0	504.0	504.0	+ 2.2	602.0	488.0	153
Dec	507.5	510.5	506.5	509.8	+ 2.0	670.0	454.0	64,881
Mr97	515.5	518.0	515.5	517.6	+ 2.0	611.0	511.0	11,120
May	520.0	522.0	520.0	522.7	+ 2.0	606.0	517.0	6,367
July		....	....	527.9	+ 2.0	655.0	522.0	4,394
Sept		....	....	533.2	+ 2.0	576.0	527.5	2,875
Dec	542.0	542.0	542.0	541.3	+ 2.0	695.0	502.0	1,372
Mr98		....	....	549.4	+ 2.0	573.0	556.0	105
July		....	....	560.1	+ 2.0	700.0	590.0	381
Dec		....	....	574.1	+ 2.0	734.0	576.0	330
Jl99		....	....	593.6	+ 2.0	660.0	588.0	350
Dec		....	....	608.7	+ 2.0	720.0	605.0	113
Est vol 9,000; vol Tu 11,976; open int 92,555, +303.								

February 1997

December 2000

Futures markets: A market in which contracts are bought or sold for the future delivery of commodities at a price to be set now.

invest through movements in interest rates and with the assistance of financial institutions. Nonetheless, the price system does not have the capacity to provide precise signals to the producers of specific goods—such as the automobile producers—far into the future. There are always problems in coordinating savings and investment decisions.

Too Little Information

In the tennis racquet–roller blade example, prices provided enough information for each producer to act properly. But as Nobel laureate Robert E. Lucas, Jr. has emphasized, prices may not always contain all the information that producers need. This can occur when there is inflation.

Producers of roller blades expanded production because the price of roller blades increased relative to the costs of production and they could earn a higher profit. If costs were rising along with the price, as in the case of inflation, there would be no incentive to expand because profits would not be increasing.

What matters to any firm is its **real price:** its price relative to all the other prices in the economy. If the firm's real price increases, it will expand its production because its profits will be higher. If the firm's price just increases with inflation, its costs will rise along with its price and there will be no incentive to expand production. This is an example of the reality principle.

Real price: The nominal price of a product adjusted for inflation.

Reality PRINCIPLE

What matters to people is the real value or purchasing power of money or income, not its face value.

Suppose, for example, that there was 5% inflation in an economy and consumer demands for tennis racquets and roller blades were unchanged. The prices of all goods in the economy would be rising by 5%: the price of tennis racquets, the price of roller blades, and the prices of inputs to the production of both goods such as labor and capital. Since each producer would find prices rising along with input costs, there would be no incentive to change production.

If there were a shift of demand away from tennis racquets to roller blades, prices of roller blades would start to increase faster than 5% and prices of tennis racquets would increase less than 5%. Since costs are still rising at 5%, the producers of roller blades would expand because their profits would go up, and the producers of tennis racquets would contract because their profits would fall. Prices would still coordinate economic activity.

Problems can occur if firms are uncertain about whether a change in their output price is an increase in the real price or only in the nominal or dollar price. In some cases, firms will not have enough information to distinguish between the two cases. In this case the price system could malfunction.

Suppose the demand for tennis racquets and roller blades does not change but inflation throughout the economy falls from 5% to 4%. Producers are not fully aware of this change but they do see that their prices are no longer rising by 5%. They must decide whether there has been a fall in the inflation rate or their product is no longer as popular. If both producers believe that demand for their product has fallen, they will both cut back production. If this happened throughout the economy, it would lead to a recession.

Firms clearly have an interest in distinguishing between increases in their real price and increases in their nominal or dollar prices. But information is not always perfect, and prices can change because of both general inflation or changes in the demand for individual products. Prices by themselves may not contain sufficient information to coordinate economic activities.

"Sticky" Prices

An important part of the tennis racquet–roller blade story is that prices were flexible and could move easily to give the proper signals to producers. If prices are "sticky" or not sufficiently flexible, prices will not coordinate activity as efficiently. Let's consider an example of the consequences of sticky prices, that is, prices that are temporarily fixed.

Figure 3

Sticky Prices in the Market for Tennis Racquets

When demand falls to D_A, prices are sticky and remain at P_0. The result is unsold production measured by the distance between E and F.

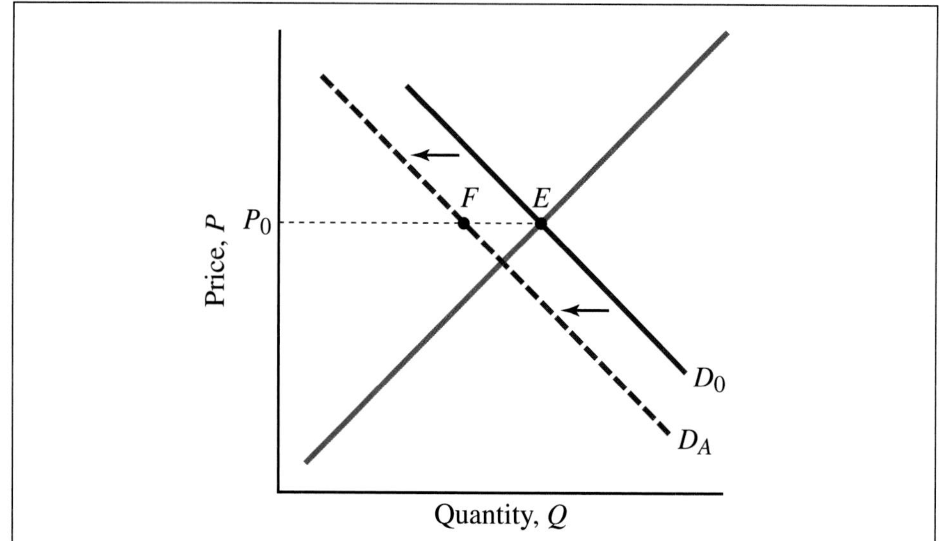

Suppose that prices were sticky in the market for tennis racquets, that is, fixed for at least some period of time. In Figure 3 the demand curve shifts to the left, from D_0 to D_A. If prices were sticky they would remain at P_0. Producers would be producing at E on their supply curve, while consumers would only be demanding a quantity of racquets at F. The result would be an excess supply of racquets, measured by the distance EF.

Since prices have not fallen in the market for tennis racquets, producers do not have an incentive to cut back production. Workers will not be released to allow the roller blade industry to expand. Similarly, if the demand for roller blades expanded but prices did not rise, there would be an excess demand for roller blades. Producers would not have the proper signal to expand their production and hire the displaced workers from the tennis racquet industry. If prices are not flexible, economic activity will not be coordinated efficiently.

In modern economies, some prices are very flexible while others are not. The economist Arthur Okun made the distinction between *auction prices*, those determined on nearly a daily basis, and *custom prices*, those that adjust rather slowly. Prices for fresh fish, vegetables, and other food products are examples of auction prices—they typically are very flexible and adjust rapidly. On the other hand, prices for industrial commodities such as steel rods or machine tools are custom prices and tend to adjust to demand changes much more slowly.

Wages, the price of labor, also adjust extremely slowly. Workers often have long-term contracts that do not allow wages to change at all during a given year. Union workers, university professors, high-school teachers, and employees of state and local governments are all groups whose wages adjust very slowly. As a general rule, there are very few workers in the economy whose wages change quickly. Perhaps movie stars, athletes, and rock stars are the exceptions: Their wages rise and fall with their popularity. But they are far from the typical worker in the economy. Even unskilled, low-wage workers are often protected from decreases in their wages by minimum wage laws.

For most firms, wages are the single most important cost of doing business. If wages are sticky, their overall costs will be sticky as well. This means that firms can allow their prices to remain sticky without having a large gap between their prices and their costs. Stickiness of wages reinforces stickiness of prices. This reduces the ability of the economy to coordinate economic activity.

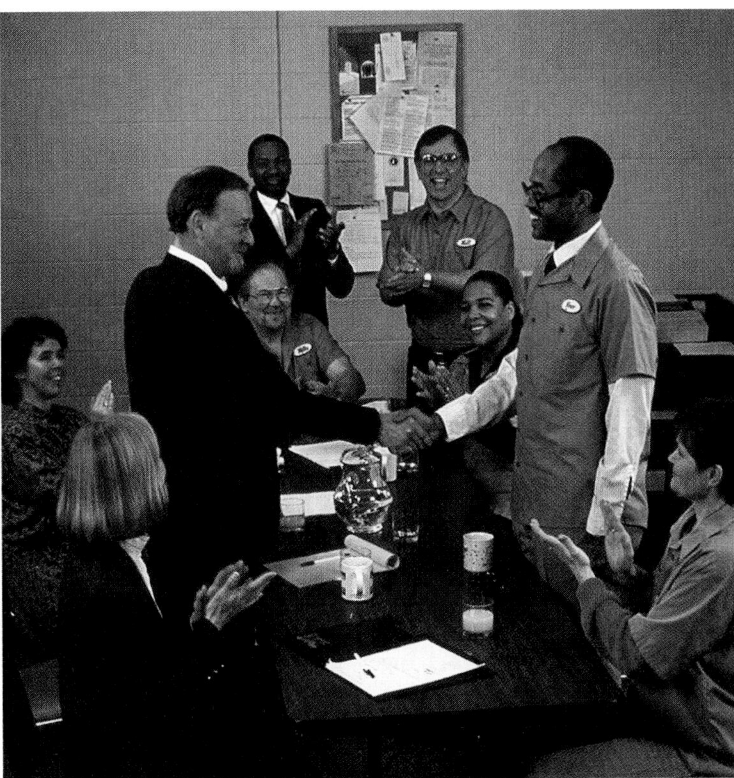

Management and labor reach agreement on a new multi-year wage contract after a long negotiation.

TEST *Your Understanding*

1 Explain why it is difficult to coordinate savings and investment decisions.

2 Complete the statement with *real* or *nominal*: A firm is interested in the ____________ price of its goods.

3 If all firms in the economy mistakenly confuse a fall in the inflation rate for a reduction in the demand for their product, what will happen to overall economic activity?

4 What types of goods and services have sticky prices?

STICKY PRICES AND DEMAND-SIDE ECONOMICS

Since prices and wages are somewhat sticky over short periods of time, prices do not fully coordinate economic activity. To assist in coordinating economic activity, firms and workers have developed alternative rules to coordinate their actions.

In general, workers and firms let demand determine the level of output in the short run. To understand this idea, consider an automobile firm that buys material from a steelmaker on a regular basis. Because the two firms have been in business with one another for a long time and have an ongoing relationship, they have negotiated a contract that keeps prices constant in the short run.

Now suppose the automobile company suddenly discovers that its cars are very popular. It needs to expand production and it needs more steel. Under their agreement, the steel company would meet this higher demand for its product and sell more steel to the automobile company without raising its price. The production of steel is totally determined by the demand from automobile producers, not by price.

On the other hand, if the automobile company discovered it had produced an unpopular car and needed to cut back on its planned production, it would require less steel. Under the agreement, the steelmaker would supply less steel but not reduce its price. Again, demand determines steel production in the short run.

Similar agreements, both formal and informal, exist throughout the economy. Typically, in the short run firms will meet changes in the demand for their products by adjusting production with only small changes in prices. The same principle also applies to workers. Suppose the automobile firm hires union workers under a contract that fixes their wages. When times are good, the automobile company will employ all the workers and perhaps even require some of them to work overtime. In bad times, however, the firm will lay off some workers and use only part of the union labor force. Wages, however, will not typically change during the period of the contract.

Over longer periods of time, prices do change. Suppose that the automobile company finds that its car remains extremely popular for a longer period of time. The steel company and automobile company will adjust the price on their contract to reflect this increased demand. These price adjustments only occur over longer periods of time; in the short run, demand determines output and prices are sticky. The *short run in macroeconomics* is the period when prices are fixed.

In the long run, prices adjust fully to changes in demand. But over short periods of time, the presence of both formal and informal contracts means that changes in demand will be reflected primarily in changes in output, not prices. We will use the term *Keynesian economics* to refer to the idea that demand determines output in the short run.

AGGREGATE DEMAND AND AGGREGATE SUPPLY

Aggregate demand: The relationship between the level of prices and the quantity of real GDP demanded.

Aggregate supply: The relationship between the level of prices and the quantity of output supplied.

We now develop an important graphical tool known as **aggregate demand** and **aggregate supply** that we can use to understand how output and prices are determined in both the short run and the long run. While there is only a single aggregate demand curve, we discuss two types of aggregate supply curves: one for the long run and another for the short run.

Aggregate Demand

Let's begin with aggregate demand. The *aggregate demand curve* plots the total *demand* for GDP as a function of price level. That is, for each price level, we ask what will be the total demand for all goods and services in the economy. As we show in Figure 4, the aggregate demand curve is downward sloping. As the price level falls, the total demand for goods and services increases. To understand the aggregate demand curve, we first learn why the curve is downward sloping and then learn what factors shift the aggregate demand curve.

The Slope of the Aggregate Demand Curve

To understand why the aggregate demand curve is downward sloping, we need to consider the supply of money in the economy. While we discuss the supply of money in more detail in later chapters, for now just think of the supply of money as the total amount of currency (cash plus coins) held by the public and the value of all deposits in checking accounts in the economy. For example, if you are holding $100 in cash and have $900 in your checking account, you have $1,000 of money.

As the price level or average level of prices in the economy changes, so does the purchasing power of your money. This is an example of the reality principle:

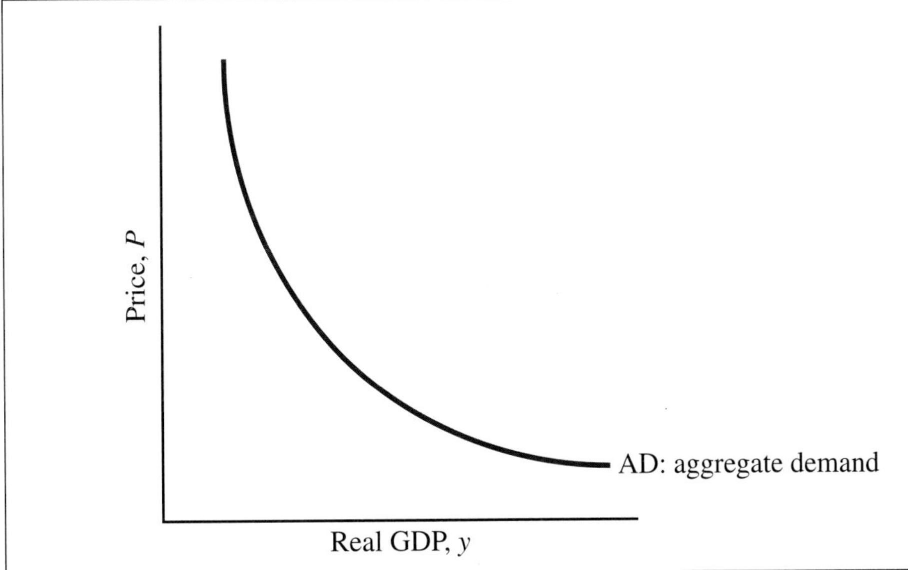

Figure 4

Aggregate Demand

The aggregate demand curve plots the total demand for real GDP as a function of the price level. The aggregate demand curve slopes downward, indicating that aggregate demand increases as the price level falls.

Reality PRINCIPLE

What matters to people is the real value or purchasing power of money or income, not its face value.

The change in the purchasing power of money will affect aggregate demand, the total demand for goods and services in the economy.

In particular, as the price level falls, the purchasing power of money will increase and your $1,000 can purchase more goods and services. As the price level falls and the purchasing power of money increases, people find that they are wealthier. With their increased wealth, they will typically want to increase their spending on goods and services. Thus, the demand for goods and services will increase as the price level falls.

Since the demand for total goods and services increases as the price level falls, this means that the aggregate demand curve is downward sloping. Conversely, when the price level increases, the real value of money decreases. With reduced wealth, there will be less total demand for goods and services. Thus, as the price level increases, total demand for goods and services in the economy decreases.

The increase in spending that occurs because the real value of money increases when the price level falls is known as the **wealth effect.** This is one of the key reasons that the aggregate demand slopes downward. Lower prices lead to higher levels of wealth. In turn, with higher levels of wealth there will be increased spending on total goods and services in the economy.

Wealth effect: The increase in spending that occurs because the real value of money increases when the price level falls.

In later chapters we will find that there are two other reasons why the aggregate demand curve is downward sloping. First, there is an *interest rate effect*. With a given supply of money in the economy, a lower price level will lead to lower interest rates. As interest rates fall, the demand for investment goods in the economy (both investment by firms and consumer durables by households) will increase.

Second, there are *effects from international trade*. In an open economy, a lower price level will mean that domestic goods become cheaper relative to foreign goods and the demand for domestic goods will increase. Moreover, as we will see, lower interest rates will affect the exchange rate to make domestic goods become relatively cheaper than foreign goods. The wealth effect, the interest rate effect, and the effects from international trade reinforce one another, leading to the downward sloping aggregate demand curve in Figure 4.

Factors That Shift the Aggregate Demand Curve

A number of different factors can shift the aggregate demand curve. At any price level, an increase in aggregate demand means that total demand for real GDP has increased and the curve shifts to the right. Similarly, factors that decrease aggregate demand will shift the aggregate demand curve to the left. At any price level, a decrease in aggregate demand means that total demand for real GDP has decreased.

Let's look at the key factors that shift the aggregate demand curve:

1. ***Changes in the supply of money.*** An increase in the supply of money in the economy will increase aggregate demand and shift the aggregate demand curve to the right. Although we will study this process in more detail in later chapters, we know that an increase in the supply of money will lead to higher demand by both consumers and firms. At any given price level, a higher supply of money will mean more consumer wealth and an increased demand for goods and services. A decrease in the supply of money will decrease aggregate demand and shift the aggregate demand curve to the left.

2. ***Changes in taxes.*** A decrease in taxes will increase aggregate demand and shift the aggregate demand curve to the right. As we will study in detail in the next chapter, lower taxes will increase income available to households and increase their spending on goods and services. Thus aggregate demand will increase as taxes are decreased. For opposite reasons, increases in taxes will decrease aggregate demand and shift the aggregate demand curve to the left.

3. ***Changes in government spending.*** An increase in government spending will increase aggregate demand and shift the aggregate demand curve to the right. Since the government is a source of demand for goods and services, higher government spending naturally leads to an increase in total demand for goods and services. Similarly, decreases in government spending will decrease aggregate demand and shift the curve to the left. We will also study this process in more detail in the next chapter.

4. ***Other factors.*** Any change in demand from households, firms, or the foreign sector will also change aggregate demand. For example, if the Japanese economy expands more rapidly than anticipated and the Japanese buy more of our goods, aggregate demand will increase. Similarly, if firms become optimistic about the future and increase their investment spending, aggregate demand will also increase. When we discuss factors that shift aggregate demand, we must not include any changes that arise from movements in the price level. These are already included in the curve and do not shift the curve. For example, the increase in consumer spending that occurs from the wealth effect when the price level falls is included in the curve and does not shift the curve.

Both Figure 5 and Table 1 summarize our discussion. Decreases in taxes, increases in government spending, and increases in the supply of money all shift the aggregate demand curve to the right. Increases in taxes, decreases in government spending, and decreases in the supply of money shift it to the left. In general, any increase in demand (not brought about by a change in the price level) will shift the curve to the right. Decreases in demand shift it to the left.

Aggregate Supply

Now let's turn to aggregate supply. The aggregate supply curve depicts the relationship between the level of prices and real GDP. We will develop two different aggregate supply curves, which correspond to the long run and the short run.

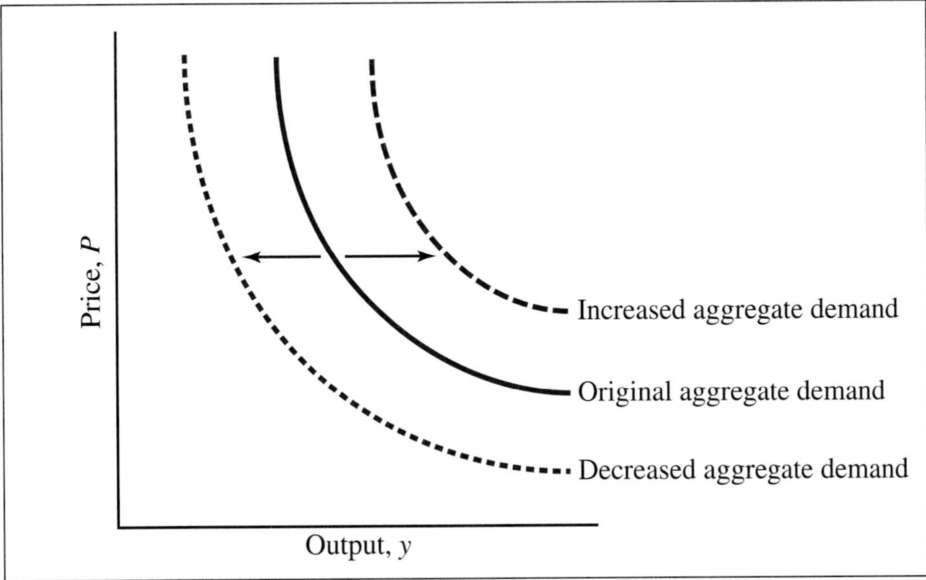

Figure 5
Shifting Aggregate Demand

Decreases in taxes, increases in government spending, or an increase in the supply of money all shift the aggregate demand curve to the right. Higher taxes, lower government spending, or a lower supply of money shift the curve to the left.

The Classical Aggregate Supply Curve

First we'll consider the aggregate supply curve for the long run when the economy is at full employment, the **classical aggregate supply curve**. In previous chapters we saw that the level of full-employment output y^* depends solely on the supply of factors—capital and labor—and the state of technology. These are the fundamental factors that determine output in the long run when the economy operates at full employment.

Classical aggregate supply curve: A vertical aggregate supply curve. It reflects the idea that in the long run, output is determined solely by the factors of production.

The level of full-employment output, however, does *not* depend on the level of prices in the economy. Since the level of full-employment output does not depend on the price level, we can therefore plot the classical aggregate supply curve as a vertical line (unaffected by the price level), as in Figure 6 on the next page.

We combine the aggregate demand curve and the classical aggregate supply curve in Figure 7 on the next page. Given an aggregate demand curve and an aggregate supply curve, the price level and level of output are determined at their intersection. At that point the total amount demanded will just equal the total amount that is supplied. The position of the aggregate demand curve will depend on the level of taxes, government spending, and the supply of money. The level of full-employment output determines the classical aggregate supply curve.

An increase in aggregate demand (perhaps brought about by a tax cut or an increase in the supply of money) will shift the aggregate demand curve to the right as in Figure 7. With a classical aggregate supply curve, the increase in aggregate demand will raise prices but leave the level of output unchanged. In general, shifts in aggregate demand curve when we have a classical supply curve do not change the level of output in the economy but only change the level of prices.

Table 1: Factors That Shift Demand

Factors That Increase Aggregate Demand	*Factors That Decrease Aggregate Demand*
Decrease in taxes	Increase in taxes
Increase in government spending	Decrease in government spending
Increase in money supply	Decrease in money supply

Figure 6

Classical Aggregate Supply

In the long run, the level of output y^* is independent of the price level.

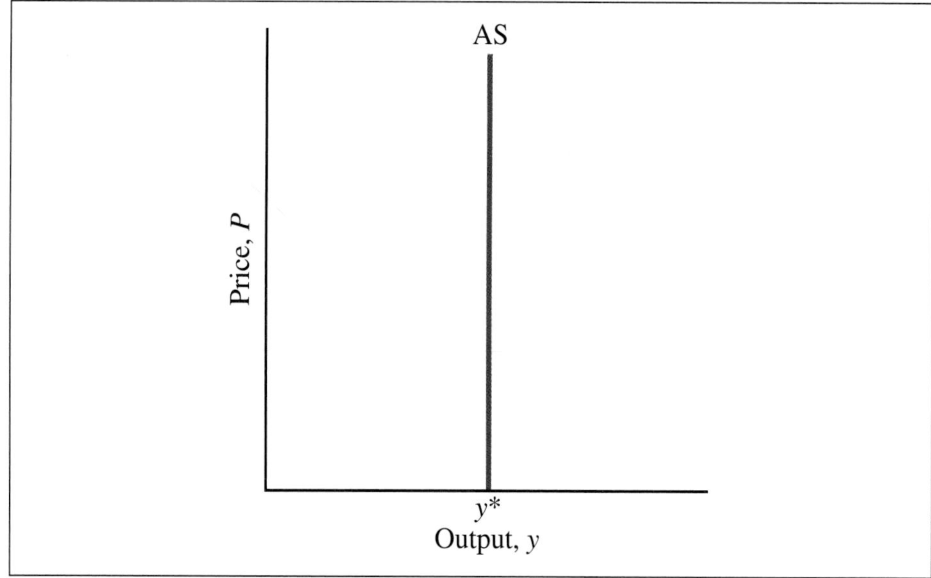

This is the key long-run result from the classical model. In the long run, output is determined solely by the supply of capital and the supply of labor. As our model of the aggregate demand curve with the classical aggregate supply curve indicates, changes in demand will affect only prices, not the level of output.

In later chapters we'll study one important application of this principle: the behavior of inflation in the long run. Suppose that the supply of money in the economy is increased year after year on a regular basis. As the supply of money increases, the aggregate demand curve will shift to the right. With a classical aggregate supply curve, the shift in the aggregate demand curve will just raise prices. Thus the consequence of continuing increases in the supply of money will be continuing increases in the level of prices, or inflation. As we will discuss in more detail, in the long run the rate of inflation will be determined primarily by the growth in the supply of money.

Figure 7

Aggregate Demand and Classical Aggregate Supply

Output and prices are determined at the intersection of AD and AS. An increase in aggregate demand leads to a higher price level.

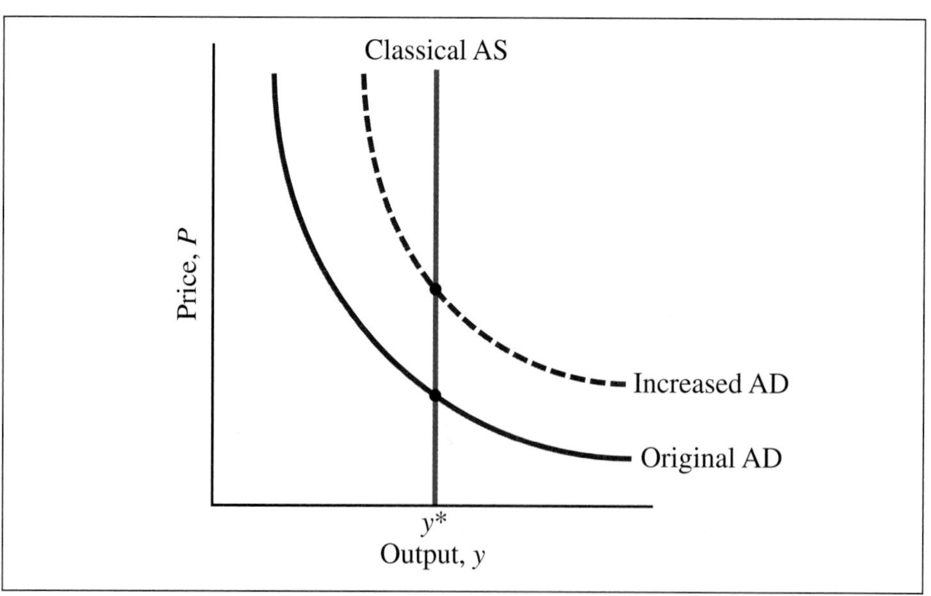

The Keynesian Aggregate Supply Curve

In the short run, prices are sticky and output is determined by demand. We can use the aggregate demand curve combined with a **Keynesian aggregate supply curve** to illustrate this idea. Figure 8 shows a horizontal Keynesian aggregate supply curve *AS*. The Keynesian aggregate supply curve is horizontal because in the short run, firms are assumed to supply all the output that is demanded at the current price. The reason the supply curve is horizontal is that the formal and informal contracts commit producers to supply all that is demanded at the going price.

Keynesian aggregate supply curve: A horizontal aggregate supply curve. It reflects the idea that prices are sticky in the short run and that firms adjust production to meet demand.

As we just explained, the Keynesian supply curve is a horizontal line because at any single point in time, firms are assumed to supply all the output that is demanded. However, as we shall see in later chapters, the entire Keynesian supply curve can shift up or down as prices adjust to their long-run levels. Our depiction of the aggregate supply curve is consistent with evidence about the behavior of prices in the economy. Most studies find that changes in demand have very little effect on prices within, say, a quarter. Thus the aggregate supply curve can be viewed as approximately flat within a limited period of time. However, changes in aggregate demand will ultimately have an effect on prices.

The intersection of the *AD* and *AS* curves determine the price level and the level of output at point E_0. Since the aggregate supply curve is horizontal, aggregate demand totally determines the level of output. In Figure 8, as aggregate demand increases, the new equilibrium will be at the same price P_0 but output will increase from y_0 to y_1.

It is important to understand that the level of output where the aggregate demand curve intersects the Keynesian aggregate supply curve *need not correspond to full-employment output*. Firms will produce whatever is demanded. If demand is very high, output may exceed full-employment output; if demand is very low, output will fall short of full-employment output. Because there are sticky prices that stem from formal and informal contracts, economic activity will not be fully coordinated. Changes in demand will lead to economic fluctuations with sticky prices and a Keynesian aggregate supply curve. Only in the long run, when prices fully adjust, will the economy operate at full employment.

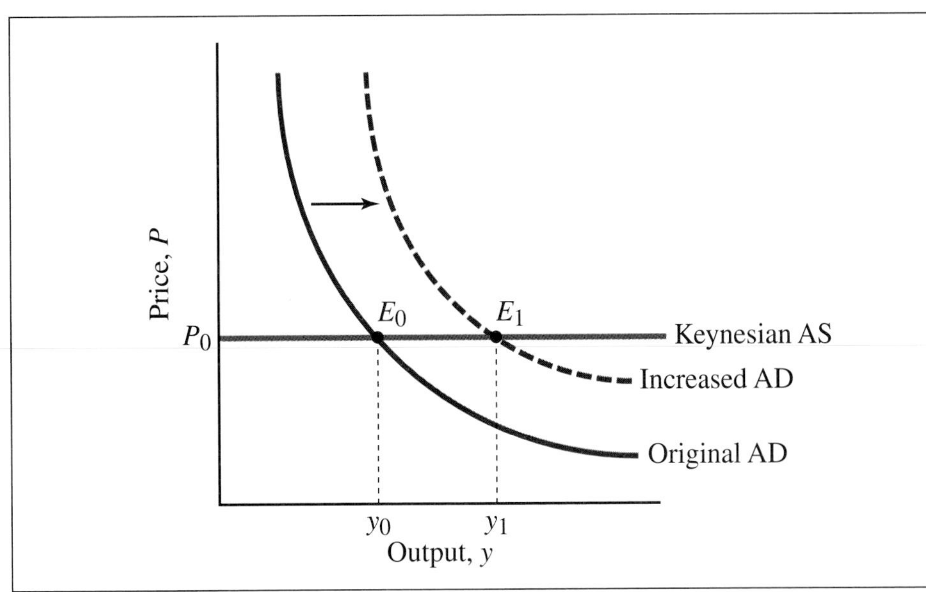

Figure 8

Aggregate Demand and Keynesian Aggregate Supply

With a Keynesian aggregate supply curve, shifts in aggregate demand lead to changes in output but no changes in prices.

Supply Shocks

Supply shocks: External events that shift the aggregate supply curve.

Up to this point we have been exploring how changes in aggregate demand affect output and prices in the short and long run. However, even in the short run it is possible for external disturbances to hit the economy and cause the Keynesian aggregate supply curve to move. We call external events that shift the aggregate supply curve **supply shocks.**

The most important illustrations of supply shocks for the world economy have been sharp increases in the price of oil that occurred in 1973 and 1979. When oil prices increased sharply, firms would no longer sell all the goods and services that were demanded at the current price. Since oil was a key input to production for many firms in the economy, the additional costs of oil reduced the profits of firms. To maintain their profit levels, firms raised their prices.

Figure 9 illustrates a supply shock that raises prices. The Keynesian aggregate supply curve shifts up with the supply shock since firms will only now supply output at a higher price. The shift of the curve raise the price level from P_0 to P_1 and lowers the level of output from y_0 to y_1. Adverse supply shocks can therefore cause a recession (a fall in output) with increasing prices. This situation corresponds closely to the events of 1973, when higher oil prices led to both a recession and rising prices for the economy.

Favorable supply shocks, such as falling prices, are also possible. In this case the Keynesian aggregate supply curve will shift down. The result will be lower prices and a higher level of output in the economy.

LOOKING AHEAD

The aggregate demand and supply models in this chapter provide a useful overview of how demand affects output and prices in both the short and the long run. The next several chapters explore more closely the process by which aggregate demand determines output in the short run. We expand our discussion of aggregate demand to see in detail how such realistic and important factors as spending by consumers and firms, government policies on taxation and spending, and foreign trade affect the demand for goods and services. In addition, we will also study the critical role that the financial system and monetary policy plays in determining demand.

Figure 9

Supply Shock

An adverse supply shock, such as an increase in the price of oil, will shift up the AS curve. The result will be higher prices and a lower level of output.

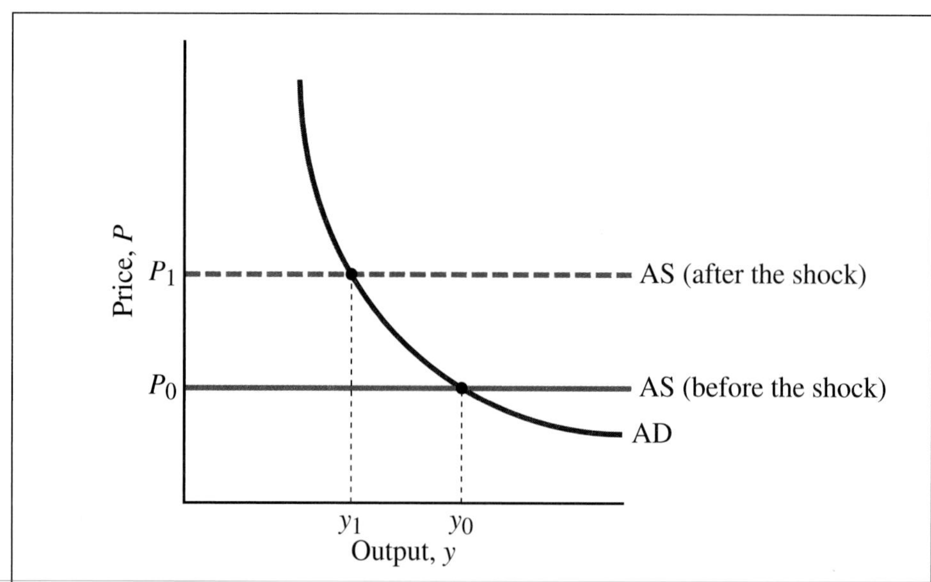

Government policy also will be a central focus of our analysis. We will see the critical role that the government plays in determining aggregate demand through its control of taxes, spending, and the supply of money.

Finally, in later chapters we will come to understand how the aggregate supply curve changes over time. As the short-run aggregate supply curve shifts over time, this will cause prices to change. In turn, the changes in prices will lead the economy on a path back to full employment. At the conclusion of our studies, we will have a complete model that we can use to analyze the behavior of prices and output in both the long run and the short run.

TEST *Your Understanding*

5 Because of both formal and informal ____________, changes in demand will often be met by changes in output rather than changes in prices.

6 If prices are sticky, what determines output in the short run?

7 Name three factors that shift the aggregate demand curve to the right.

8 Complete the statement with *vertical* or *horizontal*: The Keynesian aggregate supply curve is ____________.

9 Complete the statement with *vertical* or *horizontal*: The classical aggregate supply curve is ____________.

10 Suppose the supply of money increases. How do prices and real GDP change in both the classical and Keynesian worlds?

Using the TOOLS

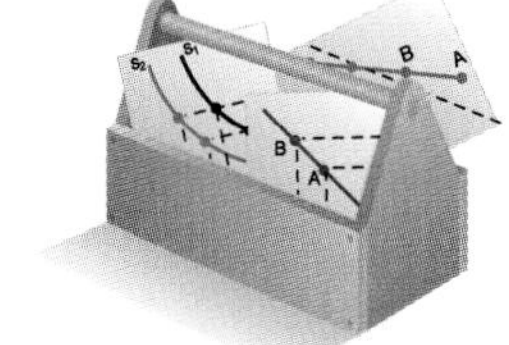

In this chapter we examined the limits of the price system in coordinating economic activity and also developed the tools of aggregate demand and aggregate supply. Take this opportunity to test your skills on economic problems.

1. ECONOMIC EXPERIMENT: *Inflation and the Price System*

Here is a game that can be played in class or electronically and that illustrates how inflation can reduce the information contained in prices. Here is how the game works: Students receive a price for their product, a number between 5 and 15. All students have the same cost of production, but this cost is unknown. However, they are told that their cost of production is random and will be chosen by the instructor, with the following probabilities:

Cost of Production	*Probability of This Cost*
8	0.05
9	0.20
10	0.50
11	0.20
12	0.05

After receiving their price, students must choose whether to produce 1 unit or not produce. They then learn their costs, which determines their net profit per unit. If they have decided to produce and they have a negative net profit, they are declared bankrupt and immediately drop out of the game. Students who are not bankrupt calculate their profits, which are equal to their net profit per unit. The game is played for three rounds. The student with the highest level of profits wins the game.

Now the game is slightly changed. This time the costs of production are chosen by the instructor according to the following table:

Cost of Production	*Probability of This Cost*
6	0.10
7	0.10
8	0.10
9	0.10
10	0.20
11	0.10
12	0.10
13	0.10
14	0.10

All other features of the game remain the same. It is also played for three rounds. After playing the game (or just reading about the game and thinking about how people might play) consider these questions.

a. Does a high price (say, 12) mean the same thing in both games?

b. In what game do people play more aggressively (that is, change their production most in response to prices)?

c. Interpret this game in terms of uncertain inflation.

2. Rationales for Sticky Wages

Think of some group of workers (for example, federal workers) that have "sticky wages." Explain why sticky wages may be convenient for both workers and employers.

3. Frugal Consumers

Suppose that households become nervous about the future and decide to increase their saving and decrease their consumption spending. How will this shift the aggregate demand curve? Using the Keynesian aggregate supply curve, what will happen to prices and output in the short run? Using the classical aggregate supply curve, what will happen to prices and output in the long run?

4. Stagflation

Suppose that oil prices suddenly increase and the economy experiences an adverse supply shock. What will happen to the price level and real GDP? Why is this sometimes called "stagflation"?

5. ECONOMIC DETECTIVE– *Did Higher Taxes Cause the Recession?*

An economy experienced a recession. The political party in power blamed an increase in the price of world commodities. Opposing politicians blamed a tax increase by the party in power for the recession. Based on aggregate demand and supply analysis, what piece of evidence would you want to look at to try to determine what caused the recession?

SUMMARY

In this chapter we emphasized difficulties in coordinating economic activity and provided the foundation for studying short-run, demand-side economics. We also developed important tools: aggregate demand and aggregate supply. Here are the main points to remember in this chapter:

1. The price system does a remarkable job of coordinating economic activity.
2. The price system, however, does not work perfectly in the short run. Coordination may fail because: (a) there are not enough prices to act as signals to producers, (b) prices do not contain sufficient information, and (c) prices are not sufficiently flexible in the short run.
3. Because of short-run coordination problems, economists find it useful to think of GDP as determined primarily by demand factors in the short run.
4. The aggregate demand curve depicts the relationship between the price level and total demand for real output in the economy. The aggregate demand curve is downward sloping because of the wealth effect, an interest rate effect, and an international trade effect.
5. Decreases in taxes, increases in government spending, and increases in the supply of money all increase aggregate demand and shift the aggregate demand curve to the right. Conversely, increases in taxes, decreases in government spending, and decreases in the supply of money decrease aggregate demand and shift the aggregate demand curve to the left. In general, anything (other than price movements) that increases the demand for total goods and services will increase aggregate demand.
6. The aggregate supply curve depicts the relationship between the price level and the level of output firms supply in the economy. Output and prices are determined at the intersection of aggregate demand and aggregate supply.
7. The classical aggregate supply curve is vertical since, in the long run, output is determined by the supply of factors of production. The Keynesian aggregate supply curve is horizontal because in the short run, when prices are fixed, output is determined by demand.
8. Supply shocks can shift the Keynesian aggregate supply curve even in the short run.

KEY TERMS

aggregate demand, *496*
aggregate supply, *496*
business cycles, *486*
classical aggregate supply curve, *499*
economic fluctuations, *486*
focal points, *491*
futures markets, *492*
invisible hand, *490*
Keynesian aggregate supply curve, *501*
Keynesian economics, *487*
real business cycle theory, *488*
real price, *493*
short run in macroeconomics, *487*
supply shocks, *502*
wealth effect, *497*

PROBLEMS AND DISCUSSION QUESTIONS

1. Prices for most goods in the future do not exist. Explain why this may cause problems in macroeconomic coordination.
2. Why should a business care about its real price rather than its nominal price?
3. Carefully explain why the classical aggregate supply curve is vertical and the Keynesian supply curve is horizontal.
4. Explain why the aggregate demand curve is downward sloping.
5. Give another example of a good or service whose prices are sticky. What factors tend to make its price sticky?
6. Futures prices exist for many agricultural commodities and metals but not for consumer goods. Can you give a reason why this occurs?
7. Suppose that in the classical model, the level of full-employment output increased. What would happen to the level of prices in the economy?
8. In the short run, with a Keynesian aggregate supply curve, what happens to the unemployment rate if aggregate demand suddenly falls?

Take It to the Net

We invite you to visit the O'Sullivan/Sheffrin page on the Prentice Hall Web site at:

http://www.prenhall.com/osullivan/

for this chapter's World Wide Web exercise.

MODEL ANSWERS FOR THIS CHAPTER

Chapter-Opening Questions

1. Inflation interferes with the price system by creating confusion about real versus nominal prices.
2. Some firms may not change their prices when demand changes because of explicit or implicit contracts.
3. Because wages and prices are slow to adjust, the economy may not always operate at full employment.
4. In the short run, output is largely determined by demand. Therefore, a sharp decrease in government spending could cause a recession.
5. In the short run, changes in the demand for goods and services primarily affect output. In the long run, they primarily affect prices.

Test Your Understanding

1. There are few prices to guide producers to make specific investment decisions.
2. real
3. There will be a fall in economic activity.
4. Prices of industrial products and most wages are sticky.
5. contracts
6. Demand determines output.
7. Three factors are increases in government spending, decreases in taxes, and increases in the supply of money.
8. horizontal
9. vertical
10. In the classical model, an increase in the money supply will raise prices but not change output. In the Keynesian model, an increase in the supply of money will increase output but not change prices.

Using the Tools

1. Economic Experiment: Inflation and the Price System

   In this experiment the price conveys more information in the first game because, in the second game, costs are more variable. You should be more willing to produce at a high price in the first game than in the second.
2. Rationales for Sticky Wages

   It would be very inconvenient and costly for employers and employees to renegotiate wages every day. Conflicts over wages would certainly arise. To keep the peace, wages are adjusted only in periodic intervals.
3. Frugal Consumers

   The decrease in consumption spending is a decrease in the demand for total goods and services and thus a decrease in aggregate demand. The aggregate demand curve shifts to the left. In the short run, prices remain the same and output falls. In the long run, prices fall and output remains at full employment.
4. Stagflation

   If the Keynesian aggregate supply curve shifts up, the result will be a lower level of output and higher prices. This is sometimes called *stagflation* because the falling output means that the economy is *stag*nating and the rising prices mean that the in*flation* rate will rise.
5. Economic Detective: Did Higher Taxes Cause the Recession?

   You would want to study what happened to prices. If an increase in taxes caused the recession, this would have shifted the aggregate demand curve to the left with no change in prices. On the other hand, if there were adverse supply shocks, prices would have increased. In practice, you would have to figure out what would have happened to prices if there had been no shocks (either tax increases or commodity price increases) in order to measure the impacts of the tax increases or commodity price increases.

CHAPTER

25

Keynesian Economics and Fiscal Policy

Movie stars, rock musicians, and starving artists have always found that one path to fame is to be a little outrageous. Some economists have learned this lesson as well.

During the Great Depression, John Maynard Keynes wanted to dramatize his controversial view that the key to ending the worldwide depression was for governments to spend more money. Rather than just writing a boring article for the newspaper, he used humor and exaggeration. He claimed that the secret of the economic success of the Ancient Egyptians was that they spent vast sums of money building pyramids. According to Keynes, pyramids were the perfect government project; a society never tired of having more pyramids.

Of course, Keynes did not really believe that the Ancient Egyptians achieved economic success because they built pyramids. But he did want to get an important message across. Particularly in times of depressed economic conditions, it is important for both the government and the private sector to purchase goods and services. Without sufficient spending, an economy will remain in depression.

In this chapter we explore Keynes's idea that spending determines output or GDP, at least over short periods of time. As we discussed in the last chapter, in macroeconomics the *short run* is defined as the period during which prices are fixed. Until prices adjust, the demand for goods and services determines the level of GDP. Producers will supply, in the short run, all the output that is demanded. This was Keynes's essential point: In the short run, the level of GDP is determined primarily by demand.

We start this chapter with the simplest case, a demand-side model that ignores the role of the government and the foreign sector. We then bring government and the foreign sector into our model and illustrate how it works with several real-world examples.

We also introduce an important tool, a graph known as the *Keynesian cross*. The Keynesian cross enables us to understand how demand determines output in the short run and how changes in demand change output. In addition to this graphical approach, we also develop simple algebraic formulas that will reinforce your understanding of the basic ideas behind demand-side models. The appendix to this chapter shows how to derive the formulas.

With the tools in this chapter, you will be able to answer the following real world questions:

1. Why do governments cut taxes to increase economic output?
2. Why is the U.S. economy more stable today than it was early in the twentieth century?
3. If consumers become more confident about the future of the economy, can this lead to faster economic growth?
4. If a government increases spending by $10 billion, could total GDP increase by more than $10 billion?
5. If a country stops buying our exports, could this lead to a recession?

THE SIMPLEST KEYNESIAN CROSS

We begin by presenting the simplest model of how demand determines output in the short run. To understand this model, we will use graphs, all of which make use of one key feature: a 45° line. Figure 1 shows a graph with the demand for goods and services on the vertical axis and output (y) on the horizontal axis. We have also drawn a 45° line that divides the angle between the two axes in half. The 45° line has the important property that from any point on it, the vertical and horizontal distances measured along the axes are equal. This is the key fact to remember.

Now we can start to build a simple demand-side model. Initially, we omit both the government and the foreign sector. Only consumers and firms can demand output: Consumers demand consumption goods and firms demand investment goods. We assume initially that consumers and firms each demand a fixed amount of goods. Let consumption demand be an amount C and investment demand be an amount I. Total demand will be $C + I$.

In the short run, demand determines output, or

$$\text{output} = \text{demand}$$

In this case,

$$\text{output} = \text{demand} = C + I$$

Figure 2 can help us understand how the level of GDP is determined. On the 45° diagram we superimpose the horizontal line marked $C + I$ (demand). In this initial case, total demand is fixed at $C + I$ and is independent of the level of GDP. Therefore, it is a horizontal line; demand does not depend on output.

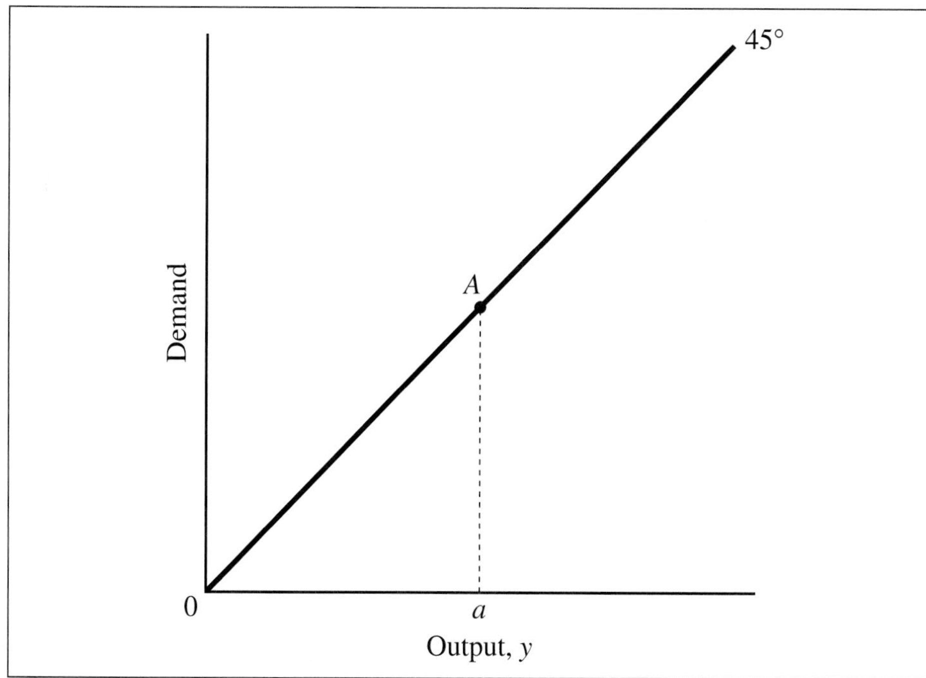

Figure 1

The 45° Line

Any point on the 45° line corresponds to the same vertical and horizontal distances. The distance $0a$ equals the distance Aa.

Equilibrium output is at y^*, the level of output at which the demand line crosses the 45° line at point E. Here output measured on the horizontal axis equals demand by consumers and firms. How do we know this? Since point E is on the 45° line, the vertical distance Ey^* equals the horizontal distance Oy^*. Recall that the vertical distance is total demand and the horizontal distance is the level of output. Therefore, at y^*, total demand equals output.

Equilibrium output: The level of GDP at which the demand for output equals the amount that is produced.

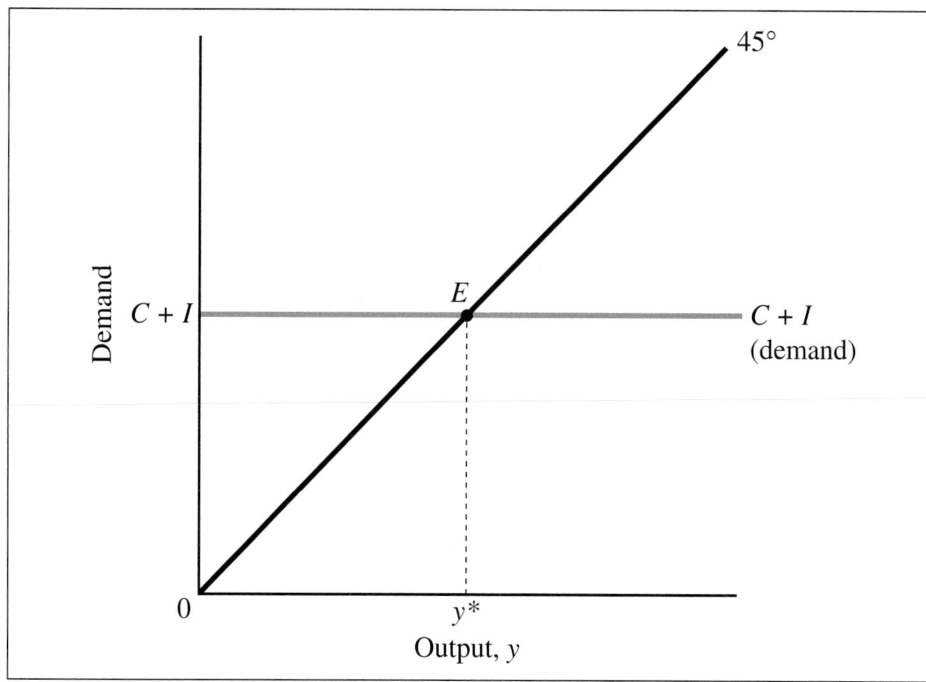

Figure 2

The Keynesian Cross

At equilibrium output y^*, total demand Ey^* equals output $0y^*$.

What would happen if the economy were producing at a higher level of output, such as y_1 in Figure 3? At that level of output, more goods and services are being produced than are desired by consumers and firms. Extra goods will pile up on the shelves of stores as demand fell short of production. Firms will react to this by cutting back on production. As the arrows in Figure 3 show, the level of output will fall until the economy reaches y^*. We see in the Closer Look box "Too Many Inventories?" that economic forecasters recognize that excess inventories often signal future cutbacks in output.

If the economy were producing at a lower level of output y_2, demand would exceed total output. Since demand now exceeds output, firms find that the demand for consumption and investment goods is greater than their current production. Inventories disappear from the shelves of stores and firms face increasing backlogs. Firms respond by stepping up production. The arrows in Figure 3 show that GDP would increase back to y^*.

To summarize, in the macroeconomic short run when prices do not change, the equilibrium level of output occurs where total demand equals production. If the economy were not producing at that level, we would find either that the demand for goods was too great relative to production or that there was insufficient demand relative to production. The economy rapidly adjusts to reach this equilibrium level of output.

THE CONSUMPTION FUNCTION AND THE MULTIPLIER

Consumer Spending and Income

Consumption function: The relationship between the level of income and consumption spending.

We now start to make consumer spending in our model more realistic. Economists have consistently found that consumer spending depends on the level of income in the economy. As you might expect, when consumers have more income, they want to purchase more goods and services. The **consumption function** describes the relationship between consumer spending and income.

Figure 3

Equilibrium Output

Given total demand, equilibrium output (y^*) is determined at E, where demand intersects the 45° line. If output were higher (y_1), it would exceed demand and production would fall. If output were lower (y_2), it would fall short of demand and production would rise.

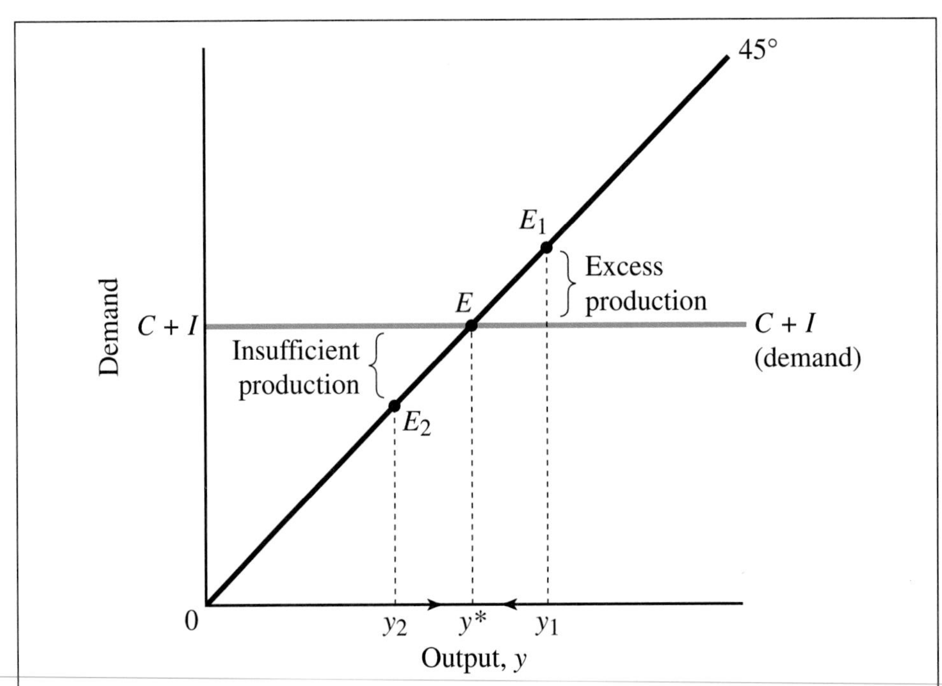

A Closer LOOK

Too Many Inventories?

Economic forecasters look carefully at the level of inventories as they prepare their forecasts. If production in the economy exceeds demand and firms accumulate unwanted inventories, they will cut back on their production. Therefore, economic forecasters often use excess inventories to predict that the economy will slow down in the future. For example, consider the following headline from the *New York Times*:

Economy Grew At a Brisk Rate in 4th Quarter

But Jump in Inventories Signals a Slowdown

But forecasters must be careful. Not all additions to inventory are unwanted: Think of stocking the shelves of a toy store before Christmas. Firms can add inventories because they expect robust growth. In this case, additional inventories are a sign that the economy will expand, not contract. The *New York Times* story did mention this possibility but said that analysts interpreted the inventory buildup as "a tailing off of consumer buying at the end of the year rather than as an intentional restocking of store shelves."

Source: After Robert Hershey, Jr., "Economy Grew at Brisk Rate in 4th Quarter: But Jump in Inventories Signals a Slowdown," *New York Times*, January 27, 1995, pp. 1, 27.

We can write a simple consumption function as

$$C = C_a + by$$

where consumption spending C has two parts. The first part, C_a, is a constant and is independent of income. For example, regardless of their current income, all consumers will have to purchase some food. Economists call this part of consumption **autonomous consumption** spending. The second part of the consumption function represents the part of consumption that depends on income. It is the product of a fraction b called the **marginal propensity to consume (MPC)** and the level of income y. For example, if $b = 0.6$, then for every \$1 that income increases, consumption increases by \$0.60.

Autonomous consumption: The part of consumption that does not depend on income.

Marginal propensity to consume (MPC): The fraction of additional income that is spent.

We plot a consumption function in Figure 4 on the next page. The consumption function is a line that intersects the vertical axis at C_a, the level of autonomous consumption spending (remember that autonomous consumption must be greater than zero, so the line does not pass through the zero point on the origin). It has a slope equal to b. Although output is on the horizontal axis, output and income in this simple economy are identical. Output generates income that is all received by households. As output rises by \$1, consumption increases by the marginal propensity to consume $(b) \times \$1$. For example, if $b = 0.6$, consumption would rise by $0.6 \times \$1$, or \$0.60. The MPC value tells us how much consumption will increase from any additional (or marginal) increase in income.

The MPC is always less than 1. If a consumer receives a dollar of income, she will spend part of it and save the rest. The fraction that the consumer spends is determined by her MPC. The fraction that she saves is determined by her **marginal propensity to save (MPS)**. The sum of the marginal propensity to consume and the

Marginal propensity to save (MPS): The fraction of additional income that is saved.

Figure 4

Consumption Function

The consumption function relates desired consumer spending to the level of income.

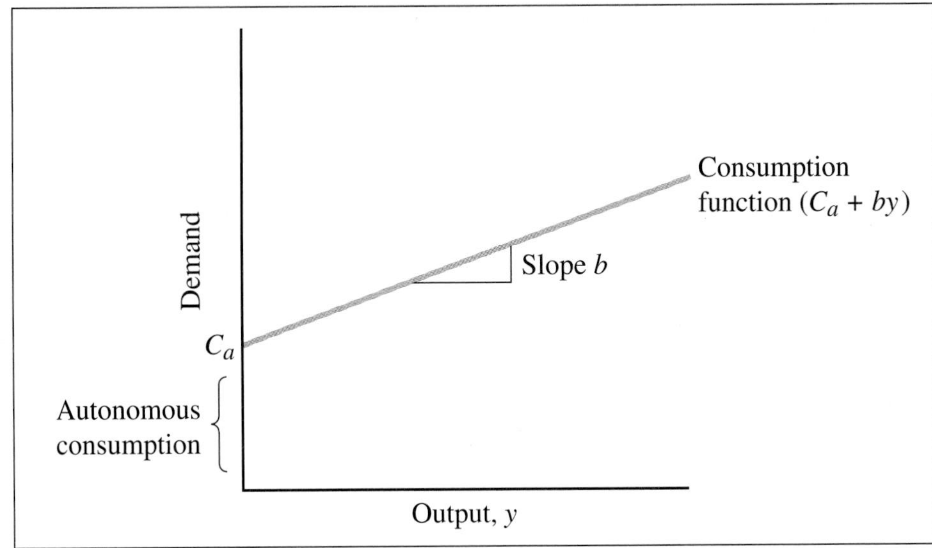

marginal propensity to save is always equal to 1. For example, if the MPC is 0.8, then the MPS must be 0.2. When a consumer receives an additional dollar, she spends \$0.80 and saves the remaining \$0.20.

Changes in the Consumption Function

The consumption function is determined entirely by the level of autonomous consumption and the MPC. Both the level of autonomous consumption and the MPC can change, thereby causing movements in the consumption function. A higher level of autonomous consumption will shift up the entire consumption function, since the intercept on the vertical axis will increase. We show an increase in autonomous consumption in panel A of Figure 5.

A number of factors can cause autonomous consumption to change. First, increases in consumer wealth will cause an increase in autonomous consumption. (Wealth consists of the value of stocks, bonds, and consumer durables. It is not the same as income, which is the amount earned in a given year.) Nobel laureate Franco Modigliani has emphasized that increases in stock prices, which raise consumer wealth, will lead to increases in autonomous consumption. Conversely, a sharp fall in stock prices would lead to a decrease in autonomous consumption. Second,

Figure 5

Movements of the Consumption Function

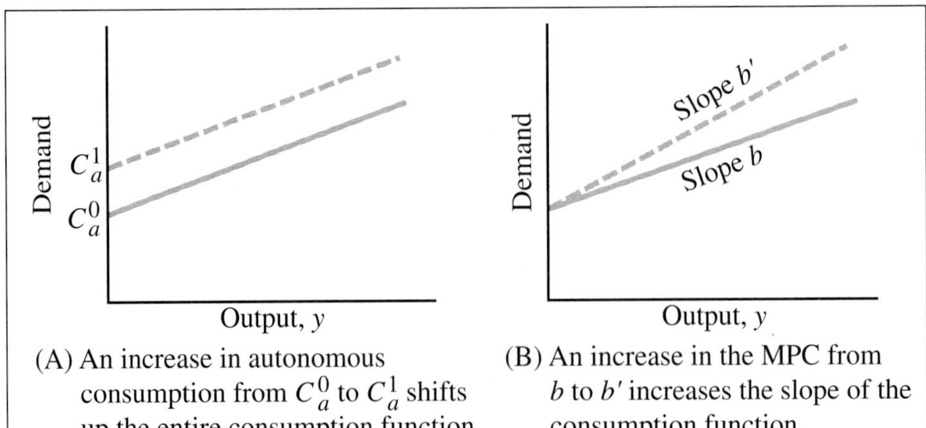

(A) An increase in autonomous consumption from C_a^0 to C_a^1 shifts up the entire consumption function.

(B) An increase in the MPC from b to b' increases the slope of the consumption function.

changes in consumer confidence will shift the consumption function. Economists have noted that increases in consumer confidence will increase autonomous consumption. Forecasters pay attention to an index of consumer confidence based on household surveys that is reported regularly in the financial press.

A change in the marginal propensity to consume will cause a change in the slope of the consumption function. We show an increase in the MPC in panel B of Figure 5. As the MPC increases, the consumption function rotates upward.

Several factors can change the MPC. First, consumers' perceptions of changes in their income affect their MPC. If consumers believe that an increase in their income is permanent, they will consume a higher fraction of the increased income than if the increase were believed to be temporary. As an example, consumers are more likely to spend a higher fraction of a permanent salary increase than they are a one-time bonus. Similarly, studies have shown that consumers save, not spend, a high fraction of one-time windfall gains such as lottery winnings. Second, as we will see later in this chapter, changes in tax rates will also change the slope of the consumption function.

Determining GDP

We are now ready to see how GDP is determined with the consumption function. As before, we assume that GDP is ultimately determined by demand. We continue to assume that investment spending, I, is a constant. The only difference between this analysis and the prior model is that we now recognize that consumption increases with the level of income.

Figure 6 shows how GDP is determined. We first plot the consumption function, C, as before. Investment is constant at all levels of income. We can therefore add the level of desired investment I vertically to the consumption function. This gives us the $C + I$ line, which is total spending in the economy. This line is upward sloping because consumption spending increases with income. At any level of income, we now know the level of total spending, $C + I$.

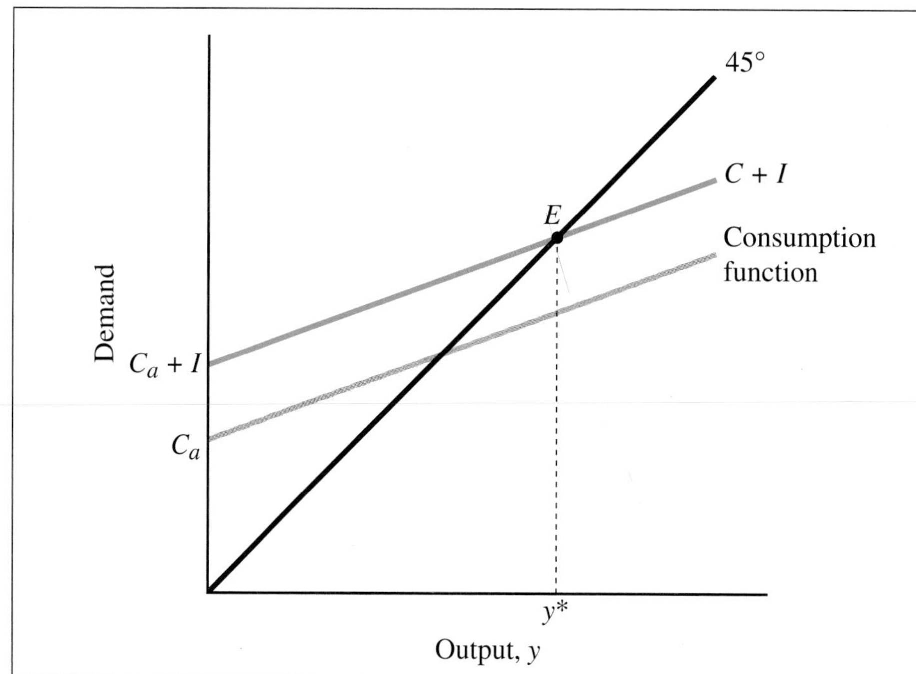

Figure 6

Determining GDP

GDP is determined where the $C + I$ line intersects the 45° line. At that level of output, y^*, desired spending equals output.

The level of equilibrium income, y^*, occurs where the spending line $C + I$ crosses the 45° line. At this level of output, total spending equals output. At any other level of production, spending will not equal output and the economy will adjust back to y^*, just as in the previous example.

In the appendix to this chapter we show that the equilibrium income in this simple economy is given by the formula

$$\text{equilibrium income} = \frac{\text{autonomous consumption} + \text{investment}}{1 - \text{MPC}}$$

or

$$y^* = \frac{C_a + I}{1 - b}$$

This expression allows us to calculate equilibrium income once we specify numerical values for C_a, I, and b. For example, suppose we have

$$C = 100 + 0.6y \qquad (C_a = 100 \text{ and } b = 0.6)$$

$$I = 40$$

Then, using our formula for equilibrium income, we have

$$y^* = \frac{100 + 40}{1 - 0.6}$$

$$= \frac{140}{0.4}$$

$$= 350$$

In equilibrium, it is also true that *saving equals investment*. In an economy without government or the foreign sector, output can only be used for consumption or investment. Whatever is not consumed must be invested. At the same time, the production of output generates an equal amount of income for the private sector. Whatever income is not consumed is, by definition, saved. Therefore, saving (income that is not consumed) must be equal to investment (output that is not used for consumption).

TEST *Your Understanding*

1. Explain why equilibrium output occurs where the demand line crosses the 45° line.
2. What happens if the level of output exceeds demand?
3. What is the slope of the consumption function called?
4. Complete the statement with *up* or *down*: An increase in autonomous consumption will shift the consumption function __________.
5. In our simple model, if $C = 100 + 0.8y$ and $I = 50$, equilibrium output will be __________.
6. If the MPC is 0.7, the marginal propensity to save must be __________.

The Multiplier

All economies experience fluctuations in investment spending. We can use the model to see what happens if there are changes in investment spending. Suppose that investment spending were originally equal to I_0 and increased to I_1, an increase we will call ΔI (the symbol "Δ," the Greek capital letter delta, stands for "change"). What happens to equilibrium income?

Figure 7 shows how equilibrium income is determined at the original and new level of investment. The increase in investment spending shifts up the $C + I$ curve by ΔI. The intersection with the 45° line shifts from E_0 to E_1. GDP increases by Δy from y_0 to y_1.

The figure shows that the increase in GDP (Δy) is greater than the increase in investment (ΔI). This is a general result; the increase in output always exceeds the increase in investment. The increase in output divided by the increase in investment is called the **multiplier**. Since output increases more than the initial increase in investment, the multiplier is greater than 1.

Multiplier: The ratio of changes in output to changes in spending. It measures the degree to which changes in spending are "multiplied" into changes in output.

Why is there a multiplier in the economy? The basic idea is really quite simple. Suppose that a computer firm invests $10 million by building a new plant. Initially, total spending increases by this $10 million paid to a construction firm. The construction workers and owners of the construction firm then spend a portion of the income they receive. To be specific, suppose that the owners and workers spend $8 million dollars on new automobiles. Producers of these automobiles will expand their production because of the increase in demand. In turn, workers and owners in the automobile industry will earn additional wages and profits. They, in turn, will spend part of this additional income on other goods and services. This is the multiplier in action.

Table 1 on the next page shows how the multiplier works in more detail. In the first round there is an initial increase of investment spending of $10 million. This additional demand leads to an initial increase in GDP and income of $10 million. Assuming that the MPC is 0.8, the $10 million of additional income will increase consumer spending by $8 million. Round 2 begins with this $8 million increase in consumer spending. Because of this increase in demand, GDP and income increase by $8 million. At the end of round 2, consumers will have an additional $8 million; with a MPC of 0.8, consumer spending will therefore increase by 0.8 × $8 million, or $6.4 million. The process continues in round 3 with an increase in consumer spending of $6.4 million. It continues, in

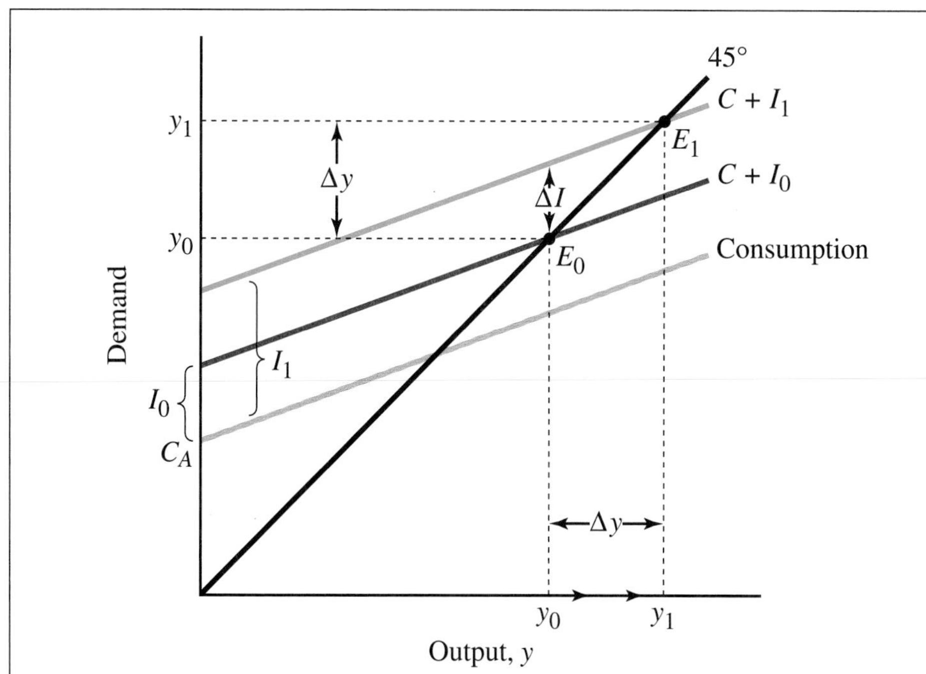

Figure 7

Multiplier

When investment increases from by ΔI from I_0 to I_1, equilibrium output increases by Δy from y_0 to y_1. The change in output (Δy) is greater than the change in investment (ΔI).

Table 1: The Multiplier in Action

Round of Spending	*Increase in Demand*	*Increase in GDP and Income*	*Increase in Consumption*
1	$10	$10	$ 8
2	8	8	6.4
3	6.4	6.4	5.12
4	5.12	5.12	4.096
5	4.096	4.096	3.277
. . .	. . .	. . .	. . .
Total	50 million	50 million	40 million

Note: All figures for increases indicate millions of dollars.

diminishing amounts, through subsequent rounds. If we add up the spending in all the (infinite) rounds, we will find that the initial $10 million of spending leads to a $50 million increase in GDP and income. In this case, the multiplier is equal to 5.

The multiplier also works in reverse. Suppose consumers become more pessimistic and cut back on their level of autonomous consumption by $10 million. Demand for GDP falls by $10 million, which means that income falls by $10 million. Consumers then cut back their spending because their incomes have fallen. This process continues in reverse. If the MPC were again 0.8, total spending would fall by $50 million.

A simple formula for the multiplier is derived in the appendix to this chapter:

$$\text{multiplier} = \frac{1}{1 - \text{MPC}}$$

To illustrate this formula, suppose that the MPC equaled 0.8; then the multiplier would be 1/(1 – 0.8), or 5.

Notice that the multiplier increases as the MPC increases. For example, if the MPC were 0.4, the multiplier would be 1.67, whereas if the MPC were 0.6, the multiplier would be 2.5. Why does this occur? Think back to our examples of the multiplier in action. The multiplier occurs because the initial increase in investment spending increases income, which, in turn, leads to higher consumer spending. With a higher MPC, the increase in consumer spending will be greater and the multiplier process will be magnified.

GOVERNMENT SPENDING AND TAXATION

Keynesian Fiscal Policy

We now make our model more realistic and useful for understanding economic policy debates by bringing in government spending and taxation. In our national economic debates, we often hear recommendations for increasing spending or cutting taxes to increase GDP. As we will explain, both the level of government spending and taxation affect GDP in the short run through their influence on the demand for goods and services in the economy. Using taxes and spending to influence the level of GDP in the short run is known as **Keynesian fiscal policy**. As we discussed in the chapter on Classical Economics, changes in taxes can also affect the supply of output in the long run by changing the incentives to work or invest. However, in this chapter we concentrate on the role of taxes and spending in determining demand for goods and services and, hence, output in the short run.

Keynesian fiscal policy: The use of taxes and government spending to affect the level of GDP in the short run.

First, let's look at the role that government spending plays in determining GDP. Government purchases of goods and services are a component of spending. Total spending, including government, is then $C + I + G$. Increases in government purchases G shift up the $C + I + G$ line just as increases in investment spending or autonomous consumption spending do. If government spending increases by \$1, the $C + I + G$ line will shift up vertically by \$1.

Panel A of Figure 8 shows how increases in government spending affect GDP. The increase in government spending from G_0 to G_1 shifts up the $C + I + G$ line and increases the level of GDP from y_0 to y_1.

As you can see, changes in government purchases have exactly the same effects as changes in investment spending or changes in autonomous consumption spending. The multiplier for government spending is also the same as for changes in investment or autonomous consumption:

$$\text{multiplier for government spending} = \frac{1}{1 - \text{MPC}}$$

If, for example, the MPC were 0.6 and the multiplier were 2.5, a \$10 billion increase in government spending would increase GDP by \$25 billion. The multiplier for government spending works just like the multiplier for investment or consumption. An initial increase in government spending raises GDP and income. The increase in income, however, generates further increases in demand as consumers increase their spending.

Now let's turn to taxes. We need to take into account that government programs affect households' **disposable personal income**, the income that ultimately flows back to households and to consumers, after subtracting any taxes that are paid and after adding any transfer payments received by households (such as Social Security, unemployment insurance, or welfare). If the government, on balance, takes \$10 out of every \$100 you make, your income after taxes and transfers is only \$90. We incorporate taxes and transfers into the model by allowing consumption spending to depend on income *after taxes and transfers*, or $y - T$, where T is *net* taxes (taxes minus transfers). For simplicity, we'll just refer to T as taxes, but remember that it is taxes less transfer payments. We can write the consumption function with taxes as

Disposable personal income: The income that ultimately flows back to households, taking into account transfers and taxes.

$$C = C_a + b\,(y - T)$$

If taxes increase by \$1, after-tax income will decrease by \$1. Since the marginal propensity to consume is b, this means that consumption will fall by $b \times \$1$, and the

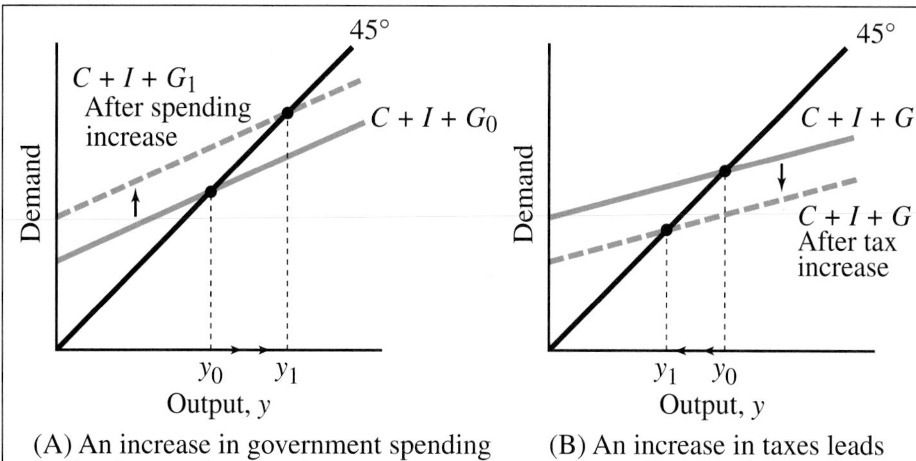

(A) An increase in government spending leads to an increase in output

(B) An increase in taxes leads to a decrease in output

Figure 8

Keynesian Fiscal Policy

$C + I + G$ line will shift down by $b \times \$1$. For example, if the MPC is 0.6, a \$1 increase in taxes will mean that consumers will have a dollar less of income and will therefore decrease consumption spending by \$0.60.

Panel B of Figure 8 shows how an increase in taxes will decrease the level of GDP. As the level of taxes increase, the demand line will shift down by the MPC × the increase in taxes. Equilibrium income will now fall from y_0 to y_1.

The multiplier for taxes is slightly different than the multiplier for government spending. If we cut government spending by \$1, the $C + I + G$ will shift down by \$1. However, if we increase taxes by \$1, consumers will only cut back their consumption by $b \times \$1$. Thus the $C + I + G$ will shift down by slightly less than \$1, or $b \times \$1$. For example, if $b = 0.6$, the demand line would only shift down by \$0.60.

Since the demand line does not shift by the same amount with taxes as it does with government spending, the formula for the tax multiplier is slightly different. In the appendix we show how to derive the formula for the tax multiplier:

$$\text{tax multiplier} = \frac{-b}{1 - b}$$

The tax multiplier is negative because increases in taxes decrease disposable income and lead to a reduction in consumption spending. If the MPC = 0.6, the tax multiplier will be $-0.6/(1 - 0.6) = -1.5$.

Notice that the tax multiplier is smaller (in absolute value) than the government-spending multiplier, which for the same MPC was 2.5. The reason is that an increase in taxes first reduces the disposable income of households by the amount of the tax. However, since the MPC is less than 1, the fall in consumer spending is less than the increase in taxes.

Finally, you may wonder what would happen if we increased government spending and taxes together by an equal amount. Since the multiplier for spending is larger than the multiplier for taxes, equal increases in both spending and taxes will increase GDP. Economists call the multiplier for equal increases in spending and taxes the *balanced budget multiplier* because equal changes in spending and taxes will not "unbalance" the budget. In the appendix we show that the balanced budget multiplier in our simple model is always equal to 1. For example, if spending and taxes are both increased by \$10 billion, then GDP will also increase by \$10 billion.

Let's look at several hypothetical examples of how we can use fiscal policy, altering taxes and government spending to affect GDP. In all these examples, suppose that GDP is \$6,000 billion, the marginal propensity to consume is 0.6, the government-spending multiplier is $1/(1 - 0.6) = 2.5$, and the tax multiplier is $-0.6/(1 - 0.6) = -1.5$.

1. Suppose policymakers want to increase GDP by 1%, or \$60 billion. By how much do policymakers have to increase spending to meet this target? Since the multiplier for government spending is 2.5, we need to increase spending by only \$24 billion. With a multiplier of 2.5, the \$24 billion increase in spending leads to a increase in GDP of \$60 billion (\$24 billion × 2.5 = \$60 billion).
2. Suppose policymakers wanted to use tax cuts rather than spending increases to increase GDP by \$60 billion. How large a tax cut would be necessary? Since the tax multiplier is −1.5, we need to cut taxes by \$40 billion. The \$40 billion tax cut times the multiplier will lead to the desired \$60 billion increase in GDP (−\$40 billion × −1.5 = \$60 billion).
3. Finally, if policymakers wanted to change taxes and spending by equal amounts so as to not affect the federal budget, how large a change would be needed to increase GDP by \$60 billion? Since the balanced budget multiplier is 1, both spending and taxes must be increased by \$60 billion.

The models we are using are, of course, very simple and leave out important factors. Nonetheless, the same basic principles apply in real-world situations. Here are two recent examples of Keynesian fiscal policy.

1. In 1993, the three members of the President's Council of Economic Advisers wrote a letter to President Clinton stating that they thought the spending cuts being proposed at the time were $20 billion too large. The economic model the council members used had a multiplier for government spending of approximately 1.5. With this multiplier, the decrease in GDP from the $20 billion spending cut would be ($20 billion × 1.5) = $30 billion. This was approximately 0.5% of GDP. If, in the absence of these cuts, GDP was expected to grow at 3% a year, with these cuts his advisers estimated that GDP would grow only at 2.5% a year. The advice of the council members, however, came too late to influence the policy decisions.

2. During 1994, the U.S. government urged the Japanese to increase public spending and cut taxes to stimulate their economy. The Japanese came up with a plan and presented it to U.S. policymakers. U.S. policymakers looked at the effects of this plan by using multiplier analysis. The United States, however, felt that this plan did not provide enough fiscal stimulus and urged the Japanese to take more aggressive actions. In 1995, the Japanese did adopt a more aggressive plan which helped end their recession.

We use some special terminology to describe actions taken by the government that effect the economy. Government policies that increase total demand and GDP are called **expansionary policies**. Government policies that decrease total demand and GDP are **contractionary policies**. Tax cuts and spending increases are examples of expansionary policies. Tax increases and spending cuts are examples of contractionary policies.

Expansionary policies: Policy actions that lead to increases in output.

Contractionary policies: Policy actions that lead to decreases in output.

Budget deficit: The difference between a government's spending and its revenues from taxation.

When a government increases spending or cuts taxes to stimulate the economy, it will increase the government's **budget deficit**, the difference between its spending and its tax collections. To take an example, suppose the budget were initially balanced (spending equaled taxes) and the government increased spending. The government would now be running a budget deficit with spending exceeding taxation. To pay for the additional spending, the government must borrow money by selling government bonds or IOUs to the public. Traditional Keynesian models assume, as a first approximation, that this borrowing has no further significant effects on the economy. In a later chapter on deficits, we study the effects of government borrowing. As we will discuss, some economists believe that government borrowing can have some important additional effects on the economy because consumers will take into account the taxes necessary to pay the interest and principal on the government IOUs. However, traditional Keynesian models do not incorporate this effect.

Although Keynesian models are very simple and naturally leave out many important factors, they do illustrate an important lesson. An increase in government spending will increase the total demand for goods and services. Cutting taxes will increase the after-tax income of consumers and will also lead to an increase in the total demand for goods and services. In the short run, the level of GDP is determined by the demand for goods and services.

TEST *Your Understanding*

7 If the MPC is 0.4, what is the government-spending multiplier?

8 Using taxes and spending to control the level of GDP in the short run is known as Keynesian ____________ policy.

9 An increase in government purchases of $10 billion will shift up the $C + I + G$ line by __________ and increase GDP by this amount times the multiplier.

10 If the MPC is 0.8, by how much will GDP decrease if taxes are increased by $10 billion?

11 If economic advisers fear that the economy is growing too rapidly, what fiscal policies should they recommend?

Keynesian Fiscal Policy in U.S. History

Although the basic elements of Keynes's theory were developed in the 1930s, it took a long time until economic policy decisions were based on Keynesian principles. Many people associate Keynesian fiscal policy in the United States with actions taken by President Franklin Roosevelt during the 1930s. But as the Closer Look box "Fiscal Policy in the Great Depression" explains, this is a misleading view.

Although Keynesian fiscal policy was not deliberately used during the 1930s, the growth in military spending at the onset of World War II increased total demand in the economy and helped to pull the economy out of its long decade of poor economic performance. But to see Keynesian fiscal policy in action, we need to turn to the 1960s. It was not until the presidency of John F. Kennedy during the early 1960s that Keynesian fiscal policy came to be accepted.

Walter Heller, the chairman of the President's Council of Economic Advisors under John F. Kennedy, was a forceful advocate of Keynesian economics. From his perspective, the economy was operating far below its potential and a tax cut was the perfect medicine to bring the economy back to full employment. When Kennedy entered office, the unemployment rate stood at 6.7%. Heller believed that the unemployment rate at full employment was approximately 4%. He convinced Kennedy of the need for a tax program to stimulate the economy and Kennedy put forth an economic program based largely on Keynesian principles.

A Closer LOOK

Fiscal Policy in the Great Depression

The Great Depression in the United States lasted throughout the 1930s and did not really end until the beginning of World War II in the early 1940s. It was precisely during this period that Keynesian economics was born. According to Keynesian economics, expansionary fiscal policy—tax cuts and increased government spending—could pull the economy out of recession. Was Keynesian fiscal policy actually employed during the Great Depression?

According to E. Cary Brown, a former economics professor at the Massachusetts Institute of Technology, "Fiscal policy, then, seems to have been an unsuccessful recovery device in the 'thirties—not because it did not work, but because it was not tried." During the 1930s, politicians did not believe in Keynesian fiscal policy, largely because they feared the consequences of government budget deficits. According to Brown, fiscal policy was expansionary only during two years of the Great Depression, 1931 and 1936. In those years Congress voted for substantial payments to veterans, over the objections of Presidents Herbert Hoover and Franklin Roosevelt. Although government spending increased during the 1930s, so did taxes, resulting in no net fiscal expansion.

Source: After E. Cary Brown, "Fiscal Policy in the Thirties: A Reappraisal," *American Economic Review*, vol. 46, December 1956, pp. 863–868.

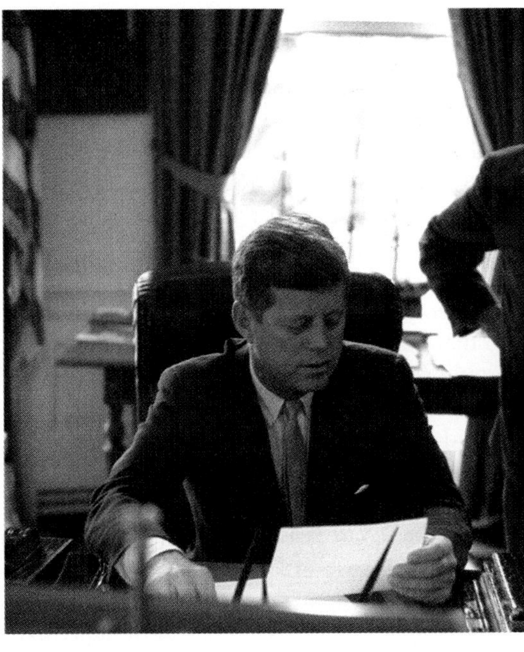

Keynesian fiscal policy was aggressively used during the presidency of John F. Kennedy.

Several other factors led the Kennedy administration to support the tax cut. First, tax rates were extremely high at the time. The top individual tax rate was 91%, compared to about 40% today. The corporate tax rate was 52%, compared to 35% today. Second, Heller convinced Kennedy that even if a tax cut led to a federal budget deficit (the gap between federal spending and taxes), it was not a problem. In 1961, the federal deficit was less than 1% of GDP and future projections indicated that the deficit would disappear as the economy grew because of higher tax revenues.

The tax cuts actually were enacted into law in February 1964, after Lyndon Johnson became president following Kennedy's assassination. The tax cuts included permanent cuts in tax rates for both individuals and corporations. Estimating the actual effects that the tax cuts had on the economy is difficult, because to have a valid comparison we need to estimate how the economy would have behaved *without* the tax cuts. The economy, however, grew at a rapid rate following the tax cuts. From 1963 to 1966, both real GDP and consumption grew at rates exceeding 4%. We cannot rule out the possibility that the economy could have grown this rapidly without the tax cuts. Nonetheless, the rapid growth during this period suggests that the tax cuts had the effect, predicted by Keynesian theory, of stimulating economic growth. (Some economists would argue that supply-side factors, such as lower marginal tax rates, could also have been important.)

The next major use of Keynesian theory in economic policy occurred in 1968. As the Vietnam war began and military spending increased, unemployment fell to very low levels. From 1966 to 1969, the overall unemployment rate fell below 4%. Policymakers became concerned that the economy was overheating and that inflationary pressures would emerge. In 1968, a temporary tax surcharge of 10% was enacted to reduce total demand for goods and services. The 10% surcharge was a tax on a tax, so that it raised tax bills by 10%. The surcharge was specifically designed to be temporary and was scheduled to expire within a year.

The surcharge did not decrease consumer spending as much as economists initially estimated. Part of the reason was that the tax increase was temporary. Economists who have studied consumption behavior have noticed that consumers

Permanent income: An estimate of a household's long-run average level of income.

often base their spending on an estimate of their long-run average income or **permanent income**, not simply on their current income.

For example, consider a salesman who usually earns $50,000 a year, although his income in any single year might be higher or lower than $50,000. Based on his permanent income, he consumes $45,000, for an MPC of 0.9 of his permanent income. If his income in one year is higher than average, say $55,000, he may still consume $45,000, as if he earned his normal $50,000, and save the rest.

The temporary, one-year tax surcharge did not have a major effect on the permanent income of households. Since their permanent income was not decreased very much by the surcharge, households that based their consumption decisions on their permanent income would be expected to maintain their prior level of consumption. Instead of reducing consumption, they would simply reduce their saving for the period that the surcharge was in effect. It appears that consumers acted in this manner, with the result that demand for goods and services did not decrease as much as economists anticipated.

During the 1970s, there were numerous changes in taxes and spending but no major fiscal policy initiatives. There was a tax rebate and other tax incentives in 1975 following the recession in 1973. However, these tax changes were relatively mild. As inflation began to increase in the 1970s, policymakers became reluctant to stimulate the economy too aggressively for fear of raising the inflation rate. We discuss economic policies toward inflation in a later chapter.

The tax cuts enacted during 1981 at the beginning of the first term of President Ronald Reagan were quite significant. However, they were not proposed on Keynesian grounds, to increase aggregate demand. Instead, the tax cuts were justified on the basis of improving economic incentives and increasing the supply of output. As we discussed in the chapter on Classical Economics, taxes can have important effects on the supply of labor, saving, and economic growth. Proponents of the 1981 tax cuts emphasized these effects and not increases in aggregate demand. Nonetheless, the tax cuts did appear to increase consumer demand and helped the economy recover from the back-to-back recessions in the early 1980s.

By the mid-1980s, large government budget deficits began to emerge. As policymakers became more concerned with budget deficits, traditional Keynesian fiscal policy took a back seat. As we noted, Keynesian fiscal policy is based on the principle that changes in taxes and government spending should be evaluated primarily on what effect they have on the economy, not what they do to the budget deficit. But as deficits grew in size and became the focus of attention, there was no longer interest in using active Keynesian fiscal policy to manage the economy. While there still were spending and tax changes in the 1980s and 1990s, relatively few of them were justified solely by traditional Keynesian thinking.

To understand economic policy in the 1980s and 1990s, we will need to turn our attention to the Federal Reserve and monetary policy as well as emerging concerns in the Congress about government budget deficits. These topics are discussed in detail in later chapters.

Automatic Stabilizers

Automatic stabilizers: Economic institutions that reduce economic fluctuations without any explicit action being taken.

With a slight addition to our basic model, we can explain one of the important facts in U.S. economic history. Figure 9 plots the rate of growth of U.S. real GDP from 1871 to 1995. It is quite apparent from the graph that the U.S. economy was much more stable after World War II than before. The reason is that government taxes and transfer payments (such as unemployment insurance and welfare payments) grew sharply after the war. Taxes and transfers act as **automatic stabilizers**, economic institutions that automatically reduce economic fluctuations.

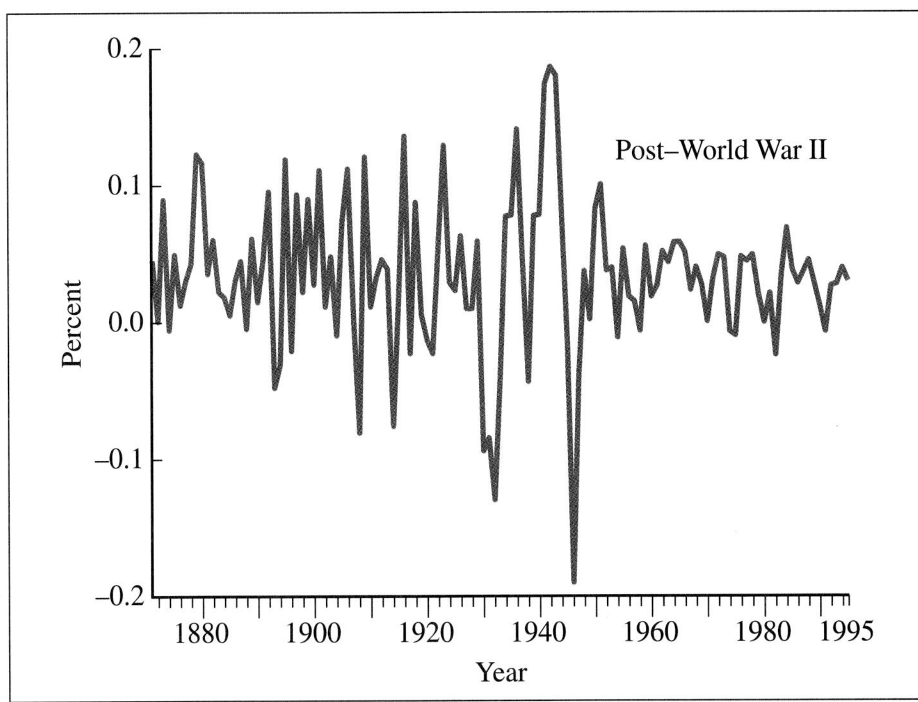

Figure 9

Growth Rate of U.S. GDP, 1871–1995

Sources: Angus Maddison, *Dynamic Forces in Capitalist Development* (New York: Oxford University Press, 1991); and the *Economic Report of the President* (Washington, DC: U.S. Government Printing Office, yearly).

Here is how the automatic stabilizers work. When income is high, the government collects more taxes and pays out less transfer payments. Since the government is taking funds out of the hands of consumers, this tends to reduce consumer spending. On the other hand, when output is low (such as during recessions), the government collects less taxes and pays out more transfer payments; this tends to increase

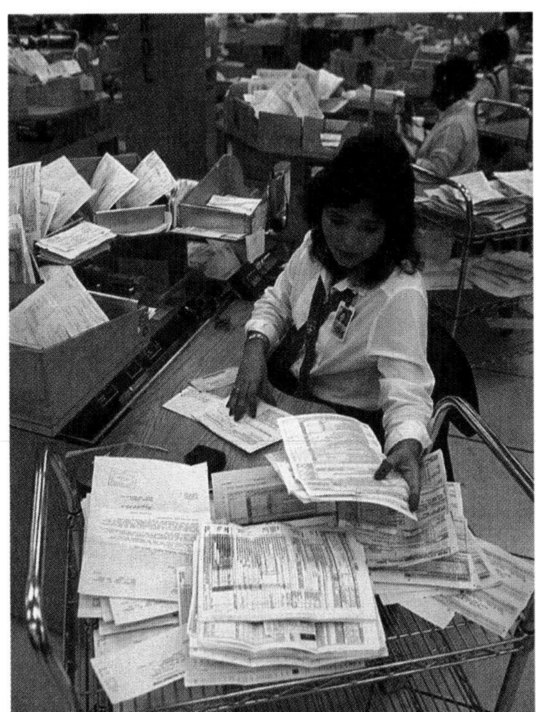

While this Internal Revenue Service worker in Austin, Texas may not realize it, she is an integral part of a process that helps to stabilize the U.S. economy.

consumer spending since the government is putting funds into the hands of consumers. The automatic stabilizers prevent consumption from falling as much in bad times and rising as much in good times. This stabilizes the economy without any need for decisions from Congress or the White House.

To see how automatic stabilizers work in our model, we must take into account that the government levies income taxes by applying a tax rate to the level of income. To simplify, suppose there were a single tax rate of 0.2 (20%) and income were \$100. The government would then collect $0.2 \times \$100 = \$20$ in taxes.

In general, we can view the total taxes collected from by the government T as a product of the tax rate, t, and output, y:

$$T = ty$$

Consumer's after-tax income will be $y - ty$ or $y(1 - t)$. If consumption depends on after-tax income, we have the consumption function:

$$C = C_a + b(1 - t)y$$

This is the consumption function with income taxes. The only difference between the consumption function *with* income taxes and *without* is that the marginal propensity to consume is now adjusted for taxes and becomes $b(1 - t)$. The reason for this adjustment is that consumers keep only a fraction $(1 - t)$ of their income; the rest goes to the government. When income increases by \$1, consumers' after-tax incomes only increase by $\$1 \times (1 - t)$, of which they spend a fraction b.

Raising the tax rate therefore lowers the MPC adjusted for taxes. Figure 10 shows the consequences of raising tax rates. With a higher tax rate, the government takes a higher fraction of income and less is left over for consumers. Recall that the slope of the $C + I + G$ line is the marginal propensity to consume. Raising the tax rate lowers the adjusted MPC and reduces the slope of this line. The $C + I + G$ line now intersects the 45° line at a lower level of income. Output falls from y_0 to y_1.

Figure 10

Increase in Tax Rates

An increase in tax rates decreases the slope of the $C + I + G$ line. This lowers output and reduces the multiplier.

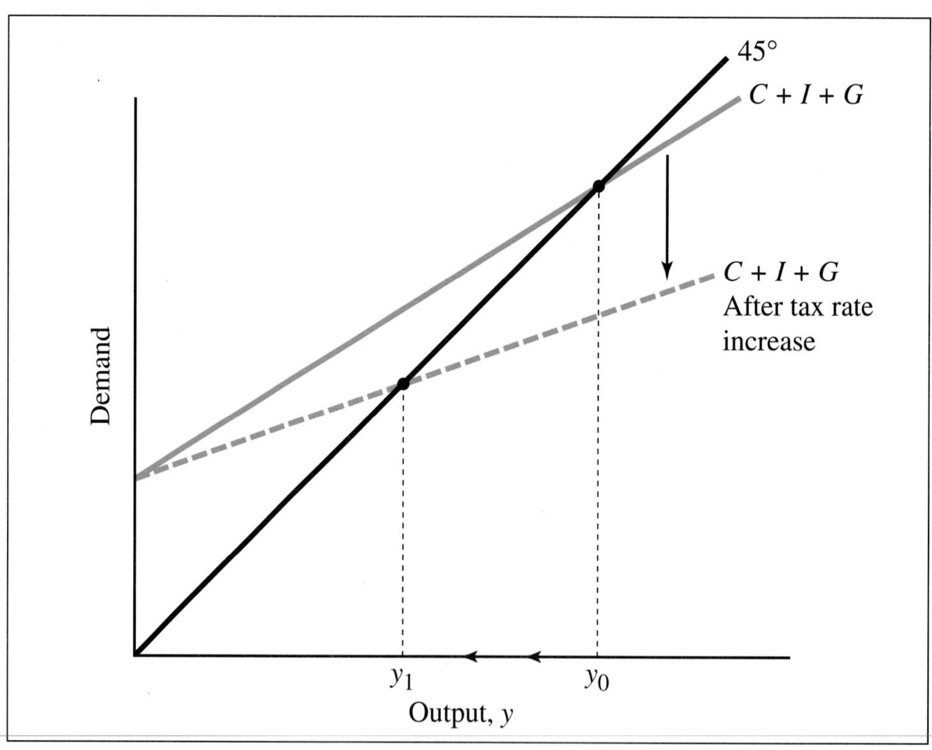

Remember that a smaller marginal propensity to consume also leads to a lower value for the multiplier. As tax rates increase and the adjusted MPC falls, the multiplier will decrease. A smaller multiplier means that any shocks to investment, for example, will have less of an impact on the economy.

Now that we have introduced income taxes into our model, we can see how automatic stabilizers work. Since World War II, taxes and transfer payments in the United States have increased sharply. As we have seen, higher tax rates will *lower* the multiplier and make the economy less susceptible to shocks. With higher taxes and transfers, there is a much looser link between fluctuations in disposable personal income and fluctuations in GDP. Since disposable personal income is more stable, consumption spending is more stable as well. Thus there is a smaller multiplier and the economy is more stable.

It is important to emphasize that automatic stabilizers work silently in the background and do their job *without* requiring explicit action by policymakers. Total tax collections rise and fall with GDP without requiring that policymakers change tax rates. The fact that the automatic stabilizers work without enacting any laws is particularly important at times when it is difficult to obtain a political consensus for taking any action and policymakers are reluctant to use active Keynesian fiscal policy.

Other factors contribute to the stability of the economy. We discussed that consumers base their spending decisions in part on their permanent income and not just on their current level of income. If households base their consumption decisions partly on their permanent or long-run income, they will not be very sensitive to changes in their current income. If their consumption does not change very much with current income, the marginal propensity to consume out of current income will be small, which will make the multiplier small as well. Thus when consumers base their decisions on long-run factors, not just on their current level of income, the economy tends to be stabilized.

EXPORTS AND IMPORTS

With international trade becoming an increasingly important economic and political issue, it is critical to understand how exports and imports affect the level of GDP. Two simple modifications of our model will allow us to understand how exports and imports affect GDP in the short run.

Exports and imports affect GDP through their influence on the worldwide demand for goods and services produced in the United States. An increase in exports will increase the demand for goods produced in the United States. Imports, on the other hand, are foreign goods purchased by U.S. residents. When we import goods rather than purchase them from our domestic producers, this will reduce the demand for U.S. goods. For example, if we spend in total \$10 billion in automobiles but import \$3 billion, only \$7 billion is spent on U.S. automobiles.

To highlight the effects from exports and imports, we will ignore government spending and taxes. In the appendix we present a complete model with both government and the foreign sector. To modify our model to allow for exports and imports, we need to take two steps:

1. Add exports, X, as another source of demand for U.S. goods and services. We assume that the level of exports (foreign demand for U.S. products) is given.
2. Subtract imports, M, from total spending by U.S. residents. We will assume that imports, like consumption, increase with the level of income.

Consumers will import more goods as income rises. We can write this as

$$\text{imports} = M = my$$

Marginal propensity to import: The fraction of additional income that is spent on imports.

where m is a fraction known as the **marginal propensity to import**. We subtract this fraction from the overall marginal propensity to consume (b) to obtain the MPC for spending on *domestic goods*, $b - m$. For example, if $b = 0.8$ and $m = 0.2$, then for every $1 that GDP increases, total consumption increases by $0.80 but spending on domestic goods increases only by $0.60 since $0.20 is spent on imports. The MPC adjusted for imports is $(0.8 - 0.2) = 0.6$.

Figure 11 shows how equilibrium income is determined in an open economy. We plot total demand for U.S. goods on our familiar 45° graph. The vertical intercept of the demand line is $(C_A + I + X)$. The slope of the line is $(b - m)$, the MPC adjusted for imports. Equilibrium output is determined where the demand line for U.S. goods crosses the 45° line.

Now let's examine an application of our model. Suppose the Japanese decide to buy another $5 billion worth of goods from the United States. What will happen to domestic output? Panel A of Figure 12 shows the effect of an increase in exports. The demand line will shift up by the increase in exports (ΔX). This will increase equilibrium income from y_0 to y_1.

The increase in income will be larger than the increase in exports because of a multiplier effect. The multiplier will be based on the MPC adjusted for trade. For example, if $b = 0.8$ and $m = 0.2$, the adjusted MPC $(b - m)$ is 0.6 and the multiplier will be $1/(1 - 0.6) = 2.5$. Therefore, a $5 billion increase in exports will lead to a $12.5 billion increase in GDP.

Suppose instead that U.S. residents become more attracted to foreign goods and, as a result, our marginal propensity to import increases. What happens to GDP? Panel B of Figure 12 depicts the effect of an increased desire to import foreign goods. The adjusted MPC $(b - m)$ will fall as the marginal propensity to import increases. This reduces the slope of the demand line, and output will fall from y_0 to y_1.

We can now understand why our domestic political leaders are so eager to sell our goods abroad. Whether it is electronics or weapons, increased U.S. exports will increase U.S. GDP and reduce unemployment in the short run. At the same time, we can also understand why politicians will find "buy American" policies attractive in

Figure 11

Determining Output in an Open Economy

Output is determined where the demand for domestic goods equals output.

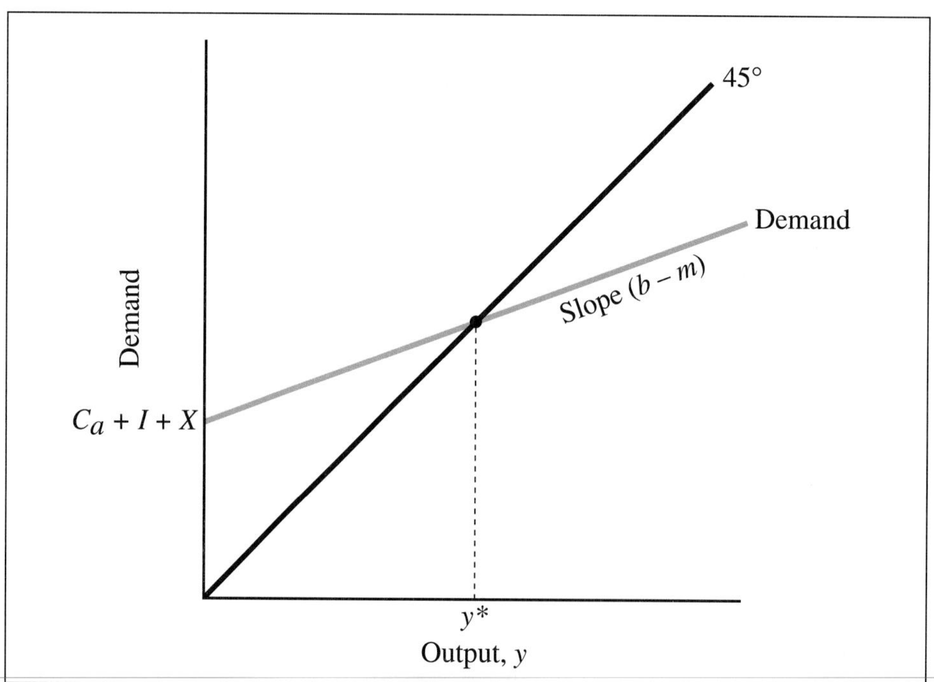

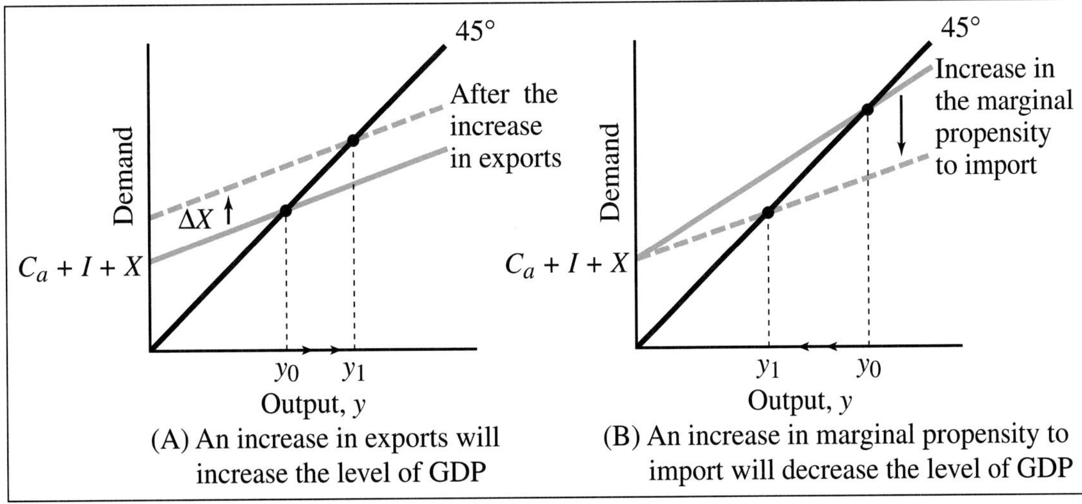

Figure 12 Increase in Exports and Imports

the short run. To the extent that U.S. residents buy U.S. goods rather than imports, we will experience a higher level of output in the short run.

FINAL REMINDER

It is important to emphasize that *all* the models in this chapter are based on short-run considerations. Policies appropriate for the short run are not necessarily appropriate for the long run. In this chapter we have seen that an increase in desired consumption spending will raise equilibrium output in the short run. But in our chapter on long run growth, we saw that higher saving (lower consumption) would increase output in the long run. The models in this chapter are designed only to analyze short-run fluctuations in output. They are not designed for long-run policy advice. In the next several chapters, we continue our study of short-run models by including interest rates and monetary policy as determinants of demand. Later, we will see how the economy makes the transition from the short run to the long run.

Using the TOOLS

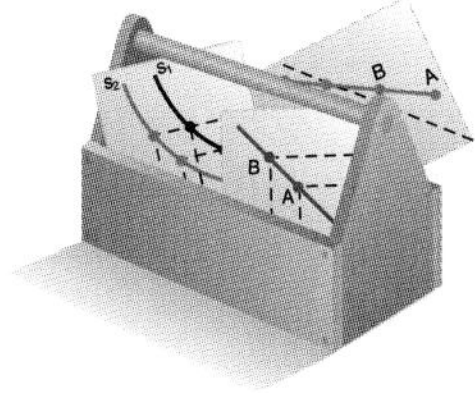

In this chapter we developed the graphical tools and formulas for Keynesian economics. Here is an opportunity to do your own economic analysis.

1. A Shock to Consumption

We can think of a "shock" to consumption as a change in autonomous consumption C_a. Economic historian Peter Temin argued that the Great Depression was caused by a negative shock to consumption. Use the graphs in this chapter to show how a negative shock to consumption can lead to a fall in output.

2. Estimating Changes to Output

a. Suppose that $C = C_a + 0.6y$ and a shock decreases C_a by \$10 billion. By how much will GDP decrease?

b. An economy has a MPC of 0.6. By how much will a \$10 billion increase in government purchases increase GDP? By how much will a \$10 billion increase in taxes decrease GDP?

3. Unemployment Insurance and Economic Fluctuations

Using the idea of automatic stabilizers, explain why states with more generous unemployment insurance programs will experience smaller fluctuations in output than states with less generous programs.

4. ECONOMIC DETECTIVE– *The Netherlands's Multiplier*

Some economists argued that the multiplier for government spending in the Netherlands was smaller than in the United States. As an economic detective, can you explain this difference? (*Hint*: Imports and exports are a higher fraction of GDP in the Netherlands.)

SUMMARY

In this chapter we explained the logic of Keynesian economics. It showed how the demand for goods and services determines GDP in the short run when prices are fixed. It also discussed the role that government taxes and spending play in determining output. Finally, we showed how the level of exports and imports can affect the economy in the short run. Here are the main points to remember from this chapter:

1. The level of GDP in the *short run* is determined by the total demand for goods and services.
2. Consumption spending consists of two parts: one part independent of income (autonomous consumption) and another part that depends on the level of income.
3. An increase in spending will typically lead to a larger increase in GDP: This effect is called the multiplier.
4. In the short run, increases in government spending lead to increases in GDP; increases in taxes lead to decreases in GDP.
5. Keynesian fiscal policies were used aggressively in the 1960s to manage the economy but concerns about budget deficits limit the use of these policies today.
6. Higher tax rates reduce fluctuations in GDP caused by shocks to spending.
7. Increases in exports lead to increases in GDP; increases in imports lead to lower GDP.

KEY TERMS

automatic stabilizer, *522*
autonomous consumption, *511*
budget deficit, *519*
consumption function, *510*
contractionary policies, *519*
disposable personal income, *517*
equilibrium output, *509*
expansionary policies, *519*
Keynesian fiscal policy, *516*
marginal propensity to consume (MPC), *511*
marginal propensity to import, *526*
marginal propensity to save (MPS), *511*
multiplier, *515*
permanent income, *522*

PROBLEMS AND DISCUSSION QUESTIONS

1. Explain the process by which GDP will increase if the current level of production is less than demand.
2. Why does equilibrium output occur where the spending line crosses the 45° line?
3. Why is there a multiplier in the economy?
4. Explain carefully how a tax cut will lead to a higher level of GDP in the short run.
5. Why would an increase in exports to Mexico raise U.S. GDP?

6. Why does a smaller multiplier for the economy typically reduce economic fluctuations?
7. Explain why Keynes suggested that building pyramids was good for the Egyptian economy. Can you think of a modern equivalent of the pyramids for our society?
8. a. Suppose that clothing stores anticipate a good season and add substantially to inventories in their stores. What will happen to GDP?
   b. Suppose an economist sees that inventories are currently increasing. Does this necessarily mean that there are increases in demand?
9. Sometimes newspapers state that if the economies of Europe and Japan grow rapidly, this will increase the growth of real GDP in the United States. Using our model with exports and imports, explain the logic of this argument.

Take It to the Net

We invite you to visit the O'Sullivan/Sheffrin page on the Prentice Hall Web site at:

http://www.prenhall.com/osullivan/

for this chapter's World Wide Web exercise.

MODEL ANSWERS FOR THIS CHAPTER

Chapter-Opening Questions

1. Cutting taxes on consumers leads to higher consumer spending which increases demand and, in the short run, increases output.
2. The U.S. economy is more stable today because of the presence of automatic stabilizers.
3. Increased consumer confidence can lead to higher consumer spending which will lead to higher GDP in the short run.
4. An increase in government spending of $10 billion will lead to an increase of GDP of more than $10 billion because of the multiplier in the economy.
5. Since exports are a component of the demand for an economy's goods and services, a reduction in exports could cause a recession.

Test Your Understanding

1. At the point where the demand line crosses the 45° line, demand equals output.
2. If production exceeds demand, inventories will pile up and firms will cut production.
3. It is the MPC.
4. up
5. 750
6. 0.3
7. The multiplier is 1.66.
8. fiscal
9. $10 billion
10. GDP will decrease by $40 billion (the tax multiplier is –4).
11. Increase taxes or cut government spending.

Using the Tools

1. A Shock to Consumption

   A decrease in autonomous consumption will shift down the vertical intercept of the $C + I + G$ line. This will lead to a fall in output. A large enough fall could, in principle, cause a major fall in output.
2. Estimating Changes to Output
   a. In this case, the multiplier is $1/(1 - 0.6) = 2.5$. Therefore, output will fall by $25 billion.
   b. With an MPC of 0.6, the multiplier is 2.5 $[1/(1 - 0.6)]$. An increase in government spending of $10 billion will therefore lead to an increase in GDP of $25 billion. With an MPC of 0.6, the tax multiplier is –1.5. Thus GDP will fall by $15 billion from a $10 billion increase in taxes.
3. Unemployment Insurance and Economic Fluctuations

   With unemployment insurance, people receive payments when they become unemployed. This reduces the drop in their income by replacing their lost wages with government subsidies. Since income does not fall by as much, neither will consumption. States with more generous programs will therefore have less fluctuations in consumption and more stable output.
4. Economic Detective: The Netherlands's Multiplier

   In the Netherlands, the marginal propensity to import, *m*, is much higher than in the United

States. This is a typical pattern for small countries. The adjusted MPC $[(b - m)]$ will tend to be lower in the Netherlands than in the United States. Since countries with a smaller adjusted MPC will have a lower multiplier, the Netherlands will have a lower multiplier.

Appendix

Formulas for Equilibrium Income and the Multiplier

In this appendix we use simple algebra to calculate a formula for equilibrium income and show how to derive the multipliers in the text. We start with the simplest model without government but also derive several multipliers for fiscal policy. Finally, we show how to derive equilibrium income with both government and the foreign sector.

To find the formula for equilibrium income, we need to use simple algebra to solve a single equation for the unknown value of y. Here are the steps to follow:

1. Equilibrium output occurs where

$$\text{output} = \text{demand} = C + I$$

2. Substitute in y for output and the expression for the consumption function:

$$y = (C_a + by) + I$$

3. Collect all terms in y on the left side of the equation:

$$y - by = C_a + I$$

4. Factor the left side:

$$y(1 - b) = C_a + I$$

5. Divide both sides by $(1 - b)$:

$$y^* = \frac{C_a + I}{1 - b}$$

This is the formula for equilibrium income in the text.

Now let's find the multiplier. What we need to do is to use our formula to calculate equilibrium income for both an initial and new level of investment and then find out how output changes with the changes in investment. For an original level of investment at I_0, we have

$$y_0 = \frac{C_a + I_0}{1 - b}$$

For a new level of investment at I_1, we have

$$y_1 = \frac{C_a + I_1}{1 - b}$$

The change in output Δy is the difference between the two levels:

$$\Delta y = y_1 - y_0$$

Substituting for the levels of income, we have

$$\Delta y = \frac{C_a + I_1}{1 - b} - \frac{C_a + I_0}{1 - b}$$

Since the denominator in both expressions is $(1 - b)$, we can subtract the numerators from another and put the difference over $(1 - b)$:

$$\Delta y = \frac{I_1 - I_0}{1 - b}$$

Finally, since $(I_1 - I_0)$ is just the change in investment, ΔI, we have

$$\Delta y = \frac{\Delta I}{1 - b}$$

or

$$\frac{\Delta y}{\Delta I} = \frac{1}{1 - b} = \text{multiplier}$$

The multiplier is the ratio of the change in income to the change in investment spending.

Here is another way to derive the expression of the multiplier which helps to illustrate its underlying logic. Suppose that investment spending increases by \$1. Since spending determines output, output will rise by \$1 as well. However, since consumption depends on income, consumption will increase by the marginal propensity to consume times the change in income. This means that as output rises by \$1, consumption will increase by $(b \times \$1)$. Since spending determines output, this additional increase in consumer demand will cause output to rise by a further $(b \times \$1)$. But again, as output and income increase, consumption will increase by the product of the MPC and the change in income, which in this case will now be $b \times (b \times \$1)$ or $b^2 \times \$1$. As we allow this process to continue, the total change in output will be

$$\Delta y = \$1 + (\$1 \times b) + (\$1 \times b^2) + (\$1 \times b^3) + \cdots$$

or

$$\Delta y = \$1 \times (1 + b + b^2 + b^3 + \cdots)$$

Using a formula from algebra for this infinite series, we have

$$\Delta y = \$1 \times \frac{1}{1 - b}$$

The change in output is the initial change in investment (in this case \$1) times the multiplier.

We can now introduce government spending and taxes. Recall that government spending becomes another determinant of demand and that consumption depends on after-tax income. Following the same steps to solve for equilibrium income as above, we have

$$\text{output} = \text{demand} = C + I + G$$

$$y = C_a + b(y - T) + I + G$$

We solve this equation for y by first collecting all terms in y on the left side and the other terms on the right side:

$$y - by = C_a - bT + I + G$$

We then factor the left side:

$$y(1 - b) = C_a - bT + I + G$$

Then divide both sides by $(1 - b)$:

$$y^* = \frac{C_a - bT + I + G}{1 - b}$$

Using this formula and the method outlined above, we can find the multipliers for changes in taxes and government spending:

$$\text{government spending multiplier} = \frac{1}{1 - b}$$

$$\text{tax multiplier} = \frac{-b}{1 - b}$$

An increase in government spending has a larger multiplier than a reduction of taxes by an equal amount. Government spending increases total demand directly but reductions in taxes first affect incomes for consumers. Since consumers will save a part of the tax cut, not all of the tax cut is spent. Therefore, the tax multiplier is smaller (in absolute value) than the government spending multiplier.

As we explained in the text, since government spending has a larger multiplier than taxes, equal increases in spending and taxes, called "balanced budget" increases, will increase total output. For equal dollar increases in both taxes and spending, the positive effects from the spending increase will outweigh the negative effects from the tax increase. To find the balanced budget multiplier, just add the government spending and tax multipliers:

$$\text{balanced budget multiplier} = \text{government spending multiplier} + \text{tax multiplier}$$

$$= \frac{1}{1 - b} + \frac{-b}{1 - b}$$

$$= \frac{1 - b}{1 - b}$$

$$= 1$$

The balanced budget multiplier is equal to 1. In other words, a \$10 billion increase in taxes and spending will increase GDP by \$10 billion.

Finally, we show how to derive equilibrium income with both government spending, taxes, and the foreign sector. First, recall that equilibrium output occurs where output equals demand. We now must include demand from both the government and the foreign sector. Demand from the foreign sector is exports minus imports:

$$\text{output} = \text{demand} = C + I + G + X - M$$

Consumption depends on disposable income:

$$C = C_a + b(y - T)$$

and imports depend on the level of output:

$$M = my$$

Substitute the equations for consumption and imports into the equation where output equals demand:

$$y = C_a + b(y - \text{T}) + I + G + X - my$$

We solve this equation for y by first collecting all terms in y on the left side and the other terms on the right side:

$$y - (b - m)y = C_a - bT + I + G + X$$

We then factor the left side:

$$y[1 - (b - m)] = C_a - bT + I + G + X$$

Then divide both sides by $[1 - (b - m)]$:

$$y^* = \frac{C_a - bT + I + G + X}{1 - (b - m)}$$

This is the expression for equilibrium income in an open economy with government. It can be used, following the method we outlined, to calculate multipliers in the open economy.

Using the **TOOLS**

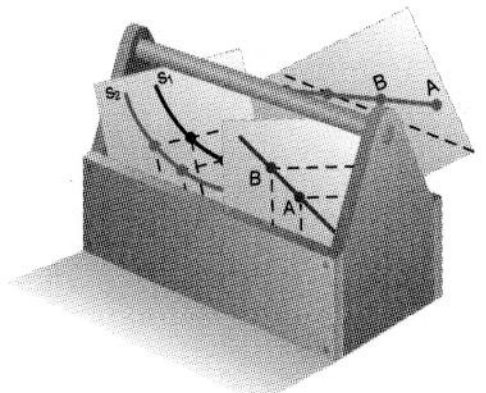

1. Find the Multiplier

An economy has a marginal propensity to consume $b = 0.6$ and a marginal propensity to import $m = 0.2$. What is the multiplier for government spending for this economy?

2. The Effects of Taxes and Spending

Suppose the economy has a marginal propensity to consume of $b = 0.4$. The government increases spending by \$2 billion and raises taxes by \$1 billion. What happens to equilibrium income?

MODEL ANSWERS FOR THIS APPENDIX

Using the Tools

1. Find the Multiplier

   Since $b = 0.6$ and $m = 0.2$, the marginal-propensity to consume adjusted for taxes is 0.4. Thus the multiplier is 1/(1 – 0.4), or 1.67. Alternatively, you could use the last formula in the appendix to derive it explicitly.

2. The Effects of Taxes and Spending

   The government spending multiplier in this case is 1/(1 – 0.4), or 1.67. The tax multiplier is –0.4/(1 – 0.4), or –0.67. Thus equilibrium income will increase by \$2 billion (1.67) – \$1 billion (0.67) = \$2.67 billion.

CHAPTER 26

Investment and Financial Intermediation

Throughout U.S. history, ordinary people have always been deeply suspicious of Wall Street. Does all that financial wheeling and dealing—the mergers, the leveraged buyouts, the trading in exotic securities, and the speculation—make the U.S. economy more productive? Or are all those New York financiers really nothing but parasites, living off the hard work of the citizens of Main Street USA? And don't they cost ordinary workers when mergers of large corporations result in downsizing and layoffs?

No one would deny that Wall Street financiers are keenly interested in making money and that some are extraordinarily greedy. Many mistakes have been made on Wall Street, just as they have in corporate boardrooms and workplaces throughout the world. But the vast frenzy in Wall Street and other financial markets of the world does contribute to the economy. It actually makes it easier for economies to invest in the future.

In this chapter we study the role of investment in the economy and the part that financial institutions play in facilitating that investment. In the previous chapter, we assumed that the level of investment was constant and we ignored the process by which investment actually takes place. In this chapter we learn about the factors that govern investment decisions and how financial markets make it easier for an economy to invest.

In this chapter we gain a number of key insights into investment and finance. For example, we will discover answers to these real-world questions:

1. Why does investment spending depend on interest rates, among other factors?
2. Why do businesses and homeowners want to borrow in inflationary times, even when interest rates are high?
3. How can banks and other financial intermediaries make risk seem to vanish into thin air?
4. Why would most investments in the economy fail to take place if there were no financial institutions?
5. Why do "runs" on healthy and profitable banks, which occurred during the Great Depression, rarely happen today?

An investment can be broadly defined as an action taken today that has costs today but provides benefits in the future. If a firm builds a new plant, it incurs costs today but will earn revenues in the future. College students incur costs to attend school now for the sake of higher earnings in the future. A government spends money today to build a dam in order to have a source of hydroelectric power in the future. All these are examples of investments. Notice that we're using the term *investment* in a broader sense than we did when discussing private domestic investment in the GDP accounts. Here an investment is an action taken by any party, such as our college student, that has costs today but provides benefits in the future.

To understand how investment decisions are made, we need to learn about interest rates. In this chapter we introduce the distinction between nominal and real interest rates. **Nominal interest rates** are the rates actually charged in the market. **Real interest rates** are nominal rates adjusted for inflation. We will see in this chapter how real interest rates affect investment. This will be an application of the reality principle: A firm will be interested in the real value of its profits.

Financial institutions such as banks, savings and loans, and insurance companies all play an important role in making it easier for an economy to invest. All these organizations receive funds from savers and channel them to investors. We will see that these institutions, which we call **financial intermediaries**, help to reduce the risks and costs associated with investment and allow a greater volume of investment to occur in the economy.

Nominal interest rates: Interest rates that are quoted in the market.

Real interest rate: The nominal interest rate minus the actual inflation rate.

Financial intermediaries: Organizations that receive funds from savers and channel them to investors.

INVESTMENT: A PLUNGE INTO THE UNKNOWN

We defined investments as actions that have costs today but provide benefits in the future. Investments are trade-offs that occur over time: Firms or individuals incur costs today in the hope of future gain. But one important aspect of investment decisions is that the payoffs occur in the future and are not known with certainty. Investments are a plunge into the unknown.

Consider a few examples. When an automobile firm builds a new plant because it anticipates future demand for its cars, it is taking a gamble. Suppose the new model proves to be unpopular, or the economy goes into a recession and consumers cut back their purchases of all cars. The firm will have made an unwise investment decision, building a new plant when it was not needed. In another example, suppose that a government builds nuclear plants but citizens decide they are unsafe and force the plants to be closed. The government in this case would have wasted resources on this investment.

Because the future is uncertain, firms and individuals are constantly revising their estimates of the future. Sometimes they may be optimistic and decide to increase their investment spending; at other times, they may turn pessimistic and cut back on investment spending. Sometimes these changes in moods can occur rather suddenly and lead to sharp swings in investment spending. John Maynard Keynes emphasized that these sharp swings in moods were often irrational and perhaps reflected our most basic, primal instincts. He often referred to what he called the *animal spirits* of investors.

In trying to estimate the future course of events, firms will look carefully at current developments. If economic growth is currently sluggish, firms may project that it will be sluggish in the future as well. On the other hand, if there is an upsurge in economic growth, firms may become more optimistic and increase their investment spending. Investment spending tends to be closely related to the current pace of economic growth. One theory of investment spending, known as the **accelerator theory**, emphasizes the role of expected growth in real GDP on investment spending. When real GDP growth is expected to be high, firms anticipate that their investments in plant and equipment will be profitable and therefore increase their total investment spending.

Accelerator theory: The theory of investment that emphasizes that current investment spending depends positively on the expected future growth of real GDP.

Projections for the future and the animal spirits of investors both are likely to move in conjunction with GDP growth. For these reasons we would expect that investment spending would be a very volatile component of GDP. As Figure 1 indicates, this is indeed the case.

Figure 1 plots total investment spending as a share of U.S. GDP from 1976 to 1995. Several points about this figure deserve emphasis. First, over this period, the share of investment in GDP ranged from a low of nearly 13% to a high of nearly 19%—a dramatic difference of 6 percentage points of GDP. Second, these swings in investment spending often occur over rather short periods. During periods of recessions, investment spending falls sharply. Investment spending is highly **procyclical**, meaning that it increases during booms and falls during recessions.

Procyclical: A component of GDP is procyclical if it rises and falls with the overall level of GDP.

Traders react rapidly as rumors and news reach the floor of the New York Stock Exchange.

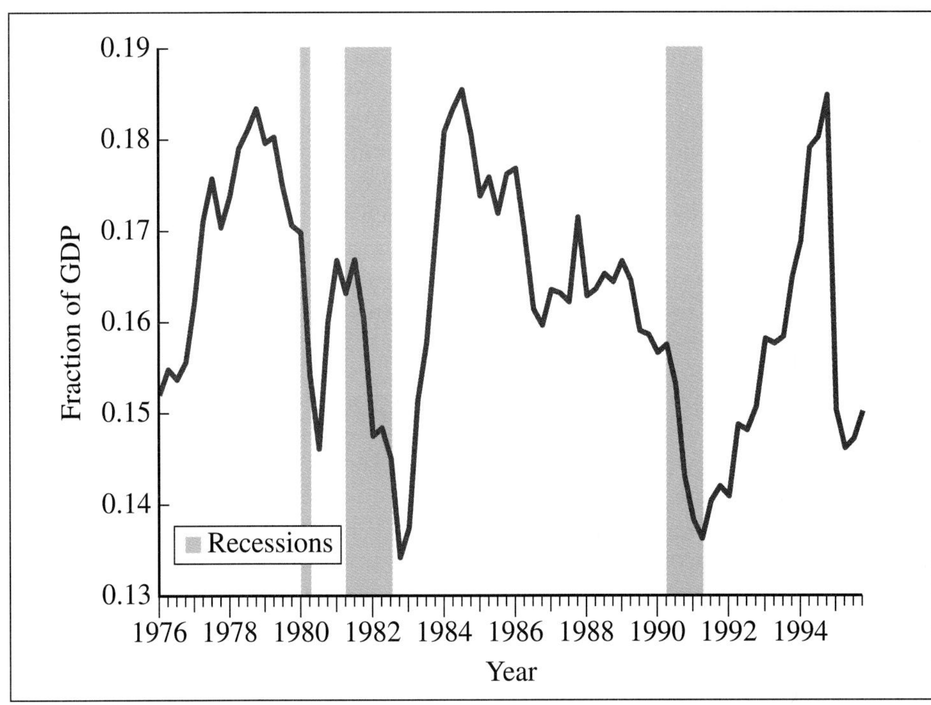

Figure 1

Investment Spending as a Share of U.S. GDP, 1976–1995

Source: Data from *Economic Report of the President* (Washington, DC: U.S. Government Printing Office, yearly).

Although investment spending is procyclical, there are often differences among different types of investment. Figure 2 shows that two important components of investment—nonresidential structures and producers' durable equipment—behaved somewhat differently during the last U.S. recession and recovery. Although both types of investment fell in 1991, investment in structures was much slower to recover, and even by 1995 it was still below its prerecession level. Since structures last a long time, firms needed to be sure that the recessionary period had truly ended before resuming their normal levels of investment. Equipment investment, however, recovered rapidly and by 1992 had reached its prerecession level.

Although investment spending is a much smaller component of GDP than consumption, its volatility makes it very important in understanding business fluctuations. Recall that changes in investment are amplified by the multiplier. If the multiplier is 1.5 and investment spending initially falls by 1% of GDP, then GDP will fall by 1.5%. However, if the fall in GDP makes firms more pessimistic than before, they may cut investment back even further. This will lead to still further reductions in GDP. In principle, a small initial fall in investment can trigger a much

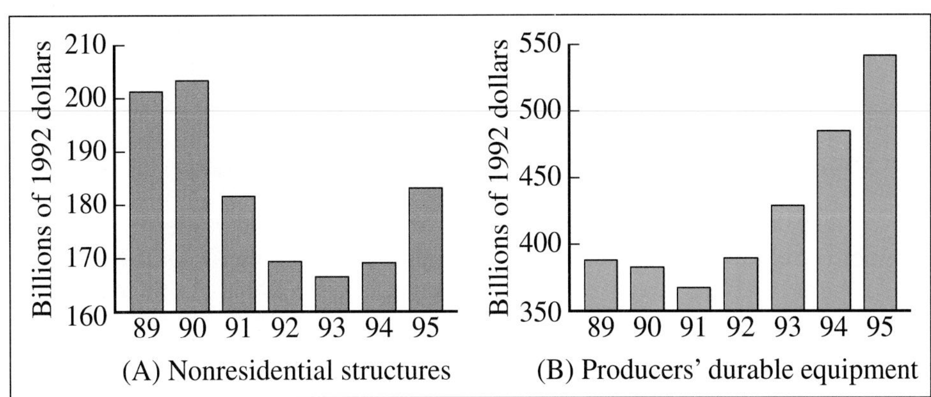

Figure 2

Investment in Structures and Equipment in the Early 1990s

Source: Data from *Economic Report of the President* (Washington, DC: U.S. Government Printing Office, yearly).

Multiplier-accelerator model: A model in which a downturn in real GDP leads to a sharp fall in investment, which, in turn, triggers further reductions in GDP through the multiplier.

larger fall in GDP. Nobel laureate Paul Samuelson emphasized these interactions with his **multiplier-accelerator model.** In this model a downturn in real GDP would lead to a sharp fall in investment, which, in turn, would entail further reductions in GDP through the multiplier for investment spending.

Investment spending does not depend just on psychology or on expectations about real GDP growth in the future. Since investments are examples of trade-offs (the present versus the future), the terms at which the firm can make the trade-off between the present and the future will also be important. To understand the price at which firms or individuals can make trade-offs between the present and the future, we now turn to a discussion of interest rates.

NOMINAL AND REAL INTEREST RATES

We are all familiar with interest rates in our everyday life. For example, if you deposit \$100 in a bank and the interest rate the bank will pay you is 6% a year, then at the end of one year you will have \$106 (\$100 × 1.06).

Bond: A promise or IOU to pay money in the future in exchange for money now.

There are many other familiar examples of interest rates. If you borrow money for college from a bank, the bank will require you to pay the funds back with interest. If a hardware store borrows money from a bank to purchase its inventory, it will have to pay the funds back to the bank with interest. Or you may buy a **bond** from the government or a corporation. A bond is a promise to pay money in the future. If you purchase a \$1,000 bond for one year at a 6% interest rate, you will receive \$1,060 (\$1000 × 1.06) next year from the issuer, to whom you have essentially lent your \$1,000.

The interest rates quoted in the market—at savings and loans, or banks or for bonds—are called *nominal interest rates*. These are the actual rates that individuals and firms pay or receive when they borrow money or lend money. There are many different interest rates in the economy, as the Closer Look box "A Variety of Interest Rates" illustrates.

When there is inflation, we have seen that it is important to correct for changes in prices to measure the true costs of borrowing or lending. This is an application of the reality principle.

Reality PRINCIPLE

What matters to people is the real value or purchasing power of money or income, not its face value.

Economists take inflation into account by distinguishing between real and nominal interest rates.

The *real rate of interest* is defined as the nominal interest rate minus the inflation rate:

$$\text{real rate} = \text{nominal rate} - \text{inflation rate}$$

For example, if the nominal rate is 6% and the inflation rate is 4%, the real rate of interest is 2% (6 – 4 = 2).

To understand what the real rate of interest means, consider this example. Suppose you have \$100 and there is 4% inflation. This means that next year you will have to hold \$104 to have the same purchasing power you have today. You now deposit the \$100 in a bank that pays 6% interest. At the end of the year, you have \$106 (\$100 × 1.06).

A Closer LOOK

A Variety of Interest Rates

There are many different interest rates in the economy. Loans vary by their riskiness and by their maturity (the length of the loan). Riskier loans and loans for longer maturities typically have higher interest rates.

A graph from the *New York Times*, reproduced below, depicts movements in three interest rates during 1995: 30-year fixed-rate mortgages (30-year loans to homeowners with a constant rate), 30-year Treasuries (loans to the U.S. government for 30 years), and six-month Treasuries (loans to the U.S. government for six months).

Notice that the 30-year mortgage rates are higher than the 30-year Treasuries: Homeowners are less likely to pay back their loans than the U.S. government. Interest rates on six-month Treasuries are less than on 30-year Treasuries, illustrating that longer-term loans carry higher interest rates.

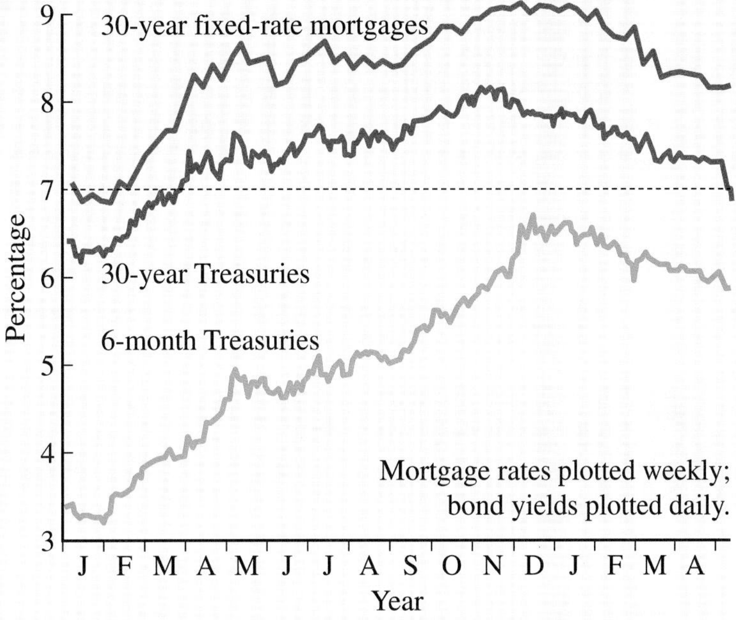

Source: From "Cheaper Borrowing," *New York Times*, May 10, 1995, p. D16.

Now let's calculate your real gain after one year. You have increased your holdings by \$6, starting with \$100 and ending with \$106. But once you take into account the \$4 you need to keep up with inflation, your gain is only \$2 (\$6 – \$4). The real rate of interest you earned, the nominal rate adjusted for inflation, is 2% or \$2, on the original \$100 deposit.

A similar calculation also applies to firms or individuals who borrow money. Suppose a firm borrows \$100 at a 10% interest rate when there is 6% inflation. The firm must pay back \$110 at the end of the year (\$100 × 1.10). But the borrower will be paying back the funds with dollars whose value has been reduced because of inflation. Since there is 6% inflation, the lender would have to receive \$106 (or six extra dollars) just to keep up with inflation. There is only a \$4 gain (\$10 – \$6). Thus the real rate of interest to the borrower is just 4%, or \$4 on the original \$100 loan, once we correct for the effects of inflation.

Expected real interest rate: The nominal interest rate minus the expected inflation rate.

We defined the real interest rate as the nominal interest rate minus the actual inflation rate. When firms or individuals borrow or lend, however, they do not know what the rate of inflation will actually be. Instead, they must form an expectation or an estimate of what they believe the inflation rate will be in the future. For a given nominal interest rate, we can define the **expected real interest rate** as the nominal rate minus the expected inflation rate. This is the real rate at which borrowers or lenders expect to make transactions.

It is difficult to determine real rates of interest precisely because we never know exactly what inflation rates people expect. One common approach to measuring expectations of inflation is to assume that individuals' expectations are based on the recent past. In Table 1 we present estimates of the expected real rate of interest based on this idea and data from the *Economist* magazine for 10 countries. In the first column we show interest rates on three-month loans, and in the second column we show the inflation rate over the last three months. In the last column we present estimates of the expected real rate of interest in each country by subtracting the inflation rate from the interest rate. Our assumption is that people expect the inflation rate that prevailed in the last three months to continue unchanged for the next three months.

Table 1 shows that it is important to distinguish nominal interest rates from expected real rates. Spain, for example, had one of the higher levels of nominal interest rates at 9.28%, but its expected real rate of interest was one of the lowest in the group. On the other hand, Japan had the lowest nominal interest rate, but because prices fell by 1.7% over the last three months, it had a real rate of interest higher than four other countries.

TEST *Your Understanding*

1 True or false: Investment is a smaller component of GDP than consumption, but it is a more stable component.

2 True or false: Investment spending is very procyclical, moving in conjunction with GDP.

Table 1: Expected Real Rates of Interest (percent per year)

Country	*3-Month Interest Rate*	*Inflation Rate over Last 3 Months*	*Expected Real Rate of Interest*
Australia	8.12	3.3	4.82
Belgium	5.13	2.4	2.73
Canada	7.86	4.2	3.66
Denmark	6.95	2.1	4.85
France	7.80	2.3	5.50
Germany	4.65	3.9	0.75
Italy	11.00	6.3	4.70
Japan	1.36	−1.7	3.06
Spain	9.28	7.9	1.38
United States	6.08	3.3	2.78

Source: The Economist, April 19, 1995, pp. 122–123.

3 Complete the statement with *real* or *nominal*: The rate of interest that you earn in the bank is known as a ____________ or dollar rate of interest.

4 With 6% inflation, a nominal rate of interest of 10% means a real rate of interest of ____________%.

INVESTMENT SPENDING AND INTEREST RATES

To understand the link between investment spending and interest rates, we use a simple example. A firm can invest $100 today in a project and receive $104 back in the next year. Assume there is no inflation so that a dollar today and next year have the same purchasing power. Figure 3 depicts this investment. A cost is incurred in period 0 (today) and the return arises in period 1 (next year). Should the firm make this investment?

To decide whether to undertake this investment, the firm should take into account the principle of opportunity cost.

PRINCIPLE *of Opportunity Cost*

The opportunity cost of something is what you sacrifice to get it.

If the firm undertakes the investment, it must give up $100 today in order to get $104 the following year. However, the $100 could be used for other purposes. For example, suppose the interest rate in the economy were 3%. Then the firm could take the $100 and lend it at 3% and receive back $103 within a year. The interest rate provides a measure of the opportunity cost of the investment.

In this case the investment *is* worthwhile for the firm. It will earn a net return of $4 ($104 – $100) from the investment project, whereas the firm would get only $3 from lending the money. Since the net return from the investment exceeds the opportunity cost of the funds, the firm is better off investing.

Suppose, however, that the interest rate in the economy were 6%. In this case the net return on the investment of $4 would be less than the opportunity cost of $6 that could be earned by lending the money. The firm would be better off making a loan and not investing. With the higher interest rate, the investment was not the most profitable course of action.

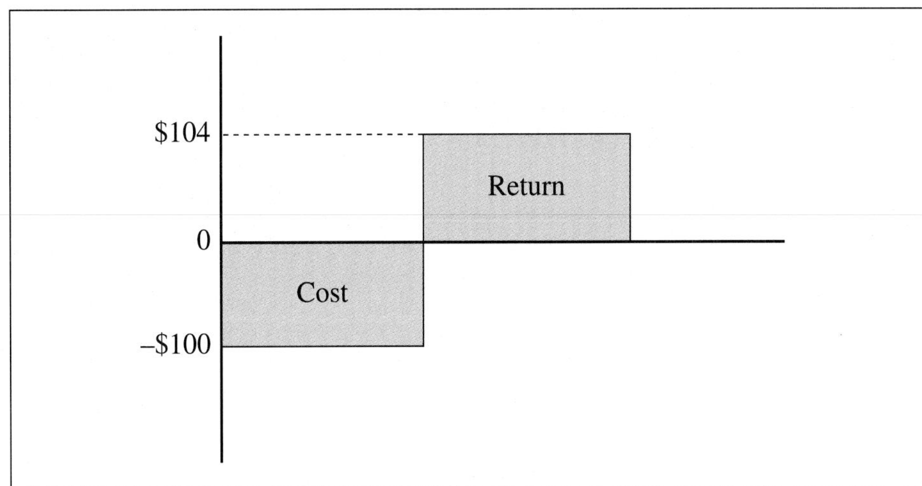

Figure 3

Typical Investment

A typical investment, in which a cost of $100 incurred today yields a return of $104 next year.

In the economy, there are millions of investment projects that can be undertaken, all with different returns. Consider this array of investments labeled A through E in Table 2. At an interest rate of 2%, only investment A is unprofitable. All the other investments have a return greater than the opportunity cost of the funds. If the interest rate increased to 4%, both A and B would now be unprofitable. Investment C would be added to the unprofitable list at an interest rate of 6%; D would be added with an 8% rate. If interest rates exceeded 9%, all the investments would become unprofitable.

Firms will compare the net return with the opportunity cost and invest as long as the net return exceeds the cost. As interest rates rise, there will be fewer profitable investments. The total level of investment spending in the economy will decline as interest rates increase. Figure 4 depicts the downward-sloping or negative relationship between interest rates and investment.

Real investment spending is in fact inversely related to the *real* interest rate. To understand this important point, let's return to our initial example. There was a $100 investment that would yield $104 next year, the interest rate was 3%, and there was no inflation. Since there was no inflation, both the nominal and real interest rates were the same. (Remember, the nominal and real rates differ only by inflation). In this case, the firm looked at the real net return on the investment of $4, compared it to the real rate of interest of 3%, and decided that the investment was profitable.

Now suppose the investment project and the real interest rate in the economy are the same but there is 2% inflation. The investment project will still cost $100, but it will pay a return of $106 in year 1. The extra $2 arises because of the 2% inflation. Nominal interest rates in the economy will be 5%, which is equal to the real rate of interest of 3% plus the inflation rate of 2%.

The firm will make precisely the same decision as before. If it compares its nominal or dollar net return of $6 to the nominal interest rate of 5%, the investment will be profitable. Since both the nominal net return and nominal interest rates in the economy increase by the rate of inflation of 2%, the firm faces the identical situation as before.

Because investment spending is negatively related to real interest rates, this means that *nominal* interest rates are not necessarily a good indicator of the true cost of investing. If nominal interest rates are 10% but inflation is 9%, the real rate of interest is a low 1%. If a firm had a project that paid a real net return greater than 1%, it would want to undertake this investment. Inflation would increase the nominal net return and the nominal interest rate equally. The firm makes its investment decisions by comparing its expected real net return from investment projects to the real rate of interest.

During the 1970s, homeowners in California understood this logic. They continued to buy homes even when they had to borrow from the bank at interest rates exceeding 10%. The reason that they were willing to borrow at such high rates is

Table 2: Returns on Investment

Investment	*Cost*	*Return*
A	$100	$101
B	100	103
C	100	105
D	100	107
E	100	109

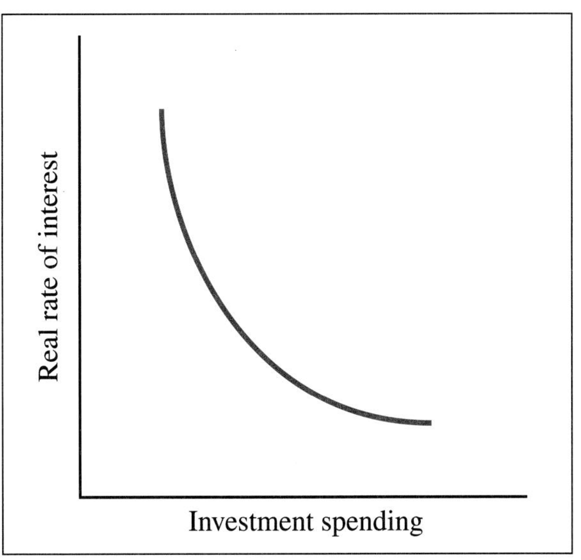

Figure 4

Interest Rates and Investment

As the real interest rate declines, investment spending in the economy increases.

that they had seen housing prices rise by more than 10% and were projecting this high return to continue in the future. If, for example, they expected housing prices to rise by 12% a year, they could earn a 2% return just by borrowing at 10% and watching their homes appreciate in value at 12%. They calculated that their real interest rate was actually –2%. In effect, they thought the banks were actually paying them to take their money! This fed a housing boom in California that lasted until housing prices stopped rising at such high rates.

Several different theories of aggregate investment spending emphasize, either directly or indirectly, the role of interest rates. In the **neoclassical theory of investment**, pioneered by Dale Jorgenson of Harvard University, real interest rates and taxes play a key role in determining investment spending. Jorgenson used his theory to analyze the responsiveness of investment to a variety of tax incentives, including investment tax credits that are subsidies to investment.

Neoclassical theory of investment: A theory of investment that emphasizes the role of real interest rates and taxes.

The **Q-theory of investment**, originally developed by Nobel laureate James Tobin of Yale University, looks a bit different from the neoclassical theory on its surface. The Q-theory states that investment spending increases when stock prices are high. If a firm's stock price is high, it can issue new shares of its stock at an advantageous price and use the proceeds to undertake new investment. Recent research has shown a close connection between the Q-theory and neoclassical theory and highlighted the key role that real interest rates and taxes play in the Q-theory as well.

Q-theory of investment: The theory of investment that links investment spending to stock prices.

TEST *Your Understanding*

5 Complete the statement with *increases* or *decreases*: As real rates of interest increase in the economy, real investment spending ____________.

6 Complete the statement with *real* or *nominal*: Both the ____________ rate of interest and the ____________ return on investment increase with the inflation rate.

7 The ____________ cost of funds is the interest that can be earned by lending the funds.

8 If a project costs $100 today and pays a return of $107 next year, what is the highest interest rate at which the project should still be undertaken?

How Financial Intermediation Facilitates Investment

Investment spending in an economy must ultimately come from savings. When households earn income, they consume part of this income and save the rest. These savings become the source of funds for investment in the economy.

Why Financial Intermediaries Emerge

Households that are saving for the future have different motivations than the firms that are investing. A typical household might be saving for the children's education or for security in later life. Such households often do not want to undertake risky investments that could jeopardize their life savings. In addition, they want their savings to be readily accessible in case of emergencies, or in other words to be what economists call **liquid**. Funds deposited in a bank account, for example, provide a source of liquidity for households—these funds can be obtained at any time.

Liquid: Easily convertible to money on short notice.

Firms and business managers who make investments in the economy are of a rather different sort. Typically, they are risk-takers; they are gambling that their vision of the future will come true and make them vast profits. They often need funds that can be tied up for a long time. For example, an entrepreneur who wants to build skyscrapers or large casinos may need financing for several years before the projects even get off the ground.

Now suppose that individual entrepreneurs had to obtain funds directly from individual savers. What a nightmare that would be! First, the entrepreneur would have to negotiate with thousands of savers to obtain sufficient funds for a large-scale project. These negotiations would be very costly. Second, the savers would face extraordinary risks if they lent all their funds to a single entrepreneur who had a risky project to undertake. Not only would all their funds be tied up in a single project; they would also have difficulty monitoring investor's decisions. How would they know the entrepreneur would not run off with the money? Finally, this investment would not be liquid. If the funds were tied up in an major project, households would not be able to obtain access to them in case of emergencies.

In these circumstances, households would demand extraordinarily high interest rates to compensate them for the costs of negotiation, risk, and lack of liquidity. These high interest rates would make it impossible for an entrepreneur to make a profit and no one would want to invest. Society would not be able to turn its savings to profitable investment projects. Figure 5 depicts this dilemma. How can society solve its coordination problem?

What society needs are institutions that can reduce costs, monitor investments, reduce risks, and provide liquidity. Fortunately, modern economies have developed precisely such institutions: *financial intermediaries*. Financial intermediaries are

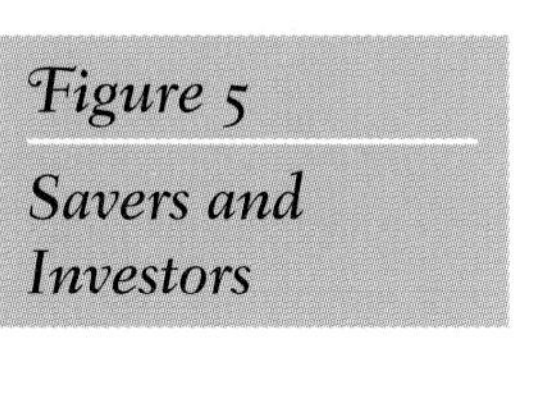
Figure 5

Savers and Investors

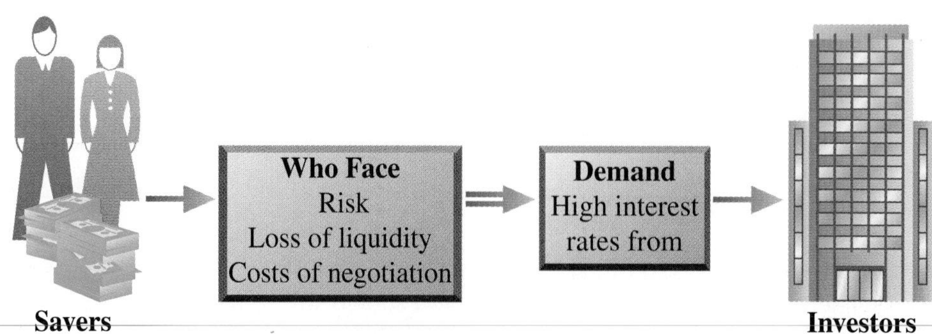

institutions such as banks, savings and loans, insurance companies, money market mutual funds, and many other types of financial institutions. These institutions accept funds from savers and make loans to businesses and individuals. For example, a local bank accepts deposits from savers and uses the funds to make loans to local businesses. Savings and loan institutions will accept deposits in savings accounts and use these funds to make loans, often for housing. Insurance companies accept premium payments from individuals in exchange for insurance. They lend the premiums to businesses to earn returns from investments so that they can pay off the insurance claims of individuals. Figure 6 shows how financial intermediaries create an interface between savers and investors.

These institutions pool the funds of savers. By pooling funds and making loans to individual businesses, financial intermediaries reduce the costs of negotiation. They also acquire expertise in both evaluating and monitoring investments. In addition, some financial intermediaries, such as banks, provide liquidity to households. Since in normal circumstances households do not all converge on a bank to take out their money at the same time, the bank can lend most of its funds to business and still have funds on hand to meet emergency withdrawals by depositors.

By pooling funds and gaining expertise, financial intermediaries can reduce costs and provide liquidity, but how do they reduce risk? Financial intermediaries reduce risk by *diversification*, that is, by not putting all their eggs in one basket.

The secret to reducing risk is to invest in a large number of projects whose returns, although uncertain, are independent of one another. By *independence* we mean that the return from one investment is unrelated to the return on another investment. Consider a bank investing in a large number of projects that on average earn an 8% return. Each project, however, is risky and could pay either a higher or lower return. As long as the returns on these projects are independent, the number of projects with higher returns will be matched by an equal number of projects with lower returns. Good fortune on some projects will be coupled with bad luck on others. With a large number of projects, the bank can be confident that it will earn an 8% return.

Financial intermediaries reduce risk with precisely this mechanism. Using the funds they receive from households, financial intermediaries invest in a large number of projects. Every household has a small stake in many projects. No one household would be able to do this. But if many households deposit their funds in financial intermediaries, the financial intermediaries can invest in a wide range of projects and reduce risk for the households.

Insurance works on the same principle. A fire insurance company accepts premiums from many individuals and uses the power of diversification to reduce its risk. Not

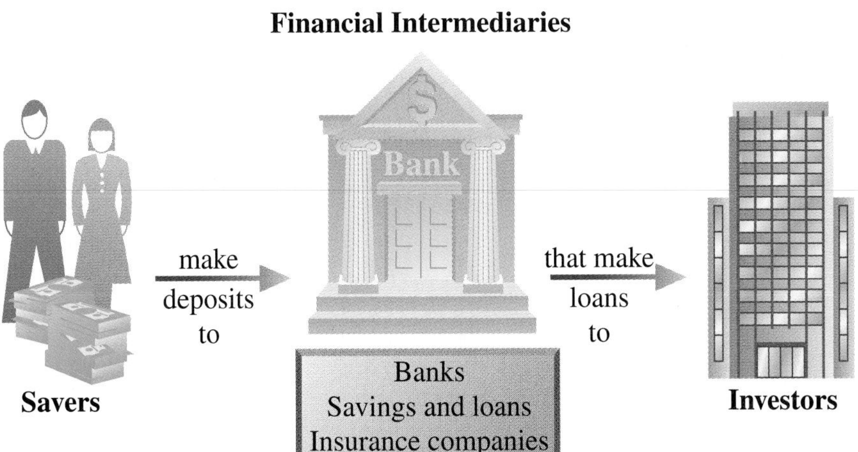

Figure 6

Financial Intermediaries

all houses will burn down in the same year! Banks also use this principle when they accept deposits. While individual depositors may want to withdraw funds on a given day, banks can be confident that not all depositors will come in on the same day.

Of course, diversification works well only when events are independent. Some events are not independent and not very insurable. For example, an insurance company would be unwise to write earthquake insurance policies for just the Los Angeles area. If an earthquake did occur, the firm would be faced with making many payments. Even bank loans are not fully independent. During a recession, many firms will be "unlucky" simultaneously in bad times, and banks will face many firms that have difficulties meeting their loan obligations.

When Financial Intermediation Malfunctions

While financial intermediation may seem like a marvelous social invention, it can sometimes go wrong. And when it does, the economy suffers as coordination of economic activity breaks down. There are several important examples of the failure of financial intermediation: commercial bank failures during the Great Depression and the savings and loans crisis of the 1980s.

During the 1930s in the early days of the Great Depression, many banks in the United States, particularly in rural areas, made loans to farmers or local business managers that turned out not to be profitable. This worried depositors, and rumors started that banks would soon be closing their doors and depositors would lose all their funds. This triggered "runs" on the banks, widespread panic in which all the depositors tried to withdraw their deposits simultaneously.

No bank, profitable or unprofitable, can survive a run. As financial intermediaries, banks make profits by lending out their deposits. They never keep 100% of these funds on hand. Thus the runs on banks closed down thousands of healthy banks and destroyed the entire banking system in large parts of the country. Many farmers and businesses could no longer find a source of loans. As economist Ben Bernanke has emphasized, this failure in the financial system helped to make the Great Depression as severe as it was.

To prevent this from happening again, the U.S. government began to provide deposit insurance for banks and savings and loans. This insurance now guarantees that your savings are secure up to $100,000. Since everyone knows that their deposits are secure, runs on banks no longer occur.

During the Great Depression, bank failures occurred throughout the world. In 1931, a dramatic panic broke out after the collapse of Creditanstalt, Austria's largest bank. Banking panics occurred throughout other countries in Europe, including Belgium, France, Germany, Italy, and Poland. Studies have shown that the countries with the most severe banking panics were particularly hard hit by the Depression. Today, most countries have some form of deposit insurance to help stem panics.

Ironically, deposit insurance indirectly helped to create the savings and loan crisis in the United States during the 1980s. In the early 1970s, savings and loan institutions throughout the country made mortgage loans to households at relatively low interest rates. In the late 1970s, nominal interest rates rose sharply as inflation increased. The savings and loans were in trouble: They had to pay high interest rates to attract deposits, but they were earning interest at low rates from their past investments. Many of these institutions were essentially bankrupt.

The government tried to assist the saving and loan industry by reducing regulations and allowing it to make investments in assets other than housing in the hope of gaining more profits. Depositors were not concerned because they were insured. Savings and loans soon became aggressive investors in speculative real estate and

Depositors gathered anxiously outside as banks closed during the Great Depression.

other risky projects. Many unsavory types were attracted to the savings and loan industry. Unfortunately, many investment projects collapsed and the government was forced to bail out the many savings and loans at a cost of nearly $100 billion to the U.S. economy. Depositors, however, were protected through deposit insurance and did not suffer directly from the collapse of their savings and loan institutions.

Japan suffered from similar problems in the 1990s. Seven of the eight largest mortgage lenders fell victim to falling real estate markets and essentially were bankrupt by 1995. The government chose to use nearly $13 billion dollars in taxpayer funds to rescue these companies and prevent further disruptions in the financial market.

As these three examples illustrate, financial intermediation does not always work perfectly. There is a lively debate on the role that government should play in investment decisions for the economy. The Closer Look box on the next page, "Should the Government Force Socially Responsive Investment?", discusses one aspect of this debate.

Using the **TOOLS**

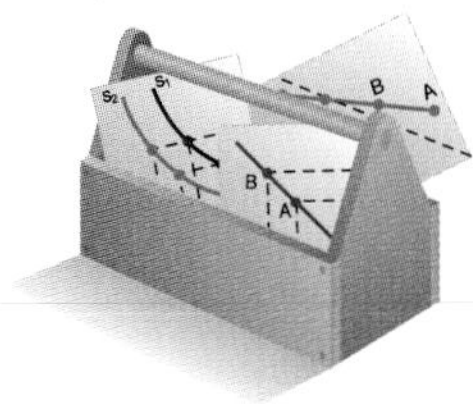

In this chapter we studied investment and financial intermediation and examined the factors that affect firms' investment decisions. Take this opportunity to do your own economic analysis.

1. ECONOMIC EXPERIMENT: *Diversification*

This classroom exercise can illustrate the power of diversification. After hearing a game described, you will be asked to vote on whether you would want to participate under different circumstances. The instructor will then discuss the game with you. To play the game, all you need to recall is one familiar lesson from basic statistics: If you flip a coin, the fraction of heads that results approaches one-half as the number of tosses you make increases.

A Closer LOOK

Should the Government Force Socially Responsive Investment?

Like other profit-making institutions, financial intermediaries do not deliberately make loans to depressed areas or to poor communities. They make their decisions on lending based on one primary criterion: the opportunity to earn as much money as possible.

Both federal and state governments often have other goals in mind. Many states require that state pension funds invest a large fraction of their assets in projects within the states, to promote jobs. At the federal level, banking laws require that financial institutions make a sufficient number of loans within their local region. Some activists argue that these laws should go much further and require investment in socially favored projects.

Although these laws may sound reasonable, they impose a cost. A study found that pension funds that are forced to invest large amounts of funds within the state will earn lower returns and face higher risks.* Future pension recipients pay the price for these restrictions. Similarly, banks that are required to lend locally may be less profitable and more risky with these restrictions. Some economists believe that if governments want to solve social problems, they should pay for solutions directly and not make investors pay the price.

*Olivia Mitchell and Ping Lung Hsin, "Public Pension Governance and Performance," *National Bureau of Economic Research Working Paper 4632*, January 1994.

You are offered a chance to play a game of tossing a coin in which you receive a payoff according to the following formula:

$$\text{payoff} = \$10 + \$100\left(\frac{\text{no. heads}}{\text{no. tosses}} - 0.5\right)$$

In this game you first get $10 but you either win or lose additional funds, depending on whether the fraction of heads that comes up exceeds one-half.

To understand this game, suppose you tossed the coin only once. Here are the outcomes depending on whether the coin came up either heads or tails:

$$\text{Heads:} \qquad \$10 + \$100\left(\frac{1}{1} - 0.5\right) = \$60$$

$$\text{Tails:} \qquad \$10 + \$100\left(\frac{0}{1} - 0.5\right) = -\$40$$

If the coin came up heads, you would win $60, but if it came up tails, you would lose $40 dollars.

The game does have a positive expected payoff or return. The expected or average payoff for this game is the probability of getting a head (1/2) times $60 if a head results plus the probability of getting a tail (1/2) times –$40 if a tail results. This is

$$\text{expected payoff} = (0.5)\$60 + (0.5)(-\$40) = \$10$$

Thus, on average, this game would pay $10. But it is risky if you can toss the coin only once. Now that you understand the game, answer the following questions:

- Would you play this game with one toss?

Now suppose you could toss the coin 1,000 times. For example, if you tossed the coin 1,000 times and received 450 heads, you would receive

$$\$10 + \$100\left(\frac{450}{1{,}000} - 0.5\right) = \$5$$

- Would you play this game if you could toss 1,000 times?
  a. Did a higher percentage of the class agree to play the game with 1,000 tosses? How does this illustrate the principle of diversification?
  b. If you toss the coin 1,000 times, what is the expected payoff?
  c. If you toss the coin 1,000 times and receive less than 400 heads, you will lose money. What do you think the probability is of this occurring?

2. Animal Spirits

Use the $C + I + G$ diagram to show the effects of increased "animal spirits" that leads to higher investment in the economy.

3. ECONOMIC DETECTIVE: *High Interest Rates and High Levels of Investment Spending*

Some journalists were puzzled that a country had high market interest rates but also had high levels of investment. As an economic detective, could you explain this phenomenon?

4. Understanding Banks

How can a bank invest in illiquid loans and still provide liquid deposits?

SUMMARY

In this chapter we discussed investment spending, interest rates, and financial intermediation. As we saw, investment spending is very volatile and depends on expectations about the future. We also explained why investment spending depends inversely on real interest rates. Finally, we examined how financial intermediaries play a crucial role in modern economies in channeling funds from savers to investors, reducing interest rates and promoting investment. Here are the main points to keep in mind from this chapter.

1. Investments are actions that incur costs today but provide benefits in the future.
2. Investment spending is a very volatile component of GDP, primarily because investment decisions are made with an eye to the ever-changing future. Keynes thought that much investment activity was irrational and governed by the animal spirits of investors.
3. Investment spending depends inversely on real interest rates.
4. Financial intermediaries reduce risk and costs through their expertise and by pooling the funds of savers.

KEY TERMS

accelerator theory, *536*
bond, *538*
expected real interest rate, *540*
financial intermediaries, *535*
liquid, *544*
multiplier-accelerator model, *538*
neoclassical theory of investment, *543*
nominal interest rates, *535*
procyclical, *536*
Q-theory of investment, *543*
real interest rate, *535*

PROBLEMS AND DISCUSSION QUESTIONS

1. Why does investment spending rise and fall with the overall level of GDP in the economy?
2. Explain the difference between real and nominal interest rates.
3. "When real interest rates are high, so is the opportunity cost of funds." What does this statement mean?
4. A stock market mutual fund will often purchase thousands of stocks. How does a stock market mutual fund reduce risk?
5. Why should we be concerned if financial intermediaries fail?
6. Explain why some insurance companies have been interested in programs for nationwide disaster insurance for floods, earthquakes, and hurricanes.
7. The components of investment spending include plant and equipment, housing, and inventories. Give a reason why each component may be volatile.
8. A business borrows from a bank at 10% but expects 8% general inflation in the economy. What are the nominal and real rates of interest facing this borrower?

Take It to the Net

We invite you to visit the O'Sullivan/Sheffrin page on the Prentice Hall Web site at:

http://www.prenhall.com/osullivan/

for this chapter's World Wide Web exercise.

MODEL ANSWERS FOR THIS CHAPTER

Chapter-Opening Questions

1. Interest rates represent the opportunity cost of an investment. The higher the opportunity cost, the less investment.
2. Borrowing depends on the real interest rate, the market or nominal interest rate adjusted for inflation. In inflationary periods, there may be a high nominal rate but a low real rate.
3. Diversification of independent risks allow financial intermediaries to reduce risk.
4. Without financial institutions, it would be too costly for individuals to make loans directly to firms.
5. Federal deposit insurance prevents the "runs" on banks that occurred during the Great Depression.

Test Your Understanding

1. False.
2. True.
3. nominal
4. 4%
5. decreases
6. nominal, nominal
7. opportunity
8. The highest rate is 7%.

Using the Tools

1. Economic Experiment: Diversification

   A higher percentage of the class should agree to play the game when the coin was tossed 1,000 times than when it was tossed a single time because the expected payoff is the same ($10) but the risk is much less. In fact, there is less than 1 chance in a million of coming up with less than 400 heads out of 1,000 and losing money!
2. Animal Spirits

   The increase in investment will lead to a vertical shift in the $C + I + G$ demand line. This will lead to higher output.
3. Economic Detective: High Interest Rates and High Levels of Investment

   The theory of investment says that investment is negatively related to the *real* rate of interest. If the inflation rate in the economy is high, a low real rate of interest may be associated with a high nominal rate of interest.
4. Understanding Banks

   Using basic statistics, a bank can estimate that only a fraction of its depositors will ask for withdrawals on any given day. Therefore, the bank can allocate a large fraction of the deposits to illiquid loans.

Money, the Banking System, and the Federal Reserve

We all have fantasies from time to time. It is a rare person who has not thought about winning the lottery and receiving the grand prize of $1 million.

Here's an even better fantasy. Imagine you had a checkbook that allowed you to write as many checks as you wished for any amount you desired. There is no need to worry about the balance in your account and the checks will always be cashed, regardless of what you spend. Too good to be true? Of course. No person has an account like this, but the Federal Reserve in Washington, our nation's central bank, has similar powers.

In this chapter we begin to learn about the key role of money and our banking system. For economists, "money" has a special meaning, so we'll look carefully at how economists define money and the role that it plays in the economy.

The supply of money in the economy is determined primarily by the banking system and the actions of the Federal Reserve, our nation's central bank. We will see how the Federal Reserve, operating through the banking system, can create and destroy money. We also study how the Federal Reserve operates, and who controls it.

The supply of money is very important for the economy's performance. In our discussion of aggregate demand, we indicated how increases in the supply of money increase aggregate demand. In the short run, when prices are fixed, increases in the money supply will raise total demand and output. In the long run, continuing money growth leads to inflation. Therefore, changes in the supply of money have important effects on both output and prices. In this chapter we explain in detail how the supply of money in the economy is determined.

After reading this chapter, you should be able to answer the following questions:

1. Why do all societies have some form of money?
2. Why do banks play a special role in our economy?
3. Can banks really create money through computer entries?
4. When the Federal Reserve uses its special powers to buy and sell government bonds, how does this affect the supply of money in the economy?
5. Why is it true that the chairman of the Federal Reserve is one of the most powerful people in the country?

WHAT IS MONEY?

In this part of the chapter we first discuss the definition and role of money and then see how it is defined in the U.S. economy.

Definition of Money

Money: Anything that is regularly used in exchange.

Economists define **money** as anything that is regularly used in economic transactions or exchanges. Let's consider some examples of the use of money.

In everyday life we use money all the time. For instance, in an ice cream store we hand the person behind the counter some dollar bills and coins and in turn receive an ice cream cone. This is an example of an economic exchange—one party hands over goods and services (the ice cream cone) and the other party hands over currency—the dollar bills and the coins.

Why do the owners of ice cream stores accept the dollar bills and coins in payment for the ice cream? The reason is that they in turn will be making other economic exchanges. For example, suppose they take the currency they receive from selling the ice cream and pay their supplier with it. The ice cream cones cost $1.50 and 100 are sold in a day. The seller then has $150 in currency. If the ice cream costs the seller $100, the seller pays $100 of the currency that was received and keeps the remaining $50 for other expenses and profits.

In the real world, actual transactions are somewhat more complicated. The ice cream store will take the currency it receives each day and deposit it into an account at its local bank. It will typically pay its suppliers with a check drawn on its account at that local bank. This is still another example of an economic exchange: The ice cream supplier sells ice cream to the store in exchange for a check.

Why does the supplier accept a check? The supplier can use the check to make further transactions. He or she can deposit the check in his or her own bank account and then either withdraw currency from this account or write checks on it.

In these examples, what is money? Recall the definition of money: anything that is regularly used in economic transaction or exchanges. Clearly, currency is money, since it was used to purchase ice cream. Checks are also money since they are used to pay the supplier.

At other times and in other societies, different items have been used as money. For example, among some ancient peoples, precious stones were used in exchanges and constituted money. In more recent times, gold bars have served as money. During World War II, prisoners of war did not have currency in their possession but they did have rations of cigarettes. The cigarettes began to be used for exchanges among the prisoners and played the role of money in the prison camps.

Three Properties of Money

Regardless of what money is in a particular society, it serves several important functions, all related to making economic exchanges easier. Here are three key properties of money:

1. Money Serves as a Medium of Exchange

As our examples illustrate, money is accepted in economic exchanges; that is, it serves as a **medium of exchange.** To appreciate the role of money as a medium of exchange, suppose that money did not exist and you had a car you wanted to sell in order to buy a boat. You could look for a person who had a boat and wanted to buy a car and then trade your car directly for a boat. This would be an example of **barter**—trading goods directly for goods.

Medium of exchange: The property of money that exchanges are made using money.

Barter: Trading goods directly for goods.

But there are obvious problems with barter. Suppose local sailors were interested in selling boats but not interested in buying your car. Unless there were a **double coincidence of wants**—that is, unless you wanted to trade a car for a boat *and* the boat owner wanted to trade a boat for your car—this economic exchange could not occur. The odds of a double coincidence of wants occurring are tiny. Even if a boat owner wanted a car, he or she might want a different type of car than you have.

Double coincidence of wants: The problem in a system of barter that one person may not have what the other desires.

By serving as a medium of exchange, money solves this problem. A car owner can sell the car to anyone who wants it and receive money in return. With the money in hand, the car owner can then find someone who owns a boat and purchase the boat for money. The boat owner can use the money in any way he or she pleases. With money, there is no need for a double coincidence of wants. This is why money exists in all societies—it makes economic transactions much easier.

2. Money Serves as a Unit of Account

Money also provides a convenient measuring rod when prices for all goods are quoted in money terms. For example, a boat may be listed for sale at $5,000, a car at $10,000, and a movie ticket at $5.00. All these prices are quoted in money. We could in principle quote everything in terms of movie tickets. The boat would be worth 1,000 tickets and the car would be worth 2,000 tickets. But since we are using money (and not movie tickets) as a medium of exchange, it is much easier if all prices are expressed in terms of money. Money is used as a **unit of account**; that is, prices are quoted in term of money. This also makes it easier to conduct economic transactions since there is a standard unit in which to do so.

Unit of account: The property of money that prices are quoted in terms of money.

3. Money Serves as a Store of Value

If you sell your car to purchase a boat, you may not be able to purchase the boat immediately. In the meantime, you will be holding the money you received from the sale of the car. Ideally, during that period, the value of the money should not change. In other words, one function of money is to be a **store of value.**

Store of value: The property of money that value is preserved between transactions.

Money is actually a somewhat imperfect store of value, thanks to inflation. Suppose that inflation is 10% a year, which means that all prices rise 10% each

Figure 1

Components of M1 for the United States

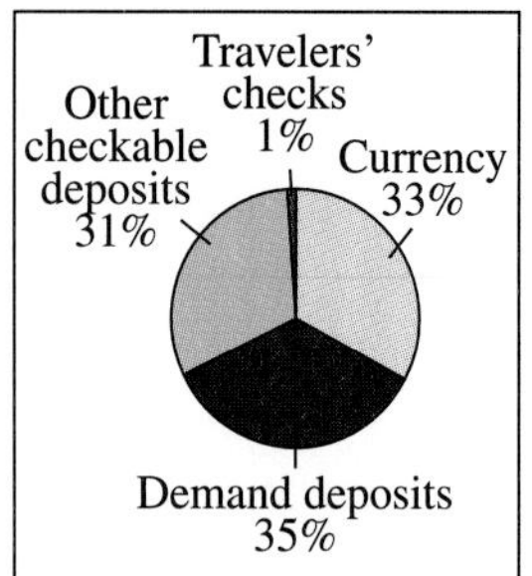

year. Let's say further that you sold a tennis racquet for $100 in order to buy 10 CDs worth $100 but that you waited a year to buy them. Unfortunately, at the end of the year, the 10 CDs now cost $110 ($100 × 1.10), or $11 each. With your $100, you can now buy only 9 CDs and get $1 in change. Money has lost some of its stored value.

As long as inflation is relatively low and you do not hold money for long periods of time, the loss in the purchasing power of money will not be a major problem. But as inflation rates increase, money becomes less useful as a store of value.

TEST *Your Understanding*

1. Money solves the problem of double coincidence of wants that would regularly occur under a system of ____________.
2. Why is money only an imperfect store of value?
3. What is the problem associated with the double coincidence of wants?
4. True or false: Because we measure all prices in monetary units, money serves as a unit of account.
5. Why are checks included in the definition of money?

MEASURING MONEY IN THE U.S. ECONOMY

In the United States and other modern economies, there are typically several different ways that economic transactions can be carried out. In practice, this leads to different definitions of money.

M1: The sum of currency in the hands of the public, demand deposits, and other checkable deposits.

The most basic official concept of money in the United States is called **M1.** Table 1 contains the components of M1 and their size for December 1995, and Figure 1 shows their relative percentages. What precisely are these components?

The first part of M1 is currency that is held by the public, that is, all currency held outside of bank vaults. The next two components are deposits in checking accounts. Economists call these *demand deposits*. Until the 1980s, checking accounts did not pay interest, and a new category entitled *other checkable deposits* was introduced in the early 1980s to describe checking accounts that did pay interest. Today this distinction is not as meaningful since many checking accounts pay interest if your account balance is sufficiently high. Finally, travelers' checks are included in M1 since they are regularly used in economic exchanges.

Approximately two-thirds of M1 consists of checking account balances (demand deposits plus other checkable deposits). The other one-third consists primarily of

Table 1: Components of M1, December 1995

Currency held by the public	$ 372 billion
Demand deposits	389 billion
Other checkable deposits	353 billion
Travelers' checks	9 billion
Total of M1	$1,123 billion

Source: Economic Report of the President (Washington, DC: U.S. Government Printing Office, 1996).

Currency held by the public is part of the official money supply.

currency. In modern economies, checking accounts have replaced currency as the means of making the majority of transactions, especially larger ones.

Let's take a closer look at the amount of currency in the economy. Since there are approximately 260 million people in the United States, the $372 billion of currency amounts to over $1,430 in currency for every man, women, and child in the United States. Do you and your friends have $1,430 of currency in your possession?

In fact, most of the currency in the official statistics is not used in ordinary commerce in the United States. Much of it is held abroad by wealthy people who want U.S. currency in case of emergencies or who use it to keep their wealth out of sight of their own governments and tax authorities. Some of it circulates in other countries along with their local currencies. Currency is also used in illegal transactions such as the drug trade. Few dealers of illegal drugs are lining up to open bank accounts that could be inspected by international law authorities. (However, they do use the international banking system to "launder" their drug profits.)

The United States is not the only country that has a large amount of currency per capita outstanding, as the Closer Look box on the next page, "Lots of Currency," explains.

M1 does not capture all the assets that are used to make economic exchanges. Economists also use a somewhat broader definition of money known as **M2**, which includes assets that are *sometimes* used in economic exchanges or can be readily turned into M1. M2 consists of all the assets in M1 plus several other assets such as deposits in money market mutual funds. These are funds in which individuals can invest; they earn interest and can be used to write checks over some minimum amount. Deposits in savings accounts are also included in M2. While deposits in savings accounts cannot generally be used directly in exchanges, they can be converted to M1 and then used. In December 1995, M2 totaled $3,780 billion.

M2: M1 plus other assets, including deposits in savings and loans and money market mutual funds.

The reason that economists use different definitions of money is that it is not always clear which assets are used primarily as money—that is, for economic exchanges—and which are used primarily for the purpose of saving and investing. For example, consider money market mutual funds, which only came into existence

A Closer LOOK

Lots of Currency

The economist Case M. Sprenkel has noted that other developed countries besides the United States have large amounts of currency per capita outstanding. In 1992, for example, while the United States had $1,096 of currency per person, measured in dollars, the Japanese had $2,228 per person and the Swiss had $3,116 per person. Austria, Belgium, Germany, Spain, and Sweden all had per capita currency holdings larger than the United States. British currency holdings per person, however, were less than half of those in the United States.

What can explain these differences? There probably are some cultural differences. The Japanese traditionally carry more currency and use it frequently for gifts. There are even automated teller machines in Japan that "press" money to remove its wrinkles. But cultural preferences are not sufficient explanation. After all, why should the British hold so much less currency than the Belgians?

Sprenkle believed that much of the currency of the countries with large currency holdings per capita was actually held abroad, in developing countries whose domestic currencies did not provide good stores of value. As he put it, "The Argentinean taxi driver or the Algerian bellhop would like to have the American tourist or businessman's dollars, but would also appreciate the Italian's lire or the Japanese's yen if that is who is arriving." Currencies from developed countries are likely to be better stores of value than currencies in many developing countries.

Source: Case M. Sprenkel, "The Case of the Missing Money," *Journal of Economic Perspectives*, Fall 1993, pp. 175–184 (quotation from p. 177).

in the late 1970s. Although individuals can use these funds to write checks and engage in economic transactions, many people use them in other ways. Some may have their wealth temporarily invested in these funds in anticipation of moving into the stock market. Others may use them to earn interest while avoiding the risks of the stock or bond market. Sometimes money market mutual funds are used like regular checking accounts, other times like savings accounts. If they are used like checking accounts, they should be in M1, but if they are used like savings accounts, they should be part of M2.

In practice, M1 may be too narrow a definition of money, since some assets, such as money market mutual funds, are not included. On the other hand, broader definitions of money will always include assets that are not necessarily used regularly in transactions. Economists use different working definitions of money because of these practical difficulties.

TEST *Your Understanding*

6 About one-third of M1 consists of __________.

7 Complete the statement with *M1* or *M2*. Economists use __________ to measure the amount of money that is regularly used in transactions.

8 Which is greater, M1 or M2?

9 How do you explain the fact that the total amount of currency divided by the U.S. population is approximately $1,430?

10 Why are money market mutual funds hard to classify?

BANKS AS FINANCIAL INTERMEDIARIES

Now we turn to the role that banks play in the creation of the supply of money. In the last chapter we discussed how financial intermediaries help bring savers and investors together. By using their expertise and the powers of diversification, financial intermediaries reduce risk to savers and allow investors in the economy to obtain funds on better terms. Commercial banks operate precisely in this manner.

A typical commercial bank will accept funds from savers in the form of deposits, for example, in a checking account. It does not leave all these funds idle; if it did, the bank could never make a profit. Instead, it turns the money around and makes loans to businesses. For example, a local hardware store might need a $100,000 loan to purchase its inventory. To make this loan, the bank would pool deposits from many savers. It will make other loans as well, reducing its risk.

To understand how banks work, it is useful to examine a simplified **balance sheet** for a commercial bank. A balance sheet shows how banks raise money and where the money actually goes.

Balance sheets have two sides: one for assets and one for liabilities. **Liabilities** are the source of funds for the bank. If you open a checking account and deposit your funds, the bank is "liable" for returning these funds to you. Your deposits are thus liabilities to the bank.

Assets are the uses of these funds. Assets generate income for the bank. Loans are examples of a bank's assets because a borrower must pay interest to the bank.

The difference between a bank's assets and liabilities is called its **net worth**:

$$\text{net worth} = \text{assets} - \text{liabilities}$$

For example, if a bank has $1,000 of assets and $900 of liabilities, it has a net worth of $100. When a bank is started, its owners must place their own funds into the bank. These funds are the bank's initial net worth. If a bank makes profits, its net worth will increase. If a bank loses money, its net worth decreases.

In Figure 2 we show the assets and liabilities of a hypothetical bank. On the liability side, we show that the bank has $2,000 of deposits. The net worth of the bank is $200. This is entered on the liability side of the balance sheet because it is also a source of funds. The total source of funds is therefore $2,200—the deposits in the bank plus its net worth.

On the asset side, the bank holds $200 in **reserves**, assets that are not lent out. Banks are required by law to hold a fraction of their deposits as reserves and not make loans with it; this fraction of deposits is called **required reserves**. Banks may choose to hold additional reserves beyond what is required; these are called **excess reserves**. A bank's reserves are the sum of its required and excess reserves. Reserves can either be cash kept in a bank's vaults or deposits with the Federal Reserve. Banks do not earn any interest on these reserves.

In our example, the bank is holding 10% of its deposits, or $200, as reserves. The remainder of the bank's assets consists of loans. In this case the bank makes $2,000 in loans.

By definition, total assets will always equal liabilities plus net worth. Balance sheets must always "balance."

Balance sheet: An account for a bank which shows the sources of its funds (liabilities) as well as the uses for the funds (assets).

Liabilities: The sources of external funds of a financial intermediary.

Assets: The uses of the funds of a financial institution.

Net worth: The difference between assets and liabilities.

Reserves: The fraction of their deposits that banks set aside in either vault cash or as deposits at the Federal Reserve.

Required reserves: The reserves that banks are required to hold by law against their deposits.

Excess reserves: Any additional reserves that a bank holds above required reserves.

Figure 2

Balance Sheet for a Bank

Assets	Liabilities
$ 200 reserves	$2,000 deposits
$2,000 loans	$ 200 net worth
Total: $2,200	Total: $2,200

THE PROCESS OF MONEY CREATION

To understand the role that banks play in determining the supply of money in the economy, let's look at a simple example. Suppose that someone walks into the First Bank of Hollywood and deposits $1,000 in cash to open a checking account. Since both currency held by the public and checking deposits are both included in the supply of money, the total money supply has not changed.

However, banks do not simply keep all the cash they receive in their safes. For a bank to make a profit, it must make loans. Let's assume that the banks are required to keep 10% of deposits as reserves and hold no excess reserves. In this case, the **reserve ratio**—the ratio of reserves to deposits—will be 0.1. Our hypothetical bank, First Bank of Hollywood, will then keep $100 in reserves and make loans totaling $900. The top panel in Figure 3 shows the change in the bank's balance sheet after it has made its loan.

Reserve ratio: The ratio of reserves to deposits.

Suppose the First Bank of Hollywood lent the funds to an aspiring movie producer. It opens a checking account for the producer who needs the funds to buy some equipment. The producer buys the equipment from a supplier who deposits the check in the Second Bank of Burbank. The next panel in Figure 3 shows what happens to the balance sheet of the Second Bank of Burbank. Liabilities increase by the deposit of $900. The bank must hold $90 in reserves (10% of the $900 deposit) and can lend out $810. Suppose it lends the $810 to an owner of a coffeehouse and opens a checking account for her. She then purchases coffee from a supplier who deposits the check into the Third Bank of Venice.

Figure 3

Process of Deposit Creation: Changes in Balance Sheets

First Bank of Hollywood

Assets	Liabilities
$100 reserves	$1,000 deposit
$900 loans	

Second Bank of Burbank

Assets	Liabilities
$90 reserves	$900 deposit
$810 loans	

Third Bank of Venice

Assets	Liabilities
$81 reserves	$810 deposit
$729 loans	

Fourth Bank of Pasadena
Fifth Bank of Compton

The Third Bank of Venice receives a deposit of $810. It must keep $81 in reserves and can lend out $729. This process continues throughout the Los Angeles area with new loans and deposits. The Fourth Bank of Pasadena will receive a deposit of $729, hold $72.90 in reserves, and lend out $656.10. The Fifth Bank of Compton will receive a deposit of $656.10 as the process goes on.

The original $1,000 cash deposit has created checking account balances throughout Los Angeles. What total amount of checking account balances has been created? Adding up the new accounts in all the banks (even the ones we have not named), we have

$$\$1{,}000 + \$900 + \$810 + \$729 + \$656.10 + \cdots = \$10{,}000$$

How did we come up with this sum? In the appendix to this chapter we derive the simple formula

$$\text{increase in checking account balances} = (\text{initial cash deposit})\left(\frac{1}{\text{reserve ratio}}\right)$$

In our example, the reserve ratio was 0.1, so that the increase in checking account balances was 1/0.1, or 10 times the initial cash deposit. The initial $1,000 deposit led to an increase in checking account balances of $10,000.

Recall that the money supply, M1, is the sum of deposits at commercial banks plus currency held by the public. Therefore, the *change* in the money supply, M1, will be the change in deposits in checking accounts plus the change in currency held by the public. Although in our example deposits increased by $10,000, the public now holds $1,000 less of currency because they deposited the currency in the bank. Therefore, the money supply, M1, increased by $9,000 ($10,000 – $1,000). No single bank lent out more than it had in deposits. Yet for the banking system as a whole, the money supply expanded by a multiple of the initial cash deposit.

The term *1/reserve ratio* in the formula is called the **money multiplier**. It tells us what the total increase in checking account deposits would be for any initial cash deposit. You may recall the multiplier for government spending in our demand side models. An increase in government spending led to larger increases in output through the multiplier. The government spending multiplier arose because additional rounds of consumption spending were triggered by an initial increase in government spending. In the banking system, an initial cash deposit triggers additional rounds of deposits and lending by banks. This leads to a multiple expansion of deposits.

Money multiplier: An initial deposit leads to a multiple expansion of deposits. In the simplified case: increase in deposits = (initial deposit) × (1/reserve ratio).

As of 1995 in the United States banks were required to hold 3% reserves against checkable deposits up to $54 million and 10% on all checkable deposits exceeding $54 million. Since large banks would face a 10% reserve requirement on any new deposits, you might think, based on our formula, that the money multiplier would be approximately 10.

However, the money multiplier for the United States is between 2 and 3, much smaller than the value of 10 implied by our simple formula. The primary reason is that our formula assumed that all loans made their way directly into checking accounts. In reality, people hold part of their loans as cash. When people hold cash, the funds are not available for the banking system to lend out. Since fewer deposits are created, this decreases the money multiplier. The money multiplier would also be less if banks held excess reserves.

The money creation process also works in reverse. Suppose that you go to your bank and ask for $1,000 in cash from your checking account. The bank must pay you the $1,000. Its liabilities fall by $1,000 but its assets must also fall by $1,000. If the reserve ratio is 0.1, the bank will reduce its reserves by $100 and reduce its loans by $900. With fewer loans there will be fewer deposits in other banks. The money multiplier will work in reverse and the money supply will decrease.

Up to this point, our examples have always started with an initial cash deposit. However, suppose that Paul receives a check from Fred and Paul deposits it into his bank. Paul's bank will eventually receive payment from Fred's bank. When it does, it will initially have an increase in both deposits and reserves, just as if a cash deposit were made. Since Paul's bank only has to hold a fraction of the deposits as reserves, it will be able to make loans with the remainder.

However, there is one crucial difference between this example and the cash deposit. When Paul receives the check from Fred, the money supply will not be changed. When the check is deposited in Paul's bank, the money supply will begin to expand, but when Fred's bank loses its deposit, the money supply will start to contract. The expansions and contractions offset each other when private citizens and firms write checks to one another.

TEST *Your Understanding*

11 Banks are required by law to keep a fraction of their deposits as __________.

12 Define *net worth*.

13 Why does a bank prefer to make loans rather than keep reserves?

14 If the reserve ratio is 0.2 and a deposit of $100 is made into a bank, the bank will lend out __________.

15 If the reserve ratio is 0.2, the simplified money multiplier will be __________.

16 Why is the actual money multiplier much smaller than in our simple formula?

THE ROLE OF THE FEDERAL RESERVE IN THE MONEY CREATION PROCESS

Banks can only expand the money supply if new reserves come into the banking system. As we saw, when private citizens and firms write checks to one another, there will be no net change in the supply of money in the system. Since the total amount of reserves in the system is unchanged, the money supply cannot expand. There is one organization, however, that has the power to change the total amount of reserves in the banking system: the Federal Reserve.

Open Market Operations

Open market purchases: The purchase of government bonds by the Fed, which increases the money supply.

Open market sales: Sales of government bonds to the public, which decreases the money supply.

The Federal Reserve (the Fed) can increase or decrease the total amount of reserves in the banking system through open market operations. There are two types of open market operations: open market purchases and open market sales. In **open market purchases**, the Federal Reserve buys government bonds from the private sector. In **open market sales**, the Fed sells government bonds to the private sector.

To understand how the Fed can increase the supply of money, let's trace the consequences of an open market purchase. Suppose the Federal Reserve purchases $1 million worth of government bonds from the private sector. It writes a check for $1 million and presents it to the party who sold the bonds. The Federal Reserve now owns the bonds.

The party who sold the bonds now has a check written on the Federal Reserve for $1 million. He deposits this check into his bank. The bank credits his account, and now it has a check for $1 million written against the Federal Reserve. Here is the key: *Checks written against the Federal Reserve count as reserves for banks.* As soon as the bank presents the check to the Federal Reserve, the bank will have $1 million in new reserves. If the reserve requirement is 10%, the bank must keep $100,000 in reserves, but it can make loans for $900,000. The process of money creation thus begins. Open market purchases increase the money supply.

As we explained at the beginning of the chapter, the Federal Reserve has powers that ordinary citizens and even banks do not have. It can write checks against itself to purchase government bonds without having any explicit "funds" in its account for the purchase. Banks accept these checks because they count as reserves for the bank.

As you might expect, open market *sales* will decrease the supply of money. Suppose the Federal Reserve sells $1 million worth of bonds to a Wall Street trading

Key economic policy decisions are made inside the imposing Federal Reserve building in Washington, DC.

firm. The firm will pay for the bonds with a check for $1 million drawn on its bank and give this check to the Federal Reserve. The trading firm now owns the bonds.

The Federal Reserve presents this check to the Wall Street firm's bank. The bank must either hand over $1 million in cash or, more likely, reduce its reserve holding with the Federal Reserve by $1 million. (Banks keep accounts with the Fed, and in this case the Fed would reduce the bank's account balance by $1 million.) Since the bank's reserves have fallen, it must decrease its loans to increase reserves to their required levels. Thus the process of money destruction begins. Open market sales will therefore decrease the money supply.

In summary, if the Federal Reserve wishes to increase the money supply, it engages in open market purchases and buys government bonds from the private sector. If it wishes to decrease the money supply, it engages in open market sales and sells government bonds to the private sector.

Other Tools

Open market operations are by far the most important means by which the Federal Reserve changes the supply of money. The Federal Reserve has two other tools it can use: changes in reserve requirements and changes in the discount rate.

If the Federal Reserve wishes to increase the supply of money, it can reduce reserve requirements for banks. Banks would then have to hold a smaller fraction of their deposits as reserves and could make more loans, thereby allowing the money supply to expand. Similarly, to decrease the supply of money, the Federal Reserve could raise reserve requirements.

Although changing reserve requirements can be a strong tool, the Federal Reserve does not use it very often because it is disruptive to the banking system. Suppose, for example, that a major bank whose clients were multinational corporations held exactly 10% of its deposits as reserves and the remainder as loans. If the Federal Reserve suddenly increased its reserve requirement to 20%, the bank would be forced to call in or cancel many of its loans. Its multinational clients would not take kindly to this! For these reasons, the Federal Reserve today does not make sharp changes in reserve requirements. However, in the past the Fed did change reserve requirements sharply, as the Closer Look box on the next page, "Why Did Banking Reserves Increase in the Great Depression?", discusses.

The Federal Reserve does allow banks to borrow reserves from it at an interest rate called the **discount rate**. Suppose, for example, that a major customer comes to the bank and asks for a loan. Unless the bank could find an additional source of funds, it would have to refuse to make the loan. Banks are reluctant to turn away major customers. They first look to see whether they can borrow reserves from other banks through the **federal funds market**, a market in which banks borrow or lend reserves to each other. If the federal funds rate seemed too high to the bank, it could borrow from the Federal Reserve itself at the discount rate.

Discount rate: The interest rate at which banks can borrow from the Fed.

Federal funds market: The market in which banks borrow and lend reserves to one another.

By changing the discount rate, the Federal Reserve can influence the amount of borrowing done by banks. For example, if the Fed raised the discount rate, banks would be discouraged from borrowing reserves because it has become more costly. Similarly, lowering the discount rate will induce banks to borrow additional reserves.

In principle, the Federal Reserve could use the discount rate as an independent tool of monetary policy: lowering the rate to expand the money supply and raising the rate to reduce the money supply. In practice, the Fed keeps the discount rate close to the federal funds rate to avoid large swings in borrowed reserves by banks. Changes in the discount rate, however, are quite visible to financial markets. Participants in the financial markets often interpret these as revealing clues about the Federal Reserve's intentions for future monetary policy.

A Closer LOOK

Why Did Banking Reserves Increase in the Great Depression?

During the bleak economic times of the 1930s in the United States, banks held substantial excess reserves beyond those required. They held these reserves for two reasons. First, economic conditions were bad and it was hard to find borrowers who would be likely to pay back their loans. Second, banks were worried about banking panics and wanted to have cash on hand in case depositors all came to the banks at once to withdraw their funds.

The Federal Reserve saw that banks were holding these extra reserves and became worried that the extra cash might cause inflation sometime in the future. In 1937, the Fed raised reserve requirements for the banks. Banks, however, cut back their loans even further to hold excess reserves. As an economic detective, can you explain why banks did this?

The reason they cut back their loans even further was that they were still fearful of banking panics and possible runs on banks. Excess reserves were held precisely for this possibility, despite the fact that banks would lose some potential profit from reducing their loans. The ultimate result of the Federal Reserve policy was to reduce lending in the economy and to precipitate a recession in 1937–1938. Since that time the Fed has learned not to make sharp increases in reserve requirements.

TEST *Your Understanding*

17 Complete the statement with *increases* or *decreases*. When the Federal Reserve buys bonds, it ____________ the money supply.

18 Complete the statement with *sale* or *purchase*. An open market ____________ will lead to a reduction of reserves in banks.

19 Who borrows and lends in the federal funds market?

20 What is the discount rate?

THE STRUCTURE OF THE FEDERAL RESERVE

Central bank: A banker's bank; an official bank that controls the supply of money in a country.

Lender of last resort: A name given to policies of central banks that provide loans to banks in emergency situations.

The Federal Reserve System was created in 1913 following a series of financial panics. During these panics, depositors became fearful of the health of banks and started to withdraw their funds. That meant that banks could no longer make loans to businesses, resulting in severe economic downturns. Congress created the Federal Reserve System to be a banker's bank or a **central bank**. One of its primary jobs was to serve as a **lender of last resort**. If there was a panic in which depositors wanted to withdraw their funds, the Federal Reserve would be there to lend funds to banks, thereby reducing some of the adverse consequences of the panic.

All countries have central banks. The German central bank is known as the Bundesbank. In the United Kingdom, it is the Bank of England. Central banks serve as lenders of last resort to the banks in their countries and also provide the levers through which the money supply is changed.

Congress was aware that it was creating an institution with vast powers, and it deliberately created a structure in which, at least on paper, power was spread throughout different groups and across the country. To understand the structure of the Federal Reserve today, you should keep in mind its three distinct subgroups: Federal Reserve Banks, the Board of Governors, and the Federal Open Market Committee.

The United States was divided into 12 Federal Reserve districts, each of which has a **Federal Reserve Bank**. These district banks provide advice on monetary policy, take part in decision making on monetary policy, and provide a liaison between the Fed and the banks in their districts.

Federal Reserve Banks: One of 12 regional banks that are an official part of the Federal Reserve System.

Figure 4 contains a map of the United States with a list of the Federal Reserve Banks. At the time the Federal Reserve was created, economic and financial power in this country was concentrated in the east and midwest. This is no longer true. What major western city does not have a Federal Reserve Bank?

The **Board of Governors of the Federal Reserve** is the true seat of power over the monetary system. Headquartered in Washington, DC, the seven members of the board are appointed for staggered 14-year terms by the President and must be confirmed by the Senate. The chair of the Board of Governors, the principal spokesman for monetary policy in the country, serves a four-year term as chair. This position is so important that the chair is carefully watched by financial markets throughout the world. An inadvertent slip of the tongue could cause a worldwide financial panic.

Board of Governors of the Federal Reserve: The seven-person governing body of the Federal Reserve system in Washington, DC.

Decisions on monetary policy are made by the **Federal Open Market Committee (FOMC)**. The FOMC is a 12-person board consisting of the seven members of the Board of Governors, the president of the New York Federal Reserve bank, plus the presidents of four other regional Federal Reserve Banks. (Presidents of the regional banks other than New York serve on a rotating basis; the seven nonvoting bank presidents attend the meetings and provide their views). The chair of the Board of Governors also serves as the chair of the FOMC. The FOMC makes the actual decisions on changes in the money supply. Its members are assisted by vast teams of professionals at the Board of Governors and at the regional Federal Reserve Banks. The structure of the Federal Reserve System is depicted in Figure 5 on the next page.

Federal Open Market Committee (FOMC): The group that decides on monetary policy and consists of the seven members of the Board of Governors plus five of 12 regional bank presidents on a rotating basis.

The chair of the Board of Governors is also required to report to Congress on a regular basis. Although the Federal Reserve operates with independence, it is a creation of Congress. The U.S. Constitution gives Congress the power to "coin

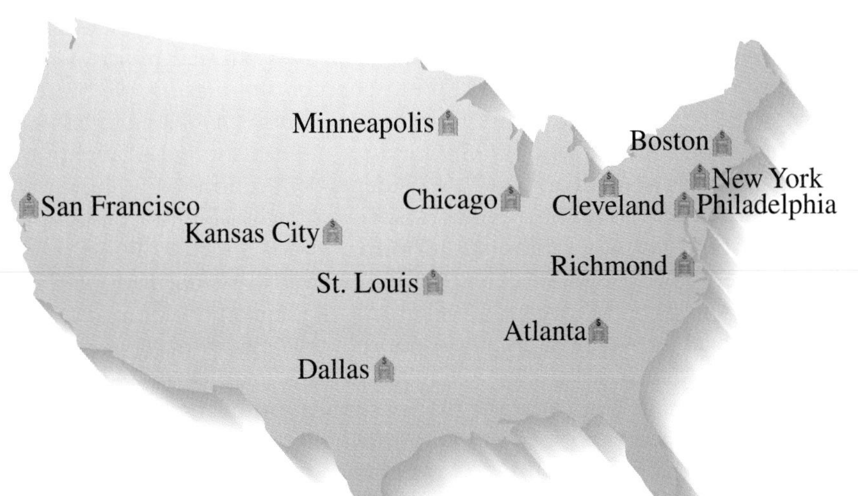

Figure 4

Federal Reserve Banks of the United States

Figure 5

Structure of the Federal Reserve

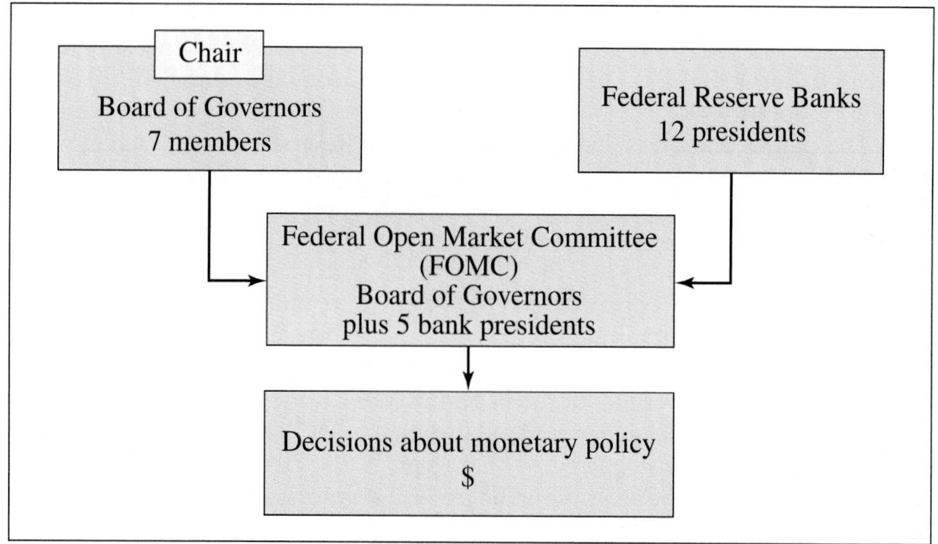

money and regulate the value thereof." In practice, the Fed takes its actions first and reports to Congress after the fact. The chair of the Federal Reserve often will meet with members of the executive branch to discuss economic affairs.

On paper, the powers of monetary policy appear to be spread throughout the government and the country. In practice, however, the Board of Governors and especially the chair have the real control. The Board of Governors operates with considerable independence. Presidents and members of Congress can bring political pressures on the Board of Governors, but 14-year terms do provide some insulation from external pressures.

Countries differ in the degree to which the central bank is independent of political authorities. In both the United States and Germany, the central banks operate with considerable independence. In other countries, such as the United Kingdom, the central bank is part of the Treasury department of the government and potentially subject to more direct political control.

There is a lively debate among economists and political scientists as to whether more independent central banks (with less external political pressures) show better economic performance. In our chapter on inflation, we present some evidence that countries with more independent central banks have less inflation over long periods of time without any sacrifice in terms of higher unemployment.

Even if there is an advantage to an independent central bank, however, there still is an important issue: In a democratic society, why should we allow there to be an important and powerful institution that is not directly subject to political control? There is an ongoing debate over the control of the Fed, as the Closer Look box "Politics and Power: Who Controls the Bankers?" indicates.

In this chapter we have discussed the role that money plays in the economy, how commercial banks play a key role in the deposit creation process, and how the Fed exercises ultimate control of the money supply. Although decision making over monetary policy appears to be dispersed throughout the government, in practice it is highly concentrated in the Board of Governors and with the chair of the Fed. In the next chapter, we will see that the Fed can also determine short-term interest rates and thereby influence the level of economic activity.

A Closer LOOK

Politics and Power: Who Controls the Bankers?

Federal Reserve Bank presidents help determine monetary policy through their participation in the Federal Open Market Committee. These bank presidents are chosen by the directors of their banks. At each bank, six of the directors are elected from the member banks in their district and three are appointed by the Board of Governors.

Some members of Congress have worried about the participation of the bank presidents on the FOMC, particularly because they have tended to be more conservative than members of the Board of Governors. While members of the Board of Governors are nominated by the President and confirmed by the Senate, bank presidents are neither appointed by elected officials nor confirmed by the Senate. While the Board of Governors does influence their selection, they represent an independent voice for the member banks in their district and the financial community. Should these bank presidents play such an important role in the determination of monetary policy?

Supporters of the current system argue that the bank presidents provide important insights from outside the narrow confines of Washington, DC and are in closer touch to business developments in their regions. Opponents claim that this gives the financial elite in our country too much power in the design of monetary policy. The current system has been in place since 1935 and Congress is unlikely to change it in the near future.

Using the TOOLS

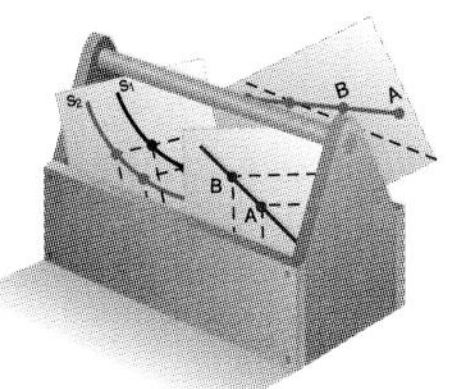

In this chapter we studied the money creation process as it works through the banking system. Take this opportunity to do you own economic analysis.

1. California Money?

In 1992 the state of California ran out of funds and could not pay its bills. It issued IOUs, called *warrants*, to its workers and suppliers. Only large banks and credit unions accepted the warrants. Should these warrants be viewed as money?

2. Bad Loans to South America

During the 1980s, U.S. banks made loans to South American countries. Many of these loans were found to be worthless. How did this discovery affect the assets, liabilities, and net worth of these banks?

3. Reserve Requirements as a Tax

Left on their own, most banks would reduce their reserve requirements far below 10%. Consequently, banks view reserve requirements as a "tax" on their holdings of deposits. Explain how a 10% reserve requirement could be viewed as a 10% tax.

4. High-Powered Money

Economists define high-powered money as the reserves at banks plus the currency held by the public. The Federal Reserve is often said to control the stock of high-powered money. Does the stock of high-powered money change when:

a. Currency is deposited into a bank?

b. A bank makes a loan?

c. The Federal Reserve buys government bonds?

SUMMARY

In this chapter we first examined the role that money plays in the economy and how economists define "money." We then took a closer look at banks as their role as financial intermediaries. We saw how banks can "create" money through the process of deposit creation. In addition, we learned how the Federal Reserve can control the supply of money through open market purchases and sales and other policies. Here are the main points to remember from this chapter.

1. Money consists of anything that is regularly used in making exchanges, that is, buying and selling goods and services. In modern economies it consists primarily of currency and deposits in checking accounts.
2. Banks are financial intermediaries that earn profits by accepting deposits and making loans. Deposits, which are liabilities of banks, are included in the money supply.
3. Banks are required by law to hold a fraction of their deposits as reserves, either in cash or in deposits with the Federal Reserve. Total reserves consists of required reserves plus excess reserves.
4. If there is an increase in reserves in the banking system, the supply of money will expand by a multiple of the initial deposit. This multiple is known as the money multiplier.
5. The Federal Reserve's primary tool for increasing or decreasing the total amount of reserves in the banking system is through open market purchases of government bonds (which increase reserves) or open market sales (which decrease reserves).
6. The Federal Reserve can also change the supply of money by changing reserve requirements or changing the discount rate.
7. Decisions about monetary policy are made at the Federal Open Market Committee (FOMC), which includes the seven members on the Board of Governors and the president of the New York Federal Reserve Bank, as well as four of the 11 other regional bank presidents, who serve on a rotating basis.

KEY TERMS

assets, *557*
balance sheet, *557*
barter, *553*
Board of Governors of the Federal Reserve, *563*
central bank, *562*
discount rate, *561*
double coincidence of wants, *553*
excess reserves, *557*
federal funds market, *561*
Federal Open Market Committee (FOMC), *563*
Federal Reserve Banks, *563*
lender of last resort, *562*
liabilities, *557*
M1, *554*
M2, *555*
medium of exchange, *553*
money, *552*
money multiplier, *558*
net worth, *557*
open market purchase, *560*
open market sale, *560*
required reserves, *557*
reserve ratio, *558*
reserves, *557*
store of value, *553*
unit of account, *553*

PROBLEMS AND DISCUSSION QUESTIONS

1. Why are all the three functions of money important?
2. Why are travelers' checks classified as money?
3. Both insurance companies and banks are financial intermediaries. Why do macroeconomists study banks more intensively than insurance companies?
4. What is the opportunity cost of holding excess reserves?
5. Why would an increase in reserve requirements lower the money supply?
6. Explain carefully why an open market purchase by the Federal Reserve will increase the money supply.
7. How does an increase in the discount rate affect the money supply?
8. Occasionally, some economists or politicians suggest that the Secretary of the Treasury become a

member of the Federal Open Market Committee. How do you think this would affect the independence of the Fed?

9. Suppose the Federal Reserve purchased gold or foreign currency. How would this purchase affect the domestic money supply? (*Hint*: Think about open market purchases of government bonds.)

10. The Federal Reserve has traditionally conducted open market operations through the purchase and sale of government bonds. In principle, could the Federal Reserve conduct monetary policy through the purchase and sale of stocks on the New York Stock Exchange? Do you see any possible drawbacks to such a policy?

Take It to the Net

We invite you to visit the O'Sullivan/Sheffrin page on the Prentice Hall Web site at:

http://www.prenhall.com/osullivan/

for this chapter's World Wide Web exercise.

MODEL ANSWERS FOR THIS CHAPTER

Chapter-Opening Questions

1. All societies have money because it makes it much easier to conduct trade.
2. Banks play a special role in our economy because the liabilities of banks are part of the supply of money.
3. The banking system as a whole can create money through the process of multiple expansion. However, this depends on the actions of the Federal Reserve.
4. When the Federal Reserve purchases bonds from the public, it increases reserves in banks and leads to an increase in the supply of deposits and loans. When the Federal Reserve sells bonds to the public, the supply of loans and deposits decrease.
5. The chairman of the Federal Reserve is the most powerful person in the Federal Reserve System which determines the supply of money in the economy.

Test Your Understanding

1. barter
2. Inflation makes money an imperfect store of value.
3. Without money you would need to find someone who had the good that you wanted to buy and also wants to trade for the good that you have.
4. True.
5. Checks are counted as money since they are regularly used in economic exchanges.
6. currency held by the public
7. M1
8. M2 is greater.
9. A "typical" person in the United States does not hold this amount of currency. Some currency is held abroad and some is held for illegal purposes.
10. Money market mutual funds are used both for making transactions and savings.
11. reserves
12. Net worth is assets minus liabilities.
13. Banks do not earn interest on reserves, but they do on loans.
14. $80
15. 5
16. The simplified formula does not take into account that individuals hold some cash from their loans.
17. increases
18. sale
19. Banks borrow and lend.
20. The discount rate is the interest rate at which banks can borrow from the Fed.

Using the Tools

1. California Money?

   The warrants in California were only partly money. Although banks did accept them, other merchants did not. Thus they were not used regularly in exchange.
2. Bad Loans to South America

   Bad loans will reduce the assets of a bank. Since they do not change the liabilities of a bank (its deposits), the net worth of the bank must also fall along with the value of its assets. If the net worth of a bank falls too far, the bank can be closed.

3. Reserve Requirements as a Tax

   Since a bank earns no interest on reserves, the reserve requirement acts as a tax. For example, suppose the bank held no reserves at all and could earn 20% interest on loans. A 10% reserve requirement means that the bank could only earn 20% interest on 90% of its deposits. This is equivalent to a tax of 10%.

4. High-Powered Money

   The stock of high-powered money only changes when the Federal Reserve buys a government bond. In this case the total of reserves plus currency increases. If the public deposits currency in the bank, currency held by the public falls but the currency held by the bank (which counts as reserves) increases. When a bank makes a loan, the total reserves in the banking system do not change.

Appendix

Formula for Deposit Creation

In this appendix we derive the formula in the text for deposit creation using the example in the text. We showed that with 10% held as reserves, a $1,000 deposit led to total deposits of

$$\$1{,}000 + \$900 + \$810 + \$729 + \$656.10 + \cdots$$

Let's find the total sum of all these deposits. Since each bank had to hold 10% in reserves, the next bank in the chain only received 0.9 of the deposits of the prior bank. Therefore, we can write the total for the deposits in all the banks as

$$\$1{,}000 \times (1 + 0.9 + 0.9^2 + 0.9^3 + 0.9^4 + \cdots)$$

We need to find the sum of the terms in parentheses. Using a formula for an infinite sum,

$$1 + b + b^2 + b^3 + b^4 + \cdots = \frac{1}{1-b}$$

the expression becomes

$$1 + 0.9 + 0.9^2 + 0.9^3 + 0.9^4 + \cdots = \frac{1}{1-0.9} = \frac{1}{0.1} = 10$$

Therefore, the total increase in deposits will be

$$\$1{,}000 \times 10 = \$10{,}000$$

To derive the general formula, note that if the reserve ratio is r, the bank will lend out $(1 - r)$ per dollar of deposits. Following the steps outlined above, we find that the infinite sum will be $1/[1 - (1 - r)] = 1/r$ or 1/reserve ratio. Therefore, in general, we have the formula

$$\text{increase in checking account balances} = (\text{initial deposit})\left(\frac{1}{\text{reserve ratio}}\right)$$

CHAPTER

28

Monetary Policy in the Short Run

Economic news and policy often seem to be centered around the potential actions of the Federal Reserve. Consider these examples:

- President Bill Clinton is about to make his first State of the Union address. An unusual guest accompanies the wives of the President and Vice-President. Who is it? None other than the chairman of the Federal Reserve, Alan Greenspan.
- A major Wall Street firm announces it has hired a former member of the Fed's Board of Governors at an astronomical salary to provide insights and "scoops" to its clients. This former governor joins the many other "Fed watchers" on Wall Street, who are there to help Wall Street interpret monetary policy.
- Your sister is about to buy a new house but she is worried about interest rates. Her banker has offered her two options for a loan. The first is a fixed-rate mortgage loan in which the interest rate is constant for the entire life of the mortgage. The second option is a variable-rate mortgage. The interest rate on this loan is lower than the fixed-rate mortgage but will increase or decrease with the general level of interest rates in the economy. If she believes interest rates will rise in the near future, your sister will take the fixed-rate option; if not, she will take a variable-rate loan. Your sister knows that you are currently studying economics and asks you, "What is the Fed going to do with interest rates?"

In this chapter we will learn why everyone is so interested in the actions of the Federal Reserve. In the *short run* when prices are temporarily fixed, the Federal Reserve has the ability to influence the level of interest rates in the economy. When the Federal Reserve lowers interest rates, investment spending and GDP increase. On the other hand, increases in interest rates will reduce investment spending and GDP. It is this power to affect interest rates in the short run that makes presidents extend invitations to the Fed chair, provides lucrative employment to former Fed officials, and explains why your sister wants to know what actions the Federal Reserve is likely to take in the near future.

After reading this chapter, you will be able to answer the following questions about the economy:

1. Why do short-term interest rates rise after the Federal Reserve decides to conduct open market sales?
2. Why do prices for bonds usually fall when the Federal Reserve raises interest rates?
3. How does the housing and construction industry respond after the Federal Reserve decides to increase the money supply?
4. Why might the Federal Reserve refuse to lower interest rates even if everyone agrees that the economy is in a slump?

The Federal Reserve influences the level of interest rates in the short run by changing the supply of money through open market operations. As we explain in this chapter, interest rates are determined in the short run by the supply and demand for money. The supply of money is determined largely by the Federal Reserve. The demand for money comes from the private sector. Using two principles of economics, *opportunity cost* and the *reality principle*, we will explain the factors that determine the demand for money. Putting demand and supply together, we will see how interest rates are determined in the short run.

Changes in interest rates, in turn, affect total spending and output in the economy. For example, an open market purchase that increases the money supply will lead to lower interest rates and increased investment spending. A higher level of investment spending will ultimately lead to a higher level of GDP. Here is the chain of events to keep in mind as you read this chapter:

open market purchase → money supply increase → fall in interest rates →
rise in investment spending → increase in GDP

All but one piece of this chain should be familiar from the preceding chapters. We have already seen that open market purchases increase the money supply, decreases in interest rates increase investment spending, and higher investment spending leads to higher levels of GDP. In this chapter we add the link from money supply increases to decreases in interest rates and complete the chain.

This process also works in reverse: Open market sales will reduce the money supply, raise interest rates, and lower investment and GDP. In this chapter we also discuss additional channels for monetary policy in an open economy.

Although the Federal Reserve has immense power, there are limits to the extent that it can effectively control the economy. First, as we have discussed, in the long run increases in the money supply affect only prices and not the level of output. Second, even in the short run when prices are fixed, there are important limits to the powers of the Federal Reserve. Our lack of knowledge about the strength and timing of both monetary and fiscal policy actions makes it difficult to execute effective policies. In this chapter we explore the limits of monetary and fiscal policy in the short run.

MODEL OF THE MONEY MARKET

We begin by learning the factors that determine the demand for money by the public. Once we understand the demand for money, we can then see how actions taken by the Federal Reserve determine interest rates in the short run.

The Demand for Money

To understand the demand for money, it is useful to think of money as simply one part of wealth. Suppose your total wealth is valued at $1,000. In what form will you hold your wealth? Should you put all your wealth into the stock market, or perhaps the bond market? Or should you hold some of your wealth in money, that is, currency and checking accounts?

If you invest your wealth in assets such as stocks or bonds, you earn returns on your investment. Stocks pay dividends and increase in value, while bonds pay interest. On the other hand, if you hold your wealth in currency or a checking account, you receive either no interest or very low interest. Holding your wealth in the form of money means that you sacrifice some potential returns.

Money does, however, provide valuable services. It facilitates transactions. If you go to a grocery store to purchase some cereal, the store will accept currency or a check, but it will not allow you to purchase the cereal with your stocks and bonds. People hold money primarily for this basic reason: Money makes it easier to conduct transactions. Economists call this reason for holding money the **transactions demand for money**.

Transactions demand for money: The demand for money based on the desire to facilitate transactions.

To understand the demand for money, we rely on the principle of opportunity cost.

PRINCIPLE *of Opportunity Cost*

The opportunity cost of something is what you sacrifice to get it.

If you hold more of your wealth in terms of money, it makes it easier to conduct everyday business. On the other hand, you sacrifice income by not investing in assets (such as stocks and bonds) that earn returns.

The opportunity cost of holding money is the return that you could have earned by holding your wealth in other assets. We measure the opportunity cost of holding money by the interest rate. Suppose the interest rate available to you on a long-term bond is 6%. If you hold $100 of your wealth in the form of this bond, you earn $6 a year. If you hold currency instead, you earn no interest. So the opportunity cost of holding $100 in currency is $6 or 6%.

As interest rates increase in the economy, the opportunity cost of holding money also increases. Economists have found that as the opportunity cost of holding money increases, the public will demand less money. In other words, the demand for money will decrease with an increase in interest rates.

In Figure 1 on the next page we draw a demand for money curve, M^d, as a function of the interest rate. At higher interest rates, individuals will want to hold less money than at lower interest rates since the opportunity cost of holding money is higher. As interest rates rise from r_0 to r_1, the demand for money falls from M_0 to M_1.

The demand for money also depends on two other important factors. One factor is the level of prices in the economy. The demand for money will increase as the level of prices increases. If prices for your groceries are twice as high, you will need to have twice as much money to purchase them. The amount of money people typically hold during any period of time will be closely related to the dollar

Figure 1

Demand for Money

As interest rates increase from r_0 to r_1, the quantity of money demanded falls from M_0 to M_1.

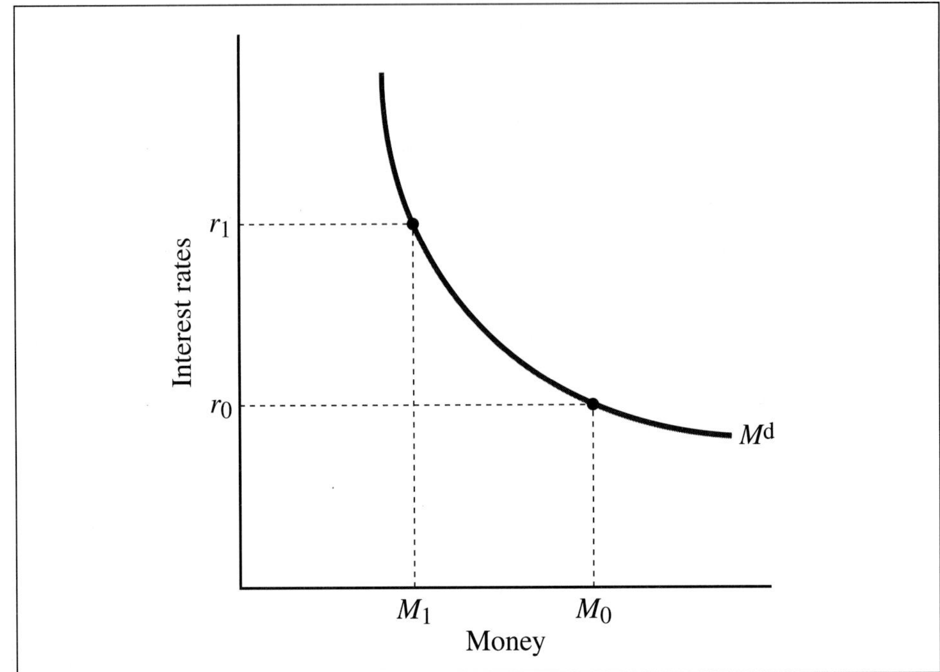

value of the transactions that they make. This is an example of the reality principle in action.

Reality PRINCIPLE

What matters to people is the real value or purchasing power of money or income, not its face value.

The other factor that influences the demand for money is the level of real GDP or real income. It seems obvious that as income increases, individuals and businesses will make more purchases. Thus, as real GDP increases, individuals and businesses will be making more transactions. To facilitate these transactions, they will want to hold more money.

Figure 2 shows how changes in prices and income affect the demand for money. Increases in money demand will shift the curve to the right. Panel A shows how the demand for money shifts to the right as the price level increases. At any interest rate, people will want to hold more money as prices increase. Panel B shows how the demand for money shifts to the right as real GDP increases. At any interest rate, people will want to hold more money as real GDP increases. These graphs are both showing the same result. An increase in prices or an increase in real GDP will increase money demand.

Liquidity demand for money: The demand for money that arises so that individuals or firms can make purchases on short notice without incurring excessive costs.

Traditionally, economists have identified other motives, besides transactions, for individuals or firms to hold money. If you hold your wealth in the form of property, such as a house or a boat, it is costly to sell the house or boat on short notice if you need to obtain funds. These forms of wealth are illiquid—that is, they are not easily transferable into money. On the other hand, if you hold your wealth in currency or checking accounts, you do not have this problem. Thus economists recognize that individuals have a **liquidity demand for money**; that is, they hold money in order to be able to make transactions on quick notice.

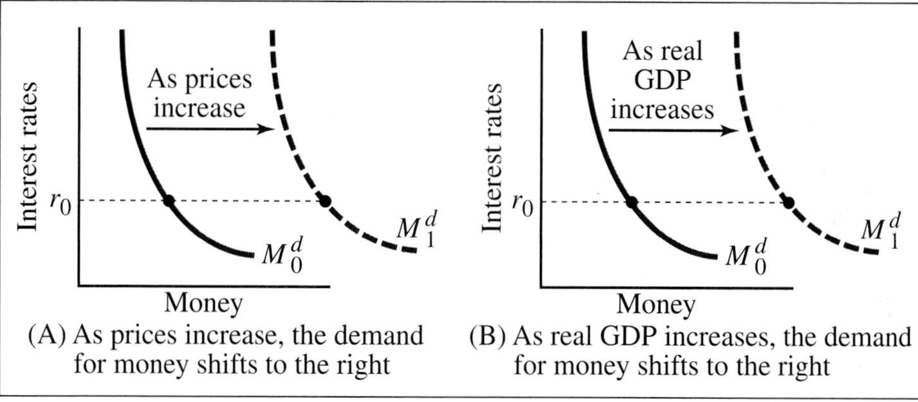

Figure 2

Shifting the Demand for Money

Individuals may also wish to hold some types of money, particularly savings accounts and other assets that are contained in M2, because they pay interest but are less risky than holding stocks or bonds. Particularly over short periods of time, individuals may not wish to hold stocks or bonds because prices of stocks and bonds might fall. Holding your wealth in a savings account is safer. The demand for money that arises because it is safer than other assets is called the **speculative demand for money.**

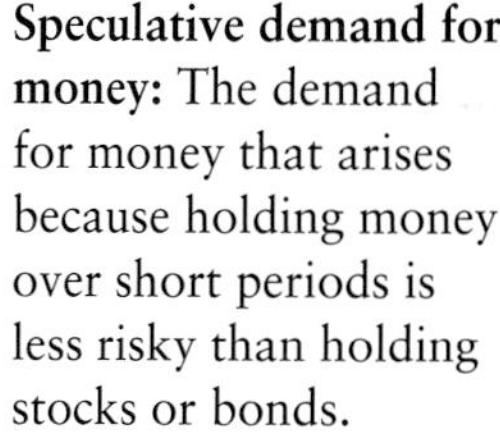
Speculative demand for money: The demand for money that arises because holding money over short periods is less risky than holding stocks or bonds.

The demand for money, in practice, will be the sum of transactions, liquidity, and speculative demands. As we indicated, the demand for money will depend positively on the level of income and prices and negatively on interest rates.

Interest Rate Determination

As we have discussed, the Federal Reserve determines the supply of money. Combining the supply of money with the demand for money, we can see how interest rates are determined in the short run in a demand and supply model of the money market.

Figure 3 depicts a model of the money market. The supply of money is determined by the Federal Reserve and we assume for simplicity that it is independent of interest rates. We show this independence by drawing a vertical supply curve for

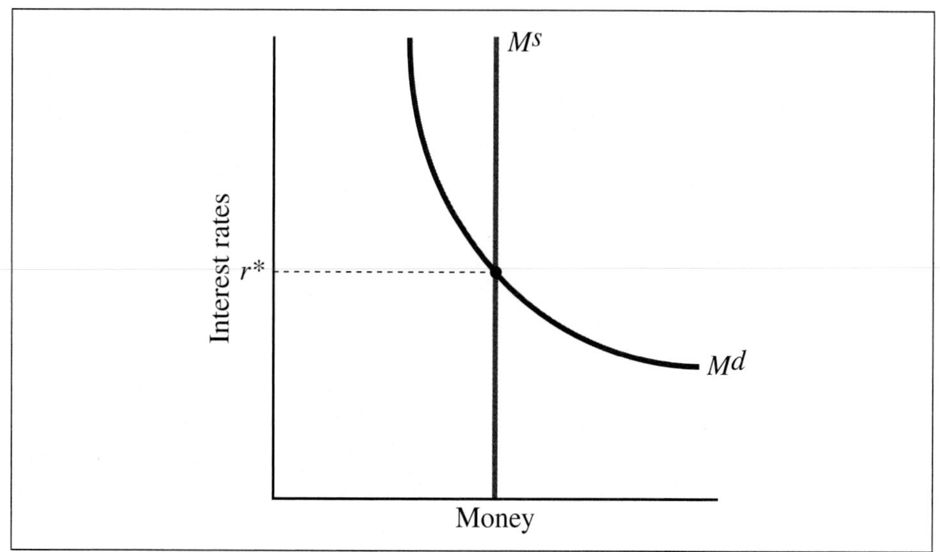

Figure 3

Equilibrium in the Money Market

Equilibrium in the money market occurs at an interest rate of r^* at which the quantity of money demanded equals the quantity of money supplied.

money, M^s. We now draw the demand for money for money M^d in the same graph. Market equilibrium occurs where the demand and supply for money are equal, at an interest rate of r^*.

At this equilibrium interest rate of r^*, the quantity of money demanded by the private sector equals the quantity of money supplied by the Federal Reserve. At a higher interest rate, the quantity of money demanded would be less than the quantity supplied, there would be an excess supply of money, and interest rates would fall. Similarly, if interest rates were below r^*, there would be an excess demand for money and interest rates would rise back to r^*. As you can see, money market equilibrium follows the same logic as any other economic equilibrium.

We can use this simple model of the money market to understand the power of the Federal Reserve. Suppose the Federal Reserve increased the money supply through an open market purchase. In panel A of Figure 4, an increase in the supply of money would shift the money supply curve to the right and lead to lower interest rates. Similarly, a decrease in the money supply through an open market sale, as depicted in panel B of Figure 4, will decrease the supply of money, shift the money supply curve to the left, and increase interest rates.

We can also think of the process from the vantage point of banks. Recall our discussion of money creation through the banking system. After an open market purchase, banks will find that they have additional reserves and will want to make loans. To entice businesses to borrow from them, they will lower the interest rates they charge on their loans. After an open market purchase, interest rates will fall throughout the entire economy.

Now we understand why potential new homeowners and even the President of the United States want to know what actions the Federal Reserve is likely to take in the near future. The Federal Reserve exerts direct control over interest rates in the short run. If the Fed decides that interest rates should be lower, it conducts open market purchases and increases the supply of money. If it wants higher interest rates, it conducts open market sales and decrease the money supply. In the short run, the actions of the Federal Reserve determine interest rates. The Fed takes these actions to influence the level of GDP and inflation in the economy.

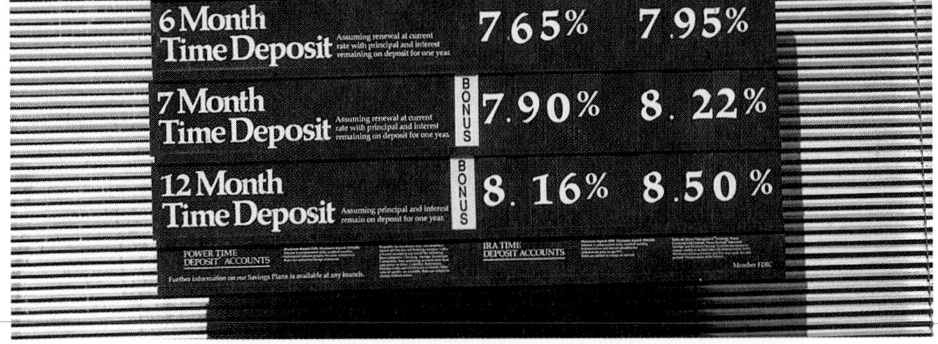

Interest rates are determined by the demand for and supply of money.

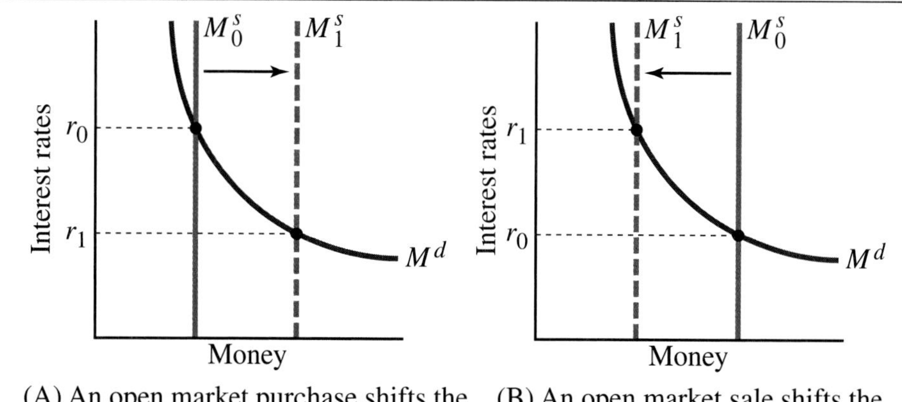

(A) An open market purchase shifts the supply of money to the right and leads to lower interest rates

(B) An open market sale shifts the supply of money to the left and leads to higher interest rates

Figure 4

Federal Reserve and Interest Rates

Bond Prices and Interest Rates

When interest rates rise in the economy, bond prices fall. Recall that bonds are promises to pay money in the future. If you own a bond, you are entitled to receive payments in the future. Why do the prices of bonds move in the opposite direction from interest rates?

For a bond that promises to pay money one period in the future, there is a simple formula that summarizes the relationship between interest rates and bond prices:

$$\text{price of bonds} = \frac{\text{promised payment}}{1 + \text{interest rate}}$$

The price of a bond is the promised payment divided by 1 plus the interest rate. To illustrate the formula, suppose the promised payment next year were \$106 and the interest rate were 6%. Then, using the formula, the price of the bond would be

$$\text{price of bond} = \frac{\$106}{1.06} = \$100$$

In this case, the bond would cost \$100.

There is an easy way to understand how this formula originates. If you had \$100 today and invested it at a 6% interest rate, you would have \$106 at the end of next year. Therefore, a bond that promises to pay you \$106 dollars next year is worth exactly \$100 today if you can invest at 6%. Thus the price of the bond will be the amount you would be willing to pay for the promised payment next year, or \$100.

The formula shows that bond prices move in the opposite direction from interest rates; that is, bond prices rise when interest rates fall and fall when interest rates rise. Let's consider two examples. Suppose the promised payment is still \$106 but the interest rate falls from 6% to 4%. Using the formula, the price of the bond is \$106/1.04, or \$101.92. The price of the bond rose in this case because, at the lower interest rate, you would need \$101.92 today to invest at 4% to have \$106 next year.

On the other hand, suppose interest rates rose from 6% from 8%. In this case the price of the bond would fall to \$106/1.08, or \$98.15. The reason the price of the bond fell is that you need only \$98.15 to invest at 8% to have \$106 next year. Thus, as interest rates rose, the price of the bond fell.

In financial markets there are many types of complex bonds that pay different sums of money at different times in the future. However, all bonds share one key feature: They are all promises to pay money in the future. Thus, as interest rates rise, investors need less money to match the promised payments in the future and the price of bonds falls. Similarly, as interest rates fall, investors need to have more money to match the promised payments. Therefore, prices of bonds will rise as interest rates fall. The same logic that applied to simple one-period bonds applies to more complex bonds as well.

There is another way to understand why bond prices and interest rates move in opposite directions. We know that when the Federal Reserve conducts an open market purchase, interest rates fall. But think about what the Federal Reserve is doing when it conducts the open market purchase. The Federal Reserve is buying bonds from the public. As it buys bonds, it increases the demand for bonds and raises their price. Thus prices of bonds rise as interest rates fall.

Similarly, interest rates rise following an open market sale. But when the Federal Reserve conducts an open market sale, it is selling bonds and thereby increasing the supply of bonds in the market. With an increase in the supply of bonds, the price of bonds will fall. Thus prices of bonds fall as interest rates increase.

Since the Federal Reserve can change interest rates and bond prices in the short run, you can now see why Wall Street firms hire "Fed watchers" to try to predict the actions of the Federal Reserve. If a Wall Street firm had an inside scoop that the Fed would surprise the market and lower interest rates, it could buy millions of dollars of bonds for itself or its clients and make a vast profit as bond prices subsequently rose.

The Federal Reserve is well aware of the importance of its deliberations and strives for secrecy. Sometimes it even calls on the law for help. In September 1996, some newspapers reported they had learned that eight regional bank presidents favored interest rate increases at the next meeting. The Federal Reserve actually called in the Federal Bureau of Investigation to explore whether there were leaks to the press. (As it turned out, the Federal Reserve did not raise interest rates that month.)

We can also use our understanding of bond prices and interest rates to explain a puzzling phenomenon about the bond market. The Closer Look box "Why Is Good News for the Economy Bad for the Bond Market?" explains this phenomenon using the tools we have developed.

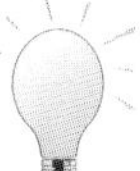

TEST *Your Understanding*

1 How do we measure the opportunity cost of holding money?

2 Complete the statement with *increase* or *decrease*: The quantity of money demanded will ____________ as interest rates increase.

3 Complete the statement with *increase* or *decrease*: Both increases in the price level and increases in real GDP will ____________ the demand for money.

4 What will happen to interest rates if the Fed conducts an open market sale?

5 If interest rates are 3%, what will be the price of a bond that promises to pay $109 next year?

INTEREST RATES, INVESTMENT, AND OUTPUT

To show how the Fed's actions affect the economy, we expand our short-run, demand model of the economy to include money and interest rates. There are three ingredients to the model.

1. The supply and demand for money, which determines interest rates in the economy

A Closer LOOK

Why Is Good News for the Economy Bad for the Bond Market?

As the *New York Times* article at right indicates, prices in the bond market often fall in the face of good economic news, such as an increase in real output. Why is good news for the economy bad news for the bond market?

We can understand the behavior of the bond market by thinking about the demand for money. When real GDP increases, the demand for money will increase. As the demand for money increases, this will shift the money demand curve to the right. From our model of the money market, we know that this will increase interest rates. Bond prices move in the opposite direction from interest rates. Therefore, good news for the economy is bad for the bond market.

High GDP growth may also lead to expectations of higher inflation in the future. This will tend to push up nominal interest rates as investors try to protect themselves against future inflation. Higher interest rates will again mean lower bond prices and bad news for the bond market.

Finally, despite the good news in the economy, stock prices still can fall, as the article indicates they did on July 5. As interest rates rise on bonds, it becomes more attractive to own bonds and the demand for stocks (a competing asset) falls. The result may be lower stock prices. Sometimes, however, stock prices do increase in the face of good news if this leads investors to think that profits (and thus future dividends from holding the stock) will be very high in the future.

U.S. JOBLESS RATE FOR JUNE AT 5.3%; LOWEST IN 6 YEARS

STOCKS AND BONDS DROP

Strong Labor Data Stir Fears of a Federal Reserve Move to Raise Interest Rates

By ROBERT D. HERSHEY Jr.

WASHINGTON, July 5 — The nation's unemployment rate dropped to 5.3 percent in June, its lowest point in six years, as signs of inflation appeared suddenly to mount, Labor Department figures showed today.

The fall in the unemployment rate was three-tenths of a percentage point, from 5.6 percent in May. The stunningly strong report, the first broad gauge of the economy's performance for the month, touched off sharp declines in the securities markets, where fears have been building of over-rapid growth that would produce rising wage demands and higher prices and prompt the Federal Reserve to tighten credit to keep inflation in check.

Interest rates surged across the board, with the yield on long-term Treasury bonds rocketing one-quarter point, to 7.18 percent, and the Dow Jones industrial average skidding 114.88 points, or slightly more than 2 percent, in a session shortened by the holiday weekend. [Page 17.]

bad news for bond market

good news

signs of inflation

interest rates rise

stock prices fall

Source: From Robert Hershey, Jr., "U.S. Jobless Rate for June at 5.3%; Lowest in 6 Years," *New York Times*, July 6, 1996, p. 1.

2. An investment function, which shows that investment spending decreases when interest rates increase
3. A demand-side $C + I + G + NX$ model in which we can find the level of output at which total demand equals total production using the 45°-line graph

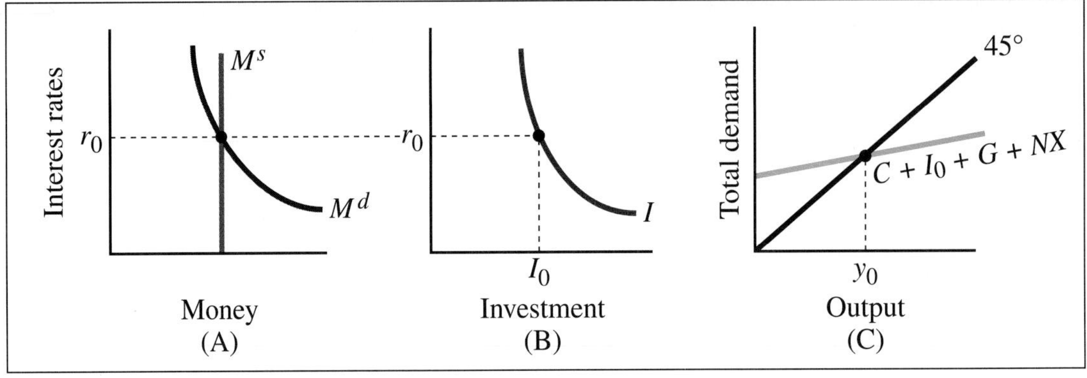

Figure 5 Demand-Side Model with Money

In panel A, the demand and supply for money determines the interest rate r_0*. At this interest rate, panel B shows investment spending at* I_0*. Finally, in panel C, output is determined where the total demand line, with investment at* I_0*, intersects the 45° line.*

In this model, the rate of interest is determined in the money market. The rate of interest, in turn, determines the level of investment in the economy. Finally, knowing the level of investment, we can find the level of output at which total demand for goods and services equals total output.

Figure 5 shows how the model works. In panel A we have the demand and supply for money, which determines the rate of interest, in this case r_0. In panel B, we plot investment as a decreasing function of the interest rate. At the interest rate of r_0, we find that investment spending will be I_0. Finally, panel C shows how the level of demand $C + I_0 + G + NX$ determines equilibrium output at y_0 using our familiar 45°-line graph. The level of investment spending we use in the 45°-line graph is the same level of investment we find from the two other panels.

Before illustrating how monetary policy works in this model, we should note that consumption as well as investment can depend on interest rates. Spending on consumer durables, such as automobiles or refrigerators, will also depend negatively on the rate of interest. Consumer durables are really investment goods for the household: If you buy an automobile, for example, you incur the cost today and receive benefits (the ability to use the car) in the future. As interest rates rise, the opportunity costs of investing in the automobile will rise. Consumers will respond to the increase in the opportunity cost by purchasing fewer cars. In the remainder of this chapter, we discuss how changes in interest rates affect investment but keep in mind that purchases of consumer durables will be affected as well.

Monetary Policy

Through its actions, the Federal Reserve can change the level of output in the short run. How does it do it? Consider an open market purchase. The Federal Reserve buys government bonds from the public and increases the supply of money. With an increase in the supply of money, interest rates fall. As we explained in the chapter, "Financial Intermediation and Investment," lower interest rates stimulate additional investment spending. Output or GDP increases by the multiplier.

Figure 6 shows how an open market purchase works in the economy. In panel A the supply of money increases from M_0^s to M_1^s and interest rates fall from r_0 to r_1. Investment spending increases from I_0 to I_1 or by ΔI. The increase in investment spending shifts up the total demand line by ΔI. GDP increases from y_0 to y_1 or by Δy.

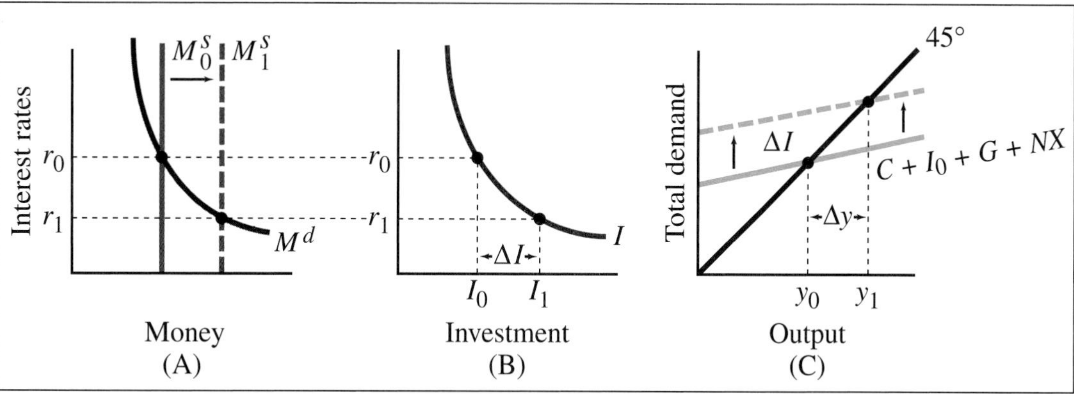

Figure 6 Open Market Purchase

An open market purchase increases the supply of money, decreases interest rates, and increases the level of output.

An open market sale works precisely in reverse. In an open market sale, the Federal Reserve sells bonds to the private sector, thereby reducing the money supply. Interest rates increase in the money market. With higher interest rates, firms will reduce their investment spending. The decrease in investment spending decreases the total demand for goods and services in the economy. The reduced demand for goods and services leads to a reduction in GDP. We can summarize this entire chain of events:

open market sale → money supply decrease → rise in interest rates →
fall in investment spending → decrease in GDP

Step back and think of the chain of events by which the Federal Reserve can affect the level of GDP in the short run. It all starts in the financial markets. By buying and selling government bonds, the Federal Reserve can change the supply of money and the level of interest rates. In making their investment decisions, firms and individuals are influenced by the level of interest rates. Finally, changes in the demand for goods and services will affect the level of GDP in the short run. The chain may be a bit indirect, but it is powerful.

The Federal Reserve can also influence the level of output through other tools that we discussed in the last chapter, such as changes in reserve requirements or changes in the discount rate. Actions taken by the Federal Reserve to influence the level of GDP are known as **monetary policy**.

Monetary policy: The range of actions taken by the Federal Reserve to influence the level of GDP or the rate of inflation

This model can be used to understand why bank failures are harmful to the economy. During the Great Depression, for example, there were severe bank failures throughout the world. How did these affect the level of GDP? Since deposits are part of the money supply, bank failures reduce the supply of money. As banks closed, they could no longer make loans, and as loans decreased, so did the amount of deposits into other banks. Bank failures therefore led to a contraction of the money supply. The effects of bank failures are thus similar to the effects of an open market sale. This decrease in the supply of money will reduce the level of output in the economy. In addition, when banks fail, there is less financial intermediation in the economy. The economy will become less efficient and the ultimate result will be less investment spending. Some economists believe that bank failures were an important reason why the Great Depression was so severe in the United States.

In an open economy, monetary policy will affect the level of imports, such as these Japanese cars arriving at Newark, New Jersey.

Monetary Policy in an Open Economy

Up until this point we have been discussing monetary policy without taking into account international trade or international movements of capital across countries. Once we bring in these international considerations, we will see that monetary policy operates through an additional channel.

Suppose the Federal Reserve conducts an open market operation and lowers U.S. interest rates. Investors in the United States will now be earning lower interest rates and will seek to invest some of their funds abroad. To invest abroad they will need to sell dollars and buy foreign currency. This will affect the **exchange rate**—the rate at which one currency trades for another in the market. In this case, as investors sell their dollars to buy foreign currency, the exchange rate or value of the dollar will fall. A fall in the exchange rate or a decrease in the value of a currency is called a **depreciation.** Therefore, lower U.S. interest rates will cause the dollar to depreciate or decline in value.

Exchange rate: The rate at which one currency trades for another in the market.

Depreciation: A fall in the exchange rate or a decrease in the value of a currency.

The lower value of the dollar will mean that U.S. goods become relatively cheaper on world markets. For example, suppose that the exchange rate was 2 German marks per 1 dollar, meaning that you received 2 German marks for every dollar. If a U.S. machine tool sold for $100,000, the machine tool would cost the Germans 200,000 marks. Suppose the value of the dollar fell so that you received only 1 mark for each dollar. The same machine tool would now cost the Germans only 100,000 marks. The lower value of the dollar makes U.S. goods cheaper to foreigners. With U.S. goods being less expensive, foreign residents will want to buy more of our goods. Thus we will export more to foreign countries.

The lower value of the dollar will also make it more expensive for U.S. residents to buy foreign goods. If the exchange rate were 2 German marks per dollar and a German car cost 60,000 marks, the car would cost a U.S. resident $30,000. However, if the exchange depreciates to 1 mark per dollar, the same car will now cost $60,000. Thus, as the U.S. exchange rate falls, imports become more expensive and U.S. residents will tend to import fewer goods.

As we have seen as the exchange rate falls, U.S. goods become cheaper and foreign goods become more expensive. This will mean that the United States will export more goods and import fewer goods. Since both exports increase and imports decrease, net exports will increase. The increase in net exports increases the demand for U.S. goods and increases GDP in the short run. We can summarize this entire chain of events:

open market purchase → money supply increase → fall in interest rates →
fall in exchange rates → increase in net exports → increase in GDP

The new links in the chain are from interest rates to exchange rates and, finally, to net exports.

This process also works in reverse. If the Fed raises interest rates, investors from around the world will want to invest in the United States. As they buy dollars, the exchange rate will increase and the dollar will increase in value. An increase in the value of a currency is called an **appreciation**. The appreciation of the dollar will make U.S. goods more expensive to foreigners and make imports cheaper for U.S. residents. For example, if the exchange rate appreciates to 3 marks per dollar, the machine tool will increase in price to the Germans to 300,000 marks, while the German car will fall in price to U.S. residents to $20,000.

Appreciation: A rise in the exchange rate or an increase in the value of a currency.

We thus expect exports to decrease and imports to increase. Net exports will therefore decrease. The decrease in net exports will decrease the demand for U.S. goods and lead to a fall in output in the short run.

The international channel for monetary policy reinforces the normal domestic channel that operates through investment. An increase in interest rates will reduce both investment spending (including consumer durables) and net exports. Similarly, a decrease in interest rates will increase investment spending and net exports. Monetary policy is even more powerful in an open economy than in a closed economy.

TEST ***Your Understanding***

6 Complete the statement with *higher* or *lower*: When the Federal Reserve conducts an open market sale, it leads to ____________ levels of investment and output in the economy.

7 Complete the statement with *sale* or *purchase*: To increase the level of output, the Fed should conduct an open market ____________.

8 What are all the events in the chain from an open market purchase to a change in output?

9 Complete the statement with *appreciate* or *depreciate*: An increase in the supply of money will ____________ a country's currency.

10 Explain the additional channel of monetary policy in an economy open to trade.

LIMITS TO DEMAND-SIDE POLICIES

Now that we have brought money into our model, we can see that the government has two different types of tools to change the level of GDP in the short run. The government can use either *fiscal policy*—changes in the level of taxes or government spending—or *monetary policy*—changes in the supply of money and interest rates—to alter the level of GDP. If the current level of GDP is below full employment or potential output, the government can use **expansionary policies** such as tax cuts, increased spending, or increases in the money supply to raise the level of GDP and reduce unemployment. If the current level of GDP exceeds full employment or potential output, the economy will overheat and inflation will break out. To avoid this, the government can use **contractionary policies** to reduce the level of GDP back to full employment or potential output. Both expansionary and contractionary policies are examples of **stabilization policies**, actions to move the economy closer to full employment or potential output.

Expansionary policies: Policies that aim to increase the level of GDP.

Contractionary policies: Policies that aim to decrease the level of GDP.

Stabilization policy: Policy actions taken to move the economy closer to full employment or potential output.

On paper, this sounds quite simple. In practice it is extremely difficult for two principal reasons. First, there are significant lags or delays in stabilization policy. Lags arise because decision makers are often slow to recognize and respond to changes in the economy and because monetary and fiscal policies take time to operate. Second, economists simply do not know enough about the economy to be accurate in all their forecasts.

Lags

Lags in policies are important because ill-timed policies can actually magnify economic fluctuations. Suppose that GDP was currently below full employment but would return to full employment on its own within one year. Also suppose that stabilization policies took a full year to become effective. If policymakers tried to expand the economy today, their actions would only take effect a year from now, when the economy would normally be back at full employment. The economy would then experience an unnecessary stimulus and output would exceed full employment.

Figure 7 illustrates the problem caused by lags. Panel A shows an example of successful stabilization policy. The solid line represents the behavior of GDP in the absence of policies. Successful stabilization policies can dampen economic fluctuations, lowering output when it exceeds full employment and raising output when it falls below full employment. If there were no lags in policy, this would be an easy task to accomplish. The dotted line shows how successful policies can reduce economic fluctuations.

Panel B shows the consequences of ill-timed policies. Again assume that policies take a year before they are effective. In year 0 the economy is below potential. If policymakers engaged in expansionary policies at that time, the change would not take effect until year 1. This would raise output even higher above full employment. Ill-timed stabilization policies can magnify economic fluctuations.

Inside lags: Lags in implementing policy.

Outside lags: The time it takes for policies to work.

Where do the lags in policy come from? Economists recognize two broad classes of lags: inside lags and outside lags. **Inside lags** are the lags in implementing policy; **outside lags** refer to the time it takes for policies to actually work. An analogy may help you understand the two types of lags. Imagine that you are steering a large ocean liner and are in charge of looking out for possible collisions with hidden

Figure 7

Possible Pitfalls in Stabilization Policy

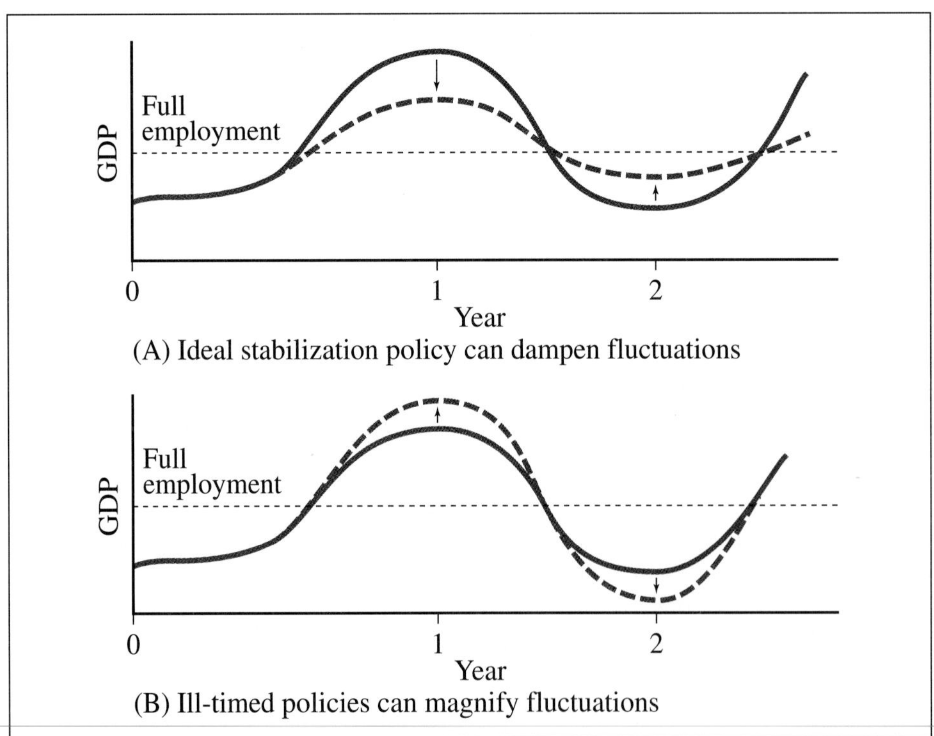

icebergs. The time it takes you to spot an iceberg, communicate this information to the crew, and initiate the process of changing course is the inside lag. Because ocean liners are large and have lots of momentum, it will take a long time before the ocean liner begins to turn—this is the outside lag.

Inside Lags

Inside lags occur for two basic reasons. First, it takes time to identify and recognize a problem. For example, the data available to policymakers may be poor and is often conflicting. Some indicators of the economy may look fine whereas others appear worrisome. It often takes several months or even a year before it is clear that there is a serious problem with the economy.

A good example of this problem occurred during the most recent recession in 1990. Today we date the beginning of the recession from July 1990, a month before Iraq invaded Kuwait. After the invasion, there was some concern that higher oil prices and the uncertainty of the political situation would trigger a recession. However, Alan Greenspan, the chairman of the Federal Reserve, testified before Congress as late as October 1990 that the economy had not yet slipped into a recession. Not until December did Greenspan declare that the economy had entered into a recession. Yet, looking back, we now know that a recession had started five months earlier.

Another example of an inside lag occurred at the beginning of the Great Depression. Although the stock market crashed in October 1929, we know through newspaper and magazine accounts that business leaders were not particularly worried about the economy for some time. Not until late in 1930 did the public begin to recognize the severity of the depression.

A second reason for inside lags is that once a problem has been diagnosed, it still takes time before any actions can be taken. This problem is most severe for fiscal policy in the United States. Any changes in taxes or spending must be approved by both houses of Congress and by the President. In recent years, the political system has been preoccupied with fights about the size and role of government. In this environment it is difficult to obtain a consensus for tax or spending changes in a timely manner.

For example, soon after he was elected, President Bill Clinton proposed a "stimulus package" as part of his overall budget plan. This stimulus package contained a variety of spending programs and was designed to increase the level of GDP and avoid the risks of a recession. However, his plan was attacked as wasteful and unnecessary government spending and did not survive. As it turned out, the stimulus package was not necessary in any case, as the economy grew rapidly in the next several years. Nonetheless, this episode illustrates how difficult it is to conduct an active fiscal policy.

Monetary policy is not subject to the same long inside lags. In a smaller group it is easier to reach a consensus. The Federal Open Market Committee meets eight times a year and can decide on major policy changes at any time. The FOMC can even give the chair of the Board of Governors some discretion between meetings.

Outside Lags

Both monetary and fiscal policy are subject to outside lags, the time it takes for policy to be effective. Consider monetary policy: The Federal Reserve can increase the money supply and lower interest rates fairly rapidly, but firms must change their investment plans before monetary policy can be effective.

To gain some perspective on the outside lags for monetary policy, we can examine the results from several well-respected **econometric models**, statistical-based computer models that economists build to capture the actual dynamics of

Econometric models: Statistical-based computer models that economists build to capture the actual dynamics of the economy.

Figure 8

Fall in GDP from One Percentage Point Increase in Interest Rates: Results from Four Econometric Models

Source: Glenn Rudebusch, "What Are the Lags in Monetary Policy?" *Federal Reserve Bank of San Francisco Weekly*, February 3, 1995.

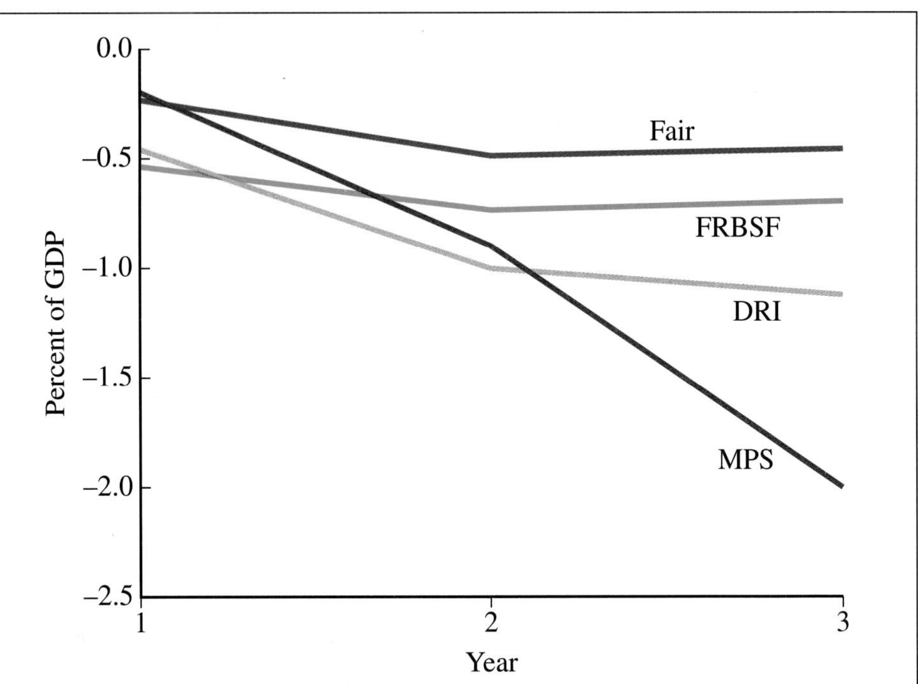

the economy. Figure 8 presents estimates of the lags in monetary policy from four different econometric models of the economy. Since these models have been built by different organizations and individuals who rely on somewhat different interpretations of macroeconomic theory and who use different statistical methods to build their models, they provide different estimates of the effects of monetary policy.

In Figure 8 we show for each of these models the effects on real GDP of a 1 percentage point increase in short-term interest rates (from 4% to 5%) after one, two, and three years. (The data for Figure 8 are given in Table 1.) That is, with each model we calculate what would happen to real GDP if we raise short-term interest rates by 1 point and then display the results in the figure. As we can see from the figure, after one year the models predict that GDP would fall between one-fourth and one-half percentage point. This means that if GDP growth were 3.0% per year before interest rates were increased, the models predict that GDP would grow at a rate between 2.5 and 2.75%. At least for the first year, the predictions of the models are quite similar.

However, the models differ sharply in their predictions for later years. The MPS model (used at the Board of Governors at the Fed) has GDP falling by 2 percentage points after three years, while the Fair model (developed by Yale economist Ray Fair) shows only a ½ percentage point fall in output after three years. The predictions from

Table 1: Fall in GDP from a One Percentage Point Increase in Interest Rates (percent)

	Model			
Year	*DRI*	*Fair*	*FRBSF*	*MPS*
1	0.47	0.24	0.55	0.20
2	1.00	0.49	0.74	0.90
3	1.13	0.46	0.70	2.00

the other two models, DRI (Data Resources) and FRBSF (Federal Reserve Bank of San Francisco), fall in between. As Figure 8 suggests, the outside lag for monetary policy can be long and is also uncertain.

Fiscal policy also is subject to outside lags. If taxes are cut, individuals and businesses must change their spending plans before any effects will be felt in the economy. It also takes some time before increases in desired spending raise GDP. While fiscal policy has a much longer inside lag than monetary policy, its outside lag is shorter. For example, the MPS model predicts that an increase in government spending will increase GDP by its maximum effect after just six months.

Forecasting Uncertainties

In addition to the problem of lags, economists are simply not terribly accurate in forecasting the economy. For example, a classic problem that policymakers face when the economy appears to be slowing down is knowing whether the slowdown is temporary or will persist. In addition to using econometric models, the Fed also relies on a variety of other information, as the Closer Look box "Science or Intuition?" explains.

Unfortunately, stabilization policy cannot be very effective without accurate forecasting. If economic forecasters predict an overheated economy and the Federal Reserve adopts a contractionary policy, the result could be disastrous if the economy weakened before the policy took effect. Today, most economic policymakers understand these limitations and are cautious in using activist policies.

Looking Ahead

The demand-side models we developed in this section are *applicable only in the short run*, when prices do not change. Monetary policy can affect output in the short run when prices are sticky, but in the long run changes in the money supply only affect inflation. The Federal Reserve cannot control real interest rates in the long run. In the next part of the book we study how prices change over time and how the economy makes the transition from the short to the long run.

A Closer LOOK

Science or Intuition?

Are the decisions of the Federal Reserve based on scientific economic models or are they largely guesswork? The Federal Reserve does use econometric models to help forecast the economy and evaluate the consequences of alternative policies. The staff of the Federal Reserve provides the members of the Federal Open Market Committee with its latest forecasts and predictions from its own model of the economy.

Members of the FOMC, however, are skeptical of the predictions of any one model. They prefer to use information from a variety of different, and sometimes conflicting, models as well as from various indicators of the economy. They even rely on anecdotal evidence about demand from trade groups in various parts of the economy.

Changes in the U.S. economy make it difficult for the FOMC to rely on a single model. Large statistical models of the economy must be based on historical data. If the economy undergoes structural change, these past relationships may no longer be reliable. For example, with computers many firms keep better track of their inventories and are not so slow in making adjustments as in the past. The Fed believes that making monetary policy is not a science but requires guesswork, judgment, and intuition.

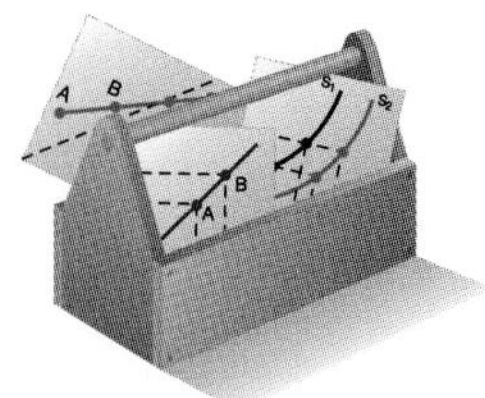

Using the **TOOLS**

In this chapter we developed the money demand curve, which enabled us to understand how interest rates are determined. We then integrated money demand, money supply, and investment spending into a complete demand-side model of the economy with money. Here is an opportunity to use the tools developed in this chapter.

1. Interest Rates on Checking Accounts

During the 1980s banks started to pay interest (at low rates) on checking accounts for the first time. Given what you know about opportunity costs, how would this affect the demand for money?

2. Pegging Interest Rates

Suppose the Federal Reserve wanted to fix or "peg" the level of interest rates at 6%. Using a simple supply and demand diagram, show how increases in money demand would change the supply of money if the Federal Reserve pursued the policy. Use your answer to explain this quote: "If the Federal Reserve pegs interest rates, it loses control of the money supply."

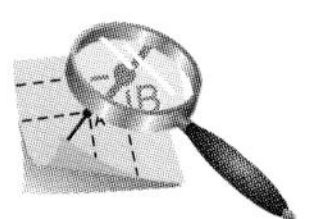

3. ECONOMIC DETECTIVE– *The Mystery of Increasing Interest Rates and Economic Recovery*

Economists have often noticed that as an economy recovers from a recession, interest rates start to rise. Some observers felt that this was mysterious because they believed that higher interest rates were associated with lower output. Using the demand and supply for money diagram, explain why interest rates can rise during an economic recovery.

4. The Presidential Praise and Blame Game

Presidents like to take credit for good economic performance. If there are lags in policies, explain why presidents may not deserve all the credit (or blame) for economic policies.

SUMMARY

This chapter brought money and monetary policy into a demand-side model of the economy for the short run. The Fed can control the level of interest rates by open market operations. Changes in interest rates will in turn affect investment and output. In an open economy, exchange rates and net exports are also affected by interest rates. We also discussed the limits to conducting successful stabilization policy. Here are the main points from the chapter:

1. The demand for money depends negatively on the interest rate and positively on the level of prices and GDP.
2. The level of interest rates is determined in the money market by the demand and supply for money.
3. To increase the level of GDP, the Federal Reserve conducts open market purchases. To decrease the level of GDP, the Federal Reserve conducts open market sales.
4. An increase in the money supply will decrease interest rates, increase investment spending, and increase output. A decrease in the money supply will increase interest rates, decrease investment spending, and decrease output.

5. In an open economy, a decrease in interest rates will depreciate the exchange rate and lead to an increase in net exports. An increase in interest rates will appreciate the exchange rate and lead to a decrease in net exports.
6. Both lags in economic policies and our own uncertainties about the economy make successful stabilization policy extremely difficult in practice.

KEY TERMS

appreciation, *581*
contractionary policies, *581*
depreciation, *580*
econometric models, *583*
exchange rate, *580*
expansionary policies, *581*
inside lags, *582*
liquidity demand for money, *572*
monetary policy, *579*
outside lags, *582*
speculative demand for money, *573*
stabilization policy, *581*
transactions demand for money, *571*

PROBLEMS AND DISCUSSION QUESTIONS

1. Explain carefully why the interest rate is the opportunity cost of holding money.
2. If you strongly believed that the Federal Reserve were going to surprise the markets and raise interest rates, would you want to buy or sell bonds?
3. If investment spending became less sensitive to interest rates, how would this affect the strength of monetary policy?
4. Compare the relative lengths of the inside and outside lags for monetary and fiscal policy.
5. Describe how well-meaning attempts to stabilize the economy could actually destabilize the economy.
6. Why is monetary policy stronger in an open economy?
7. Some members of the Board of Governors have looked to prices of commodities such as gold or copper as "early warning signs" of inflation. What policies would they recommend if they saw the price of gold beginning to rise? Can you think of any reasons, not related to the general inflation rate, why the price of gold might start to increase?

Take It to the Net

We invite you to visit the O'Sullivan/Sheffrin page on the Prentice Hall Web site at:

http://www.prenhall.com/osullivan/

for this chapter's World Wide Web exercise.

MODEL ANSWERS FOR THIS CHAPTER

Chapter-Opening Questions

1. When the Federal Reserve conducts open market sales, the money supply decreases. Given the demand for money, this raises interest rates.
2. The price of bonds is inversely related to interest rates. Since bonds are promises to pay money in the future, these promises are worth less today when interest rates rise.
3. If the Federal Reserve increases the supply of money, interest rates will fall. Lower interest rates will lead to more production of housing and increased construction.
4. It takes time for lower interest rates to stimulate the economy. If the Federal Reserve believed that a slump was only temporary, it would be reluctant to reduce interest rates for fear of creating

too much demand at the time when the economy recovered.

Test Your Understanding

1. We use the interest rates to measure the opportunity cost of holding money because the alternative to holding money is holding assets that pay interest.
2. decrease
3. increase
4. Interest rates will increase.
5. The price will be $109/1.03 = $105.83.
6. lower
7. purchase
8. An increase in the money supply will lower interest rates, raise investment, and raise output.
9. depreciate
10. An increase in the money supply will lower interest rates, depreciate the exchange rate, raise net exports, and raise output.

Using the Tools

1. Interest Rates on Checking Accounts

   When interest is paid on checking accounts, it lowers the opportunity costs of holding wealth in these accounts. With a lower opportunity cost, the demand for money will increase.
2. Pegging Interest Rates

   Start with a demand and supply for money graph where the equilibrium interest rate is 6%. An increase in the demand for money will shift the demand curve to the right and raise interest rates above 6%. To prevent this from occurring, the Federal Reserve must increase the supply of money. Similarly, a decrease in the demand for money will lower interest rates below 6% unless the Federal Reserve decreases the demand for money. In either case the Federal Reserve will lose control of the supply of money. If there are shifts in the demand for money, the Federal Reserve cannot control interest rates and the supply of money at the same time.
3. Economic Detective: The Mystery of Increasing Interest Rates and Economic Recovery

   During a recovery GDP increases, which increases the demand for money. As the demand for money increases, interest rates rise.
4. The Presidential Praise and Blame Game

   Lags make it difficult to tell whether a president is truly responsible for economic developments. If there is a two-year lag in policies, the fate of a new president for the first half of his or her term is largely determined by his or her predecessor.

CHAPTER

Part 10 ■

Inflation, Unemployment, and Government Deficits

29

From the Short Run to the Long Run

In the long run, we are all dead.
John Maynard Keynes, *A Tract on Monetary Reform*

I don't try to forecast short-term changes in the economy. The record of economists in doing that justifies only humility.
Milton Friedman

One of the great unresolved debates in macroeconomics centers on the importance of short-run versus long-run considerations for macroeconomic policy. Up to this point we have discussed the economics of the long run (classical economics) and the economics of the short run (Keynesian economics) separately. In this chapter we explain how the economy evolves over time so that the short run becomes the long run. The relationship between the short run and the long run is one of the most important ingredients in modern macroeconomics.

These are some of the real-world questions we answer in this chapter:

1. Why do we often see wages in all sectors of the economy rising or falling together?
2. Why does expansionary monetary policy raise output in the short run but only lead to higher prices in the long run?

3 Why has the job of the Federal Reserve been described as "taking the punch bowl away at the party?"

4 Why might tax cuts have beneficial effects for the economy now but have harmful effects in the future?

DEFINITIONS

To understand how the short run and the long run are related, let's first recall how we define the long run and short run in macroeconomics:

Long Run

In the long run when prices are fully flexible, the level of GDP is determined by the demand and supply for labor, the stock of capital, and technological progress. The economy operates at full employment. With the supply of output fixed at full employment, increases in government spending must come at the expense of other uses of output. We also saw in our chapter on aggregate demand and supply that increases in the supply of money (or any other increase in aggregate demand) only increase the level of prices in the long run and not the level of output.

Short Run

In the short run when prices are sticky, the level of GDP is determined by the total level of demand for goods and services. Increases in the supply of money lower interest rates, stimulate investment, and increase GDP. Increases in government spending or cuts in taxes will also lead to increases in GDP.

Should economic policy be guided by the short run or the long run? To answer this question, we need to know two things:

1. How is the short-run behavior of the economy linked to the long run?
2. How long is the short run?

The links between the short run and the long run are provided by the adjustment of wages and prices. In the short run, wages and prices are sticky and do not move immediately with changes in demand. Over time, however, wages and prices adjust and the economy reaches its long-run equilibrium.

Short-run, Keynesian economics applies to the period when wages and prices have not adjusted substantially. Long-run, full-employment economics applies after wages and prices have largely adjusted to changes in demand. Wage and price adjustment provide the links between Keynesian and classical economics.

WAGE AND PRICE ADJUSTMENTS

Wages and prices change every day in our economy. If the demand for roller blades rises at the same time as the demand for tennis racquets falls, we would expect to see a rise in the price of roller blades and a fall in the price of tennis racquets. Wages in the roller blade industry would also tend to increase while wages in the tennis racquet industry would tend to fall.

Sometimes, however, we see wages and prices in all industries rising or falling together. For example, prices for steel, automobiles, food, and fuel may all rise together. Why does this occur? Wages and prices will all tend to increase together during booms when GDP exceeds its full-employment level or potential output. On the other hand, wages and prices will fall together during periods of recessions when GDP falls below full employment or potential output.

If the economy is producing at a level above full employment, firms will find it increasingly difficult to hire and retain workers. Unemployment will be below its natural rate. Workers, on the other hand, will find it easy to obtain a job and easy to change jobs. To attract workers to their firms and to prevent their own workers from quitting, firms will have to raise wages to try to outbid their competitors. As one firm raises its wage, other firms will have to raise their wages even higher to attract workers. The actions of firms start a process in which wages increase through the economy.

For most firms, wages are the largest single cost of production. As their labor costs increase, they have no choice but to increase their prices as well. As prices rise, workers know they need higher dollar or nominal wages to maintain their real wage. This is an illustration of the reality principle:

Reality PRINCIPLE

What matters to people is the real value or purchasing power of money or income, not its face value.

This process by which rising wages cause higher prices and higher prices feed higher wages is known as a **wage–price spiral**. It occurs when the economy is producing at a level of output that exceeds potential output.

Wage–price spiral: The process by which changes in wages and prices reinforce each other.

When the economy is producing below full employment or potential output, the process works in reverse. Unemployment will exceed the natural rate and there will be excess unemployment. Firms will find that it is easy to hire and retain workers and even that they can offer less than other firms and still find skilled workers. As all firms cut wages, the average level of wages in the economy falls. Since wages are the single largest component of costs, prices start to fall as well. The wage–price spiral works in reverse.

Table 1 summarizes our discussion of unemployment, output, and changes in wages. The movements in wages and prices that occur when the economy is not producing at full employment are typically changes away from an underlying trend in inflation in the economy. For example, suppose the economy had been experiencing 6% inflation. If output exceeds full employment, prices will rise at a faster rate than 6%. On the other hand, if output is less than full employment, prices will rise at a slower rate than 6%. For the remainder of this chapter we ignore this underlying trend and concentrate on movements away from it. In the next chapter, we discuss changes in the trend rate of inflation.

If employers have a difficult time in finding new workers, wages will begin to rise.

In summary, when output exceeds potential output, wages and prices throughout the economy will rise above previous inflation rates. If output is less than potential output, wages and prices will fall relative to previous inflation rates.

Table 1: Unemployment, Output, and Wage and Price Changes

When unemployment is below *the natural rate . . .*	*When unemployment is* above *the natural rate . . .*
Output is above potential	Output is below potential
Wages and prices rise	Wages and prices fall

AGGREGATE DEMAND, AGGREGATE SUPPLY, AND ADJUSTMENT

The transition between the short run and the long run is easy to understand. If GDP is higher than potential output, the economy starts to overheat and wages and prices increase. This increase in wages and prices will push the economy back to full employment.

We can illustrate the process by which the economy moves from a short-run equilibrium to the long run by using a graphical analysis that employs aggregate demand and aggregate supply. Before showing the adjustment process, let's review the aggregate demand and supply graphs:

Aggregate demand curve: The relationship between the price level and the quantity of real GDP demanded.

Classical aggregate supply curve: The vertical aggregate supply curve at full employment.

Keynesian aggregate supply curve: The horizontal aggregate supply at the current level of prices.

1. *Aggregate demand.* The **aggregate demand curve** is plotted with the price on the vertical axis and real output on the horizontal axis. It shows the total level of demand for goods and services for any level of prices.

2. *Aggregate supply.* We have discussed two aggregate supply curves. The **classical aggregate supply curve** (long run) is a vertical line at the full-employment level of output. The **Keynesian aggregate supply curve** (short run) is a horizontal line at the current level of prices. It is horizontal because, as economists typically find, changes in demand lead to very small changes in prices over short periods of time.

Figure 1 shows an aggregate demand curve and the two aggregate supply curves. In the short run, output and prices are determined where the aggregate demand curve intersects the Keynesian aggregate supply curve at point *A*. This corresponds to a level of real output y_0 and a price level P_0.

In the long run, the level of prices and output is given by the intersection of the aggregate demand curve and the classical aggregate supply curve. This occurs at point *D* in the diagram. Output is at full employment y_F while prices are at P_F. How does the economy move from point *A* in the short run to point *D* in the long run?

At point *A* the current level of output y_0 exceeds the full employment level of output y_F. With output exceeding full employment, the unemployment rate is below

Figure 1

Aggregate Demand and Aggregate Supply

The aggregate demand curve *AD* intersects the Keynesian aggregate supply curve at point *A* and the classical aggregate supply curve at point *D*.

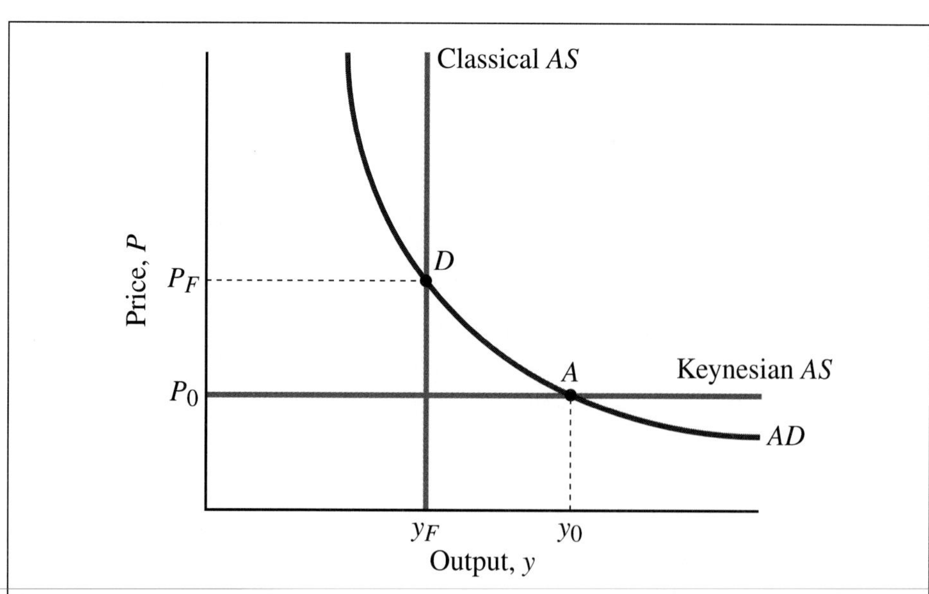

the natural rate. Firms find it difficult to hire and retain workers and the wage–price spiral begins. As the level of prices increases, the Keynesian aggregate supply curve shifts up over time. The Keynesian aggregate supply curve shifts up because increases in wages raise costs for firms. With higher costs, firms must charge higher prices in order to avoid losing money.

This shift in the Keynesian aggregate supply curve will bring the economy to long-run equilibrium. In Figure 2 we illustrate this process. The economy initially starts at point A, with output exceeding full employment. As prices rise, the aggregate supply curve shifts up from AS_0 to AS_1. The aggregate demand and the new aggregate supply curve now intersect at point B. This corresponds to a higher level of prices and a lower level of real output. Nonetheless, the level of output still exceeds full employment. Wages and prices will continue to rise, shifting up the Keynesian aggregate supply curve. At point C the aggregate supply curve AS_2 intersects the aggregate demand curve at a still higher level of price and lower level of output. As the aggregate supply curve continues to shift up, it will intersect the aggregate demand curve at higher level of prices and lower levels of output.

Eventually, the aggregate supply curve will shift to AS_3 and the economy will reach point D. This is also the intersection of the aggregate demand curve and the classical aggregate supply curve. At this point the adjustment process stops. The economy is now at full employment and the unemployment rate is at the natural rate. With unemployment at the natural rate, the wage–price spiral comes to an end. The economy has made the transition to the long run. Note that the end result is the one predicted by the classical model. Prices are higher and output returns to full employment.

If the current level of output is below full employment, wages and prices will fall to return the economy to its long-run equilibrium at full employment. Figure 3 on the next page illustrates this process. The economy originally starts at point A, at a level of output below full employment. With unemployment above the natural rate and excess unemployment, the level of wages and prices will fall. As the aggregate supply curve shifts from AS_0 to AS_1, the economy moves from point A to point B and closer to full employment. The process comes to an end when the aggregate supply curve shifts to AS_2 and the economy returns to full employment at point D. This is how an economy recovers from a recession or a downturn.

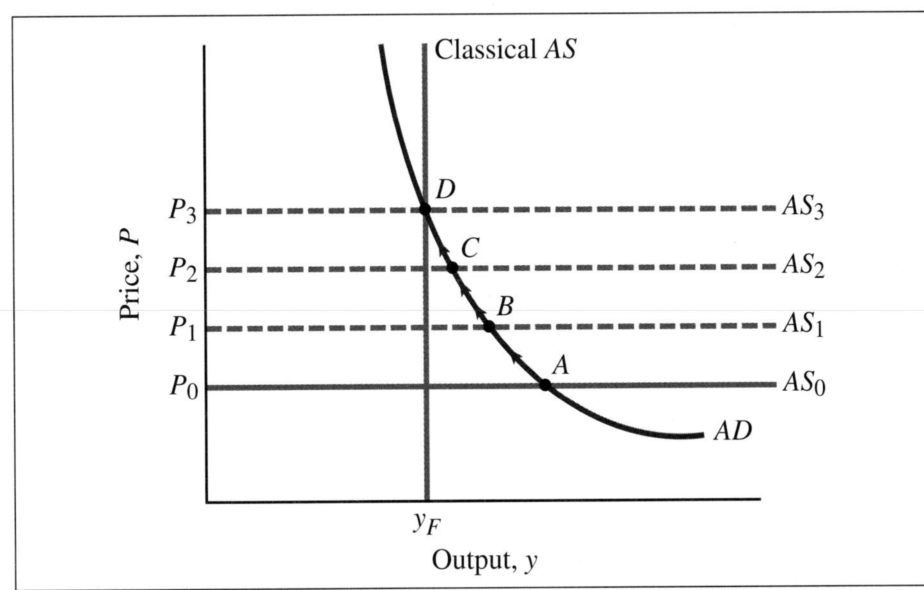

Figure 2

Shifts in the Keynesian Aggregate Supply

As prices rise in the economy, the Keynesian aggregate supply curve shifts up. The economy moves from point A to point B. The process will continue until the economy reaches the long run equilibrium at point D.

Figure 3

Returning to Full Employment

If the initial level of output is less than full employment, wages and prices will fall. As the aggregate supply curve shifts down, the economy returns to full employment at point *D*.

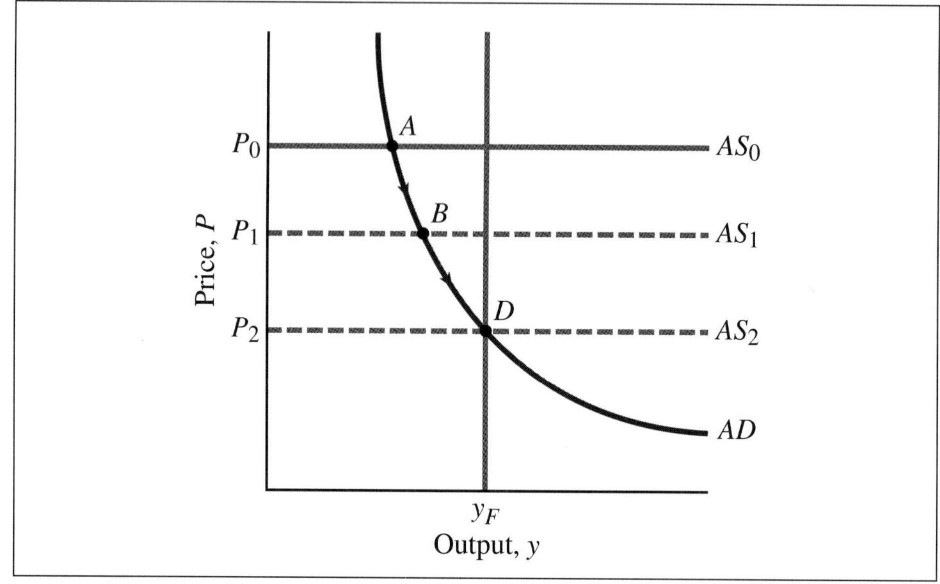

In summary, the economy will eventually return to full employment. If output exceeds full employment, prices will rise and output will fall back to full employment. If output is less than full employment, prices will fall as the economy returns to full employment.

TEST *Your Understanding*

1 True or false: Wages and prices will increase when unemployment exceeds the natural rate.

2 In what direction does the Keynesian aggregate supply curve move if output is below its potential?

THE SPEED OF ADJUSTMENT AND ECONOMIC POLICY

How long does it take to move from the short run to the long run? Economists disagree on this point, with their estimates for the U.S. economy ranging from two to six years. Since the adjustment process can operate slowly, there is room, in principle, for policymakers to step in and guide the economy back to full employment.

Suppose the economy were operating below full employment at point *A* in Figure 4 on the next page. One alternative would be to simply do nothing and allow the adjustment process, with falling wages and prices, to return the economy to full employment at point *D*. However, this may take several years. During that time the economy will experience excess unemployment and a level of real output below potential.

A second alternative would be to use expansionary policies (open market purchases, increases in government spending, or tax cuts) to shift the aggregate demand curve to the right. In Figure 4 we show how expansionary policies could shift the aggregate demand curve from AD_0 to AD_1 and move the economy to full employment at point *E*. Notice that the price level is higher at point *E* than it would be at point *D*.

Demand policies can also be used to prevent a wage–price spiral from emerging if the economy is producing at a level of output above full employment. Rather than

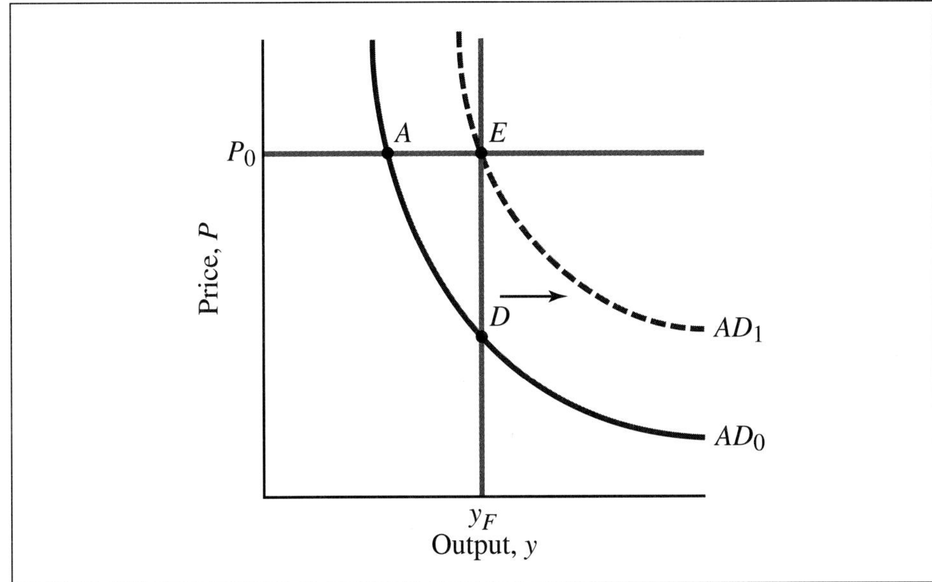

Figure 4

Using Economic Policy to Fight a Recession

Rather than letting the economy naturally return to full employment at point D, we can increase aggregate demand from AD_0 to AD_1 to bring the economy to full employment at point E.

letting an increase in wages and prices bring the economy back to full employment, we can reduce aggregate demand. Either contractionary monetary policy (open market sales) or contractionary fiscal policy (cuts in government spending or tax increases) can be used to reduce aggregate demand and the level of GDP until it reaches potential output.

Stabilization policies always look simple on paper or on graphs. In practice, the lags and uncertainties we discussed in the previous chapter make the task difficult. For example, suppose that just as we decided to increase aggregate demand, the Keynesian aggregate supply curve shifted down and intersected the original aggregate demand curve at full employment. This might occur if the adjustment process operated rapidly. In that case wages would quickly fall and the lower wages would rapidly lead to lower prices as firms' costs fell. Our economic policy would then destabilize the economy. As the aggregate demand curve shifted to the right, it would push the economy past full employment, leading to a wage–price spiral.

Active economic policies are more likely to destabilize the economy if the adjustment process operates quickly. Economists who believe the economy adjusts rapidly to full employment generally oppose using monetary or fiscal policy to try to stabilize the economy. Economists who believe the adjustment process operates slowly are more sympathetic to using monetary or fiscal policy to stabilize the economy. It is also possible for the speed of adjustment to vary over time, making decisions about policy even more difficult.

As an example, economic advisers for President Bush had to decide whether the economy needed any additional stimulus after the recession of 1990. Based on the view that the economy would recover on its own, only some minor steps were taken. However, the economy recovered completely at the very end of his administration but too late for his reelection prospects.

Up to this point we have assumed that the economy could always recover from a recession without active policy, although it might take a long period of time. Keynes expressed doubts about whether a country could recover from a major recession without active policy. He feared that falling prices could hurt business. Japan's recession in 1993–1995 illustrates some of the difficulties raised by Keynes, as the Closer Look box on the next page, "Japan's Bumpy Road to Recovery," explains.

A Closer LOOK

Japan's Bumpy Road to Recovery

Japan's rapid postwar economic growth came to a halt around 1992, and by 1993–1994 the country was suffering from a recession. Inflation started to fall as part of the adjustment process. By 1995, inflation had virtually disappeared from the economy, and wholesale prices had fallen for several years.

Yet the reduction in inflation caused problems for the economy. Real estate prices fell nearly 50% starting in 1990. Large banks that were major investors in real estate lost vast sums of money and became reluctant to make loans for other investments. Inflation rates were lower than businesses and household borrowers had anticipated. This raised the burden of debt for both businesses and households and made them more reluctant to purchase goods and services. With fewer loans from banks for new investment and reluctant households and firms, aggregate demand for goods and services was weak.

For several years the United States urged Japan to increase its public spending to stimulate the economy. Japan was reluctant to expand its public sector simply to stimulate the economy, but it finally did increase government spending in 1995. For most of the recession, Japan decided to allow the adjustment process to work. But it was a bumpy road to recovery. It was not until 1996 that the process of recovery and faster economic growth finally began.

While the lights may have been bright in Tokyo, the Japanese economy experienced difficult times in the 1990s.

A CLOSER LOOK AT THE ADJUSTMENT PROCESS

We have emphasized that changes in wages and prices restore the economy to full employment in the long run. But exactly how does this mechanism work? We can answer this question using the model of demand with money from the last chapter.

In Figure 5 on the next page, we show the three graphs that make up the model: the money market, the investment schedule, and the 45° line demand diagram. Interest rates are determined by the demand and supply for money. In turn, interest rates determine the level of investment spending in the economy. Investment spending—along with consumption, government spending, and net exports—determines the level of GDP.

The part of this diagram that we want to focus on now is money demand. Recall the reality principle:

Reality PRINCIPLE

What matters to people is the real value or purchasing power of money or income, not its face value.

Using this principle, the amount of money that people want to hold will depend on the price level. If prices are cut in half, you need to hold only half as much money to purchases the same goods and services. Decreases in the price level will cause the money demand curve to shift to the left.

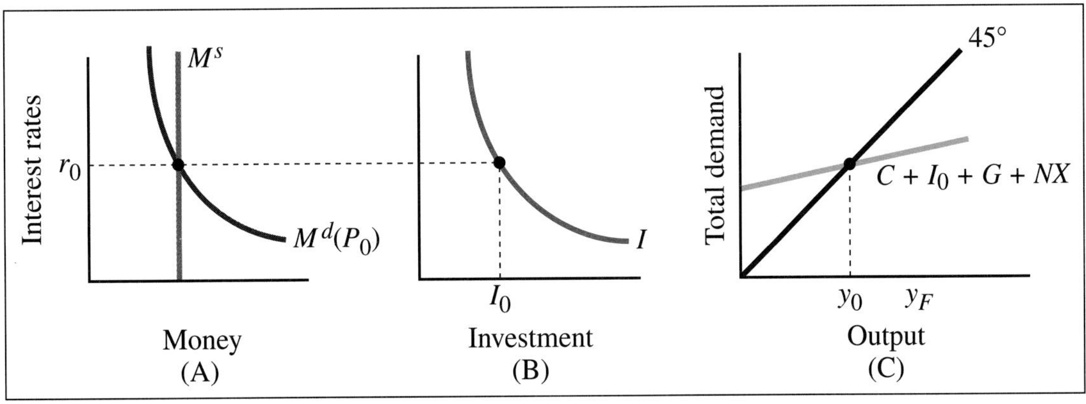

Figure 5 Model of Demand with Money

At the current price level P_0*, the economy is producing at a level of output* y_0 *that is below full employment* y_F.

In Figure 5, the price level is P_0. At that price level, interest rates are at r_0, investment spending is at I_0, and the economy is producing at y_0. This level of output is below full employment. With output below full employment, unemployment will exceed the natural rate and there will be excess unemployment. Wages and prices will start to fall.

The fall in the price level will decrease the demand for holding money. In Figure 6 on the next page, as the price level decreases from P_0 to P_1, the demand for money shifts to the left. Interest rates fall from r_0 to r_1, which increases investment spending from I_0 to I_1. As the level of investment spending in the economy increases, the total demand line shifts up and raises the level of output in the economy.

This process will continue until the economy reaches full employment. As long as output is below full employment, prices will continue to fall. A fall in the price level reduces money demand and interest rates. Lower interest rates stimulate investment spending and push the economy back toward full employment.

This process works in reverse if current output exceeds potential. In this case the economy is overheating and wages and prices rise. A higher price level will increase the demand for money and raise interest rates. Higher interest rates will decrease investment spending and reduce the level of output. This process continues until the economy returns to full employment.

We can now see why changes in wages and prices restore the economy to full employment. The key is that changes in wages and prices will change the demand for money and interest rates. In turn, changes in interest rates affect investment and the level of GDP in the economy.

LONG-RUN NEUTRALITY OF MONEY

We can use the model of demand with money to understand one of the key questions of modern macroeconomics: How is it that the Federal Reserve can change the level of output in the short run but only affect prices in the long run? Why is the short run different from the long run?

Figure 7 on the next page can help us understand these questions. The economy starts at full employment y_F. Interest rates are at r_F and investment spending is at I_F. Now suppose that the Federal Reserve increases the money supply from M_0^s to M_1^s. In the short run, the increase in the supply of money will reduce interest rates to r_0.

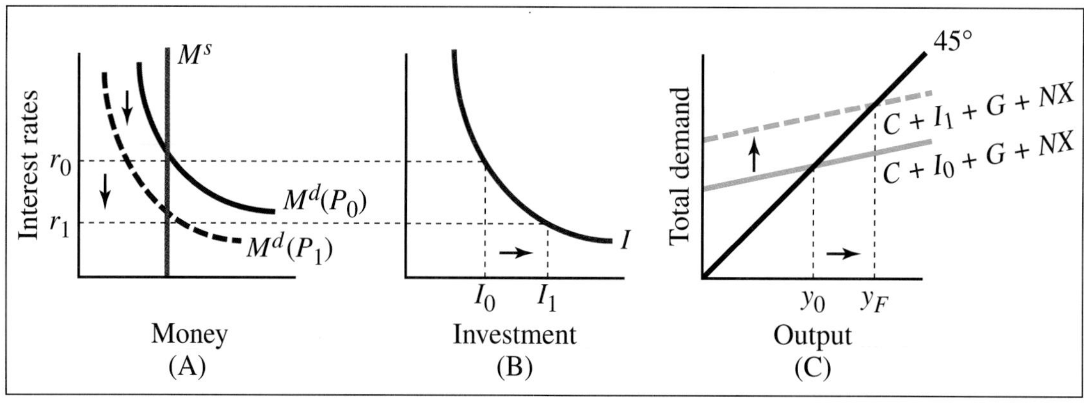

Figure 6 Returning to Full Employment

When output is below full employment, the price level falls. This reduces the demand for money and interest rates. Lower interest rates increase investment and stimulate spending. The economy returns to full employment.

The level of investment spending will increase to I_0. The increased demand for output will raise output above full employment to y_0. All this occurs in the short run. The single-headed arrows in Figure 7 show these movements.

However, now output exceeds full employment and wages and prices will start to increase. As the price level increases, the demand for money will increase. This will start to increase interest rates. Investment will start to fall as interest rates increase and this leads to a fall in output. The double-headed arrows in Figure 7 show the transition as prices increase. As long as output exceeds full employment, prices will continue to rise, money demand will continue to increase, and interest rates will continue to rise. Where does this process end? It ends only when interest rates return to their original level of r_F. At that level of interest rates, investment spending will have

Figure 7 Neutrality of Money

Starting at full employment, an increase in the supply of money will initially reduce interest rates from r_F *to* r_0*, raise investment spending from* I_F *to* I_0*, and increase output above full employment from* y_F *to* y_0 *(single-headed arrows). As wages and prices increase, the demand for money increases, restoring interest rates, investment, and output to full employment (double-headed arrows).*

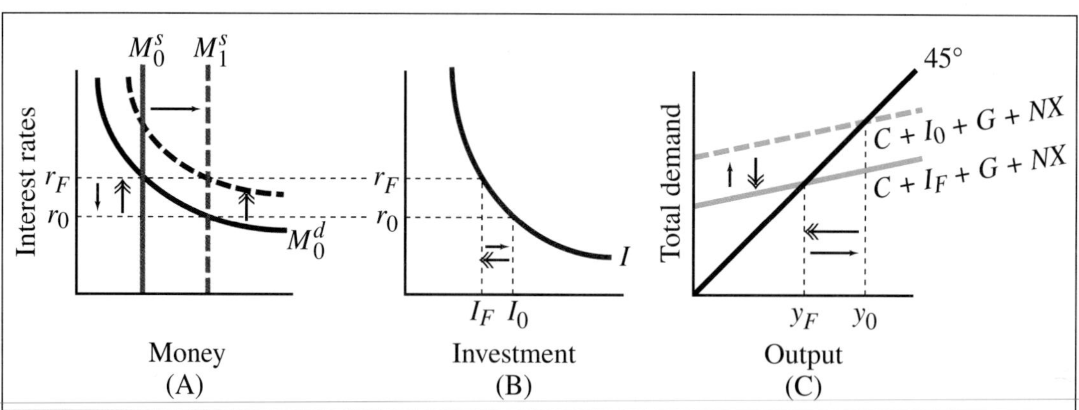

returned to I_F. This is the level of investment that provides the total level of demand for goods and services that keeps the economy at full employment.

Notice that when the economy returns to full employment, the level of real interest rates, investment, and output are precisely the same as they were before the Federal Reserve increased the supply of money. The increase in the supply of money had no effect at all on real interest rates, investment, and output. Economists call this the **long-run neutrality of money**. In the long run, increases in the supply of money have no effect on real variables, only on prices.

Long-run neutrality of money: An increase in the supply of money has no effect on real interest rates, investment, or output in the long run.

To better understand the idea of the long-run neutrality of money, consider this thought experiment. Suppose that one morning the government announced we would replace all our normal green currency with blue currency. Every green dollar bill would be replaced by two blue dollars. What would happen to prices now quoted in blue currency? You should easily be able to see that if all wages and prices in blue dollars doubled, everything would essentially be the same as before. Although everyone has twice as many (blue) dollars, prices are twice as high, so that the purchasing power of money is the same. Moreover, since wages and prices have doubled, real wage rates will be the same as before. This currency conversion will have no effect on the real economy and will be neutral.

This example points out how, in the long run, it really does not matter how "much" money there is in circulation because prices will adjust to the amount of nominal money available. Whether additional money comes from an open market purchase or a currency conversion, it will be neutral in the long run.

Money is, however, *not* neutral in the short run. In the short run, changes in the supply of money do affect interest rates, investment spending, and output. The Federal Reserve does have strong powers over real GDP but they are ultimately temporary. In the long run, all the Federal Reserve can do is to determine the level of prices in the economy.

Now we can understand why the job of the Federal Reserve had been described by William McChesney Martin, Jr., a former Federal Reserve chairman, as "taking the punch bowl away at the party." The punch bowl at the party is monetary policy: It can increase output or give the economy a brief "high." But if the Federal Reserve is worried about increases in prices in the long run, it must take the punch bowl away. If the Federal Reserve continues to increase the supply of money in the economy, the result will be continuing increases in prices, or inflation.

TEST ***Your Understanding***

3 What happens to the demand for money and interest rates as the price level increases in the economy?

4 True or false: If output is below full employment, we expect wages and prices to fall, money demand to decrease, and interest rates to fall.

5 True or false: An increase in the money supply will have no effect on the interest rate in the long run.

CROWDING OUT IN THE LONG RUN

Keynesian economists often advocate increased government spending to stimulate the economy. Critics of Keynesian economists say that these increases in spending provide only temporary relief and ultimately harm the economy. We can now use our model to understand this important debate.

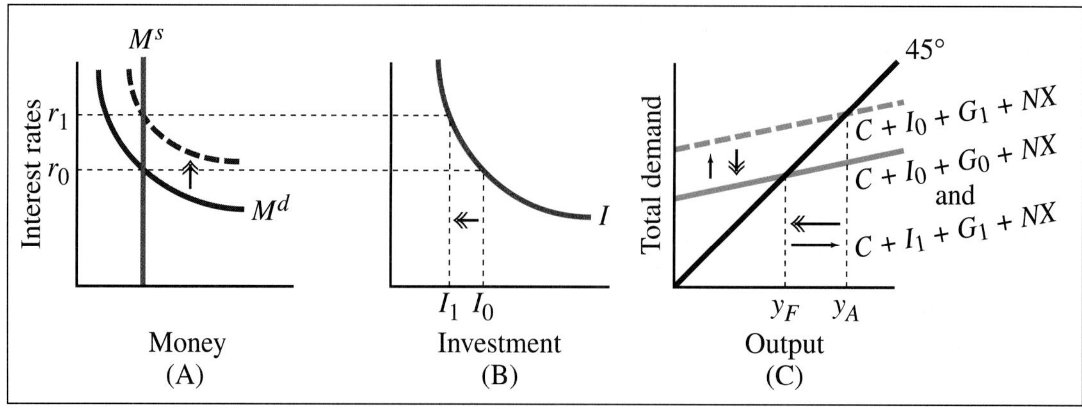

Figure 8 Crowding Out in the Long Run

Starting at full employment, an increase in government spending from G_0 to G_1 shifts up the total demand line and raises output above full employment (single-headed arrows). As wages and prices increase, the demand for money increases, raising interest rates from r_0 to r_1 and reducing investment from I_0 to I_1. The economy returns to full employment but with a higher level of interest rates and a lower level of investment spending (double-headed arrows).

In Figure 8, the economy starts at full employment and government spending is increased from G_0 to G_1: say, to stimulate the economy. In panel C, we see that the total demand line ($C + I + G + NX$) shifts up (the single-headed arrow) and output increases in the short run, just as the Keynesian demand models claim. However, now the economy is operating above full employment and wages and prices begin to increase. The increase in the price level raises both the demand for money and the level of interest rates. Higher interest rates reduce the level of investment. As investment spending falls, the level of output returns to that of full employment. The double-headed arrows in Figure 8 show the final adjustment of the economy following the increase in government spending. Interest rates increase to r_1 and investment spending falls to I_1 in the long run.

Crowding out: The reduction of investment (or other component of GDP) in the long run caused by an increase in government spending.

In the long run, the increase in government spending had no long-run effect on the level of output. Instead, the increase in government spending displaced or **crowded out** investment spending. The increase in government spending led to a higher level of interest rates, which reduced the incentives for investment in the economy. We first encountered crowding out in the chapter on classical economics. As we have discussed, the economy adjusts in the long run to the equilibrium predicted by the classical model. In this case, higher government spending crowds out investment spending. In turn, the reduction in investment will have further effects on the economy. As we saw in earlier chapters, a reduction in investment spending will reduce capital deepening and lead to lower levels of real income and wages in the future.

The idea of crowding out is actually quite simple to grasp. Since the economy ultimately returns to full employment in the long run, a higher level of government spending must come at the expense of some other component of spending. In Figure 8 we showed how investment spending would be crowded out. In other situations it is possible for consumption or net exports to be crowded out along with investment spending. Keynesian demand policy will increase GDP but only in the short run.

Crowding in: The increase of investment (or other component of GDP) in the long run caused by a decrease in government spending.

Decreases in government spending will **crowd in** investment in the long run. Initially, a decrease in government spending will cause a decrease in real GDP. But as prices fall, the demand for money will decrease and interest rates will fall. Lower interest rates will crowd in investment as the economy returns to full employment. In the very long run, the higher investment spending will raise living standards through capital deepening.

Crowding out and crowding in provide clear examples of the main theme of this chapter, namely, that the short-run effects of policy will generally differ from the long-run effects. Just as an increase in the money supply will only increase output in the short run, changes in government spending have different effects in the short run than they do in the long run.

POLITICAL BUSINESS CYCLES

Since the long-run effects of policy can differ from the short-run effects, it is possible that politicians may try to take advantage of this to get reelected. Using monetary and fiscal policy in the short run to improve reelection prospects may generate what is known as a **political business cycle.**

Political business cycle: The effects on the economy of using monetary or fiscal policy to stimulate the economy before an election to improve reelection prospects.

Here is how a political business cycle might work. About a year or so before an election, a politician might use expansionary monetary or fiscal policy to stimulate the economy and lower unemployment. If voters respond favorably to lower unemployment, the incumbent politician may be reelected. However, after reelection, the politician now faces the prospect of higher prices or crowding out. To avoid this, he or she may engage in contractionary policies. Thus we have a classic political business cycle: Because of actions taken by politicians for reelection, the economy booms before an election but then contracts after the election. Good news comes before the election and bad news comes later.

The evidence in favor of the classic political business cycle's existence is quite mixed. There are episodes that fit the description, such as President Nixon's reelection campaign in 1972. However, there are also counterexamples such as President Carter's deliberate attempt to reduce inflation at the end of his term. According to the theory, Carter would not have adopted policies with adverse consequences just before the election. Although the evidence on the classic political business cycle is mixed, there may be links between elections and economic outcomes. More recent research has investigated the systematic differences that may exist between political parties and economic outcomes. All this research takes into account both the short- and long-run effects of economic policies.

Using the TOOLS

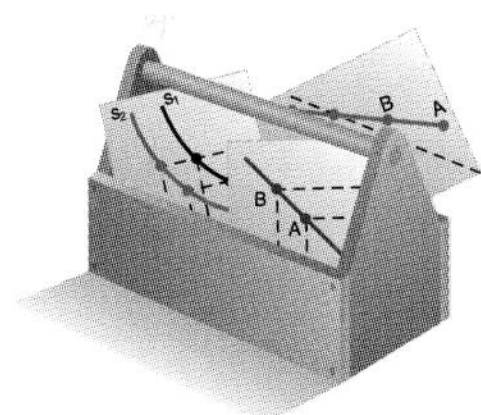

In this chapter we developed a complete model showing the transition from the short run to the long run. Take this opportunity to deepen your understanding of the ideas and tools in this chapter.

1. Economic Policies and Supply Shocks

a. Recall that in a previous chapter, we discussed supply shocks, sudden increases in the prices of commodities such as oil or food. These shocks shift the Keynesian aggregate supply curve. For example, an increase in oil prices will shift up the Keynesian aggregate supply curve because firms' costs have risen and firms must charge higher prices to avoid losing money.

   Suppose the economy were operating at full employment, and foreign countries raised the world price of oil. Assuming that policymakers do not take any action, describe what will happen to prices and output in the short run and the long run.

b. Suppose the Federal Reserve decided it wanted to offset any adverse effects on output. What actions could it take? What would be the consequences for the price level if the Fed used monetary policy to fight unemployment?

c. Economists claim that supply shocks create a dilemma for the Federal Reserve that shocks to demand (for example, from investment) do not create. Explain this point using your answer to part (b) and the aggregate demand and supply diagram.

2. ECONOMIC DETECTIVE– *Understanding Japanese Fiscal Policy*

During the early 1990s, the Japanese were suffering from a recession and some economists advocated expansionary fiscal policy. The finance ministry agreed to income tax cuts but only if national sales taxes were increased several years later. As an economic detective, explain the logic of the finance ministry using your understanding of the short- and long-run effects of fiscal policy. What was the finance ministry trying to prevent?

3. Optimistic Firms in the Long Run

Suppose the economy were operating at full employment and firms became increasingly optimistic about the future. They increase their investment spending; that is, their investment schedule shifts to the right. What happens to real GDP in the short run? Describe what happens to interest rates, investment, and real GDP in the long run. How is the investment boom self-correcting?

SUMMARY

This chapter explained how the economy makes the transition from the short run to the long run. It also highlighted why monetary and fiscal policies have different effects in the short run than they do in the long run. Understanding the distinction between the short and the long run is critical to evaluating economic policy. Here are the main points to remember from this chapter:

1. When output exceeds full employment, wages and prices rise faster than their past trends. If output is less than full employment, wages and prices fall relative to past trends.
2. The price changes that occur when the economy is away from full employment push the economy back to full employment. Economists disagree on the length that this adjustment process takes, with estimates ranging from two to six years.
3. If the economy is operating below full employment, falling wages and prices will reduce money demand and lower interest rates. The fall in interest rates will stimulate investment and lead the economy back to full employment.
4. The reverse situation occurs when output exceeds full employment. Increases in wages and prices will increase money demand and interest rates. As investment spending falls, the economy returns to full employment.
5. In the long run increases in the supply of money are neutral; that is, they do not affect real interest rates, investment, or output.
6. Increases in government spending will raise real interest rates and crowd out investment in the long run. Decreases in government spending will lower real interest rates and crowd in investment in the long run.
7. Politicians can potentially take advantage of the difference between the short- and long-run effects of economic policies to improve their chances of being reelected. However, evidence as to whether such political business cycles exist is mixed.

KEY TERMS

aggregate demand curve, *592*
classical aggregate supply curve, *592*
crowding in, *600*
crowding out, *600*
Keynesian aggregate supply curve, *592*
long-run neutrality of money, *599*
political business cycle, *601*
wage–price spiral, *591*

PROBLEMS AND DISCUSSION QUESTIONS

1. When the unemployment rate fell below 4% in the late 1960s, many economists became worried about an increase in inflation. Explain their concern.
2. Economists who believe that the transition from the short run to the long run occurs rapidly do not generally favor active use of stabilization policy. Why not?
3. During an economic boom, interest rates rise, while investment spending will rise and then fall. Explain why this pattern of economic activity occurs.
4. Countries that have high money growth for long periods of time do not grow more rapidly than countries with low money growth. Why?
5. Explain why advocates for the housing industry (an industry very sensitive to interest rates) might want to advocate lower government spending for the long term.
6. Explain why falling wages and prices lead to lower interest rates.

Take It to the Net

We invite you to visit the O'Sullivan/Sheffrin page on the Prentice Hall Web site at:

http://www.prenhall.com/osullivan/

for this chapter's World Wide Web exercise.

MODEL ANSWERS FOR THIS CHAPTER

Chapter-Opening Questions

1. Wages and prices will rise together when the economy is operating at a level of output exceeding full employment. Conversely, they will fall (relative to trend) when the output level of the economy is below full employment.
2. In the short run, the higher demand from lower interest rates will raise output. But since prices rise when output exceeds full employment, the long run effect is just higher prices.
3. The Federal Reserve is responsible for preventing inflation from emerging or increasing. This may require high interest rates to reduce output at a time when the economy is producing at too high a level.
4. Tax cuts stimulate consumer demand and lead to higher output in the short run. However, in the long run, the increased consumer spending will crowd out investment spending. Lower investment means a lower capital stock in the future and reduced future output.

Test Your Understanding

1. False; 2. The curve moves down; 3. Money demand increases, interest rates increase; 4. True; 5. True.

Using the Tools

1. Economic Policies and Supply Shocks
   a. A supply shock shifts the Keynesian aggregate supply curve up. Prices will rise and output will fall in the short run. With output below full employment, prices will fall. The economy will return to full employment at the initial price level.
   b. The Federal Reserve could increase the supply of money (open market purchases) and shift the aggregate demand curve. The price level would remain at the higher level.
   c. Unlike shocks to aggregate demand, if the Federal Reserve tries to offset the output or unemployment effects of an adverse supply shock, the price level will remain permanently higher.
2. Economic Detective: Understanding Japanese Fiscal Policy

   The Japanese finance ministry was worried about crowding out of investment in the long run. They hoped that the income tax cut would stimulate spending in the short run and pull the economy out of a recession. Later, however, they wanted to reduce consumer spending so that it would not displace investment spending.
3. Optimistic Firms in the Long Run

   With an investment boom, real GDP would increase with the additional investment spending. However, as output exceeds full employment, prices would rise, leading to increased money demand and interest rates. The higher interest rates would cut back on investment, lowering real GDP.

CHAPTER

30 The Dynamics of Inflation and Unemployment

In the early 1980s, the Federal Reserve in Washington, DC began to receive some unusual packages. From all over the country, large crates of boards and timber were being unloaded on the steps of the elegant, marble building that houses the Federal Reserve. Why did this deluge of forest products occur?

The timber was sent by representatives of the housing industry throughout the country. At that time the Federal Reserve was trying to fight inflation. During the late 1970s, the inflation rate had increased substantially and most policymakers believed inflation had to be reduced. The Federal Reserve was cutting back on the growth of the money supply, and interest rates rose sharply. In 1981, the *prime rate of interest*—the rate charged on short-term loans by banks to their best customers—rose to over 18%.

With interest rates at these levels, the housing industry was affected dramatically. It became increasingly difficult for anyone to afford to take out a loan to buy a house. The construction of new housing and new office buildings ground to a halt. Workers in the construction industry were laid off and many firms went bankrupt. Boards and logs were sent to the Federal Reserve in protest.

In this chapter we explain the problems that arise in controlling and fighting inflation. Two important themes that we've been stressing are now integrated. We have seen that in the short run, changes in money growth affect real output and real GDP. However, in the long run the rate of money growth determines the rate of inflation and not real GDP. This chapter brings these two themes together.

Our economic policy debates often concern inflation and unemployment. We take a careful look at the relationships between inflation and unemployment and apply our knowledge to examine macroeconomic developments in the United States in the 1980s. We also explore why heads of central banks typically appear to be strong enemies of inflation.

Although the United States had serious difficulties fighting inflation in the 1970s and 1980s, other countries have, at times, had much more severe problems with inflation. We study the origins of dramatic inflations and their links to government budget deficits. Finally, we take a close look at the costs that unemployment and inflation impose on a society.

In this chapter we address these real-world questions:

1. Why do countries with lower rates of money growth have lower interest-rate levels than those of countries with higher rates of money growth?
2. Why is the relationship between lower unemployment and higher inflation only temporary?
3. Why are the heads of central banks (such as the Chairman of the Board of Governors of the Federal Reserve) typically very conservative, in that they prefer to risk increasing unemployment rather than risk increasing the inflation rate?
4. Why do countries with large budget deficits often suffer from massive inflation?
5. Why do societies deliberately increase unemployment in order to reduce the rate of inflation? Is the pain of increased unemployment worth the benefit of reduced inflation?

MONEY GROWTH, INFLATION, AND INTEREST RATES

An economy can, in principle, be producing at full employment with any inflation rate. There is no "magic" inflation rate that is necessary to sustain full employment. To understand this point, consider the long run when the economy operates at full employment. As we have seen, in the long run, money is neutral. If the Federal Reserve increases the money supply at 5% a year, there will be 5% inflation; that is, prices in the economy will rise by 5% a year.

Let's think about how this economy looks. The nominal or dollar wages of workers are all rising at 5% a year. However, since prices are also rising at 5% a year, **real wages**—wages adjusted for changes in purchasing power—remain constant. Some workers may feel "cheated" by the inflation. They might believe that without the inflation they would experience real wage increases, since their nominal wages are rising by 5% a year. Unfortunately, they are wrong. They suffer from what economists call **money illusion**, a confusion of real and nominal magnitudes. The only reason their nominal wages are rising by 5% a year is the general 5% inflation. If there were no inflation, their nominal wages would not increase at all.

After some period of time, everyone in the economy would begin to expect that the 5% inflation would continue. Economists say that in this situation, individuals hold **expectations of inflation**. These expectations affect all aspects of economic life. For example, automobile producers will on average expect their prices to be

Real wages: Nominal or dollar wages adjusted for changes in purchasing power.

Money illusion: Confusion of real and nominal magnitudes.

Expectations of inflation: The beliefs held by the public about the likely path of inflation for the future.

5% higher next year. They will also expect their costs—labor and steel, for example—to increase by 5% a year. Workers would begin to understand that their 5% increases in wages would be matched by a 5% increase in the prices of the goods that they buy. Continued inflation becomes the normal state of affairs. Expectations of inflation become ingrained in decisions made in all aspects of life.

When the public holds expectations of inflation, real and nominal interest rates will differ. We first encountered real and nominal interest rates in an earlier chapter. Here we emphasize the important role for expectations of inflation. Recall that nominal interest rates are the rates quoted in the market. The **expected real rate of interest** is the nominal rate adjusted for expectations of inflation. They are linked by the equation

Expected real rate of interest: The nominal rate of interest minus expected inflation.

$$\text{expected real rate} = \text{nominal rate} - \text{expectations of inflation}$$

To understand this equation, consider a simple example. Suppose the nominal interest rate is 10% and the public expects 6% inflation for the next year. The expected real rate of interest will then be 4 (10 – 6)%. If you invest \$100, you will receive \$110 at the end of the year, for a gain of \$10. However, if you expect 6% inflation, you need an additional \$6 just to maintain your purchasing power. The real gain that you anticipate from the original \$100 is only \$4 or a 4% real rate of interest.

As we discussed in the last chapter, in the long run the real rate of interest does *not* depend on monetary policy because money is neutral. However, nominal rates of interest depend on the rate of inflation, which in the long run is determined by the growth of the money supply. Monetary policy therefore does affect the nominal interest rate in the long run. If two countries had the same real rate of interest but one had a higher inflation rate, it would also have a higher nominal interest rate. As Nobel laureate Milton Friedman pointed out, countries with higher money growth typically have higher nominal interest rates than those in countries with lower money growth rates because of the differences in inflation across the countries.

Money demand will also be affected by expectations of inflation. If the public expects 6% inflation a year, its demand for money will also increase by 6% a year. Recall the reality principle:

Reality PRINCIPLE

What matters to people is the real value or purchasing power of money or income, not its face value.

Using this principle, we can say that the public cares about the real value of its transactions. When prices rise at 6% a year, so does the value of transactions. The public will need to hold 6% more money each year for these transactions. As long as the Federal Reserve allows the supply of money to increase by 6%, the demand and supply for money will grow at the same rate. With both the demand and supply for money growing at the same rate, real and nominal interest rates will remain constant.

In the short run, however, changes in the growth rate of money *will* affect real interest rates. To continue with our example, suppose that the public expects 6% inflation and both the supply of money and money demand grow at 6% a year. Now let the Federal Reserve suddenly decrease the growth rate of money to 4% while the public continues to expect 6% inflation. Since money demand grows at 6% but the supply of money now grows at only 4%, the growth in the demand for money will exceed the growth in the supply. Since demand grows faster than supply, the result will be an increase in both real and nominal interest rates. Higher real rates of interest will reduce investment spending by firms and consumer durable spending by households.

With reduced demand for goods and services, real GDP will fall and unemployment will rise. The reduction in the growth rate of the money supply is contractionary.

In the long run, however, the economy will eventually adjust to the lower rate of money growth. Output will return to full employment through the adjustment process described in the last chapter. Since money is neutral in the long run, the real rate of interest will return to its previous value. In the long run, inflation will fall to 4%, the rate of growth of the money supply. Since the real rate has returned to its prior value and inflation has fallen, nominal interest rates will also fall.

This basic pattern fits U.S. history in the late 1970s and early 1980s. At that time, the Federal Reserve sharply decreased the rate of growth of the money supply and interest rates rose. By 1981, interest rates on three-month Treasury bills rose to over 14% from 7% in 1978. The economy went into a severe recession, with unemployment exceeding 10%. By the mid-1980s, however, the economy returned to full employment with lower interest rates and lower inflation rates. By 1986, Treasury bill rates were below 6%.

Here is another example where the long-run effects of policy actions differ from their short-run effects. In the short run, a policy of "tight money" (slower money growth) raised interest rates. But in the long run, reduced money growth led to reduced inflation and lower interest rates.

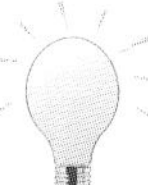

TEST *Your Understanding*

1 True or false: The expected real rate of interest is the nominal interest rate minus the expected inflation rate.

2 Explain why in the long run an inflation rate of 10% per year will lead to an increase in the demand for money of 10% per year.

Expectations and the Phillips Curve

One of the key regularities in U.S. economic data is that inflation increases when economic activity booms and unemployment falls below its natural rate. Similarly, the rate of inflation falls when the economy is in a recession and unemployment exceeds the natural rate. This relationship between unemployment and inflation is known as the **expectations Phillips curve.**

Expectations Phillips curve: The relationship that describes the links between inflation and unemployment, taking into account expectations of inflation.

The expectations Phillips curve is just a refined version of the adjustment mechanism for the economy that we described in the last chapter. There we discussed how prices and wages rise if output is above potential output and unemployment is below the natural rate. Wages tend to rise during boom periods as firms compete for workers and prices rise along with wages. Similarly, prices fall when output is below potential and unemployment exceeds the natural rate. During recessions, high levels of unemployment lead to falling wages and prices.

However, once we take into account ongoing inflation, we need to modify this story slightly. Wages and prices can now change for two reasons. First, just as before, wages and prices will tend to rise during booms and fall during recessions. Second, workers and firms will have expectations of ongoing inflation. Both workers and firms will raise their nominal wages and prices to the extent that they expect ongoing inflation, to maintain the same level of real wages and real prices.

If the economy is operating at full employment, wages and prices will rise at the rate of inflation expected by workers and firms. If unemployment exceeds the natural rate, the high level of unemployment will put downward pressure on wages and prices, and inflation will fall relative to what was expected. Similarly, if unemployment were below the natural rate, employers would bid aggressively for workers and wages and prices would rise faster than what was expected previously.

If we make the convenient assumption that expectations of inflation are based on last year's inflation rate, the expectations Phillips curve becomes a relationship between the *change* in the inflation rate and the level of unemployment. If the actual unemployment rate exceeds the natural rate of unemployment, inflation will fall below last year's level. On the other hand, if the actual unemployment rate is below the natural rate, the inflation rate will rise above last year's level.

Let's consider an example. Suppose the economy were at full employment and there had been 5% money growth for many years. The inflation rate of 5% is fully expected by everyone in the economy. If the Federal Reserve cuts the money growth rate to 3%, real interest rates will rise as the growth in the demand for money (still at 5%) exceeds the growth in the supply (now at 3%). Real interest rates will rise, reducing investment spending. Real GDP will fall and unemployment will exceed the natural rate. The increase in unemployment above the natural rate will reduce the inflation rate. In the long run, the inflation rate falls from 5% to a long-run level of 3%, consistent with the lower level of money growth. This is the expectations Phillips curve in action.

Figure 1 plots the change in the inflation rate against the unemployment rate for the years 1954 to 1995. To help see this relationship, we draw a line through the points to represent our best guess of the true underlying relationship. At point *A* on this line we can see that when the unemployment rate is approximately 6%, there is no change in the inflation rate. This is an estimate of the natural rate of unemployment for the United States based on these data. The slope of the graph also tells us that if unemployment falls below the natural rate by 1 point for a year, the rate of inflation will rise by approximately ½% per year.

Figure 1

Unemployment and the Change in Inflation, 1954–1995

Source: Authors' calculations based on data from *Economic Report of the President* (Washington, DC: U.S. Government Printing Office, yearly).

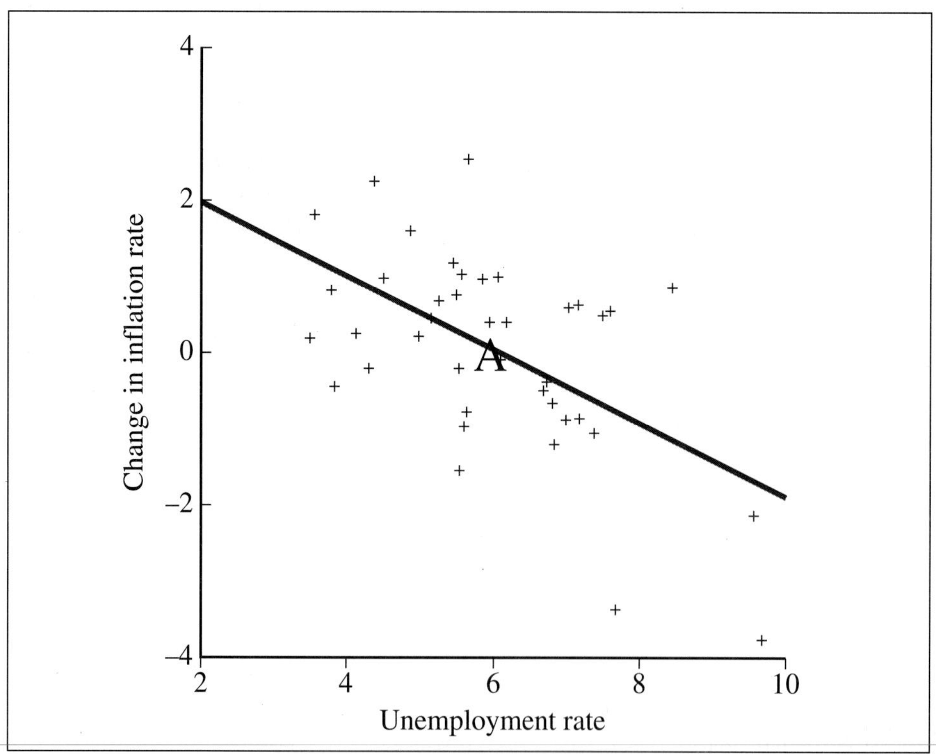

Here is how to use the expectations Phillips curve to predict inflation. Suppose the natural rate is 6% and the current inflation rate is 8%. Unemployment rises suddenly to 9% and remains at that level for two years before returning to 6%. Inflation will fall by ½% per year for each point by which the unemployment rate exceeds the natural rate. Since unemployment will exceed the natural rate by 3 percentage points for two years (for a total of 6 points), inflation will fall by 3 percentage points, from 8% to 5%.

The expectations Phillips curve differs from initial attempts to explain the relationship between inflation and unemployment. In the late 1950s, an engineer named A. W. Phillips noticed that there seemed to be a negative relationship between the level of inflation and unemployment in British data. He found lower unemployment to be associated with higher wage inflation. This relationship became known as the *Phillips curve*. In the early 1960s, Nobel laureates Paul Samuelson and Robert Solow found a similar relationship between unemployment and level of the inflation rate in the United States.

These original studies examined periods of history when there was no significant underlying trend inflation rate and did not take into account expectations of inflation. As we have seen, once we take into account expectations of ongoing inflation, the *expectations* Phillips curve describes how *changes* in the inflation rate are related to unemployment.

It is important to make the distinction between the level of inflation and the change in the inflation rate. An inflation rate could fall but nonetheless be at a high level. Suppose inflation were 20% and unemployment exceeded the natural rate, and inflation then fell to 15%. Although the inflation rate has fallen by 5 percentage points, it is still high.

Up to this point we have assumed that the natural rate of unemployment does not change very much over time. In the United States, changes in the natural rate of unemployment have been very slow to occur and we can safely view it as varying within a relatively small range, perhaps between 5 and 6.5%. In Europe, however, there have been sharp increases in the natural rate of unemployment. Some of the reasons for this are explained in the Closer Look box on the next page, "Europe's Increase in the Natural Rate."

U.S. Inflation and Unemployment in the 1980s

We can use the expectations Phillips curve to help describe the patterns of inflation and unemployment in the 1980s. To set the background, let's first discuss the late 1970s.

When President Jimmy Carter took office at the beginning of 1977, the inflation rate was approximately 6.5% and unemployment exceeded 7%. By 1980, however, inflation had risen to 9.4%. There were two reasons for this increase. First, unemployment had been steadily reduced during the Carter administration and fell below 6% by 1979. Since the natural rate was close to 6%, this led to an increase in the inflation rate. Next, there was a second oil shock in 1979 that also contributed to higher inflation.

Fears of even higher inflation led President Carter to appoint a well-known inflation fighter, Paul Volcker, as the chair of the Federal Reserve. Volcker immediately began to institute a "tight money" policy and interest rates rose sharply by 1980. When President Ronald Reagan took office, he supported Volcker's policy. Eventually high real interest rates took their toll and unemployment rose to over 10% by 1983. As unemployment exceeded the natural rate, the inflation rate fell, just as predicted by the expectations Phillips curve. By 1986, the inflation rate fell to approximately 2.7% with unemployment at 7%. The severe recession had done its job in reducing the inflation rate.

A Closer LOOK

Europe's Increase in the Natural Rate

In 1977 a doctoral student in economics at the Massachusetts Institute of Technology completed a thesis that tried to explain why unemployment rates in Europe were below those in the United States. Prior to that time, unemployment rates in Europe were typically in the 2 to 3% range, while U.S. unemployment rates were 4 to 5%.

How times have changed! Now the United States is the envy of Europe. While our natural rate is currently in the neighborhood of 5 to 6.5%, in Europe the natural rate has risen to between 8 and 11%. Since unemployment disproportionately affects the young and less skilled, unemployment has also become a social crisis in Europe. What changed in the last two decades?

Studies of European unemployment cite a variety of different factors.* One of the most important is that labor markets in Europe are less flexible than in the United States and unions are more powerful. Strong unions can maintain high wages for workers even during bad economic times, at the expense of the unemployed. European employers also face more restrictions on firing workers, which makes them reluctant to hire them in the first place. Finally, European countries are much more generous than the United States in paying unemployment insurance. Eventually, these factors caught up with the Europeans and led to the sharp increase in the natural rate.

High unemployment was the root cause of many demonstrations in Europe during the 1990s.

*See Charles Bean, "European Unemployment: A Survey," *Journal of Economic Literature*, vol. 32, June 1994, pp. 573–619.

However, as we can see in Figure 2, after 1986 the unemployment rate began to fall again. As it fell below the natural rate, inflation began to increase again. By 1989, inflation had risen to 4.5%. This led the Federal Reserve to increase unemployment to bring down the inflation rate. By 1992, the unemployment rate had increased to 7.4%, and by 1993 inflation had been brought down below 3% again.

President George Bush suffered the consequences of this episode of fighting inflation. By the time he took office in 1989, unemployment was below the natural rate, inflation had been rising, and the Federal Reserve was about to start slowing the economy. While the rate of inflation was eventually reduced, the recovery back to full employment came too late in his term to be fully appreciated by the voters and he lost his bid for reelection.

TEST *Your Understanding*

3 If the natural rate of unemployment were 6% and inflation were 3%, what would inflation be in the United States if the unemployment rate for the next two years fell to 4%?

4 Which statement is true?

a. If unemployment is high, inflation is low.

b. If unemployment is high, inflation falls.

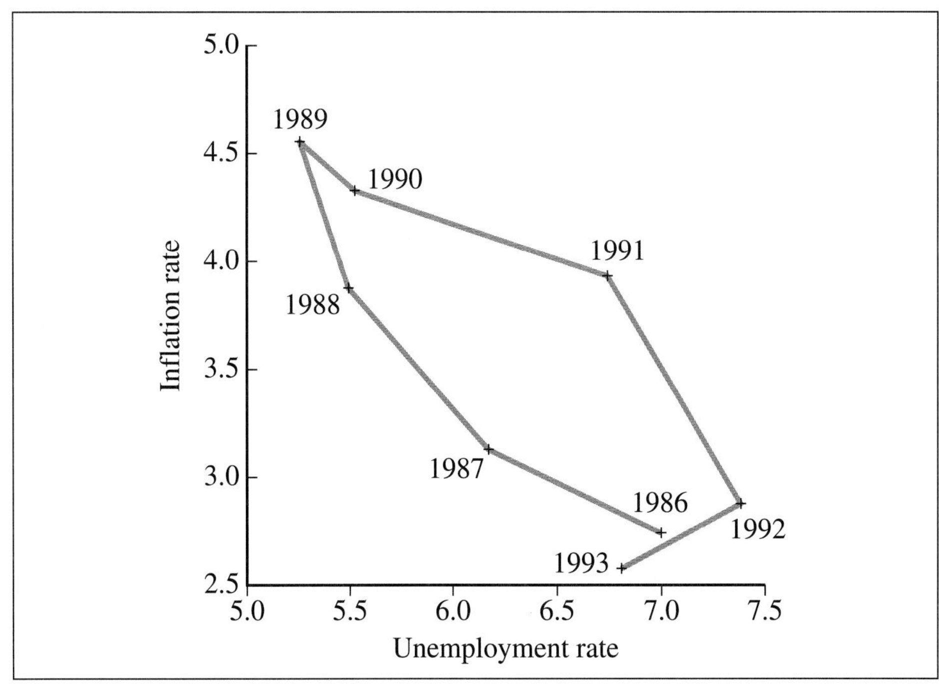

Figure 2

Dynamics of Inflation and Unemployment, 1986–1993

Source: Data from *Economic Report of the President* (Washington, DC: U.S. Government Printing Office, yearly).

CREDIBILITY AND INFLATION

Why are the heads of central banks (such as the chair of the Board of Governors) typically very conservative and constantly warning about the dangers of inflation? The basic reason is that these monetary policymakers can influence expectations of inflation. Expectations of inflation, in turn, will influence actual behavior. For example, workers will want higher nominal wages if they anticipate inflation. If policymakers are not careful, they can actually make it difficult to fight inflation in a society.

Let's consider a simple example. A large union is negotiating wages for workers in important sectors of the economy, for example automobiles and steel. If they negotiate a very high nominal wage, other unions will follow along with high wages, and prices will inevitably rise. Because of these wage settlements, the Fed will begin to see inflation emerge. The Fed had been keeping the money supply constant. What can it do in these circumstances?

We depict the Fed's dilemma in Figure 3 on the next page. By setting a higher nominal wage, the union shifts the aggregate supply curve from AS_0 to AS_1. The Fed then has a choice. It can keep the money supply and aggregate demand at AD_0. The economy will initially fall into a recession but would eventually return to full employment at the original price level. On the other hand, the Fed could increase the money supply and raise aggregate demand from AD_0 to AD_1. This will keep the economy at full employment but lead to higher prices.

The actions of the union will depend on what its leaders expect the Fed to do. If they believe the Fed will not increase aggregate demand, their actions will trigger a recession, and they know it. In this case they may be reluctant to negotiate a high wage. If they do not increase nominal wages, the economy will remain at full employment and experience no increase in prices. On the other hand, if its leaders believe the Fed will increase aggregate demand, the union has nothing to lose and will increase the nominal wage. The result will be higher prices in the economy.

As this example illustrates, expectations about the Fed's determination to fight inflation will affect behavior in the private sector. If the Fed is credible or believable in

Figure 3

Choices for the Fed

If workers push up their nominal wages, the aggregate supply curve will shift from AS_0 to AS_1. If the Fed keeps aggregate demand constant at AD_0, a recession will occur at A and eventually the economy will return to full employment at E. If the Fed increases aggregate demand, the economy remains at full employment at F but with a higher price level.

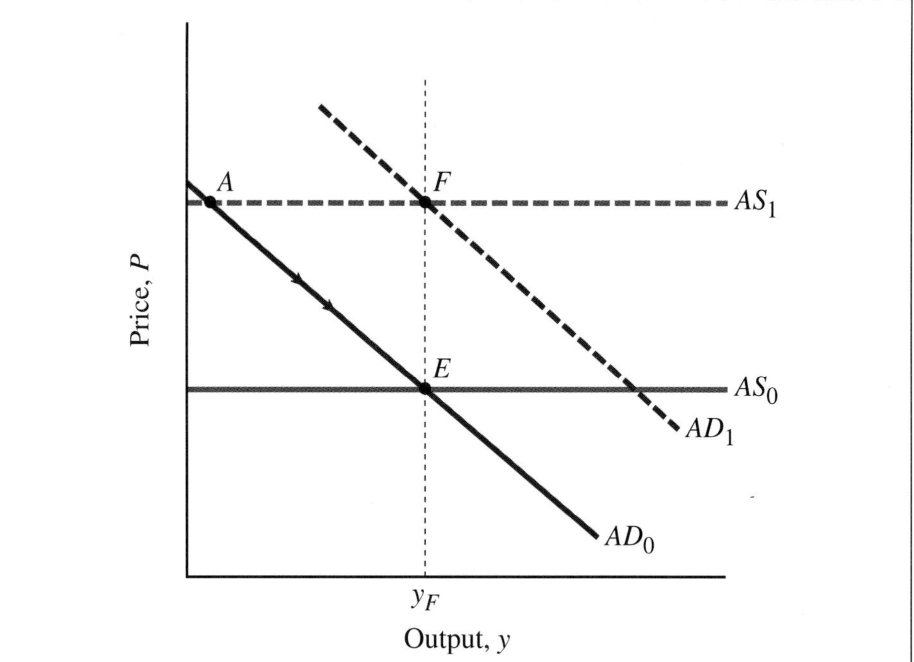

its desire to fight inflation, it can deter the private sector from taking aggressive actions that drive up prices. This is the reason we often see very conservative heads of central banks who prefer taking the risks of increasing unemployment rather than risking an increase in inflation. For example, having a conservative chair of the Federal Reserve who strongly detests inflation sends a signal that the Fed will be unlikely to increase the money supply regardless of what actions are taken in the private sector.

New Zealand took a different approach to ensure the credibility of its central bank. Since 1989, the central bank has been operating under a law which specifies that its only goal is to attempt to maintain stable prices, which, in practice, requires it to keep inflation between zero and 2% a year. Although this policy sharply limits the central bank's ability to stabilize real GDP, it does signal to the private sector that the central bank will not be increasing the money supply, regardless of the actions taken by wage setters or unions.

Our example suggests that with a credible central bank, a country can have lower inflation without experiencing extra unemployment. Some political scientists and economists have suggested that central banks which have true independence from the rest of the government, and are therefore less subject to political influence, will be more credible in their commitment to fighting inflation.

There is some evidence to support this conjecture. Figure 4 on the next page plots an index of independence against average inflation rates from 1955 to 1988 for 16 countries. The points appear to lie along a downward-sloping line, meaning that more independence is associated with lower inflation. Germany and Switzerland, the most independent central banks, had the lowest inflation rates. This same study found no association between GDP growth and central bank independence.

As our discussion illustrates, expectations about central bank behavior are important for understanding the behavior of output and prices for the economy. In the last two decades, economists have paid increasing attention to the role of expectations in many different areas of economics. They have recognized that people develop their expectations in complex ways that take into account the information they have available.

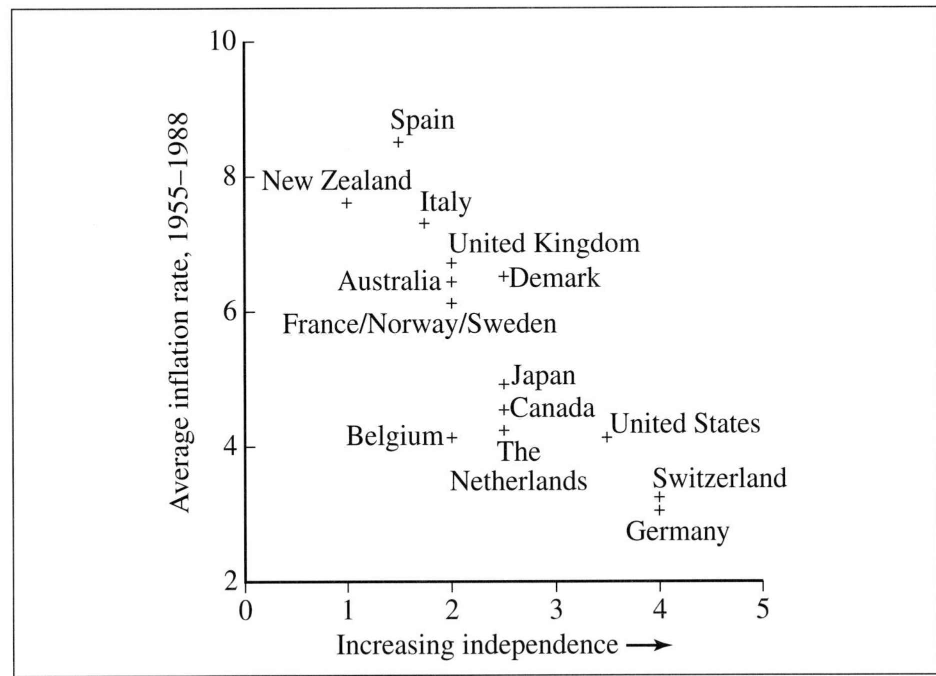

Figure 4

Inflation versus Central Bank Independence

Source: Data from Alesina and Summers, "Central Bank Independence and Macroeconomic Performance," *Journal of Money, Credit, and Banking*, May 1993.

In the 1970s, a group of economists led by Nobel laureate Robert E. Lucas, Jr. from the University of Chicago developed the theory of **rational expectations,** which analyzes how firms and individuals may base their expectations on all the information they have available to them. According to the theory of rational expectations, individuals form their expectations such that, on average, they anticipate the future correctly. Although they may make mistakes in specific instances, on average their expectations are rational or correct. The theory of rational expectations has been used extensively in many areas of economics, including the example with the union and the Fed that we discussed. In our example, rational expectations implies that the union will, on average, anticipate whether the Fed will adopt a policy of expanding the money supply in the face of wage increases. A credible Fed, therefore, will tend to deter wage increases. Although not all economists believe that the public is fully rational in economic affairs, insights from this theory have heavily influenced economic research in many different areas.

Rational expectations: The economic theory that analyzes how people form expectations in such a manner that, on average, they forecast the future correctly.

Expectations play an important role in almost all areas of economics. For example, as we have seen, both lenders and borrowers must form expectations about future inflation rates in setting nominal interest rates. There are many other examples as well. Prices of stocks of firms will depend on investors' expectations about future dividends that the firm will pay. Even your decision to buy a home or rent will depend on your expectation about the future prices of homes. If you believe that home prices will rise sharply in the future, you will be more likely to buy a home and earn a profit from the investment. Economists study how expectations are formed in all these markets, whether they are rational or not, and how expectations influence actual market outcomes.

INFLATION AND THE VELOCITY OF MONEY

Countries sometimes experience extremely dramatic inflation rates. For example, in a period of 16 months from August 1922 to November 1923, the price level in Germany rose by a factor of 10 billion! To explain these extremely high inflation rates and to

Velocity of money: Nominal GDP divided by the money supply. It is also the rate at which money turns over during the year.

provide more insight into the links between money growth and inflation, we now introduce a concept closely related to money demand called the **velocity of money.**

The velocity of money is defined as the ratio of nominal GDP to the money supply:

$$\text{velocity of money} = \frac{\text{nominal GDP}}{\text{money supply}}$$

One useful way to think of velocity is that it is the number of times the money supply has to turn over during a given year to purchase nominal GDP.

To understand this, consider a simple example. Suppose that nominal GDP in a country were \$5 trillion per year and the money supply were \$1 trillion. Then the velocity of money in this economy will be

$$\begin{aligned}\text{velocity} &= \frac{\$5 \text{ trillion per year}}{\$1 \text{ trillion}} \\ &= 5 \text{ per year}\end{aligned}$$

In this economy, the \$1 trillion money supply has to turn over on average five times a year to purchase the \$5 trillion of nominal GDP.

If the money supply turns over five times a year, this means that people are holding each dollar of money for 365 days/5 = 73 days a year. If velocity is very high, individuals turn over money very quickly and do not hold money on average for a very long time. If velocity is low, they turn over money slowly and hold onto money for a longer period of time.

To further understand the role of money and velocity, let's rewrite the definition of velocity as

$$\text{money supply} \times \text{velocity} = \text{nominal GDP}$$

or

$$M \times V = P \times y$$

Quantity equation: The equation that links money, velocity, prices and real output. In symbols, we have: $M \times V = P \times y$.

where M is the money supply, V is the velocity of money, P is a measure of the average price level (for example, the chain-type price index for GDP), and y is real GDP. Together P and y equal nominal GDP. This equation is known as the *equation of exchange* or the **quantity equation.** On the right side is nominal GDP, the product of the chain-type price index and real GDP. This is the total value of spending. On the left side, the money supply is multiplied by V, the velocity of money.

The quantity equation links the money supply and velocity to nominal GDP. If velocity is relatively predictable, we can use the quantity equation and the supply of money to predict nominal GDP. However, the velocity of money does vary over time. For example, in the United States between 1959 and 1995, the velocity of M2 varied between 1.4 and 1.9. In other words, the stock of M2 turned over between 1.4 and 1.9 times a year to purchase nominal GDP for each year during this period.

The basic quantity equation can be used to derive a closely related formula that is useful for understanding inflation in the long run:

Growth version of the quantity equation: An equation that links the growth rates of money, velocity, prices, and real output.

$$\begin{matrix}\text{growth rate} \\ \text{of money}\end{matrix} + \begin{matrix}\text{growth rate} \\ \text{of velocity}\end{matrix} = \begin{matrix}\text{growth rate} \\ \text{of prices}\end{matrix} + \begin{matrix}\text{growth rate} \\ \text{of real output}\end{matrix}$$

We will call this the **growth version of the quantity equation.** Here is how to use this formula. Suppose that money growth is 10% a year, the growth of real output is 3% a year, and velocity has zero growth (it is constant). Then the rate of growth of prices, the inflation rate, is

$$10 + 0 = \text{growth rate of prices} + 3$$

$$7 = \text{growth rate of prices} = \text{inflation}$$

Inflation will be 7% a year. This formula allows for real economic growth and for growth in velocity. For example, if velocity grew during this period at the rate of 1% a year, the inflation rate will be 1% higher, or 8 (10 + 1 – 3) % a year.

This formula enables us to make strong predictions. As long as the growth rates of real income and velocity do not change very much over time, changes in the growth rate of money should lead to corresponding changes in the rate of inflation. How closely are money growth and inflation linked in practice? Figure 5 contains data for the average growth of M2 and inflation for each decade since the 1950s for the United States.

There is a definite link between increases in the growth of money and the rate of inflation. Inflation was lowest in the 1950s, when money growth was lowest. It was also highest in the 1970s, when money growth was highest. The link is not perfect because real GDP and velocity grew at different rates during the decades. But years of economic research have revealed that sustained increases in money growth will lead to inflation.

The links between money growth and inflation are particularly dramatic when money growth is extremely high. But what leads countries to vast increases in their money supply?

TEST *Your Understanding*

5 Complete the statement with *real* or *nominal*: The velocity of money is equal to ____________ GDP divided by the money supply.

6 If the growth of the money supply is 6% a year, velocity decreases by 1%, and there is no growth in real GDP, what is the inflation rate?

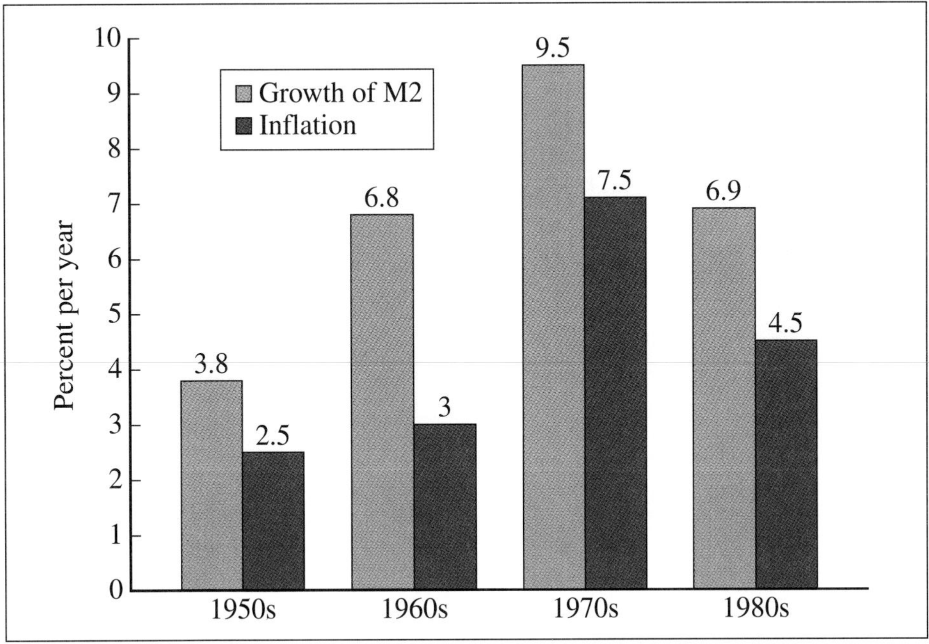

Figure 5

Money Growth and Inflation for the United States

BUDGET DEFICITS AND HYPERINFLATIONS

Hyperinflation: An inflation rate exceeding 50% per month.

The inflation rates observed in the United States in the last 40 years are insignificant in comparison to some of the experiences around the world throughout history. Economists call very high inflation rates, over 50% per month, **hyperinflation**. One of first studies of hyperinflations was conducted by Phillip Cagan of Columbia University. Table 1 presents selected data from his study.

Greece, Hungary, and Russia are three countries that have experienced hyperinflation. According to the data in Table 1, for a period of one year Greece had a *monthly* inflation rate of 365%. A monthly inflation rate of 365% per month means that the price level must rise by a factor of 4.65 each month. [If the price level rises by 4.65, its percent increase is (4.65 – 1)/1 = 3.65, or 365%.] To understand what this means, suppose we had inflation of this magnitude in the United States. At the beginning of the month, $1 could buy a large order of French fries. Since prices are rising by a factor of 4.65 each month, by the end of the month it will take $4.65 to buy the same French fries, and the dollar by the end of the month would be worth only 1/4.65 = 0.215, or 21.5 cents.

This process continues month after month. After two months, a dollar is only worth (.215) × (.215) = 0.046 of its original value, or 4.6 cents. After one year, a dollar bill is only worth 1 millionth of 1 cent! In hyperinflations, money does not hold its value very long.

In Hungary after World War II, prices rose by an unbelievable 19,800% each month. The hyperinflation in Russia in the early 1920s seems moderate by comparison. In Russia prices rose by 57% per month. Still, at that rate of inflation, $1 will be worth only 0.4 cents after a year.

Based on the quantity theory, we suspect that these hyperinflations must be all caused by money growth. We can see this in the data. For example, in Greece, the monthly inflation of 365% was accompanied by 220% money growth. In Hungary, the monthly inflation of 19,800% was caused by 12,200% money growth.

As we have seen, the value of money deteriorates sharply during hyperinflations. Money no longer serves as a good store of value. In these extreme circumstances we will expect people will not want to hold money very long but will immediately try to spend it. In other words, we will expect the velocity of money to increase sharply during hyperinflations. This is precisely what happens.

Table 1: Some Classic Hyperinflations

Country	*Dates*	*Monthly Rate of Inflation (%)*	*Monthly Rate of Money Growth (%)*	*Approximate Increase in Velocity*
Greece	November 1943 to November 1944	365	220	14.00
Hungary	August 1945 to July 1946	19,800	12,200	333.00
Russia	December 1921 to January 1924	57	49	3.70

Source: Adapted from Phillip Cagan, "The Monetary Dynamics of Hyperinflation," in *Studies in the Quantity Theory of Money*, edited by Milton Friedman (Chicago: University of Chicago Press, 1956) p. 26.

The last column of Table 1 shows how velocity increases during hyperinflations. In the hyperinflation in Greece, velocity increased by a factor of 14. In the dramatic hyperinflation in Hungary, velocity increased by over 333 times.

Hyperinflations have also have occurred in recent times. Table 2 presents data on three hyperinflations during the 1980s in Bolivia, Argentina, and Nicaragua—all averaging about 100% per month.

During hyperinflations, money no longer works very well in facilitating exchange. Since prices are changing so fast and unpredictably, there is typically massive confusion about the true value of commodities. Different stores may be raising prices at different rates, and the same commodities may sell for radically different prices. Everyone spends all their time hunting for bargains and finding the lowest prices, which becomes very costly in human terms. No country can easily live very long with hyperinflations. Governments are forced to put an end to hyperinflation before it totally destroys their economies.

The cause of all hyperinflations is excessive money growth. But why do governments allow the money supply to grow so fast and cause these economic catastrophes? The answer lies in understanding how some governments finance their deficits.

A government deficit must be covered in some way. If a government wants to spend $1,000 but is only collecting $800 in taxes, where can it get the extra $200? One option is to borrow the $200 from the public. The government will then issue government bonds—IOUs—to the public for $200. In the future, the government would have to pay back the $200 plus any interest on the bonds.

An alternative to borrowing from the public is simply to print $200 worth of new money. All governments have the ability to run the printing presses and come up with $200 in new currency.

In principle, governments could use a mix of borrowing and printing money as long as the deficit is covered:

government deficit = new borrowing from the public + new money created

Now we are in a position to understand how hyperinflations originate. Consider Hungary after World War II. Its economy was destroyed by the war and its citizens were demanding government services. The government had limited ability to collect taxes because of the poor state of the economy, but it gave in to the demands from its citizens for spending at levels that far exceeded what it could collect. The result was a large deficit. But then the government faced a problem: How would this large deficit be financed? No individuals or governments wanted to buy bonds or IOUs from Hungary (that is, lend Hungary money) because its economy was in such poor shape that it would be unlikely to pay off any debts in the near future. Without an option to borrow, Hungary resorted to printing money at a massive rate. The result was hyperinflation.

During Germany's hyperinflation in the 1920s, it was cheaper to start a fire with currency than it was to purchase wood for kindling.

Table 2: High Inflations in the 1980s

Country	*Year*	*Rate of Inflation (%)* Yearly	*Rate of Inflation (%)* Monthly	*Monthly Money Growth Rate (%)*
Bolivia	1985	1,152,200	118	91
Argentina	1989	975,500	95	93
Nicaragua	1988	302,200	115	66

Source: *International Financial Statistics Yearbook*, 1992. (Washington, DC: International Monetary Fund).

Hyperinflations always occur in countries that have large deficits but cannot borrow and are forced to print new money. Large deficits can arise in a variety of circumstances. For example, Argentina in the 1980s had large state-run firms that consistently lost vast sums of money. Because Argentina had a history of past inflations, it could not borrow easily and resorted to printing money. A similar fate befell the Ukraine after it achieved independence following the breakup of the Soviet Union. In 1994, inflation in the Ukraine was over 5,000% per year. Large, money-losing state enterprises and limited ability to borrow combined to bring money creation and hyperinflation.

To stop hyperinflations, it is necessary to eliminate the government deficit, which is the fundamental cause. Either taxes must be increased or spending must be cut, both of which cause some economic pain, but there is no other remedy. Once the deficit has been cut and the government stops printing money, the hyperinflation will end. Without money growth to feed it, hyperinflation will quickly die of starvation.

Monetarists: Economists who emphasize the role of money in determining nominal income and inflation.

Economists who traditionally emphasized the important role that the supply of money played in determining nominal income and inflation were often called **monetarists**. The most famous monetarist is Nobel laureate Milton Friedman, who studied sophisticated versions of the quantity equation and explored the role of money in all aspects of economic life. Friedman had many influential students, such as Philip Cagan, who is best known for his work on hyperinflations. They, along with other monetarist economists, did pioneering research on the link between money, nominal income, and inflation. Today, most economists agree with the monetarists that, in the long run, inflation is caused by growth in the money supply.

THE COSTS OF UNEMPLOYMENT AND INFLATION

While we can understand why societies cannot tolerate hyperinflations, it is less clear what problems occur with lower inflation rates. Why do societies deliberately create recessions and unemployment in order to lower the rate of inflation? In this section we take a closer look at the costs of unemployment and inflation to better understand the options facing policymakers.

Costs of Unemployment

When there is excess unemployment (unemployment above the natural rate), both society and individuals suffer economic loss. From a social point of view, excess unemployment means that the economy is no longer producing at its potential. The resulting loss of resources can be very large. For example, in 1983 when the unemployment rate averaged 9.6%, typical estimates of the shortfall of GDP from potential were near 6%. Simply put, this meant that society was wasting 6% of the total resources at its disposal.

Unemployment insurance: Payments received from the government upon becoming unemployed.

That social loss translates into reduced income and employment for individuals. When unemployment increases, more workers are fired or laid off from their existing jobs, and individuals seeking employment find fewer opportunities available. To families with fixed obligations such as mortgage payments, the loss in income can bring immediate hardships. **Unemployment insurance**, payments received from the government upon becoming unemployed, can cushion the blow to some degree, but unemployment insurance is typically only temporary and does not replace a worker's full earnings.

The effects of unemployment can also linger into the future. Workers who suffer from a prolonged period of unemployment are likely to lose some of their skills. For example, an unemployed stockbroker might be unaware of the latest developments and trends in financial markets. This will make it more difficult for him or her to find a job in the future. Economists who have studied the high rates of unemployment among young people in Europe point to the loss of both skills and good work habits (such as coming to work on time) as key factors leading to long-term unemployment.

The costs of unemployment are not strictly financial. In our society, a person's status and position are largely associated with the type of job held. Losing a job can impose severe psychological costs. Some studies, for example, have found that increased crime, divorce, and suicide are all associated with increased unemployment.

Costs of Inflation

Economists typically separate the costs of inflation into two categories. The first includes costs associated with fully expected or **anticipated inflation**. The second category is the costs associated with unexpected or **unanticipated inflation**. While inflation causes both types of costs, it is convenient to discuss each case separately.

Anticipated inflation: Inflation that is expected.

Unanticipated inflation: Inflation that is not expected.

Anticipated Inflation

Let's consider the costs of anticipated inflation first. Suppose the economy had been experiencing 4% inflation for many years and everyone was fully adjusted to it. Workers knew that nominal wage increases of 4% were not real wage increases because prices will rise by 4%. Investors earning a 7% rate of interest on their bonds knew their real return would be only 3% after adjusting for inflation.

Even in this case there are still some costs to inflation. First, there are the actual physical costs of changing prices, which economists call **menu costs**. Restaurant owners, catalog producers, and any other business that must post prices will have to incur costs to change their prices because of inflation. Economists believe these costs are relatively small for the economy.

Menu costs: Costs of inflation that arise from actually changing prices.

Second, people will hold less real cash balances when there is inflation. The cost of holding money is its opportunity cost, which is best measured by the nominal rate of interest. Since an increase in inflation will raise the nominal rate of interest, it will raise the cost of holding cash or checking accounts that do not pay interest. People will respond by holding less cash at any one time. If they hold less cash, they must visit the bank or their ATM more frequently because they will run out of cash sooner. Economists use the term **shoe-leather costs** to refer to the additional wear and tear necessary to hold less cash. Economists who have estimated these costs find that they can be large, as much as 1% of GDP.

Shoe-leather costs: Costs of inflation that arise from trying to reduce holdings of cash.

In practice, our tax system and financial system do not fully adjust even to fully anticipated inflation. It is difficult for the government and businesses to change their normal rules of operation when inflation changes. As an example, consider the tax system. Our tax system is based on nominal income, not real income. Suppose the inflation rate is 3% and nominal interest rates are 7% and that you have $100 in a savings account. At the end of the year, you will have earned $7. Your income taxes will be based on the full $7, and not $4, which is your earnings adjusted for inflation. This can make a considerable difference. If your tax rate is 50%, you pay $3.50 in taxes, giving you a nominal return after taxes of 3.5% on your original $100 [($7 – $3.50)/$100]. Taking into account the 3% inflation, your real return is thus only 0.5% (3.5 – 3).

On the other hand, suppose there were no inflation, the real rate were still 4%, and the tax rate were again 50%. Your taxes will be $2, which in the absence of inflation, will give you a higher real return after taxes of 2% [($4 – 2)/$100]. Inflation lowered your real after-tax return because the tax system is based on nominal, not real income. This increase in taxes was not a deliberate action of the legislature—it is solely a creature of inflation.

There are other tax examples as well. In the United States prior to 1986, inflation could have pushed you into a higher tax bracket, for example, from 15% to 28%, with the result that the government took a higher fraction of your income. Since 1986, tax brackets have been adjusted for inflation, eliminating this particular problem. Even today, however, you pay taxes when you sell a stock whose price has increased solely because of inflation even if the real value of the stock did not increase. The government can also lose from inflation as well. Homeowners can deduct their nominal interest payments on their mortgages—not their real interest payments—from their taxes. Higher inflation gives homeowners more deductions and lowers their income tax bills.

Usury laws: Laws that do not allow interest rates to exceed specified ceilings.

Many financial markets are also not fully adjusted for inflation. For example, some states have **usury laws** or ceilings on interest rates. These ceilings are on nominal rates, not real rates. At times of high inflation, some lenders may require nominal rates above the usury ceilings to provide them with an adequate real return. If they cannot lend at rates above the ceiling, the market may actually disappear.

The column in Table 3 on anticipated inflation summarizes our discussion. If the economy can adjust fully to inflation, the only costs of fully anticipated inflation are the relatively small menu and shoe-leather costs. But if institutions such as the tax system do not adjust, there will be other costs, such as distortions in the tax system, as well.

Unanticipated Inflation

The last column in Table 3 shows the costs of unexpected or unanticipated inflation. The first cost of unanticipated inflation is arbitrary redistributions of income. Suppose the public had been accustomed to 4% inflation and inflation reaches 6%. Who would gain and who would lose? Lenders would lose and borrowers would gain. If lenders and borrowers agreed to a real rate of interest of 3% and expected 4% inflation, the nominal rate will have been 7%. However, with 6% inflation, the real rate actually paid falls to 1%. Borrowers will rejoice but lenders will despair.

Anyone making a nominal contract to sell a product will lose. For example, workers who set nominal wages based on expected inflation will earn a lower real wage. Buyers with nominal contracts, such as firms setting nominal wages, will gain. These are unfair redistributions of income, or transfers, caused by unanticipated inflation.

These redistributions eventually impose real costs on the economy. Consider an analogy. Suppose you live in a very safe neighborhood where no one locks their doors. If a rash of burglaries (transfers between you and the crooks) starts to occur, people will invest in locks, alarms, and more police. You and your community will incur real costs to prevent these arbitrary redistributions.

The same is true for unanticipated inflation. If a society experiences unanticipated inflation, individuals and institutions will change their behavior. For example, potential homeowners will not be able to borrow for long periods of time at fixed

Table 3: Costs of Inflation

	Anticipated Inflation	*Unanticipated Inflation*
Institutions do not adjust	Distortions in the tax system, problems in financial markets	Unfair redistributions
Institutions adjust	Cost of changing prices, shoe-leather costs	Institutional disintegration

rates of interest but will be required to have loans whose rates can be adjusted as inflation rates change. This imposes more risk on homeowners. If unanticipated inflation becomes extreme, individuals will spend more of their time trying to profit from inflation rather than working at productive jobs. As inflation became more volatile in the late 1970s in the United States, many people devoted their time to speculation in real estate and commodity markets to try to beat inflation. The economy becomes less efficient when people take actions based on beating inflation. Latin American countries that have experienced high and variable inflation rates know all too well these costs from inflation.

When inflation becomes a problem, some societies have tried to *index* nominal contracts, that is, adjust the nominal amounts for inflation. For example, if you had an indexed wage of $10.00 an hour and there was 15% inflation, your wage would rise to $11.50 to compensate you for the inflation ($10.00 × 1.15 = $11.50). The U.S. government has now joined other countries in providing indexed bonds to protect investors from inflation.

In practice, countries find that indexing is not a perfect solution to the problems caused by inflation. First, some policymakers worry that indexing lowers the resolve to fight inflation and therefore could lead to higher inflation. Second, we know that price indices are far from perfect and are extremely difficult to construct when prices are increasing rapidly. Finally, some economists believe that indexing builds inflation into the economic system and makes it difficult to reduce inflation. If price increases automatically lead to wage increases, it becomes difficult to stop wage–price spirals. In 1995, for example, Brazil began to dismantle its very extensive system of indexing precisely for this reason.

Although Table 3 is useful for discussing the different costs of inflation, it is important to note that inflations cannot easily be separated into anticipated and unanticipated. Most inflations are a mixture of the two. Moreover, in all countries, institutions can adjust to inflation only partially. Thus all the costs outlined in Table 3 may apply to any episode of inflation.

These costs are compounded as inflation rises. Studies have shown that as inflation rises, both anticipated and unanticipated inflation increase. At high inflation rates, these costs grow rapidly, and at some point, policymakers are forced to engineer a recession to reduce the inflation rate. Although unemployment and recessions are quite costly to society, they sometimes become necessary in the face of high inflation.

Using the **TOOLS**

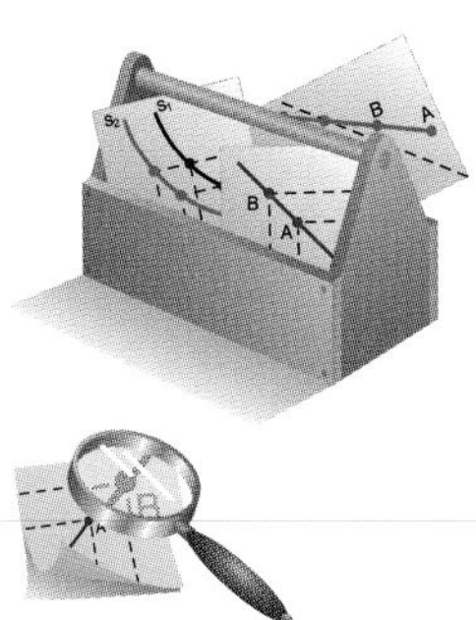

In this chapter we examined the process by which inflation becomes embedded into expectations and the problems in taming inflation. Take this opportunity to do your own economic analysis.

1. ECONOMIC DETECTIVE– *Mysteries of Short-Term versus Long-Term Interest Rates*

To stop inflation, a central bank cut back sharply on the rate of money growth. When it cut back, short-term nominal interest rates rose, but long-term rates (those on 30-year government bonds) did not change. After one month in which the central bank continued its tight money policy and short-term rates remained high, long-term rates began to fall. As an economic detective, explain the different behavior of short- and long-term nominal interest rates. (*Hint*: Long-term nominal interest rates will reflect expectations of inflation in the long run.)

2. Tax Indexation

An economy has two income tax brackets for individuals, with a tax rate of 10% for the first $30,000 of income and then 20% for any income exceeding $30,000.

a. A family earns $40,000. How much tax does it pay?

b. Suppose prices now double. The family earns $80,000. How much tax does the family pay?

c. How does the tax as a percentage of income change with the increase in prices? How could the tax system be "fixed" to ensure that the percentage of income that goes to the tax collector does not change with the level of prices?

3. Public Pronouncements and Fed Officials

When Alan Blinder, a Princeton University professor of economics, was appointed vice-chair of the Federal Reserve in 1994, he gave a speech to a group of central bankers and monetary policy specialists. In that speech he repeated one of the lessons in this chapter: In the long run, the rate of inflation is independent of unemployment and depends only on money growth, but in the short run, lower unemployment can raise the inflation rate. Blinder's speech created an uproar in the financial press. He was attacked by some commentators as being not sufficiently vigilant against inflation. Use the idea of credibility to explain why an apparently innocent speech would cause such an uproar in the financial community.

SUMMARY

In this chapter we explored the key role that expectations of inflation play in the economy and how societies deal with inflation. Both interest rates and changes in wages and prices reflect expectations of inflation. These expectations depend both on the past history of inflation and expectations about central bank behavior. To reduce inflation, policymakers must increase unemployment above the natural rate. We also looked at the ultimate causes of hyperinflations. Finally, we discussed the costs of unemployment and inflation and why policymakers sometimes deliberately cause recessions in order to reduce the rate of inflation. Here are main points to remember from this chapter:

1. In the long run, higher money growth leads to higher inflation and higher nominal interest rates.
2. A decrease in the growth rate of money will initially lead to higher real and nominal interest rates. Real rates will eventually return to their prior levels. Nominal rates will be permanently decreased with the decrease in inflation.
3. The rate of inflation increases when unemployment falls below the natural rate and decreases when unemployment exceeds the natural rate. This relationship is known as the expectations Phillips curve.
4. Monetary policymakers need to be cautious in their statements and pronouncements since they can influence expectations of inflation. Conservative central bankers can dampen expectations of inflation.
5. The quantity equation and the growth version of the quantity equation show the relationship between money, velocity, and nominal income.
6. Governments sometimes resort to printing money to finance large portions of their budget deficits. When they do, the result is rapid inflation.
7. The costs of unemployment include the loss of output for society and economic and psychological hardships for individuals.
8. The costs of inflation arise from both anticipated and unanticipated inflation. In practice, both types of costs rise with the inflation rate.

KEY TERMS

anticipated inflation, *619*
expectations of inflation, *605*
expectations Phillips curve, *607*
expected real rate of interest, *606*
growth version of the quantity equation, *614*
hyperinflation, *616*
menu costs, *619*
monetarists, *618*
money illusion, *605*
prime rate of interest, *604*
quantity equation, *614*
rational expectations, *613*
real wages, *605*
shoe-leather costs, *619*
unanticipated inflation, *619*
unemployment insurance, *618*
usury laws, *620*
velocity of money, *614*

PROBLEMS AND DISCUSSION QUESTIONS

1. Interpret this statement: "High interest rates are the evidence of loose monetary policy, not tight monetary policy."
2. Why will an increase in the rate of growth of the money supply initially lead to lower nominal rates of interest but eventually to higher rates?
3. Why can different levels of inflation be compatible with the same rate of unemployment?
4. Why does the inflation rate rise relative to its trend when unemployment falls below the natural rate?
5. Why does velocity increase when inflation increases?
6. Some economists have argued that international aid can reduce the severity of hyperinflations. Explain this argument.
7. Describe the costs of anticipated and unanticipated inflation.
8. Many people find owning their own home an attractive investment during times of inflation. Interest payments for the house can be deducted from income before calculating income taxes. When a house is sold at a price that has risen through inflation, most of the profit from owning it is free of tax. Why does an increase in inflation increase the attractiveness of owning a house? Why do people often buy larger houses during periods of high inflation than they normally would?

Take It to the Net

We invite you to visit the O'Sullivan/Sheffrin page on the Prentice Hall Web site at:

http://www.prenhall.com/osullivan/

for this chapter's World Wide Web exercise.

MODEL ANSWERS FOR THIS CHAPTER

Chapter-Opening Questions

1. Countries with lower rates of money growth will have lower inflation rates than countries with higher money growth. Nominal interest rates (which reflect inflation) will also be lower.
2. In the long run, unemployment returns to the natural rate and inflation is largely determined by money growth. Therefore, lower unemployment will lead to higher inflation but unemployment will return to the natural rate.
3. It is prudent to have conservative heads of central banks because the private sector will be less tempted to aggressively raise wages and prices.
4. Budget deficits must be financed by either issuing debt or creating money. When deficits are very large, it is difficult to issue debt, so money is created, causing massive inflation.
5. Inflation poses real costs on the economy which is why societies sometimes cause recessions to reduce inflation. However, there are costs to

unemployment as well and these need to be balanced against the costs of inflation.

Test Your Understanding

1. True.
2. This is an application of the reality principle. If prices rise, people will want to hold more money to make transactions.
3. The unemployment rate will exceed the natural rate by 2 points for two years, a total of 4 points. Since inflation rises by 0.5% for each point the unemployment rate falls below the natural rate, the inflation rate will rise from 3% to 5%.
4. b
5. nominal
6. Use the growth version of the quantity equation: 6 – 1 = inflation + 0. Inflation is thus 5%.

Using the Tools

1. Economic Detective: Mysteries of Short-Term versus Long-Term Interest Rates

   Short-term rates rose because of the increase in the real rate of interest. Since it took a while before inflation fell, expectations of inflation in the near term did not change. However, the market did expect inflation to fall over the long term. This drop in long-term expected inflation meant that nominal interest rates did not have to rise with tighter money. Indeed, they fell as market participants foresaw lower inflation.
2. Tax Indexation
   a. The family pays $5,000 in taxes ($3,000 on the first $30,000 and another $2,000 on the next $10,000).
   b. Now the family pays $13,000 in taxes ($3,000 on the first $30,000 and another $10,000 on the next $50,000).
   c. In the first case, the family pays 12.5% in taxes. In the second case, the family pays 16.3%, although their real income before taxes was the same in both cases. To prevent this, the level at which the higher rate takes effect should be adjusted or "indexed" for the price level. If the level of income at which the 20% rate took effect was raised to $60,000, then the family will pay $10,000 in taxes or 12.5% of their income.
3. Public Pronouncements and Fed Officials

   The financial markets reacted negatively to Blinder's comments because they perceived that it signaled he was soft on inflation. A conservative central banker will typically not even mention that lower unemployment could increase inflation because that might leave the impression that they might not be aggressive in fighting inflation.

CHAPTER

31

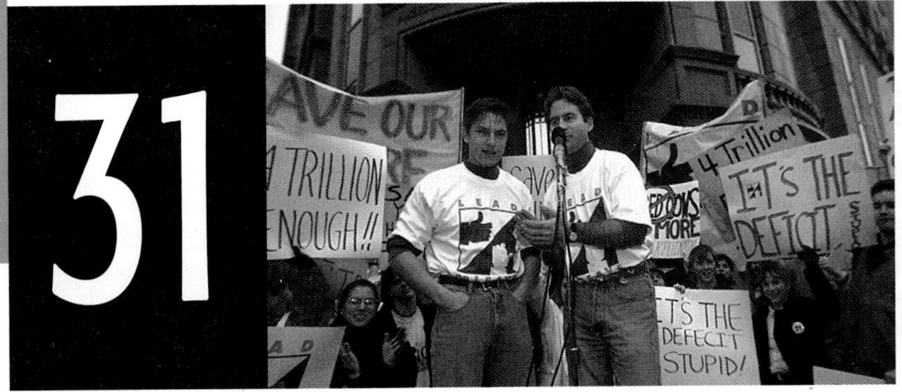

Ten Questions (and Answers) about Government Debt and Deficits

If you had a penny for every time a politician complained about the government budget deficit, you would have no trouble paying your college fees. Politicians, journalists, and "experts" of all types regularly complain that deficits are ruining our country. But are they right? How exactly do government deficits affect our everyday life? How do they affect the things we care about in macroeconomics: unemployment, growth, and inflation?

In this chapter we take a close look at government deficits. As we will see, the relationships between government deficits and the economy is not so simple as the politicians may lead you to believe. To understand the various relationships between government deficits and the economy, we will ask and answer 10 questions about deficits. Understanding these questions and answers will prepare you for the political debate about the deficit.

After reading this chapter, you will be able to answer the following real-world questions:

1. Do deficits cause inflation?
2. How can deficits pose a burden on future generations?
3. Would a constitutional amendment to balance the budget really work?
4. Do budget deficits always cause trade deficits?

1. WHAT EXACTLY ARE DEBT AND DEFICITS?

Deficit: The excess of total expenditures over total revenues.

Surplus: The excess of total revenues over total expenditures.

Balanced budget: The situation when total expenditures equals total revenues.

Government expenditure: Spending on goods and services plus transfer payments.

Fiscal year: The calendar on which the federal government conducts its business, which runs from October 1 to September 30.

Government debt: The total of all past deficits.

Governments run a **deficit** when they spend more than they currently receive in either taxes or fees. A **surplus** occurs when revenues exceed spending. Governments run a **balanced budget** when spending equals revenues. They can spend money on either purchases of goods and services or transfer payments. As you may recall, purchases of goods and services are included in GDP, but transfer payments such as Social Security, welfare payments, and interest on the federal debt are not. To measure total spending by the government, we must include both types of spending. We use the term **government expenditure** to include both purchases of goods and services and transfer payments.

The federal government runs its books on a **fiscal year** basis, which differs from the normal calendar year. Fiscal year 1997, for example, begins October 1, 1996 and ends September 30, 1997. Table 1 contains estimates made by the Congressional Budget Office in August 1996 of total expenditures, total revenues, and the deficit for fiscal years 1996 to 2006. The top part of the table contains the actual numbers and the bottom part measures everything as a percent of GDP.

Taking the year 2000 as an example, total expenditure by the government is projected to be $1,925 billion, while total revenues will be $1,681 billion, leaving a deficit of $244 billion. Expressed as a percent of GDP, expenditure, revenues, and the deficit are 21.3, 18.6, and 2.7%, respectively. Throughout the entire period, the deficit is projected to rise from 1.9% to 3.4% of GDP.

The **government debt** is the total of all its deficits. For example, if a government initially had a debt of $100 billion and then ran deficits for the next three years of $20, $30, and $50 billion, the government's total debt at the end of this period

Table 1: Estimates of Government Expenditures, Revenues, and the Deficit

	1996	*1997*	*1998*	*1999*	*2000*	*2001*	*2002*	*2003*	*2004*	*2005*	*2006*
					Billions of dollars						
Total expenditures	1,572	1,654	1,737	1,828	1,925	2,016	2,125	2,242	2,365	2,500	2,636
Total revenues	1,428	1,483	1,544	1,609	1,681	1,758	1,840	1,931	2,033	2,124	2,232
Deficit	144	171	193	219	244	258	285	311	342	376	403
					As percent of GDP						
Total expenditures	21.0	21.1	21.1	21.2	21.3	21.3	21.4	21.5	21.6	21.8	21.9
Total revenues	19.1	18.9	18.8	18.7	18.6	18.5	18.5	18.5	18.5	18.5	18.5
Deficit	1.9	2.2	2.3	2.5	2.7	2.8	2.9	3.0	3.1	3.3	3.4

Source: Congressional Budget Office, *Reducing the Deficit: Spending and Revenue Options* (Washington, DC: U.S. Government Printing Office, August 1996), p. 2.

would be $200 billion ($100 + $20 + $30 + $50 = $200). If a government ran a surplus, it would decrease the total stock of debt.

In fiscal year 1995, the debt in the hands of the public totaled approximately $3,600 billion. This amounted to approximately $14,500 for every person in the United States. You may wonder why the deficit and debt are so large when politicians so often talk about the budget cuts they have made. But as the Closer Look box "Do Budget Cuts Actually Reduce Expenditures?" explains, what is called a "cut" in Washington, DC may not always be a true cut in expenditures.

2. HOW ARE GOVERNMENT DEFICITS FINANCED?

As we discussed in the previous chapter, a government deficit must be covered in some way. If a government wants to spend $2,000 but is collecting only $1,600 in taxes, where can it get the extra $400? One option would be to borrow the $400 from the public in return for government bonds (in effect IOUs). In the future, the government would have to pay back the $400 plus any interest on the bonds. An alternative is simply to print $400 worth of new money.

In principle, governments could use a mix of borrowing or printing money, as long as the total covers its deficits:

government deficit = new borrowing from the public + new money created

In the United States, the Treasury Department always issues government bonds to finance the deficit. The Federal Reserve, however, has the option of buying existing government debt (including the new issues). If the Federal Reserve does purchase bonds, it takes the government debt out of the hands of the public and creates money through its purchase. Economists call the purchase by a central bank of newly created government debt **monetizing the deficit.** This has precisely the same effect as if the Treasury had printed money to finance the government deficit.

Monetizing the deficit: Purchases by a central bank of newly issued government bonds.

A Closer LOOK

Do Budget Cuts Actually Reduce Expenditures?

In everyday life, if we say that we cut our spending, our actual spending is reduced. With the government budget, "cuts" need not really cut spending.

Until 1995, when the Congress and the executive branch prepared their budgets, they used a procedure called *baseline budgeting.* They first estimated what they would need to spend to maintain existing programs. For example, if the price of food has increased, then under baseline budgeting, expenditures for food stamps would have to be increased. If Congress reduced expenditures from this higher level, they could claim that they were "cutting" their budget. But if the baseline budget increased by 10% and expenditures were "cut" by 5% from this higher level, then actual expenditures would have increased by 5%.

Of course, if the price of food has increased, the same level of expenditures could not support the same level of food for recipients of food stamps. In this sense there would be "cuts" in the services provided by food stamps. Baseline budgeting does provide useful information.

In 1995, Congress decided not to use baseline budgeting, but the executive branch still does. Both normal and baseline budgeting should be used on a regular basis. The public should know whether actual spending has been increased or decreased. It should also know whether government services have changed.

We have seen that if governments choose to finance deficits by creating new money, the result will be inflation. In the United States, we finance only a very small portion of our deficits by creating money. For example, between 1992 and 1993, the Federal Reserve purchased only $15 billion of a government deficit of approximately $270 billion for that period. The remainder of the debt was financed by issuing new government bonds to the public.

If a country has no options other than creating money to finance deficits, deficits will inevitably cause inflation. As we discussed in detail in the last chapter, hyperinflations occur when economies run large deficits and monetize them. Germany and Russia after World War I, Bolivia and Argentina in the 1980s, and the Ukraine in the 1990s are just some of the countries that have experienced massive inflations through monetizing their deficits. However, large stable countries that can borrow from the public, such as the United Kingdom, the United States, and Japan, do not have to monetize their deficits. For these countries, deficits do not have to lead inevitably to inflation.

3. WHAT IS THE U.S. HISTORY WITH DEBTS AND DEFICITS?

To determine whether government debt today or in the future is "too high," it is useful to have some basis for comparison. The best single measure of the debt held by the public is as a percent of GDP. Figure 1 plots this percentage for the United States for over two centuries, from 1791 to 1995.

The figure shows a number of different episodes in U.S. history with periods of both high and low debt. The debt burden was lowest in 1835 and 1836, when the total outstanding debt was only $38,000 or about .02% of GDP. As you can see, debt typically rose sharply during wars as the country ran budget deficits to

Figure 1

Debt as a Percent of GDP, 1791–1995

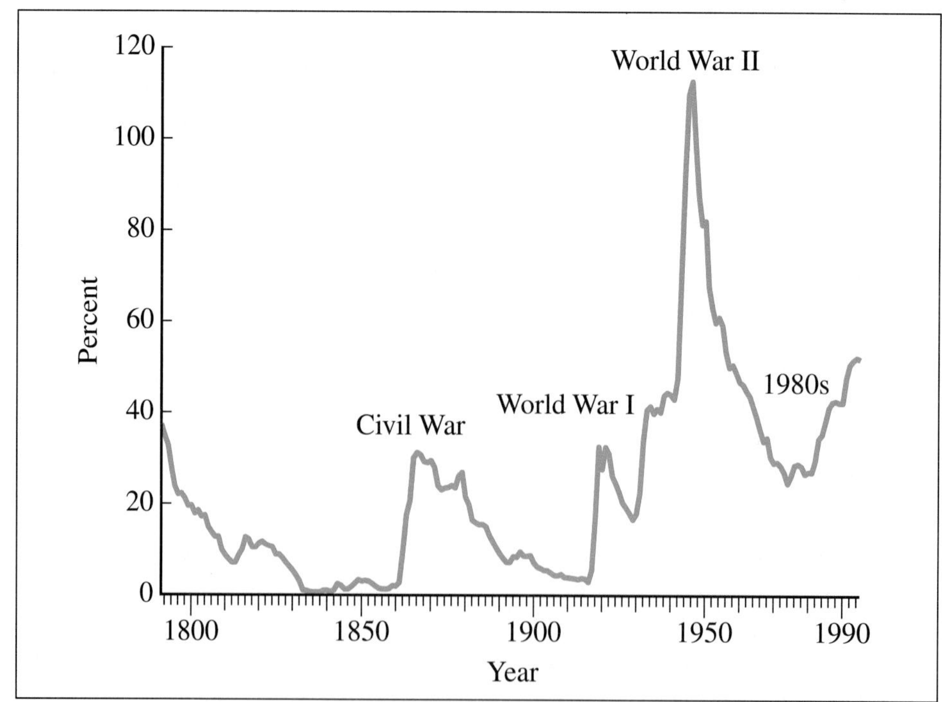

Sources: Data from *Economic Report of the President* (Washington, DC: Government Printing Office, yearly); *Historical Statistics of the United States* (Westport, CT: Greenwood Press, 1993); Thomas Senior Berry, *Estimated Annual Variations in Gross Domestic Product, 1789–1909* (Richmond, VA: Bostwick Press, 1968).

finance the wars. After the wars, debt falls as a percent of GDP. The largest increase in debt relative to GDP occurred during World War II, when the total debt outstanding exceeded the value of GDP for a year. Since that time the ratio has fallen, leveling off in the 1970s and rising again in the 1980s and 1990s. In 1995, debt was approximately 52% of GDP—less than half the percentage at its peak at the end of World War II.

Scholars who have studied deficits and debt for other countries have also found that the total level of debt relative to GDP generally rises during wars and then falls during peacetime. Starting in the 1980s, however, the United States began to run large peacetime deficits. These deficits resulted from actions taken during the first few years of the presidency of Ronald Reagan. The fight to lower inflation caused a deep recession and lowered tax revenues. Reagan's administration also pushed through increases in defense expenditures and decreases in personal and corporate taxes. While some categories of federal spending were cut, spending on entitlements and other mandatory programs (such as Medicare, Medicaid, and Social Security) were not decreased. As the debt began to grow, interest on the debt also became a significant expenditure. The combination of these factors—tax cuts, a recession, increased defense expenditures, and lack of other expenditure cuts—led to large deficits and a high percentage of total debt to GDP for a peacetime era.

Figure 2 shows some of the key components of the budget picture from 1970 to 1995 based on data from the Congressional Budget Office. You can see deficits (the gap between outlays and revenues) begin to emerge in the mid-1970s and 1980s. As a percent of GDP, revenues in 1995 were approximately the same as in 1970, while outlays were somewhat higher. Entitlement spending, however, shows the biggest change. It started in 1970 at 7.2% of GDP but reached 11.7% by 1995. As we discuss later in the chapter, the growth in entitlement spending is the primary budgetary challenge for the next century.

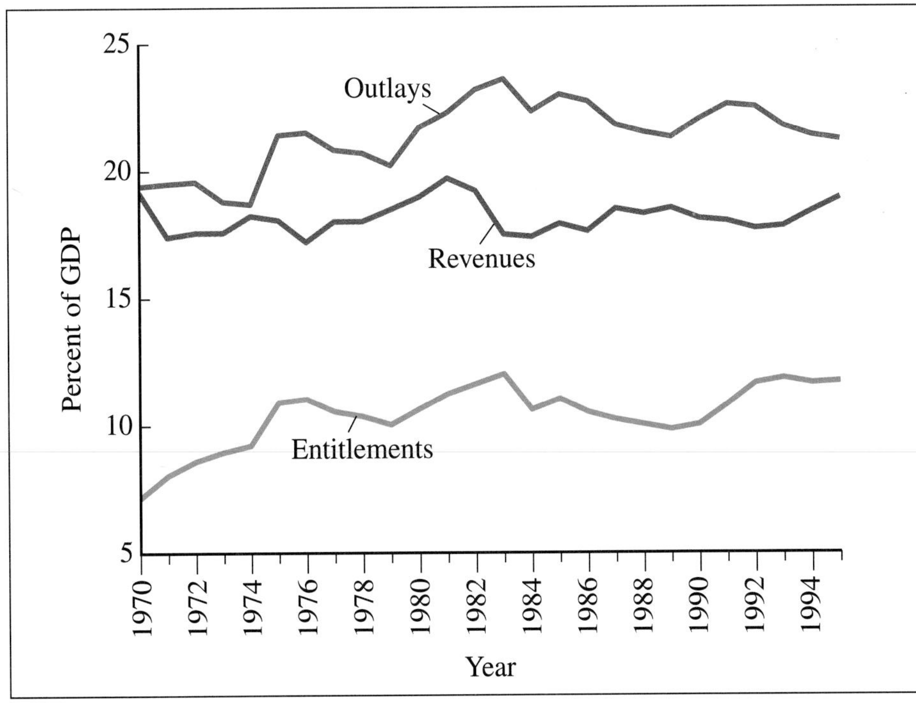

Figure 2

Federal Outlays, Revenues, and Entitlements, 1970–1995

Source: "The Economic and Budget Outlook: Fiscal Years 1997–2006" (Congressional Budget Office, 1996).

TEST *Your Understanding*

1 True or false: The government debt is the difference between the current level of total expenditures and revenues.

2 What are the two methods that governments can use to finance a deficit?

4. CAN DEFICITS BE GOOD FOR THE COUNTRY?

At times, deficits can be good for a country. They can provide a safety valve for the economy during economic downturns by stimulating private-sector spending in bad times. Governments may also deliberately create deficits to pull the economy out of a recession.

Automatic stabilizers: The changes in taxes and transfer payments that occur automatically as economic activity changes. These changes in taxes and transfers dampen economic fluctuations.

We have encountered both of these ideas before in our chapter on Keynesian economics. The increase in the deficit during economic downturns shows the **automatic stabilizers** of the economy in action, putting additional income into the hands of the public during bad economic times. This additional income allows people to avoid drastic cuts in their consumption spending. Since total spending does not fall as much, the severity of recessions is decreased.

How do automatic stabilizers work? As incomes fall during a recession, so do tax payments. Moreover, transfer payments such as welfare and food stamps rise. Since government spending increases while tax revenues fall, the deficit must rise. Figure 3 plots the deficit as a percent of GDP and the unemployment rate for the period 1970–1995. Since increases in the unemployment rate signal bad economic times, we expect the deficit to rise and fall along with the unemployment rate. This is precisely what Figure 3 shows.

The deficit can also change if the government tries to stabilize the economy through fiscal policy. For example, if a government engages in expansionary fiscal

Figure 3

U.S. Deficit and Unemployment Rate, 1970–1995

Sources: Data from U.S. Department of Commerce; and *Economic Report of the President* (Washington, DC: U.S. Government Printing Office, yearly).

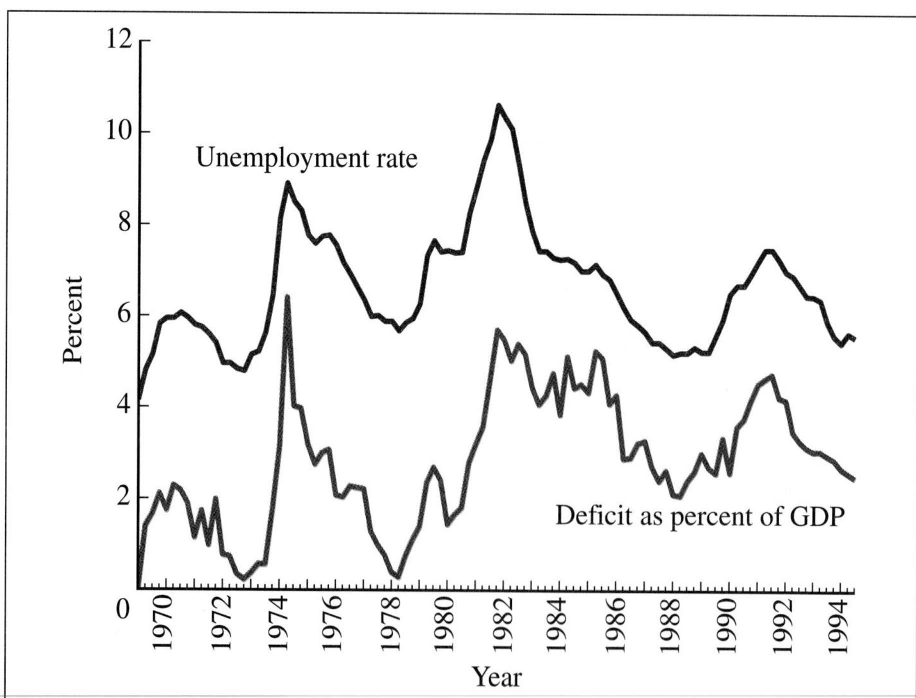

policy to pull the economy out of a recession, cutting taxes or increasing spending, the result will be to increase the deficit. However, during a recession this may be the appropriate means to steer the economy back to full employment.

When economists measure whether fiscal policy has been expansionary or contractionary, they control for the fact that the deficit rises during bad economic times and falls during good economic times. Although expansionary fiscal policy will increase the deficit, the deficit will also increase during economic downturns, without the government's taking any explicit actions.

To measure changes in fiscal policy due to economic policy, economists use a concept known as the **full-employment deficit**, also known as the **structural deficit**. The full-employment or structural deficit is an estimate of what the deficit would be *if* the economy were operating at full employment. This concept isolates the effects of fiscal policy changes from movements in GDP that affect the deficit. Increases in the full-employment deficit provide a quantitative measure of expansionary fiscal policy. The full-employment deficit is also the proper measure to use when trying to decide whether a deficit is too large, because it takes into account that deficits will be temporarily high when an economy is in a recession and temporarily low when the economy is experiencing a boom.

Full-employment deficit: An estimate of what the federal budget deficit would be if the economy were operating at full employment.

Structural deficit: Another term for the full-employment deficit.

To understand how the full-employment deficit concept works in practice, consider what would happen if the economy fell into a recession but policymakers took no actions. In this case the full-employment deficit would be unchanged because the government would still be collecting the same amount of revenue *if* (contrary to fact) the economy were operating at full employment. The actual deficit, however, would increase with the fall in tax revenue caused by the recession. The fact that the full-employment deficit did not change tells us that fiscal policy was not used during this recession.

The existence of automatic stabilizers and the use of expansionary fiscal policy during recessions suggest that we should not worry about short-run government deficits. Over short time periods, deficits can help the economy cope with shocks and give the government some room to maneuver out of a recession. Most economists believe that automatic stabilizers have reduced economic fluctuations during the twentieth century.

5. WHAT IS THE BURDEN OF THE NATIONAL DEBT?

The *national debt* (another commonly used term for total government debt) can pose two different burdens for society, both of which fall on future generations. First, a large debt can reduce the amount of capital in the economy and thereby reduce future incomes and real wages. Second, a large national debt will mean that future generations will have to pay higher taxes to finance the interest on the debt.

An economy increases its capital stock through the savings of individuals and institutions. These savings flow into capital formation. For example, if savers purchase new stock issued by a company, they provide the funds that allow the company to invest in plant and equipment. Savers hold the shares of stock as assets, which they can use for retirement or pass on to future generations.

When governments run deficits and increase the national debt, they finance these deficits by selling bonds to the public. These bonds must be bought by the very same individuals and institutions who are saving in the economy. Individuals and institutions now will be saving both by purchasing stock in companies *and* by buying government bonds. Savers will hold both shares of stock and government bonds as assets for retirement. If the level of total level of savings in the economy is given, the additional government bonds must come at the expense of shares of new stock. For example, suppose that desired savings are $1,000. If there are $200 in new bonds, only $800 is available for savings in new shares. The $200 in bonds "crowds out" $200 in new shares.

The result of government deficits is that less savings are available to firms for investment. As we have discussed in earlier chapters, reduced saving will ultimately reduce the stock of private capital in society. There will be less capital deepening. With lower capital per worker, real incomes and real wages will be lower.

Servicing the debt: Paying interest on existing debt.

The second burden of the national debt on future generations is the additional taxes they must pay toward **servicing the debt**, that is, paying interest on the national debt. This actually affects us today. According to the Congressional Budget Office, we will spend about $240 billion on interest on the debt in fiscal year 1996. These interest payments arise because we borrowed in the past and ran up a large debt. Just like your college loans, the bill eventually comes due.

Some people say that these interest payments are not a real burden because we owe the national debt to ourselves. Let's first imagine a circumstance in which this were really true. Today, the national debt is about $15,000 per person in the United States. Suppose that we all owned this debt equally, that is, all taxpayers actually had in their possession $15,000 in government bonds. In this case the taxes we pay to service the debt would come right back to us as interest payments. It would go out of one pocket into the other and not pose any burden.

In reality, we do not equally share in owning the national debt. Some of it is held by foreigners. Most of it is held by older, wealthy individuals or institutions, which at one point lent the government money and now want to be paid back. All working people must pay taxes to service the debt, but they do not earn all the interest. This is a price we pay for running deficits in the past.

Moreover, even if we shared equally in owning the national debt, it would still pose a burden if we held the debt at the expense of holding capital. From an individual point of view, a saver earns a return from holding either debt or capital. But from a social point of view, if society holds debt rather than capital, the stock of capital available for use in production will be smaller and our living standards reduced correspondingly.

Ricardian equivalence: The proposition that it does not matter whether government expenditure is financed by taxes or by debt.

Some economists do not believe that government deficits or debt impose a burden on a society. These economists believe in **Ricardian equivalence**, the proposition that it does *not* matter whether government expenditure is financed by taxes or by issuing debt. To understand the case for Ricardian equivalence, consider this example. A government initially has a balanced budget. It then cuts taxes and issues new debt to finance the deficit. The public understands that the government will have to raise taxes in the future to service the debt and increases their saving to pay for the taxes that will be raised in the future. If private saving rises sufficiently, the public would be able to purchase the new debt without reducing funds for investment. Since investment does not decline, there will be no burden of the debt.

As you can see, Ricardian equivalence requires that private savings increase when the deficit increases. Do savers behave in this fashion? It is actually quite difficult to provide a definitive answer to this question since many other factors must be taken into account in any empirical study of saving. However, during the early 1980s, it appears that private saving decreased somewhat when government deficits increased. This is precisely opposite to what Ricardian equivalence predicts. Nonetheless, the evidence on this topic is mixed and it is an area of active research today.

6. WHEN DOES A NATIONAL DEBT BECOME TOO LARGE?

There are two different warning signs of an excessive government debt: high inflation and low national investment. Countries with limited abilities to finance their deficits through issuing bonds (because of either poor economic prospects or political instability) will soon find that they must monetize their deficits. The inevitable result is inflation. This problem has afflicted many countries around the world, including the former Soviet Union and many Latin American nations. Once a country has developed a reputation for generating inflation, it becomes increasingly difficult to borrow. In these cases, even relatively small deficits must be financed by money creation with the resulting inflation.

For countries that do have a good track record of avoiding inflation, one danger of an excessive national debt is a low level of investment. As we noted, one of the burdens of the debt is that it reduces the level of investment. When governments run large deficits, savers must purchase the new government bonds that are issued. These bonds displace new investment.

One common measure of a country's debt burden is the ratio of debt to GDP. This ratio measures the past effects of running deficits relative to GDP. Figure 4 depicts some ratios for 1992. Italy and Belgium have the highest ratios of this group, comparable to the United States after World War II. Korea has the lowest, and Japan has a higher debt to GDP ratio than the United States.

However, these figures do not tell the entire story. Deficits are more of a problem when a country has a low saving rate, as does the United States. Countries with high saving rates can more easily absorb the deficits. Italy, for example, has frequently run deficits of nearly 10% of GDP. But its investment rate is close to 20% of GDP (higher than the United States at roughly 15%) because its high saving rate allows it to absorb the new bonds issued by the government.

7. DOES THE NATIONAL DEBT MEASURE THE TOTAL BURDEN ON FUTURE GENERATIONS?

A higher government debt means that future generations must pay higher interest payments to service the debt. But interest is not the only financial burden that governments can impose on future generations. Let's consider an example. Suppose the government invents a new program that promises everyone over the age of 65 a retirement pension (largely free of tax) and subsidized medical care. These benefits are to be paid through payroll taxes on workers. It does not show up as an official government deficit, but clearly this program would pose a burden on future generations who must pay for it.

This is precisely the situation we face today. Social Security and Medicare, programs that promise retirement and health benefits to retirees in the United States,

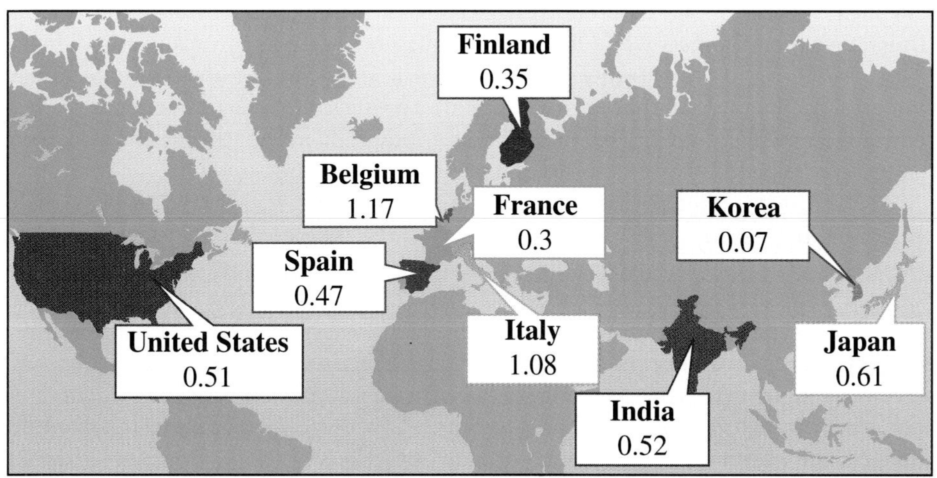

Figure 4

International Debt to GDP Ratios, 1992

Source: *International Financial Statistics*, International Monetary Fund, 1995.

are financed through payroll taxes on current workers, not the past contributions of the retirees.

Generational accounting: Methods that assign the tax burden of government debt and other programs to different generations.

Laurence Kotlikoff, an economist at Boston University, has developed a new way to measure the full burden on future generations from all government programs, not just government deficits. His approach, called **generational accounting**, provides estimates of the burdens on future generations from all the past actions taken by the government. His study indicates bad news for future generations: In the era since World War II, we have promised large benefits for future retirees that will have to be paid by future generations. According to one of Kotlikoff's estimates, male workers born today would have to hand over nearly 80% of their income to pay for all these benefits! If future workers resist this high rate of taxation, the benefits must change.

If the government raised the retirement age or cut back on promises of future medical care, this would reduce the burden on future generations of workers without showing up in the official deficit statistics. Kotlikoff's main point is that we should not become fixated on one number called the *deficit*. Other government programs can have profound effects on the burden on future generations.

Kotlikoff's numbers have been criticized because they rely on a number of special assumptions. For example, he assumes that spending programs will not be changed in the future and that the entire burden of financing these programs will fall on the newly born. Neither of these outcomes will necessarily occur. Nonetheless, Kotlikoff provides a valuable warning about our current trends in spending and the potential burden that may fall on future generations.

TEST ***Your Understanding***

3 Why do deficits rise during recessions?

4 True or false: The full-employment deficit will remain unchanged if personal income tax rates are cut.

5 True or false: Social Security and Medicare are fully paid by the past contributions of retirees.

8. WHY DO STATES USUALLY BALANCE THEIR BUDGETS BUT THE FEDERAL GOVERNMENT DOES NOT?

All 50 states have some requirement to balance their budgets. Why do states manage to balance their budgets while the federal government always seems to run deficits? There are three answers to this question: (1) The states do not always balance their budgets, (2) the budgets that they balance are not the same type of budget as the federal government's, and (3) balanced budget requirements work but they do force states to cut spending and raise taxes during poor economic times.

Most states require that the budget a governor and legislature propose at the beginning of the year be in balance. However, if the state's economy turns down and the actual budget runs a deficit, there need not be any immediate correction and the state can borrow to cover the deficit. Moreover, some states can carry over deficits for several years. For example, in the early 1990s the state of California borrowed $5 billion over several years to cover multiyear deficits.

Operating budgets: Budgets for day-to-day expenditures.

Capital budgets: Budgets for long-term investments.

The most important difference between state governments and the federal government is in the nature of the budgets. States have two types of budgets: **operating budgets** and **capital budgets**. The day-to-day operations of the government—salaries, supplies, maintenance—are included in the operating budget. These expenditures are financed by taxes. The capital budget refers to all major investment expenditures, such as roads or buildings. These are financed through long-term borrowing, which is the only borrowing that states are typically permitted to do. The balanced budget requirements apply only to their operating budgets.

The federal government, however, has only one budget and does not divide its accounts into operating and capital expenditures. A deficit in the federal budget could reflect capital expenditures—such as a new military base—or operating expenditures such as the salaries of Congress and the executive branch. Some economists have suggested that the federal government should follow the states and have two budgets, but there has not been much interest in this option. In any case, "balancing the budget" means balancing only the operating budget for states, but the entire budget for the federal government.

State legislators may succeed in balancing their budgets, but the budgets they balance differ in important dimensions from the federal budget.

Balanced budget requirements in the states do change the behavior of politicians, who are forced to decide whether to raise taxes to cover programs or cut the programs to stay within their budget limits. States do differ in the severity of their balanced budget limitations. Research by economist James Poterba at the Massachusetts Institute of Technology has shown that states with "strong antideficit rules" are more likely to cut spending in the face of unanticipated events than are states with weaker antideficit rules. However, even states with weak balanced budget limitations cannot run large deficits for long periods of time. Legal requirements to balance state budgets cannot be totally evaded by politicians.

9. HOW WELL WOULD A BALANCED BUDGET AMENDMENT REALLY WORK?

For many years, there has been interest in a constitutional amendment to balance the federal budget. In early 1995, Congress came very close to passing such an amendment and sending it back to the states for ratification. It passed in the House of Representatives but failed by a single vote in the Senate. How would a balanced budget amendment actually work? What are the pros and cons of such an amendment?

Many different budgetary constitutional amendments have been proposed. They all require that after a phase-in period, Congress propose in each fiscal year a budget in which total revenues (excluding borrowing) cover total expenditures. The amendments also have various "escape" clauses, for example, to allow borrowing during wartime. Some amendments also allow Congress to suspend the requirement for other reasons, such as during a recession when deficits naturally emerge. Finally, some versions of the amendment would limit the rate of spending increases to the growth rate of GDP, but this is actually an expenditure limitation and not a balanced budget requirement.

Proponents of the balanced budget amendment contend that it will finally exert discipline on the federal government and prevent it from running large deficits in peacetime. We thus can avoid the adverse effects of deficits, namely reduced capital formation and a shift in the burden of taxation to future generations. The proponents point to the experience of the states with balanced budget requirements and contrast it to the federal government.

Critics of a balanced budget amendment point to many different problems, among them:

- There may not be enough flexibility to deal with recessions. Under some versions of the amendment, unless three-fifths of Congress votes to suspend requirements, the government would have to cut expenditures or raise taxes during a recession. This would make the recession worse and limit the ability of the government to use fiscal policy to stabilize the economy.

- The Constitution is not the right mechanism to try to enforce complicated budget rules. As various interested parties challenge the actions of Congress, the courts would become heavily involved in federal budget matters.
- Congress could devise special budgets to get around the requirement, for example, by taking some types of spending "off budget," that is, simply not count it as part of the official budget.
- Congress could also find other nonbudgetary ways to carry out the policies that it desires. For example, it could issue more regulations or impose **mandates** or requirements on business or other governments to carry out its will.

Mandate: A requirement imposed by government on lower levels of government or on the private sector.

In reality, we do not know how a balanced budget amendment would work in practice. As the Closer Look box "Gramm–Rudman Deficit Reduction Laws" explains, we have some experience with laws that the Congress has passed to try to force itself to eliminate deficits. These laws proved not to be very successful and raised doubts about the enforceability of a balanced budget amendment. However, a law to reduce the deficit is not the same as a constitutional amendment. Congress can always change a law it does not like; it is much more difficult to amend the Constitution.

10. IS THE BUDGET DEFICIT RELATED TO THE TRADE DEFICIT?

Twin deficits: The association between increases in the federal budget deficit and the trade deficit.

At the same time that large peacetime deficits emerged during the 1980s, so did large trade deficits. The simultaneous rise in the budget and trade deficits became known as the **twin deficits**. Figure 5 on the next page compares the trade and budget deficits from 1980 through 1993. As you can see, the trade and budget deficits did increase together in the mid-1980s and fall together in the late 1980s. However,

A Closer LOOK

Gramm–Rudman Deficit Reduction Laws

Frustrated by their inability to control the U.S. budget deficit, lawmakers in the 1980s enacted a series of laws to try to force themselves to reduce the budget deficit. These laws, known as "Gramm–Rudman" after the two Senators who sponsored them, called for automatic, across-the-board cuts in the federal expenditures unless certain deficit targets were met. The idea was that these automatic cuts in expenditures would be so drastic and undesirable that Congress would be forced to meet the targets set forth in the law for the deficit.

The Gramm–Rudman laws were in effect for fiscal years 1986 to 1990. Automatic cuts did go into effect the first year, but these were quite small. In 1987 the initial version of the law was declared unconstitutional, but Congress nonetheless tried to meet the targets. While there were some real cuts in budgets, the Congress also resorted to many accounting gimmicks that did not really reduce the deficit. In 1988 the law was revised and Congress revised the deficit targets, making them easier to meet. Congress met the targets for fiscal years 1988 and 1989 with a combination of cuts and gimmicks. By 1990, however, the cuts required by the law were so large that gimmicks would no longer suffice. Fearing the automatic cuts, Congress abandoned the law and adopted new budget procedures.

The Gramm–Rudman experience showed the sheer difficulty of writing enforceable budget laws and the ingenuity that politicians demonstrate in finding ways around limits. It was a sobering experience for advocates of a balanced budget amendment to the Constitution.

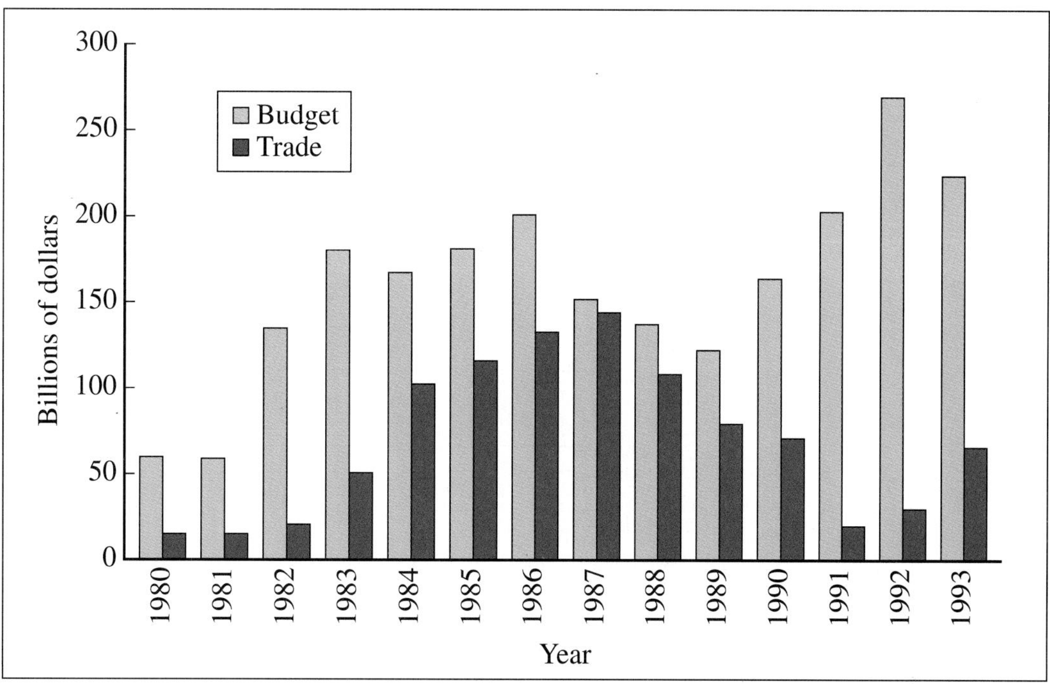

Figure 5

U.S. Trade and Budget Deficits

Source: Data from *Economic Report of the President* (Washington, DC: U.S. Government Printing Office, yearly).

in the early 1990s, the trade deficit fell while the budget deficit increased. How do we explain these patterns?

In an economy closed to trade and operating close to full employment, government deficits will lead to reduced saving available for domestic investment. As savers purchase the newly issued government bonds, there is less money available for domestic investment. In an open economy it is possible to maintain the same level of investment by importing goods from abroad and running a trade deficit. If an economy runs a trade deficit, it must either sell assets (stocks, bonds, land) or borrow from abroad. The sale of assets or borrowing from abroad enables the economy to provide the funds necessary for domestic investment despite the increased borrowing arising from government budget deficits.

These connections can explain the behavior of the U.S. economy in the mid- to late 1980s. During this period the economy was operating close to full employment and the federal government increased its deficits. The level of investment spending remained largely unchanged. To maintain the level of investment in the U.S. economy while our budget deficit was absorbing our domestic savings, we were forced to run trade deficits and borrow from abroad. As the government deficits rose and fell in the 1980s, so did the trade deficits.

These links were broken in the early 1990s because of a recession that developed. The economy no longer was at full employment and with the recession, total investment spending fell sharply. Despite the large budget deficit, our domestic savings were sufficient to finance both the budget deficit and the reduced level of investment with only minimal borrowing from abroad. Thus our trade deficit (which is also the amount we borrow from abroad) actually fell.

The lesson is that twin deficits need not always emerge. When an economy is operating at full employment and maintains its level of investment spending, higher budget deficits will lead to higher trade deficits. During recessions, however, the reduced level of investment spending breaks the links between budget and trade deficits.

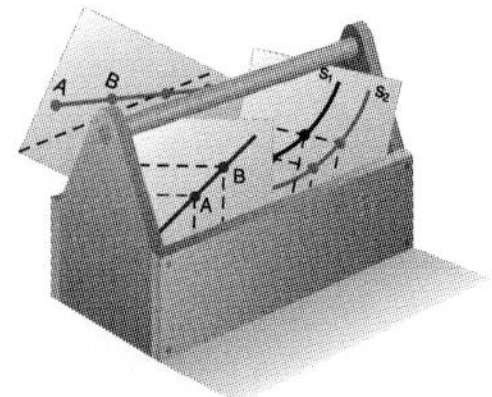

Using the TOOLS

In this chapter we explored government debt and deficits using a variety of different tools. Take this opportunity to do your own economic analysis.

1. Full Employment and Actual Deficits

The Congressional Budget Office publishes both actual deficit numbers and full-employment deficit numbers. Suppose you saw the following deficit figures (as a percent of GDP) in one of their tables:

	1989	*1990*
Actual deficit	2.9	3.5
Full-employment deficit	2.9	2.9

a. How would you interpret these figures? What happened between 1989 and 1990?

b. Suppose the full-employment deficit also increased between 1989 and 1990. How would this change your interpretation of the numbers?

2. Debt and Deficits in Belgium

Here are some data for Belgium in 1989.

GDP:	6160 billion Belgium francs
Debt:	6500 billion Belgium francs
Deficit:	380 billion Belgium francs
Interest rate on bonds:	8.5 percent

Use these data to answer the following questions:

a. What are the deficit/GDP and debt/GDP ratios? How do they compare to the United States today? The debt/GDP ratio in Belgium corresponds to what period in U.S. history?

b. Approximately how much of the budget in Belgium is devoted to interest payments on the debt? If Belgium could just wipe out its debt overnight, what would happen to its current budget deficit?

c. In 1989, Belgium had a trade surplus and investment as a share of GDP was approximately 19%, higher than the United States for the same year. How did Belgium manage this trade surplus and a high level of investment with its deficits?

SUMMARY

In this chapter we explained government budget deficits and debt from many different perspectives. We first defined deficits and debt and reviewed our historical experience. We then looked at the economic effects of budget deficits and found that they can sometimes be valuable, such as during recessions, but do pose a burden in other times. We explored the experience of the states in balancing their budgets and the pros and cons of a constitutional amendment. Finally, we analyzed the links between budget deficits and trade deficits. Here are the main points from this chapter:

1. A deficit is the difference between expenditures and revenue. The government debt is the sum of all past deficits.

2. Deficits can be financed either by issuing new debt or by creating money.
3. In most countries the ratio of government debt to GDP rises sharply during wars and then typically falls. In the United States, debt as a percent of GDP rose to its highest level during World War II, fell until the 1970s, and then rose during the 1980s. It is now approximately one-half the level it was during World War II.
4. Deficits can be good for a country. Automatic stabilizers and expansionary fiscal policy both work through the creation of deficits.
5. There are two burdens of the national debt. It can reduce the amount of capital in an economy, leading to lower levels of income. It can also raise taxes on future generations of workers. Not all economists believe that the national debt imposes a burden.
6. A national debt becomes too large when it either causes inflation through money financing or leads to low levels of investment spending and capital.
7. The national debt does not measure the total financial burden on future generations. Programs whose future costs are not included in the official deficit, such as Social Security or Medicare, can impose a burden on future generations.
8. States have balanced budget requirements, but these requirements apply to operating and not to capital budgets.
9. A balanced budget amendment would require Congress to propose only balanced budgets. Proponents contend that it would force Congress to cut expenditures or raise taxes. Opponents believe it would lead to accounting gimmicks and burdensome intervention by the courts.
10. When an economy is operating near full employment and can borrow from abroad to finance its investment spending, government budget deficits will be associated with trade deficits. This link is broken during recessions because investment spending is sharply reduced.

KEY TERMS

automatic stabilizers, *630*
balanced budget, *626*
capital budgets, *634*
deficit, *626*
fiscal year, *626*
full-employment deficit, *631*
generational accounting, *634*
government debt, *626*
government expenditure, *626*
mandate, *636*
monetizing the deficit, *627*
operating budgets, *634*
Ricardian equivalence, *632*
servicing the debt, *632*
structural deficit, *631*
surplus, *626*
twin deficits, *636*

PROBLEMS AND DISCUSSION QUESTIONS

1. Why are large government deficits more serious in countries with:
   a. limited ability to borrow?
   b. low saving rates?
2. In what ways could a balanced budget requirement limit the ability of the government to conduct fiscal policy? Do you think this is a serious loss?
3. Are the lessons from the states applicable to a balanced budget requirement for the federal government?
4. How can a large debt reduce the amount of capital available in a society?
5. How is a decrease in the age at which workers are eligible for Social Security similar to an increase in the government deficit?
6. Although the ratio of debt to GDP in the United States increased in the 1980s, it was still far below the levels in the early 1950s. Why were people concerned about the increase in the deficit in the 1980s?
7. How can the federal government view a $10 billion increase in spending on a program as a "cut"?

Take It to the Net

We invite you to visit the O'Sullivan/Sheffrin page on the Prentice Hall Web site at:

http://www.prenhall.com/osullivan/

for this chapter's World Wide Web exercise.

MODEL ANSWERS FOR THIS CHAPTER

Chapter-Opening Questions

1. Deficits only cause inflation if governments finance them by creating money. If deficits are financed by issuing bonds, then they do not lead to inflation.
2. Deficits can create a burden on future generations if they lead to reductions in investment. This will occur if the government bonds displace purchases of new stocks and bonds issued by firms.
3. In principle, a constitutional amendment could force the Congress and the president to balance the budget. However, past experience has shown that there are many accounting tricks and other devices that could be used to avoid the limits imposed by laws.
4. In recent U.S. history, we have had periods in which budget deficits were associated with trade deficits and periods in which they were not. During recessions, investment spending is low and private savings can finance both private investment and the budget deficit without leading to trade deficits. However, if investment spending increases, private savings will no longer be able to finance investment and the budget deficit. Some of the investment spending must then be financed by borrowing from abroad or, in other words, by running a trade deficit.

Test Your Understanding

1. False. This is the definition of a deficit.
2. Deficits can be financed by either issuing bonds or by monetizing the deficit.
3. In a recession, tax revenues fall and expenditures on welfare and unemployment insurance rise.
4. False.
5. False.

Using the Tools

1. Full Employment and Actual Deficits
   a. The economy went into a recession in 1990. Since the full-employment budget did not change, there were no changes in either taxes or spending policies. But in a recession, tax revenues from existing tax rates fall, increasing the actual deficit.
   b. If the full-employment deficit also increased, this would indicate that either spending policies or tax policies had become more expansionary.
2. Debt and Deficits in Belgium
   a. The deficit/GDP ratio is 6.2% and the debt/GDP ratio is 1.06. The debt/GDP ratio resembles that in the United States during World War II.
   b. With a debt of 6,500 and an interest rate of 0.085, interest payments are approximately $6{,}500 \times 0.085 = 552$. Since the budget deficit is 380, if the debt disappeared, the budget would have a surplus of 172.
   c. Belgium must be saving a higher fraction of GDP than the United States. That is the only way, with their larger budget deficits, that they can have a higher investment ratio without a trade deficit.

International Trade and Public Policy

Vilfredo Pareto had been in the mediation business for over 20 years, but he had never confronted such a complex dispute. Seated around the table were three people who wanted to do something about the country's restrictions on the apparel imports. Vilfredo's job was to develop a new trade policy that would make everyone happy. He started the session by letting everyone speak, starting with the consumer representative:

> These trade restrictions increase the price of clothing and cost the typical family about $400 per year. If we eliminate the restrictions, the total (nationwide) savings for consumers would be $400 million per year.

The representative of apparel workers spoke next:

> The elimination of these import restrictions would decrease employment in the apparel industry by 10,000 jobs. What would you do with all the people who lose their jobs?

The representative of the country's high-technology industry spoke next:

> Many countries have trade restrictions on computers, semiconductors, and medical equipment, in part to retaliate for our country's restrictions on apparel imports. If we eliminated our apparel restrictions, we could export more computers, semiconductors, and medical equipment.

After doing some quick calculations, Vilfredo had a solution. "The trade restrictions cost consumers \$400 million per year and save 10,000 jobs. This means that there is a cost of \$40,000 per apparel job saved, which exceeds the average wage of apparel jobs (\$30,000). The following plan should make everyone happy."

1. **Eliminate the trade restrictions, saving each family about \$400 per year.**
2. **Impose a temporary (two-year) tax of \$300 per family and use the revenue from this tax to pay the salaries of the 10,000 displaced workers for two years. During this two-year period, these workers will enroll in training programs to prepare them for jobs in the high-technology industry.**

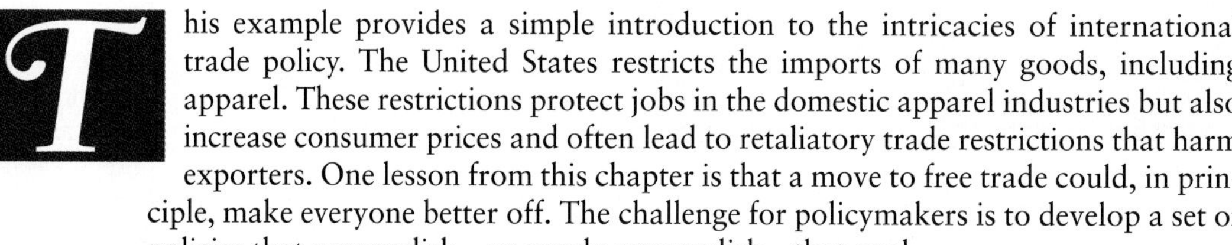

This example provides a simple introduction to the intricacies of international trade policy. The United States restricts the imports of many goods, including apparel. These restrictions protect jobs in the domestic apparel industries but also increase consumer prices and often lead to retaliatory trade restrictions that harm exporters. One lesson from this chapter is that a move to free trade could, in principle, make everyone better off. The challenge for policymakers is to develop a set of policies that accomplish—or nearly accomplish—that goal.

In this chapter we discuss the rationale for international trade and explore the effects of policies that restrict trade. Here are some of the practical questions we answer.

1. What are the trade-offs associated with free trade? Who wins and who loses?
2. Why is a tariff (a tax on an imported good) superior to an import quota?
3. Why might a firm's export price be less than its domestic price (the price charged in the domestic market)?
4. Do trade laws inhibit environmental protection?
5. Does trade increase income inequality?

BENEFITS FROM SPECIALIZATION AND TRADE

If you were put in charge of your nation, would you pursue a policy of national self-sufficiency? If your nation produced everything it consumed, it would not be dependent on any other nation for its economic livelihood. Although self-sufficiency may sound appealing, it actually would be better to specialize in some products and trade with other nations for the goods your nation doesn't produce itself. We saw in Chapter 3 that specialization and exchange can make both parties better off. In this chapter we use a simple example to explain the benefits of specialization and international trade between two nations.

Let's consider a pair of nations that produce and consume two goods, computer chips and shirts. Table 1 shows the daily output of the two goods for the two nations, which we'll call Shirtland and Chipland. In a single day, Shirtland can produce either 108 shirts or 36 computer chips, while Chipland can produce either 120 shirts or an equal number of chips. The last two rows of the table show the opportunity costs of the two goods. Recall the principle of opportunity cost:

PRINCIPLE ***of Opportunity Cost***

The opportunity cost of something is what you sacrifice to get it.

Table 1: Output and Opportunity Cost

	Shirtland	*Chipland*
Shirts produced per day	108	120
Chips produced per day	36	120
Opportunity cost of shirts	⅓ chip	1 chip
Opportunity cost of chips	3 shirts	1 shirt

In Chipland, there is a one-for-one trade-off of shirts and chips, so the opportunity cost of a shirt is one chip and the opportunity cost of a chip is one shirt. In Shirtland, people can produce three times as many shirts as chips in a given amount of time, so the opportunity cost of a chip is 3 shirts: by producing a chip, we sacrifice 3 shirts. Conversely, the opportunity cost of a shirt is one-third of a chip.

Production Possibilities Curve

Let's start by seeing what happens if each nation is self-sufficient. Each nation can use its resources (labor, land, buildings, machinery, equipment) to produce its own shirts and chips. The **production possibilities curve** shows all the feasible combinations of the two goods, assuming that the nation's resources are fully employed. This curve, which we discussed in earlier chapters, provides a sort of menu of production options. To keep things simple in this chapter, we assume the curve is a straight line, indicating a constant trade-off between the two goods. As shown by Shirtland's production possibilities curve in Figure 1 on the next page, the following combinations of chips and shirts are possible.

Production possibilities curve: A curve showing the combinations of two goods that can be produced by an economy, assuming that all resources are fully employed.

1. ***All shirts and no chips*: *point r*.** If Shirtland uses all its resources to produce shirts, it will produce 108 shirts per day.
2. ***All chips and no shirts*: *point t*.** If Shirtland uses all its resources to produce chips, it will produce 36 chips per day.
3. ***Equal division of resources*: *point h*.** Shirtland could divide its resources between shirt production and chip production and produce 54 shirts and 18 chips.

All the other points on the line connecting points *r* and *t* are also feasible. For example, one option is point *s*, with 28 chips and 24 shirts. The slope of the curve is the opportunity cost of computer chips (3 shirts).

Figure 1 also shows the production possibilities curve for Chipland. This nation can produce 120 shirts per day (point *b*), or 120 chips per day (point *d*), or any combination of chips and shirts between these two points. In Chipland, the trade-off is one shirt per computer chip: The opportunity cost of a chip is one shirt, so the slope of the production possibilities curve is 1.0.

Each nation could decide to be self-sufficient in chips and shirts. In other words, each nation could pick a point on its production possibilities curve and produce everything it wants to consume. For example, Shirtland could pick point *s* (28 chips and 24 shirts) and Chipland could pick point *c* (60 chips and 60 shirts). In the language of international trade, this is a case of **autarky** or self-sufficiency (in Greek, *aut* means "self" and *arke* means "to suffice").

Autarky: A situation in which each country is self-sufficient, so there is no trade.

Comparative Advantage and the Terms of Trade

Would the two nations be better off if each specialized in the production of one good and traded with the other? To decide which nation should produce a particular

Figure 1

Production Possibilities Curve

The production possibilities curve shows the combinations of two goods that can be produced with a nation's resources. For Chipland, there is a one-for-one trade-off between the two goods. For Shirtland, the trade-off is 3 shirts for every computer chip. In the absence of trade, Shirtland picks point *s* (28 chips and 24 shirts) and Chipland picks point *c* (60 chips and 60 shirts).

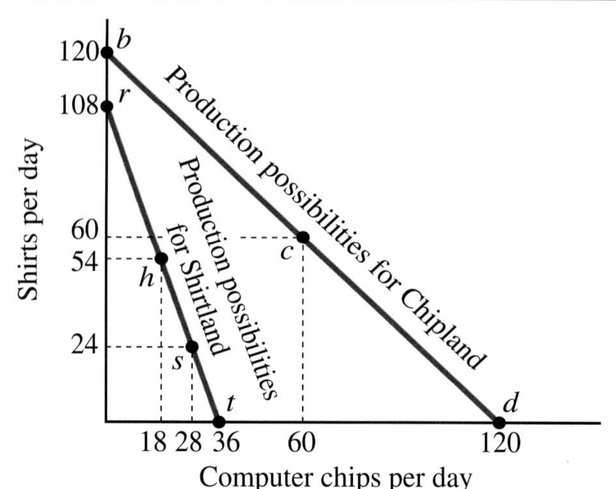

Shirtland Possibilites

Point	Shirts	Chips
r	108	0
h	54	18
s	24	28
t	0	36

Chipland Possibilities

Point	Shirts	Chips
b	120	0
c	60	60
d	0	120

Comparative advantage: The ability of one nation to produce a particular good at an opportunity cost lower than the opportunity cost of another nation.

good, we figure out which nation has a lower opportunity cost for that good. As we saw in Chapter 3, the nation with the lower opportunity cost has a **comparative advantage** in producing that good.

1. ***Chips produced in Chipland.*** The opportunity cost of chips is 1 shirt in Chipland and 3 shirts in Shirtland, so Chipland has a comparative advantage in the production of chips. Because Chipland sacrifices fewer shirts to produce a chip, Chipland should produce chips.
2. ***Shirts produced in Shirtland.*** The opportunity cost of a shirt is 1 chip in Chipland and ⅓ chip in Shirtland, so Shirtland has a comparative advantage in the production of shirts. Shirtland sacrifices fewer chips to produce a shirt, so Shirtland should produce shirts.

Terms of trade: The rate at which two goods will be exchanged.

Trade will allow people in each specialized nation to consume both goods. At what rate will the two nations exchange shirts and chips? To determine the **terms of trade**, let's look at how much Shirtland is willing to pay to get a chip and how much Chipland is willing to accept to give up a chip.

1. To get a chip, Shirtland is willing to pay up to 3 shirts because that's how many shirts it would sacrifice if it produced its own chip (the opportunity cost of a chip is 3 shirts). For example, if the nations agree to exchange 2 shirts per chip, Shirtland could rearrange its production, producing 1 less chip but 3 more shirts. After exchanging 2 of the extra shirts for a chip, Shirtland will have the same number of chips but one additional shirt.

2. To give up a chip, Chipland is willing to accept any amount greater than 1 shirt (its opportunity cost of a chip). For example, if the nations agree to exchange 2 shirts per chip, Chipland could rearrange its production, producing one more chip and one less shirt. After it exchanges the extra chip for 2 shirts, it will have the same number of chips but one additional shirt.

There is an opportunity for mutually beneficial trade because the willingness to pay (3 shirts by Shirtland) exceeds the willingness to accept (1 shirt by Chipland). One possibility is that the two countries will split the difference between the willingness to pay and the willingness to accept, exchanging 2 shirts per chip.

The Consumption Possibilities Curve

A nation that decides to specialize and trade will no longer be limited to the options shown by its own production possibilities curve. The **consumption possibilities curve** shows the combinations of two goods (computer chips and shirts in our example) that a nation can consume when it specializes in one good and trades with another nation.

Consumption possibilities curve: A curve showing the combinations of two goods that can be consumed when a nation specializes in a particular good and trades with another nation.

Figure 2 shows the consumption possibilities curve for our two hypothetical nations, assuming they exchange 2 shirts per chip. In panel A, Chipland will specialize in the good for which it has a comparative advantage (chips), so it produces 120 chips (point *d*). Given the terms of trade, Chipland can exchange 40 chips for 80 shirts, leading to point *x* on the consumption possibilities curve. In panel B, Shirtland specializes in shirts (producing at point *r*) and can exchange 80 shirts for 40 chips, leading to point *y* on its consumption possibilities frontier.

How do the outcomes with specialization and trade compare to the autarky outcomes? Chipland moves from point *c* (autarky) to point *x*, so trade increases the consumption of each good by 20 units. Shirtland moves from point *s* to point *y*, so the nation consumes 12 additional chips and 4 additional shirts. In Figure 2 each consumption possibilities curve lies above the nation's production possibilities curves, meaning that each nation has more options under specialization and trade. In most cases, a nation picks a point on the consumption possibilities curve that provides more of each good.

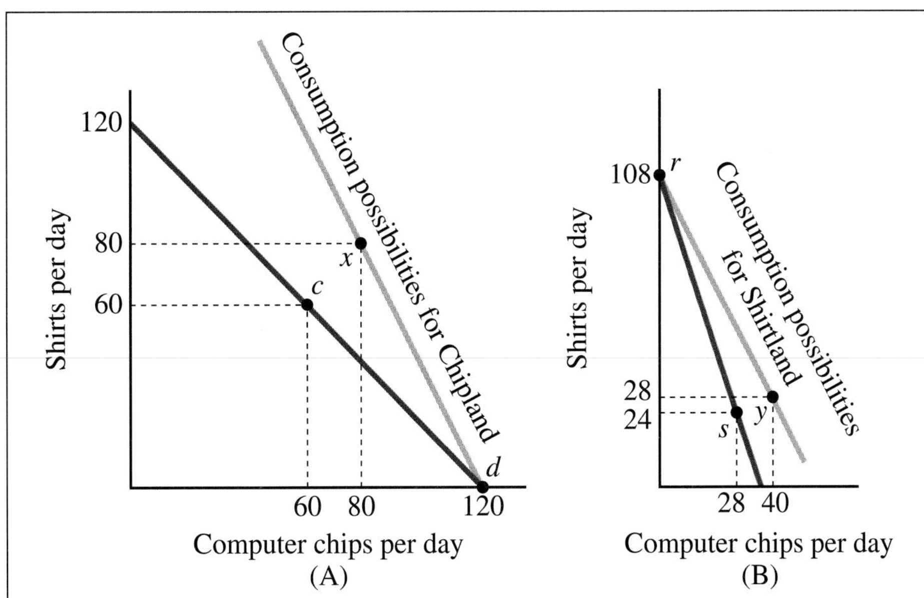

Figure 2

Consumption Possibilities Curve

The consumption possibilities curve shows the combinations of computer chips and shirts that can be consumed if each country specializes and trades. In panel A, Chipland produces 120 chips and trades 40 of these chips to Shirtland for 80 shirts. In panel B, Shirtland produces 108 shirts and trades 80 of these shirts to Chipland for 40 chips.

The Employment Effects of Free Trade

We've seen that trade allows each nation to consume more of each good, but we haven't discussed the effects of trade on employment. Under free trade, each country will begin to specialize in a single good, causing dramatic changes in the country's mix of employment. In Chipland, the chip industry doubles in size (output increases from 60 chips per day to 120 chips per day), while the shirt industry disappears. This means that workers and other resources will leave the shirt industry and move to the chip industry. In Shirtland, the flow is in the opposite direction, with workers and other resources moving from the chip industry to the shirt industry.

Figure 3 shows some of the changes in U.S. employment resulting from international trade for the period 1970–1980. Competition from imports decreased employment in footwear, motor vehicles, and several other industries. On the other hand, growing exports created many jobs in construction and mining equipment, engines, office and computing machines, aircraft, and other industries. The lesson is clear: An increase in trade changes the mix of employment, with some industries growing at the expense of others.

Is free trade good for everyone? A switch from self-sufficiency to specialization and trade increases consumption in both countries, so on average, people in each country will benefit from free trade. Some people will be harmed by free trade. In

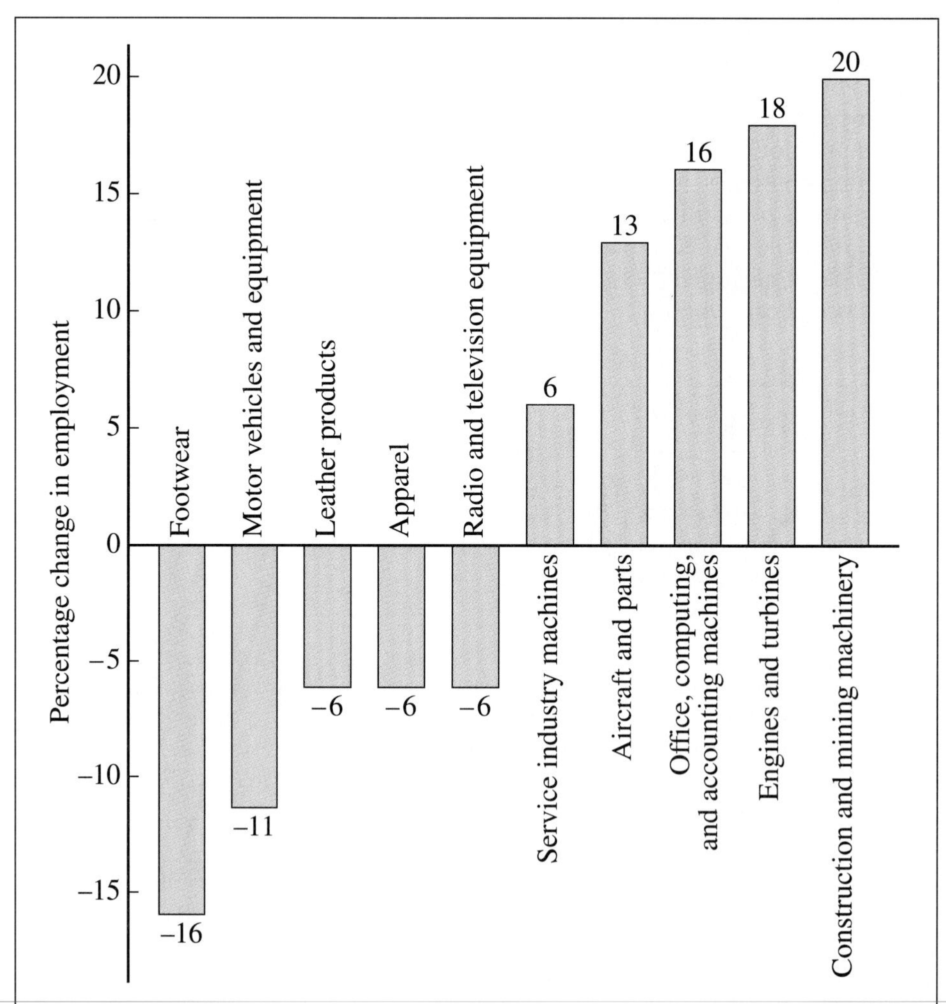

Figure 3

Percentage Change in Employment in U.S. Manufacturing Resulting from Foreign Trade, 1970–1980

Source: R. Z. Lawrence, *Can America Compete?* (Washington, DC: The Brookings Institution, 1984), pp. 58–59.

Chipland, people in the shirt industry will lose their jobs when the shirt industry disappears. Some workers can easily switch to the expanding computer-chip industry, and for these workers free trade is likely to be beneficial. Other shirt workers will be unable to make the switch to the chip industry, and they will be forced to accept lower-paying jobs or face unemployment. Free trade is likely to make these displaced workers worse off.

There is an old saying that "where you stand on an issue depends on where you sit." In our example, a person sitting at a sewing machine is likely to oppose free trade because the worker is likely to lose his or her job. In contrast, a person sitting at a work station in a computer-chip fabrication facility is likely to support free trade because the resulting increase in computer-chip exports will generate more employment opportunities in the industry.

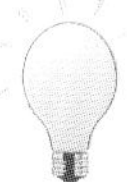

TEST *Your Understanding*

1. Use Figure 1 near the beginning of this chapter to complete the following statements with numbers: If Chipland starts at point c and decides to produce 10 more chips, it will produce ____________ shirts. If Shirtland produces only 10 chips, it will produce ____________ shirts.
2. In nation H, the opportunity cost of tables is 5 chairs, while in nation B, the opportunity cost of tables is only 1 chair. Which country should produce tables, and which should produce chairs?
3. Nations H and B split the difference between the willingness to pay for tables and the willingness to accept. What are the terms of trade?
4. List the two bits of information you need to draw the consumption possibilities curve for a particular nation.
5. In Figure 2 (two pages back), suppose the nations agree to exchange 1 shirt for each chip. Will the consumption possibilities curve for Chipland still be above its production possibilities curve?

PROTECTIONIST POLICIES

Now that you know the basic rationale for specialization and trade, we can explore the effects of public policies that restrict trade. We will consider four common import-restriction policies: an outright ban on imports, an import quota, voluntary export restraints, and a tariff.

Import Ban

To show the market effects of an import ban, let's start with an unrestricted market. Figure 4 on the next page shows the market for shirts in Chipland, a nation with a comparative advantage in computer chips, not shirts. The domestic supply curve shows the quantity of shirts supplied by firms in Chipland. Looking at point m, we see that Chipland firms will not supply any shirts unless the price is at least \$17. The total supply curve, which shows the quantity supplied by both domestic and foreign (Shirtland) firms, lies to the right of the domestic curve. At each price, the total supply exceeds the domestic supply because foreign firms supply shirts, too. Point x shows the free-trade equilibrium: The demand curve intersects the total supply curve at a price of \$12 and a quantity of 80 shirts. Because this price is below the minimum price for domestic firms, all the shirts are imported from Shirtland.

Figure 4

Effects of an Import Ban

In the free-trade equilibrium, demand intersects the total supply curve at point x, with a price of $12 and a quantity of 80 shirts. If shirt imports are banned, the equilibrium is shown by the intersection of the demand curve and the domestic supply curve (point c). The price increases to $23.

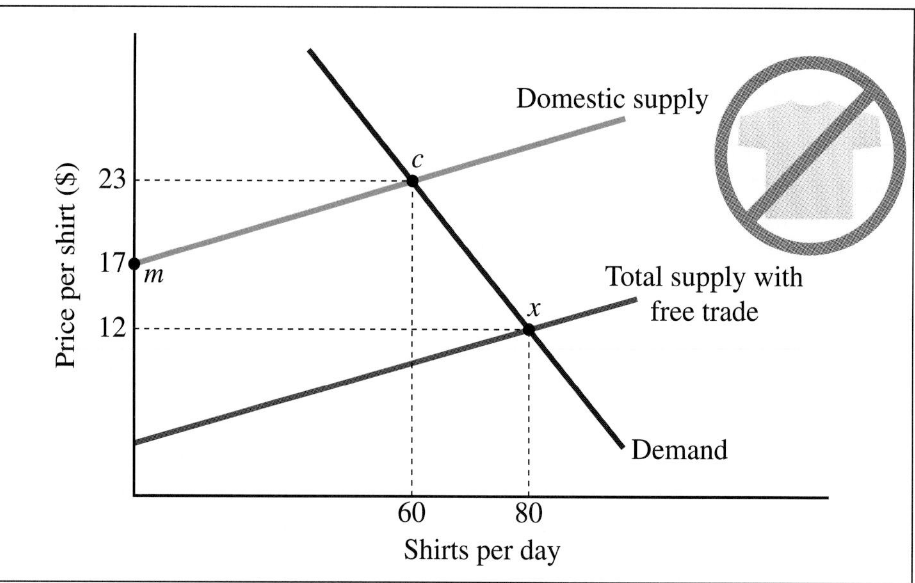

What will happen if Chipland bans imported shirts? Foreign suppliers will disappear from the market, so the total supply of shirts will be the domestic supply. In Figure 4, point c shows the new equilibrium: The demand curve intersects the *domestic* supply curve at a price of $23 and a quantity of 60 shirts. In other words, the decrease in supply resulting from the import ban increases the price and decreases the quantity of shirts.

Quotas and Voluntary Export Restraints

Import quota: A limit on the amount of a good that can be imported.

An alternative to a import ban is an **import quota**, defined as a limit on the amount of a good that can be imported. An import quota is a sort of intermediate policy between free trade and an import ban: Imports are decreased but not eliminated. This intermediate policy generates a price between the price under free trade ($12) and the price under an import ban ($23).

Figure 5 shows the effect of an import quota. Starting from the free-trade equilibrium at point x, an import quota will shift the total supply curve to the left: At each price there will be a smaller quantity of shirts because foreign suppliers cannot supply as many. The new total supply curve will lie between the domestic supply curve and the total supply curve under free trade. The new equilibrium occurs at point q, where the demand curve intersects the new total supply curve. The price with the import quota ($20) exceeds the minimum price of domestic firms ($17), so domestic firms supply 22 shirts (shown by point e).

Voluntary export restraint (VER): A scheme under which an exporting country "voluntarily" decreases its exports.

Under a **voluntary export restraint (VER)**, an exporting country "voluntarily" decreases its exports in an attempt to avoid more restrictive trade policies. A VER has the same effect as an import quota, which is illegal under the rules of the World Trade Organization (WTO), an organization with over 100 member nations that oversees the General Agreement on Tariffs and Trade (GATT) and other international agreements. Although VERs *are* legal under WTO rules, they violate the spirit of international trade agreements. Like a quota, a VER increases the price of the restricted good, allowing domestic firms to participate in the market.

A quota or a VER produces winners and losers. The winners include foreign and domestic shirt producers. In our example, foreign firms can sell shirts at a price of $20 instead of $12. In some cases, the government issues import licenses to some

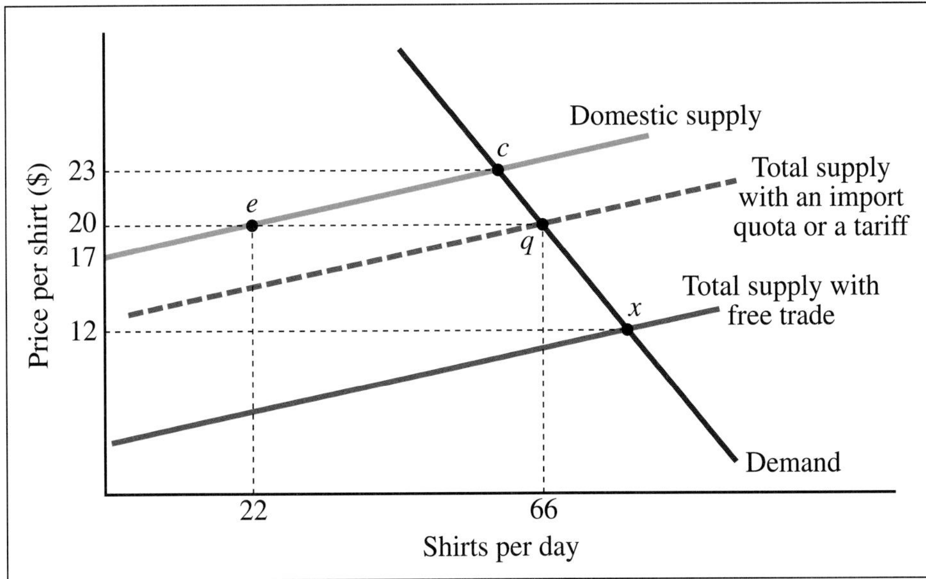

Figure 5

Market Effects of a Quota, a VER, or a Tariff

An import quota shifts the supply curve to the left. The market moves upward along the demand curve to point q, which is between point x (free trade) and c (an import ban). We can reach the same point with a tariff that shifts the total supply curve to the same position.

citizens, who can then buy shirts from foreign firms at a relatively low price ($12 in our example) and sell the shirts at the artificially high domestic price ($20 in our example). In addition, the import restrictions allow domestic shirt firms to participate in the market, generating benefits for the firms and their workers. The losers are consumers, who pay a higher price for shirts.

Price Effects of Quotas and VERs

We know that consumers pay higher prices for goods that are subject to protectionist policies, but how much more? In the United States, voluntary export restraints for Japanese automobiles in effect in 1984 increased the price of Japanese cars by about $1,300 and the price of domestic cars by about $660.[1] In 1990, U.S. consumers incurred a total cost of $70 billion as a result of the nation's protectionist policies, about $270 per person per year.[2] The largest costs resulted from protectionist policies for apparel (about $84 per person) and textiles (about $13 per person).

Many European nations used VERs to limit the market shares of Japanese automobiles. Figure 6 on the next page shows the cost of these policies in terms of their effects on the price of Japanese automobiles in several nations. For example, in France the VERs increased the price of Japanese automobiles by 35%, compared to 1% in Germany and 55% in Italy.

Tariffs

An alternative to a quota or a VER is an import **tariff**, which is a tax on an imported good. We know from our earlier discussion of the market effects of taxes that a tax shifts the supply curve to the left and increases the equilibrium price. In Figure 5, suppose the tariff shifts the total supply curve, so that it intersects the demand curve at point q. In other words, we reach the same point we reached with the quota: Consumers pay the same price ($20), and domestic firms produce the same quantity (22 shirts).

Tariff: A tax on an imported good.

There is one fundamental difference between a quota and a tariff. An import quota allows importers to buy shirts from foreign suppliers at a low price ($12) and sell them at the artificially high price ($20). In other words, importers make money from the quota. Under a tariff, the government makes money, collecting $8 per shirt from foreign suppliers. Citizens in Chipland will prefer the tariff to the quota

Figure 6

Price Effects of VERs for Japanese Cars

Many European nations uses VERs to limit the number of Japanese cars imported. The VERs increase the price of Japanese cars.

Source: Alasdair Smith and Anthony J. Venables, "Cost of Voluntary Export Restraints in the European Car Market," Chapter 10 in *International Trade and Trade Policy*, edited by Elhanan Helpman and Assaf Razin (Cambridge, MA: MIT Press, 1991).

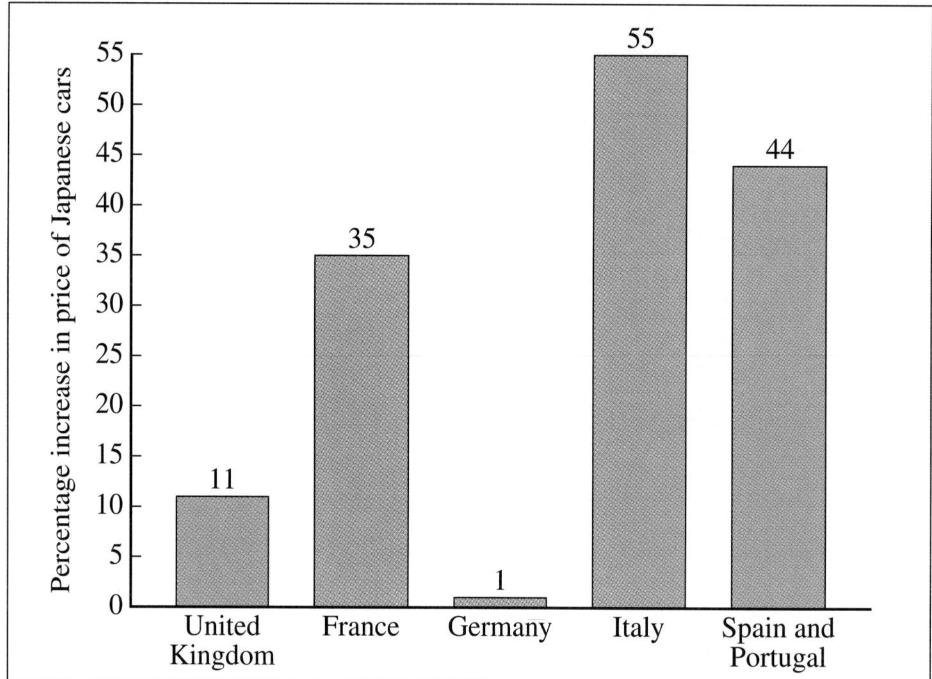

because the government can use the revenue from the tariff to cut other taxes or expand public programs.

Responses to Protectionist Policies

A restriction on imports is likely to cause further restrictions on trade. For example, if Chipland bans shirt imports, the shirt industry in Shirtland may call for retaliation in the form of a ban on computer chips from Chipland. A trade war of this sort could escalate to the point that the two nations return to self-sufficiency (autarky). Looking back at Figure 2 earlier in this chapter, Chipland would move from point x to point c, and Shirtland would move from point y to point s. This sort of retaliatory policy is common, meaning that the protection of one industry is likely to harm a country's export industries. Chipland's shirt industry may grow at the expense of its computer-chip industry.

There are many examples of import restrictions that led to retaliatory policies and a substantial decrease in trade.

1. ***Smoot–Hawley tariff of 1930.*** When the United States increased its average tariff to 59%, its trading partners retaliated with higher tariffs. The trade war decreased international trade and deepened the worldwide depression of the 1930s.[3]
2. ***Chicken tariff of 1963.*** The European Economic Community (EEC, the predecessor of the European Union) imposed a large tariff on frozen chickens from the United States, cutting U.S. imports in half. The United States retaliated by increasing its tariffs on expensive brandies (from France), potato starch (from Holland), and light trucks (from Germany).[4]
3. ***Pasta tariff of 1985.*** The United States imposed tariffs on pasta from the EEC, and the EEC retaliated by increasing its tariffs on lemons and walnuts from the United States.[5]

The threat of retaliatory policies may persuade a nation to loosen its protectionist policies. In 1995 the United States announced that it would impose 100% tariffs on Japanese luxury cars (with total sales of $6 billion per year) if Japan didn't ease its restrictions on imported auto parts. Just hours before the tariffs were to take effect, the two nations reached an agreement that is expected to increase the sales of U.S. auto parts to Japanese firms by about $9 billion per year.[6]

Import restrictions also create an incentive to smuggle goods. The restrictions create a gap between the cost of purchasing the restricted goods abroad and the price of goods in the protected economy, so there is a profit to be made from smuggling. For an example, read the Closer Look box "Forbidden Fruit in Europe: Latin Bananas Face Hurdles."

A Closer LOOK

Forbidden Fruit in Europe: Latin Bananas Face Hurdles

Bogota, Colombia — The French Embassy in Ecuador has been pelted with bananas. Workers in Colombia's principal banana-growing region have lost their jobs. In Panama, the President was forced to announce that he could not close the canal to vessels with European flags, much as the people might like that.

Latin America is in revolt against Europe over bananas. The European Community recently adopted a package of quotas and tariffs aimed at cutting by more than half Europe's banana imports from Latin American.

Europe wants to help some former banana-growing colonies of European nations in Africa and the Caribbean by waving through their bananas tariff free while imposing steep taxes on the Latin fruit. . . .

Until recently, growing bananas for northern markets was a multi-billion dollar bright spot for Land America's struggling economies. About half of the region's banana exports have traditionally gone to Europe, and growers calculate that the new restrictions, announced in February and effective July 1, will cost the region $1 billion and 170,000 jobs by 1995. . . .

Under Lomé Convention Rules first negotiated in the 1960's, Europe's former colonial powers give trade preference to 66 former 20th century colonies in Africa, the Caribbean and the Pacific.

Latin American growers, with their low labor costs and large expanses of flat tropical land near port cities, grow bananas at half the cost of growers favored by the European Community. . . .

Growers here hope that the European plan will cause a consumer backlash against high-priced, poor-quality bananas. And there has already been dissent in Europe.

Germany and Belgium are suing to overturn the decision in the European Court of Justice in Luxembourg. And Spaniards, faced with eating stubby, expensive bananas from the Canary Islands, cherish Colombian bananas like a forbidden fruit. In three raids since January, Spanish authorities have confiscated 37 tons of Colombian bananas, and news reports use language usually reserved for confiscations of cocaine.

In one recent banana shipment from Colombia, which was hidden among potato boxes from the Netherlands, the Spanish press described the seized contraband as having "a street value" of $13,000.

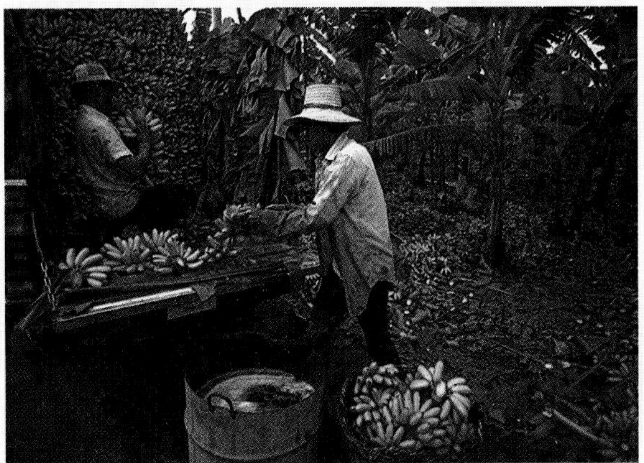

The import restrictions adopted by the European Union cut banana imports from Latin America in half.

Source: Reprinted from James Brooke, "Forbidden Fruit in Europe: Latin Bananas Face Hurdles," *New York Times*, April 5, 1993, p. A1.

Table 2: Trade Data for the United States and Mexico

Year	U.S. Imports from Mexico (billions)	U.S. Exports to Mexico (billions)	Exchange Rate: Pesos per Dollar	U.S. Trade Surplus (+) or Deficit (–) with Mexico (billions)
1993	$40	$42	3.12	$ +2
1994	49	51	3.11	+2
1995	62	46	5.33	–16

Source: U.S. Department of Commerce, *Statistical Abstract of the United States 1996* (Washington, DC: U.S. Government Printing Office, 1996).

ECONOMIC DETECTIVE– *NAFTA and the Giant Sucking Sound*

The North American Free Trade Agreement (NAFTA), which took effect in January 1994, will gradually phase out tariffs and other trade barriers between the United States, Canada, and Mexico. In the spirited debates over the effects of NAFTA on trade between the United States and Mexico, economists predicted that NAFTA would increase both imports from Mexico *and* exports to Mexico. This is sensible because NAFTA decreases the tariffs and trade barriers of both nations. Because the pre-NAFTA tariffs between the United States and Mexico were relatively low (about 4%), no one expected any dramatic changes in trade patterns, but instead, moderate growth in both imports and exports.

Table 2 provides some trade data for the United States and Mexico for the years surrounding the NAFTA agreement. Several observers—including two presidential candidates—used the figures for 1993 and 1995 to claim that NAFTA was responsible for turning a small trade surplus ($2 billion in 1993) into a huge trade deficit ($16 billion in 1995). One candidate suggested that NAFTA caused a "giant sucking sound" as jobs moved from the United States to Mexico. Who is right, the economists who predicted that NAFTA would cause moderate growth in both imports and exports, or the presidential candidates?

The clues we need to solve this puzzle are shown in the fourth column of Table 2. The exchange rate in 1994 was about the same as it was in 1993, so in the first year of NAFTA, imports and exports grew at about the same rate (22%), just as predicted by economists. The following year was quite different: The exchange rate rose from 3.11 pesos per dollar to 5.33. As we saw in Chapter 3, an increase in the exchange rate (more pesos per dollar) will make U.S. goods more expensive for Mexican consumers, so U.S. exports to Mexico will drop. At the same time, Mexican goods will become less expensive for U.S. consumers, so U.S. imports from Mexico will rise. Looking back at Table 2, that's exactly what happened: Imports increased by $13 billion and exports dropped by $5 billion. This suggests that the U.S. trade deficit with Mexico was caused by the devaluation of the peso, not by NAFTA.

TEST *Your Understanding*

6 Complete the statement: If a country bans the importation of a particular good, the market equilibrium is shown by the intersection of the ____________ curve and the ____________ curve.

7 Complete the statement with *above* or *below*: The equilibrium price under an import quota is ____________ the price that occurs with an import ban and ____________ the price that occurs with free trade.

8 From the perspective of consumers, which is better, a tariff or a quota?

9 Under the quota system underlying Figure 5 (four pages back), what fraction of the shirt market is supplied by domestic firms?

RATIONALES FOR PROTECTIONIST POLICIES

What are the rationales for protectionist policies such as an import ban, an import quota, a voluntary restraint, or a tariff? We will discuss three possible motivations for policies that restrict trade.

1. To shield workers from foreign competition
2. To nurture "infant" industries until they mature
3. To help domestic firms establish monopolies in world markets

To Shield Workers from Foreign Competition

One of the most basic arguments for protectionism is that it protects workers in industries that would be hurt by trade. For example, suppose that relative to the United States, nations in the Far East have a comparative advantage in producing textiles. If the United States reduced existing tariffs for the textile industry, domestic manufacturers could not compete. They would have to close their factories and lay off workers. In an ideal world, the laid-off workers would take new jobs in other sectors of the economy. In practice, however, this is difficult. Many workers don't have the skills to work in other sectors, and obtaining these skills takes time. Moreover, the textile industry is heavily concentrated in the southeastern part of the United States. Politicians from that region will try to keep tariffs in place to prevent the dislocations that free trade would cause. The result of this protection, of course, is less efficient production, higher prices, and lower consumption for the United States. For a discussion of the trade-offs between job protection and consumer prices, read the Closer Look box on the next page, "The Cost of Protecting Jobs."

To Nurture Infant Industries

During World War II the United States built hundreds of boats for the Navy called Liberty Ships. As more and more of these ships were built, each required fewer hours to complete because workers learned from their experiences, acquiring knowledge during the production process. Engineers and economists called this phenomenon **learning by doing**. You experience learning by doing when you learn a new game, such as Ping-Pong. At first you may find it difficult to play, but your skills improve as you go along.

Learning by doing: The knowledge gained during production that increases productivity.

Infant industry: A new industry that is protected from foreign competitors.

Tariffs and other protectionist policies are often defended on the grounds that they protect new or **infant industries** in the early stages of learning by doing. A tariff shields a young industry from the competition of its more mature rivals. After the infant industry grows up, the tariff can be eliminated because the industry is able to compete.

In practice, infant industries rarely become competitive with their foreign rivals. During the 1950s and 1960s, many Latin American countries used tariffs and other policies to protect their young manufacturing industry from foreign

A Closer LOOK

The Cost of Protecting Jobs

What's the trade-off between protecting domestic jobs and higher prices for consumers? As shown in the table below, protectionist policies for textiles and apparel imposed an annual cost of over $10 billion and saved 56,464 jobs, for a cost per job of $177,759, which is over eight times the average wage in the industry. The cost per job was even higher for dairy products, motor vehicles, sugar, and meat.

Industry Protected	*Annual Cost (millions)*	*Jobs Protected*	*Cost per Job*
Textiles and apparel	$10,037	56,464	$ 177,759
Dairy products	1,013	2,038	497,056
Motor vehicles	925	3,419	270,547
Sugar	661	1,663	404,776
Meat	185	45	4,111,111
Nonrubber footwear	147	1,316	111,702

Source: Update of *The Economic Effects of Significant U.S. Import Restraints* (Washington, DC: U.S. International Trade Commission, initial report in 1993; update in 1996).

competition. Unfortunately, the domestic industries never became as efficient as foreign suppliers, and the Latin American countries that tried this policy suffered. Another problem with protecting an infant industry is that once an industry is given tariff protection, it is difficult to take it away. For an interesting discussion of the merits of protecting an industry from "unfair" competition, read the Closer Look box "Protection for Candle Makers."

To Help Domestic Firms Establish Monopolies in World Markets

If the production of a particular good has very large scale economies, the world market will support only a few firms. A nation might be tempted to adopt policies to capture the monopoly profits for itself. For example, suppose the commercial aircraft industry can support only one large firm: If two firms enter the industry, both will lose money. A nation that decides to get into this industry—and earn monopoly profits—could agree to provide financial support to a domestic firm to guarantee that the firm will make a profit. With such a guarantee, the domestic firm will enter the industry. Knowing this, a foreign firm will be reluctant to enter, so the domestic firm will capture the monopoly profit.

One example of this approach is the Airbus, an airplane produced in Europe. Several European countries provided large subsidies for firms producing the Airbus. These subsidies allowed the Airbus firms to underprice some of their rivals in the United States, and at least one U.S. manufacturer of commercial airplanes was forced out of business.

What could go wrong with these monopoly-creation policies? If both nations subsidize their domestic firms, both firms will enter the market and lose money. The taxpayers in both countries will then have to pay for the subsidies. In addition, a nation may pick the wrong industry to subsidize. Together, the British and French subsidized an airplane known as the Concorde to provide supersonic travel between

A Closer LOOK

Protection for Candle Makers

In response to the spread of protectionism, the French economist Frédéric Bastiat (1801–1851) wrote the following fictitious petition in which French candle makers ask for protection from "unfair" competition.

> We are suffering from the intolerable competition of a foreign rival, placed, it would seem, in a condition so far superior to ours for the production of light, that he absolutely inundates our national market at a price fabulously reduced. The moment he shows himself, our trade leaves us—all of our customers apply to him; and a branch of native industry, having countless ramifications, is all at once rendered completely stagnant. This rival . . . is not other than the sun.
>
> What we pray for is, that it may please you to pass a law ordering the shutting up of all windows, sky-lights, dormerwindows, curtains, blinds, bull's eyes; in a word all openings, holes, chinks, clefts, and fissures, by or through which the light of the sun has been in use to enter houses, to the prejudice of the meritorious manufactures with which we . . . have accommodated our country—a country which, in gratitude, ought not to abandon us now. . . .
>
> Does it not argue to the greatest inconsistency to check as you do the importation of coal, iron, cheese, and goods of foreign manufacture, merely because . . . their price approaches zero, while at the same time you freely admit, and without limitation, the light of the sun, whose price is during the whole day at zero?

Source: Frédéric Bastiat, *Economics Sophisms* (Edinburgh: Oliver & Boyd, 1873) pp. 49–53.

Europe and the United States. Although the Concorde captured the market, the market was not worth capturing: The Concorde lost money because it was very costly to develop, and people are not willing to pay a very large premium for supersonic travel. Although the Concorde continues to fly, it will never raise enough money to cover its costs.

TEST *Your Understanding*

10 Comment on the following statement: If we eliminated our textile tariffs, the dislocated workers could easily switch to other jobs.

11 Explain the infant-industry argument.

12 List the two problems associated with subsidizing an industry in the hope of establishing a worldwide monopoly.

RECENT POLICY DEBATES AND TRADE AGREEMENTS

In this final part of this chapter, we discuss three recent policy debates concerning international trade.

1. Are foreign producers dumping their products?
2. Do trade laws inhibit environmental protection?
3. Does trade cause income inequality?

We also discuss some recent trade agreements that have lowered trade barriers and increased international trade.

Are Foreign Producers Dumping Their Products?

Dumping: A situation in which the price a firm charges in a foreign market is lower than either the price it charges in its home market or the production cost.

In the recent negotiations among members of WTO, there was considerable progress in reducing tariffs, but several areas of controversy remained, including the rules on dumping. A firm is **dumping** when the price it charges in a foreign market is lower than either the price it charges in its home market or its production cost. Dumping is illegal under international trade agreements, and hundreds of cases of alleged dumping are presented to WTO authorities each year. Here are some recent cases in which the WTO concluded that dumping had occurred: Hong Kong VCRs sold in Europe; Chinese bicycles sold in the United States; Asian TV sets sold in Europe; steel from Brazil, India, Japan, and Spain sold in the United States; American beef sold in Mexico; Chinese computer disks sold in Japan and the United States. Under the current provisions of WTO, a nation can impose "antidumping duties" on products that are being dumped.

Why would a firm engage in dumping, charging a relatively low price in the foreign market? The first reason is price discrimination. If a firm has a monopoly in its home market but faces strong competition in a foreign market, the firm will naturally charge a higher price in the home market. The foreign price looks low, but only because we compare it to a very high monopoly price in the home market. The firm uses its monopoly power to discriminate against consumers in its home market, so the problem is in the home market, not the foreign market.

To illustrate how international price discrimination works, let's look at the case of Korean VCRs.[7] In the 1980s there were only three firms (all Korean) selling VCRs in Korea but dozens of firms selling them in Europe. The lack of competition in Korea generated very high prices for Korean consumers: They paid much more than European consumers for identical Korean VCRs. In other words, Korean firms used their market power to discriminate against Korean consumers. When international trade authorities concluded that Korean firms were dumping VCRs in Europe, the Korean firms responded by cutting prices in their home market. They *did not* increase their prices in Europe—much to the dismay of European producers and the delight of European consumers.

The second reason for dumping is predatory pricing, the practice of cutting prices in an attempt to drive rival firms out of business. The predatory firm sets its price below its production cost: The price is low enough that both the predator and its prey (a firm in the foreign market) lose money. After the prey goes out of business, the predator increases its price to earn monopoly profit. This is also known as *predatory dumping*.

Although the rationale for antidumping laws is to prevent predatory dumping, it is difficult to determine whether low prices are the result of predatory pricing or price discrimination. Many economists are skeptical about how frequently predatory pricing actually occurs and they suspect that many nations use their antidumping laws as protectionist policies in disguise. Because WTO rules limit tariffs and quotas, some nations may be tempted to substitute antidumping duties for these traditional protectionist policies.

Do Trade Laws Inhibit Environmental Protection?

In recent trade negotiations, a new player appeared on the scene: environmental groups. Starting in the early 1990s, environmentalists began to question whether policies that liberalized trade could harm the environment. The issue that attracted their attention was the killing of dolphins by tuna fishers.

Anyone who catches tuna with a large net will also catch the dolphins that swim with the tuna, and most of the captured dolphins will die. In 1972, the United

States outlawed the use of tuna nets by U.S. ships. A short time later, ships from other nations—including Mexico—began netting tuna and killing dolphins. The United States responded with a boycott of Mexican tuna caught with nets, and the Mexican government complained to an international trade authority that the tuna boycott was an unfair trade barrier. The trade authority agreed with Mexico and forced the United States to remove the boycott.

Under current WTO rules, a country can adopt any environmental standard it chooses, as long as it does not discriminate against foreign producers. For example, the United States can limit the exhaust emissions of all cars that operate in the United States. As long as emissions rules apply equally to all cars—domestic and imports alike—the rules are legal under WTO rules. An international panel recently upheld U.S. fuel efficiency rules for automobiles on this principle.[8]

The tuna boycott was a violation of WTO rules because killing dolphins does not harm the U.S. environment directly. For the same reason, the United States could not ban imported goods that are produced in factories that generate air or water pollution in other countries. It is easy to understand why WTO rules do not allow countries to restrict trade based on the methods used to produce goods and services. Countries differ in the value they place on the environment. For example, a poor nation may be willing to tolerate more pollution if it means attaining a higher standard of living.

If trade restrictions cannot be used to protect the dolphins and deal with other global environmental problems, what else can we do? International agreements have been used for a variety of different environmental goals, from limiting the harvest of whales to eliminating the chemicals that deplete the ozone layer. These agreements are difficult to reach, however, and some nations will certainly be tempted to use trade restrictions to pursue environmental goals. If they do so, they will encounter resistance because WTO rules mean that a nation can pursue its environmental goals only within its own borders.

Does Trade Cause Income Inequality?

Inequality in wages has been growing in the United States since 1973. Wages of skilled workers have risen faster than the wages of unskilled workers. World trade has also boomed since 1973. Could there be a connection between increased world trade and income inequality?

Trade theory suggests that there may indeed be a link between increased trade and increased wage inequality. Here is how it might work. Suppose that the United States produces two types of goods: one using skilled labor (for example, airplanes) and one using unskilled labor (for example, textiles). The United States is likely to have a comparative advantage in products that use skilled labor, while developing countries are likely to have a comparative advantage in products that use unskilled labor. An increase in world trade will increase both exports and imports. An increase in U.S. exports means that we'll produce more goods that require skilled labor, so the domestic demand for skilled labor will increase, pulling up the wage of skilled labor. At the same time, an increase in U.S. imports means that we'll import more goods produced by unskilled labor, so the domestic demand for unskilled labor will decrease, pulling down the wage of unskilled labor. As a result, the gap between the wages of the two types of workers will increase.

Economists have tried to determine how much trade has contributed to growing wage inequality. As usual, there are other factors that make such a determination difficult. It is difficult, for example, to distinguish between the effects of trade and those of technical progress. Technical change, such as the rapid introduction and use of computers, will also tend to increase the demand for skilled workers and decrease the demand for unskilled workers. Economists have noted, however, that the exports of goods using skilled labor and the imports of goods using unskilled labor have both increased—just as the theory predicts. At least some of the increased wage inequality is caused by international trade.

One response to this undesirable side effect of trade is to use trade restrictions to protect industries that use unskilled workers. An alternative approach is to ease the transition to an economy with a larger fraction of skilled jobs. In the long run, workers will move to industries that use skilled workers, so they will eventually earn higher wages. The government could facilitate this change by providing assistance for education and training.

Recent Trade Agreements

In the last few decades, there has been considerable progress in lowering the barriers to international trade. Here are some examples of international trade agreements.

1. *North American Free Trade Agreement (NAFTA)*. This agreement took effect in 1994 and will be implemented over a 15-year period. The agreement will eventually eliminate all tariffs and other trade barriers between Canada, Mexico, and the United States. NAFTA may soon be extended to other nations in the western hemisphere.

2. *World Trade Organization (WTO)*. This organization has more than 120 member nations and oversees the General Agreement on Tariffs and Trade (GATT) and other international trade agreements. There have been eight rounds of tariff negotiations, resulting in much lower tariffs among the member nations. For example, between 1930 and 1995, the average tariff in the United States has dropped from about 59% to about 5%. The last set of negotiations, the so-called Uruguay round completed in 1994, decreased tariffs by about a third. WTO promotes trade in other ways as well: It has eliminated many import quotas, reduced agricultural subsidies, and outlawed restrictions on international trade in services such as banking, insurance, and accounting.

3. *European Union (EU)*. In Europe, a total of 15 nations have joined the European Union, an organization designed to remove all trade barriers within Europe and create a "single market." In addition, the nations are trying to develop a single currency for all the member nations, tentatively labeled the "euro."

4. *Asian Pacific Economic Cooperation (APEC)*. In 1994, the leaders of 18 Asian nations signed a nonbinding agreement to reduce trade barriers between their nations.

These agreements have reduced trade barriers and increased international trade. For example, the most recent round of trade negotiations (the Uruguay round) is expected to increase the volume of world trade by at least 9% and perhaps as much as 24%.[9]

TEST *Your Understanding*

13 What is dumping?

14 What restrictions do WTO rules place on a nation's environmental policies?

15 Consider a nation that has a comparative advantage in the production of goods using *unskilled* labor. What types of workers will benefit from increased trade, and what type will lose?

Using the **TOOLS**

In this chapter we've discussed the trade-offs associated with protectionist policies and used supply and demand curves to show the market effects of protectionist policies. Here are some opportunities to do your own economic analysis.

1. ECONOMIC EXPERIMENT: *Protectionist Policies*

Recall the market-equilibrium experiment from Chapter 4. We can modify the experiment to show the effects of protectionist policies on equilibrium prices and quantities. On the supply side of the market, there are domestic and foreign apple producers, and domestic producers have higher unit costs. After several trading periods without any government intervention, you can change the rules as follows.

a. Apple imports are banned: Foreign producers cannot participate in the market.

b. There is a tariff (a tax on imports) of $5 per bushel.

2. Incentives for Smuggling

The banana-smuggling story suggests that protectionist policies will lead to smuggling. Suppose Chipland bans shirt imports, causing some importers to bribe customs officials, who then "look the other way" as smugglers bring shirts into Chipland. Your job is to combat shirt smuggling. Use the information in Figure 4 (earlier in this chapter) to answer the following questions.

a. Suppose importers can sell their shirts on the world market at a price of $12. How much is an importer willing to pay to get customs officials to look the other way?

b. What sort of change in trade policy would make your job easier?

3. Vilfredo Pareto and Import Restrictions

In the opening paragraphs of the chapter, we discussed a policy scheme under which the restrictions on apparel imports would be eliminated. Would you expect all three people to be happy with this scheme? If not, how would you modify the scheme to make everyone happy?

4. Ban on Shoe Imports

Consider a country that initially consumes 100 pairs of shoes per hour, all of which are imported. The initial price of shoes is $40. Depict graphically the market effects of a ban on shoe imports.

SUMMARY

In this chapter we have discussed the benefits of specialization and trade and explored the trade-offs associated with protectionist policies. There is a basic conflict between consumers—who prefer free trade because it decreases prices—and workers in the protected industries—who want to keep their jobs. Here are the main points of the chapter.

1. If one country has a comparative advantage over a second country in producing a particular good (a lower opportunity cost), specialization and trade will benefit both countries.
2. An import ban or a quota increases the prices of the restricted good and shifts resources from an export industry into the protected domestic industries.
3. Because the victims of protectionist policies often retaliate, the protection of a domestic industry may harm an exporting industry.

4. A tariff (a tax on imports) generates revenue for the government, while a quota (a limit on imports) generates revenue for foreigners.
5. In principle, the laws against dumping are designed to prevent predatory pricing. In practice, it is difficult to prove predatory pricing, and the laws are often used to shield a domestic industry from competition.
6. Under WTO rules, each country may pursue its environmental goals only within its own borders.
7. International trade has contributed to the widening gap between the wages of low-skilled and high-skilled labor.

KEY TERMS

autarky, *643*
comparative advantage, *644*
consumption possibilities curve, *645*
dumping, *656*
import quota, *648*
infant industry, *653*
learning by doing, *653*
production possibilities curve, *643*
tariff, *649*
terms of trade, *644*
voluntary export restraint (VER), *648*

PROBLEMS AND DISCUSSION QUESTIONS

1. In Figure 2 within this chapter, suppose the two countries trade 35 chips for 70 shirts. For each country, compute the amounts of chips and shirts consumed.
2. Consider two countries, Tableland and Chairland, both of which are capable of producing table and chairs. Chairland can produce the following combinations of chairs and tables.
   - All chairs and no tables: 36 chairs per day.
   - All tables and no chairs: 18 tables per day.

   Tableland can produce the following combinations of chairs and tables.
   - All chairs and no tables: 40 chairs per day.
   - All tables and no chairs: 40 tables per day.

   In each country, there is a fixed trade-off of tables for chairs.
   a. Draw the two production possibilities curves, with chairs on the vertical axis and tables on the horizontal axis.
   b. Suppose that each country is initially self-sufficient and each country divides its resources equally between the two goods. How much does each country produce and consume?
   c. Which nation has a comparative advantage in tables? Which one has a comparative advantage in chairs?
   d. If the two countries split the difference between the buyer's willingness to pay for chairs and the seller's willingness to accept, what are the terms of trade (in chairs per table)?
   e. Draw the consumption possibilities curves.
   f. Suppose that each country specializes in the good for which it has a comparative advantage, and exchange 14 tables for some quantity of chairs. Compute the consumption bundles (consumption of tables and chairs) for each country.
3. The current approach to restricting automobile imports is to use voluntary export restraints. Evaluate the wisdom of this approach and propose an alternative policy.
4. In the Chipland/Shirtland example in Question 2, suppose the initial terms of trade involve one-half a shirt for each chip. Will both nations be willing to exchange chips and shirts under these terms of trade? If not, how would you expect the terms of trade to change?
5. The European Union is committed to eliminating most of the trade barriers among its 15 member nations. What types of people will benefit and which will lose?

Take It to the Net

We invite you to visit the O'Sullivan/Sheffrin page on the Prentice Hall Web site at:

http://www.prenhall.com/osullivan/

for this chapter's World Wide Web exercise.

MODEL ANSWERS FOR THIS CHAPTER

Chapter-Opening Questions

1. The winners are consumers, who pay lower prices, and workers in export industries. The losers are people who lose their jobs as imports replace domestically produced goods.
2. A tariff generates revenue for the government, while a quota generates profits for importers.
3. First, if a firm has a monopoly in its home market but faces strong competition in a foreign market, the firm will naturally charge a higher price in the home market (price discrimination). Second, a firm may be engaging in predatory pricing, the practice of cutting prices in an attempt to drive rivals out of business.
4. Under current WTO rules, a country cannot adopt any environmental standard that discriminates against foreign producers. For example, the U.S. cannot impose an import ban on goods produced in polluting factories in other nations. This rule means that global environmental issues must be resolved with international agreements, not trade restrictions.
5. Although trade increases income inequality, it is unclear just how much of the recent increase in inequality can be attributed to the expansion of trade.

Test Your Understanding

1. 50, 78 (108 – 30)
2. B should produce tables and H should produce chairs.
3. 3 chairs per table: H is willing to pay 5 chairs, and B is willing to accept 1 chair.
4. We need to know the maximum output of the good for which the nation has a comparative advantage and the terms of trade.
5. No. The consumption curve will be the same as the production curve.
6. demand, domestic supply
7. below, above
8. Importers make money because of the quota, while the government collects revenue from a tariff which can then be used to finance public programs or cut taxes.
9. Domestic firms supply 22 units, which is one-third of the total quantity (66).
10. This is false. Some workers do not have the skills to work in other sectors and obtaining new skills takes time.
11. It takes some time for a new industry to learn by doing, so it may be sensible to protect the industry when it is young and vulnerable to competition from foreign firms.
12. If two nations subsidize firms in the same industry, each nation could lose money. In addition, a nation might pick the wrong industry to subsidize.
13. A foreign firm is dumping when it sells a product in another country at a price below the price it charges in its own market. It is difficult to determine whether dumping is occurring, and many countries used dumping laws as a disguised form of protectionism.
14. A nation's environmental laws must not discriminate against imported goods: The laws must apply equally to imports and domestic goods.
15. The wage of unskilled labor will increase, while the wage of skilled labor will decrease.

Using the Tools

2. Incentives for Smuggling
   a. Importers are willing to pay a bribe up to $11 per shirt (the difference between the equilibrium price with the import ban and the world price).
   b. If the import ban were replaced by a tariff of $11, the smuggling problem might diminish, although there would still be an incentive to smuggle shirts to avoid the tariff.
3. Vilfredo Pareto and Import Restrictions

   Consumers would gain $400 per family per year from lower apparel prices and pay $300 per year in additional taxes for two years. The net gain would be $100 per year for the first two years and $400 per year thereafter. The apparel workers would receive a transitional payment equal to their wages for two years. To make them better off, we must be sure that they find jobs in other industries within two years. The high-technology people will be better off if the retaliatory trade barriers are lifted.

4. Ban on Shoe Imports

In Figure A we move from point *x* (price = $20 and quantity = 100) to point *m* (price = $30 and quantity = 70).

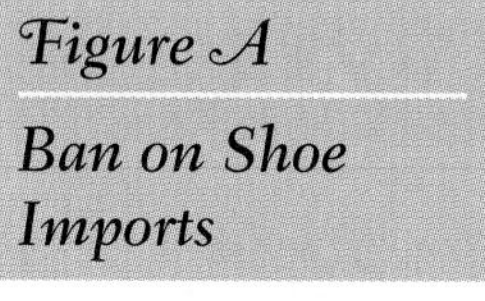

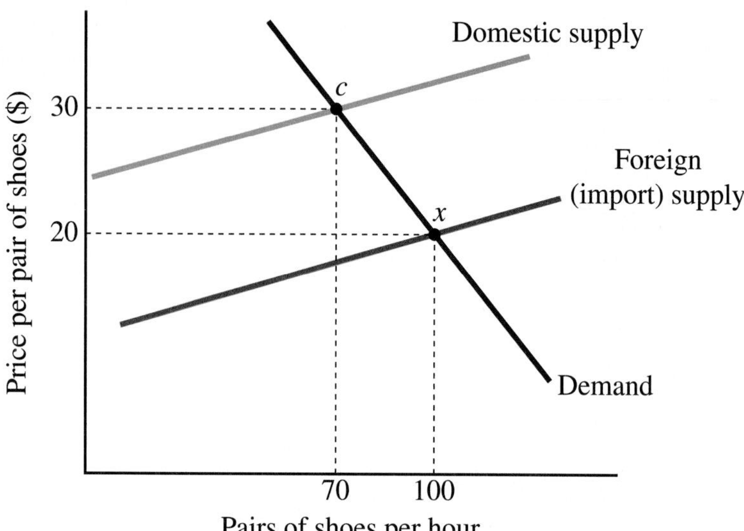

NOTES

1. *A Review of Recent Developments in the U.S. Automobile Industry Including an Assessment of the Japanese Voluntary Restraint Agreements* (Washington, DC: U.S. International Trade Commission, February 1985).
2. Gary C. Hufbauer, Diane T. Berliner, and Kimberly A. Elliot, *Measuring the Cost of Protectionism in the United States* (Washington, DC: Institute for International Economics, 1994).
3. Charles Kindleberger, *The World in Depression 1929–1939* (London: Allen lane, 1973).
4. John A. C. Conybeare, *Trade Wars* (New York: Columbia University Press, 1987).
5. Conybeare, *Trade Wars.*
6. Helene Cooper and Valerie Reitman, "Averting a Trade War, U.S. and Japan Reach Agreement on Autos," *Wall Street Journal*, June 29, 1995, p. 1.
7. Taeho Bark, "The Korean Consumer Electronics Industry: Reaction to Antidumping Actions," Chapter 7 in *Antidumping: How It Works and Who Gets Hurt*, edited by J. Michael Finger (Ann Arbor, MI: University of Michigan Press, 1993).
8. "GATT Panel Supports U.S.," *New York Times*, October 1, 1994, p. A49.
9. Norman S. Fieleke, "The Uruguay Round of Trade Negotiation: An Overview," *New England Economic Review*, May/June 1995.

CHAPTER

33

The World of International Finance

Today, the world currency markets are always open. When foreign exchange traders in New York are sound asleep at 3:00 A.M., their counterparts in London are already on the phones and at their computers at 8:00 A.M. Meanwhile, in Tokyo, the day is just ending, at 6:00 P.M. By the time Tokyo traders return home after their long commutes, the New York traders are back at work. The currency markets keep working even when mere human beings take a break.

In this world market, all currencies are traded 24 hours a day. The value of every currency depends on news and late breaking developments throughout the world. News from Singapore, South Africa, or Sweden can easily affect the price at which currencies trade, for example, the price of U.S. dollars in terms of Japanese yen. A slip of the tongue by the U.S. Secretary of the Treasury reverberates instantly throughout the world. Modern communications—fax, E-mail, video-conferencing, satellite transmissions—accelerate the process.

How do movements in the value of currencies affect the U.S. economy? In this chapter we explain the links between exchange rates and the performance of the economy, an understanding that will help you interpret the often complex news from abroad. For example, if the value of the dollar starts to fall against the Japanese yen, what does it mean, and is this good news or bad news for the economy?

After reading this chapter, you should be able to answer the following real-world questions:

1. If U.S. interest rates increase, how will this affect the exchange rate between U.S. dollars and German marks? What will this do to the cost of a summer trip to Europe?
2. If the dollar increases in value against the Japanese yen, how will this affect the balance of trade between the United States and Japan?
3. Why do governments intervene in the foreign exchange market by buying and selling currencies?
4. Why are some European countries considering adopting a common currency?
5. How do international financial crises emerge?

How Exchange Rates Are Determined

In this section we examine how the value of a currency is determined in world markets. We then take a careful look at the factors that can change the value of a currency.

What Are Exchange Rates?

Exchange rate: The rate at which one currency can be exchanged for another.

Let's start by reviewing some key concepts we introduced in Chapter 3. In order to conduct international transactions between countries with different currencies, it is necessary to exchange one currency for another. The **exchange rate** is defined as the rate at which we can exchange one currency for another. For example, suppose a U.S. songwriter sells the rights of a hit record to a Japanese producer. The U.S. songwriter agrees to be paid \$50,000. If the exchange rate between U.S. dollars and Japanese yen is 100 yen per dollar, it will cost the Japanese producer 5,000,000 yen to purchase the rights to the song. Since international trade occurs between nations with different currencies, the exchange rate, the price at which a currency trades, is an important determinant of the trade in both goods and assets.

Appreciation: An increase in the value of a currency.

An increase in the value of a currency is called an **appreciation.** If the exchange rate between the dollar and the yen increases from 100 yen per dollar to 110 yen per dollar, 1 dollar will purchase more yen. Since the dollar has increased in value, we

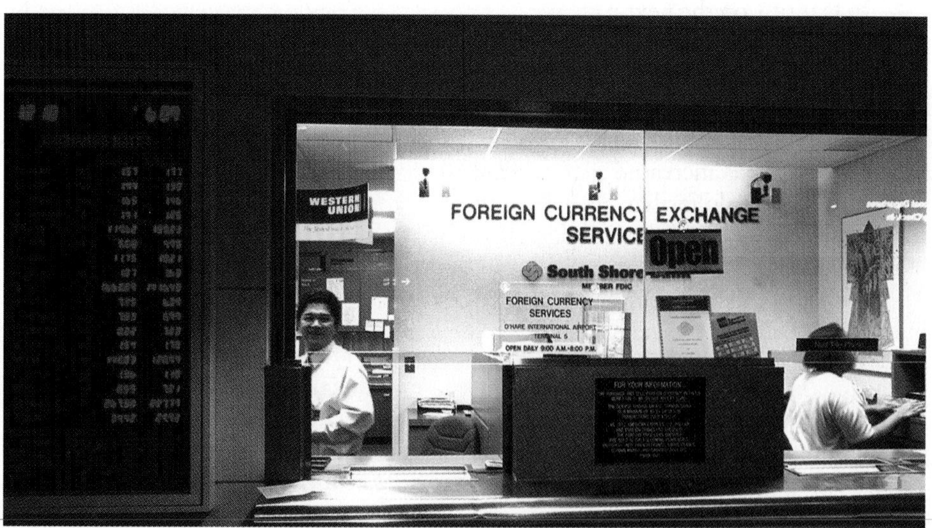

At international airports you can purchase a wide range of foreign currencies.

say that the dollar has appreciated against the yen. A **depreciation** is a reduction in the value of a currency. If the exchange rate fell to 90 yen per dollar, we get fewer yen for each dollar and we say that the dollar has depreciated against the yen.

Depreciation: A decrease in the value of a currency.

Throughout this chapter we measure the exchange rate in units of foreign currency per dollar, that is, as 100 yen per dollar or 2 marks per dollar. We can thus think of the exchange rate as the price of dollars in terms of foreign currency. If the dollar appreciates from 100 yen per dollar to 110 yen per dollar, the price of dollars in terms of yen has increased, that is, the dollar has become more expensive in terms of yen. An appreciation of the dollar, therefore, is an increase in the price of dollars in terms of yen. Similarly, a depreciation of the dollar against the yen is a decrease in the price of dollars in terms of yen.

Note that if the dollar appreciates against the yen, the yen must depreciate against the dollar. If we get more yen in exchange for the dollar, each yen will trade for fewer dollars. If the dollar appreciates from 100 to 110 yen per dollar, 100 yen will exchange for $0.91 rather than $1.00. Similarly, if the dollar depreciates against the yen, the yen must appreciate against the dollar. If we get less yen per dollar, each yen will exchange for more dollars. If the dollar depreciates from 100 yen to 90 yen per dollar, 100 yen will exchange for $1.11 rather than $1.00.

The exchange rate enables us to convert prices in one country to values in another country. Let's review a simple example to illustrate how an exchange rate works. Suppose you want to buy a cuckoo clock from Germany and need to know what a clock would cost. You call the store in Germany and they tell you the clock sells for 300 German marks. The store owners live in Germany and want to be paid in German marks. In order to figure out what it will cost you in dollars, you need to know the exchange rate between marks and dollars. If the exchange rate is 2 marks per dollar, the clock would cost you $150, since 300 marks/2 marks per dollar equals $150. If the exchange rate were 3 marks per dollar, the clock would cost only $100. The exchange rate allows you to convert the value of the clock (or any other good or service) from marks to dollars.

Supply and Demand

How are exchange rates actually determined? The price between U.S. dollars and German marks is determined in the foreign exchange market, the market in which dollars trade for German marks. To understand this market, we can use normal supply and demand analysis.

In Figure 1 on the next page we plot the demand and supply curves for dollars in exchange for German marks. On the vertical axis, we have the exchange rate, e, between marks and dollars. As we discussed, we will measure e by how many marks trade for a dollar. For example, if you receive 2 marks per dollar, then $e = 2$ marks/dollar. If e increases, this means that a dollar buys more marks and the price of dollars in terms of marks has increased. For example, if e increases from 2 marks/dollar to 2.5 marks/ dollar, the dollar has become more valuable or appreciated against the mark. Similarly, if the exchange rate fell to 1.5 marks/dollar, the dollar has depreciated in value against the mark and the price of dollars in terms of marks has decreased.

Note that if the dollar appreciates against the mark, the mark has depreciated against the dollar. If the exchange rate increases from 2 to 2.5 marks/dollar, a single mark falls in value from $0.50 to $0.40.

Figure 1 shows the supply and demand curves for dollars in exchange for marks. The supply curve in Figure 1 is the supply of dollars in exchange for marks. Individuals or firms that want to buy German goods or assets will need to exchange dollars for marks. For example, to invest in the German stock market, a U.S. investor must first trade dollars for marks because German sellers of stocks or bonds

Figure 1

Demand for and Supply of Dollars

Market equilibrium occurs where demand equals supply.

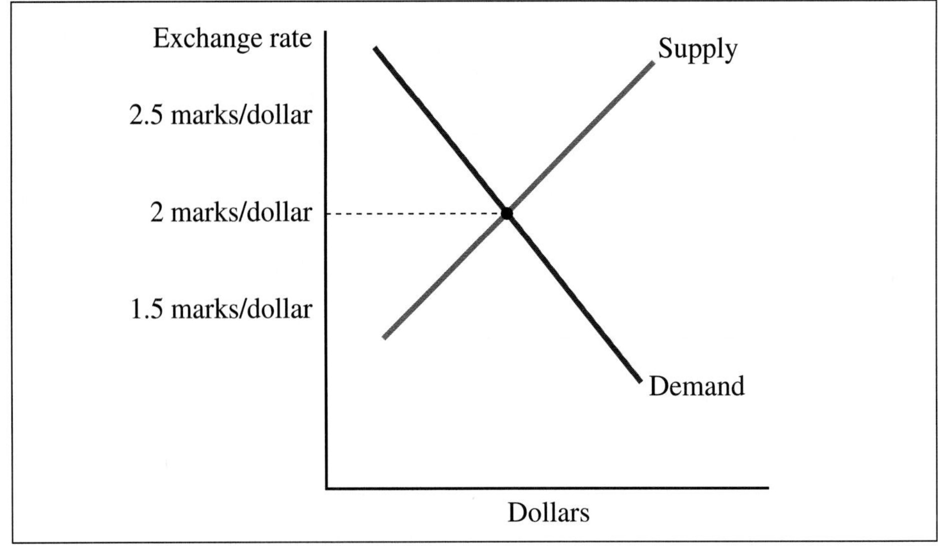

want to be paid in their own currency. Recall that we have defined the exchange rate as marks per dollar, so that an increase in the exchange rate means that each dollar exchanges for more marks and marks become cheaper relative to dollars. The supply curve is drawn under the assumption that as marks become cheaper, total spending on German goods and assets will increase. Therefore, the supply curve is upward sloping: As the value of the dollar increases, more dollars will be supplied to the market in exchange for marks.

The demand curve represents the quantity demanded of dollars in exchange for marks. Individuals or firms in Germany that want to buy U.S. goods or assets must trade marks for dollars. For example, to visit Disneyland, a German family must exchange marks for dollars. As the exchange rate falls, dollars become relatively cheaper in terms of marks. This makes U.S. goods and assets less expensive for German residents because each German mark purchases more U.S. dollars. As these goods and assets become cheaper, we assume that more German residents will want to trade marks for dollars. Therefore, the demand curve is downward sloping: Total demand for dollars will increase as the price of the dollar falls or depreciates against the mark.

Equilibrium in the market for foreign exchange occurs where the demand curve intersects the supply curve. In Figure 1 this occurs at an exchange rate of 2 marks/dollar. At this price, the desire to trade dollars for marks just matches the desire to trade marks for dollars. The foreign exchange market is in balance.

Changes in Demand and Supply

Changes in demand and supply will change equilibrium exchange rates. In Figure 2 we show how an increase in demand, a shift of the demand curve to the right, will increase or appreciate the exchange rate. U.S. dollars will become more expensive relative to German marks as the price of U.S. dollars in terms of marks increases.

Two key factors will shift the demand curve for dollars. First, higher U.S. interest rates will lead to an increased demand for dollars. With higher returns in U.S. markets, investors throughout the world will want to buy dollars to invest in U.S. assets. Second, lower U.S. prices will also lead to an increased demand for dollars. For example, if prices at Disneyland fell, there would be an overall increase in the demand for dollars because more tourists would want to visit Disneyland.

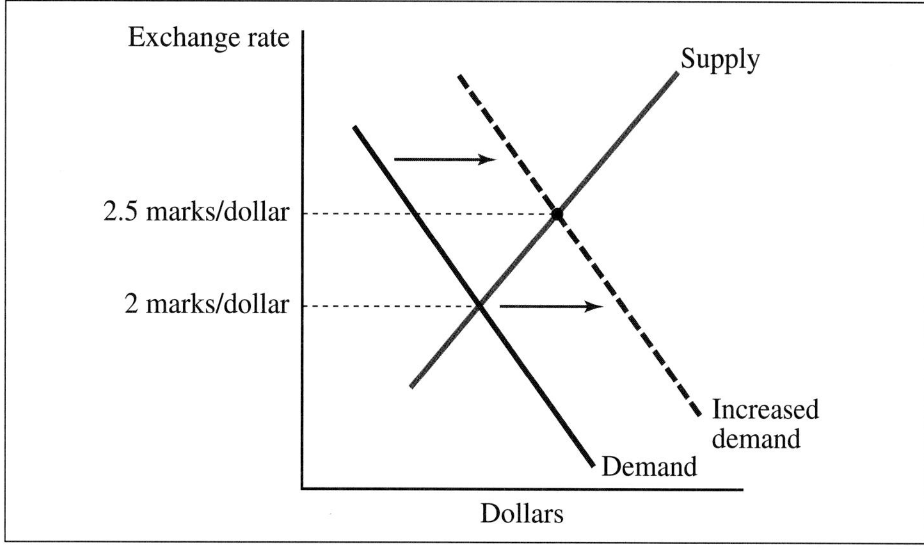

Figure 2

Shifts in Demand for Dollars

An increase in the demand for dollars will increase (appreciate) the exchange rate. Higher U.S. interest rates or lower U.S. prices will increase the demand for dollars.

Figure 3 shows the effects of an increase in supply of dollars, a shift in the supply curve to the right. This will lead to a fall or depreciation of the value of dollar against the mark. What will increase the supply of dollars in the market? Again, the two key factors are interest rates and prices. Higher German interest rates will lead U.S. investors to purchase German bonds or other assets. This will require them to supply dollars for marks, which will drive down the exchange rate for dollars. Lower German prices will also lead to an increase in the supply of dollars for marks.

Let's summarize the key facts about the foreign exchange market, using German marks as our example:

1. The demand curve for dollars represents the demand for dollars in exchange for marks. It is downward sloping. As the dollar depreciates, there will be an increase in the quantity demanded of dollars in exchange for marks.
2. The supply curve for dollars is the supply of dollars in exchange for marks. It is upward sloping. As the dollar appreciates, there will be an increase in the quantity supplied of dollars in exchange for marks.

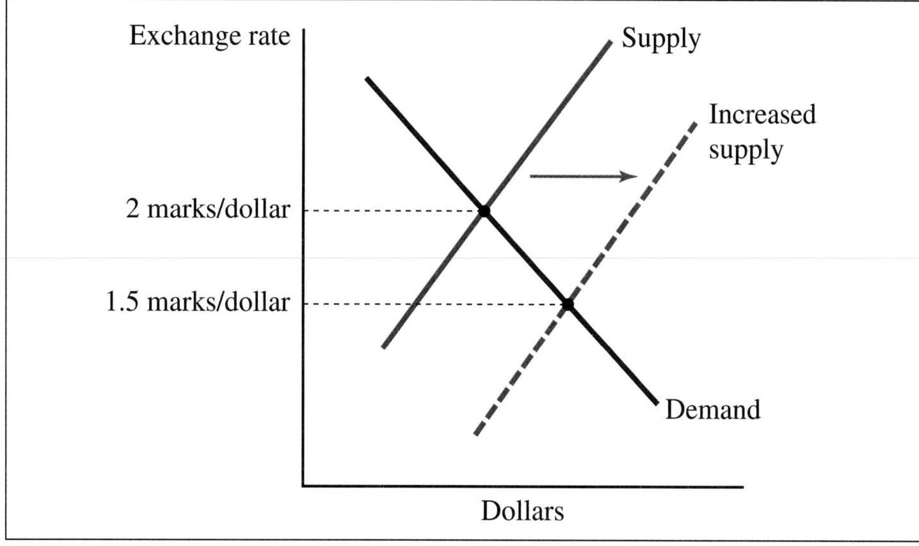

Figure 3

Shifts in the Supply of Dollars

An increase in the supply of dollars will decrease (depreciate) the exchange rate. Higher German interest rates or lower German prices will increase the supply of dollars.

3. Increases in U.S. interest rates and decreases in U.S. prices will increase the demand for dollars, leading to an appreciation of the dollar.
4. Increases in German interest rates and decreases in German prices will increase the supply of supply of dollars in exchange for marks, leading to a depreciation of the dollar.

TEST *Your Understanding*

Use demand and supply analysis to determine whether the dollar will appreciate or depreciate against the mark in each of these cases.

1. Banks cut interest rates in Germany.
2. Interest rates fall in the United States.
3. Inflation increases from 4% to 6% in the United States.
4. The German inflation rate falls from 5% to 3%.

REAL EXCHANGE RATES

As our examples of German cuckoo clocks and Disneyland indicate, changes in market exchange rates can affect the desirability of a country's goods and services. However, we have been assuming that the price of cuckoo clocks and trips to Disneyland did not change. In general, prices do change over time and we need to adjust the exchange rate that is determined in the foreign exchange market in order to take into account changes in prices. This is an application of the reality principle.

Reality PRINCIPLE

What matters to people is the real value or purchasing power of money or income, not its face value.

Real exchange rate: The market exchange rate adjusted for prices.

Economists have developed an important concept that adjusts the market exchange rates for changes in prices: It is called the real exchange rate. The **real exchange rate** is defined as the price of all U.S. goods and services relative to all foreign goods and services expressed in a common currency. We measure it by expressing U.S. prices for goods in services in foreign currency and comparing them to foreign prices. To illustrate this idea, let's just consider a single good. Suppose the price of German cars in marks was 30,000 marks and the price of U.S. cars was $15,000. If the exchange rate between marks and dollars were 2 marks/dollar, then the real exchange rate for cars would be

$$\begin{aligned}\text{real exchange rate for cars} &= \frac{\text{exchange rate} \times \text{price of U.S. cars in dollars}}{\text{price of German cars in marks}} \\ &= \frac{(2\text{ marks/dollar}) \times (\$15{,}000\text{ for a U.S. car})}{30{,}000\text{ marks for a German car}} \\ &= \frac{30{,}000\text{ marks}}{30{,}000\text{ marks}} \\ &= 1\end{aligned}$$

According to this calculation, the real exchange rate for cars is equal to 1, which means that cars cost the same in the United States as they do in Germany. An increase in the real exchange rate for cars would mean that U.S. cars had become more expensive relative to German cars.

We can apply the same type of calculation to *all* German and U.S. goods and services. Instead of just using the price of cars in both countries, we determine the real exchange rate using the overall level of prices for both countries, or:

$$\text{real exchange rate} = \frac{\text{exchange rate} \times \text{U.S. price level}}{\text{German price level}}$$

The real exchange rate is the ratio of the price of all U.S. goods and services compared to the price of German goods and services, using the exchange rate to express them in a common currency. If the real exchange rate between German and U.S. goods increases, U.S. goods will become more expensive compared to German goods.

We can use this formula to help us understand the factors that change the real exchange rate. First, an increase in U.S. prices will raise the real exchange rate. If U.S. automobiles become more expensive, holding everything else constant, the price of U.S. goods relative to German goods will increase. Similarly, a decrease in German prices will also increase the real exchange rate.

Finally, if the dollar appreciates against the mark, the real exchange rate will increase. Consider the automobile example. If the exchange rate increased from 2 to 2.5 marks/dollar, the real exchange rate would now be

$$\text{real exchange rate for cars} = \frac{(2.5 \text{ marks/dollar}) \times (\$15{,}000 \text{ for a U.S. car})}{30{,}000 \text{ marks for a German car}}$$

$$= 1.25$$

which is an increase from the previous real exchange rate of 1.0. The appreciation of the dollar has made it more costly for U.S. autos to compete with German autos in Germany, because to buy the U.S. auto Germans must acquire dollars that have become more expensive.

The real exchange rate is an important concept because it controls for changes in a country's prices. Suppose that country A had an inflation rate of 20% while country B had no inflation at all. Moreover, the exchange rate of country A fell or depreciated 20% against the country B. In this case there would be *no change* in the real exchange rate between the two countries. Although prices in country A would have increased by 20%, its currency is 20% cheaper. From the point of view of residents of country B, nothing has changed at all—it would still cost the same to buy the goods in country A.

Economists have found that a country's net exports (exports minus its imports) will decrease when its real exchange rate increases. For example, if the U.S. real exchange rate increases, the price of U.S. goods will increase relative to foreign goods. This will reduce U.S. exports because our goods have become more expensive; it will also increase imports to the United States because foreign goods have become relatively cheaper. As a result of the decrease in U.S. exports and increase in U.S. imports, net exports will decline.

Figure 4 on the next page plots an index of the real exchange rate for the United States against net exports for the decade of the 1980s. This index is based on an average of real exchange rates with all U.S. trading partners and is called a **multilateral real exchange rate**. Notice that when the multilateral real exchange rate increased, U.S. net exports fell. Net exports increased after 1984 as the real exchange rate began to decrease.

Multilateral real exchange rate: An index of the real exchange rate with a country's trading partners.

Figure 4

Real Exchange Rate and Net Exports in the United States, 1980–1990

Source: Data from *International Financial Statistics* (International Monetary Fund) and *Economic Report of the President* (Washington, DC: U.S. Government Printing Office, yearly).

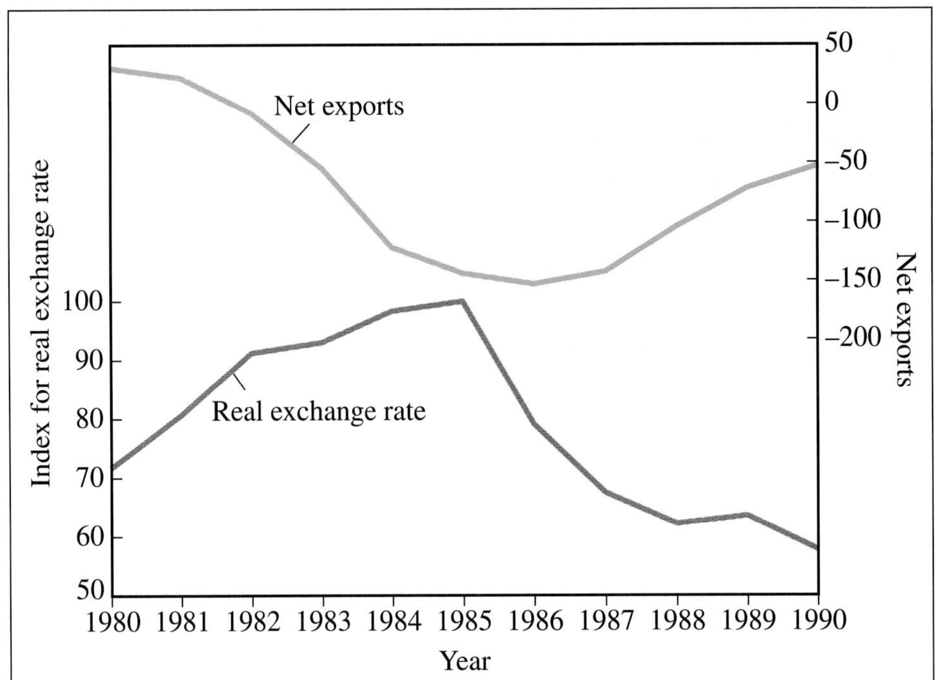

TEST *Your Understanding*

5 What is the key difference between the real exchange rate and the market exchange rate?

6 Holding everything else constant, how will the real exchange between Germany and the United States be affected by:

a. A depreciation of the dollar?

b. Higher inflation in the United States than in Germany?

c. An appreciation of the mark?

PURCHASING POWER PARITY

The real exchange rate measures the price of domestic goods relative to foreign goods. As Figure 4 shows, real exchange rates do vary over time. But for goods that are traded easily across countries (such as gold bars), we would expect the price to be the same when expressed in a common currency. For example, the price of gold bars sold in France should be virtually identical to the price of gold bars sold in New York. If the price were higher in France, demand would shift to New York, raising the price in New York and lowering the price in France until they were equal.

The tendency for goods that are easily tradeable to sell at the same price when expressed in a common currency is known as the **law of one price.** Metals, agricultural commodities, computer chips, and other tradeable goods follow the law of one price.

Law of one price: The theory that goods which are easily tradeable across countries should sell at the same price expressed in a common currency.

If all goods were tradeable and the law of one price held exactly, exchange rates would reflect no more than the differences in the way the price levels are expressed in the two countries. For example, if a basket of goods in France costs 3,000 francs and the identical basket cost $1,000 in the United States, an exchange rate of 3 francs/dollar would make the costs the same in either currency.

One theory of how market exchange rates are determined states that market exchange rates simply reflect differences in the overall price levels between countries. This theory is known as **purchasing power parity**. In our France–United States example, the theory of purchasing power parity predicts a market exchange rate of 3 francs/dollar. At that exchange rate, French and U.S. goods would sell for the same price if their products are expressed in a common currency.

Purchasing power parity: A theory of exchange rates that states that the exchange rate between two currencies is determined by the price levels in the two countries.

Research has shown that purchasing power parity does not hold precisely. A dramatic example of this has been created by the magazine *The Economist*, which measured the price of a Big Mac throughout the world and checked to see whether the law of one price held. Table 1 contains the results for selected countries.

Big Macs sell for dramatically different prices around the globe compared to the $2.32 they go for in the United States. They are a bargain in Hong Kong at $1.23 but quite expensive in Japan at $4.65. The price in Singapore of $2.10 is similar to the price in the United States.

Table 1 also contains the market exchange rate predicted by the theory of purchasing power parity. To obtain this exchange rate, divide the price of Big Macs in the foreign country by the dollar price. For example, for Japan the purchasing power exchange rate is 169 yen/dollar (391 yen/$2.32 = 169). At this exchange rate, the Big Mac in Japan would cost the same as in the United States. The actual value for the yen in April 1995 when these prices were computed was 84.2 yen/dollar, so the Big Mac was much more expensive in Japan.

Clearly, purchasing power parity does not give accurate predictions. The reason is that many goods are not traded across countries. For example, housing and services (such as haircuts) are not traded across countries. The law of one price does not hold for nontraded goods, which comprise approximately 50% of the value of production in an economy. There is some truth to purchasing power parity since exchange rates do reflect differences in the price level between countries, but as the Big Mac example shows, purchasing power parity is not a reliable guide to exchange rate levels when nontraded goods are important.

Economists have successfully used purchasing power parity theory in other settings. Countries that had been experiencing hyperinflation but then brought the inflation to a halt often need assistance in setting an appropriate exchange rate. Purchasing power parity provides a reasonable guide in this case. Problems associated with nontraded goods are negligible compared to the vast increases in the price level caused by the hyperinflation.

Table 1: The Big Mac around the World

Country	*Price of Big Mac in Local Currency*	*Price of Big Mac Expressed in Dollars*	*Predicted Purchasing Power Exchange Rate (foreign currency/dollar)*	*Actual Exchange Rate (foreign currency/dollar)*
United States	*2.32 dollars*	*$2.32*		
Belgium	109.00 francs	$3.84	47.00	28.40
Hong Kong	9.50 HK dollars	$1.23	4.09	7.73
Israel	8.90 shekels	$3.01	3.84	2.95
Mexico	10.90 pesos	$1.71	4.70	6.37
Singapore	2.95 S. dollars	$2.10	1.27	1.40
Japan	391.00 yen	$4.65	169.00	84.20

Source: Data from *The Economist*, April 15, 1995, p. 74.

THE CURRENT ACCOUNT AND THE CAPITAL ACCOUNT

Current account: The sum of net exports (exports minus imports), net income received from investments abroad, and net transfers from abroad.

Capital account: Minus the value of country's net acquisition (purchases less sales) of foreign assets. A purchase of a foreign asset is a deficit item on the capital account while a sale of a domestic asset is a surplus item.

Economists find it useful to divide international transactions into two types. A country's **current account** is the sum of its net exports (exports minus imports), net income received from investments abroad, and net transfer payments from abroad. If a country has a positive current account, we say that its current account is in surplus; if it has a negative current account, we say that its current account is in deficit. If the income from investments abroad and net transfer payments is negligible, the current account becomes equivalent to a country's net exports.

We measure a country's transactions in existing assets on its **capital account.** The capital account is defined as minus the value of the country's net acquisition (purchases less sales) of foreign assets. That is, if the United States acquired \$100 billion in net foreign assets, its capital account would be –\$100 billion. If the value on the capital account is positive, we say the country has a surplus on the capital account. Similarly, if the value on the capital account is negative, we say that is has a deficit on the capital account.

Here is a simple rule for understanding transactions on both the current account and the capital account: Any action that gives rise to a *demand* for foreign currency is a *deficit* item on either the current or capital account. Any action that gives rise to a *supply* of foreign currency is a *surplus* item on the current or capital account. Let's apply this rule to the current and capital accounts, taking the point of view of the United States.

1. ***Current account.*** A U.S. import is a deficit (negative) item on the current account because we need to demand foreign currency to acquire the import. On the other hand, with a U.S. export, foreign currency is supplied to the United States in exchange for dollars, so it gives rise to a surplus (positive item) on the current account. Income from investments abroad and net transfers received are treated like exports since they result in a supply of foreign currency for dollars. Summarizing, we have

U.S. current account surplus = U.S. exports – U.S. imports + net income from foreign investments + net transfers from abroad

2. ***Capital account.*** The purchase of a foreign asset by a U.S. resident gives rise to a deficit (negative) item on the capital account because it requires a demand for foreign currency. (You can think of the purchase of a foreign asset as "importing" capital.) On the other hand, a purchase of a U.S. asset by a foreign resident leads to a supply of foreign currency and a surplus (positive) item on the current account. (This can be thought of as "exporting" capital.) Summarizing, we have

U.S. capital account surplus = foreign purchases of U.S. assets – U.S. purchases of foreign assets

The current account and the capital account of a country are linked by a very important identity:

current account + capital account = 0

The current account plus the capital account must sum to zero.

The current account and the capital account must sum to zero because any excess demand for foreign currency that arises from transactions in goods and services (the current account) must be met by an excess supply of foreign currency arising from asset transactions (the capital account). For example, if the United States had a current account deficit of \$50 billion, it would have an excess demand of foreign exchange of \$50 billion. This excess demand could only be met by a supply of foreign exchange from $50 billion of net purchases of U.S. assets. The $50 billion net purchase of U.S. assets is a $50 surplus on the U.S. capital account. Thus the current account deficit is offset by the capital account surplus.

Let's look at this from a slightly different angle. Consider again the case in which the United States is running a current account deficit because imports from abroad exceed exports. (For simplicity, transfers and income earned from investments abroad are both zero.) The current account deficit means that, on net, foreign residents and their governments are the recipients of dollars since they have sold more goods to the United States than they have purchased.

What do they do with these dollars? They can either hold them or use them to purchase U.S. assets. In either case, foreign residents and their governments have acquired U.S. assets, either dollars or other U.S. assets. The value of these assets is the U.S. current account deficit. Since a sale of a U.S. asset to a foreign resident is a surplus item on the U.S. capital account, the value of the capital account will be equal to minus the value of the current account. Thus the current account and the capital account must sum to zero.

On the other hand, if a country runs a current account surplus, it acquires foreign exchange. It can either keep the foreign exchange or use it to buy foreign assets. In either case, the change in its net foreign assets will equal its current account surplus. Since the capital account is minus the value of the change in net foreign assets, the current account and capital account will again sum to zero.

Since 1982 the United States has run a current account deficit every year. This means that the United States has run a capital account surplus of equal value for these years as well. Since a capital account surplus means that foreign nations acquire a country's assets, the United States has, on net, reduced its holding of foreign assets. In 1986, the U.S. Department of Commerce estimated that the United States had a **net international investment position** of $136 billion, meaning that U.S. holdings of foreign assets exceeded foreign holdings of U.S. assets by $136 billion. Because of its current account deficits, the U.S. net international investment position fell every year. By 1994 it was –$584 billion, meaning that foreign residents owned $584 billion more U.S. assets than U.S. residents owned foreign assets. You may have heard the United States referred to as a net debtor—this is just another way of saying that the U.S. net international investment position is negative.

Net international investment position: Domestic holdings of foreign assets minus foreign holdings of domestic assets.

Table 2 on the next page shows the current account and capital account for the United States for 1994. The current account is comprised of the merchandise account (trade in goods), the service account (trade in services), net investment income, and net transfers. In 1994 all elements of the current account but the service component were negative. The capital account includes net increases in U.S. holdings abroad (negative entries in the capital account) and foreign holdings of U.S. assets (positive entries in the capital account). Since the current account and capital account data are collected separately, there is a statistical discrepancy. Once we include this statistical discrepancy, the current account plus the capital account sum to zero.

The capital account is defined to include purchases and sales of assets by both governments as well as private individuals. As we will see in the next section, governments will often buy or sell foreign exchange to influence the exchange rate for their currency.

FIXING THE EXCHANGE RATE

If a country's exchange rate appreciates or increases in value, there are two distinct effects. First, the increased value of the exchange rate makes imports cheaper for the residents of the country. For example, if the U.S. dollar appreciates against the

Table 2: U.S. Current Account and Capital Account, 1994 (billions)

Current account	
Merchandise account	–$166
Service account	59
Net investment income	–9
Net unilateral transfers	–35
Total on current account	–151
Capital account	
Increases in U.S. holdings abroad	–126
Increases in foreign holdings in the United States	291
Total on capital account	165
Statistical discrepancy	**-14**
Sum of current account, capital account, and statistical discrepancy	0

Source: *Economic Report of the President* (Washington, DC: U.S. Government Printing Office, 1995).

French franc, French wines will become less expensive. Consumers would clearly like this because it would lower their cost of living. The increased value of the exchange rate, however, does make U.S. goods more expensive on world markets. This will increase imports (like French wine) and decrease exports (such as California wine). Overall, net exports will decrease.

If a country's exchange rate depreciates, there are again two distinct effects. For example, if the U.S. dollar depreciated against the Japanese yen, Japanese imports would become more expensive in the United States, thereby raising the U.S. cost of living. At the same time, U.S. goods would become cheaper on world markets. With exports increasing and imports decreasing, net exports would increase.

Sometimes countries do not want their exchange rate to change. They may want to avoid sharp increases in their cost of living from an exchange rate depreciation or a reduction in net exports through an exchange rate appreciation. To prevent the value of the currency from changing, governments can enter the foreign exchange market to try to influence the price of foreign exchange. Economists call these efforts **foreign exchange market intervention**.

Foreign exchange market intervention: The purchase or sale of currencies by governments to influence the market exchange rate.

In the United States the Treasury Department has the official responsibility for foreign exchange intervention, although it conducts its activities in conjunction with the Federal Reserve. In other countries, the arrangements may vary. We will ignore these institutional details and just say that "governments" intervene in the foreign exchange market.

To influence the price at which one currency trades for another, governments have to affect the demand or supply for that currency. For example, to increase the value of a currency, governments must increase the demand for that currency. Similarly, to decrease the value of a currency, governments must increase the supply of that currency.

In Figure 5 we show how governments can fix or *peg* the price of a currency. Suppose the U.S. and German governments want the exchange rate to be 2 marks/dollar. The price at which demand and supply are equal, however, is currently 1.5 marks per dollar. To raise the price of dollars, the governments need to increase the demand for them. To do this, either government can simply go into the

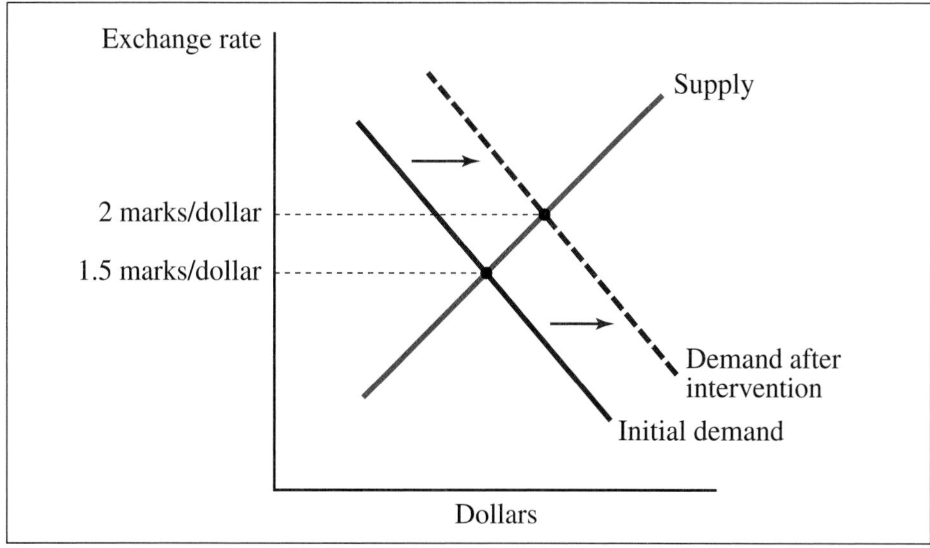

Figure 5

Intervention to Raise the Price of Dollars

To increase the price of dollars, the U.S. government sells marks in exchange for dollars. This shifts the demand curve for dollars to the right.

market for foreign exchange and sell marks in exchange for dollars. This will shift the demand curve for dollars to the right until the price of dollars has risen to 2 marks/dollar.

Similarly, if the free market price exceeded 2 marks/dollar, the governments would have to buy marks in exchange for dollars. By selling dollars in exchange for marks, they would make the supply of dollars increase and the exchange rate would fall.

Note that to lower the price of dollars (raise the value of the mark), the U.S. government has to buy marks in exchange for dollars. The U.S. government therefore acquires or stockpiles marks anytime it tries to raise the price of marks. On the other hand, the U.S. government must sell marks from its stockpile in order to raise the price of dollars (lower the value of the mark). What would happen if the United States ran down its stockpile and no longer had any marks to sell? In this case it could borrow marks from the German government or persuade Germany to sell marks for dollars. In either case, it would need the cooperation of the German government.

In theory, foreign exchange intervention is easy to describe. In practice, successful interventions are difficult, as explained in the Closer Look box on the next page, "What Does Foreign Exchange Intervention Cost?"

FIXED VERSUS FLEXIBLE EXCHANGE RATES

In this section we first discuss two different types of exchange rate systems. Then we will take a brief look at the U.S. history on exchange rate policy and exchange rate systems in the world today.

Fixed Exchange Rates

Whether you are in California, New York, or Indiana, all prices are quoted in dollars. No one asks whether your dollar came from San Francisco or Miami. Within the United States, a dollar is just a dollar.

Suppose, on the other hand, that every state in the United States had its own currency. For example, there might be a California dollar (with a picture of the Golden Gate Bridge), an Oregon dollar (with pictures of tall trees), and a Florida dollar (with pictures of Disneyworld). In principle, these "dollars" might trade at

A Closer LOOK

What Does Foreign Exchange Intervention Cost?

Trillions of dollars are traded in the foreign exchange market. If a government decides to intervene to move the price of its currency, how much will it have to spend?

In the mid-1990s, the U.S. government intervened periodically to prevent the dollar from falling too quickly against the Japanese yen. In one episode the U.S. government spent about $2 billion selling yen and buying dollars to prop up the dollar. What was the result? According to the *Wall Street Journal,* "The greenback still looks like a wet noodle." The intervention did not work.*

In general, economists are skeptical of attempts by governments to intervene in the foreign exchange markets. On some occasions, carefully planned and timed intervention can be effective. However, unless the intervention is matched by new monetary or fiscal policies that change underlying fundamentals in the economy, exchange rates will be largely unaffected by periodic purchases or sales of currency. Markets are too big today to be dominated very easily. Even $2 billion may not be enough.

*See Michael Sesit, "Dollar Stays Weak Despite Intervention," *Wall Street Journal*, November 7, 1994, p. C1.

different rates depending on the supply and demand for that currency. For example, in one year, the Texas dollar might be worth more than the Michigan dollar, trading for 1.2 Michigan dollars.

Think how much more complicated it would be to do business if each state had different currencies. To buy goods from a mail-order company in Maine, for example, you would have to find out the exchange rate between your local dollar and the Maine dollar. Any large business operating in all 50 states would be overwhelmed by its efforts to keep track of all exchange rate movements across the states. The economy would become less efficient as individuals and businesses focused all their attention on exchange rates.

These same ideas apply across nations. Wouldn't it be nice if all countries either used the same currency or fixed their exchange rates against one another so no one would have to worry about exchange rate movements? Currency systems in which governments try to keep constant the values of their currencies against one another are called **fixed exchange rate** systems.

Fixed exchange rates: A system in which governments peg exchange rates.

In a typical fixed exchange rate system, one country stands at the center and other countries fix or peg their exchange rates to the currency of this center country. They must intervene in the foreign exchange market, if necessary, to keep the exchange rate constant. A government will have to intervene if, at the fixed exchange rate, the private demand and supply for its currency are not equal.

Suppose, for example, that the supply of a country's currency exceeds the demand at the fixed exchange rate. When there is an excess supply of a country's currency at the fixed exchange rate, this is known as a **balance of payments deficit.** A balance of payments deficit will occur whenever there is a deficit on the current account that is not matched by net sales of assets to foreigners by the *private* sector. With an excess supply of a country's currency in the market, the currency would fall in value without any intervention. To prevent the currency from depreciating in value and to maintain the fixed exchange rate, the government must sell foreign exchange (that is, foreign currency) and buy its own currency. As we saw in our discussion of foreign exchange intervention, if a country sells foreign exchange, its holdings of foreign exchange will fall. Thus, when a country runs a balance of payments deficit, it will decrease its holdings of foreign exchange.

Balance of payments deficit: Under a fixed exchange rate system, a situation in which the supply of a country's currency exceeds the demand for the currency at the current exchange rate.

On the other hand, a country could be in a situation in which the demand for its currency exceeds the supply at the fixed exchange rate. When there is an excess demand for a country's currency at the fixed exchange rate, this is known as a **balance of payments surplus.** A balance of payments surplus arises when there is a current account surplus that is not matched by net purchases of foreign assets by the *private* sector. With an excess demand of a country's currency in the market, the currency would rise in value without any intervention. To prevent the currency from appreciating in value and to maintain the fixed exchange rate, the government must buy foreign exchange and sell its own currency. Since it is buying foreign exchange, its holdings of foreign exchange will increase. Thus, when a country runs a balance of payments surplus, it will increase its holding of foreign exchange.

Balance of payments surplus: Under a fixed exchange rate system, a situation in which the demand of a country's currency exceeds the supply for the currency at the current exchange rate.

Under a fixed exchange rate system, countries that run persistent balance of payments deficits or surpluses must take corrective actions. If domestic policy actions (such as changing taxes, spending, or the supply of money) do not cure the problem, it will eventually become necessary to change the level at which the exchange rate is fixed. A country facing a balance of payments deficit can lower the value at which the currency is pegged in order to increase its net exports. This is called a **devaluation.** Conversely, a country facing a balance of payments surplus can increase the value at which its currency is pegged and reduce its net exports. This is called a **revaluation.**

Devaluation: A decrease in the exchange rate to which a currency is pegged in a fixed rate system.

Revaluation: An increase in the exchange rate to which a currency is pegged.

The U.S. Experience with Fixed and Flexible Exchange Rates

After World War II, the countries of the world operated under a fixed exchange system known as Bretton Woods, after the town in New Hampshire in which the system was adopted. The United States operated at the center of this system: All countries fixed or pegged their currencies against the U.S. dollar.

The Bretton Woods system lasted until the early 1970s when the world abandoned it and went to the current system—a **flexible exchange rate** system—in which free markets primarily determine exchange rates; that is, the exchange rate of a currency is determined by the supply and demand for it.

Flexible exchange rates: A currency system in which exchange rates are determined by free markets.

If a fixed exchange rate system makes it easier to trade, why did it break down in the early 1970s? Fixed exchange rate systems do provide benefits but require countries to maintain similar economic policies. In particular, they have to maintain similar inflation rates and interest rates.

To understand this point, suppose the exchange rate between the United States and Germany were fixed but that the United States had an inflation rate of 6% compared to no inflation in Germany. Since prices in the United States would be rising by 6%, the U.S. real exchange rate against Germany would also be increasing at 6% a year. This would cause a trade deficit to emerge in United States as U.S. goods became more expensive on world markets. As long as the differences in inflation continued and the exchange rate remained fixed, the U.S. real exchange rate would continue to appreciate and the U.S. trade deficit would grow even worse. Clearly, this course of events could not continue.

In the late 1960s, inflation in the United States began to exceed inflation in other countries and a U.S. balance of payments deficit emerged. In 1971, President Nixon surprised the world and devalued the U.S. dollar against the currencies of all the other countries. This was a sharp departure from the rules underlying Bretton Woods, in which the United States was at the center of the system and other countries were supposed to make adjustments, if necessary, against the dollar. Nixon hoped, however, that a one-time devaluation of the dollar would alleviate the U.S. balance of payments deficit and maintain the underlying system of fixed exchange rates.

However, the U.S. devaluation did not stop the U.S. balance of payments deficit. As Germany tried to maintain the fixed exchange rate with the United States by purchasing U.S. dollars in the foreign exchange market, it would actually "import" inflation from the United States. With the U.S. balance of payments deficit continuing, Germany was required to buy U.S. dollars to keep the mark from appreciating. As Germany bought these dollars for German marks which were then put into circulation, the German supply of marks in their country would increase. This would raise the inflation rate in Germany.

This is precisely what happened in the early 1970s. Private-sector investors, moreover, knew that Germany did not wish to run persistent trade surpluses and import U.S. inflation. They bet that Germany would revalue the mark against the dollar, that is, raise its value against the dollar. These speculators bought massive amounts of German assets, trading dollars for marks to purchase them. Their actions forced the German government to buy even more dollars! The flow of financial capital into Germany was so massive that eventually the German government gave up all attempts to keep its exchange rate fixed to the dollar and let its exchange rate be determined in the free market. This marked the end of the Bretton Woods system.

Exchange Rate Systems Today

Fixed exchange rates require governments to keep their inflation rates and interest rates within narrow bands or be overwhelmed by inflows or outflows of funds from the private sector. Today, the world is characterized by a mixture of fixed and flexible rates. Within Europe, for example, a number of countries—including Germany and France—maintain exchange rates with one another within narrow bands called target zones. This arrangement is known as the *exchange rate mechanism*. The United Kingdom participated in this arrangement for awhile but did not want to keep its interest rates in line with those of other countries. The major currencies of the world—the U.S. dollar, the German mark, and the Japanese yen—have their values determined against one another in the market.

The flexible exchange rate system has worked reasonably well since the breakdown of Bretton Woods. World trade has grown at a rapid rate. Moreover, the flexible exchange rate system managed to handle many diverse situations, including two major oil shocks, large U.S. budget deficits in the 1980s, and large current account surpluses by the Japanese. Many scholars find it difficult to imagine that Germany, the United States, and Japan could have maintained fixed exchange rates throughout all these periods.

In addition, during the Bretton Woods period, many countries placed restrictions on flows of financial capital, for example, by not allowing their residents to purchase foreign assets or by limiting purchases of domestic assets by foreigners. By the 1970s, however, these restrictions began to be eliminated and private-sector transactions in assets grew extremely rapidly. With massive amounts of funds being traded in financial markets, it becomes very difficult to fix or peg an exchange rate.

Nonetheless, countries whose economies are closely tied together might want the advantages of fixed exchange rates. One way to avoid some of the difficulties of fixing exchange rates between countries is to abolish individual currencies and establish a single currency. This is precisely the long-run plan for the major countries in Europe. Their stated goal is to have a single currency throughout Europe and a single central bank to control the supply of the currency. The common currency has been named the *euro*. With a single currency, European countries hope to capture the benefits of a large market such as within the United States.

However, achieving this goal will be difficult because economic conditions differ across the countries. As a precondition for adopting a single currency, the European countries have, under the Maastricht treaty, set strict conditions (known as *convergence conditions*) for inflation, deficits, and debt. In particular, a country's inflation cannot exceed that of the best three performing countries by more than 1.5%, its deficits cannot exceed 3% of GDP, and the total debt of its public sector must be less than 60% of GDP. The rationale for these conditions is that to sustain a common currency, countries must have similar underlying economic fundamentals.

Meeting these conditions will be difficult for many European countries. As of late 1996, only Luxembourg easily met the debt and deficit criteria, although France, Germany, and Finland were all close. However, a number of countries whose fiscal situations were more problematic appeared willing to cut their budget deficits to meet the conditions.

There is also a large psychological component that makes it difficult to join into a common currency. To many residents of Europe, abandoning their currency may seem like abandoning their culture, and many wonder whether a common currency is worth the sacrifice.

MANAGING FINANCIAL CRISES

Hardly a year goes by without some international financial crisis. In 1994, for example, Mexico experienced a particularly severe financial crisis. How do these crises originate and what policies can be taken to prevent or alleviate them?

Let's consider the Mexican case as an example. During the late 1980s and early 1990s, Mexico decided to fix or peg its exchange rate to the U.S. dollar. It chose to do so to signal to investors throughout the world that Mexico was serious about controlling inflation and would take the necessary steps to keep its inflation rates in line with the United States. Mexico also opened up its markets to let in foreign investors and seemed to be on a solid path to development.

However, in some sense the policies proved to be too successful in encouraging foreign investment. As funds poured into the country, the demand for goods increased and prices started to rise. This rise in prices caused an increase in Mexico's real exchange rate, and the rise in the real exchange rate caused a large trade deficit to emerge. From January 1988 to February 1994, the real exchange rate for Mexico with the United States (the price of Mexican goods relative to U.S. goods) increased by 67%.

Initially, this did not cause any difficulties for the Mexican government. Since foreign investors were willingly trading foreign currencies for Mexican pesos to buy Mexican securities, the government in Mexico did not have any problem maintaining its pegged exchange rate with the United States. Although the Mexicans were importing more than they were exporting, they could obtain the necessary dollars to finance this trade imbalance from foreign investors who were purchasing Mexican securities. The government did not have to intervene in the foreign exchange market to keep the price of the peso constant against the dollar. In other words, Mexico did not have a balance of payments deficit.

But then internal political difficulties arose in Mexico. Following an assassination of a political candidate and a rural uprising, foreign investors became nervous and started to pull some of their funds out of Mexico. At this point, the Mexican government made a crucial mistake. Instead of trying to reduce its trade deficit by taking steps to reduce prices, it allowed the trade deficit to continue. Moreover, both the government and the private-sector began to find that they had to borrow in dollars rather than in pesos, because foreign investors thought that Mexico might be forced to devalue the peso. If a devaluation did occur, any lender who lent in pesos would suffer a loss because the debt would be paid back at a lower exchange rate. Consequently, Mexican borrowers were forced to borrow in loans denominated in dollars.

Eventually, more political turmoil caused investors to pull out their funds, selling pesos for dollars. The Mexican central bank spent nearly $50 billion buying these pesos in an effort to keep the exchange rate constant. The $50 billion was not enough. Mexico literally ran out of dollars. Since it could no longer buy pesos to maintain the exchange rate, it had to devalue the peso to put it more in line with its market value.

The devaluation created even more turmoil because the government and the private-sector had borrowed billions in dollars. When the peso was devalued against the dollar, the burden of these debts measured in pesos increased sharply—more pesos were needed to pay the dollar-denominated debts. Mexico faced the prospect of massive bankruptcies and the potential collapse of its economy.

To prevent a financial collapse that could easily spread to many other developing countries throughout the world, the U.S. government (along with other international financial institutions) arranged for Mexico to borrow dollars with an extended period for repayment. This allowed Mexican banks and corporations to avoid bankruptcies and prevented a major disaster. In 1996 the Mexican government was able to pay off nearly three-fourths of the loan from the United States.

The Mexican example highlights many of the ingredients of a financial crisis. With our vast global capital markets, funds can move quickly from country to country and economic policies sometimes do not keep pace with changing political and economic developments. It can be extremely difficult to maintain a fixed exchange rate in this environment. The flow of funds, moreover, is often so large that financial failures could cause major global disruptions in trade and commerce. The major countries of the world are searching for institutions to assist in financial crises. Historically, the International Monetary Fund has played a key role in assisting countries that ran into financial difficulties. However, in the Mexico situation, the sums were so large that the United States was forced to take the lead in resolving this situation. The International Monetary Fund and other international financial institutions did assist in these efforts.

Not all sharp movements in currencies are the results of financial crises; some may be based on fundamentals. Consider the evidence in the Closer Look box "Was There a Conspiracy against the Ruble?"

As world capital markets continue to grow, there will be additional trials and tribulations. Governments throughout the world will almost surely be tested through new and often unpredictable financial crises. They will need to anticipate and react to rapid changes in the economic and political environment to maintain a stable financial environment for trade.

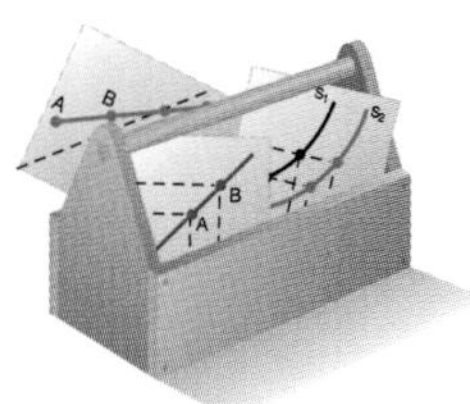

Using the **TOOLS**

In this chapter we developed several tools, including the demand and supply for foreign exchange and the real exchange rate. Take this opportunity to do your own economic analysis.

1. The Real Exchange Rate between Germany and the United States

Consider the following data for the United States and Germany:

	Germany GDP Deflator	*U.S. GDP Deflator*	*Market Exchange Rate*
1980	85.7	76.0	2.49 marks/dollar
1990	113.4	119.6	2.12 marks/dollar

A Closer **LOOK**

Was There a Conspiracy against the Ruble?

On a day in October 1994 that the Russians call "Black Tuesday," the Russian ruble fell 25% against the U.S. dollar. The President of Russia, Boris Yeltsin, blamed unnamed enemies and saboteurs and ordered the secret police to find out who was behind this devastating fall. Later, he fired key top officials.

But *was* this a dark conspiracy, or was there a simple explanation for the ruble's fall? Here are some facts. Although Russia had made some attempts to control its inflation, the inflation rate had increased just prior to Black Tuesday to a rate of about 8% a month or 150% a year. The Russian Central Bank had been increasing the money supply by making loans to state enterprises, and more inflation was inevitable. In prior weeks the government had been buying rubles to prop up their value, but even the government was wary of selling too many dollars for rubles. In case the ruble did fall against the dollar and the government had bought rubles, it would suffer a financial loss. As an economic detective, what do you think caused the fall in the ruble?

The fall in the ruble is not very mysterious given the underlying inflation in Russia, which sharply reduced demand for the currency. Perhaps it did not have to occur all in one day. But when markets sense weakness, they act quickly. Conspiracies in Russia are quite common, but inflation is a more plausible explanation for the drop of the ruble.

Was there a conspiracy lurking behind these St. Petersburg towers?

a. By what percent did the dollar depreciate against the mark over this period?

b. Using the formula for the real exchange rate,

$$\text{real exchange rate} = \frac{\text{exchange rate} \times \text{U.S. price level}}{\text{German price level}}$$

compute the real exchange rate for 1980 and 1990.

c. By how much did the real exchange rate change over this period? Compare your answer to part (a).

2. Exchange Rate Depreciation and the Returns from Investing

A newspaper headline said, "Foreign Investors Fear Dollar Depreciation: U.S. Interest Rates Rise."

a. Suppose you were a German citizen and had invested in a one-year U.S. bond that yielded 6%. The bond cost $1,000 and paid $1,060 at the end of the year. At the time you bought the bond, the exchange rate was 2 marks/dollar. How many marks did the bond cost? If the exchange rate remained at 2 marks/dollar when you received your payment, how many marks would you have? What would be your percentage return in marks for the year?

b. Suppose the dollar fell against the mark during the year from 2 marks to 1.5 marks/dollar. At the end of the year, how many marks would you have? What would be your percentage return in marks for the year?

c. Using your answers to parts (a) and (b), explain the newspaper headline.

3. Changes in Japanese Financial Policies

Until the early 1980s, Japan had required its large insurance companies to invest all their vast holdings in Japanese securities. At the prompting of the United States they relaxed the restrictions and allowed them to invest anywhere in the world, including the United States. What effect do you think this had on the exchange rate between the Japanese yen and the United States? On the trade balance between the two countries?

4. Pressures on the Bank of England

During the late 1980s, the United Kingdom had fixed exchange rates with other countries in Europe, including Germany. To fight inflationary pressures after East and West Germany were reunited, the German central bank raised interest rates sharply.

a. Let's figure out why the United Kingdom had to raise interest rates along with Germany. First, if it did not raise interest rates, what would investors do with their funds? Second, what effect would this movement of funds have had on the British pound? To prevent these changes in the British pound, what would the British central bank have had to do?

b. In fact, speculators in foreign exchange believed that the Bank of England would not be willing to raise interest rates. Why did speculators sell British pounds in massive amounts? Why did this force the British government to abandon its fixed exchange rates with Germany?

SUMMARY

In this chapter we examined the world of international finance. We saw how exchange rates are determined in markets and how governments can influence these markets. We also learned how the real exchange rate affects the trade deficit. Lying behind the often complex world of international financial transactions are a few simple ideas:

1. Exchange rates are determined in foreign exchange markets by supply and demand.
2. The real exchange rate—the market exchange rate adjusted for prices—is the relative price of a country's goods and services on world markets.
3. The current account is equal to net exports plus net income from existing investments abroad and net transfers from abroad. The capital account is minus the value of a country's net acquisition of foreign assets. The sum of the current account plus the capital account is zero.
4. Governments can attempt to change the value of currencies by buying or selling currencies in the foreign exchange market. Purchasing a currency will raise its value; selling a currency will decrease its value.
5. A system of fixed exchange rates can provide a better environment for business but requires that countries keep their inflation rates and interest rates within narrow limits.

KEY TERMS

appreciation, *664*
balance of payments deficit, *676*
balance of payments surplus, *677*
capital account, *672*
current account, *672*
depreciation, *665*
devaluation, *677*
exchange rate, *664*
fixed exchange rates, *676*
flexible exchange rates, *677*
foreign exchange market intervention, *674*
law of one price, *670*
multilateral real exchange rate, *669*
net international investment position, *673*
purchasing power parity, *671*
real exchange rate, *668*
revaluation, *677*

PROBLEMS AND DISCUSSION QUESTIONS

1. Consider the market for British pound. What are the sources of demand for British pounds and what are the sources of supply for British pounds?
2. How would decreases in U.S. interest rates and increases in U.S. prices affect the value of the dollar?
3. Why do economists use the real exchange rate, as opposed to the market or nominal exchange rate, to measure how expensive a country's goods and services are on world markets?
4. Suppose the newspapers report that the U.S. Treasury has increased its holdings of foreign currencies from last year. What does this tell you about the foreign exchange policies that the United States had engaged in during the year?
5. What would be necessary for the countries of the world to resume globally fixed exchange rates? Do you think it is feasible in the near future?
6. Why did Mexican inflation lead to a rise in Mexico's real exchange rate with the United States?
7. Explain why apartments rent for different prices around the globe while gold sells for a single price (measured in a common currency).

Take It to the Net

We invite you to visit the O'Sullivan/Sheffrin page on the Prentice Hall Web site at:

http://www.prenhall.com/osullivan/

for this chapter's World Wide Web exercise.

MODEL ANSWERS FOR THIS CHAPTER

Chapter-Opening Questions

1. An increase in U.S. interest rates will raise the value of the dollar against the German mark. This will decrease the cost of a summer trip to Europe.
2. If the dollar increases in value against the Japanese yen, it will make our exports more expensive and Japanese imports less expensive. This will reduce our trade balance with Japan.
3. Governments intervene in the market for foreign exchange because they prefer to have a different exchange rate than the one that would come from pure market transactions.
4. Some European countries are considering a single currency because they feel it would reduce the costs of trade by creating a single large market with no worries of exchange rate changes.
5. Financial crises emerge when private investors suddenly wish to withdraw funds from a country and the governments do not take the appropriate action to facilitate this adjustment.

Test Your Understanding

1. Dollar will appreciate.
2. Dollar will depreciate.

3. Dollar will depreciate.
4. Dollar will depreciate.
5. The nominal exchange rate is the market exchange rate; the real exchange rate controls for the level of prices.
6. a. It will lower the real exchange rate.
   b. It will raise the real exchange rate.
   c. It will lower the real exchange rate.

Using the Tools

1. The Real Exchange Rate between Germany and the United States
   a. The dollar fell by 14.8% [(2.12 – 2.49)/2.49 = –0 .148].
   b. The real exchange rate increased from 2.208 to 2.236.
   c. Although the dollar depreciated, prices rose more in the United States than in Germany, so that the real exchange rate actually increased.
2. Exchange Rate Depreciation and the Returns from Investing
   a. At 2 marks/dollar, the bond costs 2,000 marks and pays 2,120 marks, for a 6% return.
   b. If the dollar fell to 1.5 marks/dollar, at the end of the year you would only have (1,060)(1.5) = 1,590 marks and your return on your 2,000-mark investment would be –20.5%.
   c. If the dollar falls, returns measured in marks will decrease and foreign investors will find dollar investments less attractive. To keep investors from withdrawing funds from the United States, interest rates would have to increase.
3. Changes in Japanese Financial Policies

   Japanese insurance companies began to buy U.S. assets, which bid up the value of the dollar. The appreciation of the dollar contributed to a decrease in our net exports to Japan.
4. Pressures on the Bank of England
   a. If the British did not raise interest rates, investors would have sold British securities to buy German securities. This would have depreciated the pound. The British government would have been forced to sell marks for pounds, decreasing the money supply and raising British interest rates.
   b. If speculators believed that Britain would not do this, the British pound would fall against the mark. To profit from this, speculators would sell pounds and buy German marks. The massive selling of pounds would put further pressure on the British and require either massive purchases of pounds and even higher interest rates. The British were not willing to do this and let the pound's value be determined in the market.

GLOSSARY

Absolute advantage The ability of one person or nation to produce a particular good at a lower absolute cost than that of another person or nation.

Accelerator theory The theory of investment that emphasizes that current investment spending depends positively on the expected future growth of real GDP.

Accounting profit Total revenue minus explicit costs.

Adverse-selection problem The uninformed side of the market must choose from an undesirable or adverse selection of goods.

Aggregate demand The relationship between the level of prices and the quantity of real GDP demanded.

Aggregate demand curve The relationship between the price level and the quantity of real GDP demanded.

Aggregate production function Shows how much output is produced from capital and labor.

Aggregate supply The relationship between the level of prices and the quantity of output supplied.

Aid to Families with Dependent Children (AFDC) A government poverty program that provides assistance to families with children under the age of 18.

Anticipated inflation Inflation that is expected.

Appreciation A rise in the exchange rate or an increase in the value of a currency.

Asian Pacific Economic Cooperation (APEC) organization An organization of 18 Asian nations that attempts to reduce trade barriers between their nations.

Assets The uses of the funds of a financial institution.

Asymmetric information One side of the market—either buyers or sellers—has better information about the good than the other.

Autarky A situation in which each country is self-sufficient, so there is no trade.

Automatic stabilizers The changes in taxes and transfer payments that occur automatically as economic activity changes. These changes in taxes and transfers dampen economic fluctuations.

Autonomous consumption The part of consumption that does not depend on income.

Average-cost pricing policy A regulatory policy under which the government picks the point on the demand curve at which price equals average cost.

Average fixed cost (AFC) Fixed cost divided by the quantity produced.

Balanced budget The situation when total expenditures equals total revenues.

Balance of payments deficit Under a fixed exchange rate system, a situation in which the supply of a country's currency exceeds the demand for the currency at the current exchange rate.

Balance of payments surplus Under a fixed exchange rate system, a situation in which the demand for a country's currency exceeds the supply of the currency at the current exchange rate.

Balance sheet An account for a bank which shows the sources of its funds (liabilities) as well as the uses for the funds (assets).

Barter Trading goods directly for other goods.

Benefit-tax approach The idea that a person's tax liability should depend on how much he or she benefits from government programs.

Board of Governors of the Federal Reserve The seven-person governing body of the Federal Reserve system in Washington, DC.

Bond A promise or IOU to pay money in the future in exchange for money now.

Budget deficit The difference between a government's spending and its revenues from taxation.

Budget line The line connecting all the combinations of two goods that exhaust a consumer's budget.

Budget set A set of points that includes all the combinations of two goods that a consumer can afford, given the consumer's income and the prices of the two goods.

Business cycles Another name for economic fluctuations.

Capital The buildings, machines, and equipment used in production.

Capital account Minus the value of country's net acquisition (purchases less sales) of foreign assets. A purchase of a foreign asset is a deficit item on the capital account while a sale of a domestic asset is a surplus item.

Capital budgets Budgets for long-term investments.

Capital deepening Increases in the stock of capital per worker.

Carbon tax A tax based on a fuel's carbon content.

Cartel A group of firms that coordinate their pricing decisions, often by charging the same price.

Central bank A banker's bank; an official bank that controls the supply of money in a country.

Centrally planned economy An economy in which a government bureaucracy decides how much of each good to produce, how to produce the goods, and how to allocate the products among consumers.

Ceteris paribus Latin for "other variables are held fixed."

Chain index A method for calculating the growth in real GDP or the chain-type price index for GDP that uses data from neighboring years.

Chain-type price index for GDP A measure of the average level of prices of the goods and services contained in GDP.

Change in demand A change in quantity resulting from a change in something other than the price of the good; causes the entire demand curve to shift.

Change in quantity demanded A change in quantity resulting from a change in the price of the good; causes movement along a demand curve.

Change in quantity supplied A change in quantity resulting from a change in the price of the good; causes movement along a supply curve.

Change in supply A change in quantity resulting from a change in something other than the price of the good; causes the entire supply curve to shift.

Classical aggregate supply curve A vertical aggregate supply curve. It reflects the idea that in the long run, output is determined solely by the factors of production.

Classical economics The study of the economy when it operates at or near full employment.

Closed economy An economy without international trade.

Command-and-control policy A pollution-control policy under which the government commands each firm to produce no more than a certain volume of pollution and controls the firm's production process by forcing the firm to use a particular pollution-control technology.

Community rating In a given community or metropolitan area, every firm pays the same price for medical insurance.

Comparable worth A policy under which the government specifies a minimum wage for some occupations.

Comparative advantage The ability of one person or nation to produce a good at an opportunity cost that is lower than the opportunity cost of another person or nation.

Complements Two goods for which an increase in the price of one good decreases the demand for the other good.

Concentration ratio A measure of the degree of concentration in a market; the four-firm concentration ratio is the percentage of output produced by the four largest firms.

Constant-cost industry An industry in which the average cost of production is constant, so the long-run supply curve is horizontal.

Consumer Price Index (CPI) A price index that measures the cost of a fixed basket of goods chosen to represent the consumption pattern of individuals.

Consumer surplus The difference between the maximum amount a consumer is willing to pay for a product and the price the consumer pays for the product.

Consumption expenditures Purchases of newly produced goods and services by households.

Consumption function The relationship between the level of income and consumption spending.

Consumption possibilities curve A curve showing the combinations of two goods that can be consumed when a nation specializes in a particular good and trades with another nation.

Contestable market A market in which the costs of entering and leaving are very low, so the firms in the market are constantly threatened by the entry of new firms.

Contractionary policies Policies that aim to decrease the level of GDP.

Convergence The process by which poorer countries "catch up" with richer countries in terms of real GDP per capita.

Corporate or government bond A promissory note issued by a corporation or a government when it borrows money.

Corporate stock A certificate that reflects ownership in a corporation and gives the holder the right to receive a fraction of the corporation's profit.

Corporation A legal entity that is owned by people who purchase stock in the corporation.

Cost-of-living adjustments Automatic increases in wages or other payments that are tied to a price index.

Craft union A labor organization that includes workers from a particular occupation, for example, plumbers, bakers, or electricians.

Creative destruction The process by which competition for monopoly profits leads to technological progress.

Credit rationing The practice of limiting the amount of credit available to individual borrowers.

Cross elasticity of demand A measure of the responsiveness of the quantity demanded to changes in the price of a related good; computed by dividing the percentage change in the quantity demanded of one good (X) by the percentage change in the price of another good (Y).

Crowding in The increase of investment (or other component of GDP) in the long run caused by a decrease in government spending.

Crowding out Reductions in consumption, investment, or net exports caused by an increase in government purchases.

Current account The sum of net exports (exports minus imports), net income received from investments abroad, and net transfers from abroad.

Cyclical unemployment The component of unemployment that accompanies fluctuations in real GDP.

Deadweight loss from taxation The difference between the total burden of a tax and the amount of revenue collected by the government.

Decreasing-cost industry An industry in which the average cost of production decreases as the industry grows.

Deficit The excess of total expenditures over total revenues.

Demand curve A curve showing the relationship between price and the quantity that consumers are willing to buy during a particular time period.

Demand curve for loanable funds A curve that shows the relationship between the interest rate and the quantity of loanable funds demanded by borrowers.

Dependency ratio The ratio of the population over 65 years of age to the population between 20 and 65.

Depreciation A fall in the exchange rate or a decrease in the value of a currency.

Depression The common name for a severe recession.

Derived demand The demand for an input such as labor is derived from the demand for the final product.

Devaluation A decrease in the exchange rate to which a currency is pegged in a fixed rate system.

Diminishing returns As one input increases while the other inputs are held fixed, output increases but at a decreasing rate.

Discount rate The interest rate at which banks can borrow from the Fed.

Discouraged workers Workers who left the labor force because they could not find jobs.

Diseconomies of scale A situation in which an increase in the quantity produced increases the long-run average cost of production.

Disposable personal income The income that ultimately flows back to households, taking into account transfers and taxes.

Dividends The part of a corporation's profit paid to stockholders.

Dominant strategy An action that is the best choice under all circumstances.

Double coincidence of wants The problem in a system of barter that one person may not have what the other desires.

Dumping A situation in which the price a firm charges in a foreign market is lower than either the price it charges in its home market or the production cost.

Duopolists' dilemma A situation in which both firms would be better off if they chose a high price but each chooses a low price.

Durable goods Goods that last for a long period of time, such as household appliances.

Earned income tax credit (EITC) A tax subsidy given to low-wage workers.

Econometric models Statistical-based computer models that economists build to capture the actual dynamics of the economy.

Economic cost The sum of explicit and implicit costs.

Economic fluctuations Movements of GDP above or below normal trends.

Economic growth Sustained increases in the real production of an economy over a period of time.

Economic profit Total revenue minus the total economic cost (the sum of explicit and implicit costs).

Economics The study of the choices made by people who are faced with scarcity.

Economies of scale A situation in which an increase in the quantity produced decreases the long-run average cost of production.

Efficient market A market in which there are no additional transactions that would benefit a buyer, a seller, and any third parties affected by the transactions.

Entrepreneur A person who has an idea for a business and coordinates the production and sale of goods and services, taking risks in the process.

Entrepreneurship Effort used to coordinate the production and sale of goods and services.

Entry deterrence A scheme under which a firm increases its output and accepts a lower price to deter other firms from entering the market.

Equilibrium output The level of GDP at which the demand for output equals the amount that is produced.

European Union (EU) An organization of European nations that has reduced trade barriers within Europe.

Excess burden The difference between the total burden of a tax and the amount of revenue collected by the government.

Excess reserves Any additional reserves that a bank holds above required reserves.

Exchange rate The rate at which one currency trades for another in the market.

Expansionary policies Policies that aim to increase the level of GDP.

Expectations of inflation The beliefs held by the public about the likely path of inflation for the future.

Expectations Phillips curve The relationship that describes the link between inflation and unemployment taking into account expectations of inflation.

Expected real interest rate The nominal interest rate minus the expected inflation rate.

Experience rating Each firm pays a different price for medical insurance, depending on the past medical bills of the firm's employees.

Explicit costs The firm's actual cash payments for its inputs.

Export A good produced in the "home" country (for example, the United States) and sold in another country.

External benefit Another term for spillover benefit.

External cost The part of production cost that is external to the organization that decides how much of a particular good to produce.

Factors of production Labor and capital used to produce output.

Family A group of two or more individuals related by birth, marriage, or adoption who live in the same housing unit.

Federal funds market The market in which banks borrow and lend reserves to one another.

Federal Open Market Committee (FOMC) The group that decides on monetary policy and consists of the seven members of the Board of Governors plus five of 12 regional bank presidents on a rotating basis.

Federal Reserve Banks One of 12 regional banks that are an official part of the Federal Reserve System.

Financial intermediaries Organizations that receive funds from savers and channel them to investors.

Firm's short-run supply curve A curve showing the relationship between price and the quantity of output supplied by a firm.

Fiscal year The calendar on which the federal government conducts its business, which runs from October 1 to September 30.

Fixed cost Costs that do not depend on the quantity produced.

Fixed exchange rates A system in which governments peg exchange rates.

Flexible exchange rates A currency system in which exchange rates are determined by free markets.

Focal points Obvious points of agreement in bargaining situations.

Foreign exchange market A market in which people exchange one currency for another.

Foreign exchange market intervention The purchase or sale of currencies by governments to influence the market exchange rate.

Franchise or licensing scheme A policy under which the government picks a single firm to sell a particular good.

Free-rider problem Each person will try to get the benefit of a public good without paying for it, trying to get a free ride at the expense of others.

Frictional unemployment The part of unemployment associated with the normal workings of the economy, such as searching for jobs.

Full employment The level of employment that occurs when the unemployment rate is at the natural rate.

Full-employment deficit An estimate of what the federal budget deficit would be if the economy were operating at full employment.

Full-employment or potential output The level of output that results when the labor market is in equilibrium.

Futures markets A market in which contracts are bought or sold for the future delivery of commodities at a price to be set now.

Game tree A visual representation of the consequences of different strategies.

General Agreement on Tariffs and Trade (GATT) An international agreement that has lowered trade barriers between the United States and other nations.

Generational accounting Methods that assign the tax burden of government debt and other programs to different generations.

Government debt The total of all past deficits.

Government expenditure Spending on goods and services plus transfer payments.

Government failure A situation in which the government fails to make an efficient choice in providing public goods or subsidies.

Government purchases Purchases of newly produced goods and services by all levels of government.

Grim trigger A strategy under which a firm responds to underpricing by choosing a price so low that each firm makes zero economic profit.

Gross domestic product (GDP) The total market value of all the final goods and services produced within an economy in a given year.

Gross investment Actual investment purchases.

Gross national product (GNP) GDP plus net income earned abroad.

Growth accounting A method to determine the contribution to economic growth from increased capital, labor, and technological progress.

Growth factor 1 plus the growth rate.

Growth rate The percentage rate of change of a variable.

Growth version of the quantity equation An equation that links the growth rates of money, velocity, prices, and real output.

Guaranteed price matching A scheme under which a firm guarantees that it will match a lower price by a competitor; also known as a meet-the-competition policy.

Horizontal equity The notion that people in similar economic circumstances should pay similar taxes.

Household A group of related family members and unrelated individuals who live in the same housing unit.

Human capital The knowledge and skills acquired by a worker through education and experience and used to produce goods and services.

Hyperinflation An inflation rate exceeding 50% per month.

Imperfectly competitive market A market in which firms are large enough that they affect market prices.

Implicit costs The opportunity cost of nonpurchased inputs.

Import A good produced in a foreign country and purchased by residents of the "home" country (for example, the United States).

Import quota A limit on the amount of a good that can be imported.

Import restriction A law that prohibits the importation of a particular good.

Income effect The change in consumption resulting from an increase in the consumer's real income.

Income elasticity of demand A measure of the responsiveness of the quantity demanded to changes in consumer income; computed by dividing the percentage change in the quantity demanded by the percentage change in income.

Increasing-cost industry An industry in which the average cost of production increases as the industry grows, so the long-run supply curve is positively sloped.

Indifference curve A curve showing the combinations of two goods that generate the same level of utility or satisfaction.

Indirect taxes Sales and excise taxes.

Individual demand curve A curve that shows the relationship between the price of a good and the quantity that a single consumer is willing to buy (the quantity demanded).

Indivisible input An input that cannot be scaled down to produce a small quantity of output.

Industrial union A labor organization that includes all types of workers from a single industry, for example, steelworkers or autoworkers.

Inefficient market A market in which there is an additional transaction that would benefit a buyer, a seller, and any third parties affected by the transaction.

Infant industry A new industry that is protected from foreign competitors.

Inferior good A good for which an increase in income decreases demand.

Inflation The percentage rate of change of the price level in the economy.

Input-substitution effect The change in the quantity of labor demanded resulting from a change in the relative cost of labor.

Insecure monopoly A monopoly faced with the possibility that a second firm will enter the market.

Inside lags Lags in implementing policy.

Interest rate The amount of money paid for the use of a dollar for a year.

Intermediate good Goods used in the production process that are not final goods or services.

Invisible hand The term that economists use to describe how the price system can efficiently coordinate economic activity without central government intervention.

Keynesian aggregate supply curve A horizontal aggregate supply curve. It reflects the idea that prices are sticky in the short run and that firms adjust production to meet demand.

Keynesian economics Models in which demand determines output in the short run.

Keynesian fiscal policy The use of taxes and government spending to affect the level of GDP in the short run.

Kinked demand model A model under which firms in an oligopoly match price reductions by other firms but do not match price increases.

Labor Human effort used to produce goods and services, including both physical and mental effort.

Labor force The employed plus the unemployed.

Labor-force participation rate The fraction of the population over 16 years of age that is in the labor force.

Labor productivity The amount of output produced per worker.

Labor union An organized group of workers, the main objective of which is to improve working conditions, wages, and fringe benefits.

Laffer curve A relationship between tax rates and tax revenues that illustrates that high tax rates may not always lead to high tax revenues if high tax rates discourage economic activity.

Law of demand The lower the price, the larger the quantity demanded.

Law of diminishing marginal utility As the consumption of a particular good increases, marginal utility decreases.

Law of one price The theory that goods which are easily tradeable across countries should sell at the same price expressed in a common currency.

Law of supply The higher the price, the larger the quantity supplied.

Learning by doing The knowledge gained during production that increases productivity.

Learning effect The increase in a person's wage resulting from the learning of skills required for certain occupations.

Lender of last resort A name given to policies of central banks that provide loans to banks in emergency situations.

Liabilities The sources of external funds of a financial intermediary.

Licensing or franchise scheme A policy under which the government picks a single firm to sell a particular good.

Liquid Easily convertible to money on short notice.

Liquidity demand for money The demand for money that arises so that individuals or firms can make purchases on short notice without incurring excessive costs.

Long run A period of time long enough that a firm can change all the factors of production, meaning that a firm can modify its existing production facility or build a new one.

Long-run average cost (LAC) Total cost divided by the quantity of output when the firm can choose a production facility of any size.

Long-run demand curve for labor A curve showing the relationship between the wage and the quantity of labor demanded in the long run.

Long-run neutrality of money An increase in the supply of money has no effect on real interest rates, investment, or output in the long run.

Long-run supply curve A curve showing the relationship between price and quantity supplied in the long run.

M1 The sum of currency in the hands of the public, demand deposits, and other checkable deposits.

M2 M1 plus other assets, including deposits in savings and loans and money market mutual funds.

Macroeconomics The branch of economics that looks at the economy as a whole.

Managed competition A health system in which organizations such as HMOs compete for patients.

Mandate A requirement imposed by government on lower levels of government or on the private sector.

Marginal benefit The extra benefit resulting from a small increase in some activity.

Marginal cost The additional cost resulting from a small increase in some activity.

Marginal product of labor The change in output per unit change in labor.

Marginal propensity to consume (MPC) The fraction of additional income that is spent.

Marginal propensity to import The fraction of additional income that is spent on imports.

Marginal propensity to save (MPS) The fraction of additional income that is saved.

Marginal rate of substitution (MRS) The rate at which a consumer is willing to substitute one good for another.

Marginal revenue product of labor (MRP) The extra revenue generated from 1 more unit of labor; equal to price of output times the marginal product of labor.

Marginal utility The change in utility from one additional unit of the good.

Market An arrangement that allows buyers and sellers to exchange things. A buyer exchanges money for a product, while a seller exchanges a product for money.

Market equilibrium A situation in which the quantity of a product demanded equals the quantity supplied, so there is no pressure to change the price.

Market for loanable funds A market in which savers (the suppliers of funds) and borrowers (the demanders of funds) interact to determine the equilibrium interest rate (the price of loanable funds).

Market supply curve for labor A curve showing the relationship between the wage and the quantity of labor supplied.

Market system A system under which individuals and firms use markets to facilitate the exchange of money and products.

Marketable pollution permits system A system under which the government picks a target pollution level for a particular area, issues just enough pollution permits to meet the pollution target, and allows firms to buy and sell the permits.

Median-voter rule A rule suggesting that the choices made by government will reflect the preferences of the median voter.

Medicaid A program that provides medical services to the poor.

Medicare A government program that provides health benefits to those over 65 years of age.

Medium of exchange The property of money that exchanges are made using money.

Menu costs Costs of inflation that arise from actually changing prices.

Merger A process in which two or more firms combine their operations.

Microeconomics The study of the choices made by consumers, firms, and government, and how these decisions affect the market for a particular good or service.

Minimum efficient scale The output at which the long-run average cost curve becomes horizontal.

Mixed economy An economic system under which government plays an important role, including the regulation of markets, where most economic decisions are made.

Monetarists Economists who emphasize the role of money in determining nominal income and inflation.

Monetary policy The range of actions taken by the Federal Reserve to influence the level of GDP or the rate of inflation

Monetizing the deficit Purchases by a central bank of newly issued government bonds.

Money Anything that is regularly used in exchange.

Money illusion Confusion of real and nominal magnitudes.

Money multiplier An initial deposit leads to a multiple expansion of deposits. In the simplified case increase in deposits = (initial deposit) ÷ (1/reserve ratio).

Monopolistic competition A situation in which each firm has a monopoly in selling its own differentiated product, but competes with firms selling similar products.

Monopoly A market in which a single firm serves the entire market.

Monopsony A market in which there is a single buyer of an input.

Multilateral real exchange rate An index of the real exchange rate with a country's trading partners.

Multinational corporation An organization that produces and sells goods and services throughout the world.

Multiplier The ratio of changes in output to changes in spending. It measures the degree to which changes in spending are "multiplied" into changes in output.

Multiplier-accelerator model A model in which a downturn in real GDP leads to a sharp fall in investment, which, in turn, triggers further reductions in GDP through the multiplier.

National income Net national product less indirect taxes.

Natural monopoly A market in which there are large economies of scale, so a single firm will be profitable but a pair of firms would lose money.

Natural rate of unemployment The level of unemployment at which there is no cyclical unemployment.

Natural resources Things created by acts of nature and used to produce goods and services.

Negative relationship A relationship in which an increase in the value of one variable decreases the value of the other variable.

Neoclassical theory of investment A theory of investment that emphasizes the role of real interest rates and taxes.

Net exports Exports minus imports.

Net international investment position Domestic holdings of foreign assets minus foreign holdings of domestic assets.

Net investment Gross investment minus depreciation.

Net national product (NNP) GNP less depreciation.

Net worth The difference between assets and liabilities.

Nominal GDP The value of GDP in current dollars.

Nominal interest rates Interest rates that are quoted in the market.

Nominal value The face value of a sum of money.

Nondurable goods Goods that last for short periods of time, such as food.

Normal accounting profit An accounting profit equal to the firm's implicit costs.

Normal good A good for which an increase in income increases demand.

North American Free Trade Agreement (NAFTA) An international agreement that lowers barriers to trade between the United States, Mexico, and Canada (signed in 1994).

Oligopoly A market served by a few firms.

Open economy An economy with international trade.

Open market purchases The purchase of government bonds by the Fed, which increases the money supply.

Open market sales Sales of government bonds to the public, which decreases the money supply.

Operating budgets Budgets for day-to-day expenditures.

Output effect The change in the quantity of labor demanded resulting from a change in the quantity of output.

Outside lags The time it takes for policies to work.

Patent The exclusive right to sell a particular good for some period of time.

Pay-as-you-go A retirement system that pay benefits to the old with taxes currently levied on the young.

Peak The time at which a recession begins.

Perfectly competitive market A market with a very large number of firms, each of which produces the same standardized product and is so small that it does not affect the market price of the good it produces.

Permanent income An estimate of a household's long-run average level of income.

Personal disposable income Personal income after taxes.

Personal income Income (including transfer payments) that is received by households.

Physical capital Objects made by human beings and used to produce goods and services.

Political business cycle The effects on the economy of using monetary or fiscal policy to stimulate the economy before an election to improve reelection prospects.

Pollution tax A tax or charge equal to the spillover cost per unit of waste.

Positive relationship A relationship in which an increase in the value of one variable increases the value of the other variable.

Potential or full-employment output The level of output that results when the labor market is in equilibrium.

Poverty budget The minimum amount the government estimates that a family needs to avoid being in poverty.

Predatory pricing A pricing scheme under which a firm decreases its price to drive a rival out of business, and increases the price when the other firm disappears.

Present value The maximum amount a person is willing to pay today for a payment to be received in the future.

Price ceiling A maximum price; transactions above the maximum price are outlawed.

Price discrimination The process under which a firm divides consumers into two or more groups and picks a different price for each group.

Price elasticity of demand A measure of the responsiveness of the quantity demanded to changes in price; computed by dividing the percentage change in quantity demanded by the percentage change in price.

Price elasticity of supply A measure of the responsiveness of the quantity supplied to changes in price; computed by dividing the percentage change in quantity supplied by the percentage change in price.

Price fixing An arrangement in which two firms coordinate their pricing decisions.

Price floor A minimum price; transactions below the minimum price are outlawed.

Price leadership An arrangement under which one firm sets a price and other firms in the market match the leader's price.

Price level An average of all the prices in the economy.

Price-support program A policy under which the government specifies a minimum price above the equilibrium price.

Prime rate of interest The rate of interest that large banks charge to their best customers on short-term loans.

Principle A simple truth that most people understand and accept.

Private good A good that is consumed by a single person or household.

Private investment expenditures Purchases of newly produced goods and services by firms.

Privatizing The process of selling state firms to individuals.

Procyclical A component of GDP is procyclical if it rises and falls with the overall level of GDP.

Producer surplus The difference between the market price of a product and the minimum amount a producer is willing to accept for that product; alternatively, the difference between the market price and the marginal cost of production.

Production possibilities curve A curve that shows the possible combinations of goods and services available to an economy, given that all productive resources are fully employed and efficiently utilized.

Public choice A field of economics that explores how governments actually operate.

Public good A good that is available for everyone to consume, regardless of who pays and who doesn't.

Purchasing Power Parity A theory of exchange rates that states that the exchange rate between two currencies is determined by the price levels in the two countries.

Q-theory of investment The theory of investment that links investment spending to stock prices.

Quantity equation The equation that links money, velocity, prices and real output. In symbols, we have $M \times V = P \times y$.

Rational expectations The economic theory that analyzes how people form expectations in such a manner that, on average, they forecast the future correctly.

Real business cycle theory The economic theory that emphasizes the role of technology shocks as a cause of economic fluctuations.

Real exchange rate The market exchange rate adjusted for prices.

Real GDP A measure of GDP that controls for changes in prices.

Real GDP per capita Inflation-adjusted gross domestic product per person. It is the usual measure of living standards across time and between countries.

Real income Consumer's income measured in terms of the goods it can buy.

Real interest rate The nominal interest rate minus the actual inflation rate.

Real price The nominal price of a product adjusted for inflation.

Real value The value of a sum of money in terms of the quantity of goods the money can buy.

Real wage rate The wage rate paid to workers adjusted for inflation.

Real wages Nominal or dollar wages adjusted for changes in purchasing power.

Recession Six consecutive months of negative economic growth.

Rent control A policy under which the government specifies a maximum rent that is below the equilibrium rent.

Rent seeking The process under which a firm spends money to persuade the government to erect barriers to entry and pick the firm as the monopolist.

Required reserves The reserves that banks are required to hold by law against their deposits.

Reserve ratio The ratio of reserves to deposits.

Reserves The fraction of their deposits that banks set aside in either vault cash or as deposits at the Federal Reserve.

Revaluation An increase in the exchange rate to which a currency is pegged.

Ricardian equivalence The proposition that it does not matter whether government expenditure is financed by taxes or by debt.

Saving Total income minus consumption.

Scarcity A situation in which resources are limited and can be used in different ways, so we must sacrifice one thing for another.

Screening or signaling effect The increase in a person's wage resulting from the signal of productivity provided by completing college.

Services Reflect work done in which people play a prominent role in delivery, ranging from haircutting to health care.

Servicing the debt Paying interest on existing debt.

Shoe-leather costs Costs of inflation that arise from trying to reduce holdings of cash.

Short run A period of time over which one or more factors of production is fixed; in most cases, a period of time over which a firm cannot modify an existing facility or build a new one.

Short-run average total cost (SATC) Short-run total cost divided by the quantity of output.

Short-run average variable cost (SAVC) Variable cost divided by the quantity produced.

Short-run demand curve for labor A curve showing the relationship between the wage and the quantity of labor demanded in the short run.

Short run in macroeconomics The period of time that prices are fixed.

Short-run marginal cost (SMC) The change in total cost resulting from a 1-unit increase in output from an existing production facility.

Short-run marginal cost curve A curve showing the change in cost from producing just one more unit of output in an existing facility.

Short-run market supply curve A curve showing the relationship between price and the quantity of output supplied by an entire industry in the short run.

Short-run production function Shows how much output is produced from varying amounts of labor, holding the capital stock constant.

Shortage A situation in which consumers are willing to buy more than producers are willing to sell.

Shut-down price The price at which the firm is indifferent between operating and shutting down.

Signaling or screening effect The increase in a person's wage resulting from the signal of productivity provided by completing college.

Slope The change in the variable on the vertical axis resulting from a one-unit increase in the variable on the horizontal axis.

Social insurance A system that compensates individuals for bad luck, low skills, or misfortune.

Social Security A government program that provides retirement, survivor, and disability benefits.

Speculative demand for money The demand for money that arises because holding money over short periods is less risky than holding stocks or bonds.

Spillover A cost or benefit experienced by people who are external to the decision about how much of a good to produce or consume.

Stabilization policy Policy actions taken to move the economy closer to full employment or potential output.

Stock of capital The total of all the machines, equipment, and buildings in the entire economy.

Store of value The property of money that value is preserved between transactions.

Structural deficit Another term for the full-employment deficit.

Structural unemployment The part of unemployment that results from the mismatch of skills and jobs.

Substitutes Two goods for which an increase in the price of one good increases the demand for the other good.

Substitution effect The change in consumption resulting from a change in the price of one good relative to the price of other goods.

Sunk cost The cost a firm has already paid—or has agreed to pay some time in the future.

Supplemental Security Income (SSI) A special program for the aged, the blind, and the permanently disabled.

Supply curve A curve showing the relationship between price and the quantity that producers are willing to sell during a particular time period.

Supply curve for loanable funds A curve that shows the relationship between the interest rate and the quantity of loanable funds supplied by savers.

Supply shocks External events that shift the aggregate supply curve.

Supply-side economics The school of thought that emphasizes the importance of taxation for influencing economic activity.

Supply-siders Economists who believe that taxes have strong adverse affects on the economy.

Surplus A situation in which producers are willing to sell more than consumers are willing to buy.

Tariff A tax on an imported good.

Taxi medallion A license to operate a taxi.

Technological progress An increase in output without increasing inputs.

Terms of trade The rate at which two goods will be exchanged.

Thin market A market in which some high-quality goods are sold, but fewer than would be sold in a market with perfect information.

Tit-for-tat A strategy under which the one firm starts out with the cartel price and then chooses whatever price the other firm chose in the preceding period.

Total revenue The money the firm gets by selling its product; equal to the price times the quantity sold.

Total value of a market The sum of the net benefits experienced by consumers and producers; equal to the sum of consumer surplus and producer surplus.

Trade barriers Rules that restrict the free flow of goods between nations, including tariffs (taxes on imports), quotas (limits on total imports) voluntary export restraints (agreements between governments to limit imports), and nontariff trade barriers (subtle practices that hinder trade).

Trade deficit The excess of imports over exports.

Trade surplus The excess of exports over imports.

Transactions demand for money The demand for money based on the desire to facilitate transactions.

Transfer payments Payments to individuals from governments that do not correspond to the production of goods and services.

Transition The process of shifting from a centrally planned economy toward a mixed economic system, with markets playing a greater role in the economy.

Trough The time at which output stops falling in a recession.

Trust An arrangement under which the owners of several companies transfer their decision-making powers to a small group of trustees, who then make decisions for all the firms in the trust.

Twin deficits The association between increases in the federal budget deficit and the trade deficit.

Unanticipated inflation Inflation that is not expected.

Underemployed Workers who hold a part-time job but prefer to work full time or hold jobs that are far below their capabilities.

Underground economy Economic activity that should be in the GDP accounts but does not show up because the activity is either illegal or unreported.

Unemployed People who are looking for work but do not have jobs.

Unemployment insurance Payments received from the government upon becoming unemployed.

Unemployment rate The fraction of the labor force that is unemployed.

Unit of account The property of money that prices are quoted in terms of money.

Usury laws Laws that do not allow interest rates to exceed specified ceilings.

Utility The satisfaction or pleasure the consumer experiences when he or she consumes a good, measured as the number of utils.

Utility-maximizing rule Pick the affordable combination of consumer goods that makes the marginal utility per dollar spent on one good equal to that of a second good.

Value added The sum of all the income (wages, interest, profits, rent) generated by an organization.

Variable A measure of something that can take on different values.

Variable costs Costs that vary as the firm changes its output.

Velocity of money Nominal GDP divided by the money supply. It is also the rate at which money turns over during the year.

Vertical equity The notion that people with higher income or wealth should pay higher taxes.

Voluntary export restraint (VER) A scheme under which an exporting country "voluntarily" decreases its exports.

Wage–price spiral The process by which changes in wages and prices reinforce each other.

Wealth effect The increase in spending that occurs because the real value of money increases when the price level falls.

World Trade Organization (WTO) An organization that oversees GATT and other international trade agreements.

Worldwide sourcing The practice of buying components for a product from nations throughout the world.

Solutions to Selected Problems and Discussion Questions

Chapter 1

1. Buying a used car: It is difficult to determine the quality of the car. Providing health insurance: It is difficult to determine whether the customer will have large or small medical expenses.
3. The fixed variables are the number of lectures attended and the hours of sleep the night before the exam.
5. move along; shift

Appendix to Chapter 1

1. a. See Figure A.
   b. The slope is 5.
   c. The monthly bill will increase by $15.
3. 10%, –2%, 6%
5. The number of burglaries will decrease by 4.

Chapter 2

1. The real cost is what you give up by not having this money yourself. If you could have kept the money in a savings account that earns 5% interest per year, the real cost is $50 (5% of $1,000).
3. False. This statement ignores the opportunity cost of using the land for the stadium instead of for some other facility, such as a library or office building. Another option for the university might be to sell the land, in which case the opportunity cost is the potential selling price.
5. People whose spare time has a relatively low opportunity cost will wait in line for the cheap gasoline.
7. The marginal cost is the cost of equipping and paying one more officer. The officer would presumably decrease crime, and the marginal benefit is determined by the reduction in crime resulting from the additional officer. If you can measure the marginal cost and the marginal benefit, you should continue to hire officers until the marginal benefit equals the marginal cost.
9. In the long run, the firm can modify its production facility or build a new one.
11. Eventually, we expect output to increase at a decreasing rate because more and more workers share the copy machine.
13. Salaries increased faster than the price of consumer goods.

Figure A Relationship between Hours of Tennis and the Monthly Tennis Club Bill

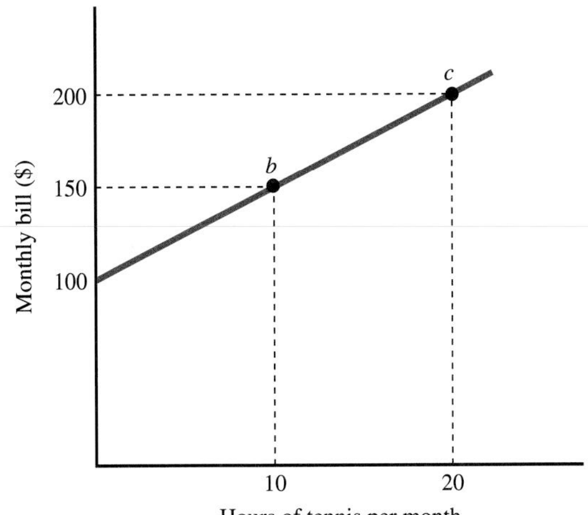

Chapter 3

1. Even if a country is less efficient in producing all goods, there will always be some goods in which it has a lower opportunity cost of production. Review the example of shirt and bread production.
3. a. Mexican goods are now less costly and therefore more attractive. If an American wants to buy a good that costs 5 pesos, he or she must spend $0.25 to get the pesos to pay for the good (5 pesos times the price of $0.05 per peso), compared to $0.50 before (5 pesos times the price of $0.10 per peso).
   b. U.S. goods are now more costly and therefore less attractive. If a Mexican wants to buy a good that costs $1, he or she must spend 20 pesos to get the dollar to pay for the good ($1 divided by the price of $0.05 per peso), compared to only 10 pesos before ($1 divided by the price of $0.10 per peso).

Chapter 4

1. a. *w*, $150, 200 per day
   b. shortage, increase
   c. surplus, decrease
3. a. The cost of producing computers will decrease, so the production of computers will be more profitable and firms will supply more of them. The supply curve will shift to the right, decreasing the equilibrium price.
   b. The tax increases the production cost, shifting the supply curve to the left and increasing the equilibrium price.
5. Education at private and public schools are substitutes, so the tuition hike will shift the demand for private education to the right, increasing the equilibrium price and quantity.
7. If price and quantity both increase, we know from Table 1 that demand has increased. We shift the demand curve to the right, increasing the price and quantity.

Chapter 5

1. The price elasticity is 1.30, the percentage change in quantity (13%) divided by the percentage change in price (10%).
3. Each brand has many substitute goods (all the other brands), so the demand for a specific brand will be more elastic than the demand for running shoes in general.
5. Inelastic: An increase in price increases total revenue, while a decrease in price decreases total revenue.
7. Using the elasticity formula, the 10% increase in the price of beer will decrease the quantity of beer consumed by 13%, decreasing the highway death rate by the same percentage. Therefore, the number of highway deaths will decrease by 13(13% of 100).

9. Use the price-change formula: The predicted change in price is 1% = 4%/(1 + 3). In the graph we shift the supply curve to the left, so the restrictions increase the price from $100,000 to $101,000 and decreases the equilibrium quantity.

Chapter 6

1. We assume that there are no spillover benefits. This assumption is likely to be violated for national defense, space exploration, public radio, and education. We also assume there are no spillover costs. This assumption is likely to be violated for goods that generate pollution, such as paper, transportation (auto and bus), and electricity.
3. We can use the elasticity formulas to compute the percentage changes in the quantity supplied and quantity demanded.

   The quantity supplied increases by 10%: 2.0 = 10%/5%
   The quantity demanded decreases by 4%: 0.80 = 4%/5%

   The quantity supplied increases by 10%, from 50 billion pounds to 55 billion pounds. The quantity demanded decreases by 4%, from 50 billion pounds to 48 billion pounds. Therefore, the surplus is 7 billion pounds.
5. a and b. The prices of dry cleaning and housing good will increase, just as the price of taxi service increased as a result of taxi medallions. See Figure 4.
   c. The price of clothing will increase, just as the price of sugar increased as a result of an import ban. See Figure 5.
7. The supply of these other goods to an individual city are much more elastic, so price controls would decrease the quantity supplied by a larger amount. In addition, everyone would have to wait in line to get these other goods. In contrast, people who occupy rent-control apartments don't have to find a new apartment every week, so they avoid most of the queuing and search costs. Although they are likely to vote for continued rent controls, they are unlikely to vote for price controls on food.
9. In the market equilibrium, there are 100 taxis and the price of taxi service is $3.00, which is just high enough to cover the cost of providing taxi service. If 101 taxis each provided 10 miles of service per hour, the quantity of taxi service would increase to 1,010 miles per hour. From the market demand curve, the price would drop below $3.00, meaning that the price would not be high enough to cover the $3.00 cost of taxi service. If the government issues more than 100 medallions, no one will use the extra medallions and the medallion policy will have no effect on the market: The price of taxi service will be $3.00 and the price of a medallion will be zero.

Chapter 7

1. As shown in Figure B, at a price of $3, Bob demands 8, Betty demands 4, and Popey demands 4, so the total demand is 16.
3. Using the *marginal principle*: The marginal benefit of a CD is 60 utils (the marginal utility), while the marginal cost is 30 utils [the number of tapes sacrificed per CD (2) times the marginal utility of tapes (15)]. Since the marginal benefit exceeds the marginal cost, you should buy more CDs.

   Using the *utility-maximizing rule*: The marginal utility per dollar spent on CDs is 6 utils (60 utils divided by $10), while the marginal utility per dollar spent on tapes is 3 utils (15 divided by $5). CDs generate a larger bang per buck, so you should spend more on CDs and less on tapes.
5. income, tastes, price of other goods, number of people
7. At a price of $20, the consumer surplus is $250 = ½ of $5 × 100. At a price of $15, the consumer surplus is $1,000 = ½ of $10 × 200. The consumer surplus increases by $750. The original consumers save $5 on each of the 100 CDs purchased, for a savings of $500. The change in consumer surplus is larger because of the law of demand: The decrease in the price increases the quantity demanded, and consumers get additional consumer surplus from the 101st through the 200th CDs.
9. See Figure C.
   a. The demand curve is negatively sloped, with a vertical intercept of 40 cents, a slope of −1, and a horizontal intercept of 40 trips. At the original price, Otto takes 10 trips per month. At the new price, he would take 20 trips per month.
   b. The change in consumer surplus is $1.50 per month: The consumer surplus at the original price of 30 cents is $0.50 and the surplus with a price of 20 cents is $2.00. The change in consumer surplus exceeds the extra tax liability, so he will support the highway.

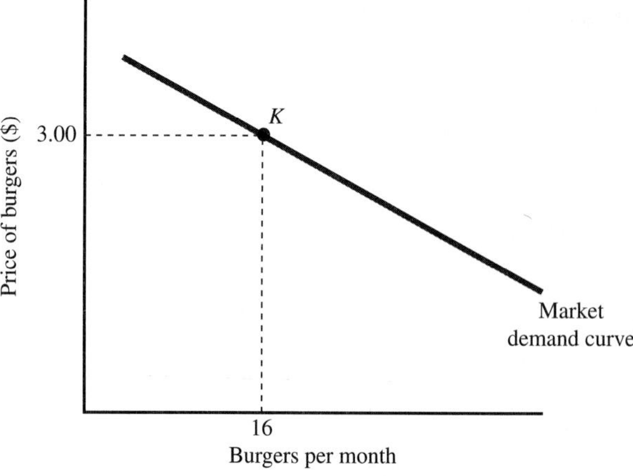

Figure B Individual to Market Demand

Figure C Consumer Surplus for Highway

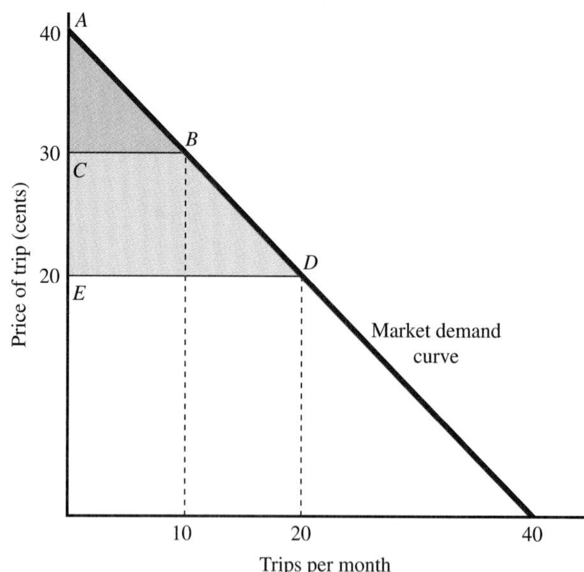

Appendix to Chapter 7

1. The vertical intercept of the budget line is 40 violets, and the horizontal intercept is 10 hats.
   a. The slope is the price of hats divided by the price of violets, or 4.0.
   b. An indifference curve that intersects the budget line is not the highest (most northeasterly) possible indifference curve.
   c. The second indifference curve should be tangent to the budget line.
   d. the marginal rate of substitution
3. Carla's MRS is 2.0, which exceeds the price ratio of ⅓. Therefore, she should pick an auto with more horsepower and less interior space.

Chapter 8

1. See Figure D. The average cost is $15 for 40 shirts, $9 for 100 shirts, $7 for 200 shirts, and $6 for 400 shirts.
3.

	Number of Tables		
	10	30	50
Fixed cost ($)	1,200	1,200	1,200
Fixed cost per table ($)	120	40	24
Labor hours	25	225	625
Labor cost ($)	250	2,250	6,250
Labor cost per table ($)	25	75	125
Material cost per table ($)	20	20	20
Average cost ($)	165	135	169

5. The marginal cost is defined as the change in total cost when the third bus is added, or $80 = $780 – 700. The $260 figure is the average cost, not the marginal cost. To compute the marginal cost, we subtract, we don't divide.
7. Diseconomies of scale occur in the long run: As output increases, average cost increases because of coordination problems and perhaps higher input costs. Diminishing returns is a short-run phenomenon, a result of packing more and more workers into a given production facility. The long-run cost curves we've seen suggest that diseconomies of scale are mild: The average cost curve is negatively sloped or horizontal over most quantities and has a slight positive slope. The marginal cost curves are steep over most quantities of output, reflecting diminishing returns.

Chapter 9

1. See Figure E for the marginal cost curve and the short-run supply curve. The supply curve is just the marginal cost curve above the shut-down price (above points).
3.

Tables per Hour	Number of Workers	Additional Workers	Additional Labor Cost	Additional Material Cost	Marginal Cost
3	15				
4	18	3	$15	$20	$35
5	23	5	25	20	45
6	33	10	50	20	70

The first and the last columns show three points on the firm's short-run supply curve: ($35, 4 tables), ($45, 5 tables), ($50, 6 tables). Multiplying the quantities by the number of firms (100), the points on the supply curve are: ($35, 400 tables), ($45, 500 tables), ($50, 600 tables).

5. a. The marginal cost ($45) exceeds the marginal revenue (price = $22), so the firm is not maximizing its profit: The firm is producing too much output. At the profit-maximizing output, the total revenue may exceed variable cost. We cannot decide whether the firm should shut down until we know the average variable cost at the profit-maximizing quantity.
   b. In Figure F on page S-4, the firm is actually profitable at the profit-maximizing quantity (60 units of output).
7. See Figure G on page S-4. At the higher price, consumers demand only 1,000 chairs (point *d*). The policy decreases consumer surplus and increases producer surplus, and decreases the total value of the market by the area bounded by points *d*, *z*, and *w*.

Figure D Long-Run Average Cost for Shirts

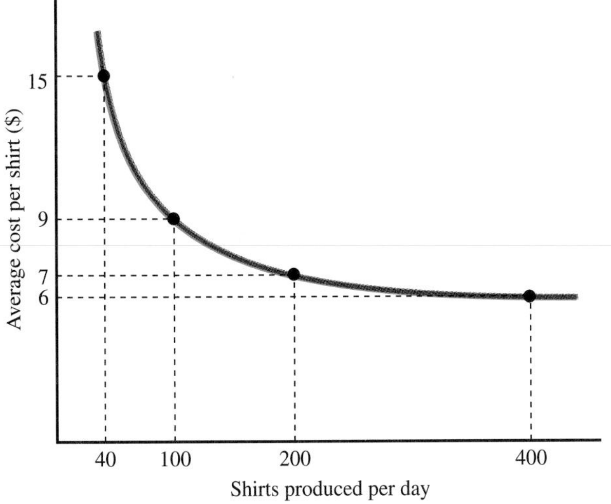

Figure E Marginal Cost Curve and Short-Run Supply Curve

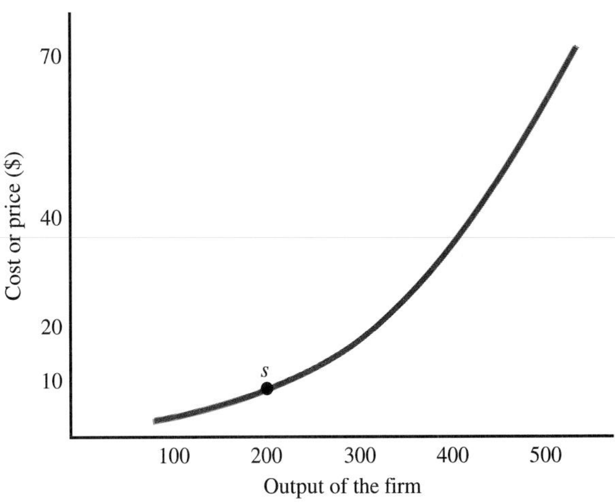

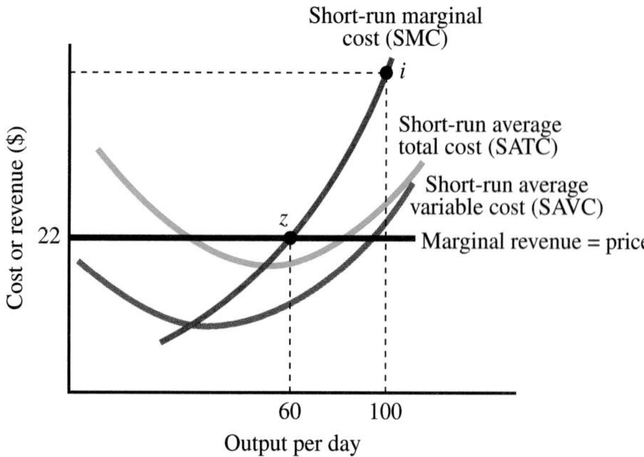

Figure F Firm Picks the Wrong Quantity of Output

Chapter 10

1.

Number of Firms	Industry Output	Total Cost for Typical Firm	Average Cost per Lamp
40	400	$300	$30
80	800	360	36
120	1,200	420	42

We have three points on the long-run supply curve: At a price of $30, the quantity is 400 lamps; at a price of $36, the quantity is 800 lamps; at a price of $42, the quantity is 1,200 lamps.

3. Any firm that did not adopt the low-cost technology would lose customers to other firms that could produce the good at a lower cost—and sell the good at a lower price.

Figure G Effects of a Minimum Price

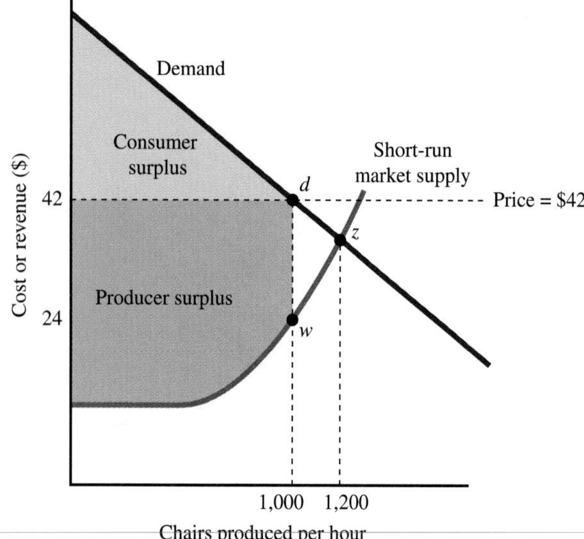

5. Because the industry uses such tiny amounts of the relevant inputs, the prices of these inputs won't change as the industry grows. Therefore, the average cost per haircut does not depend on the quantity of haircuts. The long-run supply curve is horizontal, for example, at a constant cost of $10 per haircut.
7. The short-run supply curve is relatively steep because of diminishing returns. The long-run supply curve is flatter than the short-run curve because firms enter the industry and build new factories, so there are no diminishing returns. This distinction is important because it tells us that following an increase in demand, the price will jump up a large amount (a result of movement along the short-run curve), but then gradually drop until we reach the price shown by the long-run curve.

Chapter 11

1. To maximize profit, the restaurant will pick the quantity at which marginal revenue equals marginal cost. Using the marginal revenue formula, we can compute the marginal revenue at each price and quantity:

Price	$10	$9	$8	$7
Quantity	30	40	50	60
Marginal revenue	$7	$5	$3	$1

Marginal revenue equals marginal cost at a price of $8 and a quantity of 50 meals.

3. On average, the payback per dollar spent on these lottery games is about 50 cents. In other words, for every $100 spent by players, the state pays $50 in prizes.* The commercial gambling games have much higher paybacks: The payback per dollar is 81 cents for horse racing and 89 cents for slot machines. The lottery games have lower paybacks because each state has a monopoly on lottery games: The state outlaws commercial lotteries. If the state allowed other organizations to offer lottery games, the competition between commercial and state lottery games would increase the payback from lottery games.
5. The artificial barrier to entry will generate higher prices and a smaller quantity demanded. If we eliminated the barriers, there would be more teams and ticket prices would fall, increasing total attendance.
7. The basic idea is to offer lower prices for people who are not willing to pay the regular price. You could put coupons in the local newspaper, sell tickets far in advance at lower prices, or set up a hierarchy of seating and ticket prices (lower prices for seats farther from the action).
9. This price-discrimination scheme is based on the notion that bargain hunters are early birds: The large discounts for early fabric purchases attract consumers who would otherwise not buy fabric at the regular price.

Chapter 12

1. The slope of the demand curve is $1/20 = $.05. We can use the marginal revenue formula to compute marginal revenue for each combination of price and quantity. Figure H on page S-5 shows the demand curve and marginal revenue curve with two points identified on each curve. For a quantity of 180, the price is $16 and the marginal revenue is $7. For a quantity of 120, the price is $19 and the marginal revenue is $13.

Price	$20	$19	$18	$17	$16
Quantity	100	120	140	160	180
Marginal revenue	$15	$13	$11	$9	$7

*Charles T. Clotfelter and Philip J. Cook, "On the Economics of State Lotteries," *Journal of Economic Perspectives*, vol. 4, Fall 1990, pp. 105–119.

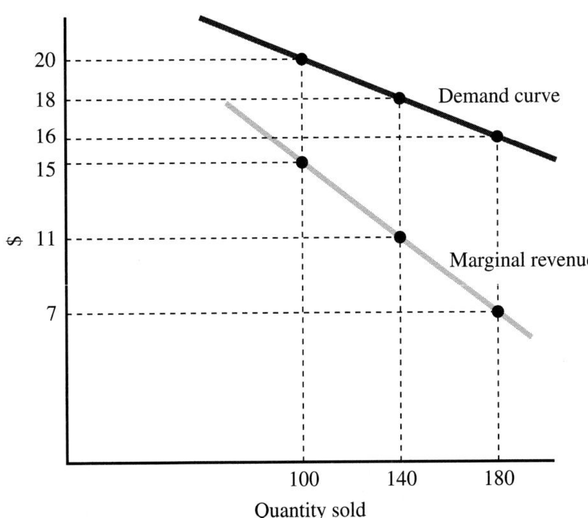

Figure H *Monopolist's Demand and Marginal Revenue Curves*

If marginal cost is $9, marginal cost equals marginal revenue at a quantity of 160 and a price of $17.

3. At a price of $60, the total demand for wigs is 40. We know this because Jean-Luc sells 30 wigs per week at a price of $70 and the slope of the demand curve is $1.00, so a $10 decrease in price increases the quantity demanded by 10 wigs. Therefore, Jean-Luc and Sinead would each sell 20 wigs at a price of $60. The average cost of selling 20 wigs is $55 (the average cost of 30 wigs is $35, and the average cost increases by $2 for every 1-unit decrease in the number of wigs sold by the firm). Therefore, each person would earn a profit of $5 per wig ($60 – $55).
5. As a regulated monopoly, the BPA charges a price that is high enough to cover all its costs. The fish-protection program will increase BPA's cost, and government regulators will increase the price of electricity.

Chapter 13

1. See Figure I. The profit per firm under the duopoly outcome is $500 (a profit of $5 per passenger times 100 passengers). The profit per firm under the cartel is $750 (a profit of $10 per passenger times 75 passengers). Each firm will pick the low price: The path of the game is square X to square Z to rectangle 4.
3. One reason for low prices at these sales is that there is no punishment for underpricing the other firm. Any prior arrangement for cartel pricing would evaporate when one firm knows it will soon go out of business.

Chapter 14

1. a. No. Bertha is willing to pay the most ($100), but she is willing to pay less than the cost ($120).
   b. No. The cost per citizen will be $40, so Bertha is the only one willing to pay more than the cost per capita.
   c. Suppose that each citizen pays $10 less than his or his willingness to pay: Bertha pays $90; Marian pays $20; Sam pays $10. This scheme raises $120 and benefits each citizen.
3. The specific answer depends on the church.
5. a. The benefit is $8,000 (80,000 citizens times $0.10 per person), which exceeds the cost of $5,000. Since the benefit exceeds the cost, the provision of the additional litter is socially efficient.
   b. No. The benefit to the rancher ($0.10) is less than the cost ($5,000).
   c. The citizens could contribute to a wolf-preservation fund to provide the rancher with enough money to offset the cost of a litter of wolves. For example, if each citizen contributed $0.07 (70% of his or her benefit), they could raise a total of $5,600. By paying this amount to the landowner who hosts the wolf litter, the rancher would be better off by $600, and each of the citizens would be better off by $0.03.
7. There are spillover benefits from the programs supported by these organizations (programs that help the poor, medical research), and the subsidy increases the amount contributed and amount of money spent on these programs.
9. a. Input suppliers do not respond to changes in the price of land, so the entire tax will be shifted to landowners. If consumers faced any price exceeding the initial price, there would be a surplus of land and the price would drop.
   b. No. Because the supply of land is fixed, the tax would not change anyone's behavior, meaning that the equilibrium quantity of land would not change. The total burden of the tax would equal the revenue collected, so there would be no excess burden.

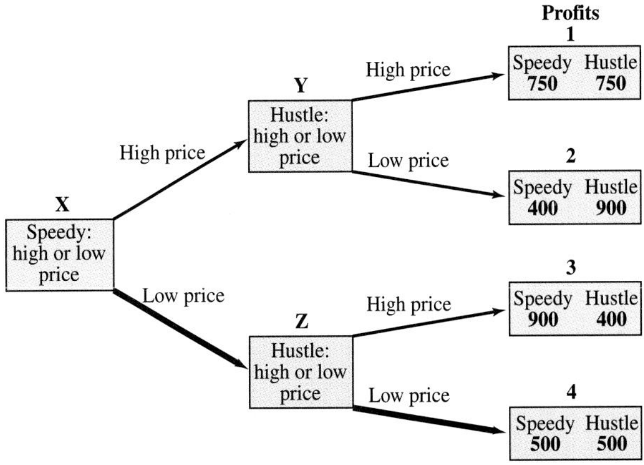

Figure I *Game Tree for Airporter Price-Fixing Game*

Chapter 15

1. See Figure J on page S-6. The market equilibrium is shown by point *i*: The demand curve intersects the supply curve at 20 units per day. The pollution tax shifts the supply curve by such a large amount that the supply curve lies entirely above the demand curve. For this to occur, the spillover cost from the pollutant must be very high, the cost of abatement must be very high, and the demand for the good must be relatively low.
3. a. From Table 1, the production cost per ton with zero pollution is $116.
   b. The marginal cost associated with going from 1 gallon to 0 gallons is $20. For firms to make this choice the marginal benefit of abatement (the tax savings) must be at least $20.
5. The supply curve will shift to the left as some of the cars are destroyed. The equilibrium price will increase and the equilibrium quantity will decrease.

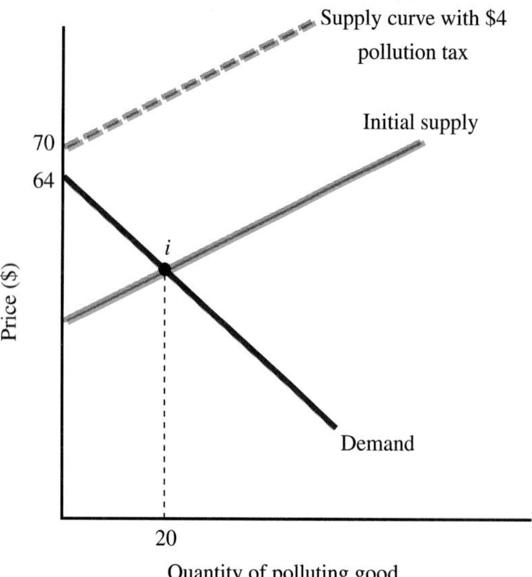

Figure J Pollution Tax Makes the Equilibrium Quantity of a Polluting Good Zero

7. We could adjust other taxes to mitigate any undesirable effects on the poor. For example, we could decrease the sales tax rate or adjust the income tax rates.

Chapter 16

1. Suppose that Groucho wants to join a social club to associate with people who are richer than he is and he assumes that other people join clubs for the same reasons. A club will invite him to join only if he would increase the average income of the club. In other words, Groucho will only be invited to join groups in which most people are poorer than he is, clubs with an adverse selection of people. The same reasoning applies if Groucho wants to associate with people who are more witty than he is and he assumes other people feel the same way. A club that asks him to join will have an average wit level that is less than his, so he will be forced to interact with dimwits.
3. a. Suppose that you're willing to pay the average value of the two types of cameras ($60) for a 50% chance of getting a plum. If you expect a greater than 50% chance of getting a plum, it will be wise to buy a used camera.
   b. Given the adverse-selection problem, your chance of getting a plum is likely to be less than 50%.
5. The detector eliminates the imperfect information problem, so the two types of used cars will be sold in separate markets, with one price for lemons ($2,000 in our example) and another price for plums ($4,000). There is no adverse selection because each buyer knows exactly what type of car he or she will get.
7. Like the lie detector, the genetic tests eliminate the adverse-selection problem, this time for insurance companies. The insurance companies will charge higher prices to those who are likely to contract the diseases and *lower* prices to those who are not. This will strike many people as unfair.

Chapter 17

1. The payroll tax shifts the supply curve to the left: At every price, a smaller quantity is supplied. The leftward shift of the supply curve increases the equilibrium wage to a wage above $10.
3. Some people will work fewer hours, so they will pay less in taxes: They pay a lower rate on fewer hours. Other people will work the same number of hours and also pay less in taxes: They pay a lower rate on the same number of hours. Even a person who works more hours could pay less in taxes: If the increase in hours is small relative to the decrease in the hourly tax rate, the tax bill (hours times the tax rate) will actually decrease. The only people who will pay more in taxes are the workers who increase their hours by an amount that is large relative to the decrease in the hourly rate.
5. a. The supply of teachers is large relative to demand, so wages are relatively low. This could result from the psychological rewards from teaching, the work hours, or the free summers.
   b. This is effectively a minimum wage for teachers, and it has the same effect as a minimum wage for any occupation: The increase in the wage will decrease the quantity demanded, so some teachers will lose their jobs.
7. Let's assume that the program is paid for by government, not coal companies. The program will increase the supply of coal workers, shifting the supply curve to the right. The equilibrium wage will decrease.

Chapter 18

1. It depends on personal preferences. Some people will save more, whereas others will save less, and others will save the same amount.
3. Here are the present values for the five payments: $10 million for today's payment, $9.10 million for the payment received in one year, $8.26 million for the payment received in two years, $7.52 million for the payment received in three years, and $6.85 million for the payment received in four years. The total is $41.73 million.
5. With an interest rate of 5%, the present value of 40 years of an annual benefit of $10,000 is about $98,000, which is less than the cost of $140,000. Therefore, unless there are some other benefits from college, it would not be sensible to get a degree.

Chapter 19

1. This policy would increase the monetary cost of becoming a father, and it might discourage teen pregnancy.
3. This policy will increase the supply of college graduates, increasing competition for jobs requiring a college education. As a result, we would expect lower wages for college graduates and a smaller gap between the wages of college graduates and high-school graduates (smaller than we would observe otherwise).
5. If health coverage is provided through employment, problems will always emerge when workers change jobs.
7. In a pay-as-you-go system, individuals will not receive any sums upon retirement; therefore they must save on their own.

Chapter 20

1. Macroeconomics deals with the economy as a whole; microeconomics focuses on individual markets.
3. If real GDP falls, its growth will be negative.
5. The same process of search and matching occurs in both the market for jobs and the market for housing. Apartment owners want to find good tenants and renters want to find good apartments.
7. The statement confuses high prices with rising prices. Inflation occurs when prices rise.

Chapter 21

1. The French do take more leisure than Americans. This is not accounted for in GDP. Unemployment is higher in France than in the United States. The French believe this is a serious problem.
3. The downside to trade deficits is that the deficit country must sell its assets to foreign countries.
5. In 1987 computer prices were higher relative to other goods than they were in subsequent years. Measuring growth using 1987 prices would therefore put more weight on computer growth in calculating real GDP than using prices from later years.
7. When the economy starts to boom, people who were not previously in the labor force might start to look for work. Since both employment and the labor force would increase, the unemployment rate could remain unchanged.

Chapter 22

1. Supply-siders are interested in the adverse effects of taxation on employment. High unemployment in Europe could be caused by high payroll taxes.
3. Restricting the number of young workers will reduce the supply of labor and may raise real wages for union members.
5. A immigrants come into a region, the supply of labor increases and wages will fall.
7. With credit cards, people find it easier to borrow against future earnings and buy goods. Limiting credit cards could reduce consumption and free up more goods for investment.

Chapter 23

1. We collect price data on many commodities in the United Kingdom and the United States in their own currencies. We then use the "exchange rate" for each commodity to calculate expenditures in dollars.
3. We can measure the contribution of technological progress indirectly. We first measure output growth and measure the contributions to that growth from labor and capital. The difference between the two is technological progress.
5. You would have to determine whether the trade deficit promoted domestic investment spending.

Chapter 24

1. Without prices it is difficult to determine when to increase or decrease production. If people postpone their spending to the future, it is not clear to producers the types of goods consumers will be buying in the future.
3. The classical aggregate supply curve is vertical because output in the long run does not depend on the price level, just the supply of factors. The Keynesian aggregate supply curve is horizontal because in the short run output depends only on demand and prices are sticky.
5. Rents on apartment are sticky in that most tenants have leases that are for at least a month and often for a year. Since it is costly to move, most renters want to have some security that their rent will not be changed too frequently.
7. The level of prices would fall.

Chapter 25

1. Firms will find their inventories being depleted and step up their production.
3. An initial increase in income leads to a rise in consumer spending, which, in turn, leads to further increases in income.
5. The increase in exports raises demand for U.S. goods and firms will increase their output.
7. When the Egyptian government built the pyramids, there was increased demand for goods and services and output therefore was increased. Perhaps building roads and highways are our modern-day equivalents.
9. Higher growth in Europe or Japan will raise incomes in these areas of the world. This will increase their imports. Some of these imports will be goods exported from the United States. Increases in U.S. exports will lead to an increase in U.S. GDP.

Chapter 26

1. If a firm projects a current increase in GDP into the future, it may want to invest in anticipation of high demand. Similarly, if GDP falls and firms believe this means that future GDP will also be low, this will decrease investment spending.
3. If real interest rates are high, an investor can earn a high rate of return by lending money. Thus the opportunity cost of putting the funds into an investment is high.
5. If financial intermediaries fail, investors will find it more costly to obtain funds from savers and the overall level of investment spending in the economy will decline.
7. All three components of investment are volatile. Plant and equipment investment will be sensitive to changes in the growth rate in the economy as well as swings in animal spirits. Housing investment will be sensitive to movements in interest rates. Inventory investment will depend both on firm's expectations about future consumer demand and on actual consumer purchases.

Chapter 27

1. All three functions make it easier to conduct transactions. As a medium of exchange, money prevents the problems that occur with barter. If money did not serve as a store of value, no one would accept it in exchange. It is also convenient for prices to be quoted in terms of the medium of exchange.
3. Macroeconomists study banks more than insurance companies because deposits in banks are part of the supply of money.
5. With higher reserve requirements, banks are able to lend less and thus not create as many deposits.
7. An increase in the discount rate reduces attractiveness of borrowing reserves from the Fed. Banks will not borrow as many reserves and the money supply will fall.
9. Whenever the Federal Reserve makes a purchase and pays for it with a check, it creates reserves. The money supply increases with these purchases.

Chapter 28

1. If you hold money, you sacrifice the interest you could have earned by holding bonds that pay interest.
3. Monetary policy would become weaker because investment would respond less to changes in interest rates.
5. If an action taken to stimulate the economy takes effect only when the economy has already returned to full employment by itself, your action could destabilize the economy.
7. If you believed that gold prices provide an early warning for inflation, you would want to tighten monetary policy (make open market sales) if the price of gold began to rise. Gold prices could rise for other reasons. For example, there could be a shift in fashion to gold jewelry, a disaster in a gold mine, or other factors that narrowly affect the demand or supply for gold.

Chapter 29

1. They became worried that unemployment was below the natural rate and inflation would increase.
3. Investment spending rises during a boom as firms became more optimistic. But as output exceeds full employment,

wages and prices will rise, raising interest rates and eventually cutting back investment.

5. Lower government spending will mean lower interest rates in the long run and more housing investment.

Chapter 30

1. When nominal interest rates are high, this is usually due to high expectations of inflation. These expectations are caused by high actual rates of money growth and thus "loose" monetary policy, not tight money.
3. In the long run, the economy operates at the natural rate of unemployment and inflation is determined by money growth. If money growth changes, so will inflation in the long run.
5. Inflation raises the costs of holding money, so people will "turn over" their money more frequently.
7. The costs are outlined in Table 3.

Chapter 31

1. a. Governments with a limited ability to borrow must resort to money finance that will cause inflation.
   b. Countries with low saving rates will find that deficits reduce investment.
3. One key difference between the states and the federal government is that the states have separate operating and capital budgets. But the limits do force politicians to raise taxes and cut expenditures when necessary.
5. Both increase the burden on future generations in terms of requiring higher taxes.
7. If the government uses baseline budgeting and the program would increase more than $10 billion in the absence of changes in law, a $10 billion increase would be cut relative to the baseline.

Chapter 32

1. Chipland produces 120 chips and exchanges 35 of them for 70 shirts, ending up with 85 chips and 70 shirts. Shirtland produces 108 shirts and exchanges 70 of them for 35 chips, ending up with 35 chips and 38 shirts.
3. If the VERs were replaced with a tariff, the government would collect revenue. Under VERs, importers earn large profits.
5. Consumers will benefit because prices will decrease. As each nation shifts its production to the goods for which it has a comparative advantage, workers in expanding industries will benefit, while workers in other industries will lose. The challenge for policymakers is to facilitate workers' transition to a more specialized economy.

Chapter 33

1. The demand for British pounds comes from individuals or firms that want to buy British goods or assets. The supply of pounds come from British residents who wish to purchase goods or assets outside Britain.
3. The real exchange rate takes into account difference in prices between two countries. If the dollar depreciates by 10% but prices rise by 10% more in the United States than overseas, the cost to foreigners of U.S. goods has not changed.
5. For the world to resume a fixed exchange rate system, countries must be willing to keep their inflation rates within narrow bands. This seems highly unlikely today.
7. Rents for apartments are based on a number of factors, including an important nontraded good, land. Since land prices are not equal across countries, neither will be rentals on apartments. Gold is traded in a world market and must sell for a single price.

INDEX

F

H

I

M

N

Q

R

T

U

V

W

X

Y

PHOTO CREDITS

Chapter 1, page 1, Melanie Carr/Index Stock Photography, Inc.; page 8, Mary Ellen Mark Library; page 8, Chuck Savage/The Stock Market

Chapter 2, page 22, Werner Krutein/Gamma—Liason, Inc.; page 24, Richard Shock/Gamma—Liason, Inc.; page 25, Ilene Perlman/Stock Boston

Chapter 3, page 37, Spencer Grant/Gamma—Liason, Inc.; page 40, Bob Daemmrich/Stock Boston; page 53, Y. Forestier/Sygma

Chapter 4, page 57, Amy C. Etra/PhotoEdit; page 63, Joe Towers/The Stock Market; page 63, Tom Bross/Studio 20/Stock Boston; page 75, Vaughn Fleming/Science Photo Library/Photo Researchers, Inc.

Chapter 5, page 81, Joe Sohn/Chronosohn/The Stock Market; page 86, Dan Sundberg/The Image Bank; page 89, Les Stone/Sygma

Chapter 6, page 100, Antonio M. Rosario/The Image Bank; page 107, Dennis Cox/ChinaStock; page 114, Joseph Nettis/Stock Boston

Chapter 7, page 124, Jack Fields/Photo Researchers, Inc.; page 134, Robert Brenner/PhotoEdit; page 135, RB Studio 96/The Stock Market

Chapter 8, page 150, Catherine Ursillo/Photo Researchers, Inc.; page 155, Paul Shambroom/Science Source/Photo Researchers, Inc.; page 162, Marilyn Katsmers—SharkSong/Dembinsky Photo Associates

Chapter 9, page 170, Jim Bertoglio/Index Stock Photography, Inc.; page 179, Michael Newman/PhotoEdit; page 185, David Young-Wolff/PhotoEdit

Chapter 10, page 192, Charles Campbell/Westlight; page 198, David Young-Wolff/PhotoEdit; page 203, Walter Michot/Miami Herald Publishing Co.

Chapter 11, page 208, Robert Brenner/PhotoEdit; page 222, Stephen Frisch/Stock Boston; page 223, Ricardo Azoury/SABA Press Photos, Inc.

Chapter 12, page 229, Cynthia Johnson/Gamma—Liason, Inc.; page 230, Weizenbach/The Stock Market; page 240, Willie L. Hill, Jr./FPG International

Chapter 13, page 246, Mary Kate Denny/PhotoEdit; page 263, Benn Mitchell/The Image Bank

Chapter 14, page 271, Rob Atkins/The Image Bank; page 280, Chase Swift/Westlight; page 284, Jeff Greenberg/PhotoEdit

Chapter 15, page 294, Kaz Mori/The Image Bank; page 298, Porter Gifford/Gamma—Liason, Inc.; page 310, Owen Franken/Stock Boston

Chapter 16, page 316, Michael Newman/PhotoEdit; page 320, Markova/The Stock Market; page 324, Bryan Yablonsky/Duomo Photography

Chapter 17, page 332, Steve Starr/SABA Press Photos, Inc.; page 341, P & G Bowater/The Image Bank; page 351, Ford Motor Company

Chapter 18, page 361, David Young-Wolff/PhotoEdit; page 371, Jose L. Pelaez/The Stock Market

Chapter 19, page 376, Michael Newman/PhotoEdit; page 389, Stephen Agricola/Stock Boston; page 395, Pete Saloutos/The Stock Market

Chapter 20, page 401, Techmap/Westlight; page 403,Culver Pictures, Inc.; page 415, L. Downing/Sygma

Chapter 21, page 422, Dallas & John Heaton/Westlight; page 426, AP/Wide World Photos; page 432, Ken Graham/Ken Graham Agency—Alaska!

Chapter 22, page 443, Peter Gridley/FPG International; page 449, Michael Newman/PhotoEdit; page 452, Vera Lentz/Black Star

Chapter 23, page 462, Porterfield-Chickering/Photo Researchers, Inc.; page 467, Greg Girard/Contact Press Images; page 477, Florent Flipper/Unicorn Stock Photos

Chapter 24, page 486, Brown Brothers; page 491, SuperStock, Inc.; page 495, Steve Skjold/PhotoEdit

Chapter 25, page 507, Stock Connection/FPG International; page 521, Elliot Erwitt/Magnum Photos, Inc.; page 523, Bob Daemmrich/Stock Boston

Chapter 26, page 534, L.M. Otero/AP/Wide World Photos; page 536, Will & Deni McIntyre/Photo Researchers, Inc.; page 547, UPI/Corbis—Bettmann

Chapter 27, page 551, James A. Finley/AP/Wide World Photos; page 555, Photo Aventurier/Gamma—Liason, Inc.; page 560, Mark Burnett/Stock Boston

Chapter 28, page 569, Chase Swift/Westlight; page 574, Mike Mazzaschi/Stock Boston; page 580, Michael Hirsch/Gamma—Liason, Inc.

Chapter 29, page 589, Doug Wilson/Westlight; page 591, Jeff Greenberg/PhotoEdit; page 596, SuperStock, Inc.

Chapter 30, page 604, Paul Conklin/PhotoEdit; page 610, Buu-Simon/Gamma—Liason, Inc.; page 617, UPI/Corbis—Bettmann

Chapter 31, page 625, Cynthia Johnson/Gamma—Liason, Inc.; page 635, SuperStock, Inc.

Chapter 32, page 641, Laure' Communications; page 651, Ping Amranand/SuperStock, Inc.

Chapter 33, page 663, Telegraph Colour Library/FPG International; page 664, Churchill & Klehr Photography; page 681, Index Stock Photography, Inc.

ABOUT THE AUTHORS

Arthur O'Sullivan

Arthur O'Sullivan is a professor of economics at Oregon State University. After receiving his B.S. in economics at the University of Oregon, he spent two years in the Peace Corps, working with city planners in the Philippines. He received his Ph.D. in economics from Princeton University in 1981, and then spent 11 years at the University of California, Davis, where he won several teaching awards. At Oregon State University, he teaches microeconomics at different levels, from the introductory course to advanced courses for doctoral students. He is the author of the best-selling textbook, *Urban Economics*, currently in its third edition.

Professor O'Sullivan's research explores economic issues concerning urban land use, environmental protection, and public finance. His articles appear in many economics journals, including *Journal of Urban Economics*, *Journal of Environmental Economics and Management*, *National Tax Journal*, and *Journal of Public Economics*.

Professor O'Sullivan lives with his wife and two children in Corvallis, Oregon. He enjoys outdoor activities, including the kids' sport du jour (soccer, basketball, baseball, badminton, lawn hockey, or football). Indoors, he is learning how to play the fiddle, much to the dismay of his family and the delight of the neighborhood dogs.

Steven M. Sheffrin

Steven M. Sheffrin is professor of economics and director of the Center for State and Local Taxation at the University of California, Davis. He has been a visiting professor at Princeton University, Oxford University, and the London School of Economics and served as a financial economist with the Office of Tax Analysis of the United States Department of Treasury. He has been on the faculty at Davis since 1976 and served as the Chairman of the Department of Economics. He received his B.A. from Wesleyan University and his Ph.D. in economics from the Massachusetts Institute of Technology.

Professor Sheffrin is the author of five other books and over 70 articles in the fields of macroeconomics, public finance, and international economics. His most recent books include *Rational Expectations* (Second Edition) and *Property Taxes and Tax Revolts: The Legacy of Proposition 13* (with Arthur O'Sullivan and Terri Sexton), both from Cambridge University Press.

Professor Sheffrin teaches macroeconomics at all levels, from large lectures of principles (classes of 400) to graduate classes for doctoral students. He is the recipient of the Thomas Mayer Distinguished Teaching Award in economics.

He lives with his wife Anjali (also an economist) and his two children in Davis, California. In addition to a passion for current affairs and travel, he plays a tough game of tennis.

The Components of Nominal GDP, 1959–1995 (Billions of Dollars)

Year	Gross Domestic Product	Personal Consumption Expenditures	Gross Private Domestic Investment	Net Exports	Government Consumption Expenditures and Gross Investment
1959	507.2	318.1	78.8	–1.7	112.0
1960	526.6	332.2	78.8	2.4	113.2
1961	544.8	342.6	77.9	3.4	120.9
1962	585.2	363.4	87.9	2.4	131.4
1963	617.4	383.0	93.4	3.3	137.7
1964	663.0	411.4	101.7	5.5	144.4
1965	719.1	444.3	118.0	3.9	153.0
1966	787.8	481.9	130.4	1.9	173.6
1967	833.6	509.5	128.0	1.4	194.6
1968	910.6	559.8	139.9	–1.3	212.1
1969	982.2	604.7	155.0	–1.2	223.8
1970	1,035.6	648.1	150.2	1.2	236.1
1971	1,125.4	702.5	176.0	–3.0	249.9
1972	1,237.3	770.7	205.6	–8.0	268.9
1973	1,382.6	851.6	242.9	.6	287.6
1974	1,496.9	931.2	245.6	–3.1	323.2
1975	1,630.6	1,029.1	225.4	13.6	362.6
1976	1,819.0	1,148.8	286.6	–2.3	385.9
1977	2,026.9	1,277.1	356.6	–23.7	416.9
1978	2,291.4	1,428.8	430.8	–26.1	457.9
1979	2,557.5	1,593.5	480.9	–24.0	507.1
1980	2,784.2	1,760.4	465.9	–14.9	572.8
1981	3,115.9	1,941.3	556.2	–15.0	633.4
1982	3,242.1	2,076.8	501.1	–20.5	684.8
1983	3,514.5	2,283.4	547.1	–51.7	735.7
1984	3,902.4	2,492.3	715.6	–102.0	796.6
1985	4,180.7	2,704.8	715.1	–114.2	875.0
1986	4,422.2	2,892.7	722.5	–131.5	938.5
1987	4,692.3	3,094.5	747.2	–142.1	992.8
1988	5,049.6	3,349.7	773.9	–106.1	1,032.0
1989	5,438.7	3,594.8	829.2	–80.4	1,095.1
1990	5,743.8	3,839.3	799.7	–71.3	1,176.1
1991	5,916.7	3,975.1	736.2	–20.5	1,225.9
1992	6,244.4	4,219.8	790.4	–29.5	1,263.8
1993	6,553.0	4,454.1	871.1	–62.7	1,290.4
1994	6,935.7	4,700.9	1,014.4	–94.4	1,314.7
1995	7,253.8	4,924.9	1,065.3	–94.7	1,358.3

Source: Economic Report of the President, 1997, Table B-1, pp. 300–301.